T0348871

# Handbook of
# COMPUTABLE GENERAL EQUILIBRIUM MODELING

VOLUME *1A*

# INTRODUCTION TO THE SERIES

The aim of the *Handbooks in Economics* series is to produce Handbooks for various branches of economics, each of which is a definitive source, reference and teaching supplement for use by professional researchers and advanced graduate students. Each Handbook provides self-contained surveys of the current state of a branch of economics in the form of chapters prepared by leading specialists on various aspects of this branch of economics. These surveys summarize not only received results but also newer developments, from recent journal articles and discussion papers. Some original material is also included, but the main goal is to provide comprehensive and accessible surveys. The Handbooks are intended to provide not only useful reference volumes for professional collections but also possible supplementary readings for advanced courses for graduate students in economics.

**Kenneth J. Arrow and Michael D. Intriligator**

# Handbook of
# COMPUTABLE GENERAL EQUILIBRIUM MODELING

VOLUME $1A$

Edited by

**Peter B. Dixon**
*Centre of Policy Studies, Monash University*

**Dale W. Jorgenson**
*Harvard University*

Amsterdam • Boston • Heidelberg • London
New York • Oxford • Paris • San Diego
San Francisco • Singapore • Sydney • Tokyo

North-Holland is an imprint of Elsevier

ELSEVIER

North-Holland is an imprint of Elsevier
The Boulevard, Langford Lane, Kidlington, Oxford, OX5 1GB, UK
225 Wyman Street, Waltham, MA 02451, USA

First published 2013

Copyright © 2013 Elsevier B.V. All rights reserved.

No part of this publication may be reproduced or transmitted in any form or by any means, electronic
or mechanical, including photocopying, recording, or any information storage and retrieval system, without
permission in writing from the publisher. Details on how to seek permission, further information about
the Publisher's permissions policies and our arrangement with organizations such as the Copyright
Clearance Center and the Copyright Licensing Agency, can be found at our website: www.elsevier.com/
permissions

This book and the individual contributions contained in it are protected under copyright by the Publisher
(other than as may be noted herein).

**Notices**
Knowledge and best practice in this field are constantly changing. As new research and experience
broaden our understanding, changes in research methods, professional practices, or medical treatment may
become necessary.

Practitioners and researchers must always rely on their own experience and knowledge in evaluating and
using any information, methods, compounds, or experiments described herein. In using such information
or methods they should be mindful of their own safety and the safety of others, including parties for
whom they have a professional responsibility.

To the fullest extent of the law, neither the Publisher nor the authors, contributors, or editors, assume
any liability for any injury and/or damage to persons or property as a matter of products liability, negligence
or otherwise, or from any use or operation of any methods, products, instructions, or ideas contained in
the material herein.

**British Library Cataloguing in Publication Data**
A catalogue record for this book is available from the British Library

ISBN Vol 1A: 978-0-444-53634-1
ISBN Vol 1B: 978-0-444-59556-0
SET ISBN: 978-0-444-59568-3

For information on all North-Holland publications
visit our website at **store.elsevier.com**

Working together to grow
libraries in developing countries

www.elsevier.com | www.bookaid.org | www.sabre.org

ELSEVIER    BOOK AID
            International    Sabre Foundation

# CONTENTS OF VOLUME *1A*

# CONTENTS OF VOLUME *1B*

# CONTRIBUTORS

**Philip D. Adams**
Centre of Policy Studies, Monash University

**Kym Anderson**
School of Economics and Crawford School, Australian National University,
University of Adelaide

**Edward J. Balistreri**
Division of Economics and Business, Colorado School of Mines

**Stefan Boeters**
CPB, Netherlands Bureau for Economic Policy Analysis, Den Haag

**François Bourguignon**
Paris School of Economics

**Maurizio Bussolo**
World Bank

**Elisabeth Christen**
Universität Innsbruck and Johannes Kepler Universität Linz

**Martin Cicowiez**
CEDLAS-Universidad Nacional de La Plata

**Shantayanan Devarajan**
World Bank

**John W. Diamond**
Tax and Expenditure Policy Program, Baker Institute for Public Policy, Rice University

**Carolina Diaz-Bonilla**
World Bank

**Peter B. Dixon**
Centre of Policy Studies, Monash University

**Hans Fehr**
University of Wuerzburg

**Joseph Francois**
Johannes Kepler Universität, Linz and Centre for Economic Policy Research, London

**James A. Giesecke**
Centre of Policy Studies, Monash University

**Richard J. Goettle**
Northeastern University

**Thomas Hertel**
Center for Global Trade Analysis, Purdue University

**Russell Hillberry**
Department of Economics, University of Melbourne

**Mun S. Ho**
Harvard University

**Bernard Hoekman**
World Bank

**Erling Holmøy**
Research Department, Statistics Norway

**Mark Horridge**
Centre of Policy Studies, Monash University

**David Hummels**
Purdue University and National Bureau of Economic Research

**Hui Jin**
International Monetary Fund

**Sabine Jokisch**
Ulm University

**Dale W. Jorgenson**
Harvard University

**Manuel Kallweit**
University of Wuerzburg

**Fabian Kindermann**
University of Wuerzburg

**Robert B. Koopman**
US International Trade Commission

**Laurence J. Kotlikoff**
Boston University and National Bureau of Economic Research

**Hans Lofgren**
World Bank

**John R. Madden**
Centre of Policy Studies, Monash University

**Miriam Manchin**
University College London

**Will Martin**
Development Research Group, World Bank

**Warwick J. McKibbin**
The Australian National University and The Brookings Institution

**Alex Meeraus**
GAMS Development Corporation, Washington DC

**Dominique van der Mensbrugghe**
Food and Agriculture Organization of the United Nations

**William Nordhaus**
Department of Economics and Cowles Foundation, Yale University and the National Bureau of Economic Research

**Brian R. Parmenter**
Queensland Competiton Authority

**Ken Pearson**
Centre of Policy Studies, Monash University

**Maureen T. Rimmer**
Centre of Policy Studies, Monash University

**Sherman Robinson**
International Food Policy Research Institute (IFPRI)

**Thomas F. Rutherford**
Agricultural and Applied Economics, University of Wisconsin—Madison

**Luc Savard**
GREDI, Department of Economics, Université de Sherbrooke

**Sebastian Schmidt**
Goethe University of Frankfurt and Institute for Monetary and Financial Stability

**Daniel T. Slesnick**
University of Texas, Austin

**Birger Strøm**
Research Department, Statistics Norway

**David G. Tarr**
World Bank

**Volker Wieland**
Goethe University of Frankfurt and Institute for Monetary and Financial Stability

**Peter J. Wilcoxen**
Syracuse University and The Brookings Institution

**Kun-Young Yun**
Yonsei University

**George R. Zodrow**
Economics Department and Tax and Expenditure Policy Program, Baker Institute for Public Policy, Rice University and Centre for Business Taxation, Oxford University

# PREFACE

The *Handbook of Computable General Equilibrium Modeling* was conceived at a lunch a few years ago that one of us had with Mike Intriligator. Mike likes a good story, especially if it involves economic analysis with a few unexpected twists. Computable general equilibrium (CGE) modeling is a great source of such stories. By the end of the lunch, Mike had suggested that CGE modeling needed its own Handbook in the prestigious *Handbooks in Economics* series that he edits with Ken Arrow.

We thank Mike for his enthusiastic support throughout the preparation of the CGE Handbook. We also thank Ken for his encouragement.

Preparation of a Handbook is not trivial. The first requirement is to persuade leading experts to participate. That we have done well on this task will be obvious to anyone familiar with CGE modeling who looks at our author list. Of course, getting agreement from top people to participate is only a necessary condition for an authoritative Handbook, not a sufficient one. Moving them from agreement to delivery is also required.

To facilitate this process we arranged a 3-day authors' conference. This was held in June 2011 at the World Bank headquarters in Washington, DC. A preliminary version of each chapter was presented by one of its authors. After the presentation, there was general discussion led by a discussion opener (an author of another chapter) who had read the draft chapter before the conference. Not only did the conference generate constructive feedback for authors, it was also effective in giving the whole project sufficient momentum to take it through to a successful completion. We thank the attending authors for their positive attitude to the conference. They gave considerable time and effort to it, and made their own arrangements regarding travel and accommodation expenses. We also thank Dominique van der Mensbrugghe for paving the way at the World Bank, and Kathy Rollins for a superb job in organizing the World Bank facilities to optimize productivity and comfort. The Centre of Policy Studies (CoPS) at Monash University paid for the conference meals and other venue charges. We thank CoPS Director, Philip Adams, for authorizing these expenditures and CoPS Administrative Officer, Louise Pinchen, for providing excellent logistical support.

All chapters were refereed, in most cases by authors of other chapters. We thank the referees for performing this valuable service. We especially thank Maureen Rimmer who took a heavy refereeing load and assisted in all aspects of our editorial work.

Scott Bentley and Kathie Paoni of Elsevier provided high-quality professional support. We thank them.

Both of us were students of Wassily Leontief. His input-output system was the pioneering contribution to empirical economy-wide modeling. We think that he would have been pleased with the contributions to this Handbook. They show how CGE modeling, built around his input-output table, has enormously broadened and deepened the application of economy-wide analysis.

**Peter B. Dixon**, *Monash University*
**Dale W. Jorgenson**, *Harvard University*
May 2012

# CHAPTER 1

# Introduction

**Peter B. Dixon\*, Dale W. Jorgenson\*\***
\*Centre of Policy Studies, Monash University
\*\*Harvard University

## 1.1 OVERVIEW

Computable general equilibrium (CGE) modeling is a challenging field. It requires mastery of economic theory, meticulous preparation of data and familiarity with underlying accounting conventions, knowledge of econometric methods, and an understanding of solution algorithms and associated software for solving large equation systems. However, the most important requirement is the ability to communicate. CGE modeling is primarily about shedding light on real-world policy issues. For CGE analyses to be influential, modelers must explain their results in a way that is comprehensible and convincing to their fellow economist, and eventually to policy makers.

While CGE modeling is challenging, it is also rewarding. CGE models are used in almost every part of the world to generate insights into the effects of policies and other shocks in the areas of trade, taxation, public expenditure, social security, demography, immigration, technology, labor markets, environment, resources, infrastructure and major-project expenditures, natural and man-made disasters, and financial crises. CGE modeling is the only practical way of quantifying these effects on industries, occupations, regions and socioeconomic groups.

In 2010, CGE modeling had its 50th birthday, marked by a celebration in Oslo commemorating the publication in 1960 of Leif Johansen's *A Multisectoral Study of Economic Growth*.[1] In that book, Johansen describes a 22-sector model of Norway which is generally recognized as the first CGE model. What distinguishes his model from other economy-wide models of that time is the explicit identification of behavior by separate agents. In Johansen's model, households maximize utility subject to their budget constraints, industries choose their inputs to minimize the costs of producing the level of output that will satisfy demand and capitalists allocate the economy's capital stock between industries so that rates of return reflect historical relativities. The behavior of these individual agents is coordinated through prices determined by interaction of demand and supply. In contrast to Johansen's multiple-agent approach, earlier and

---

[1] The papers presented at the celebration will be published at a special issue of the *Journal of Policy Modeling*.

© 2013 Elsevier B.V.
All rights reserved.

contemporaneous economy-wide models in the 1960s [e.g. the input-output and linear programming systems of Leontief (1936, 1941), and Sandee (1960) and Manne (1963)] visualized the economy as a single agent. In those models, the *economy* produced the output vector necessary to satisfy exogenous final demands or to optimize an economy-wide welfare function.

Fifty years on, CGE modeling is an established field. It has textbooks [e.g. Dervis *et al.,* (1982), Dixon *et al.,* (1992) and Burfisher (2011)], survey articles [e.g. Shoven and Whalley (1984), Robinson (1989), Bandara (1991), and Partridge and Rickman (1998, 2010)] and conference volumes [e.g. Kelley *et al.,* (1983), Scarf and Shoven (1984), Bergman *et al.,* (1990), and Mercenier and Srinivasan (1994)]. It is the subject of many monographs and journal articles, and provides the substance of thousands of consultancy reports. So what is added by the *Handbook of Computable General Equilibrium Modeling*?

This Handbook is not a textbook, a survey or a conference volume. It is a collection of chapters setting out the experience of leading CGE modelers. Each chapter contains essential knowledge but just as importantly, each chapter points to new horizons. As evidenced in the Handbook, CGE modeling embraces new problems as they arise in a real-world context. Important current focuses are aging, greenhouse gases and global financial imbalances.

In planning the Handbook we had a four-part structure in mind: single-country models; global models; technical aspects of CGE modeling covering data, parameter estimation, computation and validation, and current cutting-edge methodological areas. Broadly, this is how things worked out; but of course chapters that were initially planned for one section describe contributions that fit into other sections as well.

## 1.2 SINGLE-COUNTRY MODELS

Norway and Australia are the two countries in which CGE modeling has had its highest profile in policy formation. Both these countries have long-standing CGE modeling projects with continuous histories up to the present day. In Norway, the MSG (multi-sectoral growth) project located in the Norwegian government's statistical agency (Statistics Norway) goes back to Johansen in the 1960s. In Australia, the MONASH project, currently located in Monash University's Centre of Policy Studies, goes back to the setting up in the Australian government bureaucracy of the IMPACT project in 1975. The MSG and MONASH projects are related. The MONASH project adopted and extended Johansen's techniques and carried his style of CGE modeling to the rest of the world.

As explained in Chapter 2 by Peter Dixon, Bob Koopman and Maureen Rimmer, creation of the first MONASH model, ORANI, involved a series of enhancements to Johansen's model, including: (i) a computational procedure that eliminated Johansen's linearization errors without sacrificing simplicity, (ii) endogenization of trade flows by introducing into CGE modeling imperfect substitution between imported and domestic varieties (the Armington assumption), (iii) increased dimensionality allowing for policy-relevant detail such as transport margins, (iv) flexible closures, and (v) complex functional forms to specify production technologies. ORANI was a large-scale comparative statical model used in Australia's tariff debate of the 1970s. Modern MONASH models are dynamic. They have proved remarkably flexible and operate in numerous countries on a wide variety of policy issues. As well as broad theoretical features of MONASH models, the chapter covers data preparation and introduces the GEMPACK purpose-built CGE software, discussed in detail in Chapter 20.

To a large extent MONASH models have evolved to meet the needs of clients in government and business. The models can be used for four modes of analysis: historical, decomposition, forecast and policy. Historical simulations produce up-to-date data, and estimate trends in technologies, preferences and other naturally exogenous but unobservable variables. Decomposition simulations explain historical episodes and place policy effects in historical context. Forecast simulations provide baselines using extrapolated trends from historical simulations together with specialist forecasts. Policy simulations generate the effects of policies as deviations from baselines. To emphasize the practical orientation of MONASH models, the chapter starts with a MONASH-style policy story on the effects on the US economy of restricting the number of illegal immigrants working in the US. The story is told in a way that is typical of policy briefs provided by MONASH modelers to government-sector economic advisors. It is a *quantitative* story that exposes the main mechanisms and data items that drive the results but does not require advisors to have a CGE background. Among the factors identified in the story is the Occupation-mix effect. This is the idea that a reduction in low-skilled immigrant employment creates job vacancies for legal residents at the low-skilled end of the occupational ladder, while closing off vacancies at the top end. In the long run, this causes a deterioration in the occupational mix of employment of legal US residents.

In Chapter 3, Erling Holmøy and Birger Strøm consider applications of MSG6, the most recent version of the MSG model of Norway originally developed by Leif Johansen (1960, 1974). Holmøy (2012) has traced the development of successive generations of the MSG model over the past half century. Although the different versions of MSG have common features, such as integration with the Norwegian national accounts and an emphasis on long-term trends, the current version bears relatively little resemblance to Johansen's model. In place of constant returns to scale and perfect competition for individual industries, as in Johansen's approach, individual industries in MSG6 are modeled as imperfectly competitive with increasing returns to scale. Second, the model incorporates a detailed microsimulation model for Norway in order to capture the role of changing demographics and the distributional impact of alternative policies.

Holmøy and Strøm consider applications of MSG6 to assessments of the fiscal sustainability of government tax and spending programs in Norway. Despite Norway's massive revenues from the sale of petroleum and natural gas in buoyant international markets, the Norwegian economy faces a severe problem of fiscal sustainability in the future. This can be traced to the relatively high level of government services, the aging of the Norwegian population and the eventual depletion of oil and gas resources. This finding is robust to variations in assumptions about productivity growth, the level of petroleum prices, longevity of the Norwegian population, immigration policies and health of the elderly. The authors emphasize the crucial role of general equilibrium effects in the outcomes of the policy simulations. General equilibrium modeling is particularly important for distinguishing between the transitory impact of large petro-leum revenues and the long-term effects of an aging population on the Norwegian economy.

Apart from public sector institutions in Norway and Australia, another institution that has had a long-standing involvement in CGE modeling is the World Bank. Chapters 4, 5 and 6 discuss some of the Bank's current and past single-country CGE modeling. Later chapters (Chapters 13, 14 and 21) cover the Bank's contributions to global modeling.

In Chapter 4, Hans Lofgren, Martin Cicowiez and Carolina Diaz-Bonilla describe the World Bank's program to develop a standardized modeling approach for assessing progress toward the Millennium Development Goals (MDGs). These goals were established at the UN Millennium Summit in 2000, and called for halving poverty rates, achieving universal primary education, reducing under-5 and maternal mortality rates, and reducing the share of the population without access to improved sources of water and sanitation, all by 2015. In 2004 the World Bank established the MAMS (Maquette for MDG Simulations) framework for CGE modeling of the MDGs and launched a pilot project for Ethiopia. This framework has now been applied to more than 40 countries by the World Bank staff, the staff of the UN Department of Social and Economic Affairs and national researchers in emerging economies. Applications have been extended beyond the MDGs to include alternative targets, additional issues and longer time horizons.

Lofgren, Cicowiez and Diaz-Bonilla describe the MAMS framework, its imple-mentation in the GAMS software package and the development of an Excel-based front end to make the model results accessible to a wider range of users. A major finding from cross-country comparisons is that achievement of the MDGs is heavily dependent on each country's initial situation. This leads to the conclusion that countries may be better off pursuing country-specific goals for poverty reduction and human development. A relatively balanced development program consisting of public infrastructure and human development services generates the most desirable outcomes. Second, a focus on human development programs such as education and health generates large demands for highly educated labor and undesirable distributional effects. The MAMS framework has also been used to analyze the potential for currency appreciation from foreign aid that could undermine competitiveness. The authors present a relatively detailed model for Yemen to illustrate the CGE approach and its application to development policy.

Chapter 5 is a reflective piece by Shanta Devarajan and Sherman Robinson. It draws on their long experience in applying CGE models in developing countries on behalf of the World Bank and other organizations. The chapter provides a taxonomy of CGE models (stylized versus detailed; static versus dynamic; recursive versus perfect foresight) and identifies model characteristics necessary for addressing different policy problems in developing countries. The chapter then discusses the ways in which CGE models have been used in policy formulation and the lessons learned from past experience. An interesting conclusion is that the process of policy making in many developing countries is becoming more democratic and that this should change the way in which CGE models are used. Rather than being a tool purely for government technocrats, CGE models should become relevant and accessible to different groups in the political/economic debate. This may require modelers for developing countries to broaden the range of questions they address and to rethink their communication strategies.

Chapter 6 by David Tarr describes a World Bank CGE-based study on Russian accession to the World Trade Organization (WTO). The chapter starts with a stylized model in which services in a country are produced by domestic-owned and foreign-owned firms located in the country. The foreign-owned firms have a much more efficient technology than domestic-owned firms. However, domestic-owned firms can survive because foreign-owned firms face extremely high discriminatory taxes and red-tape requirements. When discrimination is removed, foreign-owned firms drive out domestic firms. Large welfare benefits result. Having established his main ideas via the stylized model, Tarr moves on to a detailed empirical model. Simulations with the detailed model show that the major benefit of WTO accession for Russia would be liberalization of foreign direct investment, allowing highly efficient foreign service providers to dramatically expand their operations. The projected welfare gains generated from improved service provision are about 5% of GDP, with the total benefits of all aspects of WTO accession being about 7% of GDP. As with Devarajan and Robinson in Chapter 5, Tarr emphasizes the importance of effective public communication. He cites evidence of the impact of the World Bank study on moving public opinion in favor of WTO accession.

In many countries, especially federations, the regional dimension is a key aspect in the discussion of economic policies. Consequently, in countries such as Australia, Canada and the US, an early development in national CGE modeling was the creation of facilities for working out the implications of policies for states and provinces. Chapter 7 is a comprehensive introduction to and survey of regional CGE modeling. In this chapter, James Giesecke and John Madden start with a discussion of applications. They distinguish between those concerned with national shocks, such as changes in tariffs, for which top-down (national to regional) methods are adequate and those concerned with region-specific shocks, such as major events in particular states, for which bottom-up (regional to national) methods are required. Bottom-up modeling introduces theoretical and data challenges in the handling of interregional trade and factor mobility, cross-border ownership of productive assets, the regional location of margin providers, intergovernmental finances and agglomeration economies. A "typical" multiregional CGE model is set out in the chapter to explain how these challenges are being met. Throughout the chapter, Giesecke and Madden emphasize result interpretation. They demonstrate the use back-of-the-envelope (BOTE) models to explain results from regional CGE calculations and show how intuitive explanations can be deepened and checked through regression analyses.

Chapters 8 and 9 describe CGE models for the US and Australia that have been used in high profile studies of climate policies.

In Chapter 8, Dale Jorgenson, Richard Goettle, Mun Ho and Peter Wilcoxen present their Intertemporal General Equilibrium Model (IGEM) for analyzing energy and environmental policies in the US. This model has been employed in a series of policy studies by the US Environmental Protection Agency. A distinctive feature of the IGEM model is that the behavioral responses of producers and consumers to changes in policy are obtained from econometric estimates. The econometric methods used in IGEM are discussed in more detail in Chapter 17. Jorgenson, Goettle, Ho and Wilcoxen compare a base-case simulation of the US economy, based on no change in energy and environmental policies, with alternative cases corresponding to specific policy changes. They evaluate these policy changes by means of equivalent variations in the wealth of individual households. These are defined in terms of differences between the wealth required to achieve the time path of lifetime consumption under the policy case with the wealth required under the base case, both evaluated at prices of the base case. If the difference is positive, the policy change can be recommended for implementation; if not, the current policy is preferred and no change in policy is recommended.

Jorgenson, Goettle, Ho and Wilcoxen focus on market-based environmental policies, such as environmental taxes or tradable permits. Each policy regime corresponds to an intertemporal equilibrium of the US economy. This consists of a market equilibrium between supply and demand for commodities and factors of production achieved through the price system. Markets can be extended by incorporating environmental taxes or tradable emissions permits. Supply—demand balance in each period is linked to similar balances in future periods by arbitrage conditions that assure equality between the current price of an asset and the present value of its future services. Supply—demand balance is linked to the past through the accumulation of assets from past investments. Heterogeneity of energy producers and consumers is critical for the evaluation of energy and environmental policies. To capture this heterogeneity it is necessary to distinguish among different commodities, industries and households. Econometric methods are particularly useful for summarizing information on different industries and different consumer groups in a form suitable for policy evaluation.

In Chapter 9, Philip Adams and Brian Parmenter use a CGE model to project the effects for Australia of entering a worldwide emissions trading scheme. Their chapter emphasizes the importance in the policy process of identifying winners and losers. They achieve the required level of detail for doing this in three ways.

First, they start with a bottom-up regional model for Australia that already has an impressive level of detail: 50 industries operating in each of eight regions. This work-horse model is supplemented by a top-down facility for projecting results from the eight regions to 57 subregions and by a subsidiary dataset of carbon dioxide emissions by industry. The workhorse model generates a year-on-year baseline informed by forecasts from organizations concerned with various aspects of the economy and by trends in industry technologies, consumer tastes and world trading conditions. Policy effects are generated as deviations from the baseline. Second, they modify the workhorse model in various ways to enhance its ability to encapsulate greenhouse issues. For example, they disaggregate electricity generation into six industries defined by fuel input. Third, they make links between the workhorse model and two other models: a specialist electricity model, which provides baseline paths and policy responses for several electricity variables, and a global model, which generates projections for the world price of carbon dioxide emissions. The chapter is an example of CGE modeling at its practical best. It shows how CGE modeling can support a comprehensive study of a real-life policy issue. By embedding in their CGE framework information from specialist models, Adams and Parmenter produce analysis with high credibility and widespread acceptance in policy circles.

In Chapter 10, Dale Jorgenson and Kun-Young Yun present an intertemporal general equilibrium model of the US economy for evaluating alternative tax reforms. The model has similar features to the IGEM model described in Chapter 8, but radically simplifies the analysis of tax policy by including only a single production sector and a single representative consumer. In the US, as in many other countries, income from corporate assets is taxed at both the corporate and the individual level, income from non-corporate assets is taxed at the individual level, and income from owner-occupied housing is not taxed at all.

Differences in tax policy are incorporated in the model by distinguishing among corporate, non-corporate and household capital services. For each reform proposal an intertemporal price system clears markets for outputs of consumption and investment goods and inputs of capital and labor services. This price system links the past and the future through markets for investment goods and capital services. The government sector is coupled to the commodity markets through the tax system. Parameters that describe the economic responses of households and businesses to changes in tax policy are estimated econometrically.

Jorgenson and Yun illustrate their approach to policy evaluation by comparing proposals that would remove barriers to efficient allocation of capital and labor inputs. They have analyzed the economic impact of major US tax legislation, such as the Tax Reform Act of 1986, as well the potential impact of alternative tax reform proposals. These proposals are based on two broad approaches to reform: (i) to remove discrepancies in the tax treatment of different categories of income and (ii) to shift the tax base from income to consumption. Jorgenson and Yun identify Efficient Taxation of Income as the most effective approach to tax reform. This involves equalizing tax burdens on business and household assets, especially income on assets held in the corporate sector and the imputed income from owner-occupied housing. A second feature of Efficient Taxation of Income is that the graduated tax on labor income would be replaced by a proportional tax and equity would be preserved by imposing different tax rates on capital and labor incomes. Another effective approach would be to substitute a European-style value-added tax for the corporate and personal income taxes, but this would involve a serious loss in equity.

In Chapter 11, John Diamond and George Zodrow present their dynamic, overlapping generations (OLG) CGE model for the analysis of the economic effects of tax reforms. This model is especially well-suited to analyzing both the short-run transitional and the long-run dynamic macroeconomic effects of these reforms. These effects include changes in the time paths of labor supply, saving and investment induced by changes in tax policy, as well as the distributional effects of these reforms within and across generations. This important line of research was initiated by the seminal contribution of Auerbach and Kotlikoff (1987). This work has been extended to include multiple goods and multiple individuals by Fullerton and Rogers (1993), and now includes the analysis of open economies, human capital accumulation and economic uncertainty discussed in Chapter 27. The application of OLG models has focused on changes in capital income taxation, especially on the replacement of capital income taxes by a consumption-based tax system.

Diamond and Zodrow describe their model in considerable detail. This is characterized by 55 age cohorts with 12 income groups within each cohort. The model includes four production sectors and provides explicit calculations for changes in asset values resulting from changes in tax policy. This is particularly valuable for the analysis of the substitution of a consumption-based tax for income taxes, which could produce a substantial fall in the value of residential housing. The chapter includes numerous applications of the Diamond–Zodrow model to important issues in tax policy. Examples range from incremental reforms in specific provisions of tax law to substantial changes in tax policy, such as deficit-financed tax cuts like those instituted in the US in the early years of the George W. Bush Administration. Diamond and Zodrow analyze the effects of substituting a consumption tax for individual and corporate income taxes. They also consider the addition of a consumption-based value-added tax to the existing system of income taxes as a means of reducing government deficits and slowing or reversing the increase in US government debt.

## 1.3 GLOBAL MODELS

Analysis of several major contemporary issues including: climate change, multilateral and bilateral trade agreements, immigration, and international financial imbalances, can benefit from a global perspective. CGE modelers have responded over the last twenty years with several multicountry model-building projects. Chapters 12–16 describe some of these efforts.

Chapter 12 by Tom Hertel describes GTAP (Global Trade Analysis Project) run at Purdue University. This is a remarkable project operating on a small budget with limited staff. It provides a global database for 113 countries (or in some cases regions) and 57 sectors. The data include input-output tables for each country, trade flows, tariffs and tariff equivalents of other trade restrictions, immigration flows, and greenhouse gas emissions. Since the inception of the project in 1992, the number of people participating in it as users of GTAP data and models, as contributors of data, and as presenters at GTAP conferences has grown rapidly. The GTAP network now includes 10,000 people from almost every country in the world. Surely it must be the largest cooperative network of researchers ever assembled in economics. Hertel describes the profound influence that the GTAP has had on trade negotiations and policy and its spreading influence in the area of climate policy negotiations. He also describes how the GTAP data and model are being used by economists working at the cutting edge of developments in trade theory.

The obvious question is: how did GTAP happen? Hertel credits Alan Powell and his IMPACT Project in Australia as an inspirational force in the organization of GTAP. He also credits technical developments in Australia [particularly the SALTER global model, which was derived from the first MONASH-style model (see Chapter 2) and was implemented using GEMPACK software (see Chapter 20)] as giving him a great starting point. He outlines the GTAP strategy of providing a unifying database but encouraging the creation of many models that use that database. The development of these models, focusing on aspects of the world economy of interest to particular organizations and researchers, is facilitated by the provision of a generic GTAP model. Hertel and his colleagues have emphasized openness and the provision of training. They have combined this with early and effective use of the worldwide web as a communication medium.

In Chapter 13, Kym Anderson, Will Martin and Dominique van der Mensbrugghe describe their DAI (Distortions to Agricultural Incentives) database that quantifies tariffs on imports as well as subsidies and taxes on exports and production for many countries and commodities. They compare the DAI and GTAP databases on trade-distorting policies by conducting a series of simulations with LINKAGE (a global CGE model that has been used for the past decade by the World Bank in preparing growth and trade projections for the world economy, see Chapter 14). The LINKAGE results show the effects of removing distortions as represented in the two databases. The results cover a wide variety of variables including welfare and poverty effects by country and region. A striking feature of the results is the dominance of agriculture in trade distortions.

The chapter emphasizes three points regarding simulations of trade liberalization in global CGE models: (i) accurate representation of trade-distorting policies is necessary, (ii) it is important to think about where trade-distorting policies would go in the absence of trade liberalization—it is not clear that the no-change baseline assumption is appropriate and (iii) aggregation matters. Analysts using global CGE models are restricted to about 60 commodity categories within which distortions applying to subcommodities may differ widely. Anderson, Martin and van der Mensbrugghe discuss the aggregation problem and show its importance by comparing results from liberalization simulations in which category tariff rates reflect fixed import weights with simulations in which optimal variable-weight tariff rate aggregation is used.

In Chapter 14, Dominique van der Mensbrugghe presents the ENVISAGE model of the world economy. ENVISAGE is a successor of LINKAGE (see Chapter 13), which served as the macro/industry component of the World Bank's GIDD model (see Chapter 21) for analyzing the evolution of world income distribution. ENVISAGE is a recursive-dynamic CGE model, but does not generate an intertemporal equilibrium like the models discussed in Chapters 8, 10 and 11. It is calibrated to the GTAP database described in Chapter 12. The current version of this database, release 7.1, has a base year of 2004, provides 57-sector input-output tables for 113 regions/countries and contains detailed data on bilateral trade among all these regions/countries. ENVISAGE and related models have been used to analyze international trade, the Doha Development Agenda and structural change in the world economy. The model has also been employed to construct forward-looking scenarios for agriculture and energy, to analyze the regional implications of international migration, and to study climate change and its potential impacts on the world economy.

The main application described by van der Mensbrugghe in Chapter 14 is the development of forward-looking scenarios for agriculture in the light of the sharp rise in world food prices in 2007/2008 that preceded the financial and economic crisis of 2007—2009. Construction of a forward-looking scenario for world agriculture begins with world population projections prepared by the UN. These are used to project growth of the labor force for all regions/countries. Productivity growth for agriculture is based on modeling by the International Food Policy Research Institute (IFPRI). In the baseline scenario for world agriculture presented in Chapter 14, food prices rise and land use increases in response to growth in world income and changed patterns of consumption. This reverses a long-term trend toward lower food prices in inflation-adjusted terms. These conclusions are robust to changes in assumptions about population growth, land use and agricultural productivity growth. Chapter 14 concludes with a brief discussion of applications of ENVISAGE to the analysis of climate policy.

Warwick McKibbin and Peter Wilcoxen present their G-Cubed model for analyzing energy and environmental policy in Chapter 15. This is a multiregion, multicommodity, intertemporal general equilibrium model of the world economy. In each period the model links economic activity in twelve subregions of the world economy through bilateral trade flows. Like the models presented in Chapters 8, 10 and 11, the G-Cubed model contains forward-looking links among supply−demand balances at different periods of time through rational expectations about asset prices. The model also contains backward-looking links through capital accumulation resulting from past investments. From the point of view of international trade theory, an innovative feature of the model is the distinction between physical and financial capital for each region. Financial capital is perfectly mobile among regions and investment is driven by forward-looking investors who respond to arbitrage possibilities. Physical capital, by contrast, is perfectly immobile once installed. An intertemporal budget constraint is imposed on trade for each country, so that trade deficits must eventually be repaid by accumulating trade surpluses. Saving and investment in each region of G-Cubed are determined by forward-looking households that optimize intertemporal utility functions and forward-looking investors that maximize the stock market value of their equity. Another distinctive feature of G-Cubed is that parameters describing economic behavior are determined by econometric estimation rather than calibration. Finally, G-Cubed incorporates important features of macroeconomic models such as liquidity-constrained agents, a transaction-based money demand function and slow nominal wage adjustment. These features are also included in the dynamic stochastic general equilibrium (DSGE) models discussed in Chapter 22.

The G-Cubed model has been used extensively in analyzing the impacts of climate policies on the world economy. These impacts include changes in trade patterns and capital flows. McKibbin and Wilcoxen have shown that trading in global emissions permits the possibility of greenhouse gases, like those considered in the Kyoto Protocol, producing dramatic transfers in wealth among regions. These could lead to substantial capital flows as different regions react to changes in world climate policy. G-Cubed has also been used to simulate the effects on the world economy of a variety of other policies, including international trade agreements, monetary and fiscal policies, and, most recently, the impacts of financial and economic crises on subregions of the world economy and the world economy as a whole.

In Chapter 16, William Nordhaus presents integrated assessment models (IAMs) of the world economy employed for evaluating alternative climate policies. These models integrate global economic models with physical models of the global atmosphere. The two types of models interact through the generation of emissions of greenhouse gases, such as carbon dioxide, from economic activity. These emissions effect temperatures through the well-known greenhouse effect. The resulting changes in temperature and in patterns of precipitation effect future levels of economic activity. The chapter begins with a brief overview of the physical basis for climate change. This leads to a consideration of climate policies and their likely effects. These policies include two of the principal international agreements on climate change, the Kyoto Protocol, also discussed in Chapter 15, and the Copenhagen Accord of 2009. With this essential background Nordhaus turns to economic modeling of climate change using IAMs. The economic components of these models are increasingly based on CGE models with features that capture economic behavior over the time horizon relevant for the evaluation of climate policies. The physical components of IAMs are summary representations of elaborate global circulation models used for simulations of future changes in the global atmosphere.

To illustrate the construction and application of IAMs, Nordhaus provides a detailed discussion of the DICE/RICE family of models that he originated. The DICE model (Dynamic Integrated model of Climate and the Economy) is based on a neoclassical growth model with a single sector representing the world economy. Investments in capital reduce current consumption, but provide enhanced opportunities for future consumption. The novel feature of the DICE model is the incorporation of the natural capital of the climate system. By reducing emissions of greenhouse gases today, the world economy sacrifices current consumption in order to maintain future levels of consumption. Nordhaus has used this model and the closely related RICE (Regional Integrated model of Climate and the Environment) to evaluate alternative climate policies, including the Kyoto Protocol and the Copenhagen Accord. A general finding is that the range of climate policies that produce benefits that exceed the costs is relatively limited. Many climate policies actively under discussion have costs that exceed the benefits. Nordhaus has also designed optimal policies, i.e. policies that maximize an intertemporal social welfare function. He has shown how to implement these policies using a carbon tax or tradable permits for emissions of greenhouse gases. Finally, using the RICE model, Nordhaus has analyzed the likely outcomes of negotiations among subregions of the world economy to arrive at international agreements on climate policy.

## 1.4 TECHNICAL ASPECTS OF CGE MODELING: DATA, PARAMETER ESTIMATION, COMPUTATION AND VALIDATION

Behind any policy-relevant CGE result is an enormous amount of background work on data, estimation and computation. Ideally, the result is also supported by model validation. In the early days, each modeling group performed all this background work itself. Nowadays, modelers are often able to draw on shared resources. One such resource is the GTAP database described in Chapter 12. Chapters 17—20 discuss other background efforts required to support CGE modeling: econometric parameter estimation, validation and software creation.

Chapter 17 by Dale Jorgenson, Hui Jin, Daniel Slesnick and Peter Wilcoxen and Chapter 18 by Russell Hillberry and David Hummels are devoted to econometric methods for general equilibrium modeling. However, it must be recognized at the outset that calibration of the parameters that determine behavioral responses to economic policy changes is much more common than econometric estimation. This is due in part to the lack of suitable data for econometric modeling of production. However, this obstacle is beginning to disappear with the rapid development of comprehensive datasets for individual industries within the framework of a time series of input–output tables, so-called capital-labor-energy-materials-services (KLEMS) datasets. These are now available for more than 40 countries and many countries, including the US, have incorporated these datasets in their systems of national accounts. Another important source of data for general equilibrium modeling of preferences is cross-section and panel datasets for individual households. These datasets are particularly valuable in capturing the heterogeneity of consumer behavior that is a common finding in microeconometric research.

In Chapter 17, Jorgenson, Jin, Slesnick and Wilcoxen present econometric methods for modeling producer behavior that have been implemented from a KLEMS-type dataset for the US for the period 1960–2006. These methods facilitate the separation of substitution among inputs from technical change as sources of variations in patterns of output, input and productivity for the industrial sectors of IGEM — the model presented in Chapter 8. Technical change is separated into components associated with the rate and biases of technical change. The rate of technical change is defined as the rate of decline of the price of output, holding the prices of the inputs constant. Biases are changes in the shares of inputs in the value of output, again holding the prices of inputs constant. Jorgenson, Jin, Slesnick and Wilcoxen also present econometric methods for modeling consumer behavior. These methods incorporate demographic characteristics of households as determinants of their expenditure patterns. Aggregation over the population transforms the demographic characteristics into the relative shares of different consumer groups in determining aggregate expenditure. Additional determinants include prices and statistics that describe the distribution of total expenditure.

An important ancillary benefit of econometric methods for general equilibrium modeling is that confidence intervals for the outcomes of policy simulations can be derived from econometric estimates of parameters that describe economic behavior. These confidence intervals make it possible to formulate and test the implications of general equilibrium models as statistical hypotheses. Jorgenson, Jin, Slesnick and Wilcoxen illustrate this approach in Chapter 17 by deriving confidence intervals for the outcomes of IGEM simulations. These confidence intervals must be carefully distinguished, for the intervals describe ranges for model outcomes corresponding to different parameter values and different values of the exogenous variables. These ranges reflect the sensitivity of the model outcomes to the underlying determinants but do not involve probability statements. Confidence intervals are associated with probability statements that can be used as the basis for statistical tests and, at least potentially, can provide a powerful new methodology for testing the specifications of general equilibrium models.

In Chapter 18, Hillberry and Hummels point out that CGE models of international trade typically rely on econometrically estimated trade elasticities as model inputs. Major trade-focused CGE models draw elasticities from many different econometric studies. These econometric studies use very different data samples, response horizons and estimating techniques, and arrive at elasticities as much as an order of magnitude different from each other. There is no consensus on which elasticities to use. Hillberry and Hummels review the literature on estimating trade elasticities, focusing on several key considerations: what are the identifying assumptions used to separate supply and demand parameters? What is the nature of the shock to prices employed in the econometrics? And what is the time horizon over which trade responds to this shock? The discussion in Chapter 18 ranges from older reduced form approaches that use time-series variation in prices to more recent work that identifies demand elasticities from trade costs or uses instruments in cross-section or panel data. Hillberry and Hummels consider prominent applications that separately identify supply and demand parameters in the absence of instruments.

They also discuss recent theoretical developments from the literature on heterogeneous firms that complicate the interpretation of all the parameter estimates. They focus on Melitz (2003) who considers monopolistically competitive firms that have different levels of productivity and face fixed costs of domestic production and of exporting. The most productive firms choose to sell domestically and to export; less productive firms sell only to domestic markets and the least productive firms exit. An upward-sloping export supply curve arises through expansion of export sales via the entry of marginally less productive firms charging higher prices. Hillberry and Hummels briefly survey a literature on structural estimation and link this to recent attempts to incorporate such theories in CGE applications (see also Chapter 23). By elucidating the differences and similarities in various approaches to estimation they provide a useful guide to CGE practitioners in choosing elasticity estimates. The authors favor elasticities taken from econometric exercises that employ identifying assumptions and exploit shocks that are similar in nature to those imposed in the model experiment.

In Chapter 19, Peter Dixon and Maureen Rimmer discuss validation. This topic is a key issue for policy advisors who want to know how much reliance they can place on a particular CGE analysis. Many CGE modelers respond to the reliance question with numerical sensitivity computations. Dixon and Rimmer argue that what is really required is evidence that the analysis under consideration is based on accurate up-to-date data for the relevant part of the economy and adequately captures the crucial behavioral and institutional characteristics. They advocate the use of BOTE models. A well-designed BOTE model has two properties: (i) it reveals the roles of the major behavioral, institutional and data assumptions in causing a model to generate a given result, and (ii) it is small enough to be managed with pencil and paper (on the back of an envelope) and to be presented in a limited timeframe to policy advisors.

In addition to BOTE modeling, the chapter describes three other forms of validation. The first of these is computational validation. Dixon and Rimmer describe test simulations and demonstrate that the value of these simulations goes beyond computational checking. Test simulations are a practical way to become familiar with a model and often reveal modeling weaknesses. The second is consistency with history. Dixon and Rimmer focus on historical simulation. This is a technique whereby a CGE model is reconciled with periods of history by allowing it to determine endogenously movements in technologies, preferences and other shift variables. These implied movements can then be assessed against other information leading to a process of model improvement. The final form of validation discussed in the chapter is the testing of baseline forecasts against reality. The chapter demonstrates that CGE models can produce forecasts at a highly disaggregated level that comfortably beat non-model-based trend forecasts. It also demonstrates that there is considerable potential for more accurate CGE forecasts through conscientious data work and improved methods for projecting trends from historical simulations into forecasting simulations.

Chapter 20 describes and compares the two dominant general-purposes software platforms used for solving CGE models: GEMPACK and GAMS. These two rival platforms are represented in the authorship: Ken Pearson and Mark Horridge for the GEMPACK team and Alex Meeraus and Tom Rutherford for the GAMS team. It is to the credit of the two teams that they were able to cooperate to produce a fascinating chapter. Both GEMPACK and GAMS have made an enormous contribution to CGE modeling since the mid-1980s by largely relieving modelers of the burden of acquiring advanced computing skills and knowledge of solution algorithms. The platforms have also facilitated communication between modelers, allowing effortless transfers of models between sites.

CGE modelers are typically highly committed to their chosen platform, be it GEMPACK or GAMS. Vigorous debate with claims and counterclaims about the relative merits of the two platforms and their change or levels format are a perennial feature of CGE gatherings. This chapter will be compulsory reading for committed modelers. The chapter will also make interesting reading for non-CGE modelers who are contemplating a start in the field. To bring the chapter to life, the authors incorporated a comparison of computational speed between GEMPACK and GAMS. Both platforms were presented with a standard model. In the first comparison, the standard model was given 100 sectors and the respective platforms solved it to a required degree of accuracy. In seven more comparisons the sectoral dimension was gradually increased to 500. GEMPACK outperformed GAMS at all dimensions from 100 to 500 sectors with the time difference at high dimensions being dramatic. Of course, speed is not the only criterion for comparing software platforms. The chapter also discusses the ranges of model features (e.g. complementarity conditions) that can be handled by the two platforms and the available supplementary programs for preparing data and analyzing solutions.

## 1.5 CURRENT CUTTING-EDGE METHODOLOGICAL AREAS

There is a two-way flow of ideas and techniques between CGE modeling and other branches of economics. The final group of chapters in this Handbook surveys some of the areas from which CGE modeling is currently drawing inspiration, including trade theory with imperfect competition, DSGE modeling and the theory of labor markets. It also includes a pair of chapters showing how the CGE perspective, integrated with micro datasets, can contribute to the understanding of issues in income distribution, aging and social insurance.

In Chapter 21, Francois Bourguignon and Maurizio Bussolo present the World Bank's Global Income Distribution Dynamic (GIDD) model, combining a microsimulation model with the LINKAGE CGE model of the world economy (Chapters 13 and 14). Microsimulation models are based on survey data for individual households. These models have been used for studying reforms of tax-benefit systems, the delivery of public goods like education or healthcare, or changes in the regulation of the labor markets through alterations in the retirement age and the minimum wage or other policy instruments. The GIDD model includes survey data for 132 countries, covering more than 90% of the world population. Macroeconomic models are typically used to analyze the potential impact of reforms in tax, trade, finance or monetary policies on the structure of the economy, the level of employment and wages, and their distribution by skill levels and the returns to capital. By linking this aggregate information to the distributional detail of a microsimulation model, the distribution of gains and losses from policy changes can be analyzed.

Versions of the GIDD framework have been used to study the distributional effects of trade policy reforms, financial crises, reforms of the financial sector, subsidies on agricultural production prices, workfare programs, cash transfer programs and scaling up of other poverty alleviation policies, as well as others. Bourguignon and Bussolo emphasize that different variants of the model focus on different issues, such as behavioral responses, imperfections in markets and longer-term effects. The choice of the model depends on the policy issue under consideration. For example, in analyzing the short-term impact of reductions in tariffs, a static CGE model linked to simple micro accounting may be the best methodological choice. The interaction of trade liberalization with labor markets, sectoral adjustment of the economy, and the growth and distribution effects of trade reform may require a dynamic model. Bourguignon and Bussolo illustrate the application of the GIDD model to the projection of the world distribution of income in 2030. They find that even with significant changes of within-country inequality levels, the potential reduction of global inequality can be accounted for mainly by the projected convergence in growth rates of average incomes across countries. The aggregate impact of the changes of the within-countries component of inequality appears to be minor. The main cause of changes in within-country inequality is adjustment of factor rewards.

In Chapter 22, Sebastian Schmidt and Volker Wieland present a detailed introduction to the construction and estimation of New Keynesian models and their applications in macroeconomic policy analysis. Two key ingredients of the New Keynesian model that distinguish it from traditional Keynesian models are that the decision rules of economic agents are based on optimization subject to constraints and agents' views of the future behavior of variables are formed under rational expectations. Agents' decision rules inevitably vary with changes in policy and this dependence becomes explicit in the system of reduced-form equations. The Lucas critique, named after Robert E. Lucas and formulated in Lucas (1976), criticizes policy evaluation exercises based on estimated reduced-form relationships that fail to recognize this dependence. Lucas argues that this type of econometric model is unsuitable for policy analysis because the estimated parameters are not policy-invariant. In Chapter 22, building blocks of current-generation DSGE models are discussed in detail. These models address the Lucas critique by deriving behavioral equations systematically from the optimizing and forward-looking decision making of households and firms subject to well-defined constraints. Finally, Schmidt and Wieland review a new approach to model comparison that helps to identify robust policies under model uncertainty. This comparative approach could also be of benefit to practical model-based policy making in other arenas including international trade, economic development and climate change.

In their chapter, Schmidt and Wieland present state-of-the-art methods for solving and estimating DSGE models, using standard software packages such as DYNARE. The chapter also provides a framework for model comparison along with a database that includes a wide variety of macroeconomic models. This offers a convenient approach for comparing new models to available benchmarks and for investigating whether particular policy recommendations are robust to model uncertainty. To illustrate this idea, the authors evaluate the performance of simple policy rules across a range of recently estimated models, including some with financial market imperfections. Medium- to large-scale DSGE models are routinely used by economists at central banks and international institutions to evaluate monetary and fiscal stabilization policies. In the course of the recent financial crisis commentators have criticized the DSGE approach for its failure to predict the financial turmoil and the implications for the real economy. Indeed, the type of models that were used prior to the crisis in general did not include a realistic treatment of the banking sector and the involved macroeconomic risks. In response to this criticism, proponents of the DSGE approach have started to enhance the existing benchmark models to allow for a more detailed treatment of financial market frictions and the role of the banking sector in causing and propagating shocks to the macroeconomy.

In Chapter 23, Ed Balistreri and Tom Rutherford set out the Krugman (1980) and Melitz (2003) models of international trade. These provide alternatives to the Armington (1969) specification which has been the standard in CGE models since its introduction via Australia's ORANI model in the 1970s (Dixon *et al.*, 1977, 1982). In earlier economy-wide trade-oriented models (e.g. Evans, 1972) imported and domestic varieties of a given commodity were treated as perfect substitutes. This led to "flip-flop"—import shares in domestic markets flipping between zero and one in response to seemingly minor changes in relative prices. By treating imported and domestic varieties as imperfect substitutes, the Armington specification dealt with this problem in a practical and empirically justified fashion.[2] Starting in the late 1980s, many modelers questioned the Armington specification. They were disappointed with Armington-based simulations that often show a welfare loss for a country that undertakes a unilateral reduction in tariffs, with the terms-of-trade loss outweighing the efficiency gain. Both the Krugman and Melitz specifications assume large-group monopolistic competition. This gives the potential for generating more favorable welfare results from a tariff cut than can be generated with the Armington specification. Under the Krugman specification, there are two additional sources of welfare change from a tariff cut: (i) cost reductions in the domestic economy through economies of scale and (ii) increased variety through extra imports (which may or may not be offset by a reduction in domestic varieties). Melitz adds another source of welfare change. In the Melitz model, tariff cuts can increase productivity by weeding out inefficient domestic firms.

Balistreri and Rutherford build a small-scale multicountry CGE model that incorporates the Melitz specification, with the Armington specification as a special case. Using this model, they compare results under the two specifications for the effects of tariff cuts and for climate policies. They find the use of the Melitz specification produces significantly different results from those obtained under the Armington specification. So far Melitz simulations have been conducted in small models with stylized parameter values. A major challenge remains to establish the empirical significance of the mechanisms in the Melitz approach.

Chapter 24 by Joe Francois, Miriam Manchin and Will Martin also explores imperfect competition in trade-oriented CGE modeling. In contrast to the large-group, monopolistic competition specifications of Chapter 23, Francois, Manchin and Martin focus on oligopoly specifications. For them, large-group, monopolistic competition is

---

[2] Early econometrics estimates of Armington elasticities were obtained at a detailed level by Alaouze (1976) and used in the ORANI model.

a special case. However, unlike Chapter 23, most of the discussion in Chapter 24 concentrates on the case of symmetrical firms within an industry (the Krugman case in which each firm produces its own variety but no firm is inefficient relative to other firms). Each of the symmetric firms within an industry prices according to the Lerner rule: the markup over marginal cost as a fraction of price is the reciprocal of the magnitude of the firm's perceived elasticity of demand for its product. Calibration for CGE modeling of perceived elasticities of demand and their relationship to the number of firms in an industry is discussed in detail. The calibration of marginal costs is also discussed. Another challenge that must be met in CGE modeling with oligopoly is the determination of pure profits. The chapter discusses this issue and suggests relationships between pure profits and the number of firms in an industry.

Francois, Manchin and Martin not only present calibration hints but they also provide computational hints and a discussion of some results from imperfect competition models. A valuable computational hint for modelers wanting to try imperfect competition/ increasing returns to scale specifications is to start with a vanilla perfect competition/ constant returns to scale model and then to introduce markups as phantom indirect taxes. This is also a hint for interpreting results. Understanding the equivalence[3] between indirect taxes and markups reflecting imperfect competition is the key to understanding why procompetitive, markup-reducing policies have strong positive effects on real wages.

In Chapter 25, Elizabeth Christen, Joe Francois and Bernard Hoekman discuss the treatment of services trade in a CGE framework. Services are a rapidly increasing component of international trade, now representing more than 20% of world trade on conventional measures and a considerably higher percentage if services sales by foreign affiliates are treated as trade. While trade in goods can be visualized in terms of trucks, ships and planes moving physical items across international borders, trade in services conjures up a more complex and varied picture. As set out in the General Agreement on Trade in Services (GATS), services trade can be classified into four modes: mode 1, in which neither suppliers (exporters) nor buyers (importers) are required to change their physical locations (e.g. call-center services supplied from India to US households); mode 2, in which the buyer travels to the country of the supplier to receive the service (e.g. international tourism); mode 3, in which the supplier provides the service through an affiliate or branch office in the buyer's country (e.g. foreign airline desk services at US airports); and mode 4, in which individuals temporarily move to the buying country to provide services (e.g. consulting services provided in the US by an employee of a firm based in Australia).

In the chapter, Christen, Francois and Hoekman describe barriers to services trade, pointing out that these are often less transparent than those that restrict goods trade. They

---

[3] Equivalence here refers to resource allocation effects not distributional effects.

then review CGE studies of the effects of lowering barriers to services trade. Such studies show that the welfare gains from liberalizing services trade are potentially greater than those which would flow from removing the remaining barriers to goods trade. They illustrate this point with a study of Italy, which complements the study of Russia in Chapter 6. For convincing CGE analysis of issues in services trade, the chapter emphasizes the importance of: (i) mobilizing detailed and accurate data, (ii) understanding the special circumstances that apply to trade in each type of service, (iii) taking account of the market structure of service industries in importing countries and (iv) distinguishing the effects of trade liberalization on dead-weight losses from those on rents. As an interesting example of the complexities of services trade, Christen, Francois and Hoekman mention the role of health insurance: policies that require home-country treatment inhibit trade in health services.

Chapter 26 by Stefan Boeters and Luc Savard is about the labor market in CGE models. In most models, the treatment of the labor market is rudimentary: either exogenous aggregate employment with an endogenous wage or an exogenous wage with endogenous aggregate employment. As argued by Boeters and Savard, these rudimentary approaches may be adequate for analyses of many policies, but not for those that impinge directly on labor supply such as changes in marginal income tax rates and immigration.

The chapter presents a portfolio of approaches for specifying the labor market in CGE models. It organizes the literature on the topic by starting with a discussion of the various economic issues that might motivate a desire to add labor market detail to a CGE model. Methodologies for doing this are then set out in three sections: (i) labor supply, (ii) labor demand, and (iii) coordination of labor demand and supply. Among other things, these sections provide detailed discussions on: modeling labor supply via a single representative household, multiple representative households and microsimulation; modeling labor demand via cost-minimizing problems with nested production functions distinguishing labor types by characteristics such as occupation, education, gender, age and part-time/full-time; and modeling labor market coordination and involuntary unemployment via search theory, efficiency wage and collective bargaining. The chapter will be a valuable resource for CGE modelers wishing to improve their modeling of the labor market within their own models.

In Chapter 27, Hans Fehr, Sabine Jokisch, Manuel Kallweit, Fabian Kindermann and Laurence Kotlikoff examine the micro- and macroeconomic effects of polices that affect different generations differently. For this purpose they use both closed- and open-economy CGE models that incorporate an OLG model similar to that presented in Chapter 11. The models illustrate the broad array of demographic, economic and policy issues that can be simultaneously incorporated within models of economic growth. The policy issues include country-specific tax, spending, social security, healthcare and deficit policies. The demographic issues comprise age- and country-specific mortality, age-specific fertility, age-specific morbidity, lifespan uncertainty, and age- and skill-specific emigration and immigration. Finally, economic issues embrace earnings inequality driven by skill differences and idiosyncratic labor earnings uncertainty, capital adjustment costs, international trade, international capital flows, trade specialization, and trade policy.

Fehr, Jokisch, Kallweit, Kindermann and Kotlikoff begin their chapter with an exposition of the dynamic OLG model of Auerbach and Kotlikoff (1987). They present two detailed applications. The first is with a single-country, closed-economy model characterized by an intertemporal equilibrium like that of Diamond and Zodrow (Chapter 11). This single-country model is calibrated for Germany and used to analyze the consequences of alternative pension reform proposals. The simulations demonstrate that increases in the retirement age under public pension programs are an important policy instrument for distribution of resources to future cohorts. The authors then turn to an open-economy model, featuring five regions—the US, Europe, Japan and other Asian countries, China, and India, producing six goods, some of which are traded. The transition path of this global model shows that government pay-as-you-go healthcare and pension systems in the developed countries will come under increasing stress requiring extraordinary increases in tax rates unless policies are significantly changed and done so quickly. The most obvious reform to overcome the effects of population aging is a partial or complete switch to a funded pension system. This induces the strongest redistribution toward future cohorts, and induces a significant increase in retirement ages and substantial reductions in future payroll and consumption taxes. A second major message from the model is that wage inequality in developed countries will substantially increase over the course of the century. As successive cohorts of Chinese and Indian workers reach the job market with higher levels of productivity in unskilled occupations, the worldwide effective endowment of unskilled workers rises relative to that of high skilled workers. This will put downward pressure on unskilled worker wages in the developed world thanks to factor price equalization.

## REFERENCES

Alaouze, C.M., 1976. Estimates of the Elasticity of Substitution between Imported and Domestically Produced Intermediate Inputs. IMPACT Preliminary Working Paper OP-07. Centre of Policy Studies, Monash University.

Armington, P.S., 1969. A theory of demand for products distinguished by place of production. IMF Staff Papers 16, 159—178.

Auerbach, A.J., Kotlikoff, L.J., 1987. Dynamic Fiscal Policy. Cambridge University Press, Cambridge.

Bandara, J.S., 1991. Computable general equilibrium models for development policy analysis in LDCs. J. Econ. Surv. 5, 3—69.

Bergman, L., Jorgenson, D.W., Zalai, E. (Eds), 1990. General Equilibrium Modeling and Economic Policy Analysis. Basil Blackwell, Oxford.

Burfisher, M., 2011. Introduction to Computable General Equilibrium Models. Cambridge University Press, New York.

Dixon, P.B., Parmenter, B.R., Ryland, G.J., Sutton, J., 1977. ORANI, a General Equilibrium Model of the Australian Economy: Current Specification and Illustrations of Use for Policy Analysis, Volume 2 of the First Progress Report of the IMPACT Project. Australian Government Publishing Service, Canberra.

Dixon, P.B., Parmenter, B.R., Sutton, J., Vincent, D.P., 1982. ORANI: A Multisectoral Model of the Australian Economy, Contributions to Economic Analysis 142. North-Holland, Amsterdam.

Dixon, P.B., Parmenter, B.R., Powell, A.A., Wilcoxen, P.J., 1992. Notes and Problems in Applied General Equilibrium Economics. North-Holland, Amsterdam.

Dervis, K., de Melo, J., Robinson, S., 1982. General Equilibrium Models for Development Policy. Cambridge University Press, Cambridge.

Evans, H.D., 1972 A General Equilibrium Analysis of Protection: The Effects of Protection in Australia. Contributions to Economic Analysis 76. North-Holland, Amsterdam.

Fullerton, D., Rogers, D.L., 1993. Who Bears the Lifetime Tax Burden? Brookings Institute Press, Washington, DC.

Holmøy, E. The development and use of CGE models in Norway. Journal of Policy Modeling, forthcoming.

Johansen, L., 1960. A Multisectoral Study of Economic Growth. Contributions to Economic Analysis 21. North-Holland, Amsterdam.

Johansen, L., 1974. A Multisectoral Study of Economic Growth, second enlarged ed. Contributions to Economic Analysis 21'. North-Holland, Amsterdam.

Kelley, A.C., Sanderson, W.G., Williamson, J.G. (Eds), 1983. Modeling Growing Economies in Equilibrium and Disequilibrium: Proceedings of the IIASA Meeting of November 1980. Duke University Press, Durham, NC.

Krugman, P., 1980. Scale economies, product differentiation and the pattern of trade. Am. Econ. Rev. 70, 950–959.

Leontief, W.W., 1936. Quantitative input-output relations in the economic system of the United States. Rev. Econ. Stat. 18, 105–125.

Leontief, W.W., 1941. The Structure of the American Economy 1919–1929. Harvard University Press, Cambridge, MA.

Lucas, R.E., 1976. Econometric policy evaluation: a critique. Carnegie-Rochester Conference Series on Public Policy 1, 19–46.

Manne, A.S., 1963. Key sectors of the Mexican economy 1960–1970. In: Manne, A.S., Markowitz, H.M. (Eds), Studies in Process Analysis. Wiley, New York, pp. 379–400.

Melitz, M.J., 2003. The impact of trade on intra-industry reallocations and aggregate industry productivity. Econometrica 71, 1695–1725.

Mercenier, J., Srinivasan, T.N. (Eds), 1994. Applied General Equilibrium and Economic Development: Present Achievements and Future Trends. University of Michigan Press, Ann Arbor, MI.

Partridge, M.D., Rickman, D.S., 1998. Regional computable general equilibrium modeling: a survey and critical appraisal. Int. Reg. Sci. Rev. 21, 205–248.

Partridge, M.D., Rickman, D.S., 2010. Computable general equilibrium (CGE) modeling for regional economic development analysis. Reg. Stud. 44, 1311–1328.

Robinson, S., 1989. Multisectoral models. In: Chenery, H., Srinivasan, T.N. (Eds), Handbook of Development Economics, Vol. 2. North-Holland, Amsterdam, pp. 885–947.

Sandee, J., 1960. A Long-Term Planning Model for India. Asia Publishing House, New York/(Statistical Publishing Company, Calcutta).

Scarf, H.E., Shoven, J.B. (Eds), 1984. Applied General Equilibrium Analysis. Cambridge University Press, New York.

Shoven, J.B., Whalley, J., 1984. Applied general-equilibrium models of taxation and international trade: an introduction and survey. J. Econ. Lit. 22, 1007–1051.

# CHAPTER 2

# The MONASH Style of Computable General Equilibrium Modeling: A Framework for Practical Policy Analysis

**Peter B. Dixon∗, Robert B. Koopman∗∗, Maureen T. Rimmer∗**
∗Centre of Policy Studies, Monash University
∗∗US International Trade Commission

## Abstract

MONASH models are descended from Johansen's 1960 model of Norway. The first MONASH model was ORANI, used in Australia's tariff debate of the 1970s. Johansen's influence combined with institutional arrangements in their development gave MONASH models distinctive characteristics, facilitating a broad range of policy-relevant applications. MONASH models currently operate in numerous countries to provide insights on a variety of questions including:

*the effects on:*

macro, industry, regional, labor market, distributional and environmental variables

*of changes in:*

taxes, public consumption, environmental policies, technologies, commodity prices, interest rates, wage-setting arrangements, infrastructure and major-project expenditures, and known levels and exploitability of mineral deposits (the Dutch disease).

MONASH models are also used for explaining periods of history, estimating changes in technologies and preferences and generating baseline forecasts. Creation of MONASH models involved a series of enhancements to Johansen's model, including: (i) a computational procedure that eliminated Johansen's linearization errors without sacrificing simplicity; (ii) endogenization of trade flows by introducing into computable general equilibrium (CGE) modeling imperfect substitution between imported and domestic varieties (the Armington assumption); (iii) increased dimensionality allowing for policy-relevant detail such as transport margins; (iv) flexible closures; and (v) complex functional forms to specify production technologies. As well as broad theoretical issues, this chapter covers data preparation and introduces the GEMPACK purpose-built CGE software. MONASH modelers have responded to client demands by developing four modes of analysis: historical, decomposition, forecast and policy. Historical simulations produce up-to-date data, and estimate trends in technologies, preferences and other naturally exogenous but unobservable variables. Decomposition simulations explain historical episodes and place policy effects in historical context. Forecast simulations provide baselines using extrapolated trends from historical simulations together with specialist forecasts. Policy simulations generate effects of policies as deviations from baselines. To emphasize the practical orientation of MONASH models, the chapter starts with a MONASH-style policy story.

*Handbook of CGE Modeling - Vol. 1 SET*
ISSN 2211-6885, http://dx.doi.org/10.1016/B978-0-444-59568-3.00002-X
© 2013 Elsevier B.V.
All rights reserved.

## Keywords

MONASH computable general equilibrium models, flexible closures, computable general equilibrium forecasting, policy-oriented modeling, telling a computable general equilibrium story, Johansen's computable general equilibrium influence

## JEL classification codes

C68, C63, D58, F16, F14

## 2.1 INTRODUCTION

This chapter describes the MONASH style of CGE modeling, which started with the ORANI model of Australia (Dixon *et al.*, 1977, 1982). MONASH models are directly descended from the seminal work of Leif Johansen (1960). The influence of Johansen combined with the institutional arrangements under which MONASH models have been developed has given them distinctive technical characteristics, facilitating a broad range of policy-relevant and influential applications. MONASH models are now operated on behalf of governments and private sector organizations in numerous countries, including Australia, the US, China, Finland, Netherlands, Malaysia, Taiwan, Brazil, South Africa and Vietnam.[1] The MONASH approach underlies the worldwide Global Trade Analysis Project (GTAP) network (see Chapter 12 by Hertel in this Handbook).

The practical focus of MONASH models reflects their history. ORANI was created in the IMPACT Project — a research initiative of the Industries Assistance Commission (IAC). The IAC was the agency of the Australian government with responsibility for advising policy makers on the economic and social effects of tariffs, quotas and other protective devices against imports.

To understand why the IMPACT Project was established and why it produced a model such as ORANI, we need to go back to the federation of the Australian colonies. Before federation in 1901, the dominant British colonies on the Australian continent were New South Wales, which followed a free trade policy, and Victoria, which adopted high tariffs against manufactured imports. After a heated debate,[2] the federated nation adopted what was close to the Victorian policy, setting protection of manufacturing industries at an average rate of about 23%. Protection increased during the 1930s and continued to rise after World War II, reaching rates of more than 50% for some industries. Resentments about protection persisted and intensified as rates rose, especially in the export-oriented state of Western Australia. By the 1960s,

---

[1] A complete technical exposition of a modern MONASH model is Dixon and Rimmer (2002) together with supporting web material at http://www.monash.edu.au/policy/monbook2.htm. See also Honkatukia (2009).

[2] See Glezer (1982, chapter 1).

Australia's protectionist stance was being challenged analytically by leading economists such as Max Corden (e.g. Corden, 1958) and by the 1970s, there was demand by policy makers for a quantitative tool for analyzing protection. Policy makers wanted to know how people whose jobs would disappear with lower protection could be reabsorbed into employment. The IAC responded in 1975 by setting up the IMPACT Project with the task of building an economy-wide model that could be used to trace out the effects of changes in protection for one industry on employment prospects for other industries.

The arrangements for the IMPACT Project maximized the probability of a successful outcome. It had a sharp focus on a major policy problem (protection), thereby attracting policy-oriented, ambitious economists. It had an outstanding initial director, Alan A. Powell, who was a highly respected applied econometrician. Without blunting its practical orientation, Powell conducted the Project at arms length from the bureaucracy. Under his leadership, IMPACT was an open environment that allowed talented young economists to flourish. The outcome was the ORANI model, the first version of which was operational in 1977. By providing detailed quantification of the effects of cuts in protection on winners as well as losers, and by showing where jobs would be gained as well as lost, ORANI helped in the formation of an anti-protection movement that eventually prevailed and converted Australia from high protection in the mid-1970s to having almost free trade by the end of the century.

With changes in political circumstances, the IMPACT Project left the IAC in 1979. The IMPACT team was split between the University of Melbourne and La Trobe University. Nevertheless, it continued to work as a group and in 1984 was reunited at the University of Melbourne. Since 1991 the team has operated as the Centre of Policy Studies (CoPS) at Monash University. Throughout its 37-year history, CoPS/IMPACT has maintained an extraordinary level of staff cohesion. Three researchers have been with the Project continuously for 37 years, six others have devoted more than 20 years to the Project, while many others have served more than 10 years. Seven researchers have been promoted at the Project to the rank of Full Professor. What explains the Project's success and longevity?

One factor is that since its beginning, when Powell set the standards, the Project has been an enjoyable place to work with high levels of cooperation between researchers and generous treatment of colleagues. A second factor is that the Project has generated a continuous stream of challenging, satisfying inter-related activities. These include: data management and preparation; formulation of solution algorithms; development of software; translation of policy questions into forms amenable to modeling; creation of theoretical specifications to broaden the range of CGE applications and improve existing applications; checking of model solutions; interpretation of results and deducing their policy significance; and delivery of persuasive reports.

The third and perhaps the most important factor underlying the Project's success and longevity is the adaptability of MONASH models, which are its main product. After the initial work on protection, these models have provided insights on an enormous variety of questions including:

*the effects on*:

macro, industry, regional, labor market, distributional and environmental variables

*of changes in:*

taxes, public consumption, social-security payments, environmental policies, technologies, international commodity prices, interest rates, wage-setting arrangements and union behavior, infrastructure and major-project expenditures, and known levels and exploitability of mineral deposits (the Dutch disease).

In addition, MONASH models are used for: explaining periods of history; estimating changes in technologies, consumer preferences and other unobservable variables; and creating baseline forecasts. With this flexibility of its central product, the Project has maintained the long-term interest of its researchers. Model flexibility has also been critical to the financing of the Project. Starting in the 1980s, the Project has been increasingly reliant on the sale of contract and subscription services. In 2010, these services accounted for 80% of the budget of CoPS, which had a professional and support staff of 20. Without application flexibility, CoPS could not have remained viable as a predominantly commercial entity within a university.[3]

The rest of this chapter is organized as follows. In Section 2.2 we tell a MONASH-style policy story. We start this way for four reasons.

**(i)** We want to emphasize that the primary purpose of MONASH models is practical policy analysis.

**(ii)** Before presenting technical details, we want to demonstrate the ability of MONASH models to generate policy-relevant results that can be communicated in a convincing way to people without CGE backgrounds.

**(iii)** We want to illustrate the technique of explaining CGE results in a macro-to-micro manner that avoids circularity. This requires finding an 'exogenous' starting point.

**(iv)** We want to motivate the study of CGE modeling by providing a thought-provoking analysis that illustrates its strengths.

Section 2.3 starts by outlining Johansen's model. It then describes Johansen's legacy to MONASH modelers. This includes: the representation of models as rectangular systems of linear equations in changes and percentage changes of the variables; a transparent solution procedure that directly generates a solution matrix showing the elasticities of endogenous variables with respect to exogenous variables; a mode of analysis and result

---

[3] More detailed accounts of the history of the IMPACT Project and its reincarnation at CoPS can be found in Powell and Snape (1993) and Dixon (2008).

interpretation built around the solution matrix; and the use of back-of-the-envelope (BOTE) models to aid interpretation and management of the huge volume of results that flow from a full-scale CGE model. The final part of Section 2.3 describes five innovations that were made in the journey from Johansen's model to ORANI: (i) implementation of a Johansen/Euler procedure that eliminates linearization errors without sacrifice of simplicity and interpretability; (ii) endogenization of trade flows by the introduction of imperfect substitution between imported and domestic varieties of the same commodity and downward-sloping foreign demand curves; (iii) vastly increased dimensionality that allows the incorporation of policy-relevant detail such as transport and trade margins; (iv) flexible closures; and (v) the use of complex functional forms such as CRESH to specify production technologies.

Section 2.4 is the most technically demanding part of the chapter. Sections 2.4.1 and 2.4.2 set out the mathematical structure of MONASH models. A supporting Appendix contains the mathematics that underlies the multistep Johansen/Euler solution procedure. Section 2.4.3 demonstrates that we can always find an initial solution for a MONASH model mainly via the input-output database. There is no need to explicitly locate this solution, but the fact that it exists means that derivative methods, such as the Johansen/Euler procedure, can be used to compute required solutions (i.e. solutions with required values for the exogenous variables). Section 2.4.4 shows how the percentage change equations that form Johansen's rectangular system are derived from levels equations. Section 2.4.5 is an overview of GEMPACK.[4] This suite of programs solves MONASH models, and is used for interrogating data and results. Section 2.4.6 discusses problems in transforming published input-output tables into databases for policy-relevant CGE models. We take as an example the transition from tables published by the Bureau of Economic Analysis (BEA) to a database for USAGE, a MONASH-style model of the US. Conventions and definitions adopted in published input-output tables vary from country to country. Consequently, the specifics of our experience are not immediately transferable outside the US. However, the general principle that CGE modelers need to work hard to understand input-output conventions is broadly applicable. Among other things, they need to figure out conventions adopted by their statistical agency concerning: valuations (basic prices versus producer prices versus purchasers prices); reconciliation with the national accounts; imports (direct or indirect allocation); investment (commodity versus industry); self-employment; and the treatment of imputed rents in housing.

Section 2.5 describes how MONASH models have evolved in response to demands by consumers of CGE modeling services. These consumers are concerned primarily with current policy proposals. From modelers they want results showing policy effects on finely defined constituent groups, not just effects on macro variables and coarsely defined sectors. They want results from models that have up-to-date data, detailed disaggregation

---

[4] GEMPACK is described fully in Horridge *et al.* in Chapter 20 of this Handbook.

and accurate representation of relevant policy instruments. In trying to satisfy these demands, MONASH modelers have developed four modes of analysis: historical, decomposition, forecast and policy. Historical simulations are used to produce up-to-date data for MONASH models as well as estimates of trends in technologies, preferences and other naturally exogenous but unobservable variables. Decomposition simulations are used to explain periods of history and to place the effects of policy instruments in an historical context. Forecast simulations provide a baseline picture of likely future developments in the economy using extrapolated trends from historical simulations and forecasts from specialists on different parts of the economy. Policy simulations generate the effects of policies as deviations from baseline forecasts.

Section 2.6 summarizes the main ideas in the chapter.

To a large extent the sections are self-contained. Consequently, readers can choose their own path through the chapter. Some of the material in Section 2.4, particularly Section 2.4.6 on input-output accounting, would be difficult to read passively straight through. Input-output conventions are important, but tortuous and slippery. We hope that by scanning this subsection readers will get an idea of what is involved. They may then find it useful to return to the material if they are constructing or assessing a detailed policy-relevant model.

## 2.2 TELLING A CGE STORY

One of our graduate students recently asked us how to cope with skeptics: who will not believe anything from a model unless all the parameters are estimated by time-series econometrics; who harp on about the input-output data being outdated; who highlight what they see as the absurdity of competitive assumptions and constant returns to scale; who insist that general equilibrium means that all markets clear, thus ruling out real-world phenomena such as involuntary unemployment; and who claim that, like a chain, CGE models are only as strong as their weakest part.

Our advice is to get the results up front. Do not start by telling the audience about general features of the model. The idea is to tell a story that is so interesting and engaging that general-purpose gripes about CGE modeling are at least temporarily forgotten in favor of genuine enquiry about the application under discussion. The assumptions that really matter for the particular application can then be drawn out. The aim is to lead the audience to an understanding of what specific things they need to believe about behavior and data if they are to accept the results and policy conclusions being presented.

Here, we will try to follow our own advice. We will tell a CGE story without explicitly describing the model. We will use BOTE calculations to identify assumptions and data items that matter for the results. We will rely on explanatory devices such as demand and supply diagrams that are accessible to all economists, not just those with a CGE background. Only when we have given an illustration of what a MONASH-style

CGE application can deliver will we turn our attention in the rest of the chapter to the technicalities of MONASH modeling.

Our illustrative CGE story concerns the effects on the US economy of tighter border security to restrict unauthorized immigration. This is a good CGE topic for two reasons. First, it is a contentious policy issue with many people in the political debate demanding greater government efforts to improve border security and reduce unauthorized immigration. Popular opinion is that unauthorized immigrants do economic damage to legal residents of the US by generating a need for increased public expenditures and by taking low-skilled jobs. However, these opinions may not be the whole story. This brings us to the second reason that tighter border security is a good CGE topic. To get beyond popular opinions we need to look at interactions between different parts of the economy (i.e. we need to adopt a general equilibrium approach). We need to quantify the effects of varying the supply of unskilled foreign workers; on wage rates and employment opportunities of US workers in different occupations; on output, employment and international competitiveness in different industries; on public sector budgets; and on macroeconomic variables including the welfare of legal US residents.

## 2.2.1 Tighter border security

In 2005 there were about 7.3 million unauthorized foreign workers holding jobs in the US, about 5% out of total employment of 147 million. On business-as-usual assumptions unauthorized employment was expected to grow to about 12.4 million in 2019, about 7.2% out of total employment of 173 million. As unauthorized immigrants have low-paid jobs, their share in the total wage bill is less than their employment share. In the business-as-usual forecast, their wage bill share goes from 2.69% in 2005 to 3.64% in 2019.

In our CGE policy simulation we analyze the effects of a reduction in unauthorized employment caused by a restriction in supply. Specifically, we imagine that starting in 2006 the US implements a successful policy of tighter border security that has a long-run effect (2019) of reducing unauthorized employment by 28.6%: from 12.4 million in the baseline (business-as-usual situation) to 8.8 million in the policy situation. We have in mind policies that increase the costs and dangers of unauthorized entry to the US. These policies are represented in our model as a preference shift by foreign households against US employment. However, the exact nature and size of the policy is not important. Our focus is on the long-run effects of a substantial reduction in supply of unauthorized employment, however caused.

### 2.2.1.1 Macroeconomic effects

In the long run, we would not expect a policy implemented in 2006 to have a significant effect on the employment rate of legal workers. Thus, we would expect the policy to reduce total employment in 2019 by about 3.6 million ($= 12.4 - 8.8$). That is, we would expect a reduction in total employment in the US of about 2.1% ($= 100 * 3.6/173$).

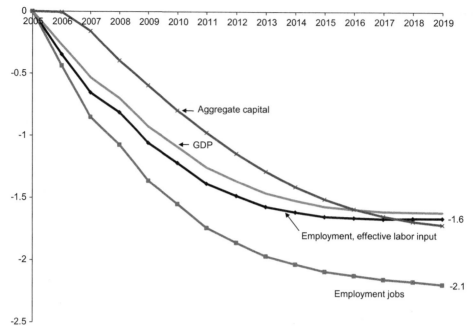

**Figure 2.1** GDP, employment and capital with tighter border security (percentage deviations from baseline).

This is confirmed by the 'Employment jobs' line in Figure 2.1 that shows results from our CGE model for the effects on employment of the tighter border security policy as percentage deviations from the business-as-usual forecast.

Higher up the page in Figure 2.1 we can see the line showing deviations in 'Employment, effective labor input'. In this measure, aggregate employment falls if the economy gains a job in a low-wage occupation but loses a job in a high-wage occupation. Under the assumption that wage rates reflect the marginal product of workers, deviations in effective labor input show the effects of a policy on the productive power of the labor input. With unauthorized immigrants concentrated mainly in low-wage occupations it is not surprising that Figure 2.1 shows smaller percentage reductions in effective labor input than in number of jobs. Whereas our tighter-border policy reduces jobs in the long run by 2.1%, it reduces effective labor input by only 1.6%.

In the long run, we would not expect a tighter border-security policy to have an identifiable effect on the US capital/labor ratio, that is the amount of buildings and machines used to support each unit of effective labor input. Underlying this expectation is the assumption that rental per unit of capital equals the value of the marginal product of capital:

$$\frac{Q}{P_g} = A * F_k\left(\frac{K}{L}\right), \tag{2.1}$$

where $Q$ is the rental rate for a unit of capital, $P_g$ is the price of a unit of output (the price deflator for GDP), $A$ represents technology, $K$ and $L$ are aggregate inputs of capital and effective labor, and $A * F_k$ is a monotonically decreasing function derived by differentiating an aggregate constant-returns-to-scale production function $[A * F(K,L)]$ with respect to $K$.

On the assumption that the cost of making a unit of capital (the asset price) moves in line with the price of a unit of output, the left-hand side of (2.1) is closely related to the rate of return on capital. In the long run we would not expect changes in border policy to affect rates of return.[5] These are determined by interest rates and perceptions of risk, neither of which is closely linked to border policy. Thus we would expect little long-run effect on the left-hand side of (2.1). On the right-hand side we would not expect any noticeable impact of border policy on US technology, represented by $A$. We can conclude that $K/L$ will not be affected noticeably by changes in border policy. This is confirmed in Figure 2.1 where the long-run reduction of 1.6% in effective labor input is approximately matched by the long-run percentage reduction in capital. Figure 2.1 shows that the long-run deviation in GDP is also about −1.6%. This is consistent with both $K$ and $L$ having long-run deviations of about −1.6%, together with our assumption that border policy does not affect technology ($A$).

Figure 2.2 shows the deviations in the expenditure components of GDP. In the long run these are all negative and range around that for GDP. The long-run deviations in private consumption, public consumption and imports are less negative than that for GDP while those for exports and investment are more negative than that for GDP.

We can understand these results as a sequence. The first element is that tighter border security improves the US terms of trade. This is a benefit from having a 1.6% smaller economy that demands less imports (thereby lowering their price) and supplies less exports (thereby raising their price). The second element is that terms-of-trade improvement allows private and public consumption to rise (as shown in Figure 2.2) relative to GDP. This is because an improvement in the terms of trade increases the prices of the goods and services produced by the US relative to prices of the goods and services consumed by the US, allowing the US to sustain a higher level of consumption for any given level of output (GDP).

The third element in understanding the long-run results in Figure 2.2 concerns investment. In the very long run, the change in immigration policy that we are considering will have little identifiable effect on the growth rate of labor input. Consequently it will have little effect on the growth rate of capital and therefore on the

---

[5] As will be explained shortly, there is a long-run increase in the terms of trade. Despite this, the cost of making a unit of capital (which includes import prices but not export prices) does not fall relative to $P_g$ (which includes export prices but not import prices). This is mainly because in the long run the construction industry suffers an increase in its labor costs relative to other industries reflecting its intensive use of unauthorized labor.

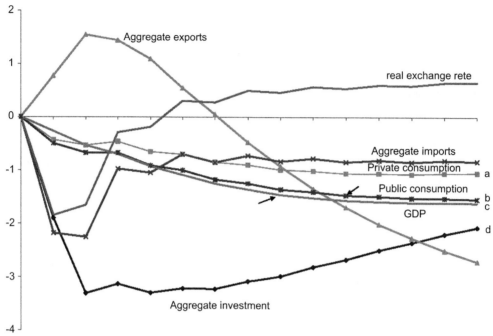

**Figure 2.2** Expenditure aggregates with tighter border security (percentage deviations from baseline).

ratio of investment to GDP.[6] As can be seen in Figure 2.1, the deviation line for capital is still falling slightly in 2019 indicating that the capital stock has not fully adjusted to the 1.6% reduction in labor input.[7] With capital still adjusting downwards in 2019, the investment to GDP ratio is still below its eventual long-run level. However, in terms of contributions to GDP, the positive gaps in 2019 between the consumption and GDP deviations outweigh the negative gap between the investment and GDP deviation (the **ac** and **bc** gaps in Figure 2.2 weighted by private and public consumption easily outweigh the **dc** gap weighted by investment). This explains why the long-run deviation in imports in Figure 2.2 is less negative than that in exports.

The fourth element concerns the long-run relationships between the GDP deviation and the trade deviations. Although we have now understood why Figure 2.2 shows a long-run increase in imports relative to exports, we have not explained why these two

---

[6] The rate of growth of capital is given by $k = (I/Y) * (Y/K) - \delta$, where $I$ and $Y$ are investment and GDP, and $\delta$ is the rate of depreciation (treated as a constant). Under our assumptions, the change in immigration policy does not affect $k$ or $Y/K$ in the long run. Therefore, it does not affect $I/Y$.

[7] It is apparent that the $K/L$ ratio is heading to a slightly lower long-run value than in the baseline. This is because the cost of making a unit of capital increases slightly in the long run relative to the price deflator for GDP, reflecting the intensive use of unauthorized labor in the construction industry.

deviations straddle the GDP deviation. If a reduction in the supply of unauthorized immigrants were particularly harmful (cost increasing) to export-oriented industries then it would be possible for both the import and export deviation lines at 2019 to be below that of GDP. Similarly, if a reduction in the supply of unauthorized immigrants were particularly harmful to import-competing industries then it would be possible for both the import and export deviation lines at 2019 to be above that of GDP. As shown in Dixon *et al.* (2011), the long-run effects of reduced unauthorized immigration on the industrial composition of activity are quite small, with no pronounced bias against or in favor of either export-oriented or import-competing industries. The lack of bias is a consequence of unauthorized employment being spread over many industries and representing only a small share of costs in almost all industries. Thus, the required gap between imports and exports is achieved with the import deviation line above that of GDP in the long run and the export deviation line below that of GDP.

Two further points about the effects of reduced unauthorized immigration on trade are worth noting. (i) The increase in imports relative to exports is in quantity terms. With an improvement in the terms of trade there is no deterioration in the balance of trade. (ii) The increase in imports relative to exports is facilitated, as shown in Figure 2.2, by a long-run increase in the real exchange rate (an increase in the nominal exchange rate relative to the foreign/US price ratio).

The final aspect of the long-run results in Figure 2.2 that we will explain is the relative movements in public and private consumption. Public consumption falls relative to private consumption because consumption of public goods by unauthorized immigrants is high relative to their consumption of private goods. In the baseline forecast for 2019, unauthorized immigrants account for 3.7% of public consumption, but only 2.4% of private consumption.

The short-run results in Figure 2.2 are dominated by the need for the economy to adjust to a lower capital stock than it had in the baseline forecast. In the short run, the policy causes a relatively sharp reduction in investment. With US investment at the margin being financed mainly by foreigners, a reduction in investment weakens demand for the US dollar. Consequently, a reduction in investment weakens the US exchange rate. This temporarily stimulates exports and inhibits imports. As the downward adjustment in the capital stock is completed, investment recovers, causing the real exchange rate to rise, exports to fall and imports to rise.

### 2.2.1.2 Effects on the occupational composition of legal employment

The starting point for the explanation of the long-run macroeconomic results was the finding that a 28.7% cut in unauthorized employment reduces effective labor input by 1.6%. But why 1.6? Recall that in the baseline forecast the share of the US wage bill accounted for by unauthorized employment in 2019 is 3.64%. This suggests that a 28.7% cut in unauthorized employment should reduce effective labor input by only

1.0% (= 3.64 * 0.287). The explanation of the discrepancy (1.0 versus 1.6) hinges on changes in the occupational mix of legal US employment.

Table 2.1 gives occupational data for 2005 and deviation results for 2019. Column (1) shows the share of unauthorized immigrants in the wage bill of each US occupation. The occupational classification was chosen to give maximum detail on employment of unauthorized immigrants, with about 90% of their employment being spread across the first 49 occupations. The last occupation, 'Services, other', accounts for about 60% of US employment, but only 10% of unauthorized employment. Columns (2) and (3) show the long-run effects of the supply-restriction policy on employment and real wage rates of legal US workers by occupation. In broad terms, the employment results in Table 2.1 show a long-run transfer of legal workers from 'Services, other', an amalgam of predominantly high-skilled, high-wage jobs, to the occupations that currently employ large numbers of unauthorized immigrants. The correlation coefficient between the deviations in jobs for legal workers (column 2) and unauthorized shares (column 1) is close to one. In occupations vacated by unauthorized immigrants, legal workers not only gain jobs, but also benefit from significant wage increases. The correlation coefficient between the employment and wage results in columns (2) and (3) is also close to one. The long-run change in occupational mix implied by column (2) does not mean that existing US workers change their occupations. For each occupation, restricting the supply of unauthorized workers presents legal workers with opportunities to replace unauthorized workers. On the other hand, the economy is smaller, generating a negative effect on employment opportunities for legal workers. The positive replacement effect dominates in the low-wage occupations that currently employ large numbers of unauthorized immigrants. The negative effect of a smaller economy dominates in high-wage occupations that currently employ few unauthorized immigrants. Thus, there is an increase in vacancies in low-wage occupations relative to high-wage occupations, allowing low-wage occupations to absorb an increased proportion of new entrants to the workforce and unemployed workers. Another way of understanding the change in the occupation mix of legal workers is to recognize that the labor market involves job shortages. At any time, not everyone looking for a job in a given occupation can find a job in that occupation. So people settle for second best. The college graduate who wants to be an economist settles for a job as an administrative officer; the high-school graduate who wants to be a police officer settles for a job in private security; the unemployed person who wants to be a chef settles for a job as a short-order cook; and so on. Through this shuffling process, a reduction in supply of unauthorized immigrants reduces the skill composition of employment of legal workers. It lowers the contribution of these workers to effective labor input, explaining the 1.0 versus the 1.6 discrepancy. We refer to this as a negative Occupation-mix effect. The idea of an Occupation-mix effect will be familiar to students of the history of US immigration. As described by Griswold (2002, p. 13), the inflow of low-skilled immigrants early in the twentieth

**Table 2.1** Occupational data for 2005 and deviation results for 2019

| | Unauthorized immigrants: % of labor costs in 2005 | % deviation in 2019 | |
| | | Legal jobs | Legal real wage |
| Occupation | (1) | (2) | (3) |
|---|---|---|---|
| 1. Cooks | 15.6 | 4.20 | 1.89 |
| 2. Grounds maintenance | 24.8 | 7.45 | 3.19 |
| 3. House keeping and cleaning | 22.0 | 6.56 | 2.82 |
| 4. Janitor and building cleaner | 10.4 | 2.31 | 1.19 |
| 5. Miscellaneous agriculture worker | 34.3 | 10.70 | 4.55 |
| 6. Construction laborer | 23.9 | 7.10 | 3.16 |
| 7. Transport packer | 24.6 | 7.37 | 3.19 |
| 8. Carpenter | 15.1 | 3.90 | 1.92 |
| 9. Transport laborer | 7.2 | 1.09 | 0.71 |
| 10. Cashier | 4.7 | 0.31 | 0.43 |
| 11. Food serving | 6.4 | 0.88 | 0.62 |
| 12. Transport driver | 4.0 | −0.09 | 0.25 |
| 13. Waiter | 5.7 | 0.64 | 0.53 |
| 14. Production, miscellaneous assistant | 8.3 | 1.07 | 0.72 |
| 15. Food preparation worker | 13.3 | 3.42 | 1.61 |
| 16. Painter | 24.9 | 7.46 | 3.31 |
| 17. Dishwasher | 22.7 | 6.83 | 2.86 |
| 18. Construction, helper | 24.8 | 7.42 | 3.30 |
| 19. Retail sales | 2.4 | −0.50 | 0.11 |
| 20. Production, helper | 20.4 | 5.54 | 2.52 |
| 21. Packing machine operator | 23.6 | 6.88 | 3.01 |
| 22. Butchers | 21.0 | 6.20 | 2.74 |
| 23. Stock clerk | 4.6 | 0.26 | 0.40 |
| 24. Child care | 5.2 | 0.56 | 0.51 |
| 25. Miscellaneous food preparation | 14.5 | 3.80 | 1.74 |
| 26. Dry wall installer | 35.8 | 11.43 | 4.87 |
| 27. Nursing | 2.8 | −0.01 | 0.29 |
| 28. Industrial truck operator | 8.5 | 1.47 | 0.87 |
| 29. Transport, cleaners | 15.8 | 4.24 | 1.93 |
| 30. Automotive repairs | 6.3 | 0.88 | 0.64 |
| 31. Sewing machine operator | 18.8 | 4.95 | 2.39 |
| 32. Concrete mason | 22.6 | 6.61 | 3.00 |
| 33. Roofers | 28.2 | 8.64 | 3.78 |
| 34. Plumbers | 7.1 | 1.07 | 0.80 |
| 35. Personal care | 5.7 | 0.91 | 0.66 |
| 36. Shipping clerk | 5.2 | 0.35 | 0.43 |
| 37. Brick mason | 22.5 | 6.56 | 2.97 |
| 38. Carpet installer | 21.4 | 6.21 | 2.82 |
| 39. Laundry | 15.5 | 4.22 | 1.93 |

(*Continued*)

**Table 2.1** Occupational data for 2005 and deviation results for 2019—cont'd

| | Unauthorized immigrants: % of labor costs in 2005 | % deviation in 2019 | |
| | | Legal jobs | Legal real wage |
| Occupation | (1) | (2) | (3) |
|---|---|---|---|
| 40. Other production workers | 9.1 | 1.57 | 0.91 |
| 41. Maintenance and repairs | 2.2 | −0.71 | −0.01 |
| 42. Repair, helper | 16.8 | 4.56 | 2.09 |
| 43. Welder | 6.2 | 0.31 | 0.41 |
| 44. Supervisor, food preparation | 3.4 | −0.20 | 0.22 |
| 45. Construction supervisors | 3.4 | −0.27 | 0.27 |
| 46. Farm/food/clean, other | 6.1 | 0.61 | 0.53 |
| 47. Construction, other | 5.5 | 0.38 | 0.49 |
| 48. Production, other | 4.6 | −0.11 | 0.21 |
| 49. Transport, other | 3.2 | −0.40 | 0.13 |
| 50. Services, other | 0.4 | −1.27 | −0.13 |
| Total | 2.6 | −0.16 | −0.46 |

century induced native-born US residents to complete their education and enhance their skills. In our terms, that was a positive Occupation-mix effect.

Before leaving Table 2.1, it is worth commenting on the deviations shown in the 'Total' row. The reduction (0.16%) in employment of legal workers is caused by the shift in the composition of their employment towards low-skilled occupations. These occupations have relatively high equilibrium rates of unemployment, which we have assumed are unaffected by immigration policy. It is sometimes asserted that cuts in employment of unauthorized immigrants would reduce unemployment rates of low-skilled legal workers. While our modeling suggests that there would be increases in the number of jobs for legal workers in low-skilled occupations, this does not mean that unemployment rates in these occupations would fall. With cuts in unauthorized immigration, low-skilled legal workers might find themselves under increased pressure from higher-skilled workers who can no longer find vacancies in higher-skilled occupations.

The overall reduction of 0.46% in the wage rate of legal workers seems surprising at first glance. Column (3) of Table 2.1 shows an increase or a negligible decrease in wage rates for legal workers in all occupations except 'Services, other' in which the wage rate is reduced by 0.13%. However, the average hourly wage rate of legal workers is reduced by the shift in the occupational composition of their employment to low-wage jobs.

### 2.2.1.3 Effects on the welfare of legal households

The headline number that policy makers are often looking for from a CGE study is the effect on aggregate welfare. In the present study, we take this as referring to long-run

**Table 2.2** Long-run (2019) percentage effects of tighter border security on consumption of legal residents

| F1 | Direct effect | −0.29 |
|---|---|---|
| F2 | Occupation-mix effect | −0.31 |
| F3 | Legal-employment effect | −0.11 |
| F4 | Capital effect | −0.24 |
| F5 | Public-expenditure effect | 0.17 |
| F6 | Terms-of-trade effect | 0.23 |
| BOTE totals | | −0.55 |
| CGE result | | −0.52 |

(2019) private and public consumption by legal US residents. We find that a reduction of 28.7% in unauthorized employment caused by tighter border security would generate a sustained annual welfare loss for legal residents of 0.52% (about $80 billion in 2009 dollars).

This result can be explained in terms of the six factors indicated in Table 2.2 by F1—F6. As detailed in Dixon *et al.* (2011), each of these factors can be quantified by a BOTE calculation. The total of the BOTE calculations (−0.55) is an accurate estimate of the CGE result (−0.52). This gives us confidence that we have adequately identified the data and mechanisms in our model that explain the result. Here, we briefly describe the factors and their quantification.

### F1: Direct effect

With a reduction in supply, the wage rate of unauthorized workers will rise. This is illustrated in Figure 2.3 in which DD is the demand curve for unauthorized labor in 2019, **SS** is the supply curve in the baseline forecast and **S′S′** is the supply curve with the tighter security policy in place. The numbers shown in the diagram are taken from our simulation: the policy reduces unauthorized employment in 2019 from 12.4 to 8.8 million and increases annual wage rates for unauthorized workers by 9.2%, from $52,660 to $57,500 (2019 dollars).

If workers are paid according to the value of their marginal product then the loss in output (represented by GDP) from reducing employment is the change in the area under the demand curve, area (**abcd**) in Figure 2.3. The change in the total cost to employers of unauthorized immigrants is area (**gaef**), the increase in costs associated with the increase in the unauthorized immigrant wage rate, minus area (**ebcd**), the reduction in costs associated with employment of less unauthorized immigrants. Ignoring taxes, the analysis so far suggests that the Direct effect of cutting illegal employment (the change in GDP less the change in the costs of employing illegal workers) is a loss represented by area (**abfg**). As indicated in Figure 2.3, this area is worth $51.5 billion. Taxes complicate the situation in two ways. (i) The change in the area under the demand curve is an

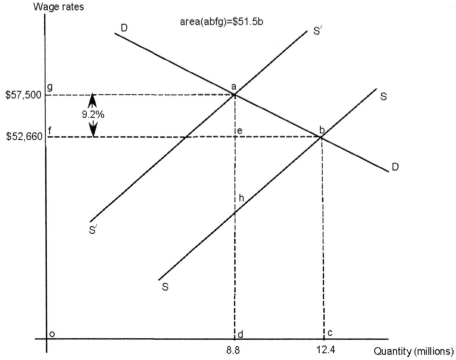

**Figure 2.3** Demand for and supply of illegal immigrants in 2019.

underestimate of the loss in GDP because indirect taxes mean that wage rates are less than the value of the marginal product of workers. (ii) Unauthorized immigrants pay income taxes. Consequently, area (**ebcd**) overstates the saving to the US economy associated with paying wages to 28.6% fewer unauthorized immigrants and area (**gaef**) overstates the cost to the US economy of paying higher wage rates to unauthorized immigrants who remain in employment. After adjusting for taxes, the final estimate that Dixon *et al.* (2011) obtained for the Direct effect was a loss of $77.3 billion. This causes a 0.29% reduction in consumption by legal households (row 1, Table 2.2).

### F2: Occupation-mix effect

Restricting the supply of unauthorized immigrants changes the occupational mix of employment of legal workers, reducing their average hourly wage rate by 0.46% (Table 2.1). In the baseline forecast for 2019, wages are 66% of the total income of legal residents.[8] A 0.46% reduction in average wage rates translates into a 0.31% ($= 0.46 * 0.66$) reduction in the ability of legal residents to consume private and public goods.

---

[8] This is GNP (i.e. GDP less net income flowing to foreign investors) minus post-tax income accruing to unauthorized immigrant.

## F3: Legal-employment effect

As explained in Section 2.2.1.2, we assume that equilibrium rates of unemployment are higher for low-skilled occupations than for high-skilled occupations, leading in our simulation to a reduction in legal employment of 0.16% (Table 2.1). With wages being 66% of the total income of legal residents, this reduces their income and consumption by 0.11%.

## F4: Capital effect

If a change in immigration policy had no effect on savings by legal residents (including the government) *up to* 2019, then it would have no effect on US ownership of capital *in* 2019. In this case, if a change in immigration policy led to a reduction in the stock of capital in the US, then it would lead to a corresponding reduction in the stock of foreign-owned capital, with little effect on capital income accruing to legal households. Nevertheless, they would suffer a welfare loss because the US treasury would lose taxes paid by foreign owners of US capital. Via the Direct effect and other negative effects in Table 2.1, the tighter border-security policy reduces saving by legal households throughout the simulation period. Thus, in the policy run, legal households own less US capital in 2019 than they had in the baseline forecast and lose the full-income of this lost capital. As explained in Section 2.2.1.1, the policy causes a long-run reduction in US capital stock of about 1.6%. This is split approximately evenly between reductions in foreign-owned and US-owned capital. Taking account of the tax effects of the loss of foreign-owned capital and the full-income effects of the loss of US-owned capital, we find that the 1.6% reduction in capital contributes −0.24% to sustained long-run welfare of legal households.

## F5: Public-expenditure effect

With a reduction in the number of unauthorized immigrants working in the US, the public sector would cut its expenditures, particularly on elementary education, emergency healthcare and correctional services. This would allow either cuts in taxes or increased provision of public services to legal households. This effect contributes 0.17% to sustained long-run welfare of legal households.[9] It should be noted that F5 encompasses only public sector expenditures and does not take account of taxes paid by illegal immigrants. These taxes are accounted for in F1 where we compute the Direct contribution of illegal immigrants to GDP net of their *post-tax* wages.

## F6: Terms-of-trade effect

In our simulation, the cut in unauthorized immigration reduces the prices of the goods and services that are consumed in the US relative to the prices of goods and services that

---

[9] The underlying data on public expenditures on unauthorized immigrants were taken from Rector and Kim (2007) and Strayhorn (2006).

are produced in the US. In 2019, the policy-induced reduction in the price index for private and public consumption relative to that for GDP is 0.23%. This increases the consuming power of legal households by 0.23%. The main reason for the relative decline in the price of consumption is the improvement in the terms of trade, discussed in Section 2.2.1.1. A terms-of-trade improvement generally reduces the price index for consumption (which includes imports, but not exports) relative to that for GDP (which includes exports, but not imports).

## 2.2.2 Engaging the audience: hoped-for reactions

When we present a CGE story to an audience we are hoping for certain reactions. We want the audience to engage on the topic, not on prejudices and general views about CGE modeling. Whether we get the desired reaction depends on how well we have told the story in terms of mechanisms that are accessible to people without a CGE background.

In the case of our tighter border-security story, we hope that the audience is enthusiastic enough to want to know about extensions. For example, what would happen if the reduction in unauthorized employment were achieved by restricting demand through more rigorous prosecution of employers rather than restricting supply? More radically, what would happen if we replaced unauthorized immigrants by low-skilled guest workers? If we have told our story sufficiently well then audiences or readers of our papers can go a long way towards answering these questions without relying on our model.

The effects of demand restriction can be visualized in terms of Figure 2.3 as an inward movement in **DD** rather than **SS**. If the demand policy were scaled to achieve the same reduction in unauthorized employment as in the supply policy, then we would expect similar results for F2—F6. which depend primarily on the reduction in the number of unauthorized workers. At first glance we might expect the Direct effect (F1) for demand-side restriction to be more favorable than that for supply-side restriction: with demand-side restriction, wage rates for unauthorized workers fall rather than rise. However, when we think of the gap between the supply-restricted wage (**da** in Figure 2.3) and the demand-restricted wage (**dh**) as being absorbed by prosecution-avoiding activities, then we can conclude that even the Direct effect will be similar under the demand- and supply-side policies. Thus, on the basis of F1—F6 we would expect little difference in the effects of equally scaled demand- and supply-side policies. This is confirmed in Dixon *et al.* (2011).

The guest-worker question arose from comments by Dan Griswold of the Cato Institute (a free-trade think tank in Washington, DC). After seeing a presentation on the negative welfare result in Table 2.2, he asked whether welfare would increase if there were more low-skilled immigrants employed in the US rather than less. This led to a consideration of a program under which US businesses could obtain permits to legally employ low-skilled immigrants. In terms of Figure 2.3, we can envisage such a program as shifting the supply curve outward — at any given wage, more low-skilled immigrants would be willing to enter the US under a guest-worker program than under the present situation in which they incur considerable costs from illegal entry. The outward shift in the supply curve would reverse the signs of the six effects identified in Table 2.2. As shown in Dixon and Rimmer (2009), a permit charge paid by employers could be used to control the number of low-skilled immigrants. It would also be a useful source of revenue, effectively transferring to the US treasury what are currently the costs to immigrants of illegal entry.

A second hoped-for reaction from audiences is well-directed questions about robustness and sensitivity. By this we mean questions about data items and parameter values that can be identified from our story as being important for our results. In presentations of our work on unauthorized immigration, we welcome questions concerning: our baseline forecasts for unauthorized employment (7.3 million in 2005 growing to 12.4 million in 2019); our data on the occupational and industrial composition of unauthorized and legal employment; our assumptions about the level of public expenditures associated with unauthorized employment; our choice of values for the elasticities of demand and supply for unauthorized workers; our adoption of a one-country framework that ignores effects outside the US; and other key ingredients of our story. When questions are asked about the existence, uniqueness and stability of competitive equilibria, then we suspect that our presentation has not effectively led the audience to understand how they should assess what we are saying.

A third satisfying reaction is curiosity about results for other dimensions. In our story here we have concentrated on macro and occupational results but for an interested audience we could also report industry results: our simulations were conducted at a 38-industry level. Greater industrial disaggregation can be introduced for organizations with a particular industry focus. For example, in a current study on unauthorized workers in agriculture, the US Department of Agriculture has expanded the industrial dimension to 70, emphasizing agricultural activities.

For readers of this chapter, we hope that our story has done two things. (i) We hope that it has demonstrated how CGE results can be explained in non-circular, macro-to-micro fashion. As in this story, we have found that in explaining most CGE results the best starting point is the inputs to the aggregate production function. In this case we started with what a cut in unauthorized immigration would do to aggregate employment. We then moved to the effect on aggregate capital. From there we went to the expenditure side of GDP. Eventually we worked down to employment by occupation. (ii) We hope that our story has aroused curiosity about some methodological issues. We have mentioned the business-as-usual forecast or baseline. How is this created in a MONASH model? We have reported policy-induced deviations. How are policy simulations conducted and what is their relationship to baseline simulations? We have worked with considerable labor market disaggregation: 50 occupations by two birth-places by two legal statuses by 38 industries. How do we cope with large dimensions? We have shown year-by-year results. How do we handle dynamic mechanism such as capital accumulation that provide connections between years?[10] These are among the issues discussed in the rest of this chapter.

## 2.3 FROM JOHANSEN TO ORANI

Modern CGE modeling has not evolved from a single starting point and there are still quite distinct schools of CGE modeling. While Johansen (1960) made the first CGE model, there were several other largely independent starting points including the contributions of Scarf (1967, 1973), Jorgenson and associates (e.g. Hudson and Jorgenson, 1974) and the World Bank group (e.g. Adelman and Robinson, 1978; Taylor *et al.*, 1980). Each of these later contributors adopted a style quite distinct from that of Johansen: different computational techniques, estimation methods, approaches to result analysis and issue focuses. In the case of the MONASH models, the ancestor is Johansen. His style was simple, effective and adaptable. It facilitated the inclusion of policy-relevant detail in CGE models and opened a path to result interpretation via BOTE explanations. In this section we describe Johansen's model and the extensions that were made in creating the ORANI model.

### 2.3.1 Johansen model

Johansen presented his 22-commodity/20-industry model of Norway as a system of 86 linear equations connecting 86 endogenous and 46 exogenous variables:

$$A_X * x + A_Y * y = 0, \tag{2.2}$$

where $x$ and $y$ are $46 \times 1$ and $86 \times 1$ vectors of exogenous and endogenous variables, and $A_X$ and $A_Y$ are matrices of coefficients of dimensions $86 \times 46$ and $86 \times 86$ built mainly from Norwegian input-output data for 1950 supplemented by estimates of income elasticities for consumer demand.

The 46 exogenous variables are: aggregate employment (1); aggregate capital (1); population (1); Hicks-neutral primary factor technical change in each industry (20); exogenous demand for each commodity (22); and the price of non-competing imports (1).[11] The 86 endogenous variables are: labor input and capital input by industry (2 × 20); output and prices by commodity (2 × 22); the average rate of return on capital

---

[10] For dynamic mechanisms that are specific to our immigration work, such as vacancy-induced occupational shuffling, we refer readers to Dixon and Rimmer (2010a).

[11] We are sometimes asked about the numéraire in Johansen's model. It is the nominal wage rate which is exogenously fixed on zero growth and then omitted from the model.

(1); and aggregate private consumption (1). All of the variables in Johansen's system are growth rates or percentage growth rates. Johansen derived the equations in (2.2) from underlying levels forms. For example, in (2.2) he represented the Cobb–Douglas relationship:

$$Z_j = N_j^{\gamma_j} * K_j^{\beta_j} * e^{\varepsilon_j * t}, \tag{2.3}$$

between the output in industry $j$ ($Z_j$) and labor and capital inputs ($N_j$ and $K_j$) as:

$$z_j - \gamma_j * n_j - \beta_j * k_j - \epsilon_j = 0, \tag{2.4}$$

where $z_j$, $n_j$ and $k_j$ are percentage growth rates in $Z_j$, $N_j$ and $K_j$, and $\epsilon_j$ is the rate of technical progress.

From (2.2) Johansen solved his model, i.e. expressed growth rates in endogenous variables in terms of exogenous variables, as:

$$y = b * x, \tag{2.5}$$

where $b$ is the $86 \times 46$ matrix given by:

$$b = -A_Y^{-1} * A_X. \tag{2.6}$$

Johansen was fascinated by the $b$ matrix in (2.6) and devoted much of his book to discussing it. The $b$ matrix shows the sensitivity (usually an elasticity) of every endogenous variable with respect to every exogenous variable. Johansen regarded the 3956 entries in the $b$ matrix as his basic set of results and he looked at every one of them. His management strategy for coping with 3956 results was to use a simple one-sector BOTE model as a guide. The BOTE model told him what to look for and what to expect in his full-scale model.

For example, the BOTE model suggested that the entries in the $b$ matrix referring to the elasticities of industry outputs with respect to movements in aggregate capital and labor should lie in the (0,1) interval. This follows from a macro version of equation (2.4).[12] With one exception, this expectation was fulfilled: the $b$ matrix shows a negative entry for the elasticity of equipment output with respect to an increase in aggregate employment. Following up and explaining exceptions is an important part of the BOTE methodology. In this way we can locate result-explaining mechanisms in the full model that are not present in the BOTE model. In other words, we can figure out what the full model knows that the BOTE model does not know. In the case of the equipment-output/employment elasticity, the explanation of the negative result is that an increase in aggregate employment changes the composition of the economy's capital stock in favor of structures and against equipment. This morphing of the capital stock reduces

---

[12] That is $z = \gamma * n + \beta * k + \epsilon$, where $\gamma$ and $\beta$ are parameters with values between 0 and 1.

maintenance demand for equipment, thereby reducing the output of the equipment industry.[13]

One of the most interesting parts of *b* is the submatrix relating movements in industry outputs to movements in exogenous demands. At the time when Johansen was writing, Leontief's input-output model, with its emphasis on input-output multipliers, was the dominant tool for quantitative multisectoral analysis. In Leontief's model, if an extra unit of output from industry *j* is required by final users, then production in *j* must increase by at least one unit and production in other industries will increase to provide intermediate inputs to production in *j*. Further rounds of this process can be visualized with suppliers to *j* requiring extra intermediate inputs. Thus, in Leontief's picture of the economy, developed in the depressed 1930s,[14] industries are in a complementary relationship, with good news for any one industry spilling over to every other industry. Johansen, working in the booming 1950s challenged this orthodoxy. His industry-output/exogenous-demand submatrix implies diagonal effects that in most cases are less than one and off-diagonal effects and are predominantly negative. Rather than emphasizing complementary relationships between industries, Johansen emphasized competitive relationships. In Johansen's model, expansion of output in one industry drags primary factors away from other industries. Only where there are particularly strong input-output links did Johansen find that stimulation of one industry (e.g. food) benefits another industry (e.g. agriculture).

Having examined the *b* matrix, Johansen used it to decompose movements in industry outputs, prices and primary factor inputs into parts attributable to observed changes in exogenous variables. In making his calculations he shocked all 46 exogenous variables with movements representing average annual growth rates for the period around 1950. In discussing the results of his decomposition exercise, Johansen paid particular attention to agricultural employment. This was a contentious issue among economists in 1960. On the one hand, diminishing returns to scale suggested that relative agricultural employment would grow with population and perhaps even with income despite low expenditure elasticities for agricultural products. On the other hand, agriculture was experiencing rapid technical progress, suggesting that employment in agriculture might not only fall as a share of total employment but might even fall in absolute terms. Johansen was able to separate and quantify these conflicting forces. He found that growth in capital, employment and population around 1950 caused relatively strong increases in agricultural employment, consistent with diminishing returns to scale interacting with increased consumption of food. However, the dominant effect on agricultural employment was technical change. This was strongly negative, leaving agriculture with net declining employment.

---

[13] For a fuller explanation of Johansen's negative equipment-output/employment elasticity, see Dixon and Rimmer (2010c, p. 7).

[14] Leontief (1936).

In another exercise, Johansen performed a validation test. He compared observed average annual growth rates around 1950 in endogenous variables such as industry outputs, employment and capital inputs with the total effects calculated in his decomposition exercise. He used this comparison to pinpoint weaknesses in his model and to organize a discussion of real-world developments. For agriculture, he found that the computed growth rate in output closely matched reality, but that the computed growth rate in employment was too high while that in capital was too low. This led to a discussion of reasons, not accounted for in the model, for exodus of rural workers to the cities. For forestry, the computed growth rates for output and primary factor inputs were too high. He thought that the income elasticity of demand for forestry products may have been set too high and also that there may have been a taste change, not included in his model, against the use of forestry products as fuel. By going through his results in this way, Johansen developed an agenda for model improvement.

## 2.3.2 Building on the Johansen legacy: creating the ORANI model

MONASH modelers owe an enormous intellectual debt to Johansen.[15] (i) They presented their models as linear systems in changes and percentage changes, Johansen's equation (2.2). This simplified the interpretation of their models and facilitated teaching. (ii) They adopted Johansen's solution equations (2.5) and (2.6). This enabled them to solve models in the 1970s and 1980s with much larger dimensions than was possible with other styles of CGE modeling. Johansen's use of BOTE models was also taken up and extended in the MONASH paradigm. (iii) MONASH modelers followed Johansen in using the $b$ matrix to understand properties of their models, to explain periods of history via decomposition analysis (see Section 2.5) and to perform validation exercises (see Dixon and Rimmer in Chapter 19 of this Handbook).

While Johansen's techniques were simple and effective, adopting them came at a cost. His solution equations (2.5) and (2.6) give only an approximation to effects implied by the underlying non-linear model: (2.5) and (2.6) produce solutions that are subject to linearization errors.[16] At the time that Johansen was developing his model, incurring this cost was a computational necessity. Later CGE pioneers were keen to avoid linearization errors and perhaps this caused them to overlook the strengths of Johansen's approach to CGE modeling. In any case, sustained development of Johansen's style of CGE modeling was not undertaken until work commenced in Australia on the ORANI model, a decade

---

[15] In their overview of the IMPACT Project's first 10 years of operation, Powell and Lawson (1990, pp. 265–266) identify the decision to use Johansen strategies as a key ingredient in the Project's success.

[16] Johansen recognized this problem and reported (Johansen, 1974) experience with a method implemented in the late 1960s by Spurkland (1970) for calculating accurate solutions. Spurkland's method used (2.5) and (2.6) to obtain an approximate solution, and then moved to an accurate solution via a general non-linear equation method such as Newton's algorithm. Spurkland's method sacrificed Johansen's simplicity and was rather awkward to implement. It was not widely adopted.

and a half after the publication of Johansen's book.[17] As described in Section 2.4.1, linearization errors were avoided in ORANI and later MONASH models without sacrificing Johansen's simplicity and interpretability. This was done by adopting a multistep extension of Johansen's solution method.

The multistep solution method was not the only innovation in the creation of ORANI. As outlined in Sections 2.3.2.1—2.3.2.4, other innovations were: the treatment of imports and competing domestic products as imperfect substitutes; the incorporation of policy-relevant detail requiring large dimensionality; allowance for closure flexibility; and inclusion of complex functional forms.

### 2.3.2.1 Imperfect substitution between imports and domestic products: the Armington specification

Johansen paid little attention to trade, simply setting net exports exogenously for all commodities except non-competing imports, which were handled as Leontief inputs to production.[18] For a trade-focused model, a more elaborate approach is required. The builders of ORANI turned to Armington (1969, 1970) who had built a 15-country trade model in which each country produced just one good, but consumed all 15 goods, treating the goods from different countries as imperfect substitutes. In ORANI, imports were disaggregated by commodity rather than country of origin. For each using agent (industries, capital creators, households and government), imports of a commodity were specified as constant elasticity of substitution (CES) substitutes for the corresponding domestic commodity.

The import/domestic substitution elasticities (named Armington elasticities in Dixon *et al.* 1982) were econometrically estimated for about 50 commodities by Alaouze *et al.* (1977) and Alaouze (1977) using a quarterly database assembled for this purpose on import and domestic prices and quantities for the period 1968(2) to 1975(2). This work is summarized in Dixon *et al.* (1982, pp. 181—189).[19] With its Armington specification, ORANI produced results in which imports responded in a realistic manner to changes in the relative prices of imported and domestic goods, avoiding import-domestic 'flip-flop'. This refers to extreme and unrealistic movements in the share of a country's demands for a commodity that are satisfied by imports. It occurs in long-run simulations with models in which import/domestic price ratios are allowed to play a role in import/domestic

---

[17] There were some important one-off flurries using Johansen's techniques in the mid-1970s (see, e.g. Taylor and Black, 1974; Staelin, 1976; Bergman, 1978; and Keller, 1980).

[18] This exogenous treatment of trade was also the approach of Hudson and Jorgenson (1974) for the US. Adelman and Robinson (1978) in their study of Korea set exports of some commodities exogenously and fixed the share of exports in domestic output for other commodities. For most imports, Adelman and Robinson fixed the import share in domestic demand. Taylor *et al.* (1980, chapter 7) in their study of Brazil exogenized exports and related imports to industry outputs and final demands via exogenous coefficients.

[19] For an overview on recent work on Armington elasticities and other elasticities used in modeling international trade, see Hillberry and Hummels in Chapter 18 of this Handbook.

choice and imported and domestically produced units of a commodity are treated as perfect substitutes. Flip-flop can also be a problem with exports. When export prices are taken as given and long-run supply curves are flat, there is a tendency for models to show extreme and unrealistic specialization in the commodity composition of exports. The ORANI modelers avoided export flip-flop by the introduction of downward-sloping export demand curves (Dixon *et al.* 1982; pp. 195−196; Dixon and Rimmer, 2002; pp. 222−225).[20] Even for a small country, downward-sloping export demand curves can be justified by attributing Armington behavior to foreigners (i.e. by assuming that they treat imports of any given commodity from different countries as imperfect substitutes).

Following ORANI, the Armington specification has been adopted almost universally in CGE models, although there is some dissatisfaction with this approach. The Armington specification with elasticity values in the empirically relevant range leads to negative terms-of-trade effects that outweigh efficiency gains for countries undertaking unilateral tariff cuts even from quite high levels (e.g. 30%) (Brown, 1987). This is worrying to people who believe that low tariffs are always better than high tariffs. For a discussion of the relevant issues, see Dixon and Rimmer (2010b). While no alternative to Armington for practical CGE modeling has emerged, incorporation of ideas from Melitz (2003) seems promising, see Fan (2008) and Balistreri and Rutherford in Chapter 24 in this Handbook. The Melitz specification introduces productivity differences between firms within industries. Efficiency effects of tariff cuts are increased by allowing for elimination of low-productivity firms. However, potentially large terms-of-trade effects remain.

### 2.3.2.2 Incorporation of policy-relevant detail requiring large dimensionality

Policy makers want detail. They want results for identifiable industries (e.g. motor vehicle parts), not vague aggregates (e.g. manufacturing). They want results for regions, not just the nation. Consequently, ORANI was designed from its outset to encompass considerable detail. The first version had 113 industries (Dixon *et al.*, 1977) and was quickly endowed with a facility for generating results for Australia's eight states/territories (Dixon *et al.*, 1978).[21] Later, this facility was extended to 56 substate regions, Fallon (1982). The imperative of providing results that were persuasive in policy circles meant that ORANI was equipped not only with industry and regional detail, but also with detail in other areas that were normally ignored by academics. For example, from its outset ORANI had a detailed specification of margin costs (road transport, rail transport, air transport, water transport, wholesale trade and retail trade). Recognition of margin

---

[20] As recognized by Johansen (1974), Taylor and Black (1974) avoided extreme flip-flop in their trade-oriented model by adopting a short-run closure (fixed capital in each industry), thereby giving supply curves a positive slope. With his focus on long-run tendencies, Johansen could not adopt the Taylor and Black approach. Instead, he continued to treat exports and competitive imports exogenously.

[21] Also see Giesecke and Madden in Chapter 7 of this Handbook.

costs is important in translating the effects of tariff changes (that impact basic prices) into implications for purchasers prices (that influence demand responses). Attention to such details was important in providing results that could be believed by policy makers.

Detail expands dimensionality. In ORANI, the dimensions of the $A_Y$ matrix in (2.2) were far too large to allow direct solution via (2.6). This dimensionality problem was overcome by a process of condensation in which high-dimension variables were substituted out of the computational form of the model. For example, consider the variable $x(i,s,j,k,r)$, which represents the percentage change in the use of margin commodity $r$ (e.g. road transport) to facilitate the flow of commodity $i$ from source $s$ (domestic or imported) to industry $j$ for purpose $k$ (current production or capital creation). In a model with 100 commodities/industries and 10 margin commodities this variable has 400,000 components. These were explained in ORANI by 400,000 Johansen-style linear percentage change equations:

$$x(i, s, j, k, r) = x(i, s, j, k) + a(i, s, j, k, r), \tag{2.7}$$

where $x(i,s,j,k)$ is the percentage change in flow $(i,s,j,k)$ and $a(i,s,j,k,r)$ is the percentage change in the use of margin $r$ per unit of flow $(i,s,j,k)$. In many ORANI simulations variables such as $a(i,s,j,k,r)$ were interpreted as changes in technology.

To reduce the computational dimensions of ORANI, (2.7) was used to substitute out $x(i,s,j,k,r)$, i.e. (2.7) was deleted and $x(i,s,j,k,r)$ was replaced by the right-hand side of (2.7) wherever it appeared in the rest of the model. By this process, the dimensions of the matrix to be inverted in (2.6) were reduced to a manageable size: about $200 \times 200$ in the 1977 version of ORANI and about $400 \times 400$ in the 1982 version.[22]

While variables and equations disappear from a model during condensation, no information is lost. Results for eliminated variables can be recovered by backsolving using the eliminated equations. One implication of this is that eliminated variables are necessarily endogenous.

Through condensation in a Johansen linear framework, problems of dimensionality were largely removed. This gave two advantages: (i) the full dimensionality of available input-output tables could be used and (ii) computational–theoretical compromises were reduced. For example, in ORANI there was no inhibition on computational grounds about including a high-dimension equation such as (2.7) if this was considered the theoretically appropriate specification.

### 2.3.2.3 Closure flexibility in the Johansen framework

Johansen used just one closure. However, his framework was readily extended to encompass closure flexibility. This was done in ORANI by leaving the allocation of

---

[22] The condensations of the two versions are described in Sutton (1976, 1977) and Dixon *et al.* (1982, pp. 207–229).

variables between $y$ (endogenous) and $x$ (exogenous) in Johansen's equation (2.2) as a user choice. This imparted an important degree of flexibility.

If, for example, the focus was on the short-run effects of a policy, then capital in each industry was treated exogenously, unaffected in the short-run. At the same time, rates of return were treated endogenously. Simulations conducted under this closure were thought to reveal effects that would emerge after about 2 years.[23] If a long-run focus were required, then the closure was reversed. It was assumed that deviations in rates of return would be temporary. Thus, in long-run simulations, rates of return were exogenous while capital stocks adjusted endogenously to allow rates of return to be maintained at their initial levels.

An early ORANI study that took advantage of closure flexibility was that by Dixon *et al.* (1979). This was commissioned by the Crawford Group, set up by the Australian Government in 1977 to report on macro and industry policies to achieve a broad-based industry and regional recovery from what was then a deeply recessed situation. To widen the appeal of the ORANI results and defuse criticism, simulations were conducted under two closures. In both closures real wages were treated exogenously, reflecting their determination in what was at the time a legalistic, centralized system that could produce outcomes with little resemblance to those that would be expected from market forces. The closures differed with respect to capital utilization and exports.

In what was referred to as a neoclassical closure, capital used in each industry was set exogenously to fully employ the capital available to the industry. Rental rates adjusted endogenously to ensure compatibility between demand for capital and the exogenously given levels of capital usage. Exports in the neoclassical closure were determined by the interaction of production costs in Australia and price-elastic foreign demands.

In what was referred to as a neo-Keynesian closure,[24] the rental rate on capital was treated as a profit mark-up and linked exogenously in each industry to variable costs per unit of production.[25] Capital in use was treated endogenously. Exports were assumed rigid and to make this computationally possible, a phantom export subsidy was endogenized for each commodity.

Despite these seemingly radical differences in closure, the policy implications of the two sets of simulations were the same: a combination of reduction in the real costs of employing labor and an expansion in demand offered the best prospect for a broad-based recovery. Real cost reduction would stimulate trade-exposed industries and regions while demand expansion would stimulate the rest of the economy. Naturally, the

---

[23] This was worked out by Cooper and McLaren (1983) who compared ORANI comparative static short-run results with those produced by a continuous-time macro model. See also Breece *et al.* (1994) and Dixon (1987).

[24] The terms neoclassical and neo-Keynesian have been used by a number of authors, but never in quite the same way. For a discussion of closure possibilities in early CGE models with associated nomenclature, see Rattso (1982) and Robinson (2006).

[25] For a more recent application of this idea in a dynamic setting, see Dixon and Rimmer (2011).

question arose as to what policies could reduce labor costs in an acceptable way while expanding demand. One answer, illustrated by ORANI simulations in Corden and Dixon (1980), was a wage-tax bargain under which workers forego wage increases in return for tax cuts or improvements in social capital. Such bargains were an important part of Australian economic policy in the 1980s.

In the 1990s, the idea of flexible closures was extended in dynamic MONASH models to allow for four modes of analysis: historical, decomposition, forecast and policy. These are described in Section 2.5.

### 2.3.2.4 Complex functional forms in the Johansen framework

Early CGE modelers outside the Johansen school worried that the use of the Johansen linear percentage-change format was limiting with respect to model specification. For example, Dervis *et al.* (1982, p. 137) comment that:

> Johansen linearized the general equilibrium model (in logarithms) and so was able to solve it by simple matrix inversion. ... Since then there have been advances in solution methods that permit CGE models to be solved directly for the levels of all endogenous variables and so permit model specifications that cannot easily be put into log-linear forms.

Far from being limiting, the Johansen framework simplified the introduction into CGE modeling of the advanced functional forms that were being developed in this period. For example, consider the CRESH[26] cost-minimizing problem:

choose $X_i, i = , \ldots n$

to minimize :

$$\sum_{i=1}^{n} P_i * X_i \tag{2.8}$$

subject to:

$$\sum_{i=1}^{n} \left(\frac{X_i}{Z}\right)^{h_i} * \frac{Q_i}{h_i} = \alpha, \tag{2.9}$$

where $Z$ is output, $P_i$ and $X_i$ are input prices and quantities, and the $Q_i$, $h_i$ and $\alpha$ are parameters, with the $Q_i$ values being positive and summing to one and the $h_i$ values being less than one but not precisely zero.

On the basis of problem (2.8)–(2.9) it is difficult to obtain an intuitive understanding of the input-demand functions: they have no closed form levels representation. Given values for $h_i$, values for $Q_i$ and $\alpha$ can be determined on the basis of input-output data, but

---

[26] CRESH was introduced as a generalization of CES by Hanoch (1971).

this is technically awkward. By contrast, the Johansen-style percentage change representation of the input-demand functions is readily interpretable and easily calibrated. As shown in Section 2.4.4, (2.8)−(2.9) leads to:

$$x_i = z - \sigma_i * (p_i - p), \quad i = 1, \ldots, n, \tag{2.10}$$

where $x_i$, $z$ and $p_i$ are percentage changes in the variables represented by the corresponding uppercase symbols, $\sigma_i$ is a positive substitution parameter defined by $\sigma_i = 1/(1 - h_i)$, and $p$ is a weighted average of the percentage changes in all input prices defined by:

$$p = \sum_{k=1}^{n} S_k^{\#} * p_k. \tag{2.11}$$

The weights $S_k^{\#}$ are modified cost shares of the form:

$$S_k^{\#} = \frac{S_k * \sigma_k}{\sum_{i=1}^{n} S_i * \sigma_i}. \tag{2.12}$$

where $S_k$ is the share of $k$ in costs.

Reflecting constant returns to scale, (2.10) implies that a 1% increase in output, holding input prices constant, causes a 1% increase in demand for all inputs. An increase in the price of $i$ relative to the average price of all inputs causes substitution away from $i$ and towards other inputs. The sensitivity of demand for $i$ with respect to its relative price is controlled by the parameter $\sigma_i$. If this parameter has the same value for all $i$, then (2.10) takes the familiar CES form. However, if we wish to introduce differences between inputs in their price sensitivity then this can be done by adopting different values for $\sigma_i$. Once values have been assigned for $\sigma_i$, calibration can be completed on the basis of cost shares ($S_k$) from input-output data.

Dixon et al. (1992, pp. 124−148) give derivations of Johansen-style demand and supply equations for a variety of optimizing problems based on CES, CET, Translog, CRESH and CRETH functions. In all these cases, the Johansen-style input-demand functions or output-supply functions look like (2.10): the percentage change in the particular input (output) equals the percentage change in the relevant activity variable minus (plus) a substitution (transformation) term that compares the percentage change in the particular price with a share-weighted average over the percentage changes in the prices of all the substitutes (transformates).

More generally, all differentiable input demand functions and output supply functions can be represented in a Johansen format. Usually the Johansen representation is more transparent than the levels representation. Perhaps reflecting this, rapid progress was made in the adoption of sophisticated functional forms in the ORANI model.

## 2.4 EXTENDING JOHANSEN'S COMPUTATIONAL FRAMEWORK: THE MATHEMATICAL STRUCTURE OF A MONASH MODEL

This section is a broad technical overview of MONASH modeling. We start in Section 2.4.1 by describing a MONASH model as a system of $m$ equations in $n$ variables. We emphasize two points: (i) the variables and equations are concerned with a single period, usually thought of as year $t$, and (ii) we always have an initial solution, i.e. a set of values for the $n$ variables that satisfy the $m$ equations. Starting from the initial solution, other solutions can be obtained by derivative methods. We describe the Johansen/Euler method used for MONASH models. Section 2.4.2 shows how periods are linked in MONASH models to make them dynamic. Section 2.4.3 establishes the existence of the initial solution for each year $t$. MONASH models are written largely as equations in which the variables are percentage changes in prices and quantities in year $t$ away from their initial solution. The derivation of percentage change equations from underlying levels equations is discussed in Section 2.4.4. An overview of the GEMPACK software used in building, solving and analyzing MONASH models is presented in Section 2.4.5. Section 2.4.6 provides some notes on the creation of a database for a MONASH-style CGE model.

### 2.4.1 Theory of the Johansen/Euler solution method

A MONASH model can be represented as a system of $m$ equations in $n$ variables:

$$F(X, Y) = 0, \qquad (2.13)$$

where $F$ is a vector of $m$ functions, $X$ is the vector of $n - m$ variables chosen to be exogenous and $Y$ is the vector if $m$ variables chosen to be endogenous.

In discussing (2.13) it is convenient to assume that we are dealing with a national model with annual periodicity.[27] In such a model the vector $(X,Y)$ includes flow variables for year $t$ at the national level representing quantities and values of demands and supplies. Other variables in $(X,Y)$ refer to stocks or levels at an instant of time, examples being capital stocks at the start of year $t$ and at the end of year $t$, and the level of the exchange rate at the start and end of year $t$. $(X,Y)$ also includes lagged variables, e.g. the lagged consumer price index for year $t$, which is the consumer price index for year $t - 1$.

The $m$ equations include links between flow variables in year $t$ provided by market-clearing conditions, zero-pure-profit conditions and demand and supply equations derived from optimizing problems. The equations also impose links between stock and

---

[27] MONASH-style regional and multicountry models are discussed by Giesecke and Madden in Chapter 7 and Hertel in Chapter 12 of this Handbook. MONASH models with quarterly periodicity can be found in Adams *et al.* (2001) and Dixon *et al.* (2010).

flow variables. For example, end-of-year capital stocks are linked to start-of-year capital stocks via investment and depreciation during the year. Lagged adjustment processes may be included among the equations. For example, wage rates in year $t$ might be related to lagged consumer prices in year $t$.

This brings us to the first critical point in understanding the MONASH paradigm. A MONASH model is a system of equations connecting variables for year $t$. These can be current variables, lagged variables, stock variables or flow variables, but they are all variables for year $t$.

To solve the model for year $t$ we need a method for computing the value for the $Y$ vector in (2.13) corresponding to the year $t$ value for the $X$ vector. If (2.13) were small and sufficiently simple we might contemplate solving it explicitly to obtain the relationship:

$$Y = G(X), \qquad (2.14)$$

However, in realistic practical CGE models (2.13) consists of many thousands of variables connected by non-linear relationships. In these circumstances, solution via discovery of an explicit form for $G$ is out of the question.

This brings us to the second critical point in understanding the MONASH paradigm. While we can rarely have an explicit form for the solution function $G$, we can always have an initial solution, i.e. a vector $(\bar{X}(t), \bar{Y}(t))$ that satisfies:

$$F(\bar{X}(t), \bar{Y}(t)) = 0 \text{ or equivalently } \bar{Y}(t) = G(\bar{X}(t)). \qquad (2.15)$$

As will be discussed in Section 2.4.3, $(\bar{X}(t), \bar{Y}(t))$ usually represents the situation in a particular year, often year $t - 1$. With an initial solution in place, and assuming that $F$ is differentiable,[28] further solutions can be computed by derivative methods. These involve estimation of the partial derivatives, $G_X$, of the $G$ function but not explicit representation of $G$ itself. With $G_X$ we can estimate the effects on $Y$ of moving $X$ from its initial value, $\bar{X}(t)$, to its required value for year $t$, $X(t)$.

The derivative method used in MONASH models to move from the initial solution for year $t$ to the final solution is the Johansen/Euler method.[29] We named this method in recognition of the contributions of Johansen (1960) who, as described in Section 2.3, applied a one-step version of it to solve his CGE model of Norway, and Euler, the eighteenth century mathematician who set out the theory of the method as an approach to numerical integration.[30]

---

[28] Non-differentiabilities associated with complementarity conditions are discussed in Horridge *et al.* in Chapter 20 of this Handbook.

[29] Other derivative methods are described in Dervis *et al.* (1982, pp. 491−496).

[30] Early followers of Johansens's one-step method include Taylor and Black (1974), Staelin (1976), Dixon *et al.* (1977), and Keller (1980). The multistep version or the Johansen/Euler method was developed by Dixon *et al.* (1982). Another early application of the multistep approach is Bovenberg and Keller (1984).

In Johansen/Euler computations we start by replacing the original system of non-linear equations in $X$ and $Y$ with a linear system in which the variables are changes in $X$ and $Y$:

$$F_X(\bar{X}(t), \bar{Y}(t)) * \Delta X + F_Y(\bar{X}(t), \bar{Y}(t)) * \Delta Y = 0, \qquad (2.16)$$

where $F_X(\bar{X}(t), \bar{Y}(t))$ and $F_Y(\bar{X}(t), \bar{Y}(t))$ are the $m \times (n - m)$ and $m \times m$ matrices of first-order partial derivatives of $F$ with respect to $X$ and $Y$ evaluated at $(\bar{X}(t), \bar{Y}(t))$ and $\Delta X$ and $\Delta Y$ are $(n - m) \times 1$ and $m \times 1$ vectors of deviations in the values of the variables away from $(\bar{X}(t), \bar{Y}(t))$. The left-hand side of (2.16) is an approximation to the vector of changes in the $F$ functions caused by changing the variable values from $(\bar{X}(t), \bar{Y}(t))$ to $(\bar{X}(t) + \Delta X, \bar{Y}(t) + \Delta Y)$. As we are looking for a new solution to (2.13), we put the vector of approximate changes in $F$ equal to zero. We recognize that in going from the initial solution for year $t$ to the new solution, we must leave the values of the $F$ functions unchanged from zero.

From (2.16), we obtain:

$$\Delta Y = B(\bar{X}(t), \bar{Y}(t)) * \Delta X, \qquad (2.17)$$

where $B(\bar{X}(t), \bar{Y}(t))$ is the $G_X$ matrix evaluated at $(\bar{X}(t), \bar{Y}(t))$ and computed according to:[31]

$$B(\bar{X}(t), \bar{Y}(t)) = -F_Y(\bar{X}(t), \bar{Y}(t))^{-1} * F_X(\bar{X}(t), \bar{Y}(t)). \qquad (2.18)$$

Equation (2.17) is a version of Johansen's linear approximation of the true relationship between changes in $X$ and changes $Y$. By setting $\Delta X$ at $X(t) - \bar{X}(t)$ we can estimate the required value for $Y$ in year $t$ as:

$$Y_1^1(t) = \bar{Y}(t) + B(\bar{X}(t), \bar{Y}(t)) * \Delta X, \qquad (2.19)$$

where $Y_1^1(t)$ is the estimate obtained in the first step (superscript) of a one-step (subscript) procedure.

The linearization errors generated in the application of (2.19) are illustrated in Figure 2.4 for a two-variable, one-equation model in which **abcd** is the true relationship between $X$ and $Y$ and **ebf** is Johansen's linear approximation — a straight line tangent to the true relationship at the initial solution. In using (2.19) to compute the effect of moving $X$ from its initial value $\bar{X}(t)$ to its final value $X(t)$, the linearization error is **fc**, i.e. the gap between the Johansen solution, $Y_1^1(t)$, and the true solution, $Y(t)$.

---

[31] We assume that $F_Y(\bar{X}(t), \bar{Y}(t))$ is non-singular. Via the implicit functions theorem, this is equivalent to assuming the existence of a unique $G$ function such that $F(X(t), G(X(t)) = 0$ for all $X$ in a neighborhood of $\bar{X}(t)$. If $F_Y(\bar{X}(t), \bar{Y}(t))$ is singular, then the Johansen method will fail. However, this is not a computational problem. Any method should fail because the model does not imply that movements in $Y$ are uniquely determined by movements in $X$ in the neighborhood of $\bar{X}(t)$.

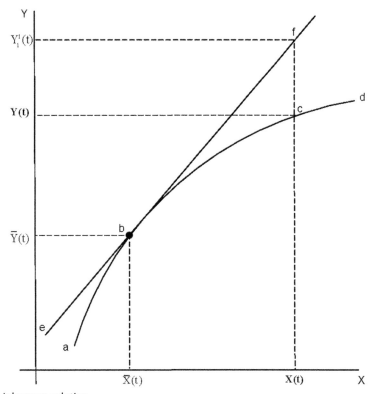

**Figure 2.4** Johansen solution.

The reason for linearization errors in the use of (2.19) to solve (2.13) can be found in (2.16), which led to (2.19). The left-hand side of (2.16) only approximates the vector of changes in the $F$ functions caused by changes in $X$ and $Y$. As we move away from $(\bar{X}(t), \bar{Y}(t))$, the partial derivatives of the $F$ functions are also moving. On the left-hand side of (2.16), we evaluate the effects on the $F$ functions of movements in the variables with the partial derivatives fixed at their initial values. More accurate solutions of (2.13) can be achieved by multistep Johansen/Euler calculations where we allow for changes in the partial derivatives of $F$.

In a two-step Johansen/Euler computation, we impose the change, $\Delta X$, in the exogenous variables in two equal steps. In the first step we use (2.19) to compute:

$$Y_2^1(t) = \bar{Y}(t) + B(\bar{X}(t), \bar{Y}(t)) * \frac{\Delta X}{2}.\tag{2.20}$$

$Y_2^1(t)$ is an estimate of the solution of (2.13) at $X = X_2^1(t)$, where:

$$X_2^1(t) = \bar{X}(t) + \Delta X/2,\tag{2.21}$$

and the superscript 1 and the subscript 2 in (2.20) and (2.21) denote values reached at the end of the first step in a two-step procedure. In the second step we re-evaluate the partial derivatives of $F$ at $(X_2^1(t), Y_2^1(t))$, recompute the $B$ matrix according to:

$$B(X_2^1(t), Y_2^1(t)) = -F_Y(X_2^1(t), Y_2^1(t))^{-1} * F_X(X_2^1(t), Y_2^1(t)), \tag{2.22}$$

and obtain our two-step estimate $[Y_2^2(t)]$ of the required year $t$ value of $Y$ as:

$$Y_2^2(t) = Y_2^1(t) + B(X_2^1(t), Y_2^1(t)) * \frac{\Delta X}{2}. \tag{2.23}$$

We can expect the two-step answer, $Y_2^2(t)$, to be considerably closer to one-step than the one-step answer, $Y_1^1(t)$. This is illustrated in Figure 2.5 in which the linearization error for the two-step computation, **sc**, is much smaller than that for the one-step computation, **fc**. In drawing Figure 2.5 we have assumed that $B(X_2^1(t), Y_2^1(t))$ is a good approximation to $B(X_2^1(t), G(X_2^1(t)))$. In other words, we have assumed that moving off the solution line **abwcd** in the first step does not invalidate formula (2.22) as an

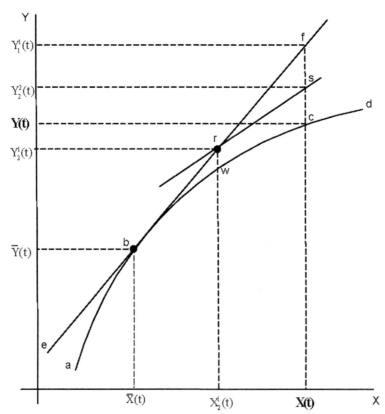

**Figure 2.5** Two-step Johansen/Euler solution.

approximation to the slope of the solution line at $X_2^1(t)$. The formal justification of this assumption is given in the Appendix: it depends on the derivatives of $B$ with respect $Y$ being bounded so that $B$ does not move too far away from the slope on the solution line as $Y$ moves away from the solution line.

Another feature of Figure 2.5 worthy of comment is that **sc** is about half of **fc**, i.e. as we double the number of steps (from 1 to 2) the linearization error is halved. This is not just an artifact of the particular illustration in Figure 2.5. As discussed in the Appendix, it is a quite general phenomenon. It can be exploited via Richardson's extrapolation to obtain highly accurate solutions from a small number of low-step computations. For example, with:

$$Y_2^2(t) - Y(t) \approx 0.5(Y_1^1(t) - Y(t)),\qquad(2.24)$$

we can often generate a highly accurate extrapolated estimate of Y(t) on the basis of one- and two-step solutions as:

$$Y_{\text{extrap}}^{1,2}(t) = 2 * Y_2^2(t) - Y_1^1(t).\qquad(2.25)$$

Even more accurate solutions can be obtained via higher-step computations and associated extrapolations.[32]

As an alternative to working with a system of equations such as (2.16) connecting *changes* in variables, it is usually more convenient to work with a system in which most of the variables are *percentage changes*. Johansen's model was mainly in percentage changes as are MONASH models. The advantage of percentage changes is that they are immediately interpretable without worrying about units. However, for some variables, those that may pass through zero in a simulation, percentage changes are not an option.

Starting from (2.16) we can produce a mixed system in which some variables are changes and some are percentage changes by replacing relevant components, $\Delta X_i$ and $\Delta Y_j$, of $\Delta X$ and $\Delta Y$ with percentage change variables:

$$x_i = 100 * \frac{\Delta X_i}{\bar{X}_i(t)} \quad \text{and} \quad y_j = 100 * \frac{\Delta Y_j}{\bar{Y}_j(t)},\qquad(2.26)$$

and relevant columns of $F_X$ and $F_Y$ by:

$$[0.01 * \bar{X}_i(t) * F_{X,i}(\bar{X}(t), \bar{Y}(t))] \quad \text{and} \quad [0.01 * \bar{Y}_j(t) * F_{Y,j}(\bar{X}(t), \bar{Y}(t))],\qquad(2.27)$$

where $F_{X,i}(\bar{X}(t), \bar{Y}(t))$ and $F_{Y,j}(\bar{X}(t), \bar{Y}(t))$ are the $m \times 1$ vectors of derivatives of $F$ with respect to the *i*th component of $X$ and the *j*th component of $Y$.

---

[32] Equation (2.25) is the simplest version of Richardson's extrapolation. For other versions, see Dahlquist *et al.* (1974, p. 269).

Using the mixed system we can proceed to a linearized form of our model (corresponding to equation 4.5) that can be written as:

$$y = b(\bar{X}(t), \bar{Y}(t)) * x, \qquad (2.28)$$

where $b(\bar{X}(t), \bar{Y}(t))$ is derived using matrices incorporating (2.27), and $y$ and $x$ are deviation vectors with percentage changes for most variables but changes for some variables such as the balance of trade for which zero is a realistic value.

With minor changes in the calculation of $(X, Y)$ at the end of each step, the mixed linearized system can be used in a multistep Johansen/Euler computation in the same way as the pure change system.

### 2.4.2 Linking the periods: dynamics

Assume that we have a solution, $(X(0), Y(0))$, for our model depicting the situation in year 0. Then we can use this as an initial solution for year 1:

$$(\bar{X}(1), \bar{Y}(1)) = (X(0), Y(0)). \qquad (2.29)$$

From here we can use the Johansen/Euler technique to generate the required solution for year 1 by applying shocks reflecting the difference between $X(0)$ and $X(1)$. The changes $dY$ in the endogenous variables generated in this process can be interpreted as growth between year 0 and year 1. As shown in Figure 2.6, we can create a sequence of solutions showing year-on-year growth through any desired simulation period.

In a year-on-year sequence of solutions, start-of-year stock variables in the required solution for year $t$ adopt the values of end-of-year stock variables in the required solution

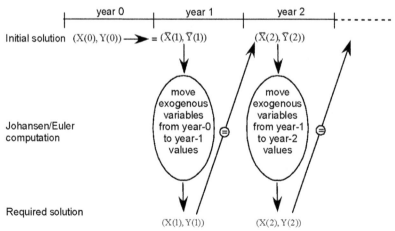

**Figure 2.6** Sequence of solutions using the required solution for year $t - 1$ as the initial solution for year $t$.

for year $t-1$. Consider, for example, a situation in which the start-of-year and end-of-year quantities of capital in industry $j$ in year $t-1$ are given by:

$$K_j^{\text{start}}(t-1) = 10 \quad \text{and} \quad K_j^{\text{end}}(t-1) = 12. \tag{2.30}$$

In the initial solution for year $t$, we have:

$$\bar{K}_j^{\text{start}}(t) = 10 \quad \text{and} \quad \bar{K}_j^{\text{end}}(t) = 12. \tag{2.31}$$

In using the Johansen/Euler method to generate the required solution for year $t$, we must make sure that the start-of-year capital stock for industry $j$ moves up by 20%, from its initial value of 10 to its required value of 12. If we include start-of-year stock variables among the components of $X$, then the required year-to-year changes can be imposed exogenously via shocks. More convenient methods are available via the use of homotopy equations. For example, we can include in (2.13) equations of the form:

$$K_j^{\text{start}}(t) = \bar{K}_j^{\text{start}}(t) + (\bar{K}_j^{\text{end}}(t) - \bar{K}_j^{\text{start}}(t)) * U. \tag{2.32}$$

where the barred coefficients referring to the initial solution are treated as parameters, and $U$ is a variable (known as a homotopy variable) whose initial value is zero and final value is one.

With $U$ on zero, (2.32) is satisfied by the initial solution (i.e. $K_j^{\text{start}}(t) = \bar{K}_j^{\text{start}}(t)$). When $U$ moves to one, $K_j^{\text{start}}(t)$ moves to its required value, $K_j^{\text{start}}(t) = \bar{K}_j^{\text{end}}(t)$.

The sequence of annual solutions depicted in Figure 2.6 is recursive (i.e. the solution for year 1 uses year 0 as a starting point, the solution for year 2 uses year 1 as a starting point, etc.) In models with forward-looking expectations, a simple recursive approach will not work: in computing the solution for year 1 we need information on year 2. Nearly all MONASH calculations have been conducted with static or adaptive expectations so that the recursive approach is adequate. However, as described in Dixon et al. (2005), it is possible to handle forward-looking expectations by an iterative method while retaining an essentially recursive approach. First, we set the model up with static expectations and solve it recursively for years 1, 2, ..., $T$. This gives us the basis for guessing values for variables in years $t+1$ and beyond when we are computing the solution for year $t$. With these guesses in place, we repeat the recursive sequence of solutions. The guesses for forward-looking variables are refined from sequence to sequence.[33]

---

[33] Another method of solving models with forward-looking variables is to compute all years simultaneously. This method was developed by Wilcoxen (1985, 1987) and Bovenberg (1985). See also Malakellis (1998, 2000). A disadvantage of simultaneous-solution methods is that they are feasible only if the underlying model is small.

Many MONASH computations are not concerned with the year-on-year evolution of the economy. For example, in a decomposition analysis we may wish to use a MONASH simulation to explain economic developments across a period of several years, say 1992–1998. In this case, the initial solution for 1998 is the situation in 1992, i.e.:

$$(\bar{X}(1998), \bar{Y}(1998)) = (X(1992), Y(1992)), \qquad (2.33)$$

and the simulation consists of looking at the effects on the endogenous variables of moving the exogenous variables from their 1992 values to their 1998 values. In such a simulation, it is no longer appropriate to assume that start-of-year stock values in the required solution equal end-of-year stock values in the initial solution. In our example, this would entail the unwarranted assumption that stock values at the start of 1998 were the same as stock values at the end of 1992.

### 2.4.3 Developing a solution for year 0 from the input-output data

#### 2.4.3.1 Solution for year 0: overview

To implement the Johansen/Euler method (or any other derivative method) we need a starting point, $(X(0), Y(0))$, which is a solution for year 0. As explained earlier, once we have a starting solution we can generate other solutions. However, how do we get a starting solution?

Most of the components in $(X(0), Y(0))$ can be derived from input–output or social accounting data for year 0. We start by explaining this in general terms. Then we will look more specifically at the input–output database for a typical MONASH model.

Input–output data are normally given as values. To separate out prices and quantities we can adopt quantity units that are compatible with all prices in year 0 being one. For example, if the price of a bushel of wheat is $4, then we adopt the quarter bushel as the quantity unit for wheat. If the input–output data shows a flow of $1 billion of wheat from farmers to bakers, then we say that 1 billion units (quarter bushels) of wheat are sold to bakers.

Given the balance conditions in input–output data, we can be sure that the quantities and prices derived in this way are compatible with demand/supply equality and zero pure profits. What about equations derived from utility maximization and cost minimization problems? These are satisfied with prices on one and the resulting quantities implied by input–output data via calibration of the parameters or the introduction of shift variables. For example, if households maximize a Cobb–Douglas utility function so that demand for commodity $i$ ($C_i$) is related to the price of commodity $i$ ($P_i$) and to total consumption ($CTOT$) by:

$$C_i = \alpha_i * \frac{CTOT}{P_i} \text{ for all commodities } i, \qquad (2.34)$$

then the parameter $\alpha_i$ is calibrated or estimated as:

$$\alpha_i = \frac{C_i(0) * P_i(0)}{CTOT(0)} \text{ for all commodities } i, \qquad (2.35)$$

where $P_i(0)$ is set at one, and $C_i(0)$ and $CTOT(0)$ are obtained from the household column of the input-output data. With $\alpha_i$ set via (2.35), it is clear that the input-output values for $C_i$, $P_i$ and $CTOT$ satisfy (2.34). More generally, all of the demand and supply equations in MONASH models (and models built in other input–output/social-accounting-matrix traditions) contain sufficient free parameters and shift variables so that they can be satisfied by the initial input-output data.

Input-output tables may not cover all of the flow variables in a model. For example, MONASH models include variables making up the balance of payments and the public sector budget. Additional data tables are necessary to provide an initial solution for these variables (see Dixon and Rimmer, 2002; pp. 212–219). As well as flow variables, MONASH models contain stock variables. Year 0 data are required for variables such as start-of-year capital stocks by industry, start-of-year foreign debts and assets and start-of-year public sector liabilities. Values for end-of-year stock variables in year 0 can be derived from start-of-year values and relevant year 0 flow variables.

### 2.4.3.2 Solution for year 0 and the input-output database for a MONASH model

The input-output database for a typical MONASH model is illustrated in Figure 2.7. These data not only provide the bulk of the year 0 solution, but they also give an immediate impression of the model's properties. By looking at the input-output data we can see the levels of commodity, industry and occupational disaggregation. We can also see: whether imported and domestic good $i$ are treated as distinct varieties; whether margins and indirect taxes are taken seriously and a distinction is made between purchasers' and producer prices; and whether there are industries that produce more than one commodity (multiproduct industries) and commodities that are produced by more than one industry (multi-industry products).

The data in Figure 2.7 has three parts: an absorption matrix; a joint-production matrix; and a vector of import duties. The first row of matrices in the absorption matrix, BAS1, …, BAS6, shows flows in year 0 of commodities to producers, investors, households, exports, public consumption and inventory accumulation. Each of these matrices has $C \times S$ rows, one for each of $C$ commodities from $S$ sources. $C$ can be large. For example in USAGE, a MONASH-style model of the US, there are over 500 commodities.[34] $S$ is usually 2: domestic and imported. However, it can be larger to facilitate analyses in which it is important to identify imports from different countries. For example, the US International Trade Commission (2007, 2009) uses a version of

---

[34] See US International Trade Commission (2004) and Dixon and Rimmer (2004).

| Absorption Matrix | | | | | | | |
|---|---|---|---|---|---|---|---|
| | | 1 | 2 | 3 | 4 | 5 | 6 |
| | | Prod-ucers | Invest-ors | House-holds | Exports | Govern-ment | Invent-ories |
| | Size | $\leftarrow I \rightarrow$ | $\leftarrow I \rightarrow$ | $\leftarrow 1 \rightarrow$ | $\leftarrow 1 \rightarrow$ | $\leftarrow 1 \rightarrow$ | $\leftarrow 1 \rightarrow$ |
| Basic Flows | $\uparrow$ $C{\times}S$ $\downarrow$ | BAS1 | BAS2 | BAS3 | BAS4 | BAS5 | BAS6 |
| Margins | $\uparrow$ $C{\times}S{\times}N$ $\downarrow$ | MAR1 | MAR2 | MAR3 | MAR4 | MAR5 | MAR6 |
| Sales Taxes | $\uparrow$ $C{\times}S$ $\downarrow$ | TAX1 | TAX2 | TAX3 | TAX4 | TAX5 | TAX6 |
| Labor | $\uparrow$ $M$ $\downarrow$ | LABOR | | | | | |
| Capital | $\uparrow$ 1 $\downarrow$ | CAPITAL | | | | | |
| Land | $\uparrow$ 1 $\downarrow$ | LAND | | | | | |
| Production Taxes | $\uparrow$ 1 $\downarrow$ | TAX0 | | | | | |

$C$ = Number of commodities
$I$ = Number of industries
$S$ = Number of sources, usually 2 (dom & imp)
$M$ = Number of occupations
$N$ = Number of commodities used as margins

| Joint Production Matrix | |
|---|---|
| Size | $\leftarrow I \rightarrow$ |
| $\uparrow$ $C$ $\downarrow$ | MAKE |

| Import Duty | |
|---|---|
| Size | $\leftarrow 1 \rightarrow$ |
| $\uparrow$ $C$ $\downarrow$ | TARIFF |

**Figure 2.7** Input-output database for a typical MONASH model.

USAGE with 23 import sources ($S = 24$) to capture the effects of country-specific import quotas.

BAS1 and BAS2 each have $I$ columns, where $I$ is the number of industries (usually approximately the same as the number of commodities). The typical component of BAS1 is the value of good $i$ from source $s$ [good $(i,s)$] used by industry $j$ as an input to current production, and the typical component of BAS2 is the value of $(i,s)$ used to create capital for industry $j$. As shown in Figure 2.7, BAS3, ..., BAS6 each have one column. Most MONASH-style models recognize one household, one foreign buyer, one category of public demand and one category of inventory demand. These dimensions can be extended in work concerned with income distribution, free trade agreements and multiple levels of government.

All of the flows in BAS1, ..., BAS6 are valued at basic prices. The basic price of a domestically produced good is the price received by the producer (that is the price paid by users excluding sales taxes, transport costs and other margin costs). The basic price of an imported good is the landed-duty-paid price, i.e. the price at the port of entry just after the commodity has cleared customs.

Costs separating producers or ports of entry from users appear in the input-output data in the margin matrices and in the row of sales-tax matrices. The margin matrices, MAR1, ..., MAR6, show the values of $N$ margin commodities used in facilitating the flows identified in BAS1, ..., BAS6. Typical margin commodities are the domestic varieties of wholesale trade, retail trade, road transport, rail transport, water transport, air transport, natural gas and other pipelines. Each of the matrices MAR1, ..., MAR6 has $C \times S \times N$ rows corresponding to the use of $N$ margin commodities in facilitating flows of $C$ commodities from $S$ sources. The sales tax matrices TAX1, ..., TAX6 show collections of sales taxes (positive) or payments of subsidies (negative) associated with each of the flows in the BAS matrices.

Payments by industries for $M$ occupational groups are recorded in Figure 2.7 in the matrix LABOR. In models and applications focusing on labor market issues, such as training needs and immigration, $M$ can be large. For example, some versions of the USAGE model distinguish 750 occupations.

In most MONASH models, payments by industries for the use of capital and land are recorded in the input-output data as vectors: CAPITAL and LAND in Figure 2.7. However in studies concerned with food security and biofuels, the land dimension has been disaggregated (see, e.g. Winston, 2009). The vector TAX0 shows collections of taxes net of subsidies on production.

The final two data items in Figure 2.7 are TARIFF and MAKE. TARIFF is a $C \times 1$ vector showing tariff revenue by imported commodity. The joint-product matrix, MAKE, has dimensions $C \times I$. Its typical component is the output (valued in basic prices) of commodity $c$ by industry $i$.

Together, the absorption and joint-production matrices satisfy two balance conditions. (i) The column sums of MAKE, which are values of industry outputs, are identical to the values of industry inputs. Hence, the $j$th column sum of MAKE equals the $j$th column sum of BAS1, MAR1, TAX1, LABOR, CAPITAL, LAND and TAX0. (ii) The row sums of MAKE, which are basic values of outputs of domestic commodities, are identical to basic values of demands for domestic commodities. If $i$ is a non-margin commodity, then the $i$th row sum of MAKE is equal to the sum across the ($i$,'dom')-rows of BAS1 to BAS6. If *i* is a margin commodity, then the *i*th row sum of MAKE is equal to the direct uses of domestic commodity *i*, i.e. the sum across the (*i*,'dom')-rows of BAS1 to BAS6, plus the margins use of commodity *i*. The margins use of *i* is the sum of the components in the (*c*,*s*,*i*)-rows of MAR1 to MAR6 for all commodities *c* and sources *s*.

To obtain a year 0 solution for MONASH flow variables from a database such as that in Figure 2.7, we start by defining quantity units for commodities as the amounts that had a *basic* price of one. Now we can read from BAS1, …, BAS6 and MAR1, …, MAR6 both values and quantities of commodity demands. Similarly, we can read from MAKE both values and quantities of commodity supplies. With basic prices of commodities assigned the value one, the input-output data quickly reveals purchasers prices for year 0. For example, the year 0 purchasers price for good *i* from source *s* bought by industry *j* for use in current production is

$$P1(i, s, j) = [BAS1(i, s, j) + \sum_{n=1}^{N} MAR1(i, s, j, n) + TAX1(i, s, j)]/BAS1(i, s, j).$$

(2.36)

Do year 0 prices and quantities defined in this way satisfy MONASH equations specifying that:

Quantity demanded of domestic product *i* = quantity supplied    (2.37)

Value of output from industry *j* = value of *j*s inputs plus production taxes    (2.38)

Purchasers values = basic values plus margins and sales taxes?    (2.39)

The balancing properties of the input-output data ensure that the values we have assigned to year 0 prices and quantities satisfy (2.37) and (2.38). Equation (2.39) is satisfied via definitions of year 0 purchasers prices such as (2.36).

MONASH models contain many more equations connecting input-output variables than those indicated by (2.37)–(2.39). All of these additional equations contain either free parameters and/or free variables. That is, they contain parameters or variables for which we are free to assign values that allow the equations to be satisfied by our year 0 values for prices and quantities. For example, consider the equation:

$$X1MARG(i, s, j, r) = X1(i, s, j) * A1MARG(i, s, j, r),$$    (2.40)

where $X1MARG(i,s,j,r)$ is the use of margin-commodity *r* (e.g., road transport) to facilitate the flow of intermediate input *i* from source *s* (domestic or imported) to industry *j*, $X1(i,s,j)$ is the use of good *i* from source *s* by industry *j* as an intermediate input and $A1MARG(i,s,j,r)$ is the use of margin-commodity *r* per unit of flow of intermediate input (*i*,*s*) to industry *j*.

From our input-output data, we have already assigned year 0 values to $X1MARG(i,s,j,r)$ and $X1(i,s,j)$. However, $A1MARG(i,s,j,r)$ is free. If $X1(i,s,j)$ is non-zero, then we ensure that (2.40) is satisfied by the year 0 quantities read from our input-output data by choosing the year 0 value for $A1MARG(i,s,j,r)$ to be the ratio of the year 0 values of $X1MARG(i,s,j,r)$ and $X1(i,s,j)$. If $X1(i,s,j)$ is zero, then $A1MARG(i,s,j,r)$ can be assigned any value provided $X1MARG(i,s,j,r)$ is also zero. If $X1(i,s,j)$ is zero but $X1MARG(i,s,j,r)$ is not zero, then we have a data error requiring correction.

Now consider a less trivial example. Part of the theory of MONASH models is that industry $j$ chooses its current inputs of domestic and imported good $i$ to minimize costs subject to a CES constraint in which the industry's requirements for good $i$ are proportional to its activity level, $Z(j)$, i.e. industry $j$ chooses:

$$X1(i, s, j), \ s = \{\text{dom, imp}\},$$

to minimize:

$$\sum_s P1(i, s, j) \, X1(i, s, j), \tag{2.41}$$

subject to:

$$Z(j) = \left[ \sum_s X1(i, s, j)^{-\rho(i,j)} \delta1(i, s, j) \right]^{-1/\rho(i,j)}, \tag{2.42}$$

where the $\delta1(i,s,j)$ are non-negative parameters summing to one over $s$ and $\rho(i,j)$ is a substitution parameter assigned a value greater than $-1$ (but not precisely zero) reflecting econometric estimates or views about import/domestic substitution.

Problem (2.41)–(2.42) leads to equations for the ratio of domestic to imported inputs of the form:

$$\frac{X1(i, \text{dom}, j)}{X1(i, \text{imp}, j)} = \left[ \frac{\delta1(i, \text{dom}, j)}{\delta1(i, \text{imp}, j)} * \frac{P1(i, \text{imp}, j)}{P1(i, \text{dom}, j)} \right]^{1/(1+\rho(i,j))}. \tag{2.43}$$

Values can be assigned to the parameters $\delta1(i,s,j)$, $s =$ dom and imp, to ensure that (2.43) is satisfied by the year 0 values for $X1(i,s,j)$ and $P1(i,s,j)$, together with the value for the substitution parameter $\rho(i,j)$.

A few examples is not a proof of the existence of a year 0 solution, $(X(0), Y(0))$, to (2.13). A complete proof for any model involves working through every equation, identifying free parameters or variables. This is not difficult, but it is tedious.

## 2.4.4 Deriving change and percentage change equations

MONASH models are represented as linear systems of the form:

$$A(V) * v = 0, \tag{2.44}$$

where $V$ is an $n \times 1$ vector of initial values or values generated during a multistep process for the variables (denoted as $(X, Y)$ in the previous subsection), $A$ is an $m \times n$ matrix of coefficients each of which is a function of $V$ and $v$ is a vector of changes and percentage changes in the variables away from their values in $V$.

In this subsection we describe how equations that make up the change/percentage change system (2.44) can be derived from the levels system (2.13).

Most equations in (2.44) can be derived from the corresponding equation in (2.13) by the application of the three rules in Table 2.3. For example, the multiplication and power rules applied to (2.43) give the percentage change equation:

$$x1(i, \mathrm{dom}, j) - x1(i, \mathrm{imp}, j) = \sigma(i, j) * (p1(i, \mathrm{imp}, j) - p1(i, \mathrm{dom}, j)), \qquad (2.45)$$

where the lowercase $x$ and $p$ are percentage changes in the variables represented by the corresponding uppercase symbols and $\sigma(i, j)$, which equals $1/(1 + \rho(i, j))$, is the elasticity of substitution in industry $j$ between domestic and imported units of commodity $i$.

In representing optimization problems in system (2.44), it is often convenient to use percentage change versions of the first-order conditions. For example, in the optimization problem (2.8)–(2.9), the first-order conditions are:

$$P_i = \Lambda * \frac{X_i^{h_i - 1}}{Z^{h_i}} * Q_i, \ i = 1, \ ..., n, \qquad (2.46)$$

where $\Lambda$ is the Lagrangian multiplier, together with the constraint (2.9). These conditions can be represented in (2.44) as:

$$p_i = \lambda + (h_i - 1) * x_i - h_i * z, \ i = 1, ..., n, \qquad (2.47)$$

$$\sum_j (x_j - z) * S_j = 0, \qquad (2.48)$$

**Table 2.3** Rules for deriving percentage-change equations

| | Levels | | Percentage changes |
|---|---|---|---|
| | | | **Representation in** |
| Multiplication rule | $U = RW$ | $\Rightarrow$ | $u = r + w$ |
| Power rule | $U = R^\alpha$ | $\Rightarrow$ | $u = \alpha r$ |
| Addition rules | $U = R + W$ | $\Rightarrow$ | $Uu = Rr + Ww$ |
| | | | or $u = S_r r + S_w w$ |

$U$, $R$ and $W$ are levels of variables, $u$, $r$ and $w$ are percentage changes, $\alpha$ is a parameter and $S_r$ and $S_w$ are shares evaluated at the current solution. In the first step of a Johansen/Euler computation, the current solution is the initial solution. Hence, $S_r = R(0)/U(0)$ and $S_w = W(0)/U(0)$. In subsequent steps, $S_r$ and $S_w$ are recomputed as $U$, $R$ and $W$ move away from their initial values.

where again we use lowercase symbols to represent percentage changes in the variables denoted by the corresponding uppercase symbols and:

$$S_j = \left(\frac{X_j}{Z}\right)^{h_j} * Q_j / \left[\sum_k \left(\frac{X_k}{Z}\right)^{h_k} * Q_k\right], \quad j = 1, \ldots, n. \tag{2.49}$$

It is apparent from (2.46) that $S_j$ is the share of total costs accounted for by input $j$.

While (2.47) and (2.48) can be used in (2.44) to represent optimization problem (2.8)–(2.9), we may prefer to eliminate the percentage change in the Lagrangian multiplier, $\lambda$. After a little algebra we can obtain (2.9) and (2.11).[35]

Not all of the equations in (2.44) can be derived by the simple rules in Table 2.3. Occasionally more complicated differentiations are required. For example, consider the levels equation

$$R = R_{\text{norm}} + C * \ln\left\{\frac{G - G_{\text{min}}}{G_{\text{max}} - G} * \frac{G_{\text{max}} - T}{T - G_{\text{min}}}\right\}. \tag{2.50}$$

Variants of this equation are used in MONASH models to relate an industry's capital growth ($G$) through year $t$[36] to the industry's expected rate of return ($R$) and its normal rate of return ($R_{\text{norm}}$).[37] In (2.50), $G_{\text{min}}$, $G_{\text{max}}$, $T$ and $C$ are parameters with $C$ positive and $G_{\text{min}} < T < G_{\text{max}}$. $T$ represents a trend rate of growth of capital. If $R$ equals $R_{\text{norm}}$ then via (2.50) the growth in capital through the year is at its trend value ($G = T$). Capital growth will exceed trend ($G > T$) if the expected rate of return is greater than the normal rate of return ($R > R_{\text{norm}}$). Capital growth will never move above $G_{\text{max}}$ (as $R \to \infty$, $G \to G_{\text{max}}$). Similarly capital growth will never move below $G_{\text{min}}$ (as $R \to -\infty$, $G \to G_{\text{min}}$). By choosing suitable values for $G_{\text{min}}$ and $G_{\text{max}}$, we can ensure that our model always implies growth rates for capital in a realistic range. To obtain a form of (2.50) suitable for inclusion in (2.44) we can totally differentiate both sides. This gives

$$\text{del\_}R - \text{del\_}R_{\text{norm}} - C * \left\{\frac{1}{G - G_{\text{min}}} + \frac{1}{G_{\text{max}} - G}\right\} * \text{del\_}G = 0. \tag{2.51}$$

In (2.51), del_R, del_R$_{\text{norm}}$ and del_G are *change* variables and form part of the $v$ vector in (2.44). We use change variables because $R$, $R_{\text{norm}}$ and $G$ are variables for which zero is a sensible value. The coefficients on del_R, del_R$_{\text{norm}}$ and del_G in the relevant row of the $A$ matrix are 1, $-1$ and $-C^*\{1/(G - G_{\text{min}}) + 1/(G_{\text{max}} - G)\}$.

---

[35] The first move in deriving (2.10) and (2.11) from (2.47) and (2.48) is to multiply (2.47) by $S_i/(h_i - 1)$ and then sum over $i$.

[36] $G$ is $J - 1$, where $J$ the ratio of capital at the end of year $t$ to capital at the start of year $t$.

[37] Details on the MONASH treatment of capital growth are in Dixon and Rimmer (2002, pp. 189–198).

### 2.4.5 Introduction to the GEMPACK programs for solving and analyzing MONASH models

MONASH models are built, solved and analyzed using GEMPACK. The existence of this software explains much of the popularity of MONASH-style models throughout the world. GEMPACK is described in detail by Horridge *et al.* in Chapter 20 of this Handbook. In this subsection we start with some brief comments on GEMPACK's history. Then we look at the structure of how model solutions are computed via GEMPACK. This will be helpful in summarizing the technical material that has been covered so far in this section.

The computer code for the first MONASH model (the ORANI model) was developed by Sutton (1977). This code was effective and handled what was for the time a very large CGE model. However, Sutton's programs were model specific: they solved the ORANI model. In 1980 Ken Pearson started work on GEMPACK. His objective was to create a suite of programs that could be used to solve any CGE model in the Johansen/MONASH tradition. The first version of GEMPACK was used for teaching in 1984 and shortly after that was adopted by Australian CGE modelers. The first GEMPACK manuals were published in 1986 (see Codsi and Pearson, 1986). Early journal descriptions of GEMPACK are Pearson (1988) and Codsi and Pearson (1988). Evidence of the success of GEMPACK is its adoption over the last 25 years by thousands of CGE modelers.

The structure of a GEMPACK solution of a MONASH model is illustrated in Figure 2.8. GEMPACK users start by presenting their model in TABLO code. This is a language close to ordinary algebra. For example, assume that model (2.13) consists of three equations and nine variables:

$$DTOT(i) = \sum_{j=1}^{2} D(i,j), \ i = 1, 2, 3, \tag{2.52}$$

where $DTOT(i)$ is total demand for good $i$ and $D(i,j)$ is demand for $i$ by user $j$. In percentage-change form the model is:

$$dtot(i) = \sum_{j=1}^{2} S(i,j) * d(i,j), \ i = 1, 2, 3, \tag{2.53}$$

where lowercase symbols are percentage changes in variables represented by the corresponding uppercase symbols and $S(i,j)$ is the share of user $j$ in the total demand for good $i$. Largely self-explanatory TABLO code for the model is shown in Table 2.4.

TABLO code has two main roles in GEMPACK. The first is to give a set of instructions for reading a database, which we can think of as revealing a value for $V$, and using it to evaluate $A(V)$ in (2.44). In the example in Table 2.4 the declaration of

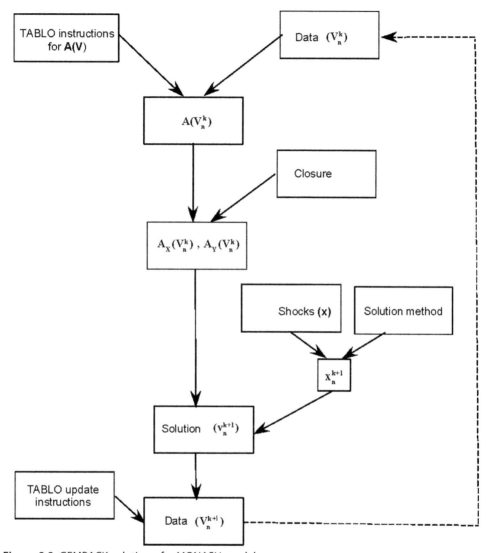

**Figure 2.8** GEMPACK solution of a MONASH model.

variables is an instruction to create an $A$ matrix with nine columns, called $d(C1,U1)$, ..., $d(C3,U2)$, $dtot(C1)$, ..., $dtot(C3)$. The command starting with '*Equation*' is an instruction that the $A$ matrix should have three rows called $E\_dtot(C1)$, ..., $E\_dtot(C3)$. The equation itself is an instruction that the row $E\_dtot(Ci)$ should contain 1 in the $dtot(i)$ column and $-S(i,j)$ in the $d(i,j)$ column. The *Read* and *Formula* commands contain instruction on how to evaluate $S(i,j)$ from a dataset (e.g. input-output data of the form shown in Figure 2.7). In Figure 2.8 we show the data to be used in the $k+1$th step in an $n$-step sequence as Data $(V_n^k)$, $k = 0$, ..., $n - 1$.

**Table 2.4** Sample of TABLO code

```
File DATA # Data file #;
Set COM # Commodities # (C1–C3);
Set USER # User # (U1–U2);
Coefficient ! Declaration of coefficients !
  (All,i,COM)(All,j,USER) BAS(i,j) # Data for demand for i by j #;
  (All,i,COM) TBAS(i) # Total demand for i #;
  (All,i,COM)(All,j,USER) S(i,j) # Share of j in demand for i #;
Read BAS from file DATA Header "BAS";
Formula
  (All,i,COM) TBAS(i) = Sum(j,USER, BAS(i,j) );
  (All,i,COM)(All,j,USER) S(i,j) = BAS(i,j)/TBAS(i);
Variable ! Declaration of variables !
  (All,i,COM)(All,j,USER) d(i,j) # Demand for i by j #;
  (All,i,COM) dtot(i) # Total demand for i #;
Equation E_dtot
  (All,i,COM) dtot(i) = Sum(j,USER, S(i,j)*d(i,j));
Update
  (All,i,COM)(All,j,USER) BAS(i,j) = d(i,j);
```

Having evaluated $A(V)$ with the initial database to obtain $A(V_n^0)$, we introduce the closure. This can be done via a subprogram that lists the exogenous variables. GEMPACK can now split the $A$ matrix into $A_X(V_n^0)$ and $A_Y(V_n^0)$.

The next two subprograms introduce the shocks (movements in exogenous variables) and specify the solution method (e.g. Johansen/Euler with $n$ steps). From these subprograms, GEMPACK can compute the shocks to be applied in the first step of the $n$-step sequence. All the information has now been assembled to enable GEMPACK to compute the movements in the endogenous variables in the first step of the $n$-step sequence.

This brings us to the second main role of TABLO. It provides instructions for updating to a new database, Data $(V_n^1)$, that incorporates the movements in the variables imposed and generated in the first step. In Table 2.4, the update instruction says that the data item BAS($i,j$) should be increased by $d(i,j)$%. Once Data $(V_n^1)$ has been created, GEMPACK is ready to undertake the second step of the $n$-step sequence, and so on through the $n$ steps.[38]

The core set of programs outlined in Figure 2.8 has been supplemented since the mid-1980s by an ever-expanding set of wonderfully useful GEMPACK features contributed by Ken Pearson and his colleagues including George Codsi, Mark

---

[38] Apart from the two roles described here, TABLO also provides instructions for condensation, see Section 2.3.2.2.

Horridge, Jill Harrison and Michael Jerie. For example, AnalyseGE allows GEM-PACK users to see the value of any coefficient (i.e. any function of database items) or any variable in a particular solution via point-and-click applied to the TABLO representation of the model. ViewSOL allows GEMPACK users to see a series of simulation results in a variety of styles (e.g. year-on-year growth, cumulative growth from an initial year or cumulative difference between two series of results) and a variety of formats (graphs or numbers). These aids greatly enhance the user's ability to undertake MONASH-style modeling.

### 2.4.6 Creating a database for a MONASH model

One of the most difficult and least teachable CGE skills is the compilation of a database for year 0. For MONASH models, the central components are a set of input-output accounts as illustrated in Figure 2.7 and estimates of capital stock by industry.[39] What makes compilation of these data so hard is that, for the most part, they must be gleaned from bulletins prepared by statistical agencies for purposes far removed from CGE modeling. The accounting conventions adopted by the agencies are often opaquely documented and tortuous to follow.

Here, we flag some of the difficulties, drawing on our experience in preparing a year 0 database for the USAGE model of the US. However, experience for the US may not be directly relevant for other countries. In creating a practical, policy-relevant CGE model for any country, there is no substitute for the time-consuming work of looking at the data presented by the statistical agencies, thinking about what it means, working out the underlying accounting conventions, and contacting the agencies and asking questions.[40] The practice adopted by some CGE modelers of delegating the data preparation task to research assistants is inappropriate for models intended for serious policy analysis.

#### 2.4.6.1 Input-output data published by the BEA

The starting point for the USAGE database was the $498 \times 498$ input-output data for 1992 published by the BEA (Bureau of Economic Analysis, 1998). The first challenge in using these data was to sort out the meaning of mysterious rows and columns designed by the BEA to give desired row and column sums. For example, the BEA wanted the household consumption and export columns to add to total household consumption and total exports as shown in the National Income and Product Accounts (NIPA) for 1992.

---

[39] Other data items required for year 0 include the balance of payments and the public sector budget. These are not discussed here but are described in Dixon and Rimmer (2002, pp. 212–219).

[40] For the US, the main statistical agency supplying data relevant for CGE modeling is the BEA. Their officers, particularly Karen Horowitz, were extremely helpful in answering the numerous questions that arose as we prepared the database for the USAGE model.

In making estimates for their input-output tables of consumption expenditures dis-aggregated by commodity, the BEA felt unable to distinguish between expenditures by residents and expenditures by visitors. They recorded all consumption expenditures on each commodity in the household consumption column and did not include expenditures by visitors in the export column. On the other hand, NIPA data excludes total visitor expenditure from the estimate of total household consumption and includes it in total exports. To achieve their objective of NIPA compatibility, the BEA included in their input-output tables a row and corresponding user column labeled 'Rest-of-world adjustment to final use'. The row contains two non-zero entries: a negative entry in the household column representing expenditures by visitors and a positive entry in the export column representing the same thing. The column consists entirely of zeros. Initially in using the BEA data we deleted both the column and row for 'Rest-of-world adjustment to final use'. Eventually we dealt with the issue satisfactorily by using data from the BEA's Tourism Satellite Accounts (Okubo and Planting, 1998) to itemize visitor expenditures which we reallocated from the household consumption column to a new industry, Export tourism. We modeled the output of this industry as being entirely exported.

After further adjustments we were able to present the BEA input-output data in the form shown in Figure 2.9 where: PV1, ..., PV6 represent direct uses of commodities (not identified by import/domestic source) valued in producer prices; MAR1, ..., MAR6 represent margins on the flows in PV1, ..., PV6; PVM represents imports; LAB, TAX0 and OVA are a breakdown of value added into compensation of employees, indirect taxes and other value added. MAKE represents commodity outputs by industries. The sum down a column of [PV1, MAR1, LAB, TAX0, OVA] matches the corresponding column sum of MAKE. For non-margin commodities the row sums of [PV1, PV2, ..., PV6, −PVM] match the corresponding row sums of MAKE. Finally, for any commodity $n$ which is a margin, the sum across the $n$-row of PV1, ..., −PVM plus all the $n$-entries in MAR1, ..., MAR6 matches the commodity $n$-row sum in MAKE.

To move from Figure 2.9 to a MONASH-style input-output database of the form shown in Figure 2.7 it was necessary to consider conventions in the BEA data concerning: valuation of flows and the recording of indirect taxes; imports; public sector demands, particularly the use of negative entries; investment; and value added. The following subsections describe some of these conventions and our efforts to cope with them. However, in the space available we cannot be comprehensive. Many important details must be omitted concerning, for example, the BEA treatment of: real estate agents and home ownership; royalties; scrap and used and second hand goods; auto rental; secondary production; capital stocks in public sector enterprises; and foreign ownership of US capital.[41]

---

[41] Documentation on these issues is available from the authors.

| | | Absorption Matrix | | | | | | |
|---|---|---|---|---|---|---|---|---|
| | | Prod-ucers | Invest-ors | House-holds | Exports | Govern-ment | Invent-ories | -Imports |
| | Size | ← $I$ → | ← 1 → | ← 1 → | ← 1 → | ← 35 → | ← 1 → | ← 1 → |
| Commod-ity flows | ↑ $C$ ↓ | PV1 | PV2 | PV3 | PV4 | PV5 | PV6 | -PVM |
| Margins | ↑ $C \times N$ ↓ | MAR1 | MAR2 | MAR3 | MAR4 | MAR5 | MAR6 | 0 |
| Labor | ↑ 1 ↓ | LAB | | | | | | |
| Taxes | ↑ 1 ↓ | TAX0 | | | | | | |
| Other value added | ↑ 1 ↓ | OVA | | | | | | |

$C$ = Number of commodities (= 483)
$I$ = Number of industries (= 493)
$N$ = Number of commodities used as margins (= 8)

| | Joint Production Matrix |
|---|---|
| Size | ← $I$ → |
| ↑ $C$ ↓ | MAKE |

**Figure 2.9** Schematic representation of BEA benchmark input-output data for 1992.

### 2.4.6.2 Valuation and treatment of indirect taxes

All commodity flows in the BEA data, and therefore in Figure 2.9, are valued at producer prices, i.e. basic values (prices accruing to producers) plus sales and excise taxes. In tables at producer prices, the indirect tax row (TAX0) normally represents taxes paid on the sales of the industry's products together with production taxes and taxes on the use of primary factors.[42] Hence, we expected to find large entries in the Tobacco and Petrol columns of TAX0. However, these entries were only moderate, whereas the entries in the Wholesale and Retail columns were surprisingly large. We found that in the BEA tables, taxes are recorded in the column of the industry that collects the taxes. Apparently, tobacco and petrol taxes are collected largely by wholesalers and retailers.

In these circumstances, we expected large amounts of wholesale and retail margins to be associated with sales of tobacco and petrol, reflecting large taxes associated with the wholesaling and retailing of these products. For sales to consumers we did, in fact, find large wholesale and retail margins in MAR3 associated with sales of tobacco and

---

[42] For a description of the standard types of input-output tables (basic values, producer values and purchasers values with either direct or indirect allocation of imports), see Dixon *et al.* (1992, chapter 2).

petrol. For example, wholesale and retail margins on petrol sales to households were $58.7 billion on a producer value of only $51.4 billion. We suspected that most of the $58.7 billion was tax paid by wholesalers and retailers on their sales of petrol to households. On petrol sales to industries the ratio of wholesale and retail margins to producer value was only about 28%, i.e. about a quarter of the value of the ratio applying to petrol sales to consumers. We suspected that this was the result of two factors: (i) lower taxes on industry use of petrol than on household use, and (ii) lower payments by industry than by households to wholesalers and retailers per gallon of petrol, i.e. genuinely lower margins.

More generally, the practice of allocating taxes to the collecting industry is unsatisfactory for CGE purposes. For example, without knowing the tax content of retail and wholesale margins associated with consumer purchases of tobacco and petrol, we cannot project effects on tax collections and retail and wholesale activity of changes in consumer demands for these products. For USAGE we needed to reclassify indirect taxes so that they were excluded from wholesale and retail margins and so that they were associated (as in Figure 2.7) with the purchases which give rise to them. In doing this we were assisted by the BEA who gave us about 10 000 items of unpublished data showing indirect taxes by commodity and user. In most cases the BEA indicated where the item was placed in their published producer value input-output tables. This enabled us to work out, for example, how much of PV3(Cigarettes), MAR3(Cigarettes, Wholesale) and MAR3(Cigarettes, Retail) in Figure 2.9 were in fact sales taxes. With this information, we reduced these three flows to basic values and made corresponding adjustments to TAX3(Cigarettes) and to the values of Cigarettes, Wholesale and Retail outputs in the MAKE matrix.

### 2.4.6.3 Imports

The BEA input-output tables adopt indirect allocation of imports. Consequently in PV1, ..., PV6 in Figure 2.9, competing imports are aggregated with output from domestic producers. Imports valued at producer prices (which for the BEA tables are landed-duty-paid prices) are shown as negative entries in a single import column (−PVM). The first problem we noticed with the BEA's treatment of imports is that three of the entries in the import column were positive, seemingly implying negative levels of imports for Wholesale trade, Water transport and Non-ferrous metal ores.

After inquiries with the BEA we found that import duties were recorded as if they were negative imports of Wholesale trade. This treatment has a column and row logic, but it is opaque for CGE modeling. The column logic is that the BEA wanted the total of the import column to reflect the cost to the US of imports (payment to foreigners). As part of achieving this they needed to deduct duties from the total of the landed-duty-paid values recorded in the import column. The row logic is that the BEA recorded duties as a tax (part of TAX0 in Figure 2.9) on the sales of the Wholesale industry, the industry they deemed to have collected the import duties. With the producer value of the output of the Wholesale industry inflated in this way, the BEA needed to inflate the value of sales of the Wholesale industry. Negative imports of wholesale services achieved this purpose. The BEA supplied us with an unpublished disaggregation of import duties by commodity, enabling us to form the Tariff vector in Figure 2.7, and to undo the BEA's treatment of import duties by zeroing out the Wholesale entry in the import column and making corresponding deductions from TAX0 in the Wholesale column and from the (Wholesale, Wholesale) entry in the MAKE matrix.

For Water transport, the seemingly negative value of imports arose from the BEA's treatment of water transport services provided by US shipping in delivering imports to US ports. The cost of these services is embedded in the landed-duty-paid value of imports recorded in the import column. Treating US-provided water transport services on imports as negative imports rather than as exports was motivated by the objective of ensuring that the total for the import column reflected the cost to the US of imports. Using unpublished data provided by the BEA we were able to reclassify negative imports of Water transport as positive exports, leaving only genuine imports of Water transport (e.g. cruises by US residents on foreign ships) in the import column. Similar adjustments were necessary for Air transport, although the problem was less obvious in the BEA data because the Air transport entry in the import column had the expected sign, negative: genuine imports of Air services outweighed US-provided air services embedded in US imports.

In the case of Non-ferrous metal ores the negative value for imports was due to the BEA's treatment of gold. For this item, the BEA is willing to estimate net imports, but not imports and exports separately. For 1992 the BEA estimated that net imports of gold were negative. We reclassified these negative imports as exports.

The second problem with the BEA's treatment of imports is that it provides no disaggregation of imports by using industry or final demander. Such a disaggregation is required for a MONASH-style database, see Figure 2.7. Again the BEA came to the rescue with unpublished data enabling us to turn the import column into an import matrix.

### 2.4.6.4 Public sector demands

The BEA tables give 35 columns of government expenditures: there are 35 columns in PV5 and MAR5 in Figure 2.9. Fourteen of these columns refer to government consumption activities and have labels such as *Federal Government consumption expenditures, national defense.* The remaining 21 columns refer to government investment activities and have labels such as *Federal Government gross investment, national defense.* Of the 21 investment activities, 14 are investment counterparts of the 14 consumption activities.

For each of the 35 activities the corresponding column in Figure 2.9 shows the commodity composition of public expenditure. For example, the column for *State and local government consumption expenditures, elementary and secondary public school systems* (column 9800C1) shows expenditures totaling $224.107 billion accounted for mainly by expenditure of $186.326 billion on *General government* (commodity 820000). While most of the expenditures in PV5 are positive, some are negative. In column 9800C1 of PV5, for example, there are expenditures of: −$2.680 billion on *Eating and drinking places* (commodity 740000), −$3.078 billion on *Elementary and secondary schools* (commodity 770401), and −$0.002 billion on *Pens, etc.* (commodity 640501). In response to our queries the BEA explained that negative entries in the government vectors are government sales, e.g. sales of Eating and drinking (lunch program) by State and local government schools. In their input-output tables, the BEA follows the convention of making the row sum for a commodity across PV1, ..., PV6, −PVM,[43] equal to the value of domestic *non-government* production.[44] The restriction to non-government production is achieved by the negative entries in PV5.

For CGE modeling it is inappropriate to treat only non-government enterprises as producers and it is counter-intuitive to treat government outputs as negative demands. Consequently we dropped the BEA convention. We converted the 14 columns for government consumption activities and the seven investment columns with no consumption counterpart into industries. (The treatment of the remaining 14 government investment activities is described in Section 2.4.6.5.) In creating these 21 new government industries we regarded the positive entries from the original BEA columns as inputs and the negative entries as outputs. Thus, we interpreted the data in column 9800C1 of PV5 and MAR5 as showing that government industry 9800C1 produced output of $229.867 billion. This was the sum of the positive entries in column 9800C1 of PV5 and MAR5. The negative entries were entered as positives in the MAKE matrix and interpreted as showing that industry 9800C1 produced $2.680 billion of *Eating and drinking places* (commodity 740000), $3.078 billion of *Elementary and secondary schools* (commodity 770401) and $0.002 billion of *Pens, etc.* (commodity 640501). In addition, industry 9800C1 produced $224.107 billion of its principal product ($= 229.867 - 2.680 - 3.078 - 0.002$), which was designated as commodity 9800C1. We assumed that the sales of industry 9800C1's principal product were entirely to a single category of government final demand. Sales of industry 9800C1's other outputs were already accounted for in Figure 2.9 in purchases by households and other demanders of commodities 740000, 770401 and 640501.

---

[43] Here we consider only non-margin commodities.
[44] An exception is the output of *General government* where the commodity row sum is entirely government production.

The BEA's government columns (PV5, MAR5) did not include any purchases of labor or other primary factor inputs. These inputs were accounted for via purchases of *General government* (commodity 820000), which is produced by industry 820000 entirely from labor and other value added. This left us unable to distinguish in our modeling between the composition of primary factor inputs in different government activities.

### 2.4.6.5 Investment by investing industry

The investment column in Figure 2.9 shows gross private fixed investment by commodity. For a MONASH-style model we need to give investment an industry dimension, see Figure 2.7. Our main data source for doing this in the case of the USAGE model was a 163 commodity by 64 industry matrix of private investment expenditures published by the BEA (BEA product NDN-0224).[45] The commodities in this matrix mapped easily to the input–output commodities for which the BEA's input–output tables showed non-zero investment. Thus, the investment matrix provided an adequate basis for giving the input–output investment column a 64-industry dimension. Within the 64 industries we allocated investment expenditures on each commodity to component industries at the detailed USAGE level (approximately 500 industries) using indicators such as other value added and employment. Thus, we assumed that all component industries within a 64-order industry had the same commodity composition of investment expenditures.

This procedure covered only private sector industries, not our 21 government industries. The BEA government investment expenditure vectors became the investment vectors for 14 of the government industries. We left the other seven government industries with no investment (zero entries in their columns of BAS2, MAR2 and TAX2 in Figure 2.7). With investment in 14 government industries, we recognized that these industries must have capital stocks with corresponding rentals. In handling this we replaced expenditures on *General government* by these 14 industries with entries in the LABOR and CAPITAL vectors in Figure 2.7. These entries represented the primary factor constituents of *General government*[46] expenditures by the 14 industries.

### 2.4.6.6 Value added, self-employment and capital stocks

The value-added section of input–output table provides the main data for CGE models on resource constraints. Perhaps reflecting the interests and times of Wassily Leontief, the originator of input–output economics, published input–output tables often lack adequate detail on value added for CGE modeling. Writing in the 1930s,[47] Leontief saw his input-

---

[45] See Bonds and Aylor (1998).
[46] Recall that the *General government* industry has only primary factor inputs.
[47] See, e.g. Leontief (1936).

output system as a means of estimating the effects on employment by industry of demand stimulation policies in an environment of high unemployment and excess capacity, a situation in which resource constraints are unimportant. Consequently, relative to the demand side of his model, Leontief gave little emphasis to value added. This bias in the presentation of input-output tables has continued even in countries in which full employment and inflationary conditions were present for much of the second half of the twentieth century making resource constraints of paramount interest. Apart from taxes which we have already discussed, the BEA input-output tables divide value added for each industry in the US into only two categories: *Compensation of employees* and *Other value added* (LAB and OVA in Figure 2.9).

For a CGE model we require the measure of labor input in each industry to be compensation of employees *plus* the value of non-payroll labor (the self employed and family helpers). Data from the Bureau of Labor Statistics (BLS) indicates that about 10% of all jobs are held by non-payroll workers and that for some industries this percentage is much higher. For example, non-payroll workers hold about half the jobs in agriculture. In developing the USAGE database, we imputed a wage (discussed below) to non-payroll workers in each industry. We then adjusted the BEA value-added data by removing the estimated values of non-payroll labor from the OVA row and adding them to the LAB row. BLS data also allowed us to disaggregate the adjusted LAB row into a large number of occupations. This has been important in studies such as that described in Section 2.2 concerned with immigration and other labor market issues.

We interpreted the entries in the adjusted OVA vector as rental on capital.[48] However, in many cases further adjustments to OVA were necessary so that our database implied reasonable values for rates of return on capital. In working out the implied rate of return for industry $j$, we divided $OVA_j$ by the value of capital stock ($K_j$) and deducted the rate of depreciation ($D_j$).

Estimates of capital stocks and depreciation rates are important in dynamic CGE models but unfortunately relevant data are scarce. For the USAGE model the main data source was the BEA's dataset NDN-0216 (see Bureau of Economic Analysis, 1999) which gives usable data for capital stocks, investment and depreciation rates for the economy divided into 55 sectors.

An unattractive feature of these data is that they are classified to sectors on a company and ownership basis. For example, the capital stock for the construction sector in NDN-0216 refers to fixed capital owned by companies whose principal activity is construction. For modeling purposes we want to know how much capital is used in construction

---

[48] In the initial version of USAGE, rental on land was not modeled. Agricultural land was included in later versions concerned with biofuels; see, e.g. Winston (2009) and Gehlhar *et al.* (2010).

activities. Capital used in construction activities can differ sharply from the NDN-0216 concept for several reasons:

- Non-construction companies may undertake construction (e.g. mining companies may drill new wells, a construction activity) and therefore own capital that is used for construction activities.
- Construction companies may operate across several non-construction activities and therefore own capital that is used for non-construction activities.
- Construction companies may hire capital from financial institutions and therefore use capital in construction activities that is not owned by construction companies.

While the capital and investment data in NDN-0216 are on a company and ownership basis, the investment data in NDN-0224 (used in our estimation of investment by industry, see Section 2.4.6.5) are on an activity basis.[49] By comparing sectoral investment from NDN-0216 with a 55 sector aggregation of our input–output investment estimates, we made an assessment of the extent to which the company/ownership capital data in NDN-0216 was likely to be a satisfactory basis for estimating capital stocks by industry defined on an activity basis. For most sectors investment on the two bases was reasonably compatible. However, for some sectors the differences were dramatic. For example, NDN-0224 showed investment in the construction sector of $32 billion, whereas NDN-0216 showed $6 billion. It appears that construction in the US is carried out to a large extent by companies that do not specialize in construction or by construction companies using rented capital.

Despite the NDN-0216 and NDN-0224 incompatibilities, we had no choice but to use NDN-0216 as the basis for the USAGE capital stock estimates. To estimate capital stocks on an activity basis at the 55 sector level, we assumed that depreciation rates ($D_j$) and capital growth ($I_j/K_j - D_j$) for sector $j$ calculated on an ownership basis from NDN-0216 also applied on an activity basis.

With sectoral capital stocks on an activity basis estimated in this way, we were able to calculate implied sectoral rates of return. This calculation gave rates of return for 26 of the 55 sectors outside the range 0–20. We considered estimates outside this range to be unrealistic and likely to cause difficulties in simulations.

Our first step in dealing with this problem was to revisit the issue of self-employment. For our initial estimates of imputed wages of self-employed workers we used the average wage rate of employees. Now for each of the 55 sectors we looked at the effects on OVA and implied rates of return of varying the self-employed/employee wage ratio between 0.5 and 4. In most sectors self-employment is

---

[49] NDN-0224 is compiled using input–output conventions. Under input–output conventions, capital is assigned to the industrial activity for which it is used. NDN-0216 is compiled using NIPA conventions. Under these conventions, capital is assigned to owning industries regardless of how it is used.

unimportant and variations in the wage ratio have little effect on estimated rates of return. However, for some sectors, we were able to make a plausible change in the wage ratio and at the same time produce a more realistic rate-of-return estimate. For health services, we raised the wage ratio to 2, thereby recognizing that self-employed health professionals are likely to be paid considerably more than health employees. This reduced the estimated rate of return in health services from 21% to a more reasonable 14%. For construction, on the other hand, we lowered the wage ratio, to 0.5. This seems reasonable because self-employed construction contractors (which include handymen) are likely to be paid considerably less than construction employees of major firms. The adjustment in the construction wage ratio increased the estimated rate of return in for the sector from an unlikely −14.3% to a less unreasonable −3.5%.

Having done as much as we could with the wage ratio, we were still had 18 sectors with estimated rates of return outside the range 0−20. For each of these 18 sectors we reset the value of capital stock. For sectors having initial estimated rates of return of over 20%, we raised our estimate of their capital stocks so that their rates of return fell to 20%. For sectors having initial estimated rates of return below zero, we lowered our estimate of their capital stocks so that their rates of return rose to zero. We then spread these final estimates of activity-based sectoral capital stocks to constituent USAGE industries mainly according to our estimates of other value added.

## 2.5 RESPONDING TO THE NEEDS OF CGE CONSUMERS: THE FOUR CLOSURE APPROACH

From their beginnings in the 1970s, MONASH models have been produced to satisfy the needs of consumers of CGE services in the public and private sectors. These are real needs expressed via willingness to pay from limited budgets. This means that the evolution of MONASH models has been largely demand driven. Section 2.5.1 describes what it is that consumers of CGE services demand. Section 2.5.2 then describes how, with MONASH models, we have tried to satisfy these demands via simulations conducted under four closures: historical, decomposition, forecast and policy.

### 2.5.1 What consumers of CGE services want

Both public and private sector consumers of services based on MONASH models are mainly concerned with current policy proposals. In assessing the quality of modeling services they assign heavy weight to: up-to-date data; detailed disaggregation in the focus area and accurate representation of relevant policy instruments; and disaggregated results. While not directly demanded by consumers, we have found that servicing their needs is made easier if we can produce forecasts showing likely developments in the economy with and without the policy under consideration and decomposition analyses quantifying the role of similar policy changes in the past.

### 2.5.1.1 Up-to-date data

Consumers are often well-informed about the latest statistics for their particular industries of interest. If they see conflict between what they know and data in a model, they lose confidence in all aspects of the model and its results. We suffered an example of this in 2006 when we were working on the US International Trade Commission's flagship publication concerned with the economy-wide effects of removing all major import restraints (US International Trade Commission, 2007). At a late stage in this work a US International Trade Commission Commissioner, who was knowledgeable about the Textile and clothing sector, drew our attention to data showing that US Apparel output in 2004 was $34 billion, yet our model's database was showing $61 billion. Our $61 billion was an estimate and overlooked data in the latest Annual Survey of Manufactures. In the context of the overall project, the problem seemed relatively minor. Nevertheless, although rectifying it involved considerable delays, this could not be avoided. It was essential for the credibility of the entire project. While satisfying consumer demands for accurate up-to-date data is a chore for CGE modelers, there is often a genuine payoff in terms of improved real-world relevance. In our example, failure to recognize that $34 billion was the right number would have led to an overstatement of the welfare gain from removing import restraints on apparel.

### 2.5.1.2 Detailed disaggregation in the focus area and accurate representation of relevant policy instruments

Policy proposals often call for the application of complicated instruments at a fine level of industry/commodity disaggregation. This sometimes causes consumers of modeling services to demand model features that stretch producers of these services to their limits or beyond. In the US, for example, our colleague Ashley Winston (Winston, 2009) has responded to demands by consumers interested in biofuel policy by extending a 500 commodity model to include as separate commodities: corn; switch grass; crop residue; cellulosic materials; organic byproducts; corn ethanol; dried distillers grains with solubles; cellulosic ethanol; advanced ethanol; gasoline; diesel; and Other fuels. Reflecting consumer demands, Winston also incorporated explicit complementarity conditions specifying the operation of tariff rate quotas on imports of Sugar and other agricultural products together with 72 types of agricultural land. To achieve all this required highly skilled theoretical, computing and data work over a long period of time. Being stretched to meet consumer demands can lead to productive and creative outcomes, as in Winston's case. However, being stretched can cause difficulties for CGE modelers in terms of budgets, time constraints and research priorities. CGE modelers must sometimes be firm in asking their customers to set the problem (e.g. work out the effects of replacing $x$% of imported oil with domestically produced biofuels) but not to dictate the way in which the modeler should tackle the problem. While a natural inclination of consumers is to think that highly elaborate modeling is called for, producers can often find shortcuts. [See, e.g. Dixon *et al.* (2007) in which the biofuel issue was tackled as a technological change in the production of motor fuels.] In these cases, the consumer is usually convinced of the adequacy of the short cut when defensible results are produced on time and within budget.

### 2.5.1.3 Disaggregated results

Consumers of modeling services want more than bottom-line aggregate welfare and GDP effects. The real policy debate is often about reallocating large revenues across industries and factors: there can be big winners and losers even when the bottom line is small. Table 2.5 is an example of the kind of information that consumers find useful. It shows results from a US International Trade Commission study on the effects of imposing a Steel Safeguard tariff. The US International Trade Commission estimated that the imposition of the tariff would result in a net loss in GDP of $30.4 million. This tiny net effect reflects large gains for the government in tariff revenue and for the Iron and steel industry in capital income, offset by losses in labor income and capital income in other industries, particularly those that use iron and steel inputs. Ability to provide disaggregated information is a CGE strength and demands by consumers for this information justifies the retention in CGE models of considerable detail.

### 2.5.1.4 Baseline forecasts

Many consumers of CGE analyses have little background in economics. It does not come naturally to them to think in terms of the effect on variable $i$ of changes in policy $j$

**Table 2.5** CGE results: income changes from an iron and steel safeguard tariff

|  |  | Income changes ($ million) |
| --- | --- | --- |
| Tariff revenue |  | 649.9 |
| Labor income |  | −386.0 |
| Capital income |  | −294.3 |
|    Iron and steel industry | 239.5 |  |
|    Input suppliers to iron and steel | 67.4 |  |
|    Other industries (including steel users) | −601.2 |  |
| GDP |  | −30.4 |

*Source*: US International Trade Commission (2003, pp. 4–5).

holding all other exogenous variables constant. A current example in Australia is the heated debate concerning the government's buyback of water rights from farmers along the Murray and Darling rivers. The aim is to increase water flow in the rivers, thereby improving the downstream environment. Implementation of the policy coincided with a severe drought and depressed conditions in rural communities. Economists' estimates showing that the effects of buyback on rural economic activity are negligible are not accepted because community leaders and their constituents are not separating the effects of buyback from the effects of drought.

We have found that the presentation of a baseline without the policy change together with a projection with the policy change helps consumers to separate out the effects of the policy change from the effects of other factors. Figure 2.10 is a diagrammatic presentation that has been used to advantage by the US International Trade Commission to explain the effects of unilateral trade liberalization by the US involving the dismantling of all major import restraints. The figure shows USAGE results for percentage changes between 2005 and 2013 in outputs of textiles and apparel in a baseline without liberalization (circles) and an alternative projection that includes liberalization (crosses). The circles immediately tell consumers that most of the textile/apparel sector is in decline and that none of it is likely to achieve growth

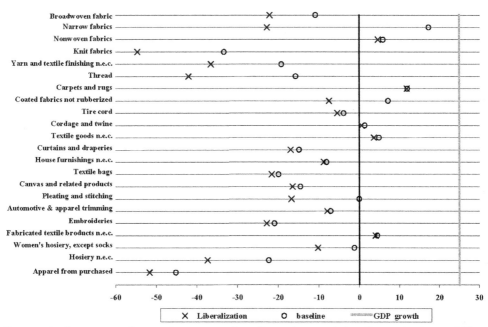

**Figure 2.10** Percentage changes in outputs of textiles and apparel, baseline projection and liberalization, 2005–2013. Source: *USAGE results presented by the US International Trade Commission (2009, p. 49).*

to match that of GDP. For about half the industries in the sector, the crosses and circles are close together indicating that liberalization would have only a minor effect on their prospects. For five industries (Narrow fabrics, Thread, Knit fabrics, Yarn and textile finishing n.e.c., and Pleating and stitching), liberalization is projected to have a severely negative effect on output growth: the gap between the crosses and circles is more than 15 percentage points. In the case of Narrow fabrics, liberalization converts relatively strong growth into contraction. For the other four industries, liberalization converts poor prospects into substantially worse prospects. As explained by the US International Trade Commission (2009) and more fully in Fox *et al.* (2008), the five textile/apparel industries worst affected by liberalization would all suffer from loss of export markets. These markets depend on rules of origin which give some countries an incentive to import textile inputs from the US. With sufficient US content in their textile/apparel exports, these countries gain access to the US market at zero tariff. With liberalization, which reduces the tariff to zero on US imports from all countries, the incentive to source intermediate inputs from the US disappears.

While a baseline is valuable from a presentational point of view, its role goes deeper than that. As discussed in Section 2.5.2.3, answers to policy questions can be improved by generating them as deviations around a realistic baseline forecast. There are at least three other reasons (discussed later in this Handbook[50]) for baseline forecasting.

(i) Consumers are interested in the baseline: they want to know where we think the economy is going, not just how the economy will be affected by a particular policy change or other shock to the economy.

(ii) A forecast is necessary in calculating adjustment costs associated with a policy change.

(iii) Forecasting opens up a possibility for model validation and model improvement.

### 2.5.1.5 Historical decomposition analyses

Another useful device for helping consumers to separate out the effects of policy changes from the effects of other factors is an historical decomposition. Table 2.6 is an example. It shows results from a 1987–1994 decomposition simulation with Australia's MONASH model undertaken to support a report by the Industry Commission (1997). The Commission was investigating the effects of reductions, proposed for 2001, in the tariff applying to imports of Motor vehicles and parts (MVP).[51] The technique of historical decomposition is described in Section 2.5.2.2. Here we will simply explain the results.

---

[50] See Section 19.6 of Dixon and Rimmer in Chapter 19 of this Handbook.

[51] Dixon *et al.* (1997) gives the details of the motor vehicle decomposition study. Another decomposition study, focused on the determinants of growth in Australia's international trade, is described in Dixon *et al.* (2000).

**Table 2.6** Output of the Australian MVP industry, 1987—1994

| Driving factor | Percentage effect |
| --- | --- |
| 1. Shifts in foreign demands and import supply curves | −4.8 |
| 2. Changes in protection | −5.6 |
| 3. Technical change | 24.4 |
| 4. Growth in aggregate employment | 16.7 |
| 5. Changes in import/domestic preferences | −4.0 |
| 6. Changes in required rates of return | −7.0 |
| 7. Other factors | −5.2 |
| Total | 14.5 |

*Source*: Extracted from results reported in table 5.5 of Dixon and Rimmer (2002).

As shown in the last row of Table 2.6, the output of Australia's MVP industry grew between 1987 and 1994 by 14.5%. Our historical decomposition simulation attributes this growth to seven factors.

The first is shifts in the positions of foreign demand curves for Australian exports and foreign supply curves for Australian imports. Between 1987 and 1994 these shifts were generally favorable. Holding constant all other exogenous variables (protection, technology, etc.) MONASH showed that the shifts in these curves gave Australia an improvement in its terms of trade of nearly 20%. However, this was bad for the MVP industry, reducing its output by 4.8%. The industry was damaged by good news for the rest of the economy via exchange rate effects. Improvement in the terms of trade strengthens Australia's real exchange rate. The MVP industry faces considerable competition from imports and real appreciation associated with terms-of-trade improvement weakened its competitive position.

The second factor is changes in protection. Between 1987 and 1994, tariff were reduced on almost all imports. The MVP tariff cut reduced the landed–duty-paid price of MVP imports by 6.5%. Although the import/domestic substitution elasticity for MVP products is high (2.55), the damage to MVP output was limited to 5.6% (row 2). The MVP industry benefited from cuts in tariffs on its inputs and from real exchange rate devaluation associated with tariff reductions more generally.

The third factor is technical change throughout the economy.[52] In the MVP industry, technical change favored intermediate inputs and capital relative to labor but there was almost no net improvement in total factor productivity. The large (24.4%) contribution to growth in MVP output attributed to technical change in Table 2.6 arises from two indirect sources. (i) Technical change is a major driver of GDP growth

---

[52] This is an amalgam of the effects of many types of technical change: input-saving for each intermediate and primary factor flow to each industry, margin-saving, and input-saving in the creation of units of capital.

which in turn contributes to growth in demand for MVP products. (ii) Between 1987 and 1994 there was a large increase throughout Australian industries in the use of MVP products per unit of output. In our calculations this was treated as an MVP-using technical change. Rather than being strictly technological, much of the increase in MVP inputs reflected the exploitation of a loophole in Australia's tax laws in this period which allowed employers to give workers tax-free use of company cars for private purposes in lieu of taxable income.

The fourth factor is growth in aggregate employment. Together with changes in technology, employment growth was responsible for most of the growth between 1987 and 1994 in GDP.[53] Thus, like row 3, row 4 of Table 2.6 shows a major contribution (16.7%) to the output of the MVP industry.

The fifth factor refers to changes in import/domestic preferences reflected by changes in import/domestic quantity ratios beyond those that can be explained by changes in import/domestic price ratios. Between 1987 and 1994, rationalization of the Australian MVP industry reduced the variety of Australian-produced cars. Simultaneously, there was an increase in the variety of imported cars available to Australian consumers.[54] This generated a strong twist in preferences in favor of imported cars. However the damage to MVP output shown in row 5 of Table 2.6 is only 4.0%. This entry includes not only the effects of the MVP twist, but the effects of all other import/domestic twists. These were generally in favor of imports. With a twist-induced increase in aggregate imports there was an associated real devaluation. This gave the MVP industry some relief against import competition.

The sixth factor is changes in required rates of return which increased between 1987 and 1994. This means that to support any given level of capital growth, investors needed to anticipate a higher rate of return in 1994 than they did in 1987. An increase in required rates of return can be caused by increases in interest rates and by reduced investor confidence. The increase in required rates of return between 1987 and 1994 reduced MVP output by 7%, mainly by reducing aggregate investment which is an MVP-intensive component of aggregate expenditure.

Decomposition simulations allow us to look at the effects of an overwhelming number of exogenous variables. Inevitably we must terminate the process by having an 'Other factors' row. In Table 2.6 this is row 7 which covers a variety of factors each having a minor effect on MVP output between 1987 and 1994. These factors include

---

[53] We can think of GDP as being specified by an aggregate production function: $Y = A * F(K,L)$. In the decomposition simulation technology ($A$, considered in row 3) and employment ($L$, considered in row 4) are exogenous. $K$ is endogenous, determined by exogenously given rates of return that are held constant in all rows except 6.

[54] Up to the mid-1980s the MVP industry was protected by quantity quotas on imports which favored the import of a narrow range of large expensive cars. After 1985, quotas were replaced by tariffs, leading to a dramatic increase in the variety of imported cars.

changes in: the average propensity to consume out of household disposable income; the ratio of public to private consumption expenditure; the commodity composition of public consumption; and shifts in export supply curves associated with increased awareness by Australian businesses of export opportunities.

In the Australian policy debate, protection is often portrayed as *the* critical variable determining the welfare of the MVP industry. Each time there is a proposal for reduced protection, supporters of the industry argue that the industry's survival would be threatened. Results such as those in Table 2.6 help to diffuse such arguments by putting the effects of past cuts in tariffs into historical context. As shown in Table 2.6, the health of the industry depends on many factors apart from protection. These include international trading conditions, technology, economy-wide employment growth, import/domestic preferences and required rates of return on capital.

## 2.5.2 Four-closure approach

Satisfying consumer demands for a high level of industry disaggregation and for presentation of results in many dimensions is facilitated in MONASH-style modeling by the adoption of the Johansen/Euler computational procedure implemented in GEMPACK software. For many years this has allowed us to handle large models without serious computing limitations. High dimensionality is also useful in satisfying consumer demands for accurate representation of policy instruments. MONASH models are equipped with tax and technology variables associated with every commodity and factor flow. Availability in MONASH models of detailed technology variables has been particularly useful in policy work concerned with microeconomic reforms, trade promotion, the environment, greenhouse gasses and other energy issues. Policies in these areas can often be represented as technological changes that alter the mix of inputs per unit of output in narrowly defined parts of the economy.

To satisfy needs for up-to-date data, baseline forecasts and historical disaggregation analysis, we have developed four broad modes of analysis with MONASH models. These are conducted with simulations under four different closures:

- The *historical* closure in which the exogenous variables are chosen so that observations at a detailed commodity/industry level on movements in consumption, investment, government spending, exports, imports, employment, capital stocks and many other variables can be introduced to the model as shocks. Computations with this closure can be used to generate up-to-date input-output tables that incorporate available statistics for years since the last published input-output table. Historical simulations also produce disaggregated estimates of movements in many naturally exogenous variables representing: industry technologies; household preferences; required rates of return on capital; and positions of export demand curves and import supply curves.

By naturally exogenous variables we mean those that are not normally explained in the type of CGE model being applied.

• The *decomposition* closure in which technology, preference and other naturally exogenous variables are exogenous so that they can be shocked with the movements estimated for them in an historical simulation. As we saw in Table 2.6, computations with this closure can be used to identify the roles in the growth of industry outputs and other naturally endogenous variables of changes in technology, changes in preferences, and changes in other naturally exogenous variables.

• The *forecast* closure which is used in simulations designed to produce a baseline picture (e.g. the circles in Figure 2.10) of the future evolution of the economy. The underlying philosophy of this closure is similar to that of the historical closure. In both closures, we exogenize variables for which we have information, with no regard to causation. Rather than exogenizing variables for which we have historical observations, in the forecast closure we exogenize variables for which we have forecasts. This might include macro variables, exports by commodity and demographic variables for which forecasts are provided by official organizations. Naturally exogenous technology, preference and trade variables in forecast simulations are largely exogenous and are given shocks that are informed by trends derived from historical simulations.

• The *policy* closure which is used in simulations designed to quantify the effects of changes in policies or other exogenous shocks to the economy. The underlying philosophy of this closure is similar to that of the decomposition closure. In both policy and decomposition closures, we are concerned with causation, with how tariff changes, for example, cause changes in employment. Thus, in policy closures, as in decomposition closures, naturally exogenous variables are exogenous and naturally endogenous variables are endogenous. In policy simulations, nearly all of the exogenous variables adopt the values that they had, either endogenously or exogenously, in the forecast simulation. The only exceptions are the policy variables of focus. For example, if we are interested in the effects of a tariff change, then the relevant tariff variable is moved away from its baseline forecast path. The effects of the tariff change on macro variables, exports by commodity and other endogenous variables are calculated by comparing their paths in the policy simulation with their paths in the baseline forecast simulation (e.g. the crosses in Figure 2.10 compared with the circles).

Connections between the four modes of analysis are illustrated in Figure 2.11. For concreteness we have drawn Figure 2.11 with reference to the US International Trade Commission study, conducted with the USAGE model, that produced the baseline forecast and policy results given in Figure 2.10.

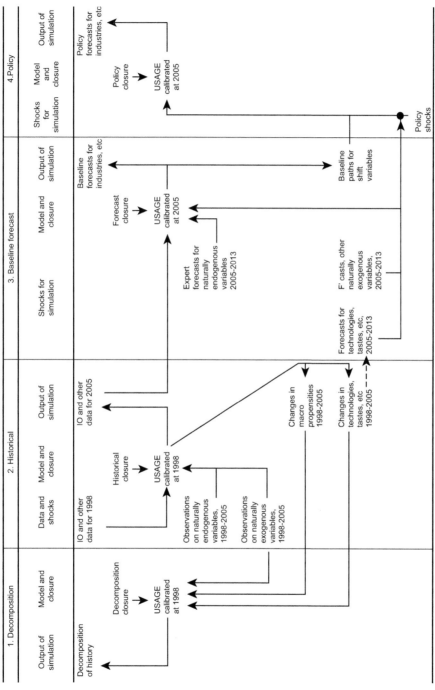

**Figure 2.11** Connections between four modes of analysis with MONASH-style models.

### 2.5.2.1 MONASH-style historical simulations

When the US International Trade Commission study was undertaken, the latest USAGE database was for 1998 and there were no published input–output data for a year beyond that date. The US International Trade Commission required a baseline and policy simulation for 2005–2013. Thus, the first job was to move the USAGE database forward to 2005. To do this, we performed an historical simulation. As shown in panel 2 of Figure 2.11, we started with USAGE calibrated with input-output and other data for 1998, and shocked it with observed movements between 1998 and 2005 in both naturally exogenous and naturally endogenous variables.

As is typical in historical simulations, the shocked naturally exogenous variables included tax rates, tariff rates, public expenditure and population. The shocked naturally endogenous variables included standard macro variables and a large number of industry and commodity variables. Absorbing macro variables requires endogenization of naturally exogenous propensities. For example, to allow growth in household consumption to be set exogenously at its observed value requires endogenization of the average propensity to consume. Absorbing micro observations requires endogenization of corresponding naturally exogenous taste, technology and trade variables. For example, data on growth in consumption of tobacco products (a naturally endogenous variable) is absorbed by allowing the model to tell us endogenously that there was a change in consumer preferences (a naturally exogenous variable) against this product. As indicated in the output column of panel 2 in Figure 2.11, the historical simulation undertaken for the US International Trade Commission produced the required up-to-date data for 2005 (including an input-output table) which, in principal, incorporated all statistical information that was available in 2005. It also produced estimates of changes between 1998 and 2005 in tastes, technologies, required rates of return and positions of export demand and import supply curves.

While the broad ideas underlying an historical simulation are straightforward, coping with the details of the data make the process time-consuming and difficult. For example, the USAGE model in our 1998–2005 historical simulation had 500 industries/commodities but data availability made it necessary to introduce micro shocks at a variety of different levels of disaggregation: 397-order export and import values from the US International Trade Commission; 160-order import prices from the BLS; 100-order export prices from the BLS; 56-order private consumption quantities and prices from the BEA; 20-order public consumption quantities and prices from the BEA; 68-order industry outputs and value-added prices from the BEA; 60-order occupational wage rates from the BEA; and 338-order industry employment from the BLS. Each of these micro data concepts were defined and absorbed in the USAGE historical simulation via special purpose equations. For example, to allow us to use BLS data on employment by 338 industries, we included in USAGE equations of the form:

$$l_{\text{BLS}}(q) = \sum_{i=1}^{500} S(i, q) * l_{\text{USAGE}}(i), \quad q = 1, 2, \ldots, 338 \qquad (2.54)$$

$$alab_{\text{USAGE}}(i) = \sum_{q=1}^{338} M(i,q) * f_{\text{BLS}}(q), \ i = 1, 2, \dots, 500, \tag{2.55}$$

where $l_{\text{BLS}}(q)$ is growth in employment in BLS sector $q$, $l_{\text{USAGE}}(i)$ is growth in employment in USAGE industry $i$, $S(i,q)$ is the share of BLS sector $q$'s employment accounted for by USAGE industry $i$, $alab_{\text{USAGE}}(i)$ is labor-saving technical change in USAGE industry $i$, $f_{\text{BLS}}(q)$ is a shift variable for BLS sector $q$, and $M(i,q)$ is a coefficient that has value 1 if USAGE industry $i$ is part of BLS sector q and zero otherwise. For simplicity we assume in this example that each USAGE industry is contained in just one BLS sector.

Equation (2.54) defines growth in employment by BLS sector $q$ in terms of growth in employment in component USAGE industries. In the historical simulation the naturally endogenous variable $l_{\text{BLS}}(q)$ was exogenized and shocked with the value implied by the BLS data on employment. Correspondingly, $f_{\text{BLS}}(q)$ was endogenized. Via (2.55), we imposed the assumption that labor-saving technical change was the same in each USAGE industry $i$ contained in BLS sector $q$.

The obvious alternative to within-model determination of USAGE industry employment growth via equations such as (2.54) and (2.55) is to assume, outside the model, that BLS sector $q$'s employment growth applied to each USAGE industry in the sector. However, we prefer the within-model approach because it allows the allocation of employment growth in sector $q$ to component USAGE industries to be informed by other information used in the historical simulation. For example, if USAGE industries 1 and 2 are both in BLS sector $q$ and other information in the historical simulation indicates that output in industry 1 grew rapidly relative that in industry 2, then it is reasonable to suppose that employment in industry 1 grew rapidly relative to employment in industry 2. This will be the result in an historical simulation under the uniform-within-sector technology assumption implemented in the model via (2.54) and (2.55) but not under the uniform-within-sector employment assumption implemented outside the model. For a more general discussion of the advantages of within-model allocation procedures, see Dixon and Rimmer (2002, pp. 200–201).

### 2.5.2.2 MONASH-style decomposition simulations

Once an historical simulation is completed, then we can perform a decomposition simulation. The decomposition simulation uses the same model and data as the historical simulation, but a different closure. All of the exogenous variables in the decomposition closure are *naturally* exogenous. As indicated by the arrows from panel 2 to panel 1 in Figure 2.11, these naturally exogenous variables were shocked in the decomposition simulation with the same values they had (either exogenously or endogenously) in the historical simulation. Consequently, the decomposition simulation produces the same results as the historical simulation.

The reason for performing decomposition simulations is that they allow us to decompose movements in macro and industry variables into parts attributable to different driving forces. This is done by partitioning the exogenous variables and separately computing the effects of the shocks for the each subset.[55] The results obtained in this way are a legitimate decomposition to the extent that the exogenous variables in the decomposition simulation can be thought of as varying independently of each other. In setting up the decomposition closure, the exogenous variables are chosen with exactly this property in mind. Thus, in the decomposition closure we find on the exogenous list variables representing policy instruments, technologies, tastes, required rates of return and positions of export demand and import supply curves. All of these can be considered as independently determined and all can be thought of as making their own contributions to movements in endogenous variables such as incomes, consumption, exports, imports, outputs, employment and investment.

### 2.5.2.3 MONASH-style forecast simulations

MONASH-style forecast simulations are conducted with models calibrated to data for a recent year. These data are often generated by an historical simulation. As indicated by the solid arrow from panel 2 to panel 3 in Figure 2.11, the 2005–2013 baseline forecast for the US International Trade Commission project was created by USAGE calibrated with data for 2005 created by our historical simulation for 1998–2005.

In creating shocks to generate a baseline forecast, we draw as much as possible on the work of specialist forecasting organizations. In many countries, well-informed forecasts are available from organizations covering different aspects of the economy. In Australia, for example, macro forecast are provided by Access Economics and the Australian Treasury; forecasts for volumes and prices of agricultural and mineral exports are provided by the Australian Bureau of Agricultural and Resource Economics; and forecasts for tourist numbers are provided by the Bureau of Tourism Resear ch. In the US, macro forecasts are provided by the Congressional Budget Office, the US Department of Agriculture and the BLS; and forecasts for an array of energy variables are provided by the Energy Information Administration. All these forecasts are prepared by large teams of economists with considerable expertise. In forecast simulations with MONASH-style models we try to take advantage of their knowledge.

We do this by exogenizing variables for which there are reputable expert forecasts and using these forecasts as shocks. To accommodate macro forecasts we endogenize macro

---

[55] Because USAGE is a non-linear system, the effect on endogenous variable $i$ of movements in exogenous variable $j$ cannot be computed unambiguously: the effects of movements in any exogenous variable depend on the values adopted for other exogenous variables. To resolve this problem we, in effect, carry out decomposition simulations in a linear system in which derivatives of endogenous variables with respect to exogenous variables are evaluated at a half-way point between the initial and final values of the exogenous variables. The computations can be done conveniently in GEMPACK, see Harrison *et al.* (2000).

propensities. To accommodate micro forecasts we endogenize corresponding micro shift variables. For example, if forecasts are available from the Energy Information Administration on the sale of electricity to US industries and households, then we endogenize electricity-using technical change in US industries and an electricity preference variable for US households. In Figure 2.11, the input of expert forecasts occurs mainly in the area in panel 3 marked 'Expert forecasts for naturally endogenous variables, 2005–2013'. We may also have expert input in the area marked 'Forecasts, other naturally exogenous variables, 2005–2013' for tariff rates and other naturally exogenous variables.

Because we know less about the future than the past, MONASH-style forecast closures are more conventional than historical closures. In forecast closures most disaggregated technology and preference variables are exogenous. In setting their forecast values, we rely heavily on extrapolations from historical simulations. This is indicated by the dotted arrow connecting panel 2 with panel 3 in Figure 2.11.

There are two outputs from a forecast simulation. The first is a baseline forecast for a potentially huge set of disaggregated variables. The forecasts start from an up-to-date database and incorporate technology, preference and trade trends derived from recent history together with expert forecasts for macro variables and for whatever micro variables are covered by specialist forecasting organizations. The second output is forecasts for movements in naturally exogenous shift variables, such as the average propensity to consume and electricity-saving technical change, that were endogenized to absorb expert forecasts.

### 2.5.2.4 MONASH-style policy simulations

Policy closures are similar to decomposition closures. In policy closures naturally endogenous variables (such as macro variables and sales of electricity) are endogenous. They must be allowed to respond to the policy change under consideration. Correspondingly, in policy closures naturally exogenous variables (such as the average propensity to consume and electricity-saving technical change) are exogenous. If there are no policy shocks, a policy simulation generates the same solution as the baseline forecast. With no policy shocks all of the exogenous variables would have the same values as in the baseline: this is indicated by the arrows from panel 3 to panel 4 in Figure 2.11. Thus the differences between results in a policy simulation and the baseline forecast are entirely due to policy shocks. Under the assumption that the non-policy exogenous variables are genuinely independent of the policy, these differences can be interpreted as the effects of the policy.

The effects of any given policy depend on the structure of the economy. For example, the removal in the US of tariffs on imports of Textiles and apparel will have a different effect on the economy if the domestic sector accounts for 0.7% of aggregate employment (as it did in 1998) than if it accounts for only 0.2% of aggregate employment (as is likely in 2015). In considering policy proposals we want to know the likely effects in the future.

These depend on the structure of the economy in the future. Thus, for policy analysis, it is a major advantage to be able to calculate policy effects in the MONASH style as deviations from a baseline that gives a plausible picture of the future structure of the economy.

## 2.6 CONCLUDING REMARKS

Here are the ideas that we hope readers will take from this chapter.

First, results from detailed CGE modeling can be explained in a convincing manner to people without CGE backgrounds. We illustrated this in Section 2.2 by explaining USAGE results for the effects of restricting the supply of unauthorized immigrants to the US workforce. Our explanation relied on elementary microeconomics (e.g. demand and supply curves) and on identifying key data items (e.g. numbers of unauthorized workers in different occupations). Explaining results in a way that is accessible to people with backgrounds in economics, but not CGE modeling, is necessary for CGE modeling to be influential in policy circles. Policy advisors cannot effectively carry our results forward unless they have confidence in them. They can only have sufficient confidence to defend our results if they understand them.

A second idea from Section 2.2 is that CGE results are often best explained in a macro-to-micro, non-circular sequence. For example, our explanation of the USAGE results for the effects of restricting the supply of unauthorized immigrants started with aggregate employment and aggregate capital. Then we moved to the expenditure side of the national accounts and eventually to occupations.

A third idea illustrated in Section 2.2 is that disaggregated CGE modeling can produce results that are credible, new, policy-relevant and not available from aggregated models. An example in Section 2.2 is the Occupation-mix effect. Identifying this effect depended on having a model with considerable labor market disaggregation. Critics, with the benefit of our explanations, sometimes suggest that our results are obvious and did not require the application of a large-scale model. Our response is that it was the model that alerted us, and we suspect them, to the result. We would not have thought of the Occupation-mix effect and numerous other subtle results, let alone quantified them, without a detailed MONASH-style model.

The main idea in Section 2.3 is that Johansen is still worth reading. His 1960 book sets out a simple effective computing technique based on a representation of a model as a rectangular system of linear equations in changes and percentage changes of the variables. He then introduces a BOTE method for interpreting results and applies it in an analysis of the matrix showing the elasticities of endogenous variables with respect to exogenous variables. He uses this matrix in several applications including a decomposition of history and a validation check of his model's forecasting performance. The addendum in his 1974 book shows Johansen's enthusiasm for having his model used, developed and scrutinized in policy departments of the Norwegian government. By starting with Johansen's simple linear framework, MONASH modelers were able to make rapid progress in the 1970s with innovations in the specification of international trade, dimensionality, closure flexibility and the use of complex functional forms. They also eliminated Johansen's linearization errors. This was done without sacrificing simplicity and transparency by introducing the Johansen/Euler multistep method.

The first key idea in Section 2.4 is that the initial solution is important. It can be derived mainly from the input-output database. Then derivative methods can be used to compute other solutions either for the same year (comparative statics) or for a linked sequence of years (dynamics). The derivative method used by MONASH models is Johansen/Euler. This can be applied routinely even for very large models using GEMPACK software.

Another idea in Section 2.4 is that creation of a database from available statistics for a detailed policy-relevant CGE model is a major task requiring skill and perseverance. It is certainly too hard for a lightly supervised research assistant.

The central idea in Section 2.5 is that the primary purpose of CGE modeling is to assist in policy formation. Policy advisors on trade, microeconomic reform, the environment, labor markets, natural resources and taxation want models with high levels of disaggregation, up-to-date data and accurate representations of policy instruments. These wishes should be respected by producers of CGE services. In trying to satisfy consumer demands, MONASH modelers have devised the four-closure approach: historical; decomposition; forecast; and policy.

The final idea is that research in CGE modeling benefits from a team environment. The enduring team at CoPS/IMPACT has facilitated the creation and application of MONASH models in several ways. First, it has allowed members of the team to adopt a degree of specialization in theory, data, computing and application. The most obvious payoff from specialization has been the development of the GEMPACK software alongside the models. The GEMPACK group, headed within CoPS/IMPACT by Ken Pearson and Mark Horridge, understands and responds to modeling needs as they emerge and anticipates future needs. However, this is not the only payoff from specialization. Team members specialize on particular countries (e.g. Australia, US and China) and particular issues (e.g. labor markets, energy and environment). While building their own specialist knowledge, they absorb general techniques (e.g. the four closure approach) from other members of the team. Transfer of knowledge within the team is of particular advantage to new members who start with fully functioning models and draw on many years of accumulated experience from people who know how to adapt models for particular applications. A second benefit of an enduring team has been the accumulation of modeling improvements. With a long collective memory, CoPS/IMPACT is able to maintain ambitious, large-scale, continuously improving models that frequently generate insights that are not available from small single-purpose models.

## APPENDIX: THEORETICAL JUSTIFICATION FOR THE JOHANSEN/EULER SOLUTION METHOD

For many people, the least convincing aspect of Figure 2.5 as an explanation of the Johansen/Euler method is the assumption that the slope of **rs** (an 'off-solution' slope) is a good approximation to the derivative of $Y$ with respect to $X$ on the solution line at **w**. Once they have doubts about that assumption, then their confidence in the theoretical underpinnings of the method is seriously eroded.

In this Appendix we provide some reassurance by proving a proposition concerning the convergence of Johansen/Euler solutions as the number of steps approaches infinity. This proposition was first proved in the context of an $n$-variable/$m$-equation CGE model by Dixon *et al.* (1982, section 35). Here we set out the proof for a two-variable/one-equation model. Nothing essential is lost from the mathematical argument by cutting down the dimensions. Being able to treat $X$ and $Y$ as scalars eliminates the need for some rather clumsy matrix notation. We also provide an explanation of the idea mentioned in Section 2.4.1 underlying Richardson's extrapolation: doubling the number of steps in a Johansen/Euler computation tends to halve the linearization error.

### A.1   Convergence proposition for the Johansen/Euler method

***Proposition.*** Assume that we are dealing with a two-variable/one-equation model in which the endogenous variable, $Y$, is a differentiable function of the exogenous variable, $X$:

$$Y = G(X). \tag{A.1}$$

While we do not know the form of $G$, assume that we do know how to evaluate a function $B(X,Y)$ which has the property that:

$$B(X, Y) = G_X(X) \quad \text{if} \quad Y = G(X), \tag{A.2}$$

where $G_X(X)$ is the Jacobian matrix of $G$ evaluated at $X$. In the scalar case we are considering, $G_X(X)$ is simply $\partial Y/\partial X$ where $Y$ is given by (A.1).

Assuming that the derivative of $G_X$ with respect to $X$ and the derivative of $B(X,Y)$ with respect to $Y$ are bounded over the relevant domain of $(X,Y)$, then the Johansen/Euler method will converge, i.e. given a starting point $(\bar{X}, \bar{Y})$ satisfying:

$$\bar{Y} = G(\bar{X}), \tag{A.3}$$

then:

$$\lim_{n \to \infty} Y_n^n = G(\bar{X} + \Delta X), \tag{A.4}$$

where $\Delta X$ is any given change in $X$ and $Y_n^n$ is the $n$-step estimate of $G(\bar{X} + \Delta X)$.

**_Proof._** We denote the values of $X$ and $Y$ reached in the $r$th step of an $n$-step computation by $X_n^r$ and $Y_n^r$. Then:

$$X_n^r = X_n^0 + \left(\frac{r}{n}\right) * \Delta X, \; r = 1, \ldots, n, \tag{A.5}$$

and:

$$Y_n^r = Y_n^{r-1} + \left(\frac{1}{n}\right) * B(X_n^{r-1}, Y_n^{r-1}) * \Delta X, \; r = 1, \ldots, n, \tag{A.6}$$

where:

$$X_n^0 = \bar{X} \text{ and } Y_n^0 = \bar{Y}. \tag{A.7}$$

We denote the true value of $Y$ corresponding to $X_n^r$ as $\bar{Y}_n^r$, i.e.:

$$\bar{Y}_n^r = G(X_n^r). \tag{A.8}$$

Note that (A.8), (A.7) and (A.3) imply that:

$$\bar{Y}_n^0 = Y_n^0 = \bar{Y}. \tag{A.9}$$

By applying Taylor's theorem we can relate the true value for $Y$ in the first step of an $n$-step procedure to the starting value of $Y$ by:

$$\bar{Y}_n^1 = \bar{Y}_n^0 + \left(\frac{1}{n}\right) * B(X_n^0, \bar{Y}_n^0) * \Delta X + \left(\frac{1}{2 * n^2}\right) * G_{XX}^{0,n}. \tag{A.10}$$

In (A.10), $G_{XX}^{0,n}$ is $(\Delta X)^2$ multiplied by the derivative of $G_X$ evaluated between $X_n^0$ and $X_n^1$. More generally, we use the notation:

$$G_{XX}^{r,n} = G_{XX}(X_{r,n}) * (\Delta X)^2, \; r = 0, 1, \ldots, n - 1, \tag{A.11}$$

where $G_{XX}$ is the derivative of $G_X$, that is the second derivative of $G$; and $X_{r,n}$ is a particular point between $X_n^r$ and $X_n^{r+1}$. Combining (A.6) and (A.10), and using (A.7) allows us to relate the true value of $Y$ in the first step of the $n$-step procedure to the estimated value by:

$$\bar{Y}_n^1 = Y_n^1 + \left(\frac{1}{2 * n^2}\right) * G_{XX}^{0,n}. \tag{A.12}$$

Again applying Taylor's theorem, we relate the true value of $Y$ in the second step in an $n$-step procedure to the true value in the first step by:

$$\bar{Y}_n^2 = \bar{Y}_n^1 + \left(\frac{1}{n}\right) * B(X_n^1, \bar{Y}_n^1) * \Delta X + \left(\frac{1}{2 * n^2}\right) * G_{XX}^{1,n}. \tag{A.13}$$

Replacing $\bar{Y}_n^1$ by the right-hand side of (A.12) and adding and subtracting $(1/n)^* B(X_n^1, Y_n^1)^* \Delta X$ gives:

$$\bar{Y}_n^2 = Y_n^1 + \left(\frac{1}{2 * n^2}\right) * G_{XX}^{0,n} + \left(\frac{1}{n}\right) * B(X_n^1, Y_n^1) * \Delta X + \left(\frac{1}{2 * n^2}\right) * G_{XX}^{1,n}$$

$$+ \left(\frac{1}{n}\right) * \left[ B\left(X_n^1, \bar{Y}_n^1\right) - B\left(X_n^1, Y_n^1\right) \right] * \Delta X. \tag{A.14}$$

Using (A.6) to replace the first and third terms on the right-hand side of (A.14) by $Y_n^2$ and applying the mean value theorem to the last term, we obtain:

$$\bar{Y}_n^2 = Y_n^2 + \left(\frac{1}{2 * n^2}\right) * G_{XX}^{0,n} + \left(\frac{1}{2 * n^2}\right) * G_{XX}^{1,n} + \left(\frac{1}{n}\right) * B_Y^{1,n} * (\bar{Y}_n^1 - Y_n^1). \tag{A.15}$$

In (A.15), $B_Y^{1,n}$ is the derivative of $B(X_n^1, Y)$ with respect to $Y$ evaluated at a particular point between $\bar{Y}_n^1$ and $Y_n^1$. More generally, we use the notation $B_Y^{r,n}$ for $r = 1, \ldots, n-1$ to denote the derivative of $B(X_n^r, Y)$ with respect to $Y$ evaluated at a particular point between $\bar{Y}_n^r$ and $Y_n^r$. Substituting from (A.12), we eliminate $\bar{Y}_n^1 - Y_n^1$ from (A.15):

$$\bar{Y}_n^2 = Y_n^2 + \left(\frac{1}{2 * n^2}\right) * \left[ \left(1 + \frac{1}{n} * B_Y^{1,n}\right) * G_{XX}^{0,n} + G_{XX}^{1,n} \right]. \tag{A.16}$$

Continuing in this way, we can show that:

$$\bar{Y}_n^3 = Y_n^3 + \left(\frac{1}{2 * n^2}\right)$$

$$* \left[ \left(1 + \frac{1}{n} * B_Y^{2,n}\right) * \left(1 + \frac{1}{n} * B_Y^{1,n}\right) * G_{XX}^{0,n} + \left(1 + \frac{1}{n} * B_Y^{2,n}\right) * G_{XX}^{1,n} + G_{XX}^{2,n} \right], \tag{A.17}$$

and ultimately that:

$$\bar{Y}_n^r = Y_n^r + \left(\frac{1}{2 * n^2}\right) * \sum_{k=0}^{r-1} \left[ \prod_{s=1}^{r-1-k} \left(1 + \left(\frac{1}{n}\right) * B_Y^{r-s,n}\right) \right] * G_{XX}^{k,n}, \tag{A.18}$$

where it is understood that $\prod_{s=1}^{0}(\ldots) = 1$.

By setting $r = n$, we can use (A.18) to obtain an expression for the gap between the *n*–step estimate, $Y_n^n$, of $G(\bar{X} + \Delta X)$ and the true value, $\bar{Y}_n^n$. To show that the limit of this gap as $n$ approaches infinity is zero, we invoke our boundedness assumptions, i.e. there exists $v$ and $u$ sufficiently large that:

$$|G_{XX}| \leq u \quad \text{and} \quad |B_Y| \leq v, \tag{A.19}$$

where $G_{XX}$ and $B_Y$ are evaluated at any point in the relevant domain of $(X,Y)$. We can think of this domain as covering economically meaningful prices and quantities. By this we mean prices and quantities that are greater than or equal to an arbitrarily small positive number or less than and equal to an arbitrarily large number.

By substituting from (A.19) into (A.18) we find that:

$$\left| \bar{Y}_n^n - Y_n^n \right| \le \left( \frac{1}{2*n^2} \right) * \sum_{k=0}^{n-1} u \prod_{s=1}^{n-1-k} \left( 1 + \frac{v}{n} \right) \le \left( \frac{u}{2*n^2} \right) * \sum_{k=0}^{n-1} \left( 1 + \frac{v}{n} \right)^{n-1-k}$$

$$\le \frac{u}{2*n*v} * \left\{ \left( 1 + \frac{v}{n} \right)^n - 1 \right\}. \tag{A.20}$$

Recalling that:

$$\lim_{n \to \infty} \left( 1 + \frac{v}{n} \right)^n = e^v \quad \text{and} \quad \lim_{n \to \infty} [f(n)*g(n)] = \lim_{n \to \infty} [f(n)] * \lim_{n \to \infty} [g(n)], \tag{A.21}$$

we can conclude that:

$$\lim_{n \to \infty} \left| \bar{Y}_n^n - Y_n^n \right| = 0. \tag{A.22}$$

This is sufficient to complete our proof.

## A.2   Richardson's extrapolation

Why does doubling the number of steps tend to halve the linearization error, thus often allowing Richardson's extrapolation applied with low-step solutions to give highly accurate results? Assume that $B_Y(X,Y)$ is zero. Under this assumption, (A.18) reduces for $r = n$ to:

$$\bar{Y}_n^n = Y_n^n + \left( \frac{1}{2*n^2} \right) * \sum_{k=0}^{n-1} G_{XX}^{k,n}, \tag{A.23}$$

or:

$$\bar{Y}_n^n = Y_n^n + \left( \frac{1}{2*n} \right) * G_{XX}^{\text{ave},n}, \tag{A.24}$$

where $G_{XX}^{\text{ave},n}$ is the average value over $k$ of the $G_{XX}^{k,n}$s. We would not expect $G_{XX}^{\text{ave},n}$ to be particularly sensitive to $n$. (In the case in which $G$ is quadratic $G_{XX}^{\text{ave},n}$ is completely insensitive to variations in $n$.) Thus, (A.24) suggests that the gap between the $n$-step estimate, $Y_n^n$, of $G(\bar{X} + \Delta X)$ and the true value, $\bar{Y}_n^n$ is proportional to $1/n$, implying that if we double the number of steps we will halve the error.

In CGE modeling we cannot expect $B_Y(X,Y)$ to be zero and $G_{XX}^{ave,n}$ will not be completely insensitive to $n$. However, experience over many years with Johansen/Euler computations confirms that the doubling/halving rule remains a useful approximation.

## ACKNOWLEDGMENTS

We thank Mun Ho for detailed comments on an earlier draft.

## REFERENCES

Adams, P.D., Dixon, P.B., Rimmer, M.T., 2001. The September 11 shock to tourism and the Australian economy from 2001-02 to 2003-04. Aust. Bull. Lab. 27, 241–257.

Adelman, I., Robinson, S., 1978. Income Distribution Policy in Developing Countries: A Case Study of Korea. Oxford University Press, New York.

Alaouze, C.M., 1977. Estimates of the elasticity of substitution between imported and domestically produced goods classified at the input-output level of aggregation. IMPACT Working Paper O-13. Available from: http://www.monash.edu.au/policy/elecpapr/O-13.htm.

Alaouze, C.M., Marsden, J.S., Zeitsch, J., 1977. Estimates of the elasticity of substitution between imported and domestically produced commodities at the four digit ASIC level. IMPACT Working Paper O-11. Available from: http://www.monash.edu.au/policy/elecpapr/O-11.htm.

Armington, P.S., 1969. The geographic pattern of trade and the effects of price changes. IMF Staff Papers 16, 176–199.

Armington, P.S., 1970. Adjustment of trade balances: some experiments with a model of trade among many countries. IMF Staff Papers 17, 488–523.

Bergman, L., 1978. Energy Policy in a Small Open Economy: The Case of Sweden, RR-78-16. International Institute for Applied Systems Analysis, Laxenberg. Available from: http://www.iiasa.ac.at/Admin/PUB/Documents/RR-78-016.pdf.

Bonds, B., Aylor, T., 1998. Investment in new structures and equipment in 1992 by using industries. Surv. Curr. Bus., 26–51. December.

Bovenberg, A.L., 1985. Dynamic general equilibrium tax models with adjustment costs. Math. Program. Study 23, 40–50.

Bovenberg, A.L., Keller, W.J., 1984. Non-linearities in applied general equilibrium models. Econ. Lett. 14, 53–59.

Breece, J.H., McLaren, K.R., Murphy, C.W., Powell, A.A., 1994. Using the Murphy model to provide short-run macroeconomic closure for ORANI. Econ. Rec. 70, 292–314.

Brown, D.K., 1987. Tariffs, the terms of trade, and national product differentiation. J. Pol. Model. 9, 503–526.

Bureau of Economic Analysis, 1998. Benchmark Input-Output Accounts of the United States, 1992. Bureau of Economic Analysis, Washington.

Bureau of Economic Analysis., 1999. Fixed reproducible tangible wealth in the United States, 1925–94. BEA Report. Available from: http://www.bea.gov/scb/pdf/national/niparel/Meth/wlth2594.pdf.

Codsi, G., Pearson, K.R., 1986. GEMPACK Documents 2, 3, 5–8 and 11–18. IMPACT Project, Melbourne.

Codsi, G., Pearson, K.R., 1988. GEMPACK: general-purpose software for applied general equilibrium and other economic modellers. Comput. Sci. Econ. Manage. 1, 189–207.

Cooper, R.J., McLaren, K.R., 1983. The ORANI–MACRO interface: an illustrative exposition. Econ. Rec. 59, 166–179.

Corden, W.M., 1958. Import restrictions and tariffs: a new look at Australian policy. Econ. Rec. 34, 331–346.

Corden, W.M., Dixon, P.B., 1980. A tax-wage bargain in Australia: is a free lunch possible? Econ. Rec. 56, 209—221.

Dahlquist, G., Bjorck, A., Anderson, N (translator)., 1974. Numerical Methods. Prentice-Hall, Englewood Cliffs, NJ.

Dervis, K., de Melo, J., Robinson, S., 1982. General Equilibrium Models for Development Policy. Cambridge University Press, Cambridge.

Dixon, P.B., 1987. On using applied general equilibrium models for analysing structural change. In: Pasinetti, L., Lloyd, P.J. (Eds.), Structural Change, Economic Interdependence and World Development. Structural Change and Adjustment in the World Economy 3. Macmillan Press for the International Economic Association, London, pp. 149—158.

Dixon, P.B., 2008. Trade policy in Australia and the development of computable general equilibrium modelling. J. Econ. Integrat. 23, 605—630.

Dixon, P.B., Rimmer, M.T., 2002. Dynamic General Equilibrium Modelling for Forecasting and Policy: A Practical Guide and Documentation of MONASH. Contributions to Economic Analysis 256. North-Holland, Amsterdam.

Dixon, P.B., Rimmer, M.T., 2004. The US economy from 1992 to 1998: results from a detailed CGE model. Econ. Rec. 80 (Special Issue), S13—S23.

Dixon, P.B., Rimmer, M.T., 2009. Restriction or Legalization? Measuring the Economic Benefits of Immigration Reform. Trade Policy Analysis Paper 40. Cato Institute, Washington DC. Available from: http://www.freetrade.org/node/949.

Dixon, P.B., Rimmer, M.T., 2010a. US imports of low-skilled labor: restrict or liberalize? In: Gilbert, John (Ed.), New Developments in Computable General Equilibrium Analysis of Trade Policy. Frontiers of Economics and Globalization 7. Emerald Publishing, Lewes, pp. 103—151.

Dixon, P.B., Rimmer, M.T., 2010b. Optimal tariffs: should Australia cut automotive tariffs unilaterally? Econ. Rec. 86, 143—161.

Dixon, P.B., Rimmer, M.T., 2010c. Johansen's contribution to CGE modelling: originator and guiding light for 50 years. CoPS/IMPACT Working Paper G-203. Available from: http://www.monash.edu.au/policy/ftp/workpapr/g-203.pdf.

Dixon, P.B., Rimmer, M.T., 2011. You can't have a CGE recession without excess capacity. Econ. Model. 28, 602—613.

Dixon, P.B., Parmenter, B.R., Ryland, G.J., Sutton, J., 1977. ORANI, A General Equilibrium Model of the Australian Economy: Current Specification and Illustrations of Use for Policy Analysis, Volume 2 of the First Progress Report of the IMPACT Project. Australian Government Publishing Service, Canberra.

Dixon, P.B., Parmenter, B.R., Sutton, J., 1978. Spatial disaggregation of ORANI results: a preliminary analysis of the impact of protection at the state level. Econ. Anal. Pol. 8, 35—86.

Dixon, P.B., Powell, A.A., Parmenter, B.R., 1979. Structural Adaptation in an Ailing Macroeconomy. Melbourne University Press, Melbourne.

Dixon, P.B., Parmenter, B.R., Sutton, J., Vincent, D.P., 1982. ORANI: A Multisectoral Model of the Australian Economy. Contributions to Economic Analysis 142. North-Holland, Amsterdam.

Dixon, P.B., Parmenter, B.R., Powell, A.A., Wilcoxen, P.J., 1992. Notes and Problems in Applied General Equilibrium Economics. North-Holland, Amsterdam.

Dixon, P.B., Malakellis, M., Rimmer, M.T., 1997. The Australian Automotive Industry from 1986—87 to 2009—10: Analysis Using the MONASH Model. A Report to the Industry Commission. Centre of Policy Studies and IMPACT Project, Monash University.

Dixon, P.B., Menon, J., Rimmer, M.T., 2000. Changes in technology and preferences: a general equilibrium explanation of rapid growth in trade. Aust. Econ. Paper 39, 33—55.

Dixon, P.B., Pearson, K.R., Picton, M.R., Rimmer, M.T., 2005. Rational expectations for large CGE models: a practical algorithm and a policy application. Econ. Model. 22, 1001—1019.

Dixon, P.B., Osborne, S., Rimmer, M.T., 2007. The economy-wide effects in the United States of replacing crude petroleum with biomass. Energ. Environ. 18, 709—722.

Dixon, P.B., Lee, B., Muehlenbeck, T., Rimmer, M.T., Rose, A.Z., Verikios, G., 2010. Effects on the US of an H1N1 epidemic: analysis with a quarterly CGE model. J. Homeland Security Emerg. Manage. 7 (1) article 75. Available from: http://www.bepress.com/jhsem/vol7/iss1/75.

Dixon, P.B., Johnson, M., Rimmer, M.T., 2011. Economy-wide effects of reducing illegal immigrants in US employment. Contemp. Econ. Pol. 29, 14–30.

Fallon, J., 1982. Disaggregation of the ORANI employment projections to statistical divisions – Theory, ORANI Research Memorandum, Archive OA0160, IMPACT Project, Melbourne.

Fan, Z., 2008. Armington meets Melitz: introducing firm heterogeneity in a global CGE model of trade. J. Econ. Integrat. 23, 575–604.

Fox, A., Powers, W., Winston, A., 2008. Textile and apparel barriers and rules of origin: what's left to gain after the agreement on textiles and clothing? J. Econ. Integrat. 23, 656–684.

Gehlhar, M., Somwaru, A., Dixon, P.B., Rimmer, M.T., Winston, R.A., 2010. Economy-wide implications from US bioenergy expansion. Am. Econ. Rev.: Papers Proceedings 100, 172–177.

Glezer, L., 1982. Tariff Politics: Australian Policy-making 1960–1980. Melbourne University Press.

Griswold, D.T., 2002. Willing Workers: Fixing the Problem of Illegal Mexican Migration to the United States. Trade Policy Analysis Paper 19. Cato Institute, Washington, DC. Available from: http://www.cato.org/pubs/tpa/tpa-019.pdf.

Hanoch, G., 1971. CRESH production functions. Econometrica 39, 695–712.

Harrison, W.J., Horridge, J.M., Pearson, K.R., 2000. Decomposing simulation results with respect to exogenous shocks. Comput. Econ. 15, 227–249.

Honkatukia, J., 2009. VATTAGE – A Dynamic, Applied General Equilibrium Model of the Finnish Economy. Research Report 150. Government Institute for Economic Research, Helsinki.

Hudson, E.A., Jorgenson, D.W., 1974. US energy policy and economic growth, 1975-2000. Bell J. Econ. Manage. Sci. 5, 461–514.

Industry Commission, 1997. The Automotive Industry, Volumes I and II. Industry Commission Report 58. Australian Government Publishing Service, Canberra.

Johansen, L., 1960. A Multisectoral Study of Economic Growth. Contributions to Economic Analysis 21. North-Holland, Amsterdam.

Johansen, L., 1974. A Multisectoral Study of Economic Growth, Second enlarged ed. Contributions to Economic Analysis 21. North-Holland, Amsterdam.

Keller, W.J., 1980. Tax Incidence: A General Equilibrium Approach. Contributions to Economic Analysis 134. North-Holland, Amsterdam.

Leontief, W.W., 1936. Quantitative input-output relations in the economic system of the United States. Rev. Econ. Stat. 18, 105–125.

Malakellis, M., 1998. Should tariff reductions be announced? An intertemporal computable general equilibrium analysis. Econ. Rec. 74, 121–138.

Malakellis, M., 2000. Integrated Macro–Micro-Modelling under Rational Expectations: with an Application to Tariff Reform in Australia. Physica-Verlag, Heidelberg.

Melitz, M.J., 2003. The impact of trade in intra-industry reallocations and aggregate industry productivity. Econometrica 71, 1695–1725.

Okubo, S., Planting, M., 1998. US travel and tourism satellite accounts for 1992. Sur. Curr. Bus., 8–22. July.

Pearson, K.R., 1988. Automating the computation of solutions of large economic models. Econ. Model. 5, 385–395.

Powell, A.A., Lawson, T., 1990. A decade of applied general equilibrium modelling for policy work. In: Bergman, L., Jorgenson, D., Zalai, E. (Eds.), General Equilibrium Modeling and Economic Policy Analysis. Basil Blackwell, Boston, MA, pp. 241–290.

Powell, A.A., Snape, R.H., 1993. The contribution of applied general equilibrium analysis to policy reform in Australia. J. Pol. Model. 15, 393–414.

Rattso, J., 1982. Different macro closures of the original Johansen model and their impact on policy evaluation. J. Pol. Model. 4, 85–97.

Rector, R., Kim, C., 2007. The Fiscal Cost of Low-Skill Immigrants to the US Taxpayer. Heritage Special Report SR-14. The Heritage Foundation, Washington, DC. Available from: http://www.heritage.org/Research/Immigration/sr14.cfm.

Robinson, S., 2006. Macro model and multipliers: Leontief, Stone, Keynes, and CGE models. In: de Janvry, A., Kanbur, R. (Eds.), Poverty, Inequality and Development: Essays in Honor of Erik Thorbecke. Springer, New York, pp. 205–232.

Scarf, H.E., 1967. On the computation of equilibrium prices. In: Fellner, W. (Ed.), Ten economic studies in the tradition of Irving Fisher. Wiley, New York, pp. 207–230.

Scarf, H.E., 1973. The Computation of Economic Equilibria. Yale University Press, New Haven, CT.

Spurkland, S., 1970. MSG — a tool in long-term planning. Report prepared for the First Seminar on Mathematical Methods and Computer Techniques. UN Economic Commission for Europe, Varna.

Staelin, C.P., 1976. A general equilibrium model of tariffs in a non-competitive economy. J. Int. Econ. 6, 39–63.

Strayhorn, C.K., 2006. Undocumented Immigrants in Texas: A Financial Analysis of the Impact to the State Budget and Economy. Special Report. Office of the Comptroller of Texas, Austin, TX.

Sutton, J., 1976. The Solution Method for the ORANI Module. Preliminary Working Paper OP-03. IMPACT Project, Melbourne.

Sutton, J., 1977. Computing Manual for the ORANI Model. IMPACT Computing Document C1-01. IMPACT Project, Melbourne.

Taylor, L., Black, S.L., 1974. Practical general equilibrium estimation of resource pulls under trade liberalization. J. Int. Econ. 4, 35–58.

Taylor, L., Bacha, E.L., Cardoso, E.A., Lysy, F.J., 1980. Models of Growth and Distribution for Brazil. Oxford University Press for the World Bank, New York.

US International Trade Commission, 2003. Steel: Monitoring Developments in the Domestic Industry. Investigation TA-204-9,3. Steel-Consuming Industries: Competitive Conditions with Respect to Steel Safeguard Measures. Investigation 332-452, Publication 3632. US ITC, Washington, DC. Available from: http://www.usitc.gov/publications/safeguards/3632/pub3632_vol3_all.pdf.

US International Trade Commission, 2004. The Economic Effects of Significant US Import Restraints: Fourth Update. Investigation 332-325, Publication 3701. US ITC, Washington, DC.

US International Trade Commission, 2007. The Economic Effects of Significant US Import Restraints: Fifth Update. Investigation 332-325, Publication 3906. US ITC, Washington, DC.

US International Trade Commission, 2009. The Economic Effects of Significant US Import Restraints: Sixth Update. Investigation 332-325, Publication 4904. US ITC, Washington, DC.

Wilcoxen, P.J., 1985. Numerical Methods for Investment Models with Foresight. IMPACT Project Preliminary Working Paper IP-23. IMPACT Project, Monash University, Clayton.

Wilcoxen, P.J., 1987. Investment with Foresight in General Equilibrium. IMPACT Project Preliminary Working Paper IP-35. IMPACT Project, Monash University, Clayton.

Winston, R.A., 2009. Enhancing Agriculture and Energy Sector Analysis in CGE Modelling: An Overview of Modifications to the USAGE Model. CoPS/IMPACT Working Paper G-180 Available from: http://www.monash.edu.au/policy/elecpapr/g-180.htm.

# CHAPTER 3

# Computable General Equilibrium Assessments of Fiscal Sustainability in Norway

**Erling Holmøy, Birger Strøm**
Research Department, Statistics Norway

## Abstract

The chapter demonstrates how the computable general equilibrium model MSG6, combined with special models of government expenditures, has been used to assess the long-run fiscal sustainability in Norway. The simulations suggest that Norway faces a severe fiscal sustainability problem in the long run, despite an exceptionally strong fiscal position at present. This result is found to be relatively robust to exogenous variations in productivity growth, petroleum prices, longevity, immigration and the health of the elderly. The chapter also discusses the fiscal effects of various policy responses, including the pension reform of 2011, improvements in the standards of public health services and care for the elderly, as well as a tighter fiscal policy rule. The simulation experiments demonstrate that general equilibrium mechanisms contribute significantly to the total effects.

## Keywords

Population ageing, fiscal sustainability, computable general equilibrium model, dynamic microsimulation

## JEL classification codes

H30, H55, H62

## 3.1 INTRODUCTION

Most industrial countries face fiscal sustainability challenges due to substantial increases in their demographic old-age dependency ratios after 2010. Contingent on present tax rates and welfare schemes, government expenditures are projected to grow faster than the tax base, which necessitates increases in the tax rates or cost-saving reforms of the welfare schemes. Most economies in the Organization for Economic Cooperation and Development (OECD) struggle with strained government finances already at the early stage of the ageing process of the population. The financial crisis and the expansionary fiscal measures taken to counteract it have further weakened government finances in several countries. Over the next decades, ageing will make the fiscal sustainability problems much harder to solve. The wave of pension reforms and other cost-saving reforms of

*Handbook of CGE Modeling - Vol. 1 SET*
ISSN 2211-6885, http://dx.doi.org/10.1016/B978-0-444-59568-3.00003-1

© 2013 Elsevier B.V.
All rights reserved.

public welfare schemes indicate that policy making adjusts to the prospects communicated through long-run economic projections. However, the present economic and political turbulence in several indebted European economies clearly manifest that cutting public welfare and increasing the tax burden are highly unpopular policies.

The fiscal sustainability problem is likely to be particularly severe in the Scandinavian welfare states where the government provides relatively generous and highly non-actuarial pensions and most of the health and care services. As will be argued in this chapter, this is also true for Norway although Norway's present fiscal stance looks exceptionally strong. The large but temporary petroleum rents collected by the government may obscure a sound evaluation of the potential fiscal sustainability problems facing Norway as ageing sets in. Moreover, substantial budget surpluses may stimulate further expansion of an already generous welfare state, rather than cost-saving welfare reforms. Thus, long-run analyses of fiscal sustainability are particularly important in Norway.

Realistic long-run projections of government finances based on empirical models are perhaps the only way to make politicians aware of the long-run fiscal consequences of today's decisions on pay-as-you-go tax-financed welfare schemes, including health services, long-term care and public pension systems of the defined benefit type. Population ageing makes the present and future expenditure effects of given welfare standards much larger than they were when they were implemented. A long-run perspective on tax-financed welfare policies is also imperative since history shows that it is very hard to reverse such welfare improvements.

Computable general equilibrium (CGE) modeling should play an important role in working out projections relevant for evaluation of long-run fiscal sustainability problems, and there is a large literature of CGE studies of fiscal sustainability.[1] (i) The long-run perspective makes the general equilibrium assumptions of rational responses to economic incentives, flexible relative prices and market clearing appropriate. (ii) The longer the time horizon, the more will many of the exogenous variables deviate from their values today. Moreover, changes in tax bases and government expenditures reflect changes in most markets of the economy. The relevance of general equilibrium effects is increasing in the magnitude of the exogenous changes, and in the number of agents facing these changes and their repercussions. (iii) CGE models are typically constructed for policy evaluation, especially of budget-neutral combinations of changes in policy instruments. The focus on budget neutrality obviously overlaps with the focus on total budget effects in studies of fiscal sustainability.

---

[1] See Chauveau and Loufir (1995); OECD (2001); European Commission (2001); McMorrow and Roeger (2002); and Visco (2002) for international comparisons of quantitative assessments of the fiscal and macroeconomic consequences of ageing. Kotlikoff et al., (2001); Kotlikoff (2001); and Feldstein (2005) estimate the fiscal gap in the US. Beetsma et al., (2003) and The Danish Welfare Commission (2004) estimate the need for raising the tax burden in the Netherlands and Denmark, respectively. Andersen et al., (2008) provide a review in English of the Danish Welfare Commission.

There is a strong tradition in Norway for using empirical large-scale models in economic planning and policy making. Bjerkholt (1998) discusses how institutional features distinguish the use of macroeconomic models in Norway from that of other countries. The shift from a high degree of central government planning in the first decades after World War II to the use of market-based mechanisms has changed, but not reduced, the use of empirical large-scale models. In particular, such models have become increasingly important in order to evaluate long-run fiscal sustainability problems. They were probably important for the wide political acceptance of the fiscal policy rule adopted in 2001, which has imposed quite tight restrictions on the annual use of the petroleum rents. They were also explicitly used in the process that provided acceptance of the cost-saving Norwegian pension reform implemented in 2011.

Empirical analyses of long-run trends and supply-side policy reforms in Norway have usually employed the model called MSG (an abbreviation of multisectoral growth) or, more precisely, one of the several versions of this family of models. Bjerkholt and Tveitereid (1985) and Schreiner and Larsen (1985) describe the use of MSG in the Norwegian planning system. In order to exploit the maximum of available information, MSG is often combined with more partial and specialized models, which determine the demographic development, labor force and public pension expenditures. Since the late 1990s, different versions of the sixth generation of MSG, MSG6, have been used, both in academic research and for policy making by the Norwegian Ministry of Finance (NMF). MSG6 has little in common with the original MSG model, MSG1, developed by Leif Johansen as an integral part of his pioneering thesis on MSG presented in Johansen (1960). According to Jorgenson (1984), MSG was the first successful implementation of a CGE model without the assumption of fixed input-output coefficients. The background and importance of Johansen's development of MSG1 is discussed in Dixon and Rimmer (2010) and Bjerkholt (2009). Holmøy (2011) also describes the CGE modeling carried out after Johansen's work within the "MSG project," focusing on how and why new generations of MSGs have been developed.

The sophistication of MSG and other CGE models have increased dramatically since 1960. The research topics are also different. However, the main motivation for the CGE approach is in principle still the same. Johansen saw that, in analyses of the expansion of several industries in a growing economy, clear and interesting results can not typically be derived analytically in general equilibrium models with more than two sectors. However, by exploiting the power of computers, instead of only pen and paper, he was able to solve much richer and more complex models. This allowed him to exploit much more of the available relevant information, which drastically improved the relevance and realism of the analysis.

However, a tradeoff between transparency and realism/relevance seems unavoidable. The lack of transparency has been a key argument for criticizing the CGE approach, and other large-scale empirical macroeconomic models, for not meeting standard criteria for good science. The main point in this criticism is that it is hard for outsiders to check the results. However, a quotation from Mankiw (2006) seems appropriate when discussing this matter:

> ... the subfield of macroeconomics was born not as a science but more as a type of engineering. God put macroeconomists on earth not to propose and test elegant theories but to solve practical problems.

Johansen made important contributions to economic theory, but his MSG book clearly shows that he had the engineer's attitude to CGE modeling. It seems fair to say that the "engineering" attitude has dominated the CGE literature, not least the MSG project.

This chapter demonstrates how CGE modeling has been used to assess to what extent Norway faces long-running problems of fiscal sustainability. It also analyses the fiscal effects of various policy responses, including the pension reform of 2011, improvements in the standards of public health services and care for the elderly, as well as a tighter fiscal policy rule. The exposition emphasizes the importance of the general equilibrium effects. More specifically, Section 3.2 describes the structure and properties of MSG6, focusing on what is most relevant when examining fiscal sustainability issues. A more comprehensive and detailed description is relegated to the Appendix. Heide *et al.,* (2004) provide detailed explanations of how MSG6 works. Section 3.3 assesses the fiscal sustainability problem in a baseline scenario. Sections 3.4, 3.5, 3.6 and 3.7 examine how the picture of the fiscal prospects depend on, respectively, higher productivity in the private sector, the oil price, the pension system, the mortality and health of the elderly, the standard of tax-financed health services and old-age care, immigration, and the tightness of the fiscal rule. Section 3.8 makes some final remarks.

## 3.2 MODEL STRUCTURE

Conceptually and empirically, the system of national accounts forms the base for MSG6. The model has been constructed to analyze a wide range of issues. In addition to long-run projections of macroeconomic growth and government finances, these issues include social efficiency and reallocation effects of industry and trade policy, tax reform and the links between economic activity, energy markets and the environment. The importance of different parts of the model depends of course on the issues being analyzed. The following exposition emphasizes the parts and properties that are most relevant in studies of long-run fiscal sustainability.

### 3.2.1 Demography, labor force, government consumption and public pensions

The demographic development is exogenous in MSG6. It is set equal to the projection regarded by the demographic experts as the most plausible one among the latest available official demographic projections. These are provided by Statistics Norway.

MSG6 specifies six government production sectors, where the factor shares are exogenous. Following the national accounts, government consumption equals the production costs in government sectors, plus the purchases of products from private industries, minus the revenues from user fees and sales of government services. Government purchases of final goods from private industries are exogenous. The government revenues from user fees and sales depend endogenously on the demand from households and private firms. However, these revenues cover a relatively small share of the total government consumption expenditures. Labor costs are the major cost component in government consumption. These expenditures are therefore basically driven by the assumptions that determine the demand for labor in government service sectors.

Employment in the sectors *Administration* and *Defense* is assumed to grow proportionally to the total population. The other four government sectors specified in MSG6 include: *Education*, *Health services*, *Child care* and *Long-term care*. Government consumption in these sectors was 19.5% of the Norwegian Mainland-GDP[3] in 2010. These sectors are split into 12 subsectors, all producing individual services. The employment growth in each subsector is determined by the corresponding labor demand, which equals the product of changes in the following components: (i) Labor productivity, (ii) the age- and gender-specific service standard, measured by man-hours per user, (iii) the age- and gender-specific user rate, measured by the number of users relative to the relevant population, and (iv) the number of males and females, respectively, in each age group. The age- and gender-specific user rates may be used to simulate changes in the health conditions of the different age groups.

The *Old-age* and the *Disability* pensions are by far the most important public pension schemes in a long-run fiscal perspective. In 2010, the expenditures of these pensions equaled 9.0% of the Norwegian Mainland-GDP. Most fiscal sustainability studies based on MSG6, including all those presented in this chapter, have incorporated highly detailed projections of public pension expenditures. However, it would be unfeasible to incorporate calculations of public pension expenditures in MSG6 that are sufficiently realistic and detailed with respect to the pension rules and population heterogeneity, to be interesting in operational pension policy discussions. Instead, MSG6 is combined with the dynamic microsimulation model MOSART, which is especially designed for simulating individual pension entitlements, benefits and government pension expenditures (Fredriksen, 1998). MOSART has been regularly used by the government to compute government pension expenditures. In particular, the model was intensively used under the preparation of the public pension reform implemented in 2011.

MOSART includes accurate descriptions of most elements in the existing and alternative pension systems. Specifically, it accounts for the complex interplay between minimum guarantees and earnings-dependent pensions. The model simulates the

---

[3] The Mainland sector is equal to the total economy except the off-shore petroleum sectors and ocean transport.

economic life courses of a representative cross-section equal to 1% of the Norwegian population, using a set of transition probabilities to determine the occurrence of sociodemographic events, including births, migration, deaths, marriages, divorces, educational activities, retirement, and labor force participation. Figure 3.1 shows the structure of this model. The probabilities of transition between states over the life course are functions of individual characteristics, which are estimated from observations in a recent period, mostly cross-sectional data. In analyses of fiscal sustainability, the relevant outcome of the MOSART projections are the time paths of the number of various types of pensioners, average individual pension benefits, total public pension expenditures and the total labor force. Pension benefits and total pension expenditures are calculated in real terms, i.e., in terms of the wage rate in a base year.

Age profiles of labor market participation and labor market earnings constitute a central part of MOSART, since the age profiles of earnings are crucial for the computations of individual pension entitlements and benefits. These age profiles differ between population groups defined by *inter alia* gender, education and country background. Aggregating man-hours over the individuals in MOSART, and adjusting for the sample size, generates the total labor force, which can be interpreted as the potential labor supply.

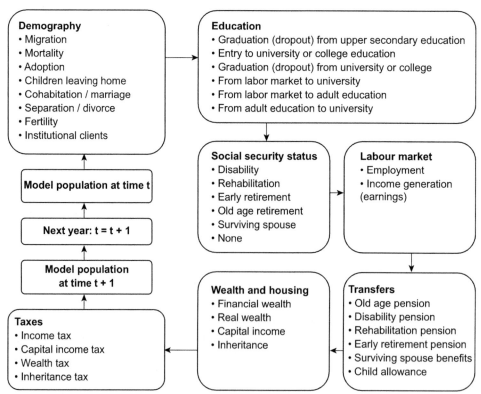

**Figure 3.1** Structure of the dynamic microsimulation model MOSART.

This is an increasing function of educational attainment at both the intensive and the extensive margin. Specifically, individuals with relatively low education become disability pensioners earlier and at a higher degree compared with individuals with high education. The microsimulations capture the increasing trend of female education and labor supply, which implies a surge in the future old-age entitlements of women.

Contrary to MOSART, MSG6 includes endogenous labor supply behavior. As will be described in more detail below, a representative consumer maximizes in each year a constant elasticity of substitution (CES) utility function defined over material consumption and leisure subject to a budget constraint. This reflects the assumption that all individuals have the same labor supply response to given changes in economic incentives. Thus, MSG6 adds the real consumer wage rate, real non-labor income and taxes to the demographic labor supply determinants specified in MOSART. The MSG6 projections take the development of the labor force determined by MOSART as a starting point in the determination of aggregate labor supply. Typically, the baseline scenario of total man-hours is set equal to the MOSART projection. In this particular projection, any labor supply effects of growth in the after tax real wage rate and the real non-labor income are neutralized by changes in the utility function parameter governing "productivity" of leisure. One rationale for this procedure is to make the baseline scenario transparent and easy to explain. Moreover, the net labor supply effect of realistic growth in both the real wage rate and non-labor income is relatively small. However, when MSG6 is used to simulate other scenarios, which are compared with the baseline, preference parameters are exogenous and equal to their baseline values, whereas labor supply responds to changes in the real wage rate and non-labor income.

Except for special studies, such as the effects of a public pension reform, there is no feedback from the economic development simulated by MSG6 on the MOSART projections. This implies that one neglects the effects on public pension expenditures caused by changes in labor supply incentives, which affect employment, earnings and pension entitlements. This is a weakness. It can be mitigated by iterative simulations between MSG6 and MOSART. As a matter of fact, this has actually been done in studies of the public pension reform, see Section 3.5, where pension expenditures are at the heart of the analysis. In the other studies, we have reasons to believe that the neglected effects on pension expenditures are relatively small and highly uncertain. In our view, the gains in terms of accuracy and relevance by taking the MOSART projections into account outweigh the importance of the lack of complete consistency between the comparable projections generated by the two models.

## 3.2.2 Brief overview of MSG6

The calculations outlined above of the demographic development, labor force, number of pensioners, individual pension benefits and public pension expenditures *ex ante* wage indexation, and real government consumption enter MSG6 as exogenous variables. One might say that the main role of MSG6 in analyses of fiscal sustainability is to calculate the tax bases and the relative prices, especially the price element in the various government expenditure components relatively to the price element in the sources of government revenues. All tax bases are endogenous in MSG6. As the model specifies 60 commodities and 40 production sectors, the calculation of the revenue from indirect taxation of households and firms captures important details of the tax system.

Changes in the wage rate and prices will in general not be budget-neutral, since they induce disproportionate effects on the nominal tax bases and the nominal government expenditures. Specifically, the direct and indirect share of wages is higher in the expenditures than in the tax bases, even when the petroleum taxes are exempted. One of the reasons for this is that almost all cash transfers to households are indexed by the wage rate. This reflects that Norway is an egalitarian welfare state with small income differentials between employed and unemployed individuals. This property of the Norwegian economy gives rise to important general equilibrium repercussions in most of the simulation experiments presented in Sections 3.4—3.7.

MSG6 models the Norwegian economy as too small to affect world prices and the international interest rate, and the exchange rate is fixed. Goods and factors are perfectly mobile between industries. Supply equals demand in all markets in all periods. All agents have access to international capital markets. The economy as a whole obeys an intertemporal budget constraint formalized as a non-Ponzi game condition for the accumulation of foreign debt. This national budget constraint reflects that households and the government obey their intertemporal budget constraints. The corporate sector is assumed to distribute all after tax profits to the owners of the companies, which include the households, the government and foreigners.

The standard version of MSG6 includes a submodel of intertemporal consumer behavior, where a representative consumer with an infinite time horizon and perfect foresight maximizes an additively intertemporal utility function over an infinite horizon subject to an intertemporal budget constraint and a time constraint in each period. However, such a model is irrelevant in fiscal sustainability studies, involving *inter alia* ageing and pensions. All studies summarized in this chapter ignore intertemporal consumer behavior, but they maintain the abovementioned intertemporal budget constraint for the economy as a whole. Rather, the time path of total private consumption is determined from the supply side; households consume what is left of production and net imports after the demand from firms and government sectors have been satisfied. The time profile of private consumption is reasonable compared to historic trends in our projections and changes in this profile have small effects on our evaluations of fiscal sustainability.

As noted above, consumers decide in each period on labor supply and the composition of private consumption according to standard consumer theory. The utility obtained in each period corresponds to the concept Full Consumption, which is a homothetic CES utility function in leisure and an aggregate of all types of consumer goods referred to as Material Consumption. The elasticity of substitution is set to 0.6. The initial budget share of leisure has been set to 0.5 based on studies of time spending by Norwegian households. Combined with the base year levels of non-labor income, these parameter values imply a direct Cournot wage elasticity of labor supply equal to 0.1. Such an order of magnitude is in line with the empirical properties of the micro-econometric model estimated by Aaberge *et al.,* (1995).

MSG6 distinguishes between the behavior of the individual firms and the aggregate industry behavior. Output and input in an industry can change through adjustments at the firm level and through entry or exit of firms. All private firms are run by managers with perfect foresight, who maximize the present value of cash flow. The private profitability is affected by indirect taxation of inputs, capital income taxation, and a rich menu of subsidies and government transfers. Producers of manufactures and tradable services allocate their output between the domestic and the foreign market. The cost of changing the composition of these deliveries is captured by assuming that output is a constant elasticity of transformation (CET) function of deliveries to the export market and deliveries to the domestic market.

Whereas exports are sold at fixed world prices, domestic consumers regard products from different firms within the same industry as close but imperfect substitutes. MSG6 employs the model of the Large Group case of Monopolistic Competition (LGMC) to formalize the market structure for domestic deliveries. The elasticities of substitution between the varieties in different industries are calibrated to be consistent with the estimated markup ratios between the output price and marginal costs in Klette (1999). None of the markup ratios exceeds 1.05. Entry (exit) takes place in an industry if the variable after tax profit increases (decreases) relative to the fixed entry cost. The model of monopolistic competition in MSG6 differs from the standard textbook model by allowing productivity differentials between firms within the same industry, which generates an *asymmetric* equilibrium (see Holmøy and Hægeland, 1997).

For inputs, the separability assumptions allows all inputs to be perfectly aggregated into one index of aggregate input through a system of nested constant returns to scale CES functions. Labor is homogeneous, whereas the capital goods and intermediaries are Leontief aggregates of the commodities specified in the model. The production function of the firm is assumed to exhibit decreasing returns to scale. The scale elasticities range from 0.85 to 1.00, which implies a small negative bias compared to those estimated in Klette (1999). This bias was introduced in order to avoid unrealistic specialization patterns of the industry structure.

Most imported manufactures and a few tradable services are close but imperfect substitutes for the corresponding domestic products. Thus, the import shares of these products are modeled according to the Armington assumption. Commodities produced by primary industries are assumed to be regarded as homogenous by both Norwegian and foreign consumers. In the absence of any trade restriction, the prices of these commodities would be equal to the corresponding exogenous world prices, and the model would determine only net imports as the residual between domestic production and domestic demand. Import protection is captured by nominal tariffs and non-tariff barriers modeled either as additional costs for foreign producers when exporting to the Norwegian market, or quantitative restrictions, such as import quotas.

Since all world prices of Norwegian exports and imports are exogenous, there is no scope for endogenous terms-of-trade effects caused by changes in Norwegian prices. The single wage rate is the only endogenous primary factor price. The model avoids the possibility that only one traded good sector survives the competition in the product and factor markets that ensures full exploitation of comparative advantages. This well-known "specialization problem" is avoided by the assumption of decreasing returns to scale, which causes increasing supply curves of exports. However, the price sensitivities of exports are large, and the dynamics of export adjustments are unrealistic. Table 3.1 summarizes the differences between the textbook Small Open Economy (SOE) model and MSG6. Despite the differences, the logic underlying the SOE model remains instructive when interpreting the results generated by MSG6.

In particular, this applies to the wage rate determination. Although this results from a highly complex simultaneous model structure, one may still say that the wage rate adjustment is *the* basic mechanism that ensures that the economy meets the intertemporal external balance constraint. In a long-term scenario, nominal wage growth will be close to the sum of the exogenous growth in world prices and the parameters reflecting factor productivities — a property consistent with the Scandinavian Model of Inflation. However, contrary to the textbook SOE model, MSG6 includes some interdependence between the determination quantities and relative prices. This can be exemplified by considering an exogenous increase in the labor force, raising employment. The additional income of increased employment is spent on both traded and non-traded goods. As long as exports do not change, increased demand for traded goods raises imports in all years, which violates the external balance constraint represented by the non-Ponzi game condition on net foreign debt. Recall that world prices of exports are exogenous. Thus, a real depreciation is required in order to restore the external balance. The real depreciation is obtained by a fall in the wage rate. This makes it profitable for firms to increase exports and the import shares will decline in all kinds of demand.

**Table 3.1** MSG6 compared with the standard model of a SOE

| SOE | MSG6 |
|---|---|
| 1. Firms maximize profits: exogenous world product price = marginal cost, which is independent of the scale of production, due to:<br>a. Constant returns to scale.<br>b. Exposed sectors with comparative advantage survive and "determine" prices of internationally immobile factors.<br>c. Prices on non-traded goods determined by unit costs.<br>d. Prices are independent of quantities (factor price equalization).<br>e. "Extreme" specialization of the exposed sector. | 1. Firms maximize profits, but:<br>a. (Weakly) decreasing returns to scale.<br>b. Imports and domestic products are imperfect substitutes.<br>c. Prices of internationally immobile factors are *mainly* determined by the exposed sectors; downsizing increases the ability to remunerate factors.<br>d. Prices on non-traded goods determined by markups over marginal costs.<br>e. Less "extreme" specialization of the exposed sector, but exporting industries are sensitive to changes in costs. |
| 2. Full employment of all resources.<br>3. Households receive the factor income, which is allocated on consumer goods through utility maximization.<br>4. Non-traded goods: domestic production = domestic demand. | 2–4. As in the SOE model, but more details. |
| 5. Balanced trade. | 5. Trade is balanced in present value terms. |
| 6. Given the set of active industries, resource rents do not affect factor prices. | 6. Resource rents increase factor prices. |

## 3.3 EVALUATING FISCAL SUSTAINABILITY

### 3.3.1 Key exogenous assumptions

The baseline scenario is simulated from 2006 until 2050. The focus on long-run fiscal sustainability makes the exogenous demographic development particularly relevant. The baseline scenario is based on the median alternative in the population projections from 2008 (Statistics Norway, 2008). This projection assumes:

- The fertility rate equals 1.85.
- Annual net immigration was set to 40,000 in the first years, which is about two-thirds of an average cohort of newborns. Net immigration gradually declines and equals 20,000 from 2030. The main share of immigrants is 20–39 years old.
- The average longevity of men and women increases annually by 0.14 years. Thus, over the period 2005–2050 average longevity for newborn men and women increases by nearly 6.5 years.

- The demographic dependency ratio measured by the number aged 20–66 relative to the number of those aged 67 and older will decrease from 4.7 in 2005 to 2.7 in 2050.
- With respect to changes in pension expenditures, it is particularly important that the remaining life expectancy for both men and women aged 62 years increases by 4 years from 2010 until 2050.
- The demographic dependency ratio, measured by the sum of individuals being younger than 20 years or older than 65 years divided by the rest of the population, will stay at about 68% until 2016. The ratio rises and stays at approximately 83% between 2037 and 2046. It then rises further, passing 88% around 2060.
- The public expenditures on health services and long-term care depend primarily on the number of elderly more than 80 years old. The share of this age group in the total population declines from 4.6% in 2007 to 4.1% in 2015. Then it starts to grow continuously, passing 4.6% again in 2020 and 9% in 2055.

In addition to the demographic development, the following exogenous assumptions are key determinants of the growth in macroeconomic variables and the government budget components:

(i) *Total labor supply in the baseline scenario* is determined in the dynamic micro-simulation (see Section 3.2.2) by adding up each person's labor force participation rate and expected working hours. It depends on age- and gender-specific assumptions about education, disability, early retirement, unemployment and working hours. Aggregate labor supply grows by 0.3% per year in the baseline. As mentioned in Section 3.2.2, the MSG6 simulations allow aggregate labor supply to change endogenously away from the baseline.

(ii) *Total factor productivity* (TFP) grows by 1.3% per year in private industries, which is in line with historical trends. Labor productivity in government sectors grows by 0.5% per year.

(iii) *World prices*, except prices of crude oil and natural gas, grow by 1.5% annually.

(iv) The *nominal interest rate* stays constant at 5.5%.

(v) The *government petroleum revenues* are based on the regularly updated production forecasts carried out by the Norwegian Petroleum Directorate. The oil price grows by 2% annually from the average level of 2007 of $71 (2007 dollars) per barrel. The price of natural gas follows the oil price.

(vi) The *public welfare policies* applying in the base year are prolonged, which implies no real growth in the standards of individual public welfare benefits, including both government cash transfers to individuals, as well as the role of the government in producing and financing individual welfare services, including *Health services, Social care* and *Education*. This assumption is probably not the most realistic one. Rather, it has been chosen for technical reasons. Especially, it provides a benchmark for analyzing the effects of the pension reform implemented in 2011, as well as other potential welfare policy changes. More precisely, the assumption means that all cash transfers are indexed by the growth in the average wage rate. It also implies prolongation of the base year age specific user ratios and the standard of the welfare services. The service standard is defined as the use of labor and other resources per user of the services.

**(vii)** *Employment in the sectors producing public goods*, i.e. *Defense* and *Administration*, is in per capita terms the same as in the base year. This also applies to the ratios between labor and other inputs.

**(viii)** The *fiscal policy* follows a strict interpretation of the fiscal rule introduced in 2001. It isolates the government petroleum revenues measured as the net cash flow ($P$) from the rest of the budget. The government petroleum revenues are saved in the Government Pension Fund (GPF). Among several restrictions on the investment policy, the GPF capital cannot be invested in Norwegian assets. The government is allowed an annual out-take, which should equal the expected real rate of return ($r$) on the GPF capital ($B$) as an average over the cycle. So far, this real rate has been set to 4.0%, which is assumed to equal the long-run difference between the expected nominal returns on the GPF capital ($i$) and the expected general growth in world prices ($\pi$). The annual public budget constraint is defined by equality between the out-take of 4% of the accumulated GPF capital and the non-petroleum primary deficit ($D$). Formally, the public budget constraint in year $t$ is $D_t = (i - \pi)B_{t-1}$. Then the GPF capital accumulates according to $B_t = (1 + \pi)B_{t-1} + P_t$. Since $i$, $\pi$ and $P$ are exogenous variables in MSG6, the time paths of $B$ and $D$ are effectively exogenous.

**(ix)** *Endogenous pay-as-you-go adjustments of the payroll tax rate* are to used meet the public budget constraint. All other tax rates remain constant in real terms. As any choice of a budget-neutral policy response, this choice is somewhat arbitrary. It has the following motivation: (a) If the long-run scenarios are supposed to quantify the problems of fiscal sustainability, it is hard to rationalize that policies aiming at reducing the growth in specific government expenditure components should be neutralized by raising other government expenditures. (b) If taxes rather than expenditures adjust, it is rather uncontroversial that the tax burden effectively will be carried by labor in a SOE. (c) Most contributions to mandatory public or private pension schemes are formally paid by the employer as a fixed share of wages. In fact, the payroll tax was introduced as a social security premium. (d) Other taxes are more complex than the payroll tax. Changing these would imply some kind tax reforms and explaining these would take the focus away from the discussion of fiscal sustainability.

These assumptions imply an average annual growth in real GDP of 1.7%. This growth projection is weak compared to historical trends. The most important reasons are slow projected growth in the labor force and the drag on aggregate productivity growth caused by the reallocation of resources from private to government sectors.

### 3.3.2 Necessary fiscal adjustments

Figure 3.2 summarizes the dynamics of government finances until 2050 in terms of the pay-as-you-go adjustments of the payroll tax rate that would be necessary to meet the fiscal policy rule, given the partly hypothetical policy assumptions in the baseline. The tax rate falls (increases) when the base of government revenues increases faster (more slowly) than government expenditures. The present fiscal rule implies that the base of government revenues in a given year includes all tax bases in the Mainland economy and 4% of the capital in the GPF.

The base of government revenues grows faster than the expenditures until 2020, and the payroll tax rate can therefore be reduced from the present level of 13%.[4] Negative payroll tax rates around 2020 suggest that there is fiscal scope for cutting other taxes as well. After 2020 government expenditures outgrows the base of government revenues, and the payroll tax rate must be raised by 0.4 points every year.

The U-shaped time profile of the payroll tax rate in Figure 3.2 will reappear several times in the subsequent sections. However, the position of this curve will vary somewhat. These variations reflect that the different studies have been carried out at different

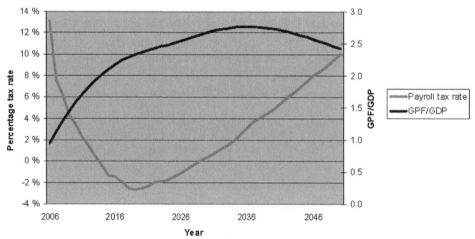

**Figure 3.2** No-reform scenario: necessary payroll tax rate (left axis) and the GPF/GDP ratio measured in current prices (right axis).

---

[4] The Norwegian payroll tax rate differs between regions. Today, the average rate is slightly above 13%.

times, and some of the exogenous assumptions have been revised. In particular, the exogenous prices of oil and the natural gas are highest in the most recent studies. Higher petroleum revenues contribute to reduce the tax burden. Also, the demographic projections have been updated, basically by increasing immigration and the average life expectancy.

The model simulations allow a closer examination of the contributions to the U-shaped time profile of the payroll tax rate. Table 3.2 reports the growth rate of the main components of the primary government expenditures and sources of revenues given the fiscal rule. Recall that fiscal rule does not allow direct spending of government petroleum revenues. Instead, 4% of the GPF can be used. Also, note that the figures do not include the effects of the endogenous adjustments of the payroll tax rate, because the point of the table is to examine the forces that contribute to make this adjustment necessary. Table 3.2 reveals the following main reasons for the U-shaped time profile of the payroll tax rate: (i) Most of profitable oil reserves are rapidly depleted before 2020 and most of the profits from the petroleum production are saved in the GPF. Thus, the capital in the GPF grows much faster "today" than it will in the future, especially after 2020, and so does the 4% out-take from the fund permitted by the fiscal rule. (ii) The growth in employment slows down. Almost all tax bases are positively

**Table 3.2** Growth in government primary expenditures and sources of government primary revenues, given the baseline assumptions except adjustments of the payroll tax rate (average annual growth rates, %)

|  | 2006–2020 | 2021–2050 |
| --- | --- | --- |
| Total expenditures | 4.6 | 5.0 |
| Government consumption | 4.1 | 4.7 |
| Employment | 0.9 | 1.0 |
| Health and old-age care | 1.4 | 2.0 |
| Labor cost per hour | 4.4 | 4.4 |
| Cash transfers to households | 6.3 | 5.5 |
| Public old-age pensions | 8.1 | 6.3 |
| Old-age pensioners | 2.3 | 1.7 |
| Average benefit *ex ante* indexation | 0.7 | 0.0 |
| Wage indexation | 4.6 | 4.5 |
| Sources of revenues | 5.6 | 4.4 |
| Tax bases, Mainland sector | 5.3 | 4.6 |
| 4% of the GPF | 7.0 | 3.0 |
| Gap between the growth rates of expenditures and sources of revenues | −1.0 | 0.6 |
| *Memo* |  |  |
| Total employment | 0.9 | 0.6 |
| GDP, Mainland sector (current prices) | 5.6 | 4.6 |

related to employment. (iii) The reallocation of labor from private industries to the government health and old-age care sectors implies a negative drag on the tax base, because there are no indirect taxes on public services and the effective tax payroll tax base is the wages in the private sector only. (iv) The growth in the number of elderly aged 80 or more accelerates from 2020. This group is the heaviest user of tax-financed health services and old-age care.

Figure 3.2 may be used to argue that Norway does not face severe fiscal sustainability problems. The present rather generous welfare state could be financed with a lower tax burden than today in all years until 2050. Simultaneously, the fiscal policy rule implies an unprecedented accumulation of financial assets. The GPF/GDP ratio rises from close to 1 in 2007 to a peak at 2.8 in 2036. Thus, judged by the *levels* of government expenditures and tax bases within a 40- to 50-year perspective, Norway's fiscal future looks bright. In particular, it looks much brighter than it did when the pension reform process was initiated, at that time one expected a real oil price of $25 (2004 dollars). Fiscally, Norway appears to be an outlier in the OECD.

However, Figure 3.2 can also be used to argue that Norway faces severe fiscal sustainability problems in the long run. This conclusion is based on the *growth trends* after 2020 rather than the *levels* of government revenues and expenditures within a more or less arbitrarily chosen period. After 2020, government expenditures grow faster than the total tax base. This imbalance between the growth rates of government expenditures and revenue bases is not a temporary phenomenon; no available information suggests that the necessary tax burden would stabilize if the simulation period were extended beyond 2050.

Furthermore, the projection underlying Figure 3.2 can be criticized for under-rating the future tax burden. One reason is the implausible assumption of no further growth in public service standards. The political pressure for improving standards of public health and care services will be strong when private consumption *per capita* grows by 2—3% annually. The demographic trends imply that the main users will represent a radically larger share of the voters. Thus, the scope for expansionary fiscal policy until 2020 may be used to expand spending instead of tax cuts. Indeed, this has been the policy so far. In particular, child care and old-age care have been given high priority. This policy implies that growth in the payroll tax rate starting in 2020 will be accelerated, since increases in the public spending per elderly interacts with the growth in the number of elderly (see Section 3.6).

A natural response to the U-shaped time path of the required payroll tax rate in Figure 3.2 is that the time path of the tax burden should be smoothened through more prefunding. This would require a tighter fiscal policy rule than the present one. It is questionable if it is politically feasible to increase government savings beyond the ambitious plan implied by the fiscal policy rule. Section 3.7 examines the effects on the tax burden dynamics of increased government saving.

## 3.4 SENSITIVITY OF THE FISCAL PROSPECTS TO VARIATIONS IN ECONOMIC GROWTH AND TERMS OF TRADE

### 3.4.1 Accelerated economic growth[5]

With a few exceptions, international literature leaves the impression that productivity growth in the private sector, *cet. par.*, has a positive government budget effect. The underlying logic is that higher productivity raises the tax bases, and that this effect dominates any price effects on government expenditures. This reasoning underlies the so-called OECD method of assessing fiscal sustainability, which draws on Blanchard *et al.*, (1990). This method uses the ratio between government debt and GDP to indicate the degree of fiscal sustainability. Cronin and McCoy (2000) claim that this debt ratio is the conventional indicator of fiscal sustainability.[6]

In addition, most studies based on generational accounting or CGE models find that productivity growth contributes, *cet. par.*, improves fiscal sustainability through the expansion of tax bases. For example, Gokhale and Raffelhüschen (1999) suspect budget projections for the US to be too optimistic because they find the projected productivity growth to be higher than warranted by US experience. Using a large CGE model, Kotlikoff *et al.*, (2001) find that a productivity-driven decline (increase) in the real wage growth contributes to the increase (decrease) in the future tax rates necessary to meet the intertemporal government budget constraint. With reference to these simulation studies, Kotlikoff (2001, p. 37) concludes: "A higher rate of technological progress improves, but doesn't fundamentally alter, the demographic transition." Heald (2005) reviews long-run projections for the UK (HM Treasury, 2004), which show that higher productivity reduces the future need for fiscal tightening. Cronin and McCoy (2000) find the same pattern in alternative long-run projections of the Irish economy.

These results may leave the impression that a positive correlation between productivity growth in the private sector and the fiscal stance is a robust empirical "law." Policy makers may even consider future fiscal sustainability problems to be over-rated to the extent that they regard productivity growth projections to be negatively biased.

However, government expenditures are also positively related to the productivity level in private sectors. It is a rather uncontroversial insight that competition will shift the cost-saving effect of productivity growth in an industry from the capital owners to the employees. Over time, the wage growth will be spread to other sectors, including the government sectors. In addition to the increase in the government wage bill, wage indexation of government cash transfers implies that the additional income caused by higher productivity in specific industries are automatically shared by all citizens, not only

---

[5] This section is a condensed exposition of Holmøy (2006b).

[6] Roux (1993); Hemming and Miranda (1991); and Cronin and McCoy (2000) represent examples of this method of measuring fiscal sustainability. Goldfajn (2002) and Bentz and Fetzer (2004) discuss the OECD method.

by the more productive workers. It is easily verified (Holmøy, 2006b) that the tax rate necessary to maintain exact primary budget balance is independent of productivity in all private sectors if total employment is fixed, all industries exhibit constant returns to scale, and all government budget components are equally affected by wage rate adjustments.

It unlikely that actual economies meet all these conditions. An important example is public debt services, which are significant in most OECD economies. These expenditures are independent of the wage rate. Eventually public debt services must be financed by a primary budget surplus. If the wage shares in all primary budget components are equal, an increase in the wage rate induces a proportional increase in the primary budget surplus. For economies where the government collects positive wage independent net revenues, the opposite results apply. This is the case in Norway and other countries where the government collects significant resource rents and interest on public wealth.

However, even if wage rate adjustments have fiscal effects, the link between the wage rate and productivity changes is not obvious. In the textbook model of the SOE the wage rate depends positively on the exogenous world prices of outputs and the productivity in the sectors producing traded goods (T-sectors), and no other variables. In particular, productivity growth in sectors producing non-traded goods (N-sectors) will not affect the wage rate. Instead, the cost effect is shifted forwards to lower product prices. Thus, the budget effect of productivity growth in N-sectors depends on the budget share of N-goods in government expenditures.

In general, the fiscal effect of productivity growth is therefore ambiguous, depending on economy specific characteristics. Such an ambiguity is a perfect challenge for CGE modeling: a multitude of interacting effects must be weighted together according to their empirical importance in the actual economy being examined. The remaining part of this section presents the results presented in Holmøy (2006b) of using MSG6 to simulate the fiscal effects of productivity changes in the Norwegian economy.

The simulation experiment considers a partial permanent 10% increase in the TFP index in a selection of T- and N-sectors. The fiscal effect is measured by the adjustment of the payroll tax rate necessary to restore the baseline path of the government budget surplus. The sectors experiencing the TFP shift are selected so that this shift affects the same base of resources in the T- and N-sectors. The simulation results reported in Table 3.3 confirm that the two TFP shifts have almost equal effects on the macroeconomic aggregates, such as private consumption, employment and the real wage rate. However, the productivity shift in the N-sector turns out to have the strongest growth effects over time. The primary reason is that the N-sector grows faster in terms of inputs than the selected T-sectors in the baseline scenario, so that the 10% TFP shift gradually affects a larger resource base than in the T-scenario. This difference is magnified by the difference in general equilibrium effects on labor supply.

Table 3.3 shows that higher TFP in private industries has an adverse fiscal effect. The endogenous increase in the wage rate turns out to have a stronger effect on government

**Table 3.3** Long-run macroeconomic effects in Norway of a 10% increase in TFP in T-sectors and N-sectors (percentage deviations from the baseline scenario unless otherwise stated)

|  | T-scenario | N-scenario |
|---|---|---|
| Pay roll tax (percent) | 1.5 | 0.5 |
| Total revenues, of which | 5.4 | 0.3 |
|    Indirect taxes | 3.4 | −0.2 |
|    Direct taxes, net of petroleum revenues | 7.2 | 0.5 |
| Total expenditures, of which | 5.9 | 0.3 |
|    Government consumption | 6.2 | 0.8 |
|    Cash transfers to households | 5.2 | 0.3 |
| Private consumption | 1.5 | 1.7 |
| Employment | −0.7 | −0.4 |
| Wage cost per hour | 6.5 | 0.8 |
| Wage rate | 5.4 | 0.4 |
| Consumer real wage rate | 1.6 | 2.0 |

expenditures than on the tax bases along the baseline. This reflects primarily that the government uses a significant share of its wage independent petroleum revenues to finance government expenditures. It also reflects that the government production sectors are labor intensive and that almost all government cash transfers are indexed by the average wage growth in Norway. Andersen and Pedersen (2006a,b) obtain the same result in a similar CGE analysis for Denmark. This suggests that the MSG6 results do not only reflect that the petroleum revenues make Norway's fiscal position exceptionally strong.

When TFP is raised by 10% in traded goods sectors accounting for 6.6% of total gross production value (in 2005), the payroll tax rate must be raised from 31 to 32.5% in 2050. If the same TFP shift takes place in a non-traded goods sector of the same size, the corresponding increase in the payroll tax rate is only a third (i.e. 0.5%). Compared to the macroeconomic effects, the differences in fiscal effects are strikingly large. Especially, the effects on gross revenues and gross expenditures are much greater in the T-scenario. The wage adjustment explains most of the difference between the fiscal effects of the two TFP shifts and it demonstrates that much of the textbook logic of the SOE model also holds in MSG6. The profit effect of higher TFP in the T-sector is shifted over to the wage rate — the only immobile resource. TFP growth in the N-sector reduces the prices of domestically produced intermediaries and capital goods. This allows a relatively small increase in the competitive wage rate consistent with trade balance. In the textbook SOE model, the possibility of this wage effect is ruled out by simplifying the assumptions.

The MSG6 results suggest that equilibrium effects on labor supply are relatively small. The labor supply falls although the consumer real wage rate increases and the uncompensated labor supply elasticity is positive (0.1). The dominance of the income effects over the substitution effects reflects that the income effects include not only the higher consumer real wage, but also higher capital income and higher wage indexed cash transfers.

Higher productivity in the form discussed in this paper is manna from heaven. By definition, it allows improved average welfare in the countries experiencing it. The possible adverse fiscal effect of productivity growth does not change this. However, although productivity growth makes life easier for the average person, it is an important policy lesson that politicians cannot rely on growth to solve fiscal sustainability problems. It should be stressed that the conclusions above are confined to fiscal effects of productivity shifts in the private business sector. Obviously, productivity growth in government service production can improve the fiscal stance if it is used to reduce costs. However, according to the hypothesis underlying the term "Baumol's (cost) disease," the technological scope for productivity improvements is on average significantly lower in the service production typically provided by the government than in other sectors.

### 3.4.2 Increased petroleum wealth[7]

It is at least a widespread impression that the financial fundament for much of the welfare and fiscal policy in Norway hinges on the oil price. In both 2009 and 2010, petroleum share of total Norwegian exports equaled 46% and the GDP share of the sector equaled 22%. Between 85 and 90% of the net cash flow from sales of oil and gas is collected by the central government through indirect and direct taxes, surplus accruing directly to the state, and dividends from companies. The cash flow collected by the central government from the petroleum sector increased from 11 to 13% from 2009 to 2010. However, oil and gas are non-renewable resources, which should be regarded as wealth. By the end of 2007, 36.4% of the total resources had been depleted. If the present production were maintained, the oil and gas reserves would be depleted after, respectively, 6 and 22 years. Realistic production profiles imply a much longer production period.

A recurrent issue in the Norwegian policy debate is the time path for oil and gas production and the intertemporal plan of spending the petroleum wealth. The policy target has been to obtain permanent benefits from the resource rents, i.e. to avoid "Dutch Disease" problems. As explained above, the fiscal rule adopted in 2001 isolates the petroleum cash flow government petroleum revenues from the government budget. It is directly invested in the Central GPF — Global and the annual 4% out-take from the fund should equal to the non-petroleum budget deficit over the cycle.

An important premise for avoiding "Dutch Disease" is to obtain realistic estimates of the petroleum wealth and to communicate to these the public. The fiscal effect of permanent changes in the oil and gas price can be measured by the adjustments in the tax

---

[7] The general equilibrium mechanisms discussed in this section are analyzed in a stylized analytical model in Holmøy (2006a).

burden needed to meet the annual budget constraint implied by the fiscal rule. Subsequently, these adjustments are computed by changes in the payroll tax rate. The real oil price stays at $71 (2007 dollars) in the baseline. In order to examine non-linearity, the budget-neutral paths for the payroll tax rate have also been estimated for $30, $120, $200 and $250 (2007 dollars). The gas price changes are proportional to the oil price changes.

The empirical significance of the general equilibrium effects on the tax rate adjustments can be elucidated by comparing them with corresponding naïve estimates. The naïve estimate ignores all equilibrium effects. It simply divides the additional government revenue by the relevant tax base. The additional revenue is given by the fiscal rule as 4% of the higher capital in the GPF. The relevant base of the payroll tax is the wage sum in the private sector. The naïve estimate is based on the same projections of all relevant variables as the CGE estimate. Following this naïve procedure, it would be possible to cut the payroll tax rate by as much as 24.8 percentage points in 2050 if the real oil price stayed at $120 rather than $30 from 2010.

The MSG6 simulations verify the obvious result that higher oil and gas prices improves the Norwegian fiscal stance, but the positive slope of the tax rate trend after 2020 is not reduced. However, interesting information lies in the estimated orders of magnitude. Two points deserve explanation because they are substantively important and because they involve interesting general equilibrium repercussions: (i) The scope for tax cuts is much smaller than the naïve estimate and (ii) the scope for tax cuts decreases as the petroleum price increases.

The simulated payroll tax cut made possible by moving from the $30 to the $120 scenario is 11.3 percent in 2050 (Figure 3.3 and Table 3.4). This is less than half of the naïve estimate. Thus, general equilibrium effects imply a striking modification of the scope for tax cuts. In other words, there is a great risk of over-rating the scope for fiscal expansion that which can be financed by additional petroleum revenues if one neglects the insights from the CGE analysis.

The by far most important general equilibrium effect is the effect of wage rate adjustments, which affect government expenditures and the tax bases differently. Thus, the nature of the equilibrium effects in this simulation experiment is analogous to those induced by higher productivity growth explained in the previous section. Since Norway is a net exporter in present value terms of oil and gas, higher prices of oil and gas imply a terms-of-trade gain. A real appreciation is required in order to meet the same intertemporal external balance as in the baseline. In the case where the oil price increase permanently from $30 to $120 (2007 dollars) in 2010, the equilibrium real appreciation corresponds to a 26% increase in the labor cost per hour in 2050 relative to the non-petroleum world prices (Table 3.5). The increase in the wage rate raises government expenditures more than the tax bases, foremost because a wage independent out-take equal to 4% of the GPF is used to finance government expenditure. The budget-neutral reductions in the payroll tax rate are passed over to labor, raising

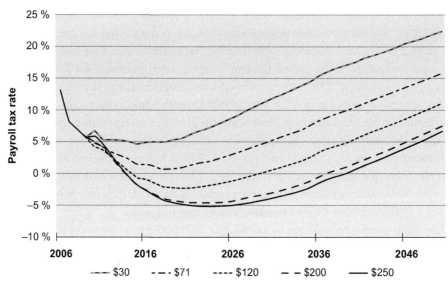

**Figure 3.3** Payroll tax rate in different oil price scenarios (%).

**Table 3.4** Government revenues and expenditures measured in current prices in 2050 for different oil prices (% unless otherwise indicated)

|  | $30 | $71 | $100 | $120 | $150 | $250 |
|---|---|---|---|---|---|---|
| Pay roll tax rate (%) | 22.3 | 15.7 | 12.6 | 11.0 | 9.2 | 6.5 |
| Total expenditures (1000 NOK *per capita*)[1] | 910.8 | 989.2 | 985.6 | 1112.0 | 1204.6 | 1584.6 |
| *Financed by (percentage shares)* |  |  |  |  |  |  |
| 4% out-take of the GPF capital | | 6.3 | 12.2 | 16.6 | 17.4 | 19.8 | 24.4 |
| Non-petroleum revenues | | 93.7 | 87.8 | 83.4 | 82.6 | 80.2 | 75.6 |

**Table 3.5** Macroeconomic development under different oil prices; fixed prices unless otherwise indicated (2050 levels relative to the $30 scenario)

|  | $71 | $120 | $200 | $250 |
|---|---|---|---|---|
| Private consumption | 1.07 | 1.14 | 1.26 | 1.32 |
| Employment (man-hours) | 0.99 | 0.98 | 0.96 | 0.94 |
| Payroll tax rate | 0.70 | 0.49 | 0.33 | 0.29 |
| Labor costs | 1.10 | 1.26 | 1.61 | 1.87 |
| Net imports | 1.65 | 2.44 | 3.79 | 4.65 |

the consumer wage rate more than the labor cost. This reduces the scope for lowering the tax burden. When all equilibrium effects are taken into account, the payroll tax rate has fallen from 22.3 to 11.0% in 2050. The corresponding increase in the consumer wage rate equals 35.2%.

The results demonstrate that real appreciation represents an important channel through which increased higher government wealth is automatically rebated to households. This automatic rebatement significantly reduces the room for tax rate reductions. The potential importance of this redistribution mechanism is especially high in economies similar to the so-called "Scandinavian Model." Such economies are characterized by relatively strong egalitarian norms, which imply a relatively strong impact of wage rate adjustments on government expenditures for two reasons: (i) A relatively high degree of centralized wage formation ensures that wage changes rapidly spread to the government sectors, and (ii) the relatively generous public pension benefits and most other government transfers to households are indexed to the average wage level.

Reduced labor supply is another general equilibrium effect, which contributes to reduce the scope for cutting tax rates, since most tax bases are positively related to employment. However, this effect is relatively modest; employment falls by 1.3% in 2050. It reflects that on balance the income effects caused by the terms-of-trade gain weakly dominate the substitution effect of the strong increase in the real consumer wage rate. The income effect captures that both labor and non-labor income increase. On the other hand, the terms-of-trade gain allows for an expansion of private consumption, which reinforces the tax rate reduction as the average indirect consumption tax rate is close to 20% in Norway. In 2050, private consumption in fixed prices would be 10.2% above the baseline scenario.

The simulations also demonstrate that there are "diminishing fiscal returns" of increasing the oil price in terms of budget-neutral reductions of the tax burden (Figure 3.3 and Table 3.5). A higher oil price implies a higher capital in the GPF. Consequently, the out-take of 4% from the fund can finance a higher wage dependent non-petroleum deficit. Table 3.5 shows how the share of government expenditures that can be financed by the 4% out-take of the GPF capital increases with the oil price. As the wage-dependent deficit grows, the equilibrium increase in the wage rate brings about a successively greater automatic expansion of the non-petroleum deficit. This non-linearity explains why the long-run scope for tax cuts is diminishing in the petroleum wealth.

The strength of the fiscal effect of wage rate adjustments is likely to differ significantly between countries and over time, because it depends on both the magnitude of the change in the wage rate, and the initial wage dependent government net revenues. Norway is a special case, because the large government petroleum wealth finances a substantial deficit of wage-dependent government net revenues, and because government expenditures are highly wage dependent. In countries where both the government and the economy as a whole must serve substantial debt, wage-dependent government net revenues may be positive. In such economies, an exogenous increase in government non-tax revenue in the form of traded goods (e.g. a drop in the interest rate) will have the opposite effects of those examined above.

The equilibrium wage growth compatible with the external balance constraint will, in this case, magnify the direct fiscal improvement.

The magnitude of the changes in the wage rate depends crucially on the degree of decreasing returns to scale in the traded goods sector. This assumption may be disputed, but decreasing returns is a realistic implication of productivity heterogeneity within the specified industries and it rests on empirical evidence (Klette, 1999). This approach to modeling industry adjustments and international trade also seems to imply a good compromise between a realistic degree of specialization of industries producing traded goods and the widespread view that small economies cannot affect world prices in the long-run. The approach also meets the criticism raised in Kehoe (2003) against alternative applied modeling approaches of exports and imports.

### 3.4.3 Higher returns to foreign investments

As the petroleum wealth is gradually transferred from the North Sea to the GPF, the rate of return to foreign investments will overtake much of the same role for the Norwegian economy as the prices of oil and gas have played during the years with large petroleum production and exports. One effect of globalization is improved access to profitable international investment projects, raising the opportunity costs of domestic investments. Having net foreign financial wealth, an increase in the international rate of return implies the same kind of income effect for Norway as an increase in the oil price. Moreover, the central government collects most of the additional income. As with changes in petroleum prices, changes in the international rate of return will affect relative prices of goods and production factors, since it will strongly influence the capital costs facing both firms and consumers. With government net financial assets reaching nearly 3 times current GDP around 2035, one would expect significant fiscal effects of permanent changes in the world interest rate. For the government finances, the terms-of-trade gain and the direct government revenue effect are by far most important.

Heide et al., (2006) examined the fiscal effects obtained by MSG6 of increasing the world interest rate permanently from 5.5 to 6.5%. However, in this study the income effects were relatively modest since the real oil price was assumed to prevail at $25 (2004 dollars), which generated a much smaller capital in the GPF than in the baseline presented in Section 3.3. In Holmøy and Kravik (2008), the real oil price was assumed to be $50 (2004 dollars). The payroll tax rate can then be 4.5 points lower than in a reference scenario in 2050. The key mechanisms were explained above. However, as for the effect of higher petroleum prices, the quantitative effects depend strongly on when the exogenous variables deviate. The fiscal effect of a higher oil price will be negative and relatively small if the shift takes place after the profitable oil resources have been depleted. Analogously, the fiscal effect of a higher world interest rate increases as long as the GPF grows relatively to government expenditures.

## 3.5 NORWEGIAN PUBLIC PENSION REFORM

Estimates of pension reform effects typically belong to one of three strands of literature: (i) Highly detailed dynamic microsimulation of purely mechanical effects on individual benefits and government pension expenditures; (ii) econometric studies of behavioral effects of particular elements of pension system, especially labor supply; and (iii) CGE estimates of the long-run effects of rather stylized reforms on employment, fiscal sustainability and the inter-generational welfare distribution. Recent examples of CGE estimates include *inter alia* Beetsma *et al.,* (2003); Bovenberg and Knaap (2005); Fehr and Habermann (2006); Fehr *et al.,* (2003); Fehr (2000); Kotlikoff *et al.,* (2001); Lindbeck and Persson (2003); McMorrow and Roeger (2002) and Miles (1999).

Holmøy and Stensnes (2008) integrate these three approaches when simulating the effects of the Norwegian pension reform of 2011 by combining the microsimulation model MOSART and MSG6. This section draws on this paper's assessments of how the reform can be expected to perform when evaluated against two inter-related goals shared by most other recent pension reforms: (i) Improving fiscal sustainability and (ii) stimulating employment.[8] MOSART includes a nearly accurate description of the details in the different pension systems, as well as a representative sample of the heterogeneous individual earning profiles and other aspects of individual life courses. On the other hand, the MSG6 model captures many relevant aspects of behavioral adjustments and general equilibrium repercussions. The models are run iteratively to ensure consistency. This strategy seeks to exploit the maximum of available information relevant for analyzing pension reform in Norway.

### 3.5.1 Main reform elements

The old public pension system was established in 1967 as a mandatory, defined benefit, pay-as-you-go pension system. The total benefit combined a flat-rate universal benefit, a means-tested supplement and an earnings-related income benefit. The income benefit was based on pension entitlements accrued through labor market earnings after 1967 and some other criteria. Both entitlements and benefits have, in principle, been wage indexed. In the stylized case where an individual earns the average wage for 40 years, the after-tax replacement ratio of the public old-age benefit would be about 65%.[9] Due to several complex non-actuarial elements, including a best-years rule, the old system implied a relatively weak income dependent on pension benefits. According to MOSART simulations, increasing earnings by 1 NOK raised the average present value of

---

[8] Since this paper was written, some elements of the pension reform have been modified. However, the reform proposal discussed in this section still captures the most important reform elements.

[9] Special tax rules for pension benefits makes the after-tax replacement ratio about 15 percent higher than the corresponding pretax ratio. Income from private pension schemes and special pension schemes for public employees come in addition to this figure.

future pension benefits by 0.10 NOK (Stensnes, 2007). The formal retirement age was 67 years. More than 40% of the population receives disability benefits at this age, and about 60% of the (still) employed are entitled to early retirement from the age of 62. Thus, the effective retirement age averages about 60 years in Norway. Note that early retirement through these arrangements did not reduce future pension benefits at any point in time. Both disability pensioners and early retirees obtain entitlements as if they remained working until the age of 67.

The new system continues to be financed on a pay-as-you-go basis. The pension benefit continues to include a minimum income guarantee at the same level as before, as well as an earnings-based benefit. Contrary to the basic benefit in the old system, however, it is means-tested against the income based pension benefit.

The expenditure risk associated with increases in longevity is shifted from taxpayers onto each cohort of pensioners through an actuarial mechanism. With some qualifications, the new system converts the implicit pension wealth of accumulated entitlements into an annuity over the average expected remaining lifetime. An increase in the expected number of retirement years reduces the annual benefit such that the present value of total pension benefits is nearly invariant to changes in current remaining life expectancy and retirement age. The statutory retirement age and current early retirement arrangements are phased out and replaced with a flexible retirement age from the age of 62 years, available to everyone. If life expectancy increases by one year, an additional eight months of labor market participation will be needed to maintain the annual benefit. The mechanism increases the individual cost of early retirement. Labor supply is also stimulated by a stronger dependency between earnings and pension benefits. The income based benefit is 1.35% of lifetime labor market earnings below an annual wage-indexed threshold. The reform strengthens the incentives to retire as a disability pensioner, but the present analysis takes as given both the disability scheme and observed rates of transition into disability.

The new system is not intended to be cost saving for the government at the time of implementation. Over time, it will be cost saving compared to the old system due to the actuarial life expectancy adjustment and the less generous indexation of benefits in payment. Income dependent entitlements will still be indexed by wage growth until retirement, but benefits will be indexed to an average of the growth in wages and consumer prices in payment.[10]

## 3.5.2 Fiscal effects

The model simulations suggest that the pension reform is likely to be highly successful in achieving a lower tax burden and stimulating employment. Compared to the no-reform

---

[10] In practice, the reform implements the less generous indexation in payment as a fixed annual deduction of 0.75 percent relative to wage indexation.

path, i.e. the baseline, the scope for cutting the payroll tax rate increases gradually after reform implementation, passing as much as 9.5 points in 2050 (Figure 3.4). Towards 2020, the reform boosts employment by 8% relative to the no-reform path, rising further to 11% in 2050. The following explanation of the results is intended to demonstrate that one would seriously underestimate the fiscal effects of the pension reform if behavioral effects and equilibrium repercussions were ignored.

Table 3.6 shows that the scope for tax rate reductions results from a rather complex mix of changes in government expenditure and revenue components. The reform is indeed cost saving: public old-age pension expenditures would be 12.2% below the no-reform scenario in 2050. On the other hand, it invokes two mechanisms which raise

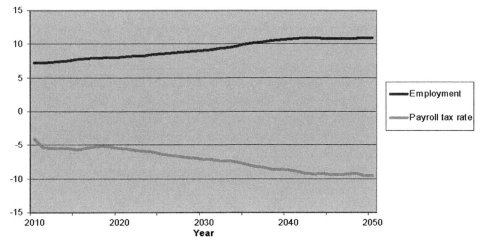

**Figure 3.4** Deviation between reform and no-reform scenarios for the payroll tax rate (%) and employment (%).

**Table 3.6** Reform effects on tax bases and government expenditures in 2050, measured in current prices (deviations from the baseline scenario)

|  | Billions NOK | Percent |
| --- | --- | --- |
| 1. Total revenues | −315 | −5.1 |
| a. Given baseline tax rates | 262 | 4.2 |
| b. Including the tax base effect of changed tax rates | 399 | 6.4 |
| c. Residual (=1 − 1b) | −714 | −11.5 |
| 2. Total expenditures | −328 | −5.9 |
| a. Transfers to households | −113 | −3.6 |
| i. Public old-age pensions | −210 | −12.2 |
| ii. Other transfers | 97 | 6.8 |
| b. Government consumption | −224 | −8.7 |
| 3. Net financial investment (=1 − 2) | 13 | 1.9 |

other government cash transfers by 6.8% in 2050: the reform transfers some of the early retirees into disability and sickness schemes, rather than work. This reclassification of beneficiaries raises transfers by 4.7 points. The remaining effects are due to the increase in the pretax wage rate, which reflects that most transfers are indexed to wage growth. In absolute terms, lower labor costs in public service production account for the greatest contribution to lower expenditures. However, this is a bookkeeping effect, reflecting that the government pays less payroll tax to itself.

On the revenue side, the scope for cutting tax rates levied on labor income reflects the reduction in government expenditure, as well as the expansion of most tax bases. The tax base expansion can be decomposed into a pure reform effect and an indirect effect induced by lower tax rates on labor income. The pure reform effect on the tax base can be estimated to 4.2% in 2050 by simulating the reform scenario while keeping the payroll tax rate at the no-reform path and neglecting the government budget constraint (Table 3.6, row 1a). This tax base expansion is driven by the stronger labor supply incentives at the intensive and extensive margins. The CGE model captures that higher employment expands almost all tax bases. The indirect effect of realizing the scope for tax cuts by reducing the payroll tax rate magnifies the tax base expansion from 4.2 to 6.4% through a further expansion of labor supply. The residual in row 1c in Table 3.6 should be interpreted as the direct and indirect revenue effect of tax rate reduction.

The surge in the pretax wage rate contributes to raise both government expenditures and the tax bases. As explained in Sections 3.4.1 and 3.4.2, the net budget effect is negative, because the direct and indirect wage share in government expenditures exceeds the wage share in the tax bases.

Table 3.7 decomposes the total reform effects on the tax rate and employment measured in 2050 into partial contributions from key reform elements: delayed retirement, stronger income dependency of benefits and reduced average old-age benefits.

**Table 3.7** Decomposition of the reform effects in 2050 (deviations from the baseline scenario in % unless otherwise indicated)

|  | Employment | Payroll tax rate (%) | Consumer real wage, including stronger income dependency |
|---|---|---|---|
| 1. Increased retirement age | 6.6 | −6.9 | 3.8 |
|    Direct effect | 4.5 |  |  |
| 2. Stronger income dependency of benefits | 3.8 | −2.8 | 5.6 |
|    Direct wage effect | 2.5 |  | 5.1 |
| 3. Reduced average benefits | 0.4 | −1.0 | 0.8 |
| 4. Interaction effects (=5 − 1 − 2 − 3) | 0.2 | 1.2 | −0.7 |
| 5. Total effect | 11.0 | −9.5 | 9.5 |

These contributions are identified by simulating the effects of each one separately. In 2050, delayed retirement corresponds to a 4.5% increase in employment. The equilibrium effects of such a shift, including the budget-neutral cut in the payroll tax rate, raises the employment effect to 6.6%, which accounts for 60% of the total surge in employment.

Stronger income dependency of benefits works as if a larger share of the tax rate on earnings is perceived as compulsory savings. This effect allows a 2.8 points cut in the payroll tax rate and employment goes up by 3.8%; 2.5 points of the employment effect is a direct response to the stronger link between earnings and benefits, the remaining 1.3 points are caused by the real wage effect following the cut in the payroll tax rate.

A striking example of the importance of behavioral and equilibrium effects is the finding that the reform leaves the average benefit unaffected. Table 3.8 reports the contributions from mechanical reform effects and equilibrium repercussions. *Cet. par.*, the new entitlement structure raises the compensation by 7%, for given earnings histories. Over time, however, increased life expectancy and less generous indexation reduce the average benefit for given earnings and retirement. In 2050, these effects would have reduced the average benefit to 0.889 of the no-reform benefit. However, labor supply responses, mainly through delayed retirement, counteract the mechanical effects, brings this ratio up to 0.976. This ratio is brought back to 1 when accounting for the partial effect of indexing entitlements to the endogenous wage growth. The labor supply responses shift most of the cost-saving effect of the reform from lower annual benefits to fewer old-age pensioners and expanded tax bases. In 2050 delayed retirement would reduce the number of old-age pensioners by 10.4% (from 1.249 to 1.119 million) compared to the no-reform scenario.

Table 3.8 Reform effects on public old-age pension expenditures, average old-age benefit and number of old-age recipients (cumulative contributions from different effects in 2050; indexes, 2050 levels in the no-reform scenario = 1)

|  | Number of old-age recipients | Old-age benefit | Public old-age pension expenditures |
|---|---|---|---|
| 1. No-reform scenario | 1 | 1 | 1 |
| 2. Mechanical reform effects |  |  |  |
| a: 1 + New entitlement structure | 1 | 1.070 | 1.070 |
| b: 2a + Actuarial benefit adjustment | 1 | 0.955 | 0.955 |
| c: 2b + New indexation of benefits | 1 | 0.889 | 0.889 |
| 3. Behavioral and equilibrium effects |  |  |  |
| a: 2c + Delayed retirement | 0.896 | 0.963 | 0.863 |
| b: 3a + Increased labor supply at the intensive margin | 0.896 | 0.976 | 0.874 |
| c: 3b + indexation of entitlements to new wage rate = *Total effects* | 0.896 | 1.000 | 0.896 |

Section 3.3 pointed out that the main long-run fiscal sustainability problem in Norway lies in a gap between the growth rates of government expenditures and the total tax base after 2020. The simulated growth rates reported in Table 3.9 suggest that the reform makes a surprisingly small contribution to resolve this problem. The reform shrinks this gap from 0.99 to 0.92 percent and the annual increase in the payroll tax after 2020 drops from 0.42 to 0.29%. This kind of dynamic fiscal improvement can be completely attributed to accelerated growth in the tax base, whereas the reform has practically no effect on the annual growth rate of total expenditures after 2020. Interestingly, and contrary to the explicit goal of the reform, this conclusion also applies to the growth rate of public old-age pension expenditures. Accordingly, the reform can indeed be expected to have strong cost-saving effect on future public pension expenditures, but this effect reflects a shift in the expenditure *level* — not a lower long-run *growth rate*. The small reform effects on the growth rates of the tax base and the government expenditure components, including the old-age pensions, are quite robust to alternative exogenous assumptions on demography and labor supply responses.

The general equilibrium repercussions need, however, some qualifications. First, most of the wage rate adjustments result from the choice of the payroll tax rate as the endogenous budget-neutral fiscal policy instrument. This mechanism reflects that the determination factor price in MSG6 is very close to the textbook SOE model of the SOE, and it was explained in Sections 3.4.1 and 3.4.2. The reform effects would have been different if the government budget constraint were met by other fiscal adjustments. There is also obvious scope for modeling improvements. Specifically, there is scope for

**Table 3.9** Average growth rates in the period 2020–2050 of government budget components measured in current prices (%)

|  | Present system | New system |
|---|---|---|
| 1. Total government expenditures | 4.45 | 4.46 |
| Government consumption | 4.39 | 4.44 |
| Transfers to households | 4.77 | 4.84 |
| Total public old-age pension expenditures | 5.57 | 5.56 |
| Number of old-age pensioners | 1.47 | 1.25 |
| Average annual benefit |  |  |
| *ex ante* indexation | 0.12 | 0.21 |
| indexation with wage growth | 3.94 | 4.06 |
| Total tax base, no-reform tax rates | 3.46 | 3.62 |
| 2. Total tax base, tax rates after reform | 3.46 | 3.54 |
| 3. Gap between growth in expenditures and tax base (2−1) | 0.99 | 0.92 |
| Gap between growth in public old-age pension expenditures and tax bas | 2.11 | 2.02 |
| Employment | 0.19 | 0.28 |
| Payroll tax rate (%) | 0.42 | 0.29 |

improving tradeoff between theoretical consistency and a detailed description of system details and population heterogeneity. Moreover, the importance of the employment effects suggest that labor supply behavior at both the intensive and the extensive margins should modeled in more detail.

## 3.6 DEMOGRAPHIC UNCERTAINTY[11]

### 3.6.1 Increased longevity

Demographic projections have regularly underestimated the reduction in mortality among the elderly. The baseline rests on the assumption that the average expected lifetime for newborn boys and girls increases by 0.14 years *per annum* for men and women. In an alternative "High population growth scenario" the average longevity increases by 0.19 years *per annum*, which translates to an increase in average expected lifetime for men and women of 2.2 years in 2050 compared to the baseline. The reductions in mortality rates will have potentially significant effects on fiscal sustainability in the long run, since they are experienced by the elderly. The resulting additional population growth will have small effects on the number of children and the labor force, but it will be almost equal to the growth in the population of old-age pensioners, who are also the heaviest users of tax-financed health services and long-term care.

Lower mortality among the elderly raises the question of the health conditions of the elderly. The baseline scenario assumes no changes in the age specific demand for health and social care services. This is a pessimistic assumption, but it serves the role of a transparent benchmark for sensitive analyses. It is maintained in this subsection. Section 3.6.2 examines the effects when increased longevity is accompanied by improved health among the elderly.

Figure 3.5 shows how employment in the public health and long-term sector will develop under different assumptions. In 2050, the baseline this employment would be 2.14 times the corresponding 2004 level. Recall that this growth reflects changes in the size and the age composition of the population only. Age-specific service standards and user ratios are constant. The increase in longevity described above contributes *cet. par.* to raise the required employment in this sector to 2.38, which is 11.0% higher than the baseline level in 2050. Inputs of other factors increase by the same proportion, and the mix between tax financing and user fees is not changed.

The MSG6 simulations account for the increase in government employment. They also account for direct changes in the number pensioners and the labor force caused by increased longevity. As pointed out in Section 3.5, the Norwegian pension reform is especially designed to make the public pension expenditures more invariant to changes

---

[11] This section draws on Holmøy and Nielsen (2008).

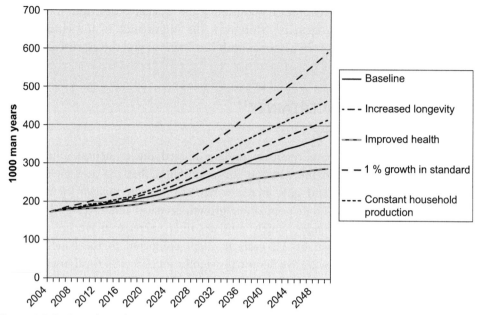

**Figure 3.5** Projected employment in public health and long-term care under different assumptions: 1000 normal man-years.

in longevity. To what extent this will be the case is examined below by computing the effects of increased longevity for both the old and the new public pension system.

Given the old pension system, the MSG6 simulation shows that the payroll tax rate must increase gradually compared with the baseline path in order to meet the government budget constraint implied by the fiscal rule. The required increase becomes higher as the difference between the numbers of elderly in the two scenarios gradually grows (Figure 3.6). It passes 4.2 percent in 2050. The figures in Table 3.10 allow a more detailed examination of the mechanisms driving this result. The 11% increase in government health and long-term care employment entails an increase in real government consumption of 7.9%. The increase in cash transfers in current prices may seem surprisingly small (0.5%) since public old-age pension expenditures amount to more than one-third of total cash transfers. However, almost all of these transfers are wage indexed and the wage rate falls by 3.7%. Thus, old-age pensions deflated by the wage rate are about 12.6% higher than in the baseline in 2050.[12]

---

[12] Let $X$ be the percentage change in old-age pensions measured in fixed wages. The share of old-age pensions in total transfers is one-third, the remaining transfers are the same in both scenarios, the wage rate falls by 3.7%, and the increase in total transfers measured in current prices is 0.5%. It then follows that $(1/3) * (-3.7 + X) + (2/3) * (-3.7) = 0.5 \leftrightarrow X = 12.6$.

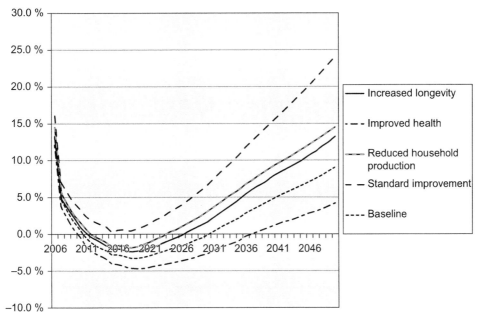

**Figure 3.6** Payroll tax rate in different oil price scenarios (%).

The wage rate adjustment is a general equilibrium effects that modifies the need for raising the payroll tax rate. As explained in Sections 3.4.1 and 3.4.2 the reason is that the share of wages is greater in government expenditures than in government revenues. The fall in the wage rate reflects the changes in the payroll tax rate and the labor cost per hour. First, a given increase in the payroll tax rate implies higher labor cost per hour for a given consumer wage rate. *Cet. par.* this means a deterioration of the international competitiveness that is inconsistent with the external balance constraint. In the textbook SOE model, the labor cost must remain constant by a decline in the consumer wage rate. This mechanism is important in MSG6, but there is some scope for changes in the labor cost since there are increasing marginal costs in the production of traded goods. The increase in consumption of health and long-term care services crowds out consumption of other goods, which reduces the average import share in total demand. This effect does not depend on the degree of public provision of these services. Thus, in order to maintain external balance, the traded goods sector must be lower in the scenario with the largest number of elderly. This is realized by a real appreciation in the form of an increase in labor cost per hour equal to 1.7%.

Other equilibrium mechanisms have also affected the need for raising the tax burden. A given change in labor supply has a strong effect on total tax revenues, since most tax bases are positively related to employment. However, total employment is almost unaffected, since the negative substitution effect of the decline in the real consumer wage

**Table 3.10** Effects of changes in demography and in determinants of the demand for health and long-term care services

| | Increased longevity | | Improved health | | 1% growth in standard | | Constant household production | |
|---|---|---|---|---|---|---|---|---|
| | 2020 | 2050 | 2020 | 2050 | 2020 | 2050 | 2020 | 2050 |
| Total government expenditures (current prices) | 1.4 | 3.5 | −1.7 | −3.6 | 4.6 | 10.0 | 1.9 | 4.0 |
| Government consumption (fixed prices) | 2.1 | 7.9 | −3.1 | −13.5 | 7.8 | 34.4 | 3.1 | 14.0 |
| Government employment | 1.0 | 4.0 | −1.9 | −8.3 | 4.8 | 21.0 | 1.9 | 8.8 |
| Employment in public health and long-term care | 3.4 | 11.0 | −7.0 | −22.9 | 17.3 | 58.0 | 7.0 | 24.3 |
| Cash transfers to households (current prices) | 0.4 | 0.5 | 0.6 | 4.0 | −1.4 | −10.2 | −0.7 | −3.9 |
| Payroll tax rate (%) | 1.0 | 4.2 | −1.5 | −4.9 | 4.1 | 15.0 | 1.7 | 5.5 |
| Total employment | −0.1 | 0.2 | 0.4 | −0.4 | −1.3 | 1.0 | −0.6 | 0.5 |
| Consumer wage rate | −0.5 | −3.7 | 0.6 | 4.2 | −1.3 | −10.8 | −0.6 | −4.1 |
| Private consumption (fixed prices) | 0.1 | −2.0 | 0.5 | 3.5 | −0.9 | −9.0 | −0.3 | −3.5 |

rate is nearly neutralized by the income effect, which also include lower profits and wage indexed transfers.

However, the tax revenue also depends on the allocation of labor between the private and the government sector. Almost all the increase in government employment is taken from the private sector, since labor supply is almost equal in the two scenarios. In 2050, this reduces private consumption by 2.0% from the baseline level. This shrinks the indirect tax base, and the average indirect tax rate on private consumption is close to 20% in Norway. In addition, the effective base of the payroll tax rate is the wages in the private sector only, since the payroll taxes paid by government production represent an identical component of government labor costs. Thus, the crowding out of private consumption and employment contributes to increase the necessary tax hike.

### 3.6.2 Increased longevity under a more actuarial pension system

As explained in Section 3.5, one of the most important elements in the Norwegian pension reform of 2011 is the actuarial mechanism supposed to neutralize the effects of changes in longevity on public old-age pension expenditures. Holmøy and Stensnes (2008) analyze how well the reform lives up to this intention by comparing a no-reform and a reform scenario under the assumption that average longevity increases by 0.19 years rather than 0.14 *per annum*.

The simulations demonstrate that the reform indeed works as intended (Table 3.11). In 2050, the increase in longevity would magnify the reduction in public old-age pension expenditures from 12.2 to 17.1%. This reflects that prolongation of the existing non-actuarial system is more costly the longer people live as pensioners. The corresponding feasible cut in the payroll tax rate increases from 9.5 to 13.6%. Stronger labor supply incentives at both the extensive and intensive margin contribute to the magnified scope for tax cuts.

**Table 3.11** Pension reform effects under alternative assumptions on demographics and labor supply (deviations from respective reference scenarios in 2050; % unless otherwise indicated)

|  | Main alternative | Longevity |
|---|---|---|
| Changes from main alternative |  | 2.2 extra years |
| Total government expenditures (current prices) | −5.9 | −8.1 |
| Cash transfers to households (current prices) | −3.6 | −5.9 |
| Old-age pension expenditures (current prices) | −12.2 | −17.1 |
| Payroll tax rate (%) | −9.5 | −13.6 |
| Total employment | 11.0 | 13.4 |
| Consumer real wage rate (including stronger dependency between earnings and pensions) | 9.4 | 11.5 |
| Pretax wage rate | 2.0 | 4.1 |
| Total tax base (current prices) | 6.4 | 8.8 |

As pointed out in Section 3.5, the simulated reform effects on the growth rate of key variables after 2020 are quite insensitive to changes in exogenous assumptions. The exception is variation in longevity. With the old pension system, the required payroll tax rate grows annually by 0.42% on average between 2020 and 2050. Under the same longevity assumptions, the corresponding growth in the pay roll tax rate is reduced by 0.13 points from the baseline. When the reform is combined with increased longevity the growth in the pay roll tax rate can be 0.21 points lower than in the baseline.

### 3.6.3 Immigration

The substantial increase in immigration to Norway over the last years has demonstrated that this variable is notoriously hard to predict. The following sensitivity analysis incorporates an increase in net immigration of 8000 persons per year, which is 50% above the net immigration in the main demographic alternative. The extra immigrants are assumed to behave as Norwegians with the lowest education. Accordingly, it reduces *cet. par.* the average labor market participation rate, earnings and pension entitlements. Immigrants are also assumed to have the same age- and gender-specific user ratios of public services as natives, and they get the same (constant) service standards. Government consumption of public goods increases proportionally to the changes in the total population.

On balance, additional immigration improves government finances (Table 3.12). However, this reflects that we do not compute effects after 2050. Few of the additional immigrants become elderly within 2050. Extending the simulation period would therefore show less positive fiscal effects. In 2050, the payroll tax rate can be 3.0% below the corresponding baseline level without violating the fiscal rule. The government revenues from increasingly higher tax bases dominate the increase in government consumption and cash transfers. Table 3.13 reports the changes in the main primary budget components measured in current prices.

**Table 3.12** Effects on the size and the age composition of the population of increasing net immigration by 8000 (50%) per year (deviations from the baseline scenario; % unless otherwise indicated)

|  | 2025 | 2050 |
|---|---|---|
| Total population, absolute change (1000 persons) | 163 | 467 |
| Total population | 3.1 | 8.0 |
| 0–19 years | 4.3 | 9.8 |
| 20–66 years | 3.4 | 9.2 |
| 67 years or older | 0.4 | 2.9 |
| Demographic dependency ratio (%) | −0.5 | −1.7 |

**Table 3.13** Effects on government finances of increasing net immigration by 8000 (50%) per year (current prices; deviations from the baseline scenario; % unless otherwise indicated)

|  | 2025 | 2050 |
|---|---|---|
| Total government expenditures | −1.1 | 2.5 |
| Cash transfers | −0.8 | 2.7 |
| Government consumption | −1.7 | 1.3 |
| Total government primary revenues | −0.7 | 2.4 |
| Taxes, Mainland sector | −1.1 | 2.7 |
| Petroleum sector | 0.7 | 1.5 |
| Payroll tax rate (%) | −2.8 | −3.0 |

The reason why higher immigration cause a fall in several budget components is the negative equilibrium effect on the wage rate, which has a strong impact on all budget components in Table 3.13 except the petroleum revenues. As explained above, the wage rate reduction contributes to reinforce the positive budget effect of higher immigration. The wage rate reduction is required because a larger population expands the demand for traded goods, which *cet. par.*, violates the external balance constraint.

In 2050, the additional immigration has contributed to raise government employment by 6.5% compared to the baseline (Table 3.14), whereas the corresponding increase in total employment equals 10.0%. It also raises the number of recipients of cash transfers from the government. The simulations have incorporated the empirical regularity that immigrants will to a greater extent than natives qualify for disability pension, since they are assumed to have the lowest degree of education.

The macroeconomic changes vary around the relative change in the size of the total population. The deviations are basically due to a higher average labor market participation rate among immigrants. However, this reflects that on average the extra immigrants are younger than natives. As noted above, this effect would be weakened if the simulation period had been extended. Controlling for age, the average immigrants work less than the average native. However, even before 2050 higher immigration causes a reduction in the

**Table 3.14** Effects on age dependent determinants of government expenditures of increasing net immigration by 8000 (50%) per year (deviations from the baseline scenario %)

|  | 2025 | 2050 |
|---|---|---|
| Number of pensioners | 1.3 | 4.7 |
| Old-age | 0.7 | 3.0 |
| Disabled | 1.0 | 7.8 |
| Government employment | 2.8 | 6.5 |
| Education | 4.2 | 9.8 |
| Health and care | 3.1 | 8.0 |

**Table 3.15** Effects on macroeconomic aggregates *per capita* of increasing net immigration by 8000 (50%) per year (fixed prices; deviations from the baseline scenario; %)

|  | 2025 | 2050 |
|---|---|---|
| Employment | 2.6 | 2.0 |
| *Per capita*, age 20–66 years | 2.3 | 0.8 |
| GDP | 0.0 | −0.8 |
| Real disposable income | 0.9 | −0.4 |
| Private consumption | −1.9 | −1.0 |

*per capita* levels of real disposable income and private consumption (Table 3.15). The reason is simply that more inhabitants will share the petroleum wealth, including both the capital in the GPF and the remaining undepleted resources, since this is owned by the government.

The effects can also be measured relatively to the change in the number of immigrants, as in Table 3.16. The ratios between the reported percentage deviations from the baseline and the percentage increase in the total population are significantly lower than unity. The most significant reason is that the variables are measured in current prices and the wage rate falls. However, the ratio associated with the number of pensioners is also as small as 0.1 in 2050. On the other hand, the corresponding ratio for government employment exceeds unity.

**Table 3.16** Effects on government finances of increasing net immigration by 8000 (50%) per year: elasticities (measured by the percentage deviation from the baseline effects divided by the percentage increase in population caused by the increased immigration)

|  | 2025 | 2050 |
|---|---|---|
| Population growth (%) | 3.1 | 8.0 |
| Government expenditures (current prices) | −0.4 | 0.3 |
| Cash transfers | −0.3 | 0.3 |
| Number of pensioners | 0.4 | 0.1 |
| Old–age | 0.2 | 0.1 |
| Disabled | 0.3 | 0.2 |
| Government consumption | −0.5 | 0.2 |
| Government employment | 1.8 | 1.3 |
| Education | 1.4 | 1.2 |
| Health and care | 1.0 | 1.0 |
| Government revenues (current prices) | −0.2 | 0.3 |
| Taxes, Mainland sector | −0.4 | 0.3 |
| Petroleum sector | 0.2 | 0.2 |

### 3.6.4 Improved health among the elderly

The majority of international projections of government health expenditures assume that lower mortality among the elderly reflects improved health. More precisely, the simulation of this alternative assumes that the age-specific demand for health and social care services is reduced so that the individual use of these services on average remains constant over the individual lifetime. This implies, for example, that the 70-year-old average individual is almost 30% more healthy in 2050 than he would have been at the same age in 2006. This would significantly slow down the growth in the required employment in the government health and long-term care sectors. In 2050, this employment is 23% lower than in the baseline and 34% lower than in the case where longevity increases with no health improvements. The required payroll tax rate would be 4.9% below the baseline level in 2050. The equilibrium effects are qualitatively the same as those explained above, but they are weaker.

### 3.6.5 Increased household production

Based on time used surveys household production of care services is roughly estimated to about one-third of the employment in the government *Health and social care* sector in 2005. The baseline scenario assumes that household production of care services grows at the same rate as government production of these services. This assumption may be positively biased. The scope for further outsourcing of household production of these services is limited due to increased female market labor participation historically, and this is continued in the baseline scenario. Table 3.10 and Figures 3.5 and 3.6 show the effects of alternatively assuming no growth in household production from the present level. The fiscal effects are significant and nearly symmetrical to the effects of improved health among the elderly described above. Government employment would be 8.8% higher in 2050 than the baseline in order to provide the same service standards. The corresponding increase in the payroll tax rate would have to be 5.5%.

### 3.6.6 Improved service standards

The baseline assumption of constant service standards would break the trend observed over the last decades in Norway and all other OECD countries (Holmøy and Nielsen, 2008). There is a strong correlation between improved living standards and the standard of public health services measured by inputs per user. Hall and Jones (2007) argue that this reflects a causal relationship. The most common assumption in international projections is to let the standard of health services growth as least as rapid as GDP *per capita*. For long-term care, the assumptions are more varied. The "Improved standard" alternative reported in this section assumes that the standard of both health services and long-term care grows by 1% annually.

The long-running effects are strong. In 2020, employment in this sector would be 17% above the corresponding baseline level and this deviation passes 58% in 2050. The increasing slope of the payroll tax rate path after 2020 becomes steeper and has become 15% higher than the baseline rate in 2050. An interaction between the growth in standards and the number elderly users contributes to this, and it causes a stronger growth in the necessary payroll tax rate than in the baseline also after the standard improvements are halted. Thus, the highly plausible policy of further, but rather moderate, improvements in the standard of health services and long-term care will dramatically reinforce the long-run problems of financing the Norwegian welfare state. On the other hand, such improvements will be politically hard to resist as the share of elderly in the voters increases and private consumption *per capita* continues to grow at an even higher rate.

On balance, general equilibrium effects significantly modify the budget effect. The effect of wage rate reduction and a slight increase in labor supply dominate the negative tax base effects of the reallocation of labor and consumption from the private to the government sector. However, if government consumption of individual goods entered the individuals' utility functions, the income effects on labor supply would have been weaker.

## 3.7 INCREASING PREFUNDING THROUGH A STRICTER FISCAL POLICY RULE

The U-shaped curve of the tax burden in Figure 3.2 triggers questions about tax smoothing. This would require more prefunding compared to what follows from the present fiscal rule, which is equivalent to a slower phasing in of the petroleum wealth in the Norwegian economy. A stronger correlation between the out-take from the fund and the ratio between government expenditures and the tax bases of the Mainland economy would result in a smoother time path for the tax burden. However, although no other alternative policy has been tried out, it is a widespread opinion that the present fiscal rule has worked well. It has disciplined the politicians, and with one exception, all political parties accept the rule. Without such a rule more, rather than less, of the petroleum wealth would have been spent before population ageing hits the welfare state hard after 2020. Accordingly, if frequent changes in the fiscal rule are accepted, there is a risk that the respect for any rule will vanish. The public budget constraint may then in practice become very soft as long as the government is highly liquid. The result would be the opposite of more tax smoothing. This line of reasoning suggests that more tax smoothing should be obtained without fundamentally changing the fiscal rule.

One way of doing this is to reduce the parameter interpreted as the expected real rate of return to the GPF assets, from the present 4% which is best interpreted as an estimate of the rate of return in terms of imports. This underlies the baseline assumptions presented in Section 3.3: the exogenous nominal international (risk free) interest rate is set to 5.5% and all world prices grow by 1.5%. Consequently, setting the real rate of return to 4% is reasonable if the nominal capital returns are spent on imports. This is the relevant choice if one wants to calculate the aggregate gain from an increase in the petroleum wealth, because the only way that the economy as a whole can benefit from a higher petroleum wealth is to spend it on imports within the external balance constraint.

However, the petroleum wealth accrues to the government in the first hand. One rationale for linking the out-take from the GPF to the *real* rate of return is to prefund the part of expenditure growth attributable to growth in prices. The share of import prices in the relevant price index for government expenditures is very small. Rather, it is very close to the average wage rate. Almost all cash transfers are wage indexed and wages are by far the dominating cost component in the production of public services. In most of the scenarios described in the previous sections the wage growth is close to 4%. Replacing the growth in world prices by the wage growth implies that the growth in the GPF capital will be equal to the wage growth when the inflow of petroleum revenues stops. Thus, such a tightening of the fiscal rule represents a step towards elimination of the growth gap between government expenditures and the tax bases.

Figure 3.7 shows the results of using MSG6 to simulate how the payroll tax rate would have to adjust if the fiscal rule were tightened. In the "tighter rule" scenario, the

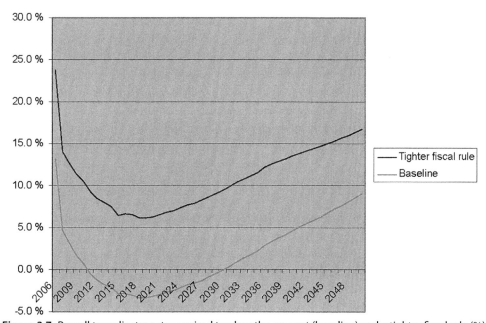

**Figure 3.7** Payroll tax adjustments required to obey the present (baseline) and a tighter fiscal rule (%).

annual rate of out-take from the GPF is reduced from the present 4 to 1.5%, which is close to the difference between the world interest rate and the simulated wage growth. After 2020 the payroll tax rate must be 7—8% points higher than in the baseline. As explained in the previous sections, the simulation accounts for several potentially important equilibrium effects, including the positive budget effect of the reduced wage rate caused by the higher payroll tax rate, and a negative effect on labor supply induced by the reduced consumer real wage rate.

The effects shown in Figure 3.7 should of course not be taken too literally. Especially, it has never been the ambition when constructing different MSG models to provide realistic short run adjustments. Therefore, Figure 3.7 gives a highly stylized picture of the tax smoothing effect of delaying spending of the petroleum wealth. The need for compensating the reduced out-take from the GPF by a higher tax burden is quite strong. The benefits in terms of lower taxes in the future — when 1.5% of a greater GPF exceeds 4% of the baseline GPF belongs to a future which is beyond 2050. The payroll tax rate can grow more slowly after 2020 under the tighter rule than in the baseline, but the returns to higher prefunding in terms of lower future tax burden appears to be rather modest. The basic reason is that after 2020 the difference between the interest rate and the growth rate of the primary fiscal deficit is less than 1 percent. Such a low growth adjusted rate of return implies that the prefunding needed to bring about a given reduction in the future tax burden must be very high.

## 3.8 FINAL REMARKS

This paper has employed the CGE model, called MSG6, of the Norwegian economy to assess the problems of financing the Norwegian welfare state until 2050. MSG6 has been developed for different purposes. In the analyses of fiscal sustainability issues it has been combined iteratively with other models, especially a microsimulation model of labor market participation and public pension expenditures. In this way, the simulations capture both consistent equilibrium repercussions and individual effects that cannot be calculated without a detailed description of population heterogeneity, income histories and the pension system. Thus, the simulations have exploited most of the available detailed information required to project long-term growth in government expenditures and revenues in Norway.

The main substantive conclusion is that the fiscal prospects for Norway are gloomy if one takes a careful look beyond the first couple of decades. This is true despite the fiscal rule adopted in 2001, which is an ambitious plan for transforming large government petroleum revenues into higher consumption for both the present and all future generations. Ageing will be costly in the generous Norwegian welfare state and the permitted out-take from the GPF will decelerate as the petroleum resources are gradually depleted. The petroleum wealth is far from sufficient to finance the *increase* in government expenditures permanently when a rapidly growing number of elderly switch roles from contributors to clients of the welfare state after 2020.

The baseline assumptions imply that a relatively broad tax on wages such as the payroll tax rate must be continuously raised after 2020 in order to obey the fiscal rule. This is not a realistic projection. It is rather supposed to stimulate the debate on policy reforms by demonstrating quantitatively that prolongation of the current policy is indeed unrealistic; it is probably unfeasible. This big unpleasant difference between the fiscal presence and the distant fiscal future makes long-run fiscal sustainability assessments even more important in Norway than in other countries, where strained budgets already trigger unpopular cost-saving reforms.

The gloomy fiscal prospects are quite, but far from completely, robust to variations in exogenous key determinants of government revenues and expenditures. An important insight is that productivity growth in the private sector will reduce the primary budget surplus through wage growth. This result differs from corresponding assessments for other economies. In some cases, this difference reflects different modeling approaches, but they are also a consequence of economy specific characteristics. Compared to models designed to be solved analytically with the help of just pen and paper, the obvious advantage of computational models is the ability to account for much relevant information.

Fundamentally, the adverse fiscal effect in Norway of productivity growth reflects the strong position of egalitarian preferences in Norway. Specifically, centralized wage formation and wage indexation of the pension benefits and most other cash transfers ensure that productivity gains in private firms are distributed automatically to all inhabitants, including civil servants and pensioners.

Wage rate adjustment is an uncontroversial general equilibrium effect in long-run analyses of productivity changes. However, the MSG6 simulations discussed in the chapter demonstrate that wage rate adjustments also strongly influence the fiscal effects of other exogenous changes. This is perhaps most strikingly demonstrated in the analyses of an increase in oil prices. The scope for budget-neutral tax reductions were reduced by an order of magnitude when taking the wage rate adjustment and other general equilibrium effects into account. The wage effect is a good example of how CGE modeling can add relevant insight and information about the plausible empirical significance of the multitude of effects and arguments being mentioned in the fiscal sustainability debate.

The pension reform of 2011 is intended to be a major part of a solution of the fiscal sustainability problems facing Norway. The reform has incorporated actuarial mechanisms in order to neutralize much of the trend-driven expenditure growth, especially increased longevity. It also includes several incentives that stimulate labor supply. It would be peculiar if the intended large effects could be obtained without complex and significant equilibrium repercussions. The combined CGE and microsimulations confirm that the pension reform is likely to significantly improve government finances in the long-run. Moreover, they demonstrate that one would seriously underestimate the fiscal effects of the pension reform if behavioral effects and equilibrium repercussions were ignored. Interestingly, most of the fiscal improvement is achieved by an expansion of the tax bases due to increased labor supply. However, these are primarily level effects. The reform makes a surprisingly small contribution to reduce the gap between the long-run *growth rates* of government expenditures and the tax base, which appear to be the root of the Norwegian fiscal sustainability problem.

The big unresolved fiscal sustainability problem is the growth in government health and care expenditures. Health services and care for the elderly will probably be the fastest growing sector in the Norwegian economy after 2020, irrespective of the mix between public and private provision of these services. Given the present dominant role of the government sector in producing and financing these services, the growth in government health and care expenditures is the most important source to growing primary non-petroleum budget deficit after 2020. This is true even in the unrealistic case when today's service standards are not improved. A standard growth of 1% is moderate compared to both historical trends in Norway and to corresponding assumptions in projections for other countries. However, the simulations suggest that such a scenario this will necessitate a much stronger growth in the tax burden or cuts in other expenditures after 2020 than in the baseline scenario.

Despite the exceptional solid fiscal stance in Norway, the majority of politicians and the public have accepted both a cost-saving pension reform, as well as a fiscal rule that distributes the petroleum wealth to all future generations, not only to the one who found and produced it. Economists may argue that the implemented pension reform should have included even stronger labor supply incentives, and that the fiscal rule should have been tighter. However, these examples indicate that the fiscal policymaking in Norway does take long-term problems into account. In order to establish understanding of the importance of long-run issues, quantitative projections have played an important role. This is both a consequence of and a premise for the tradition for the continuous development of large scale computational models used for both research and policy making. Probably, numbers are the best adjectives to make the distant future count in decisions made today.

## APPENDIX

## A.1 More detailed picture of MSG6

Heide *et al.,* (2004) provide a more comprehensive description of MSG6 and detailed explanations of how the model works.

### A.1.1 Aggregation

MSG6 specifies 60 commodity groups, including nine that are non-competing imports and 12 Government services. Different proportions of the remaining 39 goods are produced in the private business sector, which is split into 32 industries. The description of taxes and subsidies is detailed in order to make the model operational for policy analyses.

### A.1.2 Household behavior

The model user may choose between different submodels of intertemporal consumer behavior. The standard version of MSG6 includes endogenous intertemporal consumer behavior. In this model the time profiles of labor supply and consumption of the specified goods are derived from the decisions of one representative price-taking household with perfect foresight. It maximizes an additively intertemporal utility function over an infinite horizon subject to an intertemporal budget constraint and a time constraint in each period. The intertemporal elasticity of substitution is constant and equal to 0.3, which is within the range spanned by the estimates used in the literature (see, e.g. Steigum, 1993). The rate of subjective time preference is exogenous as well as the after-tax interest rate. It is a well-known property of this kind of model that a steady state solution requires these exogenous rates must be equal. This restriction is not necessarily problematic in practice since it is only required in the last part of the simulation period, which may be very distant from the years of interest for the analysis.

As pointed out in Section 3.2, the intertemporal model based on a representative consumer with an infinite life expectancy is irrelevant in studies of fiscal sustainability, where, for example, ageing and pensions are key elements. In these studies the savings of the households adapts passively so that private consumption absorbs what is left of the production and net imports after the demands from firms and government sectors have been satisfied. However, the economy maintains an intertemporal budget constraint on net foreign debt.

The utility obtained in each period corresponds to the concept Full Consumption, which is a homothetic CES utility function in leisure and an aggregate of all types of consumer goods referred to as Material Consumption. The elasticity of substitution is set to 0.6. The initial budget share of leisure has been set to 0.5 based on studies of time spending by Norwegian households. Combined with the base year levels of non-labor income, these parameter values imply a direct Cournot wage elasticity of labor supply equal to 0.1. Such an order of magnitude is in line with the empirical properties of the microeconometric model estimated by Aaberge et al., (1995).

Material Consumption is an aggregate of 19 types of consumer goods, each being a Leontief composite of the specified commodities in the model. Within this aggregate the substitution possibilities are specified by a nested separable structure of origo adjusted CES subutility functions. The origo adjustment of the CES functions allows non-homotheticity without violating the conditions for sequential budgeting associated with the specified nests. The estimation of the parameters has been based on panel data.

Aasness and Holtsmark (1995) provide further details on the nested CES structure and on the estimation results.

### A.1.3 Market structure, producer behavior and exports

MSG6 distinguishes between the behavior of the individual firms and the aggregate industry behavior. Output and input in an industry can change because of adjustments at the firm level and as a result of entry or exit of firms. All private firms are run by managers with perfect foresight, who maximize the present value of the cash flow. The private profitability is affected by indirect taxation of inputs, capital income taxation and a rich menu of subsidies and government transfers.

Producers of manufactures and tradable services allocate their output between the domestic and the foreign market. The cost of changing the composition of these deliveries is captured by assuming that output is a CET function of deliveries to the export market and deliveries to the domestic market. Exports are sold at fixed world prices. On the other hand, domestic consumers regard products from different firms within the same industry, as close but imperfect substitutes. MSG6 employs the model of the LGMC to formalize the market structure for domestic deliveries. The elasticities of substitution between the varieties in different industries are calibrated to be consistent with the estimated markup ratios between the output price and marginal costs in Klette (1999). None of the markup ratios exceeds 1.05. Entry (exit) takes place in an industry if the variable after tax profit increases (decreases) relatively to the fixed entry cost. The model of monopolistic competition in MSG6 differs from the standard textbook model by allowing productivity differentials between firms within the same industry, which generates an *asymmetric* equilibrium (see Holmøy and Hægeland, 1997).

For inputs, the separability assumptions allows all inputs to be perfectly aggregated into one index of aggregate input through a system of nested constant returns to scale CES functions. Labor is homogeneous, whereas the capital goods and intermediaries are Leontief aggregates of the commodities specified in the model. The production function of the firm is assumed to exhibit decreasing returns to scale. The scale elasticities range from 0.85 to 1.00, which implies a small negative bias compared to those estimated in Klette (1999). This bias was introduced in order to avoid unrealistic specialization patterns of the industry structure.

### A.1.4 Imports

The Armington assumption holds for manufactures and a few tradable services, i.e. imports are considered as a close but imperfect substitute for the corresponding differentiated product supplied by the domestic industry. The import shares depend negatively on the ratio between the price of imports and the price of corresponding domestic deliveries. The elasticities of substitution have been set in accordance with the stationary time series estimates reported in Naug (1994). Commodities produced by primary industries, including Agriculture, Forestry, Fishery, production of Electricity, Crude Oil and Natural Gas, are assumed to be regarded as homogenous by both Norwegian and foreign consumers. In the absence of any trade restriction, the prices of these commodities would be equal to the corresponding exogenous world prices, and the model would determine only net imports as the residual between domestic production and domestic demand. Import protection is captured by nominal tariffs and non-tariff barriers modeled either as additional costs for foreign producers when exporting to the Norwegian market, or quantitative restrictions, such as import quotas.

## A.2 Stylized one-sector version of the standard version of MSG6

### A.2.1 Consumer behavior

A representative price taking consumer with perfect foresight decides on consumption, savings and labor supply. Treating time as a continuous variable, the intertemporal utility function has the common additively separable CES form:

$$W_0 = \int_0^\infty e^{-\rho t} U(D, T - L)^{1 - \frac{1}{\sigma}} dt. \tag{3.1}$$

The intratemporal utility function, $U$, is a homothetic CES function with $\sigma$ as the elasticity of substitution, $D$ is consumption, and $T$ is the hours that can be allocated to leisure or labor, $L$, per year. $T - L$ is leisure. The ideal CES price index for $U$ takes the general form:

$$P_U = P_U((1 - t_W)W, (1 + t_C)P), \tag{3.2}$$

where $W$ is the pretax wage rate, $t_W$ is the marginal tax rate on wage income, $P$ is a price index for consumption, $t_C$ is the indirect tax on consumption. The consumer and firms consider imports to be an imperfect substitute for the domestic product. The ideal price index for the composite of imports and the domestic product is given by the CES price index:

$$P = P(P_H, (1 + t_I)P_I), \tag{3.3}$$

where $P_H$ is the price index for the domestic product, $t_I$ is the tariff rate and $P_I$ is the c.i.f. (cost, insurance and freight) price of imports. The consumer consider the product supplied by different domestic firms within the same industry to be imperfect substitutes, which can be aggregated into a composite via a CES function as in the Dixit–Stiglitz model of monopolistic competition. Assuming a continuum of domestic product variety, the price index for the domestic differentiated product takes the form:

$$P_H = \left[ \int_0^n (P_{iH})^{1 - \nu} di \right]^{\frac{1}{1 - \nu}}. \tag{3.4}$$

The intertemporal budget consumer constraint is:

$$\int_0^n e^{-(1-t_\pi)r}[(1+t_C)PD + (1-t_W)W(T-L) + (1-t_\pi)\pi + Y]dt = V_0, \quad (3.5)$$

where $D = D(D_H, D_I)$ is the volume index (subutility) of the composite of domestic varieties, $D_H$, and imports, $D_I$. $\pi$ is profits, all of which is distributed to the consumer in this stylized exposition of the model. $t_\pi$ is the tax rate on profits, which in this exposition is levied on all types of capital income. $Y$ is net transfers from the government and $V_0$ is the net wealth at time 0. $r$ is the exogenous interest rate, assumed constant here.

Choosing units so that preferences are symmetric at the nests in the utility function, utility maximization yields the following demand functions:

$$U = (\mu P_U)^{-\sigma_C} \quad (3.6)$$

$$D = \left(\frac{(1+t_C)P}{P_U}\right)^{-\sigma_F} U \quad (3.7)$$

$$L = T - \left(\frac{(1-t_L)W}{P_U}\right)^{-\sigma_F} U \quad (3.8)$$

$$D_H = \left(\frac{P_H}{P}\right)^{-\sigma_I} D \quad (3.9)$$

$$D_I = \left(\frac{(1+t_I)P_I}{P}\right)^{-\sigma_I} D \quad (3.10)$$

$$D_{iH} = \left(\frac{P_{iH}}{P_H}\right)^{-\nu} D_H, \quad (3.11)$$

where $\mu$ is the shadow price of total wealth owned by the consumer, which is equal to the inverse of the intertemporal ideal price index of welfare. Note that $\mu$ is endogenous but constant. $D_{iH}$ is the demand for the domestic variety $i$.

### A.2.2 Behavior of firms and aggregate industries

A representative firm is a price taker in all factor markets and in the export market, whereas the domestic market is characterized by monopolistic competition. Each firm has perfect foresight and maximizes the present value of the after-tax cash flow. This exposition ignores intermediary inputs, capital depreciation and the capital income taxation. The value of the $i$th firm at time 0 is:

$$V_{i0} = \int_0^\infty e^{-(1-t_C)rt}(\pi_i - P\dot{K} - F)dt, \tag{3.12}$$

where $\dot{K}$ is investment and $F$ is a fixed cost associated with entry. Operating profits are defined as:

$$\pi_i = P_{iH}X_{iH} + P_W X_{iW} - (1 + t_L)wL_i, \tag{3.13}$$

where $X_{iH}$ is output delivered to the domestic market, $X_{iW}$ is exports and $P_W$ is the common exogenous world price of exports. The perceived demand function facing each firm is consistent with the large group case of monopolistic competition:

$$X_{iH} = E(P_{iH})^{-\nu}, \tag{3.14}$$

where $E$ is a demand parameter regarded by the firm as given. The transformation function between outputs and inputs has the separable structure:

$$[(X_{iH})^\rho + (X_{iW})^\rho]^{\frac{1}{\rho}} = [A_i f(L_i, K_i)]^s, \tag{3.15}$$

where $s < 1$. Tractability is considerably increased by assuming $1/\rho = s$. The variable cost function of a firm then takes the form:

$$C_i = c_i \left[ \left( X_{iW} \right)^{\frac{1}{s}} + (X_{iH})^{\frac{1}{s}} \right]. \tag{3.16}$$

$c_i$ is the dual price index of the composite CES input of labor and capital:

$$c_i = \frac{1}{A_i} \left[ ((1 + t_L)W)^{1-\sigma_K} + ((1 + t_K)(rP - \dot{P}))^{1-\sigma_K} \right]^{\frac{1}{1-\sigma_K}}. \tag{3.17}$$

Here, $A_i$ is TFP and $t_K$ is the effective tax rate of capital services, which captures non-neutral capital income taxation. Firms are ranked according to decreasing TFP. The structure of TFP heterogeneity is formalized by:

$$A_i = A_0 e^{-ti}, \ t > 0.$$

After integrating (3.12) (by parts) and appropriate substitutions, the dynamic maximization problem of the firm can be transformed into a sequence of static problems where the firm maximizes:

$$\pi'_i = P_{iH}X_{iH} - c_i(X_{iH})^{\frac{1}{s}} + P_W X_{iW} - c_i(X_{iH})^{\frac{1}{s}} - F,$$

with respect to $P_{iH}$ and $X_{iW}$. The export supply function becomes:

$$X_{iW} = \left( \frac{sP_W}{c_i} \right)^{\frac{s}{1-s}}, \tag{3.18}$$

The exponential structure of TFP heterogeneity implies the following relationship between export supplies from firm $i$ and the most efficient firm, $i = 0$, respectively:

$$X_{iW} = X_{0W} e^{\frac{-sti}{1-s}}. \tag{3.19}$$

Optimal price setting for domestic deliveries implies the markup rule:

$$P_{iH} = \frac{mc_i}{s}(X_{iH})^{\frac{1}{s}-1}, \tag{3.20}$$

where $m = v/(v-1)$ is the markup factor. Consistency between perceived demand and supply for product $i$ implies:

$$P_{iH} = \frac{mE^{\frac{1}{s}-1}c}{s}e^{ti}(P_{iH})^{-v\left(\frac{1}{s}-1\right)}. \tag{3.21}$$

Inserting the relative product price structure back into the perceived demand function yields the relationship between domestic deliveries from different firms:

$$X_{iH} = X_{0H} e^{\frac{-mti}{m/s-1}}, \tag{3.22}$$

where the markup formula has been used. $X_{0H} = \left(\dfrac{mc}{s}\right)^{-\left(\frac{m}{m/s-1}\right)} E^{\frac{m-1}{m/s-1}}.$

For a given number, $n$, of firms and products the industry output variables are easily calculated. Defining $h_H = \dfrac{m/s-1}{t}$ and $h_W = \dfrac{1/s-1}{t}$ yields:

$$X_H = \int_0^n X_{iH}\, di = X_{0H}\frac{h_H}{m}\left(1 - e^{\frac{-mn}{h_H}}\right) \approx X_{0H}\frac{h_H}{m} \tag{3.23}$$

$$X_W = \int_0^n X_{iW} di = X_{0W} h_W\left(1 - e^{\frac{-n}{h_W}}\right) \approx X_{0W} h_W. \tag{3.24}$$

The approximations at the end of the expressions are better the greater are the number of active firms. They are not made in the real MSG6, but will be used in this exposition for the sake of simplicity. It corresponds to an infinite number of firms. Since the share of output and input of a firm $i$ decreases with $i$ due to the ranking and heterogeneity, the difference between the finite and infinite integrals is small when $n$ is large (Holmøy and Hægeland, 1997) for a detailed discussion of this approximation.

### A.2.3 Equilibrium

In the real MSG6, the number of firms is determined by the standard absence of entry/exit condition, which can be written:

$$\left(\frac{m}{s} - 1\right)c_n(X_{nH})^{\frac{1}{s}} + \left(\frac{1}{s} - 1\right)c_n(X_{nW})^{\frac{1}{s}} = F. \tag{3.25}$$

Employing the approximation defined above, the price index of the composite domestic good can be written:

$$P_H \approx b P_{0H},\tag{3.26}$$

where:

$$0 < b = \left(\frac{t}{m/s - 1}\right)^{m-1} < 1,$$

due to the "love of variety" preferences, which dominates the effect of including higher prices than $P_{0H}$ in the ideal index. Moreover, the perceived domestic demand function can now be written:

$$X_{0H} = b^\nu E (P_H)^{-\nu}.\tag{3.27}$$

Equilibrium in the domestic product market requires $X_{iH} = D_{iH} + J_{iH}$, where:

$$J_{iH} = \left(\frac{P_{iH}}{P_H}\right)^{-\nu} \left(\frac{P_H}{P}\right)^{-\sigma_I} \dot{K},$$

is the investment of the $i$th domestic variety. This equilibrium condition can be written:

$$X_{0H} = b^\nu \left(\frac{P_H}{P}\right)^{-\sigma_I} (D + \dot{K}).\tag{3.28}$$

Aggregate demand for capital and labor becomes:

$$K = \left(\frac{(1 + \tau_K)(rP - \dot{P})}{c}\right)^{-\sigma_K} \left[h_H (X_{0H})^{\frac{1}{s}} + h_W (X_{0W})^{\frac{1}{s}}\right]\tag{3.29a}$$

$$L = \left(\frac{(1 + \tau_L)W}{c}\right)^{-\sigma_K} \left[h_H (X_{0H})^{\frac{1}{s}} + h_W (X_{0W})^{\frac{1}{s}}\right].\tag{3.29b}$$

Labor market equilibrium implies:

$$T - \left(\frac{(1 - t_L)W}{P_U}\right)^{-\sigma_F} U = \left(\frac{(1 + \tau_L)W}{c}\right)^{-\sigma_K} \left[h_H (X_{0H})^{\frac{1}{s}} + h_W (X_{0W})^{\frac{1}{s}}\right].\tag{3.30}$$

Net foreign wealth, $B$, develops according to:

$$\dot{B} = rB + P_W X_W + O - P_I (D_I + J_I),\tag{3.31}$$

where $O$ is the value of oil and gas exports and $J_I$ is the investment of imported goods, which is given by:

$$J_I = \left(\frac{(1 + t_I)P_I}{P}\right)^{-\sigma_I} \dot{K}.$$

following transversality condition on net foreign wealth accumulation implies a national intertemporal budget constraint for the economy as a whole:

$$\lim_{t \to \infty} Be^{-rt} = 0. \tag{3.32}$$

The exogenous variables are: $r$, $P_I$, $P_W$, $O$ and $T$. In addition the tax rates are exogenous if a public budget constraint is met through endogenous lump sum transfer. If transfers are exogenous, one of the tax rates is endogenous.

## REFERENCES

Aaberge, R., Dagsvik, J.K., Strøm, S., 1995. Labour supply responses and welfare effects of tax reforms. Scand. J. Econ. 97, 635–659.

Aasness, J., Holtsmark, B., 1995. Effects on consumer demand patterns of falling prices in telecommunication. Working Paper 1995, vol. 8. Center for International Climate and Environmental Research (CICERO), Oslo.

Andersen, T.M., Jensen, S.E.H., Pedersen, L.H., 2008. The Welfare State and Strategies towards Fiscal Sustainability in Denmark. In: Neck, R., Sturm, J.E. (Eds.), Sustainability of Public Debt. MIT Press, Cambridge Mass., 161–192.

Andersen, T.M., Pedersen, L.H., 2006a. Assessing fiscal sustainability and the consequences of reforms. European Economy, vol. 248. European Commission, Brussels.

Andersen, T.M., Pedersen, L.H., 2006b. Financial restraints in a mature welfare state—the case of Denmark. Oxf. Rev. Econ. Pol. 22, 313–329.

Beetsma, R., Bettendorf, L., Broer, P., 2003. The budgeting and economic consequences of ageing in the Netherlands. Econ. Model. 20, 987–1013.

Bentz, U., Fetzer, S., 2004. Indicators for measuring fiscal sustainability: A comparative application of the oecd-method and generational accounting. Discussion Paper 118/04. Institut für finanzwissenschaft, der Albert-Ludwigs-Universität, Freiburg im Breisgau.

Bjerkholt, O., Tveitereid, S. 1985. The use of the MSG-model in preparing a "Perspective Analysis 1980–2000" for the Norwegian economy. In: Førsund, F.R., Hoel M., Longva, S. (Eds.), Production, Multi-Sectoral Growth and Planning. Contributions to Economic Analysis 154, North-Holland, Amsterdam, 271–287.

Bjerkholt, O., 1998. Interaction between model builders and policy makers in the Norwegian tradition. Econ. Model. 15, 317–339.

Bjerkholt, O., 2009. The making of the Leif Johansen multi-sectoral model. Hist. Econ. Ideas XVII, 3.

Blanchard, O., Chouraqui, J.C., Hagemann, R.P., Sartor, N., 1990. The sustainability of fiscal policy: New answers to an old question. OECD Economic Studies, vol. 15. OECD, Paris.

Bovenberg, L., Knaap, T., 2005. Ageing, funded pensions and the dutch economy. CESifo Working Paper, vol. 1403. CESifo, Munich.

Chauveau, T., Loufir, R., 1995. The future of public pensions in the seven major economies. OFCE Working Paper. Research Department, OFCE, Paris.

Cronin, D., McCoy, D., 2000. Fiscal sustainability when time is on your side. Technical Paper 4/RT/00. Central Bank of Ireland, Dublin.

Dixon, P.B., Rimmer, M.T., 2010. Johansen's contribution to CGE modelling: Originator and guiding light for 50 years. CoPS/IMPACT Working Paper G-203. Available at: http://www.monash.edu.au/policy/ftp/workpapr/g-203.pdf.

European Commission, 2001. Budgetary challenges posed by ageing populations. The impact on public spending on pensions, health care for the elderly and possible indicators of the long-term sustainability of public finances. Report of the Working Group on Ageing Populations to the Economic Policy Committee. European Commission, Brussels.

Fehr, H., Habermann, C., 2006. Pension reform and demographic uncertainty: The case of Germany. J. Pension Econ. Finance 5, 69–90.

Fehr, H., Sterkeby, W.I., Thøgersen, Ø, 2003. Social security reforms and early retirement. J. Popul. Econ. 16, 345–361.

Fehr, H., 2000. Pension reform during the demographic transition. Scand. J. Econ. 102, 419–443.

Feldstein, M., 2005. Structural reform of social security. NBER Working Paper 11098. NBER, Washington, DC.

Fredriksen, D., 1998. Projections of population, education, labour supply and public pension benefits. Analyses with the dynamic simulation model MOSART. Social and Economic Studies 101. Statistics Norway, Oslo.

Gokhale, J., Raffelhüschen, B., 1999. Population ageing and fiscal policy in Europe and the United States. Econ. Rev. 35 (4), 10–20.

Goldfajn, I., 2002. Are there reasons to doubt fiscal sustainability in Brazil?. Banco Central do Brasil Technical Notes, No. 25.

Heald, D., 2005. Fiscal sustainability: The case of the United Kingdom. Paper Presented to the Conference on the Long-Term Budget Challenge: Public Finance and Fiscal Sustainability in the G-7, Washington, DC. Available at: http://www.davidheald.com/.

Hemming, R., Miranda, K., 1991. Interest payments. In: Chu, K., Hemming, R.(Eds.), Public Expenditure Handbook: A Guide to Public Policy Issues in Developing Countries. IMF, New York, pp. 68–74.

Hall, R.E., Jones, C.I., 2007. The value of life and the rise in health spending. Q. J. Econ. 122, 39–72.

Heide, K.M., Holmøy, E., Solli, I.F., Strøm, B., 2006. A welfare state funded by nature and OPEC: A guided tour on Norway's path from an exceptionally impressive to an exceptionally strained fiscal position. Discussion Paper 464. Statistics Norway, Oslo.

Heide, K.M., Holmøy, E., Lerskau, L., Solli, I.F., 2004. Macroeconomic properties of the norwegian applied general equilibrium model MSG6. Reports 2004/18. Statistics Norway, Oslo.

HM Treasury, 2004. Long-term public finance report: An analysis of fiscal sustainability – December 2004. HM Treasury, London.

Holmøy, E., 2003. Aggregate industry behaviour in a monopolistic competition model with heterogeneous firms. Discussion Paper 352. Statistics Norway, Oslo.

Holmøy, E., 2006a. Can welfare states outgrow their fiscal sustainability problems?. Discussion Paper 487. Statistics Norway, Oslo.

Holmøy, E., 2006b. Real appreciation as an automatic channel for redistribution of increased government non-tax revenue. Discussion Paper 471. Statistics Norway, Oslo.

Holmøy, E., 2011. The development and use of CGE models in Norway, Paper Presented at the International Symposium in Memory of Professor Leif Johansen, Oslo. Forthcoming as Discussion Paper from Statistics Norway, Oslo.

Holmøy, E., Hægeland, T., 1997. Aggregate productivity effects of technology shocks in a model of heterogeneous firms: The importance of equilibrium adjustments. Discussion Paper 198. Statistics Norway, Oslo.

Holmøy, E., Kravik, E., 2008. Virkninger på norsk næringsstruktur av endringer i generelle rammebetingelser. Betydningen av generelle likevektseffekter (Effects on the Norwegian industry structure of changes in general economic conditions: The importance of general equilibrium adjustments). Reports 2008/7. Statistics Norway, Oslo. (In Norwegian).

Holmøy, E., Nielsen, V.O., 2008. Velferdsstatens langsiktige finansieringsbehov. (The long run sustainability of the Norwegian welfare state). Economic Surveys 4/2008. Statistics Norway, Oslo, pp. 44-52. (In Norwegian).

Holmøy, E., Stensnes, K., 2008. Will the norwegian pension reform reach its goals? An integrated micro—macro assessment. Discussion Paper 557. Statistics Norway, Oslo.

Johansen, L., 1960. A multi-sectoral study of economic growth. North-Holland, Amsterdam.

Jorgenson, D.W., 1984. Econometric methods for applied general equilibrium analysis. In: Scarf, H., Shoven, J.B.(Eds), Applied General Equilibrium Analysis. Cambridge University Press, Cambridge, pp. 139—203.

Kehoe, T.J., 2003. An evaluation of the performance of applied general equilibrium models of the impact of NAFTA. Research Department Staff Report 320. Federal Reserve Bank of Minneapolis, Minneapolis, MN.

Klette, T.J., 1999. Market power, scale economies and productivity: estimates from a panel of establishment data. J. Ind. Econ. 110, 451—475.

Kotlikoff, L., 2001. The Coming Generational Storm. Available at: http://www.bu.edu/econ/workingpapers/papers/Laurence%20J.%20Kotlikoff/GenerationalStorm.pdf.

Kotlikoff, L., Smetters, K., Walliser, J., 2001. Finding a way out of America's demographic dilemma. NBER Working Paper 8258. NBER, Cambridge, MA.

Lindbeck, A., Persson, M., 2003. The gains from pension reform. J. Econ. Lit. XLI, 74—112.

Mankiw, N.G., 2006. The macroeconomist as scientist and engineer. J. Econ. Perspect. 20 (4), 29—46.

McMorrow, K., Roeger, W., 2002. EU pension reform—an overview of the debate and an empirical assessment of the main policy reform options. DG ECFIN Economic Papers 162. European Commission, Brussels.

Miles, D., 1999. Modelling the impact of demographic change upon the economy. Econ. J. 109, 1—36.

Naug, B., 1994. En økonometrisk analyse av utviklingen i importandelene for industrivarer 1968—1990. Social and Economic Studies, vol. 84.. Statistics Norway, Oslo.

OECD, 2001. Fiscal implications of ageing: Projections of age-related spending. OECD Economic Outlook, vol. 69. OECD, Paris.

Roux, A., 1993. The public debt: a medium-term perspective. The S. Afr. J. Econ. 61, 324—333.

Schreiner, P., Larsen, K.A., 1985. On the introduction and application of the MSG-model in the Norwegian planning system. In: Førsund, F.R., Hoel M., Longva, S. (Eds), Production, Multi-Sectoral Growth and Planning. Contributions to Economic Analysis 154, North-Holland, Amsterdam, 241—269.

Steigum, E., 1993. Accounting for long run effects of fiscal policy by means of computable overlapping generations models. In: Honkapohja, S., Ingeberg, M.(Eds), Macroeconomic Modelling and Policy Implications. Elsevier, Amsterdam, pp. 45—71.

Stensnes, K., 2007. Equity versus efficiency in public pension schemes. Microsimulating the trade-off. Discussion Paper, vol. 515. Statistics Norway, Oslo.

Statistics Norway, 2008. Demographic projections. Available at: http://www.ssb.no/english/subjects/02/03/.

The Danish Welfare Commission, 2004. Analyserapport—Fremtidens velfærd kommer ikke af sig selv (The future public welfare does not come by itself). Available at: www.velfaerd.dk. (In Danish)

Visco, I., 2002. Ageing populations: economic issues and policy challenges. In: Siebert, H.(Ed.), Economic Policy for Ageing Societies. Springer, Berlin, pp. 9—47.

# CHAPTER 4

# MAMS — A Computable General Equilibrium Model for Developing Country Strategy Analysis

**Hans Lofgren*, Martin Cicowiez**, Carolina Diaz-Bonilla***

*World Bank
**CEDLAS-Universidad Nacional de La Plata

## Abstract

This chapter presents MAMS (Maquette for MDG Simulations), a recursive-dynamic CGE model developed at the World Bank for analysis of medium- to long-run country strategies for low- and middle-income countries, including strategies aimed at improving MDG (Millennium Development Goals) outcomes. Compared to other CGE models, MAMS offers a unique combination of new and policy-relevant features, most importantly disaggregation of the government services by function, broad and integrated coverage of MDGs and endogenous links between education and the labor market. The chapter provides a detailed description of MAMS, the policy insights that it has generated, exemplified by a case study of Yemen and the lessons learned from developing and applying MAMS to a large number of countries.

## Keywords

Computable general equilibrium model, millennium development goals, human development, fiscal policy

## JEL classification codes

C68, E62, O15, O21, H50

## 4.1 INTRODUCTION

At the United Nations (UN) Millennium Summit in 2000, the leaders of the world committed themselves to the achievement by 2015 of a set of ambitious global goals, termed the Millennium Development Goals (MDGs) and related to poverty, education, health, gender equality, the environment and the creation of a global partnership for development.[1] Since then, the pursuit of policies aimed at achieving these goals have figured prominently on the agendas of developing country governments and the

---

[1] For the eight goals and related data, see www.worldbank.org/mdgs, http://unstats.un.org/unsd/mdg and www.undp.org/mdg. The World Bank and the International Monetary Fund produce an annual Global Monitoring Report devoted to MDGs (go.worldbank.org/UVQMEYED00), while different UN organizations produce and sponsor a wide range of global, regional and national reports (see www.undp.org/mdg).

*Handbook of CGE Modeling - Vol. 1 SET*
ISSN 2211-6885, http://dx.doi.org/10.1016/B978-0-444-59568-3.00004-3
© 2013 Elsevier B.V.
All rights reserved.
159

international community. Such policies may often have significant economy-wide repercussions due to their consequences for government budgets, the balance of payments and domestic markets for factors, goods and services. Such repercussions may be particularly pronounced in low-income countries where the most rapid progress is sought. Against this background and given its economy-wide perspective, computable general equilibrium (CGE) modeling presented itself quite naturally as an appropriate tool for analysis of MDG-related issues (along with more sector-specific approaches).

In 2004, the World Bank, at the initiative of its then Chief Economist Francois Bourguignon, embarked on the development of a country-level CGE-based modeling framework baptized MAMS (Maquette for MDG Simulations), developed with GAMS[2] as the core software and designed for the analysis of strategies aimed at achieving the MDGs, with Ethiopia as the pilot study.[3] In its framework, MAMS has focused on the MDGs that appeared as the best candidates for consideration in a country-level economy-wide model — MDG 1 (represented by the target of halving poverty rates), 2 (achieving universal primary schooling), 4 (reducing under-5 mortality rates by two thirds), 5 (reducing maternal mortality rates by three quarters) and 7 (halving the population shares without access to improved sources of water and sanitation), in all cases (except for MDG 2) relative to 1990 figures.[4]

Since the start of this work in 2004, MAMS has been applied to more than 40 countries. Together with the World Bank, the UN Department of Economic and Social Affairs (UN-DESA) it has played a leading role in many country applications, typically with a strong involvement from national researchers. After an initially exclusive focus on strategies and the requirements for achieving the MDGs by 2015, later applications have been more diverse, responding to the analytical demands from developing-country governments, World Bank country teams and different UN agencies. As examples, in addition to MDG analyses, client interest has frequently led to a focus on tradeoffs between alternative targets given limited (domestic or foreign) financing, consideration

---

[2] The GAMS software, developed at the World Bank in the 1980s, is documented in Brooke *et al.* (2010).

[3] The authors would like to thank many other colleagues for valuable inputs into the development of MAMS, including François Bourguignon, Maurizio Bussolo, Denis Medvedev, Dominique van der Mensbrugghe, Marco V. Sánchez Cantillo, Hans Timmer and Rob Vos. Institutionally, Enrique Ganuza of the UN Development Programme (UNDP) played a key role by paving the way for collaboration between the World Bank and the UN system, leading to a large number of MAMS country applications, especially in Latin America.

[4] Among the goals that have not been prioritized in MAMS, MDG 8 (to develop a global partnership for development) is not relevant for an individual developing country, while MDG 3 (focused on the achievement of gender equality in primary and secondary education) is highly demanding in terms of data and modeling yet the required policies are likely to be relatively low in cost (primarily requiring changes in attitudes and institutional rules), as a consequence having relatively limited economy-wide effects. In response to demands, future analyses may attach priority to MDG 6 (to combat HIV/AIDS, malaria and other diseases) even though this may, like MDG 3, also be highly demanding analytically and in terms of data. A study of Ethiopia considered gender issues related to education, labor markets and time use (Ruggeri Laderchi *et al.*, 2010).

of additional issues (like demography and effects of the global financial crisis) and simulation periods that are dictated by national strategies and thinking, often extending beyond 2015.

This chapter provides a detailed description of MAMS, the policy insights that it has generated and the broader lessons learned, in a relatively non-academic, operational context, from developing and applying a CGE model to a large number of countries. Like other chapters in this Handbook, its primary audience is researchers and analysts who are developing, using or interacting with CGE models. In outline, Section 4.2 positions MAMS in the broader context of the evolution of CGE modeling, while Section 4.3 discusses key aspects of the model's design and evolution since 2004. A detailed presentation of MAMS' mathematical structure is covered in Section 4.4 and the content of a country-level database is described in Section 4.5. Section 4.6 presents a user-friendly Excel-based interface that has been developed with the aim of facilitating productive use of MAMS by a larger group of analysts while Section 4.7 provides an overview of the applications of MAMS and their major findings together with a detailed account of an analysis of development prospects for Yemen. Section 4.8 concludes. Among these sections, Section 4.4 is aimed at readers interested in the details of model structure, whereas the other sections also are aimed at broader audiences.

## 4.2 CONTEXT AND MAIN CONTRIBUTIONS OF MAMS

Since Johansen's pioneering CGE model of Norway in the late 1950s, which was used to explore issues related to long-run economic development, the evolution of CGE models has been strongly influenced by the evolution of policy concerns in the broader economics discipline and in different country contexts. Due to their versatility, CGE models have been able to respond to demands for policy insights in many different areas, including international trade, taxation, poverty and income distribution, sector policies (often with a focus on agriculture), natural resources, energy and the environment (in recent years including global warming). The issues have been analyzed with different regional treatments, ranging from single-region village models to multiregion global models, with single-region country models as the most common species.

In this broader context, MAMS is a single-region country model with a focus on policies related to the achievement of time-bound international MDG targets and, more broadly, how government spending and taxation, foreign aid and exogenous conditions (including world markets) together influence and are influenced by human development. In terms of model structure and computer implementation, MAMS is a recent example of a long tradition of CGE modeling among researchers related to the World Bank. Research in the second half of the 1970s and the early 1980s, with the volumes by Adelman and Robinson (1978) and Dervis *et al.* (1982) as the most prominent examples, played a pioneering role in CGE modeling in general and in applications to developing countries in particular. The structural features that characterize current incarnations of this tradition, some of which originated in Johansen's original model or later work in the Johansen tradition in Australia, include: the treatment of international trade with Armington and constant elasticity of transformation (CET) functions, wage differentials across producing sectors, neoclassical flexibility between primary factors but Leontief coefficients for intermediates, homogenous capital (as opposed to a vintage treatment), a preference for a recursive treatment of dynamics, variables defined in levels and model implementation using the GAMS software. For MAMS, the more recent starting points in terms of structure and computer code are the static "IFPRI Standard Model" (Lofgren *et al.*, 2002) and dynamic extensions of this model (Thurlow, 2004; Lofgren and Robinson, 2008).[5]

Nevertheless, in order to meet the analytical challenges at hand, a fair amount of innovations were required, often drawing on formulations from other economic models, especially in the CGE area, i.e. a case of "normal science" in the Kuhnian sense.[6] With the notable exception of poverty, indicators related to the MDGs and the mechanisms through which they are determined were (and are still) very rarely covered in CGE models, especially from a concrete public finance angle that links policies and their resource requirements to outcomes while also considering other factors that influence these outcomes. This gap in the literature is surprising considering the importance of these issues in development policy.

In the broader economic literature, education and health have more commonly been considered in the context of human capital in which production- (often productivity)-enhancing investments can be made, i.e. without reference to explicit labor categories differentiated by education (or other characteristics). While the human-capital perspective may be fruitful for some purposes, it is not sufficiently concrete for Ministries of Finance and Education as they consider education at different levels, student enrollment, demography and related budgetary issues. In the MDG-related areas, the closest antecedents to MAMS may be found in manpower planning models that link education and labor, but suffer from a largely exogenous treatment of the broader economic context in which education and the labor market operate (Hopkins, 2002).[7] Another model with which MAMS has some affinity is SSELMA (Social Security, Education, Labor and the Macroeconomy), built by Marouani (see, e.g. Marouani and Robalino,

---

[5] In addition to Lofgren *et al.* (2002), Robinson *et al.* (1999) and van der Mensbrugghe (2005) present the structure and GAMS implementation of a World Bank-type CGE model.

[6] Kuhn (1962, pp. 24–25) refers to "normal science" as the phase of day-to-day puzzle solving by scientists working within a central paradigm. This phase is distinct from the preceding preparadigm phase and the succeeding phase of revolutionary science.

[7] Hopkins is part of an International Labour Organization-based group that in the late 1970s and early 1980s developed and applied a country-level dynamic input-output model with fixed prices to analyze basic needs; in its emphasis on human development, their model may be seen as a precursor to MAMS; for a summary, see Hopkins and van der Hoven (1982).

2008). SSELMA, which does not cover MDGs, is characterized by a highly detailed treatment of the labor market (in terms of skill levels and in terms of distinctions between permanent and temporary employment) with a link to a separate model that (without interactions) feeds SSELMA with labor-supply growth by skill, i.e. as opposed to MAMS, disaggregated labor supplies by education are not endogenous to the model. At a level of aggregation similar to that of MAMS, Jung and Thorbecke (2003) endogenize the supply of labor by education (none, primary or higher) as the outcome of optimal household decisions influenced by public education spending but with a stylized treatment of public finance aspects. In a static model, Cloutier et al. (2008) treat households as making income-maximizing decisions with respect to investment in higher (non-basic) education considering (exogenous) wage gaps, as well as the opportunity and direct costs of education. At the most aggregate end, the MDG Monitoring Framework may be the only CGE model other than MAMS that is explicitly developed for the purpose of MDG analysis (Agénor et al., 2005). It has the advantage of demanding little data but the drawback of providing less information and can only address a relatively limited set of issues.[8]

As will be apparent from the detailed presentation in Section 4.4, MAMS draws on a wide range of models, including some of those referred to above. Nevertheless, the analytical demands put on MAMS has required the development of a tool with a unique combination of new and policy-relevant features, most importantly broad and integrated coverage of MDGs, endogenous links between education and the labor market, disaggregation of the government spending by function into current and investment and coverage of government capital stocks. More concretely, as opposed to virtually all analyses of human development, MAMS accounts for interactions between different outcomes (e.g. the fact that increased access to safe water and sanitation contributes to better health outcomes), permits services to be supplied by both government and private producers, using for each technologies that may evolve over time and change as the costs of different inputs change. The fact that MAMS links education to the labor market, and positions both in a broader economic context, permits it to consider how growth and its sectoral features influence the payoffs from educational policies — a significant improvement relative to the standard practice of evaluating today's investments in education on the basis of historical micro level benefits and costs from such investments. More broadly, MAMS addresses the striking inability of most CGE models to address not only the costs but also the benefits from government spending and how these benefits differ across different functions (cf. spending on infrastructure and education). A key

---

[8] The MDG Monitoring Framework is fundamentally a single-sector macro model. The only labor input is educated labor, the quantity of which is a function of raw labor (with exogenous growth) and the stock of education capital, financed via the government budget. Most of the MDGs are treated in a top-down fashion, post-calculated in equations based on cross-country econometric estimates.

aspect of the model design is rigorous separation of model code and country database, permitting the same model code to be applied to multiple country databases without any changes, including databases with widely differing degrees of disaggregation and length of simulation periods. Partly automated procedures for aggregation of existing databases have also enhanced modeling productivity.

MAMS has numerous limitations, many of which are shared with other CGE models and broader classes of economic models and which also are hard to overcome, including the difficulty of objectively assessing the validity of a given model structure for a specific analytical task. The areas in which MAMS has made its major contributions (discussed above) are probably also the areas in which there is most room for improvements with great payoffs. Among other issues, MDG and education outcomes are modeled on the basis of what may be termed a production function approach with a limited representation of micro structure. While this is convenient, especially in terms of data requirements, it may be preferable to consider alternative approaches that more explicitly account for the role of households as demanders of human development services.[9]

## 4.3 MODEL DESIGN

As noted in the preceding section, the core development of MAMS has taken place in an operational, time-constrained and demand-driven context at the World Bank, initially focusing on strategies for achieving time-bound MDG targets in a given country context (that of Ethiopia), but over time evolving into applications to a wider range of issues and time frames in other countries. Nevertheless, while the settings have varied, most applications have addressed the effects of alternative scenarios for government spending (level and allocation across functions) and resource mobilization (from taxes, borrowing and foreign aid) on poverty and human development with a medium- to long-run time frame (in the range of 5–40 years). Given this, model extensions and solutions to modeling and data issues in an earlier application are almost invariably relevant to future applications. In order to work effectively in this context, it was imperative to avoid using an unchanging bare-bones model as the starting point for the different applications; this would have required repeated reinvention of the wheel. Instead, an attempt was made to ensure, in a systematic fashion, that new applications would benefit from preceding model developments and refinements, resulting in what may be termed an expanding-purpose generic model with earlier versions representing special cases. In other words, new model features are introduced without precluding replication of the simulation results of an earlier model structure and its database.

---

[9] For example, for health, it may be fruitful to apply the Mosley-Chen framework, which distinguishes between proximate (direct) and socioeconomic (indirect) determinants of child mortality (Mosley and Chen, 1984; Lay and Robilliard, 2009).

Technically, a critical feature of the resulting research design was strict separation between, on the one hand, generic model code (in GAMS) and, on the other hand, application-specific files (almost exclusively in Excel) that contain the database and the specification of simulations.[10] The generic GAMS model code covers everything that is common across applications, including declarations of sets, variables and parameters; declarations and definitions of equations and models; solve statements; and definitions of parameters for reports and diagnostic tests (capturing errors in the database, model solutions, or reports). A database includes all application-specific definitions of parameters and sets (which, *inter alia*, provide the domains of most parameters), including the items that are used to select among alternative, preprogrammed assumptions and define alternative simulations. In practice, this means that each database controls the disaggregation of the building blocks of the model (sectors, factors and institutions), the choice between core and MDG versions of the model, the time frame for simulations and selected assumptions about the functioning of the economy, including factor markets, macro balances and payments (split into government and non-government payments depending on whether the government is or is not involved, either as payer or payee). The MDG version can be run only if the database includes data required to cover at least a subset of the MAMS MDGs and/or links between education and the labor market. In this setting, the analyst is able to develop a tailormade application, controlled from the application database, using a generic model code. Powerful features of the GAMS software made this design feasible and attractive, including the fact that it is set-driven and able to exchange data with other software, including Excel.

As part of the modeling routine, new applications use the current version of the generic model code and database structure as its starting point. Apart from developing a database, new applications may also require changes in the model structure and/or provide lessons for diagnostic tests. Whenever such new developments have been deemed to be of interest to a non-negligible subset of future applications, they have been introduced into the generic model code in a manner that does not impose the new feature but rather offers the analyst the option of selecting it (via the application-specific database). To provide some concrete examples, the changes that have been introduced as part of this process have led to more flexibility in terms of closures and rules for macro balances and factor markets, specifications for targeting of MDG and education outcomes (selection of indicators, numerical targets and timing, with a specification echoing the international targets as one option) and policy (including easier coverage of demographic issues).

In order to ensure robustness, any modifications of the code are tested on multiple databases (currently around a dozen, typically permitting applications of the core and MDG versions of the model) — a process that often has required minor changes in the

---

[10] For a detailed description of the MAMS file structure, see Lofgren (2011).

structure of earlier databases. In this manner, the capabilities of a generic and increasingly robust framework have gradually been growing without sacrificing backward compatibility to earlier databases. While these are important advantages, the main disadvantage of this approach is increased complexity of the model code, significantly increasing the entry cost for users who would like to be able to modify the model structure. Given this, the two primary target groups for analytical work with the model are a small group of core users (who have the knowledge and experience required to adjust or further develop the model) and a larger group who work within the existing capabilities of the framework. Up until recently, analysts using MAMS have been required to specify information in Excel files and call up GAMS separately to run the model. To reduce skill requirements (including knowledge of GAMS) and facilitate use of MAMS by a potentially much larger group of analysts, a transition is under way toward primary reliance on a user-friendly interface called ISIM-MAMS, which permits the analyst to run MAMS from Excel (see Section 4.6).

## 4.4 MATHEMATICAL STRUCTURE OF MAMS

In this section we present the mathematical structure of MAMS. Mathematically, MAMS may be divided into two modules — a core CGE module and an MDG module — both of which are integrated in a simultaneous system of linear and non-linear equations, including some mixed-complementary relationships. We start our discussion with the core module, after that turning to the MDG module. As with other CGE models, poverty and inequality analysis can be performed in several ways; in the last part of this section, we briefly discuss the optional poverty module (which offers alternative representative household approaches), as well as microsimulation approaches that may be used with MAMS.

For each time period, the core CGE module gives a comprehensive and consistent account of decisions and related payments involving production (activities producing outputs using factors and intermediate inputs), consumption (by households and the government), investment (private and government), trade (both domestic and foreign), taxation, transfers between institutions (households, government and the rest of the world) and the distribution of factor incomes to institutions (reflecting endowments). This module also considers the constraints under which the economy operates (the budget constraints of institutions and producers; macro balances; and market constraints for factors and commodities). In addition to these standard features of a static CGE model, the core CGE module in MAMS also updates selected parameters (including factor supplies, population and factor productivity) on the basis of exogenous trends and past endogenous variables.

The MDG module captures the processes that determine MDG achievement in the human development area, most importantly the provision of services in the areas of education, health and water and sanitation. Specifically, the MDG module typically covers MDG 2 (primary education completion), 4 (under-5 mortality rate), 5 (maternal mortality rate) and 7 (rates for access to safe water and improved sanitation). The size and skill composition of the labor force is endogenized, in large measure depending on the evolution of the education system. The MDG module has feedback effects into the rest of the economy, primarily via the labor market.

The poverty module provides relatively basic, yet quick, welfare estimations. As with other CGE models, poverty and inequality analysis can be performed in several ways. The simplest but least desirable method uses an elasticity calculation for poverty given changes in *per capita* household consumption. Representative-household or survey-based microsimulation approaches are preferable. The former assumes fixed distributions of income or consumption within each household group, providing welfare estimations directly from the CGE model results. The latter type of approach can be either top-down, feeding CGE simulation results to a separate household model, or integrated, with the household model built directly into MAMS. In addition, the top-down approach may either use microsimulations based on randomized allocation (simpler) or based on econometric analysis to determine wages and/or sector of work.

In the model, growth depends on the accumulation of production factors (labor at different educational levels, private capital and other factors such as land, if singled out in the database) and changes in factor productivity, which may be influenced by the accumulation of government capital stocks and openness to foreign trade. The structure is recursive: the decisions of economic agents depend on the past and the present, not the future; in other words, the model does not consider forward-looking behavior.

The disaggregation of MAMS is data-driven and flexible in most areas: subject to computer memory constraints, there is no upper limit on the number of primary factors, households, production activities and commodities. Some minimum disaggregation of government human development functions is needed to permit the model to address MDGs in a meaningful manner; in most applications, the government has been split into education (disaggregated by cycle or level), health, water and sanitation and other public infrastructure, in addition to a residual sector for other government. To ensure that MDG achievement in education has explicit dynamic feedback effects on labor supply, the labor force is disaggregated by educational achievement, typically into three types: those who have completed tertiary, completed secondary but not completed tertiary and less than completed secondary. Further disaggregation of labor categories is straightforward and has been implemented in some applications.

MAMS may be solved with both the core and the MDG modules (in full or only selected parts) or with only the core module; in either case, the poverty module may be included or excluded. If the MDG module is excluded, MAMS is similar to other recursive-dynamic CGE models, applicable to a more limited set of policy issues but with very limited minimum data requirements. MAMS may be solved in "multipass" mode (year by year) or in "single-pass" mode (simultaneously for all periods; often faster but less robust).[11]

The applicability of the model to specific policy issues depends in large part on the degree of disaggregation. For example, the analysis of issues related to poverty requires a relatively detailed breakdown of household income sources (from factor endowments and the production activities in which they are employed). Similarly, it is likely preferable to disaggregate non-government production into multiple sectors and commodities, as it will provide more specific results of the sectoral employment and income effects of an MDG strategy, pursued on its own or in conjunction with other policies.

The mathematical statement of MAMS is presented in Tables 4.1–4.10 (notation and equations for the core CGE module) and Tables 4.11–4.14 (notation and equations for the MDG Module).[12] The following notational conventions apply in Tables 4.1–4.14 and various parts of the main text: uppercase Latin letters are used for variables; exogenous variables have a bar on top, endogenous variables do not. Parameters have Greek or lowercase Latin letters. Subscripts refer to set indices. A "0" superscript is used to refer to base-year variable values. Otherwise, superscripts are exponents (i.e. not part of the name of the variable or parameter). In the presence of the "0" superscript, the time subscript ($t$) has been suppressed. The fact that an item is a variable and not a parameter signals that, at least under certain model assumptions, its value is endogenous. In Tables 4.5–4.10 and 4.14, the domain column, which follows the column with the equations, is an important part of the mathematical statement — it indicates the set elements to which each equation applies.[13]

### 4.4.1 Core module

The notation used for the core CGE module — its sets, parameters and variables — is presented in Tables 4.1–4.4. The equations of the module are divided into blocks covering prices, production and trade, domestic institutions, investments, system constraints and macro variables and stock updating and productivity;[14] each block is presented in Tables 4.5–4.10. The presentation will briefly explain in more technical terms the equations in each of these blocks, with a focus on non-standard characteristics, including links between government services and government capital stocks, a relatively

---

[11] A potential advantage of the single-pass mode is that, if some adjustments are introduced in the formulations determining agent (government or non-government) decisions, MAMS may incorporate forward-looking behavior.

[12] In tables with equations, verbal explanations in brackets are included under the mathematical expressions; this style of notation, designed to facilitate understanding, was originated by Alan Manne (Kendrick, 1996, p. 306).

[13] For example, in Table 4.5, the domain column of Equation (4.1) shows that this equation does not apply to all commodities; it is limited to commodities with imports.

[14] Apart from the fact that variables are time indexed, most of the core CGE module is similar to the IFPRI standard, static CGE model described in Lofgren *et al.* (2002). That document provides more detail and references to the CGE modeling literature.

**Table 4.1** Sets for core MAMS module

| Symbol | Explanation | Symbol | Explanation |
|---|---|---|---|
| $a \in A$ | activities | $f \in FCAP(\subset F)$ | capital factors |
| $a \in ALEO(\subset A)$ | activities with Leontief function between value added and intermediate inputs | $f \in FCAPGOV(\subset FCAP)$ | government capital factors |
| $c \in C$ | commodities | $f \in FEXOG(\subset F)$ | factors with exogenous growth rates |
| $c \in CD(\subset C)$ | commodities with domestic sales of domestic output | $f \in FLABN(\subset F)$ | non-labor factors |
| $c \in CDN(\subset C)$ | commodities not in $CD$ | $f \in FUEND(\subset F)$ | factors with endogenous unemployment |
| $c \in CE(\subset C)$ | exported commodities | $h \in H(\subset INSDNG)$ | households (including NGOs) |
| $c \in CEN(\subset C)$ | commodities not in $CE$ | $i \in INS$ | institutions (domestic and rest of world) |
| $c \in CECETN(\subset C)$ | exported commodities without CET function | $i \in INSD(\subset INS)$ | domestic institutions |
| $c \in CINF(\subset C)$ | infrastructure commodity | $i \in INSDNG(\subset INSD)$ | domestic non-government institutions |
| $c \in CM(\subset C)$ | imported commodities | $i \in INSNG(\subset INS)$ | non-government institutions |
| $c \in CMN(\subset C)$ | commodities not in $CM$ | $(f, a) \in MFA$ | mapping showing that disaggregated factor $f$ is used in activity $a$ |
| $c \in CT(\subset C)$ | transaction service commodities | $t \in T$ | time periods |
| $f, f' \in F$ | factors | | |

comprehensive treatment of government financing, links between total factor productivity (TFP) by activity and accumulation of selected capital stocks, as well as the option of deviating from neoclassical assumptions for selected sectors (sometimes useful for regulated utilities and export-oriented production based on natural resources).

### 4.4.1.1 Price block

Most of the equations in the price block, Table 4.5; Equations (4.1)–(4.11) define prices that can be expressed as functions of other endogenous variables (as opposed to being free variables

**Table 4.2** Parameters (Latin letters) for core MAMS module

| | | | |
|---|---|---|---|
| $capcomp_{c,f,t}$ | quantity of commodity $c$ per unit of new capital $f$ | $pwse_{c,t}$ | world price for export substitutes (FCU) |
| $cwts_c$ | weight of commodity $c$ in the CPI | $qdst_{c,i,t}$ | quantity of stock (inventory) change |
| $depr_f$ | depreciation rate for factor $f$ | $\overline{qe}_{c,t}$ | export demand for $c$ if $PWE = pwse$ (world price for subs) |
| $dwts_c$ | domestic sales price weights | $qfhhtot_{f,t}$ | total household stock of exogenous, non-labor factors |
| $fdebtrelief_{i,t}$ | foreign debt relief for domestic institution $i$ | $qfinsadj_{i,f,t}$ | exogenous factor stock adjustment |
| $fdi_{i,t}$ | FDI by institution $i$ (rest of world) (FCU) | $qfpc_{i,f,t}$ | *per capita* quantity of exogenous-supply factor $f$ by institution $i$ and year $t$ |
| $fintrat_{i,t}$ | interest rate on foreign debt for domestic institution $i$ (paid) | $qg01_{c,c',t}$ | parameter linking government consumption growth across commodities |
| $fintratdue_{i,t}$ | interest rate on foreign debt for domestic institution $i$ (due) | $qggrwbar_{ac,t}$ | growth in government consumption or capital stock $ac$ in $t$ |
| $fprd_{f,a,t}$ | productivity of factor $f$ in activity $a$ | $shii_{i,i'}$ | share of net income of $i'$ to $i$ ($i' \in INSDNG$) |
| $gfcfshr_{f,i,t}$ | share of gross fixed capital formation for institution $i$ in capital factor $f$ | $ta_{a,t}$ | tax rate for activity $a$ |
| $gintrat_{i,t}$ | interest rate on government bonds for domestic institution $i$ | $te_{c,t}$ | export tax rate |
| $ica_{c,a}$ | quantity of $c$ as intermediate input per unit of aggregate intermediate in activity $a$ | $tf_{f,t}$ | direct tax rate for factor $f$ |
| $icd_{c,c',t}$ | trade input of $c$ per unit of commodity $c'$ produced and sold domestically | $tfp01_{a,t}$ | 0–1 parameter for activities with endogenous TFP growth |
| $ice_{c,c',t}$ | trade input of $c$ per unit of commodity $c'$ exported | $tfpelasqg_{a,f,t}$ | elasticity of TFP for $a$ w.r.t. to government capital stock $f$ |
| $icm_{c,c',t}$ | trade input of $c$ per unit of commodity $c'$ imported | $tfpelastrd_a$ | elasticity of TFP for $a$ w.r.t. to GDP trade share |
| $ifa_{f,a}$ | quantity of capital $f$ per unit of government activity $a$ | $tfptrdwt_{t,t'}$ | weight of period $t'$ in tfp-trade link in $t$ |
| $igf_{c,f,t}$ | quantity of government consumption per unit of infrastructure capital stock $f$ | $tgap_{t,t'}$ | gap between $t$ and $t'$ (years used for calculation of expected growth rate for QA) |

*(Continued)*

**Table 4.2** Parameters (Latin letters) for core MAMS module—cont'd

| | | | |
|---|---|---|---|
| $inta_a$ | quantity of aggregate intermediate input per unit of activity $a$ | $tins01_i$ | 0—1 parameter with 1 for institutions with potentially flexed direct tax rates |
| $iva_a$ | quantity of value-added per unit of activity $a$ | $tinsbar_{i,t}$ | exogenous component in direct tax rate for domestic institution $i$ |
| $mps01_i$ | 0—1 parameter with 1 for institutions with potentially flexed direct tax rates | $tm_{c,t}$ | import tariff rate |
| $mpsbar_{i,t}$ | exogenous component in savings rate for domestic institution $i$ | $tq_{c,t}$ | rate of sales tax |
| $poptot_t$ | total population by year | $tva_{a,t}$ | rate of tax on value added for activity $a$ |
| $pwm_{c,t}$ | import world price of $c$ (FCU) | | |

**Table 4.3** Parameters (Greek letters) for core MAMS module

| | | | |
|---|---|---|---|
| $\alpha_c^{ac}$ | shift parameter for domestic commodity aggregation function | $\gamma_{a,c,h}^{h}$ | *per capita* household subsistence consumption of home commodity $c$ from activity $a$ |
| $\alpha_{a,t}^{vag}$ | exogenous component of efficiency (TFP) for activity $a$ | $\gamma_{c,h}^{m}$ | *per capita* household subsistence cons of marketed commodity $c$ |
| $\alpha_c^{q}$ | Armington function shift parameter | $\varphi_{*,f}$ | elasticity of reservation wage for $f$ w.r.t. $*$, where $* = qhpc$ (household *per capita* consumption), *uerat* unemployment rate) or *cpi* (CPI) |
| $\alpha_c^{t}$ | CET function shift parameter | $\rho_c^{ac}$ | domestic commodity aggregation function exponent |
| $\beta_{a,c,h}^{h}$ | marginal share of household consumption on home commodity $c$ from activity $a$ | $\rho_c^{q}$ | Armington function exponent |
| $\beta_{c,h}^{m}$ | marginal share of household consumption spending on marketed commodity $c$ | $\rho_i^{sav}$ | elasticity of savings rate with respect to *per capita* income for institution (household) $h$ |
| $\delta_a^{ac}$ | share parameter for domestic commodity aggregation function | $\rho_c^{t}$ | CET function exponent |
| $\delta_c^{q}$ | Armington function share parameter | $\rho_a^{va}$ | CES value-added function exponent |
| $\delta_c^{t}$ | CET function share parameter | $\theta_{a,c}$ | yield of output $c$ per unit of activity $a$ |
| $\delta_{f,a}^{va}$ | CES value-added function share parameter for factor $f$ in activity $a$ | $\alpha_i^{sav}$ | intercept of savings fn for domestic institution $i$ |

**Table 4.4** Variables for Core MAMS module

| Variable | Description | Variable | Description |
|---|---|---|---|
| $ALPHAVA_{a,t}$ | efficiency parameter in the CES value-added function | $PWE_{c,t}$ | export world price of $c$ (FCU) |
| $ALPHAVA2_{a,t}$ | endogenous TFP trend term by $a$ | $PX_{c,t}$ | aggregate producer price for commodity $c$ |
| $CALTFPG_t$ | calibration factor for TFP growth | $PXAC_{a,c,t}$ | price of commodity $c$ from activity $a$ |
| $CPI_t$ | CPI | $QA_{a,t}$ | quantity (level) of activity $a$ |
| $DKGOV_{f,t}$ | gross government investment in $f$ | $QD_{c,t}$ | quantity sold domestically of domestically produced $c$ |
| $DKINS_{i,f,t}$ | gross change in capital stock (investment in) $f$ for institution $i$ | $QE_{c,t}$ | quantity of exports of commodity $c$ |
| $DMPS_t$ | uniform point change in savings rate of selected domestic institutions | $QF_{f,a,t}$ | quantity demanded of factor $f$ by activity $a$ |
| $DPI_t$ | producer price index for non-traded output | $QFINS_{i,f,t}$ | real endowment of factor $f$ for institution $i$ |
| $DTINS_t$ | uniform point change in direct tax rate of selected domestic institutions | $QG_{c,t}$ | quantity of government consumption of commodity $c$ |
| $EG_t$ | government expenditures | $QGGRW_{c,t}$ | real government consumption growth of $c$ in $t$ relative to $t-1$ |
| $EH_{h,t}$ | consumption spending for household | $QH_{c,h,t}$ | quantity consumed by household $h$ of marketed commodity $c$ |
| $EXR_t$ | exchange rate (LCU per unit of FCU) | $QHA_{a,c,h,t}$ | quantity consumed of home commodity $c$ from act $a$ by household $h$ |
| $FBOR_{i,t}$ | foreign borrowing for domestic institution $i$ | $QINTA_{a,t}$ | quantity of aggregate intermediate input used by activity $a$ |
| $FDEBT_{i,t}$ | foreign debt for domestic inst $i$ | $QINT_{c,a,t}$ | quantity of commodity $c$ as intermediate input to activity $a$ |
| $FGRANT_{i,t}$ | foreign grants to domestic institution $i$ (FCU) | $QINV_{c,t}$ | quantity of investment demand for commodity $c$ |
| $GBOR_{i,t}$ | change in holding of government bonds for domestic institution $i$ | $QM_{c,t}$ | quantity of imports of commodity $c$ |
| $GBORTOT_t$ | total change in holding of government bonds | $QQ_{c,t}$ | quantity of commodity $c$ supplied to domestic market (composite supply) |
| $GBORMS_{i,t}$ | government monetary system borrowing (deficit monetization) burden for institution $i$ | $QT_{c,t}$ | quantity of trade and transport demand for commodity $c$ |
| $GBORMSTOT_t$ | total government monetary system borrowing (deficit monetization) | $QVA_{a,t}$ | quantity of (aggregate) value-added |

| | | | | |
|---|---|---|---|---|
| $GDEBT_{i,t}$ | endowment of government bonds for $i$ | | $QX_{c,t}$ | aggregated quantity of domestic output of commodity |
| $GDPREAL_t$ | real GDP at market prices | | $QXAC_{a,c,t}$ | quantity of output of commodity $c$ from activity $a$ |
| $GDPREALFC_t$ | real GDP at factor cost | | $SHIF_{i,f,t}$ | share of institution $i$ in income of factor $f$ |
| $GSAV_t$ | government savings | | $TINS_{i,t}$ | direct tax rate for domestic non-government institution $i$ |
| $INSSAV_{i,t}$ | savings of domestic non-government institution $i$ | | $TINSADJ_t$ | direct tax scaling factor |
| $INVVAL_{i,t}$ | investment value for institution $i$ | | $TRDGDP_t$ | foreign trade as share of GDP |
| $MPS_{i,t}$ | marginal propensity to save for domestic non-government institution $i$ | | $TRII_{i,i',t}$ | transfers from institution $i'$ to $i$ (both in the set $INSDNG$) |
| $MPSADJ_t$ | savings rate scaling factor | | $TRNSFR_{ac,i,t}$ | transfers from non-household institution $i$ to $i$ non-household institution or factor $ac$ |
| $PA_{a,t}$ | activity price (unit gross revenue) | | $TRNSFRPC_{i,i',t}$ | per capita transfers from institution $i'$ to household institution $i$ |
| $PDD_{c,t}$ | demand price for commodity $c$ produced and sold domestically | | $WF_{f,t}$ | economy-wide wage of factor $f$ |
| $PDS_{c,t}$ | supply price for commodity $c$ produced and sold domestically | | $WFDIST_{f,a,t}$ | wage distortion factor for factor $f$ in activity $a$ |
| $PE_{c,t}$ | export price (domestic currency) | | $WFRES_{f,t}$ | reservation wage for factor $f$ |
| $PINTA_{a,t}$ | aggregate intermediate input price for activity $a$ | | $YF_{f,t}$ | income of factor $f$ |
| $PK_{f,t}$ | price of new capital stock $a$ | | $YG_t$ | government revenue |
| $PM_{c,t}$ | import price (domestic currency) | | $YI_{i,t}$ | income of domestic non-government institution |
| $POP_{i,t}$ | population by household | | $YIF_{i,f,t}$ | income to domestic institution $i$ from factor $f$ |
| $PQ_{c,t}$ | composite commodity price | | $YIINT_{i,t}$ | net interest income of institution $i$ |
| $PVA_{a,t}$ | value-added price (factor income per unit of activity) | | | |

**Table 4.5** Price block equations

$(4.1)$

$$PM_{c,t} = pwm_{c,t} \cdot (1 + tm_{c,t}) \cdot EXR_t + \sum_{c' \in C} \left( PQ_{c',t} \cdot icm_{c',c,t} \right)$$

$$\begin{bmatrix} import\ price \\ (LCU) \end{bmatrix} = \begin{bmatrix} import\ price \\ (FCU) \end{bmatrix} \cdot \begin{bmatrix} tariff \\ adjustment \end{bmatrix} \cdot \begin{bmatrix} exchange\ rate \\ (LCU\ per\ FCU) \end{bmatrix} + \begin{bmatrix} transaction \\ costs \end{bmatrix}$$

Import price

$c \in CM$

$t \in T$

$(4.2)$

$$PE_{c,t} = \overline{PWE}_{c,t} \cdot (1 - te_{c,t}) \cdot EXR_t - \sum_{c' \in C} \left( PQ_{c',t} \cdot ice_{c',c,t} \right)$$

$$\begin{bmatrix} export\ price \\ (LCU) \end{bmatrix} = \begin{bmatrix} export\ price \\ (FCU) \end{bmatrix} \cdot \begin{bmatrix} tariff \\ adjustment \end{bmatrix} \cdot \begin{bmatrix} exchange\ rate \\ (LCU\ per\ FCU) \end{bmatrix} - \begin{bmatrix} transaction \\ costs \end{bmatrix}$$

Export price

$c \in CE$

$t \in T$

$(4.3)$[15] (a)

$$PDS_{c,t} \geq PE_{c,t}$$

$$\begin{bmatrix} domestic\ supply \\ price \end{bmatrix} \geq \begin{bmatrix} export\ price \\ (LCU) \end{bmatrix}$$

(b)

$$QE_{c,t} \geq 0$$

$$\begin{bmatrix} export \\ quantity \end{bmatrix} \geq [0]$$

$c \in$

$(CD \cap CECETN)$

$t \in T$

For non-CET exportables with domestic sales: (a) domestic floor price, (b) non-negative export quantity constraints and (c) related complementary-slackness relationship

(c)

$$(PDS_{c,t} - PE_{c,t})(QE_{c,t} - 0) = 0$$

$$\begin{bmatrix} \text{Complementary slackness relationship:} \\ \text{1. If domestic price exceeds export price then export quantity is zero.} \\ \text{2. If export quantity exceeds zero, then domestic price equals export price.} \end{bmatrix}$$

(4.4)

$$PDD_{c,t} = PDS_{c,t} + \sum_{c' \in C} \left( PQ_{c',t} \cdot icd_{c',c,t} \right)$$

$$\begin{bmatrix} \text{domestic demander} \\ \text{price} \end{bmatrix} = \begin{bmatrix} \text{domestic supplier} \\ \text{price} \end{bmatrix} + \begin{bmatrix} \text{transaction} \\ \text{costs} \end{bmatrix}$$

$c \in CD$

$t \in T$

Domestic demander price for domestic commodity

(4.5)

$$PQ_{c,t} \cdot \left( 1 - tq_{c,t} \right) \cdot QQ_{c,t} = PDD_{c,t} \cdot QD_{c,t} + PM_{c,t} \cdot QM_{c,t}$$

$$\begin{bmatrix} \text{absorption} \\ \text{(at demand prices} \\ \text{net of sales tax)} \end{bmatrix} = \begin{bmatrix} \text{domestic demander} \\ \text{price times} \\ \text{domestic sales quantity} \end{bmatrix} + \begin{bmatrix} \text{import price} \\ \text{times} \\ \text{import quantity} \end{bmatrix}$$

$c \in (CD \cup CM)$

$t \in T$

Domestic demand value

(Continued)

**Table 4.5** Price block equations—cont'd

(4.6)
$$PX_{c,t} \cdot QX_{c,t} = PDS_{c,t} \cdot QD_{c,t} + PE_{c,t} \cdot QE_{c,t}$$

$$\begin{bmatrix} producer\ price \\ times\ marketed \\ output\ quantity \end{bmatrix} = \begin{bmatrix} domestic\ supplier \\ price\ times \\ domestic\ sales\ quantity \end{bmatrix} + \begin{bmatrix} export\ price \\ times \\ export\ quantity \end{bmatrix}$$

$c \in (CD \cup CE)$    Marketed output value

$t \in T$

(4.7)
$$PA_{a,t} = \sum_{c \in C} PXAC_{a,c,t} \cdot \theta_{a,c}$$

$$\begin{bmatrix} activity \\ price \end{bmatrix} = \begin{bmatrix} producer\ prices \\ times\ yields \end{bmatrix}$$

$a \in A$    Activity price

$t \in T$

(4.8)
$$PINTA_{a,t} = \sum_{c \in C} PQ_{c,t} \cdot ica_{c,a}$$

$$\begin{bmatrix} aggregate \\ intermediate \\ input\ price \end{bmatrix} = \begin{bmatrix} intermediate\ input\ cost \\ per\ unit\ of\ aggregate \\ intermediate\ input \end{bmatrix}$$

$a \in A$    Aggregate intermediate input price

$t \in T$

(4.9)

$$PA_{a,t} \cdot (1 - ta_{a,t}) \cdot QA_{a,t} = PVA_{a,t} \cdot QVA_{a,t} + PINTA_{a,t} \cdot QINTA_{a,t}$$

$$\begin{bmatrix} \text{activity price} \\ \text{(net of taxes)} \\ \text{times activity level} \end{bmatrix} = \begin{bmatrix} \text{value} - \text{added} \\ \text{price times} \\ \text{quantity} \end{bmatrix} + \begin{bmatrix} \text{aggregate intermediate} \\ \text{input price times quantity} \end{bmatrix}$$

$a \in A$

Activity revenue and costs

(4.10)

$$\overline{CPI_t} = \sum_{c \in C} PQ_{c,t} \cdot cwts_c$$

$$[CPI] = \begin{bmatrix} \text{prices times} \\ \text{weights} \end{bmatrix}$$

$t \in T$

CPI

(4.11)

$$DPI_t = \sum_{c \in CD} PDS_{c,t} \cdot dwts_c$$

$$\begin{bmatrix} \text{price index for} \\ \text{non-tradables} \end{bmatrix} = \begin{bmatrix} \text{supplier price for output} \\ \text{marketed domestically} \\ \text{times weights} \end{bmatrix}$$

$t \in T$

Price index for non-tradables

---

[15]Among Equations (4.3a–c), only part (a) is an explicit equation in the GAMS code. The non-negativity constraint (b) on $QE_{c,t}$ is handled via a lower limit of zero on this variable. The complementary-slackness condition (c) is imposed via the GAMS model definition in which Equation (a) is associated with $QE_{c,t}$. MAMS also includes complementary-slackness conditions for government investment, the labor market constraint and MDG targeting (in the core module blocks for investment and other system constraints and the MDG module, respectively). In terms of the GAMS code, the treatment is similar to the case of exports with perfect transformability.

that perform market-clearing functions). Among these prices, it is worth noting that trans-actions costs (the cost of moving the commodity between the border and demanders or suppliers, or between domestic demanders and suppliers) are accounted for in the definitions of demander (domestic-currency) import prices, supplier (domestic-currency) export prices and demander prices for domestic output sold domestically, Equations (4.1), (4.2) and (4.4).

Whereas most outputs with exports have imperfect transformability between exports and domestic sales, the model also allows for the case of perfect transformability, using a complementary-slackness formulation, Equation (4.3). Perfect transformability is useful for commodities that are relatively homogeneous, with only small differences depending on whether the demander is domestic or foreign (like grains). Equation (4.3) has three components: (i) The constraint that domestic supplier prices are larger than or equal to export prices in local currency units (LCU); (ii) the constraint that exports are larger than or equal to zero (i.e. zero is a possible outcome); and (iii) a complementary-slackness relationship according to which at least one of (i) and (iii) has to hold as a strict equality — domestic supplier prices only exceed export prices if exports are zero or, if exports are above zero, then the two prices are equal. In terms of economics, this means that the export price is a floor price and that producers prefer to sell at the highest price that is offered. If the domestic price is above the export price, then nothing is exported. If, in the absence of exports, the price would have fallen below the export price, then exports will be positive, preventing a decline below the export price.[16]

Various aggregative prices — for composite supplies, for produced commodities and value-added — are derived from relationships that define total revenue or costs as the sum of disaggregated receipts or payments, Equations (4.5–4.7) and (4.9). The price of the aggregative intermediate commodity for any activity depends on its commodity composition and the prices of the commodities involved, Equation (4.8). The model is homogeneous of degree zero in prices, with the consumer price index (CPI) serving as the model numéraire, Equation (4.10). Alternatively, the price index for non-tradables may serve as numéraire, Equation (4.11).[17]

### 4.4.1.2 Production and trade block

This block (Table 4.6; Equations (4.12–4.27)) includes the first-order conditions for profit-maximizing production and transformation decisions as well as cost-minimizing domestic demand decisions. Given available technology and market prices (taken as given

---

[16] In GAMS, a model formulated as an MCP (mixed-complementarity problem) can handle a combination of equations that are: (i) Strict equalities and (ii) non-strict inequalities linked to variables with lower limits in a mixed-complementarity relationship.

[17] The GAMS code permits the user to choose either the CPI or the price index for non-tradables as numéraire. As long as the model is homogeneous of degree zero in prices, this choice has no impact on the equilibrium values of real variables. This homogeneity condition is not met under macro closures with fixed savings or domestic borrowing for the government. In these cases, it is implicitly assumed that the fixed variables are indexed to the numéraire.

in a perfectly competitive setting), producers maximize profits.[18] The technology is defined by a nested, two-level structure. At the top, output is a Leontief aggregation of real value-added and a real aggregate intermediate, Equations (4.12 and 4.13).[19] At the bottom, these are linked to a constant elasticity of substitution (CES) aggregation of primary factors (a value-added function) and a Leontief aggregation of intermediate inputs, Equations (4.14–4.16). Given that the national accounts rarely attribute value-added to government capital, the CES value-added functions for government production do not include capital factors. Typically, government value-added is limited to labor.[20]

Note that, at the activity level, the wage paid is the product of $WF_{f,t}$ and $WFDIST_{f,a,t}$, cf. Equation (4.15). $WFDIST_{f,a,t}$, a distortion (or differential) term that typically is exogenous, reflects relative wage differences across activities. In some cases it may be desirable to impose an exogenous time path for the employment of specific factors in selected activities (drawing on other pieces of information, e.g. data on the expected evolution of sectors based on the exploitation of natural resources). For the factor–activity–time combination in question, the analyst only has to flex the wage distortion variable ($WFDIST_{f,a,t}$) and fix the employment variable ($QF_{f,a,t}$). Such an assumption can coexist with factor markets with or without endogenous unemployment.

Each activity produces one or more outputs with fixed yield coefficients, Equation (4.17). Any commodity may be produced and marketed by more than one activity. A CES approach, assuming profit-maximizing producer behavior, is used to aggregate market sales of any commodity from different activities, Equations (4.18 and 4.19). Production is transformed into exports and domestic sales on the basis of a CET function. The profit-maximizing, optimal ratio between the quantities of exports and domestic sales is positively related to the ratio between the corresponding supply prices, Equations (4.20 and 4.21). A less complex relationship applies to production without exports or without domestic sales, Equation (4.22). Government and private social services are typically non-traded, i.e. they have no exports and all of the supply is from domestic producers. For any exported commodity, two alternatives are possible for export demand: (i) Exogenous prices in

---

[18] In some applications MAMS has included a private regulated sector (typically a utility) for which behavior deviates from the assumption of profit-maximizing output and input demand (including capital use) given market prices and rents. Each regulated activity has its own capital stock. (Otherwise, there is only one private capital stock, which is mobile across private activities.) For regulated activities, output prices, investment and capital use are exogenous; production is demand-driven at fixed output prices. Their capital stocks earn an endogenous, residual share of value-added which most likely deviates from the market rent; other factors earn market wages.

[19] MAMS also permits the alternative of a CES aggregation of the real aggregates of value-added and intermediates. The choice does not tend to have a major impact on results. Most applications have used the Leontief alternative.

[20] Nevertheless, the model accounts for the fact that government capital stocks indeed are needed in government activities by imposing investments derived from a Leontief-relationship between government activity levels and related capital stocks, with the stocks being defined on the basis of initial stocks, investment and depreciation (see Equation (4.45). In the exceptional cases when the SAM indicates that government capital earns value-added, this value-added is a fixed share of the total value-added of the activity (in effect equivalent to a tax on value-added), not related to any market rent.

**Table 4.6** Production and trade block equations

(4.12)

$$QVA_{a,t} = iva_a \cdot QA_{a,t}$$

$$\begin{bmatrix} demand\ for \\ value\text{-}added \end{bmatrix} = f \begin{bmatrix} activity \\ level \end{bmatrix}$$

$a \in ALEO$

$t \in T$

Demand for aggregate value-added

(4.13)

$$QINTA_{a,t} = inta_a \cdot QA_{a,t}$$

$$\begin{bmatrix} demand\ for\ aggregate \\ intermediate\ input \end{bmatrix} = f \begin{bmatrix} activity \\ level \end{bmatrix}$$

$a \in ALEO$

$t \in T$

Demand for aggregate intermediate input

(4.14)

$$QVA_{a,t} = ALPHAVA_{a,t} \cdot \left( \sum_{f \in F} \delta_{f,a}^{va} \cdot \left( fprd_{f,a,t} \cdot QF_{f,a,t} \right)^{-\rho_a^{va}} \right)^{-\frac{1}{\rho_a^{va}}}$$

$$\begin{bmatrix} quantity\ of\ aggregate \\ value\text{-}added \end{bmatrix} = CES \begin{bmatrix} factor \\ inputs \end{bmatrix}$$

$a \in A$

$t \in T$

Value-added

(4.15)

$$WF_{f,t} \cdot \overline{WFDIST}_{f,a,t} = PVA_{a,t} \cdot (1 - tva_{a,t}) \cdot QVA_{a,t}$$

$$\cdot \left( \sum_{f' \in F} \delta^{va}_{f',a} \cdot \left(fprd_{f',a,t} \cdot QF_{f',a,t}\right)^{-\rho^{va}_a} \right)^{-1} \cdot \delta^{va}_{f,a} \cdot fprd_{f,a,t}^{-\rho^{va}_a} \cdot QF_{f,a,t}^{-\rho^{va}_a - 1}$$

$$\left[ \begin{array}{c} \textit{marginal cost of} \\ \textit{factor f in activity a} \end{array} \right] = \left[ \begin{array}{c} \textit{marginal revenue product} \\ \textit{of factor f in activity a} \end{array} \right]$$

Factor demand

$a \in A$

$f \in F$

$t \in T$

(4.16)

$$QINT_{c,a,t} = ica_{c,a} \cdot QINTA_{a,t}$$

$$\left[ \begin{array}{c} \textit{intermediate demand} \\ \textit{for commodity c} \\ \textit{from activity a} \end{array} \right] = f \left[ \begin{array}{c} \textit{aggregate intermediate} \\ \textit{input quantity} \\ \textit{for activity a} \end{array} \right]$$

Disaggregated intermediate input demand

$c \in C$

$a \in A$

$t \in T$

(4.17)

$$QXAC_{a,c,t} + \sum_{h \in H} QHA_{a,c,h,t} = \theta_{a,c} \cdot QA_{a,t}$$

$$\left[ \begin{array}{c} \textit{quantity of output} \\ \textit{of commodity c} \\ \textit{from activity a} \end{array} \right] + \left[ \begin{array}{c} \textit{quantity consumed of} \\ \textit{home commodity c} \\ \textit{from activity a in} \\ \textit{all households} \end{array} \right] = \left[ \begin{array}{c} \textit{activity-specific} \\ \textit{marketed} \\ \textit{production of} \\ \textit{commodity c} \end{array} \right]$$

Commodity production and allocation between market and home

$a \in A$

$c \in C$

$t \in T$

*(Continued)*

**Table 4.6** Production and trade block equations—cont'd

(4.18)

$$QX_{c,t} = \alpha_c^{ac} \cdot \left( \sum_{a \in A} \delta_{a,c}^{ac} \cdot QXAC_{a,c,t}^{-\rho_c^{ac}} \right)^{-\frac{1}{\rho_c^{ac}}}$$

$$\left[ \begin{array}{c} \textit{aggregate marketed} \\ \textit{production of} \\ \textit{commodity } c \end{array} \right] = CES \left[ \begin{array}{c} \textit{output of commodity } c \\ \textit{from activity } a \end{array} \right]$$

$c \in$
$(CE \cup CD)$
$t \in T$

Output aggregation function

(4.19)

$$\frac{PXAC_{a,c,t}}{PX_{c,t}} = QX_{c,t} \cdot \sum_{a' \in A} \left( \delta_{a',c}^{ac} \cdot QXAC_{a',c,t}^{-\rho_c^{ac}} \right)^{-1} \cdot \delta_{a,c}^{ac} \cdot QXAC_{a,c,t}^{-\rho_c^{ac}-1}$$

$$\left[ \begin{array}{c} \textit{ratio of price of commodity } c \\ \textit{from activity } a \textit{ to} \\ \textit{average output price} \end{array} \right] = f \left[ \begin{array}{c} \textit{aggregate marketed commodity} \\ \textit{output and output of commodity } c \\ \textit{from activity } a \end{array} \right]$$

$a \in A$
$c \in C$
$t \in T$

Ratio of prices for output aggregation function

(4.20)

$$QX_{c,t} = \alpha_c^{t} \cdot \left( \delta_c^{t} \cdot QE_{c,t}^{\rho_c^{t}} + (1 - \delta_c^{t}) \cdot QD_{c,t}^{\rho_c^{t}} \right)^{\frac{1}{\rho_c^{t}}}$$

$$\left[ \begin{array}{c} \textit{aggregate marketed} \\ \textit{domestic output} \end{array} \right] = CET \left[ \begin{array}{c} \textit{export quantity, domestic} \\ \textit{sales of domestic output} \end{array} \right]$$

$c \in (CD \cap$
$CECET)$
$t \in T$

Output transformation (CET) function

(4.21)

$$\frac{QE_{c,t}}{QD_{c,t}} = \left(\frac{PE_{c,t}}{PDS_{c,t}} \cdot \frac{1 - \delta_c^t}{\delta_c^t}\right)^{\frac{1}{\rho_c^t - 1}}$$

$$\begin{bmatrix} export\text{-}domestic \\ supply\ ratio \end{bmatrix} = f \begin{bmatrix} export\text{-}domestic \\ price\ ratio \end{bmatrix}$$

Export-domestic supply ratio

$c \in (CDN \cap CECET)$

$t \in T$

(4.22)

$$QX_{c,t} = QD_{c,t} + QE_{c,t}$$

$$\begin{bmatrix} aggregate \\ marketed \\ domestic\ output \end{bmatrix} = \begin{bmatrix} domestic\ market \\ sales\ of\ domestic \\ output\ [unless \\ c \in (CEN \cap CDN)] \end{bmatrix} + \begin{bmatrix} exports\ [unless \\ c \in (CDN \cap CEN)] \end{bmatrix}$$

Output transformation for outputs without exports, exports without domestic sales and non-CET exports with domestic sales

$c \in$
$(CDN \cap CEN) \cup$
$(CEN \cap CDN) \cup$
$(CDN \cap CECETN),$

$t \in T$

(4.23)

$$QE_{c,t} = \overline{qe}_{c,t} \cdot \left(\frac{PWE_{c,t}}{pwse_{c,t}}\right)^{\rho_c^e}$$

$$\begin{bmatrix} export \\ demand \end{bmatrix} = f \begin{bmatrix} trend\ export\ quantity,\ world\ price \\ for\ exports\ relative\ to\ world \\ price\ for\ export\ substitutes \end{bmatrix}$$

Export demand with CE demand function

$c \in CED$

$t \in T$

(Continued)

**Table 4.6** Production and trade block equations—cont'd

(4.24)

$$QQ_{c,t} = \alpha_c^q \cdot \left( \delta_c^q \cdot QM_{c,t}^{-\rho_c^q} + \left( 1 - \delta_c^q \right) \cdot QD_{c,t}^{-\rho_c^q} \right)^{-\frac{1}{\rho_c^q}}$$

$$\begin{bmatrix} composite \\ supply \end{bmatrix} = CES \begin{bmatrix} import\ quantity,\ domestic \\ use\ of\ domestic\ output \end{bmatrix}$$

$c \in$
$(CM \cap CD)$

$t \in T$

Composite supply (Armington) function

(4.25)

$$\frac{QM_{c,t}}{QD_{c,t}} = \left( \frac{PDD_{c,t}}{PM_{c,t}} \cdot \frac{\delta_c^q}{1 - \delta_c^q} \right)^{\frac{1}{1+\rho_c^q}}$$

$$\begin{bmatrix} import\text{-}domestic \\ demand\ ratio \end{bmatrix} = f \begin{bmatrix} domestic\text{-}import \\ price\ ratio \end{bmatrix}$$

$c \in$
$(CM \cap CD)$

$t \in T$

Import-domestic demand ratio

(4.26)

$$QQ_{c,t} = QD_{c,t} + QM_{c,t}$$

$$\begin{bmatrix} composite \\ supply \end{bmatrix} = \begin{bmatrix} domestic\ use\ of \\ marketed\ domestic \\ output\ [for \\ c \in (CD \cap CMN)] \end{bmatrix} + \begin{bmatrix} imports\ [for \\ c \in (CM \cap CDN)] \end{bmatrix}$$

$c \in$
$(CD \cap CMN)$
$\cup$
$(CM \cap CDN)$

$t \in T$

Composite supply for non-imported outputs and non-produced imports

(4.27)

$$QT_{c,t} = \sum_{c' \in C'} \left( icm_{c,c',t} \cdot QM_{c',t} + ice_{c,c',t} \cdot QE_{c',t} + icd_{c,c',t} \cdot QD_{c',t} \right)$$

$$\begin{bmatrix} trade\ and\ transport \\ demand\ for\ commodity\ c \end{bmatrix} = [from\ imports] + [from\ exports] + \begin{bmatrix} from\ marketed \\ domestic\ output \end{bmatrix}$$

$c \in CT$
$t \in T$

Demand for transaction services

foreign currency units (FCU) combined with an infinitely elastic demand or (ii) price-sensitive export demands (defined by constant-elasticity functions) with the FCU prices linked to domestic conditions and the exchange rate, Equation (4.23) applies to the constant-elasticity case). Given that, in equations other than Equation (4.23), $PWE_{c,t}$ (the export world price) has a bar on top, we assume that the set $CED$ is empty and that Equation (4.23) is not used.

Domestic demanders are assumed to minimize the cost of imperfectly substitutable imports and commodities from domestic production according to an Armington (CES aggregation) function, Equations (4.24 and 4.25). For commodities with only one of the two supply sources (domestic or import), the supply from this source equals the composite supply, Equation (4.26). The transaction (trade and transport) demand for any service commodity is the sum of demands arising from domestic sales, exports and imports, each of which is the product of the quantity traded and a fixed input coefficient (showing the quantity of the service commodity per unit of trade, Equation (4.27).

Government service sectors typically produce single outputs, and have fixed coefficients for intermediate inputs and capital (typically without any value-added payment; also see discussion in Section 4.4.14), but labor demands that respond to relative wage changes. The demanders (often only the government) pay a price that covers the cost of labor and intermediates, i.e. excluding capital.

### 4.4.1.3 Domestic institution block

This block, Table 4.7; Equations (4.28–4.44) account for the receipts and expenditures of all domestic institutions, both government and non-government (households) as well as current, non-trade payment flows to and from the rest of the world (i.e. factor incomes and transfers). When they represent inflows of foreign currency, these payments tend to be fixed (in FCU). The equations are structured to accommodate databases with any number of households, one government and one entity representing the rest of the world. The payments in this block are highly inter-related since institutions often are both at the receiving and paying ends. Transfers between any two institutions may flow in both directions; however, if so, the analyst may often find it more convenient to net these in the initial model social accounting matrix (SAM).

Turning to the equations, factor incomes are defined as a function of domestic wages (which may vary across activities) and employment levels, augmented by factor incomes from the rest of the world, Equation (4.28) and allocated across different institutions (domestic and foreign), net of direct factor taxes, in value shares that depend on endogenous factor endowment shares, Equations (4.29 and 4.30). Domestic non-government institutions: (i) Earn net interest incomes, defined as the difference between net interest earnings from loans to the government and net interest payments to the rest of the world on foreign debt, Equation (4.31), with all interest rates assumed to be exogenous; (ii) transfer fixed shares of their incomes (net of direct taxes and savings) to

**Table 4.7** Domestic institution block equations

(4.28)

$$YF_{f,t} = \sum_{a \in A} WF_{f,t} \cdot \overline{WFDIST}_{f,a,t} \cdot QF_{f,a,t} + \overline{TRNSFR}_{f,row,t} \cdot EXR_t$$

$$\begin{bmatrix} income\ of \\ factor\ f \end{bmatrix} = \begin{bmatrix} sum\ of\ activity\ payments \\ (activity - specific\ wages \\ times\ employment\ levels) \end{bmatrix} + \begin{bmatrix} income\ to\ factor\ f \\ from\ rest\ of\ world \end{bmatrix}$$

$f \in F$

$t \in T$

Factor income

(4.29)

$$SHIF_{i,f,t} = \frac{QFINS_{i,f,t}}{\sum\limits_{i \in INS} QFINS_{i,f,t}}$$

$$\begin{bmatrix} share\ of\ institution\ i\ in \\ the\ income\ of\ factor\ f \end{bmatrix} = \begin{bmatrix} endowment\ of\ institution\ i\ of\ factor\ f \\ divided\ by\ total\ endowment\ of\ factor\ f \end{bmatrix}$$

$i \in INS$

$f \in F$

$t \in T$

Institutional
shares in factor
incomes

(4.30)

$$YIF_{i,f,t} = SHIF_{i,f,t} \cdot \left[ \left( 1 - tf_{f,t} \right) \cdot YF_{f,t} \right]$$

$$\begin{bmatrix} income\ of \\ institution\ i \\ from\ factor\ f \end{bmatrix} = \begin{bmatrix} share\ of\ income \\ of\ factor\ f\ to \\ institution\ i \end{bmatrix} \cdot \begin{bmatrix} income\ of\ factor\ f \\ (net\ of\ tax) \end{bmatrix}$$

$i \in INS$

$f \in F$

$t \in T$

Institutional
factor incomes

(Continued)

**Table 4.7** Domestic institution block equations—cont'd

(4.31)

$$YIINT_{i,t} = gintrat_{i,t} \cdot GDEBT_{i,t} - fintrat_{i,t} \cdot FDEBT_{i,t} \cdot EXR_t$$

$$\begin{bmatrix} net\ interest \\ income\ of \\ institution\ i \end{bmatrix} = \begin{bmatrix} interest\ earnings \\ on\ government \\ bonds \end{bmatrix} - \begin{bmatrix} interest \\ payments \\ on\ foreign\ debt \end{bmatrix}$$

$i \in INSDNG$
$t \in Tv$

Institutional net interest income

(4.32)

$$TRII_{i,i',t} = shii_{i,i'} \cdot (1 - MPS_{i',t}) \cdot (1 - TINS_{i',t}) \cdot YI_{i',t}$$

$$\begin{bmatrix} transfer\ from \\ institution\ i'\ to\ i \end{bmatrix} = \begin{bmatrix} share\ of\ net\ income \\ of\ institution\ i' \\ transfered\ to\ i \end{bmatrix} \cdot \begin{bmatrix} income\ of\ institution \\ i',\ net\ of\ savings\ and \\ direct\ taxes \end{bmatrix}$$

$i \in INS$
$i' \in INSDNG$
$t \in T$

Intra-institutional transfers

(4.33)

$$YI_{i,t} = \sum_{f\in F} YIF_{i,f,t} + \sum_{i'\in INSDNG} TRII_{i,i',t} + YIINT_{i,t}$$

$$\begin{bmatrix} income\ of \\ institution\ i \end{bmatrix} = \begin{bmatrix} factor \\ income \end{bmatrix} + \begin{bmatrix} transfers\ from\ other \\ domestic\ non-government \\ institutions \end{bmatrix} + \begin{bmatrix} net \\ interest \\ income \end{bmatrix}$$

$$+ \overline{TRNSFR}_{i,gov,t} \cdot \overline{CPI}_t + tmsfrpc_{i,gov,t} \cdot POP_{i,t} \cdot \overline{CPI}_t$$

$$+ \begin{bmatrix} transfers\ from\ government \\ to\ non-household\ institutions \end{bmatrix} + \begin{bmatrix} transfers\ from \\ government\ to\ households \end{bmatrix}$$

$$+ \overline{TRNSFR}_{i,row,t} \cdot EXR_t + tmsfrpc_{i,row,t} \cdot POP_{i,t} \cdot EXR_t$$

$$+ \begin{bmatrix} transfers\ from\ Rest\ of\ World \\ to\ non-household\ institutions \end{bmatrix} + \begin{bmatrix} transfers\ from \\ Rest\ of\ World\ to\ households \end{bmatrix}$$

$i \in INSDNG$
$t \in T$

Income of domestic, non-government institutions

(4.34)

$$TINS_{i,t} = tinsbar_{i,t} \cdot \left(1 + \overline{TINSADJ}_t \cdot tins01_i\right) + DTINS_t \cdot tins01_i$$

$$\begin{bmatrix} \text{direct tax} \\ \text{rate for} \\ \text{institution } i \end{bmatrix} = \begin{bmatrix} \text{exogenous rate adjusted} \\ \text{for scaling for} \\ \text{selected institutions} \end{bmatrix} + \begin{bmatrix} \text{point change} \\ \text{for selected} \\ \text{institutions} \end{bmatrix}$$

$i \in INSDNG$

$t \in T$

Direct tax rates for domestic non-government institutions

(4.35)

$$MPS_{i,t} = mpsbar \cdot \left(\frac{(1 - TINS_{i,t}) \cdot YI_{i,t}}{POP_{i,t}}\right)^{\rho_i^{sav}} \cdot \left(1 + \overline{MPSADJ}_t \cdot mps01_i\right)$$
$$+ \overline{DMPS}_t \cdot mps01_i$$

$$\begin{bmatrix} \text{marginal} \\ \text{propensity} \\ \text{to save} \end{bmatrix} = \begin{bmatrix} \text{exogenous} \\ \text{term} \end{bmatrix} \cdot \begin{bmatrix} \text{adjustment for} \\ \text{per capita} \\ \text{post-tax income} \end{bmatrix} \cdot \begin{bmatrix} \text{scaling adjustment} \\ \text{for selected} \\ \text{institutions} \end{bmatrix}$$
$$+ \begin{bmatrix} \text{point-change} \\ \text{adjustment for} \\ \text{selected institutions} \end{bmatrix}$$

$i \in INSDNG$

$t \in T$

Savings rates for domestic non-government institutions

(4.36)

$$INSSAV_{i,t} = \alpha_i^{sav} \cdot \overline{POP}_{i,t} + MPS_{i,t} \cdot (1 - TINS_{i,t}) \cdot YI_{i,t}$$

$$\begin{bmatrix} \text{savings for} \\ \text{institution } i \end{bmatrix} = \begin{bmatrix} \text{intercept of} \\ \text{savings function} \end{bmatrix} + \begin{bmatrix} \text{marginal} \\ \text{propensity} \\ \text{to save} \end{bmatrix} \cdot \begin{bmatrix} \text{income of} \\ \text{institution } i \\ \text{(net of direct taxes)} \end{bmatrix}$$

$i \in INSDNG$

Savings for domestic non-government institutions

(Continued)

**Table 4.7** Domestic institution block equations—cont'd

(4.37)
$$EH_{h,t} = \left(1 - \sum_{i \in INSDNG} shii_{i,h}\right) \cdot (1 - MPS_{h,t}) \cdot (1 - TINS_{h,t}) \cdot YI_{h,t}$$

$$\begin{bmatrix} household\ income \\ disposable\_for \\ consumption \end{bmatrix} = \begin{bmatrix} household\ income,\ net\ of\ direct \\ taxes,\ savings\ and\ transfers\ to \\ other\ non-government\ institutions \end{bmatrix}$$

$h \in H$
$t \in T$

Household consumption expenditure

(4.38)
$$QH_{c,h,t} = \overline{POP}_{h,t} \cdot \left( \gamma_{c,h}^m + \frac{\beta_{c,h}^m \cdot \left( \left[ \dfrac{EH_{h,t}}{\overline{POP}_{h,t}} \right] - \sum_{c' \in C} PQ_{c',t} \cdot \gamma_{c',h}^m - \sum_{a \in A}\sum_{c' \in C} PXAC_{a,c',t} \cdot \gamma_{a,c',h}^h \right)}{PQ_{c,t}} \right)$$

$$\begin{bmatrix} quantity\ of \\ household\ demand \\ for\ commodity\ c \end{bmatrix} = f \begin{bmatrix} household \\ consumption \\ spending,\ prices \end{bmatrix}$$

$c \in C$
$h \in H$
$t \in T$

Household consumption demand for commodities from market

(4.39)
$$QHA_{a,c,h,t} = \overline{POP}_{h,t} \cdot \left( \gamma_{a,c,h}^h + \frac{\beta_{a,c,h}^h \cdot \left( \left[ \dfrac{EH_{h,t}}{\overline{POP}_{h,t}} \right] - \sum_{c' \in C} PQ_{c',t} \cdot \gamma_{c',h}^m - \sum_{a \in A}\sum_{c' \in C} PXAC_{a,c',t} \cdot \gamma_{a,c',h}^h \right)}{PXAC_{a,c,t}} \right)$$

$$\begin{bmatrix} quantity\ of\ household\ demand \\ for\ commodity\ c\ from\ activity\ a \end{bmatrix} = f \begin{bmatrix} household\ consumption \\ spending,\ prices \end{bmatrix}$$

$a \in A$
$c \in C$
$h \in H$
$t \in T$

Household consumption demand for own production

(4.40)

$$YG_t = \sum_{i \in INSDNG} TINS_{i,t} \cdot YI_{i,t} + \sum_{f \in F} tf_{f,t} \cdot YF_{f,t} + \sum_{a \in A} ta_{a,t} \cdot PA_{a,t} \cdot QA_{a,t}$$

Government
current
revenue

$t \in T$

$$\begin{bmatrix} government \\ revenue \end{bmatrix} = \begin{bmatrix} direct\ taxes \\ from\ institutions \end{bmatrix} + \begin{bmatrix} direct\ taxes \\ from\ factors \end{bmatrix} + [activity\ tax]$$

$$+ \sum_{a \in A} tva_{a,t} \cdot PVA_{a,t} \cdot QVA_{a,t} + \sum_{c \in CM} tm_{c,t} \cdot pwm_{c,t} \cdot QM_{c,t}$$

$$+ [value - added\ tax] + [import\ tariffs]$$

$$+ \sum_{c \in CE} te_{c,t} \cdot \overline{PWE}_{c,t} \cdot QE_{c,t} \cdot EXR_t + \sum_{c \in C} tq_{c,t} \cdot PQ_{c,t} \cdot QQ_{c,t}$$

$$+ [export\ taxes] + [sales\ tax]$$

$$+ \sum_{f \in F} YIF_{gov,f,t} + \sum_{i \in INSDNG} TRII_{gov,i,t} + \overline{TRNSFR}_{gov,row,t} \cdot EXR_t$$

$$+ [factor\ income] + \begin{bmatrix} transfers\ from \\ domestic\ institutions \end{bmatrix} + [transfers\ from\ rest\ of\ world]$$

(Continued)

**Table 4.7** Domestic institution block equations—cont'd

(4.41)

$$EG_t = \sum_{c \in C} PQ_{c,t} \cdot QG_{c,t} + \sum_{i \in INSDNH} \overline{TRNSFR}_{i,\text{gov},t} \cdot \overline{CPI}_t$$

$$\left[\begin{matrix}\textit{government}\\\textit{spending}\end{matrix}\right] = \left[\begin{matrix}\textit{government}\\\textit{consumption}\end{matrix}\right] + \left[\begin{matrix}\textit{transfers to domestic}\\\textit{non-household institutions}\end{matrix}\right]$$

$$+ \sum_{h \in H} trnsfrpc_{h,\text{gov},t} \cdot \overline{POP}_{h,t} \cdot \overline{CPI}_t + \overline{TRNSFR}_{\text{row;gov},t} \cdot EXR_t$$

$$+ \left[\begin{matrix}\textit{transfers to domestic}\\\textit{households}\end{matrix}\right] + \left[\begin{matrix}\textit{transfers to}\\\textit{rest of world}\end{matrix}\right]$$

$$+ \sum_{i \in INS} gintrat_{i,t} \cdot GDEBT_{i,t} + fintrat_{\text{gov},t} \cdot FDEBT_{\text{gov},t} \cdot EXR_t$$

$$+ \left[\begin{matrix}\textit{interest payment}\\\textit{on domestic debt}\end{matrix}\right] + \left[\begin{matrix}\textit{interest payment}\\\textit{on foreign debt}\end{matrix}\right]$$

$t \in T$

Government recurrent expenditures

(4.42)

$$QG_{c,t} = QG_{c,t-1}$$

$$\cdot \left(1 + qggrowbar_{c,t} + \sum_{c' \in C} qg01_{c,c',t} \cdot \overline{QGGRW}_{c',t}\right)$$

$$\left[\begin{matrix}\textit{real}\\\textit{government}\\\textit{consumption}\\\textit{of c in t}\end{matrix}\right] = \left[\begin{matrix}\textit{real}\\\textit{government}\\\textit{consumption}\\\textit{of c in t}-1\end{matrix}\right] \cdot \left(1 + \left[\begin{matrix}\textit{growth rate}\\\textit{of c in t}\\\textit{(exogenous}\\\textit{part)}\end{matrix}\right] + \left[1 + \left[\begin{matrix}\textit{growth adjustment}\\\textit{for c (if c is linked to}\\\textit{c' via qg01 and if}\\\textit{QGGRW}_{c'}\textit{is endogenous)}\end{matrix}\right]\right]\right)$$

$c \in C$

$c \notin CINF$

$t \in T$

$t > 1$

Real government consumption (excluding infrastructure services)

(4.43)

$$QG_{c,t} = \sum_{\substack{i\in INS \\ f\in F}} igf_{i,f,t} \cdot QFINS_{i,f,t}$$

$$\begin{bmatrix} \text{real government} \\ \text{consumption} \\ \text{of } c \text{ in } t \end{bmatrix} = \begin{bmatrix} \text{quantity of gov consumption} \\ \text{per unit of gov infrastructure} \\ \text{capital stock } f \end{bmatrix} \cdot \begin{bmatrix} \text{real endowment of} \\ \text{factor } f \text{ for} \\ \text{institution } i \end{bmatrix}$$

$c \in CINF$   Real government consumption of infrastructure services
$t \in T$
$t > 1$

(4.44)

$$GSAV_t = YG_t - EG_t$$

$$\begin{bmatrix} \text{government} \\ \text{savings} \end{bmatrix} = \begin{bmatrix} \text{government} \\ \text{recurrent revenue} \end{bmatrix} - \begin{bmatrix} \text{government} \\ \text{recurrent expenditures} \end{bmatrix}$$

$t \in T$   Government savings

other institutions (domestic or foreign), Equation (4.32); (iii) earn total gross incomes defined as the sum of factor incomes, net interest incomes and transfers from other institutions, where the treatment of the latter differs depending on the nature of the sending institution (government, the rest of the world, or another domestic non-government institution) and the receiving institution (household or non-household), Equation (4.33); (iv) pay direct taxes according to rates that are fixed unless adjusted as part of the government closure rule, Equation (4.34); note that all right-hand-side terms are exogenous; and (v) save out of incomes net of direct taxes according to marginal (and average) rates that are endogenous, depending on changes in *per capita* incomes if the elasticity of savings with respect to *per capita* income is different from zero, Equation (4.35 and 4.36).[21] In Equation (4.36), the savings of domestic non-government institutions are a linear function of their respective income, Equation (4.36) allows for the marginal propensity to save to be different from the average propensity to save.[22] Alternatively, for any given institution, the savings and/or direct tax rate may be adjusted as part of the savings–investment and government closure rules. If direct taxes are adjusted as part of the government closure rule, selected institutions face changes in their rates, either via uniform scaling ($TINSADJ_t$) or via a uniform point change ($DTINS_t$). As suggested by the absence of a bar above $DTINS_t$, this mathematical statement assumes that changes in direct tax payments via adjustments in $DTINS_t$ clear the government budget. The marginal propensity to save can be adjusted through similar alternative mechanisms (through $MPSADJ_t$ or $DMPS_t$) as part of the savings–investment rule.

For households, incomes net of direct taxes, savings and transfers to other institutions, defined in Equation (4.37) are allocated across different commodities according to demand functions belonging to a linear expenditure system (LES), defined in *per capita* form with separate equations for demands from the market and from own-production, see Equations (4.38 and 4.39). If the database explicitly considers transactions costs, then market demands include these whereas demands for own production do not.

For the remaining domestic institution, the government, current incomes come from taxes (which are disaggregated into a wide range of categories), factor endowments (the government may own non-labor factors) and transfers from other domestic institutions and the rest of the world, Equation (4.40); transfers from the rest of the world may be endogenous, clearing the government budget as part of the government closure rule.

---

[21] Drawing on empirical evidence and a formulation used in van der Mensbrugghe (2005b), the model code for Equation (4.35) has been expanded to permit an optional link between changes in youth and old-age dependency ratios and the marginal propensity to save, using a constant-elasticity formulation. This may be particularly relevant in analyses of demographic issues.

[22] If the database does not include independent information about the marginal propensity save, then the intercept vanishes and the initial average and marginal savings propensities become equal. An independent estimate of the marginal propensity is required if base-year savings are negative.

(If so, direct taxes do not perform this role.) The current expenditures of the government are divided into consumption, transfers to domestic institutions (CPI-indexed) and the rest of the world (fixed in FCU) and interest payments on domestic and foreign debt, Equation (4.41). For each period except the first, real government consumption, disaggregated by commodity (excluding consumption for infrastructure), is defined as the level in the previous year times a growth factor that consists of multiple terms, Equation (4.42). In the mathematical statement, the right-hand side terms are all exogenous or lagged; in simulations with other rules for determining government consumption (including simulations targeting MDGs), one of the exogenous terms is endogenous.[23] Real government consumption of infrastructure services, also for each period except the first, is defined as the quantity of government consumption per unit of the government infrastructure capital stock times the real endowment of that capital stock by the government, i.e. the size of the capital stock determines consumption (which may represent maintenance, administration and so on, see Equation (4.43). Finally, government savings is simply the difference between current revenues and current expenditures, Equation (4.44).

### 4.4.1.4 Investment block

This block, Table 4.8; Equations (4.45–4.53) covers the determination of government and private investment [including foreign direct investment (FDI)] and how these are financed.

Government investment demand by capital stock ($DKGOV_{f,t}$) is defined in Equation (4.45), which consists of three parts, including a complementary-slackness relationship (cf. above discussion of Equation (4.3) for outputs with perfect transformability between exports and domestic sales). Different treatments are applied to service capital (used in the production of government services) and infrastructure capital (which requires government support services), see Equation (4.45a). For service capital, growth in service production is the driving force; investment demand is determined as the difference between: (i) The anticipated capital demand next year (assuming that production growth will be the same as last year and using a fixed capital-input coefficient) and (ii) the capital stock that would remain if no investments were made.[24] For infrastructure capital, government investment demand is determined as the difference between: (i) An exogenous growth term times the infrastructure capital stock in $t$, similar to Equation (4.21) and (ii) the capital stock that

---

[23] MAMS permits government demand for a commodity $c$ to be endogenous for several reasons: the demand is an exogenous share of GDP or absorption; demand adjusts as part of outcome targeting with the provision of commodity $c$ as the tool; demand adjusts to clear the government budget — if so, the variable $QGGRWC_{c,t}$ is flexible. For the most straightforward case, $qg01_{c,c',t}$, a parameter for mapping one $c$ to another, is 1 when $c = c'$ and zero otherwise. If the analyst wants one or more kinds of government consumption to grow in tandem with another (e.g. as part of budget clearing), more than one $c$ may have a value of one for any given $c'$. In either case, each $c$ is linked to only one $c'$.

[24] In GAMS, the treatment is more general, giving the user the option to assume that the rate of expected output growth is the same as the rate of simulated output growth during the last one, two or three years.

**Table 4.8** Investment block

(4.45) (a)

$$DKGOV_{f,t} \geq \sum_{a \in A\big|_{(f,a)\in MFA}} ifa_{f,a,t} \cdot QA_{a,t} \cdot EXP\left(\ln\left(\frac{QA_{a,t}}{QA_{a,t-1}}\right)\right)\Bigg|_{f \in FCAPGOVSER}$$

$$\begin{bmatrix} \text{government investment} \\ \text{demand for capital } f \end{bmatrix} \geq \begin{bmatrix} \text{demand for government service capital in } t+1: \\ \text{capital coefficient times expected activity level in } t+1 \end{bmatrix}$$

$$+ \left(\left(1 + qggrwbar_{f,t} + \sum_{c \in C} qg01_{f,c,t} \cdot \overline{QGGRW}_{c,t}\right) \cdot QFINS_{\text{gov} f,t}\right)\Bigg|_{f \in FCAPGOVINF}$$

$$+ \begin{bmatrix} \text{demand for government infrastructure capital in } t+1: \\ \text{growth rate   times infrastructure capital stock in } t \end{bmatrix}$$

$$- QFINS_{\text{gov} f,t} \cdot (1 - depr_{f,t}) - \begin{bmatrix} \text{remaining capital stock } (\text{after dep-}) \\ \text{reciation}) \text{ in } t+1 \text{ if no investment in } t \end{bmatrix}$$

$f \in$    Real government
FCAPGOV   demand for
$t \in T$   investment in
$t > 1$    capital stock f

(b)

$$DKGOV_{f,t} \geq 0$$

$$[\text{government investment}] \geq [\text{zero}]$$

(c)

$$(DKGOV_{f,t} - DKGOVDEM_{f,t}) \cdot (DKGOV_{f,t} - 0) = 0$$

where $DKGOVDEM_{f,t}$ = right-hand of part (a) of Equation 4.45

$$\begin{bmatrix} Complementary\ slackness\ relationship: \\ \text{1. If government investment exceeds its demand then this investment level is zero.} \\ \text{2. If the government investment level is above zero, then it equals its demand.} \end{bmatrix}$$

(4.46)

$$DKINS_{gov,f,t} = DKGOV_{f,t}$$

$$\begin{bmatrix} gross\ investment\ in\ f\ of \\ government \end{bmatrix} = \begin{bmatrix} gross\ government\ investment \\ demand\ for\ capital \end{bmatrix}$$

$f \in FCAPGOV$

$t \in T$

$t > 1$

Real government investment in capital stock f (investment by destination)

(4.47)

$$PK_{f,t} = \sum_{c \in C} capcomp_{c,f} \cdot PQ_{c,t}$$

$$\begin{bmatrix} price\ of\ new \\ capital\ stock \end{bmatrix} = \begin{bmatrix} total\ value\ of\ commodities\ c \\ per\ unit\ of\ new\ capital \end{bmatrix}$$

$f \in FCAP$

$t \in T$

Price of new capital stock

(4.48)

$$\sum_{f \in FCAPGOV} PK_{f,t} \cdot DKINS_{gov,f,t} = GSAV_t - \sum_{c \in C} PQ_{c,t} \cdot qdst_{c,gov,t} + \overline{GBORTOT}_t$$

$$\begin{bmatrix} government\ fixed \\ investment\ value \end{bmatrix} = \begin{bmatrix} government \\ savings \end{bmatrix} - \begin{bmatrix} spending\ on \\ stock\ changes \end{bmatrix} + \begin{bmatrix} total\ change\ in\ holdings \\ of\ government\ bonds \end{bmatrix}$$

$$+ \overline{GBORMSTOT}_t + (\overline{FBOR}_{gov,t} + \overline{FGRANT}_{gov,t}) \cdot EXR_t$$

$$+ \begin{bmatrix} Government\ monetary\ system \\ borrowing\ (deficit\ monetization) \end{bmatrix} + \begin{bmatrix} foreign\ borrowing\ and\ foreign \\ grants\ (transformed\ into\ LCU) \end{bmatrix}$$

$t \in T$

Government investment value and financing

(Continued)

**Table 4.8** Investment block—cont'd

(4.49)

$$GBOR_{i,t} = \overline{gbor}_{i,t} + \left(\overline{GBORTOT}_t - \sum_{i' \in INSDNG'} \overline{gbor}_{i',t}\right) \cdot \frac{INSSAV_{i,t}}{\sum_{i' \in INSDNG'} INSSAV_{i',t}}$$

$$\begin{bmatrix} \text{change in holdings} \\ \text{of government} \\ \text{bonds by} \\ \text{institution } i \end{bmatrix} = \begin{bmatrix} \text{exogenous} \\ \text{borrowing from} \\ \text{institution } i \end{bmatrix} + \begin{bmatrix} \text{remaining} \\ \text{total} \\ \text{borrowing} \end{bmatrix} \cdot \begin{bmatrix} \text{share of} \\ \text{institution } i \text{ in} \\ \text{total savings} \end{bmatrix}$$

$i \in INSDNG$

$t \in T$

Allocation of government bond borrowing across domestic non-government institutions

(4.50)

$$GBORMS_{i,t} = \overline{gborms}_{i,t} + \left(\overline{GBORMSTOT}_t - \sum_{i' \in INSDNG'} \overline{gborms}_{i',t}\right) \cdot \frac{INSSAV_{i,t}}{\sum_{i' \in INSDNG'} INSSAV_{i',t}}$$

$$\begin{bmatrix} \text{burden of government} \\ \text{monetary} \\ \text{system borrowing} \\ \text{allocated to} \\ \text{institution } i \end{bmatrix} = \begin{bmatrix} \text{exogenous} \\ \text{burden for} \\ \text{institution } i \end{bmatrix} + \begin{bmatrix} \text{remaining} \\ \text{monetary} \\ \text{system} \\ \text{borrowing} \end{bmatrix} \cdot \begin{bmatrix} \text{share of} \\ \text{institution } i \text{ in} \\ \text{total savings} \end{bmatrix}$$

$i \in INSDNG$

$t \in T$

Allocation of the burden of monetary system borrowing across domestic non-government institutions

(4.51)

$$INVVAL_{i,t} = INSSAV_{i,t} - \sum_{c \in C} PQ_{c,t} \cdot qdst_{c,i,t} - GBOR_{i,t}$$

$$- GBORMS_{i,t} + (\overline{FBOR}_{i,t} + fdi_{i,t}) \cdot EXR_t$$

$$\begin{bmatrix} \text{non-government fixed} \\ \text{investment value} \end{bmatrix} = [\text{savings}] - \begin{bmatrix} \text{stock} \\ \text{changes} \end{bmatrix} - \begin{bmatrix} \text{change in holdings of} \\ \text{government bonds} \end{bmatrix}$$

$$- \begin{bmatrix} \text{Government Central} \\ \text{Bank borrowing} \end{bmatrix} + \begin{bmatrix} \text{foreign borrowing and} \\ \text{FDI (transformed into LCU)} \end{bmatrix}$$

$i \in INSDNG$

$t \in T$

Investment financing for non-government institutions

(4.52)

$$PK_{f,t} \cdot DKINS_{i,f,t} = gfcfshr_{f,i,t} \cdot INVVAL_{i,t}$$

$$\begin{bmatrix} non\text{-}government\ spending \\ on\ capital\ stock\ f \end{bmatrix} = \begin{bmatrix} total\ fixed\ investment\ value \\ times\ share\ for\ capital\ stock\ f \end{bmatrix}$$

$i \in INSNG$   Non-government investment by capital stock (investment by destination)
$f \in FCAP$
$t \in T$

(4.53)

$$QINV_{c,t} = \sum_{f \in FCAP} \left( capcomp_{c,f,t} \cdot \sum_{i \in INS} DKINS_{i,f,t} \right)$$

$$\begin{bmatrix} real\ investment\ demand \\ for\ commodity\ c \end{bmatrix} = \begin{bmatrix} demand\ for\ c\ for\ each\ type\ of\ capital, \\ summed\ over\ all\ institutions\ and\ capital\ types \end{bmatrix}$$

$c \in C$   Total real investment demand by commodity (investment by origin or source)
$t \in T$

would remain if no investments were made.[25] A non-negativity constraint is also imposed for government investment, Equation (4.45b). A complementary-slackness condition, Equation (4.45c) imposes that (i) if $DKGOV_{f,t}$ is positive, then Equation (4.45a) must hold as an equality, and (ii) if the right-hand side of Equation (4.45a) is negative, then $DKGOV_{f,t}$ will be zero and Equation (4.45a) will hold as a strict inequality. This treatment is used to avoid a negative investment value ($DKGOV_{f,t} < 0$) in the exceptional case of an anticipated production *decline* that is larger than the depreciation rate. Equation (4.46) transfers the value of $DKGOV_{f,t}$ to investment by institution, $DKINS_{gov,f,t}$ (for the government), a variable that is used elsewhere in the model for investment across all capital stocks.[26]

The prices of new capital stocks (disaggregated by type) depend on their composition and market prices, Equation (4.47). The resulting fixed government investment value (defined on the basis of the price and quantity information generated in the preceding equations) is financed by some combination of government savings (net of spending on stock changes), sales of government bonds (i.e. new interest-bearing borrowing), borrowing via the monetary system, foreign borrowing and foreign capital grants (which is separate from current government transfers from the rest of the world), Equation (4.48). Returning to the equations, government bond sales and borrowing via the monetary system are allocated across households on the basis of their savings shares adjusted for an exogenous, household-specific term in each equation, see Equations (4.49) and (4.50).[27]

Equation (4.48) concludes the series of equations that summarize the government budget, see also Equations (4.40), (4.41) and (4.44). The choice of mechanism for clearing the budget (the government closure rule) is often an important part of the simulations. As noted above, in this mathematical statement it is assumed that changes in the variable $DTINS_t$, see Equation (4.34) and adjust direct tax payments sufficiently to clear the budget. The other terms in the expressions for government receipts and outlays are exogenous or determined via other mechanisms. Under alternative government closures, $DTINS_t$ is exogenous while some other variable is endogenous, clearing the government budget, e.g. government bond sales ($GBORTOT_t$) or government borrowing from the rest of the world ($FBOR_{gov,t}$).

Each alternative closure has specific macroeconomic repercussions. Increases in government bond sales reduces the amount of financing that is available for private

---

[25] For public infrastructure, actual $QG_{c,t}$ (government service level) is determined by the current capital stock, see Equation (4.43). In Equation (4.45), the exogenous growth variable $QGGRWC_{c,t}$ (which is defined over $c$, where the relevant $c$ may be public infrastructure services) is mapped to the capital stock $f$ associated with $c$ and drives the expansion in the capital stock.

[26] In order to permit smoothing of year-to-year changes investment quantities, the GAMS code permits the user to define $DKINS_{gov,f,t}$ as a weighted average between $DKGOV_{f,t}$ and $DKINS_{gov,f,t}$ in the previous year.

[27] The burden of monetary system borrowing is felt by other agents since it extracts real purchasing power from them by reducing the value of the old money that they hold. In the absence of an explicit treatment of money in this model, this burden is here allocated across households on the basis of their savings shares. The terms $\overline{gbor}_{i,t}$ and $\overline{gborms}_{i,t}$ are non-zero in the initial year in so far as observed shares for government borrowing deviate from savings share.

investment, *cf.* Equation (4.51) while increases in foreign grants or foreign borrowing tend to permit more rapid growth in GDP and private final demand (consumption and investment). Reliance on foreign resources also tends to bring about real exchange rate appreciation, slower export growth and more rapid growth in imports and production of non-tradables. The strength of these effects depends on the growth impact of the expansion in government spending as well as on whether the new spending has high or low import shares. If the country later needs to reverse the switch toward production of non-tradables (e.g. because of a decline in foreign grants in the future), and its structure is rigid, it may end up suffering from "Dutch Disease." Expansion in foreign borrowing is less favorable than grants since it drives up the foreign debt (which, in the absence of debt relief, eventually has to be repaid) and related interest payments (more or less burdensome depending on loan conditions). The alternative of raising direct taxes tends to be less favorable to growth in GDP and private final demand than reliance on foreign resources. However, given that most of the cut in household disposable income is born by consumption as opposed to savings and investment, the direct tax alternative is more favorable than domestic government borrowing for long-run growth in GDP and private final demand.

Equation (4.51) defines the fixed investment values for non-government institutions — all terms do not apply to each institution — as own savings, net of spending on stock changes and lending to the government and augmented by borrowing, capital grants and FDI from the rest of the world.[28] For the latter, the fixed investment value is simply the value of FDI (fixed in FCU) times the exchange rate. (The FDI term is invariably fixed at zero for domestic institutions.) Implicitly, Equation (4.51) shows a rule for ensuring that total savings and total investment are equal: given that government and households savings, government investment and FDI all are determined by rules, the clearing variable is private household investment ($INVVAL_{h,t}$).

For each non-government institution, real investment in different capital stocks (investment by destination) is determined by its total fixed investment values, the prices of capital goods and exogenous value shares by capital stock; the value share is unity if the database only specifies a single private capital type, Equation (4.52).[29]

The final equation in this block defines total investment demand by commodity source (often referred to as investment by origin). It is defined on the basis of real gross fixed capital formation (both private and government; investment by destination) and the capital composition parameter, Equation (4.53).

---

[28] Note that MAMS does not cover borrowing and related debts obligations that only involve domestic non-government institutions (i.e. without involvement from the government or the rest of the world).

[29] Typically, the model will only have one private capital stock, i.e. the value of the share parameter is unity for this capital type. If the model has more than one private capital stock, the allocation between the different stocks may be endogenized, possibly deviating from the base-level allocation in response to changes in relative profit rates — a relationship that would need to be specified in one or more additional equations.

### 4.4.1.5 Other system constraints: foreign exchange, factors and commodities

In the preceding, we discussed alternative mechanisms for clearing two of the macro constraints of the model, the government budget and the savings—investment balance. The current block, see Table 4.9; Equations (4.54—4.58), includes the remaining system constraints: the balance of payments and the markets for factors and commodities.

The balance of payments (or foreign exchange constraint) Equation (4.54) imposes equality between foreign exchange uses (spending on imports, factor incomes and transfers to the rest of the world and interest payments on foreign debts) and sources (export revenues, transfers, factor incomes, borrowing, capital grants and FDI).[30] In practice, the only plausible assumption for medium- and long-run analysis tends to be that the (real) exchange rate ($EXR_t$) clears this balance. For example, other things being equal, depreciation (an increase in $EXR_t$) will remove a deficit by raising supplies for export relative to supplies for home sales while reducing domestic use of imports relative to domestic use of local output.[31]

The market constraint for factors, Equation (4.55), which applies to all factors except government capital, states that total demand for any factor (the left-hand side) equals the total endowment times the employment rate (1 — the unemployment rate). This is straightforward if the unemployment rate is exogenous — if so, in any time period, the economy-wide wage variable ($WF_{f,t}$) will clear the market by influencing the quantities demanded.

On the other hand, for factors with endogenous unemployment (in the set *FUEND*; typically including labor), Equations (4.56) and (4.57) are also included.[32] Using labor as an example, workers have a reservation (minimum) wage ($WFRES_{f,t}$) below which they will not work, Equation (4.56). It is defined as a function of the economy-wide wage in the base year, and the ratios between current and base-year values for the unemployment rate, household consumption *per capita* (as an indicator of real living standards) and the CPI. The ratio terms are raised to elasticities that determine their importance (an elasticity of zero implies that a term has no importance in the application in question). Equation (4.57) consists of three parts: (4.57a) the constraint that the economy-wide wage for each factor cannot fall below the endogenous reservation wage, (4.57b) the constraint that the unemployment rate cannot fall below an exogenous minimum ($ueratmin_{f,t}$)[33] and (4.57c) a complementary slackness condition, which states that either (a) or (b) but not both are slack (non-

---

[30] Implicitly, an additional system constraint, the savings—investment balance, also holds: by channeling domestic savings and the terms that make up foreign savings to investment, the model equations ensure that total savings and total investment are equal.

[31] Alternative assumptions (e.g. that foreign grants or borrowing clear the balance) typically seem farfetched and may also cause sharp imbalances for the domestic institution that is involved (in this example as recipient of foreign grants or loans).

[32] This formulation draws on van der Mensbrugghe (2005, pp. 20—21). See also Agénor (2007, Chapter 1).

[33] The level of the base-year unemployment rate relative to the minimum unemployment rate indicates the potential for employment growth over and above the growth rate of the labor stock.

**Table 4.9** Constraints for foreign exchange, factors and commodities

(4.54)

$$\underbrace{\sum_{c \in CM} pwm_{c,t} \cdot QM_{c,t}}_{\begin{bmatrix} import \\ spending \end{bmatrix}} + \underbrace{\frac{\sum_{f \in F} YIF_{row,f,t}}{EXR_t}}_{\begin{bmatrix} factor\ income \\ to\ RoW \end{bmatrix}} + \underbrace{\frac{\sum_{i \in INSDNG} TRII_{row,i,t}}{EXR_t}}_{\begin{bmatrix} transfers\ from\ domestic \\ non\text{-}government\ institutions\ to\ RoW \end{bmatrix}}$$

$$+ \underbrace{\overline{TRNSFR}_{row,gov,t}}_{\begin{bmatrix} transfers\ from \\ government\ to\ RoW \end{bmatrix}} + \underbrace{\sum_{i \in INSD} fintrati_{i,t} \cdot FDEBT_{i,t}}_{\begin{bmatrix} interest\ payment \\ on\ foreign\ debt \end{bmatrix}} =$$

$$\underbrace{\sum_{c \in CE} \overline{PWE}_{c,t} \cdot QE_{c,t}}_{\begin{bmatrix} export \\ revenue \end{bmatrix}} + \underbrace{\sum_{i \in INSDNH} \overline{TRNSFR}_{i,row,t}}_{\begin{bmatrix} transfers\ from\ RoW\ to\ domestic \\ non\text{-}household\ institutions \end{bmatrix}} + \underbrace{\sum_{h \in H} trnsfrpc_{h,row,t} \cdot \overline{POP}_{h,t}}_{\begin{bmatrix} transfers\ from\ RoW\ to \\ domestic\ households \end{bmatrix}}$$

$$+ \underbrace{\sum_{f \in F} \overline{TRNSFR}_{f,row,t}}_{\begin{bmatrix} factor\ income \\ from\ RoW \end{bmatrix}} + \underbrace{\sum_{i \in INSD} \overline{FBOR}_{i,t}}_{\begin{bmatrix} borrowing \\ from\ RoW \end{bmatrix}} + \underbrace{fdi_{row,t}}_{\begin{bmatrix} grants \\ from\ RoW \end{bmatrix}} + \underbrace{}_{\begin{bmatrix} foreign\ direct \\ investment \end{bmatrix}}$$

Balance of payments (in FCU)

$t \in T$

(Continued)

**Table 4.9** Constraints for foreign exchange, factors and commodities—cont'd

(4.55)

$$\sum_{a\in A} QF_{f,a,t} = (1 - UERAT_{f,t}) \cdot \sum_{i\in INS} QFINS_{i,f,t}$$

$$\begin{bmatrix} demand\ for \\ market\ factor\ f \end{bmatrix} = \begin{bmatrix} 1 - unemployment\ rate \\ (i.e.\ employment\ rate) \end{bmatrix} \cdot \begin{bmatrix} sum\ of\ all\ institutional \\ endowments\ of\ factor\ f \end{bmatrix}$$

$f \in F$

$t \in T$

Factor markets

(4.56)

$$WFRES_{f,t} = WF_f^0 \cdot \left(\frac{QHPC_t}{QHPC^0}\right)^{\varphi_{qhps,f}} \cdot \left(\frac{UERAT_{f,t}}{UERAT_f^0}\right)^{\varphi_{uerat,f}} \cdot \left(\frac{CPI_t}{CPI^0}\right)^{\varphi_{cpi,f}}$$

$$\begin{bmatrix} reservation\ wage \\ for\ factor\ f \\ in\ year\ t \end{bmatrix} = \begin{bmatrix} economy\text{-}wide\ wage \\ for\ factor\ f\ in \\ the\ base\ year \end{bmatrix} \cdot \begin{bmatrix} adjustment\ due\ to:\ percapita \\ household\ consumption, \\ unemployment\ rate\ and CPI \\ (all\ relative\ to\ base\ year\ values) \end{bmatrix}$$

$f \in FUEND$

$t \in T$

Reservation wage

(4.57)(a)

$$WF_{f,t} \geq WFRES_{f,t}$$

$$\begin{bmatrix} economy\text{-}wide \\ wage\ for\ factor\ f \\ in\ year\ t \end{bmatrix} \geq \begin{bmatrix} reservation \\ wage\ for\ factor \\ f\ in\ year\ t \end{bmatrix}$$

(b)

$$UERAT_{f,t} \geq ueratmin_{f,t}$$

$$\begin{bmatrix} unemployment \\ rate\ for\ factor \\ f\ in\ year\ t \end{bmatrix} \geq \begin{bmatrix} minimum\ unemployment \\ rate\ for\ factor\ f \\ in\ year\ t \end{bmatrix}$$

$f \in FUEND$

$t \in T$

For factors with endogenous unemployment: (a) wage and (b) unemployment constraints; and (c) related complementary-slackness relationship

(c)

$$(WF_{f,t} - WFRES_{f,t}) \cdot (UERAT_{f,t} - ueratmin_{f,t}) = 0$$

$$\left[\begin{array}{l}\textit{Complementary slackness relationship :}\\\textit{1. If wage exceeds reservation wage then unemployment rate is at its minimum.}\\\textit{2. If unemployment rate exceeds its minimum, then wage equals reservation wage.}\end{array}\right]$$

(4.58)

$$QQ_{c,t} = \sum_{a\in A} QINT_{c,a,t} + \sum_{h\in H} QH_{c,h,t} + QG_{c,t}$$

$$\left[\begin{array}{c}\textit{composite}\\\textit{supply}\end{array}\right] = \left[\begin{array}{c}\textit{intermediate}\\\textit{use}\end{array}\right] + \left[\begin{array}{c}\textit{household}\\\textit{consumption}\end{array}\right] + \left[\begin{array}{c}\textit{government}\\\textit{consumption}\end{array}\right]$$

$$+ QINV_{c,t} + \sum_{i\in INS} qdst_{c,i,t} + QT_{c,t}$$

$$+ \left[\begin{array}{c}\textit{fixed}\\\textit{investment}\end{array}\right] + \left[\begin{array}{c}\textit{stock}\\\textit{change}\end{array}\right] + \left[\begin{array}{c}\textit{trade and}\\\textit{transport}\end{array}\right]$$

$c \in C$
$t \in T$

Composite
commodity
markets

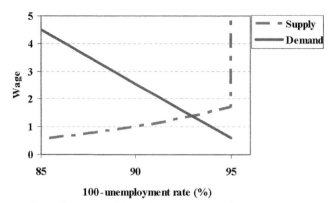

**Figure 4.1** Labor market adjustment with endogenous unemployment.

binding). In other words, if the unemployment rate is above its minimum, then the wage must be at the reservation level; if the wage is above the reservation level, then the unemployment rate must be at its minimum.

Figure 4.1 illustrates the functioning of factor markets with endogenous unemployment. The supply curve is upward–sloping, reflecting that, *cet. par.*, workers request higher wages as the labor market gets tighter. When the market reaches "full employment," i.e. when the minimum unemployment rate is reached (which here is set at 5%), the supply curve turns vertical. When the factor market is below full employment, market-clearing changes in the economy-wide wage variable ($WF_{f,t}$) brings about changes, not only on the demand side but also on the supply side of the labor market; at full employment, only the demand side responds. Unemployment should be seen as broadly defined, representing the degree of underutilization of the factor (and the potential for increased utilization), due to a combination of full or partial unemployment (i.e. also considering underemployment) *cf.* above discussion of Equation (4.3) for outputs with perfect transformability between exports and domestic sales, which also includes a complementary-slackness condition.

For each composite commodity, the supply is set equal to the sum of demands, Equation (4.58). As noted earlier, composite supplies stem from two sources, imports and domestic supplies to domestic markets, *cf.* Equation (4.24); for each commodity with both sources, demand is allocated between them on the basis of relative prices. The market-clearing variables are the quantity ($QM_{c,t}$) for imports and, for domestic output, the price ($PDS_{c,t}$ for suppliers and $PDD_{c,t}$ for demanders, with a wedge between the two in the presence of transactions costs).

### 4.4.1.6 Asset stock updating and productivity block

The equations in this block update institutional stocks of assets and liabilities and TFP by activity, Table 4.10; Equations (4.59)−(4.66). Except for equations defining

**Table 4.10** Asset stock updating and productivity block

(4.59)

$$QFINS_{i,f,t} = (1 - depr_{f,t-1}) \cdot QFINS_{i,f,t-1} + DKINS_{i,f,t-1} + qfinsadj_{i,f,t-1}$$

$$\begin{bmatrix} stock\ of\ capital \\ type\ f\ held \\ by\ institution\ i \end{bmatrix} = \begin{bmatrix} non\text{-}depreciated \\ capital\ stock \end{bmatrix} + \begin{bmatrix} fixed\ investment \\ in\ t-1 \end{bmatrix} + \begin{bmatrix} exogenous\ adjustment \\ in\ capital\ stock \end{bmatrix}$$

$i \in INS$   Capital stocks by institution
$f \in FCAP$
$t \in T$
$t > 1$

(4.60)

$$FDEBT_{i,t} = FDEBT_{i,t-1} + FBOR_{i,t-1}$$
$$+ (fintratdue_{i,t-1} - fintrat_{i,t-1}) \cdot FDEBT_{i,t-1} - fdebtrelief_{i,t-1}$$

$$\begin{bmatrix} foreign \\ debt\ in\ t \end{bmatrix} = \begin{bmatrix} foreign \\ debt\ in\ t-1 \end{bmatrix} + \begin{bmatrix} foreign \\ borrowing\ in\ t-1 \end{bmatrix} + \begin{bmatrix} unpaid\ interest\ on \\ foreign\ debt\ in\ t-1 \end{bmatrix} - \begin{bmatrix} foreign\ debt \\ relief\ in\ t-1 \end{bmatrix}$$

$i \in INSD$ Foreign debt of domestic institutions
$t \in T$
$t > 1$

(4.61)

$$GDEBT_{i,t} = GDEBT_{i,t-1} + GBOR_{i,t-1}$$

$$\begin{bmatrix} stock\ of\ government \\ bond\ held\ by \\ institution\ i \end{bmatrix} = \begin{bmatrix} redistributed\ holdings\ of \\ stock\ of\ government\ bond \\ held\ by\ institution\ i\ in\ t-1 \end{bmatrix} + \begin{bmatrix} government \\ borrowing \\ from\ i\ in\ t-1 \end{bmatrix}$$

$i \in INSDNG$ Government bond holdings of domestic institutions
$t \in T$
$t > 1$

*(Continued)*

**Table 4.10** Asset stock updating and productivity block—cont'd

(4.62)

$$GDPREAL_t = \sum_{c \in C} \sum_{h \in H} PQ_c^0 \cdot QH_{c,h,t} + \sum_{a \in A} \sum_{c \in C} \sum_{h \in H} PXAC_{a,c}^0 \cdot QHA_{a,c,h,t}$$     $t \in T$     Real GDP at market prices

$$[real\ GDP] = \left[\begin{array}{c} household\ market \\ consumption \end{array}\right] + \left[\begin{array}{c} household\ own \\ production\ consumption \end{array}\right]$$

$$+ \sum_{c \in C} PQ_c^0 \cdot QG_{c,t} + \sum_{c \in C} PQ_c^0 \cdot QINV_{c,t} + \sum_{c \in C} \sum_{i \in INS} PQ_c^0 \cdot qdst_{c,i,t}$$

$$+ \left[\begin{array}{c} government \\ consumption \end{array}\right] + \left[\begin{array}{c} fixed \\ investment \end{array}\right] + \left[\begin{array}{c} stock \\ change \end{array}\right]$$

$$+ \sum_{c \in CE} EXR^0 \cdot PWE_c^0 \cdot QE_{c,t} - \sum_{c \in CM} EXR^0 \cdot PWM_c^0 \cdot QM_{c,t}$$

$$+ [exports] - [imports]$$

(4.63)

$$TRDGDP_t = \frac{\sum_{c \in CE} EXR^0 \cdot PWE_c^0 \cdot QE_{c,t} + \sum_{c \in CM} EXR^0 \cdot PWM_c^0 \cdot QM_{c,t}}{GDPREAL_t}$$     $t \in T$     Real Trade-GDP ratio

$$\left[\begin{array}{c} ratio\ of \\ trade\ to\ GDP \end{array}\right] = \frac{[real\ trade]}{[real\ GDP]}$$

(4.64)

$$ALPHAVA_{a,t} = ALPHAVA2_{a,t} \cdot \prod_{f \in FCAP} \left[ \frac{\sum_{i \in INS} QFINS_{i,f,t}}{\sum_{i \in INS} QFINS^0_{i,f}} \right]^{tfpelasg_{a,f,t}}$$

$$\cdot \left( \frac{\sum_{t' \in T} tfptrdwt_{t,t'} \cdot TRDGDP_t}{TRDGDP^0} \right)^{tfpelastrd_a}$$

$a \in A$
$t \in T$
$t > 1$

Efficiency (TFP) by activity

$$\begin{bmatrix} efficiency \\ term\ for \\ activity\ a \end{bmatrix} = \begin{bmatrix} trend \\ term\ for \\ activity\ a \end{bmatrix} \cdot \begin{bmatrix} product\ of: \\ current\ real\ capital \\ endowments\ f\ to\ initial \\ value,\ raised \\ to\ the\ relevant\ elasticity \end{bmatrix} \cdot \begin{bmatrix} weighted\ avg.\ (over\ time) \\ of\ ratios\ of\ openness \\ to\ initial\ value,\ raised \\ to\ the\ relevant\ elasticity \end{bmatrix}$$

(4.65)

$$ALPHAVA2_{a,t} = ALPHAVA2_{a,t-1} \cdot \left(1 + \alpha^{vag}_{a,t} + \overline{CALTFPG}_t \cdot tfp01_{a,t}\right)$$

$a \in A$
$t \in T$
$t > 1$

TFP trend term by activity

$$\begin{bmatrix} trend\ term\ for \\ activity\ a\ in\ t \end{bmatrix} = \begin{bmatrix} trend\ term\ for \\ activity\ a\ in\ t-1 \end{bmatrix} \cdot \begin{bmatrix} growth\ adjustment \\ factor \end{bmatrix}$$

(4.66)

$$GDPREALFC_t = \sum_{a \in A} PVA^0_a \cdot \left(1 - tva^0_{a,t}\right) \cdot QVA_{a,t}$$

$t \in T$

Real GDP at factor cost

$$\begin{bmatrix} real\ GDP \\ at\ factor\ cost \end{bmatrix} = \begin{bmatrix} value\text{-}added \\ net\ of\ taxes \end{bmatrix}$$

arguments for the definition of TFP, all equations in this block include lagged relationships. They do not apply to the first year, for which the values of the variables defined in this block are fixed.

Implicitly, this mathematical statement assumes that MAMS has a single representative household.[34] For capital, the stock of any institution (household, government and rest of world) is defined as the sum of its previous-period stock (adjusted for depreciation), new investments and exogenous adjustments (which may reflect the impact of natural disasters or institutional changes, removing parts of the capital stock from production), Equation (4.59). The evolution of labor endowments is defined in Equation (4.79).[35] For other factors (e.g. agricultural land), the growth in institutional endowments ($QFINS_{i,f,t}$) is exogenous. Except for the absence of depreciation, the relationships that hold for foreign debt, Equations (4.60) and government bonds, Equations (4.61) are identical to those used for capital. For foreign debt, the treatment is potentially more complex since the model allows for the possibility of non-paid interest (which is added to the debt) and debt relief.

This block includes further a set of equations used to define TFP for each activity. For this purpose, Equations (4.62) and (4.63) define real GDP at market prices and the real trade-to-GDP ratio. In Equation (4.64), the TFP of each activity (a variable that appears in Equation (4.14), the CES value-added function) is defined as the product of a trend term, changes due to capital accumulation and changes due to variations in economic openness (defined by the real trade-to-GDP ratio). The effects of capital accumulation and changes in openness depend on the values of exogenous elasticities — if they are set at zero, the effect is zero and then only the trend term matters. In the definition of the trend term, Equation (4.65), the first of the trend growth terms, $\alpha_{a,t}^{vag}$ is invariably exogenous and set at unity unless it is changed as part of an experiment. The second term, $CALTFPG_t$ is endogenized when a certain GDP level is targeted (a typical assumption for the base run). In this context, the parameter $tfp01_{a,t}$ has been used to control relative TFP growth rates across activities; given that only relative values matter, its values may conveniently range between zero and unity. However, apart from the base simulation, all right-hand terms are

---

[34] For applications with multiple households, the GAMS representation of MAMS specifies how the population of each household evolves over time. Given that it adds complexity, this aspect is suppressed in this chapter. Briefly, the general principle is that the household types that exist in the base-year (characterized by patterns for generation and spending of incomes) continue to exist but grow at different rates depending on the types of labor that they control. The capital endowments of each household are updated on the basis of new investment and the size of the non-depreciated stock of the previous period, adjusted for population changes and economy-wide constraints. Other (non-labor, non-capital) factor endowments are defined as the initial *per capita* endowment, scaled upwards or downwards to ensure that total endowments across all household equals the economy-wide endowment total.

[35] In the absence of a link between education and the labor market, the core version of MAMS simplifies the evolution of labor stocks; each stock grows at an exogenous rate with the total economy-wide stock in each period being scaled to ensure that it matches an exogenous rate of labor force participation among the population in labor force age (typically 15—64).

typically either exogenous or lagged while GDP is endogenous.[36] The trade-to-GDP ratio, an indicator of economic openness (in terms of outcome, not policy stance) is defined in real terms (to avoid the impact of nominal changes, e.g. due to exchange rate depreciation) and with a potential lag (to avoid unrealistically large immediate productivity effects of changes in openness): in any time period, the numerator in the last term of Equation (4.64) is a weighted average of current and past trade-to-GDP ratios. The parameter for the length of the lag is part of the country-specific database. The final equation in this block, Equation (4.66), defines real GDP at factor cost; it is flexible unless $CALTFPG_t$ is fixed.

The fact that the elasticity parameters in Equation (4.64) are disaggregated (by activity for trade and by activity and function for capital) make it possible to specify different channels and magnitudes for the productivity effects of trade and of different types of capital stocks. Depending on the degree of disaggregation of these capital stocks and activities, the productivity effects can be more or less finely targeted. For example, if irrigation and road capital stocks are singled out, these could meaningfully be linked to agriculture (especially crop activities) and transportation services, respectively; other sectors would only be influenced indirectly by these productivity changes.[37] On the other hand, if infrastructure capital is a single capital stock, the selection of targeted sectors would have to be more general (implicitly reflecting some assumed composition of this broader spending type).

## 4.4.2 MDG and education module

The MDG and education module, Equations (4.67)–(4.81) specifies the mechanisms that determine the values for the indicators related to the different MDGs and educational outcomes as well as the size and disaggregation (by educational achievement) of the labor force. The rest of the economy, which was presented in the preceding sections, influences the evolution of the MDGs and the educational sector through variables related to household consumption, the provision of different types of MDG-related services, labor wages and capital stocks in infrastructure. In its turn, the MDG module influences the rest of the economy through its impact on the size, composition and productivity of the labor force. In addition, the evolution of one set of MDGs can influence other MDGs. The notation and the equations of the MDG module are, respectively, presented in Tables 4.11–4.14.

---

[36] When developing the model base run, $CALTFPG_t$ may be endogenous or exogenous. If it is endogenous, real GDP (at factor cost) should be fixed (growing exogenously over time). If so, the analyst should review the resulting economy-wide growth in TFP as well as efficiency growth in different activities ($ALPHAVA_{a,t}$) and, if needed, adjust the targeted real GDP levels. On the other hand, if $CALTFPG_t$ is exogenous (and real GDP endogenous), the analyst should monitor overall GDP growth and, if needed, adjust either $CALTFPG_t$ or $\alpha_{a,t}^{vag}$. The estimates of initial capital stocks and depreciation rates may also have to be revisited. For non-base runs, the determinants of trend TFP growth ($ALPHAVA2_{a,t}$) are typically fixed, while real GDP growth is determined by growth in factor employment and endogenous TFP changes.

[37] The GAMS representation of the model also permits productivity disaggregated by factor and activity to be influenced by these determinants as well as MDG indicators; the latter may, for example, permit inks between health indicators and labor productivity.

**Table 4.11** Sets for MDG and education module

| Symbol | Explanation | Symbol | Explanation |
|---|---|---|---|
| $a \in A$ | activities | $i \in INSNGAGG$ | aggregate (domestic) non-government institution |
| $b \in B$ | student behavioral characteristics = {$rep$ = repeater; $dropout$ = dropout; $prom$ = promotion; $grdcont$ = continuing graduate; $grdexit$ = exiting graduate; $neting1$ = net (in-cohort) intake to grade 1} | $b, b' \in MBB$ | mapping between $b$ (in *BRES*) and $b'$ (in *BLOG*): = {($rep, dropout$),$grd$, $grdexit.grdcont$} |
| $b \in BLOG$ ($\subset B$) | student behavior determined by logistic function = {$prom, grdcont, neting1$} | $b, b' \in MBB2$ | mapping between $b$ (also in *BRES*) and all elements $b'$ (also in *BRES*) that are related to the same element(s) in *BLOG*: = {$rep.(rep, dropout)$, $dropout.(rep, dropout)$, $grdexit.grdexit$} |
| $b \in BRES$ ($\subset B$) | student behavior determined by residual scaling = {$rep$ = repeater; $dropout$ = dropout; $grdexit$ = exiting graduate} | $c, c' \in MCE$ | mapping private and public education into 1 education commodity, by cycle = {$c$-$edup$. ($c$-$edup$, $c$-$edupng$)} where $c$-$edupng$ is private primary; similarly for $c$-$edup2$, $c$-$edus$ and $c$-$edut$. |
| $c \in C$ | commodities | $c, c' \in MCHDC$ | human development service $c$ is aggregated to $c'$ |
| $c \in CEDU$ ($\subset C$) | education services = {$c$-$edup$ = primary cycle; $c$-$edus$ = secondary cycle; $c$-$edut$ = tertiary cycle}; may include both private and public education | $c, c' \in MCM$ | mapping between aggregate (CMDG) and disaggregated MDG service commodities (CHLTH and CWTSN) = {$c$-$hlt$.($c$-$hlt1g$, $c$-$hlt2g$, $c$-$hlt3g$, $c$-$hlt1ng$, $c$-$hlt2ng$, $c$-$hlt3ng$)} and {$c$-$wtsn$.($c$-$wtsn$)} |
| $c \in CEDUP$ ($\subset C$) | primary education services = {$c$-$edup$} | $mdg \in MDG$ | selected MDG indicators = {$mdg2$, $mdg4$, $mdg5$, $mdg7w$, $mdg7s$} |

| Set | Description |
|---|---|
| $c \in CEDUT$ ($\subset C$) | tertiary education services = {c-edut} |
| $c \in CHLTH$ ($\subset C$) | health services (public) = {c-hlt1g = low-tech; c-hlt2g = medium-tech; c-hlt3g = high-tech}; corresponding private health services labeled with "ng" |
| $cmdg \in CMDG$ | aggregate MDG (non-education) service commodities = {c-hlt = aggregate health in MDG functions, not in C; c-wtsn = water–sanitation services} |
| $c \in CWTSN$ ($\subset C$) | water–sanitation service commodities {c-wtsn = water–sanitation services} |
| $eduarg \in EDUARG$ | arguments in constant-elasticity function for educational behavior = {edu-qual = quantity of services per student; w-prem = skilled–unskilled wage ratio; w-prem2 = superskilled–skilled wage ratio; mdg4 = under-5 mortality rate; fcapinf = infrastructure capital stocks; qhpc = per capita household consumption} |
| $f \in FEXOG$ | factors with exogenous growth |
| $c, b, t', t \in MCYC$ | MDG2 in $t$ is defined as the product over selected combinations of $b$ and $t'$ (where $t' \in T11$) = {prom, neting1} |
| $mdg \in MDGSTD$ | MDG indicators = {mdg4 = under-5 mortality rate; mdg5 = maternal mortality rate; mdg7w = access to safe water; mdg7s = access to basic sanitation} |
| $f, c \in MFC$ | mapping between labor types and cycles of education = {flab-n.(c-edup1, c-edup2); flab-s.(c-edus); flab-t.(c-edut)} |
| $c, g \in MCGLAB$ | students in cycle c, grade g are in labor force age |
| $c, g \in MCGLABENT$ | students in cycle c, grade g are in labor force entry age |
| $c, g \in MCGMAX$ | grade g is the last (maximum) grade in cycle c |

(Continued)

**Table 4.11** Sets for MDG and education module—cont'd

| | | |
|---|---|---|
| $f \in FLAB$ | labor factors {f-labn = less than 12 years of education; f-labs = 12–14 years of education (secondary education or 2 years of tertiary); f-labt = more than 14 years of education (at least 3 years of tertiary) | |
| | $c, g \in MCGMIN$ | grade $g$ is the first (minimum) grade in cycle $c$ |
| $g \in G$ | grade (in a cycle of schooling) | |
| | $mdgarg \in MDGARG$ | arguments in constant-elasticity function for MDGs = {cmdg = aggregate commodities; mdg = different MDGs; fcapinf = infrastructure capital stocks; hhdconspc = per capita household consumption} |
| $h \in H$ | households (excl. NGOs) = {h = the single household} | |
| | $t \in T$ | time periods |
| $i \in INSG$ | government institution | |
| | $t \in T11$ | time periods including preceding years for MDG2 calculation |

**Table 4.12** Parameters for MDG and education module

| | | | |
|---|---|---|---|
| $\alpha_{b,c}^{edu}$ | constant in logistic function for educational behavior | $ext_{b,c}^{edu}$ | maximum share for educational behavior $b$ in cycle $c$ |
| $\alpha_{b,c}^{educe}$ | constant in constant-elasticity function for educational behavior | $ext_{mdg}^{mdg}$ | maximum value for MDG 7w and 7s; minimum value for MDG 4 and 5 |
| $\alpha_{mdg}^{mdg}$ | constant in logistic function for MDG achievement | $grdcont_{c,c'}$ | 0—1 constant showing that for $c'$ next cycle is $c$ |
| $\alpha_{mdg}^{mdgce}$ | constant in constant-elasticity function for intermediate MDG variable | $pop_t^{g1}$ | population in age cohort entering grade 1 |
| $\alpha_c^{hd}$ | efficiency term in CES aggregation function for human development | $pop_t^{lab}$ | population of labor force age (often 15—64) |
| $\beta_{b,c}^{edu}$ | constant in logistic function for educational behavior | $pop_t^{labent}$ | population in age cohort entering labor force |
| $\beta_{mdg}^{log}$ | constant in logistic function for MDG achievement | $pop_t^{tot}$ | total population in $t$ |
| $\delta_{c,i}^{hd}$ | share parameter for human development CES function | $qenr_{c,g,t}^{newoth}$ | other new entrants to cycle $c$, grade $g$ |
| $\varphi_{b,c,eduarg}^{edu}$ | elasticity of behavior $b$ in cycle $c$ w.r.t. argument *eduarg* in educational constant-elasticity function | $shif_{i,f,t}^0$ | share of domestic institution $i$ in income of factor $f$ |
| $\varphi_{mdg,mdgarg}^{mdg}$ | elasticity of *mdg* w.r.t. argument *mdgarg* in constant-elasticity function for MDG | $demot_{c,c'}$ | 0—1 parameter showing that for dropouts from $c'$ the highest cycle is $c$ |
| $\gamma_{b,c}^{edu}$ | parameter in logistic function for education | $shr_{b,c}^{edu0}$ | base-year share for behavioral indicator behav in cycle $c$ |
| $\gamma_{mdg}^{mdg}$ | parameter in logistic function for non-education MDGs | $shr_{c,t}^{labent}$ | share of drop-outs and leavers in cycle $c$ that enter the labor force |
| $\rho_c^{hd}$ | exponent in CES aggregation function for human development | $shr_{f,t}^{labent2}$ | share of labor type $f$ of labor force entrants without education |
| $demot_{c,c'}$ | cycle $c$ is the cycle preceding $c'$ | $yrcyc_c$ | years in school cycle for each education cycle $c$ |
| $depr_{f,t}$ | depreciation rate for factor $f$ | | |

**Table 4.13** Variables for MDG and education module

| | | | |
|---|---|---|---|
| $EDUQUAL_{c,t}$ | educational quality in cycle $c$ in year $t$ | $QFACINS_{i,f,t}$ | endowment of labor type $f$ for institution $i$ in $t$ |
| $EG_t$ | government expenditures | $QH_{c,h,t}$ | consumption of commodity $c$ in $t$ by household $h$ |
| $INVVAL_{i,t}$ | investment value for institution $i$ | $QHA_{a,c,h,t}$ | quantity consumed of home commodity $c$ from activity $a$ by household $h$ |
| $MDGVAL_{mdg,t}$ | value for MDG indicator $mdg$ in $t$ | $QHPC_t$ | *per capita* household consumption in $t$ |
| $PQ_{c,t}$ | price of commodity $c$ in $t$ | $QQ_{c,t}$ | quantity of goods supplied to domestic market (composite supply) |
| $PXAC_{a,c,t}$ | price of commodity $c$ from activity $a$ | $SHR^{edu}_{b,c,t}$ | share of students in cycle $c$ with behavior $b$ in $t$ |
| $QENR_{c,t}$ | total number of students enrolled in cycle $c$ in year $t$ | $WF_{f,t}$ | economy-wide wage for factor $f$ in $t$ |
| $QENR^{old}_{c,t}$ | number of old students enrolled in cycle $c$ in year $t$ | $ZEDU_{b,c,t}$ | intermediate variable for educational outcome (defined by constant-elasticity function; entering logistic function) |
| $QENR^{new}_{c,t}$ | number of new students enrolled in cycle $c$ in year $t$ | $ZMDG_{mdg,t}$ | intermediate variable for standard MDGs (4—5—7w—7s) (defined by constant-elasticity function; entering logistic function) |

MAMS focuses on the MDGs that typically are most costly and have the greatest interactions with the rest of the economy: universal primary school completion (MDG 2; measured by the net primary completion rate), reduced under-5 and maternal mortality rates (MDG 4 and 5) and increased access to improved water sources and basic sanitation (part of MDG 7).[38] The poverty MDG (MDG 1) is not targeted given the absence of tools (in MAMS and in most real-world, developing-country contexts) that policy makers realistically could use to fine-tune poverty outcomes.

MDG outcomes depend on government and private sector provision of MDG-related services as well as demand conditions for those services. Table 4.15 lists the determinants that have been included in a typical country application of MAMS, identified on the basis of available evidence, preferably sector studies underpinned by

---

[38] Implicitly, when MDG 4 and 5 are achieved, the expansion in health services and other determinants may be sufficient to achieve MDG 6 (to halt and reverse the spread of HIV/AIDS, malaria and other diseases). MDG 3 (elimination of gender disparity in education and empowering women) was not addressed due to data issues. However, note that, if MDG 2 is achieved, gender equality is achieved in primary education.

**Table 4.14** Equations for MDG and education module

(4.67)
$$QHD_{c,i,t} = \sum_{c' \in C}\Bigg|_{\substack{(c,c') \in MCHDC \\ i \in INSG}} QG_{c',t} + \sum_{c' \in C}\Bigg|_{\substack{(c,c') \in MCHDC \\ i \in INSNGAGG}} (QQ_{c',t} - QG_{c',t})$$

$$\left[\begin{array}{l} demand\ for\ HD\ (MDG\ or\ educ) \\ service\ c\ by\ aggregate\ demander\ i \end{array}\right] = \left[\begin{array}{l} sum\ of\ gov\ and\ non-gov \\ demand\ for\ HD\ service \end{array}\right]$$

$c \in C$
$i \in I$
$t \in T$

Separation of human development (HD) services into government and non-government

(4.68)
$$QHDAGG_{c,t} = \alpha_c^{hd} \cdot \sum_{i \in INS} \left(\delta_{c,i}^{hd} \cdot QHD_{c,i,t}^{-\rho_c^{hd}}\right)^{-\frac{1}{\rho_c^{hd}}} \Bigg|_{c \in CHDCES}$$
$$+ \sum_{i \in INS} QHD_{c,t,g} \Bigg|_{c \in CHDPRFSUB}$$

$$\left[\begin{array}{l} aggregate\ demand\ for\ HD \\ (MDG\ or\ educ)\ service\ ac \end{array}\right] = \left[\begin{array}{l} aggregation\ of\ HD\ demand\ as\ imperfect\ substit- \\ utes\ (CES)\ or\ as\ perfect\ substitutes\ (summed) \end{array}\right]$$

$c \in C$
$i \in I$
$t \in T$

Aggregation of human development (HD) services (i.e. MDG and education)

(4.69)
$$QHPC_t = \frac{\sum_{c \in C}\sum_{h \in H} PQ_c^0 \cdot QH_{c,h,t} + \sum_{a \in A}\sum_{c \in C}\sum_{h \in H} PXAC_{a,c}^0 \cdot QHA_{a,c,h,t}}{pop_t^{tot}}$$

$$\left[\begin{array}{l} real\ household \\ consumption\ per\ capita \end{array}\right] = \left[\begin{array}{l} total\ household\ consumption\ at\ base- \\ year\ prices\ divided\ by\ total\ population \end{array}\right]$$

$t \in T$

Real household consumption per capita

*(Continued)*

**Table 4.14** Equations for MDG and education module—cont'd

(4.70)

$$EDUQUAL_{c,t} = \frac{QHDAGG_{c,t}}{\sum_{g \in G} QENR_{c,g,t}} \Big/ \frac{QHDAGG_t^0}{\sum_{g \in G} QENR_{c,g}^0}$$

$$\begin{bmatrix} \text{educational quality} \\ \text{in cycle } c \text{ in year } t \end{bmatrix} = \begin{bmatrix} \text{real services per student} \\ \text{in cycle } c \text{ in } t \end{bmatrix} \div \begin{bmatrix} \text{real services per student} \\ \text{in cycle } c \text{ in base} - \text{year} \end{bmatrix}$$

Educational quality

$c \in CEDU$
$t \in T$
$t > 1$

(4.71)

$$QENR_{c,g,t}^{old} = \sum_{g' \in G \,|\, (g,g') \in mgg2} SHR_{pass,c,t-1}^{edu} \cdot QENR_{c,g',t-1} + SHR_{rep,c,t-1}^{edu} \cdot QENR_{c,g,t-1}$$

$$\begin{bmatrix} \text{number old students} \\ \text{enrolled in cycle } c, \text{ grade } g \text{ in } t \end{bmatrix} =$$

$$\begin{bmatrix} \text{passers from preceding grade} \\ g' \text{ in the same cycle } c \text{ in } t-1 \end{bmatrix} + \begin{bmatrix} \text{repeaters from last year still} \\ \text{enrolled in cycle } c, \text{ grade } g \end{bmatrix}$$

Old enrolled students

$c \in CEDU$
$g \in G$
$t \in T$
$t > 1$

(4.72)

$$QENR_{c,g,t}^{new} = SHR_{neting1,c,t-1}^{edu} \cdot pop_t^{g1} \Big|_{\substack{(c,g) \in mgmin \\ c \in CEDUP}} + qenr_{c,g,t}^{newoth}$$

$$+ \sum_{c' \in C} SHR_{cont,c,t-1}^{edu} \cdot grdcont_{t,c'} \cdot SHR_{prom,c',t-1}^{edu} \cdot \sum_{g' \in G \,|\, (c',g') \in mgcmax} QENR_{c',g,t-1} \Big|_{\substack{(c,g) \in mgmin \\ c \notin CEDUP}}$$

$$\begin{bmatrix} \text{number of new students} \\ \text{enrolled in cycle } c, \text{ grade } g \text{ in } t \end{bmatrix} =$$

$$\begin{bmatrix} \text{(cohort) students entering} \\ \text{cycle } c \ (c = primary), \text{ grade } 1 \end{bmatrix} + \begin{bmatrix} \text{(non-cohort) students from outside} \\ \text{school system entering cycle } c, \text{ grade } g \end{bmatrix}$$

$$+ \begin{bmatrix} \text{enrolled in last grade } g \text{ in preceding (non-primary)} \\ \text{cycle } c' \text{ in } t-1 \text{ who were promoted and entered first grade of } c \end{bmatrix}$$

New enrolled students

$c \in$
$CEDU$
$g \in G$
$t \in T$
$t > 1$

(4.73)

$$QENR_{c,g,t} = QENR_{c,g,t}^{old} + QENR_{c,g,t}^{new}$$

$$\begin{bmatrix} \text{total number enrolled} \\ \text{in cycle } c, \text{ grade } g \text{ in } t \end{bmatrix} = \begin{bmatrix} \text{enrolled old students} \\ \text{in cycle } c, \text{ grade } g \text{ in } t \end{bmatrix} + \begin{bmatrix} \text{enrolled new students} \\ \text{in cycle } c, \text{ grade } g \text{ in } t \end{bmatrix}$$

$c \in CEDU$

$g \in G$

$t \in T$

$t > 1$

Total enrollment

(4.74)

$$SHR_{b,c,t}^{edu} = ext_{b,c}^{edu} + \frac{\alpha_{b,c}^{edu}}{1 + EXP(\gamma_{b,c}^{edu} + \beta_{b,c}^{edu} \cdot ZEDU_{b,c,t})}$$

$$\begin{bmatrix} \text{student share with} \\ \text{behavior } b \text{ in cycle } c \end{bmatrix} = \begin{bmatrix} \text{logistic function of intermediate} \\ \text{behavior variable}(ZEDU_{b,c,t}) \end{bmatrix}$$

$b \in BLOG$

$c \in CEDU$

$t \in T$

Student behavior (logistic function)

(4.75)

$$ZEDU_{b,c,t} = \alpha_{b,c}^{educ} \cdot (EDUQUAL_{c,t})^{\varphi_{b,c,edu-qual}^{edu}}$$

$$\cdot \left(\frac{WF_{f-labt,t}}{WF_{f-labn,t}}\right)^{\varphi_{b,c,w-prem}^{edu}} \cdot \left(\frac{WF_{f-labt,t}}{WF_{f-labs,t}}\right)^{\varphi_{b,c,w-prem}^{edu}} \cdot MDGVAL_{mdg4,t}^{\varphi_{b,c,mdg4}^{edu}}$$

$$\cdot \prod_{f \in FCAPGOVINF} \left(\sum_{i \in INS} QFINS_{i,f,t}\right)^{\varphi_{b,c,f}^{edu}} \cdot QHPC_t^{\varphi_{b,c,qhpc}^{edu}}$$

$$\begin{bmatrix} \text{intermediate variable for student} \\ \text{share with behavior } b \text{ in cycle } c \end{bmatrix}$$

$$= \begin{bmatrix} \text{exogenous} \\ \text{trend value} \end{bmatrix} \cdot \begin{bmatrix} \text{influence of}: \text{ education quality (service per student);} \\ \text{wage premia (for } c \leq \text{ secondary and } c \geq \text{ tertiary, respectively);} \\ \text{student health (proxied by MDG4); of infrastructure; and per capita house} \end{bmatrix}$$

$b \in BLOG$

$c \in C$

$t \in T$

Student behavior (constant-elasticity function defining intermediate variable)

*(Continued)*

**Table 4.14** Equations for MDG and education module—cont'd

(4.76)

$$SHR_{b,c,t}^{edu} = \left(1 - \sum_{\substack{b' \in BLOG \\ (b,b') \in MBB}} SHR_{b',c,t}^{edu}\right) \cdot \frac{SHR_{b,c}^{edu0}}{\sum_{\substack{b' \in BRES \\ (b,b') \in MBB2}} SHR_{b',c}^{edu0}}$$

$$\begin{bmatrix} student\ share \\ with\ behavior \\ b\ in\ cycle\ c \end{bmatrix} = \begin{bmatrix} residual\ value\ (1\ less\ sum \\ of\ shares\ for\ related \\ elements\ in\ BLOG) \end{bmatrix} \cdot \begin{bmatrix} initial\ share\ of\ b\ in \\ total\ shares\ for\ related \\ residual\ elements \end{bmatrix}$$

$b \in BRES$
$c \in CEDU$
$t \in T$

Student behavior (defined residually, given left-hand side of the logistic function for education)

(4.77)

$$MDGVAL_{mdg2,t} = SHR_{neting1,cedup,t}^{edu} \cdot SHR_{prom1,cedup,t}^{edu} \cdot ytcy_{cedup}$$

$$\begin{bmatrix} primary\ school \\ net\ completion\ rate \end{bmatrix} = \begin{bmatrix} product\ of\ current\ primary\ rates \\ of\ net\ intake\ and\ promotion \end{bmatrix}$$

$t \in T$

MDG 2

(4.78)

$$labpartrat_t = \frac{\sum_{i \in INS} QFINS_{i,f,t}}{\substack{f \in FLAB \\ pop_t^{lab} - \sum_{c \in CEDU} \sum_{\substack{(c,g) \in \\ moglab}}^{g \in G} QENR_{c,g,t}}}$$

$$\begin{bmatrix} labor\ force \\ participation\ rate \end{bmatrix} = \frac{[labor\ force]}{[population\ in\ labor\ force\ age - enrollment\ in\ labor\ force\ age]}$$

$t \in T$
$t > 1$

Labor force participation rate

Labor supply

$i \in INS$
$f \in FLAB$
$t \in T$
$t > 1$

(4.79)

$$QFINS_{i,f,t} = shif^{0}_{i,f,t}$$

[endowment of labor type $f$ for institution $i$ in $t$] = [share of $i$ in labor type $f$]

$$\cdot \left\{ (1 - depr_{f,t-1} \cdot QFLABADJ_t) \cdot \sum_{i \in INS} QFINS_{i,f,t-1} \right.$$

$$\cdot \left\{ [non - retired\ labor\ from\ previous\ year] \right.$$

$$+ \sum_{\substack{c,c' \in C \mid (f,c) \in MFC \\ c' \notin CEDUT}} demot_{c,c'} \cdot shr^{labent}_{c,t}$$

$$\cdot SHR^{edu}_{gdexit,c',t-1} \cdot \sum_{\substack{c \in C \mid (c,g) \in \\ mgmax}} SHR^{edu}_{prom,c,t-1} \cdot QENR_{c,g,t-1}$$

$$+ \left[ \begin{array}{l} enrolled\ in\ non\text{-}tertiary\ cycle\ in\ t-1\ who\ were\ promoted\ from \\ their\ last\ grade,\ exit\ the\ school\ system,\ and\ enter\ labor\ force\ in\ t \end{array} \right]$$

$$+ \sum_{\substack{c \in C \mid (f,c) \in MFC \\ c \in CEDUT}} demot_{c,c'} \cdot shr^{labent}_{c',t} \cdot \sum_{\substack{c \in C \mid (c,g) \in \\ mgmax}} SHR^{edu}_{prom,c,t-1} \cdot QENR_{c,g,t-1}$$

$$+ [enrolled\ in\ tertiary\ cycle\ in\ t-1,\ who\ graduate\ and\ enter\ the\ labor\ force\ in\ t]$$

$$+ \sum_{\substack{c \in C \mid (f,c) \\ \in MFC}} demot_{c,c'} \cdot shr^{labent}_{c',t} \cdot \sum_{\substack{g \in G \mid (c',g) \in \\ mgdab}} SHR^{edu}_{dropout,c',t-1} \cdot QENR_{c',g,t-1}$$

$$+ [enrolled\ in\ school\ in\ t-1,\ who\ drop\ out\ and\ enter\ labor\ force\ in\ t\ at\ next\ lower\ level\ c]$$

$$+ shr^{labent2}_{f,t} \cdot \left( pop^{labent}_t - \sum_{c \in CEDU} \sum_{\substack{g \in GRD \mid (c,g) \in \\ mgdlabent}} QENR_{c,g,t} \right)$$

$$+ [entrants\ from\ outside\ educational\ system\ who\ are\ of\ labor - force\ age] \}$$

(Continued)

**Table 4.14** Equations for MDG and education module—cont'd

(4.80)
$$MDGVAL_{mdg,t} = ext_{mdg}^{mdg} + \frac{\alpha_{mdg}^{mdg}}{1 + EXP(\gamma_{mdg}^{mdg} + \beta_{mdg}^{mdg}\, ZMDG_{mdg,t})}$$

$$\begin{bmatrix} MDG \\ value \end{bmatrix} = \begin{bmatrix} logistic\ function\ of\ intermediate \\ MDG\ value(ZMDG_{mdg,t}) \end{bmatrix}$$

$mdg \in MDGSTD$

$t \in T$

MDG 4, 5, 7w and 7s (logistic function)

(4.81)
$$ZMDG_{mdg,t} = \alpha_{mdg}^{mdgce} \cdot \prod_{\substack{cmdg \in \\ CMDG}} \left( \sum_{\substack{c \in C\,|\,(cmdg,c) \\ \in MCM}} \frac{QQ_{c,t}}{pop_t^{tot}} \right)^{\varphi_{mdg,cmdg}^{m}}$$

$$\cdot \prod_{\substack{f \in \\ FCAPGOVINF}} \left( \sum_{i \in INS} QFINS_{i,f,t} \right)^{\varphi_{mdg,f}^{m}}$$

$$\cdot \left( \prod_{\substack{mdg \in \\ MDGSTD}} MDGVAL_{mdg,t}^{\varphi_{mdg,mdg'}^{m}} \right) \cdot QHPC_t^{\varphi_{mdg,hhconpc}^{m}}$$

$$\begin{bmatrix} intermediate \\ variable\ for \\ MDG\ 4\ and\ 5 \end{bmatrix} = \begin{bmatrix} exogenous \\ parameter \end{bmatrix} \cdot \begin{bmatrix} influence\ of:\ real\ value\ for\ services \\ per\ capita;\ level\ of\ infrastructure; \\ water\ and\ sanitation\ MDGs; \\ household\ consumption\ per\ capita \end{bmatrix}$$

$mdg \in MDGSTD$

$t \in T$

MDG 4, 5, 7w and 7s (constant-elasticity function defining intermediate variable)

**Table 4.15** Determinants of non-poverty MDGs

| MDG | Service delivery | Household consumption *per capita* | Wage incentives | Public infrastructure | Other MDGs |
|---|---|---|---|---|---|
| 2: Primary education | × | × | × | × | 4 |
| 4: Under-5 mortality | × | × | | × | 7w, 7s |
| 5: Maternal mortality | × | × | | × | 7w, 7s |
| 7w: Access to safe water | × | × | | × | |
| 7s: Access to basic sanitation | × | × | | × | |

econometric analysis and subject to the constraints of an economy-wide model like MAMS (including the fact that it is difficult to include finely disaggregated actions, like increasing coverage of certain types of vaccinations).[39] Beyond *per capita* real service delivery (either public or a combination of public and private), the determinants include other MDGs (e.g. better access to water and sanitation may improve health outcomes — MDG 4 and 5), as well as public infrastructure, *per capita* household consumption and wage incentives (through the ratio of labor wages of different educational levels). Other determinants should be added when evidence suggests that the effect is significant during the time frame of the analysis. One possible candidate is the impact of education on health, which may be important in long-run analyses if the educational status of the population changes significantly. The MDG and education functions may be seen as "production functions" with inputs at a level of aggregation that is similar to other parts of a typical MAMS database; while this is convenient considering the objective of applying MAMS in settings without more detailed information, it means that MAMS is not a substitute for disaggregated analysis of human development policies, which often would have to consider more additional determinants.

In the equations of this module, the treatment of the education MDG (2) is separate from the treatment for the remaining MDGs (4, 5, 7w and 7s) since, rather than targeting

---

[39] Econometric analysis for several countries in Latin America show that the relationships between the determinants and the non-poverty MDGs in the MAMS model tend to hold from a statistical point of view. Kamaly (2006) provides examples of the literature on health and education whose findings, although sometimes contradictory, show broad support also in sub-Saharan Africa for the inclusion of the determinants referred to in Table 4.15. Lofgren (2010) reviews the cross-country literature on MDG and education determinants.

MDG 2 directly, the model defines (and may target) specific educational behavioral outcomes that jointly determine the value for MDG 2.

### 4.4.2.1 Definitions for the MDG and education block

The first three equations define arguments that enter both education and MDG functions. Equations (4.67) and (4.68) in Table 4.14 define aggregate human development services (which include both MDG and education services). For each service type, Equation (4.67) separates demand into two aggregates — government and non-government, according to who is paying for the service. Typically, services paid for by the government (non-government) are also supplied by a government (non-government) activity, but this is not necessarily the case. Equation (4.68) generates an economy-wide aggregate (which below is fed into the determination of MDG and education outcomes), permitting two alternative assumptions: services paid for by government and non-government are perfect substitutes (simply summed) or imperfect substitutes (according to a CES function). Equation (4.69) defines average real household consumption *per capita* ($QHPC_t$) as total household consumption (both marketed and home commodities) at base-year prices divided by total population.

### 4.4.2.2 Education block

The educational component consists of Equations (4.70)–(4.79) in Table 4.14. It is disaggregated by cycle (with three cycles as a typical level of disaggregation). For each cycle, educational quality ($EDUQUAL_{c,t}$) is defined as the ratio between real services per student (aggregated services divided by total enrolment) in the current year and in the base year, i.e. in the base year, educational quality is indexed to one, Equation (4.70).

Within any cycle, the model endogenizes the following aspects of student behavior (or outcomes):

- The shares of the enrolled that are promoted from their current grade, drop out or repeat the grade next year (referred to as *prom*, *dropout* and *rep*). The sum of these shares is unity, i.e. during the school year, a student must either be promoted, drop out or become a repeater (this applies to each grade and for each cycle as a whole). Note that the term "*prom*" throughout this paper and the model refers both to students who successfully complete a grade and continue to a higher grade within the cycle and to students who successfully finish the last year of a given education cycle (and thus graduate).
- The shares among the promotees from their current grade (*prom*) who graduate from their current cycle (*grdcyc*) or continue to a higher grade within this cycle (*contcyc*). In terms of shares: *grdcyc* + *contcyc* = *prom*.
- The shares among cycle graduates who exit the school system (*grdexit*) or continue to next cycle (*grdcont*). The sum of these shares is also unity. For graduates from the last cycle, the share of those who exit is unity.
- The share of the cohort of the first year in primary school that enters school (*neting1*).

Drawing on the above information, we can define the number of enrolled students by cycle, grade and year. Note that, as a simplification, the rates of promotion, dropout and repetition are not grade-specific, but averages at the level of each cycle. Equation (4.71) defines the number of "old" enrolled students (i.e. those who were enrolled in the same cycle last year) as the sum of those who: (i) Continue within the cycle after successful completion of an earlier grade and (ii) repeat the grade they were in last year. The number of "new" enrolled students is defined in Equation (4.72) as the sum of (i) cohort entrants (only for the first primary cycle), (ii) other, non-cohort entrants entering any cycle in the educational system and (iii) graduates from the relevant earlier cycle last year who chose to continue.[40] The total number of enrolled students by cycle, grade and year is the sum of old and new students, Equation (4.73).

Equations (4.74)—(4.78) model the share variables that identify different aspects of student behavior. For each cycle, a logistic function, Equation (4.74) defines $SHR^{edu}_{b,c,t}$, the shares for first year in-cohort entry, for promotees from the current grade and for promotees from the last grade who decide to continue to next cycle (i.e. *neting1*, *prom* and *grdcont*, the elements of the set *BLOG*).[41] The logistic form was selected since it makes it possible to impose extreme values for the function (e.g. for education it is a maximum of one — representing 100%) and to incorporate extraneous information about elasticities and conditions under which target values are achieved. Another advantage is that it allows for segments of increasing and decreasing marginal returns to improvements in the determinants of educational behavior. The only endogenous variable in the logistic function ($ZEDU_{c,d,t}$), is defined in a constant-elasticity function, Equation (4.75) as determined by: (i) Educational quality, (ii) wage incentives, defined as relative wage gains from continued schooling (i.e. the relative wage gain that students can achieve if they complete a cycle that is sufficiently high to enable them to climb to the next higher level in the labor market), (iii) the under-5 mortality rate (a proxy for the health status of the school population); (iv) the size of the infrastructure capital stock, and (v) household consumption *per capita*.[42] Figure 4.2 illustrates the logistic functional form

---

[40] This category includes non-cohort entrants to the first primary year of primary school (who may represent a significant number during a transitional period of primary school expansion). It may also include immigrants from other countries.

[41] The $\alpha$ and $\beta$ parameters in the logistic functions, Equations (4.74) and (4.80) are calibrated so that: (i) Under base-year conditions, the left-hand side variables (showing student behavior shares or MDG values) will replicate base-year values and (ii) under conditions for achieving target values for MDG and education indicators derived from supporting studies, the left-hand side variables will take on values indicative of or compatible with reaching these targets.

[42] In the computer program, Equations (4.75) and (4.81) (constant-elasticity functions defining intermediate variables for educational behavior or MDG achievement) are more complex in two respects: (i) The terms that are raised to exponents, which represent elasticities, are all divided by base-year values. This formulation was preferred given our desire to simulate scenarios with changes in elasticities but without any changes in simulated base-year values for left-hand-side variables. (ii) For the element *grdcont* ∈ *BLOG*, the decision to continue to the next education cycle depends on the values for the right-hand side variables that correspond to the next cycle.

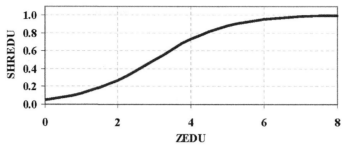

**Figure 4.2** Logistic function for education.

for education. The observed base-year value for $SHR_{b,c,t}^{edu}$ is generated at the base-year value for $ZEDU_{c,d,t}$. The parameters of the function have to be defined such that the maximum share is one, the base-year elasticities of $SHR_{b,c,t}^{edu}$ with respect to each determinants of $ZEDU_{c,d,t}$ is replicated and, under values for the determinants of $ZEDU_{c,d,t}$ identified in the database, a target level for $SHR_{b,c,t}^{edu}$ is realized. In terms of the algebra, the parameters in Equations (4.74) and (4.75) are selected as follows:

- The parameter $ext_{b,c}^{edu}$ shows the extreme (maximum) value (here unity) to which the behavior share should converge as the value of the intermediate variable approaches infinity.
- The parameter $\alpha_{b,c}^{edu}$ is calibrated so that, under base-year conditions, the behavioral share replicates the base-year value.
- The parameters $\beta_{b,c}^{edu}$ and $\varphi_{b,c,ac}^{edu}$ are calibrated so that the two equations: (i) Replicate the base-year elasticities of the behavioral share ($SHR_{b,c,t}^{edu}$) with respect to the arguments of the constant-elasticity function and (ii) achieve a behavioral target (e.g. a share very close to one for *neting1*, the share of the relevant age cohort that enters first grade) under a set of values for the arguments of the constant-elasticity function that have been identified by other studies.
- The value of the parameter $\gamma_{b,c}^{edu}$ determines how the base-year point on the logistic function is positioned relative to the inflection point (where the curve switches from increasing to decreasing marginal returns as the determinants of educational behavior improve).

Equation (4.75) is calibrated so that, in the base year (under base-year conditions), $ZEDU_{b,c,t} = SHR_{b,c}^{edu0}$; note that the left-hand-side term enters the denominator of the second term in Equation (4.74).

Drawing on the shares defined in the preceding equations, the shares for repeaters, dropouts and cycle graduates exiting from the school system (*rep, dropout* and *grdexit*; elements in the set *BRES*) are defined residually, Equation (4.76). The formulation considers the fact that, as noted above, selected shares have to sum to unity. If more than one variable in *BRES* has to be adjusted in relation to one or more elements in *BLOG* (as is the case for the adjustment of shares for repeaters and dropouts in response to changes in the share of promotes), then all adjusted variables are scaled up or down by the same factor.[43]

Alternative indicators may be used to define MDG 2. It is here, Equation (4.77) defined as the net completion rate expressed as a period measure, i.e. the share of the population that enters the first primary grade in the current year that would graduate on time given the current rates of net entry (*neting1*) and promotion (*prom*), i.e. the measure uses current rates assuming that the rate of promotion of the current year prevails throughout their primary cycle (typically the current year and five more years).[44,45]

The labor force participation rate is defined as the labor force ($QFINS_{i,f,t}$) divided by the population in labor force age that is not enrolled in secondary and tertiary cycles, Equation (4.78).[46] Institutional labor endowments ($QFINS_{i,f,t}$ for labor) are defined as the sum of the following components, Equation (4.79): (i) Remaining labor from the preceding year, (ii) new labor force entrants among students who exited from the school system in the previous year (with separate terms for non-tertiary graduates, tertiary graduates and dropouts) and (iii) new labor force entrants from the non-student population who reach the age at which they, to the extent that they seek work, become part of the labor force. Depending on their highest completed grade, the new labor force entrants are allocated to a specific labor category.

### 4.4.2.13 Non-education MDG block

The treatment underlying MDG 4, 5, 7w and 7s is similar but less complex. For these, a logistic function directly defines the MDG indicators as a function of an intermediate variable that is defined in a related constant-elasticity function, see Table 4.14; Equations (4.80) and (4.81). The values for the parameters $ext_{mdg}^{mdg}$, $\alpha_{mdg}^{mdg}$, $\beta_{mdg}^{mdg}$ and $\varphi_{mdg,ac}^{mdg}$ are defined following the same principles as the corresponding parameters in the logistic and constant-elasticity functions for education. The arguments of the constant-elasticity function are similar except for that the relevant service supply is expressed in *per capita* form (not per enrolled student).

---

[43] The equation is formulated so that it works for cases with one or more than one term in any of the sums over related shares (defined by the mappings *MBB* and *MBB2*) in either of the sets *BRES* and *BLOG*.

[44] Given that we do not generate separate promotion rates for students in the relevant cohort (as opposed to students outside this cohort), we assume that the rates for in-cohort students are identical to the over-all rates for students in the cycle. In order to get a rate of 100%, the rates of net intake and promotion must both be 100%. In other words, in order for 100% of the cohort to complete the primary cycle on time, it is necessary that all of them enter at the time of their first year and then that all manage to pass each year (i.e. successfully complete each grade) up to the final year of the cycle.

[45] Many MAMS applications have used a cohort variant of the net completion rate, i.e. the share of the population of theoretical primary graduation age that graduates in the current year. This is more data-demanding — assuming a six-year cycle, it requires information about the net intake rate six years earlier and the promotion rates in each year since then.

[46] It is assumed that, as an acceptable approximation, students in secondary and above are in labor force age. If not, this definition should be adjusted.

### 4.4.3 Poverty module and alternative approaches

Poverty and inequality indicators can be computed on the basis of MAMS simulation results either through the built-in MAMS poverty module or through microsimulation modeling. The MAMS poverty module offers a choice between the following approaches, each of which is linked to the representative households (one or more) that are included in any application database and may use either household income or consumption as its welfare measure:[47]

**(i)** Constant elasticity of poverty with respect to *per capita* welfare for each model household.[48]

**(ii)** Log-normal distribution of *per capita* welfare within each model household.

**(iii)** Distribution of *per capita* welfare within each model household follows a real-world household survey.

Under (i), the poverty module computes the headcount poverty rate; under (ii) and (iii) it also computes the poverty gap, the squared poverty gap and the Gini coefficient.

As described in Section 4.5, if approach (i) or (ii) is selected, then the analyst has to provide data for each model household (or for an aggregation of model households); if approach (iii) is selected, microdata from a household survey is also needed. In all three cases, the change in *per capita* welfare (household income or consumption) derived from MAMS is used as an input (the "linking aggregate variable") in the module that computes poverty and inequality indicators. In case (i), the constant growth elasticity of poverty approach, the change in welfare *per capita* for each model household is used to estimate the change in the corresponding and national poverty rates. In case (ii), the log-normal approach, a synthetic household survey is generated based on a log-normal distribution with mean and standard deviation derived from the user-supplied data. Once the synthetic household survey is generated, poverty and inequality computations follow an "arithmetic microsimulation" computation in which changes in welfare *per capita* of each model household are used to estimate the counterfactual distribution of *per capita* welfare. Then, poverty and inequality indicators are easily computed. Case (iii), the real-world household survey approach, applies the second and third steps of the approach in case (ii) to microdata from a household survey.

The MAMS poverty module has the advantage of quickly generating poverty and inequality results that are fully integrated with the MAMS simulations. Among its three built-in approaches, the first, a growth elasticity of poverty, is by far the simplest but also most likely to be misleading; empirically, it is unlikely that the poverty elasticity of growth remains constant if *per capita* welfare changes significantly

---

[47] For a discussion of the representative household approach, see Lofgren *et al.* (2003) and Agénor *et al.* (2004).

[48] The use of other distributions (like the $\beta$ distribution) seems less compelling since they are dominated by the survey approach and require econometric estimation.

(see, e.g. Bourguignon, 2003).[49] The remaining two approaches — (ii) and (iii) — are both based on the assumption that the distribution of welfare within the population represented by each model household does not change over time. Whether this assumption detracts from the empirical value of the analysis may depend on the disaggregation of the MAMS database, especially income sources and households; disaggregation into multiple households that are homogeneous in terms of the income sources of the database may be preferable. Whether this assumption represents a drawback may also depend on whether it is reasonably well understood how within-group distributions are likely to change; if it is not well understood, then the assumption of an unchanging distribution may be appropriate. Among approaches (ii) and (iii), the latter may be preferred since the assumption reflects the observed distribution of each household group; however, it is more data-intensive and computations may be more time-consuming (depending on survey size). The second alternative, a log-normal distribution, demands less data and computation time. It is widely accepted that it provides a good approximation for within-country income and consumption distributions (Bourguignon, 2003; Easterly, 2009); however, for any model household, it is dominated by the third approach.

Alternatively, poverty and inequality results can be generated using a microsimulation model (see Bourguignon *et al.*, 2008; Bussolo and Cockburn, 2010), either top-down, feeding CGE simulation results to a separate household model, or integrated, with the household model built directly into MAMS. In addition, the top-down approach may either use microsimulations based on randomized allocation (simpler) or based on econometric analysis to determine wages and/or sector of work. For example, the microsimulation methodology described in Vos and Sanchez (2010), which is based on randomized allocation, has been used in conjunction with MAMS in a large number of applications (see Section 4.7). The use of a microsimulation model has the advantage of relying on less restrictive assumptions but adds further complexity and is more demanding in terms of data and computation time. The empirical gain from using microsimulation analysis may critically depend on the extent to which the disaggregation of income sources in the micro database matches that of the CGE model.

## 4.5 MAMS DATABASE

As noted, for each application, the bulk of the MAMS database resides in one or two Excel files; one includes data needed both for the core and MDG versions and a second

---

[49] As noted by Easterly (2009, pp. 28—29): (i) Empirical cross-country analysis indicates that the higher the initial poverty rate, the lower the poverty elasticity of growth and (ii) the absolute value of the simulated poverty-elasticity of growth with a log-normal distribution is inversely related to the initial poverty rate and positively related to *per capita* income.

file data that only is needed for the MDG version.[50] The size of the database of a MAMS application varies widely, not only depending on model version (core or MDG), but also on the extent to which the database is disaggregated. In this section we will briefly survey the data requirements and highlight key steps and procedures involved in constructing the database.[51]

### 4.5.1 Data requirements

#### *4.5.1.1 SAM*

The basic accounting structure and much of the underlying data of MAMS, like other CGE models, is derived from a SAM; unless the database imposes aggregation of selected SAM accounts, the model will follow the disaggregation of the SAM.[52] Most features of a SAM for MAMS are familiar from SAMs used for other models. However, a MAMS SAM has some unconventional features related to the explicit treatment of financial flows and, for the MDG version of MAMS, a relatively detailed disaggregation of sectors (activities and commodities; government and, often, non-government) for MDG- and education-related services. Table 4.16 shows a stylized and aggregated version of a SAM designed for MAMS. Table 4.17 shows the notation that is used.[53]

As in a typical SAM, the activity accounts represent the entities that carry out production, allocating sales receipts to intermediates, factors (value-added) and (indirect) taxes. The commodities are activity outputs, either exported or sold domestically and imports. The row entries of the commodity accounts represent payments from commodity demanders; the column entries show payments to the suppliers and indirect taxes (tariffs on imports and/or a sales tax on domestic sales irrespective of whether the commodity is of foreign or domestic origin). For the MDG version of MAMS, the accounts for the government activity and commodity are disaggregated by function, matching the requirements for the analysis of the MDGs and the educational system. In

---

[50] In addition, MAMS simulations (other than the reference simulation) are defined in a third Excel file; it is not discussed here, but could also be considered as part of the database.

[51] The MAMS User Guide (Lofgren, 2011) provides a detailed explanation of the data required and suggests procedure for generating required data.

[52] For background on SAMs, see, e.g. Round (2003) and Pyatt and Round (1985).

[53] The SAMs in applied databases are more disaggregated. For the core version of MAMS, the only *required* change in the SAM of Table 4.16 is the disaggregation of the tax account into separate accounts for direct, import, export, value-added and other domestic indirect taxes (of course, in some of the applications, some of these tax types may not exist). For the MDG version of MAMS, the accounts for government activities, commodities and investment accounts are split by government function. Irrespective of model version, the SAM (and MAMS) may also include accounts and entries representing home consumption and transactions costs of commodity marketing (disaggregated into importation, exportation and domestic sales). For details, see Lofgren *et al.* (2002, pp. 3–7). In the SAM, any activity may sell (and produce) multiple commodities while any commodity may be sold by multiple activities.

**Table 4.16** Stylized macro SAM for MAMS

| | act-prv | act-gov | com-prv | com-gov | f-lab | f-capprv | hhd | gov | row | taxes | interest | cap-hhd | cap-gov | cap-row | inv-prv | inv-gov | dstk | Total |
|---|---|---|---|---|---|---|---|---|---|---|---|---|---|---|---|---|---|---|
| act-prv | | | output | | | | | | | | | | | | | | | |
| act-gov | | | | output | | | | | | | | | | | | | | |
| com-prv | interm | interm | | | | | cons | | exports | | | | | | inv | inv | dstk | |
| com-gov | | | | | | | | cons | | | | | | | | | | |
| f-lab | va | va | | | | | | | | | | | | | | | | |
| f-capprv | va | | | | | | | | yrow | | | | | | | | | |
| hhd | | | | | va | va | | trnfr | trnfr | | int-dom | | | | | | | |
| gov | | | | | | va | trnfr | | trnfr | taxes | | | | | | | | |
| row | | | imports | | | va | trnfr | trnfr | | | int-row | | | | | | | |
| taxes | | | taxes | | | | taxes | | | | | | | | | | | |
| int-dom | | | | | | | | int-dom | | | | | | | | | | |
| int-row | | | | | | | int-row | int-row | | | | | | | | | | |
| cap-hhd | | | | | | | sav | | | | | | | | | | | |
| cap-gov | | | | | | | | sav | | | | bor | | bor | | | | |
| cap-row | | | | | | | | | sav | | | | | | | | | |
| inv-prv | | | | | | | | | | | | inv | | inv | | | | |
| inv-gov | | | | | | | | | | | | | inv | | | | | |
| dstk | | | | | | | | | | | | dstk | | | | | | |
| Total | | | | | | | | | | | | | | | | | | |

**Table 4.17** Accounts and cell entries in stylized macro SAM for MAMS

| Account | Explanation | Cell entry | Explanation |
|---|---|---|---|
| act-prv | Activity—private production | bor | Borrowing |
| act-gov | Activity—government production | cons | Consumption |
| com-prv | Commodity—private production | dstk | Stock change |
| com-gov | Commodity—government production | exports | Exports |
| f-lab | Factor—labor | imports | Imports |
| f-capprv | Factor—private capital | int-dom | Interest on domestic government debt |
| hhd | Household | int-row | Interest on foreign debt |
| gov | Government | interm | Intermediate inputs |
| row | Rest of world | inv | Investment (gross fixed capital formation) |
| taxes | Taxes—domestic and trade | output | Production |
| int-dom | Interest on domestic debt | sav | Savings |
| int-row | Interest on foreign debt | taxes | Taxes (direct and indirect) |
| cap-hhd | Capital account—household | trnsfr | Transfers |
| cap-gov | Capital account—government | va | Value added |
| cap-row | Capital account—rest of world | yrow | Factor income from rest of world |
| inv-prv | Investment—private capital | | |
| inv-gov | Investment—government capital | | |
| dstk | Stock change | | |

particular, these government accounts usually include: primary, secondary and tertiary education; health; water and sanitation; infrastructure (one or more); and other government. The accounts for the non-government activity and commodity are flexible, depending on the purpose of the analysis and data availability and when relevant often include MDG- and education-related sectors.

The row entries of the factor accounts in the SAM indicate that they earn value-added from domestic production activities and, for private capital, income from the rest of the world (this is less common for labor since it only applies to income from abroad for workers resident in the country of the SAM). In the factor columns, value-added is distributed to the owners of the factors.[54] The MDG version requires

---

[54] In addition to the current entries, it is not uncommon that the government owns part of private capital and earns part of its value-added.

labor to be disaggregated by educational achievement, typically into three segments with the following achievements: less than completed secondary, completed secondary, completed tertiary. MAMS is designed to have a single factor (and SAM account) for private capital (i.e. capital used in activities that are not part of the functions of the general government).[55] MAMS includes one type of government capital per government activity (i.e. the activities that are part of the functions of the general government). However, typically, government capital does not earn value-added and, given this, it is not represented in the SAM. Lastly, the SAM may also include other optional factors, such as land or other natural resources.

The SAM includes three institutions: household, government and rest of world.[56] The household may be disaggregated further. Each institution has a current account and a capital account linked to investment accounts and the capital accounts of other institutions. This treatment is significantly different from the more common treatment where savings and investments are handled by a unified institutional account.

In the rows of their current accounts, these institutions receive value-added, transfers from other institutions, interest (for households and rest of world), taxes (for the government) and payments for the imports of the SAM country (for the rest of the world). Along their columns, the outlays of the institutions are allocated to commodity purchases (consumption for the household and the government; and the exports of the SAM country for the rest of the world), direct taxes (for the household), interest payments (for indebted institutions) and savings. It is also possible to include one or more additional institutions that carry out the functions of an off-budget donor or a non-governmental organization (NGO) — receiving transfers from other institutions (typically the rest of the world and/or the government) and using these resources to purchase services related to health and/or education. The tax account (which in MAMS applications is disaggregated according to tax type) passes on its receipts from activities, commodities and households (along the row) to the government (along the column).[57]

---

[55] While this in some contexts may be a drawback, it has the advantage of removing the need to model how the endowments and investments of different institutions (households, government and the rest of the world) are allocated across different private capital types (perhaps disaggregated by sector); this is a key advantage given limited knowledge of this distribution and of the mechanisms that determine how it evolves over time.

[56] MAMS does not separate enterprises from other domestic institutions. In the SAM, these would have been linked to factors (enterprises receive factor incomes, reflecting their ownership of non-labor factors), "other" institutions (direct tax payments and transfers reflecting institutional ownership of the enterprise) and enterprise capital accounts (which spend on investments). In the database, these "other" institutions (primarily households) directly receive the factor transfers while assuming the savings and direct tax payments that otherwise would have been done by the enterprises. Other SAM payments are not affected.

[57] The SAM and MAMS may also include direct taxes levied on factor incomes (represented by payments from factor accounts to the tax account).

The (domestic and foreign) interest accounts pass on payment from the (net) borrowers to the (net) lenders. Note that the SAM (and MAMS) only captures interest payments (and related debts) of domestic institutions to the rest of the world and of the government to households. It does not capture interest payments and debts linking domestic non-government institutions.[58]

For each institutional capital account, the receipts are savings (from the current account of the same institution) and net borrowing from the capital accounts of selected other institutions (for the government from the rest of the world and the household; for the household, from the rest of the world). In addition to lending to (funding the net borrowing of) selected institutions, the outlays of the institutional capital accounts include investments of two types: payments to private and government investment accounts (one investment account per capital stock) representing gross fixed capital formation; and payments to the account for stock changes. The payments from the capital account of the rest of the world to the private investment account are FDI. This structure makes it possible for MAMS to capture, in a simple way, the structure of institutional assets (different types of capital and financial claims) and liabilities (financial debt) and how the evolution of this structure differs under alternative scenarios, including the fact that households with more rapid income growth tend to save more and acquire increasing shares of private capital and government debt.

Like most other CGE models, MAMS is a "real" model in which inflation does not matter (only relative prices matter). Given this, there is no significant gain from having a separate monetary sector. Implicitly, in the SAM, the current account of the monetary sector is merged with service activities and commodities while its capital account is merged with the government capital account. Given this, in the merged government capital account, the cells for net government borrowing from other institutions are made up of multiple items. The cell for net borrowing by the government from the household is the sum of (i) net direct borrowing by government from household (net sales of government bonds on which the government pays interest) and (ii) net increases in the claims of the household sector on the monetary sector (the differences between changes in broad money holdings and monetary sector credit to the household). In MAMS (but not in the SAM), the two items in this cell are treated separately, making it possible to consider the fact "(i)" gives rise to interest payments and a debt whereas "(ii)" is a grant to the government, providing it with "seignorage" (as the one who spends this new money first). The cell for net borrowing by government from the rest of the world is the difference between (i) net direct borrowing by the government from the rest of the world and (ii) the increase in foreign

---

[58] The decision not to include these financial links reflects the context-specific assessment that the benefits from this extension (in the form of insights) fall short of the costs (in the form of additional data and complexity).

exchange reserves. In MAMS, these two items are not treated separately.[59] While this treatment remains simple, it captures the important fact that the government, by means of money creation, appropriates part of private savings. Given the fact that the model does not consider effects of and private sector responses to high general inflation, MAMS should not be used for scenarios under which the resources obtained via the monetary sector are so large that inflation would accelerate. The assessment of what is a prudent upper limit for this type of borrowing should draw on expertise on the macroeconomics of each country; a few percent of GDP is often a reasonable figure.

Finally, the investment and stock change accounts transform receipts from institutional capital accounts to commodity demands. For the investment accounts, these payments show the value composition of new capital stocks. The SAM for MAMS includes several investment accounts: one for the private sector and one for each government service; this disaggregation implies that investment by sector of origin and by sector of destination have to be specified. The payments of the stock change account may be negative and should be limited to goods accounts — it is not possible to stock services.

### 4.5.1.2 Non-SAM data

Beyond the SAM, MAMS also requires other data that is common to most CGE models. Most importantly, the required data includes elasticities to capture: substitutability between factors in production; transformability of output between exports and domestic sales; substitutability between imports and domestic commodities in domestic demand; and responses in household consumption to income changes. The required data also includes (i) debt stocks, such as domestic government debt by non-government institutions and foreign debt by domestic institutions; (ii) data on production factors — stocks, unemployment and employment (disaggregated by activity); and (iii) population data (the base-year population of each representative household, and projections for total population and population in labor-force age (typically 15—64 years old). For private capital, base-year stocks may be defined on the basis of base-year data for rents, profit rates and depreciation rates.[60] For each type of government capital, various devices may

---

[59] Macro consistency matrices that treat the monetary sector as an intermediary often do not have any separate current account for the monetary sector. To verify the statements in this paragraph, note that the balances for government and monetary sector capital accounts can be written as (i) $I_g = S_g + B_{gm} + B_{gh} + B_{gr}$ and (ii) $B_{gm} + B_{hm} + \Delta R = \Delta M$, respectively, where g = government, m = monetary sector, h = household and r = rest of the world, $I$ = investment, $B$ = borrowing by first index from second index, $R$ = foreign reserves and $M$ = broad money. By solving (ii) for $B_{gm}$, substituting the resulting expression for $B_{gm}$ into (i) and rearranging, we get the merged government—monetary sector capital account: $I_g = S_g + (\Delta M - B_{hm}) + B_{gh} + (B_{gr} - \Delta R)$, where the capital account payments to the merged government—monetary sector from the household and the rest of the world are $(\Delta M - B_{hm}) + B_{gh}$ and $(B_{gr} - \Delta R)$, respectively. For more details, see Agénor (2004, pp. 11—22), Rao and Nallari (2001, pp. 25—32, 176 and 168) and Barth and Hemphill (2000, pp. 71—74 and 101—106).

[60] The following formula is used to define the base-year private capital stock: $qfcap = samrent/(netprfrat + deprrat)$, where $qfcap$ = the stock, $samrent$ = total VA to private capital in SAM, $netprfrat$ = the net profit rate (in decimal form) and $deprrat$ = the depreciation rate (also in decimal form).

be used to approximate base-year stocks. The MAMS default is to define these stocks on the basis of historical data on service growth, investments, depreciation rates and the assumption that the capital stock over time has grown at the same rate as real services. Alternatively, government capital stocks may be defined using the perpetual inventory method (PIM) or drawing on data on average capital-output ratios (ACORs) for government services.[61] For other factors such as agricultural land and natural resources, base-year stocks can typically be defined so that base-year rents are normalized to unity; data on future stock growth is also needed — as opposed to labor and capital, growth for these factors is exogenous.

The data requirements for the (optional) MAMS built-in poverty module include the headcount poverty rate for an identified year for each representative household or any aggregation of representative households; the base simulation will endogenously generate a poverty line that is calibrated to replicate the observed poverty rate for the identified year. Other representative household-specific data requirements vary depending on the approach that is followed. For the simplest (but least satisfactory approach), the only requirement is the growth elasticity (the elasticity of poverty with respect to changes in real household *per capita* consumption or income). For the log-normal approach, the user has a choice between providing the same elasticity (for the calibration year), the standard deviation of the distribution or the Gini coefficient. In case the real-world household survey approach is selected for poverty and inequality computations, the analyst has to provide microdata on the *per capita* welfare indicator, individual weights and a mapping that indicates to which model household each individual observation in the microdata belongs.

The remaining data requirements are specific to the MDG module of MAMS. This data is due to extensions to include MDG indicators and their determinants, an extended education module and relatively detailed government accounts. Both for education (for each of the three levels) and for the non-education MDGs other than poverty (labeled 4, 5, 7w and 7s), it is necessary to provide data for base-year outcomes. In education, each educational level requires rates for promotion, repetition, dropout and entry (among graduates from the previous cycle, or, in the case of primary education, out of the relevant age cohort). For education, base-year enrollment by cycle and grade and additional population data (identifying age groups relevant to education) are also required. To model how these outcomes change over time, two additional pieces of information are needed. (i) Base-year elasticities, linking outcomes to determinants, are

---

[61] The extent to which estimates of government capital stocks matter depend on the details of the model; while estimates tend to be highly approximate, it is nevertheless empirically important to include these in order to make it possible to capture links between service expansion and required investments as well as links between infrastructure investments and required spending on operations and maintenance.

required for MDG and education rates (other than repetition and dropout rates, which are scaled residuals) with respect to a set of explanatory variables. (ii) For logistic MDG and education functions (that cover the same rates as those referred to above), a vector is required showing a non-base point — a combination of values for the outcome and the explanatory variables. This point is typically a business-as-usual projection or a projection derived from a strategy for achieving an MDG or education target. This information is used to calibrate the functions so that they replicate base-year outcomes and elasticities, reach each MDG under specified conditions and have the upper or lower limits that were specified exogenously.

### 4.5.2  Data sources

Within available space, it is only possible to provide a brief outline of steps involved when constructing the MAMS database; to a large extent, the details tend to be country-specific.

When constructing a SAM for MAMS or some other CGE model, the main sources tend to be existing SAMs, input-output tables and supply-and-use tables and other standard databases (both country-specific and those of international organizations, covering national accounts, fiscal data and the balance of payments). Given the need for a relatively disaggregated treatment of accounts for the government as well as human development services, government fiscal publications, public expenditure reviews and focused analysis of human development and infrastructure sectors are particularly important for the development of a MAMS SAM. A typical procedure is to start with a relatively aggregate SAM that, in a stepwise fashion is disaggregated, drawing on additional data in different areas. Tools have been developed to construct a macro SAM in Excel and to estimate a balanced, more detailed SAM from an imbalanced starting point (using cross-entropy methods).[62]

Sources with data relevant for parameters other than the SAM tend to include publications (both academic and non-academic, from governments and international organizations) and websites with analysis and statistics on trade, production sectors, private consumption, population, human development (including MDG and education sectors), infrastructure, as well as surveys (of households, labor and health conditions).[63] [See Lofgren (2011) for more detail.] In some applications, econometric analysis was undertaken when available studies did not provide satisfactory values for required elasticities (for an example, see Section 4.7).

---

[62]  For more on the cross-entropy approach to SAM estimation, using GAMS as software, see Robinson *et al.* (2001) and Robinson and El-Said (2000).

[63]  To exemplify, the UNESCO Institute for Statistics (www.uis.unesco.org) and the World Bank Edstats (http://go. worldbank.org/ITABCOGIV1) constitute two international sources for enrollment and other education data needed for MAMS. National data sources often provide more detail.

## 4.6 USER-FRIENDLY INTERFACE

The skills required to make productive use of CGE models in policy analysis are considerable, *inter alia* including strength in economics, modeling and a variety of software. The purpose behind the development of a user-friendly interface for MAMS was to reduce the skills required in terms of modeling and software, permitting the analyst to focus on policy and economics, thereby making MAMS-based policy analysis more cost-effective.[64] The analyst who uses the interface, named ISIM-MAMS, works exclusively in an Excel environment and receives substantial guidance throughout the analytical process. Knowledge of GAMS (the software in which MAMS is coded) and an editor (GAMS-IDE or other) is no longer needed.[65]

This section briefly describes the structure of ISIM-MAMS, how users at different skill levels may use and interact with it and the major steps involved in a typical application with a predefined dataset. It is aimed at practitioners interested in applying the MAMS framework or developing similar interfaces for other models.

### 4.6.1 Overview of the interface

ISIM-MAMS was developed using Visual Basic as an add-in for Excel 2007, later updated to also work with Excel 2010. The user is required to work in a current Windows environment and to have Excel 2007 or 2010 and GAMS installed on the computer.[66] The reason for using Excel as the front-end is that the Excel environment is familiar for most analysts, in effect removing the initial barrier for users to start working with ISIM-MAMS.

ISIM-MAMS is packaged with a set of datasets defined by country and year, often available in two versions: core and MDG (*cf.* Section 4.4). These datasets have been developed by a core team drawing on the databases of existing GAMS-MAMS applications (i.e. applications for MAMS run using GAMS and Excel without the interface). Most users of ISIM-MAMS are simply expected to do policy analysis using one or more applications, each of which is associated with an existing dataset and includes a preprogrammed reference scenario. However, advanced users may also develop a database and a reference scenario working in GAMS-MAMS and, after reading in the database as a new dataset for ISIM-MAMS (using its *Expert Mode*), shift

---

[64] Reducing the skills required to develop and apply economic models was also a major reason behind the initial development of GAMS (Bussieck and Meeraus, 2003, p. 138). The RunGTAP software for the GTAP model was developed with the same objective (Pearson and Horridge, 2005).

[65] ISIM is short for "I simulate." ISIM-MAMS is designed to belong to the suite of models of iSimulate — a framework developed by the World Bank's Development Economics Prospects Group. For more information, see http://go.worldbank.org/2BB8HIAHU0. ISIM-MAMS was developed by Martin Cicowiez, Fernando Consigli and Enrique Gallego.

[66] One likely drawback of relying on Excel is that reprogramming of parts of ISIM-MAMS may be required to maintain compatibility with future Excel versions.

to ISIM-MAMS for policy analysis, perhaps collaborating with a broader group of analysts. The aim is that every user, irrespective of background, finds it more convenient to carry out the policy analysis step in ISIM-MAMS rather than using the traditional GAMS-MAMS alternative.

Assuming that GAMS and Excel 2007 or 2010 are already installed on the user's computer, the first step is to install ISIM-MAMS, which comes in the form of an .exe file that, when activated, runs a standard installation routine. After installation, Excel has a new tab called ISIM-MAMS that, when selected, opens an intuitive interface ribbon with user-friendly buttons. To run ISIM-MAMS for an application (once defined), the user simply has to click on the *Run* button on the ISIM-MAMS ribbon. The ISIM-MAMS interface is connected to a database that, for each dataset, stores definitions of sets (including commodities, activities, factors and institutions) and parameters (including default elasticities, closure and rules/policies) that are used to define scenarios. The rest of the relevant country dataset (other than the application database) is stored in the ISIM-MAMS installation folder, mostly in Excel files.

Assuming that the user is satisfied to work with one of the existing datasets, the next steps are to: (i) Open Excel 2007;[67] (ii) create a new application and associate it with one of the available datasets; (iii) select the ISIM-MAMS tab (see Figure 4.3); (iv) run and optionally modify the predefined reference scenario; (v) define and run additional scenarios such as "base" (that may be identical to the reference scenario) and, most likely, other scenarios of interest; and (vi) access the results inside the same Excel file, presented in tables and graphs. Throughout the process, parameters and other items are hyperlinked to relevant segments in the MAMS User Guide (Lofgren, 2011), which is included with ISIM-MAMS. Each application resides in an Excel file (named by the user) that can be used by others who have ISIM-MAMS installed.

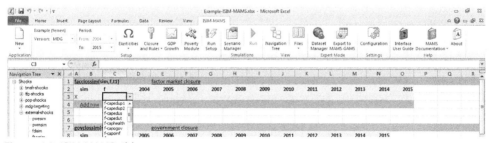

**Figure 4.3** ISIM-MAMS ribbon.

---

[67] The steps enumerated throughout Section 4.6 are the same if using Excel 2010.

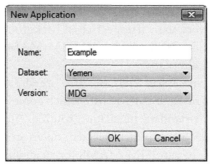

**Figure 4.4** New application dialog box.

## 4.6.2  Using ISIM-MAMS

### 4.6.2.1  Selection of database and model version

This section shows how to create an MDG ISIM-MAMS application named "example" based on the "Yemen" dataset and using the MDG version of the model (see Figure 4.4).[68] ISIM-MAMS will load into Excel 2007 the data needed to define scenarios for the selected application, including the elements in the sets that are used to define shocks (e.g. the elements in the set of exported commodities are loaded to define world export prices or the elements in institution sets so as to define inter-institutional transfers).

ISIM-MAMS permits changes in and creation of application databases; the user can change selected elements of these datasets, like elasticities, closures and rules. To facilitate the navigation across the different sections of the Excel file, the user is provided with a button for the *Navigation Tree*, where the analyst can click on the element of interest (see Figure 4.3).

In addition, (advanced) users can add new country datasets to ISIM-MAMS and change other aspects of the MAMS program by editing relevant files in the MAMS installation folder, using Excel 2007 and a text editor.

### 4.6.2.2  Reference scenario

The first step in performing counterfactual simulations with ISIM-MAMS is the construction of a (dynamic) baseline scenario. To help the user carry out this task, ISIM-MAMS includes, for each country dataset, a predefined reference scenario. Key parameters of this scenario can be changed inside ISIM-MAMS, including the GDP growth rate, a subset of model elasticities (including those related to trade, household expenditure, the reservation wage and the impact of share of trade in real GDP on TFP), as well as closures and other rules, the latter covering the government budget, the balance

---

[68] As explained in Section 4.4, two versions of MAMS exist: core (a standard, dynamic-recursive CGE model) and MDG (an extended dynamic-recursive CGE model designed for MDG and human development analysis).

of payments, the savings–investment balance, factor markets and various payments, split into government and non-government depending on whether the government is involved or not. The rule chosen for any payment is overwritten if, according to the related closure setting, the payment in question is a free variable (e.g. the specification that direct taxes are determined on the basis of exogenous tax rates is overwritten if, according to the government closure rules, changes in direct taxes clear the government budget). In addition, the user can configure the MAMS Poverty Module (see Section 4.4). Specifically, the parameters of the Poverty Module allow the user to change (i) the approach to compute poverty, (ii) the welfare index (income/consumption), (iii) the initial poverty rate and (iv) the growth elasticity of poverty.

To exemplify, Figure 4.5 demonstrates how the analyst can change the elasticities of substitution between primary factors of production; the default values can always be restored. Once defined, the reference scenario can be run by clicking the *Run Setup* button; ISIM-MAMS will automatically call GAMS in order to run MAMS.

### 4.6.2.3 Defining and running scenarios for analysis

By default, ISIM-MAMS generates a scenario called *base*. The user can define additional scenarios and introduce policy changes and exogenous shocks, including changes in

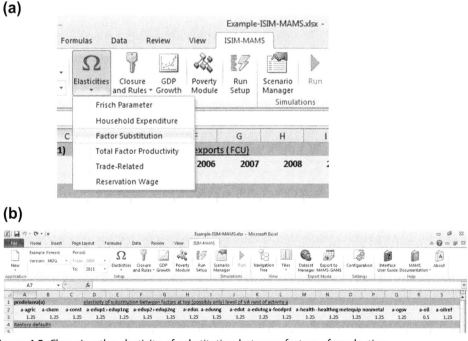

**Figure 4.5** Changing the elasticity of substitution between factors of production.

world prices of exports and imports, foreign aid, taxation and public spending and its allocation. All the defined counterfactual scenarios are saved in the ISIM-MAMS application-specific Excel file. The types of changes that can be introduced relative to the reference scenario reflect what seemed relevant in light of experience from a large number of MAMS applications. The interface validates the input from the user in order to reduce the likelihood that simulations will fail to run without error.

To create a new simulation or delete an existing one, the user clicks on the *Scenario Manager* button, opening the window shown in Figure 4.6. By clicking or unclicking the box in front of each scenario, the user decides which simulations to run (there is no need to run all the defined scenarios). By right-clicking above any scenario, the user can edit the name and the explanatory text of the simulation and select the mode (whether the scenario is solved single-pass or multipass, indicated by [S] or [M] at the end of the explanatory text for each simulation). In the example, the pwm-2 simulation will be run, while the pwe-2 will not. The elements under Shocks and Closure and Rules in the *Navigation Tree* show what can be changed in the definition of the non-reference scenarios. If no changes are made for a scenario, then it is identical to the reference scenario. In order for the base scenario to function as the benchmark to which other scenarios are compared, it may be preferable to leave it unchanged (i.e. identical to the reference scenario).

More specifically, the user can make changes in a set of items, grouped into the following categories:

- External shocks: changes in (i) the world price of exports and imports, (ii) FDI and (iii) foreign borrowing.
- Total productivity shocks: changes in (i) TFP, by activity and time period, and (ii) real GDP at factor cost.

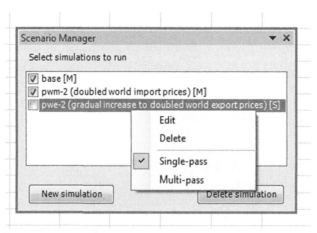

**Figure 4.6** Scenario manager.

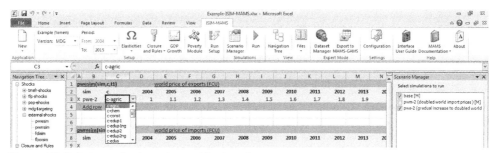

**Figure 4.7** Defining a shock to the world price of exports.

- Demographic shocks: changes in (i) population size, by representative household or other population segment, and (ii) changes in the growth rate of non-labor (all) factors (core version only).
- Transfers shocks: changes in (i) transfers non-household institutions or factors and (ii) *per capita* transfers to households.
- Closures and rules: changes in closures and rules — similar to the setting of closures and rules for the preprogrammed reference scenario. Among other things, the rules section allows defining scenarios with changes in (i) government spending and receipts, and (ii) transfers between institutions.
- Targeting of MDG and/or education outcomes (only for the MDG version of the model); the analyst can impose the targeting of one or more MDG goals and/or education outcomes. The available drop-down menus help the user to select scenario name and MDG or education outcome.

As an example, Figure 4.7 shows how to define a 50% increase in the world price of agricultural exports during 2005—2008 using an application based on the "Yemen" dataset; the other shocks can be similarly defined.

### 4.6.2.4 Review and further processing of simulation results

Once the selected scenarios have been run with success, results can be accessed via the ISIM-MAMS interface by clicking on *Reports* via the *Navigation Tree*. In addition to providing simulated variable results as levels, growth rates and GDP shares (all accessible through a pivot table inside Excel as well as GAMS .GDX files), the interface generates predefined tables and figures (see Figure 4.8 for an example of a predefined figure). By clicking on the *Configuration* button, the user can select which preprogrammed tables are generated, start and end years for these tables, the order in which the result tables will appear and whether or not to generate a pivot table and chart with raw model results. Irrespective of the settings under *Configuration | Reports*, the user can access all simulation results using the report .GDX files through the *View | Files* menu option.

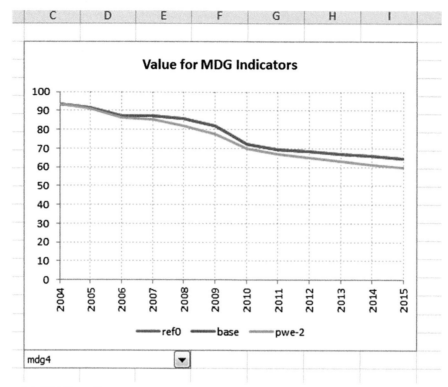

**Figure 4.8** MAMS results.

### 4.6.2.5 Input validation and error messages

Before calling GAMS to run a selected simulation, ISIM-MAMS validates the definition of shocks, elasticities and/or closures and rules. In case errors are found, messages appear in pop-up windows and the user will have to check the red Excel cells, located in the sheets whose label also turned to red (see Figure 4.9). Besides, an error summary sheet shows the list of generated validation errors. In case the solution of ISIM-MAMS ends with an error, the user is offered the chance to inspect the ISIM-MAMS log file or the GAMS listing file (see Figure 4.10). The log and listing file viewer allows the user to navigate through the ISIM-MAMS and/or GAMS errors. The log file is intended for users with no GAMS knowledge. On the other hand, the GAMS listing file provides the raw GAMS results and error messages. In case MAMS is successfully solved, ISIM-MAMS will add or update the report sheets (i.e. it will add extra worksheets in Excel).

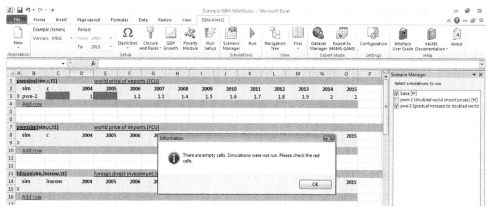

**Figure 4.9** Validation errors in ISIM-MAMS.

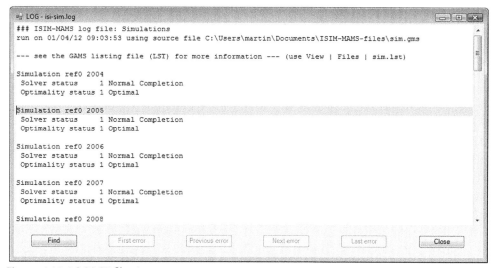

**Figure 4.10** LOG/LST file viewer.

## 4.7 APPLICATIONS: POLICY ISSUES AND INSIGHTS

This section provides an overview of the applications of MAMS and the insights that the analyses have generated, together with a detailed account of a development prospects analysis for Yemen. Section 4.7.1 summarizes policy issues addressed, the institutional contexts of MAMS-based analysis and how the model has evolved in tandem with both the evolution of issues and the incorporation of lessons from earlier applications. Section 4.7.2 provides the reader a recent case study for Yemen while Section 4.7.3 summarizes the main insights from the wider range of studies.

### 4.7.1 Policy issues, institutional context and evolution of model structure

Since the initial development of MAMS in 2004 with its pilot application to Ethiopia, the framework has been applied to a large number of countries and a variety of issues. Table 4.18 lists a total of 65 MAMS applications (completed or in progress) spread over 45 countries throughout the developing world but with the strongest focus on Latin America and Sub-Saharan Africa. In terms of institutional sponsorship, these applications are roughly evenly divided between World Bank-led projects and projects in which UN-DESA has been the leading institution, typically working with the World Bank, the UNDP and developing-country analysts. Projects led by UN-DESA have invariably had a strong training component with extensive interaction with small country teams during an extended period (two years or more); World Bank-led projects have also offered extensive training to researchers from some countries, including Ghana and Uganda. The applications for which the UN had a leading role have focused on scenarios that are geared toward the objectives of the UN Millennium Declaration of 2000: reaching the MDGs by 2015. To study the possible economy-wide effects of the pursuit of these objectives, the scenarios targeted full achievement of the non-poverty MDGs by 2015 under alternative assumptions regarding the source of the required additional financing (foreign grants, foreign borrowing, domestic taxes or domestic borrowing), while tracking the resulting effect on the poverty MDG as well. After a set of initial Ethiopia applications also focused on targeting MDGs, the World Bank-led applications have been more diverse, although without departing from the overarching concern of analyzing links between fiscal policy, exogenous shocks, poverty reduction and other aspects of human development; the details of each application have reflected the priorities of World Bank country teams and developing-country governments. As shown in Table 4.18, applications have addressed often inter-related topics similar to gender, demography, foreign aid, debt sustainability, mining exports, labor markets, FDI and fiscal policy, in the latter area often simulating tradeoffs related to alternative spending allocations and their impact on poverty versus non-poverty MDGs. With few exceptions, the findings from MAMS-based applications have been presented in each country to policy makers and researchers. Among developing-country governments, those of Ethiopia and Uganda have relied on simulation results from MAMS for their MDG Needs Assessment Report and their current National Development Plan, respectively (Government of Ethiopia, 2005, pp. 45–52 and 65–66; Musisi, 2009, pp. 15–29; Government of Uganda, 2010, p. 58).

When MAMS has been applied to new issues or countries, it has typically been necessary to extend the model and its computer code. The initial Ethiopia application

**Table 4.18** MAMS applications and references by country, issue, model version and context

| Country | Issue | Version | Context | Key references/ status |
|---|---|---|---|---|
| Afghanistan | Growth, aid and mining exports | Core | A | In progress |
| Argentina | MDG targeting | MDG | B | Cicowiez *et al.* (2008, 2010) |
| Benin | MDG targeting | MDG | C | Republic of Benin and UNDP (2010) |
| Bolivia | MDG targeting | MDG | B | Jimenez *et al.* (2008, 2010) |
| | Financial crisis and MDGs | MDG | D | Jimenez (2010); United Nations (2011) |
| Brazil | MDG targeting | MDG | B | Ulyssea and Le Boulluec (2008; 2010) |
| Burkina Faso | Fiscal tradeoffs; demography | MDG | A | Gottschalk *et al.* (2009); World Bank (2011) |
| Chile | MDG targeting | MDG | B | O'Ryan *et al.* (2008, 2010) |
| | Financial crisis and MDGs | MDG | D | O'Ryan *et al.* (2010) |
| Colombia | MDG targeting | MDG | B | Nuñez *et al.* (2008) |
| Congo (Democratic Republic) | Debt sustainability | Core | A | World Bank (2007b, 2008a) |
| | Fiscal tradeoffs | MDG | A | Nielsen and Lofgren (2011) |
| Costa Rica | MDG targeting | MDG | B | Sanchez (2008, 2010) |
| Cuba | MDG targeting | MDG | B | Ferriol *et al.* (2008) |
| Dominican Republic | MDG targeting | MDG | B | Diaz-Bonilla *et al.* (2008) |
| | National Development Strategy | MDG | A | Diaz-Bonilla (2009) |
| Ecuador | MDG targeting | MDG | B | Leon *et al.* (2008, 2010) |
| | Financial crisis and MDGs | MDG | D | Rosero and Leon (2010); United Nations (2011) |
| Egypt | MDG targeting | MDG | B | Khorshid *et al.* (2012) |

*(Continued)*

**Table 4.18** MAMS applications and references by country, issue, model version and context—cont'd

| Country | Issue | Version | Context | Key references/ status |
|---------|-------|---------|---------|------------------------|
| El Salvador | MDG targeting | MDG | B | Acevedo (2008) |
| Ethiopia | Gender | MDG | A | Ruggeri Laderchi *et al.* (2010); World Bank (2009a) |
| | MDG targeting; fiscal tradeoffs | MDG | A | Lofgren and Diaz-Bonilla (2008) |
| | Absorptive capacity | MDG | A | Sundberg and Lofgren (2006); Bourguignon and Sundberg (2006a, 2006b) |
| | Demography | MDG | A | World Bank (2007a) |
| | Labor markets | MDG | A | World Bank (2007c) |
| | Public finance | MDG | A | World Bank (2006); Lofgren and Abdula (2006) |
| | Macro analysis of MDG Strategy | Core | A | Government of Ethiopia (2005) |
| Ghana | Growth; fiscal tradeoffs | MDG | A | Bogetic *et al.* (2008); Bussolo and Medvedev (2008a); World Bank (2007d) |
| Guatemala | MDG targeting | MDG | B | Vázquez (2008) |
| Honduras | MDG targeting | MDG | 1, 2 | Bussolo and Medvedev (2008a, 2008b); World Bank (2007e) |
| Jamaica | MDG targeting | MDG | B | King and Handa (2008) |
| Kenya | Poverty and inequality | MDG | A | World Bank (2009b) |
| | Growth | Core | A | World Bank (2008b); Lofgren and Kumar (2007) |
| | MDG targeting | MDG | 5 | Kiringai and Levin (2008) |
| Kyrgyz Republic | MDG targeting | MDG | D | Mogilevsky and Omorova (2012) |
| Liberia | Poverty reduction; growth | MDG | A | In progress |

*(Continued)*

**Table 4.18** MAMS applications and references by country, issue, model version and context—cont'd

| Country | Issue | Version | Context | Key references/ status |
|---|---|---|---|---|
| Malawi | Policy tradeoffs | MDG | A | World Bank (2007f) |
| Mexico | MDG targeting | MDG | B | Ortega and Székely (2008; 2010) |
|  | Financial crisis and MDGs | MDG | D | Ortega (2011) |
| Moldova | Remittances; food and oil prices | Core | A | In progress |
| Mongolia | Mineral exports | Core | A | Unpublished |
| Morocco | MDG targeting | MDG | B | Khellaf et al. (2011) |
| Nicaragua | MDG targeting | MDG | B | Sanchez and Vos (2008, 2010) |
|  | Financial crisis and MDGs | MDG | D | Sanchez and Vos (2010); United Nations (2011) |
| Paraguay | MDG targeting | MDG | B | Biedermann and Corvalán (2008) |
| Peru | MDG targeting | MDG | B | Castro and Yamada (2008; 2010) |
| Philippines | MDG targeting | MDG | D | Briones et al. (2012) |
| Rwanda | Policy tradeoffs | MDG | A | Lofgren et al. (2009) |
| Senegal | MDG targeting | MDG | E | Robilliard and Chemingui (2011) |
|  | MDG targeting | MDG | B | Diagne et al. (2012) |
| South Africa | MDG targeting | MDG | B | Kearney and Odusola (2012) |
| Syria | Policy tradeoffs | MDG | A | In progress |
| Tunisia | MDG targeting | MDG | B | Chemingui and Sanchez (2012) |
| Uganda | Oil exports | MDG | A | In progress |
|  | Demography | MDG | A | In progress |
|  | MDG targeting | MDG | B | Matovu et al. (2011) |
|  | Demography | MDG | A | Kinnunen et al. (2009) |
|  | Fiscal tradeoffs | MDG | A | World Bank (2007g); Lofgren and Diaz-Bonilla (2006) |
|  | National Development Strategy | MDG | A | Musisi (2009); Government of Uganda (2010) |
| Uruguay | MDG targeting | MDG | B | Laens and Llambi (2008) |

*(Continued)*

**Table 4.18** MAMS applications and references by country, issue, model version and context—cont'd

| Country | Issue | Version | Context | Key references/ status |
|---|---|---|---|---|
| | Financial crisis and MDGs | MDG | D | Llambí and Laens (2011) |
| Uzbekistan | MDG targeting | MDG | D | Olimov and Fayzullaev (2012) |
| Yemen | MDG targeting; fiscal tradeoffs | MDG | B | See Section 4.7.2 |
| Zimbabwe | FDI, government and domestic private investment | Core | A | In progress |
| Archetype resource-poor low-income country | Aid, policy (spending, taxation) and TFP | MDG | A | World Bank (2010, pp. 107–119) |
| Archetype resource-rich low-income country | Aid, policy (spending, taxation) and TFP | MDG | A | World Bank (2010, pp. 107–119) |

Issues:

- MDG targeting = Full achievement of one or more non-poverty MDGs by 2015 with alternative sources of additional financing.
- Fiscal tradeoffs = Within fiscal space limits, analysis of tradeoffs related to different spending priorities (typically infrastructure versus human development).
- Demography = Effects of alternative demographic scenarios (often UN projections; sometimes associated with policy changes) on MDGs and other indicators.

Versions:

- Core = Version without non-poverty MDG indicators and links between education and the labor market.
- MDG = Version with one or more non-poverty MDG indicators and links between education and the labor market.

Contexts:

- A = World Bank staff or consultants as part of World Bank analytical work; coordinated with government with in-country presentations; sometimes with full government collaboration and/or training.
- B = Developing country analysts in joint projects with UN-DESA, UNDP, World Bank and consultants; extensive training.
- C = Developing country analysts in joint project with UNDP, Gesellschaft für Technische Zusammenarbeit and consultants.
- D = Developing country analysts in joint project with UNDP, UN-DESA and consultants.
- E = Developing country analysts in joint project with UN Economic Commission for Africa and consultants.

The MAMS website at www.worldbank.org/mams may also include links to other versions of the same studies, including working papers.

had been limited to the essentials of what was needed given the priorities at hand and constraints on data and time. With few exceptions, the extensions that have been introduced in the context of different applications have been brought into the standard code as optional features (i.e. adding to the flexibility of the framework without imposing changes in the content and results of earlier applications).[69]

Accordingly, the initial model structure, developed for the Ethiopia application, was focused on MDG targeting.[70] Relative to most CGE models, the features of the initial Ethiopia application that may be non-standard and that were significant for the analysis include:

- Endogenization of the MDG and the education outcomes typically covered by MAMS (cf. Section 4.4) using nested logistic — constant-elasticity functions with links to the labor market.
- Disaggregated treatment of government human development and infrastructure services to capture human development and growth impacts of government actions.
- Targeting of MDG outcomes: flexing of real government service levels combined with fixing of MDG outcomes. For cases where the number of targets exceeded the number of policy tools, a mixed-complementarity formulation was used to ensure that all targets were achieved exactly for one target per tool combined with likely overshooting for other targets.[71]
- Introduction of a non-competitive import commodity in the SAM to ensure that the implicit import share of investment demand matched available data — no changes were required in the model structure relative to the static model in Lofgren et al. (2002), on which MAMS draws. Import intensity matters as it has strong implications for the impact of simulated spending expansion on the real exchange rate and production of tradables (including potential "Dutch Disease" effects).

As an example of a path not taken, in the context of the initial Ethiopia analysis, some simulations minimized the present value of government costs of achieving the MDGs (requiring a model solution in the single-pass mode); however, this was not pursued in later applications considering the nature of the MDG targets (which, strictly speaking,

---

[69] So far, the only exceptions are in Kinnunen et al. (2009) and Ruggeri Laderchi et al. (2010) where the extensions, related to demography and gender (in time use, education and the labor markets), respectively, were deemed too data-demanding to be desirable in a larger number of applications at the same time as their introduction as special cases would have added unduly to the complexity of the model code.

[70] Prior to the development of the general equilibrium version of MAMS, a top-down macro–micro framework was developed in which a separate macro model fed data into a partial equilibrium MDG module in which the outcomes for MDG 2, 4, 5 and 7 were computed without feedback from the MDG module to the rest of the economy. The MDG module had more detail on health (distinguishing between different types of health services) while the treatment of education was limited to primary education (Bourguignon et al., 2004)

[71] As noted in Section 4.4, in effect no application has had more than one excess target per tool — water and sanitation MDGs are targeted with aggregate government water-sanitation services as the policy tool; and under-5 and maternal mortality rates are targeted with aggregate government health services as the policy tool.

only are concerned with outcomes in 2015) and the fact that our understanding of time lags in the links between human development determinants and outcomes is very limited.[72]

After the initial Ethiopia analysis, MAMS was applied to a large number of countries in Latin America and the Caribbean, confronting the framework with a wider range of country features that required higher degrees of flexibility and robustness as well as various extensions relative to a model designed to work for a specific country like Ethiopia. *Inter alia*, MAMS was modified to include:

- Sectors that deviate from the default assumption that production decisions (including production quantities) are driven by profit maximization in a perfectly competitive setting. These non-standard sectors belong to two categories: (i) Natural resource-based sectors for which production volumes and factor quantities are exogenous, with a natural resource factor earning residual value-added while factors, intermediate inputs and outputs are subject to market rents and prices and (ii) utilities for which a private operator has agreed to satisfy market demand at an exogenous price and to undertake an agreed-upon investment plan (sufficient to produce demanded quantities).

- Imposition of exogenous aggregate rates of labor force participation among the population in labor-force age outside school. This was needed to ensure that education-specific attrition rates for labor generated macro outcomes that matched available trends for labor force growth.

- Reservation wages and endogenous unemployment rates for selected factors (typically limited to labor factors). By spreading responses to changing labor market conditions across employment and wages, this extension had the effect of reducing sometimes excessive year-to-year wage variations that resulted when employment was fixed; obviously, it also permits the model to generate endogenous changes in unemployment.[73]

- Optional non-government service providers in MDG- and education-related sectors, typically financed like other non-government sectors and contributing to MDG and education outcomes as perfect or imperfect substitutes of government services. This extension, also present in later Ethiopia applications, was particularly important for

---

[72] To provide an example, if health outcomes in year *t* merely depend on the levels *in the same year t* for government services and other determinants of health outcomes, then the cost-minimizing policy for achieving the health MDGs would involve postponing expansion of government spending on health and other determinants until 2015, the final year. To avoid such outcomes, simulations targeting MDG outcomes have tended to impose gradual progress over time for the MDG indicators at rates consistent with constant growth rates for the different determinants (government services and other). In the real world, lags are likely to vary strongly depending on country context and the kinds of micro-level interventions that are pursued.

[73] In addition, imposition of the assumption that labor productivity growth increases with the level of education has often been necessary to counter the tendency for less educated labor to enjoy implausibly rapid relative wage growth given its relatively slow stock growth.

Latin America and Caribbean countries where the private sector tends to play a major role in these sectors.

In addition to these changes in the model structure, various background changes were crucial to make it feasible to apply MAMS to a rapidly growing number of countries (including the simultaneous application of MAMS to 18 countries in the Latin America and Caribbean region), *inter alia*, including the programming of a large number of diagnostic checks on the databases (aborting the program if data was missing or inconsistent) and the creation of additional parameters in Excel data files that facilitate user control of an expanded number of parameters on a year-to-year basis.[74]

The more recent World Bank-led applications, which have been more diverse, have been done in close collaboration with government and World Bank country teams. Instead of imposing targets and exploring what is needed by way of financing, the emphasis has been on determining what can be achieved under alternative scenarios for financing and allocations of government spending. The changes in the model structure are numerous but have not changed the overall structure; they include:

- Fine-tuning of government closures with budget clearing via spending adjustments (via a percentage-point adjustment in real growth for one or more selected government functions that, in each period, is uniform across these functions). To exemplify, an exogenous increase in grant aid may be combined with uniform upward adjustment in human development and infrastructure services within the limits of fiscal space or, alternatively, exogenous adjustments in spending on infra-structure services may be combined with endogenous real growth adjustments in human development services.

- Creation of auxiliary equations and related variables (potentially exogenous) that permit analysts to control real growth rates and shares of GDP or absorption for the different receipts and outlays of the government as well as different non-government payments (e.g. FDI or remittances to households from the rest of the world). These extensions were often driven by the need to replicate observed macro data during the initial simulation years, which typically cover recent history, with counterfactual scenarios starting for a year in the near future.[75]

- The development of the built-in poverty module (beyond the initial formulation with a fixed growth elasticity of poverty; see Section 4.4.3).

- Broadened optional targeting of MDG and education outcomes to cover a wider range of indicators (also higher levels of education) and permit a flexible setting of target years. These extensions have been useful when the analyst has desired to

---

[74] To provide just a few examples, diagnostic checks verify that (i) all SAM entries are legal, (ii) if data is provided for a multiyear parameter (e.g., a set of annual growth rates), then coverage is complete over the simulation period and (iii) the activity disaggregation of factor employment data is consistent with that of SAM payments to factors.

[75] In order to avoid imposing inconsistent pieces of information, it has often been convenient to construct a very aggregate macro SAM for the most recent year with comprehensive macro data.

impose outcomes from one scenario on subsequent scenarios, constraining welfare-related changes to a smaller number of variables (private consumption and incomes, poverty and inequality).

- Disaggregation of student stocks by grade and cycle instead of only by cycle to better capture the dynamics of the educational system (including graduation and transition from one cycle to next).

The Yemen application that is presented next is based on the current MAMS version and thus is able to draw on these more recent changes in model structure.

## 4.7.2 Case study

### 4.7.2.1 Policy issues

The purpose of this section is to demonstrate a practical application of MAMS, using Yemen as a case study.[76] Yemen is one of the poorest countries in the Arab region with a *per capita* GDP of US$1160 for 2008 (WDI, 2010) and faces a wide range of developmental challenges, amplified in 2011 by deepened domestic conflict. In 2007, the country was ranked 140 out of 182 according to the Human Development Index (HDI) (UNDP, 2009). Ever since reunification in 1990, Yemen's relative position on the HDI has remained more or less unchanged and its progress towards attaining the MDGs has been very slow. At 3%, the country has one of the highest population growth rates globally, with the population expected to double in 23 years to around 40 million. This increases the demand for educational and health services, drinking water and employment opportunities. Yemen faces a severe water shortage, with available ground water being depleted at an alarming rate. Its oil production and reserves are declining with severe budgetary consequences. Moreover, the political crisis that erupted in 2011 threatens to make Yemen's prospects for rapid growth and progress on MDGs even bleaker. The case study was conducted to provide guidance to policy making once at least the minimum requirements for stability and policy making have been restored.

Social development indicators, such as child malnutrition, maternal mortality and education attainment remain discouraging. The *Fourth Five-Year Socio-Economic Development Plan for Poverty Reduction 2011–2015* (see MOPIC, 2011) indicates that about 42.4% of the population live below the national poverty line.[77] Yemen's first and second

[76] The Yemen case study is part of the project "Assessing Development Strategies to Achieve the Millennium Development Goals in the Arab Region," carried out by the UNDP/RBAS (Regional Bureau for the Arab States), UN/DESA (Department of Economic and Social Affairs), the World Bank and country teams for Egypt, Jordan, Morocco, Tunisia and Yemen. The members of the Yemen team are Mohamed Ahmed Al-Hawri (team leader; Ministry of Planning and International Cooperation), Abdulmajeed Al-Batuly (Ministry of Planning and International Cooperation), Anwar Ahmed Farhan (Central Statistical Organization), Ali Shatter (Ministry of Finance), Mohammad Pournik (UNDP), Martin Cicowiez, Ana Pacheco and Hans Lofgren.

[77] The *Fourth Five-Year Socio-Economic Development Plan for Poverty Reduction 2011–2015* is an official document that, among other things, provides projections for several variables useful for generating the MAMS reference scenario as further explained below.

MDG Reports of 2003 and 2010 concluded that Yemen was off track with respect to meeting the MDGs (see MOPIC, 2003, 2010).

MAMS for Yemen (MAMS applied to a Yemeni database) is here used to run a set of simulations that explore the economic impact of different options for creating and using fiscal space — the former refers to mobilizing resources and the latter to their possible uses.[78] In these simulations, exogenous increases are introduced for foreign aid, government allocative efficiency or TFP in the production of government services. The government makes use of the resulting addition to fiscal space to expand spending and service delivery in infrastructure and human development. The results suggest that substantial improvements could be achieved if, as a result of one (or more) of these exogenous changes, fiscal space would increase. The simulated effects differ depending on the size of the simulated exogenous shock and on how the government uses the additional resources. For the simulations that involve increased access to foreign aid, the gains are more substantial, including a reduction in the poverty rate, reductions in the under-five mortality rate, as well as a significant improvement in on-time completion of primary schooling. In general, emphasis on infrastructure leads to more rapid growth for GDP and absorption, but has less significant improvements for the MDG indicators. In addition to key MDG indicators (related to poverty, health, primary education and water and sanitation), the analysis covers the impact of the strategy on national account aggregates, major macroeconomic balances (including the government budget and the balance of payments), the size of the government relative to the rest of the economy, as well as production and trade in different sectors. In addition, our analysis confirms the importance of considering synergies and economy-wide constraints and repercussions in the analysis of major government policy changes such as an MDG strategy.

### 4.7.2.2 Database development

MAMS for Yemen was calibrated to a 2004 SAM and other data, developed following the procedures described in Section 4.5. The main source of information for the construction of the Yemeni SAM was the supply and in use tables for the same year. In addition, information from the Balance of Payments was the most important input to build the external accounts of the SAM. For the government accounts, data for 2004 from the 2008 Bulletin of Government Finance Statistics was used. In order to complete the SAM, data computed from the 2005 Household Budget Survey was also used. Like other MAMS SAMs, the Yemeni SAM offers a relatively detailed treatment of investment and its financing (*cf.* Section 4.5). Table 4.19 shows the accounts in the 2004 Yemeni SAM, which determine the size (i.e. disaggregation) of the model. The government is disaggregated into eight activities: four cycles of education (basic grades

---

[78] Heller (2005) defines fiscal space as "room in a government's budget that allows it to provide resources for a desired purpose without jeopardizing the sustainability of its financial position or the stability of the economy."

**Table 4.19** Accounts in the Yemen 2004 SAM

| Sectors (25) | Tax accounts (4) |
|---|---|
| *Private (17)* | Commodity taxes |
| Agriculture | Factor taxes |
| Crude oil, gas and other mining | Direct taxes |
| Food and beverages | Import taxes |
| Textiles | **Institutions (3)** |
| Wood, paper and press | Households |
| Liquid petroleum products | Government |
| Chemical products | Rest of the world |
| Non-metal industry | **Interest payments (3)** |
| Metal and equipment | Domestic interest payments |
| Other manufactures | Foreign interest payments |
| Construction | **Capital accounts (3)** |
| Other services | Households |
| Health private | Government |
| Basic education grade 1—6 | Rest of the world |
| Basic education grade 7—9 | **Investment accounts (9)** |
| Secondary education | *Private (2)* |
| Tertiary education | Gross capital formation |
| *Government (8)* | Stock changes |
| Water and sanitation | *Government (8)* |
| Other infrastructure | Water and sanitation |
| Health government | Other infrastructure |
| Basic education grade 1—6 | Health government |
| Basic education grade 7—9 | Basic education grade 1—6 |
| Secondary education | Basic education grade 7—9 |
| Tertiary education | Secondary education |
| Other government | Tertiary education |
| **Factors of production (13)** | Other government |
| Unskilled labor | |
| Semi-skilled labor | |
| Skilled labor | |
| Private capital | |
| Natural resource | |
| Government capital (8) | |

1—6, basic grades 7—9, secondary and tertiary cycles), health, water and sanitation, other public infrastructure and other government services.[79] In the following, the basic grades 1—6 are referred to as primary education (following international standards for the length of primary education). Owing to the focus of MAMS on MDGs, in addition to other private services, the private service sector is disaggregated into four education activities

---

[79] As can be seen, the official basic education cycle was split into two subcycles; the first includes grades 1—6 and the second includes grades 7—9.

(with the same cycles as in government education) and a private health activity.[80] The rest of the economic activities (agriculture and industry) are disaggregated into the 12 sectors shown in Table 4.19.

Among the factors of production, there are three types of labor: those with less than completed secondary education (unskilled), with completed secondary education but not completed tertiary (semi-skilled) and with completed tertiary (skilled). Each of these labor types is therefore linked directly to an educational cycle. The growth in the labor force and changes in its composition will in part depend on the functioning of the education system in the model.[81] The remaining factors include public capital stocks by government activity, a private capital stock and a natural resource used in oil and gas extraction.

The institutions include the government, a household (the private domestic institution, which represents both households and domestic enterprises) and the rest of the world. Each institution has its own capital account. Taxes have been disaggregated into direct, import and commodity taxes/subsidies. There is one private investment account and eight public investment accounts (one for each government sector). Lastly, the SAM includes accounts for domestic and foreign interest payments.

As explained in Section 4.5, apart from the SAM, the MAMS database includes data related to the different MDGs, the labor market and various elasticities. Most importantly, the first two data types include levels of service delivery required to meet the different MDGs, number of students at different educational cycles, student behavioral patterns in terms of promotion rates and other indicators and number of workers and initial unemployment rates by skill level (i.e. educational achievement). The elasticities include those in production, trade, consumption and in the different MDG functions. This implementation of MAMS covers MDG 2 (primary education), 4 (under-five mortality) and 7 (water and sanitation access).[82] The elasticities for the MDG functions are informed by two studies done for Yemen by Sanchez and Sbrana (2009) and Sbrana (2009) for education and water and sanitation, respectively. However, rather than using the exact point estimates from the econometric partial equilibrium analysis, we use the relative importance of the determinants in choosing the (general equilibrium) elasticities. In addition, the MAMS elasticities were adjusted in order to generate plausible trends under baseline conditions — and this procedure was, in fact, entirely used to define plausible elasticity values for MDG 4 in view of a lack of empirical studies and data to better inform the definition of these elasticities. Reflecting these adjustments, Table 4.20 shows the determinants in the MAMS

---

[80] According to official estimates, the share of students in private institutions is 2.3, 2.0 and 14.9% for basic, secondary and high education, respectively.

[81] Notice that workers are classified as "unskilled" labor unless they have completed secondary education or higher.

[82] MDG 5 (maternal mortality) can also be considered in MAMS, but was left out as data was insufficient.

**Table 4.20** Elasticities for the determinants of MDGs

| MDG | Per student or per capita service delivery | Per capita household consumption | Wage premium | Public infrastructure | Other MDGs[a] |
|---|---|---|---|---|---|
| Basic education (grades 1–6) | | | | | |
| First grade net intake rate | 1.563 | 0.195 | 0.004 | 0.781 | −0.031 |
| Promotion rate | 0.466 | 0.039 | 0.001 | 0.155 | −0.004 |
| Continuation rate[b] | 0.733 | 0.105 | 0.001 | 0.105 | −0.020 |
| Under-5 mortality rate | −0.865 | −0.087 | | −0.087 | −0.084 |
| Access to safe water | 0.261 | 0.010 | | 0.010 | −0.084 |
| Access to basic sanitation | 1.201 | 0.120 | | 0.120 | −0.105 |

[a]Refers to MDG 4 for education and MDG 7w and 7s for health.
[b]To grades 7–9 among students who were promoted from grade 6.

functions that define MDG outcomes and the corresponding elasticities used in the model.[83]

The determinants in the MDG functions include the provision of relevant services (in education, health and water and sanitation) and other indicators as *per capita* consumption and the size of the capital stock in public infrastructure, also allowing for the presence of synergies between MDGs, i.e. the fact that achievements in terms of one MDG can have an impact on other MDGs. For example, improvements in water and sanitation (i.e. MDG 7) will reduce under-5 mortality (MDG 4). In the cases of health and water and sanitation (i.e. MDG 4, 7w and 7s), service provision is expressed relative to the size of the population. For MDG 2, the treatment is slightly more complex. The arguments in Table 4.20 determine the shares of children that enter basic school (out of the cohort of 6-year olds) and successfully complete their current grade (among those enrolled in the first basic cycle). The shares that repeat their current grade or drop out from it are determined residually. The service level is measured per enrolled student — an indicator of educational quality. MDG 4 is included as a proxy for the health status of those enrolled. Wage incentives — an indicator of payoffs from continued education — are expressed as the ratio between the wages for labor at the next higher and the current levels of education.

[83] Sensitivity analysis for the elasticities shows that the overall qualitative results do not change. In addition to the primary education elasticities shown in Table 4.20, the database includes the same set of data points for the higher educational levels (except for that no continuation rate is defined for tertiary education, this being a terminal level).

For the secondary and tertiary cycles, the same set of arguments enter functions that determine the shares of enrolled students that pass as well as the shares of graduates from the previous cycle that enter the first grade of these two cycles. The only differences are that the arguments for services (per enrolled student) and wage incentives are redefined to be relevant to these higher cycles and that no continuation rate is defined for the tertiary cycle (as it is viewed as a terminal cycle).

MAMS typically focuses on the net (on-time) primary completion rate as its main MDG 2 indicator; the net enrolment rate, which is the official indicator, is a less informative measure of the extent to which the relevant age group is able to complete the six-year primary cycle.[84] More specifically, in any year, the net completion rate is defined as the share of the students that would complete primary school on time if this year's net intake and grade promotion rates were to prevail during the coming six years.[85] In addition, MAMS reports other indicators related to the primary cycle, the gross enrollment rate and the gross completion rate; the latter is used by the World Bank as an alternative MDG 2 indicator.

Generally speaking, the functions for educational outcomes and the other (i.e. non-education) MDGs have all been calibrated to ensure that, under base-year conditions, base-year indicators are replicated and that, under a set of other conditions identified in the *Yemen Needs Assessment Report* (see MOPIC, 2005), the target is fully achieved. Specifically, the *Yemen Needs Assessment Report* provides estimates of government sectoral spending needs (current and capital) for the period 2006—2015, which are used to calibrate the logistic functions in the MDG module of MAMS.

Finally, the MAMS Poverty Module was calibrated under the assumption that the household income distribution follows a log-normal distribution (see Section 4.4). Specifically, a poverty rate of 42.4% for 2010 and a Gini coefficient of 0.411 were used (see Government of Yemen *et al.*, 2007; MOPIC, 2011); these two pieces of information were used to estimate the shape of the log-normal distribution and the value of the poverty line. As explained, this approach assumes that the income distribution within the representative household does not change over time.

---

[84] According to the UN Millennium Declaration, the primary schooling target is to "ensure that, by the same date [2015], children everywhere, boys and girls alike, will be able to complete a full course of primary schooling and that girls and boys will have equal access to all levels of education" (http://www.un.org/millennium/declaration/ares552e.htm).

[85] Mathematically, $NPCR_t = NIR_t \cdot (PR_t)^\gamma$, where $NPCR$ = net primary completion rate, $NIR$ = net intake rate $(0 \leq NIR \leq 1)$, $PR$ = promotion rate $(0 \leq PR \leq 1)$ and $\gamma$ = number of grades in the primary cycle. As a simplification, MAMS assumes a uniform PR for all primary grades. This is a period measure; the corresponding cohort measure would use the relevant rates over a six-year period.

### *4.7.2.3 Implementation of simulations*

This section presents the simulations while the next analyzes their results. The first simulation (base) is a "business as usual" scenario, which reflects current policies and trends. Taking this base scenario as a benchmark, the other simulations consider different alternatives for creating and using fiscal space.[86] This set of simulations was designed with the aim of capturing what may be feasible once Yemen has emerged from the current political impasse. In these simulations, more fiscal space is created through exogenous increases for foreign aid or government efficiency. The government makes use of the resulting addition to fiscal space to expand spending and service delivery in infrastructure and human development. Specifically, the following simulations were implemented:

- **aid–hd**: an increase in transfers from the rest of the world to the government so that they reach an average of US$69 *per capita* for the period 2011–2015, close to the average for low income countries in 2007 — aid *per capita* is increased from US$13.7 in 2010 to US$71.4 in 2011 and US$66.7 in 2015. In terms of GDP, aid reaches an average of around 10% for the period 2011–2015. The increase in government receipts is used to finance an increase in government consumption of (demand for) MDG-related services (primary education, health and water and sanitation). In addition, post-primary education also expands sufficiently to keep the same educational quality (defined as real spending per enrolled student) as in the base scenario as the sector faces increases in the number of graduates from primary school.

- **aid–infra**: similar to the previous scenario, but the increase in government spending is used to finance an increase in the public infrastructure capital stock.

- **eff–hd**: gains in the allocative efficiency of government spending via a 50% cut in the growth rate for other government expenditures (i.e. expenditures not related to human development or infrastructure) during 2011–2015 with an expansion in human development-related spending sufficient to make use of the resulting fiscal space. Thus, we assume that cost savings are realized through efficiency gains such as elimination of overlapping government functions and/or of functions that do not contribute to production in other areas.

- **eff–infra**: similar to the previous scenario but the increase in government spending is used to finance an increase in investment in public infrastructure.

The non-base simulations only deviate from the base for the period 2011–2015; during the period 2004–2010, the baseline scenario is designed to capture the main developments of the Yemeni economy. For these simulations, an underlying assumption is that

---

[86] In Abdulmajeed *et al.* (2011), simulations are used to assess the changes in government spending that would be needed to achieve the MDGs as well as the economy-wide effects of pursuing such an MDG strategy; their main finding is not surprising considering the magnitude of the MDG challenge: full, on-time, MDG achievement does not appear a realistic objective. In fact, the authors estimate that the required financing is unlikely to be available and, if it were, it would be extremely challenging for the government to bring about the required increases in real service delivery without strong sacrifices in efficiency.

the conflict that erupted in 2011 can be resolved promptly, permitting Yemen's government to assume its developmental functions at a level of efficiency that is similar to what has prevailed in the past.

### 4.7.2.4 Analysis of results
#### 4.7.2.4.1 Base scenario

This section concentrates on the period 2011–2015. As explained, during the period 2004–2010, the baseline scenario is designed to capture the main developments of the Yemeni economy. The non-base simulations only deviate from the base for the period 2011–2015.

For the base scenario, which serves as a benchmark for comparisons, we impose the observed growth rates in real GDP at factor cost for the period 2005–2010, and an average growth of 5.2% starting from 2011, based on projections from the *Fourth Five-Year Socio-Economic Development Plan for Poverty Reduction 2011–2015*. The exogenous part of TFP growth is adjusted to generate such a growth path. GDP growth is endogenous for all non-base scenarios. In addition, we impose a decrease in the exploitation of the natural resource factor in the oil and gas extraction sector; this reflects the recent evolution and prospects of the oil and gas sector in Yemen.

In the base scenario, government consumption of education and non-education services is kept fixed as a share of absorption (total domestic final demand) at the base-year value. Transfers from government to households are kept fixed as a share of GDP. Tax rates are fixed over time, while the amount spent on commodity subsidies (basically, refined oil products) decreases gradually between 2011 and 2015, according to official projections. The ratio between domestic government debt stock and GDP increases from 10% in 2004 to about 17% during 2011–2015; domestic borrowing is adjusted accordingly. The foreign debt-to-GDP ratio increases from 30% in the base year to 33.6% in 2015, being 23% in 2009. These assumptions generate results that are consistent with recent trends (see Central Bank of Yemen, 2010).

For the base, the government fiscal account is balanced via adjustments in foreign borrowing. The base assumption for private investment is that it is fixed as a share of domestic absorption; given this, adjustments in private savings clear the savings–investment balance (i.e. savings is investment-driven). Across all simulations, the real exchange rate equilibrates inflows and outflows of foreign exchange by influencing export and import quantities. The non-trade-related payments in the balance of payments (transfers and foreign investment) are non-clearing, determined by their own rules — exogenous shares of GDP are assumed. The CPI is the model numéraire.

The rule for keeping the government account in balance is modified for non-base simulations; the counterfactual model closure rule assumes that adjustments in public spending on human development or infrastructure clear the government budget. In addition, for non-base scenarios, private investment adjusts endogenously to maintain balance between total savings (from different sources) and total investment (i.e. the model becomes savings-driven). Consequently, the model will capture the crowding-out of private investment when domestic sources of financing are used to achieve the MDGs trough increased government spending.

Among factor stocks, growth is driven by investment and depreciation for the different capital types, by a combination of demographic factors and the functioning of the educational system for the different labor categories and by an exogenous growth rate for natural resources used in the oil extraction sector. For the different types of government capital, markets are not specified; however, it is required that investment be sufficient to ensure that stocks grow at the same pace as the services that are produced. For other factors, flexible wages (or rents) clear the markets. For the different labor types, the model replicates observed unemployment rates in the base year. In other years, the unemployment rate and the wage will typically both change following a "wage-curve" formulation (see Section 4.4); declines in the unemployment rate will be combined with wage increases and *vice versa* unless unemployment is at the minimum level (set at 5%), at which point wage movements will clear the labor market in question; for the other factors with wage-clearing, supply curves are vertical leaving the adjustments to the demand side.

In the base scenario, the economy evolves according to recent trends, with most macro aggregates growing at 5–6% per year, at the upper end of this range for public consumption and investment and at the lower end for exports. Relative to GDP, export and import decrease. *Per capita* household consumption grows at a rate of 1.9% per year. The exchange rate depreciates over time, reflecting the decrease in (real) oil exports. As explained, the foreign debt-to-GDP ratio reaches 33.6% in 2015 — a level that is within the range observed for other countries at Yemen's income level. This increase in foreign borrowing brings about a net improvement in the non-trade balance (in foreign currency) and an increase in the trade deficit (also in foreign currency). However, the decline in oil exports is so large that some depreciation is still required to keep the trade deficit within the permitted limit.

As a result of growth in GDP, government service provision and household *per capita* consumption, the indicators for MDG 2 (completion of primary education), 4 (under-5 mortality rate), 7w (water access) and 7s (sanitation access) as well as poverty, all improve (see Table 4.21).[87] However, Yemen is not on track to achieve any of these MDGs by the 2015 deadline. Figure 4.11 shows the 2015 targets and the paths over time for the different MDGs.

---

[87] The tables and graphs that follow are automatically generated by ISIM-MAMS — the Excel Interface for MAMS.

**Table 4.21** Yemen simulation results

| Macroeconomic aggregates | 2004 | Base scenario | Non-base scenarios | | | |
|---|---|---|---|---|---|---|
| | | | aid-hd | aid-infra | eff-hd | eff-infra |
| | Billion YR[a] | Percent average annual growth rate, 2010–2015 | | | | |
| Absorption | 2536 | 4.9 | 7.1 | 7.3 | 4.9 | 5.0 |
| Consumption—private | 1691 | 4.3 | 5.5 | 5.3 | 4.4 | 4.3 |
| Consumption—government | 326 | 6.0 | 11.1 | 6.4 | 6.4 | 3.5 |
| Fixed investment—private | 274 | 4.6 | 6.3 | 6.0 | 4.7 | 4.6 |
| Fixed investment—government | 263 | 7.5 | 11.3 | 19.1 | 6.7 | 10.8 |
| Exports | 931 | 2.2 | −0.3 | 1.3 | 2.0 | 2.7 |
| Imports | 909 | 3.7 | 6.2 | 7.2 | 3.6 | 4.1 |
| GDP at factor cost | 2635 | 5.2 | 5.7 | 6.1 | 5.2 | 5.3 |
| Total factor employment (index) | | 2.9 | 3.7 | 4.2 | 2.9 | 3.0 |
| Total factor productivity (index) | | 2.3 | 1.9 | 1.9 | 2.3 | 2.3 |
| Real exchange rate (index) | | 2.2 | −0.1 | 0.7 | 2.2 | 2.5 |
| **Government consumption** | **Billion YR[a]** | **Percent average annual growth rate, 2010–2015** | | | | |
| Water and sanitation | 0.1 | 5.2 | 22.8 | 5.2 | 15.7 | 5.2 |
| Other infrastructure | 0.2 | 5.6 | 5.6 | 18.3 | 5.6 | 11.1 |
| Health | 19.6 | 5.4 | 23.0 | 5.4 | 15.9 | 5.4 |
| Basic education (grade 1–6) | 55.8 | 4.7 | 22.3 | 6.2 | 15.3 | 5.3 |
| Basic education (grade 7–9) | 16.0 | 6.9 | 9.7 | 7.8 | 8.2 | 7.2 |
| Secondary education | 19.5 | 7.0 | 7.5 | 7.7 | 7.1 | 7.3 |
| Tertiary education | 18.0 | 7.0 | 8.1 | 7.4 | 7.3 | 7.0 |
| Other government | 196.3 | 6.2 | 6.2 | 6.2 | 1.7 | 1.7 |
| Total | 325.4 | 6.0 | 11.1 | 6.4 | 6.4 | 3.5 |
| **MDG indicator[b]** | **Value** | **Value in 2015** | | | | |
| MDG 1: Poverty rate[c] | 42.4 | 39.2 | 36.1 | 36.6 | 38.9 | 39.0 |
| MDG 2: Net completion rate in basic education | 16.8 | 55.2 | 88.7 | 70.4 | 78.9 | 62.4 |
| MDG 4: Under-5 mortality rate | 93.4 | 64.6 | 52.1 | 59.3 | 57.8 | 63.2 |
| MDG 7w: Access to safe water | 43.9 | 48.2 | 49.0 | 49.3 | 48.4 | 48.5 |
| MDG 7s: Access to improved sanitation | 15.9 | 24.1 | 25.5 | 26.9 | 24.4 | 24.9 |

[a]YR = Yemeni Rials.
[b]Units: % for MDG 1, 2, 7w and 7s; per 1000 for MDG 4.
[c]Base year is 2010.
*Source*: Authors' estimates.

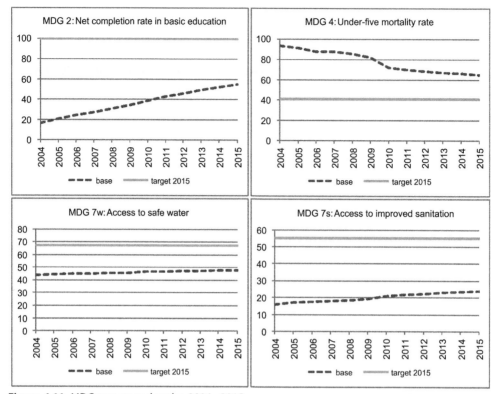

**Figure 4.11** MDG targets and paths, 2004—2015.

### 4.7.2.4.2 Aid scenarios

In the scenarios **aid–hd** and **aid–infra**, foreign transfers are increased to around 10% of GDP during 2011—2015. In the **aid–infra** scenario, GDP growth gains 0.9 percentage points and is accompanied by expansion, not only in government demands, but also in private consumption and private investment as additional infrastructure stocks permit private incomes and savings to grow more rapidly with a positive feedback into the growth process (see Table 4.21). The appreciation of the real exchange rate strengthens this process by adding to domestic purchasing power. It represents a response to the fact that, due to the aid, Yemen is now able to have a more negative trade balance, importing more and/or exporting less. As described in Sundberg and Lofgren (2006) for the case of Ethiopia, such aid-induced "Dutch Disease" effects can be a serious concern if, in the future, these trade deficits are unsustainable and if the economy becomes locked into a structure that is unable to expand production of tradables. However, these concerns should be weighed against the benefits of foreign aid, indicated by the simulation results.

For the **aid–hd** scenario, the acceleration of growth in GDP is weaker — the GDP growth rate increases by 0.5 percentage points. MDG 2, 4, 7w and 7s all improve more strongly, as government consumption of primary education, health and water and sanitation increases. The average GDP share of government current and capital spending in MDG-related commodities reaches 10.5% during 2010—2015, starting from the 4.5% for the baseline scenario. The additional public spending in education and health (i.e. scenario **aid-hd**) has a positive impact on the relative demand for skilled workers, pushing up their relative wage. In fact, the wage gap between skilled and unskilled workers is (on average) 11% higher than in the base scenario — this result reflects a bottleneck in the form of a shortage of highly educated labor (e.g. teachers and nurses) to provide these services. In the long run, beyond 2015, the end-year of our simulations, however, the combination of increased education spending and high wages for highly educated labor, both of which make it attractive for students to remain in school and obtain secondary and tertiary education degrees, would lead to an increase in the supply of highly educated labor and a decreasing wage gap between skilled and unskilled workers.

In the **aid-infra** scenario, infrastructure spending promotes growth and the MDGs. Infrastructure has a direct positive impact on education and health MDG indicators because it facilitates the delivery of these services (e.g. more infrastructure lowers the cost of getting to schools for both teachers and students). There is also an indirect effect through higher growth — higher *per capita* income increases private demand for education and health services.

In both aid scenarios, the 2015 poverty rate is lower than for the baseline, mainly as a result of a decrease in unemployment, a higher average wage, a decrease in the wage gap between unskilled and semi-skilled labor and an increase in non-labor income. Moreover, the poverty effect would be larger if a multidimensional measure of poverty were considered instead of only monetary poverty.

In this set of scenarios, it is important to consider the tradeoff between the eventual competitiveness loss caused by aid induced "Dutch Disease" and the long-term gains of improving MDGs.

### 4.7.2.4.3 Efficiency scenarios

For the **eff-infra** scenario, annual growth in GDP accelerates by 0.1 percentage points. The government reallocates spending from consumption to investment, as infrastructure is more capital-intensive than other government services. MDG 2, 4, 7w (water) and 7s (sanitation) all improve. For the **eff-hd** scenario, the acceleration of growth in GDP is weaker (i.e. positive, but less than 0.1 percentage points). The government provision of primary education, health and water and sanitation services grows 5.7 percentage points more than in the base scenario. Certainly, this expenditure shift helps to promote the MDGs. The resulting improvements are stronger for MDG 2 and 4 and less so for MDG 7w and 7s. By 2015, the poverty rate is 0.3 percentage points lower than for the base.

Interestingly, the simulations show that spending on human development is better for poverty reduction than spending on infrastructure, in spite of more rapid GDP growth in **aid–infra** and **eff–infra** compared to **aid–hd** and **aid–infra**, respectively. This result reflects that, relatively speaking, the human development scenarios benefit labor incomes and that labor is owned by the households, whereas the infrastructure scenarios benefit capital and natural resource incomes, which to a significant extent are owned by the government and the rest of the world. As a consequence, in the infrastructure scenarios an important share of income leaks into spending that has a weaker link to household consumption and poverty reduction.

Overall, according to our results, under "business-as-usual" conditions up to 2015, Yemen will not reach the targets for the MDGs that are covered by our analysis. However, important improvements can be achieved if additional resources are spent on infrastructure and/or human development without losses in efficiency. In addition, progress can also be made if government spending efficiency is improved. Under some of the scenarios (**aid–hd** and **aid–infra**), there is a "Dutch Disease" effect, which may harm growth in the production of tradables during the period of these simulations. In future analysis, it would be important to assess the effects of different policies over a longer time horizon, in particular considering the fact that indicators related to human development should lead to stronger gains in future decades.

### 4.7.3 Summary of insights from MAMS applications

The MAMS country applications may be divided into two groups, with the first focused on an analysis of requirements and general equilibrium repercussions of pursuing full achievement of key MDGs by 2015 and the second being more eclectic, but typically looking at the impact of alternative scenarios for public spending (in terms of total resource envelopes and sector priorities), financing (domestic and foreign) and efficiency of public service production and delivery. The Yemen analysis presented above belongs to the second group.

With regard to MDG strategies, the many applications confirm that initial country conditions are the major determinant of whether achievement of the MDGs is feasible or not. For countries, like Ethiopia, for which full MDG achievement would require progress at speeds that go far beyond the historical record of virtually any other country, on-time achievement would accordingly require rates of expansion in grant aid and government services that seem infeasible, at least without a serious deterioration in government efficiency and would create imbalances between government and private sector growth (Lofgren and Diaz-Bonilla, 2008). This outcome is a reflection of the manner in which the targets are defined, and suggests that countries in this category may be better off pursuing poverty and human development targets that are home-grown, reflecting the initial situation, government priorities and plausible scenarios for foreign aid and domestic resource mobilization (*cf.* Easterly, 2009). At the other end of the spectrum of developing countries, comparative cross-country analysis of MAMS results for countries in the Latin America and Caribbean region (which tend to be more middle income) indicate that, even if the prospects for achieving each MDG vary considerably across countries, the required additional financing (which often has to be domestic) of well-conceived programs (covering human development services and infrastructure) are relatively modest and feasible, especially in settings with good income growth for the poorer groups in the population (Vos *et al.*, 2010, pp. 9—12).

Across the board, the second, eclectic group of applications has generated relatively uniform findings related to sectoral allocation of government spending, domestic versus foreign financing, foreign aid and "Dutch Diseases" and government efficiency. These insights may be summarized as follows:

- *Spending on human development versus infrastructure.* The findings in this area indicate that: (i) Marginal changes in infrastructure spending tend to have a more positive impact on production and income growth than human development (i.e. health, education and water—sanitation) spending, especially within a shorter time frame (e.g. within the next five years); (ii) while strategies that on the margin expand spending on human development tend to have more positive human development outcomes than scenarios expanding infrastructure spending, the fact that they tend to generate reduced growth in household incomes noticeably mitigates the gains in human development outcomes while reducing the pace of poverty reduction; and (iii) a relatively balanced expansion of government spending in multiple areas with identified gains (especially public infrastructure and human development services) tend to generate overall outcomes that seem more attractive to policy makers. Such scenarios may also be more feasible politically since they permit a larger number of government functions to expand in real terms, albeit at different rates.

- *Income distribution.* A major short- to medium-run effect of scenarios focused on scaled-up human development spending is a switch in relative wages in favor of the more educated, reflecting that an expansion of health and education sectors leads to a disproportionate increase in demand for relatively educated labor. A byproduct of such scenarios is a general increase in the wages of educated labor throughout the economy (also in the private sector), putting sectors that are intensive in educated labor at a relative disadvantage. In the long run, this relative-wage switch may be reversed as scaled up education spending raises the supply of educated labor, giving rise to the opposite long-run challenge of absorbing rapidly growing highly educated labor stocks with acceptable wage growth, something that requires rapid economic growth and structural changes that, in different sectors, permit productive use of more educated labor.

- *Domestic financing versus foreign aid.* Reliance on domestic financing (taxes or borrowing) to cover rapid expansions in government spending on human development tends to give rise to difficult tradeoffs between the poverty and non-poverty MDGs as the former tend to suffer while the latter gain, reflecting the reallocation of resources from private demand (consumption and investment) to government demand. Reliance on grant aid for marginal financing makes it easier to address these tradeoffs; whether receipt of sufficient additional grant aid is likely or not depends on country context.
- *Foreign aid and "Dutch Disease".* Whether foreign aid expansion leads to "Dutch Disease" effects is an empirical question, primarily depending on the marginal import share of government spending. "Dutch Disease" effects may be stronger for scenarios that emphasize human development spending given that human development sectors are relatively non-traded, with domestic wages representing a large share of input costs, whereas investment spending often has a large import share. The symptoms of "Dutch Disease" are a decline in export growth and an increase in import growth. Whether this should be viewed as a disease depends on whether, in the future, an export/import growth reversal is both needed and difficult to bring about.
- *Government efficiency (allocative and productive).* Simulations suggest that improvements in allocative efficiency, via seemingly feasible marginal reallocations over time of government resources from areas with little or no return to human development and/or infrastructure can lead to noticeable improvements in performance. The same applies to increases in productive government efficiency in different areas of service delivery except for that it is difficult to assess the extent to which such efficiency improvements are feasible.

These findings have been generated by a consistent framework that incorporates a fair amount of economic behavior. They also seem intuitive, supported by basic economic logic. Nevertheless, given the complexity of these issues and uncertainty about parameter values, it is important not to take the exact quantitative results at face value but rather to view the results as aids to thinking that should be cross-checked against insights based on other methods and pieces of analysis. The development of streamlined validation procedures could add to our confidence in the results generated by MAMS and other CGE models.

## 4.8 CONCLUSION

This chapter presented MAMS, a CGE model created for strategy analysis in developing countries: the context in which it was developed, its design features, mathematical structure, database and user-friendly interface. In our discussion of applications, we survey the countries and issues that have been covered and summarize the findings generated, also including a detailed presentation of a Yemeni case study. In addition to the policy-relevant findings, the MAMS experience has also taught lessons of broader relevance to policy-oriented CGE modeling:

- Contrary to frequent assertions, our experience confirms that applications of CGE-based policy analysis are not necessarily time–consuming or high-cost.[88] Model-based analysis would be very costly if, for every study, a new model were built from scratch. However, this is rarely done and should in effect only be done as part of a training program. Data intensity and time needed for data work are highly dependent on the issues addressed, country context and previous experience. We find no reason to think that it is significantly different for CGE modeling compared to other approaches that try to respond to a similar set of questions. Advances in data availability and computational technology should permit streamlining of the development of the bulk of the required datasets.

- Instead of starting new applications using a relatively unchanging bare-bones model, productivity of model-based analysis can over time be enhanced significantly if a framework is applied repeatedly and gradually enhanced as part of a learning process. The benefits may include reduced coding time; fewer and more easily corrected errors (as corrections are carried over to subsequent work and diagnostic checks can be built into the code); higher payoffs from the development of supporting materials (such as manuals and interfaces).

- When interacting with clients in governments and elsewhere, the relevance and persuasiveness of the analysis often depends on the ability of the model to replicate data (frequently expressed in terms of real growth or GDP shares) for years more recent than the model base year and, as a starting point for the analysis, to generate scenarios that match those of other frameworks (e.g. International Monetary Fund projections). In order for this to be feasible, the CGE model must include a wide range of alternative rules for defining payments and related quantities (if any). Similarly, in order to be able to address fiscal policy questions in a flexible manner, it is important to be able to quickly draw on a wide range of alternative clearing mechanisms for the government budget, covering individual or combinations of receipt or spending items.

- The relatively extensive skill set that is required (economics, policy, software and programming) remains a major barrier in the way of a fuller exploitation of the potential of CGE modeling as workhorses for the analysis in areas

---

[88] For example, World Bank (2003, p. 82 and 88) states that the time required to do analysis with a CGE model ranges from "a few months to a year, depending on the existence of a SAM, or of another CGE model built to address a different [sic] question" and, with specific reference to a CGE model with representative households along the lines of Lofgren *et al.* (2002), that "between six months and a year is needed to collect data and work with simulations …."

where they have a comparative advantage (*cf.* the roles of the IS-LM and monetary programming models of Hicks and Polak, respectively, in open-economy macro analysis). In order to permit policy analysts to focus on economics, policy and communication, other requirements should be minimized. One promising avenue may be the development of applications that permit the conduct of simulation analysis over the internet without requiring installation of (or familiarity with) specialized software. This would require fuller exploitation of advances in computational technology and internet-based communication as well as increased division of labor and teamwork among researchers.

## REFERENCES

Acevedo, C., 2008. El Salvador. In: Vos, R., Ganuza, E., Lofgren, H., Sánchez, M.V., Díaz-Bonilla, C. (Eds), Políticas Públicas para el Desarrollo Humano: ¿Cómo lograr los Objetivos de Desarrollo del Milenio en América Latina y el Caribe? Uqbar and UNDP. UNDP, UN-DESA and World Bank, Washington, DC, pp. 419–449.

Adelman, I., Robinson, S., 1978. Income Distribution Policy in Developing Countries. World Bank Research Publication. Oxford University Press and World Bank, Washington, DC.

Agénor, P.-R., Chen, D.H.C., Grimm, M., 2004. Linking representative household models with household surveys for poverty analysis: a comparison of alternative methodologies. Policy Research Working Paper.3343. World Bank, Washington, DC.

Agénor, P.-R., Bayraktar, N., Pinto Moreira, E., El Aynaoui, K., 2005. Achieving the Millennium Development Goals in Sub-Saharan Africa: a macroeconomic monitoring framework. Policy Research Working Paper 3750. World Bank, Washington, DC.

Al-Batuly, A., Al-Hawri, M., Cicowiez, M., Lofgren, H., Pournik, M., 2012. Yemen. In: Sánchez, M.V., Vos, R. (Eds), Financing Human Development in Africa, Asia and the Middle East. Bloomsbury, London, forthcoming.

Barth, R., Hemphill, W., 2000. Financial Programming and Policy: The Case of Turkey. International Monetary Fund, Washington, DC.

Biedermann, G., Corvalán, J., 2008. Paraguay. In: Vos, R., Ganuza, E., Lofgren, H., Sánchez, M.V., Díaz-Bonilla, C. (Eds), Políticas Públicas para el Desarrollo Humano: ¿Cómo lograr los Objetivos de Desarrollo del Milenio en América Latina y el Caribe? Uqbar and UNDP. UNDP, UN-DESA and World Bank, Washington, DC, pp. 607–633.

Bjerkholt, O., 1998. Interaction between model builders and policy makers in the Norwegian tradition. Econ. Model. 15, 317–339.

Bogetic, Z., Bussolo, M., Medvedev, D., 2008. Achieving accelerated and shared growth in Ghana: a MAMS-based analysis of costs and opportunities. World Bank Policy Research Paper 4523. World Bank, Washington, DC.

Bourguignon, F., 2003. The growth elasticity of poverty reduction; explaining heterogeneity across countries and time periods. In: Eicher, T.S., Turnovsky, S.J. (Eds), Inequality and Growth: Theory and Policy Implications. MIT Press, Cambridge, MA, pp. 3–26.

Bourguignon, F., Bussolo, M., Pereira da Silva, L.A., 2008. Introduction: evaluating the impact of macroeconomic policies on poverty and income distribution. In: Bourguignon, F., Maurizio, B., Pereira da Silva, L.A. (Eds), The Impact of Macroeconomic Policies on Poverty and Income Distribution: Macro–Micro Evaluation Techniques And Tools. World Bank and Palgrave Macmillan, Basingstoke, pp. 1–23.

Bourguignon, F., Bussolo, M., Pereira da Silva, L.A., Timmer, H., van der Mensbrugghe, D., 2004. MAMS—MAquette for MDGs Simulation: A Simple Macro-Micro Linkage Model for a Country-Specific Modeling of the Millennium Development Goals or MDGs. World Bank, Washington, DC.

Briones, R.M., Quimba, F., Bungcayao, J.B., Paglingayen, J.B., Libunao, I., Asuncion, M.B., 2012. Philippines. In: Sánchez, M.V., Vos, R. (Eds), Financing Human Development in Africa, Asia and the Middle East. Bloomsbury, London, forthcoming.

Brooke, A., Kendrick, D., Meeraus, A., Raman, R., 2010. GAMS: A User's Guide. GAMS Development Corporation, Washington, DC.

Bussieck, M., Meeraus, A., 2004. General Algebraic Modeling System (GAMS). In: Kallrath, J. (Ed), Modeling Languages in Mathematical Optimization. Kluwer, Norwell, MA, pp. 137–157.

Bussolo, M., Medvedev, D., 2008a. Challenges to MDG achievement in low income countries: lessons from Ghana and Honduras. In: Cockburn, J., Valdivia, M. (Eds), Reaching the MDGs: An International Perspective. Poverty and Economic Policy (PEP) Research Network, pp. 65–96.

Bussolo, M., Medvedev, D., 2008b. Honduras. In: Vos, R., Ganuza, E., Lofgren, H., Sánchez, M.V., Díaz-Bonilla, C. (Eds), Políticas Públicas para el Desarrollo Humano: ¿Cómo lograr los Objetivos de Desarrollo del Milenio en América Latina y el Caribe? Uqbar and UNDP. UNDP, UN-DESA and World Bank, Washington, DC, pp. 477–509.

Bussolo, M., Medvedev, D., 2010. Honduras. In: Sánchez, M., Vos, R., Ganuza, E., Lofgren, H., Díaz-Bonilla, C. (Eds), Public Policies for Human Development: Achieving the Millennium Development Goals in Latin America. Palgrave Macmillan, Basingstoke, pp. 279–306.

Bussolo, M., John, C., 2010. Macro–micro analytics: a guide to combining computable general equilibrium and microsimulation modelling frameworks. Int. J. Microsimulation 3 (1) Special Issue.

Castro, J.F., Yamada, G., 2008. Perú. In: Vos, R., Ganuza, E., Lofgren, H., Sánchez, M.V., Díaz-Bonilla, C. (Eds), Políticas Públicas para el Desarrollo Humano: ¿Cómo lograr los Objetivos de Desarrollo del Milenio en América Latina y el Caribe? Uqbar and UNDP. UNDP, UN-DESA and World Bank, Washington, DC, pp. 635–660.

Castro, J.F., Yamada, G., 2010. Pru. In: Sánchez, M., Vos, R., Ganuza, E., Lofgren, H., Díaz-Bonilla, C. (Eds), Public Policies for Human Development: Achieving the Millennium Development Goals in Latin America. Palgrave Macmillan, Basingstoke, pp. 365–385.

Central Bank of Yemen, 2010. Annual Report 2009. Central Bank of Yemen, Sana'a.

Chemingui, M.A., Sánchez, M.V., 2012. Tunisia. In: Sánchez, M.V., Vos, R. (Eds), Financing Human Development in Africa, Asia and the Middle East. Bloomsbury, London, forthcoming.

Cicowiez, M., Di Gresia, L., Gasparini, L., 2008. Argentina. In: Vos, R., Ganuza, E., Lofgren, H., Sánchez, M.V., Díaz-Bonilla, C. (Eds), Políticas Públicas para el Desarrollo Humano: ¿Cómo lograr los Objetivos de Desarrollo del Milenio en América Latina y el Caribe? Uqbar and UNDP. UNDP, UN-DESA and World Bank, Washington, DC, pp. 159–195.

Cicowiez, M., Di Gresia, L., Gasparini, L., 2010. Argentina. In: Sánchez, M., Vos, R., Ganuza, E., Lofgren, H., Díaz-Bonilla, C. (Eds), Public Policies for Human Development: Achieving the Millennium Development Goals in Latin America. Palgrave Macmillan, Basingstoke, pp. 127–158.

Cloutier, M.-H., Cockburn, J., Decaluwé, B., 2008. Education and poverty in Vietnam: a computable general equilibrium analysis. CIRPEE Working Paper 08-04. CIRPEE, Montreal.

Dervis, K., de Melo, J., Robinson, S., 1982. General Equilibrium Models for Development Policy. World Bank Research Publication. Cambridge University Press and World Bank, New York.

Diagne, A., Cabral, F.J., Cissé, F., Robilliard, A.-S., 2012. Senegal. In: Sánchez, M.V., Vos, R. (Eds), Financing Human Development in Africa, Asia and the Middle East. Bloomsbury Publishing, London forthcoming.

Diaz-Bonilla, C., 2009. Objetivos de Desarrollo del Milenio en la República Dominicana: Insumo a la Estrategia Nacional de Desarrollo. World Bank, Washington, DC.

Diaz-Bonilla, C., Lofgren, H., Cicowiez, M., 2008. República Dominicana. In: Vos, R., Ganuza, E., Lofgren, H., Sánchez, M.V., Díaz-Bonilla, C. (Eds), Políticas Públicas para el Desarrollo Humano: ¿Cómo lograr los Objetivos de Desarrollo del Milenio en América Latina y el Caribe? Uqbar and UNDP. UNDP, UN-DESA and World Bank, Washington, DC, pp. 661–693.

Dixon, P.B., Rimmer, M.T., 2010. Johansen's contribution to CGE modelling: originator and guiding light for 50 years. General Paper G-203. Centre of Policy Studies, Monash University.

Easterly, W., 2009. How the Millennium Development Goals are unfair to Africa. World Dev. 37, 26–35.

Ferriol, Á, Hernández, A., Álvarez, P., Rosales, S., 2008. Cuba. In: Vos, R., Ganuza, E., Lofgren, H., Sánchez, M.V., Díaz-Bonilla, C. (Eds), Políticas Públicas para el Desarrollo Humano: ¿Cómo lograr los Objetivos de Desarrollo del Milenio en América Latina y el Caribe? Uqbar and UNDP. UNDP, UN-DESA and World Bank, Washington, DC, pp. 349—380.

Fox, T., Fullerton, D., 1991. The irrelevance of detail in a computable general equilibrium model. Econ. Lett. 36, 67—70.

Gottschalk, J., Manh Le, V., Lofgren, H., Nouve, K., 2009. Analyzing fiscal space using the MAMS model: an application to Burkina Faso. IMF Working Paper 09/227. IMF, Washington, DC.

Government of Ethiopia, 2005. Ethiopia: The Millennium Development Goals (MDGs) Needs Assessment Synthesis Report. Development Planning and Research Department, Ministry of Finance and Economic Development, Government of Ethiopia, Addis Ababa.

Government of Uganda, 2010. National Development Plan 2010/11—2014/15. Government of Uganda, Kampala.

Government of Yemen, World Bank, United Nations Development Program, 2007. Yemen Poverty Assessment. Government of Yemen, Washington, DC and Sana'a.

Heller, P.S., 2005. Back to basics — fiscal space: what it is and how to get it. IMF Finance Dev. 42 (2).

Hopkins, M., 2002. Labour Market Planning Revisited. Palgrave Macmillan, Basingstoke.

Hopkins, M., van der Hoven, R., 1982. Policy analysis in a socioeconomic model of basic needs applied to four countries. J. Pol. Model. 4, 425—455.

Jiménez, W., 2010. Crisis mundial y cumplimiento de los ODM en América Latina y el Caribe: El caso de Bolivia. Final Project Report (unprocessed). UNDP and UN-DESA, New York.

Jiménez, W., Mariscal, M., Canavire, G., 2008. Bolivia. In: Vos, R., Ganuza, E., Lofgren, H., Sánchez, M.V., Díaz-Bonilla, C. (Eds), Políticas Públicas para el Desarrollo Humano: ¿Cómo lograr los Objetivos de Desarrollo del Milenio en América Latina y el Caribe? Uqbar and UNDP. UNDP, UN-DESA and World Bank, Washington, DC, pp. 197—225.

Jiménez, W., Mariscal, M., Canavire, G., 2010. Bolivia. In: Sánchez, M., Vos, R., Ganuza, E., Lofgren, H., Díaz-Bonilla, C. (Eds), Public Policies for Human Development: Achieving the Millennium Development Goals in Latin America. Palgrave Macmillan, Basingstoke, pp. 159—183.

Johansen, L., 1960. A Multi-Sector Study of Economic Growth. North-Holland, Amsterdam.

Jung, H.-S., Thorbecke, E., 2003. The impact of public education expenditure on human capital, growth, and poverty in Tanzania and Zambia: a general equilibrium approach. J. Pol. Model. 25, 701—725.

Kamaly, A., 2006. On the Determinants of Selected Health and Education Outcomes in sub-Saharan Countries: A Quantitative Analysis. World Bank, Washington, DC.

Kearney, M., Odusola, A., 2012. South Africa. In: Sánchez, M.V., Vos, R. (Eds), Financing Human Development in Africa, Asia and the Middle East. Bloomsbury, London, forthcoming.

Kendrick, D., 1996. Sectoral economics. In: Amman, H., Kendrick, D. (Eds), Handbook of Computational Economics. Elsevier, Amsterdam, pp. 296—332.

Khellaf, A., Belhachmi, E., Karim, M., 2011. Assessing development strategies to achieve the MDGs in The Kingdom of Morocco. Country Study Project Realizing the Millennium Development Goals through Socially Inclusive Macroeconomic Policies. UN Department for Social and Economic Affairs, New York.

Khorshid, M., Kamaly, A., El-Laithy, H., Abou El-Enein, S., 2012. Egypt. In: Sánchez, M.V., Vos, R. (Eds), Financing Human Development in Africa, Asia and the Middle East. Bloomsbury, London, forthcoming.

King, D., Handa, S., 2008. Jamaica. In: Vos, R., Ganuza, E., Lofgren, H., Sánchez, M.V., Díaz-Bonilla, C. (Eds), Políticas Públicas para el Desarrollo Humano: ¿Cómo lograr los Objetivos de Desarrollo del Milenio en América Latina y el Caribe? Uqbar and UNDP. UNDP, UN-DESA and World Bank, Washington, DC, pp. 511—539.

Kinnunen, J., Lofgren, H., Merotto, D., 2009. Family planning, human development and growth in Uganda. Paper presented at the Twelfth Annual Conference on Global Economic Analysis, Santiago.

Kiringai, J., Levin, J., 2008. Achieving the MDGs in Kenya with some aid and reallocation of public expenditures. Working Paper 10. Swedish Business School, Örebro University, Örebro.

Kuhn, T., 1962. The Structure of Scientific Revolutions. University of Chicago Press, Chicago, IL.

Laens, S., Llambí, C., 2008. Uruguay. In: Vos, R., Ganuza, E., Lofgren, H., Sánchez, M.V., Díaz-Bonilla, C. (Eds), Políticas Públicas para el Desarrollo Humano: ¿Cómo lograr los Objetivos de Desarrollo del Milenio en América Latina y el Caribe? Uqbar and UNDP. UNDP, UN-DESA and World Bank, Washington, DC, pp. 695–726.

Lay, J., Robilliard, A.-S., 2009. The complementarity of MDG achievements: the case of child mortality in Sub-Saharan Africa. Policy Research Working Paper 5062. World Bank, Washington, DC.

León, M., Rosero, J., Vos, R., 2008. Ecuador. In: Vos, R., Ganuza, E., Lofgren, H., Sánchez, M.V., Díaz-Bonilla, C. (Eds), Políticas Públicas para el Desarrollo Humano: ¿Cómo lograr los Objetivos de Desarrollo del Milenio en América Latina y el Caribe? Uqbar and UNDP. UNDP, UN-DESA and World Bank, Washington, DC, pp. 381–417.

León, M., Rosero, J., Vos, R., 2010. Ecuador. In: Sánchez, M., Vos, R., Ganuza, E., Lofgren, H., Díaz-Bonilla, C. (Eds), Public Policies for Human Development: Achieving the Millennium Development Goals in Latin America. Palgrave Macmillan, Basingstoke, pp. 245–277.

Llambí, C., Laens, S., 2010. Crisis mundial y cumplimiento de los ODM en América Latina y el Caribe: El caso de Uruguay. Final Project Report (unprocessed). UNDP and UN-DESA, New York.

Lofgren, H., 2010. What determines the evolution of MDG indicators? A selective review of the literature. World Bank, Washington, DC.

Lofgren, H., 2011. MAMS: A Guide for Users. World Bank, Washington, DC.

Lofgren, H., Diaz-Bonilla, C., 2006. Patterns of growth and public spending in Uganda: Alternative scenarios for 2003–2020. Background paper for Uganda: Moving Beyond Recovery—Investment & Behavior Change, For Growth. Country Economic Memorandum, World Bank, Washington, DC.

Lofgren, H., Diaz-Bonilla, C., 2008. Foreign aid, taxes, and government productivity: alternative scenarios for Ethiopia's Millennium Development Goal strategy. In: Go, D.S., Page, J. (Eds), Africa at a Turning Point? Growth, Aid, and External Shocks. World Bank, Washington, DC, pp. 267–300.

Lofgren, H., Kumar, P., 2007. The challenges of achieving Kenya's Vision 2030: a macro perspective. Background paper for Kenya: Accelerating and Sustaining Inclusive Growth. Policy Note. Report 42844-KE. World Bank, Washington, DC.

Lofgren, H., Abdula, R., 2006. Domestic policies and foreign aid: alternative scenarios for Ethiopia, 2006–2010. Background paper for Ethiopia: Review of Public Finance. Poverty Reduction and Economic Management, Africa Region, World Bank, Washington, DC.

Lofgren, H., Robinson, S., 2008. Public spending, growth, and poverty alleviation in Sub-Saharan Africa: a dynamic general equilibrium analysis. In: Fan, S. (Ed), Public Expenditures, Growth, and Poverty: Lessons from Developing Countries. Johns Hopkins University Press, Baltimore, MD, pp. 184–224.

Lofgren, H., Harris, R.L., Robinson, S., with assistance from El-Said, M., Thomas, M., 2002. A standard computable general equilibrium (CGE) model in GAMS. Microcomputers in Policy Research 5. IFPRI, Washington, DC.

Lofgren, H., Robinson, S., El-Said, M., 2003. Poverty and inequality analysis in a general equilibrium framework: the representative household approach. In: Bourguignon, Pereira da Silva, L.A. (Eds), The Impact of Economic Policies on Poverty and Income Distribution: Evaluation Techniques and Tools. World Bank and Oxford University Press, New York, pp. 325–337.

Marouani, M.A., Robalino, D.A., 2008. Assessing interactions among education, social insurance, and labor market policies in a general equilibrium framework: an application to Morocco. Policy Research Working Paper 4681. World Bank, Washington, DC.

Matovu, J.M., Twimukye, E., Musisi, A., Levine, S., 2012. Uganda. In: Sánchez, M.V., Vos, R. (Eds), Financing Human Development in Africa, Asia and the Middle East. Bloomsbury, London, forthcoming.

Mogilevsky, R., Omorova, A., 2012. Kyrgyzstan. In: Sánchez, M.V., Vos, R. (Eds), Financing Human Development in Africa, Asia and the Middle East. Bloomsbury, London, forthcoming.

MOPIC, 2003. Millennium Development Goals: Progress Report for Yemen. Ministry of Planning and International Cooperation. MOPIC, Sana'a.

MOPIC, 2005. Millennium Development Goals Needs Assessment. Yemen Country Report. Ministry of Planning and International Cooperation. MOPIC, Sana'a.

MOPIC, 2010. The Second National Millennium Development Goals Report. Ministry of Planning and International Cooperation. MOPIC, Sana'a.

MOPIC, 2011. Fourth Five-Year Socio-Economic Development Plan for Poverty Reduction 2011–2015. Ministry of Planning and International Cooperation. MOPIC, Sana'a.

Mosley, W.H., Chen, L., 1984. An analytical framework for the study of child survival in developing countries. Popul. Dev. Rev. 10, 25–48 (Supplement: Child Survival: Strategies for Research).

Musisi, A.A., 2009. NDP macroeconomic framework, investment and financing options 2010/11–2014/15. Background Paper for the National Development Plan (NDP). Theme – Growth, Employment and Prosperity for Social-Economic Transformation. Revised Draft (Updated), August. Government of Uganda, Kampala.

Nielsen, N., Lofgren, H., 2011. How important is the efficiency of government investment? The case of the Republic of Congo. Policy Research Working Paper 5901. World Bank, Washington, DC.

Núñez, J., González, N., Hernández, G., 2008. Colombia. In: Vos, R., Ganuza, E., Lofgren, H., Sánchez, M.V., Díaz-Bonilla, C. (Eds), Políticas Públicas para el Desarrollo Humano: ¿Cómo lograr los Objetivos de Desarrollo del Milenio en América Latina y el Caribe? Uqbar and UNDP. UNDP, UN-DESA and World Bank, Washington, DC, pp. 283–312.

O'Ryan, R.L., Pereira, M., de Miguel, C., 2010. Crisis mundial y cumplimiento de los ODM en América Latina y el Caribe: El caso de Chile. Final Project Report (unprocessed). UNDP and UN-DESA, New York.

Olimov, U., Fayzullaev, Y., 2012. Uzbekistan. In: Sánchez, M.V., Vos, R. (Eds), Financing Human Development in Africa, Asia and the Middle East. Bloomsbury, London, forthcoming.

Ortega Díaz, A., 2011. Crisis mundial y cumplimiento de los ODM en América Latina y el Caribe: El caso de México. Final Project Report (unprocessed). UNDP and UN-DESA, New York.

Ortega, A., Székely, M., 2008. México. In: Vos, R., Ganuza, E., Lofgren, H., Sánchez, M.V., Díaz-Bonilla, C. (Eds), Políticas Públicas para el Desarrollo Humano: ¿Cómo lograr los Objetivos de Desarrollo del Milenio en América Latina y el Caribe? Uqbar and UNDP. UNDP, UN-DESA and World Bank, Washington, DC, pp. 541–567.

Ortega, A., Székely, M., 2010. Mexico. In: Sánchez, M., Vos, R., Ganuza, E., Lofgren, H., Díaz-Bonilla, C. (Eds), Public Policies for Human Development: Achieving the Millennium Development Goals in Latin America. Palgrave Macmillan, Basingstoke, pp. 307–327.

O'Ryan, R., de Miguel, C., Lagos, C., 2008. Chile. In: Vos, R., Ganuza, E., Lofgren, H., Sánchez, M.V., Díaz-Bonilla, C. (Eds), Políticas Públicas para el Desarrollo Humano: ¿Cómo lograr los Objetivos de Desarrollo del Milenio en América Latina y el Caribe? Uqbar and UNDP. UNDP, UN-DESA and World Bank, Washington, DC, pp. 251–281.

O'Ryan, R., de Miguel, C., Lagos, C., 2010. Chile. In: Sánchez, M., Vos, R., Ganuza, E., Lofgren, H., Díaz-Bonilla, C. (Eds), Public Policies for Human Development: Achieving the Millennium Development Goals in Latin America. Palgrave Macmillan, Basingstoke, pp. 185–211.

Pearson, K., Horridge, M., 2005. Hands-on Computing with RunGTAP and WinGEM to Introduce GTAP and GEMPACK. Centre of Policy Studies and Impact Project. Monash University.

Pyatt, G., Round, J.I. (Eds), 1985. Social Accounting Matrices: A Basis for Planning. A World Bank Symposium. World Bank, Washington, DC.

Rao, M.J.Manohar., Raj Nallari., 2001. Macroeconomic Stabilization and Adjustment. Oxford University Press, New Delhi.

Republic of Benin (Ministry of Economy and Finance) and UNDP., 2010. Strategies de Financement pour l'Atteinte des OMD au Benin: Politique Fiscale et Aide Publique au Développement [Financing Strategy for Achieving MDGs in Benin: Fiscal Policy and Public Development Aid]. Government of Benin and UNDP, Porto Novo.

Robinson, S., El-Said, M., 2000. GAMS code for estimating a social accounting matrix using cross entropy (CE) methods. Trade and Macroeconomics Division Discussion Paper 64. IFPRI, Washington, DC.

Robinson, S., Cattaneo, A., El-Said, M., 2001. Updating and estimating a social accounting matrix using cross entropy methods. Econ. Systems Res. 13, 47–64.

Robinson, S., Yúnez-Naude, A., Hinojosa-Ojeda, R., Lewis, J.D., Devarajan, S., 1999. From stylized to applied models: building multisector CGE models for policy analysis. N. Am. J. Econ. Finance 10, 5–38.

Rosero Moncayo, J.A., León G, M., 2010. Crisis mundial y cumplimiento de los ODM en América Latina y el Caribe: El caso de Ecuador. Final Project Report (unprocessed). UNDP and UN-DESA, New York.

Round, J.I., 2003. Constructing SAMs for development policy analysis: lessons learned and challenges ahead. Econ. Systems Res. 15, 161—183.

Ruggeri Laderchi, C., Lofgren, H., Abdula, R., 2010. Addressing gender inequality in Ethiopia: trends, impacts and the way forward. In: Saba Arbache, J., Kolev, A., Filipiak, E. (Eds), Gender Disparities in Africa's Labor Market. World Bank and the Agence Française de Développement (AFD), Washington, DC, pp. 193—227.

Sánchez, M., Vos, R., 2010. Crisis mundial y cumplimiento de los ODM en América Latina y el Caribe: El caso de Nicaragua. Final Project Report (unprocessed). UNDP and UN-DESA, New York.

Sánchez, M.V., 2008. Costa Rica. In: Vos, R., Ganuza, E., Lofgren, H., Sánchez, M.V., Díaz-Bonilla, C. (Eds), Políticas Públicas para el Desarrollo Humano: ¿Cómo lograr los Objetivos de Desarrollo del Milenio en América Latina y el Caribe? Uqbar and UNDP. UNDP, UN-DESA and World Bank, Washington, DC, pp. 313—347.

Sánchez, M.V., 2010. Costa Rica. In: Sánchez, M., Vos, R., Ganuza, E., Lofgren, H., Díaz-Bonilla, C. (Eds), Public Policies for Human Development: Achieving the Millennium Development Goals in Latin America. Palgrave Macmillan, Basingstoke, pp. 213—243.

Sánchez, M.V., Sbrana, G., 2009. Determinants of Education Attainment and Development Goals in Yemen. Department of Economic and Social Affairs (DESA), United Nations, New York.

Sánchez, M.V., Vos, R., 2008. Nicaragua. In: Vos, R., Ganuza, E., Lofgren, H., Sánchez, M.V., Díaz-Bonilla, C. (Eds), Políticas Públicas para el Desarrollo Humano: ¿Cómo lograr los Objetivos de Desarrollo del Milenio en América Latina y el Caribe? Uqbar and UNDP. UNDP, UN-DESA and World Bank, Washington, DC, pp. 596—603.

Sánchez, M.V., Vos, R., 2010. Nicaragua. In: Sánchez, M., Vos, R., Ganuza, E., Lofgren, H., Díaz-Bonilla, C. (Eds), Public Policies for Human Development: Achieving the Millennium Development Goals in Latin America. Palgrave Macmillan, Basingstoke, pp. 329—364.

Sbrana, G., 2009. Technical Note on the Determinants of Water and Sanitation in Yemen. Department of Economic and Social Affairs (DESA), United Nations, New York.

Shoven, J.B., Whalley, J., 1984. Applied general-equilibrium models of taxation and international trade: an introduction and survey. J. Econ. Lit. 22, 1007—1051.

Sundberg, M., Lofgren, H., 2006. Absorptive capacity and achieving the MDGs: the case of Ethiopia. In: Isard, P., Lipschitz, L., Mourmouras, A., Yontcheva, B. (Eds), The Macroeconomic Management of Foreign Aid: Opportunities and Pitfalls. International Monetary Fund, Washington, DC, pp. 141—170.

Thurlow, J., 2004. A dynamic computable general equilibrium (CGE) model for South Africa: extending the static IFPRI model. Trade and Industrial Policy Strategies Working Paper 1-2004. Johannesburg.

Ulyssea, G., Le Boulluec, Y., 2008. Brasil. In: Vos, R., Ganuza, E., Lofgren, H., Sánchez, M.V., Díaz-Bonilla, C. (Eds), Políticas Públicas para el Desarrollo Humano: ¿Cómo lograr los Objetivos de Desarrollo del Milenio en América Latina y el Caribe? Uqbar and UNDP. UNDP, UN-DESA and World Bank, Washington, DC, pp. 227—250.

United Nations., 2011. Impact of the crisis and macroeconomic challenges to meeting the Millennium Development Goals. United Nations, World Economic Situation and Prospects, Box I.3. United Nations publication, New York.

UNDP, 2009. Human Development Report 2009: Overcoming Barriers: Human Mobility and Development. United Nations Development Program, New York.

van der Mensbrugghe, D., 2005a. Prototype Model for a Single Country Real Computable General Equilibrium Model. Development Prospects Group, World Bank, Washington, DC. Available at siteresources.worldbank.org/INTPROSPECTS/Resources/334934-1184090646382/DvdMTechRefV5.pdf.

van der Mensbrugghe, D., 2005b. LINKAGE Technical Reference Document. Version 6.1. Development Prospects Group, World Bank, Washington, DC.

Vásquez Mazariegos, W.F., 2008. Guatemala. In: Vos, R., Ganuza, E., Lofgren, H., Sánchez, M.V., Díaz-Bonilla, C. (Eds), Políticas Públicas para el Desarrollo Humano: ¿Cómo lograr los Objetivos de

Desarrollo del Milenio en América Latina y el Caribe? Uqbar and UNDP. UNDP, UN-DESA and World Bank, Washington, DC, pp. 451–476.

Vos, Rob, Sánchez, Marco V., 2010. A non-parametric microsimulation approach to assess changes in inequality and poverty. Int. J. Microsimulation 3 (Special Issue), 8–23.

WDI, 2010. World Development Indicators 2010. World Bank, Washington, DC.

World Bank, 2003. A User's Guide to Poverty and Social Impact Analysis. World Bank, Washington, DC.

World Bank, 2006. Ethiopia. Review of Public Finance. Poverty Reduction and Economic Management Unit. Country Department for Ethiopia, Africa Region. World Bank, Washington, DC.

World Bank, 2007a. Capturing the demographic bonus in Ethiopia: the role of gender equitable development and demographic actions. Sector Report 36434-ET. Poverty Reduction and Economic Management 2 (AFTP2). Country Department for Ethiopia, Africa Region. World Bank, Washington, DC.

World Bank, 2007b. Country assistance strategy for the Democratic Republic of Congo for the period FY08–FY11. World Bank Report 41474-ZR. Africa Region. World Bank, Washington, DC.

World Bank, 2007c. Urban labour markets in Ethiopia: challenges and prospects. Sector Report 38665-ET. Poverty Reduction and Economic Management, Africa Region. World Bank, Washington, DC.

World Bank, 2007d. Ghana: meeting the challenge of accelerated and shared growth. country economic memorandum. World Bank Report. 40934-GH.PREM 4. Africa Region. World Bank, Washington, DC.

World Bank, 2007e. Honduras: public expenditure review. World Bank Report 39251-HO. Poverty Reduction and Economic Management, Latin America and the Caribbean Region—Central America Department. World Bank, Washington, DC.

World Bank, 2007f. Malawi: public expenditures review 2006. World Bank Report 40145-MW. Poverty Reduction and Economic Management, Africa Region. World Bank, Washington, DC.

World Bank, 2007g. Uganda: moving beyond recovery—investment and behavior change, for growth. Country economic memorandum. World Bank Report 39221-UG. Poverty Reduction and Economic Management, Africa Region. World Bank, Washington, DC.

World Bank, 2008a. Democratic Republic of Congo: public expenditure review. World Bank Report 42167-ZR. Poverty Reduction and Economic Management, Africa Region. World Bank, Washington, DC.

World Bank, 2008b. Kenya: accelerating and sustaining inclusive growth. Policy note. Report 42844-KE. Poverty Reduction and Economic Management, Africa Region. World Bank, Washington, DC.

World Bank, 2009a. Unleashing the potential of Ethiopian women: trends and options for economic empowerment. World Bank Report 49366-ET. Poverty Reduction and Economic Management 2, Africa Region. World Bank, Washington, DC.

World Bank, 2009b. Kenya poverty and inequality assessment: executive summary and synthesis. Report 44190-KE. Poverty Reduction and Economic Management, Africa Region. World Bank, Washington, DC.

World Bank, 2010. Global Monitoring Report: The MDGs After the Crisis. World Bank, Washington, DC.

# CHAPTER 5

# Contribution of Computable General Equilibrium Modeling to Policy Formulation in Developing Countries

**Shantayanan Devarajan\*, Sherman Robinson\*\***
\*World Bank
\*\*International Food Policy Research Institute (IFPRI)

## Abstract

This chapter reviews the experience of computable general equilibrium (CGE) models from the perspective of how they have, or have not, influenced public policy in developing countries. The paper describes different classes of empirical models — from small, stylized to large, multisectoral applied models; from static equilibrium models to dynamic, perfect-foresight models — and identifies the characteristics of models best suited to address different policy problems in developing countries. The paper then discusses the different ways CGE models have been and are being used in policy formulation, the types of questions they have addressed, and the lessons learned from past experience. Finally, the paper suggests that, in light of the changing nature of policy making in developing countries, in the future CGE models should be used differently, moving from a purely technocratic exercise used by policy makers to providing an accessible empirical framework that can contribute to a widespread public debate.

## Keywords

Computable general equilibrium modeling, economic development, policy modeling, computable general equilibrium in democracy

## JEL classification codes

O2, F1, H2, Q1, Q5

## 5.1 INTRODUCTION

The first computable general equilibrium (CGE) model, developed for Norway by Leif Johansen (Johansen, 1960), was intended to be used for policy analysis and its descendants are still used by the Norwegian government today. Early applications of models of the US also focused on policy issues (in public finance, international trade and environmental policy; Shoven and Whalley, 1972, Jorgenson, 1984). In parallel, there has been an equally rich and varied tradition of applications to developing countries, starting from work with input–output and programming models, which were precursors to CGE

*Handbook of CGE Modeling - Vol. 1 SET*
ISSN 2211-6885, http://dx.doi.org/10.1016/B978-0-444-59568-3.00005-5
© 2013 Elsevier B.V.
All rights reserved.
277

models, and then CGE models.[1] These different strands of work, while initially focused on different policy issues, are all rooted in the same core of neoclassical general equilibrium theory.[2]

Many developing countries, starting with India, were initially engaged in central planning. CGE models, or their predecessor input-output and programming models, were appropriate instruments for evaluating the consistency of public investment programs and other policies with the plan's objectives.[3] As countries abandoned central planning and moved towards more market-based economies, with less direct government involvement in production and investment decisions, CGE models became even more appropriate, as they simulate the operation of market economies. Finally, inasmuch as developing countries are characterized by high levels of poverty and poverty reduction is a major goal of policy, a tool that captures the uses and sources of people's incomes (both of which are mediated through product and factor prices) is not just valuable — it is essential.

On the other hand, some observers were, and a few continue to be, skeptical about the application of CGE models to developing countries for the following reasons: (i) Developing countries are characterized by many institutional factors and rigidities (dual labor markets, thin capital markets, state-owned enterprises, controlled prices, etc.) so that a neoclassical, price-endogenous model, where agents optimize based on full information about prices and their own endowments, may not be the most suitable theoretical framework. (ii) These models require large amounts of data — across sectors and over time — in countries where even robust national accounts are a recent phenomenon. (iii) The domestic capacity to build, maintain and use CGE models was limited in most developing countries. Models built by scholars in developed countries might at best be ineffective and at worst be seen as yet another imposition from rich countries. To be sure, advances in developing countries over the past 30–40 years have allayed many of these concerns and CGE models are now widely used there as standard tools of policy analysis.

This chapter reviews the experience of applying CGE models to policy problems in developing countries. We focus on those cases where the use of models has made a contribution to policy formulation. We do not therefore look at the numerous applications that have shed light on development economics in general (Gunning and Keyzer, 1995; Robinson, 1989). In Section 5.2, we show how the above-mentioned tension between the need for a price-endogenous, general equilibrium model and some

---

[1] See, e.g. Blitzer et al. (1975), Adelman and Robinson (1978), and Dervis et al. (1982).

[2] While they shared the same underlying theory, the different strands of work initially used different approaches to solving the models empirically (see, e.g. Dixon and Parmenter, 1996). Today, solving even very large CGE models has become routine, so these differences do not concern those engaged in policy analysis with these models.

[3] The theoretical evolution from programming models to general equilibrium models was a focus of academic work on general equilibrium analysis (see, e.g. Dorfman et al., 1958).

of the features of developing countries — such as institutional rigidities and poor data — have led to particular types of CGE models being more commonly used to inform policy in developing countries. In Section 5.3, we review the main policy questions facing developing countries, and show how these models have been used to address them and the lessons learned from the experience. Section 5.4 draws the lessons learned and suggests future directions for enhancing the impact of CGE models on development policy.

## 5.2 TYPES OF CGE MODELS FOR DEVELOPMENT POLICY

### 5.2.1 Theory and empirical models

Models in general, and CGE models in particular, are used widely in economics. To understand their application to developing countries, it is useful to place CGE models along two continua: (i) analytic to applied and (ii) reduced form to deep structural.

"Analytic" refers to theoretical models that can be solved mathematically, while applied models are simulation models that are solved numerically because they are too complex to be solved analytically. "Stylized numerical models" are simulation models that stay as close as possible to their theoretical roots, are typically small and provide numerical solutions that can be used to explore the empirical implications of different theoretical mechanisms at work in the models. On the continuum, they lie between analytic and applied models. We will use the term "applied" to refer to empirical simulation models that attempt to incorporate institutional features of particular developing economies; they provide a more realistic representation of such economies than is typical of stylized models. These applied models tend to be larger and more complex than stylized models. In this continuum, "policy models" are simulation models that explicitly include policy instruments and capture the links between changes in those instruments and economic outcomes. In policy analysis, empirical policy models tend to be applied models, but, as we show below, there are many examples of stylized numerical models that incorporate policy instruments and have been used in policy debates.

In policy analysis, the credibility, applicability and realism of economic models are often subjects of debate. Simulation models have been criticized for being "black boxes" whose results are difficult or impossible to explain in terms of credible causal chains that are accessible to policy makers. The work program on the policy use of CGE models has involved, over a long period, both theoretical and empirical advances that have illuminated the black boxes. For example, the theoretical treatment of foreign trade in CGE models has been of particular concern, given the wide use of these models in the analysis of trade policy. The specification of traded goods as imperfect substitutes for domestically produced goods in the same commodity classification — the Armington insight — was viewed by some as an *ad hoc* empirical specification that was theoretically suspect.[4] Others criticized the theoretical role of exchange rates in CGE models, since a Walrasian general equilibrium model can only determine relative prices and there is no role for a "financial" exchange rate variable.[5] These theoretical debates spilled over into criticisms of the policy uses of CGE models and needed to be resolved to establish the validity of these models in policy analysis.

The theoretical issues around the Armington specification and the role of the exchange rate in CGE models were sorted out through the development of a small theoretical model — the 1—2—3 model (one country, two activities, three commodities) — that captured the theoretical core of trade-focused CGE models.[6] The 1—2—3 model is an extension of the Salter—Swan "Australian" model, which distinguished a tradable and a non-tradable commodity, with the tradable price determined in the world market and the non-tradable price determined in the domestic market. In the Salter—Swan model, the real exchange rate is the relative price of the tradable to the non-tradable commodity.

Using the Armington insight, the 1—2—3 model specifies that a country produce two commodities, one for domestic consumption and one for exports, and also consumes a third commodity, an import, which is an imperfect substitute in consumption with the domestic good. The model extends Salter—Swan in specifying degrees of tradability. Both export and import commodities are "semi-tradable" — imperfect substitutes with domestically produced goods sold on the domestic market, as in trade-focused CGE models. The 1—2—3 model is simple enough to be solved analytically, so that all its properties can be shown algebraically (and graphically).[7]

The 1—2—3 model demonstrated that CGE models are theoretical generalizations of the Salter—Swan model and that the textbook neoclassical trade theory model, with all commodities specified as both tradable and perfect substitutes with domestically

---

[4] Armington (1969) assumed imperfect substitutability of traded and non-traded goods in estimating import demand functions, and the approach was picked up by early CGE models. Deardorff (1984), in a survey for the *Handbook of International Trade*, described the use of this specification in CGE models as theoretically unsatisfactory but useful in empirical models, which would otherwise generate nonsensical results (e.g. extreme specialization).

[5] See Whalley and Yeung (1984), who carefully avoided the term "exchange rate" when discussing the "parameter" that adjusted to clear the foreign trade balance constraint in trade-focused CGE models.

[6] See de Melo and Robinson (1989), Devarajan and de Melo (1987), and Devarajan *et al*. (1990, 1993) for discussions of the 1—2—3 model. Thierfelder and Robinson (2003) extend the 1—2—3 model to include factor markets and describe the theoretical implications for the Stolper—Samuelson and Rybczynski Theorems, and the link between wages and changes in the trade balance.

[7] The technique used to solve the 1—2—3 model analytically (and graphically) is to note that a CGE model can be written as a special constrained maximization problem, maximizing social welfare subject to constraints on available resources and the trade balance — the value in world prices of total imports cannot exceed the value of total exports plus any foreign transfers. The shadow prices from the solution to this maximization problem equal the solution market prices from a CGE model. The solution real exchange rate can be seen as the shadow price of the trade-balance constraint. The use of this theoretical approach to solve CGE models is described in Ginsburgh and Keyzer (2002), and its application in models where there is a trade-balance constraint (and perhaps other aggregate "macro" constraints) is described in Ginsburgh and Robinson (1984).

produced commodities, is a special case of this model. As in the Salter—Swan model, the exchange rate in the 1—2—3 model and CGE models is a theoretically well-defined relative price of aggregates of traded to non-traded commodities. It can be seen as a signal in commodity markets and is in no sense a financial variable, since the CGE model does not contain money, financial instruments or asset markets. Conceptually, it is close to the "real effective exchange rate" calculations published by the International Monetary Fund and others (Devarajan *et al.*, 1993).

The 1—2—3 model and CGE models based on this specification have a number of realistic empirical properties compared to models assuming perfect substitutability of traded and non-traded commodities.

- The model allows two-way trade (both exports and imports) in particular commodity classifications, which is realistic given the level of aggregation usually specified in empirical models; indeed, two-way trade is observed at very detailed levels of disaggregation of trade data.
- Changes in world prices, and the impact of changes in tariffs, are only partially transmitted to domestic prices, depending on both the degree of substitutability and trade shares; again, a realistic property.
- Changes in aggregate exports and imports are related to the real exchange rate, with a real depreciation associated with an increase in aggregate exports and a decrease in imports (with the amounts depending on elasticities).
- An increase in the trade balance (i.e. aggregate imports rising relative to exports due, for example, to an increase in foreign borrowing) will always lead to an appreciation of the real exchange rate — the model replicates the "Dutch Disease" effect specified in macro models. The trade balance is monotonically related to the real exchange rate.
- The powerful links between world markets, factor prices and the sectoral allocation of resources that are evident in models with all commodities tradable are damped in the 1—2—3 model (extended to include factor markets). In particular, the magnification effects shown in the Stolper—Samuelson theorem (wages) and Rybczynski theorem (factor allocation across sectors) now depend on substitution elasticities and trade shares, and are empirically much more realistic in CGE models (Thierfelder and Robinson, 2003). If imports are poor substitutes for domestic commodities, even the sign of the Stolper—Samuelson effect of changes in world prices on factor prices is reversed.

While it was developed to contribute to the theoretical debate, the 1—2—3 model has also been implemented as the core of stylized numerical models used to understand, and explain to policy makers, the results of larger applied models. Versions of the 1—2—3 model have been used to estimate the revenue implications of trade reforms (Devarajan *et al.*, 1999) and the degree of overvaluation of the CFA Franc (Communauté Financière Africaine) in the early 1990s (Devarajan, 1997). The use of theoretically well-specified, stylized numerical models to explain the results of larger, applied policy models has greatly reduced the "black box" criticism of CGE simulation models.

The second model continuum, "reduced form to deep structural," refers to the way in which economic theory is reflected in model structure. The term "reduced form" comes from econometrics, where such models include equations linking endogenous and exogenous variables, but where it is often impossible to "identify" the underlying structural model that gives rise to the reduced form equations. In effect, such models use economic theory to motivate the specification, but end up with estimated equations and parameters only loosely linked to the theory. At the other end of this continuum, "deep structural" models such as CGE models, explicitly specify the economic actors (e.g. households and producers), their motivation (e.g. utility and profit maximization), the markets across which they interact (e.g. commodity and factor markets) and the signals to which they respond (e.g. relative prices of commodities and factors). In addition, CGE models specify aggregate resource supplies (e.g. labor and capital) and market-clearing conditions (supply equals demand in all markets) whose satisfaction determines the equilibrium solution values for commodity and factor prices, as well as all quantities.

With these continua in mind, CGE models can be seen as deep structural, empirical, market simulation models, with many examples along the continuum from stylized to applied and usually incorporating policy instruments explicitly. They have to be structural because understanding the mechanisms through which policies affect the economy is the whole purpose of the exercise. A reduced-form model, even if it forecasts the economy's aggregate variables accurately, is of little use for policy analysis, which requires explicit structural links between policy choices and economic outcomes. For policy debates and analysis, models tend to be at the applied end, incorporating institutional detail and commodity/factor disaggregation that adequately describe the economic environment and mechanisms by which policy instruments affect economic actors.

## 5.2.2 Types of equilibrium and domain of application

In addition to these continua, CGE models can be classified according to: (i) the nature of the equilibrium they embody and (ii) their domain of application. A standard static CGE model is a "neoclassical" Arrow–Debreu general equilibrium model in that it incorporates only flow equilibria in product and factor markets, and solves only for relative prices. The model contains no assets or money, and is static, with myopic agents who do not look beyond the current period in making decisions — or do not need to, if the static equilibrium can be viewed as a steady state. Walras, not Keynes, is the patron saint of CGE models. When these models incorporate financial assets, it is often in an *ad hoc* manner, departing from the neoclassical assumptions of the rest of the model.

Nevertheless, some of these departures are necessary to address the question at hand, and to incorporate characteristics of developing economies.[8]

There are two broad types of dynamic CGE models: dynamic recursive and forward-looking. Dynamic recursive models are the most commonly used in developing-country applications, with a two-step dynamic process: (i) a "within-period" static CGE model is solved, yielding a within-period set of equilibrium prices and quantities, and (ii) a "between-period" model is solved, specifying how parameters that are exogenous in the within-period model are updated between periods. Such updating may involve applying simple growth rates (e.g. labor force or total factor productivity growth) or specifying some kind of "adaptive expectations" (e.g. allocation of investment to sector of destination). While agents may adapt, there is no forward-looking equilibrium in such models (e.g. perfect foresight or rational expectations equilibrium). As we show in the case of Turkey's real exchange rate below, this admittedly imperfect way of incorporating changes over time can yield important insights for policy — especially when the alternative of a forward-looking dynamic model is not available or seems theoretically inappropriate in a particular applied setting.

There are many examples of forward-looking dynamic CGE models that essentially incorporate neoclassical growth theory.[9] These models tend to be highly stylized, but often include policy instruments and have been used to explore issues such as investment strategies or climate change where intertemporal resource allocation is salient. These models have not generally been influential in policy debates in developing countries, largely because of their stylized nature — they lack the granularity and specificity of applied models to particular country settings. Dynamic stochastic general equilibrium (DSGE) models, in cases where they include more than one sector, are close to this class of highly stylized, neoclassical dynamic CGE models.

Simulation models in general and CGE models in particular can also be characterized by their domain of applicability — the range of phenomena they incorporate. When considering the usefulness of a particular model in a particular application, it is important to judge whether the model adequately incorporates and simulates the features of an economy necessary for capturing the links under study. Model specifications that may be adequate for one purpose may be inappropriate for another. For example, many static CGE models specify simple utility functions such as Cobb–Douglas that assume unitary income elasticities of demand for all commodities. In a static model, where income does not change significantly, such an approximation may be adequate, but it is clearly

---

[8] The issues of macro features of CGE models, and of integrating macro and CGE models, have been topics of active debate throughout the history of CGE models applied to developing countries. See Rattso (1982) and Robinson (1989, 1991, 2006) for surveys of these debates.

[9] An excellent textbook treatment of empirical growth models is Roe *et al.* (2010).

inadequate for a dynamic model where incomes change over time, and Engel's law will come into play.[10]

The large number of CGE models used to analyze the implications of trade liberalization — a major policy issue in developing countries over the last two decades — is another example. Most of these models captured the changes in the intersectoral structure of demand and supply arising from trade reforms. They did not address the endogenous growth effects of lowering trade barriers, except in an *ad hoc* manner (e.g. by assuming an impact of lower tariffs on total factor productivity). These effects are better analyzed in dynamic models, although there is as yet no widespread agreement about the theoretical specification of such links. Even with a limited scope, as we illustrate with the case of India below, static CGE models have been influential in sharpening the debate on trade policy in developing countries.

The notion of domain of applicability is relevant to another model design characteristic: simplicity. There is a modeler's version of "Occam's Razor:" always use the simplest and smallest model that is adequate to the task.[11] In policy debates, this notion of model simplicity is especially important. As we discuss below, it is very important in policy debates to be able to explain model results in simple terms — avoiding the "black box" criticism discussed earlier. Models that are needlessly complex make it harder to trace and explain the causal chains between changes in policy instruments and economic outcomes. At the same time, policy makers are sometimes skeptical about models that leave out phenomena they consider important — even if, in the modeler's view, including them would make no difference to the model's results for particular policy issues.

There are many examples of CGE models linked to "auxiliary" models or relationships, which are used to trace the outcomes from the CGE model to other relevant variables. For example, the (Maquette for MDG Simulations) model at the World Bank consists of a core single-country, dynamic recursive CGE model which generates scenarios for: output, trade, employment, and income over time.[12] The model includes a set of auxiliary functions, mostly regression equations and elasticity relationships that determine the impact of the national economic changes on a set of the Millennium Development Goals (MDGs), which includes measures of poverty, nutrition status, and so on. The result is a linked set of models that are, however, viewed as a single integrated model. These extraneous relationships are not integral to the CGE model, but are linked to it in policy debates, and criticisms concerning the validity of these relationships spill

---

[10] The assumption of unitary own-price elasticities of demand in a Cobb–Douglas utility function seems unrealistic, even in simple models.

[11] Note that simplicity is not necessarily related to size. Large models may be driven by simple causal chains that are easy to explain, while small models may be theoretically very complex.

[12] See Lofgren and Diaz-Bonilla (2012) and Lofgren *et al.* in Chapter 4 of this Handbook.

over to the CGE model. In this case, it would be useful in policy applications to separate the two strands of analysis in the discussion of results.

In short, simplification should be strategic. As Einstein reportedly said: "Everything should be made as simple as possible, but no simpler."

## 5.2.3 Estimation and validation

Model estimation and validation are difficult issues for CGE simulation models. For a macro-econometric simultaneous equation model; estimation, validation and definition of the domain of applicability are all done simultaneously. Estimation of parameters and validation are done together by finding parameter values that minimize a "goodness-of-fit" distance function between the forecast values of endogenous variables and historical data. The better is the goodness of fit, the more "valid" is the model.[13] The domain of values of the historical data and the range of values of the endogenous variables define the domain of applicability of the estimated model. Using such a model to "forecast" endogenous variables for values of exogenous variables outside the domain of the historical data used to estimate the model is not statistically justified and is problematic. Validation of an econometric model for such forecasting requires information about the validity of the structural relations in the model outside of historical experience.

For deep structural CGE models of developing countries, parameter estimation and model validation are separate exercises. Typically, there are two kinds of parameters to be estimated for the various production and cost functions and expenditure equations — shares and elasticities. The shares can be estimated with confidence from data in the social accounting matrix (SAM), which is assumed to represent an equilibrium solution of the model in the base year. The various elasticities of substitution in production and demand are more difficult to estimate, since there are rarely adequate time-series data to support estimation by standard econometric methods. However, there are often scattered econometric studies from which estimates can be drawn. The specification of the deep structural model allows for a Bayesian approach, using priors for elasticities based on theoretical and empirical information about the nature of the underlying production, cost and expenditure functions. Defining the domain of applicability of the CGE model also relies on a Bayesian analysis of the specification and parameters of the deep structural model. Economic theory provides information about the validity of the relationships and related econometric studies provide information about potential parameter values, which together define the domain of applicability of the model. Given the lack of data to support standard econometric analysis, validation also often

---

[13] When feasible (e.g. with lots of data), good econometric practice is to estimate the model with one set of data and then use a separate data set to validate the model, using the estimated parameters from the first set in forecasting the endogenous variables in the second set.

involves sensitivity analysis to determine if the model results are robust over its domain of application. In an environment of poor data, as in many developing countries, this sensitivity analysis for model validation becomes increasingly important.

## 5.2.4 Modes of policy analysis

In policy analysis, CGE models have typically been used to explore different "scenarios" where policies are changed and then the model is solved to see how the changes affect the economy. The model is used as a simulation laboratory for doing controlled experiments, which are designed to explore the empirical importance of the links between policy changes and economic outcomes. The scenarios are not necessarily designed to be realistic in the sense that they are "likely" to occur. Rather, they are meant to inform policy makers about the relative strength of potential impacts of policy changes. Nor are they designed to provide "forecasts" since the variables being held constant in order to isolate important causal chains are unlikely to be constant in the real world. As illustrated in the case of a carbon tax in South Africa, it is common when exploring and comparing the distortionary impact of different tax regimes to design scenarios where tax rates are changed, but total government revenue is held constant. This assumption provides a control — a benchmark — to facilitate comparison across different tax instruments. However, it is not a realistic assumption if the goal is to provide a forecast of the impact of a proposed change in tax regime in a particular institutional setting.

In principle, a good, deep structural simulation model can be used for forecasting as well as for scenario analysis. The challenges, however, are different between the approaches. Scenarios are generally designed to isolate and quantify the importance of different causal chains linking policy changes and economic outcomes. Forecasting requires designing composite scenarios where realistic changes in all exogenous parameters and variables need to be specified and implemented simultaneously in the model, which will then be solved for the forecast of all endogenous variables. The accuracy and hence validity of the forecasted endogenous variables is conditioned on the accuracy of the forecast of all the exogenous variables and parameters.

For the purposes of policy analysis, scenario analysis is generally more relevant than forecasting — policy makers are interested in the potential impacts of the choices they are considering. In making decisions about policy choices, scenario analysis that focuses on controlled experiments to explore the links between policies and outcomes provides the relevant framework for analysis.

In scenario analysis, we distinguish four different "modes" of analysis with CGE models in empirical applications: (i) timeless comparative statics, (ii) dated comparative statics, (iii) timeless dynamics and finally (iv) dated dynamics. Dated comparative statics and dated dynamics can be seen as two forms of "projection" analysis.

In timeless comparative statics, a model calibrated for a particular year is "shocked" by changing various exogenous variables or parameters (often policy parameters) and the results are compared with the base-year solution (which is an equilibrium solution calibrated to replicate the base-year data). The analysis answers counterfactual questions of the form: "What would the economy have looked like in the base year given the particular shocks under consideration?" Since the analysis often focuses on the impact of particular policy changes, there is no attempt to generate composite experiments that incorporate changes in all the exogenous variables and parameters that changed (or are projected to change) over some actual period, historical or in the future. The results are thus "timeless" in the sense that they are not designed to reflect actual changes over a given period. They represent "what if" counterfactual experiments tied to the base year of the analysis.

Most policy analysis with CGE models has been conducted in this timeless-static mode. Work in this mode generates *ex ante* information about the empirical importance of different shocks and also is used to uncover important synergistic effects arising from simultaneous changes in a variety of policies. To test the quality of these results using *ex post* historical data is difficult because a fair test requires somehow "removing" from the actual data the impact of everything that happened *except* the particular shocks considered in the timeless-static analysis. In this case, validation cannot be done by comparing with historical data, but must be done by evaluating the appropriateness of the theoretical structure of the model and the quality of the estimated parameters of the structural relationships, given the domain of applicability of the model. This kind of validation typically employs a lot of sensitivity analysis to determine how robust the results are, given reasonable variations in parameter values and model specification (Devarajan and Robinson, 2005).

The second mode of analysis — dated comparative statics — involves solving a CGE model for a year some periods away from the base year of the model, incorporating in the solution actual changes in many exogenous variables and parameters for which there are data. This approach is a form of "projection" in which a comparative statics experiment is designed to incorporate changes (historical or projected) in important exogenous variables and parameters. The distinction between "timeless" and "dated" is the identification of the model solution with a particular year. In this mode, for a historical period, a fair test of the quality of the model is to compare the model solution with actual data from the terminal solution year. The validity of the model results is reflected in some measure of correctness of fit between the solution values of endogenous variables and actual data. These results, of course, are conditional on the values of the exogenous variables.

A judgment about the validity or quality of a dated-static model also depends on the intended domain of applicability of the model. A model with many exogenous variables is hard to compare with a more ambitious model that seeks to endogenize more effects. If almost everything is exogenous, a projection conditional on known values of all the exogenous variables should do very well. A model with more endogeneity has more variables to compare with historical values, which raises the bar on validation tests.

An early example of a model used in dated-static mode is the analysis of the causes of the Turkish foreign exchange crisis in the late 1970s by Dervis and Robinson (1982).[14] The model was calibrated using data for 1972 and then used to generate a dated-static "historical run" experiment for a year during the crisis, 1977. Exogenous variables in the simulation included the nominal exchange rate, aggregate price level, levels of foreign borrowing and remittances, degree of import rationing, and world prices of oil and other important commodities. Model validation was done by comparing the dated-static run with actual data for various endogenous macro aggregates in 1977. A series of experiments was then done to decompose the "sources" of the crisis, removing the shocks one by one by setting particular exogenous variables (domestic price level, world prices of major imports, foreign borrowing and remittances) one at a time to their 1972 levels and then solving them for the equilibrium exchange rate. The results indicated that about half, but only half, of the gap between the equilibrium real exchange rate and the actual rate — the measure of the degree of the foreign exchange "crisis" — was due to the Turkish policy decision not to adjust the nominal exchange rate given the rise in domestic prices. The rest of the gap was due, in declining degree, to the oil price rise, loss of foreign remittances and other world price rises. The results were of policy interest because the International Monetary Fund was arguing at the time that the major problem was that the Turks had failed to devalue to adjust the nominal exchange rate for differential changes in world and domestic price levels — a serious underestimate and misunderstanding of the drivers at work.

A more recent example is Kehoe et al. (1995), which tests a CGE model of Spain by comparing forecast values of a number of endogenous variables with actual data for a dated comparative simulation one year after the base year of the model. That article was narrow in focus, looking only at changes in tax rates in one year. They created a partial dated-static run where they fixed a few exogenous variables to their actual values in the next year after the base. Running the model for only one year undoubtedly helped, since, as they note, "… this time horizon is short enough to justify ignoring secular trends and the inter-sectoral impact of changes in the growth rate." They concluded that the results validated the model, which seems a reasonable conclusion for the domain of applicability of exploring the impact of changes in tax rates.

Kehoe (2005) used his Spanish exercise as an example to criticize various CGE models used in the North American Free Trade Area (NAFTA) debate in the US because the modelers did not do a similar validation exercise, comparing their model results with what happened 5 years after NAFTA was implemented. Given the low bar

---

[14] The analysis is also described in Dervis et al. (1982, Chapter 10). There are many examples of analyses by Peter Dixon and numerous coauthors using the ORANI/MONASH CGE model in dated-static mode.

that Kehoe, Polo and Sancho set for themselves, this criticism of NAFTA modelers seems especially inappropriate. The NAFTA models were all used in comparative static mode, and the period after NAFTA came into effect was characterized by a financial crisis, deep devaluation and recession in Mexico, a recession and recovery in the US, and changes in world markets — none of which were relevant to NAFTA or a concern in the policy debate. Evaluations of the NAFTA models after the fact indicated that they correctly estimated the relevant impacts of NAFTA for the policy debate at the time and were consistent with other impact studies at various levels of aggregation and detail.[15]

Some examples of timeless-dynamic models include the work with steady-state, balanced-growth, dynamic CGE models (Devarajan and Go, 1998; Diao *et al.*, 1998. Roe *et al.*, 2010). Dawkins *et al.* (2001) discuss the problems of calibrating this type of model, using as an example a real business cycle model. The calibration cannot refer to "dated" information for specific years, but they sought to specify their model "so that its steady-state properties were consistent with long-term trend data for the US."

Finally, a dated-dynamic model refers to particular years and must be calibrated for those years (Jorgenson and co-authors in Jorgenson, 1998). These models incorporate both a steady-state, balanced growth path and an adjustment path to get from the model's (benchmark) base year to the steady-state path. In principle, these models can be tested against actual historical data. Some of these papers have explicitly discussed the problems of calibrating this type of dated-dynamic model.

In sum, CGE models used for policy formulation in developing countries range along the continuum from stylized to applied numerical simulation models. They are deep structural models specifying agent behavior in product and factor markets, and attempt to capture the salient structural relationships in developing countries that are relevant for the policy problem at hand. Their estimation and validation tends to be Bayesian in spirit, drawing on information from many sources, and involving a combination of calibration and estimation of certain parameters where feasible; sensitivity analysis is widely used as a substitute for classic econometric validation. With some exceptions, these models are either timeless or dated comparative static models, although dynamic models are beginning to see more use in policy discussions.

## 5.3 CGE MODELS AND POLICY FORMULATION

Broadly speaking, the CGE models characterized in the previous section have been used in policy analysis in four main ways:

- *Measurement.* Many — although not all — policy questions require some quantitative measurement. By how much should an exchange rate be devalued? How much extra

---

[15] See Devarajan and Robinson (2005) for a review of the use of CGE models in the NAFTA debate.

revenue will a tax reform generate? How will world trade patterns change if a global trade agreement is signed? These are questions that require a consistent analytical framework (i.e. a model) for their answer. As we show below, CGE models have often proved useful in providing estimates of the magnitudes involved. Even if the estimates have been crude, they have been obtained in a transparent manner, with the assumptions and parameters lending themselves to sensitivity analysis.

- *Directions of change.* Sometimes, it is the direction rather than the magnitude of the change that is salient to the policy debate. For instance, while increased public spending will (absent a tax increase and/or Keynesian multiplier effects) raise the fiscal deficit, if that spending is on productive infrastructure that, in turn, raises the economy's growth rate, then the fiscal deficit as a share of GDP may go down over time. Likewise, if a carbon tax shifts the production mix of the economy towards heavily-taxed goods (and away from subsidized goods), then the net welfare effect may be positive. To demonstrate that these are realistic possibilities, one needs a general equilibrium framework; CGE models are one way of quantifying that framework, even though it is the direction of change that is of ultimate interest. Often CGE models are used to determine the magnitude of the crucial parameters on which the particular direction of change will depend. The simple 1–2–3 model, for instance, shows that whether the real exchange rate appreciates or depreciates in the wake of an import price shock depends on whether the elasticity of substitution between domestic and imported goods is greater or less than one (Devarajan *et al.*, 1990).

- *Evidence to nourish the public debate.* In general, policies are not decided by a single number, much less a direction of change, arising out of a CGE model simulation. Rather, they are decided by there being a domestic political consensus. And that consensus is more likely to be sustained if it is the result of an open and evidence-based debate. CGE models can contribute evidence to a debate, where evidence is also provided by other types of models as well as other sources of information. For instance, debates over whether trade liberalization lowers workers' wages — a critical debate to determine future trade reforms — can be informed by CGE model simulations. The results of these simulations can be compared with those coming from partial equilibrium models and other techniques. In addition, as we will see below, CGE models have contributed evidence to debates that would otherwise have been politically charged (e.g. black unemployment in South Africa).

- *Comparative analysis across countries.* Policy makers are often influenced not by analysis of their own country, but by the experience of other countries. CGE models have provided a way of distilling the experience of, say, tax reform in many countries, by casting it in a common analytical framework, so that differences can be analyzed in detail. The large number of studies analyzing trade liberalization's effect is a case in point. Another is the study by Mitra (1994) of adjustment in oil-importing countries.

### 5.3.1 Policy formulation in practice

All four of the above channels through which CGE models are used in policy have seen their application in developing countries. The areas of application fall under nine categories.

#### 5.3.1.1 Adjustment to external shocks

Starting in the late 1970s, these models were used to underpin the many structural adjustment programs of countries such as Turkey, Indonesia and Thailand. In some cases — Turkey is a good example — CGE models were useful in estimating the real exchange rate depreciation necessary to accommodate a simultaneous oil price increase and a shock to workers' remittances (Dervis *et al.*, 1982). A similar modeling exercise estimated the overvaluation of the CFA Franc in the early 1990s (Devarajan, 1997), which was important for the decision to devalue the CFA Franc in 1994. A recent example was the policy debate in Ethiopia about the need to devalue the currency in the face of external shocks and domestic inflation that had led to import rationing (Dorosh *et al.*, 2011). The article, which started as a discussion paper in 2009, alerted the authorities to the undesirable implications of using import rationing to manage the overvalued exchange rate.

#### 5.3.1.2 Trade reform

Most of the adjustment programs of this era involved a reduction in trade protection, especially tariffs. The reforms were resisted for a variety of reasons, one of which was the potential loss in tariff revenues. A series of CGE models of various countries estimated the loss in revenues from trade reform, concluding for the most part that it was smaller than originally thought, because of increases in the tax base. A particularly important application was Go and Mitra's (Go and Mitra, 1999) study of India — a country that even in the late 1980s had not reformed its tariffs. Their study showed that the effects of trade liberalization could be quite beneficial to the country, since the growth effects of cheaper intermediate goods outweighed any negative consequences of lower protection. The study fed into policy makers' thinking on the eve of India's 1991 trade liberalization. Subsequent work by Chadha *et al.* (1999) validates the Go—Mitra *ex ante* analysis, while showing that the gains may be even greater because of scale effects. A similar analysis of China's accession to the World Trade Organization (WTO) both quantified the gains and allayed concerns about the impacts on poverty and inequality (Bhattasali *et al.*, 2004).

In addition to revenue losses, the other problem with trade reform is that there are winners and losers. CGE models are ideally designed to identify these groups, since they can capture the impact of price and wage changes on people's sources and uses of income. Not surprisingly, therefore, there is a long tradition of CGE models being used to inform the debate about trade reform in developing countries, starting with Australia, which spent the 1940s to the 1970s arguing that it was "a developing country that happened to be rich."[16] The debate in Australia was underpinned by the ORANI model — one of the earliest CGE models used for trade policy analysis (Dixon et al., 1977, 1982). In describing Australia's early trade reform, Gary Banks (Banks, 2010), the chairman of the Productivity Commission, said:

> *A novel feature was the development of analytical tools to estimate relative (net) assistance levels across industries, and the impacts of protection not just on consumers but also on domestic (user) industries. As a result, the farmers and miners came to appreciate that, contrary to the accepted myth of "protection all around," a tax on imports was actually a tax on (their) exports. They accordingly became a countervailing political force for reform.*

### 5.3.1.3 Public finance

In addition to trade policy, another area where CGE models have played an important role in public policy is, not surprisingly, public finance (Shoven and Whalley, 1972). On the tax side, general equilibrium tax incidence analysis was used to dispel the notion that increasing energy taxes (or, equivalently, lowering energy subsidies) was regressive in the Philippines (Devarajan and Hossein, 1998), a finding that contributed to the government's decision to raise energy taxes during an election year. In a novel application, Dabla-Norris and Feltenstein (2005) used a CGE model to simulate the effects of tax evasion on the macroeconomy in Pakistan — a country where this was a major policy issue. On the expenditure side, a few papers examined whether government infrastructure expenditure crowds out private investment and exports, or crowds them "in" by lowering the costs of production. Feltenstein and Ha (1999) showed, in the case of Mexico, that the latter effect is unlikely to exceed the former. The pressure that increased infrastructure spending puts on the interest rate and inflation greatly reduces any benefits from higher infrastructure stocks. Similarly, Feltenstein and Ball (2001) looked at the general equilibrium effects of government bailouts of insolvent banks in Bangladesh. Their model was operational at the Bangladesh Ministry of Finance for several years.

CGE models have been used extensively in developing countries to explore the implications of adopting a value-added tax (VAT). A good example is Mozambique, where CGE model analysis was part of an extensive work program concerning the economic impacts of adopting a VAT system, and the problems of implementing and administering the new tax system. Tarp and Arndt (2009) describe the overall work program and Arndt et al. (2009) describe the CGE application. The model was adapted

---

[16] Will Martin, personal correspondence.

to incorporate in detail the European-style destination VAT system in Mozambique, with exempt sectors, zero-rated sectors and a complicated rebate system. The analysis focused on problems of applying the VAT and noted that, in some cases, it operated more like a tariff than a VAT, since it was easy to tax imports, but difficult to tax domestic producers of the same products.

### 5.3.1.4 Poverty

The purpose of trade and public finance reforms in developing countries is to accelerate growth, to reduce poverty and enhance human capital. Some CGE models have looked at poverty and human capital directly. Robillard *et al.* (2008) used a micro–macro model to simulate the impact of the Asian financial crisis on poverty in Indonesia, as well as to compare different policy responses. Their analysis helped shape the government's response to subsequent crises. Likewise, Devarajan and Go's (Devarajan and Go, 2003) 123PRSP model was a simple framework to underpin Poverty Reduction Strategy Papers. Among other things, it showed that, in Zambia, a negative copper price shock could have regressive consequences — even though the poor do not earn their income from copper. These papers contributed to a stronger push for safety-net programs in the wake of a negative terms-of-trade shock.

### 5.3.1.5 Agriculture

A series of agriculture-focused, micro-macro CGE models were developed at the International Food Policy Research Institute (IFPRI) to explore the impact of different agricultural development strategies on growth and poverty in a number of African countries. These models were designed to explore the Comprehensive Africa Agriculture Development Program (CAADP) funded by AID in consultation with the governments of the countries involved. The approach linked top-down microsimulation models based on household survey data with economy-wide CGE models with detailed specification of agricultural sectors. The work explored the differential impact on the poverty of different agricultural investment programs (Breisinger, *et al.*, 2009; Diao *et al.*, 2012).

Related CGE models of countries across the world have examined the extent and impact of "policy bias" against agriculture in overall development programs, using CGE models to provide general equilibrium measures of such bias; see Jensen *et al.* (2010). This work demonstrated that policy bias against agriculture had largely disappeared by the late 1990s. In addition, the work showed that partial equilibrium measures often overstated the bias, because they assumed domestic and foreign goods were perfect substitutes — a point made earlier by Devarajan and Sussangkarn (1992). This body of work has been part of the movement to rationalize policies relating to the agriculture sector (see, e.g. Anderson, 2010).

### 5.3.1.6 Human development

Turning to human development, the MAMS class of models, discussed above, looks at various determinants of poverty and the MDGs in poor countries. In Ghana, for instance, the application showed that, when account is taken of the interdependence of the MDGs (progress on the water and sanitation goal contribute to the health goals, for instance), the incremental costs of reaching all the MDGs were much smaller than previously envisioned (Bogetic *et al.*, 2008) — a finding that made a meeting among donors and the government go much more smoothly. Sussangkarn (1995) — a CGE modeler who also served as Minister of Finance — used a combined CGE and demographic model to examine the impact of an accelerated education strategy on labor market outcomes in Thailand.[17] He showed that even an ambitious education strategy would not have a significant impact on the skills of the labor force — except with a long lag. Instead, Thailand started emphasizing the upgrading of skills of the existing labor force.

### 5.3.1.7 Labor markets

Another area of growing interest is labor markets and CGE models have contributed to the public debate in several countries. Go *et al.* (2010) examined the impact on employment of a proposed wage subsidy in South Africa. They showed that the impact is likely to be very small (alternatively, the fiscal costs could be very large) because of rigidities in South Africa's labor market. The model results served as background for the Finance Minister's budget speech and subsequently for a modification of the original wage subsidy proposal. Sussangkarn (1996) took on the sensitive issue of Thailand's migrant workers (largely from Myanmar). He showed that, because these workers' presence potentially expands total economic output, even though low-educated Thais might be hurt, there are ways to compensate them with transfers so that society as a whole benefits. The simulations helped defuse a potentially tense situation.

### 5.3.1.8 International trade agreements

Beyond the single-country CGE models described up to now, there are a number of multicountry models that have had significant policy influence since they have been designed around particular international agreements, such as the Uruguay Round in multilateral trade reform. Some of the first models in this tradition calculated the welfare gains from multilateral trade liberalization (Goldin *et al.*, 1993). These estimates underpinned the arguments that Organization for Economic Cooperation and Development (OECD) agricultural subsidies were hurting developing countries — to the tune of $300 billion, about 6 times foreign aid. Likewise, Hertel *et al.* (2009) created a stir when they showed that the Doha Development Round had omitted those policy

---

[17] Another CGE modeler who served as Minister of Finance was Jaime Serra-Puche in Mexico.

reforms that would do most to reduce poverty. They described the existing policies as "transferring money from poor farmers in poor countries to rich farmers in rich countries."

### 5.3.1.9 Climate change

Finally, in keeping with greater general interest on the subject, CGE modelers have been looking at climate change recently. In Africa's first application of carbon taxation to mitigate climate change, Devarajan *et al.* (2010) examine the welfare and distributional consequences of taxes on carbon and on carbon-intensive goods and services such as coal or transport in South Africa. They show that the welfare effects are driven by the interaction with other distortions in the economy rather than the carbon tax itself. For instance, a simulation with all the labor market distortions removed results in a negligible cost of carbon taxation. Coincidentally, the carbon tax rate in the base-case scenario of the South Africa model was very close to that used in the Government's position paper, which, in turn, is being implemented now.

On adaptation to climate change, there are now examples using CGE models to analyze the effects of climate variability on agriculture and the overall economy in a few countries (see Bangladesh: Yu *et al.*, 2010; Ethiopia: Arndt *et al.*, 2011a; Mozambique: Arndt *et al.*, 2011b). The projects on Ethiopia and Mozambique were done in consultation with the governments, and have been part of the climate change policy discussion in both countries.

## 5.3.2 Lessons learned

The examples presented above of the use of CGE models in policy discussions reflect both the potential as well as some of the pitfalls of this particular technique.[18] For instance, when a numerical estimate is called for (as in the case of real exchange rate overvaluation), a CGE model is both the appropriate tool as well as a convenient one for generating that estimate. However, in other cases, one wonders whether the fact that the estimate came from a CGE model gives a false sense of precision. This might be the case for the MAMS application in Ghana, where the estimate of foreign aid required to reach the MDGs depended not on the CGE model itself but on the auxiliary equations added to the model to capture the interactions among water and health outcomes. The CGE model was not necessary to obtain the estimate, but the fact that the estimates were part of an integrated CGE/MDG model gave the estimate a sense of accuracy that was not justified from the CGE work alone — in a chain of analysis, accuracy depends heavily on the weakest link.

---

[18] For an excellent discussion of these issues, see McDougall (1993).

The cases where the CGE model was used to show directions of change also fall into two categories. The first are those cases where the CGE model was the appropriate framework, such as for instance, tax incidence or tax evasion. A multisector, multi-household, price-endogenous model is what is needed. In other cases, however, the direction of change depends mainly on the additional equations, such as the work on fiscal effects of infrastructure spending. Whether public infrastructure spending crowds-in or crowds-out private investment will depend on the importance of public infrastructure stock in the private production function. However, this is a parameter that is outside the CGE model. Nevertheless, here too the analyst can undertake sensitivity analysis and identify the critical value of the parameter that will reverse the result. In fact, this technique is one of the advantages of using a CGE model to underpin the discussion.

As the examples above show, CGE models have also contributed evidence to an ongoing policy debate. The case of trade liberalization in India is illustrative. There was a vigorous and often ideological debate on the topic throughout the 1980s. The Go and Mitra study did not enter the "big debate" of whether or not India should liberalize. Rather, they attempted to contribute evidence to a component of the debate, i.e. the impact of trade liberalization on revenues. Since their study used a CGE model, their results also shed light on the bigger debate. Whereas some of the rhetoric at the time was bemoaning the fact that existing industries will die, the Go–Mitra study showed that, on the contrary, some industries would do quite well because intermediate goods would now be cheaper. Likewise, the Sussangkarn study on migrant workers rigorously portrayed the output-enhancing effects of these workers and presented a dispassionate analysis on a charged topic.

However, here, too, there are cases where it may appear as if the main contribution was not directly associated with the CGE model, but a closer examination reveals that it was. For example, Hertel's result that most of the poverty-reducing measures had not been included in the Doha Round was driven by the profile of tariff and subsidy cuts, which were exogenous to the model. Yet it required model simulations to show that what was left out of the Doha Round was more poverty friendly than what was included. These results — especially as they created a stir at the WTO in Geneva — were more credible since they were based on a coherent analytical framework.

Where multiple CGE models and complementary detailed micro analysis (based on different models) have provided the same result, as was the case with the distributional effects of trade liberalization, the power of these models becomes evident — a point made with respect to the NAFTA debate by Devarajan and Robinson (2005). Not only are CGE models the right model to capture the salient mechanisms in the economy, but the fact that they stem from a rigorous analytical framework (e.g. the models satisfy Walras' law and are homogenous of degree zero in prices) increases the chances that the consistency of the results is saying something about the economy and not just a fluke. The statement about trade liberalization in Australia captures this phenomenon very well. To be sure, disagreement among model results can also be instructive, because they help identify differences among underlying assumptions and data (also noted by Devarajan and Robinson, 2005).

Finally, there is the question of whether the CGE model should be embedded in a government institution, as were the Bangladesh and South Africa models, or built and maintained independently, as were most of the other cases presented here. The Australian experience, which is noteworthy for its long-standing and continuous presence, is discussed in Dixon (2008). The argument for embedding in a government institution is that there will be greater ownership, and hence acceptance, of the model results, and that the analysis is more likely to be focused and timely — crucial matters in policy debates. On the other hand, their very presence in government might constrain the questions the model could ask (think of the work on tax evasio/n in Pakistan), not to mention the answers. The resolution is clearly a question of judgment and will depend on country circumstances. The typical pattern seems to be that models are developed outside government, but then adopted and used by government agencies as well as advisers and consultants to government. This may also be a moot question, given the direction that policy making in developing countries is going — a point to which we now turn.

## 5.4 CONCLUSIONS

After examining different classes of CGE models, this survey has identified the policy questions that these models can be designed to answer, the way in which the models are used to answer the questions and how such a process works out in practice. We showed how CGE models have been used in practice to inform policy making in developing countries. Looking ahead, it is apparent that policy making in developing countries is rapidly changing. With the rise of democracy and, in some cases, multiparty democracy, decisions are no longer made by an elite group of technocrats. Rather, policy is made with a view towards what the voters think. It is of course natural for politicians to think in terms of their electorate. However, it is a lesson often forgotten in CGE modeling circles, where recommendations are derived from model results without reflecting on the incentives facing politicians, who are the decision makers. The use of models to identify winners and losers arising from policy choices is often more important than more general welfare analysis.

The implication of this way of looking at policy making is that the process of using CGE models should also be changing. Rather than building and running models to serve the technocrats (who, in the past, would take the model results and interpret them to the omnipotent decision maker), modelers should be using their simulations to contribute evidence to the public debate. In turn, this statement means that the choice of questions should follow from those being debated. While this is already the case for many exercises, a clearer link between model design and use, and the burning questions of the day, would greatly enhance the models' impact.

In addition, if the goal is to contribute evidence to the public debate, the models must be publicly available and accessible by all sides of the debate. This would apply whether the model is in the government or outside.

Furthermore, the model results should be communicated in such a way that the participants in that debate — ordinary voters — can absorb them. Not only should the results be rigorously examined, but they should be presented so that average citizens can connect with them. For example, instead of presenting the incidence of taxation as a table of numbers, they could be presented as the story of five families (one in each quintile) and what the tax change means to them. The results should also be communicated by more than the standard medium of a paper or book, which is likely to be read by only a tiny fraction of the voting population. With two-thirds or more of the developing-country population having cell phones, CGE model results could be transmitted to people living in remote areas — provided we have a way of translating model results into SMS messages. To be sure, there is a danger that in such a situation the loudest voice receives the greatest credence, even if it is not correct. This is why it is particularly important that model results be scrutinized by experts — the equivalent of peer review in scholarly journals. However, the danger that modelers will be satisfied with just publishing results in journals rather than trying to get maximum impact is also significant. Either way, the model's results should be broadcast to the general public, allowing the debate to decide whether this particular set of simulations, or analysis from a completely different model, or even no model at all, plays the pivotal role in influencing the policy decisions.

## ACKNOWLEDGMENTS

We thank Peter Dixon and Thomas Hertel for valuable comments on an earlier draft.

## REFERENCES

Adelman, I., Robinson, S., 1978. Income Distribution Policy in Developing Countries: A Case Study of Korea, Stanford University Press.

Anderson, K., 2010. Agricultural Price Distortions, Inequality, and Poverty. World Bank, Washington, DC.

Armington, P.S., 1969. A theory of demand for products distinguished by place of production. IMF Staff Papers 16, 159–178.

Arndt, C., Robinson, S., Willenbockel, D., 2011a. Ethiopia's growth prospects in a changing climate: a stochastic general equilibrium approach. Global Environ. Change 21, 701–710.

Arndt, C., Strzepeck, K., Tarp, F., Thurlow, J., Fant, C., Wright, L., 2011b. Adapting to climate change: an integrated biophysical and economic assessment for Mozambique. Sustain. Sci. 6, 7–20.

Arndt, C., Byiers, B., Robinson, S., Tarp, F., 2009. VAT and economy-wide modeling. In: Tarp, F., Arndt, C. (Eds), 2009, Taxation in a Low-Income Economy: the Case of Mozambique. Routledge Studies in Development Economics. Routledge, New York, pp. 328–340.

Bhattasali, D., Li, S., Martin, W. (Eds), 2004. China and the WTO: Accession, Policy Reform and Poverty Reduction Strategy. World Bank and Oxford University Press, New York.

Banks, G., 2010. Successful Reforms: Past lessons, future challenges. Keynote Address to the Annual Forecasting Conference of Australian Business Economists.

Blitzer, C.R., Clark, P.B., Taylor, L., 1975. Economy-wide Models and Development Planning. Oxford University Press for the World Bank, Oxford.

Bogetic, Z., Bussolo, M., Medvedev, D., 2008. Achieving accelerated and shared growth in Ghana: A MAMS-based analysis of costs and opportunities. World Bank Policy Research Working Paper 4523. World Bank, Washington, DC.

Breisinger, C., Diao, X., Thurlow, J., 2009. Modeling growth options and structural change to reach middle income country status: the case of Ghana. Econ. Model. 26, 514–525.

Chadha, R., Deardorff, A.V., Pohit, S., Stern, R.M., 1999. The Impact of Trade and Domestic Policy Reforms in India: a CGE Modeling Approach. Studies in International Economics. University of Michigan Press, Ann Arbor, MI.

Dabla-Norris, E., Feltenstein, A., 2005. The underground economy and its macroeconomic consequences. J. Pol. Reform 8, 153–174.

Dawkins, C., Srinivasan, T.N., Whalley, J., 2001. Calibration. In: Heckman, J.J., Leamer, E. (Eds), Handbook of Econometrics, vol. 5. Elsevier, Amsterdam, pp. 3653–3703.

Deardorff, A., 1984. Testing trade theories and predicting trade flows. In: Kenen, P.B., Jones, R.W. (Eds), Handbook of International Economics, vol. 1. Elsevier, New York, pp. 467–517.

Dervis, K., Robinson, S., 1982. A general equilibrium analysis of the causes of a foreign exchange crisis: the case of Turkey. Weltwirtschaftliches Archiv 118, 259–280.

Dervis, K., de Melo, J., Robinson, S., 1982. General Equilibrium Models for Development Policy. Cambridge University Press, Cambridge (Reprinted by the World Bank, 1989).

Devarajan, S., 1997. Real exchange rate misalignment in the CFA zone. J. Afr. Econ. 6, 35–53.

Devarajan, S., Go, D.S., Robinson, S., Thierfelder, K., 2010. Tax policy to reduce carbon emissions in South Africa. B.E. J. Econ. Anal. Pol. 11 (1) (Topics), article 13.

Devarajan, S., Go, D.S., 1998. The simplest dynamic general-equilibrium model of an open economy. J. Pol. Model. 20, 677–714.

Devarajan, S., Go, D.S., 2003. The 123PRSP model. In: Bourguignon, F., Pereira da Silva, L. (Eds), The Impact of Economic Policies on Poverty and Income Distribution – Evaluation Techniques and Tools. Oxford University Press, Oxford.

Devarajan, S., Hossain, S.I., 1998. The Combined Incidence of Taxes and Public Expenditures in the Philippines, World Development 26 (6) (June 1998), 963–977.

Devarajan, S., de Melo, J., 1987. Adjustment with a fixed exchange rate: Cameroon, Cote d'Ivoire, and Senegal. World Bank Econ. Rev. 1, 447–487.

Devarajan, S., Robinson, S., 2005. The influence of computable general equilibrium models on policy. In: Kehoe, T., Srinivasan, T.N., Whalley, J. (Eds), Frontiers in Applied General Equilibrium Modeling: Essays in Honor of Herbert Scarf. Cambridge University Press, Cambridge Also available as TMD Discussion Paper 98. Washington, DC: International Food Policy Research Institute (2002).

Devarajan, S., Sussangkarn, C., 1992. Effective rates of protection when domestic and foreign goods are imperfect substitutes: the case of Thailand. The Rev. Econ. Stat. 74 (4), 701–711.

Devarajan, S., Lewis, J.D., Robinson, S., 1990. Policy lessons from trade-focused two-sector models. J. Pol. Model. 12, 625–657.

Devarajan, S., Lewis, J.D., Robinson, S., 1993. External shocks, purchasing power parity, and the equilibrium real exchange rate. World Bank Econ. Rev. 7, 45–63.

Devarajan, S., Go, D.S., Lewis, J.D., Pekka, S., Robinson, S., 1997. Policy lessons from a simple, open-economy model. In: Francois, J., Reinert, K. (Eds), Applied Methods for Trade Policy Analysis. Cambridge University Press, Cambridge, pp. 156–188.

Devarajan, S., Go, D.S., Li, H., 1999. Quantifying the fiscal effects of trade reform. Policy Research Working Paper 2162. World Bank, Washington, DC.

Diao, X., Roe, T., Yeldan, E., 1998. A simply dynamic applied general equilibrium model of a small open economy: transitional dynamics and trade policy. J. Econ. Dev. 23, 77–101.

Diao, X., Thurlow, J., Benin, S., Fan, S. (Eds), 2012. Agricultural Strategies in Africa: Evidence from Economy-wide Simulation Models. International Food Policy Research Institute, Washington DC.

Dixon, P.B., Parmenter, B.R., 1996. Computable general equilibrium modelling for policy analysis and forecasting. In: Amman, H.M., Kendrick, D.A., Rust, J. (Eds), Handbook of Computational Economics. Elsevier, Amsterdam, pp. 3–85.

Dixon, P.B., Parmenter, B.R., Ryland, G.J., Sutton, J., 1977. ORANI, a General Equilibrium Model of the Australian Economy: Current Specification and Illustrations of the Use for Policy Analysis, Volume 2 of the First Progress Report of the IMPACT Project. Australian Government Publishing Service, Canberra.

Dixon, P.B., Parmenter, B.R., Sutton, J., Vincent, D.P., 1982. ORANI: a Multisectoral Model of the Australian Economy, Contributions to Economic Analysis, vol. 142. North-Holland, Amsterdam.

Dixon, P.B., 2008. Trade policy in Australia and the development of computable general equilibrium modeling. J. Econ. Integrat. 23, 605–630.

Dorfman, R., Samuelson, P.A., Solow, R.M., 1958. Linear Programming and Economic Analysis. McGraw Hill, New York.

Dorosh, P., Robinson, S., Ahmed, H., 2011. Economic implications of foreign exchange rationing in Ethiopia. Ethiopian J. Econ. 18, 1–30 (2, October 2009; published in November 2011).

Feltenstein, A., Ha, J., 1999. An analysis of the optimal provision of public infrastructure: a computational model using Mexican data. J. Dev. Econ. 58, 219–230.

Feltenstein, A., Ball, S., 2001. Bank failures and fiscal austerity: policy prescriptions for a developing country. J. Publ. Econ. 82, 247–270.

Ginsburgh, V., Keyzer, M., 2002. The Structure of Applied General Equilibrium Models. MIT Press, Cambridge, MA.

Ginsburgh, V., Robinson, S., 1984. Equilibrium and prices in multisector models. In: Syrquin, M., Taylor, L., Westphal, L.E. (Eds), Economic Structure and Performance. Academic Press, New York.

Go, D.S., Kearney, M., Korman, V., Robinson, S., Thierfelder, K., 2010. Wage subsidy and labour market flexibility in South Africa. J. Dev. Stud. 46, 1481–1502. Also as Economic Research Southern Africa Working Paper 114 and World Bank Policy Research Working Paper 4871.

Go, D.S., Mitra, P., 1999. Trade liberalization, fiscal adjustment and exchange rate policy in India. In: Ranis, G., Raut, L. (Eds), Trade, Growth, and Development. North-Holland, Amsterdam, pp. 229–272.

Gunning, J.W., Keyzer, M., 1995. Applied general equilibrium models for policy analysis. In: Chenery, H., Srinivasan, T.N. (Eds), Handbook of Development Economics, vol. 3. Elsevier, Amsterdam, pp. 2025–2107.

Goldin, I., Knudsen, O., van der Mensbrugghe, D., 1993. Trade Liberalization: Global Economic Implications, World Bank and OECD, Washington and Paris.

Hertel, T., Keeney, R., Ivanic, M., Winters, L.A., 2009. Why isn't the Doha Development Agenda more poverty friendly? Rev. Dev. Econ. 13, 543–559.

Johansen, L., 1960. A Multisectoral Study of Economic Growth. North-Holland Publishing Co. Amsterdam.

Jorgenson, D.W., 1984. Econometric methods for applied general equilibrium analysis. In: Scarf, H., Shoven, J. (Eds), Applied General Equilibrium Analysis. Cambridge University Press, Cambridge, pp. 139–203.

Jorgenson, D.W., 1998. Growth: Volume 1: Econometric General Equilibrium Modeling. MIT Press, Cambridge, MA.

Jensen, H.T., Robinson, S., Tarp, F., 2010. Measuring agricultural policy bias: general equilibrium analysis of fifteen developing countries. Am. J. Agr. Econ. 92, 1136–1148.

Kehoe, T., Polo, C., Sancho, F., 1995. An evaluation of the performance of an applied general equilibrium model of the Spanish economy. Econ. Theor. 6, 115–141.

Kehoe, T., 2005. An evaluation of the performance of applied general equilibrium models of the impact of NAFTA. In: Kehoe, T.J., Srinivasan, T.N., Whalley, J. (Eds), Frontiers in Applied General Equilibrium Modeling: Essays in Honor of Herbert Scarf. Cambridge University Press, Cambridge, pp. 341–377.

Lofgren, H., Diaz-Bonilla, C., 2012. MAMS: An economy-wide model for analysis of MDG country strategies — an application to Latin America and the Caribbean. In: Sánchez, M. V., Vos, R., Ganuza, E., Lofgren, H., Díaz-Bonilla, C. (Eds), Public Policies for Human Development. Feasible Financing Strategies for Achieving the MDGs in Latin America and the Caribbean.

McDougall, R., 1993. Uses and Abuses of AGE Models. Available at: https://www.gtap.agecon.purdue.edu/resources/download/21.pdf.

de Melo, J., Robinson, S., 1989. Product differentiation and the treatment of foreign trade in computable general equilibrium models of small economies. J. Int. Econ. 27, 47—67.

Mitra, P., 1994. Adjustment in Oil-importing Countries. Cambridge University Press, Cambridge.

Rattso, J., 1982. Different macroclosures of the original Johansen model and their impact on policy evaluation. J. Pol. Model. 4, 85—97.

Robilliard, A.-S., Bourguignon, F., Robinson, S., 2008. Examining the social impact of the Indonesian financial crisis using a macro—micro model. In: Bourguignon, F., Bussolo, M., Pereira da Silva, L.A. (Eds), The Impact of Macroeconomic Policies on Poverty and Income Distribution: Macro—Micro Evaluation Techniques and Tools. World Bank and Palgrave Macmillan, New York, pp. 93—118.

Robinson, S., 1989. Multisectoral models. In: Chenery, H., Srinivasan, T.N. (Eds), Handbook of Development Economics. North-Holland, Amsterdam, pp. 885—947.

Robinson, S., 1991. Macroeconomics, financial variables, and computable general equilibrium models. World Dev. 19, 1509—1525.

Robinson, S., Yuñez-Naude, A., Hinojosa-Ojeda, R., Lewis, J.D., Devarajan, S., 1999. From stylized to applied models: building multisector CGE models for policy analysis. The N. Am. J. Econ. Finance 10, 5—38.

Roe, T.L., Smith, R.B.W., Saraqcoglu, D.S., 2010. Multisector Growth Models: Theory and Application. Springer, New York.

Shoven, J.B., Whalley, J., 1972. A general equilibrium calculation of the effects of differential taxation of income from capital in the U.S. Journal of Public Economics, Elsevier, vol. 1(3-4) 281—321, November.

Sussangkarn, C., 1995. Education, labor markets and economic development: policy simulations. Chulalongkorn J. Econ. 7, 201—253.

Sussangkarn, C., 1996. The macroeconomic impacts of migrant workers: analysis with a CGE model. TDRI Q. Rev. 11 (3), 3—11.

Tarp, F., Arndt, C. (Eds), 2009. Taxation in a Low-Income Economy: The Case of Mozambique. Routledge Studies in Development Economics. Routledge, New York.

Thierfelder, K., Robinson, S., 2003. Trade and tradability: exports, imports, and factor markets in the Salter—Swan model. Econ. Rec. 79 (244), 103—111.

Whalley, J., Yeung, B., 1984. External sector "closing rules" in applied general equilibrium models. J. Int. Econ. 16, 123—138.

Yu, W., Alam, M., Hasan, A., Khan, A., Ruane, A., Rosensweig, C., Major, D., Thurlow, J., 2010. Climate Change Risks and Food Security in Bangladesh. World Bank and Earthscan, New York.

# Putting Services and Foreign Direct Investment with Endogenous Productivity Effects in Computable General Equilibrium Models

**David G. Tarr**
World Bank

## Abstract

In this chapter I explain an innovative modeling approach that incorporates services, foreign direct investment (FDI) and endogenous productivity effects from services. I begin with a small stylized model to help understand the fundamental economics. The model shows that services liberalization yields welfare gains several multiples of the welfare gains obtained from a constant to returns to scale model. Further, the welfare gains are supported by the econometric estimates of the gains from trade or FDI liberalization. I then describe computable general equilibrium studies by my colleagues and I conducted for the Russian government on the potential effects of Russian accession to the World Trade Organization (WTO). We find that the projected welfare gains generated from liberalization of barriers against foreign direct investment are about 5% of consumption, with the total benefits of all aspects of WTO accession being about 7% of consumption. We find that almost every household in Russia would be expected to gain from WTO accession. We show, however, that a model of Russian WTO accession that fails to incorporate FDI in services and endogenous productivity effects from additional services would yield an estimated gain of less than 1% of consumption with about 7% of the households losing. Reviews of the work have indicated that the work has had a significant influence on the public debate and helped the Russian government to steer public opinion in favor of WTO accession. In the process of doing this work, T. Rutherford and I developed a technique for incorporating tens of thousands of households as agents of the model. All of the major results in the chapter are shown to be robust under sensitivity analysis.

## Keywords

Services liberalization, foreign direct investment, endogenous productivity effects, WTO accession, trade and poverty, trade policy modeling

## JEL classification codes

F12, F13, F23, C68, C63

© 2013 Elsevier B.V.
All rights reserved.      303

## 6.1 INTRODUCTION

Services now constitute about 70% of global GDP.[1] Moreover, foreign direct investment (FDI) flows have shifted toward services and now constitute almost half of the total FDI flows in developing countries.[2] Recognizing their importance and the need to have special rules to treat trade in services, the General Agreement on Trade in Services (GATS) was incorporated into the World Trade Organization (WTO) when it was formed in the mid-1990s. Further, services are now a key part of the regional agreements of both the US and the EU.

Given that services cannot be stored, FDI, to achieve a domestic presence (what is known as the proximity burden), has historically been crucial to the effective delivery of services. While technological change has progressively allowed more services to be supplied on a cross-border basis, to effectively compete in services "trade," it still is likely that it requires more of a domestic presence than trade in goods.[3] Given the key role of FDI in the effective delivery of services, commitments to foreign investors are key aspects of trade negotiations in services. With the growing importance of services trade and FDI in services, it is important to have a framework with which we can analyze the impacts of the liberalization of barriers to FDI in services.

The way my coauthors and I have modeled services builds crucially on the growing body of empirical evidence that shows that increased access to services, increased FDI in services or services liberalization increases the productivity of the manufacturing sectors and of the economy as a whole (see Rutherford and Tarr, 2008, 2010; Markusen et al., 2005a,b; Jensen et al., 2006, 2007, 2010; Balistreri et al., 2009; Jensen and Tarr, 2008, 2011; Balistreri and Tarr, 2011). Further there is evidence that increased access to imported intermediate goods increases economy-wide productivity. I summarize the computable general equilibrium (GCE) modeling literature on services in GCE modeling below, where I argue that our approach is the first to incorporate the liberalization of barriers against FDI in services where endogenous productivity impacts play an important role in the results. In our full applied models, we also incorporate the endogenous productivity impacts from increased access to intermediate goods. We have shown that in applications where liberalization of barriers against foreign investors in services is important, such as in accession to the WTO, the estimated welfare gains depend crucially on our modeling framework — the estimated welfare gains are several multiples of the estimated gains of models without FDI in services and endogenous productivity effects. Given the crucial importance of productivity impacts to our mo deling framework, I begin with a survey of the literature on the impact of services

---

[1] Francois and Hoekman (2010, p. 644).

[2] See World Bank (2004), *Global Development Finance*.

[3] Data on the sales of foreign affiliates of US firms suggests that sales through FDI are the most important channels for US firms to sell services to foreigners (Francois and Hoekman, 2010, p. 655).

liberalization on economy-wide productivity and the impact of increased access to intermediate goods on productivity.

## 6.1.1 Impact of services availability and services liberalization on productivity[4]

First, several studies using firm-level data have established a link between increased access to services and increases in productivity. Using panel-level data and controlling for FDI endogeneity, Arnold *et al.* (2011) for the Czech Republic, Fernandes and Paunov (2012) for Chile, Shepotylo and Vakhitov (2012) for Ukraine, and Arnold *et al.* (2012) for India find a significant positive relationship between FDI in services following liberalization (especially allowing foreign entry) and the performance of downstream domestic firms in manufacturing. Arnold *et al.* (2008) find a statistically significant positive relationship between productivity in a sample of over 1000 firms in 10 Sub-Saharan countries and the performance of the three service industries for which they collected data. Several papers have shown (e.g. Fink *et al.*, 2005) that openness in a range of producer or intermediate service sectors is linked to increased export competitiveness and performance for high-technology sectors, for which services tend to be an important element of total cost.

Second, using cross-country growth regressions, several studies have found that open-services regimes induce greater growth rates. Mattoo *et al.* (2006) find (after controlling for other determinants of growth) that countries with open financial and telecommunications sectors grew about 1 percent faster than other countries.[5] Eschenbach and Hoekman (2006) find that measures of services sector reform were statistically significant explanatory variables in explaining growth in their sample of 20 transition countries. Fernandes (2009) finds that liberalization of services in transition countries had a positive and significant effect on labor productivity growth that was stronger the more distant the sector was from the technological frontier.

Several other studies also show a link to services availability and productivity. Triplett and Bosworth (2004) calculate that productivity growth in distribution and financial services fueled much of the post-1995 overall expansion in US productivity. Inklaar *et al.* (2008) show that differences in aggregate productivity levels and growth rates in seven Organization for Economic Cooperation and Development (OECD) countries are largely attributable to services sectors. That is, much of the differential in their sample is due to variation in business services performance. Ciccone and Hall (1996)

---

[4] This section draws on the survey paper by Francois and Hoekman (2010). The reader should consult that source for a more complete review of the literature on the impact of services availability and services liberalization on productivity and growth.

[5] Their results are consistent with several other studies that find a positive relationship between financial sector openness and economic growth. See Levine (2005).

show that firms operating in economically dense areas are more productive than firms operating in relative isolation. Hummels (1995) shows that most of the richest countries in the world are clustered in relatively small regions of Europe, North America and East Asia, while the poor countries are spread around the rest of the world. He argues this is partly explained by transportation costs for inputs since it is more expensive to buy specialized inputs in countries that are far away. The high cost of using far-away inputs is especially true of business services that are not provided locally, as Marshall (1988) shows that in three regions in the UK (Birmingham, Leeds and Manchester) almost 80% of the services purchased by manufacturers were bought from suppliers within the same region. He cites studies which show that firm performance is enhanced by the local availability of producer services. In developing countries, McKee (1988) argues that the local availability of producer services is very important for the development of leading industrial sectors.

## 6.1.2 Endogenous productivity effects through the Dixit–Stiglitz mechanism

As early as the 1960s, the urban and regional economics literature (e.g. Chinitz, 1961; Vernon, 1960) argued that non-tradable intermediate goods (primarily producer services produced under conditions of increasing returns to scale) are an important source of agglomeration externalities that account for the formation of cities and industrial complexes, and account for differences in economic performance across regions. The more recent economic geography literature (e.g. Fujita et al., 1999) has also focused on the fact that related economic activity is economically concentrated due to agglomeration externalities. I believe it is crucial to capture this endogenous productivity effect of better access to services providers. The key mechanism used in the economic geography literature, as well as in the endogenous growth theory (e.g. Romer, 1990), is the Dixit–Stiglitz mechanism. The Dixit–Stiglitz mechanism is so widely employed because it provides a micro-foundation for the link between a change in policy and productivity growth. The models in this paper capture the productivity effects of additional service suppliers through use of the Dixit–Stiglitz–Ethier[6] mechanism, whereby additional varieties of business services increase the productivity of the firms that use the services.

Similarly, beginning with the path-breaking work of Coe and Helpman (1995), a rich literature now exists (summarized in Section 6.3 below) that has empirically shown that total factor productivity increases due to the purchase of imported intermediate goods, and the productivity impact is stronger the more technologically advanced is the country

---

[6] Ethier (1982) made the key extension of the Dixit–Stiglitz framework for our purposes; he showed how liberalization of international trade could lead to productivity increases when imports are used as intermediate inputs. We use the phrases Dixit–Stiglitz framework and Dixit–Stiglitz–Ethier framework synonymously in the paper.

that is the source of the imports. Thus, we also employ the Dixit—Stiglitz—Ethier mechanism for varieties of goods in those goods sectors that are subject to imperfect competition and increasing returns to scale. In perfectly competitive goods or services sectors, there are no productivity effects from additional trade.

## 6.1.3 Small gains from trade without productivity impacts from trade

Further, focusing on the goods trade alone in international trade liberalization analysis in combination with constant returns to scale (CRTS) models has led to very small estimated welfare gains. Typically the estimated gains are less than 1% of GDP — a result that has loosely come to be known as the "Harberger constant." However, econometric estimates of the gains from an open trade regime suggest that the gains are much larger. Rutherford and Tarr (1998, appendix A) have analytically derived the relationship between a permanent increase in the steady-state growth rate and the equivalent variation. A welfare gain of between 10 and 35% of consumption corresponds to a permanent increase in the growth rate of between 0.4 and 1%. A policy-induced change in the growth rate of this magnitude is quite plausible in the context of the actual long-term *per capita* growth rates over the 25- to 30-year period beginning in 1962 and in the context of evidence on the impact of services liberalization cited above. For example, Sachs and Warner (1995) estimate that open economies have grown about 2.45% faster than closed economies, with even greater differences for open versus closed economies among developing countries. They note that trade liberalization is often accompanied by macro stabilization and other market reforms, and their open economy variable may be picking up these other effects as well. However, they argue that trade liberalization is the *sine qua non* of the overall reform process, because other interventions such as state subsidies are often unsustainable in an open economy. Although the estimates of the gains from trade liberalization based on cross-country growth regressions are controversial, there are a few reasons to believe that the gains are very substantial. Frankel and Romer (1999) have shown that adjusting for the simultaneity bias in cross-country regression studies such as Sachs and Warner does not reduce the estimated impact of openness on growth. Further, the significant literature, starting with Coe and Helpman (1995), on the productivity gains from imported intermediates is largely unchallenged at this time. Finally, the cross-country growth regressions focus on trade in goods, so the estimates of the gains from openness to FDI in services should further contribute to the gains.

Since trade policy is inherently controversial, policy makers wonder why they should undertake the exercise if so little is at stake. CRTS models without services, by missing the productivity gains, from an open trade regime and FDI regimes in service are missing most of what is important.

### 6.1.4 Literature

Christen *et al.*, in Chapter 25 of this Handbook, provide a review of the numerical general equilibrium modeling of services. I therefore focus here on the papers most closely related to the models in this chapter. There have been a number of theoretical papers modeling FDI liberalization in services, including Markusen (1989, 1990), Francois (1990a,b) , and Markusen and Venables (1998). The modeling here incorporates a key idea of Markusen, i.e. that when multinationals engage in FDI, they bring technology or expertise to the local production process. They therefore have a different cost structure than local firms in the same sector.

Brown *et al.* (1996), Robinson *et al.* (2002) and Francois *et al.* (2005) examined the liberalization of barriers in services, but focused on cross-border trade in services. The paper by Robinson *et al.* (2002) incorporated productivity impacts from additional services, but did so through exogenous productivity shocks.[7] Francois *et al.* (2005) incorporated monopolistic competition in manufacturing and services sectors, but did not incorporate productivity impacts.

Lejour *et al.* (2008) model FDI in services, but do not incorporate productivity effects. Brown and Stern (2001) and Dee *et al.* (2003) employ multicountry numerical models with many of the same features I outline in the models below. Their models contain three sectors: agriculture, manufacturing and services, and are thus rather stylized. Results in the Brown and Stern paper depend crucially on capital flows between nations, with capital importing nations typically gaining and capital exporting nations typically losing. In Dee *et al.* (2003), multinationals are assumed to capture the quota rents initially. So, the results of liberalization depend crucially on the fact that liberalization transfers rents to capital importing countries. Since their models contain only one services sector, it is not possible to estimate barriers at the level of a particular business services sector. Moreover, it appears that the productivity impacts of additional services are not significant in their models as they are not discussed in the interpretation of results.

### 6.1.5 Outline of the chapter

In this chapter, I report on the efforts of my coauthors and I to incorporate FDI in business services with endogenous productivity effects. I show that our approach results in estimated gains from liberalization that are several orders of magnitude larger than in

---

[7] In their approach they make the coefficient that multiplies the use of capital and labor into output a function of the trade intensity. For example, if the production function in a sector is Cobb–Douglas, i.e. $Y = A^\pi K^\alpha L^{(1-\alpha)}$, they introduce a parameter $\pi$ that increases with the trade intensity of the sector and where the change in the parameter $\pi$ depends on the region of the imports. Then trade liberalization has a positive productivity impact in their model. Since the change in the trade intensity of each sector is endogenous, the extent of the productivity increase in their model is endogenous. However, the specification of the production function lacks a micro-foundation for the productivity increase; it is analogous to Hicks neutral technical change in the exogenous growth theory.

models without services and endogenous productivity effects. In order to understand the key features, I begin in Section 6.2 with a stylized model where it is relatively straightforward to describe the model mathematically, have clearly understood the FDI and endogenous productivity mechanisms that are key to the results and important differences we may obtain incorporating FDI in services with endogenous productivity effects in the model. In Section 6.3, I describe the first full economy application of this model: the case of Russian accession to the WTO, where our model of Russia contains a single representative consumer. To capture the productivity effects of a more open trade regime, I also employ the Dixit–Stiglitz–Ethier mechanism in goods sectors subject to increasing returns to scale, but do not incorporate FDI in goods sectors. In Section 6.4, I extend the model to a "real household" model by incorporating all 50 000 plus households of the Russian Household Budget Survey (HBS) as agents in the model, while retaining the modeling features introduced in the representative household model described in Section 6.3. I conclude in Section 6.5 with some extensions and other applications of these models, and a discussion of how these models impacted policy discussions in Russia, Ukraine and Kazakhstan.

## 6.2 MODELING SERVICES AND FDI IN A STYLIZED SMALL CGE MODEL[8]

In order to gain intuition into the features of models with producer services and FDI, we begin with a small stylized model in which it will be relatively straightforward to illustrate how this class of models differs from CRTS models without FDI.

### 6.2.1 Model and calibration

#### 6.2.1.1 Model

In this section, we will model producer services as intermediate inputs. In all the applied economy models in later sections, services are also used as final consumption goods. These intermediate inputs will be differentiated from one another and may also be differentiated according to whether or not they are produced domestically or by foreign firms. Both types of services are produced with increasing returns to scale due to fixed costs.

There will be two final goods, $X$ and $Y$, and two primary factors available on the domestic market, $S$ and $L$. $S$ will denote skilled labor and $L$ will denote all other factors, aggregated into a composite factor to simplify the model. $S$ and $L$ are in fixed aggregate supplies and are immobile between countries. The production function for $Y$

---

[8] This section is based on the comparative static model in Markusen *et al.* (2000, 2005), where a dynamic version of the model may also be found. The computer code and data for calibration may be found as an appendix to Markusen *et al.* (2000).

is written in Cobb–Douglas form to facilitate comparison with $X$, but in the numerical model we allow the more general constant elasticity of substitution (CES) production function. In order to illustrate the importance of the intensity of services use in final goods production, we assume that only the $X$ sector uses services as an intermediate input:

$$Y = S_y^{\alpha_y} L_y^{(1-\alpha_y)}. \tag{6.1}$$

Services are an intermediate input into $X$ production. The composite of all services inputs $Z$ enters into the production of $X$:

$$X = S_x^{\alpha_x} L_x^{\beta_x} Z_x^{(1-\alpha_x-\beta_x)}. \tag{6.2}$$

In our central parameter assumptions, we will also assume that in direct $S$ and $L$ requirements, $X$ is skilled-labor intensive relative to $Y$, in the sense that $\alpha_x/\beta_x > \alpha_y/\beta_y$.

Services are produced by imperfectly competitive firms. There is a one-to-one correspondence between the firm and their differentiated service varieties. There are both domestic and foreign firms producing services' inputs. $Z_x$ is a CES function of $ZD$ and $ZM$, each of which is in turn a CES function of the individual $ZD$ and $ZM$ varieties, $zd_i$ and $zm_j$, respectively:

$$Z_x = (ZD^\gamma + ZM^\gamma)^{1/\gamma} \tag{6.3}$$

$$ZD = \left[\sum_{i=1}^{n_d} zd_i^\delta\right]^{1/\delta} \quad ZM = \left[\sum_{i=1}^{n_m} zm_i^\epsilon\right]^{1/\epsilon} \tag{6.4}$$

where $n_d$ and $n_m$ are the number of domestic and imported service varieties, respectively. The elasticities of substitution within product groups are: $\sigma_d = 1/(1-\delta)$ and $\sigma_m = 1/(1-\epsilon)$. We require that $\delta$ and $\epsilon$ are between 0 and 1, which implies that the elasticities of substitution within product groups exceed unity.

Domestic intermediate inputs $ZD$ are produced using domestic skilled labor and the composite factor. Imported services $ZM$ are produced from domestic skilled labor, the composite domestic factor and a composite imported factor. Examples of these imported inputs, which will be denoted $V$, are: specialized technical expertise, advanced technology, management expertise and marketing expertise. The variable $V$ is thus quite general and denotes a key difference between foreign and domestic production structures.

$zd_i$ and $zm_i$ are produced with a fixed and a variable cost. Let $C^D$ and $C^M$ be the cost functions for producing individual domestic and foreign varieties. We impose a symmetry assumption within firm types, i.e., all foreign firms have identical cost structures, and all domestic firms that operate have cost structures identical to other domestic firms. $cd$ and $cm$ represent unit variable cost functions and $fd$ and $fm$ represent the fixed costs functions for domestic and foreign varieties respectively. Let $r$ be the price of $S$, $w$ be the price of $L$ and $p_v$ be the price of $V$. Cost functions for domestic and foreign intermediates are thus:

$$C^D(r, w, zd) = cd(r, w)zd + fd(r, w) \tag{6.5}$$

$$C^M(r, w, p_v, zm) = cm(r, w, p_v)zm + fm(r, w, p_v). \tag{6.6}$$

Let $n_d$ and $n_m$ as variables refer to the number of domestic and foreign service firms active in equilibrium. Recalling that the derivatives of cost function with respect to the price of factor $i$ is the input demand for factor $i$, the market clearing equations for $S$ and $L$ can then be written as:

$$L = L_y + L_x + n_d C_w^D + n_m C_w^M \tag{6.7}$$

$$S = S_y + S_x + n_d C_r^D + n_m C_r^M, \tag{6.8}$$

in which $C_w^j$ and $C_r^j$ represent the partial derivatives of unit cost for firm type $j$ with respect to the unskilled wage rate and the wage rate of skilled labor, respectively, where $j$ is equal to either D or M. (By Shephard's lemma, these are the compensated demand functions.)

The demand side of the economy consists of a representative consumer, who derives income from factor supplies and possibly from tax revenues (net of subsidies). Let subscripts c and p distinguish consumption and production of $X$ and $Y$. Preferences of the representative consumer are given by:

$$U = U(X_c, Y_c), \tag{6.9}$$

The trade balance condition requires that net exports of $X$ and $Y$ equal net payments for foreign services. Let $p_x^*$ and $p_y^*$ denote the world prices of $X$ and $Y$ (which may differ from domestic prices if there are taxes or subsidies). The trade balance is given by:

$$p_x^*(X_p - X_c) + p_y^*(Y_p - Y_c) - p_v^* V = 0, \tag{6.10}$$

where the demand for foreign services is given by the number of foreign services firms times the derivative of the cost function for a given foreign service with respect to the cost of imports:

$$V = n_m C_{p_v}^M. \tag{6.11}$$

To simplify the interpretation of results, we assume "large-group monopolistic competition." That is, individual firms believe they are too small to influence the composite price of their group. Consider first the marginal product of an individual service $zm_i$ in the aggregate output of the service sector $Z_x$.[9] From the chain rule, we have:

$$\frac{\partial X}{\partial zm_i} = \frac{\partial X}{\partial Z_x}\frac{\partial Z_x}{\partial ZM}\frac{\partial ZM}{\partial zm_i}.$$ (6.12)

Large-group monopolistic competition is the assumption that an individual firm views $Z_x$ as fixed or parametric, and here by extension views $ZM$ and $ZD$ as fixed. Thus, the individual firm views all composite prices and quantities as fixed except for its own output $zm_i$. Using Equations (6.2), (6.3) and (6.4), we have that the marginal product of $zm_i$ is:

$$\frac{\partial X}{\partial zm_i} = (1 - \alpha_x - \beta_x)S_x^{\alpha_x}L_x^{\beta_x}Z_x^{-\alpha_x-\beta_x}[ZD^\gamma + ZM^\gamma]^{\frac{1}{\gamma}-1}ZM^{\gamma-\epsilon}zm_i^{\epsilon-1}.$$ (6.13)

Let $p_x$ denote the domestic price of $X$ and $p_{zm_i}$ denote the price received by the producer of a representative $zm_i$. Since final $X$ production is assumed competitive, $p_{zm_i}$ is the value of the marginal product of $zm_i$ in producing $X$. That is:

$$p_{zm_i} = p_x(1 - \alpha_x - \beta_x)S_x^{\alpha_x}L_x^{\beta_x}Z_x^{-\alpha_x-\beta_x}[ZD^\gamma + ZM^\gamma]^{\frac{1}{\gamma}-1}ZM^{\gamma-\epsilon}zm_i^{\epsilon-1}.$$ (6.14)

Revenue of an individual producer of $zm_i$ is price times quantity:

$$zm_ip_{zm_i} = p_x(1 - \alpha_x - \beta_x)S_x^{\alpha_x}L_x^{\beta_x}Z_x^{-\alpha_x-\beta_x}[ZD^\gamma + ZM^\gamma]^{\frac{1}{\gamma}-1}ZM^{\gamma-\epsilon}zm_i^{\epsilon}.$$ (6.15)

Then marginal revenue takes a very simple form:

$$MR_{zm_i} = p_x(1 - \alpha_x - \beta_x)S_x^{\alpha_x}L_x^{\beta_x}Z_x^{-\alpha_x-\beta_x}[ZD^\gamma + ZM^\gamma]^{\frac{1}{\gamma}-1}ZM^{\gamma-\epsilon}\epsilon zm_i^{\epsilon-1} = \epsilon p_{zm_i}.$$ (6.16)

Setting marginal revenue equal to marginal cost implies that the ratio of price to marginal cost is $1/\epsilon$.

We have assumed that all foreign varieties have an identical cost structure and the demand for all foreign varieties is identical. These "symmetry" assumptions imply that the output and price of all foreign firms that operate will be identical. We can thus write $zm_i = zm$ and $p_{zm_i} = p_{zm}$ for all $i$. Similar conclusions follow for domestic firms.

Then equilibrium for a symmetric group of service firms ($zm$ or $zd$) requires that two equations are satisfied: marginal revenue equals marginal cost; and zero profits:

$$MR = MC : p_{zm}\epsilon = cm(r, w, p_v)$$ (6.17)

$$p_{zm} = AC : p_{zm} = cm(r, w, p_v) + fm(r, w, p_v)/zm.$$ (6.18)

---

[9] A similar argument applies to $zd_i$.

Solving these equations to find $zm$, output per firm, we get:

$$zm = \frac{\epsilon}{1-\epsilon} \frac{fm(r, w, p_v)}{cm(r, w, p_v)} = (\sigma_{\mathrm{m}} - 1)\frac{fm(r, w, p_v)}{cm(r, w, p_v)}. \qquad (6.19)$$

The output of a given variety is larger when fixed costs are larger relative to marginal costs (scale economies are larger) and when the varieties are better substitutes. Similar results apply for domestic type firms.

Dual to the output indices in Equation (6.4) are cost functions. When firms minimize the cost of purchasing foreign (domestic) varieties of services, the cost of one unit of the composite foreign (domestic) variety $ZM$ ($ZD$) is:

$$CM = \left[\sum_{i=1}^{n_{\mathrm{m}}} p_{zm_i}^{1-\sigma_{\mathrm{m}}}\right]^{\frac{1}{1-\sigma_{\mathrm{m}}}}, \quad \sigma_{\mathrm{m}} = \frac{1}{1-\epsilon} \qquad (6.20)$$

$$CD = \left[\sum_{i=1}^{n_{\mathrm{d}}} p_{zd_i}^{1-\sigma_{\mathrm{d}}}\right]^{\frac{1}{1-\sigma_{\mathrm{d}}}}, \quad \sigma_{\mathrm{d}} = \frac{1}{1-\delta}. \qquad (6.21)$$

Substituting the symmetry of the equilibrium into the cost functions for a unit of $ZM$ or $ZD$, implies that $CD$ *and* $CM$ can be written as:

$$CD = \frac{p_{zd}}{n_{\mathrm{d}}^{\sigma_{\mathrm{d}}-1}} \quad CM = \frac{p_{zm}}{n_{\mathrm{m}}^{\sigma_{\mathrm{m}}-1}}. \qquad (6.22)$$

Since the elasticities of substitution exceed unity, the cost of obtaining an aggregate unit of foreign or domestic services declines as the number of varieties increases. That is, additional varieties convey an externality to the final goods sector $X$ by lowering the cost of obtaining a unit of composite services. The elasticity of the cost of a unit of composite foreign services with respect to the number of foreign varieties is $(1 - \sigma_{\mathrm{m}})$. Thus, if an additional variety conveys a smaller externality on the final goods sector the better foreign varieties substitute for each other. A similar argument applies for domestic varieties.

We make the "small country assumption," that prices to the country are fixed. This means we assume, in addition to fixed prices of $X$ and $Y$, that there are a large number of potential foreign firms in production in the rest of the world so the domestic market has no "world" effect on the number of multinationals.

### 6.2.1.2 Calibration of the model

The computer code for this model (with explanations) and the social accounting matrix (SAM) for the calibration are available in an appendix to Markusen *et al.* (1999). In the initial equilibrium, the value of $Y$ is 120 and the value of $X$ is 80. $Y$ does not use services and $X$ uses 25 units of services. So services are 12.5% of the economy in the initial equilibrium. Imports of $V$ are banned in the initial equilibrium, so there are no foreign services initially. We assume that the world price of $V$ is 0.2. The model is calibrated so that when imported inputs $V$ have a price of one (a barrier of 400%), the costs of producing domestic and foreign services are equal, imported services $ZM$ have a 10% value share in $X$ production and $V$ has a 40% value share in producing $ZM$. Thus, with $p_v = 1$, $V$ has a 4.0% value share in $X$ and about 2% of the income of the home country. The various shares and elasticities are assumed without empirical support.

## 6.2.2 Modeling issues

### 6.2.2.1 Initially inactive activities

Often models avoid initial calibrations in which there are no initially inactive production activities or trade links. Or, if there is an initially inactive trade link (aircraft exports from Sri Lanka to the US), the link is omitted from the model, i.e., an inactive link is always inactive.

In this case, this is not an appropriate procedure. We want to consider initial situations in which FDI is prohibited in a sector and liberalization opens the closed sector. In a complementarity framework this is not a technical difficulty. The difficulty is economic. We would like to know how profitable the excluded activity would be if the barrier were removed. This will obviously be very quantitatively important to the results, which can range from zero in a perfectly competitive model (the barrier was redundant, the activity is not profitable with no barrier) to extremely high values. In Section 6.3 below, we explain how we have approached this problem in full models.

### 6.2.2.2 Firm-level product differentiation or differentiation by region of origin and bang-bang solutions

We have chosen a structure of production that provides for firm-type product differentiation with national differences, see Equations (6.3) and (6.4). When the elasticities of substitution are equal at all levels, i.e. $\gamma = \delta = \epsilon$, the CES function reduces to strictly firm-level product differentiation. In this case, the final good sector is completely indifferent between a domestic or foreign variety. Decreasing $n_m$ by one is perfectly matched in final sector productivity by increasing $n_d$ by one; only the total number of varieties matters. If the costs of producing domestic or foreign services are not that different, and they are collectively a small part of total GDP, then we can get bang-bang solutions in which a small change in relative costs shift is from only domestic services being produced to only foreign services. This has indeed occurred in our simulations.

On the other hand, we have set $\gamma$ less than $\delta = \epsilon$ (which may be justified by economic arguments as noted above). We have set the elasticity of substitution between aggregate domestic services and aggregate multinational services at 3, and the elasticity of substitution among services of one firm type (domestic or foreign) at 5. In this case, domestic and foreign varieties have different impacts on the productivity of the final goods sector.

The total number of varieties is not all that is important, but also the share of foreign and domestic varieties are concerned. In particular, the marginal productivity of either the domestic or foreign aggregate, $ZD$ and $ZM$, goes to infinity as its share goes to zero. Then, as long as either foreign or domestic varieties are permitted to be produced and sold, they will both exist in the market and we will not have bang-bang solutions.

The same result could be achieved by adding preference parameters to Equation (6.3) as:

$$Z_x = [\alpha ZD^\gamma + (1 - \alpha)ZM^\gamma]^{1/\gamma}. \qquad (6.23)$$

In the full model applications discussed below, we have chosen a pure firm-level product differentiation; but have added sector-specific factors of production for each firm type, which limit bang-bang solutions. See Section 6.3 below for an elaboration of these issues.

## 6.2.3 Simulation results

### 6.2.3.1 *What is the counterfactual*

There are a myriad of barriers applied against FDI by multinational services providers. These include limitations on the use of expatriate labor, domestic content requirements, restrictions on the expatriation of profits, denial of licenses to operate or sell services, restraints on how a firm can do business (such as joint venture requirements with national entities), requirements to transfer technology and simply increasing the red tape costs of multinationals. Most, but not all such barriers, are non-tariff barriers that raise the costs to multinational firms of supplying services. Recent estimates of the *ad valorem* equivalence of barriers against multinational services providers exhibit an enormous variance, but for some countries and products, the cost of domestic services may be elevated by as much as 1000% (see, e.g. Kang, 2000; Warren, 2000). We model the variable $V$ as the key input required for FDI and assume that any barriers imposed on multinational investment fall on the cost of importing $V$. In principle, the costs of barriers could fall on the output of the multinational firm or on the use of its domestic resources. However, insofar as many barriers restrain how the business operates or the nature of the firm, we prefer to assume that the cost of barriers falls on the foreign input $V$.

To understand the policy simulations requires further explanation of the value of $p_v$ and the meaning of changes in its value. Since this is a real model, all prices are relative to the numéraire, which is the cost of one unit of utility using our specified utility function. Thus, $p_v$ is the cost of a unit of $V$ in terms of the basket of goods consumed by the representative agent. Our small country assumption implies that there is a foreign supply price of $V$, which we denote $p^s_v$, where again this supply price is relative to our numéraire. We assume that there are regulatory barriers or red tape that result in a difference between the foreign supply price of $V$ and the price of a unit of $V$ to the

**Table 6.1** Impact of lowering the barriers against imported specialized inputs (skilled labor, blueprints, patents, etc.) of multinational services providers (price of specialized inputs $V^a$ to the home country or % ad valorem barrier against imported specialized inputs)

| Variables | +INF/+INF (1) | Price/% barrier | | | | |
|---|---|---|---|---|---|---|
| | | 1.00/400 (2) | 0.80/300 (3) | 0.60/200 (4) | 0.40/100 (5) | 0.20/0 (6) |
| 1. Welfare | 1.00 | 1.03 | 1.03 | 1.05 | 1.07 | 1.15 |
| 2. Real wage of skilled labor | 1.00 | 1.07 | 1.07 | 1.11 | 1.14 | 1.40 |
| 3. Real price of other primary factor (the composite factor) | 1.00 | 0.99 | 1.01 | 1.00 | 1.02 | 0.96 |
| 4. No. of domestic service firms | 1.00 | 0.45 | 0.35 | 0.24 | 0.11 | 0.03 |
| 5. No. of foreign service firms | 0.00 | 0.51 | 0.67 | 0.98 | 1.42 | 2.80 |
| 6. Net imports of $X$ | 1.00 | 0.00 | 0.00 | −0.41 | −0.63 | −3.01 |
| 7. Net imports of $Y$ | −1.00 | −0.26 | −0.31 | 0.00 | 0.11 | 2.18 |
| 8. Net imports of $V$ | 0.00 | 0.26 | 0.31 | 0.41 | 0.52 | 0.83 |

[a]We set 0.2 as the international supply price of the specialized input $V$. Prices above 0.2 are due to barriers against importing the input and represent real resource costs to the home country. The *ad valorem* equivalent of the barriers against the inputs are listed below the price of $V$.

importing country. The difference, $p_v - p^s_v$, is dissipated due to regulatory barriers. That is, $p_v$ is the real resource cost to the domestic economy of an imported unit of $V$.[10]

In our policy simulations we shall lower the value of $p_v$ toward the foreign supply price $p^s_v$. It is perhaps easier to think of this if we define $t$ as the *ad valorem* equivalent of the barriers against imported inputs into FDI in services. Then $p_v = p^s_v (1 + t)$ and our simulations can be thought of as our small open economy (SOE) lowering $t$, the *ad valorem* equivalent of its barriers against imported inputs into multinational service production.

We assume that in the initial equilibrium of the model, the barriers against imported inputs into multinational production are so high that no imported inputs are permitted, so there is no foreign production in the domestic market. That is, the *ad valorem* equivalence of the barriers against imported inputs into multinational production are infinite. The first column of Table 6.1 shows results of this initial equilibrium, when imports of $V$ are banned. Hence, the value zero is displayed in two rows of column (1): the number of foreign service firms and imports of the variable $V$. The country exports $Y$ and imports $X$, and there is no trade in $V$ (trade balance requires that the last three entries in a column sum to zero). We choose units of other variables displayed so that they are unity in the initial equilibrium.

---

[10] In our applied models of Russia below, we calculate the impact of assuming domestic rent capture of the barriers. An alternate interpretation of $p_v$ is the international "term-of-trade" for $V$. A lower $p_v$ denotes better terms of trade insofar as how much $X$ or $Y$ the country must pay for the imported input $V$. From the point of view of the *domestic* economy, either interpretation is the same.

In Table 6.1, the columns are headed by various values of $p_v$ and by the equivalent *ad valorem* barrier to imports of inputs of $V$ (in percentage terms). We set the foreign supply price $p^s_v = 0.2$. Moving from the left to the right in Table 6.1, we progressively decrease the barriers against inputs to FDI from infinite to zero. The *ad valorem* equivalent of the barriers against imported specialized inputs falls from infinite and 400% in columns (1) and (2) and to zero in column (6) where $p_v = 0.2$.

### 6.2.3.2 Comparative static results

Table 6.1 shows some simulation results from the static model. When the barriers against foreign service providers are relaxed, the cost of using $V$ in the production of services by multinationals falls and the imports of $V$ increase monotonically across row 8. If there are positive profits, entry by foreign service providers must occur until the price of foreign services is driven down to restore equilibrium. However, the lower prices by foreign service providers results in a substitution in demand away from domestic service providers and a decline in the number of domestic service providers. Hence, moving from the left to right in Table 6.1, the number of foreign service providers ($n_m$) increases (row 5) and the number of domestic service providers ($n_d$) decreases (row 4).

#### Large welfare gains from the Dixit–Stiglitz externality

As explained, additional varieties convey an externality on the final goods sector $X$ by lowering its costs of obtaining a unit of composite services. Equivalently, additional service varieties increase total factor productivity in the sector ($X$) that uses services. As the barriers against multinational service providers fall (from $p_v = 1$ to $p_v = 0.2$), the total number of varieties increases. The increase in total factor productivity from additional varieties results in an increase in welfare as shown in row 1.[11] Consider the very large changes in welfare in Table 6.1. Despite the fact that the cost of the $V$ input is only about 2% of income of the country in the first counterfactual, column (2), comparing columns (2) and (6) of row 1, a fall in the cost of $V$ from 1 to 0.2 produces a 12 percent increase in welfare (1.03 to 1.15) − result that is due to the productivity-variety effect.

#### Imported primary inputs: partial equilibrium substitute but general equilibrium complement for skilled labor

One of the most interesting results is displayed in row 2. The real wage of skilled labor rises monotonically across the row. As barriers to foreign service providers fall, the $X$ sector substitutes foreign services for domestic services and there is a substitution effect away from domestic skilled labor because foreign service providers use skilled labor less intensively than domestic service providers ($V$ economizes on domestic skilled labor in

---

[11] Although the total number of varieties decreases between columns (1) and (2), total factor productivity increases. Since there are zero foreign varieties in column (1), an additional foreign variety has higher marginal productivity than a domestic variety.

producing $ZM$). However, the reduction in the quality adjusted cost of services lowers the cost of final output in the $X$ sector and induces an output expansion there. In the simulation, the expansion of output in the $X$ sector increases the $X$-sector's direct demand for skilled labor. The output effect dominates the substitution effect resulting in an increase in the demand for skilled labor on balance. Thus, $V$ and skilled labor are partial equilibrium substitutes but general equilibrium complements. These results are particularly dramatic if we want to think of $V$ as largely consisting of imported skilled workers: they are clearly a general equilibrium complement to domestic skilled labor.

### Reversal of comparative advantage due to services liberalization

Results for the trade pattern are especially interesting. With high barriers to foreign service providers, the economy imports the service intensive good $X$ and exports $Y$. As the barriers against foreign service providers fall, the economy can produce the good $X$ more cheaply. In column (2), imports of $X$ are eliminated, and trade consists of a small export of $Y$ to pay for imported $V$. As the barriers fall further, the pattern of trade in goods is reversed in the right-hand two columns of Table 6.1. When $V$ is sufficiently cheap, the country imports $Y$ and exports $X$.

### Real prices of both labor and capital can rise

Results for the primary factor $L$, which is a composite of unskilled labor and other primary factors are displayed in row 3. These results exhibit a tradeoff between the Stolper–Samuelson effect and the Dixit–Stiglitz (1977) effect. $L$ is used intensively in $Y$ and $Y$ is the contracting sector. Thus, the Stolper–Samuelson theorem suggests that the real price of $L$, the factor used intensively in $Y$, should fall. On the other hand, increased variety lowers the cost (and therefore price) of producing a unit of the service composite, which, *ceteris paribus*, tends to reduce the price of the good of $X$ (the good that uses services intensively). These competing effects just about cancel each other in the simulations. The price of skilled labor increases *relative* to the price of $L$, consistent with Stolper–Samuelson, but unlike the usual Heckscher–Ohlin model, the real prices of both can rise due to the Dixit–Stiglitz price index effect.

### Product differentiation generates trade

Finally, column (2) of Table 6.1 in which $p_v = 1$ is a very important special case and requires some explanation. Let $w_0$ and $r_0$ be the initial equilibrium values of $w$ and $r$ in column (1), where foreign FDI is banned. For $zd = zm$ (domestic and imported varieties produced in the same quantity), we choose units of $V$ such that $p_v = 1$ is the value of $p_v$ that satisfies the equality:

$$cd(r_0, w_0)zd + fd(r_0, w_0) = cm(r_0, w_0, p_v)zm + fm(r_0, w_0, p_v).$$

That is, at the initial prices with FDI banned, $p_v = 1$ means that cost of one unit of output from a representative foreign firm is equal to cost of a unit of output from a domestic firm. This is an interesting case because, in homogeneous good competitive models, no entry would occur and the initial no-FDI equilibrium would continue to be an equilibrium once entry is permitted. However, due to the demand for both foreign and domestic varieties, both must exist in equilibrium unless they are banned. Thus, even with no cost advantage, foreign service providers will enter. In a competitive model without variety productivity effects, the second column would be identical to the first; but in our model, the second column in fact shows a welfare increase of 3%. With the Armington assumption and perfect competition, however, we would also achieve trade.

### 6.2.3.3 Conclusions

Although there is a clear trend among developing countries to liberalize their policies with respect to inward FDI (UN Conference on Trade and Development, Division on Transnational Corporations and Investment, 1995, pp. 272–275), many developing countries continue to impose restraints on FDI in general and in services in particular. These policies may be motivated by the fear that foreign service providers will harm domestic skilled workers. For example, examination of the commitments on services of WTO members in their General Agreement on Trade in Services (GATS) schedules reveals that 32 countries (mainly in Africa and Latin America) have scheduled "horizontal restrictions" that require foreign firms to use and train domestic skilled workers. In many cases these restraints may impede the foreign firm from importing the specialized people it would desire.

One of the more interesting results of our stylized model is that the real wage of domestic skilled labor increases with liberalization of policies against foreign service providers and the more foreign firms there are in the domestic market the more the real wage of domestic skilled workers increases. Thus, despite the fact that foreign firms import an input ($V$) and thereby use domestic skilled labor less intensively than domestic firms, additional foreign firms benefit domestic skilled labor. The reason is that additional foreign firms lower the cost of the intermediate service product in final goods production and thereby increase the relative importance of the final good sector ($X$), which uses services relatively intensively. Thus, in a general equilibrium sense, domestic skilled labor and the specialized foreign input $V$ are complements. One possible interpretation of this result is that the policies of certain developing countries that restrain the import of foreign inputs or force foreign multinationals to use domestic skilled factors in place of foreign inputs may not only result in lost national income, but may hurt the factor of production they are designed to assist. We show below that in a full general equilibrium model calibrated to a real economy, this result tends to hold, but not always.

We showed, with our static model, that liberalization could lead to gains of between 3 and 15% of GDP, depending on parameter assumptions. These are very large gains relative to what we might expect from a static model given that the imported input is only about 4% of $X$ output, or about half that as a share of host-country income. The source of these large gains is that additional intermediate service firms increase the productivity of the final goods sector that uses the services of these firms as intermediate inputs. More service firms allow final goods producers to use more specialized expertise, in the same way that larger markets allow for more specialized machine tools.

## 6.3 IMPACT OF LIBERALIZING BARRIERS TO FDI IN SERVICES: THE CASE OF RUSSIAN ACCESSION TO THE WORLD TRADE ORGANIZATION

### 6.3.1 Introduction

Russia applied for membership in the General Agreement on Tariffs and Trade (GATT) in June 1993 and the GATT Working Party was transformed into the WTO Working Party in 1995. It became the largest Working Party on accession in WTO history and Russia's effort at accession was the longest in the history of the WTO. In December 2011, the WTO invited Russia to become a member of the WTO and Russia became a member in August 2012.

Within Russia, numerous industrialists, policy analysts and even the former Prime Minister called for an assessment of the gains and losses from WTO accession, and for an assessment of the impact on different sectors of the economy. Russian goods providers were concerned that a fall in tariffs will imply increased competition from foreign goods providers and a decline in their market share. Russian service providers were concerned that liberalized rules on new FDI will lead to increased competition from multinational service providers in Russia. The government attempted to assure the business community that it had little to fear from WTO accession and that Russian exporters will obtain improved access to the markets of WTO member countries. However, some commentators and many in the business community remained skeptical, in part because there was a lack of quantitative estimates of the impacts and in part because the sources of the gains mentioned by the government were not well articulated.

On behalf of the World Bank, my colleagues and I responded to a request from the government of Russia to estimate the impacts of Russian WTO accession (Jensen et al., 2007). When we began the project, our assessment of the tariff regime of Russia was that the tariff barriers were not very high (about 12–13% average tariff in the first decade of the twenty-first century; see Shepotylo and Tarr, 2008). Although there were tough negotiations in some specific sectors such as aircraft and pork, on the whole we did not believe that the tariff regime would be the source of serious obstacles to Russian WTO accession. On the other hand, Russia had significant barriers to FDI in several important services sectors; and the Ministry of Trade was having enormous difficulty obtaining cooperation in its WTO accession effort from the agencies like the central bank (for banking and insurance) and the Ministry of Communications (regarding telecommunications). It appeared clear that services were going to be an area of very difficult negotiations for Russia, and we had to develop a model capable of assessing the impact of the liberalization of barriers against FDI in services for our model to be relevant to the major issues and impacts of WTO accession on Russia.

Although the government was interested in aggregate estimates of impacts on overall welfare and sector impacts at the country level, it had a much broader request for analysis. It also wanted an assessment of the household and poverty impacts; and, given the vast geographic scope of the country, impacts on the regions of Russia. We responded to the broader request with the analysis that we document in Rutherford and Tarr (2008, 2008a, 2010). In this section, we summarize Jensen et al. (2007), which was our first modeling effort to respond to the government's request; this model assesses impacts on an aggregate Russia with a single representative consumer model. We developed a 35-sector SOE comparative static CGE model of Russia that we believe was appropriate to evaluate the aggregate impacts of Russian accession to the WTO.

It is crucial to understand that WTO accession is a process. Russia implemented many of its commitments in advance of accession (such as the termination of the Rostelekom monopoly on long-distance land-line telephone services in Russia). Other commitments, such as allowing branches of foreign insurance companies 9 years after accession, will be implemented with an adjustment period following accession. The estimates of this model are intended to capture the cumulative impact of all these commitments, not just those that would be implemented on the day of accession.

We have built on the model is Section 6.2 above regarding our key modeling assumptions. That is, we assumed that a substantial portion of business services requires a domestic presence; multinational service providers import some specialized capital or labor as part of their decision to establish a domestic presence and business services supplied with a domestic presence are supplied by imperfectly competitive firms who produce a unique variety of the service. We adopted the Dixit–Stiglitz–Ethier structure for business services (and for increasing returns to scale goods) that implies endogenous productivity gains from the net introduction of new varieties. We have shown that the estimated welfare gains are 6 times the gains from a CRTS version of this model and that the inclusion of FDI in services with the Dixit–Stiglitz variety mechanism are the principle reasons for the larger estimated welfare gains.

The model in this section is innovative in a couple dimensions relative to Brown and Stern and Dee et al. papers discussed in Section 6.1. (i) It numerically assesses liberalization of barriers against foreign direct investors in business services in a model with considerable sector detail (35 sectors in our model). This allows the crucial estimates of the barriers to FDI in services to be estimated at the level of a particular business service. (ii) Unlike Brown and Stern and Dee et al., the Dixit–Stiglitz endogenous productivity effects are important in interpreting the results from the impact of service sector liberalization.[12]

---

[12] There have also been numerical estimates of the benefits of services liberalization where services trade is treated analogously to goods trade, i.e. trade in services is assumed to be entirely cross-border and subject to tariffs. See, e.g. Brown et al. (1996).

The section is organized as follows. In Section 6.3.2 we describe the model, focusing on the key extensions of the model relative to the model in Section 6.2, and issues in robustness of the model with imperfect competition and Dixit–Stiglitz effects. In Section 6.3.3, we discuss the most important data, especially how we estimate the crucial *ad valorem* equivalents of the barriers against FDI in services. In Section 6.3.3, we present and interpret the large estimated welfare gains and why WTO accession is counterproductive to the government's objective of diversifying the economy. In Section 6.3.4, we examine the impact of different modeling assumptions (or model closures) on the results. In Section 6.3.5, we present the results of our piecemeal and systematic sensitivity analysis.

## 6.3.2 Overview of the model and key data

### 6.3.2.1 Overview of the model formulation

The model is an SOE model, with Russia modeled endogenously and an aggregate rest of the world modeled as vectors of perfectly elastic supply and demand prices for the sectors in the model. An algebraic formulation of the full model is available in Jensen *et al.* (2004). Here, we provide a general description. Primary factors include skilled and unskilled labor; mobile capital; sector-specific capital in the energy sectors reflecting the exhaustible resource; sector specific capital in imperfectly competitive sectors; and primary inputs imported by multinational service providers, reflecting specialized management expertise or technology of the firm. The existence of sector specific capital in several sectors implies that there are decreasing returns to scale in the use of the mobile factors and supply curves in these sectors slope up. There are 35 sectors as shown in Table 6.2. Regardless of sector, all firms minimize the cost of production.

In all sectors, firms optimize their sales between exports and the domestic market to maximize revenue for any composite output level, based on a constant elasticity of production transformation schedules. Prices on the export markets are perfectly elastic. Total capital and labor are in fixed supply, but mobile capital and labor move freely between sectors to equilibrate the returns to these factors across sectors. The balance of trade is fixed, so any increase in imports must be matched by an increase in exports. There is a single representative consumer, who maximizes utility subject to his/her income constraints; the consumer (and firms) have a love of variety, where the gains from variety are represented by the Dixit–Stiglitz structure.

### 6.3.2.2 Structure of production

#### Competitive goods and services sectors

One category of sectors is produced under CRTS, where the price equals marginal costs with zero profits. This includes agriculture, forestry and construction. It also includes

**Table 6.2** Structure of value added in Russia: factor shares from the input-output table and after reconciliation with the Household Budget Survey (HBS)

| | Value added | Value added (%) | Input-output table | | | | Reconciled with HBS | | |
| --- | --- | --- | --- | --- | --- | --- | --- | --- | --- |
| | | | Unskilled labor (%) | Skilled labor (%) | Capital (%) | | Unskilled labor (%) | Skilled labor (%) | Capital (%) |
| *Sectors total* | *1354* | *100.0* | *28* | *12* | *61* | | *21* | *63* | *16* |
| Business services | | | | | | | | | |
| Railway transportation | 45 | 3.3 | 30 | 24 | 45 | | 11 | 85 | 5 |
| Truck transportation | 20 | 1.5 | 31 | 33 | 36 | | 8 | 88 | 4 |
| Pipelines transportation | 49 | 3.6 | 5 | 3 | 92 | | 11 | 58 | 31 |
| Maritime transportation | 4 | 0.3 | 32 | 19 | 48 | | 14 | 81 | 5 |
| Air transportation | 8 | 0.6 | 48 | 29 | 24 | | 14 | 84 | 2 |
| Other transportation | 14 | 1.1 | 21 | 20 | 59 | | 9 | 85 | 6 |
| Telecommunications | 16 | 1.2 | 31 | 16 | 53 | | 16 | 79 | 5 |
| Financial services | 21 | 1.5 | 33 | 27 | 40 | | 10 | 86 | 4 |
| Science and science servicing | 11 | 0.8 | 56 | 10 | 34 | | 35 | 61 | 4 |
| *Subtotal* | *188* | *13.9* | *2583* | *1794* | *5623* | | *1244* | *7626* | *1130* |
| Differentiated goods | | | | | | | | | |
| Ferrous metallurgy | 26 | 1.9 | 18 | 17 | 65 | | 9 | 85 | 7 |
| Non-ferrous metallurgy | 31 | 2.3 | 18 | 13 | 69 | | 12 | 81 | 7 |
| Chemical and oil–chemical industry | 24 | 1.8 | 28 | 10 | 61 | | 20 | 74 | 7 |
| Mechanical engineering and metal-working | 71 | 5.2 | 48 | 11 | 41 | | 30 | 66 | 4 |
| Timber and woodworking and pulp and paper industry | 19 | 1.4 | 37 | 17 | 45 | | 17 | 79 | 5 |
| Construction materials industry | 21 | 1.6 | 33 | 13 | 54 | | 19 | 75 | 5 |
| Light industry | 9 | 0.7 | 66 | 3 | 30 | | 63 | 32 | 5 |
| Food industry | 45 | 3.3 | 25 | 11 | 64 | | 17 | 76 | 7 |
| Other industries | 9 | 0.6 | 54 | 19 | 28 | | 22 | 76 | 3 |
| *Subtotal* | *255* | *18.8* | *3436* | *1226* | *5338* | | *2125* | *7312* | *562* |

(*Continued*)

**Table 6.2** Structure of value added in Russia: factor shares from the input-output table and after reconciliation with the Household Budget Survey (HBS)—cont'd

| | Value added | Value added (%) | Input-output table | | | Reconciled with HBS | | |
|---|---|---|---|---|---|---|---|---|
| | | | Unskilled labor (%) | Skilled labor (%) | Capital (%) | Unskilled labor (%) | Skilled labor (%) | Capital (%) |
| Extractive industries | | | | | | | | |
| Oil extraction | 39 | 2.9 | 4 | 9 | 87 | 1 | 12 | 87 |
| Gas | 12 | 0.9 | 4 | 7 | 89 | 1 | 10 | 89 |
| Coalmining | 15 | 1.1 | 13 | 41 | 47 | 2 | 52 | 47 |
| *Subtotal* | *67* | *4.9* | *581* | *1580* | *7840* | *76* | *2084* | *7840* |
| Constant returns industries | | | | | | | | |
| Electric industry | 48 | 3.6 | 19 | 17 | 64 | 9 | 84 | 6 |
| Oil processing | 10 | 0.8 | 7 | 17 | 77 | 3 | 89 | 8 |
| Other fuel industries | 0 | 0.0 | 30 | 2 | 68 | 49 | 33 | 18 |
| Construction | 116 | 8.6 | 30 | 26 | 44 | 10 | 86 | 4 |
| Agriculture and forestry | 103 | 7.6 | 25 | 2 | 73 | 47 | 31 | 22 |
| Post | 4 | 0.3 | 23 | 11 | 66 | 15 | 78 | 7 |
| Trade | 309 | 22.9 | 10 | 3 | 87 | 20 | 53 | 27 |
| Public catering | 2 | 0.1 | 67 | 28 | 5 | 19 | 81 | 1 |
| Other goods-producing sectors | 11 | 0.8 | 72 | 23 | 5 | 23 | 76 | 1 |
| Communal and consumer services | 76 | 5.6 | 24 | 9 | 67 | 19 | 72 | 9 |
| Public health and sports and social security | 42 | 3.1 | 59 | 7 | 34 | 44 | 52 | 4 |
| Education and culture and art | 54 | 4.0 | 68 | 5 | 28 | 56 | 40 | 4 |
| Geology and hydrometeorology | 3 | 0.2 | 63 | 7 | 30 | 45 | 52 | 3 |
| Administration and public associations | 65 | 4.8 | 66 | 22 | 12 | 22 | 76 | 1 |
| *Subtotal* | *844* | *62.3* | *2806* | *957* | *6237* | *2486* | *5999* | *1515* |

certain public services, like education and post office facilities, and key mineral industries.[13] In these sectors, products are differentiated by country of origin (i.e. we employ the Armington assumption). All Russian goods producing firms (including imperfectly competitive firms) can sell on the domestic market or export. Russian firms optimize their output decision between exports and domestic sales based on relative prices and their constant elasticity of transformation production function.

### Goods produced subject to increasing returns to scale

These goods are differentiated at the firm level. We assume that manufactured goods may be produced domestically or imported. Firms in these industries set prices such that marginal cost (which is constant with respect to output) equals marginal revenue and there is free entry, which drives profits to zero. For domestic firms, costs are defined by observed primary factors and intermediate inputs to that sector in the base year data. Foreigners produce the goods abroad at a constant marginal cost but incur a fixed cost of for operating in Russia. The c.i.f. (cost, insurance, and freight) import price of foreign goods is simply defined by the import price, and, by the zero profits assumption, in equilibrium the import price must cover fixed and marginal costs of foreign firms. We employ the standard Chamberlinian large-group monopolistic competition assumption within a Dixit–Stiglitz framework, which results in constant markups over marginal cost.

For simplicity we assume that the composition of fixed and marginal cost is identical in all firms producing under increasing returns to scale (in both goods and services). This assumption in a our Dixit–Stiglitz based Chamberlinian large-group model assures that output per firm for all firm types remains constant (i.e. the model does not produce rationalization gains or losses).

Due to the Dixit–Stiglitz formulation, the effective cost function for users of goods produced subject to increasing returns to scale declines in with the total number of firms in the industry.

### Services sectors that are produced in Russia under increasing returns to scale and imperfect competition

This third category of sectors includes telecommunications, financial services, most business services and transportation services. For convenience, we call these services producer services, although all services are intermediate services in production. In services sectors, we observe that some services are provided by foreign service providers on a cross-border basis analogous to goods providers from abroad. However, a large share of business services are provided by service providers with a domestic presence, both

---

[13] Although electricity and gas are monopolistically controlled, prices are controlled by the government. Thus, market-determined pricing to exploit market power is excluded by the government and we maintain the assumption of price equal to marginal costs.

multinational and Russian.[14] Our model allows for both types of foreign service provision in these sectors. There are cross-border services allowed in this sector and they are provided from abroad at constant costs — this is analogous to competitive provision of goods from abroad. Cross-border services, however, are not good substitutes for service providers who have a presence in Russia.[15]

There are also multinational service firm providers that choose to establish a presence in Russia in order to compete with Russian firms directly in the Russian market. When multinationals service providers decide to establish a domestic presence in Russia, they will import some of their technology or management expertise. That is, FDI generally entails importing specialized foreign inputs. Thus, the cost structure of multinationals differs from Russian service providers. Multinationals incur costs related to both imported primary inputs and Russian primary factors, in addition to intermediate factor inputs. Foreign provision of services differs from foreign provision of goods, since the service providers use Russian primary inputs. Domestic service providers do not import the specialized primary factors available to the multinationals. Hence, domestic service firms incur primary factor costs related to Russian labor and capital only. These services are characterized by firm-level product differentiation. For multinational firms, the barriers to FDI affect their profitability and entry. Reduction in the constraints on FDI will induce foreign entry that will typically lead to productivity gains because when more varieties of service providers are available, buyers can obtain varieties that more closely fit their demands and needs (the Dixit–Stiglitz variety effect).

### Value-added and producer services substitute for each other

In Figure 6.1, we depict how production of a representative good is produced. One departure from a standard formulation is that, as in Section 6.2, we allow producer services (services that are produced in Russia under increasing returns to scale) to substitute with value added in a CES nest. Other intermediate goods and services enter in to the production structure in the usual fixed coefficients, Leontief nests with the composite of value added and producer services. We believe that there is strong substitutability between producer services and value added which justifies this separate treatment. For example, transportation services clearly substitute well for value added. Firms have a choice of hiring a driver and buying or renting a truck for delivery services or else contracting with a trucking company or other transportation company for delivery services. With legal, accounting and most professional services, firms can employ a lawyer, accountant or engineer, or substitute for the use of their company capital and labor by purchasing these services from a firm.

---

[14] One estimate puts the worldwide cross-border share of trade in services at 41% and the share of trade in services provided by multinational affiliates at 38%. Travel expenditures 20% and compensation to employees working abroad 1% make up the difference. See Brown and Stern (2001, Table 1).

[15] Daniels (1985) found that service providers charge higher prices when the service is provided at a distance.

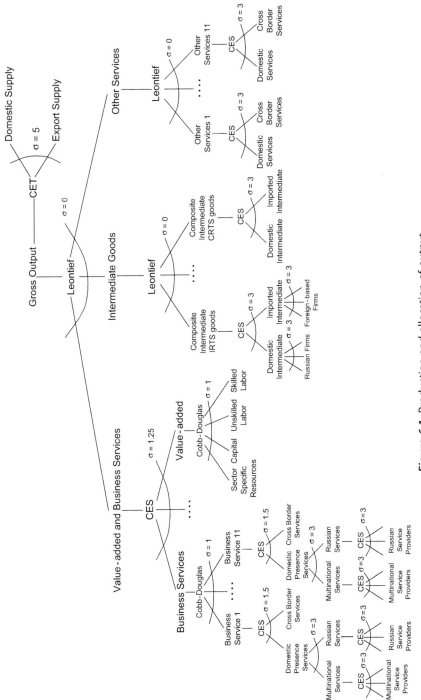

**Figure 6.1** Production and allocation of output.

### 6.3.2.3 Comparative steady-state formulation

In this version of our model, we allow the capital stock to adjust to its steady-state equilibrium along with all of the model features we employ in our WTO reference case (i.e. we allow for tariff and FDI liberalization with endogenous productivity effects as above). We call this our comparative steady-state model. In the comparative static model, we assume that the capital stock is fixed and the rental rate on capital is endogenously determined. In the comparative steady-state model, the logic is reversed. We assume that the capital stock is in its initial steady-state equilibrium in the benchmark dataset, but that the capital stock will adjust to a new steady-state equilibrium based on a fixed rate of return demanded by investors.[16] That is, if the trade policy shock happens to induce and increase in the rate of return on capital so that it exceeds the initial rate of return, investors will invest and expand the capital stock. Expansion of the capital stock drives down the marginal product of capital, i.e., it drives down the rental rate on capital, until the rate of return on capital falls back to the initial level.[17] To analyze trade policy, this comparative steady-state approach has been employed by many authors, including Harrison *et al.* (1996, 1997), Baldwin *et al.* (1999) and Francois *et al.* (1996). The approach, however, dates back to the 1970s, when both Hansen and Koopmans (1972) and Dantzig and Manne (1974) used it. The approach ignores the foregone consumption necessary to achieve the higher level of investment and thus is an overestimate or an upper-bound estimate of the long-run gains within the framework of the model assumptions.[18]

### 6.3.2.4 Empirical basis for our modeling assumptions in imperfectly competitive sectors

The model assumes: (i) that discriminatory barriers against FDI in business services exist in Russia; (ii) that WTO accession will result in the reduction or removal of these barriers; (iii) that the removal or reduction of the barriers will stimulate an increase in FDI in business services; and (iv) that additional varieties of business services (and goods in imperfectly competitive sectors) will produce productivity gains in Russia. We now address each of these issues in turn.

#### Barriers to FDI in Russian services sectors

As Russia began seriously negotiating its barriers in services as part of its WTO accession, key barriers to FDI were the following. Rostelekom had a monopoly on long-distance fixed-line telephone services. In banking and insurance, foreign banks and foreign insurance companies were restrained to a maximum of about 15% of the market. Foreign insurance

---

[16] Essentially, we use our one model, but alter the model closure rule for the rate of return on capital and the capital stock. Since the justification for allowing the capital stock to vary while keeping the rate of return on capital fixed is based on comparative long-run steady-state equilibria, we prefer to use the expression long-run steady-state model.

[17] The rate of return on investment in our model is the rental rate on capital divided by the cost of a unit of the capital good.

[18] Rutherford and Tarr (2002) have shown, however, that trade liberalization can produce considerably larger long run gains in an endogenous growth model. However, that is another model formulation.

companies were prohibited from selling insurance in the mandatory insurance markets, and branches of foreign banks and insurance companies were prohibited. In transportation services, China made liberalization of Russian barriers against its providers of truck transportation services a significant issue in its bilateral talks on Russian WTO accession. While several large multinational oil companies would like to construct a gas pipeline, only Gazprom may construct or operate a gas pipeline. Consequently, at least 20 billion cubic meters of gas that is associated with the production of oil must be flared each year.

### Will WTO accession reduce the barriers to FDI in business services?

The business services sectors have been the subject of some of the most intense negotiations associated with Russian accession. Russia has made numerous commitments in this area. Some of the key concessions are the following. Russia has agreed to increase the quota on the maximum share that foreign banks and insurance companies can attain from 15 to 50%, and Russia will phase out the prohibition on foreign participation in mandatory insurance lines. Russia agreed to terminate the Rostelekom monopoly on long-distance fixed-line telephone services as part of the Russia–EU bilateral agreement. There are multinational telephone operators already operating in the Russian mobile telephone market, but the maximum equity restriction of 49% will be lifted. Russia will ensure national treatment and market access for a wide variety of professions, including lawyers, accountants, architects, engineers, marketing specialists and healthcare professionals. Foreign-owned companies will be permitted to engage in wholesale and retail trade, franchise sectors and express courier services.[19] The EU has negotiated intensely for the rights of companies other than Gazprom to construct a gas pipeline, but did not achieve success in this area.

### Will reduction of the barriers against FDI increase FDI?

Potential foreign direct investors in Russia face many barriers including include lack of good governance in Russia, administrative barriers to investment and customs delays that inhibit Russia participating in international production chains as well as explicit barriers to FDI. Despite these problems faced by foreign investors, there are foreign providers of business services operating in Russia in virtually all of the business services sectors (estimates by our specialist service sector institutes of the shares of the market captured by multinationals are later in Table 6.5), which shows interest in the Russian market by foreign service providers.[20] And the intensity with which the negotiations have been conducted in the business services sectors is due in most cases to lobbying interests by foreign providers of services. This suggests that multinational service providers have a desire to expand operations in Russia. Consequently, it is natural to assume then that

---

[19] See Tarr (2007) for details.
[20] See Tarr and Volchkova (2007, Table 1) for data on FDI flows into Russia on an annual basis from 2000 to 2008.

a reduction of barriers against multinational providers of services will, at the margin, result in an increase in FDI in those sectors, at least given some time.[21]

## Impact of additional varieties on productivity

We have discussed the evidence on the productivity impacts of additional varieties of services in Section 6.1. Here, we focus on goods, as we employ the Dixit–Stiglitz mechanism in the imperfectly competitive goods sectors as well. As Romer (1994) has argued, product variety is a crucial and often overlooked source of gains to the economy from trade liberalization. In our model, it is the greater availability of varieties that is the engine of productivity growth, but we believe there are other mechanisms as well through which trade may increase productivity.[22] Consequently, we take variety as a metaphor for the various ways increased trade can increase productivity. Winters et al. (2004) summarize the empirical literature by concluding that "the recent empirical evidence seems to suggest that openness and trade liberalization have a strong influence on productivity and its rate of change." Some of the key articles regarding product variety are the following. Broda and Weinstein (2004) find that increased product variety contributes to a fall of 1.2% per year in the "true" import price index. Hummels and Klenow (2005) and Schott (2004) have shown that product variety and quality are important in explaining trade between nations. Feenstra et al. (1999) show that increased variety of *exports* in a sector increases total factor productivity in most manufacturing sectors in Taiwan (China) and Korea, and they have some evidence that increased input variety also increases total factor productivity. Finally, Feenstra and Kee (2004) show that export variety and productivity of a country are positively correlated.

Beginning with the path-breaking work of Coe and Helpman (1995), a rich literature now exists that has empirically shown that total factor productivity increases due to the purchase of imported intermediate goods. Coe and Helpman found that OECD countries benefit from foreign research and development (R&D), and that they benefit more from trading with countries that have a larger stock of research and development. Further, the benefits are greater the more open the country is to foreign trade. Moreover, while in large countries, the elasticity of total factor productivity (TFP) with respect to domestic R&D capital stocks is larger than that with respect to foreign R&D capital stocks, the opposite holds in small countries (i.e., foreign R&D is more important for small countries). Coe et al. (1997) extend these results based on a sample of 77 developing countries. They find developing countries that do little R&D on their own have

---

[21] More systematically, Alessina et al. (2005) find, for a sample of a large number of OECD countries, that regulatory reform, especially liberalization of the barriers against entry, plays a strong role in increasing investment in the sector.

[22] Trade or services liberalization may increase growth indirectly through its positive impact on the development of institutions (see Rodrik et al., 2004). It may also induce firms to move down their average cost curves, or import higher-quality products or shift production to more efficient firms within an industry. Tybout and Westbrook (1995) find evidence of this latter type of rationalization for Mexican manufacturing firms.

benefited substantially from industrialized country R&D through trade in intermediate products and capital equipment with industrialized countries. They find that R&D spillovers through trade with the US are the largest, since the US stock of R&D is the highest and it is the most important trading partner for many developing countries. A 1% increase in the R&D stock of the US raises total factor productivity for all 77 developing countries in their sample by 0.03%. By comparison, a 1% increase in the R&D stock of Japan, Germany, France or the UK raises total factor productivity only between 0.004 and 0.008%. Crucially, they find that countries that trade more with the US, such as the Latin American countries, get more productivity spillover increases from the US R&D stocks and that the relatively more open East Asian countries have benefited the most from foreign R&D through trade. Keller (2000) also finds that trade is an important conveyor of R&D and is especially important for small countries. Several other studies, including Lumenga-Neso *et al.* (2005), Schiff and Wang (2006), and Falvey *et al.* (2002), confirm these results. Lumenga-Neso *et al.* (2005) show that technological spillovers can occur from indirect trade with technologically advanced countries, i.e. imports from the UK embody some US technology due to UK imports from the US. Since the data show that OECD countries have the vast majority of R&D stocks,[23] it implies that it is important for small developing countries to trade with large technologically rich countries, such as the US and the EU, at least indirectly.

On the other hand, Hummels and Klenow (2005) have shown that, contrary to the standard Dixit−Stiglitz model, varieties expand less than proportionately to market size. Hummels and Logovskyy (2005) adopt an interesting approach that can explain this phenomenon: they modify the demand structure so that goods become more substitutable as more varieties enter the market; then the marginal benefit of new varieties falls with market size. In our model, varieties also expand less than proportionately with market size, but it is due to the costs of production. We assume that in each imperfectly competitive industry there are two specific factors − one used by domestic firms and one used by foreign firms. Both fixed and variable costs require the use of a specific factor. The expansion of the industry bids up the price of the specific factor, so additional varieties are acquired at increasing costs. We show in the sensitivity analysis that the welfare results are quite sensitive to the parameter in our model [$\epsilon(f_i)$] that is determined by the share of costs due to the specific factor.

### 6.3.2.5 Does the model have adequate convexity?

It is well known that monopolistic competition models do not necessarily have a general equilibrium. Arrow and Hahn (1971) have shown, however, that in an economy with both perfectly competitive and monopolistically competitive sectors, a general equilibrium can be guaranteed if the perfectly competitive sectors have enough resources available to support

---

[23] Coe *et al.* (1997) calculate that 96% of the world's R&D expenditures took place in industrial countries in 1990.

the expansion of the imperfectly competitive sectors.[24] Since we use models as a basis of policy discussions with governments who take assessments of industry output change seriously, we have a more binding constraint than the existence of an equilibrium — we must assure that the sector results are reasonable. For example, in a developmental stage of the model of Russia, we had a counterfactual equilibrium in which one sector essentially became the whole economy — an implausible result for a policy change such as WTO accession in an economy as diverse as the Russian. These issues imply that it is necessary to develop a model structure that limits potentially explosive expansions of the imperfectly competitive sectors. The following are four ways to introduce convexity in the model that we have employed in various applications. We have chosen to employ the first two in this model.

### Sector-specific factors

By assuming that some share of the labor or capital is specific to the sector, expansion of the sector bids up the price of that factor and limits the expansion of the sector. In the applied models with monopolistic competition on which I have been a coauthor, in each imperfectly competitive sector, we have assumed that some share of capital *for each firm type* is sector-specific. That is, foreign and domestic firms have a different sector-specific factor. The elasticity of supply of output of the firm type (foreign or domestic firm types in each sector in the models in this paper) in the sector with respect to the price of its output is then related to the share of sector-specific capital for that firm type. [See Balistreri and Tarr (2011) for the mathematical representation.] Assuming some sector-specific factors has advantages. (i) It is economically reasonable to assume that some factors are specific, which explains lobbying for protection. (ii) As the demand for the output of a firm type declines, the price of the sector-specific factor declines, reducing costs of the firm type and allowing the firm type to maintain a share of the market. This also contributes to a pro-competitive effect of liberalization, as domestic firms will decrease prices and costs from this effect. (iii) If the model has multiple foreign firm types, representing say firms from different regions, there will be an elasticity of firm supply parameter for each region. As we discuss below, this parameter can play a very important role in policy discussions, such as with whom should a country form a regional trade agreement.

### Excluding the Dixit–Stiglitz productivity gain for own use varieties

If a monopolistically-competitive sector has a large share of its costs due to the costs of inputs from its own sector, the Dixit–Stiglitz productivity improvement can cause an explosive expansion of the sector. That is, suppose the counterfactual shock induces an

---

[24] Arrow and Hahn (1971, p. 154) characterize their formal requirement as follows: "the extent of increasing returns there [in the monopolistic production possibility sets] is not too great relative to the resources that the competitive sector would be capable of supplying."

expansion of the sector. In monopolistic competition, this means there is an increase in varieties in the sector. The new entry has two effects — the price of the output is lowered (limiting expansion in the sector), but the additional varieties also lower the costs of the sector (inducing expansion in the sector). Entry into the sector continues as long as price exceeds average costs, but costs may fall faster than price, inducing explosive expansion. A solution to this problem was to exclude the Dixit—Stiglitz productivity gains from varieties in the same sector.

Since we have sector-specific factors of production, as the sector expands, the costs of the sector-specific factor increases and costs do not fall proportionately with varieties. In practice, we have always had an equilibrium in these models. However, in the case of the Russia model, the costs of non-ferrous metals inputs in the total costs of the non-ferrous metals sector were very high — about 40%. In the developmental stage of the model in this section, we observed dramatic expansion of the non-ferrous metals sector in our WTO accession counterfactual, while virtually all other sectors contracted. We assessed this to be due to an unrealistically large cost reduction due to the variety externality. Since businessmen, policy makers and political leaders had been calling for an assessment of the consequences of WTO accession at the sector level, it was crucial that we have results that could be explained with clear economic intuition. We modified the Dixit—Stiglitz formulation such that there was no productivity gain from additional intermediate varieties in the same sector. Subsequently, the sector results were very reasonable and easily interpreted. Moreover, surveys have revealed that policy makers and political leaders throughout Russia came to adopt the assessments of this model as their expected outcomes at the sector level of the impacts of Russian WTO accession.

### Elasticity of substitution differences or preference parameters in the demand function

It is possible to avoid highly specialized solutions (or bang-bang solutions in the dynamic version of the model in Section 6.2) by using nested CES functions with elasticities of substitution that differ by firm type, as in Equations (6.3) and (6.4) or if there are preference parameters by firm type as in Equation (6.23). Then the marginal productivity of a particular firm type goes to infinity as the use of that firm type goes to zero, assuring all firm types will be used if they exist. We have chosen pure firm level product differentiation in this model. We have found that with sector-specific factors and the exclusion of the Dixit—Stiglitz own use productivity gains, there is adequate convexity in the model to avoid highly specialized solutions.

### *6.3.2.6 Export demand*

This is a SOE model with perfectly elastic export demand in all sectors. As part of the counterfactual, the price of exports expands in a limited number of sectors, and firms in this sector increase output to supply the increased demand in the export markets. We employ a constant elasticity of transformation (CET) function between sales to the domestic and export markets that allows sales to both the domestic and export markets. However, output expansion of the sector would be less pronounced if expanding sales on the export market were tempered by a downward sloping export demand curve. In our models of Kenya (Balistreri *et al.*, 2009) and Tanzania ( Jensen *et al.*, 2010) we employ a downward sloping export demand curve in the imperfectly competitive sectors.

### 6.3.2.7 Can the large-group monopolistic competition model produce results regarding competition?

Contrary to a criticism that is sometimes leveled at the large-group monopolistic competition model, the models in this chapter exhibit the important pro-competitive effects of liberalization of barriers against foreigners. The criticism is that many of the services sectors are characterized by few firms and with large group monopolistic competition the markup of price over marginal cost is fixed by the Dixit–Stiglitz elasticity of substitution, see Equation (6.17). However, we have specific capital for each firm type in each imperfectly competitive sector. If there is entry into the sector by foreign or multinational firms, then rents to the sector-specific factor for domestic firms will decline. This will lead to a decline in both the costs and prices of the domestic firms. Further, the price charged by foreign firms will fall from the reduction of cost increasing barriers and the entry in to the sector will lead to a decline in the quality adjusted price to users of the Dixit–Stiglitz aggregate due to the Dixit–Stiglitz variety externality. Consequently, even though price-cost margins are fixed, our models capture what is crucial to consumers and firms about increased competition: a fall in foreign prices due to reduced barriers to foreigners, a fall in domestic prices due to reduced rents to the specific capital in domestic firms and a quality improvement of their products. All of these can be measured in this model. Further, the model captures what is important to producers and what can explain lobbying for protection — their own sector-specific rents.

### 6.3.2.8 Key data
*Ad valorem* equivalence of barriers to FDI in services sectors
Estimates of the *ad valorem* equivalents of barriers to FDI in services are key to the results. Consequently, we commissioned 20-page surveys from several Russian research institutes that specialize in these sectors and followed this with econometric estimates of these barriers based on these surveys.

These questionnaires provided us with data and descriptions and assessments of the regulatory environment in these sectors.[25] Using this information and interviews with

---

[25] This information was provided by the following Russian companies or research institutes: ZNIIS in the case of telecommunications; expert RA for banking, insurance and securities; Central Marine Research and Design Institute (CNIIMF) for maritime transportation services; and Infomost for air transportation services. The questionnaires are available at www.worldbank.org/trade/russia-wto. The same sources provided the data on the share of expatriate labor discussed below.

specialist staff in Russia, as well as supplementary information, Kimura *et al.* (2004a,b,c) then estimated the *ad valorem* equivalents of barriers to FDI in several Russian sectors, i.e., in telecommunications; banking, insurance and securities, and maritime and air transportation services. The process involved first converting the answers and data of the questionnaires into an index of restrictiveness in each industry. Kimura *et al.* then applied methodology explained in the volume by Findlay and Warren (2000), notably papers by Warren (2000), McGuire and Schulele (2000), and Kang (2000). For each of these service sectors, authors in the Findlay and Warren volume evaluated the regulatory environment across many countries and developed indices of trade restrictiveness for the sector they were studying in each of the countries in their sample. The price of services is then regressed against the regulatory barriers to determine the impact of any of the regulatory barriers on the price of services. Kimura *et al.* then assumed that the international regression applies to Russia. Applying that regression and their assessments of the regulatory environment in Russia from the questionnaires and other information sources, they estimated the *ad valorem* impact of a reduction in barriers to FDI in these services sectors.[26] The results of the estimates are listed in Table 6.3.[27] In the case of maritime and air transportation services, we assume that the barrier will only be cut by 15 percent since pressure from the Working Party in these sectors is not strong.

---

[26] Warren estimated quantity impacts and then using elasticity estimates was able to obtain price impacts. The estimates by Kimura *et al.* that we employ are for "discriminatory" barriers against FDI. Kimura *et al.* also estimate the impact of barriers on investment in services that are the sum of discriminatory and non-discriminatory barriers.

[27] Kimura *et al.* estimated that the prices of telecommunications services in Russia are elevated by 10% due to barriers to multinational service providers. We believe that in telecommunications it is crucial to employ a differentiated product model to characterize competition between multinational and Russian telecommunications providers. This means that we interpret the estimates of Kimura *et al.* to indicate that the discriminatory tax on multinational service providers results in a 10% increase in the *composite price* of domestic and multinational service provision. Then the *ad valorem* tax on multinationals, say at rate $x$, must be above 10% since there is no discriminatory tax on domestic service providers and the composite price is a weighted average of domestic prices (which are untaxed) and multinational prices that are taxed at a rate $x$. More precisely, if $x$ is the *ad valorem* equivalent of the barriers to multinational investment in telecommunications in Russia, $s$ is the share of the market in Russia of multinationals, 10% is the amount by which telecommunications prices are elevated due to the barriers and if we assume Russian domestic service providers prices are unaffected, then we may solve for $x$ from: $sx + (1 - s) * 0 = 0.10$. That is, $x = 0.10/s$ Our data indicate that $s = 0.15$, then $x = 0.67$ or 67%. Barriers to FDI, however, have an indirect effect on the price of Russian telecommunications services. Consequently, $sx + (1 - s) * y = 0.10$ may be more appropriate, where $y$ is the amount by which the price of Russian telecommunication services are increased in the benchmark as a result of barriers on multinational telecommunications service providers. The value of $y$ would have to be less than the value of the increase in composite services (0.1). It is likely that the indirect effect of barriers to FDI on the price of domestic Russian telecommunications services is less than 0.05, since the composite price increased by only 0.1 and lower values of $y$ yield higher estimates of $x$. However, if we take $y = 0.05$, then $x$ equals 0.38, which is approximately the value estimated for financial services, of 0.33. We take a conservative estimate here of 0.33 for telecommunications.

**Table 6.3** Tariff rates, export tax rates, estimated *ad valorem* equivalence of barriers to FDI in services sectors and estimated improved market access (*ad valorem* in %; by sector)

| | Tariff rates | Export tax rates | Estimated change in world market price | Equivalent % barriers to FDI | |
|---|---|---|---|---|---|
| | | | | Base year | Post-WTO Accession |
| Electric industry | 4.5 | 0.0 | 0.0 | | |
| Oil extraction | 0.0 | 7.9 | 0.0 | | |
| Oil processing | 3.8 | 4.6 | 0.0 | | |
| Gas | 0.5 | 18.8 | 0.0 | | |
| Coalmining | 0.0 | 0.0 | 0.0 | | |
| Other fuel industries | 2.6 | 2.6 | 0.0 | | |
| Ferrous metallurgy | 2.9 | 0.4 | 1.5 | | |
| Non-ferrous metallurgy | 7.4 | 5.3 | 1.5 | | |
| Chemical and oil−chemical industry | 7.1 | 1.6 | 1.5 | | |
| Mechanical engineering and metal-working | 7.2 | 0.0 | 0.0 | | |
| Timber and woodworking and pulp and paper industry | 9.9 | 6.9 | 0.0 | | |
| Construction materials industry | 10.6 | 1.6 | 0.0 | | |
| Light industry | 11.8 | 4.1 | 0.5 | | |
| Food industry | 11.3 | 3.1 | 0.5 | | |
| Other industries | 6.4 | 0.0 | 0.5 | | |
| Agriculture and forestry | 8.2 | 0.6 | 0.0 | | |
| Other goods-producing sectors | 0.0 | 0.0 | 0.5 | | |
| Telecommunications | | | | 33.0 | 0.0 |
| Science and science servicing (market) | | | | 33.0 | 0.0 |
| Financial services | | | | 36.0 | 0.0 |
| Railway transportation | | | | 33.0 | 0.0 |
| Truck transportation | | | | 33.0 | 0.0 |
| Pipelines transportation | | | | 33.0 | 0.0 |
| Maritime transportation | | | | 95.0 | 80.0 |
| Air transportation | | | | 90.0 | 75.0 |
| Other transportation | | | | 33.0 | 0.0 |

*Source:* Author's estimates.

### Share of expatriate labor employed by multinational service providers

In Section 6.2, we explained that imported foreign primary inputs in services production by multinationals are partial equilibrium substitutes, but could be general equilibrium complements. In our applied model, the impact of the liberalization of barriers to FDI in business services sectors on the demand for labor in these sectors will depend importantly on the share of expatriate labor used by multinational firms. We obtained estimates of the share of expatriate labor or specialized technology that is used by multinational service providers in Russia from Russian research institutes that specialize in these sectors. In general, we found that multinational service providers use mostly Russian primary factor inputs and only small amounts of expatriate labor or specialized technology. In particular, the estimated share of foreign inputs used by multinationals in Russia is: telecommunications, $10\% \pm 2\%$; financial services, $3\% \pm 2\%$; maritime transportation, $3\% \pm 2\%$; and air transportation, $12.5\% \pm 2.5\%$.

### Tariff data

For about 1700 tariff lines, Russia employs a "mixed system" in which the maximum of the *ad valorem* or specific tariff applies. Due to the acquisition of trade flow data at the tariff line level, the actual tariffs were first calculated precisely by Shepotylo and Tarr (2008), and employed in Russian WTO accession analysis by Rutherford and Tarr (2008, 2010). The tariff rates for the analysis in this section were based on trade flow data at a slightly aggregated level and were therefore not precise. Shepotylo and Tarr have shown, however, that the tariff calculations used in this paper are not subject to significant errors.

Based on a mapping (of the Russian Statistical Office) from the tariff line data of the Customs Committee to the sectors in our input-output table, we calculated a weighted average tariff rate for the sectors of our model. We calculated these rates two ways: based on all imports (where the collected tariff rate as a percentage of all imports is 8.1%) and on non-CIS (Commonwealth of Independent States) imports (where the collected tariffs as a percentage of non-CIS imports is 11.1%). The rates we employ in the model are the rates based on all imports. The rates based on all imports are lower since the base on the calculation includes CIS imports on which no tariffs are imposed. We believe collected tariff rates more closely approximate the protection a sector receives and the incentives it faces. Similar procedures are applied for export taxes. The results at the sector level are in Table 6.3.

Applying these tariff rates across all sectors implies that tariff revenue in our model is about 1.6% of GDP in the initial equilibrium. Collected tariffs in Russia are closer to 1.1% of GDP.[28] There are several reasons that the collected tariffs in Russia are less than the legal rates on most favored nation (MFN) imports. Most notably, exemptions to the Russian tariff are available for regional agreements (most notably the CIS), personal

---

[28] See International Monetary Fund (2002).

imports and shuttle trade. We adjust for the CIS trade, so we are applying the MFN rates on all imports from the non-CIS. This slightly, but not significantly biases upward the rates we employ relative to collected rates.

### Export tax data

Analogous to the import trade data, the Russian State Customs Committee publishes data on export volumes and values. Similar to the tariff data, the export taxes are sometimes *ad valorem* or sometimes the maximum of the *ad valorem* or specific tax rate. The results are reported in Table 6.3.

### Input-output table

The core input-output table for this section is the 1995 table produced by Goskomstat. [This was updated for the applications in Rutherford and Tarr (2008, 2010).] The official table contained only 22 sectors and importantly has little service sector disaggregation. Consequently, Russian input-output expert S.P. Baranov disaggregated this table into a 35-sector input-output table. Baranov used unpublished data available to Goskomstat based on the surveys that were used to construct the 1995 table. The principal elements of this disaggregation were: a split of the oil and gas sector into oil, gas and oil processing; a split of the transport sector into railroad, maritime, air, pipeline, truck and other transportation services; the breakup of communication into post services and telecommunications; and disaggregation of the data in several business services sectors regarding market and non-market activities. The documentation by Baranov is available on the website www.worldbank.org/trade/russia-wto.

## 6.3.3 Results

In our general WTO scenario, we assume that: (i) Barriers against FDI are reduced as indicated in Table 6.3, (ii) seven sectors subject to anti-dumping actions in export markets receive slightly improved market access (this is implemented as an exogenous increase in their export price as shown in Table 6.3) and (iii) the tariff rates of all sectors are reduced by 50%.[29] We first discuss (and present in Table 6.4) our estimates of the impact of Russian WTO accession on aggregate variables such as welfare and the real exchange rate, aggregate exports, the return to capital, skilled labor and unskilled labor, and the percentage change in tariff revenue. In order to obtain an assessment of the adjustment costs, we estimate the percentage of labor and mobile capital that must change industries. The gains come from a combination of effects, so we also estimate the comparative static impacts of the various components of WTO accession in order to assess their relative importance.

---

[29] Actual tariff reductions were part of the accession negotiations and were not known when this study was done. The paper was finalized in January 2012, 1 month after Russia was offered membership in the WTO. The WTO reported that the Russian average tariff will decline to 7.8%, which is a tariff cut slightly less than we had assumed.

**Table 6.4** Impact of WTO accession on economy-wide variables in Russia: policy results and decomposition of effects (results are percentage change from initial equilibrium)

| | Benchmark | WTO accession (1) | Tariff reform only (2) | Improved market access only (3) | Reform of FDI barriers only (4) | WTO accession in steady-state model (5) | WTO accession with partial reform of FDI barriers (6) | WTO accession with domestic rent dissipation (7) | WTO accession in short run model (8) |
|---|---|---|---|---|---|---|---|---|---|
| **Aggregate welfare** | | | | | | | | | |
| Welfare (*EV* as % of consumption) | | 7.2 | 1.3 | 0.6 | 5.2 | 23.6 | 4.1 | 7.7 | 5.9 |
| Welfare (*EV* as % of GDP) | | 3.3 | 0.6 | 0.3 | 2.4 | 11.0 | 1.9 | 3.6 | 2.8 |
| **Government budget** | | | | | | | | | |
| Tariff revenue (% of GDP) | 1.4 | 0.9 | 0.8 | 1.4 | 1.4 | 1.0 | 0.8 | 0.9 | 0.8 |
| Tariff revenue (% change) | | −33.4 | −38.4 | 8.4 | 10.6 | −23.3 | −35.4 | −33.2 | −35.8 |
| **Aggregate trade** | | | | | | | | | |
| Real exchange rate (% change) | | 2.6 | 2.0 | −0.5 | 1.1 | 4.8 | 1.8 | 2.7 | 3.0 |
| Aggregate exports (% change) | | 13.2 | 7.9 | 1.5 | 3.5 | 24.3 | 10.8 | 13.5 | 9.5 |
| **Returns to mobile factors** | | | | | | | | | |
| Unskilled labor (% change) | | 2.5 | 0.4 | 0.1 | 1.9 | 13.2 | 1.0 | 2.7 | 1.9 |
| Skilled labor (% change) | | 4.7 | 1.5 | 0.6 | 2.5 | 17.6 | 2.6 | 4.9 | 3.4 |
| Capital (% change) | | 4.9 | 2.0 | 0.7 | 3.1 | 19.5 | 3.6 | 4.9 | 4.3 |
| **Factor adjustments** | | | | | | | | | |
| Unskilled labor (% of non-sector specific workers who change jobs) | | 2.6 | 1.1 | 0.5 | 1.6 | 4.4 | 1.7 | 2.6 | 0.0 |
| Skilled labor (% of non-sector specific workers who change jobs) | | 2.1 | 0.4 | 0.4 | 1.5 | 2.5 | 1.0 | 2.2 | 0.0 |
| Capital | | 0.6 | 0.4 | 0.4 | 0.2 | 0.1 | 0.6 | 0.6 | 0.4 |

*Source:* Author's estimates.

First, we discuss the comparative static results. We shall also consider the results of assuming the time frame is long enough for capital to adjust to its new long run steady-state equilibrium in a scenario we call comparative steady state. In addition, we evaluate a "short-run" scenario, in which all labor is "sector-specific."

### 6.3.3.1 Aggregate welfare effects of WTO accession

We estimate that the welfare gains to Russia are equal to 7.2% of Russian consumption (or 3.3% of GDP) in the medium term. These gains derive from three key effects: (i) Improved access to the markets of non-CIS countries in selected products, (ii) Russian tariff reduction and (iii) liberalization of barriers to FDI in services sectors. We execute three scenarios that allow us to understand the relative impact of these various elements and the mechanisms through which they operate.

#### Impact of tariff reduction

The results for this scenario are presented in column (2) of Table 6.4. We lower tariffs by 50%, but there is no liberalization of the barriers to FDI or improved market access. The estimated welfare gains to the economy are 1.3% of consumption or 0.6% of GDP.

The gains to the economy from tariff reduction alone come about for two reasons. (i) The liberalization induces additional varieties in the imperfectly competitive sectors of Russia, which results in a productivity improvement for users of these goods through the Dixit–Stiglitz–Ethier effect. Additional varieties come from the fact that tariff reduction on imports in imperfectly competitive sectors raises the tariff-ridden demand curve for imports. This increases profitability for foreigners of selling in the Russian market thereby inducing new entry by foreign suppliers until zero profits are restored. Although there is a loss of domestic varieties due to increased foreign competition, there is a net increase in varieties. This result is analogous to the result found by Rutherford and Tarr (2002) in a fully dynamic model. (ii) Tariff reduction in Russia will lead to improved domestic resource allocation since tariff reduction will induce Russia to shift production to sectors where production is valued more highly based on world market prices. This is the fundamental comparative advantage effect from trade liberalization in CRTS models.

#### Impact of improved market access

In column (3) of Table 6.4, we present the results of a scenario in which we allow for improved market access (according to the terms-of-trade improvements of Table 6.3), but we do not lower tariffs or barriers to FDI in services sectors. We estimate that the impact of improved market access at 0.6% of consumption (0.3% of GDP). Gains derive from improved prices for exports. However, also a higher value for exports allows Russia to buy more imports and more varieties of imports increase productivity. Thus, the impact of improved market access is greater in a model with Dixit–Stiglitz variety effects than in a CRTS model.

### Impact of FDI liberalization in business services

In this scenario, labeled reform of FDI barriers in column (4) of Table 6.4, we eliminate or reduce the discriminatory tax on multinationals in the services sectors (as shown in Table 6.3), but there is no reduction in tariffs or improved market access. The reduction in the discriminatory tax on multinationals increases profitability for provision of services in Russia by multinationals, thereby inducing new entry by multinational service providers until zero profits are restored. Although there is a loss of domestic service varieties due to increased multinational foreign competition, there is a net increase in varieties. Russian businesses will then have improved access to the services of multinational service providers in areas like telecommunication, banking, insurance, transportation and other business services. The additional service varieties in the business services sectors should lower the cost of doing business and result in a productivity improvement for users of these goods through the Dixit–Stiglitz–Ethier effect. We estimate that the gains to Russia from liberalization of barriers to FDI in services are about 5.2% of the value of Russian consumption or about 72% of the total gains to Russia of WTO accession.

### 6.3.3.2 Sector results
#### Expanding manufacturing sectors

Sectors we estimate will expand are those that either export a relatively large share of their output, obtain an exogenous increase in export prices as a result of WTO accession, are relatively unprotected initially compared to other sectors of the economy or experience a significant reduction in the cost of their intermediate inputs, typically because they have a large share of intermediate inputs that come from sectors that experience productivity advances due to trade or FDI liberalization.

The manufacturing sectors that we estimate are likely to expand their output the most are non-ferrous metals, ferrous metals and chemicals. These three sectors are among the sectors that we assume will gain an exogenous increase in the price of its exports upon WTO accession. They are also among those that export the highest share of their output — they all export over 30% of the value of their output. Export intensity is important because a reduction in tariffs generally depreciates the real exchange rate. Since the real exchange rate depreciates, sectors that export intensively will gain more domestic goods for a unit of their exports.[30]

---

[30] The real exchange must depreciate to restore equilibrium in the balance of trade. That is, the decline in tariffs induces an increase in the demand for imported goods and the reduction in barriers to multinational investment in the services sectors induces multinationals to import more foreign skilled labor. The depreciation of the real exchange rate encourages more exports and mutes the import expansion to restore equilibrium in the balance of trade constraint.

### Declining manufacturing sectors

The sectors that contract the most are the sectors that are the most protected prior to tariff reduction and which have a relatively small share of exports. Most notably this includes machinery and equipment, food and light industry and construction materials. All of these sectors do little exporting and light industry and food are the sectors with the highest tariff rates.

### Business services sectors

Russian business and labor interests in these sectors are not the same, and we discuss the impact on labor in these sectors first. We find that skilled and unskilled employment will expand in most, but not all, of the business services sectors. This is an application to a full economy model of the result found by Markusen *et al.* (2000, 2005). They have shown in a more stylized model that even when FDI is a partial equilibrium substitute for domestic skilled labor, it may be a general equilibrium complement. The reason is as follows. As a result of a reduction in the barriers to FDI in these sectors, we estimate that there will be an expansion in the number of multinational firms who locate in Russia to provide business services from within Russia and a contraction in the number of purely Russian firms. Although multinationals also demand Russian labor, though they use Russian labor slightly less intensively than Russian firms, i.e. since multinationals import primary inputs, FDI is a partial equilibrium substitute for Russian labor. However, as more service firms enter the market, the quality adjusted price of services falls and industries that use services expand their demand for business services. On balance, the increase in labor demand from the increase in the demand for business services typically exceeds the decline in labor demand from the substitution of multinational supply for Russian supply in the Russian market. That is, FDI is a partial equilibrium substitute but a general equilibrium complement to Russian labor. Thus, we estimate that labor in the business services sectors will typically gain from an expansion in FDI and multinational provision of services in Russia.

Regarding capital, as a result of the removal of restrictions, we estimate there would be significant increase in FDI and an increase in multinational firms operating in Russia. We estimate that specific capital owners in imperfectly competitive sectors will lose from this increase in competition. We expect, however, that the increase in FDI to have diverse impacts on Russian firms. We define a firm as a multinational even if a foreign firm and a Russian firm have formed a joint venture. Multinationals will often look for Russian joint venture partners when they want to invest in Russia. Russian companies that become part of the joint ventures in the expanding multinational share of the business services market will likely preserve or increase the value of their investments. Russian capital owners in business services who remain wholly independent of multinational firms, either because they avoid joint ventures or are not desired as joint venture partners, will likely see the value of their investments decline and the least efficient will exit the industry.[31]

This suggests that domestic lobbying interests within a service sector could be diverse regarding FDI liberalization. We estimate that labor should find it in their interest to support FDI liberalization even if capital owners in the sector oppose it. However, capital owners themselves may have diverse interests depending on their prospects for acquisition by multinationals.

## 6.3.4 Sensitivity analysis

The results depend on the choice of parameters in the model as well as certain assumptions or "closures." In this section, we evaluate the impact on the results of the changing the values of the key parameters or modeling assumptions in the model. We begin with key model assumptions. We then discuss the results of "piecemeal sensitivity" analysis on the parameters. Finally we discuss the results of our "systematic sensitivity" analysis.

### 6.3.4.1 Model assumptions
Sensitivity to results to a 50% cut in the barriers to FDI

In this scenario, we simulate a cut in the barriers by one-half as much as in our central scenario (shown in column (6) of Table 6.4). However, we allow for improved market access and a 50% cut in tariff barriers. We find that the gains to the economy are reduced to about 4.1% of consumption. From Table 6.4, we can see this is slightly less than the sum of three components: (i) Half of the gains from FDI liberalization, (ii) tariff reduction and (iii) improved market access.

Rent capture or dissipation

Resource loss from rent seeking of licenses is a significant problem in Russia. In our central scenario we have ignored these costs, i.e. we assume that Russians capture the rents from the barriers without dissipation of the rents. It may be appropriate, however, to assume that those that obtain the licenses used Russian capital and labor in wasteful license seeking activities and the like. Then the *ad valorem* equivalents of the barriers to multinational investment are a real resource cost. As a result, the estimated gains from WTO accession increase from 7.2 to 7.7% of consumption (as shown in column (7) of Table 6.4) because the resources that were used to capture the rents become available for productive activities.

Similarly, if foreigners capture the rents initially, liberalization of the barriers will allow competition among foreigners that will result in a transfer of the rents from

---

[31] Exit of least-efficient firms is an inference we make outside of our model results, since we do not have a heterogeneous firms model. We assume that firms in the business services sectors must use a specific factor in order to produce output. This specific factor results in an upward-sloping supply curve in each business services sector.

foreigners to Russia. Then we estimate the gains to Russia from WTO accession will increase from our central estimate of 7.2 to 7.5% of consumption.

### Sector-specific labor

Although we have sector specific capital (varying by sector and firm type), in our central scenario all labor is mobile. To evaluate short-run effects, where a significant portion of labor will be unable to switch jobs between sectors, we assume that labor cannot move between sectors (i.e., labor is "sector-specific"). With sector-specific labor, wages of skilled and unskilled labor will vary across sectors in response to shifts in demand coming from WTO accession.

The aggregate results are presented in Table 6.4, column (8). The welfare gains fall to 5.9% of consumption. This decline in the gains is expected when labor is sector specific since when labor is immobile, it cannot move to the sectors where it is valued most highly. What is striking about this scenario is that the gains remain very substantial. This shows how important productivity effects are since without productivity effects, a model with no labor market resource reallocation would produce very small gains.

While the welfare gains are smaller, no labor changes jobs in this scenario (see the rows on factor adjustments in Table 6.4). So the "social" adjustment costs of labor are zero.[32] Despite no dislocation of labor, the wages of workers in each sector will have their wages go up or down relative to the average wage in the economy for skilled or unskilled labor; thus, there are private adjustment costs of WTO accession, even if there are no social costs of adjustment in this short-run model.[33]

### CRTS model — no productivity effects

We also executed a CRTS version of our model where we reduced tariffs by 50%, allowed improved access and lowered FDI barriers. Without the Dixit–Stiglitz structure that provides the possibility of productivity gains, the welfare gains are reduced to 1.2% of consumption.[34]

### Long-run comparative steady-state results of WTO accession

In a long-run analysis, we should allow for the fact that WTO accession could improve the investment climate in Russia. In this scenario, we employ our comparative steady-state model. As explained in Section 6.3.2, the principal feature is that we allow for the fact that accession to the WTO could increase the rate of return on investment. This

---

[32] We have not estimated the social adjustment costs, we only calculate the share of the workers in each sector that have to change jobs. See Dixon and Rimmer (2002) for an application that measures adjustment costs.

[33] See Matusz and Tarr (2000) for an elaboration of the distinction between private and social costs of adjustment.

[34] Without increasing returns to scale, removing barriers to FDI has no effect (recall that rents are not dissipated in the benchmark).

would induce an increase in the capital stock until the marginal productivity of capital declines sufficiently that the rate of return on investment is no higher than the initial steady-state equilibrium rate of return on investment.[35]

With our comparative steady-state model, we estimate that the gains to Russia from WTO accession are 23.7% of consumption (11% of GDP). This is more than 3 times the estimated comparative static welfare gains. The reason the gains are larger is that we estimate that WTO accession will induce an increase in the rental rate on capital in Russia in the comparative static model by 4.9 %. In the comparative steady-state model, this induces an expansion of the capital stock in the new equilibrium. We estimate that the capital stock will increase by about 14.4% of its initial level in the long-run steady-state equilibrium. With a higher capital stock, the economy is able to produce more output and there is more consumption. Under the assumptions of this model, we must remark that this type of model produces an overestimate or an upper-bound estimate of the welfare gains because the foregone consumption necessary to achieve the higher capital stock is not taken into account. However, this model is not the optimal tool to assess the long-run growth welfare impacts since we have not captured endogenous growth effects in our model. Rutherford and Tarr (2002) have shown that a fully dynamic model that incorporates productivity effects endogenously, and which takes into account foregone consumption from investment decisions, is likely to produce estimated welfare gains that are as large or larger than these comparative steady-state results (see Section 6.4.4 for an elaboration).

### 6.3.4.2 Piecemeal sensitivity analysis

In Table 6.5, we present the impact on welfare of varying the value of key parameters. In these scenarios, we retain the central value of all parameters except the parameter in question. In general, the gains to the economy (welfare gains) increase with an increase in elasticities, since higher elasticities imply that the economy is able to more easily shift

---

[35] It is sometimes alleged that the capital stock should not be expected to increase in the comparative steady-state model. The argument is that trade liberalization could favor labor intensive industries as easily as capital intensive ones, so there should be no presumption that the rental rate of capital will increase relative to the wage rate. I have explained in Section 6.2, however, that the pessimism of Stolper—Samuelson is overcome with Dixit—Stiglitz productivity effects. Both the rental rate on capital and the wage rate can rise relative to the price of goods. However, even in a CRTS CGE trade model, I maintain that we should normally (but not always) expect an increase in the capital stock from trade liberalization. The reason is that the rate of return on investment depends on the ratio of the rental rate on capital to the price of a unit of capital. In a model of homogeneous goods, the Stolper—Samuelson theorem implies that if the rental rate falls relative to the wage rate, the rental rate must also fall relative to the price of goods in the model. However, CGE modelers typically employ the Armington assumption. Our cost function of the capital good is produced by both domestic and imported inputs as well as labor and capital, and trade liberalization will reduce the price of imported inputs. [See Rutherford and Tarr (2003) for a mathematical characterization of the CRTS dynamic and comparative steady-state models.] Thus, there is a general presumption that the cost of the capital good will decline. Even when trade liberalization induces a fall in the rental rate of capital relative to the wage rate, the price of a unit of capital could fall more, inducing a rise in the return on investment and the capital stock in the new equilibrium.

**Table 6.5** Piecemeal sensitivity analysis—welfare effects

| Parameter[a] | Parameter value | | | Hicksian equivalent variation[b] with corresponding parameter | | |
|---|---|---|---|---|---|---|
| | Lower | Intermediate | Upper | Lower | Intermediate | Upper |
| esubs | 0.5 | 1.25 | 2.0 | 5.6 | 7.2 | 9.7 |
| esub | 2.0 | 3.0 | 4.0 | 7.3 | 7.2 | 6.8 |
| sigmadm | 2.0 | 3.0 | 4.0 | 7.1 | 7.2 | 7.3 |
| esubprimary | 0.70 | 1.00 | 1.30 | 7.1 | 7.2 | 7.2 |
| esubintermed | 0.0 | 0.0 | 0.25 | 7.2 | 7.2 | 7.4 |
| esubconsumer | 0.5 | 1.0 | 1.5 | 6.8 | 7.2 | 7.5 |
| etadx | 3.0 | 5.0 | 7.0 | 7.1 | 7.2 | 7.2 |
| etad | 5.0 | 7.5 | 10.0 | 6.9 | 7.2 | 7.4 |
| etaf | 10.0 | 15.0 | 20.0 | 5.1 | 7.2 | 8.7 |
| theta_m(i) | see table below | | | 7.1 | 7.2 | 7.2 |
| theta_fdi(i) | see table below | | | 5.2 | 7.2 | 8.4 |

[a]The piecemeal sensitivity analysis employs central values for all parameters (see below) other than the tested parameter and lump sum tax replacement.
[b]Hicksian equivalent variation as a percentage of the value of consumption in the benchmark equilibrium.

| Parameter | Central Value | Definitions of the parameter |
|---|---|---|
| esubs | 1.25 | Elasticity of substitution between value-added and business services |
| esub | 3.0 | Elasticity of substitution between firm varieties in imperfectly competitive sectors |
| sigmadm | 3.0 | "Armington" elasticity of substitution between imports and domestic goods in CRTS sectors |
| esubprimary | 0.0 | Elasticity of substitution between primary factors of production in value added |
| esubintermed | 0.0 | Elasticity of substitution in intermediate production between composite Armington aggregate goods |
| esubconsumer | 1.0 | Elasticity of substitution in consumer demand |
| etadx | 5.0 | Elasticity of transformation (domestic output versus exports) |
| etad | 7.5 | Elasticity of Russian service firm supply with respect to price of output |
| etaf | 15.0 | Elasticity of multinational service firm supply with respect to price of output |
| theta_m(i) | Varies | Share of specialized imports $V$ as a share of value added in multinational firms in sector I in the benchmark equilibrium |
| theta_fdi(i) | Varies | Share of output of service sector I captured by multinationals firms in the benchmark equilibrium |

| Parameter values for | theta_fdi(i) | | | theta_m(i) | | |
|---|---|---|---|---|---|---|
| | Low | Central | High | Low | Central | High |
| Railway transportation | 0.01 | 0.03 | 0.05 | 0.02 | 0.04 | 0.06 |
| Truck transportation | 0.03 | 0.05 | 0.07 | 0.01 | 0.03 | 0.05 |
| Pipelines transportation | 0.01 | 0.03 | 0.05 | 0.05 | 0.1 | 0.15 |
| Maritime transportation | 0.25 | 0.35 | 0.4 | 0.01 | 0.03 | 0.05 |
| Air transportation | 0.15 | 0.25 | 0.35 | 0.1 | 0.125 | 0.15 |
| Other transportation | 0.02 | 0.04 | 0.06 | 0.03 | 0.05 | 0.07 |
| Telecommunications | 0.05 | 0.15 | 0.25 | 0.08 | 0.1 | 0.12 |
| Science and science servicing (market) | 0.05 | 0.1 | 0.15 | 0.1 | 0.15 | 0.2 |
| Financial services | 0.05 | 0.1 | 0.15 | 0.01 | 0.03 | 0.05 |

to sectors or products that are cheaper after trade and FDI liberalization.[36] There are three sets of parameters in Table 6.5 that have a strong impact on the results: the elasticity of substitution between value-added and business services (*esubs*), the elasticity of multinational firm supply (*etaf*) and the vector of initial multinational shares in the services sectors *theta_fdi(i)*. A liberalization of the barriers to FDI will result in a reduction in the cost of business services, both from the direct effect of lowering the costs of doing business for multinational service providers and from the indirect effect that additional varieties of business services allow users to purchase a quality adjusted unit of services at less cost. When *esubs* (the elasticity of substitution between value-added and business services) is high, users have the greater potential to substitute the cheaper business services and this increases productivity. The elasticity of multinational and Russian firm supply (*etaf*, *etad*) is primarily dependent on the sector-specific factor for each firm type (foreign or domestic). The mathematical relationship between the elasticity of firm supply and sector-specific factors is elaborated in an appendix to Balistreri and Tarr (2011). When *etaf* is high, a reduction in the barriers to FDI results in a larger expansion in the number of multinational firms supplying the Russian market, and hence more gains from additional varieties of business services. Finally, *theta_fdi(i)* (the share of the services market captured by multinationals) has a strong effect, since a liberalization results in a larger number of new varieties introduced when multinationals have a large initial share.

### Share of expatriate labor employed by multinational service providers

The impact of liberalization of barriers to FDI in business services on the demand for labor in the business services sectors will depend on the share of expatriate labor used by multinational firms. If multinationals use mostly Russian labor, their expansion is likely to increase the demand for Russian labor in these sectors. We employed the estimates of the share of expatriate labor or specialized technology not available to Russian firms that is used by multinational service providers in Russia provided by the various Russian research institutes mentioned above. Here, we estimate the impact of employing the upper or lower bound estimates of this share in all business services sectors.

We find that the impact on the welfare estimates of lower or higher share of imported inputs in the business services sectors is only 1/10th of one percent of consumption. However, the impact on labor demand in the business services sector is more significant. For example, skilled labor demand in telecommunications increases by 6.0% with our central estimates of labor demand change, but would increase by 7.5% with the lower shares of imported inputs by multinationals and by 4.5% with higher shares of labor demand by multinationals. There is a similar range of results for labor demand in most of

---

[36] An increase in the elasticity of substitution between varieties reduces the welfare gain. This is because when varieties are good substitutes, additional varieties are worth less to firms and consumers.

the business services sectors. With sufficiently high share of expatriate labor use by the multinationals, the demand for labor in the business services sectors would decline, but based on the expert estimates of the use of expatriate labor, we expect to see an increase in the demand for labor in telecommunications, financial services and truck transportation, but a decline in air transportation services and science servicing. In all these cases, the shift in employment is less than 15% of initial employment.

### 6.3.4.3 Systematic sensitivity analysis

Piecemeal sensitivity analysis shows how the results change when we vary the value of key parameters one-by-one, with central values of all parameters except the one under consideration. In the systematic sensitivity analysis, we allow all parameters to change simultaneously. A probability distribution for each parameter is chosen. We typically choose uniform probability distributions, with the lower and upper bounds for the values of the parameters taken from the lower and upper values of the key parameters presented in Table 6.5. We furthermore assume that all distributions are stochastically independent.

We then run the model 30,000 times. Each time the program chooses a random configuration of parameters and executes the model with this configuration. For each variable in our model, we then harvest the sample distribution based on the 30,000 solutions. Consequently the sample distribution is not dependent on any particular set of parameter values, but represents results representative of the full distribution of parameter values.

We present the distribution of the results below for three key variables: welfare change as a percentage of consumption, output change and skilled employment changes. A full compendium or results with the sample distributions and confidence intervals is in Jensen *et al.* (2004). For each report variable, we calculate the percentage of solutions associated with a given result for the variable. Figure 6.2 shows that the welfare gains as a percentage of consumption are, in most cases, between 6 and 8%. The minimum value is 4.5% and the maximum value is 11.4%. The statistics show that only 6.4% of the solutions are below a welfare gain of 6% and that 13.0% are above a gain of 8%. More than 80% of the solutions yield a gain between 6 and 8%. This shows that the welfare results are very robust within the six to eight percent of the consumption range.

In Figure 6.3, we focus on the employment impacts in the six sectors where the impacts are the greatest: the three sectors with the largest increase in employment and the three sectors with the largest decline in employment. We only show the results for skilled labor, as the results for unskilled labor are very close to the results for skilled labor. We assume total employment is unchanged, so employment must expand in some sectors and contract in others. The sectors where employment expands the most are: ferrous metallurgy, non-ferrous metallurgy and chemical industry. The manufacturing sectors where employment declines the most are: mechanical engineering, light industry and

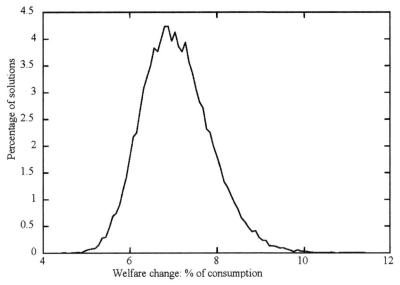

**Figure 6.2** Frequency distribution of welfare change as a percentage of consumption. More than 80% of the solutions are in the interval 6–8%; 6.4% of the solutions below 6%; 13.0% of the solutions above 8%; minimum value: 4.5%; maximum value: 11.4%; mean value: 7.1%; median value: 7.1%. *Source: Jensen* et al. *(2007).*

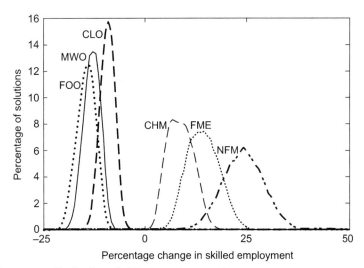

**Figure 6.3** Frequency distribution of skilled employment impacts.

food industry. The results for all six sectors show that our central results are robust to most parameter configurations, and in particular that the expanding (declining) sectors are expanding (declining) for virtually all configurations. Figure 6.3 also shows that the magnitude of the results for the expanding sectors is more uncertain than the results for

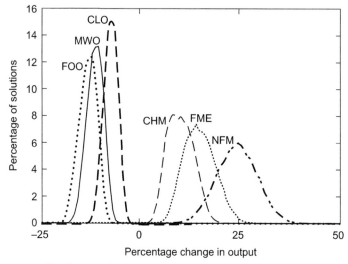

**Figure 6.4** Frequency distribution of output impacts.

the declining sectors. This is explained by the relatively greater use of business services and goods from imperfectly competitive sectors.[37]

In Figure 6.4, we display the frequency distributions of the output changes in the same six sectors. The pattern with which sectors expand or contract is the same as for employment, but the results are more positive. Whereas economy-wide employment is fixed by assumption, output increases overall. Output expands due to greater efficiency in the use of resources, and, more importantly, due to the greater productivity of factors of production from the increase in varieties of business services and differentiated goods.

Finally, in order to display systematic sensitivity results for all industries in one figure, in the upper panel of Figure 6.5, we display bars that represent 50% confidence intervals for aggregate output (export plus domestic sales) for all industries (the point on the bar is our point estimate). In the lower panel of Figure 6.5, we show 50% confidence intervals for domestic output by industry. Similar figures for other variables are in appendix B of Jensen *et al.* (2004).

## 6.3.5 Conclusions

In this section we have developed an innovative SOE CGE model of the Russian economy that is capable of assessing the impact of the liberalization of barriers against FDI. Surveys and estimates of the *ad valorem* equivalents of the barriers against FDI were prepared for this model. We find that the source of the largest gains to Russia from WTO accession is that additional multinational service providers will reduce the

---

[37] Thus, variation in the values of *etaf*, *esubs* and *theta_fdi* have a greater impact on these sectors.

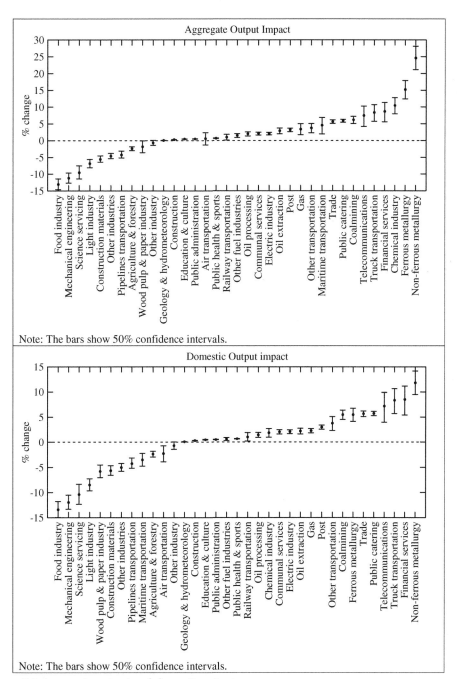

**Figure 6.5** Aggregate output and domestic output.

quality-adjusted cost of purchasing business services in Russia and that these gains are rather substantial when compared with the typical gains from CRTS models of tariff liberalization. We believe that these results are supported by the empirical literature cited in Section 6.1 that indicates that access to a diverse set of service providers with a domestic presence is crucial for growth.

## 6.4 POVERTY EFFECTS OF RUSSIA'S WTO ACCESSION: MODELING "REAL" HOUSEHOLDS WITH FDI IN SERVICES AND ENDOGENOUS PRODUCTIVITY EFFECTS

### 6.4.1 Introduction[38]

The work discussed in this section originated from a request by the Government of Russia to the World Bank for development of a methodology to assess the impact of WTO accession on poverty and social issues in Russia. In Russia, as in many countries, policy makers are concerned with not only the aggregate effects and impacts on productive sectors of the economy, but they are also concerned with impacts on the poor and other distributional effects.

We extend the model of Russia discussed above to assess the poverty and distribution effects of Russia's WTO accession. In particular, the model again incorporates FDI in imperfectly competitive business service sectors, and we adopt the Dixit–Stiglitz framework in both business services and imperfectly competitive goods sectors, which implies that we have endogenous productivity effects from additional varieties in these sectors. We show that these features are crucial to the distributional and aggregate results. What is innovative in this model is that we integrated all the 55,098 households of the Russian HBS as agents in the model. Thus, our model is a "real household" model.

Interest in the impact of trade policy on poverty has dramatically increased in recent years. Some modelers have assessed impacts with a CGE multiple representative agent approach. The pioneering papers on multihousehold models in CGE models were done by Adelman and Robinson (1978) and Piggott and Whalley (1985); recent examples include Harrison *et al.* (2003, 2004). However, this approach can mask large differences among the households within each representative household. In order to incorporate information on all available households, but given the difficulty in incorporating large household datasets as multiple agents of a CGE model, several authors (e.g. Bourguignon *et al.*, 1991; Chen and Ravallion, 2004) have adopted a sequential (also called "open-loop" or "top-down") microsimulation approach. In the first step a single representative agent CGE model is employed to obtain the estimated price changes from a trade policy change. These price changes are then fed into a microsimulation household model for predicted household effects. However, the sequential approach ignores feedback effects

---

[38] This section is based on Rutherford and Tarr (2008) and Rutherford *et al.* (2005).

of the quantity changes in the microsimulation household model on the equilibrium prices in the representative agent general equilibrium model. Moreover, although efforts are sometimes made at data reconciliation, the sequential approach does not require reconciliation of inconsistent information on household income from the National Accounts (which report factor payments) and the household surveys (which report factor income).[39] Consequently, in summarizing the state of the literature, Bourguignon and Perreira (2003, p. 343) have argued that one of the major challenges for the analysis of the impact of economic policies on poverty and income distribution is to integrate a CGE model with "real" households from the household survey rather than representative households, but they note that this is empirically difficult.

The first successful integration of a full household survey into a CGE model was by Cockburn (2001) when he integrated the 3373 households in the household survey into his CRTS CGE model of Nepal. Subsequently, Cororaton and Cockburn (2007) integrated the 24,979 households in the household survey into their CRTS model of the Philippines.[40] The solution techniques used by Cockburn and his coauthors, however, will not typically allow incorporation of larger household datasets, and increasing returns to scale models present greater challenges for robust solutions. In this section, however, we employ a new solution algorithm for an increasing returns to scale CGE model with essentially no significant bound on the number of household agents.

In our central model, we estimate that the mean welfare gains to Russia, averaged over all households, from WTO accession are a rather substantial 7.3% of Russian consumption (with a standard deviation of 2.2% of consumption) in the medium run. Decomposition analysis reveals that over 70% of the gains are due to the liberalization of barriers against foreign investors in services. We estimate that 99.9% of the households will gain from 2% to 25% of their household income. We find that poor households gain slightly more than rich households on average, since the return on capital does not increase as much as the wages of skilled and unskilled labor. We conduct both piecemeal sensitivity analysis and systematic sensitivity analysis (the latter by executing the model 30,000 times with random parameter selection), and find that our results are robust with respect to parameter specification. However, without FDI, services liberalization and Dixit–Stiglitz externalities, the welfare gains are only one-sixth of the gains in our model and 7% of the households are estimated to lose. Our results show that, while incorporating the diversity of households though a real household model is important, incorporating FDI in business services with Dixit–Stiglitz effects is as important for assessing household impacts.

---

[39] Without data reconciliation the household model and the representative agent model can produce very different results. Ianchovichina and Martin (2004) estimated that China will gain from WTO accession based on their representative agent model. However, Chen and Ravallion (2004) estimate overall losses for China from WTO accession based on their household model using price changes from Ianchovichina and Martin.

[40] See also Annabi et al. (2005), who have incorporated 3278 households into a CRTS CGE model.

We describe the model, algorithm and data in Sections 6.4.2 and 6.4.3. Results are presented in Section 6.4.4. We show the results of piecemeal and systematic sensitivity analysis in Section 6.4.5. Also in Section 6.4.5, we assess the estimation error in the sequential approach and suggest conditions under which the sequential approach may be a good approximation for our integrated approach.

## 6.4.2 The model

Since we have described the structure of that single representative agent model in Section 6.3, we only briefly describe the structure of the representative model here. Rather, we focus on the features of the model that are necessary to generalize the model to 55,098 households.

### 6.4.2.1 Household consumer demand[41]

Based on the data work described below, we aggregate individuals within each of the 55 098 households to obtain household factor income shares, expenditure shares on the commodities in our model, and transfers between the household and the government and savings. We assume each household maximizes a Cobb–Douglas utility function of the aggregate 35 goods in our model subject to its budget constraint (which is factor income net of transfers). Each of the 35 aggregate commodities is a CES ("Armington") aggregate of imported goods or services and goods or services produced in Russia. In imperfectly competitive goods sectors, imported and Russian-produced goods are Dixit–Stiglitz aggregates of the outputs of foreign or Russian firms. (Since consumer demand is analogous to firm level demand, the structure is depicted in Figure 6.1 under "Composite intermediate IRTS goods") The structure of consumer demand for imperfectly competitive services sectors (equivalent to business services in our model) is depicted on the left side of Figure 6.1 under "Business Services" (value-added does not enter the demand function of consumers). The structure of production is identical to the single representative agent model.

Consumer demand, as well as firm level demand, exhibits love of variety in imperfectly competitive goods. Given that we have weak separability and homothetic functions at all levels of consumer demand, the conditions for two-stage (or multistage) budgeting are satisfied. Given the initial data on each of the households and our assumptions on the structure of demand, we solve for the parameter values in each of the 55,098 household utility functions that are consistent with optimization by the households. Thus, the demand functions of all households are dependent on their initial choices and, in general, differ from one another.

---

[41] For a mathematical treatment of the algorithm we have developed see the appendices to Rutherford *et al.* (2005). We also provide a graphical interpretation there to intuitively explain the algorithm and why it allows us to integrate all households from any household budget survey into a general equilibrium model, i.e., it has essentially eliminated the constraint on the number of households that can be integrated into a general equilibrium model.

## 6.4.3 Data

Here, we focus on the data relevant to development of the multihousehold model. Unless otherwise specified, we use parameters and data from the single representative agent model.

### 6.4.3.1 Households

Households are modeled endogenously based on the 55 098 households of the Russian HBS. The HBS, which is representative at the regional level, has very detailed information on household consumption expenditures, and information about age, gender, education and occupation of each member of the household. It also has information about expenditures and savings, and by implication household income.

The major shortcoming of the HBS for our purposes is that it does not contain information on the sources of income of the households. For sources of household income, we must turn to the Russian Longitudinal Monitoring Survey (RLMS). The RMLS has less than 5000 observations and is not representative of the population on the regional level. However, is has extensive information on individual and household sources of income: wages and profits from first, second and third jobs; pensions and unemployment benefits; profits and dividends from accumulated assets.

We have employed both small area estimation (SAE) and Matching techniques (see Rao, 1999; Elbers *et al.*, 2003; Moriarity and Scheuren, 2003) to generate sources of income data for all 55 098 households in the HBS. We describe our procedures in appendix B of Rutherford *et al.* (2005). Results from both techniques yield similar results.

The key point is that we chose characteristics of the two datasets that are common to both datasets and which we expect influence factor shares of income. These characteristics, which can be found in both the HBS and the RLMS, are personal, household and geographic characteristics. Personal characteristics include age, gender, skilled or unskilled worker, head of the household, primary, secondary and other occupation, and income. Household characteristics are family size, members of the household who work and gender of the head of household. Geographic characteristics are the region of Russia and urban or rural.

Using the RLMS data, we then estimate regression equations where the independent variables are the characteristics mentioned above and factor shares are the dependent variables. In the SAE procedure, we assume that the estimated equations based on the RLMS data apply to all the households in the HBS. Using the data on the household characteristics in the HBS, we thereby generate factor shares for the larger HBS. Factor shares and consumption shares aggregated to deciles are presented in Rutherford *et al.* (2005).

### 6.4.3.2 Reconciliation of the National Account data and HBS data

We have two sources of data for aggregate factor incomes: data from National Accounts and data from the HBS. In our Russian data, capital's share of factor income is much larger in the National Account data than in the HBS (see Table 6.2). This is typical. Ivanic (2004) mapped income from the Living Standards Measurement Surveys (LSMS) in 14 countries into factor shares and compared factor shares with the input-output tables in these countries. Capital's average share from the LSMS surveys was 21% of household income, but it was 52% of household income based on National Account information (based on the "GTAP" dataset).[42]

We must produce a balanced SAM in order to implement our integrated model, which means we must reconcile those differences. There are biases in both the collection of National Account and HBS data so that neither source is clearly correct. A key problem with the factor share data from the National Accounts is that capital's share is calculated residually in the input-output tables. Then in sectors where labor payments are under-reported, as in agriculture (where sole proprietors do not report their labor income and temporary workers are often informal workers) and services, the share of capital is biased up. Unprofitable sectors that receive state subsidies will be reported as labor-intensive, despite the fact that in developing countries these are typically the capital-intensive sectors. Harrison *et al.* (2003) have shown that this bias can lead to perverse reporting of which sectors are labor-intensive in developing countries. On the other hand, income estimates from LSMS surveys are known to be less than income estimates from National Accounts. Deaton (2003) explains that one of the most likely explanations of the difference is that households fail to respond to the survey and that the probability of non-response plausibly increases monotonically with income. This presumed pattern of non-response to the household survey would also help explain this difference in capital's share, since the rich are likely to have more capital than the poor.

For our central model, we took total value added by sector from the National Accounts, but given our desire to preserve "real households" and our focus on poverty, we did not want to alter the HBS factor shares. Thus, we did not alter the HBS data or value-added data by industry from the National Accounts. Rather we adjusted factor shares at the industry level to be consistent with the factor payments implied by the HBS. This reconciliation of the two sets of data significantly decreased the share of capital reported by the input-output table, especially in some of the more capital intensive sectors like ferrous and non-ferrous metals (see Table 6.2).[43]

---

[42] Household income (net of taxes and transfers) in Russia exceeds household consumption for almost all households. Part of the reason is savings for investment. However, in the case of Russia, an important part of the reason is that Russia has a large current account surplus. Consistency between the macro balances and the household data in construction of the SAM implies that household factor income must be larger than household consumption for most households to allow for the transfer of capital to foreigners. It follows that the change in factor income as a percent of consumption will be larger than the change in factor income as a percent of household income.

[43] Of course as capital's share decreases, labor's share must increase, but reconciliation of data with the household data, also resulted in an increase in the relative share of skilled labor to unskilled labor. This is because, lacking more specific data at the household level, we defined all labor income as skilled labor income if the worker had any post-secondary education. Russia has a highly educated labor force, so this reconciliation resulted in an increase in the share of labor income going to skilled labor.

**Table 6.6** Impact of WTO accession in 55,098 household model on economy-wide variables in Russia—policy results and decomposition of effects (results are percentage change from initial equilibrium)

| | Benchmark | WTO accession (1) | WTO accession (equal Ruble transfers) (2) | Improved market access only (3) | Tariff reform only (4) | Reform of FDI barriers only (5) | CRTS Model (6) | WTO Accession with partial reform of FDI barriers (7) |
|---|---|---|---|---|---|---|---|---|
| Aggregate welfare | | | | | | | | |
| Mean welfare (EV as % of consumption) | | 7.3 | 7.2 | 0.7 | 1.3 | 5.3 | 1.2 | 4.1 |
| Standard deviation of EV as % of consumption[a] | | (2.2) | (2.2) | (0.5) | (0.8) | (1.5) | (0.7) | (1.3) |
| Welfare (EV as % of GDP) | | 3.4 | 3.4 | 0.3 | 0.6 | 2.4 | 0.6 | 1.9 |
| Government budget | | | | | | | | |
| Tariff revenue (% of GDP) | 1.4 | 0.9 | 0.9 | 1.4 | 0.8 | 1.4 | 0.9 | 0.8 |
| Tariff revenue (% change) | | −33.2 | −33.2 | 8.7 | −38.3 | 10.9 | −43.5 | −35.2 |
| Aggregate trade | | | | | | | | |
| Real exchange rate (% change) | | 2.6 | 2.6 | −0.5 | 2.0 | 1.1 | 0.3 | 1.8 |
| Aggregate exports (% change) | | 14.4 | 14.4 | 2.3 | 8.1 | 3.7 | 5.9 | 11.9 |

(Continued)

**Table 6.6** Impact of WTO accession in 55,098 household model on economy-wide variables in Russia—policy results and decomposition of effects (results are percentage change from initial equilibrium)—cont'd

| | Benchmark | WTO accession (1) | WTO accession (equal Ruble transfers) (2) | Improved market access only (3) | Tariff reform only (4) | Reform of FDI barriers only (5) | CRTS Model (6) | WTO Accession with partial reform of FDI barriers (7) |
|---|---|---|---|---|---|---|---|---|
| **Returns to mobile factors** | | | | | | | | |
| Unskilled labor (% change) | | 3.7 | 3.7 | 0.1 | 0.6 | 2.9 | 1.0 | 1.7 |
| Skilled labor (% change) | | 5.3 | 5.3 | 0.7 | 1.7 | 2.8 | 1.9 | 3.2 |
| Capital (% change) | | 1.8 | 1.8 | −0.6 | 1.0 | 1.4 | 0.9 | 2.2 |
| **Percent of factors that must adjust** | | | | | | | | |
| Unskilled labor | | 1.2 | 1.2 | 0.3 | 1.2 | 0.4 | 0.8 | 1.3 |
| Skilled labor | | 1.4 | 1.4 | 0.5 | 0.6 | 0.7 | 0.6 | 1.0 |
| Capital | | 0.5 | 0.5 | 0.1 | 0.3 | 0.1 | 0.3 | 0.4 |

[a]The means and standard deviations are the population weighted means and standard deviations of the 55,098 estimates.
*Source:* Author's estimates.

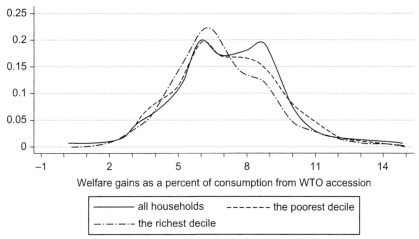

**Figure 6.6** Distributions of estimated welfare gains from Russian WTO accession for the entire sample, the poorest decile and the richest decile. Observations in the range of 0% to 5% are shown. Details are constructed to be representative of 10% of the Russian population based on the weights of the HBS.

We acknowledge that alternate methods of reconciliation are valid. For the purposes of sensitivity analysis, therefore, we have also run the model with the opposite reconciliation. That is, we adjusted factor shares at the household level to be consistent with the factor payments of the National Accounts. We report these results in the sensitivity results.

## 6.4.4 Estimated impacts of Russian WTO accession

### 6.4.4.1 Aggregate results in the full 55 098 household model

In our general WTO scenario, we make the same assumptions regarding the counterfactual changes in parameters as in Section 6.3. Aggregate results are summarized in Table 6.6. Aggregate welfare results in Table 6.6 are obtained by aggregating the equivalent variation gains (as a% of consumption) of the 55 thousand consumers, using population weights. We report both the mean and the standard deviation of the welfare results across the 55,098 households.[44] The overall results are very similar to the results for the single representative consumer model. For our central WTO scenario, column

---

[44] For each of our 55,098 households $h$, we estimate its equivalent variation $(EV_h)$ and we have the value of the household's initial consumption $(C_h)$. Define $100\ ev_h = 100(EV_h/C_h)$, which is the increase in the equivalent variation of household $h$ as a percentage of its initial consumption. To calculate the mean and standard deviation of the 55,098 values of $100\ ev_h$ we need to take into account that the households in the sample are statistically representative of the Russian population and each household in the HBS has a weight $w_h$ that reflects the number of people it represents in the overall Russian population. We normalize the household weights by defining $\alpha_h = w_h / \sum_h w_h$. The weights $\alpha_h$ for $h = 1, \ldots, 55,098$ are each household's share of the total Russian population. Thus, our estimated weighted average increase in equivalent variation as a percent of initial household consumption is $100\sum_h \alpha_h ev_h = \mu$. Calculation of the weighted average variance of the increase in equivalent variation as a percent of initial consumption follows similar principles; it is defined as: $\sum_h [\alpha_h 100^2 (ev_h - \mu)^2]$. We report the positive square root of this value in Table 6.6, i.e., the standard deviation.

(1), we obtain rather substantial aggregate gains for a comparative state trade model equal to 7.3% of aggregate consumption. To determine what is driving these results, we decompose the WTO scenario into its three components. The results are shown in columns (3)–(5). The key result is that liberalization of barriers to FDI is responsible for an estimated welfare gain of 5.3% of consumption, or over 70% of the total welfare gain.

To put these numbers in perspective, Rutherford and Tarr (2002) have analytically derived the relationship between a permanent increase in the steady-state growth rate and equivalent variation. A welfare gain of 10% of consumption corresponds to a permanent increase in the growth rate of about 0.4%. Although cross-country assessments of the impact of trade liberalization on growth have been criticized, several authors have estimated that trade liberalization could increase the growth rate by between 1 and 2.5%.[45]

Similar to the single-consumer model, if we assume CRTS in all sectors of the economy, the estimated gains, column (6) are reduced to 1.2% of consumption. These results again show that incorporating liberalization of barriers to FDI in the analysis as well as the Dixit–Stiglitz–Ethier formulation for endogenous productivity effects are both crucial in explaining the rather substantial estimated gains from Russian WTO accession.

In the WTO scenario, the wage rate of skilled labor increases by 5.3%, the wage rate of unskilled labor increases by 3.7% and the return on capital increases by 1.8%. Although the return to capital rises relative to a basket of consumption goods, it does not rise as much as wages. The return to capital increases less than wages because owners of "specific capital" in imperfectly competitive sectors that are subject to increased competition from imports or from FDI will see a reduction in the value of their returns. Returns to mobile capital increase by over 6%, even faster than returns to skilled labor because the economy shifts resources into the more capital-intensive sectors and away from more unskilled labor-intensive sectors such as light industry and mechanical engineering and metal working (see Rutherford et al., 2005, Table 6). However, the return on sector-specific capital in all imperfectly competitive sectors falls, so that the total return on capital rises less than wages. The ratio of skilled to unskilled labor in the expanding sectors is greater than in the contracting sectors. As a result, the wage of skilled labor rises faster than the wage rate of unskilled labor.

---

[45] These cross-country regression results are controversial, since trade liberalization is often accompanied by macro stabilization and other market reforms, and the open economy variable in the regressions can be picking up these other effects as well. Moreover, institutional reforms may also be rather important. However, trade reform may compel complementary reforms, such as the elimination of state subsidies, which are often unsustainable in an open economy. WTO accession also involves a number of institutional reforms. For example, liberalization of FDI in services will put great pressure on the regulatory authorities to improve the institutional environment.

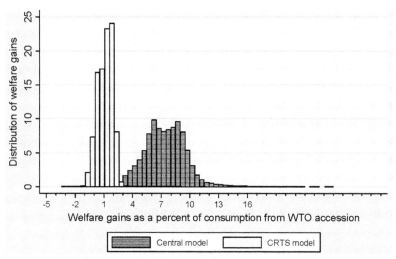

**Figure 6.7** Distributions of estimated welfare gains from Russian WTO accession. Central and CRTS models comparison. Households sampled = 55,098. Observations in the range of −5% to 25% are shown.

### 6.4.4.2 Results for individual households
#### Distribution of the results

The distribution of gains from Russian WTO accession across all 55,098 households is summarized in Figures 6.6 and 6.7. In Figure 6.6, we display the distribution of gains for the poorest and richest deciles of the population, along with the distribution of the gains for all households. We find that gains are rather evenly distributed across income groups, but we find that the poor gain slightly more than the wealthy because the wage rate of unskilled labor increases more than the rate of return on capital. The Gini coefficient is only marginally affected: it declines from 0.401 to 0.399.[46] We also find that rural households gain less than urban households because the wage rate of skilled labor increases more than the other factors of production and rural households are less endowed with skilled labor than urban households.

Figure 6.7 shows there is a distribution of income changes across the 55,098 households that is centered around a mean gain of income of 7.3%.[47] Except for 14 households, we estimate that all households will gain in the new equilibrium relative to the *status quo*.[48] These results highlight in a real household model what we showed in

---

[46] Our estimate of the Gini coefficient is virtually identical to Rostat (the statistical agency of Russia). Rostat estimates the Gini coefficient at 0.400 in 2003.

[47] Of the 55,098 households, there are 59 with gains less than 2% and seven households with gains above 25%. Thus, 99.9% of all households have gains that fall in the range of 2−25%. Fourteen households, or two-hundredths of 1% of the households, are estimated to lose.

[48] Households that depend disproportionately on specific capital that falls in return would be expected to lose from WTO accession, but the data do not allow this distinction.

Section 6.2 in a stylized model: with Dixit–Stiglitz productivity impacts, we escape the pessimism of Stolper–Samuelson. The fact that the model has FDI in business services yields Dixit–Stiglitz productivity effects from services liberalization and further contributes to increase in real returns to all mobile factors. The principal caveat to the widespread gains is the potential loss of income to owners of specific capital in sectors subject to increased competition from FDI.[49]

In Figure 6.7 we compare the results across 55,098 households based on two models. On the right side of the diagram is the histogram of results for all households from our central model. Despite diversity among households, virtually none are estimated to lose. On the left side of the diagram, we present the histogram of results for all households with a CRTS model. The CRTS distribution is centered around 1.2% of gains in consumption and about 7% of the households are estimated to lose from accession to the WTO.[50]

The striking aspect of Figure 6.7 is that the distribution of gains from our central model is centered sufficiently far to the right of the CRTS distribution that there is only a slight overlap of the two distributions in the tails. *Figure 6.7 encapsulates the central point of this section: to estimate household impacts, it is important to incorporate household diversity through a real household model. However, incorporating FDI in business services and Dixit–Stiglitz effects in imperfectly competitive sectors is as important for our policy simulation.* It is evident that incorporating FDI liberalization and endogenous productivity effects will decisively affect the results.

### 6.4.4.3 *What is left out of the analysis?*
Transition costs
We have not modeled the transition costs of achieving a new equilibrium. During a transition period it is likely that many households will lose, so the gains will be less that we estimate to that extent.

---

[49] While households that are heavily endowed with specific capital in declining sectors will lose on average from WTO accession, those who can form joint ventures with foreign investors will likely see the value of their specific capital holdings increase.

[50] The fact that only 7% of households lose with liberalization under CRTS may be surprising in view of the Stolper–Samuelson theorem. However, one should not apply intuition from Stolper–Samuelson in our model. (i) We have specific factors in our CRTS model. (ii) Ethier (1984) has shown that "the Stolper–Samuelson result in its strong form is inherently a 2 × 2 property and offers no hope for generalization." More importantly, we maintain the assumption of product differentiation by country of origin in CRTS sectors (the "Armington" assumption). To see why this is crucial, consider a two-sector CRTS model with products differentiated by country of origin. Suppose factor intensities are identical in the two sectors. Trade will exist due to the product differentiation assumption. Suppose there is one distortion: a tariff on one of the goods and it is removed. Welfare and real incomes increase on average due to the tariff removal. However, since factor intensities are identical, relative factor returns can not change and the returns to both factors increase, i.e. Stolper–Samuelson does not hold as a general principle. Stolper–Samuelson results are more likely to hold, the better the products substitute for each other and the larger the factor intensity differences across sectors.

**Table 6.7** Data reconciliation and the welfare impacts of WTO accession—with a decomposition of the impacts

| | | Skilled wages | Unskilled wages | Return to capital | Taxes and transfers | Goods prices | Aggregate EV |
|---|---|---|---|---|---|---|---|
| | | **Percentage change in _EV_ due to changes in factor prices, goods prices or transfers, by aggregated deciles[a]** | | | | | |
| Decile 1 (0—10%) — overall | unreconciled sequential approach | 5.3 | 2.2 | 0.2 | −0.5 | 0.0 | 7.2 |
| | integrated model | 5.4 | 2.8 | 0.1 | −0.3 | 0.3 | 7.6 |
| Decile 2 (11—20%) — overall | unreconciled sequential approach | 5.3 | 2.0 | 0.3 | −0.4 | 0.0 | 7.3 |
| | integrated model | 5.5 | 2.5 | 0.1 | −0.3 | 0.3 | 7.6 |
| Decile 3 (21—30%) — overall | unreconciled sequential approach | 5.8 | 1.7 | 0.5 | −0.5 | −0.1 | 7.6 |
| | integrated model | 5.9 | 2.2 | 0.2 | −0.3 | 0.2 | 7.7 |
| Decile 4 (31—40%) — overall | unreconciled sequential approach | 5.8 | 1.6 | 0.6 | −0.4 | −0.1 | 7.6 |
| | integrated model | 5.9 | 2.0 | 0.2 | −0.3 | 0.2 | 7.7 |
| Decile 5 (41—50%) — overall | unreconciled sequential approach | 5.7 | 1.5 | 0.9 | −0.4 | −0.1 | 7.8 |
| | integrated model | 5.9 | 1.8 | 0.3 | −0.3 | 0.1 | 7.7 |
| Decile 6 (51—60%) — overall | unreconciled sequential approach | 5.6 | 1.4 | 1.2 | −0.5 | −0.1 | 7.9 |
| | integrated model | 5.8 | 1.7 | 0.5 | −0.3 | 0.1 | 7.5 |
| Decile 7 (61—70%) — overall | unreconciled sequential approach | 5.7 | 1.1 | 1.6 | −0.5 | −0.1 | 8.1 |
| | integrated model | 5.8 | 1.4 | 0.6 | −0.3 | 0.0 | 7.5 |
| Decile 8 (71—80%) — overall | unreconciled sequential approach | 5.9 | 0.9 | 1.9 | −0.5 | −0.1 | 8.4 |
| | integrated model | 6.0 | 1.2 | 0.7 | −0.4 | 0.1 | 7.5 |
| Decile 9 (81—90%) — overall | unreconciled sequential approach | 5.1 | 0.9 | 2.6 | −0.5 | −0.2 | 8.3 |
| | integrated model | 5.3 | 1.1 | 1.0 | −0.3 | −0.1 | 7.2 |

(_Continued_)

**Table 6.7** Data reconciliation and the welfare impacts of WTO accession—with a decomposition of the impacts—cont'd

| | | Percentage change in *EV* due to changes in factor prices, goods prices or transfers, by aggregated deciles[a] | | | | | |
|---|---|---|---|---|---|---|---|
| | | Skilled wages | Unskilled wages | Return to capital | Taxes and transfers | Goods prices | Aggregate *EV* |
| Decile 10 (91—100%) — overall | unreconciled sequential approach | 4.4 | 0.6 | 3.8 | −0.5 | 0.0 | 8.3 |
| | integrated model | 4.5 | 0.8 | 1.4 | −0.3 | −0.3 | 6.8 |

[a]In the integrated (sequential) approach, the percentage change in skilled wages, unskilled wages and return on capital is 5.3% (5.1%), 3.7% (3.0%) and 1.8% (4.9%), respectively. All households face the same factor prices, but depending on the factor endowments of the different households, this will impact the *EV* of the households differently. Similarly, for goods price changes. We have estimated the decomposed impacts as shown in the table. Aggregate *EV* for each decile is approximately the horizontal sum of the elements in the same row.

### Intellectual property

The most important part of WTO accession that we have not modeled is the strengthening of the intellectual property regime in Russia, especially enforcement. Contrary to the transition cost issue, it is difficult to assess the direction of the impact on Russia from better intellectual property enforcement. On the one hand, Russia will have to pay more for goods like imported DVDs, software and drugs. However, Russia is a high human capital country and has the potential to significantly expand its marketable research. As President, Vladimir Putin reportedly considered the balance of these issues to favor Russia and encouraged more vigorous enforcement of intellectual property laws in Russia.

## 6.4.5 Sensitivity analysis

The results depend on the choice of parameters in the model, alternate ways of reconciling data and method of solution of the model. In this section, we begin with an assessment of the bias from the sequential approach to microsimulation analysis. We then assess the impact on the results if we adjust the household data to be consistent with the input-output data. We then turn to "piecemeal sensitivity" analysis on the parameters. Finally, we discuss the results of our "systematic sensitivity analysis."

### 6.4.5.1 Decomposition of the gains and biases from the sequential approach to microsimulation analysis

We have aggregated the households in our model into deciles, from poorest to richest. Then we have decomposed the equivalent variation gains (as a percentage of consumption) of the 10 aggregated households into changes in factor prices, goods prices and taxes and transfers. The results are in Table 6.7 labeled "integrated model." For all the deciles of aggregated households the impact of goods prices is relatively unimportant compared with the impact of factor prices. In part because households cannot easily change their factor endowments between unskilled labor, skilled labor and capital, but they can substitute among commodities consumed, impacts on factor incomes through changes in factor prices tend to dominate the household welfare impacts in these kinds of models.[51]

We have also executed a single representative consumer model based on input–output data that is not reconciled with the household data. We feed the factor and good price changes into a household model for the determination of household equivalent variation of the 55,098 households. Aggregation of the household welfare results for households within each decile provides the results at the decile level labeled "unreconciled sequential approach" in Table 6.7. We find that the richer households are estimated to gain significantly more in the unreconciled sequential approach, since the return to capital increases more in the unreconciled approach (this is not a general result). On the other hand, we find that the bias from ignoring the quantity feedback effects on prices is very small if the data are reconciled first between the household and representative consumer models. See Rutherford et al. (2005) for further details.[52]

Based on these results, we believe that a sequential approach to assess household impacts of trade policy changes is likely to be a good approximation to the results of a more difficult to implement integrated approach, provided three conditions are satisfied: (i) the household data are reconciled with National Accounts data, (ii) the factor and consumption shares of the representative agent in the sequential approach are equal to factor and consumption shares that are the sum over all households, and (iii) the representative agent and the households exhibit the same optimizing behavior. The latter implies that the first order effects are the same.

### 6.4.5.2 Alternate reconciliation of the National Account and HBS data

As opposed to our central model, in this "National Accounts"-based model we allow the household factor shares to adjust while keeping the factor shares from the National Accounts fixed. Taking a weighted average of the 55 098 household welfare gains, we get an estimated 7.2% of consumption; this is only trivially different than the 7.3% gain in our central model (and coincides with our representative agent model that is based on the national income accounts data). At the household level, we again estimate that virtually all households should gain from WTO accession.

There are, however, differences in the distribution of gains among households, the standard deviation of the estimated gains is somewhat larger and the Gini coefficient

---

[51] See, e.g. Harrison et al. (2003).

[52] We have also shown that if we are only interested in results at the decile level (as opposed to household results), running a model with thousands of households and then aggregating results to deciles (as we have done in Table 6.7) does not appear to make much difference compared with aggregating the households to 10 households first and then running the model with 10 households. See Rutherford et al. (2005) for details regarding this section.

slightly increases, rather than slightly decreases. As a result of the National Accounts-based reconciliation of the factor shares, several sectors are considerably more capital intensive, and among them are three key expanding export intensive sectors — ferrous metals, non-ferrous metals and chemicals. Consequently the return to capital expands considerably more than in our central model based on the HBS data. The percentage change in skilled wages, unskilled wages and return on capital in the National Accounts based (central model) is 4.7% (5.3%), 2.5% (3.7%) and 4.4% (1.8%), respectively. Then, since rich households depend more on capital income, we estimate slightly regressive results with the National Accounts-based model, as opposed to very slightly progressive results with our central model based on the HBS-based data reconciliation.[53]

We conclude that the aggregate results and the shape of the distribution of gains across all households are not significantly affected by the principal choice of data reconciliation. Although virtually all households gain due to the Dixit—Stiglitz variety effect, which households gain more or less, however, is affected by the choice of how we reconcile the data.

### 6.4.5.3 Piecemeal sensitivity analysis

In table 5 of Rutherford and Tarr (2008) we present the impact on welfare of varying the value of key parameters. The results are extremely close to the results presented in Table 6.5 so are not reproduced here. We have verified that in the household model as well, the same three parameters have a strong impact on the results: the elasticity of substitution between value-added and business services, *esubs*; the elasticity of multinational firm supply, etaf; and *theta_fdi(i)*, the share of output of service sector *i* captured by multinational firms in the benchmark equilibrium.

Finally, we have executed a variant of the model with land as a specific factor in agriculture; this reduced the variable capital in agriculture by 50% relative to our central model. The mean of the estimated gains is slightly reduced, from 7.3 to 7.1%, which is explained by the Le Chatelier principle.

### 6.4.5.4 Systematic sensitivity analysis

Piecemeal sensitivity analysis shows how the results change when we vary the value of key parameters one-by-one, with central values of all parameters except the one under consideration. In the systematic sensitivity analysis, we allow all parameters to change simultaneously. A probability distribution for each parameter is chosen. We typically choose uniform probability distributions, with the lower and upper bounds for the

---

[53] Results, based on the national accounts model, for *EV* as a percent of consumption by decile are: decile 1, 5.7; decile 2, 5.7; decile 3, 6.1; decile 4, 6.2; decile 5, 6.5; decile 6, 6.6; decile 7, 7.0; decile 8, 7.3; decile 9, 7.5; decile 10, 8.0. With the data reconciled based on the national accounts data, the Gini coefficient is 0.403 in this benchmark equilibrium, and it increases to 0.405 after our WTO accession scenario.

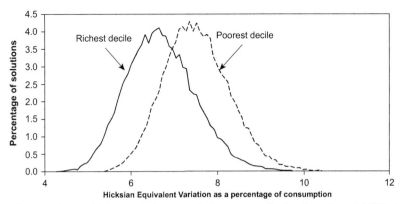

**Figure 6.8** Systematic sensitivity analysis—sample frequency distributions from 30,000 simulations for the richest and poorest deciles: 95% confidence intervals (assuming a normal distribution), poor (6.1, 9.0); rich (5.1, 8.3); 99% confidence intervals (assuming a normal distribution), poor (5.6, 9.5); rich (4.6, 8.8).

values of the parameters taken from the lower and upper values of the key parameters presented in Table 6.5. We furthermore assume that all distributions are stochastically independent.

We have executed the model with all 55,098 households 30,000 times.[54] Each time the program chooses a random configuration of parameters and executes the model with this configuration. For each variable in our model, we then harvest the sample distribution based on the 30,000 solutions. Consequently, the sample distribution is not dependent on any particular set of parameter values, but represents results representative of the full distribution of parameter values.

We present the distribution of the weighted average welfare results in Figure 6.8 for the poorest and richest deciles of the population. Results for each decile are the aggregated equivalent variations, as a percentage of consumption, for the households in the decile. Figure 6.8 shows that there is virtually no chance that the weighted average welfare gains as a percentage of consumption for the poorest decile of the population is less than 5% or more than 11%; a 99% confidence interval is 5.6—9.5%. For the richest decile, the gains are slightly smaller; a 99% confidence interval for the richest decile of the population is 4.6—8.8%. These results are consistent with the central parameter value estimates, where we had the poorest decile gaining 7.6% and the richest 6.8%.[55]

---

[54] The systematic sensitivity analysis took about 4 months to complete. We produced about 2300 solutions of the model per week on a 2.8-GHz computer dedicated fully to this task.

[55] Note that these systematic sensitivity distributions are the sample probability distributions for the weighted average welfare gains of the households in the decile being considered, based on random parameter selection; whereas the distributions of Figures 6.6 and 6.7 are distributions of welfare gains across all the different households based on our specified central parameter values.

### 6.4.6 Conclusions

We estimate that in the medium term, virtually all households will gain from Russian WTO accession. We have shown that our estimates of the distribution of gains across the 55,098 households are decisively affected the inclusion of liberalization of barriers against FDI in business services sectors and endogenous productivity effects in business services and goods.

Figure 6.7 encapsulates the key point of this section. To estimate income distribution effects, a microsimulation model is important, given that there is great diversity of impacts for trade liberalization across households. However, incorporating FDI in business services with Dixit—Stiglitz effects in imperfectly competitive sectors is as important since these modeling features displace the distribution of results across households to the right from a CRTS model based distribution.

## 6.5 POLICY IMPACTS AND OTHER MODEL APPLICATIONS AND EXTENSIONS

### 6.5.1 Policy impacts

This models and results of this paper were the core contribution in the effort of the World Bank to assist the government of Russia in its WTO accession effort, especially in its public awareness campaign. It was, however, only part of multifaceted research and dissemination effort that was sustained over several years.[56] Although the Russian government was convinced of the benefits of WTO accession, prior to this work there was widespread public skepticism and Russian businessmen were calling for an explanation of the impacts on their sectors. Russian leaders and independent internal World Bank evaluators of the work have concluded that the work was instrumental in shifting public opinion in favor of WTO accession, and in explaining to businessmen and politicians in convincing terms the consequences of WTO at the sector level. Surveys taken after this work was done showed that, regarding the impacts of WTO accession on the sectors of Russia, the views of informed laymen (such as political leaders in the regions of Russia) were coincident with the assessments of the models discussed above. The latest internal review by a World Bank evaluation team (as part of a broader review of economic work on Russia by World Bank teams) concluded the following:

> *The WTO analytical work for Russia consists of a large number of very high quality papers and publications assessing the economic and social effects of Russia's planned accession to WTO.... The body of analytical work (about 15 papers) was disseminated through training events (a number of them requested by the authorities) attended by (prospective) civil servants, representatives of labor and industry and the academic community. It has clearly made*

---

[56] Research papers included the following: Jensen *et al.* (2004, 2006, 2007); Rutherford and Tarr (2008; 2008a, 2010); Rutherford *et al.* (2005); Shepotylo and Tarr (2008); Tarr (2006, 2007, 2010a, 2010b); Tarr and Thomson (2004); Tarr and Volchkova (2010, 2012).

*a contribution to the policy dialogue and is seen as instrumental for establishing a sense that WTO accession would be beneficial for Russia among the government's trade reform team and parts of the research community. Prior to this project, editorials were rampant in the Russian press expressing fears of WTO accession and focusing on the fact that the government has not explained the consequences of WTO accession or the source of the benefits. Now polls of regional politicians reveal that they anticipate exactly the impacts suggested by the analytic studies. Moreover, polls of the public have shown progressively increasing endorsement, and now significant majority supporting WTO accession. Finally, as the analytic studies strongly empha- sized the crucial role of liberalization against barriers to FDI in business services, Russian has agreed to major openings in the business services markets as part of its bilateral market access agreements in the WTO negotiations (Tarr, 2007).*

As noted in the review, the work was very widely disseminated over a period of years.[57] Crucially the dissemination efforts involved writing several short policy papers and op-eds, where the results could be explained in clear terms understandable to a non-technical audience. We regard the extensive and sustained dissemination efforts over several years as a key aspect of the success on the policy front, possibly equally important as the innovative feature of incorporating FDI in services with endogenous productivity impacts.

In addition to the impact of this work and model in Russia, lead negotiators for WTO accession in both Kazakhstan and Ukraine became aware of the work in Russia,

---

[57] The evaluation noted that dissemination was good on several fronts. It stated: "First, the information was presented in a readable way that was easy to follow for non-experts. A selection of the materials were summarized in book form for teaching purposes and translated into Russian. Second, an intensive training course on Trade policies and WTO accession was organized with the World Bank Institute and held twice. In addition to the World Bank Institute training (attended by about 200 participants from civil service and academia), the findings were presented in several conferences in Russia and abroad. A two day workshop for Russian counterparts was organized in London in 2006 to help assist the government in formulating an international trade strategy. Two GDLN events (80 participants each) organized by the World Bank Institute linking up several Russian, one Belarusian university and one Kazak location were held in 2008 and 2009. Third, findings were reflected in the Bank's poverty assessment and highlighted in one of the country office on-line reports to the country. Fourth, a bilingual website was established listing the key outputs of this exercise and other relevant publications. www. worldbank.org/trade/russia-wto. Fifth, in order to transfer the model to Russian experts, seven days of training on the model was provided to economic modelers from Russia and the CIS during which they were provided with the software to run for the models and were given the software. Summaries and PowerPoint presentations were prepared for various audiences including a conference organized with the Ministry of Communications; the CEFIR trade conference; the New Economic School tenth anniversary conference; the CEFIR conference on telecommunications; the conference of labor, business and government officials in Saint Petersburg led by the International Labor Organization; a GDLN presentation to Russian regional officials through the RAGS network; presentations were made to: 800 participants in the conference organized by the Russian Union of Industrialists and Entrepreneurs in Moscow in 2007; to 110 Russian small and medium businessmen in Washington; to a large conference of CIS businessmen in Evian France; to the Russia–US Business Council in Washington; to the government officials representing the CAREC countries at their meetings in Mongolia in 2009, and several smaller gatherings of Russian business interests in both Moscow and visiting in Washington. Short policy papers appeared in the bilingual journal of the American Chamber of Commerce in Russia, the International Labor Organization and a short policy paper was prepared for the Ministry of Economic Development and Trade website. Two op-eds were published in Russia, and other Russian researchers, such as Ksenia Yudaeva, also wrote op-eds based on results of the analytic work. In Moscow, there were three large press conferences, several additional interviews with members of the press as well as a television interview on the network *Russia Today*."

and requested similar studies in their countries. The model was adapted and applied in Ukraine and Kazakhstan, and had a significant impact in those countries in developing a framework for assessing the gains from WTO accession. This helped the lead negotiators with their public awareness obligations.

In requesting the involvement of the team that executed this work in Russia, the Ukrainian lead negotiator said that he had people telling him the impact of WTO accession in agriculture, or in various services sectors or in manufacturing. However, he needed to know how it all fit together. This is a perspective that a general equilibrium modeler can love. Jesper Jensen and colleagues working in the Institute for Economic Research in Kiev adapted the model developed for Russia to Ukraine, and helped the lead negotiator with his public awareness need (see Copenhagen Economics *et al.*, 2006).

In Kazakhstan, Jensen and Tarr (2008) adapted the Russia model to assess the impact of WTO accession in Kazakhstan. The lead negotiator in Kazakhstan wanted to know how WTO accession could be used to increase the productivity and competitiveness of manufacturing in Kazakhstan. As in Russia, the results showed that the largest gains to Kazakhstan would come from its own liberalization in services, due to the productivity gains to industry, agriculture and services in Kazakhstan from additional providers of services. Subsequent to this work, the lead negotiator for WTO accession in Kazakhstan has repeatedly made it her message that the principal benefit to Kazakhstan from WTO accession will be the increase in productivity it will reap from the liberalization of services barriers.

### 6.5.2 Model extensions

#### 6.5.2.1 Multiregion trade model

In Rutherford and Tarr (2010), we extended the model of the single representative consumer model of Section 6.3 into a 10-region model of Russia (with a single representative consumer in each region). Russia in aggregate was modeled as a SOE, but within Russia, the model was a multiregion trade model with FDI in each of the 10 regions. The principal explanation for the differences across regions is the ability of the different regions to benefit from a reduction in barriers against FDI. The three regions with the largest welfare gains are clearly the regions with the estimated largest shares of multinational investment. Moreover, regions may gain more from WTO accession if they can succeed in creating a good investment climate.

#### 6.5.2.2 Impact of liberalization of non-discriminatory services barriers

In Balistreri *et al.* (2009) and Jensen *et al.* (2010), we applied the methodology of Section 6.3 to Kenya and Tanzania, respectively. Our empirical assessment of the barriers revealed that the most important barriers in both countries were barriers that increased costs, but which restricted both local and multinational providers of services. The estimates showed very substantial potential gains (over 10% of consumption in the case of

Kenya) from a 50% reduction of all barriers against potential providers of services (both local and multinational).

### 6.5.2.3 Preferential trade arrangements

In Balistreri and Tarr (2011) and Jensen and Tarr (2010), we extended our models of Kenya and Tanzania, respectively, to be able to assess preferential liberalization of trade and services barriers. We decomposed the rest of the world into the EU, an Africa partner region and a residual rest of the world. We show that there is an imperfect competition extension of the idea of trade diversion. That is, preferential liberalization of barriers against partner country services providers will result in fewer varieties of services from excluded countries. Immizering preferential liberalization of services is more likely the more technologically advanced the excluded regions are relative to the partner region and the greater the share of rents from the services barriers captured by the home country initially.

In Jensen and Tarr (2011), we applied this model of preferential commitments in goods and services to Armenia to assess the potential "Deep and Comprehensive Free Trade Agreement" under negotiation between Armenia and the EU. We showed that it was only the deep aspects of the agreement that would benefit Armenia, especially the trade facilitation and services liberalization aspects of the agreement.

### 6.5.2.4 Heterogeneous firms

Balistreri *et al.* (2011) have succeeded in incorporating heterogeneous firms into a multiregion trade model. It would be valuable to extend that approach to include services with FDI and endogenous productivity effects. Heterogeneous firms add another element of gain from trade liberalization; it comes from more efficient use of resources, by shifting resources from less efficient firms to more efficient firms.

However, is the welfare gain from the improved resource allocation of incorporating heterogeneous firms of the same small order of magnitude as the welfare gains from improved resource allocation in perfect competition models? Moreover, it remains to be investigated whether there are significant quantitative differences between the heterogeneous firms model, on the one hand, and a model with homogeneous monopolistically competitive firms, Dixit—Stiglitz productivity effects and sector-specific factors that give rise to increasing industry marginal costs, on the other hand.

## ACKNOWLEDGMENTS

Parts of this paper appeared in the following publications: Markusen *et al.* (2005a), Jensen *et al.* (2007), Rutherford and Tarr (2008), and Rutherford, Tarr and Shepotylo (2006). I thank my coauthors of these papers and Ed Balistreri for their many contributions to these collective works. I thank Brian Parmenter for comments as a referee of this paper, and Peter Dixon for very stimulating exchanges and comments. I thank the World Bank and the Department for International Development (DFID) of the UK for its financial support. All views expressed in this chapter are my own and do not necessarily reflect those of the World Bank, its Executive Directors, DFID or the Russian Government.

# REFERENCES

Adelman, I., Robinson, S., 1978. Income Distribution Policies in Developing Countries. Stanford University Press, Stanford, CA.

Alessina, A., Ardagna, S., Nicoletti, G., Schiantarelli, F., 2005. Regulation and investment. J. Eur. Econ. Assoc. 3, 791–825.

Annabi, N., Cisse, F., Cockburn, J., Decaluwe, B., 2005. Trade liberalization, growth and poverty in senegal: A dynamic microsimulation CGE model analysis, CEPII Research Paper. CEPII, Paris.

Arnold, J.M., Javorcik, B.S., Matoo, A., 2011. Does services liberalization benefit manufacturing firms: Evidence from the Czech Republic. J. Int. Econ. 85, 136–146.

Arnold, J.M., Javorcik, B.S., Lipscomb, M., Matoo, A., 2012. Services reform and manufacturing performance: evidence from India. World Bank Policy Research Working Paper 5948. World Bank, Washington, DC.

Arnold, J., Mattoo, A., Narciso, G., 2008. Services inputs and firm productivity in Sub-Saharan Africa: evidence from firm level data. J. Afr. Econ. 17, 578–599.

Baldwin, R.E., Forslid, R., Haaland, J., 1999. Investment creation and investment diversion: Simulation analysis of the single market programme. In: Baldwin, R., Francois, J. (Eds), Dynamic Issues in Applied Commercial Policy Analysis. Cambridge University Press, Cambridge, pp. 228–265.

Balistreri, E.J., Tarr, D.G., 2011. Services liberalization in preferential trade arrangements: the case of Kenya. World Bank Policy and Research Working Paper 5552. World Bank, Washington, DC.

Balistreri, E.J., Rutherford, T.F., Tarr, D.G., 2009. Modeling services liberalization: the case of Kenya. Econ. Model. 26, 668–679.

Balistreri, E.J., Hillberry, R.H., Rutherford, T.F., 2011. Structural estimation and solution of international trade models with heterogeneous firms. J. Int. Econ. 83, 95–108.

Baranov, S.P., 2000. Compiling the disaggregated version of "input-output" tables of the Russian Federation for 1995 year for consequent use as a basic data for building the general equilibrium model for the Russian Federation. Available at: http://siteresources.worldbank.org/INTRANETTRADE/Resources/Topics/Accession/Baranov_equilibrium.pdf

Bourguignon, F., Pereira da Silva, L., 2003. Conclusion: Where do we go from here? In: Bourguignon, F., Pereira da Silva, L. (Eds), The Impact of Economic Policies on Poverty and Income Distribution: Evaluation Techniques and Tools. World Bank and Oxford University Press, New York, pp. 1–26.

Bourguignon, F., de Melo, J., Morrison, C., 1991. Poverty and income distribution during adjustment: Issues and evidence from the OECD project. World Dev. 19, 1485–1508.

Broda, C., Weinstein, D., 2004. Variety, growth and world welfare. Am. Econ. Rev. 94, 139–144.

Brown, D., Deardorf, A., Fox, A., Stern, R., 1996. Liberalization of services trade. In: Martin, W., Winters, L.A. (Eds), The Uruguay Round and the Developing Countries. Cambridge University Press, Cambridge, pp. 292–315.

Brown, D., Stern, R., 2001. Measurement and modeling of the economic effects of trade and investment barriers in services. Rev. Int. Econ. 9, 262–286.

Coe, D.T., Helpman, E., 1995. International R&D spillovers. Eur. Econ. Rev. 39, 859–887.

Coe, D.T., Hoffinaister, A.W., 1999. Are there international R&D spillovers among randomly matched trade partners? A response to Keller, International Monetary Fund Working Paper. IMF, Washington, DC.

Coe, D.T., Helpman, E., Hoffinaister, A.W., 1997. North–south R&D spillovers. Economic Journal 107, 134–149.

Chen, S., Ravallion, M., 2004. Welfare impacts of China's accession to the WTO. World Bank Econ. Rev. 18, 29–57.

Chinitz, B., 1961. Contrast in agglomeration: New York and Pittsburgh. Am. Econ. Rev., Papers Proceedings 51, 279–289.

Ciccone, A., Hall, R., 1996. Productivity and the density of economic activity. Am. Econ. Rev. 86, 54–70.

Cockburn, J., 2001. Trade Liberalisation and Poverty in Nepal: A Computable General Equilibrium Micro Simulation Analysis, Discussion paper 01-18. Centre de Recherche en Économie et Finance Appliquées, Universite Laval, Quebec.

Copenhagen Economics, East Europe Institute of Munich and the Institute for Economic Research and Policy Consulting (2006) Analysis of Economic Impacts of Ukraine's WTO Accession to the WTO: Overall Impact Assessment, Available from: www.ier.kiev.ua.

Cororaton, C.B., Cockburn, J., 2007. Trade reform and poverty—lessons from the Philippines: A CGE micro-simulation analysis. J. Policy Model. 29, 141—163.

Daniels, P.W., 1985. Service Industries: A Geographical Appraisal. Methuen & Co, New York.

Dantzig, G., Manne, A., 1974. A Complementary algorithm for an optimal capital path with invariant proportions,. J. Econ. Theory 9, 312—323.

Dee, P., Hanslow, K., Phamduc, T., 2003. Measuring the costs of barriers to trade in services. In: Ito, T., Krueger, A. (Eds), Trade in Services in the Asia-Pacific Region. University of Chicago Press, Chicago, IL, pp. 11—46.

de Melo, J., Tarr, D.G., 1992. A General Equilibrium Analysis of US Foreign Trade Policy. MIT Press, Cambridge, MA.

Dixit, A., Stiglitz, J., 1977. Monopolistic competition and optimum product diversity. Am. Econ. Rev. 76, 297—308.

Dixon, P.B., Rimmer, M.T., 2002. Dynamic General Equilibrium Modeling for Forecasting and Policy: A Practical Guide and Documentation on MONASH. In: Contributions to Economic Analysis 256. North-Holland, AMsterdam.

Eschenbach, F., Hoekman, B., 2006. Services policy reform and economic growth in transition economies. Rev. World Econ. 142, 746—762.

Elbers, C., Lanjouw, J.O., Lanjouw, P., 2003. Micro-level estimation of poverty and inequality. Econometrica 71, 355—364.

Ethier, W.J., 1982. National and international returns to scale in the modern theory of international trade. Am. Econ. Rev. 72, 389—405.

Ethier, W., 1984. Higher dimensional issues in trade theory. In: Jones, R., Kenen, P. (Eds), Handbook of International Economics. International Trade, Vol. I. North-Holland, Amsterdam, pp. 131—184.

Falvey, R., Foster, N., Greenaway, D., 2002. Imports, exports, knowledge spillovers and growth. Econ. Lett. 85, 209—213.

Feenstra, R., Madani, D., Yang, T.H., Liang, C.Y., 1999. Testing endogenous growth in South Korea and Taiwan. J. Dev. Econ. 60, 317—341.

Feenstra, R., Kee, H., 2004. On the measurement of product variety in trade. Am. Econ. Rev. 94, 145—149.

Fernandes, A.M., 2009. Structure and performance of the services sector in transition economies. Econ. Transit. 17, 467—501.

Fernandes, A.M., Paunov, C., 2012. Foreign direct investment in services and manufacturing productivity: evidence for Chile. J. Dev. Econ. 97, 305—321.

Findlay, C., Warren, T., 2000. Impediments to Trade in Services: Measurement and Policy Implications. Routledge, London.

Fink, C., Mattoo, A., Neagu, I.C., 2005. Assessing the impact of communications costs on international trade. J. Int. Econ. 67 428—425.

Frankel, J., Romer, D., 1999. Does trade cause growth. Am. Econ. Rev. 89, 379—399.

Francois, J., McDonald, B., Nordstom, H., 1996. Assessing the Uruguay Round. In: Martin, W., Winters, L.A. (Eds), The Uruguay Round and the Developing Countries. Cambridge University Press, Cambridge, pp. 253—291.

Francois, J.F., 1990a. Trade in producer services and returns due to specialization under monopolistic competition. Can. J. Econ. 23, 109—124.

Francois, J.F., 1990b. Producer services, scale, and the division of labor. Oxf. Econ. Papers 42, 715—729.

Francois, J., Hoekman, B., 2010. Services trade and policy. J. Econ. Lit. 48, 642—692.

Francois, J., van Meijl, H., van Tongeren, F., 2005. Trade liberalization and the Doha Development Round. Econ. Policy 42, 342—379.

Fujita, M., Krugman, P., Venables, A.J., 1999. The Spatial Economy: Cities, Regions, and International Trade. MIT Press, Cambridge, MA.

Hansen, T., Koopmans, T., 1972. On the definition and the computation of a capital stock invariant under optimization. J. Econ. Theor. 5, 487–523.

Harrison, G.H., Rutherford, T.F., Tarr, D.G., 1997a. Economic implications for Turkey of a customs union with the European Union. Eur. Econ. Rev. 41, 861–870.

Harrison, G.H., Rutherford, T.F., Tarr, D.G., 1997b. Quantifying the Uruguay Round. Economic Journal 107, 1405–1430.

Harrison, G.H., Rutherford, T.F., Tarr, D.G., 2003. Trade liberalization, poverty and efficient equity. J. Dev. Econ. 71, 97–128.

Harrison, G.H., Rutherford, T.F., Tarr, D.G., Gurgel, A., 2004. Trade policy and poverty reduction in Brazil. World Bank Econ. Rev. 18, 289–317.

Holmes, T., 1995. Localization of Industry and Vertical Disintegration. Federal Reserve Bank of Minneapolis, Minneapolis, MN.

Hummels, D., 1995. Global Income Clustering and Trade in Intermediate Goods, Graduate School of Business. University of Chicago, Chicago, IL.

Hummels, D., Klenow, P., 2005. The variety and quality of a nation's trade. Am. Econ. Rev. 95, 704–723.

Hummels, D., Lugovsky, V., 2005. Trade in ideal varieties: Theory and evidence. NBER Working Paper 11828. NBER, Cambridge, MA.

Ianchovichina, E., Martin, W., 2004. Impacts of China's Aaccession to the World Trade Organization. World Bank Econ. Rev. 18, 3–27.

Inklaar, R., Timmer, M.P., van Ark, B., 2008. Market services productivity across Europe and the US. Econ. Policy 53, 139–171. 178–194.

International Monetary Fund, 2002. Russian Federation: Selected Issues and Statistical Appendix. IMF, Washington, DC.

Ivanic, M., 2004. Reconciliation of the GTAP and household survey data. GTAP Resource Memorandum 1408 Available at: http://www.gtap.agecon.purdue.edu/resources/res_display.asp?RecordID=1408.

Jensen, J., Tarr, D.G., 2003. Trade, exchange rate and energy pricing reform in Iran: Potentially large efficiency effects and gains to the poor. Rev. Dev. Econ. 7, 543–662.

Jensen, J., Tarr, D.G., 2008. Impact of local content restrictions and barriers against foreign direct investment in services: The case of Kazakhstan accession to the WTO. E. Eur. Econ. 46 (5), 5–26.

Jensen, J., Tarr, D.G., 2010. Regional trade policy options for Tanzania: the importance of services commitments. World Bank Policy and Research Working Paper 5481. World Bank, Washington, DC.

Jensen, J., Tarr, D.G., 2011. Deep trade policy options for Armenia: The importance of trade facilitation, services and standards liberalization. Economics: The Open Access-Open Assessment E-Journal 6 2012–1, Available at: http://dx.doi.org/10.5018/economics-ejournal.ja.2012-1.

Jensen, J., Rutherford, T.F., Tarr, D.G., 2004. The impact of liberalizing barriers to foreign direct investment in services: The case of Russian accession to the World Trade Organization. World Bank Policy and Research Working Paper 3391. World Bank, Washington, DC. Available at: http://econ.worldbank.org/external/default/main?pagePK=64165259&theSitePK=469372&piPK=64165421&menuPK=64166093&entityID=000012009_20040909153130.

Jensen, J., Rutherford, T.F., Tarr, D.G., 2006. Telecommunications reform within Russia's accession to the WTO. E. Eur. Econ. 44, 25–58.

Jensen, J., Rutherford, T.F., Tarr, D.G., 2007. The impact of liberalizing barriers to foreign direct investment in services: the case of Russian accession to the World Trade Organization. Rev. Dev. Econ. 11, 482–506.

Jensen, J., Rutherford, T.F., Tarr, D.G., 2010. Modeling services liberalization: the case of Tanzania. J. Econ. Int. 25, 644–675.

Kang, J.-S., 2000. Price impact of restrictiveness on maritime transportation services. In: Findlay, C., Tony, W. (Eds), Impediments to Trade in Services: Measurement and Policy Implications. Routledge, London, pp. 189–199.

Kang, J.-S., Findlay, C., 2000. Regulatory reform in the maritime industry. In: Findlay, C., Warren, T. (Eds), Impediments to Trade in Services: Measurement and Policy Implications. Routledge, London, pp. 152–188.

Kimura, F., Ando, M., Fujii, T., 2004a. Estimating the Ad Valorem Equivalent of Barriers to Foreign Direct Investment in the Telecommunications Services Sectors in Russia. World Bank, Washington, DC. Available at: http://www.worldbank.org/trade/russia-wto.

Kimura, F., Ando, M., Fujii, T., 2004b. Estimating the Ad Valorem Equivalent of Barriers to Foreign Direct Investment in the Maritime and Air Transportation Service Sectors in Russia. World Bank, Washington, DC. Available at: http://www.worldbank.org/trade/russia-wto.

Kimura, F., Ando, M., Fujii, T., 2004c. Estimating the Ad Valorem Equivalent of Barriers to Foreign Direct Investment in Financial Services Sectors in Russia. World Bank, Washington, DC. Available at: http://www.worldbank.org/trade/russia-wto.

Keller, W., 2000. Do trade patterns and technology flows affect productivity growth? World Bank Econ. Rev. 14 (1), 17—47.

Konan, D.E., Maskus, K.E., 2006. Quantifying the impact of services liberalization in a developing country. J. Dev. Econ. 81, 142—162.

Levine, R., 2005. Finance and growth: theory and evidence. In: Taylor, J.B., Woodford, M. (Eds), Handbook of Economic Growth, Vol. 1A. North-Holland, Amsterdam, pp. 865—964.

Lejour, A.M., Rojas-Romagosa, H., Verweij, G., 2008. Opening services markets within Europe: Modeling foreign establishments in a CGE framework. Econ. Model. 25, 1022—1039.

Lopez-de-Silanes, F., Markusen, J.R., Rutherford, T., 1994. Complementarity and increasing returns in imported intermediate inputs. J. Dev. Econ. 45, 101—119.

Lumenga-Neso, O., Olarreaga, M., Schiff, M., 2005. On Indirect trade related research and development spillovers. Eur. Econ. Rev. 49, 1785—1798.

Markusen, J.R., 1989. Trade in producer services and in other specialized intermediate inputs. Am. Econ. Rev. 79, 85—95.

Markusen, J.R., 1990. Derationalizing tariffs with specialized intermediate inputs and differentiated final goods. J. Int. Econ. 28, 375—384.

Markusen, J.R., Venables, A., 1998. Multinational firms and the new trade theory. J. Int. Econ. 46, 183—204.

Markusen, J.R., Venables, A.J., 2000. The general theory of endowment, intra-industry, and multinational trade,. J. Int. Econ. 52, 209—234.

Markusen, J.R., Rutherford, T., Tarr, D., 2005. Trade and direct investment in producer services and the domestic market for expertise. Can. J. Econ. 38, 758—777.

Markusen, J.R., Rutherford, T.F., Tarr, D.G., 2000. Foreign direct investment in services and the domestic market for expertise. World Bank Policy and Research Working Paper 2413. World Bank, Washington, DC.

Marshall, J.N., 1988. Services and Uneven Development. Oxford University Press, London.

Matoo, A., Rathindran, R., Subramanian, A., 2006. Measuring services trade liberalization and its impact on economic growth: An illustration. J. Econ. Int. 21, 64—98.

Matusz, Steven J, Tarr, D.G., 2000. Adjusting to trade policy reform. In: Krueger, A. (Ed.), Economic Policy Reform. University of Chicago Press, Chicago, IL, pp. 365—399.

McGuire, G., Schuele, M., 2000. Restrictiveness of international trade in banking services. In: Findlay, C., Warren, T. (Eds), Impediments to Trade in Services: Measurement and Policy Implications. Routledge, London, pp. 215—229.

McKee, D.L., 1988. Growth, Development, and the Service Economy in the Third World. Praeger, New York.

Moriarity, C., Scheuren, F., 2003. A note on Rubin's statistical matching using file concatenation with adjusted weights and multiple imputations. J. Bus. Econ. Stat. 21, 65—73.

Piggott, John, Whalley, J., 1985. UK Tax Policy and Applied General Equilibrium Analysis. Cambridge University Press, New York.

Rao, J.N.K., 1999. Some recent advances in model-based small area estimation. Surv. Method. 25, 175—186.

Robinson, S., Wang, Z., Martin, W., 2002. Capturing the implications of services trade liberalization. Econ. Syst. Res. 14, 3—33.

Rodrik, D., Subramanian, A., Trebbi, F., 2004. Institutions rule: the primacy of institutions over geography and integration in economic development. J. Econ. Growth 9, 131—165.

Romer, P., 1994. New goods, old theory and the welfare costs of trade restrictions. J. Dev. Econ. 43, 5—38.

Romer, P.M., 1990. Endogenous technological change. J. Polit. Econ. 98, 71—102.

Rutherford, T.F., 1999. Applied general equilibrium modeling with MPSGE as a GAMS subsystem: An overview of the modeling framework and syntax. Comput. Econ. 14, 1—46.

Rutherford, T.F., 1995. Extensions of GAMS for complementarity problems arising in applied economics. J. Econ. Dynam. Contr. 19, 1299–1324.

Rutherford, T.F., Tarr, D.G., 1998. Trade liberalization and endogenous growth in a small open economy. World Bank Policy and Research Working Paper 1970. World Bank, Washington, DC.

Rutherford, T.F., Tarr, D.G., 2002. Trade liberalization, product variety and growth in a small open economy: a quantitative assessment. J. Int. Econ. 56, pp. 247–272.

Rutherford, T.F., Tarr, D., 2003. Regional trading arrangements for Chile: Do the results differ with a dynamic model? Integrat. Trade 7, 117–139.

Rutherford, T.F., Tarr, D.G., 2008. Poverty effects of Russia's WTO accession: Modeling "real households" with endogenous productivity effects. J. Int. Econ. 75, 131–150.

Rutherford, T.F., Tarr, D.G., 2010. Regional impacts of liberalization of barriers against foreign direct investment in services, the case of Russia's accession to the WTO. Rev. Int. Econ. 18, 30–46.

Rutherford, T.F., Tarr, D.G., Shepotylo, O., 2005. Poverty effects of Russia's WTO accession: Modeling "real" households and endogenous productivity effects. World Bank Policy and Research Working Paper 3473. World Bank, Washington, DC.

Rutherford, T.F., Tarr, D.G., Shepotylo, O., 2006. The Impact on Russia of WTO accession and The Doha Agenda: the importance of liberalization of barriers against foreign direct investment in services for growth and poverty reduction. Reprinted in: Winters, L. A. (ed.), 2007. The WTO and Poverty and Inequality: An Elgar Reference Collection. Cheltenham: Edgar Elgar. In: Hertel, T., Winters, L.A. (Eds), Putting Development Back into the Doha Agenda: Poverty Impacts of a WTO Agreement. Palgrave McMillan and the World Bank, New York.

Sachs, J.D., Warner, A., 1995. Economic reform and the process of global integration. In: Brainard, W.C., Perry, G.L. (Eds), Brookings Papers on Economic Activity. Brookings Institution, Washington, DC, pp. 1–117.

Schiff, M., Wang, Y., 2006. North–south and south–south trade related technology diffusion: An industry level analysis of direct and indirect effects. Can. J. Econ. 39, 831–844.

Schott, P., 2004. Across-product versus within-product specialization in international trade. Q. J. Econ. 119, 647–678.

Shepotylo, O., Tarr, D.G., 2008. Specific tariffs, tariff simplification and the structure of import tariffs in Russia: 2001-2005. E. Eur. Econ. 46, 49–58.

Shepotylo, O., Vakitov, V., 2012. Impact of services liberalization on productivity of manufacturing firms: Evidence from the Ukrainian firm-level data. World Bank Policy and Research Working Paper 5944. World Bank, Washington, DC.

Stibora, J., de Vaal, A., 1995. Services and Services Trade: A Theoretical Inquiry. Tinbergen Institute, Amsterdam.

Tarr, D.G. (Ed.), 2006. Trade Policy and WTO Accession for Development in Russia and the CIS: A Handbook (in Russian). Ves Mir, Moscow.

Tarr, D.G., 2007. Russian accession to the WTO: An assessment. Eurasian Geography and Economics 48, 306–319.

Tarr, D.G., 2010a. The economic impact of export restraints on Russian gas and raw timber. In: The Economic Impact of Export Restrictions on Raw Materials. OECD, Paris, pp. 131–154.

Tarr, D.G., 2010b. The crucial role for competition in the Russian gas market: implications for Russia and Europe. IAEE Energy Forum, Fourth Quarter, 31–35.

Tarr, D.G., Thomson, P., 2004. The merits of dual pricing of Russian natural gas,. World Econ. 27, 1173–1194.

Tarr, D.G., Volchkova, N., 2010. Foreign economic policy at a crossroads. In: Aslund, A., Guriev, S., Kutchins, A. (Eds), Russia After the Global Economic Crisis. Peterson Institute for International Economics and Center for Strategic and International Studies, Washington, DC, pp. 200–222.

Tarr, D.G., Volchkova, N., 2012. Foreign trade and direct investment, patterns and policy issues. In: Alexeev, M.V., Weber, S. (Eds), Handbook of the Russian Economy. Oxford University Press, Oxford forthcoming.

Triplett, J.E., Bosworth, B.P., 2004. Productivity in the US Services Sector: New Sources of Economic Growth. Brookings Institution, Washington, DC.

Tybout, J., Westbrook, D., 1995. Trade liberalization and the dimensions of efficiency change in Mexican manufacturing industries. J. Int. Econ. 39, 53–78.

UN Conference on Trade and Development, Division on Transnational Corporations and Investment 1995. World Investment Report 1995, New York: United Nations.

Vernon, R., 1960. Metropolis 1985. Harvard University Press, Cambridge, MA.

Walmsley, T.L., Winters, L.A., 2005. Relaxing the restrictions on the temporary movement of natural persons: A simulation analysis. J. Econ. Integrat. 20, 688–726.

Warren, T., 2000. The impact on output of impediments to trade and investment in telecommunications services. In: Findlay, C., Warren, T. (Eds), Impediments to Trade in Services: Measurement and Policy Implications. Routledge, London, pp. 93–108.

Winters, L.A., McCulloch, N., McKay, A., 2004. Trade liberalization and poverty: The evidence so far. J. Econ. Lit. 42, 72–115.

# CHAPTER 7

# Regional Computable General Equilibrium Modeling

**James A. Giesecke, John R. Madden**

Centre of Policy Studies, Monash University

## Abstract

Over the past three decades the field of regional computable general equilibrium (CGE) modeling has flourished, growing from a handful of top-down, single-region and low-dimensioned multiregional models, to a mature field, in which output of large-scale general-purpose multiregional CGE models has become a standard input to policy deliberations in a growing number of countries. Researchers have ensured that innovations in theory, data construction and model application have matched growth in both computing power and the appetite of government decision makers for expanding levels of policy-relevant regional and sectoral detail. This chapter focuses on the development of the field, its current state, and its accomplishments in elucidating important research questions and policy issues in regional economics. We begin by discussing the development of regional CGE modeling as a subdiscipline of CGE modeling, expanding on the distinguishing attributes of regional CGE models. We then discuss policy applications of regional CGE models, demonstrating the power of such models to answer important policy questions and providing an application-driven motivation for our discussion of the innovations in the field. We consider the key theoretical features of multiregional CGE models, identifying the many ways researchers have modeled the behavior of economic agents in a multiregional context. The paucity of data at the regional level suitable for CGE modeling has long been a constraint and so we discuss methods for populating a multiregional model's database. We then undertake simulations with a large-scale CGE model and show how output of the model can be communicated in a way that does not presume knowledge of the details of the underlying model. We note that effective communication of the results of regional CGE modeling studies, based on a correct interpretation of the model mechanisms which underlie them, is a prerequisite for its acceptance in policy circles.

## Keywords

Regional economic modeling, computable general equilibrium, dynamic modeling, regional economic policy

## JEL classification codes

D58, R11, R13, R23, R58

## 7.1 INTRODUCTION

While computable general equilibrium (CGE) modeling started at a national level, it was not long before models with a regional dimension appeared. Early examples are Dixon

© 2013 Elsevier B.V.
All rights reserved.

*et al.*'s (1978) top-down and Liew's (1984a) bottom-up models for Australia, Whalley's (1982) multicountry model, and Hertel and Mount's (1985) single-region model for New York state. This chapter is about the modeling of subnational regions: multicountry CGE models are discussed elsewhere in this Handbook.

Many current CGE models have a regional dimension, reflecting demand by policy makers for information on regional outcomes of: national shocks (e.g. tariffs); region-specific shocks (e.g. state government fiscal policies); and regionally heterogeneous shocks (e.g. drought with varying regional intensities). Regional CGE models have been applied across the same range of issues (tax, trade, environment, etc.) as their national counterparts as well as to issues that are essentially regional, such as fiscal federalism, regional development, mega events, major disasters, transport policy and regional-government microeconomic reforms.

The focus of this chapter is those aspects that distinguish regional CGE models from national models. On the face of it, it may appear that regional CGE models are no more than national models with an extra dimension added to each of the model's agents: households in region *r* rather than just national households, and so on. However, regional CGE modeling involves several challenges beyond those in national modeling. First, factors are more mobile intranationally than internationally. A regional CGE model needs a satisfactory specification of inter-regional migration. The inter-regional mobility of labor/households has in turn implications for regional welfare analysis and inter-regional variations in preference patterns. Cross-border ownership of productive assets tends to be much higher intranationally than internationally, so that accounting for the inter-regional ownership of capital and land can be important. Second, as argued by Isard *et al.* (1998), multiregional modeling should imply the introduction of distance. Proper modeling of distance requires regionally specified margin services, such as transport and retail and wholesale trade. While a number of national CGE models contain extensive treatment of margins, the matter becomes more complex in a multi-regional setting where margins associated with a commodity flow can be supplied by the region of origin, the region of destination or by third regions. A third challenge faced by regional CGE modelers is the specification of the behavior of different tiers of government: national, provincial/state and local. A fourth challenge is to mold scanty regional data into a comprehensive regional CGE database.

The chapter is organized as follows. Sections 7.2 and 7.3 consider some major themes in the regional CGE literature.[1] Section 7.2 is about applications. We start in this way to motivate the study of methodological issues described in Section 7.3 by immediately

---

[1] Reviews of the regional CGE modeling literature include Kraybill (1993) and Partridge and Rickman (1998). A more recent review (Donaghy, 2009) largely confines its scope to a subset of regional CGE models; ones with a definite spatial orientation. In the course of their discussion of methodology in regional CGE modeling, Partridge and Rickman (2010) update their 1998 review.

demonstrating the power of regional CGE modeling to answer questions of policy relevance. Discussion of applications identifies crucial methodological developments in regional CGE modeling, and points the way to future developments required to increase the scope and quality of regional CGE analyses.

In Section 7.4, we specify key features of a state-level CGE model and focus our discussion on aspects that are special to multiregional modeling. We then examine in Section 7.5 methods for populating a multiregional model's database, before putting such a model to work in Section 7.6 on two illustrative simulations. The simulations we choose involve shocks typical of those in real-life policy applications. The aim in discussing these simulations is to demonstrate how to uncover the driving factors behind CGE results at the regional level. We do so with the aid of back-of-the-envelope (BOTE) techniques. While there are many examples of BOTE interpretations of national results, the adoption of this level of rigor in interpreting regional results is rare. In doing so, we demonstrate the essential driving mechanisms in regional CGE results in both the short and long runs.

Concluding remarks are in Section 7.7.

## 7.2 WHAT REGIONAL MODELS CAN TELL US

In this section we provide an overview of regional CGE applications in terms of the major classes of issues investigated, while adumbrating the required methodological developments to be discussed in the next section. In the course of the overview we discuss a small number of studies in a little more detail. The selected publications are good examples of regional CGE studies which answer questions that: have been keenly debated in policy fora; exhibit regional mechanisms at work in the CGE framework; and demonstrate sound interpretations of the factors underlying the results.

We start by considering policy shocks in the order of the geographical level at which they occur.[2] Thus, we begin our overview with shocks which we will term national shocks (i.e. shocks that are uniform across regions, in the sense of not actively discriminating between regions). We then look at policy applications involving region-specific shocks, starting with those where regionally non-uniform shocks tend to occur across all or most regions, before moving to policies and events that are confined to particular regions.

### 7.2.1 Regional effects from national shocks

Kraybill *et al.* (1992, p. 726) observed from a CGE simulation of the effects of the increased US federal budget and trade deficits of the first half of the 1980s, that

---

[2] We interpret policy shocks broadly to also include economic events (e.g. a world oil price rise).

"seemingly aspatial national policies may shift the geographical distribution of national output and income."[3] Such an observation may provide a motivation for regional CGE analysis of national policies. With the question of trade barriers being an intensely debated topic in the late 1970s and early 1980s, the same time that regional CGE models began to emerge, it was natural that trade studies figured prominently among early applications.[4] Early regional CGE studies (Dixon et al., 1982; Liew, 1984b; Whalley and Trela, 1986) identified those regions that were winners from trade restrictions and those that were losers, and by how much.

An important element in considering regional CGE studies is the degree to which they explain the factors driving their regional results. A study that does this well is Dixon et al. (2007). They examined the effects on US states of removing tariffs and quotas on the 45 most heavily protected of the 500 commodities in their regional CGE model. They found that the worst-affected states in terms of employment were Idaho and North Carolina, which were over-represented in adversely affected activities (sugar and dairy in the former, textiles in the latter). The most positively affected state, Washington, was over-represented in export-oriented activities (e.g. aircraft), which gained via the real devaluation that resulted from the trade liberalization. The authors used regression analysis to show that a state's commodity composition of employment, combined with percentage changes in nationwide employment producing each commodity, explained almost three-quarters of the state's employment result.[5] They then used their regression results to search for other factors underlying their state employment simulation results. They proceeded by comparing state employment results from the simulation against those predicted by the regression. They noticed that the regression strongly under-estimated aggregate employment results for a number of states that had in common the presence of a major port. While the regression equation took no account of interstate differences in employment effects for individual commodities, Dixon et al.'s (2007) regional CGE model recognized that the increased international trade arising from trade liberalization provided a bigger percentage boost for margin services (e.g. road and rail transport) in those states with a major port. Adding a port index to their regression equation increased the $R^2$ to 0.88.[6] They then searched for further factors underlying

---

[3] Their simulation is with a comparative-static two-region CGE model of the US (Virginia and Rest of US) in short-run mode.

[4] With the tariff debate a central political issue at that time, trade liberalization was also among the earliest applications with national CGE models (for an early example, see Dixon and Sutton, 1977), and also with multicountry models (for an early example, see Whalley, 1982). It has remained a major topic of CGE analysis, particularly with multicountry models (recent examples are Francois et al., 2005; Dimaranan et al., 2007).

[5] They regressed state aggregate employment impacts against an index which was computed for each state as the weighted average of the percentage changes in each commodity's employment nationally, where the weights were that region's commodity employment shares. The $R^2$ was 0.73.

[6] The port index is the ratio of the state's share of US international trade through its ports to the state's share of national employment.

their state employment results by comparing the gaps between fitted values from the *amended* regression equation and the simulation results. This revealed gaps for some other groups of states. The explanation for the gaps could be attributed successfully to sales patterns of states in the group differing in a common way from the national sales pattern. For instance, one group whose employment results the regression under-predicted were tourism-oriented states. Commodities such as restaurants and hotels in "holiday" states tend to be sold more to tourism, which is favored by real devaluation (as it leads to substitution of domestic for foreign holidays and expands foreign tourism to the US). Dixon *et al.* (2007) confirmed this as one of the factors behind the impact on the "holiday" states by adding a holiday index to the regression equation which increased the $R^2$ to 0.90.

Dixon *et al.* (2007, p. 50) state that the "most striking feature of the state employment results … is the narrowness of their range."[7] As opposed to the Kraybill *et al.* (1992) study referred to above where large macroeconomic shocks were involved, tariff reductions, even when they are across the board, tend to significantly affect only a subset of industries. For reasonably aggregated regions, such as states or provinces, the industrial structure of the regional economies, at least at the broad sectoral level, tend to have roughly similar patterns. Even with substantial regional multiplier effects, it is unlikely that the most affected industries are sufficiently over-represented in particular regions to dramatically increase the dispersion of the regional impacts.[8]

While the bulk of regional CGE studies have moved away from examining purely national shocks, the range of national shocks subjected to regional CGE analysis has increased. In the trade policy area, there have been a number of studies of the regional consequences of free trade areas (e.g. Gazel *et al.*, 1996; Haddad *et al.*, 2002a) and multilateral initiatives (Diao *et al.*, 2006; Anderson *et al.*, 2010). In the central government tax area, Giesecke (1999) examined the regional effects of the national fringe benefits tax, Cardenete and Sancho (2003) analyzed the effects of reforms to the Spanish income tax, and Dixon and Rimmer (1999) assessed the regional effects of a value-added tax. The first two studies were aimed at analyzing the effects of national tax changes on particular regions, Western Australian regions and Andalusia, respectively. On the other hand, the primary focus of Dixon and Rimmer's study was national, with regional results being one of the major disaggregated results also given attention.

Other areas where the shock has been national include: central government defense expenditure cuts (Hoffmann *et al.*, 1996); tourism (Adams and Parmenter, 1995; Blake

[7] Bröcker and Schneider (2002) similarly found a narrow range of effects across Austrian regions from increased trade between Austria and four Central European countries.

[8] Dixon *et al.* (2007) note the following. While sugar and dairy might have a share in Idaho's aggregate employment five times their share nationally, the share for Idaho is still only 0.91%. Thus, the significant employment contraction in these activities directly contributes only 0.13% towards the state's aggregate employment loss. Idaho is projected to experience the largest employment effect, but it is still only a reduction of 0.5%.

and Gilham, 2001); climate change (Madden, 1991; Li and Rose, 1995; Oladosu and Rose, 2007; Snoddon and Wigle, 2008; Garnaut Climate Change Review, 2008); foreign direct investment (Gillespie *et al.*, 2002a); and nationally-set minimum wage rates (Dixon *et al.*, 2010). Again, while most of the cited studies are concerned essentially with regional analysis, some (Adams and Parmenter, and the Garnaut Review) include regional analysis as one component of wider studies. These latter studies nevertheless can provide interesting regional results that defy commonly-held views. For instance, Adams and Parmenter (1995, p. 991) find that Queensland, the Australian state whose "economy is most oriented towards servicing overseas tourists," suffers a reduction in its Gross State Product (GSP) growth rate as a result of a uniform economy-wide increase in the growth rate of foreign tourism demand. Victoria, on the hand, the state least oriented to foreign tourism is found to be a net gainer from the tourism shock. The key explanation for this lies in Queensland being significantly over-represented, and Victoria under-represented, in traditional export industries (principally agriculture and mining). Traditional exports are strongly crowded-out by the tourism shock.[9]

## 7.2.2 Analyzing fiscal federalism

Fiscal federalism is a topic to which regional CGE models are manifestly suitable. A major focus of fiscal federalism applications relates to fiscal equalization issues. Early studies looked at the regional economic impacts of changing the allocation of federal government grants among states in Australia (Madden *et al.*, 1983) and provinces in Canada (Whalley and Trela, 1986) — the two countries with the most developed equalization systems.[10] Dixon *et al.* (1993) reported on the effects on states (and territories), and on Australia's economic efficiency, of discontinuing fiscal equalization arrangements. Dixon *et al.* (1993) found that the arrangements generated inefficiencies arising from overmigration to regions with location-specific disabilities, but they argued that this sort of inefficiency is necessarily small. They also found that discarding just the location-disability part of the fiscal equalization system would still deliver the same

---

[9] It is noteworthy that traditional exports are particularly strongly crowded-out in Adams and Parmenter's simulation due to the medium-term nature of their model closure. With the shock delivering an increase in Australia's terms of trade and the average rate of return on capital assumed fixed, real rental costs of capital to producers fall. This induces an increase in investment. With no change in aggregate employment assumed, GDP is largely constrained and as the non-investment components of gross national expenditure are also largely unaffected, the trade balance must deteriorate. While the import content of the increased investment makes a contribution towards the required trade balance deterioration, the real exchange rate must still appreciate to cause net exports to fall sufficiently. With the increased tourism exports causing an initial movement towards surplus, traditional exports must be particularly negatively affected.

[10] Under (horizontal) fiscal equalization the federal government adjusts its grants to the states away from *per capita* shares to offset state differences in tax bases (in both Australia and Canada) and the cost of providing public services (location-specific disabilities — Australia only). See Madden (2006) and Bird and Vaillancourt (2006) for a discussion of Australian and Canadian fiscal federalism arrangements.

efficiency gains, but considerably reduce the size of the large interstate migration from the states which lose from the policy change.[11]

Subsequent regional CGE studies of fiscal equalization arrangements by Dixon *et al.* (2002, 2005) found a much higher level of inter-regional inefficiency from the arrangements once the so-called "flypaper" effect is taken into account.[12] The flypaper effect refers to a tendency by subnational governments to spend a higher proportion of intergovernmental grant income than it would for any other increase in the region's income. Dixon *et al.* (2002) also found that the effects of diminishing marginal returns from labor tax reductions (and increasing marginal congestion costs) in a positively-affected state meant that the welfare benefits from a reallocation of funds towards a donor state, or away from a subsidized state, initially rise and then fall. Their simulations indicate that interstate differences in the slopes of these benefit curves means that the optimal allocation of grants (in pure economic efficiency terms) differs from equal *per capita* grants.

The implementation of fiscal equalization normally only occurs when there is a situation of vertical fiscal imbalance (VFI), i.e. where the higher tier government's share of national tax receipts is higher than its share of expenditure responsibilities. There has been only limited regional CGE modeling of the effects of changes to VFI, notable examples being Madden (1993) and Hirte (1998).[13]

## 7.2.3 Regional policies and events

The analysis of regional policies or economic events has now become the major area of regional CGE application and the range of questions examined under this broad heading has become very wide. We briefly run through the range of applications, referencing notable examples, with a short discussion of a few papers that provide compelling illustrations of the power of regional CGE models to answer key regional policy questions.

Most regional CGE modeling has been conducted for regions that correspond with subnational administrative boundaries, generally for governments with substantial areas of

---

[11] The bulk of the efficiency loss related to the Northern Territory which would lose over 20% of employment/population under complete abandonment and 15% under discarding just the location-specific disability component. The corresponding figures for Tasmania, the other state Dixon *et al.* model, were 4 and about 0.5%.

[12] Inefficiency is about 4 times greater in real terms in the new studies compared with the 1993 studies. However, as Dixon *et al.* (2002, p. 313) note, this is "only a moderate contribution to Australian welfare."

[13] In the 1990s the Australian federal government justified maintaining that nation's very high VFI in the interest of ensuring its control over macroeconomic management. Madden (1993) conducted regional CGE simulations to test possible state government fiscal reactions and concluded that a very high level of VFI is unlikely to ensure that states' reactions do not run contrary to federal government aims for fiscal contractionary policies. Hirte (1998) examined changes recommended for Germany by an advisory board to allow, *inter alia*, regional governments to levy income taxes and found that depending on institutional arrangements the welfare effects might be negative.

autonomy (as is the case with the states/provinces considered under fiscal federalism above).[14] Thus there have been many applications in the key state/provincial government policy areas of fiscal policy, regional development and infrastructure. These areas are highly inter-related, so for instance one finds tax measures modeled as an instrument for regional development and applications on infrastructure conducted under varying state government budgetary measures for providing the finance. While there are examples of regional CGE studies fundamentally relating to tax efficiency (e.g. Dixon *et al.*, 2004) and to tax incidence (Mutti *et al.*, 1989), most studies of regional government fiscal policies are concerned to a reasonable extent with their effects on regional macro-economic aggregates.[15] For instance, Seung and Kraybill (1999) examined the effects of removing Ohio's state corporate tax on the state's macroeconomic aggregates, while Morgan *et al.* (1989) investigated the effects of all regional taxes on regional growth under different factor mobility assumptions. Madden (1989) examined the efficacy of changing the Tasmanian tax mix in increasing that state's employment, while Berck *et al.* (1997) carried out a similar exercise for California.[16] Morgan *et al.* (1996) found that the degree of tax exporting (i.e. tax burden borne by out-of-region residents) does not necessarily coincide with regional growth effects, which in turn does not correspond with the effects on regional welfare. Giesecke (2003) examined whether it is within the power of an Australian state government to halt the continued decline in the share of its region (Tasmania) in national GDP through a budget-neutral rearrangement of its fiscal instruments. His results showed that to gain a temporary halt in Tasmania's relative decline would involve the introduction of unfeasibly large combinations of subsidies and taxes.[17]

Regional, and national, governments frequently use industry assistance measures as a regional development policy, but these measures have received little attention from regional CGE modelers. An example of CGE modeling of regional government assistance is Challen *et al.* (1984) who simulated labor subsidies to selected Tasmanian

---

[14] Note that subnational governments with considerable autonomy can be found in unitary as well as federal systems. This occurs where the central government has devolved powers to regions. Thus, there has been a good deal of modeling of Scotland to which the UK central government has now devolved many powers (e.g. responsibilities for health, education, justice, transport). Also, of relevance to the discussion in Section 7.2.2, is Ferguson *et al.*'s (2007) modeling of the effects of the formula for the allocation of central government funds to Scotland.

[15] Mutti *et al.* (1989) — as do Morgan *et al.* (1989) and Morgan *et al.* (1996), mentioned immediately below — use a six-region model of the US. It provides an example of where aggregated states are assumed to act as a single state.

[16] Madden (1989) also looks at changes in the state government expenditure mix, and in the fiscal mix generally. Berck *et al.*'s chief concern is the extent to which cuts in taxes on labor and capital are self-financing — a question their simulations answer in the negative.

[17] Giesecke further found that even to achieve a slight, and temporary, diminution in the rate of decline would require a change in the fiscal mix that involved the elimination of the state's major tax category, payroll tax. Other studies look at national government regional assistance policies. For instance, in a recent study Rutherford and Törmä (2010) found that *nationally-funded* reductions in taxes on labor and capital have the capacity to combat out-migration from Northern Finland. They report a slightly positive impact on the welfare of Finland as a whole.

industries financed by a tax surcharge on the region's households and by state government expenditure cuts.[18] An example of a CGE application of national government assistance to a region is Gillespie *et al.* (2001) who examined the effects on Scotland of nationally-funded regional selective assistance for Scottish industry projects.

Major industrial projects are the subject of numerous regional CGE studies commissioned by business and government. Examples of regional CGE modeling of the construction and operating phases of mining projects are Higgs and Powell (1992) and Clements *et al.* (1996). Dixon *et al.* (1992a) examined the economic effects of establishing a proposed science city, simulating its location in each of the bidding states in turn. A feature of this study was the modeling of alternative financing assumptions — two in which the nation paid for the project in the construction phase (fixed balance of trade and reductions in private and public consumption) and one in which the nation paid for the project in the operating phase. The core idea of ensuring that all debt financing of a project from foreigners is repaid within the period simulated (or that the present value of the debt enter welfare calculations) has been central to many regional (and national) CGE studies of major projects since then.

There is a large literature supporting the existence of a positive relationship between public infrastructure and regional economic development outcomes (e.g. Aschauer, 2000), as is the case nationally.[19] In countries such as Australia, much of the responsibility for the provision of public infrastructure rests with regional governments. Giesecke *et al.* (2008) evaluated a state government infrastructure project program under four alternative financing measures — three regional tax types and debt — over each year of a 25-year period. A key feature of this paper is the level of explanation of results for both the short and long terms. Giesecke *et al.* (2008) achieve this through an extended BOTE model; essentially a miniature regional CGE model parameterized using the database of the large-scale multiregional CGE. Their aim was to develop this "model of a model" sufficiently to capture the key mechanisms of the large model, but at the same time keeping it small enough for journal presentation. The authors were able to accurately reproduce the results from the main model with the miniature model and at the same time isolate the mechanisms driving their results, from the early years of the program to the long term. In Section 7.6, we undertake a similar exercise with our illustrative modern regional CGE model.

We consider that if regional CGE modeling is to influence policy, identification and explanation of the key model mechanisms underlying the results is critical. The topic of regional government financing alternatives is an important current policy question. Australia, for instance, has seen reduced spending on public infrastructure over the past

---

[18] Giesecke and Madden (1997) included industry assistance measures, as well as fiscal measures, in their examination of fully-funded regional-stimulus policies.

[19] Although debate remains on the size of the effect.

two decades, as regional governments have sought to restore their fiscal positions, following their exposure to failed government enterprises. Despite now having quite robust fiscal positions, Australian regional governments are reluctant to finance infrastructure through debt, and traditional regional taxes are seen as unpopular. Regional CGE modeling such as that undertaken by Giesecke et al. (2008) provide valuable insights to regional governments not only on the ranking of fiscal instruments, but also on the time paths of the total effects of both the infrastructure and each of the financing instruments.

Regional governments often see major events, such as the Olympic Games, as a major economic attractor to their region, leaving a legacy of inbound tourism and sporting and other infrastructure. Giesecke and Madden (2011) examined whether the large economic benefits often predicted for Olympics host countries necessarily materialize. They re-examined the Sydney 2000 Olympics via historical regional CGE modeling, taking care to avoid common sources of overestimation such as elastic factor supply assumptions and the failure to treat public inputs as costs. In particular, they conducted a simulation from 1997/98 to 2005/06 to uncover whether the Olympics did in fact give a tourism boost to the host region of New South Wales, as *ex ante* regional CGE modeling had predicted. Their historical simulation results did not provide support for the presence of an Olympics-induced tourism effect.[20] They then conducted a simulation for a no-Olympics counterfactual and find the Sydney Olympics generated a real consumption loss of $AUD2.1 billion; an economic cost against which the apparent non-use benefits from the Games could be compared.

Giesecke and Madden (1997, p. 16) suggest that: "Regional governments may have only a limited ability to influence the standard targets of regional development policy with either fiscal or industry assistance instruments" and that their ability "to influence *per capita* measures of well-being using conventional policy instruments is even more limited."[21] They note that implementing the program of microeconomic reforms as proposed under the national competition policy (NCP) agenda that was agreed to by the Australian federal, state and territory governments in 1995 would bring gains that dwarf any potential gains from industry assistance packages. Productivity Commission (1999) find that the major proposed NCP reforms would bring benefits in terms of real *per capita* regional income for states and territories ranging from 2.4% (Victoria) to 2.9% (Tasmania) and for substate regions from 1.5% (Goldfields-Esperance) to 7.4% (Gippsland).[22] Economic modeling of both national effects (Industry Commission, 1995) and regional

---

[20] Giesecke and Madden argue that this is consistent with other information on the tourism effects of mega events in established tourism destinations and that econometric results for induced tourism in host cities (such as Seoul in 1988) that are emerging tourism destinations cannot be simply transplanted to more established tourism locations.

[21] Indeed, like Morgan et al. (1996), Giesecke and Madden (1997) find that policies that have stimulatory effect on output and employment tend to have per/capita real consumption impacts of the opposite sign.

[22] For a summary of regional CGE modeling of NCP, see Madden (2004).

effects (Madden, 1995) of NCP played a valuable role in obtaining the 1995 intergovernmental agreement.

An area of regional government policy which has been subject to a good deal of regional CGE modeling is the area of transport, a topic central to regional analysis. Much of the CGE analysis of infrastructure development concerns transport projects (e.g. Dixon and Madden, 1990; Haddad *et al.*, 2010). In the case of road transport projects benefits are usually computed as savings from reduced congestion (Conrad and Heng, 2002).[23] Kim *et al.* (2004), on the other hand, model investments in inter-regional highway networks as increasing accessibility, and evaluate benefits in terms of macro-economic aggregates.

Regional CGE transport studies cover a much wider range of questions than purely infrastructure ones. These include tax-deductibility of commuting costs (Hirte and Tscharaaktschiew, 2011), freight pricing reforms (e.g. Norrie and Percy, 1983), rural development (Kilkenny, 1998) and urban spatial structure (Horridge, 1994). These applications have been associated with various extensions to the spatial aspects of regional CGE modeling, which we shall discuss in the next section.

Among the other topics to which regional CGE models have been applied are: industrial relations (Dixon and Wittwer, 2004); higher education (Giesecke and Madden, 2006); terrorism (Thissen, 2004; Giesecke *et al.*, 2012); regional resource, environmental and energy issues (e.g. Miyata, 1995; Cattaneo, 2001; Hanley *et al.*, 2009; Seung and Waters, 2010); and natural disasters (Rose and Liao, 2005; Horridge *et al.*, 2005; Wittwer *et al.*, 2005; Shibusawa and Miyata, 2011). The capability of a regional CGE model to provide convincing answers to a current controversial environmental question involving local and inter-regional issues is demonstrated in a recent paper by Dixon *et al.* (2011).

Dixon *et al.*'s (2011) paper relates to a controversial government policy to buy back irrigation water rights from farmers in the Southern Murray—Darling Basin (SMDB). The Murray—Darling Basin covers a large part of south-east Australia containing the country's most significant agricultural area.[24] Over the past two decades there has been much concern about the ecological health of the SMDB river system. In the 1990s, a cap was placed on the amount of water available to irrigators and a system of tradeable water rights was introduced. Water quality and salinity problems remained, however, and in 2010, a plan to reduce the quantity of water rights was released. This led to vehement protests in the SMDB amid fears that entire communities in the area were under threat.

---

[23] Conrad and Heng compute congestion benefits within the CGE model, but most studies (normally contract research studies) impose time, fuel and repairs savings from external transport models, with the regional CGE model's task being to compute the real consumption benefits over the construction and operating years.

[24] The Basin covers about one-seventh of Australia (an area over 1.5 times the size of Texas). Three quarters of all farming output from the Murray-Darling Basin is produced in the SMDB.

Dixon *et al.* (2011) examined a buyback scheme being implemented by the federal government that would reduce water rights by almost a quarter. Their results indicated that the scheme would actually slightly increase economic activity in the SMDB. While the scheme would sharply increase the irrigation water price and greatly reduce the output of some irrigated agricultural activities, resources would largely move from these to other SMDB farm activities, leaving total farm output in the 13 regions that make up the SMDB with reductions ranging from just over 0.5% to less than 2.5% (on average a reduction of 1.3%). Furthermore, farmers as holders of water rights, would gain from the increase in the water price, thus leading to an increase in real consumption in 10 of the SMDB regions.

With such a set of simulation results in a political environment of strong protest against the proposal, it was clearly important to be able to explain to policy makers the reasons underlying them. Dixon *et al.* (2011) start by discussing the effects of the buyback scheme on the price of water as this is the key variable in understanding the effects of the scheme. The buyback occurs in the first eight years of the simulation period of 2009—2018, with an assumed yearly purchase by government of one-eighth of the permanent water rights to be withdrawn under the scheme. While the *baseline* price rises to over \$AUD80 per megaliter (Ml) by 2009, it falls with an assumed easing of the drought to less than \$AUD20/Ml by 2018. Under the buyback scheme, which started in 2009, the price still initially falls, although at a lesser rate, before starting to climb sharply in 2013, reaching around \$AUD110/Ml by 2018. A regression equation between the simulation price results for each year to 2018 and the proportionate reduction in irrigation water supply is then estimated (yielding an $R^2 = 0.99$).[25] The authors then point out that their result of a negligible effect of the scheme on GDP (0.0059% by 2018) is to be expected. A valuation of the lost contribution to GDP from the withdrawn water rights can be computed from the entire area under the demand curve for irrigation water (already estimated) between the new and old caps. In 2018 this is equal to \$AUD97 million, or 0.0052% of GDP, which closely corresponds to the simulation result.

Dixon *et al.* (2011) provide similar reasoning as to why the impact on aggregate farm output for the SMDB is so low. \$AUD97 million is 1.1% of SMDB farm output. The rest of the simulation result of −1.3 can be attributed to a small reduction in capital usage by the SMDB farm sector, particularly capital which can be used in the SMDB only by irrigated farms (e.g. vineyards). The authors also present farm industry output impacts for 2018 by the 13 regions within the SMDB. There are 17 industries producing 10 agricultural commodities. Three commodities are produced by an irrigated industry (Rice, Grapes and Vegetables); the other seven are produced by both an irrigated industry and by a dry-land farming industry (e.g. Cereal Dry and Cereal Irrigated). In

---

[25] The authors note that their implied demand elasticity values for irrigation water (ranging from −0.13 with a low price to −0.30 with a high price) are close to those of a recent econometric study.

general, as might be expected, irrigated industries are negatively impacted, in some cases very severely, while dry-land industries are positively affected. There are exceptions, however, with some irrigated industries being positively impacted in two regions and one irrigated industry, Vegetables, being positively impacted in all regions. Also, in only five of the 13 regions is the expectation met that the relative size of the impact on a region would correlate well with the size of the region's share of irrigated industries in their total farm output. The authors observe that there are superficial explanations that can be given for each of these results. For instance, they note (Dixon et al., 2011, p. 162) that with high water prices, vegetable farming is a better use of irrigable land and water than cultivating other crops such as rice. They are not satisfied, however, with such superficial answers and proceed to develop a proper understanding of their regional farm industry results.

We provide here a detailed summary of their investigation of their results. We do so because it provides an excellent example of how to unravel regional CGE results using a regression method. Dixon et al. (2011) commence their investigations by developing an equation that regresses the output impact on a particular farm industry in a particular region in a particular year against three indices of competitiveness. These indices are: (i) The SMDB's competitiveness in producing the industry's output, (ii) the competiveness of the region against other SMDB regions in producing the industry's output and (iii) the competitiveness of the industry against other producers of its output within the region (i.e. irrigated versus dry-land industries). These competitiveness indices are computed as relative effects of the schemes' impacts on regional industry costs. For any regional industry in any year the cost impact is initially assumed to be the percentage impact on the price of water multiplied by the regional industry's share of the value of irrigation water in its total costs.[26] The authors find that this equation provides quite a good explanation of output impacts with an $R^2$ of 0.76.

There were some regional industry results, however, for which the estimated equation was inadequate in providing an explanation. In Central Murray, Rice enjoys a positive impact while in other regions its impact is negative (though there is no inter-regional dissimilarity in irrigated water intensity) and the positive output impact for Vegetables is many times that for the industry in other regions. The explanation for this, the authors surmise, involves a collapse in the rental prices for irrigable land in Central Murray. Dixon et al. (2011, p. 163) say they would "expect increases in the price of irrigation water to cause relatively sharp reductions in rental prices of irrigable land in regions with two characteristics: (a) A high ratio for the value of irrigation water to irrigable land; and (b) limited options for using irrigable land in dry-land activities." They confirmed this surmise by regressing the percentage change in the rental price of

---

[26] The percentage impact on a variable is the percentage deviation between its policy forecast level and its base case (no buyback scheme) forecast level.

irrigable land in the region at time $t$ against the percentage impact on the price of water in the region at $t$ multiplied by shares representing these two characteristics and obtaining a very close fit ($R^2 = 0.95$). In particular, it explained why the average rental price in Central Murray fell so sharply, as it was very strong in both characteristics. Cost impacts were thus recomputed as equal to an appropriately weighted sum for the regional industry of the price of water *and* the rental price of land in the region. A re-estimation of the output to cost indices equation using the new cost impact estimates increases the equation fit ($R^2 = 0.80$) and more importantly finds simulated outputs for irrigated industries much closer to the new regression line.

Thus, by following their regression procedure for interpretation the authors are able to explain an important finding of their model: "In irrigation industries based on land with limited dry-land uses, land rents rather than outputs bear much of the damage from higher water prices" (Dixon et al., 2011, p. 164). The subdued contractions in these industries are afforded by the purchase of water from other regions where irrigable land can be more easily adapted for use in dry-land activities. The fact that their model recognizes that irrigable land can be used as dry land, explains a remaining anomaly with the updated regression — it is poor in explaining the output impact on dry-land industries in Central Murray. The authors note that movements on the rental rates on irrigable and dry land in a region should show a close correspondence. When cost impacts are adjusted to also include the rental price of dry land the regression of output on cost indices yields an $R^2$ of 0.89.

Finally, the authors explain their real regional consumption results in terms of water exports, including the sale of permanent water rights to the federal government. Water which could have been used to make $AUD97 million in annual value added is sold under the scheme to the federal government for a price generating $AUD173 million in annual income. The authors also examine the case where half of these gains are not spent in the SMDB due to some farmers deciding to leave the region after permanently selling their water rights. This reduced the real consumption gains from over 0.3% to less than 0.1%, but had virtually no effect on farm outputs which direct little of their sales to local consumer demands. There are unlikely to be severe equity problems say the authors, as the owners of water rights will experience a simultaneous increase in the price of this asset and a reduction in returns to their irrigable land.

Dixon et al. (2011, p. 154) state: "No knowledge of CGE modeling is required to understand our results: they are explained in terms of familiar economic mechanisms." The above summary clearly demonstrates just how successful the authors were in this task.[27] Their article is a clear demonstration of how the intricate regional CGE model mechanisms can be

---

[27] It is true that Dixon et al. (2011) do start by alerting their readers to the agricultural production technology used in their particular model. The key aspects of this technology have been revealed in our summary, again clearly demonstrating how CGE stories can be told in a convincing way to the non-CGE modeler. We summarize the details of the technology in Section 7.3.5.5.

drawn out in such a way that a transparent account of modeling results can be presented to economists unfamiliar with CGE. It should also be clear from our summary that the essence of the story is extractable in a way that could be understood by a general audience.

### 7.2.4 Forecasting and historical analyses

We complete this section by considering regional CGE modeling as a forecasting tool and as a vehicle for explaining regional economic performance. As with national models over recent years, dynamic regional CGE models have been applied to forecasting (e.g. Adams *et al.*, 2000; Giesecke and Madden, 2003) and historical analysis (Parmenter and Welsh, 2001; Giesecke, 2002, 2008). As with national CGE models, historical modeling performs a number of purposes, including the updating of databases, uncovering trends in unobservable variables (e.g. technological and taste changes) to provide information for forecasting simulations, and detecting the major reasons underlying past movements in macroeconomic variables. Uncovering why some regional economies perform better than others has been a major research activity of regional economists for a long time. Giesecke and Madden (2010) argue that historical CGE modeling provides an avenue for obtaining a much richer set of results than more traditional methods such as shift-share analysis. They undertake an historical modeling exercise for the Australian states for the eight years to 2003/04. They isolate the key driving factors for the economies of Australia's six states and two territories. An instance of their findings is that tariff reductions, blamed by a number of commentators for the relatively slow growth of South Australia and Victoria over the period, had little effect. Rather, the "Dutch Disease" phenomenon had a far more important role, as the import-competing industries, in which South Australia and Victoria are over-represented, suffered from real appreciation resulting from the expansion of foreign demand for goods produced by the export-oriented states.

### 7.3 SHORT REVIEW OF THE DEVELOPMENT OF REGIONAL CGE MODELS

### 7.3.1 Basic regional CGE model types

In relation to their purely regional aspect, there are three basic types of regional CGE models. They are:
 (i) Regional disaggregation attachment to national CGE models ("top-down" models).
 (ii) Multiregional models of the national economy ("bottom-up" models).
(iii) Stand-alone models of single subnational regions.

There are variants of these basic types as we shall see, such as hybrid (top-down models with bottom-up elements) and multiregional models of just a part of a nation (e.g. regions of a single city). We look at each of these regional model types, including variants in the next three sections.

## 7.3.2 Top-down models

The essence of a top-down approach (in the terminology of Klein and Glickman, 1977) is the sequential running of a model at the super-regional level to obtain economy-wide results and then feeding these results into a second model that decomposes the national results into a set of regional results. The first of the regional CGE models, ORANI-ORES (Dixon et al., 1978), was of this type.[28]

ORES (ORANI Regional Equation System) is based upon a method devised by Leontief et al. (1965) — commonly referred to as the LMPST method — for the frugal use of regional data in a multiregional input-output (MRIO) system. Central to the method is a division of industries into two groups: national and local. National industries produce only commodities that are inter-regionally tradable. Local industries produce commodities that can be traded only intra-regionally. Regional shares in aggregate output of national industries are assumed to stay constant and thus in ORES the percentage change in an industry's output in each region is simply equal to the industry's percentage change nationally (which is endogenous in ORANI, but effectively exogenous to ORES).[29] ORES determines the regional output of local industries via regional market-clearing equations for local commodities. Local demands involve intra-regional sales to producers, final demanders and margin services. Right-hand-side variables of this equation involve either constant regional shares (e.g. investment in national industries move by the same percentage in all regions) or variable shares computed so as to ensure aggregation of regional to national results.[30] An example of the latter is that investment in a local industry in region $r$ moves with investment in that local industry nationally and with the movement in the ratio of the industry's output in $r$ to the industry's output nationally. Similarly, regional consumption is driven by national consumption modified by movements in the ratio of the regional wage bill to the national wage bill; which in turn is a function of industry output. The regional balance equation thus captures regional multiplier effects. If a region is over-represented in strongly performing national industries — or under-represented in poorly performing ones — demand for local goods will be relatively stronger in that region.

Given an assumption of the same input-output technology in all regions, ORES' simple sourcing assumptions mean that very little regional data is required. ORES also has the advantage of having a simple theoretical structure, possessing attractive aggregation properties and incorporating two factors likely to be central to the determination of the distribution across regions of the effects of national economic shocks. These

---

[28] For a full description of ORANI and ORES, see Dixon et al. (1982).

[29] Note that, this is equivalent to the Leontief et al. (1965) assumption that all users of a national commodity, in every region, share the same geographical sourcing mix for that commodity (for details, see Dixon et al., 1982).

[30] For a full proof of ORES aggregation properties, see Dixon et al. (1982, pp. 277–283).

factors are: (i) Inter-regional differences in the industry composition of total regional output and (ii) intra-regional multiplier effects. ORES, however, has some obvious drawbacks: (i) There is no constraint on the mobility of capital across regions, (ii) there is no regional variation in any regional prices from those determined nationally in ORANI, (iii) the inter-regional pattern of a national industry's output is not responsive to any changes in the inter-regional pattern of demand, and (iv) the dichotomy between national and local industries may not be particularly realistic.

The first two drawbacks mean that the ORES decomposition is more appropriate to the long run than the short run. Even in the short run, however, problem (i) may be serious only for a few local industries which are highly capital intensive (particularly ownership of dwellings). Australian experience suggests that ORES works quite well in the case of national shocks. Parmenter and Welsh (2001, p. 209) note that the method "gives acceptable rankings of regional economic prospects but understates inter-regional differences."[31] One reason may be that problem (iv) is unlikely to be significant in the Australian context due to an aspect of Australian geography. Australia's principal population centers are generally a long way from state boundaries, and most commonly states have been the regions to which the method has been employed.

Problem (iv) can present more serious difficulties for disaggregating to substate regions, or even to the state level, for many other countries. Dixon *et al.* (2007) note the proximity in the US of many major cities to state borders across which virtually all commodities are traded. While practically none of the traditional local commodities (services and perishables) could be classified as local in the US, they find these commodities do not fit the national classification either. Advances in regional data estimation techniques that do not require a local–national dichotomy, however, meant that Dixon *et al.* (2007) were able to develop an updated top-down method that also dispensed with the national–local division. The new method is essentially a generalization of the original LMPST method. Its core idea is that equations for domestic demands can be specified in percentage change terms as follows:[32]

$$vR(r) = v + relR(r) - \sum_{g \in \text{REG}} SHRV(g) \times relR(g), \tag{7.1}$$

where $vR$ is a regional demand variable,[33] $v$ is the corresponding national variable (essentially exogenous to the regional decomposition), $relR$ is a regional variable

---

[31] Parmenter and Welsh find that they can improve their forecasts significantly by imposing information on regional macroeconomic aggregates and the regional distribution of output for national industries. They find satisfactory results are computed for local industries.

[32] All variables beginning with a lower case letter are in percentage changes.

[33] For example $vR$ might be the percentage change in the demand by industry $j$ in region $r$ for commodity $i$ from source $s$ (domestic or foreign import) for purpose $k$ (current production or capital formation).

(determined elsewhere in the top-down system) that is an appropriate variable for determining the difference between $vR$ and $v$, and $SHRV$ is region $g$'s share in the national level of $V$. Summing Equation (7.1) across regions gives:

$$\sum_{r \in \mathrm{REG}} SHRV(r) \times vR(r) = v. \tag{7.2}$$

Thus, we see from Equation (7.2) that the method produces regional results which aggregate to the national results.

Looking briefly at the major equations of the regional equation system described by Dixon *et al.* (2007), we note that the relevant variable for material demands for current and capital formation by industry $j$ in region $r$, is the output of the industry. The relevant variable for region $r$ household demands for each commodity from each source is the region's household disposable income. The relevant variable for export goods by region of exit is a shift variable which is normally exogenous, but could be shocked to alter regional shares in place of export. Government demands can be handled similarly. For margin demands to facilitate the flows of a good produced or landed in region $r$, the relevant variable is regional supplies of the good. Similarly, for margin demands on direct demand by region $r$ for a good (by users and exit ports), the relevant variable is the region's demand for that good. Region $r$'s aggregate demand for margin $m$ is a weighted aggregation of all demands for the margin for which region $r$ is responsible for organizing. Thus, Dixon *et al.* (2007) incorporate the idea that margins on the flow of a good from supplier to user can be supplied by more than one region. Disposable income movements vary regionally with regional employment differentials, which in turn are related to commodity supply differentials. Finally, the total supply of a commodity from a region (production or port of entry) is obtained by applying sourcing shares to all regional demands and summing all demands for the region of supply.

The new top-down theory could of course have been applied to a MRIO database computed by the LMPST method, but there would have been no advantage to this. We discuss details of methods for generating MRIOs in Section 7.5, in particular the "Horridge method" (Horridge *et al.*, 2005), which by generating sourcing shares as an intermediary step allows for the latest development in top-down modeling, as well as for advances in bottom–up modeling discussed in Section 7.3.2.

We discussed Dixon *et al.*'s (2007) first results with their new top-down method in Section 7.2.1, where the capabilities of the method for regionally decomposing national model results for economy-wide shocks were evident from the richness of their analysis of the effects of a tariff cuts on US regions. Giesecke (2008) similarly displays the advantages of employing the new top-down framework for historical CGE analysis.

Notwithstanding these capabilities for regionally distributing the effects of national shocks, the top-down method provides hardly any scope for modeling shocks emanating at the regional level.[34] A proper capacity for modeling region-specific shocks within a multiregional context requires a bottom-up model. Higgs *et al.* (1988) sought to avoid the cost of full-scale bottom-up modeling by introducing a hybrid method that incorporated some modeling of regional economic agents' behavior into the top-down method. This regional dimension was accomplished by redefining some industries as being region specific. In Higgs *et al.*'s model, ORANI-TAS, they focused on the island state of Tasmania, splitting certain industries into a Tasmanian component and an Australian mainland component. This allowed for a limited range of regional shocks (to variables associated with the regionally defined industries). Higgs *et al.*'s main motivation for improving on the top-down method was to lessen the ORES problem of constant regional shares in the output of national industries. Thus they regionally specified ORANI industries where the costs or sales shares of an industry differ substantially across regions. Thus, for instance, they split the Fruit industry for which Tasmania had a foreign export share of 60% compared to an 11% share in the mainland regions and a 66% labor cost share in value added compared to 42% on the mainland. As expected, these features make the Tasmanian Fruit industry much more responsive (3.5 times in fact) in Higgs *et al.*'s tariff-cut simulation. The recent developments in top-down modeling by Dixon *et al.* (2007) greatly lessen the value of the hybrid method as far as regional divergences in sales-share patterns are concerned.

The Higgs method may still have applications, particularly where the focus is on subregional areas within a bottom-up multiregional model — the class of models we are about to discuss next. Giesecke (1999) provides an example of this use of top-down modeling in decomposing Western Australian results from a two-region version of the FEDERAL model.[35] He employed the hybrid method by modeling key components of the Pilbara region within the Western Australian component of the bottom-up CGE model. Giesecke showed that explicit modeling of certain substate cost and sales differences were important to his results. While a budget-neutral removal of the fringe benefits tax was shown to have little impact at the national level, Giesecke projected a significant positive effect on the Western Australian economy and a very substantial positive impact on the Pilbara economy.[36]

---

[34] Madden *et al.* (1983) did model a set of regional demand-side shocks with ORANI-ORES by decomposing the shocks into (small) national-level shocks to ORANI and shocks to ORES shift variables that changed regional shares in national expenditures (by government). This approach, however, basically picked up only input-output mechanisms at the regional level and, in any event, could not handle supply-side shocks.

[35] The FEDERAL model is discussed in Section 7.3.3.

[36] The fringe benefits tax is an Australian federal government tax on employer-provided non-cash benefits. Fringe benefits (and the associated tax) make up a relatively high proportion of labor costs of certain industry sectors in the remote mining region of the Pilbara.

### 7.3.3 Bottom-up models

The advent of a bottom-up multiregional CGE model in the early 1980s allowed for the possibility of a large range of supply-side shocks to be imposed at the regional level. The first such model was by Liew (1981, 1984a, 1984b) who built a six-region model of Australia, MRSMAE (Multi-Regional Multi-Sectoral Model of Australian Economy). As it turned out Liew's only application with MRSMAE was for a national shock — tariff reform. A major motivation of Liew's was to compare bottom-up with top-down modeling. He found more pronounced gross output effects regionally, and nationally, with MRSMAE than ORANI-ORES, but the reverse for employment. He intimates, however, that the differences may not be of a size sufficient to justify the extra effort of bottom-up modeling; particularly when subject to the data limitations that restricted the richness of his regional modeling.

While Liew's model was experimental, the next few years saw the advent of bottom-up multiregional CGE models that were aimed at capturing detailed regional features that would allow them to simulate a wide-range of regional questions, particularly in the area of fiscal federalism. The first of these was the six-region six-commodity model of Canada by Whalley and Trela (1986), which incorporated both regional and federal governments (each taxing and spending) plus inter-governmental transfers. A key feature was the model's handling of imperfect labor mobility across regions (which we report on in detail in Section 7.3.5.1). Whalley and Trela reported a range of simulations of national and regional reform policies and changes in fiscal federalism arrangements, although they reported only briefly on each of them. Further applications are reported in Jones and Whalley (1988 and 1989). Whalley and Trela (1986) also noted that they had constructed a 13-commodity version of their model, plus variants which treated: transport margins, returns to scale and a pure public good.

In order to realize his pioneering bottom-up model, Liew had reverted to treating margin sales as direct sales in his implemented version of MRSMAE. He also linked regional income to only wage income, treated commodity demands from a single government buyer as exogenous and did not allow for technical or taste changes.

An explicit treatment of transport as a supplier of margins is seen as being a highly desirable property for regional CGE models (Isard *et al.*, 1998). At the start of the 1990s a number of bottom-up CGE models (Madden, 1990; Buckley, 1992; Wigle, 1992) appeared that incorporated a detailed treatment of margins facilitating the delivery of goods. The latter two authors developed multiregional CGE models with a specific transport focus. Buckley's five-sector model, which covered three regions of the US, had similarities with the Jones and Whalley (1989) six-region Canadian model, with the particular inclusion of transport and wholesale margin services on direct flows being supplied by the origin and destination regions respectively.[37] Wigle aimed to capture a spatial dimension by introducing transport margins into his seven-region (six Canadian and the US) 13-commodity model. As his focus was on the importance of transport costs in trade restrictions, he kept the rest of his model simple, with goods being produced by a single technology and output distributed according to a regional production possibility frontier.

The third model to incorporate explicit modeling of margins was the FEDERAL model (Madden, 1990).[38] FEDERAL provided an early example of detailed general-purpose bottom-up multiregional modeling. Like MRSMAE, the starting point for FEDERAL's theory was the ORANI model, but unlike Liew, Madden retained all of ORANI's features, developing them into their full multiregional complexity, and then added a very detailed treatment of regional household income and a full treatment of two tiers of government.

A primary example of the multiregional complexity of FEDERAL is its handling of margins which could be supplied by both origin and destination regions on inter-regional trade. Similarly, it separately models commodity taxes levied by the federal government and each regional government (provided the good originates from or is sold in their region) with the rate varying according to the type of commodity, source of supply and class of purchaser. Detailed modeling of expenditures and revenue-raising by all governments (including intergovernmental transfers) is accompanied by a set of income and outlay accounts. These features allowed for detailed modeling of fiscal federalism and regional policy issues (e.g. Madden, 1989, 1993; Dixon et al., 1993; Giesecke and Madden, 1997). A key feature of FEDERAL is its treatment of real disposable income that was probably the most detailed for a CGE model at that time. For each regional household, it is calculated as the sum of all factor incomes earned by residents from all regions, plus all transfer income (such as unemployment benefits and interest receipts) less all direct taxes (such as income taxes, land taxes and fines) and interest payments.[39] Madden (1996) demonstrates that inter-regional variations in the extent of local ownership and the degree of reliance on social security payments can play a significant role in regional short-run results. A number of later variants of FEDERAL were constructed during the 1990s, by far the most important of which was a dynamic version, FEDERAL-F, constructed by Giesecke (2002, 2003). FEDERAL-F contains all

---

[37] While the six-region Canadian model was reported first in Whalley and Trela (1986), it is often cited in the literature as the Jones and Whalley model.

[38] FEDERAL was initially entitled TASMAIN and its theoretical structure was first outlined in Madden (1987).

[39] An aspect of FEDERAL worth noting is its treatment of investment. It incorporates a multiregional version of the ORANI investment theory, with all domestic and foreign investors allocating investment across regional industries in order to equate expected rates of return. This contrasts with the Whalley and Trela model, which does not treat investment behavior. Madden (1989) showed this distinction can be particularly important in short-run simulations of regional taxes that fall on fixed capital. As we show in Section 7.6, it is also important in correctly modeling short-run regional aggregate demand responses for a more general range of shocks.

the features required for detailed forecasting and historical, as well as policy, analysis and we discuss this in Section 7.3.5.2.

Due to computing restrictions in the late 1980s, and the increase in dimensions required to allow for margins to be supplied, and commodity taxes to be imposed, by both origin and destination regions, Madden (1990) kept his model to a two-region implementation — a region of focus (initially Tasmania) and the rest of the country — and initially kept the number of industries to nine.[40] A desire to overcome these restrictions led to the construction of an eight-region model of Australia with minimal dynamics, MMRF (Naqvi and Peter, 1996). MMRF again was fashioned on the ORANI model, and overcame the dimensionality problem from the larger number of regions by assuming margins to be supplied only by destination regions and (in the initial version) by not distinguishing governments in the imposition of indirect taxes (tax revenues being assigned to their respective government by a decomposition on the basis of base-year shares). MMRF has become the workhorse model for Australian CGE modeling, having been used in hundreds of applications over almost two decades. It too has been converted to a recursive dynamic model (Adams et al., 2000) and has been subject to continuous development, including the incorporation of extensive greenhouse gas accounting and climate change policy features, disaggregated treatment of the transport sector (including a private motor vehicle industry), and government and income modeling along similar lines to FEDERAL.[41] Multiregional CGE models for other countries, notably the B-MARIA (Haddad, 1999) model of Brazil, have used the MMRF code.

While a large-scale general purpose multiregional CGE model like MMRF provides a powerful tool for analyzing a very wide range of regional economic issues for a model containing a moderate number of regions (like the eight regions of Australia in the standard MMRF model), it suffers from problems of dimensionality when bottom-up modeling is required for a large number of regions. In order to overcome this problem Horridge et al. (2005) adopted an approach commonly used in multicountry modeling to develop TERM (The Enormous Regional Model). This involves different classes of agents being assumed to be identical in certain aspects of their technology or tastes. Horridge et al. assume that all agents in any region r source their inter-regional imports from the other regions in identical proportions.[42] This assumption allows for inter-regional sourcing and associated margins data to be stored in satellite accounts. The authors demonstrate TERM's capacity for modeling many (45) regions and many (38) sectors in an application on the effects of the

---

[40] Later versions of FEDERAL focused on other Australian states (or in the case of Dixon et al., 1990, an aggregation of two states) and featured a substantial number of industries (over 100 in the Western Australian version).

[41] As a consequence of its extensive greenhouse gas features, the dynamic version of MMRF is sometimes referred to as MMRF-GREEN. See Adams and Parmenter in Chapter 9 of this Handbook for a review of greenhouse modeling with MMRF. For detailed documentation of MMRF, see Adams, et al. (2010).

[42] This assumption carries virtually no penalty, since it is likely that in most cases there is little information on how a region's economic agents might differ in their sourcing patterns.

2002–2003 Australian drought, which had variable rainfall impacts across the country. In order to further increase the capacity of TERM to include very small regions in their multiregional structure for particular applications, Wittwer and Horridge (2010) construct a massive database for many small regions from census data, and introduce a variable aggregation facility for regions, industries and commodities.

A feature of TERM is that its use of satellite accounts reduces the dimensions of the margins matrix sufficiently to allow for margins to be imposed at origin (place of manufacture or port of entry), destination (place of use or port of exit) and by any region along the transport route. TERM has opened up a new scope of multiregional CGE modeling of individual nations. Versions have now been created for Brazil, China, Finland, Indonesia, Japan, Poland and South Africa.

Bottom-up multiregional models have become the most common general purpose type in regional CGE analysis. Outside the Australian and Brazilian general purpose multiregional CGE models, AMOSRUK — a CGE model of Scotland and the rest of the UK (McGregor et al., 1999; Gillespie et al., 2002b) — is one of the best known. We will look at a further group of multiregional CGE models in Section 7.3.5.4 relating to transport and land use.

## 7.3.4 Single-region models

A substantial number of regional CGE models have been of just one region (almost half the regional CGE models listed in Partridge and Rickman (1998) fall into this category). This would seem a very reasonable approach for models designed for specific purposes, particularly when the region is quite small — such as Churchill County, Nevada (Seung et al., 2000) or Fort Collins, Colorado (Schwarm and Cutler, 2006). It is true that once an input-output table is available for the region in question, a two-region database for the nation can be computed by a residual method (Madden, 1990), but this is likely to be an unnecessary time-consuming task for many regional CGE model applications. It is also true that single-region general-purpose CGE models can be very successful. The best known of such single-region models is the AMOS model of Scotland (Harrigan et al., 1991), which has been used continuously for the past two decades.[43]

Lofgren and Robinson (2002) express a concern that subnational single-region models "may generate misleading results since they do not allow for inter-regional and nation-region feedbacks." Experience has shown, however, that for regional economies of 10%, or even more, of the nation's output, such feedback effects are not of a large order of magnitude. For instance, McGregor et al. (1999) find the same basic results for

---

[43] A characteristic of successful single-region models is that they properly treat net migration to (or from) the region. Such migration modeling has always been a feature of the AMOS model. Inter-regional population movement is particularly important for small-region models. Examples of small-region CGE models are Seung et al. (2000) who treat inter-regional migration, and Schwarm and Cutler (2006) who also account for commuting.

Scotland for long-run simulations with AMOSRUK, as they did with AMOS (McGregor *et al.*, 1996a). In essence, they find with both models that the own-region effects of a regional demand shock in a CGE model converge on an input–output result in the long run where virtually all factors are inter-regionally mobile. The point of their 1999 paper, however, is that for the other region (rest of UK), the long-run result is nothing like an input–output result, being completely opposite in sign. This points to a potential problem with single-region models in a policy context. By concentrating on the effects on a single region resulting from, say, regional development policies that are not self-funded within the region, negative effects on other regions are ignored. This can give rise to misleading perceptions and it is important that researchers using single-region CGE models bring attention to any such qualification of their results.

## 7.3.5 Developments in incorporating key regional features

### 7.3.5.1 Regional labor markets and inter-regional migration

Regional and multiregional models have taken a variety of approaches to the treatment of inter-regional migration. A substantial number of regional CGE models assume that labor is immobile across regions, particularly single-region models (e.g. Despotakis and Fisher, 1988). This assumption is more likely to be the case when the study is just for the short run (e.g. Li and Rose, 1995). Other studies take the opposite long-run approach and allow for endogenous inter-regional migration to equalize wages (e.g. Morgan *et al.*, 1989) or utility (e.g. Groenewold *et al.*, 2003). Many other regional CGE models, however, allow for *imperfect* inter-regional labor mobility.

Whalley and Trela (1986) were the first to incorporate imperfect inter-regional labor mobility into a regional CGE model.[44] Their migration theory was developed from their observation that individuals have "direct associations with specific regions" (p. 74). They assume that there is a distribution of individuals within each region who differ only by their intensity of preference for remaining in the region. In making decisions about migration, individuals compare the utility they would receive from residing in each of the regions. The marginal individual (i.e. the individual indifferent to migrating or remaining) is assumed to treat utility as just coming from income and (as they are the marginal individual) the income receivable is the same for each region of residence.[45] All other individuals face a utility penalty from relocating, with the penalty increasing with the intensity of their location preference. If out-of-region income were to increase following some shock, out-migration would occur — until for the *new* marginal individual, home region income would just equal the income they could receive outside the region less the location penalty from shifting. That is, individuals tradeoff the extra

---

[44] A description detailing the model's migration theory can also be found in Jones and Whalley (1989).

[45] "Income" is the sum of real incomes from labor, natural resource taxes and federal government transfers to the region.

income they would receive by migrating against the loss from leaving their preferred location. Thus, in the new equilibrium inter-regional wage differentials are consistent with zero migration.

The responsiveness of inter-regional migration to inter-regional income differentials depends on the parameterization of location preferences. Jones and Whalley (1989, p. 386) point to difficulties in setting the value of this parameter to be consistent with econometrically estimated elasticities of out-migration. Other modelers use equations directly employing econometrically estimated parameters for net migration (e.g. Rickman, 1992; McGregor *et al.*, 1995, 1996b; Fry *et al.*, 1999; Rutherford and Törmä, 2010).[46] McGregor *et al.* model net migration to equalize a function of inter-regional differences in unemployment, wage rates and regional amenities, with gradual adjustment of regional wage rates to return populations to equilibrium (i.e. a zero net migration rate).[47]

In Section 7.4.11 we develop an alternative treatment of inter-regional migration. As with McGregor *et al.*, persons decide on the region they will reside in on the basis of differentials in wage and employment rates and amenities. Shocks to these differentials cause a disequilibrium in gross regional migration rates according to a logistic curve. Migration occurs until the disparities in real regional wage relativities reach a new equilibrium. The advantage of this approach is that it allows gross migration flows to be tracked. The latter is useful in keeping account of movements in regional ownership of capital and land.

Regional CGE models use a variety of regional wage setting alternatives. A feature of the AMOS model is the range of alternative labor-market closures that can be used (Harrigan *et al.*, 1991). In countries where national wage-setting institutions exist, it has often been assumed that wages are set at the national level.[48] Models with an imperfect inter-regional migration theory often incorporate some type of regional wage-bargaining mechanism. For instance, Ferguson *et al.* (2007) employs a standard econometrically estimated regional bargaining equation for AMOS. In Section 7.4.10.1 we present an alternative wage equation that returns the regional employment rate to its base case path after a number of years.

### 7.3.5.2 Dynamics

Most regional CGE models have been comparative static, but as with their national counterparts, there has been a move in regional CGE models towards a dynamic

---

[46] Berck *et al.* (1997) allow the regional working population to be affected by both migration and the participation rate, which in turn is a function of real after-tax wages.

[47] McGregor *et al.* (1996b) simulate an improvement in amenities in Scotland and find that while population, employment and output in the region are positively affected, the Scottish employment market is adversely affected. Depending on the labor market closure employed there is a fall in the real consumer wage rate and/or an increase in the unemployment rate. That is, the inducement to migrate to Scotland by the higher amenities is eventually completely offset by the region's weaker labor market, thus re-establishing a zero net migration rate.

[48] See, e.g. Madden (1993). In Australia, it is now less common to assume national wage settings as the central wage system has been very much weakened.

specification. Examples are the AMOS model (see, e.g. McGregor *et al.*, 1996) and the multiregional model of Korea by Kim and Kim (2003). In general, such models assume a base case of a steady-state growth path (e.g. Seung and Kraybill, 1999). On the other hand, the dynamics in FEDERAL and MMRF have been fashioned on the MONASH model, and therefore can be run under historical, decomposition, forecast and policy closures. These closures are discussed in Dixon *et al.* in Chapter 2 of this Handbook in this volume and thus we do not discuss them here, except to point out the advantages of this approach in: producing regional forecasts (Adams *et al.*, 2000), identifying regional adjustment issues (Giesecke and Madden, 2007) and allowing for the effects of underlying movements in the database (Dixon and Rimmer, 1999).

### 7.3.5.3 Government and intergovernmental finances

A detailed treatment of national and regional government expenditures and revenues, and intergovernmental financial transfers is usually incorporated into large-scale general-purpose multiregional models. These features are not only useful for considering fiscal federal issues and regional government fiscal policies, but also enable applications on a wide range of shocks to report impacts on regional budgets — a factor usually of quite some interest to regional policy makers. Models explicitly set up for revenue analysis are likely to contain significant regional tax details. The DRAM model (Berck *et al.*, 1996), for instance, contains separate modeling of state and local governments. They also capture a feature of the US economy that regional taxes affect federal tax liabilities. For countries with fiscal equalization arrangements, some models explicitly incorporate central-regional grant distribution formulae (e.g. Whalley and Trela, 1986).

Special-purpose regional CGE models have been constructed to introduce innovations in modeling fiscal federalism. For instance, Groenewold *et al.* (2003) constructed a small experimental model that merged a CGE component with a political-economy component that contained competitive regional governments which solve an optimization problem subject to the CGE results. In Section 7.3.2 we discussed the Dixon *et al.* (2002, 2005) simulation of changes in fiscal equalization arrangements. They constructed the CSF (Commonwealth-State Funding) model aimed at including those things important to modeling the efficiency effects of the allocation of central government grants to regional governments. CSF included: optimizing state governments that incorporated a flypaper effect in their social welfare function; a labor—leisure tradeoff; mineral resource rents; and congestion in intra-regional travel.

### 7.3.5.4 Transport, land use and agglomeration

One of the main areas of developments in regional CGE models in recent years has related to the issues of transport and agglomeration. A driving force for this has been the advent of the new economic geography (Krugman, 1991). There have now been a considerable number of multiregional CGE models constructed that incorporate agglomeration economies — essentially external economies of scale related to regional economic size and spatial compactness. The most prevalent approach to capturing agglomeration economies is by incorporating in the regional CGE model the well-known Dixit–Stiglitz specification of monopolistic completion.[49] Prominent papers are by Kilkenny (1998, 1999) and Bröcker (2001, 2002). Kilkenny (1998), for example, employs her model to show a non-monotonic relationship between relative transport costs (agriculture to non-farm transport) and the rural share of the US national workforce. The result is consistent with long-term rural–urban trends — the reduction in non-farm products transport costs gradually eroded local natural protection for manufacturing in rural areas, but as these transport costs fell further, along with the rural–urban wage rate ratio, it became profitable for certain activities such as mail-order retailers to move to cheap labor rural locations.

The above models used, like Krugman, the "iceberg" transport assumption. The RAEM model of the Netherlands (Thissen, 2005), however, incorporates a transport industry that supplies freight margins. RAEM models both commuting and migration in the computation of regional labor supply. Regional labor market behavior is based on search theory, with the outcome generating the matrix of commuting. In medium-run analysis there is limited migration, but in the long run migration acts to equalize utility across regions. Utility is a constant elasticity of substitution (CES) combination of consumption utility (itself a Stone–Geary function of non-transport consumption) and amenities utility. The latter is dependent on the ratio of a given amount of housing stock to resident population. Agglomeration economies are captured via a Dixit–Stiglitz CES aggregation of varieties of each intermediate input from regional sources.[50] Transport costs for freight, commuting and shopping, however, are computed in a separate transport model that takes into account all transport infrastructure and transport logistics.[51]

An alternative to using the Dixit–Stiglitz approach is to capture agglomeration economies through the use of an accessibility approach (Kim *et al.*, 2004; Haddad and Hewings, 2005; Madden and Gwee, 2010). Kim *et al.*, and Madden and Gwee both use a separate transport model to compute accessibility indices.[52] An improvement/

---

[49] For reviews of this class of regional CGE models, see Bröcker (2004) and Donaghy (2007).

[50] Similarly, the regional consumers' utility function allows for a love of variety.

[51] Thissen (2005) notes that shopping costs are generally non-monetary costs. He observes that, while often ignored in models treating monopolistic competition, shopping costs "are definitely not negligible in the case of services" (p. 69).

[52] There are various definitions of accessibility indices characterizing economic agglomeration. A typical index for any region $j$ is computed as the aggregation across all regions in some wider area encompassing $j$ of their regional economic size discounted by their effective travel distance from $j$. Common measures used for regional economic size are income, population and employment. Effective travel distance takes into account the cost of travel, including time.

deterioration in accessibility drives an improvement/deterioration in productivity in their multiregional CGE models.[53] Kim *et al.* (2004) found that the Korean Highway projects examined increased both economic activity and regional welfare.[54] Madden and Gwee (2010) found that the regional economic effects of the change in accessible workforce induced by a transport infrastructure shock are swamped by the conventional labor-market effects resulting from the shock.[55]

While the RAEM model takes regional housing stocks as given, Horridge (1994) constructed a model of the city of Melbourne, Australia, which explicitly models two types of residential land (houses and apartments), industrial land and other land. In Horridge's model workers decide according to a logit model where to work, where to live and the plot size of the land they reside on. Utility for each person in income class $s$ working in region $w$, residing in region $h$ on plot size $r$ is obtained from the consumption of land services and other goods. Disposable income for each person is comprised of wage income, rental and redistributed tax income less commuting transport costs. Thus a person's work location determines income before transport costs. Their choice of region of residence and plot size implies their spending on transport and land, with remaining income being available for spending on other goods. Alternative closures specify the degree to which land can be swapped between alternative uses in each of nine residential zones.

CGE models of cities, or commuting regions (e.g. the 44 regions of the Netherlands modeled in RAEM), tend to be specific to certain areas of applications (such as transport economic questions), rather than being general-purpose models. For instance, Horridge's model is for regions within one city, excludes freight costs and trade external to Melbourne. However, his model has proved powerful in uncovering the likely effects of policies designed to reduce transport costs and urban sprawl. For instance, Horridge (1994) found that taxes on travel tend to be successful as they create an incentive to work and live in the same, or geographically, close regions. He also simulated urban consolidation (an increase in apartments compared with houses) and found it led to a more compact city, but had little effect in reducing transport use.[56]

---

[53] For instance, Madden and Gwee (2010) adopt elasticities of productivity to agglomeration estimated by Graham (2007) for the UK, to compute the productivity loss from commuter congestion.

[54] In a subsequent regional CGE study of the Korean transport network, Kim and Hewings (2009) found synergy effects from a set of highway infrastructure developments across the network.

[55] Madden and Gwee (2010) use a five-region variant of the TERM model, featuring three regions in the city of Melbourne which are subject to the infrastructure shock.

[56] The reason for the smallness of the effect on transport use (and associated energy use) was partly due to geometry; travel distances do not fall at the same rate as city area. The other reason arose from the substantially lower rent payments resulting from the policy. Lower expenditure on land leaves more income for expenditure on transport, which while not directly entering utility, increases options for work and residential locations.

### 7.3.5.5 Other innovations

We look at just a further two innovations here. One is the embedding of specific-purpose modules within general-purpose regional CGE models. Examples are the inclusion of travel modules to incorporate congestions, such as in the CSF model discussed in Section 7.3.5.3 and Conrad and Heng's (2002) model referred to in Section 7.2.3. Another example is the model used by Dixon et al. (2011) to analyze a scheme to buyback water rights from farmers in the SMDB of Australia; a simulation discussed in detail in Section 7.2.3. They used a variant of the TERM model (TERM-H$_2$O). The features of this model are alluded to in our explanation of their results. In essence, their TERM-H$_2$O involved a detailed modeling of agricultural inputs. This chiefly involved a specification of each regional farm industry's production function in a way that captured the essential features of farmers' input choices. Labor was split into hired labor and farm owner-operators, and capital into specific farm capital and general capital. At the top level, primary factors is a CES aggregation of land and operator, general capital and hired labor. Land and operator is a CES aggregation of specific capital (e.g. orchards), operator labor and total land, itself a CES combination of effective land and cereal (i.e. feed for livestock). Effective land is made up of a CES combination of dry land, irrigated land and unwatered irrigable land. In turn, irrigated land is a Leontief combination of unwatered irrigable land and water. Unwatered irrigable land is allocated to an irrigated use or a dryland (i.e. unwatered) alternative according to a CET function. Water and cereal are interregionally tradable. It will be clear from our earlier discussion that the introduction of this specification of farm production is sufficient to generate a very policy-relevant set of results that meet the essential realities of farm production.

The other innovation is a top-down linkage of two CGE models — a national CGE model, MONASH, and a multiregional one, MMRF. In practice, regional CGE modelers in responding to requests from industry and government to provide policy analyses with short deadlines are at times torn between alternative models, each appropriate to aspects of the question, but no model covering all aspects. Dixon et al. (2010) were asked by the Australian government to model a proposed wage increase to Australian workers covered by federal awards and to provide detailed regional results. MONASH contained detailed modeling of labor demand and supply by award and non-award workers, but lacked the required regional dimension (top-down being inappropriate for awards that fell unevenly across states). The authors ran the models in sequence, using MONASH to compute the degree of pass-through of award wage changes to non-award wage rates. MMRF was then shocked with a set of industry by state wage rate changes, which combined award wage rate shocks together with the non-award wage rate results from MONASH, according to state-specific shares. The models were kept compatible by imposing national macroeconomic results from MONASH on MMRF.

## 7.4 A MODERN MULTIREGIONAL CGE MODEL

We now turn to look at the features of a bottom–up multiregional CGE model in more detail. In doing so, we describe the major components that comprise a typical modern multiregional CGE model. We build our explanation around a fully-dimensioned MRIO database and ancillary regional accounts, as depicted in Figures 7.1 and 7.2. The MRIO database is a helpful framework around which to discuss the structure of a multiregional CGE model. One way of conceiving of such a model is as a set of equations sufficient to describe the value flows of the MRIO database. To facilitate our use of the MRIO database to describe the equations of a multiregional CGE model, we identify in Figure 7.1 the price, quantity and tax variables underlying each value flow. These variables are described in Table 7.1. In Sections 7.4.1–7.4.13 below, we describe the decisions that builders of multiregional CGE models have made in modeling the individual variables identified in Figures 7.1 and 7.2. As we do so, we also point out specific features of the version of the dynamic multiregional CGE model, MMRF, that we use in Section 7.6 to illustrate the use of BOTE methods to describe simulation results.

### 7.4.1 Demand for inputs to current production

Examining the first column of Figure 7.1 (in conjunction with the variable descriptions in Table 7.1), we find region-specific industries requiring intermediate inputs $\left(X_{(i,s)}^{(1)(j,r)}\right)$, labor $\left(X_{(o,h,s)}^{(1)(L)(j,r)}\right)$, capital $\left(X_{(h,s)}^{(1)(K)(j,r)}\right)$ and natural resources $\left(X_{(h,s)(t)}^{(1)(N)(j,r)}\right)$ as inputs to current production. Use of these inputs generates output, or in a multiproduction model, a generalized capacity to produce output, which we describe in Figure 7.1 by $Z_{(j,r)}^{(1)}$.

The large number of inputs to any regional industry $(j,r)$'s output described in Figure 7.1 by $X_{(i,s)}^{(1)(j,r)}$, $X_{(o,h,s)}^{(1)(L)(j,r)}$, $X_{(h,s)}^{(1)(K)(j,r)}$ and $X_{(h,s)(t)}^{(1)(N)(j,r)}$ potentially introduces a very large number of substitution elasticities for which the modeler must obtain independent econometric estimates. In practice, this task is normally simplified by assuming that industries face nested production functions. Generally, the top-level of the production nests is Leontief, or fixed proportions. Thus in MMRF, which we employ in Section 7.6, industry $(j,r)$ uses effective inputs of intermediate inputs undifferentiated by source $\left(X_{(i,\cdot)}^{(1)(j,r)}\right)$ and effective inputs of primary factors undifferentiated by factor type and factor ownership $\left(X_{(\cdot)}^{(1)(\cdot)(j,r)}\right)$ in fixed proportions to produce a given level of activity $\left(Z_{(j,r)}^{(1)}\right)$.

| | Flow type | Size | (1) Producers $J \times R$ | (2) Investors $J \times R$ | (3) Household $H \times R$ | (4) Export $1$ | (5) Government $G$ |
|---|---|---|---|---|---|---|---|
| (1) | Basic flows | $I \times S$ | $BAS1_{(i,s)}^{(j,r)} =$ $P_{(i,s)}^{(0)} \cdot X_{(i,s)(j,r)}^{(1)}$ | $BAS2_{(i,s)}^{(j,r)} =$ $P_{(i,s)}^{(0)} \cdot X_{(i,s)}^{(2)(j,r)}$ | $BAS3_{(i,s)}^{(h,r)} =$ $P_{(i,s)}^{(0)} \cdot X_{(i,s)}^{(3)(h,r)}$ | $BAS4_{(i)}^{(r)} = P_{(i,r)}^{(0)} \cdot X_{(i)}^{(4)(r)}$ | $BAS5_{(i,s)}^{(g,r)} = P_{(i,s)}^{(0)} \cdot X_{(i,s)}^{(5)(g,r)}$ |
| (2) | Margins | $I \times S \times M \times R$ | $MAR1_{(i,s)(m,k)}^{(j,r)} = P_{(m,k)}^{(0)} \cdot X_{(i,s)(j,r)(m,k)}^{(1)}$ | $MAR2_{(i,s)(m,k)}^{(j,r)} =$ $P_{(m,k)}^{(0)} \cdot X_{(i,s)(j,r)(m,k)}^{(2)}$ | $MAR3_{(i,s)(m,k)}^{(h,r)} =$ $P_{(m,k)}^{(0)} \cdot X_{(i,s)(h,r)(m,k)}^{(3)}$ | $MAR4_{(i)(m,k)}^{(r)} =$ $P_{(m,k)}^{(0)} \cdot X_{(i)(r)(m,k)}^{(4)}$ | $MAR5_{(i,s)(m,k)}^{(g,r)} =$ $P_{(m,k)}^{(0)} \cdot X_{(i,s)(g,r)(m,k)}^{(5)}$ |
| (3) | Commodity taxes | $I \times S \times G \times R$ | $TAX1_{(i,s)}^{(j,r)} =$ $P_{(i,s)}^{(0)} \cdot X_{(i,s)}^{(1)(j,r)} \cdot T_{(i,s)(g)}^{(1)}$ | $TAX2_{(i,s)}^{(j,r)} =$ $P_{(i,s)}^{(0)} \cdot X_{(i,s)}^{(2)(j,r)} \cdot T_{(i,s)(g)}^{(2)}$ | $TAX3_{(i,s)}^{(h,r)} =$ $P_{(i,s)}^{(0)} \cdot X_{(i,s)}^{(3)(h,r)} \cdot T_{(i,s)(g)}^{(3)}$ | $TAX4_{(i)}^{(r)} =$ $P_{(i,r)}^{(0)} \cdot X_{(i)}^{(4)(r)} \cdot T_{(i)(g)}^{(4)}$ | $TAX5_{(i,s)}^{(g,r)} =$ $P_{(i,s)}^{(0)} \cdot X_{(i,s)}^{(5)(g,r)} \cdot T_{(i,s)(g)}^{(5)}$ |
| (4) | Labor | $O \times H \times R$ | $LABR_{(o,h,k)}^{(j,r)} =$ $W_{(o)}^{(0)} \cdot X_{(o)}^{(1)L(j,r)}$ | | | | |
| (5) | Labor taxes | $O \times H \times R \times G$ | $LABT_{(o,h,k)(g)}^{(j,r)} =$ $W_{(o)}^{(j,r)} \cdot X_{(o)}^{(1)L(j,r)} \cdot T_{(o,h,k)(g)}^{(1)L(j,r)}$ | | | | |
| (6) | Capital | $H \times S$ | $CAPR_{(h,s)}^{(j,r)} =$ $R^{(K)(j,r)} \cdot X_{(h,s)}^{(1)K(j,r)}$ | | | | |
| (7) | Capital taxes | $G \times H \times S$ | $CAPT_{(h,s)}^{(j,r)} =$ $R^{(K)(j,r)} \cdot X_{(h,s)}^{(1)K(j,r)} \cdot T_{(s)(g)}^{(1)K(j,r)}$ | | | | |
| (8) | Natural resources | $H \times S \times T$ | $NATR_{(h,s)}^{(j,r)} =$ $R_{(t)}^{(N)(j,r)} \cdot X_{(h,s)(t)}^{(1)N(j,r)}$ | | | | |
| (9) | Natural resource taxes | $G \times H \times S \times T$ | $NATT_{(h,s)}^{(j,r)} =$ $R_{(t)}^{(N)(j,r)} \cdot X_{(h,s)(t)}^{(1)N(j,r)} \cdot T_{(s)(g)}^{(1)N(j,r)}$ | | | | |
| (10) | Production taxes | $G$ | $PTAX_{(g)}^{(1)(j,r)} =$ $P_{(j,r)}^{(1)} \cdot Z_{(j,r)}^{(1)} \cdot T_{(j,r)(g)}^{(1)}$ | $PTAX_{(g)}^{(2)(j,r)} =$ $P_{(j,r)}^{(2)} \cdot Z_{(j,r)}^{(2)} \cdot T_{(j,r)(g)}^{(2)}$ | | | |

**Commodities**

| | Export | Government |
|---|---|---|
| Trade taxes | — | $TARF_{(i,imp)}^{(fed)} =$ $P_{(i,imp)}^{(0)} \cdot X_{(i,imp)}^{(fed)} \cdot T_{(i,imp)}^{(fed)}$ |

**Multi-production**

| Regional commodities | Regional industries |
|---|---|
| | $MAKE_{(i,r)}^{(i)} =$ $P_{(i,r)}^{(0)} \cdot X_{(i,r)}^{(0)(i)}$ |

**Figure 7.1** MRIO database and associated price, quantity and value variables.

| | | | |
|---|---|---|---|
| (A) | Household net interest on foreign debt | H × R | $HINT^{(h,r)}$ |
| (B) | Foreign net transfers to the private sector | H × R | $FTRN^{(h,r)}$ |
| (C) | Government transfer payments | G × H R | $GTRN^{(h,r)}_{(g)}$ |
| (D) | Private inter-regional transfers | H × R H × R | $HTRN^{(h,r)}_{(t,k)}$ |
| (E) | Inter-governmental grants | G × G | $GRNT^{(k)}_{(g)}$ |
| (F) | Household direct tax | G × H × R | $HTAX^{(h,r)}_{(g)}$ |
| (G) | Government net interest on foreign debt | G | $GINT_{(g)}$ |
| (H) | Foreign net transfers to the public sector | G | $FTRN_{(g)}$ |

*Set definitions*

*J: Set of all industries.*
*R: Set of all domestic regions.*
*I: Set of all commodities.*
*S: Set of all regions, namely, all domestic regions and foreign. Hence, S = R + 1.*
*M: Set of all margin commodities. Note that M is a subset of I.*
*G: Set of all regional governments and the federal government.*
*O: Set of all occupations.*
*T: Set of all natural resource types.*
*H: Set of all households.*

**Figure 7.2** Ancillary income and expenditure accounts.

**Table 7.1** Variable descriptions for Figures 7.1 and 7.2

| Variable | Description |
|---|---|
| $\mathrm{BAS1}^{(j,r)}_{(i,s)}$ | The value, at basic prices, of commodity $i$ from source $s$ used by industry $j$ in region $r$ for input to current production |
| $\mathrm{BAS2}^{(j,r)}_{(i,s)}$ | The value, at basic prices, of commodity $i$ from source $s$ used by industry $j$ in region $r$ for input to gross fixed capital formation |
| $\mathrm{BAS3}^{(h,r)}_{(i,s)}$ | The value, at basic prices, of commodity $i$ from source $s$ used by household $h$ in region $r$ for current consumption purposes |
| $\mathrm{BAS4}^{(r)}_{(i)}$ | The value, at basic prices, of foreign exports of commodity $i$ from domestic source $r$ |
| $\mathrm{BAS5}^{(g,r)}_{(i,s)}$ | The value, at basic prices, of commodity $i$ from source $s$ used by government $g$ for public consumption purposes in region $r$ |
| $\mathrm{CAPR}^{(j,r)}_{(h,s)}$ | Post tax capital income earned by household $h$ in region $s$ on capital rented to industry $j$ in region $r$ |
| $\mathrm{CAPT}^{(j,r)}_{(h,s)(g)}$ | Value of tax paid to government $g$ on capital income earned by household $h$ in region $s$ on capital rented to industry $j$ in region $r$ |
| $\mathrm{FTRN}^{(h,r)}$ | Domestic currency value of net foreign unrequited transfers to household $h$ in region $r$ |
| $\mathrm{FTRN}_{(g)}$ | Domestic currency value of net unrequited foreign transfers to government $g$ |
| $\mathrm{GINT}_{(g)}$ | Domestic currency value of interest payments on net foreign liabilities of government $g$ |
| $\mathrm{GRNT}^{(k)}_{(g)}$ | Inter-governmental grant, by government $g$ to government $k$ |
| $\mathrm{GTRN}^{(h,r)}_{(g)}$ | Transfer payments by government $g$ to household $h$ in region $r$ |
| $\mathrm{HINT}^{(h,r)}$ | Domestic currency value of net foreign interest payments by household $h$ in region $r$ |
| $\mathrm{HTAX}^{(h,r)}_{(g)}$ | Direct tax payments levied by government $g$ on household $h$ in region $r$ |
| $\mathrm{HTRN}^{(h,r)}_{(t,k)}$ | Transfer payments by household $t$ in region $k$ to household $h$ in region $r$ |
| $\mathrm{LABR}^{(j,r)}_{(o,h,k)}$ | Post tax value of labor payments earned by household $h$ in region $k$ working in occupation $o$ in industry $j$ in region $r$ |
| $\mathrm{LABT}^{(j,r)}_{(o,h,k)(g)}$ | Value of tax paid to government $g$ on labor payments earned by household $h$ in region $k$ working in occupation $o$ in industry $j$ in region $r$ |

(*Continued*)

| Symbol | Definition |
|---|---|
| $MAKE^{(i)}_{(j,r)}$ | Value, at basic prices, of commodity $i$ produced by industry $j$ in region $r$ |
| $MAR1^{(j,r)}_{(i,s)(m,k)}$ | The value of margin commodity $m$ produced in region $k$ used to facilitate intermediate input purchases of commodity $i$ from source $s$ by industry $j$ in region $r$ |
| $MAR2^{(j,r)}_{(i,s)(m,k)}$ | The value of margin commodity $m$ produced in region $k$ used to facilitate purchases of commodity $i$ from source $s$ for input to capital formation by industry $j$ in region $r$ |
| $MAR3^{(h,r)}_{(i,s)(m,k)}$ | The value of margin commodity $m$ produced in region $k$ used to facilitate private consumption purchases of commodity $i$ from source $s$ by household $h$ in region $r$ |
| $MAR4^{(r)}_{(i)(m,k)}$ | The value of margin commodity $m$ produced in region $k$ used to facilitate foreign exports of commodity $i$ from region $r$ |
| $MAR5^{(g,r)}_{(i,s)(m,k)}$ | The value of margin commodity $m$ produced in region $k$ used to facilitate public consumption purchases of commodity $i$ from source $s$ in region $r$ by government $g$ |
| $NATR^{(j,r)}_{(h,s)(t)}$ | Post tax natural resource rent earned by household $h$ in region $s$ on natural resource type $t$ used by industry $j$ in region $r$ |
| $NATT^{(j,r)}_{(h,s)(t)(g)}$ | Tax paid to government $g$ on resource rent earned by household $h$ in region $s$ on natural resource $t$ used by industry $j$ in region $r$ |
| $P^{(0)}_{(i,s)}$ | Basic price of commodity $i$ from source $s$ |
| $P^{(1)}_{(j,r)}$ | Average output price received by industry $j$ in region $r$ |
| $P^{(2)}_{(j,r)}$ | Purchaser's price of new units of capital installed in regional industry $j,r$ |
| $PTAX^{(1)(j,r)}_{(g)}$ | The value of production taxes levied by government $g$ on industry $j$ in region $r$ |
| $PTAX^{(2)(j,r)}_{(g)}$ | The value of per-unit or ad-valorem taxes collected by government $g$ on gross fixed capital formation in regional industry $j,r$ |
| $R^{(N)(j,r)}_{(t)}$ | Rental price of natural resource type $t$ used by industry $j$ in region $r$ |
| $R^{(K)(j,r)}$ | Rental price of capital used by industry $j$ in region $r$ |
| $T^{(1)(N)(j,r)}_{(s)(t)(g)}$ | Tax rate levied by government $g$ on rents earned on natural resource $t$ used by industry $j$ in region $r$ owned by domestic or foreign agent $s$ |
| $T^{(1)(K)(j,r)}_{(s)(g)}$ | Tax rate levied by government $g$ on rents earned on capital used by industry $j$ in region $r$ owned by domestic or foreign households in $s$ |
| $T^{(1)(L)(j,r)}_{(o,k)(g)}$ | Tax rate levied by government $g$ on wages earned by labor type $o$ supplied by residents of region $k$, employed by industry $j$ in region $r$ |
| $T^{(1)}_{(j,r)}(g)$ | Ad valorem production tax rate on output of industry $j,r$ |
| $T^{(2)}_{(j,r)}(g)$ | Ad valorem tax rate on units of new capital purchased by regional industry $j,r$ |

$T^{(1)(j,r)}_{(i,s)(g)}$ — Rate of indirect tax levied by government g on purchases of commodity i from source s by industry j in region r for input to current production

$T^{(2)(j,r)}_{(i,s)(g)}$ — Rate of indirect tax levied by government g on purchases of commodity i from source s by industry j in region r for input to capital formation

$T^{(3)(r)}_{(i,s)(g)}$ — Rate of indirect tax levied by government g on purchases of commodity i from source s by households in region r

$T^{(4)(r)}_{(i)(g)}$ — Rate of indirect tax levied by government g on exports of commodity i from region r

$T^{(5)(k,r)}_{(i,s)(g)}$ — Rate of indirect tax levied by government g on purchases of commodity i from source s by government k for public consumption purposes in region r

$T^{(fed)}_{(i,imp)}$ — Rate of duty levied by the federal government on foreign imports of commodity i

$TARF^{(g)}_{(i)}$ — Tariff revenue collected on commodity i by government g

$TAX1^{(j,r)}_{(i,s)(g)}$ — Value of indirect taxes collected by government g on purchases by industry j in region r of commodity i from source s for input to current production

$TAX2^{(j,r)}_{(i,s)(g)}$ — Value of indirect taxes collected by government g on purchases by industry j in region r of commodity i from source s for input to capital formation

$TAX3^{(h,r)}_{(i,s)(g)}$ — Value of indirect taxes collected by government g on current consumption purchases of commodity i from source s by household h in region r

$TAX4^{(r)}_{(i)(g)}$ — Value of indirect taxes collected by government g on exports of commodity i from region r

$TAX5^{(k,r)}_{(i,s)(g)}$ — Value of indirect taxes collected by government g on purchases of commodity i from source s by government k for public consumption purposes in region r

$W^{(j,r)}_{(o)}$ — Wage paid by industry j in region r for labor type o

$X_{(i,imp)}$ — Economy-wide imports of commodity i

$X^{(1)(L)(j,r)}_{(o,h,k)}$ — Inputs of labor type o, supplied by household h resident in region k, used by industry j in region r for current production purposes

$X^{(1)(K)(j,r)}_{(h,s)}$ — Inputs of physical capital to industry j in region r, owned by household h in region s

$X^{(1)(N)(j,r)}_{(h,s)(t)}$ — Inputs of natural resource type t to industry j in region r, owned by household h in region s

*(Continued)*

| Symbol | Description |
|---|---|
| $X^{(1)(j,r)}_{(i,s)(m,k)}$ | Demand for margin commodity $m$ produced in region $k$ to facilitate intermediate input purchases of commodity $i$ from source $s$ by industry $j$ in region $r$ |
| $X^{(2)(j,r)}_{(i,s)(m,k)}$ | Demand for margin commodity $m$ produced in region $k$ to facilitate purchases of commodity $i$ from source $s$ for input to capital formation by industry $j$ in region $r$ |
| $X^{(3)(h,r)}_{(i,s)(m,k)}$ | Demand for margin commodity $m$ produced in region $k$ to facilitate private consumption purchases of commodity $i$ from source $s$ by household $h$ in region $r$ |
| $X^{(4)(r)}_{(i)(m,k)}$ | Demand for margin commodity $m$ produced in region $k$ to facilitate foreign exports of commodity $i$ from region $r$ |
| $X^{(5)(g,r)}_{(i,s)(m,k)}$ | Demand for margin commodity $m$ produced in region $r$ to facilitate public consumption purchases of commodity $i$ from source $s$ in region $r$ by government $g$ |
| $X^{(0)(i)}_{(j,r)}$ | Production of commodity $i$ by industry $j$ in region $r$ |
| $X^{(1)(j,r)}_{(i,s)}$ | Inputs of commodity $i$ from source $s$, used by industry $j$ in region $r$ for current production purposes |
| $X^{(2)(j,r)}_{(i,s)}$ | Demand for commodity $i$ from source $s$ by industry $j$ in region $r$ for input to gross fixed capital formation |
| $X^{(3)(h,r)}_{(i,s)}$ | Demand for commodity $i$ from source $s$ by household $h$ resident in region $r$ |
| $X^{(4)(r)}_{(i)}$ | Demand for commodity $i$ produced in region $r$ by foreign economic agents |
| $X^{(5)(g,r)}_{(i,s)}$ | Public consumption demand in region $r$ for commodity $i$ from source $s$ by government $g$ |
| $Z^{(1)}_{(j,r)}$ | Activity level of industry $j$ in region $r$ |
| $Z^{(2)}_{(j,r)}$ | Gross fixed capital formation by industry $j$ in region $r$ |

Having defined an effective intermediate input $X_{(i,\bullet)}^{(1)(j,r)}$, the theory governing inter-regional sourcing of intermediate inputs becomes one of choosing between alternative functional forms describing how $X_{(i,\bullet)}^{(1)(j,r)}$ comprises $X_{(i,s)}^{(1)(j,r)}$ from the $R$ domestic sources ($s = 1, \ldots, R$) and the foreign source ($s = R + 1$). For example, in the FEDERAL model, single-tiered CRESH[57] aggregation functions govern regional industry ($j,r$)'s substitution possibilities across all domestic and foreign sources for commodity $i$. In MMRF, two-tiered CES aggregation functions govern commodity sourcing. In the first tier, effective inputs of commodity $i$ are assumed to be a cost-minimizing CES composite of foreign imported $i$ $\left(X_{(i,r+1)}^{(1)(j,r)}\right)$ and a domestic composite $\left(X_{(i,\mathrm{Dom})}^{(1)(j,r)}\right)$. The domestic composite in turn is assumed to be a cost-minimizing CES composite of commodity $i$ sourced from the $R$ domestic regional sources for $i$ $\left(X_{(i,s)}^{(1)(j,r)}, s \leq R\right)$.

CES, or CRESH functions, are common choices for describing substitution possibilities across primary factors.[58] Regional models differ in the detail and importance they attach to inter-regional factor ownership. In Figure 7.1, we allow for the possibility that occupation specific labor ($o$) used by industry ($j,r$) might be distinguished by both the region of residence ($k$) of the households supplying the labor and some characteristic of the household ($h$). Similarly, we allow for the possible identification of $S$ ($R$ domestic regions and foreign) ownership claims by $H$ household types on returns from the physical capital and natural resources used by each regional industry. Accounting for out-of-region ownership is a feature of only some regional CGE models.[59] The need to maintain inter-regional capital and land ownership as a standard part of a multiregional CGE model is likely to grow, for two reasons. First, the trend in regional CGE model development has been to identify a growing number of smaller regions. As the level of regional detail rises, so too does: (i) The likelihood that households resident in any given small region will source a significant proportion of their rental income from outside the region and (ii) regional heterogeneity, raising the possibility that a number of rentier regions might appear among a list of small geographic regions. Second, many countries are experiencing a strong rise in the share of their populations that are retired. A proportion of retired households finance all or part of their consumption from capital income earned on diversified portfolios. Hence, even in regional models containing a few large and thus relatively homogeneous regions, we might still anticipate that

---

[57] Constant ratios of elasticities of substitution, homothetic (Hanoch, 1971).

[58] Some smaller-scale regional CGE model have used Cobb–Douglas functions, while there has been occasional use of flexible functional forms (see Table 1 of Partridge and Rickman, 1998, for examples).

[59] Examples of models accounting for out-of-region ownership are: Morgan *et al.* (1989), Madden (1990), Buckley (1992), Rickman (1992), Giesecke (2000) and Gillespie *et al.* (2002b).

modeling of rental income sourced from outside the home region will grow in importance in countries where the aged dependency ratio is rising.

In the MMRF variant employed in Section 7.6, capital and natural resource ownership detail is suppressed. It is assumed that an effective primary factor unit $\left(X_{(\cdot)}^{(1)(\cdot)(j,r)}\right)$ is a cost-minimizing CES combination of regional-industry-specific capital $\left(X_{(\cdot)}^{(1)(K)(j,r)}\right)$, regional-industry-specific agricultural land $\left(X_{(\cdot)}^{(1)(N)(j,r)}\right)$ and a labor composite $\left(X_{(\cdot,\cdot)}^{(1)(L)(j,r)}\right)$. The labor composite is assumed to be a cost-minimizing CES combination of labor distinguished by occupation $\left(X_{(o,\cdot)}^{(1)(L)(j,r)}\right)$.

## 7.4.2 Commodity composition of regional industry output

National input-output tables often contain a supply table detailing multiproduction across industries. With multiproduction a feature of the structure of production at the national level, we might presume that it is also a feature of regional economic structure. Figure 7.1 allows for this possibility, describing the value of regional multiproduction by $\text{MAKE}_{(j,r)}^{(i)}$: the value, at basic prices $\left(P_{(i,r)}^{(0)}\right)$, of production $\left(X_{(j,r)}^{(0)(i)}\right)$ of commodity $(i)$ by regional industry $(j,r)$.[60] In models like FEDERAL and MMRF, supply functions describing how regional industry activity levels $\left(Z_{(j,r)}^{(1)}\right)$ are transformed into commodity-specific output $\left(X_{(j,r)}^{(0)(i)}\right)$ are derived from constrained revenue maximization problems in which $Z_{(j,r)}^{(1)}$ is assumed to be a CET or CRETH function of $X_{(j,r)}^{(0)(i)}$.[61]

---

[60] A common assumption is that the different industrial producers of $i$ in region $r$ receive a common basic price. Under this assumption, commodity $i$ from $r$ is assumed to be undifferentiated by its industry of production, simply entering a total supply pool for $i$ produced in $r$. However, in some applications, it may be useful to allow for the possibility that the basic price received by producers of commodity $i$ in region $r$ differs across alternative producers, $j$. For example, this may be important in dynamic simulations of models in which a given commodity may be produced by a number of different industries employing factors that are largely mobile in the long run. In such simulations, minor differences in the costs of the alternative producers of a given commodity can generate large movements in the activity levels of those producers. For example, applications of MMRF-GREEN to the study of carbon abatement policies have recognized production of a single commodity (electricity) by a variety of alternative electricity production technologies. To prevent this introducing long-run over-determination of the supply price of electricity, electricity users (and, in particular, the national electricity grid) are assumed to face imperfect substitution possibilities in their use of electricity from alternative generation technologies. More generally, purchasers of commodity $i$ from region $r$ can be assumed to minimize the cost of acquiring $i$ from the alternative $j$ producers of $i$, subject to substitution possibilities described by CES or CRESH functions. Such treatment introduces an industry $(j)$ dimension to the total demand functions for commodity $i$ produced in region $r$, and with it, an industry $(j)$ dimension to the basic price variable.

[61] Respectively, constant elasticity of transformation and constant ratio of elasticities of transformation, homothetic. See Powell and Gruen (1968) and Vincent *et al.* (1980), respectively.

### 7.4.3 Demand for inputs to capital formation

The second column block of Figure 7.1 describes the cost structure of inputs to capital formation for $J \times R$ regional industries. In identifying an industry ($j$) dimension to the investment data, Figure 7.1 recognizes that capital formation input structures can differ across regional industries. This can be important in long-run dynamic simulations, where changes in capital cost conditions eventually flow through into the supply cost of industry production. For example, in a simulation of the effects of reducing tariffs on imported machinery, a model with investment theory describing variables in the second column of Figure 7.1 will recognize that the cost of capital in the agricultural sector (which is intensive in the use of imported machinery) will fall by more than the cost of capital in the dwellings construction sector (which is intensive in the use of labor and local manufactured inputs).

In Section 7.4.10.2 we describe how regional industry gross fixed capital formation $\left( Z_{(j,r)}^{(2)} \right)$, is determined on the basis of expected rates of return on capital specific to each regional industry. For the moment, we take this variable as given, and describe the determination of inputs to capital formation $\left( X_{(i,s)}^{(2)(j,r)} \right)$. In MMRF, capital creation is subject to a three-tiered production structure. At the top level of this structure, new units of industry-specific capital in each region $\left( Z_{(j,r)}^{(2)} \right)$ are formed as a cost-minimizing combination of composite commodities that are undifferentiated by source $\left( X_{(i,\bullet)}^{(2)(j,r)} \right)$. These composite commodities are assumed to be used in fixed proportions in the composition of new units of capital, $Z_{(j,r)}^{(2)}$. Below the fixed proportions tier of the production structure sit two tiers of CES aggregation functions governing commodity sourcing. First, effective inputs of commodity $i$ are assumed to be a cost-minimizing CES composite of imported $i$ $\left( X_{(i,R+1)}^{(2)(j,r)} \right)$ and a domestic composite $\left( X_{(i,\text{Dom})}^{(2)(j,r)} \right)$. The domestic composite, in turn, is assumed to be a cost-minimizing CES composite of commodity $i$ sourced from the $R$ domestic sources for $i$ $\left( X_{(i,r)}^{(2)(j,r)} \right)$.

### 7.4.4 Demand for commodities for private consumption

The third column of Figure 7.1 identifies the basic value flows, taxes and margins associated with the purchases of source-specific commodities by each household in each region $\left( X_{(i,s)}^{(3)(h,r)} \right)$. Commonly, regional CGE models recognize a single representative household in each region.[62] In the MMRF model employed in Section 7.6, consumption

---

[62] This is the case for the MMRF model used in Section 7.6. Examples of models containing multiple households in each region are Kim and Kim (2002), Ferreira and Horridge (2006), Cutler and Davies (2007), and Decaluwé et al. (2010). Ferreira and Horridge's model is notable for linking a multiple-household 27-region CGE model of Brazil to a microsimulation model containing over 100,000 households. The models are solved iteratively to obtain consistent results.

decisions of the region $r$ household are governed by a nested three-tiered decision process. At the top tier of this process, regional households maximize a Stone–Geary or Klein–Rubin utility function by choosing among composite units of commodity $i$ $\left(X_{(i,\bullet)}^{(3)(\bullet,r)}\right)$ subject to an aggregate expenditure constraint. The next two tiers describe the manner in which households choose commodity $i$ from among the competing alternative sources for $i$. This pattern follows a structure similar to that outlined above for current production and capital formation. First, composite units of commodity $i$ $\left(X_{(i,\bullet)}^{(3)(\bullet,r)}\right)$ are modeled as cost-minimizing CES composites of imported $i$ $\left(X_{(i,R+1)}^{(3)(\bullet,r)}\right)$ and a composite of domestically-sourced $i$ $\left(X_{(i,\mathrm{Dom})}^{(3)(\bullet,r)}\right)$. The domestic composite, in turn, is modeled as a cost-minimizing CES composite of commodity $i$ sourced from the $R$ domestic regional sources for $i$ $\left(X_{(i,r)}^{(3)(\bullet,r)}\right)$.

### 7.4.5 Export demands

The fourth column of Figure 7.1 identifies the tax, margin and basic flow components of the purchaser's value of regional foreign exports. In Figure 7.1, we define the basic value of foreign export sales $\left(\mathrm{BAS4}_{(i)}^{(r)}\right)$ as the product of export volumes $\left(X_{(i)}^{(4)(r)}\right)$ and the regional basic price common to all purchasers of commodity $i$ across row 1 $\left(P_{(i,r)}^{(0)}\right)$. This is illustrative of the treatment in the MMRF variant we employ in Section 7.6, which does not distinguish between exported and domestic varieties of commodities. Many models, however, add a product transformation stage to the regional production structure, in which export and domestic product varieties are differentiated in a constrained revenue maximizing way (e.g. Hoffmann et al., 1996; Kim and Kim, 2002; Rose and Liao, 2005). From this decision problem are derived revenue-maximizing supply functions for domestic and exported varieties of each good, allowing the basic price in cell (1,4) of Figure 7.1 to differ from the basic price faced by the remaining users across row 1. This approach can be attractive in models which carry a small country assumption of highly elastic export demand. In such models, independent functions describing the supply of commodity $i$ to the domestic and foreign market are helpful in avoiding long-run overspecialization in the structure of production. The MMRF model used in Section 7.6, carries the assumption that the export volume for any given commodity $i$ from region $r$ $\left(X_{(i)}^{(4)(r)}\right)$ is inversely related to the export's f.o.b. (free on board) foreign currency price via a constant elasticity export demand function. We set export demand elasticities at around $-4$, consistent with evidence collected for Australian national models.[63]

---

[63] Dixon and Rimmer (2010) make a good case for Australian export demand elasticities in the vicinity of $-4$.

### 7.4.6 Demand for commodities for public consumption purposes

Explicit behavioral assumptions governing the composition of spending by regional and federal government levels are rare in the regional CGE literature (Groenewold et al., 2003). In most models, $X_{(i,s)}^{(5)(g,r)}$ is treated as an exogenous policy variable, or held at a constant ratio of regional consumption spending (in the case of regional government) or national consumption spending (in the case of the federal government). In our simulations discussed in Section 7.6, our default setting for the determination of real public consumption spending by regional governments is to maintain a constant ratio with real regional private consumption spending. In determining federal government spending, we impose two restrictions. At the national level, we determine real federal public consumption spending by determining exogenously the ratio of real federal public consumption spending to economy-wide real private consumption spending. To determine the regional allocation of federal consumption spending, we assume that base-period *per capita* federal spending relativities across regions are exogenous for certain relevant commodities, such as education and health. For other commodities, such as defense, we assume that the regional shares in national spending are exogenous. In our dynamic simulations with the MMRF model, this has the effect of ensuring that federal spending has a tendency to follow inter-regional population movements, but with stickiness in some regional federal spending, via the fixity of spending on certain public administration and defense functions.

### 7.4.7 Demand for commodities as margin services

Row 2 of Figure 7.1 identifies the basic value of demands for commodities as margin services to facilitate commodity purchases by each of the agents described across the figure's five columns. For example, cell (2,1) describes the value of margin services $\left( P_{(m,k)}^{(0)} \cdot X_{(i,s)(m,k)}^{(1)(j,r)} \right)$ used to facilitate intermediate input purchases. In explicitly identifying the region of margin supply, $k$, we follow Madden (1990) and Horridge *et al.* (2005). The former identified margin supply in both source and destination regions for each commodity flow. The latter allows for the possibility that certain margins, such as transport, may also be supplied by regions between the source and destination regions for the underlying commodity flow. The MMRF model employed in Section 7.6 identifies destination margins only. This reduces the effective dimension of the cells in row 2 of Figure (4.1). For example, cell (2,2), which describes demand for margin services to facilitate purchases by investors, in MMRF defines $P_{(m,r)}^{(0)} \cdot X_{(i,s)(m,r)}^{(2)(j,r)}$, since $X_{(i,s)(m,k)}^{(2)(j,r)} = 0$ if $k \neq r$.

MMRF follows the Dixon *et al.* (1982) assumption that margin services are used in fixed proportions with the underlying transaction that they facilitate. Hence, a 1% increase in the value of $X_{(i,s)}^{(3)(\bullet,r)}$ produces a 1% increase in the value of $X_{(i,s)(m,r)}^{(3)(\bullet,r)}$ for all $m$. For some applications, other assumptions may be useful. For example, Adams *et al.*

(2010) allow for price-responsive intermodal substitution in demands for transport margins, reflecting the importance of road/rail competition in the Australian long-distance transport market.

### 7.4.8 Commodity market clearing conditions

Market clearing basic prices for domestic commodities are endogenously determined by equating the supply of, and the demand for, commodity $i$ produced in region $r$. In terms of the notation in Figure 7.1, the multiregional CGE model endogenously determines the market clearing basic price for commodity $i,r$, $P_{(i,r)}^{(0)}$ via:

$$
\sum_{j\in \text{IND}} X_{(j,r)}^{(0)(i)} = \sum_{k\in \text{REG}} \left( \sum_{j\in \text{IND}} \left( X_{(i,r)}^{(1)(j,k)} + X_{(i,r)}^{(2)(j,k)} \right) + \sum_{h\in \text{HOU}} X_{(i,r)}^{(3)(h,k)} + \sum_{g\in \text{GOV}} X_{(i,r)}^{(5)(g,k)} \right)
$$
$$
+ X_{(i)}^{(4)(r)} + X_{(i,r)}^{(M)},
$$

(7.3)

where $X_{(i,r)}^{(M)}$ is the demand for $i$ produced in $r$ as a margin service, defined as:

$$
X_{(i,r)}^{(M)} = \sum_{c\in \text{COM}} \sum_{t\in \text{REG}} \left( X_{(c)(i,r)}^{(4)(t)} + \sum_{k\in \text{REG}} \left( \sum_{j\in \text{IND}} \left( X_{(c,t)(i,r)}^{(1)(j,k)} + X_{(c,t)(i,r)}^{(2)(j,k)} \right) \right. \right.
$$
$$
\left. \left. + \sum_{h\in \text{HOU}} X_{(c,t)(i,r)}^{(3)(h,k)} + \sum_{g\in \text{GOV}} X_{(c,t)(i,r)}^{(5)(g,k)} \right) \right).
$$

In determining the basic price of imported commodities ($P_{(i,\text{imp})}^{(0)}$ in Figure 7.1), a typical starting point is the exogenous determination of c.i.f. (cost, insurance and freight) foreign currency import prices. Landed duty paid domestic currency import prices are calculated endogenously, after translating c.i.f. foreign currency prices to domestic currency through the national exchange rate, and after applying federal import tariffs.

### 7.4.9 Zero-pure-profit conditions on current production, capital formation and commodity purchases

A typical regional CGE model will apply zero-pure-profit conditions on the activities of current production, the supply of commodities to domestic agents, exporting and importing. This allows the endogenous determination of all the purchaser's prices and regional industry activity levels.

Using Figure 7.1 as a template, zero-pure-profit conditions allow purchaser's prices to be determined endogenously for each of the transactions described in cells (1,1) through (1,5). For example, domestic currency purchaser's prices for exports $\left( P_{(i,r)}^{(4)} \right)$ are determined by (7.4):

$$
P_{(i,r)}^{(4)} \cdot X_{(i)}^{(4)(r)} = P_{(i,r)}^{(0)} \cdot X_{(i)}^{(4)(r)} + \sum_{m\in \text{MAR}} \sum_{k\in \text{REG}} P_{(m,k)}^{(0)} \cdot X_{(i)(m,k)}^{(4)(r)} + \sum_{g\in \text{GOV}} P_{(i,r)}^{(0)} \cdot X_{(i)}^{(4)(r)} \cdot T_{(i)(g)}^{(4)(r)}.
$$

(7.4)

With $X_{(i)}^{(4)(r)}$ largely determined by the export demand function for $(i,r)$ (see Section 7.4.5 above); $P_{(i,r)}^{(0)}$ and $P_{(m,k)}^{(0)}$ largely determined by the market clearing conditions for $(i,r)$ and $(m,k)$ (Section 7.4.8 above); $X_{(i)(m,k)}^{(4)(r)}$ determined by the margin demand functions (Section 7.4.7 above); and with export tax rates $\left( T_{(i)(g)}^{(4)(r)} \right)$ exogenous, (7.4) can be viewed as determining $P_{(i,r)}^{(4)}$.

The reader will note that cells (2,1) through (2,5) of Figure 7.1 also involve transactions in the form of purchases of margin services. In Figure 7.1 we have assumed that the cost of a margin service is its basic price. In a detailed fiscal model, more complex expressions are possible. For example, MMRF allows for the price paid for margin services to include relevant indirect taxes, such as VAT.

Again, using Figure 7.1 as a template, zero pure profits in current production can be expressed as:

$$
P_{(j,r)}^{(1)} \cdot Z_{(j,r)}^{(1)} = \sum_{g \in \text{GOV}} P_{(j,r)}^{(0)} \cdot Z_{(j,r)}^{(1)} \cdot T_{(j,r)}^{(1)(g)}
$$

$$
+ \sum_{i \in \text{COM}} \sum_{s \in \text{SRC}} \left( P_{(i,s)}^{(0)} \cdot X_{(i,s)}^{(1)(j,r)} + \sum_{m \in \text{MAR}} \sum_{k \in \text{REG}} P_{(m,k)}^{(0)} \cdot X_{(i,s)(m,k)}^{(1)(j,r)} + \sum_{g \in \text{GOV}} P_{(i,s)}^{(0)} \cdot X_{(i,s)}^{(1)(j,r)} \cdot T_{(i,s)(g)}^{(1)(j,r)} \right)
$$

$$
+ \sum_{o \in \text{OCC}} \sum_{h \in \text{HOU}} \sum_{k \in \text{REG}} \left( W_{(o,k)}^{(j,r)} \cdot X_{(o,h,k)}^{(1)(L)(j,r)} + \sum_{g \in \text{GOV}} W_{(o,k)}^{(j,r)} \cdot X_{(o,h,k)}^{(1)(L)(j,r)} \cdot T_{(o,k)(g)}^{(1)(L)(j,r)} \right)
$$

$$
+ \sum_{h \in \text{HOU}} \sum_{s \in \text{SRC}} \left( R^{(K)(j,r)} \cdot X_{(h,s)}^{(1)(K)(j,r)} + \sum_{g \in \text{GOV}} R^{(K)(j,r)} \cdot X_{(h,s)}^{(1)(K)(j,r)} \cdot T_{(s)(g)}^{(1)(K)(j,r)} \right)
$$

$$
+ \sum_{h \in \text{HOU}} \sum_{s \in \text{SRC}} \sum_{t \in \text{RES}} \left( R_{(t)}^{(N)(j,r)} \cdot X_{(h,s)(t)}^{(1)(N)(j,r)} + \sum_{g \in \text{GOV}} R_{(t)}^{(N)(j,r)} \cdot X_{(h,s)(t)}^{(1)(N)(j,r)} \cdot T_{(s)(t)(g)}^{(1)(N)(j,r)} \right).
$$

$$(7.5)$$

The $j,r$ Equations of (7.5) can, in conjunction with the market clearing conditions and commodity supply equations discussed in Sections 7.4.8 and 7.4.2 above, be viewed as largely determining regional industry activity levels, $Z_{(j,r)}^{(1)}$. Equation (7.5) introduces the average price of industry $(j,r)$'s output $\left( P_{(j,r)}^{(1)} \right)$, which is defined via:

$$
P_{(j,r)}^{(1)} \cdot Z_{(j,r)}^{(1)} = \sum_{i \in \text{COM}} P_{(i,r)}^{(0)} \cdot X_{(j,r)}^{(0)(i)}.
$$

$$(7.6)$$

The unit cost of capital in regional industry $j,r$ $\left( P_{(j,r)}^{(2)} \right)$ is determined by zero-pure-profit equations of the form:

$$P_{(j,r)}^{(2)} \cdot Z_{(j,r)}^{(2)} = \sum_{g \in \text{GOV}} P_{(j,r)}^{(2)} \cdot Z_{(j,r)}^{(2)} \cdot T_{(j,r)}^{(2)(g)}$$

$$+ \sum_{i \in \text{COM}} \sum_{s \in \text{SRC}} \left( P_{(i,s)}^{(0)} \cdot X_{(i,s)}^{(2)(j,r)} + \sum_{m \in \text{MAR}} \sum_{k \in \text{REG}} P_{(m,k)}^{(0)} \cdot X_{(i,s)(m,k)}^{(2)(j,r)} \right. \tag{7.7}$$

$$\left. + \sum_{g \in \text{GOV}} P_{(i,s)}^{(0)} \cdot X_{(i,s)}^{(2)(j,r)} \cdot T_{(i,s)(g)}^{(2)(j,r)} \right).$$

### 7.4.10 Regional factor markets

As noted in Section 7.4.1, three broad types of primary factor are identified in Figure 7.1 — labor, capital and natural resources. In Figure 7.1, we have allowed for the possibility that employees may be distinguished by occupation and region of residence. Figure 7.1 also provides for the possibility that capital and natural resources may be distinguished by the asset owner's region of residence.

#### 7.4.10.1 Regional wages and employment in the short run and long run

In thinking about how regional labor markets have been modeled in CGE models, we begin by distinguishing comparative static and dynamic models. In comparative static applications, modeling of the labor market, particularly as it relates to wage and employment flexibility, is one of the ways in which short-run and long-run analytical timeframes are commonly distinguished. In short-run applications, a common assumption is that institutional or structural features of the regional labor market generate short-run stickiness in the regional wage rate. With short-run regional wages sticky, regional labor market pressures are mainly expressed as movements in short-run regional employment. With short-run regional populations given, these short-run regional employment movements are expressed as short-run movements in the regional employment rate and/or participation rate. As stated in Section 7.3.5.1, the modeling of long-run labor markets is intertwined with assumptions governing the long-run mobility of populations across regions. For example, the long-run implementations of the MMRF model assume that long-run inter-regional wage relativities are exogenous. At the level of the regional labor market, this translates to near exogeneity of the regional wage rate, with long-run regional employment endogenously adjusting via long-run movements in regional populations.

In discussing modeling of labor markets within a dynamic CGE model, we begin with the Dixon and Rimmer (2002, p. 15) distinction between baseline and policy simulations. In its broadest sense, a baseline simulation represents a forecast of the economy, typically undertaken under an assumption that the particular policy that is the subject of the research is not implemented. The policy simulation is typically identical to the baseline simulation in all respects other than the addition of shocks representing the particular policy under analysis. In undertaking the baseline simulation with a regional CGE model, a common assumption is to allow regional labor forces to adjust endogenously each period, under an environment of given regional wage relativities. Under this closure, labor market clearing is imposed at the national level, with regional wages adjusting in tandem with the national wage so as to maintain given regional wage relativities. In policy simulations, a similar closure structure may be imposed, that is, labor market clearing occurring at the national level, with endogenous regional labor forces maintaining given regional wage relativities. An extension of this approach in standard MMRF implementations allows for short-run sticky wage adjustment at the national level, using the method outlined in Dixon and Rimmer (2002, p. 205). Under this approach, sticky or gradual adjustment of the national wage allows the level of national employment in the policy simulation to deviate from its level in the baseline simulation. Over time, gradual adjustment of the national wage returns the level of national employment in the policy simulation back to its baseline value.

In our variant of the standard MMRF model employed in Section 7.6, we allow for short-run stickiness in both regional populations and regional wage rates. Regional populations adjust slowly, via inter-regional migration, to movements in regional wage relativities. We discuss our treatment of inter-regional migration in Section 7.4.11 below; however, readers need not follow this forward reference to understand the remainder of our discussion here. In our policy simulations, we allow for limited deviations in short-run regional wages away from their baseline values. With short-run regional populations also sticky, we allow short-run labor market pressures to be mainly manifested as short-run deviations in regional employment rates. More explicitly, we allow the path of real regional consumer wages in policy simulations to be governed by:[64]

$$
\left( W_r^{(\text{Policy})} / W_r^{(\text{Baseline})} - 1 \right) = \left( W_{(t-1),r}^{(\text{Policy})} / W_{(t-1),r}^{(\text{Baseline})} - 1 \right)
$$
$$
+ \alpha \left( ER_r^{(\text{Policy})} / ER_r^{(\text{Baseline})} - 1 \right),
$$

(7.8)

where $W_r^{(\text{Baseline})}$ and $W_r^{(\text{Policy})}$ are the real consumer wage in region $r$ in the baseline and policy simulation, respectively; $W_{(t-1),r}^{(\text{Baseline})}$ and $W_{(t-1),r}^{(\text{Policy})}$ are the lagged values for the regional real wage in the baseline and policy simulations, respectively; $ER_r^{(\text{Baseline})}$ and $ER_r^{(\text{Policy})}$ are regional employment rates $(1 -$ the unemployment rate) in the baseline and policy simulations respectively; and $\alpha$ is a positive parameter.

---

[64] We define the real regional consumer wage as the ratio of the nominal regional wage to the regional household consumption deflator.

With (7.8) activated in the policy simulation, the deviation in the real regional consumer wage grows (declines) as long as the regional employment rate remains above (below) its baseline level. A value for $\alpha$ is chosen that ensures the regional employment effects of a shock in year $t$ are largely eliminated by year $t + 5$. Equation (7.8) represents an implementation at the regional level of the national sticky wage adjustment mechanism described in Dixon and Rimmer (2002, p. 205).[65] Use of a *national* sticky wage mechanism (i.e. one that imposes short-run stickiness of the national wage before transitioning to a long-run flexible national wage that gradually returns the economy-wide employment rate to its baseline level) is not appropriate in a regional model that has explicit location decision modeling, such as that discussed in Section 7.4.11 below, because it introduces a wage determination process that is independent of movements in region-specific labor forces. To introduce short-run sticky wages but long-run labor market clearing to a regional model with a regional labor supply theory that does not passively adjust to movements in regional wages, we require theory implementing short-run stickiness in region-specific wages. For example, Giesecke (2003) implements a regional variant of the Dixon and Rimmer (2002) national mechanism, one in which region-specific real wages gradually adjust in policy simulation to return the number of unemployed persons in each region to baseline. This approach has the advantage of ensuring that the national long-run employment deviation is zero, since region-specific numbers of unemployed persons are eventually returned to their baseline values. A disadvantage of this approach is that regional unemployment rates will deviate from baseline in any policy simulation that generates deviations in regional populations. Another option is to return the regional unemployment rate or the regional employment rate (1 − the unemployment rate) to baseline. This is the function of (7.8). However, in cases where baseline unemployment rates differ across regions, (7.8) can lead to small deviations in national employment when the policy shock causes the national population to move between regions.

### 7.4.10.2 *Rates of return and capital stocks in the short run and long run*

In Section 7.4.1 we discussed the derivation of cost-minimizing demands for capital inputs by regional industries. On the supply side of regional industry capital markets, comparative static regional CGE models, in common with their national counterparts, generally draw a distinction between their modeling of the short run and the long run. Typically, the short run has been defined as a period sufficiently long for firms to have time to adjust investment to changes in expected rates of return, but too short for new investment to affect installed capital. In terms of model closure, this is implemented via

---

[65] Equation (7.8) follows the basic structure of the wage adjustment equation described by Equation (24.2) in Dixon and Rimmer (2002, p. 205). The difference is that in (24.2) the national wage deviation rises (falls) so long as national employment in the policy case is above (below) its base-case level. In (7.8) the regional wage deviation rises (falls) so long as the regional employment rate is above (below) its base-case level.

the exogenous determination of regional industry capital stocks $\left(X_{(\bullet)}^{(1)(K)(j,r)}\right)$, requiring $J \times R$ market clearing capital rental prices $\left(R^{(K)(j,r)}\right)$ to be determined endogenously.

While capital stocks are, by definition, unable to adjust in the short-run, a typical short-run closure allows for adjustment of gross fixed capital formation $\left(Z_{(j,r)}^{(2)}\right)$ in response to movements in rates of return. Rates of return on regional industry capital $(\mathrm{ROR}_{(j,r)})$ may be approximated by:

$$\mathrm{ROR}_{(j,r)} = R^{(K)(j,r)}/P_{(j,r)}^{(2)} - D_{(j,r)}, \tag{7.9}$$

where $D_{(j,r)}$ is the depreciation rate on regional industry $j,r$'s capital stock.

Regional industry investment can then be determined by:

$$Z_{(j,r)}^{(2)}/X_{(\bullet)}^{(1)(K)(j,r)} = F^{(2)}\left(\mathrm{ROR}_{(j,r)}/\mathrm{RORN}_{(j,r)}, \mathrm{GN}_{(j,r)}^{(2)}\right), \tag{7.10}$$

where $F^{(2)}$ is an increasing positive function of $\mathrm{ROR}_{(j,r)}/\mathrm{RORN}_{(j,r)}$, $\mathrm{RORN}_{(j,r)}$ is an exogenously determined trend or normal rate of return, and $\mathrm{GN}_{(j,r)}^{(2)}$ is an exogenously determined trend or normal rate of capital growth. In MMRF, $F^{(2)}$ takes the inverse logistic form described in Dixon and Rimmer (2002, pp. 190−195).

The long-run in comparative static applications of regional CGE models is typically defined as a period sufficiently long that regional industry capital stocks have adjusted to return $\mathrm{ROR}_{(j,r)}$ to some exogenously specified level (such as $\mathrm{RORN}_{(j,r)}$). In practice, this is effected by exogenously determining $\mathrm{ROR}_{(j,r)}$ and endogenously determining $X_{(\bullet)}^{(1)(K)(j,r)}$. Under this closure, long-run capital rental rates $R^{(K)(j,r)}$ move with long-run capital construction costs $\left(P_{(j,r)}^{(2)}\right)$ via (7.9) and long-run real investment $\left(Z_{(j,r)}^{(2)}\right)$ moves with long-run capital stocks $\left(X_{(\bullet)}^{(1)(K)(j,r)}\right)$ via (7.10).

In dynamic simulations, MMRF follows the Dixon and Rimmer (2002) approach of linking a sequence of comparative static short-run equilibria via the addition of stock/flow accounting equations. For MMRF's investment and capital supply theory, this means including equations of the form:

$$X_{(\bullet)(t+1)}^{(1)(K)(j,r)} = X_{(\bullet)(t)}^{(1)(K)(j,r)} \times \left[1 - D^{(j,r)}\right] + Z_{(j,r)(t)}^{(2)}, \tag{7.11}$$

where $X_{(\bullet)(t)}^{(1)(K)(j,r)}$ and $X_{(\bullet)(t+1)}^{(1)(K)(j,r)}$ are regional industry capital stocks in years $t$ and $t+1$, respectively, and $Z_{(j,r)(t)}^{(2)}$ is real investment in regional industry $j,r$ in year $t$. In dynamic simulations, (7.10) and (7.11) together allow for short-run capital market pressures to be mainly expressed as movements in rates of return with gradual adjustment of capital stocks and long-run capital market pressures to be expressed as adjustment of capital stocks with rates of return deviating little from their normal values.

### 7.4.10.3 Natural resource use and rental rates in the short run and long run

Figure 7.1 distinguishes returns to physical capital from returns to natural resources, identifying $X_{(h,s)(t)}^{(1)(N)(j,r)}$, the quantity of natural resource type $t$, in region $r$, used by industry $j$ and owned by household $h$ in region $s$. In many of the large-scale general purpose models that make the distinction between capital and land rentals, the ownership dimension is absent and the resource type dimension ($t$) may be defined by the employing industry ($j$). For example, in general purpose models, non-agricultural natural resources, such as mining subsoil assets and fishery resources, may be modeled as specific to the industries in which they are employed. However, regional modelers with a specific interest in natural resource issues, particularly in agriculture, will typically expand the detail in which natural resource endowments are defined within their models. In Sections 7.2.3 and 7.3.5.5 we described the detailed treatment of agricultural land use and supply necessary to properly model water allocation policy in the SMDB region (Dixon et al., 2011). Ferreira and Horridge (2011) identify three types of region-specific agricultural land in use − forestry, crops and pasture.

Figure 7.1, identifies the natural resource rental price $R_{(t)}^{(N)(j,r)}$. By suppressing the ownership dimension on the rental rate, it is assumed that different owners receive the same rental rate on a given natural resource employed in a given regional industry. $R_{(t)}^{(N)(j,r)}$ typically serves two functions. (i) It maintains equality of supply of, and demand for, $X_{(\cdot)(t)}^{(1)(N)(j,r)}$. (ii) It guides the allocation of region $r$'s endowment of resource type $t$, across alternative uses, $j$.

In comparative static models, region $r$'s endowment of resource type $t$ is typically treated as exogenous. However, as regional models have become dynamic, model builders have begun turning their attention to modeling resource supply change. Ferreira and Horridge (2011) allow land to transition from one year to the next between forestry, crops and pasture, and for unused land to enter production via one of these three routes, in response to movements in land rental rates. Within any year, land within any one of the three categories can be applied to alternative agricultural production. For example, pasture land can be used for beef or dairy production, with the allocation across these uses changing in response to movements in the relative profitability of beef and dairy production. By modeling the transition of unused land into one of three agricultural uses, Ferreira and Horridge break with the traditional assumption of exogenous region-specific agricultural land supply.

In our application of MMRF in Section 7.6, we adopt a simple specification for natural resource supply, identifying resources that are specific to each regional industry, $X_{(\cdot)(\cdot)}^{(1)(N)(j,r)}$, with market clearing rental rates $R_{(\cdot)}^{(N)(j,r)}$. Under this specification, the $j$ dimension not only identifies the industry using the natural resource, it also defines the natural resource type. For example, natural resources used by the agriculture and mining industries represent agricultural land and subsoil assets, respectively.

## 7.4.11 Inter-regional migration

As foreshadowed in Section 7.3.5.1, we develop an alternative migration theory in this chapter. This new theory is then employed in the variant of MMRF we use to undertake the simulations reported in Section 7.6. We begin by assuming that gross inter-regional migration flows respond to movements in *per capita* regional income relativities. We call the measure of income that is relevant to the migration decision "migration income." Equation (7.12) defines migration income in region $r$ as the expected wage per worker:

$$Y_r^{(M)} = W_r \cdot E_r, \tag{7.12}$$

where $Y_r^{(M)}$ is migration income in region $r$, $W_r$ is the wage rate in region $r$ and $E_r$ is the employment rate ($1 -$ the unemployment rate) in region $r$.

We define movements in *per capita* migration income relativities via:

$$\frac{Y_d^{(M)}}{Y_o^{(M)}} = Y_{o,d}^{(\text{Diseq})} \cdot \frac{F_d^{(M)}}{F_o^{(M)}}, \tag{7.13}$$

where $Y_r^{(M)}$ is migration income in region $r$, $Y_{o,d}^{(\text{Diseq})}$ is a measure of disequilibrium in migration income relativities between migration origin region $o$ and migration destination region $d$, and $F_r^{(M)}$ is a shift-variable for calibrating migration income ratios.

We assume that a rise, say, in $Y_{o,d}^{(\text{Diseq})}$ will generate a rise in the gross emigration rate from region $o$ to region $d$ ( $GEMR_{o,d}$) and a fall in the gross emigration rate from region $d$ to region $o$ ( $GEMR_{d,o}$).

We adopt the inverse logistic function, used by Dixon and Rimmer (2002, pp. 190−193) to model capital supply, to model the relationship between $Y_{o,d}^{(\text{Diseq})}$ and $GEMR_{o,d}$. For modeling a region's gross emigration rate, this function has the useful property of allowing us to limit the minimum and maximum rates of gross emigration.[66] The inverse logistic relationship is described in Figure 7.3. The equation describing Figure 7.3 is:

$$
\begin{aligned}
Y_{o,d}^{(\text{Diseq})} =\ & 1 + F_{o,d} + \left(1/C_{o,d}\right) \\
& * \left\{ \left[ \ln\left( GEMR_{o,d} - GEMR_{o,d}^{(\text{MIN})} \right) - \ln\left( GEMR_{o,d}^{(\text{MAX})} - GEMR_{o,d} \right) \right] \right. \\
& \left. - \left[ \ln\left( GEMR_{o,d}^{(\text{TREND})} - GEMR_{o,d}^{(\text{MIN})} \right) - \ln\left( GEMR_{o,d}^{(\text{MAX})} - GEMR_{o,d}^{(\text{TREND})} \right) \right] \right\},
\end{aligned}
\tag{7.14}
$$

---

[66] We choose minimum and maximum emigration rates by examining the historical data on origin- and destination-specific gross regional emigration rates.

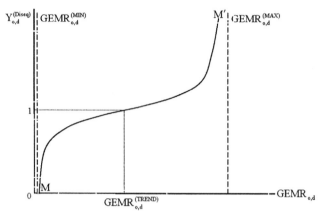

**Figure 7.3** Relationship between gross regional emigration rates and disequilibrium in regional migration income.

where $F_{o,d}$ is a parameter governing the vertical position of the function MM′ in Figure 7.3, $C_{o,d}$ is a positive parameter, governing the sensitivity of the gross emigration rate from region $o$ to region $d$ to movements in disequilibrium in the migration income ratio between region $o$ and $d$,[67] $GEMR_{o,d}$ is the gross emigration rate from region $o$ to region $d$, expressed as a proportion of region $o$'s population, $GEMR_{o,d}^{(MIN)}$ is the historically observed minimum proportion of region $o$'s population that emigrates to region $d$ each year, $GEMR_{o,d}^{(MAX)}$ is the historically observed maximum proportion of region $o$'s population that emigrates to region $d$ each year, and $GEMR_{o,d}^{(TREND)}$ is the trend or normal rate of emigration from region $o$ to region $d$.

To parameterize (7.13), we begin by calculating $Y_{o,d}^{(Diseq)}$ from (7.14) using the known initial values for $GEMR_{o,d}$ from official statistics and assuming initial values for $F_{o,d}$ of zero. With the initial values for $Y_{o,d}^{(Diseq)}$ calculated from (7.14), initial values for $F_r^{(M)}$ can be calculated from (7.13).

In year-on-year simulations, we treat $GEMR_{o,d}^{(TREND)}$ as a variable and update its value each year according to the rule:

$$\left[100/GEMR_{o,d}^{(TREND)}\right] \times \Delta GEMR_{o,d}^{(TREND)} = q_d - q, \qquad (7.15)$$

where $q_d$ is the percentage change in the population of region $d$, and $q$ is the percentage change in national population.

---

[67] We choose a value for $C_{o,d}$ that generates migration dynamics consistent with those described for Australia in Debelle and Vickery (1999). They find that net emigration from an Australian state following a relative downturn in its labor market occurs steadily over a number of years, with the bulk of the population adjustment having occurred by year four and the process largely complete by year seven.

Equation (7.15) ensures that the trend value for origin region $o$'s gross emigration rate to region $d$ moves in proportion with region $d$'s share of the national population.

To translate movements in $GEMR_{o,d}$ to movements in gross emigration numbers, we multiply the year $t$ value of $GEMR_{o,d}$ by the year $t$ population of region $o$. The resulting population flows affect start of year populations in year $t+1$. Movements in $GEMR_{o,d}$ can thus be interpreted as changes in planned emigration in year $t$, with an average 6-month lag before the population movement occurs at the beginning of year $t+1$.

## 7.4.12 Regional household income and expenditure

Figure 7.1 contains a large amount of information about the income and expenditure accounts of regional households. However, full accounting of regional household income and expenditure requires that the MRIO data of Figure 7.1 be supplemented with a set of ancillary income and expenditure accounts. These are presented in Figure 7.2. Before discussing Figure 7.2 we expand on the household accounts information contained in Figure 7.1.

Column (3) of Figure 7.1 sets out the components of regional household consumption. Calculation of private consumption at market prices by household $h$ in region $r$ ($\mathrm{CON}^{(h,r)}$) is a simple matter of aggregating the commodity, source, margin and tax detail in column (3):

$$\mathrm{CON}^{(h,r)} = \sum_{i \in \mathrm{COM}} \sum_{s \in \mathrm{SRC}} \left( \mathrm{BAS3}^{(h,r)}_{(i,s)} + \sum_{m \in \mathrm{MAR}} \sum_{k \in \mathrm{REG}} \mathrm{MAR3}^{(h,r)}_{(i,s)(m,k)} + \sum_{g \in \mathrm{GOV}} \mathrm{TAX3}^{(h,r)}_{(i,s)(g)} \right).$$
(7.16)

Rows 4, 6 and 8 of Figure 7.1 set out the components of the post-tax primary factor income of household $h$ in region $r$ ($\mathrm{PFPT}^{(h,r)}$):

$$\mathrm{PFPT}^{(h,r)} = \sum_{j \in \mathrm{IND}} \sum_{k \in \mathrm{REG}} \left[ \sum_{o \in \mathrm{OCC}} \mathrm{LABR}^{(j,k)}_{(o,h,r)} + \mathrm{CAPR}^{(j,k)}_{(h,r)} + \sum_{t \in \mathrm{RES}} \mathrm{NATR}^{(j,k)}_{(h,r)(t)} \right].$$
(7.17)

Post-tax primary factor income is an important, but not the sole, determinant of total post-tax regional household income. The remaining categories of regional household income and outlays are set out in broad terms in Figure 7.2. Via Figure 7.2, the net household income of household $h$ in region $r$ ($\mathrm{HINC}^{(h,r)}$) can be calculated as:

$$\mathrm{HINC}^{(h,r)} = \mathrm{PFPT}^{(h,r)} - \sum_{g \in \mathrm{GOV}} \mathrm{HTAX}^{(h,r)}_{(g)} + \sum_{g \in \mathrm{GOV}} \mathrm{GTRN}^{(h,r)}_{(g)}$$

$$+ \sum_{t \in \mathrm{HOU}} \sum_{k \in \mathrm{REG}} \left[ \mathrm{HTRN}^{(h,r)}_{(t,k)} - \mathrm{HTRN}^{(t,k)}_{(h,r)} \right] + \mathrm{FTRN}^{(h,r)} - \mathrm{HINT}^{(h,r)}.$$
(7.18)

Together, (7.16) and (7.18) imply household savings of:

$$\text{HSAV}^{(h,r)} = \text{HINC}^{(h,r)} - \text{CON}^{(h,r)}. \tag{7.19}$$

In a comparative static model, a working assumption for household net interest payments on foreign debt, $\text{HINT}^{(h,r)}$ is that they are exogenous. In a dynamic model, stock/flow accounting for household interest payments can be implemented via:

$$\text{HINT}^{(h,r)} = \Phi \times \text{HNFL}_t^{(h,r)} \times \rho_t \tag{7.20}$$

$$\text{HNFL}_{t+1}^{(h,r)} = \text{HNFL}_t^{(h,r)} - (1/\Phi)\left[\text{HSAV}_t^{(h,r)} - \text{HINV}_t^{(h,r)}\right], \tag{7.21}$$

where $\Phi$ is the nominal exchange rate expressed as domestic currency units per foreign currency unit, $\rho_t$ is the rate of interest on net foreign debt $\text{HNFL}_{t+1}^{(h,r)}$ and $\text{HNFL}_t^{(h,r)}$ are household net foreign liabilities in foreign currency terms in years $t+1$ and $t$, respectively, and $\text{HINV}_t^{(h,r)}$ is that part of the nation's gross fixed capital formation financed by household $h$ in region $r$.

Equations (7.20) and (7.21) suppress many potential details. (i) Equation (7.21) assumes all net financing occurs via foreign transactions, thus excluding the possibility of inter-regional domestic net liability positions. (ii) Both Equations (7.20) and (7.21) assume that claims on assets are via debt only, thus excluding the possibility of equity positions. (iii) By identifying a single interest rate on a net debt position only, Equation (7.20) excludes the possibility of differential rates of return on debt and equity positions at home and abroad. (iv) Equations (7.20) and (7.21) assume that net foreign borrowings are denominated in foreign currency terms only. These assumptions may be relaxed in a detailed large-scale model.

### 7.4.13 Government accounts

The MRIO database set out in Figure 7.1 contains many elements of the regional and federal government accounts. From column (5) we can identify aggregate public consumption at market prices by government $g$ in region $r$ as:

$$\text{GOV}_{(g)}^{(r)} = \sum_{i \in \text{COM}} \sum_{s \in \text{SRC}} \left( \text{BAS5}_{(i,s)}^{(g,r)} + \sum_{m \in \text{MAR}} \sum_{k \in \text{REG}} \text{MAR5}_{(i,s)(m,k)}^{(g,r)} + \sum_{h \in \text{GOV}} \text{TAX5}_{(i,s)(h)}^{(g,r)} \right). \tag{7.22}$$

The elements of rows 3 and 10, together with the tariff array $\text{TARF}_{(i)}^{(g)}$, allow us to identify aggregate indirect tax revenue as:

$\text{ITAX}_{(g)}$

$$= \sum_{j \in \text{IND}} \sum_{r \in \text{REG}} \left( \sum_{i \in \text{COM}} \sum_{s \in \text{SRC}} \left( \text{TAX1}_{(i,s)(g)}^{(j,r)} + \text{TAX2}_{(i,s)(g)}^{(j,r)} \right) + \text{PTAX}_{(g)}^{(1)(j,r)} + \text{PTAX}_{(g)}^{(2)(j,r)} \right)$$

$$+ \sum_{i \in \text{COM}} \left( \sum_{r \in \text{REG}} \left( \sum_{s \in \text{SRC}} \left( \sum_{h \in \text{HOU}} \text{TAX3}_{(i,s)(g)}^{(h,r)} + \sum_{k \in \text{GOV}} \text{TAX5}_{(i,s)(g)}^{(k,r)} \right) + \text{TAX4}_{(i)(g)}^{(r)} \right) + \text{TARF}_{(i)}^{(g)} \right). \tag{7.23}$$

Note that among the indirect taxes on commodity- and source-specific inputs Figure 7.1 allows for per-unit or *ad valorem* taxes levied by government $g$ on new capital formation in regional industry $j,r$, via $\text{PTAX}_{(g)}^{(2)(j,r)}$. $\text{PTAX}_{(g)}^{(2)(j,r)}$ is not a typical feature of a MRIO database. Nevertheless, in simulations investigating a new capital tax levied on the installation of new units of capital, $\text{PTAX}_{(g)}^{(2)(j,r)}$ must be recognized. For example, Giesecke *et al.* (2008), investigating the impact of a developer charge on new residential developments, model the charge as a production tax on new units of capital in the ownership of dwellings sector. In Jorgenson and Yun in Chapter 10 of this Handbook, taxation of new housing forms an important part of their tax reform package.

The elements of rows 5, 7 and 9 of Figure 7.1, together with $\text{HTAX}_{(g)}^{(h,r)}$ from the ancillary accounts, allow us to identify aggregate direct tax revenue as:

$$\text{DTAX}_{(g)} = \sum_{j \in \text{IND}} \sum_{r \in \text{REG}} \left[ \sum_{o \in \text{OCC}} \sum_{h \in \text{HOU}} \sum_{k \in \text{REG}} \text{LABT}_{(o,h,k)(g)}^{(j,r)} \right.$$

$$\left. + \sum_{h \in \text{HOU}} \sum_{s \in \text{SRC}} \left( \text{CAPT}_{(h,s)(g)}^{(j,r)} + \sum_{t \in \text{RES}} \text{NATT}_{(h,s)(t)(g)}^{(j,r)} \right) \right] + \sum_{r \in \text{REG}} \sum_{h \in \text{HOU}} \text{HTAX}_{(g)}^{(h,r)}. \tag{7.24}$$

Equations (7.22), (7.23) and (7.24), together with the ancillary revenue and expenditure items identified in Figure 7.2, allows us to identify public sector savings:

$$\text{GSAV}_{(g)} = \text{DTAX}_{(g)} + \text{ITAX}_{(g)} + \text{FTRN}_{(g)} + \sum_{k \in \text{GOV}} \text{GRNT}_{(k)}^{(g)}$$

$$- \sum_{r \in \text{REG}} \left( \text{GOV}_{(g)}^{(r)} + \sum_{h \in \text{HOU}} \text{GTRN}_{(g)}^{(h,r)} \right) - \sum_{k \in \text{GOV}} \text{GRNT}_{(g)}^{(k)} - \text{GINT}_{(g)}. \tag{7.25}$$

In a comparative static model, a working assumption for government net interest payments on foreign debt, $\text{GINT}_{(g)}$ is that they are exogenous. In a dynamic model, stock/flow accounting for government interest payments can be implemented via:

$$\text{GINT}_{(g)} = \Phi \times \text{GNFL}_{(g)}^{t} \times \rho_{(g)}^{t} \tag{7.26}$$

$$\text{GNFL}_{(g)}^{t+1} = \text{GNFL}_{(g)}^{t} - (1/\Phi) \left[ \text{GSAV}_{(g)}^{t} - \text{GINV}_{(g)}^{t} \right], \tag{7.27}$$

where $\Phi$ is the nominal exchange rate expressed as domestic currency units per foreign currency unit; $\rho_{(g)}^{t}$ is the rate of interest on net foreign debt; $\text{GNFL}_{(g)}^{t+1}$ and $\text{GNFL}_{(g)}^{t}$ are government net foreign liabilities in foreign currency terms in years $t+1$ and $t$, respectively; and $\text{GINV}_{(g)}^{t}$ is that part of the nation's gross fixed capital formation undertaken by government ($g$).

Like the stylized interest and foreign liability accounting equations identified for the household sector, (7.26) and (7.27) abstract considerably from the full national income accounting details available in official statistics. In a large applied fiscal model, more detail can be introduced on assets and liabilities distinguished by debt and equity, the currencies in which liabilities are denominated, differences in interest rates and rates of return across asset and liability categories and government levels, and valuation impacts on net asset positions.[68]

## 7.5 CONSTRUCTING (MULTI)REGIONAL DATABASES

### 7.5.1 Regional data limitations

Partridge and Rickman (1998) speculate that scarcity of regional data may lie behind the slow adoption of CGE techniques for regional modeling. Certainly, as is clear from Section 7.4, regional CGE models, particularly of the bottom-up variety, demand large amounts of regional data, of which only a meager amount is available from statistical agencies and other data sources. However, an array of estimation techniques is available to fill in the many data gaps for which no statistics have been collected.

Regional CGE models share part of their data requirements with other types of regional models and there is a considerable literature on estimating techniques in this area (e.g. Round, 1983). We limit our discussion of input-output and other social accounting data to the development of recent methods of particular use to regional CGE modelers.

### 7.5.2 Structural data

Of the three basic types of regional CGE models, bottom-up multiregional is the type which naturally has the most extensive data requirements. The structural data required for a full-blown multiregional CGE model can be seen in Figures 7.1 and 7.2 that depict MRIO, and income and government accounts, respectively. We consider estimation techniques for just the former here, since the latter tends to be peculiar to an individual country and the level of regional disaggregation.[69]

While there have been standard (largely) computerized techniques for the non-survey generation of input-output tables for several decades (e.g. Jensen *et al.*, 1979), comparable techniques for MRIO tables have been less in evidence.[70] The LMPST method referred to in Section 7.3.2 was an early method for generating an MRIO with minimal information, see Dixon *et al.* (1982) for a detailed discussion of how an

---

[68] See, e.g. Dixon and Rimmer (2002, pp. 212–219).

[69] Most regional CGE models are defined on regions which equate with jurisdictions, but these might be as aggregated as states/provinces or as disaggregated as counties or local government areas.

[70] Jensen *et al.*, provides an extensive guide to the GRIT (Generation of Input-Output Table) method. Alternatively, see West (1984) or Johns and Leat (1987).

MRIO is formed via LMPST. This method could have formed the basis for estimating a multiregional CGE database, although perhaps only after a readily-made improvement to the method's treatment of the sourcing of national commodities. LMPST assumes that all users, regardless of their region, source their purchases of a commodity in proportion to the supplying region's share in the national production of that commodity. At least for some goods in geographically spread countries such as the US, production shares might have been modified by distances between origin and destination regions. This would amount to employing the gravity method (Leontief and Stroud, 1963).

Multiregional CGE modelers have used a variety of methods to estimate the required MRIO database (Haddad *et al.*, 2002b). Here, we will address ourselves to a method developed by (Horridge *et al.*, 2005), which combines variants of previous methods, and which has been successfully applied to Australia, the US, China and other countries.

The first step in the Horridge procedure is to establish, for each industry, regional shares in nationwide output. Usually employment by regional industry figures are used, although for certain industries such as ownership of dwellings (which has zero employment) other information, like regional rental income, needs to be used. The major other information requirement is regional estimates for household and government consumption, and information on ports of import and export by commodity. Together with national input-output data, this is enough to establish total regional demands and supplies by commodity and sources. The procedure then computes a matrix of regional sourcing estimates. Diagonal elements (i.e. the degree of local sourcing of commodities) are computed for each domestic and each imported commodity by a modified location quotient expressed as:[71]

$$\text{Min} \left\{ \frac{\text{Local supply}}{\text{Local demand}}, 1 \right\} \times F, \tag{7.28}$$

where $F$ is a parameter varying between 0.5 and 1.0, with a value close to the latter where the commodity is not easily tradable. The introduction of the $F$ parameter allows for cross-hauling of commodities.

Off-diagonal elements (out-of-region sourcing) are estimated according to a gravity formula that in its general form can be represented as:[72]

$$\frac{V(r, d)}{V(\bullet, d)} \propto \frac{V(r, \bullet)}{D(r, d)^K} \, r \neq d, \tag{7.29}$$

[71] A location quotient is a ratio of an industry's share in aggregate regional output to its share in economy-wide output (see Johns and Leat, 1987).

[72] Subscripts for commodity and international source (domestic or imported) are omitted for convenience.

where $V(r,d)$ is the value of the flow from origin $r$ to destination $d$, $V(\bullet,d)$ is local demand from all sources, $V(r,\bullet)$ is the value of production, $D(r,d)$ is the distance between regions $r$ and $d$, and $K$ is a commodity-specific parameter valued between 0.5 and 2, with values being inversely related to the ease of tradability.

The $F$ parameters are adjusted and a RAS procedure undertaken to ensure all estimated flows from $r$ add to $r$'s total supply and all estimated demands by $d$ add to $d$'s total demands.

The above provides only a general summary of what is in practice a set of complex computations, particularly in relation to margin commodities. Dixon and Rimmer (2004) provide a detailed discussion of the intricacies of these computations. It is worth noting here, however, that in estimating margins, transport costs $T(r,d)$ are related to distance:

$$\frac{T(r,d)}{V(r,d)} \propto \sqrt{D(r,d)}. \tag{7.30}$$

A major advantage of the Horridge data estimation routines is that they deliver an MRIO database in suitable form for use in most CGE models. These values are in basic prices, and margins and taxes are shown separately in their full specification. This allows the purchasers' value of each flow to be computed by a simple addition of the corresponding elements of the direct flow, margins and tax matrices. This greatly enhances the ease of usability for modelers.

Similarly, Giesecke (2011) provides a method for estimating single-region input–output data for regional CGE models. While input–output data for single regions are often readily available (e.g. in the US from IMPLAN), this data often is not in a suitable format to directly use in a single-region CGE model. Giesecke (2011) provides procedures for adjusting IMPLAN single-region input–output matrices to generate the required data matrices for CGE modeling through the application of national share information to perform appropriate disaggregations.

## 7.5.3 Behavioral parameters

It is common practice for regional CGE models to use elasticities borrowed from their national counterparts (e.g. Jones and Whalley, 1989; Madden, 1990). While this is a reasonable approach in the case of most types of elasticities, frequent concern is expressed in the case of the inter-regional trade Armington elasticities (e.g. Partridge and Rickman, 2010). It is commonplace for regional CGE modelers to undertake sensitivity analysis on these latter elasticities (Turner, 2009).

In the case of many countries, there is a dearth of the regional data required to undertake econometric estimates of inter-regional trade elasticities. There have been, however, some studies (e.g. Bilgic et al., 2002; Ha et al., 2010) that econometrically estimate inter-regional Armington elasticities for the US where commodity flow surveys are undertaken by the Bureau of Transportation Statistics at 5-year intervals. Ha *et al.* compare their results for inter-regional elasticities with Bilgic *et al.*'s, and with three studies estimating Armington estimates in international trade.[73] The comparison is made for agriculture, mining and seven manufacturing commodities, and it suggests, in general, that inter-regional and international elasticities are within the same broad order of magnitude. They give no support to the often-held idea that international trade elasticities form a lower bound for the corresponding inter-regional import elasticities.

Certainly, it is an area calling for further econometric work. Examination of the movement in inter-regional twist parameters and price movements from historical multiregional CGE simulations might reveal evidence as to whether the inter-regional import elasticity estimates currently being used are reasonable. However, on the face of it, the use of inter-regional import elasticities equal to or close to their international counterparts would seem reasonable.

## 7.6 SIMULATIONS AND INTERPRETATION OF MULTIREGIONAL MODEL MECHANISMS

In this section, we use the MMRF model to investigate two regional economic shocks. The first, a supply-side shock, explores the effects of a change in regional labor productivity. The second, a demand-side shock, explores the effects of a change in the regional distribution of demand. The purpose of the section is to set out techniques for explaining regional CGE results in ways that can be readily understood by readers unfamiliar with a multiregional CGE model. To do this we explain our results in terms of a miniature or BOTE model. Use of stylized models to describe the workings of large-scale CGE models has a long tradition in the application of national CGE models.[74] However, they are found less frequently in the regional CGE literature. In presenting the BOTE model, and using it to analyze our regional shocks, we hope to demonstrate the value of the BOTE technique in explicating results from large-scale regional models.

While the BOTE model is small and aggregated, it is sufficient to explain the major regional macroeconomic outcomes of the full-scale multiregional model. The BOTE model is a stylized single-region representation of a regional macroeconomy as it operates within MMRF, with coefficient values evaluated using the MMRF database. We use an aggregated MMRF model for these simulations, one recognizing three Australian regions: north (comprising Western Australia, the Northern Territory and

---

[73] Ha *et al.*'s study is for Illinois inter-regional imports, while Bilgic *et al.*'s estimates are for inter-regional imports for the US in general. Two of the international studies were for US foreign imports, the other for the Organization for Economic Cooperation and Development (OECD) countries.

[74] See Dixon *et al.* (1984) for an early example.

Queensland), South (comprising South Australia, Victoria and Tasmania) and East (comprising New South Wales and the Australian Capital Territory).

We begin by describing the BOTE model in Section 7.6.1. Section 7.6.2 describes the closure of BOTE. Section 7.6.3 uses the BOTE equations to derive compact equations describing regional aggregate demand and aggregate supply in the short run and long run. We then proceed to investigate two region-specific shocks: a rise in regional labor productivity (Section 7.6.4) and a shift in the spatial distribution of regional sourcing preferences (Section 7.6.5). In each case, we provide BOTE explanations of the regional consequences of the shock.

## 7.6.1 BOTE: A back-of-the-envelope representation of regional CGE macroeconomic mechanisms

BOTE is described in Tables 7.2–7.5. Table 7.2 presents the BOTE equations. Variable descriptions, together with short-run and long-run closures of BOTE, are presented in Table 7.3. We use short-run (2012) and long-run (2030) values from the baseline simulation of the full-scale MMRF model to evaluate the coefficients of BOTE. These coefficients and their values are described in Tables 7.4 and 7.5.

As discussed in Section 7.4.1, in deriving primary factor input demand equations, MMRF carries the assumption that each regional industry faces primary factor substitution possibilities described by CES functional forms. These give rise to cost-minimizing input demand and unit cost equations that, expressed in terms of percentage changes, are of the form:[75]

$$x^v_{j,r} = a^v_{j,r} + y_{j,r} - \sigma\left(p^v_{j,r} + a^v_{j,r} - p_{j,r}\right) \tag{7.31}$$

$$p_{j,r} = \sum_v S^v_{j,r} \cdot \left(p^v_{j,r} + a^v_{j,r}\right), \tag{7.32}$$

where $x^v_{j,r}$ is the percentage change in demand for factor $v$ by regional industry $j,r$, $a^v_{j,r}$ is the percentage change in the technical efficiency of primary factor input $v$ in regional industry $j,r$, $y_{j,r}$ is the percentage change in the output of regional industry $j,r$, $p^v_{j,r}$ is the percentage change in the price faced by regional industry $j,r$ for factor $v$, $p_{j,r}$ is the percentage change in the average price of primary factors faced by regional industry $j,r$, $\sigma$ is the elasticity of substitution between primary factor inputs, and $S^v_{j,r}$ is the share of payments to factor $v$ in industry $j,r$'s total primary factor costs.

---

[75] See Dixon et al. (1992b, pp. 124–125) for the derivation of the percentage change form of the input demand and unit cost functions arising from a CES production function.

**Table 7.2** BOTE: A calibrated back-of-the-envelope representation of regional macroeconomic relationships in MMRF

Demand for labor
(B1) $\qquad l_r - a_r^{L} = y_r - \sigma(\{w_r + a_r^{L}\} - p_r)$
Demand for capital
(B2) $\qquad k_r = y_r - \sigma(r_r^{K} - p_r)$
Demand for natural resources
(B3) $\qquad n_r = y_r - \sigma(r_r^{N} - p_r)$
Regional GDP deflator
(B4) $\qquad p_r = S_r^{L}\{w_r + a_r^{L}\} + S_r^{K}r_r^{K} + S_r^{N}r_r^{N}$
Rate of return on capital
(B5) $\qquad ror_r = r_r^{K} - p_r^{I}$
Investment price index
(B6) $\qquad p_r^{I} = S_r^{(D)I}p_r$
Real gross regional expenditure
(B7) $\qquad e_r = S_r^{(E)C}c_r + S_r^{(E)I}i_r + S_r^{(E)S}g_r^{(S)} + S_r^{(E)F}g_r^{(F)}$
Real private consumption
(B8) $\qquad c_r = apc_r + y_r$
Gross capital growth rate
(B9) $\qquad \psi_r = i_r - k_r$
Relationship between rate of return on capital and the capital growth rate
(B10) $\qquad \psi_r = \beta_r[ror_r - \lambda_r]$
Ratio of regional government consumption to private consumption
(B11) $\qquad \lambda_r^{(S)} = g_r^{(S)} - c_r$
Federal government consumption *per capita*
(B12) $\qquad \lambda_r^{(F)} = g_r^{(F)} - q_r$
Regional expenditure-side real GDP
(B13) $\qquad y_r = S_r^{(Y)E}e_r + \left( S_r^{(Y)XF}x_r^{(F)} - S_r^{(Y)MF}m_r^{(F)} \right) + \left( S_r^{(Y)XR}x_r^{(R)} - S_r^{(Y)MR}m_r^{(R)} \right)$
Foreign export volumes
(B14) $\qquad x_r^{(F)} = -\eta_r^{(XF)}(p_r - v_r)$
Foreign import volumes
(B15) $\qquad m_r^{(F)} = y_r + \left[ \sigma_r^{(2)}S_r^{(Dom)}S_r^{(Local)} \right]p_r$
Inter-regional export volumes
(B16) $\qquad x_r^{(R)} = -\left[ \sigma^{(2)}S_{(Imp)r}^{(RoC)}S_r^{(RoC)} + \sigma^{(3)}\left( 1 - S_r^{(RoC)} \right) \right]S_r^{BAS}p_r + (1 - S_r^{(RoC)})\xi_r$
Inter-regional import volumes
(B17) $\qquad m_r^{(R)} = y_r + \left[ \sigma^{(3)}S_r^{(Local)} - \sigma^{(2)}S_r^{(Local)}\left( 1 - S_r^{(Dom)} \right) \right]p_r - S_r^{(Local)}\xi_r$
Short-run sticky wage mechanism
(B18) $\qquad w_r - p_r^{C} = \alpha \cdot er_r + f_r^{(W)}$
Consumption price index
(B19) $\qquad p_r^{C} = S_r^{(D)C}p_r$
Employment decomposition population, participation rate and employment rate
(B20) $\qquad l_r = q_r + pr_r + er_r$
Net inter-regional immigration rate
(B21) $\qquad \varphi_r = nim_r - q_r$
Relationship between inter-regional net immigration rate and expected regional wage
(B22) $\qquad \varphi_r = \phi_r\left[ w_r + er_r - f_r^{(SR)} \right]$
Regional wage relativity
(B23) $\qquad f_r^{(LR)} = w_r - w$

**Table 7.3** Variables of the BOTE model

| Variable and variable description (all variables are percentage change, unless otherwise indicated) | | Closure[a] Short-run | Long-run |
|---|---|:---:|:---:|
| $a_r^L$ | Regional labor augmenting technical change | X | X |
| $apc_r$ | Regional average propensity to consume | X | X |
| $c_r$ | Real regional private consumption spending | N | N |
| $e_r$ | Real gross regional expenditure | N | N |
| $er_r$ | Region $r$'s employment rate ($1 -$ the unemployment rate) | N | X |
| $f_r^{(SR)}$ | Shift variable on the short-run net regional immigration function | X | N |
| $f_r^{(LR)}$ | Ratio of the regional wage to the national wage | N | X |
| $f_r^{(W)}$ | Shift variable on the short-run regional wage equation | X | N |
| $g_r^{(S)}$ | Real regional government consumption spending | N | N |
| $g_r^{(F)}$ | Real federal government consumption spending | N | N |
| $i_r$ | Real regional gross fixed capital formation | N | N |
| $k_r$ | Region $r$'s capital stock | X | N |
| $l_r$ | Employment of persons in region $r$ | N | N |
| $m_r^{(F)}$ | Region $r$'s foreign import volumes | N | N |
| $m_r^{(R)}$ | Region $r$'s inter-regional import volumes | N | N |
| $n_r$ | Region $r$'s land endowment | X | X |
| $nim_r$ | Net immigration to region $r$ | N | N |
| $p_r$ | Regional GDP deflator | N | N |
| $p_r^C$ | Region $r$'s household consumption price deflator | N | N |
| $p_r^I$ | Region $r$'s investment price deflator | N | N |
| $pr_r$ | Region $r$'s participation rate | X | X |
| $q_r$ | Region $r$'s population | X | N |
| $r_r^K$ | Average capital rental price in region $r$ | N | N |
| $r_r^N$ | Region $r$'s land rental price | N | N |
| $ror_r$ | Rate of return on capital in region $r$ | N | X |
| $v_r$ | Vertical scalar on the position of the regional export demand schedule | X | X |
| $w$ | The economy-wide wage rate | X | X |
| $w_r$ | Nominal wage per person in region $r$ | N | N |
| $x_r^{(F)}$ | Region $r$'s foreign export volumes | N | N |
| $x_r^{(R)}$ | Region $r$'s inter-regional export volumes | N | N |
| $y_r$ | Real regional GDP | N | N |
| $\lambda_r$ | The normal rate of return in region $r$ | X | N |

(*Continued*)

**Table 7.3** Variables of the BOTE model—cont'd

| Variable and variable description (all variables are percentage change, unless otherwise indicated) | | Closure[a] Short-run | Long-run |
|---|---|:---:|:---:|
| $\lambda_r^{(S)}$ | Ratio of regional government public consumption to private consumption | X | X |
| $\lambda_r^{(F)}$ | Regional *per capita* federal consumption spending | X | X |
| $\xi_r$ | Cost-neutral change in regional sourcing preferences towards region $r$'s goods | X | X |
| $\varphi_r$ | Region $r$'s net inter-regional immigration rate | N | X |
| $\psi_r$ | Regional investment/capital ratio | N | X |

[a]X = exogenous; N = endogenous.

**Table 7.4** Short-run parameter and coefficient values of the calibrated BOTE model[a]

| | Parameters and coefficients of the BOTE model | North | East | South |
|---|---|:---:|:---:|:---:|
| $\sigma$ | Primary factor substitution elasticity | 0.30 | 0.30 | 0.30 |
| $S_r^N$ | Share of payments to land in regional GDP at factor cost | 0.07 | 0.07 | 0.07 |
| $S_r^K$ | Share of payments to capital in regional GDP at factor cost | 0.45 | 0.38 | 0.40 |
| $S_r^L$ | Share of payments to labor in regional GDP at factor cost | 0.48 | 0.55 | 0.54 |
| $S_r^{(D)I}$ | Share of region ($r$)-sourced inputs in region ($r$)'s investment | 0.60 | 0.64 | 0.64 |
| $S_r^{(E)C}$ | Share of private consumption in gross regional expenditure | 0.51 | 0.55 | 0.55 |
| $S_r^{(E)S}$ | Share of state government consumption in gross regional expenditure | 0.11 | 0.11 | 0.11 |
| $S_r^{(E)I}$ | Share of investment in gross regional expenditure | 0.32 | 0.27 | 0.27 |
| $S_r^{(E)F}$ | Share of federal government consumption in gross reg. expenditure | 0.06 | 0.07 | 0.07 |
| $S_r^{(Y)XF}$ | Share of foreign exports in regional GDP | 0.29 | 0.15 | 0.16 |
| $S_r^{(Y)MF}$ | Share of foreign imports in regional GDP | 0.19 | 0.19 | 0.22 |
| $S_r^{(Y)XR}$ | Share of inter-regional exports in regional GDP | 0.16 | 0.21 | 0.22 |
| $S_r^{(Y)MR}$ | Share of inter-regional imports in regional GDP | 0.23 | 0.18 | 0.18 |
| $S_r^{(Y)E}$ | Share of gross regional expenditure in regional GDP | 0.98 | 1.01 | 1.02 |
| $\eta_r^{(XF)}$ | Foreign export price elasticity of demand | 4.00 | 4.00 | 4.00 |
| $\sigma^{(2)}$ | Import/domestic substitution elasticity | 2.50 | 2.50 | 2.50 |
| $\sigma^{(3)}$ | Inter-regional substitution elasticity | 2.50 | 2.50 | 2.50 |
| $S_r^{BAS}$ | Basic value share in the purchaser's value of inter-regional exports | 0.85 | 0.86 | 0.79 |
| $S_{(Imp)r}^{(RoC)}$ | Share of foreign imports, in total traded goods use, in the rest of the country | 0.23 | 0.23 | 0.22 |
| $S_r^{(Local)}$ | Share of use of own supply in region $r$'s use of domestic goods | 0.82 | 0.80 | 0.87 |

(*Continued*)

**Table 7.4** Short-run parameter and coefficient values of the calibrated BOTE model[a]—cont'd

| | Parameters and coefficients of the BOTE model | North | East | South |
|---|---|---|---|---|
| $S_r^{(\text{Dom})}$ | Share of domestically sourced goods in region $r$'s total use of traded goods | 0.78 | 0.78 | 0.76 |
| $S_r^{(\text{RoC})}$ | Region $r$'s trade share in use of traded domestic goods in the rest of the country | 0.08 | 0.07 | 0.11 |
| $S_r^{(\text{D})\text{C}}$ | Share of region $r$-sourced goods in region $r$ private consumption | 0.79 | 0.83 | 0.84 |
| $\beta_r$ | Elasticity of regional investment to rates of return | 1.25 | 1.25 | 1.25 |
| $\phi_r$ | Elasticity of immigration rate to migration income relativity | 0.20 | 0.20 | 0.20 |
| $\alpha$ | Elasticity of the short-run regional real wage deviation to the employment rate deviation | 0.50 | 0.50 | 0.50 |
| $\Omega_r^{(1)}$ | See Equation (7.39) | 0.81 | 0.71 | 0.73 |
| $\Omega_r^{(2)}$ | See Equation (7.39) | −2.13 | −1.62 | −1.67 |
| $\Omega_r^{(3)}$ | See Equation (7.39) | 0.61 | 0.67 | 0.67 |
| $\Omega_r^{(4)}$ | See Equation (7.39) | 0.31 | 0.27 | 0.28 |
| $\Omega_r^{(5)}$ | See Equation (7.39) | 0.11 | 0.11 | 0.11 |
| $\Omega_r^{(6)}$ | See Equation (7.39) | 0.06 | 0.08 | 0.07 |
| $\Omega_r^{(7)}$ | See Equation (7.39) | 1.15 | 0.61 | 0.63 |
| $\Omega_r^{(8)}$ | See Equation (7.39) | 0.33 | 0.34 | 0.35 |
| $A_r^{(1)}$ | See Equation (7.37) | 0.04 | 0.05 | 0.04 |
| $A_r^{(2)}$ | See Equation (7.37) | 0.32 | 0.41 | 0.40 |
| $A_r^{(3)}$ | See Equation (7.37) | 1.71 | 1.92 | 1.88 |

[a]Evaluated from the short-run (year 2012) MMRF database.

**Table 7.5** Long-run parameter and coefficient values of the calibrated BOTE model[a]

| | Parameters and coefficients of the BOTE model | North | East | South |
|---|---|---|---|---|
| $\sigma$ | Primary factor substitution elasticity | 0.30 | 0.30 | 0.30 |
| $S_r^{\text{N}}$ | Share of payments to land in regional GDP at factor cost | 0.14 | 0.10 | 0.11 |
| $S_r^{\text{K}}$ | Share of payments to capital in regional GDP at factor cost | 0.35 | 0.30 | 0.31 |
| $S_r^{\text{L}}$ | Share of payments to labor in regional GDP at factor cost | 0.51 | 0.60 | 0.58 |
| $S_r^{(\text{D})\text{I}}$ | Share of region ($r$)-sourced inputs in region ($r$)'s investment | 0.60 | 0.64 | 0.63 |
| $S_r^{(\text{E})\text{C}}$ | Share of private consumption in gross regional expenditure | 0.56 | 0.59 | 0.59 |
| $S_r^{(\text{E})\text{S}}$ | Share of state government consumption in gross regional expenditure | 0.12 | 0.12 | 0.11 |

(*Continued*)

**Table 7.5** Long-run parameter and coefficient values of the calibrated BOTE model[a]—cont'd

| Parameters and coefficients of the BOTE model | North | East | South |
|---|---|---|---|
| $S_r^{(E)I}$ | Share of investment in gross regional expenditure | 0.26 | 0.22 | 0.22 |
| $S_r^{(E)F}$ | Share of federal government consumption in gross regional expenditure | 0.06 | 0.08 | 0.07 |
| $S_r^{(Y)XF}$ | Share of foreign exports in regional GDP | 0.34 | 0.20 | 0.21 |
| $S_r^{(Y)MF}$ | Share of foreign imports in regional GDP | 0.17 | 0.18 | 0.20 |
| $S_r^{(Y)XR}$ | Share of inter-regional exports in regional GDP | 0.14 | 0.21 | 0.22 |
| $S_r^{(Y)MR}$ | Share of inter-regional imports in regional GDP | 0.21 | 0.18 | 0.17 |
| $S_r^{(Y)E}$ | Share of gross regional expenditure in regional GDP | 0.90 | 0.95 | 0.96 |
| $\eta_r^{(XF)}$ | Foreign export price elasticity of demand | 4.00 | 4.00 | 4.00 |
| $\sigma^{(2)}$ | Import/domestic substitution elasticity | 2.50 | 2.50 | 2.50 |
| $\sigma^{(3)}$ | Inter-regional substitution elasticity | 2.50 | 2.50 | 2.50 |
| $S_r^{BAS}$ | Basic value share in the purchaser's value of inter-regional exports | 0.86 | 0.86 | 0.80 |
| $S_{(Imp)r}^{(RoC)}$ | Share of foreign imports, in total traded goods use, in the rest of the country | 0.23 | 0.23 | 0.22 |
| $S_r^{(Local)}$ | Share of use of own supply in region $r$'s use of domestic goods | 0.81 | 0.78 | 0.86 |
| $S_r^{(Dom)}$ | Share of domestically sourced goods in region $r$'s total use of traded goods | 0.79 | 0.77 | 0.76 |
| $S_r^{(RoC)}$ | Region $r$'s trade share in use of traded domestic goods in the rest of the country | 0.08 | 0.07 | 0.11 |
| $S_r^{(D)C}$ | Share of region $r$-sourced goods in region $r$ private consumption | 0.81 | 0.84 | 0.85 |
| $\Psi_r^{(1)}$ | See Equation (7.52) | 0.54 | 0.49 | 0.49 |
| $\Psi_r^{(2)}$ | See Equation (7.52) | −2.27 | −1.78 | −1.85 |
| $\Psi_r^{(3)}$ | See Equation (7.52) | 0.06 | 0.08 | 0.07 |
| $\Psi_r^{(4)}$ | See Equation (7.52) | 1.37 | 0.80 | 0.83 |
| $\Psi_r^{(5)}$ | See Equation (7.52) | 0.32 | 0.35 | 0.37 |
| $\Phi_r^{(1)}$ | See Equation (7.44) | 0.46 | 0.35 | 0.36 |
| $\Phi_r^{(2)}$ | See Equation (7.44) | 0.65 | 0.70 | 0.69 |
| $\Phi_r^{(3)}$ | See Equation (7.44) | 0.51 | 0.60 | 0.58 |
| $\Theta_r^{(1)}$ | See Equation (7.68) | 0.88 | 0.90 | 0.90 |
| $\Theta_r^{(2)}$ | See Equation (7.68) | 0.96 | 1.23 | 1.20 |

[a]Evaluated from the long-run (year 2030) MMRF database.

On the basis of (7.31) and (7.32), BOTE Equations (B1)–(B4) approximately hold at the regionwide level for any given region.[76]

BOTE Equation (B5) defines the percentage change in the regional rate of return on capital. (B5) introduces the percentage change in the regional cost of capital, which we define by (B6).[77]

Equation (B7) defines the percentage change in real gross regional expenditure as the share-weighted-sum of the percentage changes in regional real private consumption, real investment and real state and federal government public consumption.

Equation (B8) presents a stylized consumption function, describing regional real private consumption as a function of real regional GDP and a given regional average propensity to consume.

Equation (B9) defines the gross growth rate of the regional capital stock. Equation (B10) is a short-run investment function, relating the gross growth rate of the regional capital stock to movements in the regional rate of return on capital.

Equation (B11) defines the ratio of real regional public consumption to real regional private consumption. Equation (B12) defines regional *per capita* federal government consumption.

Equation (B13) defines the percentage change form of the regional GDP identity in constant price terms.

Equation (B14) models demand for region $r$'s foreign exports via a constant elasticity demand function.

As discussed in Section 7.4.1, MMRF carries the assumption that region-specific economic actors make their commodity sourcing decisions in a nested two stage manner: they first choose between foreign and domestic sources for each commodity, before choosing between alternative region-specific sources for the domestic commodity. At both stages of the decision process, CES functions are used to describe imperfect substitution possibilities across alternative supply sources. On the basis of this nested CES structure, we employ (B15), (B16) and (B17) to describe regional foreign imports, inter-regional imports and inter-regional exports, respectively.[78] We describe the terms in

---

[76] Let $\widehat{S}_{j,r}^{v}$ be industry $j$'s share of region $r$'s total use of primary factor $v$. Let $\widehat{S}_{j,r}^{\bullet}$ be industry $j$'s share of value added in region $r$. To derive (B1)–(B3), multiply (7.31) through by $\widehat{S}_{j,r}^{v}$ and sum over $j$. If factor intensities do not differ significantly across industries, then $\widehat{S}_{j,r}^{v} \approx \widehat{S}_{j,r}^{\bullet}$, yielding (B1)–(B3). To derive (B4), multiply (7.32) through by $\widehat{S}_{j,r}^{\bullet}$ and sum over $j$. In (B2) and (B3) we suppress technical change in capital and land usage.

[77] Note that in (B6), and other equations of BOTE, we treat the region's import prices (foreign and inter-regional) as exogenous and unshocked, and thus suitable for omission from the equation system.

[78] The derivation of (B15)–(B17) is available from the authors on request. Note that in deriving these BOTE equations, we adopt a number of simplifying assumptions. (i) We assume that the region is sufficiently small that it does not materially influence the prices it faces for foreign or inter-regional imports. (ii) We assume that the percentage change in demand for traded goods within a region, undifferentiated by source, can be approximated by the percentage change in that region's real GDP.

(B16) and (B17) relating to structural change in inter-regional sourcing preferences in Section 7.6.5.

Equation (B18) describes the operation, in the first year of a simulation, of the short-run sticky wage assumption described by Equation (7.8). Equation (B18) introduces the regional consumer price index, which we define in BOTE via (B19). Equation (B20) decomposes the percentage change in regional employment into movements in the regional population, the regional participation rate and the regional employment rate.

Equation (B21) defines the regional net immigration rate as the ratio of regional net immigration to population. Equation (B22) relates the regional net immigration rate to the expected regional wage. This equation is a stylized representation of the operation of Equations (7.12)−(7.14). Equation (B23) defines the percentage change in the ratio of the regional wage to the national wage.

## 7.6.2 Short-run and long-run closures of the BOTE model

Table 7.3 presents short-run and long-run closures of BOTE. Since MMRF is a dynamic model, the essentially comparative-static concepts of "short-run" closure and "long-run" closure do not directly apply to it. Nevertheless, these closures are very useful frameworks for understanding the operation of MMRF over the full course of a simulation, with the short-run closure being a good description of how MMRF operates within the first few years of a shock and the long-run closure being a good description of how MMRF operates a number of years following a shock.

### 7.6.2.1 Short-run closure

In describing the BOTE closures, we begin by noting that certain variables are exogenous in both the short-run and the long-run. These variables are of three types. (i) Certain elements of the closure reflect the absence in MMRF of theory, either of a short-run or long-run nature, explaining the determination of the variable in question. This explains the exogenous status of labor augmenting technical change ($a_r^L$), the regional land endowment ($n_r$), foreign willingness to pay for regional exports ($v_r$), cost-neutral shifts in inter-regional sourcing preferences ($\xi_r$) and the regional participation rate ($pr_r$). (ii) In BOTE we assume that our region is too small to exert a material influence over certain economy-wide variables. This accounts for the exogenous status of the national wage rate ($w$).[79] (iii) The exogenous status of certain variables allows us to describe particular behavioral assumptions governing the regional private and public sectors in the MMRF simulations. In MMRF, household consumption is a fixed proportion of regional income. This is represented in BOTE by the exogenous determination of $apc_r$. The MMRF simulations carry the assumption that regional governments maintain their

---

[79] It also accounts for the omission of certain otherwise exogenous and unshocked variables, such as the regional import price index.

spending as a fixed proportion of regional private consumption. In BOTE, this is described via the exogenous status of $\lambda_r^{(S)}$. To represent the MMRF modeling of federal government consumption in BOTE, $\lambda_r^{(F)}$ is exogenous.

Of the remaining variables that are exogenous in the short run, all are endogenous in the long run. These variables are of two types. The first reflect the time period with which we are concerned: a period too short for the variables in question to have time to adjust to a given shock. Variables in this category of short-run exogenous variable are the regional capital stock ($k_r$) and the regional population ($q_r$). The second category of such variables is made up of shifters whose exogenous status activate short-run mechanisms describing how the economy transitions from the short run to the long run. In this category are $\lambda_r$, $f_r^{(SR)}$ and $f_r^{(W)}$. With $\lambda_r$ exogenous, short-run movements in regional investment are related to movements in rates of return via (B10). With $f_r^{(SR)}$ exogenous, short-run movements in the region's net inter-regional migration rate are related to expected regional wages via (B22). With $f_r^{(W)}$ exogenous, short-run movements in the regional real wage are related to movements in the regional employment rate via (B18).

### 7.6.2.2 Long-run closure and operation of BOTE

The final column of Table 7.3 presents the long-run closure of BOTE. Our description of the long-run closure differs in four respects from the short-run closure described above:

(i)   Equation (7.8) of our MMRF variant (represented in BOTE by B18) ensures that the policy-case level of the regional employment rate ($er_r$) is eventually returned to its baseline level via regional wage adjustment. In BOTE, the end-point of this process is represented by long-run exogeneity of $er_r$ and endogeneity of $f_r^{(W)}$.

(ii)  The short-run operation of (B10) gradually drives rates of return towards baseline via capital adjustment. In (B10), $\lambda_r$ can be interpreted as a normal rate of return. Hence, via (B10), the regional capital growth rate will be above (below) baseline so long as the rate of return is above (below) the normal rate of return. Capital accumulation (or depreciation) gradually drives convergence of actual and normal rates of return. In Table 7.3, we describe the long-run outcome of this process as effective exogeneity of $ror_r$ and endogeneity of $k_r$.

(iii) Long-run change in the equilibrium regional capital stock requires long-run adjustment of the level of real regional investment in order to maintain the new level of capital. We describe this via the long-run exogenous status of $\psi_r$. With (B9) determining long-run real regional investment, we describe (B10) as inactive in the long run via the endogenous status of $\lambda_r$.

(iv)  The short-run operation of (7.12)−(7.14) generates movements in population that eventually return expected inter-regional wage relativities to some independently given level. In BOTE, we represent this by the long-run endogenous status of $q_r$ and exogenous status of $f_r^{(LR)}$. Once long-run regional populations have adjusted to maintain independently determined inter-regional expected wage relativities, inter-regional migration rates return to independently established values. In BOTE, this is represented by the exogenous status of $\varphi_r$. With the long-run annual value of $nim_r$ determined by (B21), we describe (B22) as inactive in the long run via the endogenous status of $f_r^{(\mathrm{SR})}$.

## 7.6.3 BOTE representations of regional aggregate demand and supply in both the short run and long run

In Sections 7.6.4 and 7.6.5, we will use BOTE to explain long-run outcomes (in the labor productivity example) and short-run outcomes (in the regional demand switching example) for the size of the regional economy as predicted by the full MMRF model. We begin by using BOTE Equations (B1)−(B23) to find reduced-form BOTE solutions for regional price and regional GDP outcomes under both short-run and long-run closures of the model.

### 7.6.3.1 Short-run regional aggregate supply

We begin by noting that in the short-run representation of BOTE, the operation of MMRF's sticky wage assumption in the first year of the simulation is described by (B18). Turning to (B20), the regional participation rate ($pr_r$) is exogenous and, we shall assume, unshocked (hence $pr_r = 0$). The regional population ($q_r$) does not deviate from baseline in the first year of the simulation, and thus $q_r = 0$. Substituting (B20) into (B18) for $er_r$ thus provides:

$$w_r - p_r^{\mathrm{C}} = \alpha \cdot l_r. \tag{7.33}$$

Substituting (B19) into (7.33) for $p_r^{\mathrm{C}}$ provides:

$$w_r = \alpha \cdot l_r + S_r^{(\mathrm{D})\mathrm{C}} p_r. \tag{7.34}$$

Substituting (7.34) into (B1) for $w_r$ provides:

$$l_r = [1/(1 + \sigma \alpha)]((1 - \sigma)a_r^{\mathrm{L}} + y_r + \sigma(1 - S_r^{(\mathrm{D})\mathrm{C}})p_r). \tag{7.35}$$

BOTE Equations (B1)−(B4) together imply the regional production function:[80]

$$y_r = S_r^{\mathrm{L}}\{l_r - a_r^{\mathrm{L}}\} + S_r^{\mathrm{K}} k_r + S_r^{\mathrm{N}} n_r. \tag{7.36}$$

Substituting (7.35) into (7.36) provides the percentage change expression for short-run regional aggregate supply:

$$y_r = A_r^{(1)} p_r - A_r^{(2)} a_r^{\mathrm{L}} + A_r^{(3)} \left(S_r^{\mathrm{K}} k_r + S_r^{\mathrm{N}} n_r\right), \tag{7.37}$$

---

[80] Multiply (B1), (B2) and (B3) through by $S_r^{\mathrm{L}}$, $S_r^{\mathrm{K}}$ and $S_r^{\mathrm{N}}$, respectively. Add the resulting expressions, and use (B4) to substitute out $p_r$. Noting that $S_r^{\mathrm{L}} + S_r^{\mathrm{K}} + S_r^{\mathrm{N}} = 1$, provides (7.36).

where:

$$A_r^{(1)} = \frac{S_r^L \sigma \left(1 - S_r^{(D)C}\right)}{S_r^K + S_r^N + \sigma\alpha}, \quad A_r^{(2)} = \frac{S_r^L \sigma(1+\alpha)}{S_r^K + S_r^N + \sigma\alpha}, \quad A_r^{(3)} = \frac{1 + \sigma\alpha}{S_r^K + S_r^N + \sigma\alpha}.$$

Table 7.4 reports values for $A_r^{(1)}$, $A_r^{(2)}$ and $A_r^{(3)}$, evaluated from the MMRF database.

### 7.6.3.2 Short-run regional aggregate demand

We turn now to the derivation of the short-run regional aggregate demand function. We start by substituting (B8), (B11) and (B12) into (B7) to produce a reduced-form expression for real gross regional expenditure:

$$e_r = \left[S_r^{(E)C} + S_r^{(E)S}\right] apc_r + \left[S_r^{(E)C} + S_r^{(E)S}\right] y_r + S_r^{(E)I} i_r + S_r^{(E)S}\lambda_r^{(S)} + S_r^{(E)F}\lambda_r^{(F)}. \tag{7.38}$$

To derive the short-run regional aggregate demand function (7.39), we substitute (7.38), (B14), (B15), (B16) and (B17) into (B13):

$$\Omega_r^{(1)} y_r = \Omega_r^{(2)} p_r + \Omega_r^{(3)} apc_r + \Omega_r^{(4)} i_r + \Omega_r^{(5)}\lambda_r^{(S)} + \Omega_r^{(6)}\lambda_r^{(F)} + \Omega_r^{(7)} v_r + \Omega_r^{(8)}\xi_r, \quad (7.39)$$

where:

$$\Omega_r^{(1)} = 1 - S_r^{(Y)E}\left[S_r^{(E)C} + S_r^{(E)S}\right] + S_r^{(Y)MF} + S_r^{(Y)MR}$$

$$\begin{aligned}\Omega_r^{(2)} = &-S_r^{(Y)MF}\left[\sigma_r^{(2)} S_r^{(Dom)} S_r^{(Local)}\right] - \left[\eta_r^{(XF)} S_r^{(Y)XF}\right] \\ &-S_r^{(Y)XR}\left[\sigma^{(2)} S_{(Imp)r}^{(RoC)} S_r^{(RoC)} + \sigma^{(3)}\left(1 - S_r^{(RoC)}\right)\right] S_r^{BAS} \\ &-S_r^{(Y)MR}\left[\sigma^{(3)} S_r^{(Local)} - \sigma^{(2)} S_r^{(Local)}\left(1 - S_r^{(Dom)}\right)\right]\end{aligned}$$

$$\Omega_r^{(3)} = S_r^{(Y)E}\left[S_r^{(E)C} + S_r^{(E)S}\right] \quad \Omega_r^{(4)} = S_r^{(Y)E} S_r^{(E)I}$$

$$\Omega_r^{(5)} = S_r^{(Y)E} S_r^{(E)S} \quad \Omega_r^{(6)} = S_r^{(Y)E} S_r^{(E)F}$$

$$\Omega_r^{(7)} = \eta_r^{(XF)} S_r^{(Y)XF} \quad \Omega_r^{(8)} = S_r^{(Y)MR} S_r^{(Local)} + S_r^{(Y)XR}\left(1 - S_r^{(RoC)}\right).$$

Table 7.4 reports values for $\Omega_r^{(1)} - \Omega_r^{(8)}$ evaluated from the MMRF database.

In (7.39) we treat real regional investment as a shift variable on the regional aggregate demand function. However, real investment is endogenous, and thus will respond to movements in regional prices and regional GDP induced by movements in the exogenous variables in (7.37) and (7.39). To derive a reduced form equation for short-run real investment, we note that in the very short-run, with capital stocks unchanged from baseline ($k_r = 0$) in the short run, (B2) implies that:

$$r_r^K = [1/\sigma]y_r + p_r. \qquad (7.40)$$

Substituting (7.40) and (B6) into (B5) provides the following short-run expression for the regional rate of return on capital:

$$ror_r = [1/\sigma]y_r + \left(1 - S_r^{(D)I}\right)p_r. \qquad (7.41)$$

Substituting (7.41) into (B10) and then substituting the resulting expression into (B9) while noting that $k_r = 0$, we have:

$$i_r = \beta_r \left[\left(1/\sigma\right)y_r + \left(1 - S_r^{(D)I}\right)p_r - \lambda_r\right], \qquad (7.42)$$

which is our BOTE expression for short-run real investment.[81]

### 7.6.3.3 Long-run regional aggregate supply

Our derivation of the long-run regional aggregate supply function begins with BOTE Equations (B5) and (B6). As discussed in Section 7.6.2.2, we describe $ror_r$ as exogenous in the long-run. Via (B5), this ensures that movements in regional capital construction costs flow into the long-run regional rental price of capital, that is $r_r^K = p_r^I$. Substituting (B6) into (B5), and substituting the resulting expression into (B4) provides:

$$p_r = \left(1 \Big/ \left(1 - S_r^K S_r^{(D)I}\right)\right)\left(S_r^L\{w_r + a_r^L\} + S_r^N r_r^N\right). \qquad (7.43)$$

On the right-hand side of (7.43) we find the regional wage, $w_r$, and regional natural resource rental prices, $r_r^N$. As discussed in Section 7.6.2.2, $f_r^{(LR)}$ is exogenous in the long-run, reflecting the MMRF assumption that long-run inter-regional population movements return inter-regional wage relativities to baseline. Hence, via (B23), $w_r = w$. To understand the long-run movement in $r_r^N$, we use (B3). Natural resource supply does not deviate from its baseline value, hence $n_r = 0$.[82] Substituting (B3) into (7.43) for $r_r^N$,

---

[81] The reader will note that with $y_r$ and $p_r$ appearing on the right-hand side of (7.42), neither regional investment ($i_r$), nor, via the appearance of $i_r$ in (7.39), regional aggregate demand, are independent of movements in the exogenous shift variables in (7.37) or (7.39). For example, a positive shock to $apc_r$, with investment held at its initial level, will, via (7.37) and (7.39), cause positive deviations in $y_r$ and $p_r$. Via (7.42), this will produce a positive deviation in real investment, and thus, via (7.39), a further 'north-easterly' shift in the regional aggregate demand schedule described by (7.39). A demonstration that this process generates convergent movements in $y_r$, $p_r$ and $i_r$ under reasonable parameter values is available from the authors on request.

[82] Naturally, we would choose to retain $n_r$ as an explicit (rather than omitted) exogenous variable in any derivation of long-run aggregate supply in which we sought to explain a multiregional CGE simulation in which natural resources were a shocked exogenous variable. Equation (7.37) is an example of the retention of $n_r$ as an exogenous variable in the derivation of short-run aggregate supply.

and substituting $w_r = w$ into (7.43) for $w_r$, provides (7.44), the BOTE representation of region $r$'s long-run aggregate supply function:

$$\Phi_r^{(1)} y_r = \Phi_r^{(2)} p_r - \Phi_r^{(3)} \{w + a_r^L\}, \tag{7.44}$$

where $\Phi_r^{(1)} = S_r^N/\sigma$, $\Phi_r^{(2)} = 1 - S_r^K S_r^{(D)I} - S_r^N$ and $\Phi_r^{(3)} = S_r^L$.

Table 7.5 reports values for $\Phi_r^{(1)} - \Phi_r^{(3)}$ evaluated from the MMRF database.

### 7.6.3.4 Long-run regional aggregate demand

To derive the BOTE representation of the long-run regional aggregate demand function, we begin with (B7). Our first task is to describe the long-run determination of the right-hand components of (B7): $c_r$, $i_r$, $g_r^{(S)}$ and $g_r^{(F)}$.

Long-run determination of real private and public consumption is relatively straightforward. With $\lambda_r^{(F)}$, $\lambda_r^{(S)}$ and $apc_r$ exogenous and unshocked (thus $\lambda_r^{(F)} = \lambda_r^{(S)} = apc_r = 0$), we have, via (B8), (B11) and (B12), respectively:

$$c_r = y_r \tag{7.45}$$

$$g_r^{(S)} = c_r \tag{7.46}$$

$$g_r^{(F)} = q_r. \tag{7.47}$$

With $\psi_r$ exogenous and unshocked in the long-run, real investment is determined by (B9), i.e.:

$$i_r = k_r. \tag{7.48}$$

In the long run, $k_r$ is endogenous and determined by (B2). Substituting (B6) into (B5), and substituting the resulting expression into (B2) for $r_r^K$, provides:

$$k_r = y_r - \sigma\left(S_r^{(D)I} - 1\right) p_r. \tag{7.49}$$

Substituting (7.49) into (7.48) provides:

$$i_r = y_r - \sigma\left(S_r^{(D)I} - 1\right) p_r. \tag{7.50}$$

Substituting (7.45), (7.46), (7.47) and (7.50) into (B7) we have:[83]

$$e_r = \left[S_r^{(E)C} + S_r^{(E)S} + S_r^{(E)I}\right] y_r + \sigma S_r^{(E)I}\left(1 - S_r^{(D)I}\right) p_r + S_r^{(E)F} q_r. \tag{7.51}$$

---

[83] Naturally, if our aim was to use BOTE to explain the long-run effects of shifts in $\lambda_r^{(F)}$, $\lambda_r^{(S)}$, $apc_r$ and $\psi_r$, we would not omit these exogenous variables from the derivation of the long-run aggregate demand schedule as we have done here. For an example of the retention of these exogenous variables in the derivation of short-run regional aggregate demand, see (7.40).

As is clear from (7.51), in the long run gross regional expenditure is inelastic to the regional GDP deflator, *cet. par.* In (7.51), the regional price level directly affects gross regional expenditure only through demand for capital, via the coefficient $\sigma S_r^{(E)I}\left(1 - S_r^{(D)I}\right)$. This coefficient recognizes that a rise in the long-run regional price level will typically signal a fall in the relative price of regional capital, since, for many regions, a large share of the cost of capital is determined by import prices.

Our next step in deriving the percentage change form for the regional aggregate demand function is to consider (B13). While gross regional expenditure may not be price elastic, overall aggregate demand at the regional level is rendered price elastic via net interstate and overseas trade. Finally, substituting (7.51), (B14), (B15), (B16) and (B17) into (B13) generates the long-run regional aggregate demand function:

$$\Psi_r^{(1)} \gamma_r = \Psi_r^{(2)} p_r + \Psi_r^{(3)} q_r + \Psi_r^{(4)} v_r + \Psi_r^{(5)} \xi_r, \tag{7.52}$$

where:

$$\Psi_r^{(1)} = 1 - S_r^{(Y)E}\left[S_r^{(E)C} + S_r^{(E)S} + S_r^{(E)I}\right] + S_r^{(Y)MF} + S_r^{(Y)MR}$$

$$\begin{aligned}
\Psi_r^{(2)} = {}& -\sigma S_r^{(Y)E} S_r^{(E)I}\left(S_r^{(D)I} - 1\right) - \eta_r^{(XF)} S_r^{(Y)XF} - \sigma_r^{(2)} S_r^{(Y)MF} S_r^{(Dom)} S_r^{(Local)} \\
& -S_r^{(Y)XR}\left[\sigma^{(2)} S_{(Imp)r}^{(RoC)} S_r^{(RoC)} + \sigma^{(3)}\left(1 - S_r^{(RoC)}\right)\right] S_r^{BAS} \\
& -S_r^{(Y)MR}\left[\sigma^{(3)} S_r^{(Local)} - \sigma^{(2)} S_r^{(Local)}\left(1 - S_r^{(Dom)}\right)\right]
\end{aligned}$$

$$\Psi_r^{(3)} = S_r^{(Y)E} S_r^{(E)F} \quad \Psi_r^{(4)} = \eta_r^{(XF)} S_r^{(Y)XF}$$

$$\Psi_r^{(5)} = S_r^{(Y)XR}\left(1 - S_r^{(RoC)}\right) + S_r^{(Y)MR} S_r^{(Local)}.$$

Table 7.5 reports values for $\Psi_r^{(1)} - \Psi_r^{(5)}$ evaluated from the MMRF database.

## 7.6.4 Regional labor-saving technical change

We investigate the regional impact of a 1% labor-saving technical change in the South region, such as might be caused by a region-specific program of microeconomic reform.[84] In this section, we use BOTE primarily as a vehicle for exploring long-run regional impacts. In Section 7.6.5, we turn BOTE to the task of exploring short-run regional impacts in particular.

We begin by noting that in BOTE, labor-saving technical change is represented by $a_r^L$, the number of units of labor required per effective labor input. A 1% labor-saving

---

[84] See, e.g. Productivity Commission (2006, pp. 349–356).

technical change in South represents a $-1\%$ shock to $a_{\text{South}}^{\text{L}}$. To trace the impact of this on short-run employment, we begin by subtracting (B2) from (B1), which provides:

$$\{l_r - a_r^{\text{L}}\} - k_r = -\sigma(\{w_r + a_r^{\text{L}}\} - r_r^{\text{K}}). \tag{7.53}$$

In the very short-run, $k_r$ does not deviate from its baseline value. Hence, (7.53) can be viewed as determining $l_r$ in the short run. Substituting (7.40) into (7.53) for $r_r^{\text{K}}$ provides:

$$l_r = (1 - \sigma)a_r^{\text{L}} + y_r - \sigma(w_r - p_r). \tag{7.54}$$

The first term of (7.54) indicates that a $1\%$ fall in $a_r^{\text{L}}$ has two direct effects on regional employment — a productivity effect and a factor price effect. (i) By reducing by $1\%$ the number of persons required to secure an effective labor unit, the productivity effect reduces employment of persons by $1\%$. (ii) By reducing the cost of acquiring an effective labor unit by $1\%$, the factor price effect increases demand for effective labor units, and with it, persons, by $\sigma$. With $\sigma = 0.3$ (see Table 7.4), the factor price effect lifts employment of persons by $0.3\%$. Hence, a region-specific $1\%$ labor-saving technical change has a *direct* short-run effect on South's employment of $-1 + 0.30 = -0.70\%$. For values of $\sigma$ less than 1, (7.54) indicates that labor-saving technical change has a negative direct short-run impact on regional employment. However, (7.54) also points to general equilibrium impacts on regional employment via changes in regional activity and/or the real producer price of labor. To explore this general equilibrium effect further, and moreover, to examine the likelihood of this effect offsetting the direct employment loss, we begin with the regional aggregate demand Equation (7.39):

$$y_r = \left[\Omega_r^{(2)}/\Omega_r^{(1)}\right]p_r + \left[\Omega_r^{(4)}/\Omega_r^{(1)}\right]i_r = \eta_r^{(1)}p_r + \eta_r^{(2)}i_r. \tag{7.55}$$

Next, we note that in the short-run, with capital stocks and natural resource endowments exogenous and unshocked, $k_r = n_r = 0$. Hence, via (B2) and (B3) it must be that $r_r^{\text{K}} = r_r^{\text{N}}$. Hence, (B4) becomes:

$$p_r = S_r^{\text{L}}\{w_r + a_r^{\text{L}}\} + (1 - S_r^{\text{L}})r_r^{\text{K}}. \tag{7.56}$$

Substitute (7.56) into (7.55):

$$y_r = \eta_r^{(1)}\left(S_r^{\text{L}}\{w_r + a_r^{\text{L}}\} + (1 - S_r^{\text{L}})r_r^{\text{K}}\right) + \eta_r^{(2)}i_r. \tag{7.57}$$

Substitute (7.56) and (7.57) into (B2):

$$r_r^{\text{K}} = \left(\frac{-\left[\eta_r^{(1)} + \sigma\right]S_r^{\text{L}}}{\left[\eta_r^{(1)}\left(1 - S_r^{\text{L}}\right) - \sigma S_r^{\text{L}}\right]}\right)\{w_r + a_r^{\text{L}}\} - \left(\frac{\eta_r^{(2)}}{\left[\eta_r^{(1)}\left(1 - S_r^{\text{L}}\right) - \sigma S_r^{\text{L}}\right]}\right)i_r. \tag{7.58}$$

Substitute (7.56) and (7.57) into the labor demand Equation (B1):

$$l_r = a_r^L + \left[\eta_r^{(1)} S_r^L - \sigma\left(1 - S_r^L\right)\right]\left\{w_r + a_r^L\right\} + \left(1 - S_r^L\right)\left[\sigma + \eta_r^{(1)}\right]r_r^K + \eta_r^{(2)} i_r. \quad (7.59)$$

Substituting (7.58) into (7.59) provides our short-run employment function:

$$l_r = \left((1 - \sigma) - \frac{\sigma S_r^L}{1/\left(1 + \sigma/\eta_r^{(1)}\right) - S_r^L}\right)a_r^L - \left(\frac{\sigma}{\eta_r^{(1)}\left(1 - S_r^L\right) - \sigma S_r^L}\right)\left(\eta_r^{(1)} w_r + \eta_r^{(2)} i_r\right). \quad (7.60)$$

Abstracting from movements in the regional wage ($w_r$) and regional investment ($i_r$), the first coefficient on the right-hand side of (7.60) identifies the direct and indirect routes via which a movement in $a_r^L$ affects regional employment. We established earlier that the direct effect, the strength of which is represented by $(1 - \sigma)$, will be negative for values of $\sigma < 1$. The value of the general equilibrium effect, the strength of which is represented by the term $-\sigma S_r^L / \left(1/\left(1 + \sigma/\eta_r^{(1)}\right) - S_r^L\right)$, is governed by three parameters: $\sigma$, $S_r^L$ and $\eta_r^{(1)}$. The value of this term is most sensitive to the values of $\sigma$ and $S_r^L$, both of which will normally be known with some confidence. The term's value is less sensitive to $\eta_r^{(1)}$, over which there may be more uncertainty given the role of Armington elasticities and export demand elasticities in determining its value.[85] For South, the value of the general equilibrium term is 0.30.[86] This is not sufficient to offset the employment loss generated by the direct effect $(1 - \sigma)$. Hence, South experiences a short-run negative deviation in employment (Figure 7.4). Certainly, with sufficient wage flexibility or a large induced investment response, the short-run employment outcome could be positive. However (7.60) suggests this is not a likely outcome under plausible parameter value ranges.

We now investigate the long-run regional consequences of region-specific labor-saving technical change. In particular, we investigate how changes in regional labor efficiency affect the long-run size of the regional economy, in terms of real GDP, population and employment. As we shall see, while regional labor-saving technical change unambiguously increases long-run real regional GDP, it may cause regional population and employment to either rise or fall. Our approach will be to find BOTE solutions for long-run regional price and real GDP outcomes by drawing on the long-run expressions for regional aggregate supply and aggregate demand derived in Section 7.6.3.

We begin by considering the consequences of the shock for the long-run regional wage. In the long-run, the inter-regional migration theory described by (7.12)–(7.14)

---

[85] $\eta_r^{(1)} = \Omega_r^{(2)}/\Omega_r^{(1)}$. Via (7.39), we see that values for inter-regional sourcing elasticities and export demand elasticities play a dominant role in determining the value of $\Omega_r^{(2)}$.

[86] $0.3 * 0.58/(1/(1 + 0.3/-2.29) - 0.58) = 0.30$.

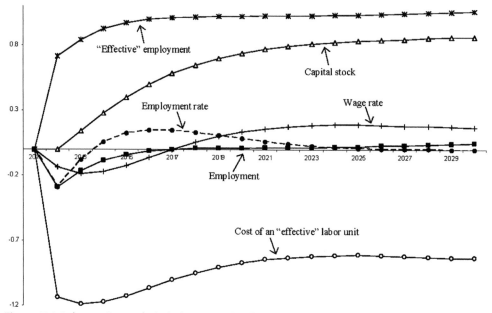

**Figure 7.4** Labor-saving technical change in South. Capital stock, employment, effective employment, wage rates per hour and effective labor unit, and employment rate for the South region (percentage deviation from baseline).

returns long-run migration income relativities to their baseline levels. In our MMRF implementation, we define migration income as expected (employment probability weighted) wage income via (7.12). Since our long-run wage adjustment mechanism returns long-run region-specific employment rates to their baseline levels, our migration theory generates a convergence of long-run wage deviations. Hence, in Figure 7.5, we find that South's long-run wage deviation eventually converges on the long-run national wage deviation. Note that the long-run national wage deviation is positive. With employment rates returning to baseline in every region, and the national population unchanged from baseline, the national employment deviation must be close to zero.[87] With capital adjusting in the long-run to return rates of return to baseline levels, the labor-saving technical change must be expressed as a rise in returns to the fixed factor, labor. This accounts for the long-run increase in the national wage (Figure 7.5).

Table 7.5 reports long-run values for the parameters and shares of our calibrated BOTE model. For the South region, the parameterized long-run regional aggregate supply and demand functions are:

$$y_{South} = 1.92\, p_{South} - 1.61\, \{ w + a^L_{South} \} \quad \text{Aggregate supply} \quad (7.61)$$

---

[87] Recall population movements between regions with differing base-case unemployment rates can generate small deviations in national employment.

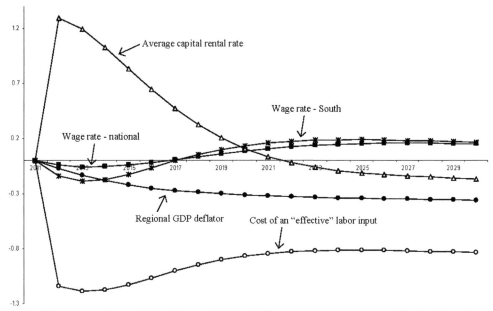

**Figure 7.5** Labor-saving technical change in South. Wage rate, wage rate per effective labor input, capital rental rate and GSP deflator for the South region (percentage deviation from baseline).

$$y_{\text{South}} = -3.78\, p_{\text{South}} + 0.143\, q_{\text{South}} \quad \text{Aggregate demand.} \tag{7.62}$$

We draw the reader's attention to $\Psi^{(2)}$ in (7.52), and in particular the collection of coefficients and parameters that determine the long-run sensitivity of demand for region $r$'s output to the price of region $r$'s output. Note that, as discussed in reference to (7.51), the value of the first term in $\Psi_r^{(2)}$, $\sigma S_r^{(Y)E} S_r^{(E)I}\left(S_r^{(D)I} - 1\right)$, is small ($-0.02$ for South). This leaves three salient behavioral parameters in $\Psi_r^{(2)}$ important to determining the price elasticity of region $r$'s aggregate demand: $\eta_r$, $\sigma_r^{(2)}$ and $\sigma^{(3)}$. Shortly, we show that these three parameters exert a strong influence on the long-run regional employment consequences of regional labor-saving technical change.

Our aim is to understand how regional labor-saving technical change affects the long-run size of the regional economy, both in terms of real GDP, and population and employment. We begin by substituting the regional aggregate demand function (7.52) into the regional aggregate supply function (7.44) and solving for $y_r$:

$$y_r = \left(\frac{\Psi_r^{(2)}}{\Phi_r^{(2)}\Psi_r^{(1)} - \Phi_r^{(1)}\Psi_r^{(2)}}\right)\left[\frac{\Phi_r^{(2)}\Psi_r^{(3)}}{\Psi_r^{(2)}}\, q_r + \Phi_r^{(3)}\left\{w_r + a_r^{\text{L}}\right\}\right]. \tag{7.63}$$

Using Table 7.5 to evaluate (7.63) for South provides:

$$y_{\text{South}} = 0.05\, q_{\text{South}} - 1.07\left\{w_{\text{South}} + a_{\text{South}}^{\text{L}}\right\}. \tag{7.64}$$

Equation (7.64) suggests that the long-run elasticity of South's real GDP at factor cost to movements in the regional effective wage rate ($w_{South} + a^L_{South}$) is a little over $-1$. The long-run deviation in South's wage per effective labor unit is $-0.83\%$ (Figure 7.5). Equation (7.64) suggests that this should generate a long-run deviation in South's real GDP at factor cost of approximately $-1.07 * -0.83 = +0.89$, which proves to be identical to that generated by MMRF (Figure 7.6). To understand the implications for regional employment and population of a 0.89% expansion in real GDP, we begin by considering BOTE Equations (B1)−(B4) which together imply the regional production function:[88]

$$y_r = S^L_r\{l_r - a^L_r\} + S^K_r k_r + S^N_r n_r. \tag{7.65}$$

Together, (7.65) and (7.53) remind us that in the long-run, regional demand for effective primary factor inputs will tend to move proportionately with movements in real regional GDP, unless there is a change in relative regional factor prices. Substituting (7.53) into (7.65) for $k_r$ provides region $r$'s long-run demand equation for effective labor inputs:

$$\{l_r - a^L_r\} = \left(\frac{1}{1 - S^N_r}\right)\left[y_r - \sigma S^K_r\left(\{w_r + a^L_r\} - r^K_r\right) - S^N_r n_r\right]. \tag{7.66}$$

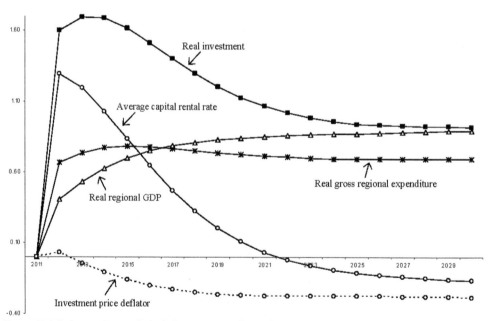

**Figure 7.6** Labor-saving technical change in South. Real investment, real gross regional expenditure, real GDP, investment price deflator and average capital rental rate for the South region (percentage deviation from baseline).

---

[88] Multiply (B1), (B2) and (B3) through by $S^L_r$, $S^K_r$ and $S^N_r$, respectively. Add the resulting expressions and use (B4) to substitute out $p_r$. Noting that $S^L_r + S^K_r + S^N_r = 1$, provides (7.65).

Using Table 7.5 to calibrate (7.66) for South provides:

$$l_{\text{South}} - a^{\text{L}}_{\text{South}} = 1.1 \, y_{\text{South}} - 0.10 \left( \left\{ w_{\text{South}} + a^{\text{L}}_{\text{South}} \right\} - r^{\text{K}}_{\text{South}} \right) + 0.12 \, n_{\text{South}}.$$

(7.67)

Via (7.64) we established that South's 1% labor-saving technical change lifts the region's real GDP by approximately 0.89% in the long-run. Via (7.67), we see that this causes demand for effective employment $\left( l_{\text{south}} - a^{\text{L}}_{\text{South}} \right)$ to rise by 0.98%, *cet. par.* However, the 1% labor-saving technical change alone provides a 1% rise in effective Southern employment. Hence, *cet. par.*, (7.67) suggests long-run employment of persons must fall by 0.02%. The true long-run employment outcome, calculated by MMRF, is a small rise of 0.05% (Figure 7.4). The difference is due to the relative factor price effect in (7.67). As discussed above, the wage per effective labor unit in South falls by −0.83%. At the same time, the long-run rental price of South's capital falls by 0.17% (Figure 7.6). This induces substitution towards labor which contributes the remaining +0.07 percentage points $(= -0.10 * \{0.17 - 1 - -0.17\})$ of South's long-run employment deviation.

    In the long-run, we assume that region-specific participation rates and employment rates do not deviate from their baseline values. Hence, with South's long-run employment 0.05% above baseline, via (B20), South's population is also 0.05% above baseline. Note that to keep our explanation of long-run employment results simple, in Equations (7.52), (7.63) and (7.64) above, we treated the regional population, $q_r$, as exogenous. Regional population appears in the long-run regional aggregate demand function because region-specific *per capita* federal government consumption spending remains at baseline levels. For South, the small long-run population increase associated with labor-saving technical change signals a second, albeit small, round of increases in aggregate demand, real GDP and employment via additional federal government consumption spending.

    We now turn to explore more generally the long-run consequences for regional employment and population of region-specific labor-saving technical change. To do so, we substitute (7.63) into (7.66) for $y_r$, which yields (7.68). To focus on the impact on regional employment of labor-saving technical change, (7.68) omits all variables other than $a^{\text{L}}_r$:

$$l_r = \left[ \Theta^{(1)}_r - \Theta^{(2)}_r \right] a^{\text{L}}_r,$$

(7.68)

where:

$$\Theta^{(1)}_r = \left( 1 - \left( \frac{\sigma S^{\text{K}}_r}{1 - S^{\text{N}}_r} \right) \right) \quad \text{and} \quad \Theta^{(2)}_r = \left( \frac{1}{1 - S^{\text{N}}_r} \right) \left( \frac{\Phi^{(3)}_r \Psi^{(2)}_r}{\Phi^{(1)}_r \Psi^{(2)}_r - \Phi^{(2)}_r \Psi^{(1)}_r} \right).$$

(7.68) identifies two routes via which labor-saving technical change affects regional employment.[89] The first, $\Theta_r^{(1)}$, recognizes the direct impact of labor-saving technical change on regional employment for a *given level* of regional GDP. The second, $\Theta_r^{(2)}$, recognizes labor productivity's indirect impact on regional employment via its impact on regional GDP, and with it, demand for labor inputs. Examining Table 7.5, we see that $\Theta_r^{(1)} \approx \Theta_r^{(2)}$. Hence, we might expect that labor-saving technical change will tend to have small effects on long-run regional employment, and that these effects will be of uncertain sign. To investigate this further, we must consider the structural and behavioral parameters that comprise $\Theta_r^{(1)}$ and $\Theta_r^{(2)}$.

In Table 7.5, we see that a typical value for $\sigma S_r^K / (1 - S_r^N)$ is small, approximately 0.10. Hence a typical value for $\Theta_r^{(1)}$ will be around 0.9. The components of $\Theta_r^{(1)}$ will normally be known with some confidence. The structural parameters $S_r^K$ and $S_r^N$ are available from regional input output data. The value for the behavioral parameter $\sigma$ may be known with less certainty, but a nevertheless plausible and limited range of values can be inferred from econometric studies of the wage elasticity of labor demand.[90]

Like $\Theta_r^{(1)}$, many of the components of $\Theta_r^{(2)}$ also relate to share parameters describing economic structure that are readily available from regional input output data. An exception is $\Psi_r^{(2)}$, which contains parameters governing the price elasticity of demand for output of the region's traded goods sector: $\eta_r$, $\sigma_r^{(2)}$ and $\sigma^{(3)}$. Increasing the values of $\eta_r$, $\sigma_r^{(2)}$ and $\sigma^{(3)}$ will increase the value of $\Theta_r^{(2)}$, generating larger regional employment gains for a given labor-saving technical change. Recall that $\sigma_r^{(2)}$ and $\sigma^{(3)}$ are international and inter-regional Armington elasticities, and implicit in estimates for $\eta_r$ are Armington elasticities in the foreign destinations for region $r$'s exports (Dixon and Rimmer, 2010). As McDaniel and Balistreri (2003) note, there is a range of estimates in the literature for these parameters.[91] While sensitivity analysis is in general not a good alternative to the BOTE analysis, the BOTE analysis that has taken us to (7.68) allows us to identify the parameters most

---

[89] (7.68) suppresses three second-order effects. The first, via population-driven movements in federal spending, is small, and is in any case determined by the outcome for regional employment via (B20) and (B12). The second, via movements in the regional wage, will also be small if the region represents a sufficiently small share of the national labor market since, via (B23), the long-run regional wage deviation will track the national wage deviation. The third indirect effect on regional employment, also small, is via movements in $r_r^K$ in (7.66). In the long-run, with rates of return exogenous, movements in the regional price level induced by labor-saving technical change will affect the user cost of capital via (B6) and (B5). The impact of this on long-run labor demand is small for three reasons. (i) With the price elasticity of long-run regional aggregate demand quite high, the scope for large relative movements in the long-run regional price level are constrained. (ii) The effect of movements in the long-run regional price level on the rental price of capital is mediated by the share $S_r^{(D)l}$ in (B6). (iii) The impact of long-run movements in the rental price of capital on labor demand is mediated by the product of $\sigma$ and $S_r^K$ in (7.66) (note that because $S_r^N$ will be small for most regions, the term $1/(1 - S_r^N)$ in (7.66) will typically be close to 1).

[90] See Dixon (2009).

[91] See also the discussion in Section 7.5.3.

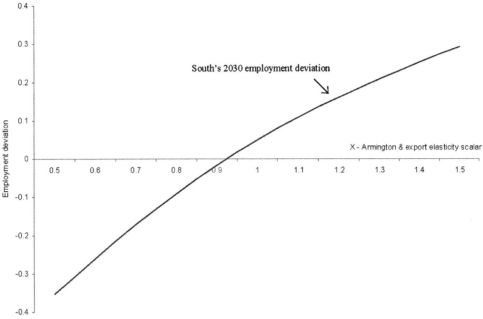

**Figure 7.7** Labor-saving technical change in South. Sensitivity analysis: Long-run (year 2030) percentage deviation in South's employment under alternative values for Armington and export elasticities.

relevant to determining the long-run employment consequences of region-specific labor-saving technical change. Equipped with this finding, (Figure 7.7) explores the sensitivity of South's long-run employment outcome to alternative values for $\eta_r$, $\sigma_r^{(2)}$ and $\sigma^{(3)}$. In determining alternative values for these parameters, we apply a uniform scalar ($X$ in Figure 7.7), ranging between 0.5 and 1.5, to our preferred values for $\eta_r$, $\sigma_r^{(2)}$ and $\sigma^{(3)}$. For example, when $X = 1$, $\eta_r$, $\sigma_r^{(2)}$ and $\sigma^{(3)}$ have the values reported in Table 7.5, and when $X = 0.5$, the values for $\eta_r$, $\sigma_r^{(2)}$ and $\sigma^{(3)}$ are half those reported in Table 7.5. The sensitivity analysis reported in Figure 7.7 confirms our conclusion from inspection of (7.68). At our preferred settings for $\eta_r$, $\sigma_r^{(2)}$ and $\sigma^{(3)}$ (i.e. when $X = 1$), the employment promoting and employment contracting impacts of region-specific labor-saving technical change, i.e. $\Theta_r^{(2)}$ and $\Theta_r^{(1)}$, are evenly balanced. Hence, even a small decrease in $\eta_r$, $\sigma_r^{(2)}$ and $\sigma^{(3)}$ away from our preferred values may change the sign of the long-run deviations in regional employment and population.

## 7.6.5 Change in the spatial distribution of domestic demand

In this section, we investigate the effects of a change in preferences over alternative sources of domestic commodity supply. We describe the change in preferences through an inter-regional sourcing twist, defined as a cost-neutral combination of changes in source-specific input requirements that, taken together, achieve a given change in the ratio of locally sourced to interstate-sourced inputs. As Dixon and Rimmer (2002, p. 173) describe, national and commodity-specific twist variables have proved valuable in forecasting and historical analysis with national CGE models. Similarly, in developing baseline forecasts with multiregional CGE models, national import/domestic twists and labor/capital twists are important in allowing the models to accommodate independent forecasts for national import volumes and the national average wage rate. Inter-regional sourcing twist variables have also proved useful in historical analysis with multiregional models (Giesecke, 2002; Giesecke and Madden, 2010). Giesecke *et al.* (2012) use twist-like revenue-neutral tax variables to model region-specific demand shifts associated with a rise in regional risk perception following a hypothetical terrorist attack. Twist variables are also valuable in simulating the effects of new projects or major events that involve economic agents transferring their purchases from one region to another. For example, in modeling domestic mineral sales by a new mining enterprise located in North, we might implement a cost-neutral twist in sourcing preferences by domestic users of the mineral, with the twist favoring greater use of the North source and lower use of alternative domestic sources. Similarly, in modeling, say, a successful domestic interstate tourism campaign by the North, we might implement a twist in sourcing preferences by households in all regions, with the twist favoring the Northern source for commodities related to tourism. In both examples, the inter-regional sourcing twist allows us to vary the spatial distribution of commodity sourcing decisions, while leaving unchanged the economy's level of technical efficiency. In this section, we explore the effects of the inter-regional sourcing twist, by modeling a 1% twist towards the Northern source for all commodities. We begin by deriving the twist variable. This derivation extends to the multiregional setting the import/domestic twist formulated by Horridge (2003). We start with (7.69), which describes the percentage change form of MMRF's cost-minimizing demand equations for region-specific commodity demands by agent $t$ in region $k$:

$$x_{(i,r)}^{(t,k)} = a_{(i,r)}^{(t,k)} + x_{(i,\text{Dom})}^{(t,k)} - \sigma^{(3)}\left(p_{(i,r)}^{(t,k)} + a_{(i,r)}^{(t,k)} - p_{(i,\text{Dom})}^{(t,k)}\right), \qquad (7.69)$$

where $x_{(i,r)}^{(t,k)}$ is the percentage change in demand for commodity $i$ from domestic region $r$ by agent $t$ located in domestic region $k$, $a_{(i,r)}^{(t,k)}$ is the percentage change in a technical efficiency variable describing the number of units of commodity $i$ from region $r$ required to sustain an effective input of $i$ from $r$ by agent $t$ located in domestic region $k$, $x_{(i,\text{Dom})}^{(t,k)}$ is the percentage change in demand by agent $t$ in region $k$ for domestic commodity $i$ irrespective of source, $\sigma^{(3)}$ is the elasticity of substitution across alternative domestic commodity sources, $p_{(i,r)}^{(t,k)}$ is the percentage change in the price faced by agent $t$ in region

$k$ for commodity $i$ from domestic source $r$, and $p_{(i,\text{Dom})}^{(t,k)}$ is the percentage change in the average price faced by agent $t$ in region $k$ for domestic commodity $i$ irrespective of source, defined as:

$$p_{(i,\text{Dom})}^{(t,k)} = \sum_{r=1}^{R} S_{(i,r)}^{(t,k)} \left( p_{(i,r)}^{(t,k)} + a_{(i,r)}^{(t,k)} \right), \tag{7.70}$$

where $S_{(i,r)}^{(t,k)}$ is the value share of commodity $i$ from domestic source $r$ in agent $(t,k)$'s total purchases of $i$ from all domestic sources.

We define a twist $\left( \xi_{(i,1)}^{(t,k)} \right)$ by agent $(t,k)$ towards region 1 as a source for commodity $i$ as:

$$\xi_{(i,1)}^{(t,k)} = x_{(i,1)}^{(t,k)} - x_{(i)^*}^{(t,k)}, \tag{7.71}$$

where the movements in the right-hand side variables $x_{(i,1)}^{(t,k)}$ and $x_{(i)^*}^{(t,k)}$ are confined to those generated by the cost-neutral combination of technical change terms defining the twist, and where $x_{(i)^*}^{(t,k)}$ is the percentage change in agent $(t,k)$'s demand for commodity $i$ from all domestic sources other than 1, defined as:

$$\left[ 1 - S_{(i,1)}^{(t,k)} \right] x_{(i)^*}^{(t,k)} = \sum_{s=2}^{R} S_{(i,s)}^{(t,k)} x_{(i,s)}^{(t,k)}. \tag{7.72}$$

Our aim is to find the combination of technical change terms $a_{(i,1)}^{(t,k)}$, and $a_{(i,2)}^{(t,k)} = a_{(i,3)}^{(t,k)} = \dots = a_{(i,R)}^{(t,k)} = a_{(i)^*}^{(t,k)}$ that achieves (7.71) while ensuring that, for given prices, the unit cost of commodity $i$ to agent $(t,k)$ remains unchanged. That is, find $a_{(i,1)}^{(t,k)}$ and $a_{(i)^*}^{(t,k)}$ such that:

$$S_{(i,1)}^{(t,k)} a_{(i,1)}^{(t,k)} + \sum_{r=2}^{R} S_{(i,r)}^{(t,k)} a_{(i)^*}^{(t,k)} = 0 \tag{7.73}$$

$$\xi_{(i,1)}^{(t,k)} = x_{(i,1)}^{(t,k)} - x_{(i)^*}^{(t,k)}. \tag{7.74}$$

To begin the derivation of the twist terms, we begin by noting that, for given prices, (7.69) simplifies to:

$$x_{(i,r)}^{(t,k)} = x_{(i,\text{Dom})}^{(t,k)} + \left( 1 - \sigma^{(3)} \right) a_{(i,r)}^{(t,k)}. \tag{7.75}$$

Substituting (7.75) for sources 2, ..., $R$ into (7.72) and noting that $a_{(i,2)}^{(t,k)} = a_{(i,3)}^{(t,k)} = \dots = a_{(i,R)}^{(t,k)} = a_{(i)^*}^{(t,k)}$ provides:

$$x_{(i)^*}^{(t,k)} = x_{(i,\text{Dom})}^{(t,k)} + \left( 1 - \sigma^{(3)} \right) a_{(i)^*}^{(t,k)}. \tag{7.76}$$

Substituting both (7.75) (for source 1) and (7.76) into (7.74) provides:

$$\xi_{(i,1)}^{(t,k)} = \left(1 - \sigma^{(3)}\right)\left(a_{(i,1)}^{(t,k)} - a_{(i)^*}^{(t,k)}\right). \tag{7.77}$$

Rearranging (7.73) we have:

$$a_{(i)^*}^{(t,k)} = -\left[S_{(i,1)}^{(t,k)} \Big/ \left(1 - S_{(i,1)}^{(t,k)}\right)\right] a_{(i,1)}^{(t,k)}. \tag{7.78}$$

Substituting (7.78) into (7.77):

$$a_{(i,1)}^{(t,k)} = \left[\left(1 - S_{(i,1)}^{(t,k)}\right) \Big/ \left(1 - \sigma^{(3)}\right)\right] \xi_{(i,1)}^{(t,k)}. \tag{7.79}$$

Substituting (7.79) into (7.73):

$$a_{(i)^*}^{(t,k)} = -\left[S_{(i,1)}^{(t,k)} \Big/ \left(1 - \sigma^{(3)}\right)\right] \xi_{(i,1)}^{(t,k)}. \tag{7.80}$$

Together, (7.79) and (7.80) constitute the combination of technical changes required to achieve the cost-neutral change in sourcing preferences described by $\xi_{(i,1)}^{(t,k)}$. Substituting (7.79) and (7.80) back into (7.69) for $a_{(i,r)}^{(t,k)}$ provides:[92]

$$x_{(i,1)}^{(t,k)} = a_{(i,1)}^{(t,k)} + x_{(i,\bullet)}^{(t,k)} - \sigma^{(3)}\left(p_{(i,1)}^{(t,k)} + a_{(i,1)}^{(t,k)} - p_{(i,\bullet)}^{(t,k)}\right) + \left(1 - S_{(i,1)}^{(t,k)}\right)\xi_{(i,1)}^{(t,k)} \tag{7.81}$$

$$x_{(i,r)}^{(t,k)} = a_{(i,r)}^{(t,k)} + x_{(i,\bullet)}^{(t,k)} - \sigma^{(3)}\left(p_{(i,r)}^{(t,k)} + a_{(i,r)}^{(t,k)} - p_{(i,\bullet)}^{(t,k)}\right) - S_{(i,1)}^{(t,k)}\xi_{(i,1)}^{(t,k)} \quad (r = 2, \ldots R). \tag{7.82}$$

Returning to the BOTE model, we now complete (B16) and (B17), first discussed in Section 7.6.1, by including twist terms. Mirroring (7.81), we complete (B16) by adding the twist term $(1 - S_r^{ROC})\xi_r$. Mirroring (7.82), we complete (B17) with the twist term $-S_r^{(Local)}\xi_r$.

In our MMRF simulation, we shock $\xi_{(i,\text{North})}^{(t,k)} = 1$. Via (B16) and (B17) we expect this to increase interstate exports from North while simultaneously reducing interstate imports into North. We see this outcome confirmed in Figure 7.8.[93] Note, however, that Figure 7.8 shows that, while the twist generates a movement towards surplus in

---

[92] In making this substitution, we assume that the technical change movements described by the $a$ terms in (7.69) can be divided into two parts: one related to the twist, and one related to all other sources of change in sourcing preferences. The latter accounts for the continued presence of the $a$ terms in (7.81) and (7.82).

[93] Note that (B16) and (B17) somewhat overestimate the MMRF outcomes for North's interstate exports and imports, because they omit prices in the rest of the country. In the MMRF simulation, by reducing demand for goods outside of North, the twist reduces the relative price of goods produced in the rest of Australia (see Figure 7.10). This damps interstate exports from North while simultaneously expanding interstate imports into North.

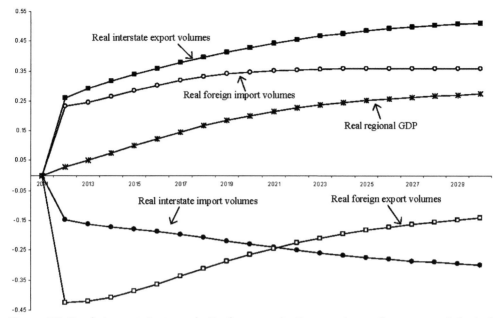

**Figure 7.8** Simulating a twist towards Northern goods. Export volumes (interstate and foreign), import volumes (interstate and foreign) and real GDP for the North region (percentage deviation from baseline).

North's interstate balance of trade, it simultaneously produces a movement towards deficit in the region's international balance of trade. As we shall find, short-run regional output is price inelastic. In the short-run, the regional demand stimulus afforded by the twist thus serves mainly to increase the regional price level, moving the region's international balance of trade towards deficit even as it moves the inter-regional balance of trade towards surplus.

To explore further the initial regional macroeconomic consequences of the shock, we begin by substituting Northern values for $y_r$, $w_r$ and $p_r$ into (B1).[94] In so doing, we see that our BOTE model predicts a deviation in 2012 Northern employment of 0.03%.[95] The true (MMRF) result is 0.06% (Figure 7.9). As Adams and Parmenter (1994) note, while (B1) holds exactly at the level of an individual industry, it is an approximation only at the economy-wide level.[96] We draw attention to (B1)'s underestimate of the employment outcome, because it will shortly prove important in explaining why (7.37), our short-run aggregate supply equation, underestimates the MMRF real GDP

---

[94] $y_{North} = 0.028$ (Figure 7.10). $w_{North} = 0.25$ (Figure 7.13). $p_{North} = 0.27$ (Figure 7.10).
[95] $0.03\% = 0.028 - 0.3 * (0.25 - 0.27)$.
[96] In our simulation (B1) underestimates short-run regional employment because employment outcomes by industry are positively correlated with the ranking of industries by labor intensity.

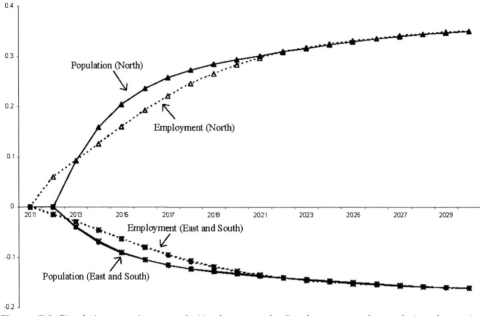

**Figure 7.9** Simulating a twist towards Northern goods. Employment and population, by region (percentage deviation from baseline).

outcome. Table 7.4 reports short–run (year 2012) values for the coefficients of (7.37). For North, the short–run aggregate supply function is:

$$y_{\text{North}} = 0.045 p_{\text{North}} - 0.32 a^L_{\text{North}} + 0.78 k_{\text{North}} + 0.12 n_{\text{North}}. \qquad (7.83)$$

In 2012, the twist causes a 0.28% deviation in North's GDP deflator (Figure 7.10). Via (7.83), we expect this to produce a positive deviation in North's real GDP of approximately 0.012%. The true result, 0.028% (Figure 7.10), is approximately twice that predicted by (7.83). Equation (7.83)'s underestimation of the GDP outcome follows from (B1)'s underestimation of the employment outcome. Despite (7.83)'s underestimation of the short–run GDP outcome, the equation makes clear that even in the presence of sticky wages, the regional short–run supply schedule is price inelastic. This follows from three characteristics of MMRF's short–run regional macro closure. (i) Land and capital cannot deviate from their baseline values in the simulation's first year. (ii) Stickiness of the real consumer wage has the effect that short–run movements in nominal wages almost keep pace with short–run movements in the GDP deflator (see B19 and B18), leaving limited scope for short–run movements in the real producer wage. (iii) Positive short–run labor market pressures begin to be expressed in short–run movements in the real regional wage via (B18). This limits the scope for short–run employment-generated movements in regional GDP.

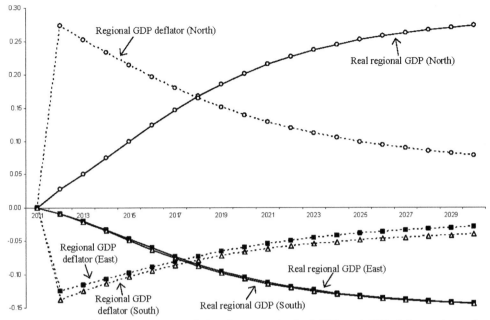

**Figure 7.10** Simulating a twist towards Northern goods. Real GDP and GDP deflators, by region (percentage deviation from baseline).

In Section 7.6.3.2 we derived (7.42), a reduced form expression for short-run real investment. Using Table 7.4 to evaluate (7.42) for North provides:

$$i_{\text{North}} = 4.17 y_{\text{North}} + 0.50 p_{\text{North}} - 1.25 \lambda_{\text{North}}. \tag{7.84}$$

With deviations in North's real GDP and GDP deflator of 0.028 and 0.27%, respectively, in the simulation's first year, (7.84) predicts a real investment deviation of 0.25%, close to the MMRF result of 0.23% (Figure 7.11).

Using Table 7.4 to evaluate (7.39), North's short-run aggregate demand function can be presented as:

$$0.81 y_{\text{North}} = -2.13 p_{\text{North}} + 0.61 apc_{\text{North}} + 0.31 i_{\text{North}} + 0.11 \lambda_{\text{North}}^{(S)} + 0.06 \lambda_{\text{North}}^{(F)}$$
$$+ 1.15 v_{\text{North}} + 0.33 \xi_{\text{North}}.$$

$$\tag{7.85}$$

Together, (7.83), (7.84) and (7.85) imply $y_{\text{North}} = 0.0076 \xi_{\text{North}}$ and $p_{\text{North}} = 0.17 \xi_{\text{North}}$. Since our shock is $\xi_{\text{North}} = 1$, BOTE anticipates $p_{\text{North}} = 0.17$ and $y_{\text{North}} = 0.0076$. Via Figure 7.10 we see that the true outcomes are $p_{\text{North}} = 0.27$ and $y_{\text{North}} = 0.028$. While our short-run BOTE model does reasonably well at reproducing the signs and relative magnitudes of the Northern price and activity outcomes, it

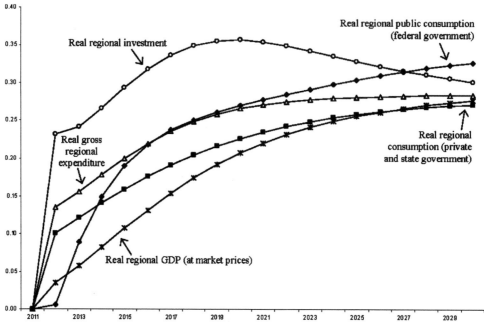

**Figure 7.11** Simulating a twist towards Northern goods. Real regional GDP (at market prices), and real gross regional expenditure and its components, for the North region (percentage deviation from baseline).

has underestimated their absolute magnitudes. The underestimation of the real GDP outcome is due in part to BOTE's underestimation of the price elasticity of the short-run aggregate supply curve, as discussed earlier in reference to (B1) and (7.37). The underestimate of the price outcome is due in part to the absence in BOTE of terms-of-trade-induced aggregate demand expansion. To keep our BOTE model simple, we have suppressed terms-of-trade effects in (B8)'s description of real consumption. However, our twist shock generates an inter-regional terms-of-trade gain for North, because it raises demand for Northern goods while simultaneously depressing demand for goods produced in the rest of the country. In Figure 7.10 this is manifested as a large short-run rise in the Northern GDP deflator relative to the GDP deflators in the other two regions. Figure 7.12 goes further, reporting the deviation in North's average (interstate and foreign) terms of trade and its components. From Figure 7.12 it is clear that North's terms-of-trade improvement is due not only to a rise in its interstate export price relative to its interstate import price, but also to a rise in its foreign export price. It is the short-run positive deviation in North's terms of trade that explains why the deviations in real private consumption and real state government consumption lie above the deviation in real GDP in Figure 7.11.

We turn now to the behavior of the short-run regional labor market. Via (7.36), a 0.028% deviation in 2012 Northern real GDP requires a short-run positive deviation in

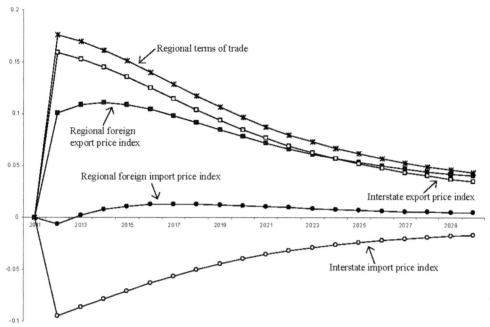

**Figure 7.12** Simulating a twist towards Northern goods. Regional terms of trade and its components, for the North region (percentage deviation from baseline).

Northern employment of 0.06% (Figure 7.9).[97] Since North's participation rate and population are unchanged from baseline values in 2012, via (B20), North's 0.06% employment deviation requires a 0.06% deviation in the Northern employment rate (Figure 7.13). Substituting (B19) into (B18), BOTE suggests that the positive deviation in the regional employment rate, together with the positive deviation in the regional price level, requires a positive deviation in the 2012 regional wage of:

$$w_{\text{North}} = \alpha \cdot er_{\text{North}} + S_{\text{North}}^{(D)C} p_{\text{North}} = 0.5{}^*0.06 + 0.79{}^*0.27 = 0.24\%. \qquad (7.86)$$

which is close to the MMRF result of 0.25% (Figure 7.13).

(B21) is a stylized representation of the operation of MMRF Equations (7.12)−(7.14). Ceteris paribus, with $er_{\text{North}} = 0.06$ and $w_{\text{North}} = 0.25$, via (B21) we might anticipate a 2012 deviation in North's net immigration rate ($\varphi_{\text{North}}$) of $\varphi_{\text{North}}(w_{\text{North}} + er_{\text{North}}) = 0.2{}^*0.31 = 0.064\%$. However, in Figure 7.9, we find the 2013 Northern population deviation is somewhat higher, at 0.09%. (B21)'s underestimate of North's immigration response can be traced to the fall in the migration income measure in the rest of Australia. Via (7.13), we see that $Y_{(o,d)}^{(\text{Diseq})}$ is a function of migration

97 $= \gamma_r / S_r^{\text{L}} = 0.028/0.48 = 0.06$

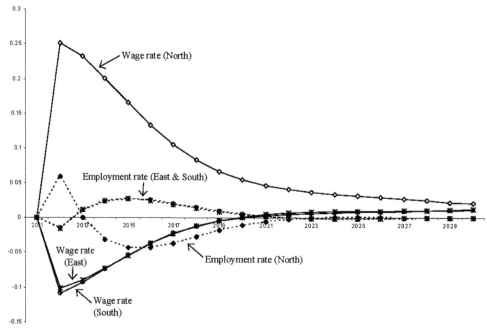

**Figure 7.13** Simulating a twist towards Northern goods. Employment rates and wage rates by region (percentage deviation from baseline).

income in both destination and origin regions. The twist causes short-run labor market conditions to deteriorate in the rest of Australia: the 2012 deviations in the employment rate and wage rate outside of North are −0.015 and −0.11, respectively (Figure 7.13). In (B21), we can represent this by setting $f_r^{(SR)} = -0.015 - 0.11 = -0.125$. This contributes the remaining 0.025% (= 0.2 * 0.125) to our BOTE outcome for $\varphi_{North}$.

We conclude by using BOTE to describe the long-run outcomes of the shift in preferences towards Northern goods. We begin with (B5), (B23), and (B4). With rates of return, regional wage relativities, and region-specific productivity variables exogenous and unshocked, BOTE suggests little scope for long-run deviations in relative regional output prices. Figure 7.10 broadly confirms this expectation, revealing long-run attenuation of the large deviations in regional GDP deflators observed in the short run. Nevertheless, it is clear from Figure 7.10 that North's GDP deflator remains above baseline in the long-run, while the GDP deflators of the remaining two regions remain below baseline. The long-run persistence in the deviations in the regional GDP deflators is due to natural resource supply ($n_r$ in BOTE), which is assumed to remain at baseline values throughout the policy simulation. The shift towards North in the spatial distribution of domestic demand places upward pressure on market clearing natural resource rental prices in North, while simultaneously depressing natural resource rental prices in the rest of the country. This is expressed as a small long-run positive deviation in the relative Northern regional GDP deflator (Figure 7.10).

With North's price level tending back towards baseline in the long-run, via (B14) we expect North's foreign exports to also tend back towards baseline in the long-run (Figure 7.8). Despite the gradual return of North's price level back to baseline, North's foreign import deviation remains positive (Figure 7.8). As described in (B15), foreign imports depend on both relative prices and regional activity. It is the long-run positive deviation in North's real GDP that keeps the foreign import volume deviation steady even as the long-run Northern price deviation declines.

We find that the long-run effects of the shift in regional preferences on North's real trade accounts is for a permanent rise in interstate export volumes, a permanent fall in interstate import volumes, a tendency towards little deviation in foreign export volumes, and an activity-induced positive deviation in foreign import volumes (Figure 7.8). In terms of (B13), the long-run deviation in the interstate trade balance is positive. With labor and capital in long-run elastic supply to the Northern economy, this causes long-run Northern real GDP to rise. This expansion in long-run regional GDP accounts for the long-run positive deviation in North's foreign import volumes.

Via (7.36), the long-run positive deviation in North's real GDP requires positive deviations in North's capital stock and employment. Via (B20), since long-run regional participation rates and employment rates do not deviate from baseline, the long-run positive deviation in North's employment requires an equivalent percentage deviation in North's population (Figure 7.9). Australia's total population is unaffected by the change in regional sourcing preferences. Hence, North's long-run population gain must be matched by long-run population loss in the rest of Australia (Figure 7.9). Again, with employment rates in all regions returning to baseline in the long-run, population loss in the rest of Australia requires employment in the rest of Australia to fall relative to baseline.

## 7.7 CONCLUDING REMARKS

Introducing a regional dimension to a CGE model comes at some cost in terms of such factors as increased data requirements that are not matched by data availability, increased model size and increased complexity in interpreting the subnational results. The imperative, however, for inter-regional and intraregional analysis is also considerable.

In this chapter, we aimed first to demonstrate the richness of analysis that can be undertaken with regional CGE models. Central to this are interpretations of model results that both reflect the underlying model mechanisms, but are explainable to policy makers outside the CGE field. It is our contention that without such explication of model results, their policy relevance is undermined. The capability of regional CGE models to produce useful results is of course dependent on the suitability of the model theory and database to the regional research question at hand. We thus review the major modeling issues particular to regional analysis and how the capacity to handle these issues has developed over time. In order to elucidate the above we summarize the general structure of large-scale multiregional CGE models, describing the range of regional attributes and inter-regional interactions treated in the regional CGE literature. We then proceed to conduct representative simulations with such a model, a variant of MMRF, in order to demonstrate the driving model mechanisms in determining regional CGE results. We interpret the results in a meticulous manner with the aid of miniature model techniques. While these techniques are now frequently used in national level modeling, their adoption in regional modeling has been quite rare.

In our discussion of regional CGE model applications we have shown three overall methods of analyzing results: (i) the BOTE technique, (ii) the use of regression analysis on model results to uncover in a step-wise fashion the driving factors underlying the key model results and (iii) sensitivity analysis. These three techniques are linked. For instance, Dixon *et al.* (2007) show that the long-run effects of a supply shock — a water buyback scheme — just depend on regional industry competitiveness. They show using regression analysis that this explains 90% of farm output results, deepening their understanding of their results as they refine their competitiveness indexes. That competitiveness indexes were the appropriate measure to use is signaled by our BOTE explanation of the effects on regional macro variables of regional supply shocks. Both regression and BOTE techniques identified the appropriate candidates for sensitivity analysis. For sensitivity analysis to be informative, it is important that it be limited to those parameters that are instrumental in determining results of the key variables.

## ACKNOWLEDGMENTS

We thank Peter Dixon, Dale Jorgenson, Luc Savard and Brian Parmenter for their valuable comments and suggestions.

## REFERENCES

Adams, P.D., Parmenter, B.R., 1994. Microeconomic reform and employment in the short-run. Econ. Rec. 70, 1—11.

Adams, P.D., Parmenter, B.R., 1995. An applied general equilibrium analysis of the economic effects of tourism in a quite small, quite open economy. Appl. Econ. 27, 985—994.

Adams, P.D., Horridge, J.M., Parmenter, B.R., 2000. Forecasts for Australian regions using the MMRF-GREEN model. Australasian J. Reg. Stud. 6, 293—322.

Adams, P.D., Dixon, J.M., Giesecke, J.A. and Horridge, J.M., 2010. MMRF: Monash Multi-Regional Forecasting Model: A dynamic multi-regional model of the Australian economy. General Working Paper G-223. Centre of Policy Studies and IMPACT Project, Melbourne.

Anderson, K., Giesecke, J.A., Valenzuela, E., 2010. How would global trade liberalization affect rural and regional incomes in Australia? Aust. J. Agric. Resour. Econ. 54, 389—406.

Aschauer, D.A., 2000. Do states optimize? public capital and economic growth. Ann. Reg. Sci. 34, 343—363.

Berck, P., Golan, E., Smith, B., 1996. Dynamic Revenue Analysis for California: Report. California Department of Finance, Sacramento, CA.

Berck, P., Golan, E., Smith, B., 1997. State tax policy, labor, and tax revenue feedback effects. Ind. Relat. 36, 399−417.

Bilgic, A., King, S., Lusby, A., Schreiner, D.F., 2002. Estimates of US regional commodity trade elasticities of substitution. J. Reg. Anal. Policy 32, 79−98.

Bird, R.M., Vaillancourt, F., 2006. Changing with the times: success, failure, and inertia in Canadian federal arrangements. In: Srinivasan, T.N., Wallack, J.S. (Eds), Federalism and Economic Reform: International Perspectives. Cambridge University Press, New York, pp. 189−248.

Blake, A., Gillham, J., 2001. A multi-regional CGE model of tourism in Spain, paper prepared for the European Trade Study Group Annual Conference, Brussels.

Bröcker, J., 2001. Spatial effects of transport infrastructure: The role of market structure. In: Roy, J.R., Schulz, W. (Eds), Theories of Regional Competition. Nomos-Verlag, Baden-Baden, pp. 181−193.

Bröcker, J., 2002. Spatial effects of European transport policy: A CGE approach. In: Hewings, G.J.D., Sonis, M., Boyce, D. (Eds), Trade, Networks And Hierarchies: Modeling Regional and Inter-Regional Economics. Springer, Berlin, pp. 11−28.

Bröcker, J., 2004. Computable general equilibrium analysis in transportation economies. In: Hensher, D.A., Button, K.J., Haynes, K.E., Stopher, P.R. (Eds), Handbook of Transport Geography and Spatial Systems. Elsevier, Amsterdam, pp. 269−292.

Bröcker, J., Schneider, M., 2002. How does economic development affect Austria's regions? a multiregional general equilibrium framework. J. Reg. Sci. 42, 257−285.

Buckley, P.H., 1992. A transportation-oriented inter-regional computable general equilibrium model of the United States. Ann. Reg. Sci. 26, 331−348.

Cardenete, M.A., Sancho, F., 2003. An applied general equilibrium model to assess the impact of national tax changes on a regional economy. Rev. Urb. Reg. Dev. Stud. 15, 55−65.

Cattaneo, A., 2001. Deforestation in the Brazilian Amazon: Comparing the impacts of macroeconomic shocks, land tenure, and technological change. Land Econ. 77, 219−240.

Challen, D.W., Hagger, A.J., Madden, J.R., 1984. Unemployment Policy Packages for Tasmania. CREA Paper RS-04. Centre for Regional Economic Analysis, University of Tasmania, Hobart.

Clements, K.W., Ahammad, H., Ye, Q., 1996. New mining and mineral-processing projects in Western Australia: Effects on employment and the macroeconomy. Res. Policy 22, 293−346.

Conrad, K., Heng, S., 2002. Financing road infrastructure by savings in congestion costs: A CGE analysis. Ann. Reg. Sci. 36, 107−122.

Cutler, H., Davies, S., 2007. The impact of specific-sector changes in employment on economic growth, labor market performance and migration. J. Reg. Sci. 47, 935−963.

Debelle, G., Vickery, J., 1999. Labour market adjustment: Evidence on interstate labour mobility. Aust. Econ. Rev. 32, 249−263.

Decaluwé, B., Lemelin, A., Bahan, D., 2010. Endogenous labour supply with several occupational categories in a bi-regional computable general equilibrium (CGE) model. Reg. Stud. 44, 1401−1414.

Despotakis, K.A., Fisher, A.C., 1988. Energy in a regional economy: A computable general equilibrium model for California. J. Environ. Econ. Manage. 15, 313−330.

Dimaranan, B.V., Hertel, T.W., Martin, W., 2007. Potential gains from post-Uruguay round table policy reforms: Impacts on developing countries. In: McCalla, A.F., Nash, J. (Eds), Reforming Agricultural Trade for Developing Countries. Quantifying the Impact of Multilateral Trade Reform, vol. 2. World Bank, Washington, DC, pp. 112−145.

Diao, X., Somwaru, A., Tuan, F., 2006. Regional and national perspectives of China's integration into the WTO: A CGE inquiry with emphasis on the agricultural sector. In: Doi, M. (Ed.), Computable General Equilibrium Approaches in Urban and Regional Policy Studies. World Scientific, Singapore, pp. 269−295.

Dixon, P.B., 2009. Comments on the productivity commission's modelling of the economy-wide effects of future automotive assistance. Econ. Pap. 28, 11−18.

Dixon, P.B., Madden, J.R., 1990. The economic impact of the very fast train. The Economics of the Very Fast Train, VFT Joint Venture, Canberra, section 7.C.

Dixon, P.B., Rimmer, M.T., 1999. The government's tax package: short run implications for employment by industry, region, occupation, age and gender' in Report of the Inquiry into the GST and a New Tax System, Senate Employment, Workplace Relations, Small Business and Education References Committee, Parliament House, Canberra, Appendix 4.

Dixon, P.B., Rimmer, M.T., 2002. Dynamic general equilibrium modelling for forecasting and policy: A practical guide and documentation of MONASH. Contributions to Economic Analysis 256. Elsevier, Amsterdam.

Dixon, P.B., Rimmer, M.T., 2004, Disaggregation of results from a detailed general equilibrium model of the US to the state level. General Working Paper G-145. Centre of Policy Studies and IMPACT Project, Melbourne.

Dixon, P.B., Rimmer, M.T., 2010. Optimal tariffs: Should Australia cut automotive tariffs unilaterally? Econ. Rec. 86 (273), 143—161.

Dixon, P.B., Sutton, J., 1977. Industry implications of international trade policy: Experiments with the ORANI model. IMPACT Project General Paper G-06. IMPACT Project, Melbourne.

Dixon, P.B., Wittwer, G., 2004. Forecasting the economic impact of an industrial stoppage using a dynamic, computable general equilibrium model. Aus. J. Lab. Econ. 7, 39—51.

Dixon, P.B., Parmenter, B.R., Sutton, J., 1978. Spatial disaggregation of ORANI results: A preliminary analysis of the impacts of protection at the state level. Econ. Anal. Policy 8, 35—86.

Dixon, P.B., Parmenter, B.R., Sutton, J., Vincent, D.P., 1982. ORANI: A Multisectoral Model of the Australian Economy. North-Holland, Amsterdam.

Dixon, P.B., Parmenter, B.R., Powell, A.A., 1984. The role of miniatures in computable general equilibrium modelling: Experience from ORANI. Econ. Model. 1, 421—428.

Dixon, P.B., Madden, J.R., Peter, M., 1990. Simulations of the economic effects of changing the distribution of general revenue assistance. Commonwealth Grants Commission Report on Issues in Fiscal Equalization vol. II. Australian Government Publishing Service, Canberra. 231—295.

Dixon, P.B., Horridge, M., Johnson, D.T., 1992a. A general equilibrium analysis of a major project: The multifunction polis. Aus. Econ. Pap. 31, 272—290.

Dixon, P.B., Parmenter, B.R., Powell, A.A., Wilcoxen, P.J., 1992b. Notes and Problems in Applied General Equilibrium Economics. North-Holland, Amsterdam.

Dixon, P.B., Madden, J.R., Peter, M., 1993. Simulations of the economic effects of changing the distribution of general revenue assistance among the Australian states. Econ. Rec. 69 (207), 367—381.

Dixon, P.B., Picton, M.R., Rimmer, M.T., 2002. Efficiency effects of inter-government financial transfers in Australia. Aus. Econ. Rev. 35, 304—315.

Dixon, P.B., Picton, M.R., Rimmer, M.T., 2004. Payroll taxes: Thresholds, firm sizes, dead-weight losses and commonwealth grants commission funding. Econ. Rec. 80, 289—301.

Dixon, P.B., Picton, M.R., Rimmer, M.T., 2005. Efficiency effects of changes in commonwealth grants to the states: A CGE analysis. Aus. Econ. Pap. 44, 82—105.

Dixon, P.B., Rimmer, M.T., Tsigas, M., 2007. Regionalising results from a detailed CGE model: Macro, industry and state effects in the US of removing major tariffs and quotas. Pap. Reg. Sci. 86, 31—55.

Dixon, P.B., Madden, J.R., Rimmer, M.T., 2010. Linking national and multi-regional models: The effects of an increase in award wage rates in Australia. Reg. Stud. 44, 1369—1385.

Dixon, P.B., Rimmer, M.T., Wittwer, G., 2011. Saving the Southern Murray—Darling Basin: The economic effects of a buyback of irrigation water. Econ. Rec. 87, 153—168.

Donaghy, K.P., 2009. CGE modeling in space: A survey. In: Capello, R., Nijkamp, P. (Eds), Handbook of Regional Growth and Development Theories. Edward Elgar, Cheltenham, pp. 389—422.

Ferguson, L., Learmonth, D., McGregor, P.G., Swales, J., Turner, K., 2007. The impact of the Barnett formula on the Scottish economy: Endogenous population and variable formula proportions. Environ. Plan. A 39, 3008—3027.

Ferreira Filho, J.B.S., Horridge, J.M., 2006. The Doha round, poverty and regional inequality in Brazil. In: Hertel, T.W., Winter, L.A. (Eds), Poverty and the WTO: Impacts of the Doha Development Agenda. Palgrave Macmillan, New York, pp. 183—217.

Ferreira Filho, J.B.S., Horridge, J.M., 2011. Ethanol expansion and the indirect land use change in Brazil. Paper prepared for the 14th Annual Conference on Global Economic Analysis, Ca' Foscari University of Venice.

Francois, J., van Meijl, H., van Tongeren, F., 2005. Trade liberalization in the Doha development round. Econ. Policy 20, 349–391.

Fry, J.M., Fry, T.R.L., Peter, M.R., 1999. Inter-regional migration in Australia: An applied economic analysis. Australasian J. Reg. Stud. 5, 111–130.

Garnaut Climate Change Review (2008) Modelling the cost of unmitigated climate change. Economic Modelling Technical Paper 5. Canberra, available at http://www.garnautreview.org.au/index.html.

Gazel, R., Hewings, G.J.D., Sonis, M., 1996. Trade, sensitivity and feedbacks: Inter-regional impacts of the US–Canada free trade agreement. In: van den Bergh, J., Nijkamp, P., Rietveld, P. (Eds), Recent Advances in Spatial Equilibrium Modeling: Methodology and Applications. Springer, Berlin, pp. 346–358.

Giesecke, J.A., 1999. Modelling the regional consequences of commomwealth policy: The case of the Fringe Benefits Tax. Australasian J. Reg. Stud. 5, 365–376.

Giesecke, J.A., 2000. The Theoretical Structure of the FEDERAL-F model. CREA Paper TS-08. Centre for Regional Economic Analysis, University of Tasmania, Hobart.

Giesecke, J.A., 2002. Explaining regional economic performance: An historical application of a dynamic multi-regional CGE model. Pap. Reg. Sci. 81, 247–278.

Giesecke, J.A., 2003. Targeting regional output with state government fiscal instruments: A dynamic multi-regional CGE analysis. Aus. Econ. Pap. 42, 214–233.

Giesecke, J.A., 2008. A top-down framework for regional historical analysis. Spatial Econ. Anal. 3, 45–87.

Giesecke, J.A., 2011. Development of a large-scale single US region CGE model using IMPLAN data: A Los Angeles county example with a productivity shock application. Spatial Econ. Anal. 6, 331–350.

Giesecke, J.A., Madden, J.R., 1997. Regional government economic policy: Assessing the policy instruments. Australasian J. Reg. Stud. 3, 3–18.

Giesecke, J.A., Madden, J.R., 2003. A large-scale dynamic multi-regional CGE model with an illustrative application. Rev. Urb. Reg. Dev. Stud. 15, 2–25.

Giesecke, J.A., Madden, J.R., 2006. A CGE evaluation of a university's effects on a regional economy: An integrated assessment of expenditure and knowledge impacts. Rev. Urb. Reg. Dev. Stud. 18, 229–251.

Giesecke, J.A., Madden, J.R., 2007. Regional adjustment to globalization: Developing a CGE analytical framework. In: Cooper, R.J., Donaghy, K.P., Hewings, G.J.D. (Eds), Globalization and Regional Economic Modeling. Springer, Berlin, pp. 229–261.

Giesecke, J.A., Madden, J.R., 2010. Uncovering the factors behind comparative regional economic performance: A multiregional CGE approach. Reg. Stud. 44, 1329–1349.

Giesecke, J.A., Madden, J.R., 2011. Modelling the economic impacts of the Sydney Olympics in retrospect — game over for the bonanza story? Econ. Pap. 30, 218–232.

Giesecke, J.A., Dixon, P.B., Rimmer, M.T., 2008. Regional macroeconomic outcomes under alternative arrangements for the financing of public infrastructure. Pap. Reg. Sci. 87, 3–31.

Giesecke, J.A., Burns, W.J., Barrett, A., Bayrak, E., Rose, A., Slovic, P., Suher, M., 2012. Assessment of the regional economic impacts of catastrophic events: CGE analysis of resource loss and behavioral effects of an RDD attack scenario. Risk Anal. 32, 583–600.

Gillespie, G., McGregor, P.G., Swales, J.K., Yin, Y.P., 2001. The displacement and multiplier effects of regional selective assistance: A computable general equilibrium analysis. Reg. Stud. 35, 125–139.

Gillespie, G., McGregor, P.G., Swales, J.K., Yin, Y.P., 2002a. The regional impact of foreign direct investment: Structure and behaviour in an ownership-disaggregated computable general equilibrium model. In: Hewings, G.J.D., Sonis, M., Boyce, D. (Eds), Trade, Networks and Hierarchies: Modeling Regional and Inter-regional Economies. Springer, Berlin, pp. 65–98.

Gillespie, G., McGregor, P.G., Swales, J.K., Yin, Y.P., 2002b. A computable general equilibrium approach to the ex post evaluation of regional development agency policies. In: Johansson, B., Karlsson, C., Slough, R.R. (Eds), Regional Policies and Comparative Advantage. Edward Elgar, Cheltenham, pp. 253–282.

Graham, D., 2007. Agglomeration, productivity and transport investment. J. Transp. Econ. Policy 41, 317–343.

Groenewold, N., Madden, J.R., Hagger, A.J., 2003. The effects of inter-regional transfers: A political-economy CGE approach. Pap. Reg. Sci. 82, 535–554.

Ha, S.J., Turner, K., Hewings, G., McGregor, P., Swales, J.K., 2010. Econometric estimation of Armington import elasticities and their system-wide impact in a regional CGE model of the Illinois economy. Stirling Economic Discussion Paper 2010-19, available at http://hdl.handle.net/1893/2707.

Haddad, E.A., 1999. Regional Inequality and Structural Change. Ashgate, Aldershot.

Haddad, E.A., Dominiques, E.P., Perobelli, F.S., 2002a. Regional effects of economic integration: The case of Brazil. J. Policy Model. 24, 453–482.

Haddad, E.A., Hewings, G.J.D., Peter, M., 2002b. Input-Output Systems in Regional and Inter-Regional CGE Modeling. In: Hewings, G.J.D., Sonis, M., Boyce, D. (Eds), Trade, Networks and Hierarchies: Modeling Regional and Inter-Regional Economics. Springer, Berlin, pp. 407–431.

Haddad, E.A., Hewings, G.J.D., 2005. Market imperfections in a spatial economy: Some experimental results. Q. Rev. Econ. Finance 45, 476–496.

Haddad, E.A., Hewings, G.J.D., Perobelli, F.S., dos Santos, R.A.C., 2010. Regional effects of port infrastructure: A spatial CGE application to Brazil. Int. Reg. Sci. Rev. 33, 239–263.

Hanley, N., McGregor, P.G., Swales, J.K., Turner, K., 2009. Do increases in energy efficiency improve environmental quality and sustainability? Ecol. Econ. 68, 692–709.

Hanoch, G., 1971. CRESH production functions. Econometrica 39, 695–712.

Harrigan, F., McGregor, P.G., Dourmashkin, N., Perman, R., Swales, K., Yin, Y.P., 1991. AMOS: A macro–micro model of Scotland. Econ. Model. 8, 424–479.

Hertel, T.W., Mount, T.D., 1985. The pricing of natural resources in a regional economy. Land Econ. 61, 229–243.

Higgs, P.J., Powell, A.A., 1992. Australia's North West Shelf project, a general equilibrium analysis of its impact on the Australian economy. Res. Policy 18, 179–190.

Higgs, P.J., Parmenter, B.R., Rimmer, M.T., 1988. A hybrid top-down, bottom-up regional computable general equilibrium model. Int. Reg. Sci. Rev. 11, 317–328.

Hirte, G., 1998. Welfare effects of regional income taxes: Results of an inter-regional CGE analysis for Germany. Ann. Reg. Sci. 32, 201–219.

Hirte, G., Tscharaktschiew, S., 2011. Income tax deduction of commuting expenses and tax funding in an urban CGE study: The case of German cities' Dresden Discussion Paper in Economics 02/11, Technische Universität Dresden, Dresden.

Hoffmann, S., Robinson, S., Subramanian, S., 1996. The role of defense cuts in the California recession: Computable general equilibrium models and interstate factor mobility. J. Reg. Sci. 36, 571–595.

Horridge, J.M., 1994. A computable general equilibrium model of urban transport demands. J. Policy Model. 16, 427–457.

Horridge, J.M., 2003. ORANI-G: A Generic Single-Country Computable General Equilibrium Model, Centre of Policy Studies, Monash University, Melbourne, available at http://www.monash.edu.au/policy/oranig.htm.

Horridge, J.M., Wittwer, G., 2008. The economic impacts of a construction project, using SinoTERM, a multi-regional CGE model of China. China Econ. Rev. 19, 628–634.

Horridge, J.M., Madden, J.R., Wittwer, G., 2005. Impact of the 2002–03 drought on Australia. J. Policy Model. 27, 285–308.

Industry Commission, 1995. The Growth and Revenue Implications of Hilmer and Related Reforms. A Report by the Industry Commission to the Council of Australian Governments. Industry Commission, Canberra.

Isard, W., Azis, I.J., Drennan, M.P., Miller, R.E., Saltzman, S., Thorbecke, E., 1998. Methods of Inter-Regional and Regional Analysis. Ashgate, Aldershot.

Jensen, R.C., Mandeville, T.D., Karunaratne, N.D., 1979. Regional Economic Planning: Generation of Regional Input-Output Analysis. Croom Helm, London.

Johns, P.M., Leat, P.M.K., 1987. The application of modified grit input-output procedures to rural development analysis in Grampian Region. J. Agric. Econ. 38, 243–256.

Jones, R., Whalley, J., 1988. Regional effects of taxes in Canada: An applied general equilibrium approach. J. Public Econ. 37, 1–28.

Jones, R., Whalley, J., 1989. A Canadian regional general equilibrium model and some applications. J. Urb. Econ. 25, 368–405.

Kilkenny, M., 1998. Transport costs and rural—urban development. J. Reg. Sci. 38, 293—312.

Kilkenny, M., 1999. Explicitly spatial rural—urban computable general equilibrium. Am. J. Agric. Econ. 81, 647—652.

Kim, E., Hewings, G.J.D., 2009. An application of an integrated transport network — multiregional CGE model to the calibration of synergy effects of highway investments. Econ. Syst. Res. 21, 377—397.

Kim, E., Kim, K., 2002. Impacts of regional development strategies on growth and equity of Korea: A multiregional CGE model. Ann. Reg. Sci. 36, 165—180.

Kim, E., Kim, K., 2003. Impacts of the development of large cities on economic growth and income distribution in Korea: A multiregional CGE model. Pap. Reg. Sci. 82, 101—122.

Kim, E., Hewings, G.J.D., Hong, C., 2004. An application of integrated transport network-multiregional CGE model: A framework for the economic analysis of highway projects. Econ. Syst. Res. 16, 235—258.

Klein, L.R., Glickman, N.J., 1977. Econometric model-building at regional level. Reg. Sci. Urb. Econ. 7, 3—23.

Kraybill, D.S., 1993. Computable General Equilibrium Analysis at the Regional Level. In: Otto, D.M., Johnson, T.G. (Eds), Microcomputer-Based Input-Output Modeling: Applications to Economic Development. Westview Press, Boulder CO, pp. 198—215.

Kraybill, D.S., Johnson, T.G., Orden, D., 1992. Macroeconomic imbalances: A multiregional general equilibrium analysis. Am. J. Agric. Econ. 74, 726—736.

Krugman, P.R., 1991. Increasing returns and economic geography. J. Polit. Econ. 99, 483—499.

Leontief, W.W., Strout, A., 1963. Multiregional Input-Output Analysis. In: Barna, T. (Ed.), Structural Interdependence and Economics Development. Macmillan, London, pp. 119—149.

Leontief, W.W., Morgan, A., Polenske, K., Simpson, D., Tower, E., 1965. The economic impact — industrial and regional — of an arms cut. Rev. Econ. Stat. 47, 217—241.

Li, P.C., Rose, A., 1995. Global warming policy and the Pennsylvania economy: A computable general equilibrium analysis. Econ. Syst. Res. 7, 151—171.

Liew, L.H., 1981. A multi-regional multi-sectoral general equilibrium model of the Australian economy. PhD Thesis, Monash University, Melbourne.

Liew, L.H., 1984a. A Johansen model for regional analysis. Reg. Sci. Urb. Econ. 14, 129—146.

Liew, L.H., 1984b. "Tops-down" versus "bottoms-up" approaches to regional modeling. J. Policy Model. 6, 351—367.

Lofgren, H., Robinson, S., 2002. Spatial-network, general-equilibrium model with a stylized application. Reg. Sci. Urb. Econ. 32, 651—671.

Madden, J.R., 1987. The Structure of the TASMAIN Model. IAESR Working Paper 11/1987. Institute of Applied Economic and Social Research, University of Melbourne, Melbourne.

Madden, J.R., 1989. Employment Policy Options: Answers from a Large-Scale Economic Model. Report to the Tasmanian Employment Summit. Parliament House, Hobart.

Madden, J.R., 1990. FEDERAL: A two-region multi-sectoral fiscal model of the Australian economy, PhD Thesis, University of Tasmania, Hobart.

Madden, J.R., 1991. Regional Impacts of Reducing $CO_2$ Emissions. In: Gordon, M.T., Gordon, B.L.J. (Eds), Regional Modelling and Regional Planning. Institute of Industrial Economics Conference Series Number 18. University of Newcastle, Newcastle, pp. 119—130.

Madden, J.R., 1993. The economics of vertical fiscal imbalance. Aus. Tax Forum 10, 75—90.

Madden, J.R., 1995. Implementing the Hilmer reforms: The effects on the national and state economies. Business Coun. B. Melbourne, 14—19. March.

Madden, J.R., 1996. FEDERAL: A two-region multisectoral fiscal model of the Australian Economy. In: Vlacic, L., Nguyen, T., Cecez-Kecmanovic, D. (Eds), Modelling and Control of National and Regional Economies. Pergamon, Oxford, pp. 347—352.

Madden, J.R., 2004. The economic impact of national competition policy on Australian regions. Eur. Plan. Stud. 12, 41—56.

Madden, J.R., 2006. Australia: Central fiscal dominance, collaborative federalism and economic reform. In: Srinivasan, T.N., Wallack, J.S. (Eds), Federalism and Economic Reform: International Perspectives. Cambridge University Press, New York, pp. 85—142.

Madden, J.R., Gwee, E., 2010. A spatial CGE model for assessing the vulnerability of regional economies to transport system failures. Paper presented to 57th Annual North American Meetings of the Regional Science Association International, Denver CO, November.

Madden, J.R., Challen, D.W., Hagger, A.J., 1983. The Grants Commission's relativities proposals: Effects on the state economies. Aust. Econ. Pap. 22, 302–321.

McDaniel, C.A., Balistreri, E.J., 2003. A review of Armington trade substitution elasticities. Économie Internationale 94–95, 301–314.

McGregor, P.G., Swales, J.K., Yin, Y.P., 1995. Migration equilibria/disequilibria and the natural rate of unemployment in a regional context. Ind. J. Manpower 16, 66–72.

McGregor, P.G., Swales, J.K., Yin, Y.P., 1996a. A long-run interpretation of regional input-output. J. Reg. Sci. 36, 479–501.

McGregor, P.G., Swales, J.K., Yin, Y.P., 1996b. Migration equilibria in regional economies: A multi-period CGE analysis of an improvement in local amenities. In: van den Bergh, J., Nijkamp, P., Rietveld, P. (Eds), Recent Advances in Spatial Equilibrium Modeling: Methodology and Applications. Springer, Berlin, pp. 346–358.

McGregor, P.G., Swales, J.K., Yin, Y.P., 1999. Spillover and feedback effects in general equilibrium inter-regional models of the national economy: A requiem for inter-regional input-output?. In: Hewings, G.J.D., Sonis, M., Madden, M., Kimura, Y. (Eds), Understanding and Interpreting Economic Structure. Springer, Berlin, pp. 167–190.

Miyata, Y., 1995. A general equilibrium analysis of the waste-economic system—a CGE modeling approach. Infrastruct. Plan. Rev. 12, 259–270.

Morgan, W., Mutti, J., Partridge, M., 1989. A regional general equilibrium model of the United States: Tax effects on factor movements and regional production. Rev. Econ. Stat. 71, 626–635.

Morgan, W., Mutti, J., Rickman, D., 1996. Tax exporting, regional economic growth and welfare. J. Urb. Econ. 39, 131–159.

Mutti, J., Morgan, W., Partridge, M., 1989. The incidence of regional taxes in a general equilibrium framework. J. Public Econ. 39, 83–107.

Naqvi, F., Peter, M.W., 1996. A multi-regional multi-sectoral model of the Australian economy with an illustrative application. Aus. Econ. Pap. 35 (66), 94–113.

Norrie, K.H., Percy, M.B., 1983. Freight rate reform and regional burden: A general equilibrium analysis of western freight rate proposals. Can. J. Econ. 16, 325–349.

Oladosu, G., Rose, A., 2007. Income distribution impacts of climate change mitigation policy in the Susquehanna river basin economy. Energy Econ. 29, 520–544.

Parmenter, B.R., Welsh, A., 2001. Historical simulations with the Monash Regional Equation system. Australasian J. Reg. Stud. 7, 209–230.

Partridge, M.D., Rickman, D.S., 1998. Regional computable general equilibrium modeling: A survey and critical appraisal. Int. Reg. Sci. Rev. 21, 205–248.

Partridge, M.D., Rickman, D.S., 2010. Computable general equilibrium (CGE) modeling for regional economic development analysis. Reg. Stud. 44, 1311–1328.

Powell, A.A., Gruen, F.H., 1968. The constant elasticity of transformation frontier and linear supply system. Int. Econ. Rev. 9, 315–328.

Productivity Commission, 1999. Modelling the Regional Impacts of National Competition Policy Reforms. Supplement to Inquiry Report, Impact of Competition Policy Reforms on Rural and Regional Australia. Productivity Commission, Canberra.

Productivity Commission, 2006. Potential Benefits of the National Reform Agenda. Report to the Council of Australian Governments. Productivity Commission, Canberra.

Rickman, D., 1992. Estimating the impacts of regional business assistance programs: Alternative closures in a computable general equilibrium model. Pap. Reg. Sci. 71, 421–435.

Rose, A., Liao, S.Y., 2005. Modeling regional economic resilience to disasters: A computable general equilibrium analysis of water services disruptions. J. Reg. Sci. 45, 75–112.

Round, J.I., 1983. Nonsurvey techniques: A critical review of the theory and the evidence. Int. Reg. Sci. Rev. 8, 189–212.

Rutherford, T.F., Törmä, H., 2010. Efficiency of fiscal measures in preventing out-migration from North Finland. Reg. Stud. 44, 465—475.

Schwarm, W., Cutler, H., 2006. Building small city and town: SAMs and CGE models revisited. In: Doi, M. (Ed.), Computable General Equilibrium Approaches in Urban and Regional Policy Studies. World Scientific, Singapore, 59—81.

Seung, D.K., Kraybill, D.S., 1999. Tax incentives in an economy with public goods. Growth Change 30, 128—147.

Seung, C.K., Waters, E.C., 2010. Evaluating supply-side and demand-side shocks for fisheries: A computable general equilibrium (CGE) model for Alaska. Econ. Syst. Res. 22, 87—109.

Seung, C.K., Harris, T.R., Englin, J.E., Netusil, N.R., 2000. Impacts of water allocation: A computable general equilibrium and recreational demand model approach. Ann. Reg. Sci. 34, 473—487.

Shibusawa, H., Miyata, Y., 2011. Evaluating the dynamic and spatial impacts of an earthquake: A CGE application to Japan. Reg. Sci. Inquiry J. 3, 13—25.

Snoddon, T., Wigle, R., 2008. Regional incidence of the costs of greenhouse policy. Can. J. Reg. Sci. 30, 313—336.

Thissen, M.J., 2004. The indirect economic effects of a terrorist attack on transport infrastructure: A proposal for a SAGE. Disaster Protect. Manag. 13, 315—322.

Thissen, M.J., 2005. RAEM: Regional applied general equilibrium model for The Netherlands. In: van Oort, F.G., et al. (Eds), A Survey of Spatial-economic Planning Models in The Netherlands: Theory, Application and Evaluation. NAi Publishers, Rotterdam, pp. 63—86.

Turner, K., 2009. Negative rebound and disinvestment effects in response to an improvement in energy efficiency in the UK economy. Energy Econ. 31, 648—666.

Vincent, D.P., Dixon, P.B., Powell, A.A., 1980. The estimation of supply response in Australian agriculture: The CRESH/CRETH production system. Int. Econ. Rev. 21, 221—242.

West, G.R., Morison, J.B., Jensen, R.C., 1984. A method for the estimation of hybrid inter-regional input-output tables,. Reg. Stud. 18, 413—421.

Whalley, J., 1982. An evaluation of the Tokyo round table agreement using general equilibrium computational methods. J. Policy Model. 4, 341—361.

Whalley, J., Trela, I., 1986. Regional Aspects of Confederation. University of Toronto Press, Toronto.

Wigle, R.M., 1992. Transportation costs in regional models of foreign trade: An application to Canada—US trade. J. Reg. Sci. 32, 185—207.

Wittwer, G., Horridge, M., 2010. Bringing regional detail to a CGE model using census data. Spatial Econ. Anal. 5, 229—255.

Wittwer, G., McKirdy, S., Wilson, R., 2005. Regional economic impacts of a plant disease incursion using a general equilibrium approach. Aust. J. Agric. Resour. Econ. 49, 75—89.

# Energy, the Environment and US Economic Growth

**Dale W. Jorgenson\*, Richard J. Goettle\*\*, Mun S. Ho\*, Peter J. Wilcoxen\*\*\***
\*Harvard University
\*\*Northeastern University
\*\*\*Syracuse University and The Brookings Institution

## Abstract

The point of departure for the study of the impact of energy and environmental policies is the neoclassical theory of economic growth formulated by Cass (1965) and Koopmans (1967). The long-run properties of economic growth models are independent of energy and environmental policies. However, these policies affect capital accumulation and rates of productivity growth that determine the intermediate-run trends that are important for policy evaluation. Heterogeneity of different energy producers and consumers is critical for the evaluation of energy and environmental policies. To capture this heterogeneity it is necessary to distinguish among commodities, industries and households. Econometric methods are essential for summarizing information on different industries and consumer groups in a form suitable for general equilibrium modeling. In this chapter, we consider the application of econometric general equilibrium modeling to the US — the economy that has been studied most intensively. The framework for our analysis is provided by the Intertemporal General Equilibrium Model (IGEM) introduced by Jorgenson and Wilcoxen (1998). The new version of the IGEM presented in this paper is employed for the evaluation of proposed legislation on climate policy by the US Environmental Protection Agency (2012b).

## Keywords

Econometric modeling, energy, environment, general equilibrium, heterogeneity, policy evaluation

## JEL classification codes

C51, C68, D58, E13, O41, O51, Q43, Q50

## 8.1 INTRODUCTION

Economic growth is a critical determinant of US demand for energy. Emissions from the combustion of fossil fuels are an important source of US requirements for pollution abatement. An essential first step in modeling the impact of energy and environmental policies is to analyze the growth of the US economy. The appropriate point of departure for modeling economic growth is the neoclassical theory of economic growth, originated by Solow (1956, 2005). The form of this theory appropriate for modeling the

© 2013 Elsevier B.V.
All rights reserved.

inter-relationships among energy, the environment and US economic growth was developed by Cass (1965) and Koopmans (1967).[1]

Maler (1974) and Uzawa (1975) have presented neoclassical theories of economic growth with pollution abatement. A recent survey by Brock and Taylor (2005) summarizes the extensive literature on this topic. Solow (1974a, 1974b) has provided a theory of economic growth that includes an exhaustible resource. The classic textbook treatment of this topic remains that of Dasgupta and Heal (1979), who also give a detailed survey of the literature. In this paper we focus on pollution abatement, since the US economy is relatively open to trade in natural resources, exporting coal and importing oil and natural gas.

In the neoclassical theory of economic growth wage rates grow at the same rate as productivity in the long run, while rates of return depend on productivity growth and the parameters that describe saving behavior. These long-run properties of economic growth are independent of energy and environmental policies. The neoclassical theory of economic growth also provides a framework for analyzing intermediate-run growth trends. These trends reflect the same determinants as long-run trends, but also depend on energy and environmental policies through their effects on capital accumulation and rates of productivity growth. In this context the "intermediate-run" refers to the time needed for the capital–output ratio to converge to a long-run stationary value. This often requires decades, so that the impact of energy and environmental policies on intermediate-run trends is critical for policy evaluation.

The slowdown of the US economy during the 1970s and 1980s, and the acceleration of growth during the 1990s and 2000s, are striking examples of changes in intermediate-run trends. Two events associated with the slowdown — the advent of more restrictive environmental policies and the increase in world petroleum prices — have led to a focus on the interactions of energy supplies and prices, environmental quality and its cost, and the sources of economic growth. Similarly, Jorgenson (2009a) has demonstrated that the rapid development of information technology is the key to more rapid growth in the 1990s and 2000s.

Nordhaus (2008, 2010) has applied the Cass–Koopmans theory of economic growth to the analysis of energy and environmental policies in his important studies of climate policy for the world economy.[2] The necessarily schematic modeling of technology limits consideration of issues that are very important in implementation of energy and environmental policies at the national level, such as the heterogeneity of different energy producers and consumers. To capture this heterogeneity we distinguish among commodities, industries and households. We employ an econometric approach to summarize information on different industries and consumer groups in a form

---

[1] Barro and Sala-i-Martin (2004) provide a standard textbook treatment.
[2] More details are given by Nordhaus (2012) in Chapter 16 of this Handbook.

suitable for general equilibrium modeling. We next consider the application of the econometric approach to the US economy.

The framework for our econometric analysis of the impact of energy and environmental policies is provided by the Intertemporal General Equilibrium Model (IGEM) introduced by Jorgenson and Wilcoxen (1998). The organizing mechanism of this model is an intertemporal price system balancing demand and supply for products and factors of production. The intertemporal price system links the prices of assets in every time period to the discounted value of future capital services. This forward-looking feature is essential in dealing with the critique of macroeconometric models by Lucas (1976).[3]

Forward-looking behavior of producers and consumers is combined with backward linkages among investment, capital stock and capital services in modeling the dynamics of economic growth. These mechanisms are also featured in the Cass—Koopmans neoclassical model of economic growth. The alternative time paths for economic growth depend on energy and environmental policies through the impact of these policies on intermediate-run trends.

In disaggregating the economic impacts of US energy and environmental policies, we preserve the key features of more highly aggregated IGEMs like those of Nordhaus. One important dimension for disaggregation is to distinguish among industries and commodities in order to measure policy impacts for narrower segments of the US economy. This makes it possible to model differences among industries in response to changes in energy prices and the imposition of pollution controls for different fuels.

A second avenue for disaggregation is to distinguish among households by level of wealth and demographic characteristics. This makes it possible to model differences in responses to price changes and environmental controls. Jorgenson *et al.* (1997, 2011) incorporate these differences in analyzing the distributional effects of energy and environmental policies. We begin our discussion of econometric intertemporal general equilibrium modeling by outlining the methodology.[4]

At the outset of our discussion it is necessary to recognize that the predominant tradition in general equilibrium modeling does not employ econometric methods. This tradition originated with the seminal work of Leontief (1951), beginning with the implementation of the static input-output model. Leontief (1953) gave a further impetus to the development of general equilibrium modeling by introducing a dynamic

---

[3] An important application of the econometric approach to general equilibrium is the G-Cubed model constructed by McKibbin and Wilcoxen (1999). A survey of applications of the G-Cubed model is presented by McKibbin and Wilcoxen in Chapter 15 of this Handbook.

[4] Econometric methodology for general equilibrium modeling is discussed in greater detail by Jorgenson *et al.* in Chapter 17 of this Handbook.

input-output model. This model can be regarded as an important progenitor of the intertemporal general equilibrium model described below. Empirical work associated with input-output analysis is based on determining the parameters that describe technology and preferences from a single interindustry transactions table.

The usefulness of the "fixed coefficients" assumption that underlies input-output analysis is hardly subject to dispute. By linearizing technology and preferences Leontief solved at one stroke the two fundamental problems that arise in practical implementation of general equilibrium models. (i) The resulting general equilibrium model can be solved as a system of linear equations with constant coefficients. (ii) The "input-output coefficients" can be estimated from a single data point. The data required are now available for all countries that have implemented the United Nations' *2008 System of National Accounts* (United Nations *et al.*, 2009).

An input-output approach to modeling environmental policy was introduced by Kneese *et al.* (1970). Their work was particularly notable for introducing a "materials balance" implied by conservation of mass for all economic activities. Materials balances bring out the fact that material not embodied in final products must result in emissions of pollutants. These emissions accumulate as solid waste or enter the atmosphere or hydrosphere and reduce air or water quality. The assumption that pollutants are generated in fixed proportions to output is a natural complement to the fixed-coefficients assumptions of Leontief's input-output models in implementing the materials balance approach.

The obvious objection to the fixed-coefficients approach to modeling energy and environmental policies is that the purpose of these policies is to change the input-output coefficients. For example, the purpose of many environmental regulations is to induce producers and consumers to substitute less polluting inputs for more polluting ones. A prime example is the substitution of low-sulfur coal for high-sulfur coal by electric utilities to comply with regulations on sulfur dioxide emissions. Another example is the dramatic shift from leaded to unleaded motor fuels in order to clean up motor vehicle emissions.

Johansen (1960, 1974) provided the first successful implementation of an empirical general equilibrium model without the fixed-coefficients assumption of input-output analysis. Johansen retained Leontief's fixed-coefficients assumption in determining demands for intermediate goods, including energy. However, he employed linear-logarithmic or Cobb–Douglas production functions in modeling the substitution between capital and labor services and technical change.

Johansen also replaced Leontief's fixed coefficients assumption for household behavior by a system of demand functions originated by Frisch (1959). Finally, he developed a method for solving the resulting nonlinear general equilibrium model for growth rates of sectoral output levels and prices and implemented this model for Norway, using data from the Norwegian national accounts. Johansen's multisectoral growth

(MSG) model of Norway is another important progenitor for the IGEM described below.[5]

Linear logarithmic production functions have the obvious advantage that the capital and labor input coefficients respond to price changes. Furthermore, the relative shares of these inputs in the value of output are fixed, so that the unknown parameters can be estimated from a single data point. In describing producer behavior Johansen employed econometric modeling only in estimating constant rates of productivity growth. Similarly, the unknown parameters of the demand system proposed by Frisch can be determined from a single point, except for a single parameter estimated econometrically.

Dixon and Parmenter (1996) and Dixon and Rimmer (2012) have surveyed the literature on Johansen-type models. The unknown parameters describing technology and preferences in these models are determined by "calibration" to a single data point. Data from a single interindustry transactions table are supplemented by a small number of parameters estimated econometrically. An important advantage of the Johansen approach, like input-output analysis, is the capacity to absorb the enormous amounts of detail available for a single data point. Dixon and Parmenter describe a model of Australia with 120 industries, 56 regions, 280 occupations and several hundred family types.

The obvious disadvantage of the calibration approach is the highly restrictive assumptions on technology and preferences required to make calibration feasible. Almost all general equilibrium models retain the fixed-coefficients assumption of Leontief and Johansen for modeling the demand for intermediate goods. However, this assumption is directly contradicted by massive empirical evidence of price-induced energy conservation in response to higher world energy prices beginning in 1973.

British Petroleum's (2011) *Energy Outlook 2030* shows that world energy use per unit of GDP peaked in the early 1970s and has fallen by more than 50% through 2010. The reductions in energy utilization induced by successive energy crises in the 1970s and the higher level of energy prices prevailing in the 1980s has been documented in great detail by Schipper *et al.* (1992). This extensive survey covers nine Organization for Economic Cooperation and Development (OECD) countries, including the US, for the period 1970–1989 and describes energy conservation in residential, manufacturing, other industry, services, passenger transport and freight transport sectors. Reductions in energy–output ratios for these activities average 15–20%.

Fixed coefficients for intermediate goods also rule out a very important response to environmental regulations by assumption. This is the introduction of pollution control equipment to treat wastes after they have been generated, substituting capital for other inputs, such as energy and materials. This is commonly known as end-of-pipe abatement

---

[5] Holmøy (2012) describes the current version of the MSG model of Norway. Holmøy and Strøm present applications of this model to financial sustainability of the Norwegian economy in Chapter 3 of this Handbook.

and is frequently the method of choice for retrofitting existing facilities to meet environmental standards.

A typical example of end-of-pipe abatement is the use of electrostatic precipitators to reduce emissions of particulates from combustion. Regulations promulgated by regulators like the US Environmental Protection Agency encourage the use of this approach by setting standards for emission on the basis of the "best available technology." Bergman (2005) surveys computable general equilibrium (CGE) models of energy and the environment.

A representation of technology and preferences that overcomes the limitations of the Johansen approach requires econometric methods. A common extension of Johansen's methodology employs constant elasticities of substitution between two inputs into production. A less restrictive approach is to generate complete systems of equations for the inputs of capital, labor, energy, materials and services (KLEMS). The current version of IGEM discussed in this chapter employs the state-space model of technical change introduced by Jin and Jorgenson (2010) and discussed in Chapter 17 of this Handbook.

As in the descriptions of technology by Leontief and Johansen, production in the econometric approach of Jin and Jorgenson is characterized by constant returns to scale in each sector. As a consequence, commodity prices can be expressed as functions of factor prices, using the non-substitution theorem of Samuelson (1951). The non-substitution theorem permits a substantial reduction in the dimensionality of the space of prices determined by the model. This greatly facilitates the solution of the new version of IGEM.

Constant returns to scale and the non-substitution theorem have been exploited in solving Johansen models by the "fixed point" methods pioneered by Scarf (1973). Johansen (1960, 1974) introduced a method of linearizing the MSG model and solving it by matrix inversion. Dixon *et al.* (1982) extended this to the "Johansen–Euler" method that eliminated the linearization errors. Dixon and Parmenter (1996) survey the extensive applications of this method. Dixon *et al.* (1992) surveys methods for solving intertemporal general equilibrium models like the IGEM model of Jorgenson and Wilcoxen (1998).

Similarly, econometric models of consumer behavior can overcome the limitations of the Frisch (1959) model of consumer demand. A common approach is to use systems of equations that incorporate the theory of consumer behavior by utilizing the notion of a representative consumer employed by Frisch. Aggregate demand functions are treated as if they could be generated by a single utility-maximizing individual. The difficulty with this approach is that aggregate demand functions must be expressed as sums of individual demand functions.

Jorgenson *et al.* (1997a) have constructed an aggregate model of consumer behavior based on Lau's (1977) theory of exact aggregation. The exact aggregation model included the demographic characteristics of individual households, as well as prices and household expenditures, as determinants of consumer behavior. The model was implemented from aggregate time series and individual household data. The demographic characteristics of the households successfully capture the enormous heterogeneity of the US population reflected in census and survey data and emphasized by Browning *et al.* (1999).

Jorgenson and Slesnick (2008) have recently extended the exact aggregation approach to include labor supply, as well as the intertemporal allocation of full wealth. Full wealth includes the value of the household's human wealth, as well as the household's tangible and financial wealth. Jorgenson and Slesnick (2008) implement this model of aggregate demand for goods and leisure for the US using 150,000 individual household observations from the consumer expenditure survey (CEX) and price data from the consumer price index (CPI) for US regions at different points of time (Bureau of Labor Statistics, 2012a, 2012b).

The exact aggregation approach to econometric modeling of data for individual households generates a model of aggregate behavior. The fact that individual demand functions can be recovered from the aggregate demand functions makes it possible to evaluate energy and environmental policies in terms of measures of individual welfare, as demonstrated by Jorgenson *et al.* (1997b). We extend these measures of household welfare to incorporate labor supply, using the model of Jorgenson and Slesnick (2008) discussed in Chapter 17 of this Handbook.

## 8.2 IGEM

In this section we describe the main features of the IGEM used in this chapter for analyzing energy, the environment and US economic growth.[6] The core of the supply side of the model is the domestic production sector modeled by Jin and Jorgenson (2010). This is augmented by models of imports from the rest-of-the-world sector. The core of the demand side is the household sector modeled by Jorgenson and Slesnick (2008). This is supplemented by models of investment and government demand and models of exports to the rest of the world.

We distinguish among 35 industries and commodities listed in Table 8.1, including the five energy-producing sectors — coal mining, petroleum and natural gas mining, petroleum refining, electric utilities, and gas utilities. Each commodity is the primary product of one of the industries. Non-comparable imports (NCIs) are a 36th commodity that is not produced domestically, but enters as an input into production. We describe the main agents in the model in turn, beginning with the household sector.

---

[6] A summary of the model is given by Environmental Protection Agency (2012b). http://www.epa.gov/climatechange/economics/modeling.html.

**Table 8.1** Industry output, energy use in 2005 and historical growth

| | | Output (billion $) | Energy share (% output) | Output growth 1960–2005 (% p.a.) | TFP growth 1960–2005 (% p.a.) |
|---|---|---|---|---|---|
| 1 | Agriculture, forestry, fisheries | 424 | 4.4 | 2.00 | 1.40 |
| 2 | Metal mining | 25 | 9.8 | 0.67 | −0.60 |
| 3 | Coal mining | 26 | 12.5 | 2.21 | 1.17 |
| 4 | Crude oil and gas extraction | 260 | 7.6 | 0.40 | −0.58 |
| 5 | Non-metallic mineral mining | 24 | 12.3 | 1.56 | 0.27 |
| 6 | Construction | 1356 | 2.7 | 1.60 | −0.61 |
| 7 | Food products | 595 | 1.8 | 2.01 | 0.52 |
| 8 | Tobacco products | 31 | 0.7 | −0.83 | −1.52 |
| 9 | Textile mill products | 60 | 3.2 | 1.17 | 1.56 |
| 10 | Apparel and other textile products | 36 | 1.4 | −0.28 | 0.97 |
| 11 | Lumber and wood products | 130 | 2.9 | 2.03 | 0.15 |
| 12 | Furniture and fixtures | 101 | 1.9 | 3.27 | 0.69 |
| 13 | Paper and allied products | 168 | 4.4 | 2.04 | 0.47 |
| 14 | Printing and publishing | 230 | 1.1 | 1.83 | −0.15 |
| 15 | Chemicals | 521 | 4.9 | 2.81 | 0.55 |
| 16 | Petroleum refining | 419 | 51.3 | 1.63 | 0.08 |
| 17 | Rubber and plastic products | 188 | 2.5 | 4.21 | 0.87 |

| | | | | |
|---|---|---|---|---|
| 18 | Leather and leather products | 6 | 2.7 | −2.36 | 0.33 |
| 19 | Stone, clay and glass products | 129 | 5.9 | 1.90 | 0.54 |
| 20 | Primary metals | 251 | 5.1 | 0.84 | 0.32 |
| 21 | Fabricated metal products | 296 | 2.2 | 1.94 | 0.51 |
| 22 | Industrial machinery | 424 | 1.3 | 5.92 | 2.65 |
| 23 | Electrical machinery | 331 | 1.4 | 6.50 | 3.81 |
| 24 | Motor vehicles | 442 | 0.9 | 3.22 | 0.27 |
| 25 | Other transportation equipment | 227 | 1.3 | 1.91 | 0.28 |
| 26 | Instruments | 207 | 1.0 | 4.32 | 1.10 |
| 27 | Miscellaneous manufacturing | 61 | 1.8 | 2.18 | 0.88 |
| 28 | Transportation and warehousing | 668 | 13.1 | 3.01 | 0.99 |
| 29 | Communications | 528 | 0.8 | 5.65 | 1.16 |
| 30 | Electric utilities (services) | 373 | 14.2 | 2.94 | 0.30 |
| 31 | Gas utilities (services) | 77 | 55.0 | −0.45 | −0.86 |
| 32 | Wholesale and retail trade | 2488 | 3.2 | 3.72 | 0.84 |
| 33 | Finance, insurance and real estate (FIRE) | 2752 | 1.2 | 4.19 | 0.77 |
| 34 | Personal and business services | 4354 | 1.7 | 3.93 | −0.27 |
| 35 | Government enterprises | 328 | 7.8 | 2.43 | 0.19 |

"Energy share" includes feedstocks.

## 8.2.1 Household behavior and demographic characteristics

Our household model has three stages. In the first stage, *lifetime full income* is allocated between consumption and savings. Full income includes leisure as well as income from the supply of capital and labor services. Consumption consists of commodities and leisure and we refer to this as *full consumption*. In the second stage, full consumption is allocated to leisure and three commodity groups — non-durables, capital services and services. In the third stage, the three commodity groups are allocated to the 36 commodities, including the five types of energy. We next describe the three stages of the household model.

### 8.2.1.1 Stage 1: intertemporal optimization

Let $V_{kt}$ denote the utility of household $k$ derived from consuming goods and leisure during period $t$. In the first stage household $k$ maximizes the expectation of an additively separable intertemporal utility function:

$$\max{}_{F_{kt}} U_k = E_t \left\{ \sum_{t=1}^{T} (1+\rho)^{-(t-1)} \left[ \frac{V_{kt}^{(1-\sigma)}}{(1-\sigma)} \right] \right\}, \tag{8.1}$$

subject to the lifetime budget constraint:

$$\sum_{t=1}^{T} (1+r_t)^{-(t-1)} PFF_{kt} \leq W_k, \tag{8.2}$$

where $PFF_{kt}$ is the value of full consumption in period $t$, the value of goods and leisure, $r_t$ is the nominal interest rate, $W_k$ is full wealth, $\sigma$ is an intertemporal curvature parameter, and $\rho$ is the subjective rate of time preference. The expectation based on the dataset at time $t$ is denoted $E_t$.

The term full wealth refers to the present value of future earnings from the supply of tangible assets and labor, plus transfers from the government, and imputations for the value of leisure. Tangible assets include domestic capital, government bonds and net foreign assets. Equations (8.1) and (8.2) are standard in growth models found in macroeconomics textbooks.[7] In describing the second stage of the household model below, we show that $V_{kt}$ is a function of the prices of goods and leisure and may be regarded as the quantity of full consumption, $V_{kt} = F_{kt}$. The price of full consumption is the value of full consumption, divided by this quantity index, $PF_{kt} = PFF_{kt}/F_{kt}$.

---

[7] See, e.g. Barro and Sala-i-Martin (2004).

The first-order condition for intertemporal optimality is expressed in the Euler equation:

$$\Delta \ln PF_{k,t+1} F_{k,t+1} = (1 - \sigma) \Delta \ln V_{k,t+1} + \Delta \ln \left( - D\left( p_{k,t+1} \right) \right)$$

$$+ \ln(1 + r_{t+1}) - \ln\left( 1 + \rho \right) + \eta_{kt}, \qquad (8.3)$$

where $D(p_{kt})$ is a function of the prices of goods and leisure. This arises from expressing $V_{kt}$ as a function of these prices (see (8.13) below); $\eta_{kt}$ is an expectational error. Jorgenson *et al.* in Chapter 17 of this Handbook describe how the household Euler equation is estimated from data for synthetic cohorts obtained by adding over all households in each cohort. From these household Euler equations we derive an aggregate Euler equation. This Euler equation is forward-looking, so that the current level of full consumption incorporates expectations about all future prices and discount rates.

In the simulations reported below we use a simplified version of the aggregate Euler equation with the curvature parameter $\sigma$ equal to one. This is used in the version of IGEM given in Jorgenson and Wilcoxen (1998), and is written simply as:

$$\frac{F_t}{F_{t-1}} = \frac{(1 + n_t)(1 + r_t)}{1 + \rho} \frac{PF_{t-1}}{PF_t}, \qquad (8.4)$$

where $n_t$ is the rate of growth of population.

### 8.2.1.2 Stage 2: goods and leisure

In the second stage of the household model, full consumption is divided between leisure time and personal consumption expenditures on commodities. Given the time endowment of the household sector, the choice of leisure time also determines the supply of labor. The allocation of full consumption employs a very detailed household demand model that incorporates demographic characteristics of the population. The database for this model includes the CEX and the CPI, and is described in greater detail in Chapter 17. Since the model is based on the National Income and Product Accounts (NIPAs), we need to distinguish the concept of personal consumption expenditures (PCE) employed there from the concept employed in the CEX. We use the "X" superscript to denote variables associated with the CEX.

Conceptually, we determine the consumption $C_{ik}^X$ of commodity $i$ for household $k$ by maximizing a utility function $U(C_{1k}^X, \ldots C_{ik}^X \ldots C_{Rk}^X; A_k)$, where $C_{Rk}^X$ is leisure and $A_k$ denotes the demographic characteristics of household $k$, such as the number of children and region of residence. We arrange the 35 distinctly identified inputs into a tier structure. This is shown in Table 8.2 along with the values of the inputs in 2005. The names of the nodes of the tier structure are capitalized. At the top tier, the utility function

**Table 8.2** Tier structure of consumption function, 2005 (billion $)

| | | | | | | |
|---|---|---|---|---|---|---|
| Full consumption | 23,423 | | | | | |
| | Non-durables | 2715 | Energy | 503 | gasoline and oil | 284 |
| | | | | | fuel-coal | 21 |
| | | | | | coal | 0.3 |
| | | | | | fuel-oil | 21 |
| | | | | | electricity | 133 |
| | | | | | gas | 65 |
| | | | Food | 1270 | food | 720 |
| | | | | | meals | 449 |
| | | | | | meals–emp | 12 |
| | | | | | tobacco | 88 |
| | | | Consumer goods | 942 | clothing-shoe | 342 |
| | | | | | shoes | 55 |
| | | | | | clothing | 287 |
| | | | | | household articles | 181 |
| | | | | | toilet articles; cleaning | 138 |
| | | | | | furnishings | 43 |
| | | | | | drugs | 265 |
| | | | | | miscellaneous goods | 154 |
| | | | | | toys | 66 |
| | | | | | stationery | 20 |
| | | | | | imports | 7 |
| | | | | | reading materials | 61 |
| | Capital Services | 1972 | | | | |
| | Consumer Services | 4303 | Housing | 536 | rental housing | 334 |
| | | | | | owner maintenance | 202 |
| | | | Household operation | 281 | water | 64 |
| | | | | | communications | 133 |
| | | | | | domestic service | 20 |
| | | | | | other household | 64 |
| | | | Transportation | 324 | own transportation | 263 |
| | | | | | transportation services | 62 |
| | | | Medical | 1491 | medical services | 1350 |
| | | | | | health insurance | 141 |
| | | | Miscellaneous services | 1670 | personal services | 116 |
| | | | | | business services | 646 |
| | | | | | financial services | 499 |
| | | | | | other business services | 147 |
| | | | | | recreation | 458 |
| | | | | | recreation | 358 |
| | | | | | foreign travel | 100 |
| | | | | | education and welfare | 451 |
| | Leisure | 14,432 | | | | |

depends on Non-durables, Capital Services, Consumer Services and Leisure; in the second tier, the Non-durables node is a function of three other subaggregates (Energy, Food and Consumer goods) and the Consumer Services node is a function of five other subaggregates:

$$U = U\left(C_{ND,k}, C_{K,k}, C_{SV,k}, C_{R,k}; A_k\right); C_{ND} = C\left(C_{EN}, C_{FD}, C_{CG}\right); C_{SV}$$
$$= C\left(C_{\text{housing}}, \dots C_{\text{misc svcs}}\right). \tag{8.5}$$

A major difference between our classification system and PCE from the US NIPAs is the treatment of consumers' durables. Purchases of new housing are included in investment in the NIPAs, while only the annual rental value of housing is included in PCE. Purchases of consumers' durables such as automobiles are treated as consumption expenditures in the PCE, but in the new architecture for the national accounts they are treated symmetrically with housing. Investment in housing and consumers' durables are included in investment and annual rental values are treated as consumption.

We first describe how the parameters of the top tier of the household model are estimated from the CEX. We then indicate how the model for individual households is aggregated to obtain the model of the household sector in IGEM. Summation over all households gives the total demand for commodity $i$:

$$PC_{it}^X C_{it}^X = \sum_k P_{ikt}^{CX} C_{ikt}^X \quad i = 1, 2, \dots, R. \tag{8.6}$$

The price $P_{ik}^{CX}$ is the price of good $i$ faced by household $k$. Similarly, total leisure demand, $PC_R C_R^X$, is the sum over all leisure demands, and the sum of goods and leisure gives full consumption:

$$PF_t F_t = \sum_i PC_{it}^X C_{it}^X + PC_R C_R^X. \tag{8.7}$$

In order to characterize substitutability among leisure and the commodity groups, we find it convenient to derive household $k$'s demands from a translog indirect utility function $V(p_k, m_k; A_k)$, where:

$$-\ln V_k = \alpha_0 + \alpha^H \ln \frac{p_k}{m_k} + \frac{1}{2} \ln \frac{p_k}{m_k}' B^H \ln \frac{p_k}{m_k} + \ln \frac{p_k}{m_k}' B_A A_k, \tag{8.8}$$

$p_k$ is a vector of prices faced by household k, $\sigma^H$ is a vector of parameters, $B^H$ and $B_A$ are matrices of parameters that describe price, total expenditure and demographic effects.[8] The value of full expenditure on leisure and the three commodity groups is:

$$m_k = P_{ND}^C C_{NDk} + P_K^C C_{Kk} + P_{SV}^C C_{SVk} + P_R^C C_{Rk}. \tag{8.9}$$

---

[8] This indirect utility function satisfies the restrictions implied by exact aggregation over households to obtain aggregate demand. These restrictions are discussed in more detail in Jorgenson and Slesnick (2008) and Chapter 17.

In (8.8) the demands are allowed to be non-homothetic, so that full expenditure elasticities are not constrained to be equal to unity.

The commodity groups in (8.5) and (8.9) represent consumption of these commodities by household $k$. The leisure consumed by household $k$ takes into account the different opportunity costs of time of different members of the household. To do this we use the after-tax wage $p_{Rk}^m$. We assume that the effective quantity of leisure of person $m$ ($R_k^m$) is non-work hours multiplied by the after-tax wage relative to the base wage, that is, multiplied by an effectiveness index: $q_k^m = p_{Rk}^m / p_R^0$.

We assume a time endowment of $\bar{H} = 14$ hours a day for each adult. The annual leisure of person $m$ is the time endowment, less hours worked $LS$; thus, effective leisure is:

$$R_k^m = q_k^m (\bar{H}_k^m - LS_k^m) = q_k^m (14 * 365 - \text{hours worked}_k^m). \tag{8.10}$$

The quantity of leisure for household $k$ is the sum over all adult members:

$$C_{Rk} = \sum_m R_k^m, \tag{8.11}$$

and the value of household leisure is:

$$P_R^C C_{Rk} = p_R^0 \sum_m R_k^m = \sum_m p_{Rk}^m (\bar{H}_k^m - LS_k^m). \tag{8.12}$$

The demand functions for commodities and leisure are derived from the indirect utility function (8.8) by applying Roy's Identity:

$$\mathbf{w}_k = \frac{1}{D(p_k)} \left( \alpha^H + B^H \ln p_k - \iota' B^H \ln m_k + B_A A_k \right), \tag{8.13}$$

where $\mathbf{w}_k$ is the vector of shares of full consumption, $\iota$ is a vector of ones and $D(p_k) = -1 + \iota' B^H \ln p_k$. For example, the demand for consumer non-durables is:

$$w_{ND,k} = -\frac{1}{D(p_k)} \left( \alpha_{ND}^H + B_{ND}^H \cdot \ln p_k - \iota B^H \ln m_k + B_{A,ND} \cdot A_k \right), \tag{8.14}$$

where $B_{ND}^H$ denotes the top row of the $B^H$ matrix of share elasticities.

The parameters of the translog indirect utility function must satisfy the restrictions:

$$B^H = B^{H'}; \iota' B^H \iota = 0, \iota' B_A = 0, \iota' \alpha^H = -1, \tag{8.15}$$

where $B^H$ are the share elasticities, $\iota' B^H$ represents the full expenditure effect and the $k$th column of $B_A$ determines how the demands of demographic group $k$ differ from the base group. These restrictions are implied by the theory of individual consumer behavior and the requirement that individual demand functions can be aggregated exactly to obtain the aggregate demand functions used in the model. The demographic characteristics of individual households employed in the model are given in Table 8.3.

**Table 8.3** Demographic groups identified in household consumption model

| Number of children | 0, 1, 2, 3 or more |
|---|---|
| Number of adults | 1, 2, 3 or more |
| Region | Northeast, Midwest, South, West |
| Location | urban, rural |
| Gender of head | male, female |
| Race of head | white, nonwhite |

**Table 8.4** Price and income elasticities

| | Uncompensated price elasticity | Compensated price elasticity | Expenditure elasticity |
|---|---|---|---|
| Non-durables | −0.727 | −0.651 | 0.673 |
| Capital services | −1.192 | −1.084 | 0.902 |
| Consumer services | −0.561 | −0.490 | 1.067 |
| Leisure | 0.014 | −0.305 | 1.063 |
| Labor supply | −0.032 | 0.713 | −2.486 |

The estimated price and income elasticities are reported in Table 8.4. The elasticities are calculated for the reference household type − two adults, two children, Northeast, urban, male head, white. They are computed at $100,000 of full consumption in 1989. The compensated own-price elasticities are negative for all goods and services, as well as for leisure.

Capital services are price elastic, while non-durables, consumer services, and leisure are price inelastic. The uncompensated wage elasticity of household labor supply is negative but close to zero, a common finding in modeling labor supply, while the compensated wage elasticity is 0.7. The full consumption elasticity for leisure is greater than one, so that leisure is classified as a luxury. Non-durables and capital services are necessities with full consumption elasticities less than one, while services are a luxury.

Table 8.5 gives the fitted shares of the four commodity groups at different levels of full consumption for the reference household. The share allocated to non-durables falls

**Table 8.5** Full expenditures and household budget shares

| Full expenditures | Non-durables | Capital | Services | Leisure |
|---|---|---|---|---|
| 7500 | 0.208 | 0.151 | 0.055 | 0.586 |
| 25,000 | 0.164 | 0.137 | 0.06 | 0.626 |
| 75,000 | 0.123 | 0.124 | 0.065 | 0.693 |
| 150,000 | 0.098 | 0.116 | 0.068 | 0.713 |
| 275,000 | 0.075 | 0.108 | 0.071 | 0.718 |
| 350,000 | 0.066 | 0.106 | 0.072 | 0.716 |

rapidly as expenditures rise while the share allocated to services rises a little. Leisure value is hours multiplied by wage rates and the share rises substantially with rising wage rates of the higher income households.

To incorporate the econometric model of household behavior in IGEM we derive an aggregate version of the household demand functions (8.13). Let $n_k$ be the number of households of type $k$. Then the vector of consumption shares for the US economy:

$$SC^X = \left( \frac{P_{ND}^{CX} C_{ND}^X}{MF^X}, \frac{P_K^{CX} C_K^X}{MF^X}, \frac{P_{SV}^{CX} C_{SV}^X}{MF^X}, \frac{P_R^{CX} C_R^X}{MF^X} \right)',$$

is obtained by aggregating over all types of households:

$$SC = \frac{\sum_k n_k m_k \mathbf{w}_k}{\sum_k n_k m_k} \tag{8.16}$$

$$= \frac{1}{D(p)} \left[ \alpha^H + B^H \ln p - \iota B^H \xi^d + B_A \xi^L \right],$$

where the distribution terms are:

$$\xi^d = \sum_k n_k m_k \ln m_k / M; \quad M = \sum_k n_k m_k \tag{8.17}$$

$$\xi^L = \sum_k n_k m_k A_k / M. \tag{8.18}$$

The national value of full consumption expenditures in CEX units is given by:

$$MF^X = \sum_k n_k m_k = P_{ND}^{CX} C_{ND}^X + P_K^{CX} C_K^X + P_{SV}^{CX} C_{SV}^X + P_R^{CX} C_R^X. \tag{8.19}$$

By constructing an aggregate model of consumer demand through exact aggregation over individual demands, we are able to incorporate the restrictions implied by the theory of individual consumer behavior. In addition, we incorporate demographic information through the distribution terms (8.17) and (8.18). For the sample period we estimate the values of these distribution terms from microeconomic data. For the period beyond the sample we project the distribution terms, using projections of the population by sex and race. More formally, we project the number of households of type $k$, $n_{kt}$, by linking the age and race of the head of household to the projected population.

A final step deals with the difference between the CEX and PCE measures of consumption. The difference in the value of expenditures on non-durables is

$PN^{\mathrm{ND}} N^{\mathrm{ND}} - P^{\mathrm{CX}}_{\mathrm{ND}} C^{\mathrm{X}}_{\mathrm{ND}}$, where $N^{\mathrm{ND}}$ denotes the quantity on non-durable consumption in PCE units and $PN^{\mathrm{ND}}$ denotes its price.[9] The CEX omits many items in the PCE, such as employer-paid health insurance. Given the rising gap between these two measures of consumption we express the gap as an AR(1) process and project this forward. The value of full consumption is the sum of expenditures on non-durables, capital, services and leisure; this sum is the same in both CEX and PCE units and it is the value that appears in the Euler Equation (8.4) in the first stage:

$$PF_t F_t = PN^{\mathrm{ND}} N^{\mathrm{ND}} + PN^{\mathrm{K}} N^{\mathrm{K}} + PN^{\mathrm{CS}} N^{\mathrm{CS}} + PN^{\mathrm{R}} N^{\mathrm{R}} = MF^{\mathrm{X}}. \qquad (8.20)$$

### 8.2.1.3 Stage 3: allocation of demands for commodities

In the third and final stage of the household model we allocate the quantities of non-durables, capital services, and other services ($N^{\mathrm{ND}}$, $N^{\mathrm{K}}$ and $N^{\mathrm{CS}}$) to the 35 commodities, NCIs and capital services, such as housing and consumers' durables. We do not employ demographic characteristics of households for this stage and allocate aggregate consumption, using a hierarchical model with the 17 nodes shown in Table 8.2. At each node $m$ we represent the demand by a translog indirect utility function, $V^m(P^{\mathrm{H}m}, m_m; t)$:

$$-\ln V^m = \alpha_0 + \alpha^{\mathrm{H}m} \ln \frac{P^{\mathrm{H}m}}{m_m} + \frac{1}{2} \ln \frac{P^{\mathrm{H}m}}{m_m}{}' B^{\mathrm{H}m} \ln \frac{P^{\mathrm{H}m}}{m_m} + f^{\mathrm{H}m} \ln \frac{P^{\mathrm{H}m}}{m_m}. \qquad (8.21)$$

$$\ln P^{\mathrm{H}m} \equiv \left( \ln PN_{m1}, \ldots, \ln PN_{mi}, \ldots, \ln PN_{m,im} \right)', \quad i \in \text{node } m.$$

There are $im$ inputs at node $m$ and the value of aggregate expenditures at $m$ is:

$$m_m = PN_{m1} N_{m1} + \ldots + PN_{m,im} N_{m,im}. \qquad (8.22)$$

The shares of full consumption derived from (8.21) are similar to (8.13), but exclude demographic characteristics and impose homotheticity. Formally, we require $\iota' B^{\mathrm{H}m} = 0$. In order to model the changes in budget shares not explained by price movements we include latent variables, $f_t^{\mathrm{H}m}$, to represent changes in preferences. These latent variables are discussed in greater detail for the production model presented in Section 8.2.2 below.

The shares of consumption at node $m$ simplify to an expression that is independent of the level of expenditures ($m_m$):

$$SN^m = \begin{bmatrix} PN_{m1} N_{m1} / PN^m N^m \\ \cdots \\ PN_{m,im} N_{m,im} / PN^m N^m \end{bmatrix} = \alpha^{\mathrm{H}m} + B^{\mathrm{H}m} \ln PN^{\mathrm{H}m} + f^{\mathrm{H}m}. \qquad (8.23)$$

---

[9] For more detail, see Fixler and Jaditz (2002).

Under homotheticity the indirect utility function reduces to:

$$- \ln V^m = \alpha^{Hm} \ln P^{Hm} + \frac{1}{2} \ln P^{Hm\prime} B^{Hm} \ln P^{Hm} + f^{Hm} \ln P^{Hm} - \ln m_m. \quad (8.24)$$

We define the price for consumption at node $m$ as:

$$\ln PN^m = \alpha^{Hm} \ln P^{Hm} + \frac{1}{2} \ln P^{Hm\prime} B^{Hm} \ln P^{Hm} + f^{Hm} \ln P^{Hm}. \quad (8.25)$$

The quantity of consumption in node $m$ is an index of utility and the value of expenditures is the price multiplied by this quantity:

$$m_m = PN^m N^m. \quad (8.26)$$

As an example, for $m = 3$ the energy aggregate is a function of $N_6$ (gasoline), $N^{FC}$ (fuel-coal aggregate), $N_{18}$ (electricity) and $N_{19}$ (natural gas). The demand shares are functions of the prices of these four components and the state variables representing the non-price trends:

$$SN^{m=3} = \begin{bmatrix} PN_6 N_6 / PN^{m=3} N^{m=3} \\ \cdots \\ PN_{19} N_{19} / PN^{m=3} N^{m=3} \end{bmatrix} = \alpha^{H3} + B^{H3} \ln PN^{H3} + f^{H3}. \quad (8.27)$$

The value of energy purchases that appears in the next higher node for non-durables ($m = 2$) is:

$$PN^{EN} N^{EN} = PN_6 N_6 + PN^{FC} N^{FC} + PN_{18} N_{18} + PN_{19} N_{19}. \quad (8.28)$$

A full set of estimates of unknown parameters of the household model for all 17 nodes is given by Jorgenson *et al.* (2009b). Most of the estimated share elasticities ($\beta_{ii}^{Hm}$) are between −0.1 and 0.1. About half are negative, i.e. the price elasticity is greater than one. The latent variables $f_t^{Hm}$ representing changes in preferences have noticeable trends in the sample period. For example, the term for electricity rises between the late 1960s and 1990 but has flattened since then.

The final step is to convert the model of household behavior based on PCE categories in the NIPAs to categories employed in the interindustry transactions tables. A major difference is that PCE is based on purchasers' prices whereas the input-output values are producers' prices and exclude trade and transportation. The PCE values are converted to input-output values by using the bridge table provided with the official benchmark input-output tables.[10] Denote the bridge matrix by **H**, where $H_{ij}$ is the share of input-output commodity $i$ in PCE item $j$. The value of total demand for commodity $i$ is:

$$VC_i = \sum_j H_{ij} PN_j N_j. \tag{8.29}$$

A similar link is required for the input-output commodity prices $(PS_i)$ and the PCE prices $(PN_j)$.

### 8.2.1.4 Leisure and household disposable income

The demand for leisure is given by the fourth element of the vector of shares of full consumption (8.16). Individual leisure is related to hours supplied to the labor market in (8.10). We construct an aggregate version of this equation by defining the aggregate time endowment $LH_t$ as an index number of the population, where individuals are distinguished by gender, age and educational attainment. Let $POP_{kt}$ denote the number of people in group $k$ at time $t$ and the price of time is the after-tax hourly wage of person $k$, $(1 - tl_t^m)P_{kt}^L$. The value of the aggregate time endowment, allocating 14 hours a day to each person, is:

$$P_t^h LH_t = VLH_t = \sum_k \left(1 - tl_t^m\right)P_{kt}^L * 14 * 365 * POP_{kt}. \tag{8.30}$$

The value of time endowment is the product of the quantity $LH$ and the price of hours, $P^h$. The Tornqvist index for the quantity of the time endowment is:

$$d \ln LH_t = \sum_k \frac{1}{2} \left(v_{kt}^L + v_{kt-1}^L\right) d \ln \left(14 * 365 * POP_{kt}\right), \tag{8.31}$$

where $v_{kt}^L$ are the value shares and the $k$ index runs over gender, age and educational attainment. In a similar manner, the quantity of aggregate leisure, $N_t^R$, is a Tornqvist index of the leisure hours in each population group, $H_{kt}^R$. The price of aggregate leisure, $PN_t^R$, is given by the value and the quantity index:

$$VR_t = PN_t^R N_t^R = \sum_k \left(1 - tl_t^m\right)P_{kt}^L * H_{kt}^R * POP_{kt}. \tag{8.32}$$

The price of aggregate time endowment $(P_t^h)$ is not the same as the price of aggregate leisure due to the differences in aggregation weights and we relate the two with an aggregation coefficient:

$$PN_t^R = \psi_{Ct}^R P_t^h. \tag{8.33}$$

---

[10] For the 1992 Benchmark in the *Survey of Current Business*, November 1997, this is given in table D, "Input-Output Commodity Composition of NIPA Personal Consumption Expenditure Categories."

Taking this aggregation coefficient into account, aggregate labor supply is time endowment less leisure:

$$LS = LH - \psi_C^R N^R. \tag{8.34}$$

The value of labor supply is equal the gross payments by employers less the marginal tax on labor income $(tl^m)$. The payment by industry $j$ $(PLD_j LD_j)$ is given below (Equation 8.42). Summing over industry $j$ gives the value of the labor supply:

$$P^h LS = P^h LH - PN^R N^R = (1 - tl^m) \sum_j PLD_j LD_j. \tag{8.35}$$

We next describe the household financial accounts. Household tangible income, $Y_t$, is the sum of after-tax capital income $(YK^{net})$, labor income $(YL)$ and transfers from the government $(G^{TRAN})$:

$$Y_t = YK_t^{net} + YL_t + G_t^{TRAN} - TLUMP_t - twW_{t-1}. \tag{8.36}$$

The term $twW_{t-1}$ represents taxes on wealth, and $TLUMP_t$ represents lump-sum taxes that are zero in the base case but may be different from zero for specific energy and environmental policies.

Labor income is the main source of household income. Labor income is employer payments less the average tax rate:

$$YL = P^h LS \frac{1 - tl^a}{1 - tl^m} = (1 - tl^a) \sum_j PLD_j LD_j. \tag{8.37}$$

We distinguish between marginal and average tax rates. The price of the time endowment and leisure refers to the marginal price, the wage rate reduced by the marginal tax rate, while income is reduced by average income taxes.

Capital income is the sum of dividend income $(DIV)$ from the private stock of physical assets and financial assets in the form of claims on the government and rest of the world.

$$YK_t^{net} = DIV - YK^{gov} + (1 - tk)(GINT_t + Y_t^{row}). \tag{8.38}$$

The components of capital income are explained in more detail below. Private household saving is income less consumption, non-tax payments to the government $(R_t^N)$ and transfers to rest of the world $(CR)$:

$$S_t = Y_t - P_t^{CC} CC_t - CR_t - R_t^N. \tag{8.39}$$

### 8.2.2 Producer behavior and endogenous technical change

A key feature of IGEM is a specification of producer behavior that captures substitution among inputs in response to price changes and changes in technology. Modeling price substitution is especially important for analyzing the economic impacts of energy and environmental policies that induce substantial price changes. However, production patterns also depend on changes in output per unit of input or *total factor productivity (TFP)* and *biases of technical change* or changes in the composition of inputs unrelated to price changes. For example, energy use may decline in intensity due to energy-saving changes in technology, as well as substitution away from higher-priced energy.

We employ a production function for each of the 35 industries in IGEM. These industries are listed in Table 8.1 and include the five energy producers. The output of each industry is produced by using capital, labor and intermediate inputs. The value of capital services consists of all property-type income — profits and other operating surplus, depreciation and taxes on property. The price of capital services is the price of the corresponding asset, multiplied by an annualization factor that we denote as the *cost of capital*. The cost of capital consists of the rate of return, the rate of depreciation, less capital gains or plus capital losses, all adjusted for taxes.

The construction of the price of capital services and the cost of capital is described in Jorgenson *et al.* (2005, Chapter 5), and is based on the detailed development in Jorgenson and Yun (2001). The quantity of capital services for each industry is an aggregate of the service flows from all asset types. Our database identifies 62 asset categories including land and inventories. We emphasize that the price of capital services is distinct from the price of capital stock. The price of capital services is an annualized rental, while the capital stock price is the price for acquiring an asset.

Similarly, the quantity of labor input for each industry is a Tornqvist aggregate over the hours of work for different demographic categories, where the weights are the hourly compensation of workers, including wages and salaries and benefits. Our database identifies seven age groups, six education groups and the two genders. The construction of the labor input indices is described in Jorgenson *et al.* (2005, Chapter 6).

The construction of capital and labor indices is a critical feature of our historical dataset. Simple sums of hours worked or asset quantities would not fully capture the substitution possibilities within each aggregate. For example, a simple sum of computers and industrial buildings would fail to reflect the impact on capital input of substitution toward information technology equipment and software as prices of these inputs decline relative to buildings. Similarly, a simple sum of hours worked would not adequately characterize the impact on labor input of the substitution toward more highly educated workers as the educational attainment of the labor force increases.

Intermediate inputs are the 35 commodity groups consisting of domestically produced goods and competitive imports. There is a 36th input consisting of NCIs, defined in the official input–output tables to include goods not produced in the US, such as coffee, natural rubber and foreign port services. The generation of our data on industry-level outputs and intermediate inputs is described by Jorgenson chapter (2005, Chapter 4).

The output of the production sector is divided among 35 commodities, each the primary product of one of the 35 industries. Many industries produce secondary products as well, e.g. the petroleum-refining industry produces refined petroleum products and secondary products that are the primary outputs of the chemicals industry. The relation between industries and commodity output is given by the *make* matrix (or supply matrix) in the official input-output accounts. We model joint production of primary and secondary products as well as substitution among inputs and technical change for each industry.

### 8.2.2.1 Top-tier production function

The production function represents output from capital services, labor services and intermediate inputs. Output also depends on the level of technology $t$, so that for industry $j$:

$$QI_j = f\left(KD_j, LD_j, QP_1^j, QP_2^j, \ldots, QP_{35}^j, QP_{NCI}^j, t\right), \quad j = 1, 2, \ldots, 35. \quad (8.40)$$

The dimensionality of this production function is intractable. We assume that the production function is separable in energy and materials inputs, so that output at the first stage of the production model depends on quantities of energy input and input of non-energy materials, as well as inputs of capital and labor services:

$$QI_j = f\left(KD_j, LD_j, E_j, M_j, t\right)$$

$$E_j = E\left(QP_3^j, QP_4^j, QP_{16}^j, QP_{30}^j, QP_{31}^j\right) \quad (8.41)$$

$$M_j = M\left(QP_1^j, QP_2^j, QP_5^j, \ldots, QP_{35}^j, QP_{NCI}^j\right).$$

In the second stage of the production model the energy and non-energy inputs depend on the components of each of the aggregates. For example, energy input depends on inputs of coal, crude oil, refined petroleum products, natural gas, and electricity. Similarly, non-energy input depends on all the non-energy commodities listed in Table 8.1, plus NCIs. Energy and materials inputs are further allocated among the detailed commodity groups by means of the tier structure of the production model is given in Table 8.6. There is a total of 13 nodes in the tier structure with 11 of them describing non-energy material input.

We assume constant returns to scale and competitive markets, so that the production function (8.41) is homogeneous of degree one and the value of output is equal to the sum of the values of all inputs:

$$PO_{jt} QI_{jt} = PKD_{jt} KD_{jt} + PLD_{jt} LD_{jt} + P_{Ejt} E_{jt} + P_{Mjt} M_{jt}$$

$$P_{Ejt} E_{jt} = PS_{3t} QP_{3t}^j + PS_{4t} QP_{4t}^j + \ldots + PS_{31t} QP_{31t}^j \quad (8.42)$$

$$P_{Mjt} M_{jt} = PS_{1t} QP_{1t}^j + PS_{2t} QP_{2t}^j + \ldots + PNCI_{jt} QP_{NCI,t}^j.$$

**Table 8.6** Tier structure of industry production function

| | Symbol | Name | Components |
|---|---|---|---|
| 1 | Q | Gross output | Capital, Labor, Energy, Materials<br>$Q = f(K,L,E,M)$ |
| 2 | E | Energy | Coal mining, Petroleum and gas mining, Petroleum refining, Electric utilities, Gas utilities<br>$E = f(X3,X4,X16,X30,X31)$ |
| 3 | M | Materials (non-energy) | Construction, Agriculture materials, Metallic materials, Non-metallic materials, Services materials<br>$M = f(X6,MA,MM,MN,MS)$ |
| 4 | MA | Agriculture materials | Agriculture, Food manufacturing, Tobacco, Textile-apparel, Wood-paper<br>$MA = f(X1,X7,X8,TA,WP)$ |
| 5 | MM | Metallic materials | Fabrication-other metals, Machinery materials, Equipment<br>$MM = f(FM,MC,EQ)$ |
| 6 | MN | Non-metallic materials | Non-metal mining, Chemicals, Rubber, Stone, Miscellaneous manufacturing<br>$MN = f(X5,X15,X17,X19,X27)$ |
| 7 | MS | Services materials | Transportation, Trade, FIRE, Services, OS<br>$MS = f(X28,X32,X33,X34,OS)$ |
| 8 | TA | Textile-apparel | Textiles, Apparel, Leather<br>$TA = f(X9,X10,X18)$ |
| 9 | WP | Wood-paper | Lumber-wood, Furniture, Paper, Printing<br>$WP = f(X11,X12,X13,X14)$ |
| 10 | OS | Other services | Communications, Government enterprises, NCIs<br>$OS = f(X29,X35,X\_NCI)$ |
| 11 | FM | Fabricated-other metals | Metal mining, Primary metals, Fabricated metals<br>$FM = f(X2,X20,X21)$ |
| 12 | MC | Machinery materials | Industrial machinery, Electric machinery<br>$MC = f(X22,X23)$ |
| 13 | EQ | Equipment | Motor vehicles, Other transport equipment, Instruments<br>$EQ = f(X24,X25,X26)$ |

Each industry $j$ is composed of many firms, each maximizing profits independently. In order to simplify the characterization of substitution and technical change for the industry we assume that these firms face the same price for commodity $i$, $PS_{it}$. Under this assumption, it is more convenient to work with the price function, rather than the production function (8.41).[11] The price function expresses the price of output as a function of the input prices and technology.

---

[11] The price function contains the same information about technology as the production function. For further details, see Jorgenson (2000).

We have chosen the translog form of the price function, so that substitutability in response to price changes can be characterized in a flexible manner and changes in technology can be represented by latent variables through the Kalman filter, as in Jin and Jorgenson (2010):

$$\ln PO_t = \alpha_0 + \sum_i \alpha_i \ln p_{it} + \frac{1}{2} \sum_{i,k} \beta_{ik} \ln p_{it} \ln p_{kt} + \sum_i \ln p_{it} f_{it}^P + f_t^P \tag{8.43}$$

$$p_i, p_k = \{PKD, PLD, P_E P_M\}.$$

$\alpha_i$, $\beta_{ik}$ and $\alpha_0$ are parameters that are separately estimated for each industry, and we have dropped the industry "j" subscript for simplicity.

The "p" superscript on the $f_{it}^P$ s denotes that these are latent variables for the production sector. There are similar variables for the consumption, investment and import demand functions. The vector of latent variables, $\xi_t = (1, f_{Kt}^P, f_{Lt}^P, f_{Et}^P, f_{Mt}^P, \Delta f_t^P)'$, is generated by a first-order vector autoregressive scheme:

$$\xi_t = F\xi_{t-1} + v_t. \tag{8.44}$$

An important advantage of the translog price function is that it generates equations for the input shares that are linear in the logarithms of the prices and the latent variables. Differentiating Equation (8.43) with respect to the logarithms of the prices, we obtain equations for the shares of inputs. For example, if we differentiate with respect to the price of capital services, we obtain the share of capital input:

$$v_K = \frac{PKD_t KD_t}{PO_t QI_t} = \alpha_K + \sum_k \beta_{Kk} \ln P_k + f_{Kt}^P. \tag{8.45}$$

The parameters $\{\beta_{ik}\}$ are *share elasticities*, giving the change in the share of the *i*th input in the value of output with respect to a proportional change in the price of the *k*th input. These parameters represent the degree of substitutability among the capital (K), labor (L), energy (E), and non-energy (M) inputs. If the share elasticity is positive, the value share increases with a change in the price of the input, while if the share elasticity is negative, the share decreases with a change in the price. A zero share elasticity implies that the value share is constant, as in a linear-logarithmic or Cobb–Douglas specification of the technology.

The price function is homogeneous of degree one, so that a doubling of input prices results in a doubling of the output price. This implies that the row and column sums of the matrix of share elasticities must be equal to zero:

$$\sum_i \beta_{ik} = 0 \text{ for each } k; \quad \sum_k \beta_{ik} = 0 \text{ for each } i. \tag{8.46}$$

Symmetry of the price effects implies that the matrix of share elasticities is symmetric. Monotonicity and concavity restrictions on the price function are discussed along with further details on estimation in Jorgenson *et al.* in Chapter 17 of this Handbook.

The level of technology $f_t^p$, together with the biases of technical change $\{f_{it}^p\}$, evolves according to equation (8.44). The latent variable $f_t^p$ represents the level of technology, a declining value corresponding to a decline in output prices or positive growth in productivity. The first difference of the level of technology takes the form:

$$\Delta f_t^p = F_{p1} + F_{pK} f_{K,t-1}^p + F_{pL} f_{L,t-1}^p + F_{pE} f_{E,t-1}^p + F_{pM} f_{M,t-1}^p + F_{pp} \Delta f_{t-1}^p + v_{pt}.$$

(8.47)

The latent variables $\{f_{it}^p\}$ describe the *biases of technical change*. For example, if the energy share declines, holding prices of all inputs constant, the bias with respect to energy is negative and we say that technical change is energy-saving. Similarly, a positive bias implies that technical change is energy-using. While the parameters describing substitution in response to price changes are constant, the biases of technical change may vary from time to time. Historical patterns of production involve both energy-using and energy-saving technical change.

The estimated parameters are given in a supplement to Jorgenson and Jin (2010).[12] The $\beta_{EE}$ coefficients for almost all the 35 industries are positive; the value share of energy rises with the price of energy, so that the quantity of energy input falls by less than the percentage rise in price. The $\beta_{LL}$ coefficients, on the other hand, show a more varied pattern, the value share of labor input may rise or fall with higher wage rates.

Table 8.7 gives the cumulative change in the bias terms for various sub-periods. A positive value in the $f_{Kt}$ column, for example, indicates a capital-using bias over this period. Most industries, 29 out of 35, have a capital-using bias in this period, that is, an increase in the use of capital beyond that explained by the fall in the cost of capital. Two-thirds of the industries had labor-saving technical change, the major exception being the labor-intensive Services and Construction industries. Eleven of the 35 industries have energy-saving technical change, while 20 industries have material-saving bias.

The major energy-intensive industries — Paper, Chemical products, Electric utilities and Gas utilities — have energy-saving technical change, while Petroleum refining, Stone, clay and glass, Primary metals, and Transportation have energy-using change. In the energy group Electric utilities have labor- and energy-saving technical change, while Petroleum refining has labor- and material-saving change. Technical change in Gas utilities is energy-saving, and capital-, labor- and material-using, while change in Coal mining is capital-using and change in Petroleum and gas mining is energy-saving.

---

[12] See: http://www.economics.harvard.edu/faculty/jorgenson/recent_work_jorgenson.

**Table 8.7** Changes in the bias of technical change latent variable

| | | 1960–2005 | | | |
|---|---|---|---|---|---|
| | | $\Delta f_{Kt}$ | $\Delta f_{Lt}$ | $\Delta f_{Et}$ | $\Delta f_{Mt}$ |
| 1 | Agriculture | 0.0436 | −0.0109 | 0.0619 | −0.0946 |
| 2 | Metal mining | 0.0250 | 0.0679 | −0.0004 | −0.0925 |
| 3 | Coal mining | 0.2528 | −0.1836 | −0.0589 | −0.0103 |
| 4 | Petroleum and gas | 0.1192 | 0.0178 | −0.2093 | 0.0722 |
| 5 | Non-metallic mining | 0.0046 | 0.0279 | 0.0588 | −0.0913 |
| 6 | Construction | 0.0309 | 0.0151 | 0.0155 | −0.0614 |
| 7 | Food products | 0.0655 | 0.0524 | −0.0012 | −0.1166 |
| 8 | Tobacco products | 0.0434 | 0.0304 | −0.0003 | −0.0735 |
| 9 | Textile mill products | 0.0007 | 0.0041 | 0.0175 | −0.0223 |
| 10 | Apparel and textiles | 0.0545 | −0.0493 | −0.0009 | −0.0043 |
| 11 | Lumber and wood | 0.0444 | −0.0509 | 0.0145 | −0.0081 |
| 12 | Furniture and fixtures | 0.0252 | −0.0384 | 0.0044 | 0.0089 |
| 13 | Paper products | 0.0176 | 0.0125 | −0.0054 | −0.0247 |
| 14 | Printing and publishing | 0.0370 | −0.0119 | 0.0020 | −0.0271 |
| 15 | Chemical products | 0.1094 | 0.1155 | −0.0232 | −0.2018 |
| 16 | Petroleum refining | 0.1058 | −0.0453 | 0.0695 | −0.1300 |
| 17 | Rubber and plastic | 0.0365 | 0.0181 | 0.0012 | −0.0557 |
| 18 | Leather products | 0.0790 | −0.0291 | 0.0132 | −0.0631 |
| 19 | Stone, clay and glass | 0.0580 | −0.0731 | 0.0097 | 0.0054 |
| 20 | Primary metals | 0.0325 | −0.0369 | 0.0262 | −0.0217 |
| 21 | Fabricated metals | 0.0874 | −0.1150 | 0.0054 | 0.0223 |
| 22 | Industrial machinery | −0.0038 | −0.0034 | 0.0031 | 0.0041 |
| 23 | Electronic and electric equipment | 0.0849 | −0.0897 | 0.0023 | 0.0025 |
| 24 | Motor vehicles | −0.0317 | 0.0151 | 0.0022 | 0.0145 |
| 25 | Other transportation equipment | 0.0008 | −0.0001 | 0.0008 | −0.0015 |
| 26 | Instruments | 0.0426 | −0.1127 | 0.0033 | 0.0667 |
| 27 | Miscellaneous manufacturing | 0.0635 | −0.1275 | 0.0021 | 0.0619 |
| 28 | Transport and warehouse | 0.0458 | −0.0903 | 0.0372 | 0.0073 |
| 29 | Communications | −0.0436 | 0.0005 | 0.0018 | 0.0413 |
| 30 | Electric utilities | 0.1013 | −0.0471 | −0.0646 | 0.0104 |
| 31 | Gas utilities | 0.0161 | 0.0180 | −0.0467 | 0.0125 |
| 32 | Trade | −0.0057 | −0.0471 | −0.0096 | 0.0625 |
| 33 | FIRE | −0.0272 | −0.0006 | 0.0041 | 0.0237 |
| 34 | Services | −0.0063 | 0.0040 | 0.0034 | −0.0011 |
| 35 | Government enterprises | 0.1797 | −0.0316 | 0.0376 | −0.1857 |

The change in the level of technology is given for the 35 industries in Table 8.8. This is calculated for the entire 1960–2005 period, the most recent decade 1995–2005 and the first 20 years of the projection period 2005–2025. While the majority of industries had falling prices and improving technology, there are nine industries with negative productivity growth over the 1960–2005 period. These poor performers include three

**Table 8.8** Changes in the level of technology, sample period and projections (negative of change in $f_t$)

| | | $-\Delta f_t$ per year | | |
|---|---|---|---|---|
| | | **1960–2005** | **1995–2005** | **2005–2025** |
| 1 | Agriculture | 0.0129 | 0.0155 | 0.0316 |
| 2 | Metal mining | −0.0059 | −0.0264 | −0.0055 |
| 3 | Coal mining | 0.0107 | 0.0237 | 0.0114 |
| 4 | Petroleum and gas | −0.0058 | −0.0147 | −0.0528 |
| 5 | Non-metallic mining | −0.0026 | −0.0065 | −0.0027 |
| 6 | Construction | −0.0066 | −0.0108 | −0.0048 |
| 7 | Food products | 0.0051 | 0.0054 | 0.0035 |
| 8 | Tobacco products | −0.0163 | −0.0336 | −0.0167 |
| 9 | Textile mill products | 0.0149 | 0.0187 | 0.0154 |
| 10 | Apparel and textiles | 0.0102 | 0.0167 | 0.0095 |
| 11 | Lumber and wood | 0.0013 | 0.0057 | 0.0010 |
| 12 | Furniture and fixtures | 0.0059 | 0.0101 | 0.0063 |
| 13 | Paper products | 0.0043 | 0.0125 | 0.0038 |
| 14 | Printing and publishing | −0.0025 | 0.0033 | −0.0046 |
| 15 | Chemical products | 0.0043 | 0.0047 | −0.0147 |
| 16 | Petroleum refining | −0.0024 | −0.0341 | −0.0053 |
| 17 | Rubber and plastic | 0.0082 | 0.0089 | 0.0074 |
| 18 | Leather products | 0.0034 | 0.0035 | 0.0015 |
| 19 | Stone, clay and glass | 0.0045 | 0.0055 | 0.0118 |
| 20 | Primary metals | 0.0024 | 0.0103 | 0.0078 |
| 21 | Fabricated metals | 0.0048 | 0.0040 | 0.0052 |
| 22 | Industrial machinery | 0.0261 | 0.0500 | 0.0338 |
| 23 | Electronic and electric equipment | 0.0375 | 0.0591 | 0.0522 |
| 24 | Motor vehicles | 0.0019 | 0.0092 | 0.0045 |
| 25 | Other transportation equipment | 0.0022 | 0.0042 | −0.0021 |
| 26 | Instruments | 0.0101 | 0.0132 | 0.0172 |
| 27 | Miscellaneous manufacturing | 0.0088 | 0.0115 | 0.0151 |
| 28 | Transport and warehouse | 0.0088 | 0.0087 | 0.0123 |
| 29 | Communications | 0.0099 | 0.0083 | 0.0121 |
| 30 | Electric utilities | 0.0011 | 0.0033 | 0.0119 |
| 31 | Gas utilities | −0.0078 | −0.0119 | −0.0046 |
| 32 | Trade | 0.0072 | 0.0063 | 0.0066 |
| 33 | FIRE | 0.0076 | 0.0082 | 0.0066 |
| 34 | Services | −0.0035 | −0.0011 | −0.0041 |
| 35 | Government enterprises | 0.0007 | 0.0042 | −0.0114 |

energy industries — Petroleum and gas Mining, Petroleum refining, and Gas utilities — and the large labor-intensive industries, Construction and Services. On the other extreme, the information technology industries — Industrial machinery and Electrical machinery, containing computers and semiconductors — have very rapid productivity growth.

### 8.2.2.2 Lower-tier production functions for intermediate inputs

In the lower tiers of the model, energy and non-energy materials inputs are allocated to the individual commodities, as summarized in Table 8.6. The energy and materials aggregates are represented in (8.41) above. As before, we work with the price dual to the production function. To illustrate the elements of the tier structure we consider the translog price function for energy input:

$$\ln P_{Et} = \alpha_0 + \sum_{i \in \text{energy}} \alpha_i \ln P_{it}^{P,E} + \frac{1}{2} \sum_{i,k} \beta_{ik} \ln P_{it}^{P,E} \ln P_{kt}^{P,E} + \sum_{i \in \text{energy}} f_{it}^{\text{node}=E} \ln P_{it}^{P,E}$$

$$P_i^{P,E} \in \left\{ PS_3, PS_4, PS_{16}, PS_{30}, PS_{31} \right\}.$$

$$(8.48)$$

The share equations are obtained by differentiating with respect to the log price, for the first input, the coal mining commodity, the share demand is:

$$v_3 = \frac{PS_3 \, QP_3}{P_E E} = \alpha_3 + \sum_{k \in \text{energy}} \beta_{3k} \ln P_k^{P,E} + f_{3t}^{\text{node}=E}. \quad (8.49)$$

The other four input demands corresponding to crude petroleum, refined petroleum products, electricity and natural gas are derived in a similar manner.

The components of the non-energy materials input include the other thirty commodities identified in IGEM, in addition to NCIs. The price functions for the subtiers (8.48) differ from the price function (8.43), since there is no latent variable representing the level of technology. This reflects the fact that the price of energy is an index number constructed from the prices of the individual components, while the price of output is measured separately from the prices of capital, labor, energy, and non-energy materials inputs. As before, the $\beta_{ik}$s are share elasticities; in the case of the energy node they represent the degree of substitutability among the five energy commodities.

The latent variables $\{ f_{it}^{\text{node}} \}$ represent the biases of technical change. For example, an increase in the latent variable $f_{30t}^{\text{node}=E}$ implies that the electricity share of total energy input is increasing, so that technical change is electricity-using, while a decrease in this latent variable implies technical changes in electricity-saving. The latent variables are generated by a vector autoregression, as in (8.44).

Our econometric method for estimating the input share Equation (8.49) is identical to that for the top tier. Homogeneity, symmetry, and concavity restrictions are imposed for the subtier price functions. As shown in Table 8.6 there are 12 nodes in the subtiers, giving a total of 106 independent parameters ($\alpha_i$ and $\beta_{ik}$) for each industry after imposing these constraints. Some inputs are zero and thus the number of estimated parameters is less than 106; however, with 35 industries, the total number of parameters to be estimated for the subtiers exceeds 3000.

To summarize the highlights of the results: there is a wide range of estimates for the share elasticities. For example, in the Electric utilities tier structure the most elastic own price term is in the Textile-apparel node with a coefficient of $-0.397$, and the most inelastic own-price term is in Machinery with a coefficient of $0.225$. This implies that the Leontief framework, imposing fixed input-output coefficients, is far too inflexible and imposes an artificially high welfare cost for policy changes.

The contribution of the bias of technical change is sizable in most cases. In the Electric utilities industry, for example, the node for Service materials (MS) has five inputs — Transportation, Trade, FIRE, Services and Other services (OS). The shares of these five inputs in 1996 were 23%, 13%, 22%, 37% and 45% respectively. The latent variable $f_{it}^{NI}$ for transportation fell by $0.274$ over this period, while FIRE rose by $0.052$ and Services rose by $0.244$.

In concluding this section we emphasize that the state-space model of producer behavior is required to capture the changes in patterns of production revealed in the data. Overly simplified formulations like the fixed coefficients of the Leontief framework would lead to inaccurate estimates of the cost of policy changes, generating costs that are far too high. Latent variables representing biases of technical change are required to track the changes in inputs that are not explained by price changes. Finally, a latent variable representing the level of technology is needed to capture differences in productivity growth rates across industries and over time.

### 8.2.2.3 Commodities, industries and output taxes

Production or sales taxes may be proportional to the value of output or expressed as a tax per unit of the quantity. We represent all taxes on production as an *ad valorem* tax that is proportional to value. In the policy simulations we introduce additional *ad valorem* or unit taxes. $PO_j$ is the seller's price given in (8.43), and we refer the post-tax price as the industry price, $PI_j$:

$$PI_j = \left(1 + tt_j^{\text{full}}\right)PO_j, \tag{8.50}$$

where the "full" superscript denotes that it is the sum of the taxes described in (8.63).

We have noted that each industry makes a primary commodity and many industries also make secondary products that are the primary outputs of other industries. We denote the price, quantity, and value of commodity $i$ by $PC_i$, $QC_i$ and $V_i^{QC}$ respectively, all from the purchasers' point of view. The shares contributed by the various industries to commodity $i$ $(m_{ji})$ are given by the make matrix, as are the shares of output of industry $j$ to the various commodities $(m_{ji}^{\text{row}})$. To model joint production we fixed these shares to the base year's make matrix.

We assume that the production function for each commodity is a linear logarithmic aggregate of the outputs from the various industries, with these base shares as weights.

That is, the price of commodity $i$ as a linear logarithmic function of the component industry prices:

$$\ln PC_i = \sum_{j=1}^{35} m_{ji} \ln PI_j, \quad i = 1, 2, \ldots, 35. \tag{8.51}$$

The value of commodity output is the sum of the contributions from all industries:

$$V_{it}^{QC} = \sum_j m_{ji}^{row} PI_{jt} QI_{jt}. \tag{8.52}$$

The quantity of commodity $i$, $QC_i$, is this value divided by $PC_i$.

### 8.2.3 Investment and the cost of capital

Capital input in IGEM is derived from data on investment in structures, producers' durable equipment, land, inventories, and consumers' durables. This differs from the definition of investment in the NIPAs, which excludes consumers' durables.[13] As in the NIPAs, we consider government-owned capital separately from private capital. There are two sides to the private capital account. The capital stock is rented to the producers, as described in Section 8.2.2, and the annual rental payment is the capital income of the household sector. The flow of investment is purchased annually to replace and augment the capital stock. We consider both aspects of the capital market.

#### 8.2.3.1 Aggregate investment and cost of capital

We assume that the supply of capital is determined by past investments; however, we assume that there are no installation or adjustment costs in converting new investment goods into capital stocks or transferring assets among industries. Under these assumptions the savings decision by the household is identical to the investment decision. We analyze the savings–investment decision in order to clarify the role of the cost of capital, a key equation of IGEM. Since capital formation is the outcome of intertemporal optimization, decisions today are based on expectations of future prices and rates of return. Policies announced today that affect future prices will affect investment decisions today.

The owner of the stock of capital chooses the time path of investment by maximizing the present value of the stream of after-tax capital income, subject to a capital accumulation constraint:

$$\text{Max} \sum_{t=u}^{\infty} \frac{(1 - tk)(PKD_t \psi^K K_{t-1} - tpPK_{t-1}) - (1 - t^{ITC})PII_t I_t^a}{\prod_{s=u}^{t} 1 + r_s} \tag{8.53}$$

---

[13] Land is not part of Investment in GDP. The rental from land is included in gross domestic income.

$$\text{s.t. } K_t = (1 - \delta)K_{t-1} + \psi^I I_t^a. \tag{8.54}$$

After-tax capital income $(1 - tk)(PKD_t\psi^K K_{t-1} - tpPK_{t-1})$ is related to the $YK^{net}$ term in household income (8.36) and the discount rate $r_s$ is the same as that in the Euler Equation (8.4).

The stock of capital available at the end of the period is $K_t$. The rental price of capital services is $PKD_t$. We require an aggregation coefficient $\psi^K$ to convert the stock measure to a flow of services. The remaining terms are $tp$, the property tax rate, $tk$, the capital income tax rate, and $PK$ the price of the capital stock. Finally, $I_t^a$ is the quantity of aggregate investment, $(1 - t^{ITC})PII_t$ is its price net of the investment tax credit, and $\psi_t^I$ is an aggregation coefficient that reconciles the different compositions of investment and capital stock.

The solution of the maximization problem gives the Euler equation:

$$(1 + r_t)\frac{(1 - t^{ITC})PII_{t-1}}{\psi_{t-1}^I} = (1 - tk)(PKD_t\psi_t^K - tpPK_{t-1}) + (1 - \delta)\frac{(1 - t^{ITC})PII_t}{\psi_t^I}. \tag{8.55}$$

There is a simple interpretation of this equation: if we were to put $(1 - t^{ITC})PII_{t-1}$ dollars in a bank in period $t-1$ we would earn a gross return of $(1 + r_t)(1 - t^{ITC})PII_{t-1}$ at $t$. On the other hand, if we used those dollars to buy one unit of investment goods $(= \psi^I$ units of capital) we would collect a rental for one period, pay taxes, and the depreciated capital would be worth $(1 - \delta)(1 - t^{ITC})PII_t$ in period $t$ prices. In a model without uncertainty these two returns are equal.

The assumption of no installation costs implies that new investment goods are perfectly substitutable for existing capital. This means that the price of capital stock is linked linearly to the price of aggregate investment:

$$PK_t = \psi_t^{PK}PII_t(1 - t^{ITC}). \tag{8.56}$$

The aggregation coefficient $\psi_t^{PK}$ plays a symmetrical role to $\psi_t^I$ and is used to reconcile the different weights of the asset types.

In equilibrium, the price of one unit of capital stock ($PK$) is the present value of the discounted stream of rental payments ($PKD$). Capital rental prices, asset prices, prices of capital stock, rates of return, and interest rates for each period are related by (8.55). This incorporates the forward-looking dynamics of asset pricing into our model of intertemporal equilibrium. The asset accumulation in Equation (8.54) imparts backward-looking dynamics.

Combining (8.56) and the Euler equation, we obtain the well-known cost of capital equation (Jorgenson, 1963):

$$PKD_t = \frac{1}{(1-tk)}\left[(r_t - \pi_t) + \delta(1 + \pi_t) + tp\right]PK_{t-1}, \tag{8.57}$$

where $\pi_t = (PK_t - PK_{t-1})/PK_{t-1}$ is the asset inflation rate. The rental price of aggregate capital equates the demands for capital by the 35 industries and households with the aggregate supply given by $K_{t-1}$.

The rental payment by industry $j$ for capital services is $PKD_j KD_j$, as specified in the industry cost function. The sum of these rental payments is the gross private capital income, $PKD_t \psi_t^K K_{t-1}$, in the objective function (8.53). This private capital income, less taxes, is the dividend income in (8.38) above:

$$DIV = (1 - tk)\left[\sum_j PKD_j KD_j - tp PK_t K_t\right]. \tag{8.58}$$

### 8.2.3.2 Investment by commodity

The quantity of total investment in period $t$ is $I_t^a$ when the price is $PII_t$. In the NIPAs this total is an aggregate of investment by detailed asset classes — structures, producer durable equipment, consumer durables and inventories. In the benchmark input–output tables, expenditures in purchasers' prices are linked to producer prices via bridge tables in a way identical to how PCE is linked to the input–output categories as described earlier in Section 8.2.1.3.[14] Using these bridge tables, we have constructed a time series of investment demands by the 35 commodity groups employed in IGEM.

We allocate investment demand $I_t^a$ to the 35 individual commodities by means of a hierarchical tier structure of production models similar to the demand for intermediate inputs in the producer model. This is given in Table 8.9, at the top tier we express aggregate investment as a function of fixed and inventory investment:

$$I^a = I\left(I^{\text{fixed}}, I^{\text{inventory}}\right)$$
$$I^{\text{fixed}} = I^f\left(IF_1, IF_2, \ldots, IF_{35}\right). \tag{8.59}$$

As in the production and consumption submodels, we use translog price functions at each of the 15 nodes of the investment tier structure. For node $m$ this is a function of the component prices $\{PII_{m1}, \ldots, PII_{m,im}\}$ and the latent variables $f_t^{Im}$. For each node $m$,

---

[14] In the 1992 Input-Output Benchmark this bridge table is Table E in the *Survey of Current Business*, November 1997.

**Table 8.9** Tier structure of investment function

| | Symbol | Name | Components |
|---|---|---|---|
| | A | Aggregate Investment | Fixed investment, Inventory investment $I^a = I(I^{FX}, I^{IY})$ |
| | IY | Inventory | All 35 commodities in flat Cobb–Douglas function $VII^{IY}$ |
| 1 | FX | Fixed | Long-lived assets, Short-lived assets $I^{FX} = I(IF^{LG}, IF^{SH})$ |
| 2 | LG | Long-lived assets | Construction, FIRE $IF^{LG} = I(IF_6, IF_{33})$ |
| 3 | SH | Short-lived assets | Vehicles, Machinery, Services $IF^{SH} = I(IF^{VE}, IF^{MC}, IF^{SV})$ |
| 4 | VE | Vehicles | Motor vehicles, Other transportation equipment $IF^{VE} = I(IF_{24}, IF_{25})$ |
| 5 | MC | Machinery | Industrial machinery, Electrical machinery, Other machinery $IF^{MC} = I(IF_{22}, IF_{23}, IF^{MO})$ |
| 6 | SV | Services | Services, Other services $IF^{SV} = I(IF_{32}, IF^{SO})$ |
| 7 | MO | Other machinery | Gadgets, Wood products, Non-metallic products, Other miscellaneous. $IF^{MO} = I(IF^{GD}, IF^{WD}, IF^{MN}, IF^{OO})$ |
| 8 | SO | Other services | Services, Transport-communications $IF^{SO} = I(IF_{34}, IF^{TC})$ |
| 9 | GD | Gadgets | Primary metals, Fabricated metals, Instruments $IF^{GD} = I(IF_{20}, IF_{21}, IF_{26})$ |
| 10 | WD | Wood products | Lumber and wood, Furniture and fixtures $IF^{WD} = I(IF_{11}, IF_{12})$ |
| 11 | MN | Non-metallic products | Chemicals, Rubber, Stone, clay and glass, Miscellaneous manufacturing $IF^{MN} = I(IF_{15}, IF_{17}, IF_{19}, IF_{27})$ |
| 12 | OO | Other miscellaneous | Mining aggregate, Textile aggregate, Paper $IF^{OO} = I(IF^{TX}, IF_{13}, IF^{MG})$ |
| 13 | TC | Transport-communications | Transportation, Communications $IF^{TC} = I(IF_{28}, IF_{29})$ |
| 14 | TX | Textile aggregate | Textile, Apparel, Leather, NCIs $IF^{TX} = I(IF_9, IF_{10}, IF_{18}, IF_{NCI})$ |
| 15 | MG | Mining aggregate | Metal mining, Petroleum mining $IF^{MG} = I(IF_2, IF_4)$ |

there are *im* inputs and the set of inputs at that node is denoted $I_{INVm}$. The price function is written in vector form as:

$$\ln PII^m = \alpha^{Im\prime} \ln P^{Im} + \frac{1}{2}\ln P^{Im\prime} B^{Im}\ln P^{Im} + \ln P^{Im\prime}f_t^{Im} + \log \lambda^I \tag{8.60}$$

$$\ln P^{Im} \equiv \left(\ln PII_{m1}, \ldots, \ln PII_{mi}, \ldots, \ln PII_{m,im}\right)' \quad i \in I_{INVm}.$$

The latent variable $f_t^{Im}$ plays a role identical to that of $f_{it}^{node}$ in (8.48) for the producer model, that is, it accounts for changes in demand patterns that cannot be explained by price movements. This vector of latent variables is also modeled as a VAR(1). The share demands corresponding to the price function are:

$$SI^m = \begin{bmatrix} PII_{m1} IF_{m1} / PII^m IF^m \\ \dots \\ PII_{m,im} IF_{m,im} / PII^m IF^m \end{bmatrix} = \alpha^{Im} + B^{Im} \ln PII^{Im} + f_t^{Im} \quad m, i \in I_{INVm}. \quad (8.61)$$

Inventory investment is a variable that fluctuates with the business cycle which we do not model and we simply specify it as an exogenous share of aggregate investment:

$$VII^{inventory} = \alpha^{IY} VII. \quad (8.62)$$

Total inventory demand is allocated to the 35 commodities using fixed shares from the base year.

### 8.2.4 Government and rest of the world

The government plays an important role in IGEM. Government spending affects household welfare directly through transfer payments and public health spending, and indirectly through tax wedges. We do not specify a model for public goods and taxation, but set tax rates exogenously and take the shares of public expenditure by commodity as exogenous. We also set the government deficit exogenously, allowing the level of real purchases to be endogenous.

The government collects revenues for the social insurance trust funds and transfers these funds to households. In the new architecture for the US national accounts discussed by Jorgenson (2009), the trust funds are treated as part of household assets. For example, social security contributions and benefits are regarded as transfers within the household sector and not accounted as government revenue and expenditures. The tax rate on labor income in IGEM thus includes federal and state and local income taxes, but not social insurance contributions.

#### 8.2.4.1 Government revenues and expenditures

The tax codes of the federal, state and local governments are very complex with progressive rates and numerous deductions and tax credits. We simplify these codes in order to obtain a tractable representation that captures the key distortions. The taxes that are explicitly recognized are sales taxes, import tariffs, capital income taxes, labor income taxes, property taxes and wealth or estate taxes.

The tax on production, $tt_j^{full}$, was introduced in (8.50) as putting a wedge between the seller's and purchasers' price, and it includes sales taxes and environmental taxes. The average sales tax rate is chosen to match the revenues collected, less subsidies. The labor taxes discussed in (8.35) give the effective price of leisure as the price paid by employers less the marginal tax rate $tl^m$. Similarly, the labor income received is the price after the average tax rate $tl^a$ is given in (8.7). While the income tax code includes standard deductions, progressive rate schedules, alternative minimum taxes and federal-state interactions, our two labor tax rates captures the key feature that marginal rates are higher than average rates.

The effective capital income tax $tk$ used in (8.38) and (8.57) shows the gap between the payments by producers and receipts by the household. The average tax rate represents the combined effect of corporate tax with personal income tax. The property tax $tp$ also appears in the cost of capital Equation (8.57); this is mostly state and local property taxes. The wealth tax $tw$ is a deduction from household income in (8.36).[15] Tariffs $tr$ are described later in (8.71). Non-tax receipts, denoted $R_t^N$, include various fees charged by governments and appear as a household expenditure in (8.39). To reiterate: the effective tax rates are chosen to replicate the actual revenues; they are close, but not identical, to the statutory rates.[16]

In addition to taxes that are currently collected we introduce new taxes as part of an energy and environmental policy. Environmental taxes may be imposed on unit values or quantities (e.g. per dollar or per gallon). The externality or environmental tax on the sales value of industry $j$'s output is denoted by $tx_j^v$, while the unit tax is $tx_j^u$. Other, non-environmental, unit taxes are denoted by $tu_j$. The result is that the total tax on a dollar of industry $j$'s output is:

$$tt_j^{full} = tt_j + tx_j^v + \frac{tu_j + tx_j^u}{PO_j} . \qquad (8.63)$$

This is the full tax on the industry output price $PO_j$ introduced in (8.50).

The model also allows for a consumption tax, i.e. a tax on personal consumption expenditures but not on intermediate purchases. Also, taxes on capital may be modified, for example, by changing the deductibility of household mortgage interest from income for tax purposes. These features allow for the simulation of tax reforms combined with environmental taxes. In policy simulations we often impose a new tax or subsidy, but wish to maintain revenue neutrality. To implement the scenario where the new subsidy is offset by a lump-sum tax we introduce the variable $TLUMP$, which is subtracted from household income in (8.36) and added to government revenues in (8.65).

---

[15] In the current NIPAs, this is a "capital transfer receipt" that affects the balance sheet but not the flow of disposable income. In IGEM we follow older conventions and account this as a reduction of household income that reduces the government's "net borrowing" account.

[16] The estimated tax rates are given in Jorgenson *et al.* (2009b, table G1).

Government expenditures fall into three major categories — goods and services purchased from the private sector, transfers to the household and foreigners, and interest payments on debt to household and foreigners. These are denoted by $VGG$, $G^{\mathrm{TRAN}} + G^{\mathrm{tran,row}}$ and $GINT + GINT^{\mathrm{row}}$. We treat subsidies as negative sales taxes and include these in the calculation of taxes on outputs in (8.63). Transfers and interest payments are set exogenously as described in Section 8.3.2 below.

Total spending on commodities, including labor and capital services, is denoted $VGG$ and this has to be allocated to individual commodities. Government consumption $VG_i$ of commodity $i$ is set to actual purchases in the sample period. For projections, these are fixed shares of total spending, using shares from the final year:

$$VG_{it} = PS_{it} G_{it} = \alpha_i^G VGG_t$$

$$PLD_{Gt} LD_{Gt} = \alpha_L^G VGG_t \tag{8.64}$$

$$VG_{GK,t} = \alpha_K^G VGG_t.$$

The quantity of public consumption $G_i$ is the value divided by the supply price. The government does not rent capital from the private sector but rather owns the stock of public capital. We follow the NIPAs in adding this imputation to both the expenditure side and the income side of the government accounts.

### 8.2.4.2 Total government accounts and deficits

The total revenue of the government is the sum of the sales tax, tariffs, property taxes, capital income taxes, labor income taxes, wealth taxes, non-tax revenues, unit output taxes, externality taxes, imputed capital consumption, income from government enterprises (industry 35) and lump-sum taxes:

$$R\_TOTAL = R\_SALES + R\_TARIFF + R\_P + R\_K + R\_L + R\_W$$
$$+ R^{\mathrm{N}} + R\_UNIT + R\_EXT + VG_{GK} + YK^{\mathrm{gov}} + TLUMP, \tag{8.65}$$

where:

$$R\_SALES = \sum_j tt_j PO_j QI_j; \quad R\_TARIFF = \sum_i tr_i PM_i M_i;$$

$$R\_P = tp PK_{t-1} K_{t-1}; \quad R\_K = tk\big(YK - R\_P\big) + tk GINT + tk Y^{\mathrm{ROW}};$$

$$R\_L = tl^a P^h LS / (1 - tl^m) = tl^a \sum_j PLD_j LD_j;$$

$$R\_W = tw(PK.K + BG + BF); \quad R\_UNIT = \sum_j tu_j QI_j;$$

$$R\_EXT = \sum_j tx_j^v PI_j QI_j + \sum_i tx_i^{rv} PM_i M_i + \sum_j tx_j^u QI_j + \sum_i tx_i^{ru} M_i;$$

$R^N$, $YK^{gov}$ and $VG_{GK}$ are non-tax receipts, government enterprise surpluses and government capital consumption. Total government expenditures are the sum of purchases, transfers and interest payments to both domestic households and to the rest of the world:

$$EXPEND = VGG + G^{tran} + G^{tran,row} + GINT + GINT^{row}. \qquad (8.66)$$

Given our treatment of the social insurance funds as household assets, the government interest payments, $GINT$, include interest to the trust funds, minus payments from the funds to the government for operating expenses. These interest payments are normally set exogenously as a function of the projected government debt. IGEM allows an alternative formulation tying the payments to the endogenous rate of return.

The public deficit is total outlays less total revenues, a concept equal to the official net borrowing requirement:

$$\Delta G_t = EXPEND_t - R\_TOTAL_t. \qquad (8.67)$$

These deficits add to the public debt which is separated between debt held by US residents and debt held by foreigners, $BG + BG^*$. The increase in the domestic debt is the total deficit less the portion financed by foreigners (negative government foreign investment, $GFI$),

$$BG_t = BG_{t-1} + \Delta G_t + GFI. \qquad (8.68)$$

Historically, there are no official accounts of this equation; however, the BEA's recent "integrated macroeconomic accounts" provides this with a statistical discrepancy item that we also include.[17] The stock of debt to the rest of the world is, similarly, the accumulation of the foreign borrowing, including the statistical discrepancy:

$$BG_t^* = BG_{t-1}^* - GFI. \qquad (8.69)$$

These deficit and stocks of debt are set to actual values for the sample period, and set to official projections beyond that.

To summarize: we set tax rates exogenously and set the deficit exogenously. The model generates economic activity and hence endogenous revenues. Government transfers and interest are also set exogenously. Thus, the remaining item, general government final purchases, $VGG$, is determined residually.

### 8.2.4.3 Rest of the world – imports, total supply and exports

Since IGEM is a one-country model, the supply of goods by the rest of the world, and the demand for US exports, are not modeled explicitly for each commodity. We follow the standard treatment and regard imports and domestic outputs as imperfect substitutes,

---

[17] See Teplin *et al.* (2006).

the Armington assumption, which is reasonable at our level of aggregation.[18] We also assume that US demand is not sufficient to change world relative prices.

The total supply of commodity $i$ at period $t$ is an aggregate of the domestic and imported varieties:

$$QS_{it} = QS(QC_i, M_i, t). \qquad (8.70)$$

Domestic commodity supply $QC_i$ is given earlier in (8.52), while $M_i$ denotes the quantity of competitive imports. The price of imports is the world price multiplied by an effective exchange rate, plus tariffs $tr$ and, possibly, new externality taxes $tx$:

$$PM_{it} = \left(1 + tr_{it} + tx_i^{\mathrm{rv}}\right)e_t PM_{it}^* + tx_i^{\mathrm{ru}}. \qquad (8.71)$$

$e_t$ is the world relative price; its role will be made clear after the discussion of the current account balance below.

We treat the total supply function in a similar manner to the model of producer behavior. The demands for domestic and imported varieties are derived from a translog price function for the total supply price:

$$\ln PS_{it} = \alpha_{ct} \ln PC_{it} + \alpha_{mt} \ln PM_{it} + \frac{1}{2}\beta_{cc} \ln^2 PC_{it} + \frac{1}{2}\beta_{mm} \ln^2 PM_{it}$$
$$+ \beta_{cm} \ln PC_{it} \ln PM_{it} + f_{ct}^{\mathrm{M}} \ln PC_{it} + f_{mt}^{\mathrm{M}} \ln PM_{it}. \qquad (8.72)$$

The demand for imports in share form derived from this cost function is:

$$\frac{PM_{it}M_{it}}{PS_{it}QS_{it}} = \alpha_{mt} + \beta_{mm} \ln \frac{PM_{it}}{PC_{it}} + f_t^{\mathrm{Mi}}. \qquad (8.73)$$

Again, when $\beta_{mm} = 0$ it implies that the demand has unit price elasticity, while a large positive value means an inelastic demand for imports. The total value of the supply of commodity $i$ to the domestic market and exports is:

$$PS_{it}QS_{it} = PC_{it}QC_{it} + PM_{it}M_{it}. \qquad (8.74)$$

Imports into the US have risen rapidly during our sample period, not only in absolute terms but as a share of domestic output. This change cannot be explained by price movements alone, so that we employ the state–space approach to modeling changes in the pattern of imports that are not induced by price movements. The right-hand side of (8.73) contains a latent variable, $f_{it}^{\mathrm{M}}$, modeled as in the producer model (8.44). The estimated parameters are given in Jorgenson *et al.* (2009b, Table 3.9). The estimated $\beta_{mm}$s are quite elastic; many are negative, so that the substitution elasticity is greater than unity. The latent

---

[18] That is, while we may regard the imports of steel of a particular type as perfectly substitutable, the output of the primary metals industry is a composite of many commodities and would have an estimated substitution elasticity that is not large.

variables play particularly large roles in Leather, Apparel, and Miscellaneous manufacturing; the imports of crude oil and refined petroleum also have significant non-price effects.

We have now closed the loop in the flow of commodities. We began with the producer model purchasing intermediate inputs at price $PS_i$ and selling output at price $PO_j$. The price of intermediates is the total supply price given in (8.24) as a function of domestic and imported commodities.

The inputs into the industry production functions include NCIs as listed in Table 8.6. In the zero-profit Equation (8.42), the value of such imports by industry $j$ is $PNCI_jQP_{NCI}^j$. Like the competitive imports, the price of NCIs is the world price multiplied by the exchange rate:

$$PNCI_{jt} = \left(1 + tr_{jt}\right)e_tPNCI_{jt}^*. \tag{8.75}$$

Beyond the sample period, world prices are projected to change at the same rate as productivity growth in US industry prices. That is, $PM_{it}^*$ is assumed to change at the same rate as the latent variable $f_{it}^p$ in the domestic output price function (8.43).

For exports we also follow the standard treatment in single country models. A translog price function with a latent state variable is used to allocate supply between domestic supply and exports. Historical data on export prices received in the sample period move differently from prices of imports into the US. We simplify IGEM by using one world price for each commodity $i$. We thus write the allocation function in terms of the import price, $PM_{it}$:

$$SX_t^i = \frac{PC_{it}X_{it}}{PC_{it}QC_{it}} = \alpha_{xt} + \beta_{xx} \ln \frac{PM_{it}}{PC_{it}} +f_{it}^X. \tag{8.76}$$

We use a latent variable to track the historical changes that cannot be explained by price movements alone. We use the import prices instead of the actual export prices. Note that this function is derived from profit maximization by the supplier, so that the implied price function is convex, not concave as in the price function used in modeling imports. The share elasticities for the manufacturing commodities are between 0.05 and 0.31, with the biggest values in Other transportation equipment and Machinery (which includes computers). The latent variable play a smaller role in the export functions compared to the import functions in general, but is substantial for Electrical equipment and Motor vehicles.

The current account balance in dollars is the value of exports less imports, plus net interest receipts, and less private and government transfers:

$$CA_t = \sum_i PC_iX_i - \sum_i e_tPM_i^*M_i - \sum_j ePNCI_j^*NCI_j + Y_t^{row}$$
$$- GINT^{row} - CR_t - G_t^{tran,row}. \tag{8.77}$$

The current account surplus, less the portion due to government foreign investment, adds to the stock of net private US foreign assets:

$$BF_t = BF_{t-1} + CA_t - GFI. \qquad (8.78)$$

Note that the total claims on the rest of the world are the private assets less the government debt, $BF_t - BG_t^*$.

The closure of the external sector is treated in various ways in different trade models. One could set the current account exogenously and let the world relative price, $e_t$, adjust. Alternatively, one could set $e_t$ exogenously and let the current account balance be endogenous. In a dynamic model the second option would require something like a portfolio choice model to determine the demand for foreign assets and hence the path of current account balances. This is beyond the scope of IGEM and we set the current account exogenously, making $e_t$ endogenous, so that (8.77) is satisfied.

### 8.2.5 Emissions

IGEM is equipped with a number of externality variables that are defined to suit the needs of a particular analysis. These can include energy consumption in BTUs, emissions of carbon dioxide from combustion and sulfur dioxide emissions. For the analysis of climate change mitigation policy below, we define a single variable — total greenhouse gas emissions from all sources and gases.

The externalities in IGEM may be process-related, depending on output, or product-related, depending of the quantity of inputs such as coal. The externality coefficients for the environment are derived from the detailed historical data in the Environmental Protection Agency (2010b), *Inventory of US Greenhouse Gas Emissions and Sinks: 1990–2008*. This emissions series is sorted and aggregated to create the emissions totals corresponding to the externality variable defined above. These totals are then allocated based on the output and inputs of each industry and final demand sector.

$$EXT_{xt} = \sum_j XP_{jx} QI_{jx} + \sum_j \sum_{i \in \text{fuels}} XC_{ijx} QP_{it}^j. \qquad (8.79)$$

The emission coefficients for the IGEM industries are described in more detail in Jorgenson *et al.* (2009b); we note here that there are trends in these industry-level aggregate coefficients due to changes in composition and other technical changes over time. For projections beyond the sample period, the emission coefficients either are set to the last sample point or, as appropriate, follow historical trends, but tapering to a steady state.

## 8.3 INTERTEMPORAL EQUILIBRIUM AND ECONOMIC GROWTH

The previous section describes all the components of supplies and demands for commodities and factor services in IGEM. This is a dynamic model with an intertemporal equilibrium, and we now characterize the equilibrium where all the supply and demand conditions are met. We present this in a manner that leads naturally to the development of the solution algorithm discussed below.

The Cass–Koopmans neoclassical model of economic growth has a saddle-path property: given the initial value of the state variable there is a unique value of the costate variable for which the model converges to a steady state that satisfies the transversality condition. In IGEM the capital stock is the state variable. The path of this stock is determined by the Euler equation derived by maximizing of the household's objective function. Full consumption is the costate variable.

Given the initial stock of capital, there is only one value of full consumption in the initial period that will be on the saddle path that satisfies the transversality condition. There are other state variables in the system, such as the government debt, claims on foreigners and the latent variables estimated by means of the Kalman filter. However, these state variables are not determined by optimizing behavior in IGEM, and are set exogenously and do not have associated costate variables.

In a disaggregated model like IGEM a well-defined steady state requires all industries to have the same rate of productivity growth in the very long run. In IGEM we focus on the intermediate term (75 years) and specify a TFP growth rate for each industry in the intermediate term that replicates the observed variety of behavior. After 75 years, we impose a zero rate of TFP growth and allow the model to converge to its steady state.

## 8.3.1 Market balance and intertemporal equilibrium

We first describe the equilibrium within each period, *given* the inherited capital stock and a guess of full consumption for that period. Under the assumptions of constant returns to scale and factor mobility the equilibrium prices clear all markets at zero profits for each period. We then describe the intertemporal equilibrium with the Euler equation linking full consumption across time periods.

In the commodity markets the demand side of the economy consists of intermediate demands by producers, household consumption, investment demand, government demand, and exports. The supply, $QS_i$, comes from domestic producers and imports as given in (8.74). In the equilibrium within each period, the industry output prices $PO_j$ equate demands and supply:

$$PS_i QS_i = \sum_j PS_i QP_{ij} + PS_i(C_i + I_i + G_i) + PC_i X_i. \tag{8.80}$$

In capital market equilibrium, the demand for capital input from all industries and households is equal to the supply from the stock of inherited capital, $K_{t-1}$. We have been careful to stress the distinction between the stock and flow of capital and how these stock and flow measures are independently aggregated.[19] Capital income is equal to the aggregate service price multiplied by the effective service flow, which in turn is given by the capital stock multiplied by the aggregation coefficient $\psi_t^K$. The equilibrium condition in value terms is:

$$PKD_t \psi_t^K K_{t-1} = \sum_j PKD_{jt} KD_{jt}. \tag{8.81}$$

Since we assume that capital is mobile across sectors, only one capital rental price is needed to clear this market. However, we observe different rates of return in the historical data. To reconcile this with our simplifying assumption of capital mobility, we treat the industry rental price as a constant times the economy-wide rental price:

$$PKD_{jt} = \psi_{jt}^K PKD_t. \tag{8.82}$$

For the sample period we calculate the $\psi_{jt}^K$ coefficients from the actual data on industry costs of capital, and for the projection period we set them equal to the last sample point. With these industry-specific adjustments, the economy-wide price $PKD_t$ equates supply and demand for capital services:

$$\sum_{j=1}^{C} \psi_{jt}^K KD_{jt} = KD_t = \psi_t^K K_{t-1}. \tag{8.83}$$

Turning to the labor market, supply $(LS_t)$ comes from the household demand for leisure given in (8.16) and the demand is the sum over the demands from the 35 industries and government $(LD_{jt})$. The equilibrium condition in value terms is:

$$P_t^h LS_t = P_t^h \left( LH_t - \psi_{Ct}^R N_t^R \right) = \left( 1 - tl_t^m \right) \sum_j PLD_{jt} LD_{jt}. \tag{8.84}$$

Recalling the discussion for the leisure price in (8.33), $\psi_C^R$ is an aggregation coefficient linking the time endowment to aggregate leisure.

As with the price of capital input, the price of labor input differs across sectors in the historical data. To reconcile this with the simplifying assumption of labor mobility, we first set the economy-wide wage rate equal to the price of the time endowment $(P^h)$, adjusted for the marginal labor tax. We then use fixed constants to scale the industry wage rates to the economy-wide wage rate:

$$PLD_j = \psi_j^L \frac{P^h}{\left( 1 - tl^m \right)}. \tag{8.85}$$

---

[19] The stocks are aggregated using asset price weights while the service flows are aggregated using the user cost of capital given in (8.59).

The price of aggregate time endowment, $P^h$, clears the market for labor:

$$LS_t = LH_t - \psi^R_{Ct}N^R_t = \sum_j \psi^L_{jt}LD_{jt}. \tag{8.86}$$

Three additional equations must hold in equilibrium. The first is the exogenous government deficit (8.67), which is satisfied allowing government spending on goods $VGG$ to be determined endogenously. The second is the exogenous current account surplus (8.77), which is satisfied by allowing the world relative price $e_t$ to be endogenous. The third is the savings and investment equilibrium:

$$S_t = P^I_t I^a_t + \Delta G_t + CA_t. \tag{8.87}$$

Household savings is first allocated to the two exogenous items — lending to the government to finance the public deficit ($\Delta G$) and lending to the rest of the world ($CA$), both adjusted for government borrowing from abroad. The remainder is allocated to investment in domestic private capital. Investment and savings decisions are not separate in IGEM, so that (8.87) holds as a result of household intertemporal optimization.

### 8.3.1.2 Intertemporal equilibrium

The steady state of the Cass–Koopmans model is reached when the state and costate variables are stationary. The two dynamic equations — capital accumulation (8.54) and the Euler Equation (8.4) — determine the steady state (ss). By setting $K_t = K_{t-1}$ and $F_t = F_{t-1}$ we obtain the two equations that determine the steady state (in addition to the equations characterizing the intraperiod equilibrium just discussed):

$$\delta K_{ss} = \psi^I_{ss} I^a_{ss} \tag{8.88}$$

$$r_{ss} = \rho. \tag{8.89}$$

The steady state obtains when investment exactly covers depreciation and the interest rate equals the rate of time preference.

Along the transition path, from the first period with the inherited state variables to the steady state, the following equations must hold: the capital accumulation Equation (8.54), the Euler Equation (8.4) linking full consumption between adjacent periods, the cost of capital Equation (8.57) linking the marginal product of capital with the rate of return and capital gains.

### 8.3.1.3 Solution algorithm

IGEM, as described so far, has some 4000 endogenous variables for each period. We approximate the steady state at $T = 120$ periods after the initial shock. We structure our algorithm to solve the model in steps that are described more fully in Jorgenson *et al.* (2009b, appendix J). Briefly, this algorithm consists of: (i) Solving for the steady state, (ii) guessing a path of full consumption, $\{F^g_t\}^T_{t=1}$, and (iii) calculating a sequence of intratemporal equilibria consistent with this guess and the initial capital stock. In the next step, (iv) the sequence of realized interest rates is used to check whether Euler Equation (8.4) holds in each period. If not, (v) the guessed vector of full consumption is revised and the process repeated. At the solution, the Euler equation holds for all $t$ and is consistent with both the initial capital stock and the sequence of period-by-period interest rates.

For each intratemporal equilibrium, we do not solve 4000 equations simultaneously but rather triangulate the system into a series of nested loops, where each loop involves only a small number of equations and unknowns. This algorithm solves the resulting system quickly and is relatively easy to debug. Once the base-case transition path is determined, alternative policy cases usually only take seconds to compute.

## 8.3.2 Exogenous Projections and the Base Case

The variables determined outside the model include the time endowment, the level of technology represented by the state variables, the government and current account deficits, world prices, and the aggregation coefficients. While these exogenous variables are major determinants of the steady state and the growth rate in the base case, they play relatively modest roles in determining the effect of policy shocks. We briefly describe here how we project these exogenous variables and the behavior of the model in the base case; the details are in Jorgenson *et al.* (2009b).

The time endowment is a function of the population composition and relative wages, as given in (8.31). This is projected using the population projection by sex and age from the Bureau of the Census (2008).[20] We assume a small improvement in the level of educational attainment over the projection period as described in Jorgenson *et al.* (2009b, Chapter 2). We also assume that the relative wages of each demographic group remains unchanged at the last sample point.

In projecting hours we have to decide on the treatment of business cycles. In particular, the near term forecasts are for a slow recovery after the Great Recession of 2009, with a period of above average unemployment rates. A simulation beginning in 2010 that extrapolates average leisure hours observed in the sample period would over-state work, output and energy use. To avoid this we make a simple adjustment of the time endowment using the Congressional Budget Office projections of unemployment rates.

The government accounts include transfers, interest payments, deficits and stocks of debt which are all set exogenously. These are projected over the first 10 years using the forecasts of the federal budget from the Congressional Budget Office (Congressional Budget Office, 2010a), augmented by straightforward assumptions about state and local government accounts. Tax rates are given implicitly by the revenue forecasts. Beyond the 10-year window in Congressional Budget Office (2010a) we use the Long-Term

---

[20] Census Bureau projections of the US population released in 2008 are available at http://www.census.gov/population/www/projections/natproj.html.

Outlook in Congressional Budget Office (2010b) to generate the trend in tax rates out 75 years. The federal revenue from individual and corporate taxes is projected to rise from 11.4% of GDP in 2011 to 21.0% in 2060 under the "baseline scenario." Beyond 2020, the deficit is assumed to fall gradually to zero by 2060 to give a smooth transition to the steady state. The share of the deficit financed by foreigners is very high in the 2000s and we make a simple assumption that this share falls gradually back to zero in 2060.

There is less expert guidance for current account forecasts, we take the five-year forecast from IMF (2010) and then assume that it falls gradually to zero by 2060 in line with our assumptions about the government borrowing requirement. Growth in energy import prices is taken from the Energy Information Administration's *Annual Energy Outlook 2010* (Energy Information Administration, 2010). Finally, we note again that the state variables in the production, consumption, investment, import and export functions are projected using VARs like those in (8.44). These determine the non-price trends in input demands, consumption, imports and exports.

### 8.3.2.2 Base case

We simulate IGEM to create a base case with the setting of exogenous variables described above. The first years, 2010−2015, represent a continuation of recent trends and recovery from the Great Recession. Then, driven by demographics, vanishing budget and current account deficits, tax policy and the state variables for production, consumption, investment, exports and imports, the US economy experiences stable but slightly modulating growth as it tracks toward its steady state over the remainder of this century. From 2100 to 2110, expansion begins to slow, achieving a zero-growth steady state over the period 2110−2130.

Table 8.10 gives the average growth rates of key economic variables for the first 50 years of this expansion, 2010−2060. GDP growth averages 2.4% annually over this interval.

**Table 8.10** Base case: macroeconomic outcomes (average annual growth in real quantities, 2010−2060, %)

| | |
|---|---|
| Real GDP | 2.4 |
|    Consumption | 2.1 |
|    Investment | 2.0 |
|    Government | 1.8 |
|    Exports | 4.0 |
|    Imports | 2.3 |
| Household full consumption (goods, services and leisure) | 1.5 |
| Capital stock | 2.1 |
| Labor demand (labor supply) | 1.0 |
| Leisure demand | 1.1 |
| Total factor productivity (value added) | 0.8 |
| Total greenhouse gas emissions (GtCO$_2$-e) | 1.5 |

Consumption and investment grow more slowly as the historically rapid expansion in household and commercial capital slows. Growth in government purchases reflects the new fiscal realities of the base-case deficit and tax rate assumptions. Import growth, as expected, aligns with the overall economy while exports signal a rebalancing as a consequence of a continuing weakened dollar early on, high productivity in key export producing sectors such as agriculture and high technology manufacturing and vanishing current account deficits.

On the supply side, growth in aggregate final net output of 2.3% annually is provided by capital, labor and TFP. The growth in the capital stock leads to growth in capital services that contributes around 0.9 percentage points to output growth. The growth in labor input at 1.0% annually contributes another 0.6 percentage points annually with the balance provided by the approximately 0.8% annual growth in productivity.

As shown in growth rates of the 35 sectors in Table 8.11, there is a changing mix of energy inputs in the base case. Electricity use grows almost exactly with GDP at 2.4% annually. The inputs into power generation change with coal, gas and capital (e.g. renewables) fueling the load. Total national coal consumption grows at 2.5% annually, slightly faster than the overall economy. With petroleum and gas use growing at much slower rates, aggregate fossil fuel use tracks the overall economy but it too grows at a slower rate. Greenhouse gas emissions grow at 1.5% *per annum* (Table 8.10) and continue their decline relative to GDP, but not at the rates observed most recently. While petroleum and gas use diminish significantly in relative importance, electricity and, hence, coal use do not. In this base case simulation, it is the intensity of coal use that accounts for the slowing rate of decline in the ratio of emissions to GDP.

For the non-energy industries and commodities, the growth rates in Table 8.11 appear plausibly in line with growth overall and with expectations arising from historical observation. For example, US agriculture continues as a comparatively high productivity growth industry with corresponding benefits for US exports and food production and consumption. Productivity growth differences also are reflected in the slower growing construction and personal services sectors and the traditionally much more rapidly growing high technology non-electric and electric machinery industries. Growth in print and publishing gives way to other forms of communications and financial services continue to outpace the general economy. Finally, we see several industries (e.g. mining and metals) that clearly benefit from the aforementioned rebalancing of the US economy toward exports.

## 8.4 WELFARE MEASUREMENT

Our methodology for measuring the welfare effects of policy changes was introduced by Jorgenson *et al.* (1997b). The household sector is comprised of infinitely-lived households that we refer to as *dynasties*. Each household takes commodity prices, wage rates

**Table 8.11** Base case: domestic industry and commodity outcomes (average annual growth in real quantities, 2010–2060, %)

| | | Production | Supply | Consumption |
|---|---|---|---|---|
| 1 | Agriculture | 4.7 | 4.5 | 4.3 |
| 2 | Metal mining | 2.9 | 2.7 | 2.5 |
| 3 | Coal mining | 2.6 | 2.5 | 2.5 |
| 4 | Petroleum and gas | 0.4 | 0.4 | 0.4 |
| 5 | Non-metallic mining | 2.8 | 2.8 | 2.7 |
| 6 | Construction | 1.6 | 1.6 | 1.6 |
| 7 | Food products | 2.9 | 2.7 | 2.6 |
| 8 | Tobacco products | 0.2 | 0.2 | 0.2 |
| 9 | Textile mill products | 3.2 | 2.9 | 2.6 |
| 10 | Apparel and textiles | 2.9 | 2.5 | 2.4 |
| 11 | Lumber and wood | 2.6 | 2.4 | 2.4 |
| 12 | Furniture and fixtures | 1.7 | 1.6 | 1.5 |
| 13 | Paper products | 2.6 | 2.4 | 2.4 |
| 14 | Printing and publishing | 1.2 | 1.2 | 1.2 |
| 15 | Chemical products | 2.2 | 2.1 | 2.0 |
| 16 | Petroleum refining | 1.1 | 1.2 | 1.2 |
| 17 | Rubber and plastic | 2.8 | 2.6 | 2.6 |
| 18 | Leather products | 2.3 | 2.0 | 2.0 |
| 19 | Stone, clay and glass | 3.1 | 2.9 | 2.8 |
| 20 | Primary metals | 3.2 | 2.7 | 2.5 |
| 21 | Fabricated metals | 2.5 | 2.4 | 2.3 |
| 22 | Industrial machinery | 6.1 | 5.6 | 4.7 |
| 23 | Electronic and electric equipment | 6.0 | 5.6 | 4.8 |
| 24 | Motor vehicles | 2.8 | 2.3 | 2.0 |
| 25 | Other transportation equipment | 2.6 | 2.4 | 1.9 |
| 26 | Instruments | 2.8 | 2.7 | 2.6 |
| 27 | Miscellaneous manufacturing | 3.5 | 3.1 | 3.0 |
| 28 | Transport and warehouse | 3.2 | 3.1 | 2.9 |
| 29 | Communications | 3.2 | 3.2 | 3.2 |
| 30 | Electric utilities | 2.5 | 2.4 | 2.4 |
| 31 | Gas utilities | 1.7 | 1.9 | 1.9 |
| 32 | Trade | 2.2 | 2.2 | 2.2 |
| 33 | FIRE | 3.0 | 2.9 | 2.9 |
| 34 | Services | 1.7 | 1.7 | 1.7 |
| 35 | Government enterprises | 1.6 | 1.6 | 1.5 |

and rates of return as given. All dynasties are assumed to face the same vector of prices $p_t$ and the same nominal rate of return $r_t$. The quantity of a com-modity, including leisure, consumed by dynasty $d$ in period $t$ is $C_{ndt}$ and the full expenditure of dynasty $d$ on consumption in period $t$ is $M_{dt}$.

We assume that each dynasty maximizes an additive intertemporal utility function of the form:

$$V_d = \sum_{t=0}^{\infty} \delta^t \ln V_{dt},$$

(8.90)

where $\delta = 1/(1+\rho)$ and $\rho$ is the subjective rate of time preference. The intratemporal indirect utility function is expressed in terms of *household equivalent members*, $N_{dt}$:

$$\ln V_{dt} = \alpha^{H'} \ln p_t + \frac{1}{2} \ln p_t' B^H \ln p_t - D(p) \ln \frac{M_{dt}}{N_{dt}},$$

(8.91)

where:

$$N_{dt} = \frac{1}{D(p_t)} \ln p_t B_A A_d,$$

and $A_d$ is a vector of attributes of the dynasty allowing for differences in preferences among households.

The utility function $V_d$ is maximized subject to the lifetime budget constraint:

$$\sum_{t=0}^{\infty} \gamma_t M_{dt}(p_t, V_{dt}, A_d) = \Omega_d$$

(8.92)

where:

$$\gamma_t = \prod_{s=0}^{t} \frac{1}{1+r_s},$$

and $\Omega_d$ is the full wealth of the dynasty. In this representation $M_{dt}(p_t, V_{dt}, A_d)$ is the intratemporal full expenditure function and takes the form:

$$\ln M_{dt}(p_t, V_{dt}, A_d) = \frac{1}{D(p_t)} \left[ \alpha^{H'} \ln p_t + \frac{1}{2} \ln p_t' B^H \ln p_t - \ln V_{dt} \right] + \ln N_{dt}.$$

(8.93)

The necessary conditions for a maximum of the intertemporal utility function, subject to the wealth constraint, are given by the discrete time Euler equation:

$$\ln V_{dt} = \frac{D_t}{D_{t-1}} \ln V_{dt-1} + D_t \ln \left( \frac{D_{t-1} \gamma_t N_{dt} P_t}{\delta D_t \gamma_{t-1} N_{dt-1} P_{t-1}} \right),$$

(8.94)

where we have used $D_t$ to denote $D(p_t)$ and the aggregate price term:

$$P_t = \exp \left( \frac{\alpha^{H'} \ln p_t + \frac{1}{2} \ln p_t' B^H \ln p_t}{D_t} \right).$$

(8.95)

The Euler equation implies that the current level of utility of the dynasty can be represented as a function of the initial level of utility and the initial and future prices and discount factors:

$$\ln V_{dt} = \frac{D_t}{D_0} \ln V_{d0} + D_t \ln \left( \frac{D_0 \gamma_t N_{dt} P_t}{\delta^t D_t N_{d0} P_0} \right), \tag{8.96}$$

We can represent dynastic utility as a function of full wealth and initial and future prices and interest rates. We begin by rewriting the intertemporal budget constraint as:

$$\sum_{t=0}^{\infty} \gamma_t N_{dt} P_t V_{dt}^{-1/D_t} = \Omega_d, \tag{8.97}$$

Substituting (8.96) into (8.97) and simplifying yields the following:

$$\ln V_{d0} = -D_0 \ln \left( \frac{\Omega_d}{N_{d0} R} \right), \tag{8.98}$$

where:

$$R = \frac{P_0}{D_0} \sum_{t=0}^{\infty} \delta^t D_t.$$

Equation (8.98) enables us to evaluate dynastic utility in terms of full wealth:

$$
\begin{aligned}
V_d &= \sum_{t=0}^{\infty} \delta^t \ln V_{dt} \\
&= \sum_{t=0}^{\infty} \delta^t \left[ \frac{D_t}{D_0} \ln V_{d0} + D_t \ln \left( \frac{D_0 \gamma_t N_{dt} P_t}{\delta^t D_t N_{d0} P_0} \right) \right] \\
&= \sum_{t=0}^{\infty} \delta^t \left[ -D_t \ln \frac{\Omega_d}{R} + D_t \ln \left( \frac{D_0 \gamma_t N_{dt} P_t}{\delta^t D_t P_0} \right) \right], \\
&= S \ln R - S \ln \Omega_d + \sum_{t=0}^{\infty} \delta^t D_t \ln \left( \frac{D_0 \gamma_t N_{dt} P_t}{\delta^t D_t P_0} \right)
\end{aligned}
\tag{8.99}
$$

where:

$$S = \sum_{t=0}^{\infty} \delta^t D_t.$$

Solving for full wealth as a function of prices and utility yields the intertemporal expenditure function of the dynasty:

$$\ln \Omega_d(\{p_t\}, \{\gamma_t\}, V_d) = \frac{1}{S}\left[ S \ln R + \sum_{t=0}^{\infty} \delta^t D_t \ln \left( \frac{D_0 \gamma_t N_{dt} P_t}{\delta^t D_t P_0} \right) - V_d \right], \quad (8.100)$$

where $\{p_t\}$ is the time profile of prices and $\{\gamma_t\}$ is the profile of discount factors.

We employ the intertemporal expenditure function (8.100) in measuring the monetary equivalent of the effect on welfare of a change in policy. We let $\{p_t^0\}$ and $\{\gamma_t^0\}$ represent the time profiles of prices and discount factors for the base-case and $V_d^0$ the resulting level of welfare. Denoting the welfare of the dynasty after the imposition of the new policy by $V_d^1$, the equivalent variation in full wealth is:

$$\Delta W_d = \Omega_d(\{p_t^0\}, \{\gamma_t^0\}, V_d^1) - \Omega_d(\{p_t^0\}, \{\gamma_t^0\}, V_d^0). \quad (8.101)$$

The equivalent variation in full wealth (8.101) is the wealth required to attain the welfare associated with the new policy at prices of the base case, less the wealth required to attain base-case welfare at these prices. If the equivalent variation is positive, the policy produces a gain in welfare; otherwise, the policy change results in a welfare loss. Equivalent variations in full wealth enable us to rank the base-case policy and any number of alternative policies in terms of a money metric of dynastic welfare.

## 8.5 EVALUATION OF CLIMATE POLICY

We next consider the evaluation of three cap-and-trade policies to control greenhouse gas emissions in the US. The caps refer to economy-wide emissions of six greenhouse gases — carbon dioxide, methane, nitrous oxide, hydrofluorocarbons, perfluorocarbons and sulfur hexafluoride. The least extreme of these policies freezes total annual greenhouse gas emissions at the 2005 level of 7.2 metric gigatonnes of carbon dioxide equivalent (GtCO$_2$-e) through 2050. The most extreme policy imposes a "cap" or cumulative emissions limit on greenhouse gas of 205.4 GtCO2-e over the period 2012–2050. The requisite trend reduction in emissions ultimately targets an emissions level in 2050 of 3.6 GtCO2-e. This is 50% of the 7.2 GtCO2-e of greenhouse gas observed in 2005 and more than 40% below the 6.1 GtCO2-e of 1990. This policy is a primary US policy scenario for the Energy Modeling Forum 24 (EMF 24). It also is very close to the central case described by Goettle and Fawcett (2009) in their contribution to EMF 22 and to the policy outcomes for total greenhouse gases arising from the US House and Senate legislative initiatives, 2007–2010.[21] Our central policy case, and

---

[21] See: http://www.epa.gov/climatechange/economics/economicanalyses.html.

the focus of much of our subsequent discussion, lies halfway between these extremes. Specifically, cumulative emissions, 2012–2050, are capped at 241.4 GtCO2-e with annual emissions tracking to 5.4 GtCO2-e by 2050.

After 2050 we opt for price rather than emissions certainty. Specifically, we hold constant the allowance prices that are necessary to achieve the 2050 emissions target. In each case, the 2050 price is fixed indefinitely in terms of constant GDP purchasing power. Were emissions to remain at 2050 levels, cumulative emissions, 2051–2060, would total 72.0, 54.0 and 36.0 GtCO$_2$-e under the progressively restrictive targets. By freezing the 2050 allowance prices, these amounts rise to 78.9, 59.1 and 39.7 GtCO$_2$-e, respectively.

In these simulations, we assume the US government auctions emissions allowances or permits and, therefore, controls all revenue collection and redistribution. Through 2050 IGEM endogenously determines the time path of allowance prices that achieves the necessary annual abatement. Figures 8.1 and 8.2 show the emissions levels and allowance prices corresponding to these three scenarios which are denoted by "2005 Level," "25% Target" and "50% Target." Figure 8.1 also shows the baseline greenhouse gas emissions path, thus providing a sense of the magnitude of required abatement.

In our central case, allowance prices begin at just under $1 (2005 dollar) per tonne in 2012 and rise exponentially to $109 per tonne by 2050. With a flat level of emissions

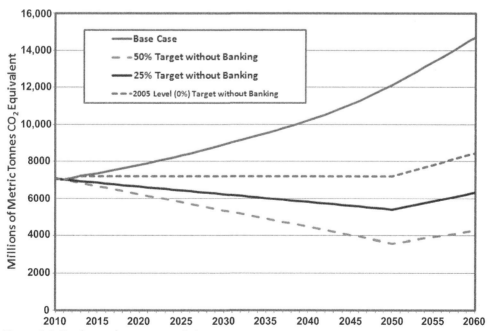

**Figure 8.1** Total greenhouse gas emission.

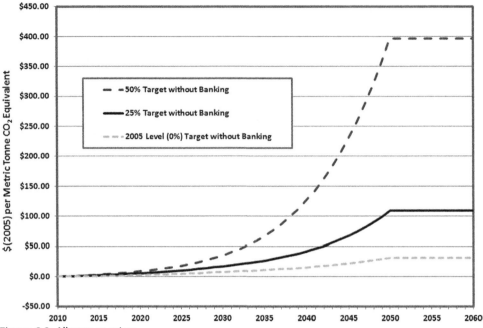

**Figure 8.2** Allowance prices.

under the least restrictive policy, the constraint is not binding until 2013, the price rising moderately from 7 cents in 2013 to $31 per tonne in 2050. As evidence that more aggressive abatement becomes increasingly more expensive, under the 50% target allowance prices again begin at under $1 per tonne in 2012 but rise to $396 per tonne by 2050. The differences in these time patterns clearly demonstrate IGEM's structure and econometric foundations exhibit anything but constant-elasticity behavior. See Figure 8.2.

Emissions abatement occurs through three mechanisms — output reductions, input substitutions and price-induced technical change. The demand functions in IGEM capture the first two effects and endogenous technical change incorporates the third. To illustrate these effects in their purest form, the simulations do not include the opportunities related to non-$CO_2$ abatement, such as bio-electricity generation, carbon capture and storage technologies, domestic sequestration and other offsets and international permit trading that characterize our earlier policy analyses. The allowance prices and economic costs are thus higher here than in the analyses that include these options.[22]

---

[22] To see the power of these external abatement opportunities in reducing allowance prices and the economic costs of mitigation policy refer to Jorgenson *et al.* (2009a) and Environmental Protection Agency (2012a).

For the same reason, our simulations of the outcomes of cap-and-trade policies are compared to a base case that is produced by the model, rather than calibrated to a particular time pattern of energy consumption (coal, oil, gas and electricity) and economic growth, as is typical of policy assessments. For example, the Environmental Protection Agency instructions to their analysts include GDP and energy forecasts from the Department of Energy. These calibrations require adjustments to the industry cost functions. Our intent in this exercise is to measure the econometrically determined impacts of climate policy in a transparent manner and thus avoid these adjustments.

IGEM's model closure and steady-state condition requires vanishing government and current account deficits, and most policy scenarios require twin deficit neutrality. By design, these closures imply that variations in US saving fully account for the variations in US investment and capital formation; there can be no crowding-out or crowding-in of private investment from these two sources. With allowance revenues as a new source of government income, a key assumption in setting the policy simulation is the treatment of the government budget.

With an endogenous tax (or transfer), either we keep nominal revenues and expenditures equal to the base case, thus preserving deficit *and* revenue neutrality, or we keep real expenditures on goods equal to the base case and preserve only deficit neutrality. Although there is no price inflation in IGEM, there are large changes in relative prices due to the policy; a dollar buys a different basket of goods in year *t* in the policy case compared to the base case. To keep welfare comparisons simple we keep an index of real aggregate government expenditures under the cap-and-trade policy equal to that of the base case.

## 8.5.1 Impact on economic growth and industry

The consequences for the economy are examined by considering the average adjustments over the period 2010—2060 as these generally are representative of what happens in any given year. As shown in Table 8.12 and Figure 8.3, the emissions constraints and resulting allowance prices adversely affect each aspect of aggregate GDP — consumption, investment, government purchases, exports and imports.

The effects on the economy are best understood by first considering the changes in industry prices. These changes include the direct effects of emissions pricing as well as their indirect general equilibrium consequences and are presented in Table 8.13 and Figure 8.4. Clearly, energy prices — coal, oil, gas and electricity — are most affected, with coal more so than any other commodity. This is not surprising in that almost 80% of all greenhouse gas emissions in the US are related to fossil fuel combustion. In addition, coal is high in carbon content in relation to the other fossil fuels and is used extensively along with gas and some oil in the manufacture of electricity.

**Table 8.12** Macroeconomic impacts

|  | 2005 Level | 25% Target | 50% Target |
|---|---|---|---|
| Emissions (GtCO$_2$-e) | | | |
| Cumulative emissions target, 2012–2050 | 280.9 | 241.4 | 205.4 |
| Cumulative emissions outcome, 2051–2060 | 78.9 | 59.1 | 39.7 |
| Allowance price ($(2005)/tonne CO$_2$ equivalent) | | | |
| 2012 | 0 | 1 | 1 |
| 2050 | 31 | 109 | 396 |
| 2051 and beyond | 31 | 109 | 396 |
| Average % change from base case, 2010–2060 | | | |
| Real GDP | −0.6 | −1.4 | −3.4 |
| Consumption | −0.4 | −0.9 | −2.2 |
| Investment | −0.9 | −2.1 | −5.0 |
| Government | 0.0 | 0.0 | 0.0 |
| Exports | −1.1 | −2.9 | −7.0 |
| Imports | −1.1 | −2.6 | −6.1 |
| GDP prices | 0.5 | 1.4 | 3.4 |
| Consumption | 0.4 | 1.1 | 2.6 |
| Investment | 0.3 | 0.8 | 1.9 |
| Government | 0.2 | 0.6 | 1.3 |
| Exports | 0.6 | 1.6 | 3.8 |
| Imports | 0.5 | 1.1 | 2.2 |
| Household full consumption (goods, services and leisure) | −0.1 | −0.1 | −0.3 |
| Capital stock | −0.5 | −1.2 | −2.7 |
| Labor demand and supply | −0.3 | −0.7 | −1.7 |
| Leisure demand | 0.1 | 0.3 | 0.7 |
| Exchange rate ($/foreign currency) | 0.5 | 1.1 | 2.3 |

Domestic crude oil and gas extraction prices decline under the condition in IGEM that approximates an upward-sloping supply curve.[23] Here, the lower domestic production that follows from reduced demand is obtained at a lower cost. This is the only price (cost) reduction that occurs. All non-energy prices increase relative to the labor price numéraire. Some prices — Agriculture, Chemicals, Plastics, Stone, clay and glass, Primary metals, Electrical machinery (semiconductors), and Services (waste management) — are affected both directly and indirectly as their emissions are "covered" by

---

[23] An exception to the treatment in equations (8.81)–(8.83) is the crude oil and gas extraction industry, industry 4. Its capital stock measure, $K_{4t}$, includes land and its resource base. Given the non-reproducible nature of this base, we allow two possible closures of its market for capital services, $KD_{4t}$: one is to treat it symmetrically with all other industries, and two is to assume that the stock of capital in this sector is fixed (no investment and no depreciation). In the second option, we have an endogenous rental price of this fixed stock of capital, $PKD_{4t}$ such that the demand for capital input is equal to the fixed supply: $KD_{4t} = KD_4$. This second option introduces behavior associated with an upward sloping supply curve.

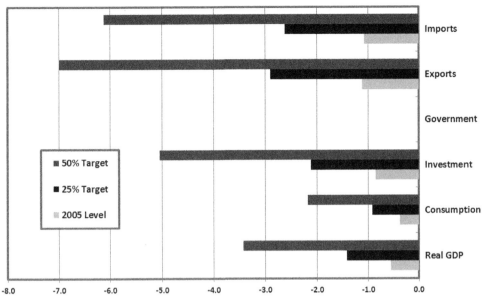

**Figure 8.3** Impacts on real final demand (average percent change from base, 2010–2060).

policy. Others like Food, Lumber and wood, Paper, Motor Vehicles, Communications, Trade, Finance, and Services are affected only indirectly.

The overall impacts on the economy are dominated by the decisions of households. Their first decision concerns the intertemporal allocation of full consumption — the expenditure on good, services *and* leisure. Households know that the price increases from abatement policy will be larger "tomorrow" than they are "today" as the emissions from a growing economy make stabilization at the target emission levels more difficult over time. Households view this as a progressive erosion of real incomes and purchasing power and redistribute full consumption toward the present.

Households next decide on the allocation of full consumption between non-durable goods, household capital services and consumer services, on the one hand, and leisure, on the other.[24] The pass-through of allowance prices makes all consumer goods and services more expensive and, so, the overall price of consumption relative to labor is higher. This prompts households to substitute leisure for consumption. Within the overall increase in near-term full consumption arising from the intertemporal effect, comparatively more is spent on leisure than is spent on goods and services.

In addition to the comparatively small consumption-related impact on aggregate demand, this second decision by households has important implications for the supply

[24] The importance of and sensitivity to the consumption-leisure tradeoff is examined in detail in Volume 1, Chapter 7 of Jorgenson *et al.* (2009b).

**Table 8.13** Industry effect (average % change from base case, 2010–2060)

|  |  | 2005 Level | | 25% Target | | 50% Target | |
|---|---|---|---|---|---|---|---|
|  |  | Price | Output | Price | Output | Price | Output |
| 1 | Agriculture | 2.5 | −3.1 | 7.5 | −8.5 | 24.0 | −20.2 |
| 2 | Metal mining | 0.9 | −0.4 | 2.0 | −2.5 | 4.5 | −8.4 |
| 3 | Coal mining | 114.1 | −44.4 | 358.3 | −61.9 | 1191.0 | −72.0 |
| 4 | Petroleum and gas | −0.5 | −0.2 | −2.1 | −0.6 | −6.1 | −1.7 |
| 5 | Non-metallic mining | 1.0 | −1.6 | 2.3 | −4.2 | 5.0 | −10.3 |
| 6 | Construction | 0.3 | −0.6 | 0.8 | −1.5 | 2.2 | −3.8 |
| 7 | Food products | 1.0 | −1.2 | 2.6 | −3.0 | 7.1 | −7.2 |
| 8 | Tobacco products | 0.4 | −0.6 | 1.2 | −1.7 | 3.1 | −4.3 |
| 9 | Textile mill products | 0.6 | −1.0 | 1.6 | −2.6 | 4.2 | −6.4 |
| 10 | Apparel and textiles | 0.4 | −0.5 | 0.9 | −1.1 | 2.2 | −2.2 |
| 11 | Lumber and wood | 0.5 | −0.9 | 1.3 | −2.2 | 3.5 | −5.4 |
| 12 | Furniture and fixtures | 0.4 | −0.7 | 0.9 | −1.6 | 2.2 | −3.7 |
| 13 | Paper products | 0.8 | −1.2 | 1.8 | −2.8 | 3.9 | −6.0 |
| 14 | Printing and publishing | 0.3 | −0.4 | 0.6 | −1.0 | 1.4 | −2.4 |
| 15 | Chemical products | 1.2 | −2.0 | 3.5 | −5.4 | 10.5 | −13.3 |
| 16 | Petroleum refining | 1.9 | −2.5 | 5.1 | −6.4 | 14.0 | −14.7 |
| 17 | Rubber and plastic | 0.7 | −1.6 | 1.9 | −3.5 | 5.5 | −7.8 |
| 18 | Leather products | 0.5 | −0.8 | 1.2 | −1.9 | 2.8 | −4.2 |
| 19 | Stone, clay and glass | −0.5 | 0.1 | 0.8 | −2.0 | 7.1 | −9.0 |
| 20 | Primary metals | 1.9 | −2.3 | 3.8 | −5.2 | 8.0 | −11.5 |
| 21 | Fabricated metals | 0.7 | −1.3 | 1.4 | −3.1 | 3.1 | −6.7 |
| 22 | Industrial machinery | 0.3 | −0.8 | 0.8 | −2.0 | 1.8 | −4.5 |
| 23 | Electronic and electric equipment | 0.3 | −0.7 | 0.8 | −1.8 | 2.1 | −4.4 |
| 24 | Motor vehicles | 0.5 | −1.2 | 1.1 | −2.8 | 2.6 | −6.2 |
| 25 | Other transportation equipment | 0.3 | −0.3 | 0.7 | −0.7 | 1.5 | −1.7 |
| 26 | Instruments | 0.2 | −0.5 | 0.4 | −1.2 | 1.0 | −3.0 |
| 27 | Miscellaneous manufacturing | 0.4 | −0.6 | 1.0 | −1.6 | 2.3 | −4.2 |
| 28 | Transport and warehouse | 0.5 | −1.1 | 1.2 | −2.7 | 3.1 | −6.7 |
| 29 | Communications | 0.2 | −0.6 | 0.6 | −1.4 | 1.3 | −3.2 |
| 30 | Electric utilities | 3.3 | −2.6 | 6.5 | −4.8 | 11.2 | −7.9 |
| 31 | Gas utilities | 4.6 | −4.0 | 13.9 | −11.4 | 43.7 | −25.6 |
| 32 | Trade | 0.3 | −0.6 | 0.8 | −1.6 | 1.8 | −3.7 |
| 33 | FIRE | 0.3 | −0.6 | 0.7 | −1.5 | 1.6 | −3.6 |
| 34 | Services | 0.3 | −0.5 | 0.6 | −1.3 | 1.5 | −3.2 |
| 35 | Government enterprises | 0.4 | −0.7 | 0.9 | −1.7 | 2.2 | −4.0 |

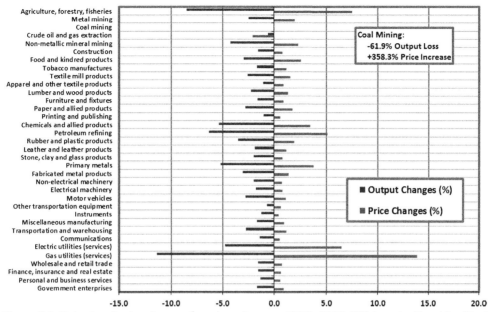

**Figure 8.4** Output and price changes from base (average 2010–2060, 25% target without banking).

side of the economy. The increase in leisure demand is a reduction in household labor supply; the magnitudes of the changes are shown in Figure 8.5. While increasing leisure is welfare improving for households, their reductions in labor supply, at prevailing wages, reduce labor and, hence, national income.

The third decision by households concerns the allocation of purchases among the variety of consumer goods and services, but within the overall level of reduced total real spending. There is a redirection of expenditure away from those goods and services incurring the larger price increases and toward those experiencing the smaller price increases. As household spending is such a large fraction of overall spending, the actions taken here strongly influence the structure of real GDP and the domestic production that supports it.

Given the reduction in real incomes, and labor and capital input, the output of all industries fall, especially those related to energy (Table 8.13 and Figure 8.4). Producers minimize the cost impact by substituting away from more costly inputs and toward relatively cheaper materials, labor and capital. Ultimately, there is still a unit cost increase that is passed through as higher prices to consumers, reducing real incomes and demand, on one hand, and reducing factor supplies on the other.

There is, however, a small net benefit on the production side that helps mitigate the economic costs of abatement policy. Beyond factor substitutions, there is also price-induced technical change (ITC) at work in each industry. Price induced patterns of innovation are discussed in Section 8.2.2 above and Chapter 17. Policy changes alter the

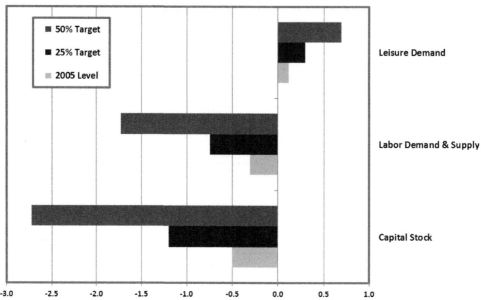

**Figure 8.5** Impacts on real value added (average percent change from base, 2010–2060).

future pattern of relative prices, and so "induces" changes in productivity through the innovation term ($f_{it}^p$ in Equation 8.43).

The effect of price-induced technical change in these simulations leads to permit prices that are marginally higher than they would be in its absence. To see the impact, we show in Figure 8.6 the size of the induced technical change for each industry and, in the top bar, the economy-wide output-weighted sum of the industry effects. The impacts are shown for 2030 and 2050. While the ITC effect of the carbon price ranges from −0.09% to +0.12% at the industry level, the overall economy-wide effect on productivity is positive. As the economy is marginally larger, greenhouse gas emissions are marginally higher and permit prices need to be higher to achieve the required abatement.

The ITC effects also have structural implications for the economy and, so too, for energy use and greenhouse gas emissions. This is best seen by focusing on four sectors in Figure 8.6 — electric utilities, petroleum refining, gas utilities and services. ITC in the electric utilities sector plays the dominant role in the overall ITC effect observed for this policy — electricity prices are lower, and demand is higher, than would be otherwise. This is due to the estimated bias as reported in Chapter 17; technical change is "energy saving" in electric utilities. In short, the estimated relationship in this sector works somewhat against the goals of this policy. Since induced technical change helps to lower electricity prices, unconstrained energy use and emissions are higher which means that permit prices also have to be higher to achieve a given emissions reduction.

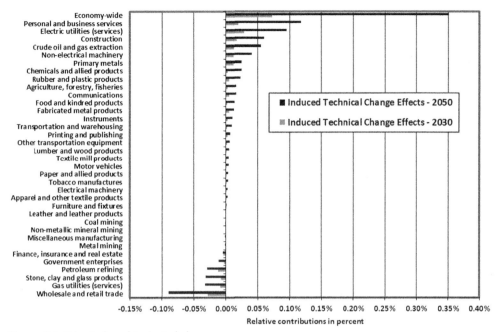

**Figure 8.6** Price-induced technical change.

On the other hand, the ITC effects in petroleum refining and gas utilities counter the effects in electricity. Here, technical change works to raise prices further leading to larger reductions in their demands and greater emissions abatement. The ITC in services has an interesting effect. It raises productivity and lowers prices, which leads to higher demand and output. However, this sector is not energy- or emissions-intensive so that this change in the composition of output yields an economy that is less energy- and emissions-intensive. Hence, the permit prices are marginally lower.

The reduction in labor income arising from the reduced labor supply, combined with lower capital income from businesses, yields a lower national income. However, in terms of the labor price numéraire, nominal personal consumption increases due to the intertemporal effect of shifting spending from the future to the present. In addition, overall real consumption gives the appearance of being price inelastic as its annual decline is less than proportional to the increase in its aggregate price (Table 8.12). With falling income and rising consumption, private saving falls unambiguously. The reduction in saving leads to a corresponding reduction in nominal private investment. With higher prices for investment goods, this lower saving leads to lower real investment and hence a lower capital stock (Table 8.12 and Figures 8.3 and 8.5). The lower supplies of capital and labor limit the economy's domestic supply possibilities following the introduction of this policy.

IGEM's saving–investment balance summarizes the net flow of funds available for investment. These funds arise from three sources. The first source, discussed above, is the domestic saving of households and businesses. The second source reflects the behavior of the government and the magnitude of its deficit. The third source is due to the interactions with the rest of the world and whether the annual current account balance is in deficit or surplus.

To eliminate government's direct effects on real investment spending through the saving–investment balance, these simulations assume deficit neutrality and unchanged real government purchases. Accordingly, as the prices rise, there occurs a proportional increase in nominal government spending. Lump-sum redistributions of allowance revenues are set so as to preserve deficit and real spending levels while accommodating all other general equilibrium effects. While there are numerous potential reactions concerning the fiscal policies of governments, the above assumptions give rise to transparent outcomes that are uncomplicated by speculations as to what governments might do to soften any adverse policy impacts.

The impacts on real exports and imports appear in Table 8.12 and Figure 8.4. The prices of US exports rise relative to goods and services from the rest of the world. As exports supplies are estimated to be price-elastic, export volumes fall by proportionally more than export prices rise. The reductions in exports occur in all sectors and contribute to a direct and indirect reduction in the global greenhouse gas emissions arising from US export activities.

Real and nominal imports also decline in all sectors except for electric utilities. Import reductions occur from the overall reductions in spending associated with a smaller economy. Import reductions also occur in those commodities directly affected by abatement policy. The cap on emissions and the corresponding emissions permits fall on all commodities that contribute to US greenhouse gases, whether they are produced domestically or imported. Thus, within total imports, there are disproportionate reductions in oil, gas and other policy-sensitive commodities as their prices rise along with those of their domestic counterparts.

Since import reductions occur in all sectors except electricity, the contributions to global greenhouse gas emissions arising from US import activities also decline. Even if the small increase in electricity imports is based entirely on fossil fuel inputs, these policies do not contribute to an increase in worldwide emissions through leakage, either on average or in a given policy year.[25] For example, in 2050, the decline in emissions associated with US export reductions is 502 million tonnes $CO_2$-e and that associated with US import reductions is 94 million tonnes.

---

[25] Since IGEM is a national model, we are unable to make inferences on emissions rising in other countries in reaction to US policy.

To neutralize the impact of lower exports and somewhat smaller reduction in imports on investment, the dollar weakens to maintain the current account balance at its pre-policy level. By affecting the terms of trade, this partially dampens the policy's export effect and dampens the loss of competitiveness in the carbon intensive goods. As illustrated in Figure 8.2, allowance prices increase more than proportionately to the size of the emission reduction. Not surprisingly, the economic costs of increasingly severe abatement requirements also rise disproportionately.

Figure 8.7 shows the impact on GDP for each of the three scenarios. Holding greenhouse gas emissions constant at their 2005 levels leads to an economy that is 1% smaller by 2050. In our central case, the impacts by 2050 are almost three times greater. This corresponds to an average reduction in annual real growth that is under 0.1%. In the most extreme policy, the losses in GDP again rise disproportionately. Achieving the 50% target results in an economy that is 8% smaller by 2050, incurring eight times the losses from holding annual emissions constant. As the 2050 allowance prices are held constant in real terms, the proportionate losses in real GDP in 2051 and beyond are virtually identical to those in 2050.

To put a dollar figure on the losses, we express them in terms of dollars per household. In 2020, with emissions held constant the loss per household is $298 (0.18%) in 2005 dollars. In the central case, this loss increases to $577 (0.35%) per household and

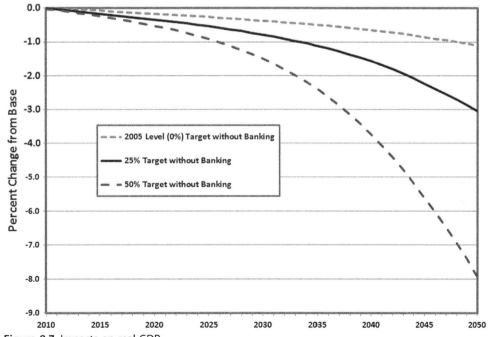

**Figure 8.7** Impacts on real GDP.

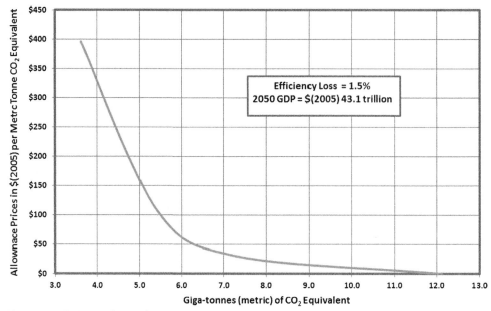

**Figure 8.8** Emission demand, 2050.

rises to $883 (0.53%) in our most extreme case. By 2050, these per household losses increase to $2,800 (1.10%), $7,718 (3.04%) and $20,158 (7.94%), respectively.

Figure 8.8 plots the 2050 allowance prices against the corresponding emissions levels for each of our three cases and the base case. This loss function has the appearance of a conventional demand curve. The first 4.9 $GtCO_2$-e of greenhouse gas abatement costs $31 in 2005 dollars, the next 1.8 $GtCO_2$-e costs $78 and the final 1.8 $GtCO_2$-e costs $287. This implies an efficiency loss of 1.5% of the $43.1 trillion GDP in 2050. Figures 8.7 and 8.8 provide clear evidence that, in IGEM, emission reductions become increasingly less elastic as targets are tightened.

### 8.5.2 Distributional impact

We next report the impacts of the cap–and–trade policies on household welfare, as given by the equivalent variation in full wealth in Equation (8.101). Recall that the equivalent variation in full wealth is the wealth required to attain the welfare associated with a new policy at base-case prices, less the wealth required to attain the base-case welfare at these same prices. We consider equivalent variations for each of the 244 household types, cross–classified by the demographic categories presented in Table 8.3.[26]

---

[26] Table 8.3 gives a total of 384 possible household types. However, in the most recent Survey underlying IGEM, the number of types with a positive number of households is only 244.

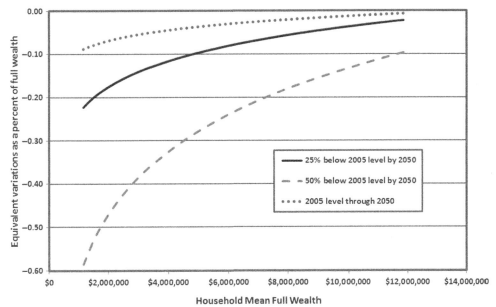

**Figure 8.9** Household welfare effects and full wealth (at mean wealth without banking, 244 household types).

In Chapter 17 we describe the wide range of full expenditure values for each demographic category. Figure 8.9 shows the welfare effects for the three policy scenarios at the mean full wealth for each of the 244 household types. The percentage losses are smaller than those for GDP because households respond to the changing prices by changing their consumption patterns. The welfare losses also are smaller because of the offsetting increases in leisure demand and the lump-sum transfers of allowance revenues.

The households with lower full wealth suffer a larger percentage loss in welfare. Smaller households and others with lower full wealth consume less leisure and have larger budget shares of consumer goods. Hence, they are more adversely affected by the direct and indirect effects of mitigation policy. Moreover, as emissions targets are tightened, the welfare losses increase at an increasing rate as mean household wealth decreases. Lower expenditure households are harmed more and, the more aggressive the abatement policy, the more they are harmed.

Figures 8.10 and 8.11 show the welfare effects associated with only the 25% target. In Figure 8.10, the 244 household types are arranged from the lowest to the highest levels of mean full wealth. In Figure 8.11, the 244 household types are arranged from the most to the least adversely affected. The principal curve is the solid line in each graph labeled "At mean wealth." This shows the welfare impact on households with the mean wealth among those with the same demographic characteristics. For mean wealth, all households experience a welfare loss ranging from −0.02 to −0.22% of full wealth are

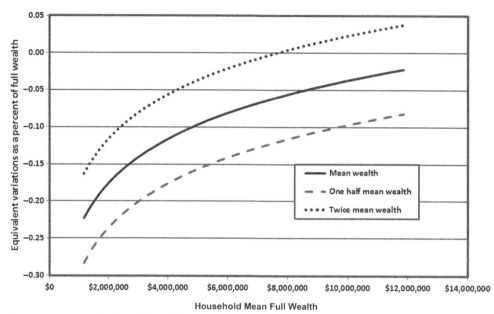

**Figure 8.10** Household welfare effects and full wealth (25% target without banking, 244 household types).

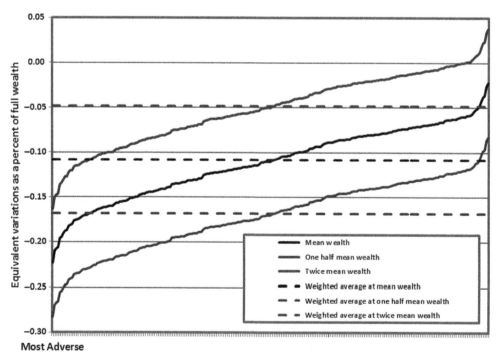

**Figure 8.11** Household welfare effects (25% target without banking, 244 household types).

included. The most negatively affected households consist of one child with one adult living in the rural South and headed by non-white females. The least negatively affected are large urban households in the West, households with three or more children and three or more adults headed by non-white males.

To illustrate how the policy affects households with different levels of full wealth, the effects in Figure 8.10 and 8.11 also are shown for half and twice mean wealth. The population-weighted average welfare effects are −0.17, −0.11 and −0.05% of lifetime expenditure at the half mean, mean, and twice mean levels, respectively, as represented by the horizontal lines in Figure 8.11. It must be emphasized that these are the average household effects. Figures 8.10 and 8.11 show that the effects of the policy change are regressive; the equivalent variations become more negative as full wealth decreases both across and within demographic groups. However, it should be noted that in all cases the welfare losses are relatively small, the worst case being under 0.3% of full wealth.

Figure 8.12 decomposes the welfare effect by isolating the impact of price changes alone. The solid line in Figure 8.12 shows the solid curves from Figures 8.9 and 8.10 for mean wealth. The dashed line below it shows the welfare effects due solely to price changes, holding household full expenditure at its base case value. In the absence of changes in expenditure, households experience net welfare losses in the range of 0.23−0.43% of their full wealth. However, the lump-sum redistributions required to

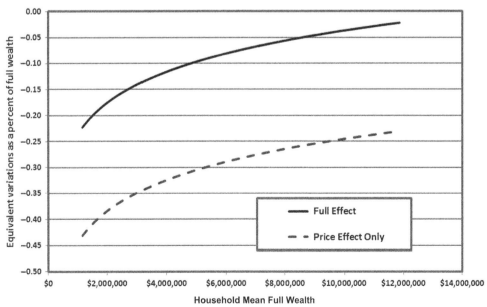

**Figure 8.12** Decomposition of household welfare effects (25% target without banking, at mean full wealth).

hold real government spending at its base-case levels partially compensate the price effects.

With leisure such a large share of household budgets, there is a natural concern as to the influence of family size on the findings summarized above. Accordingly, we examine the two most populous segments of the household sample — households with two adults and no children (28.8% of all households), and households with one adult and no children (29.5%). The dominance of leisure in full wealth is evident here. In Figures 8.9, 8.10 and 8.12, single-person adult households are concentrated at the lower end of the spectrum for lifetime expenditure while two-person adult households are concentrated in its middle range. However, what matters most here are the robust findings of regressivity when controlling for leisure this manner. For both groups, climate policy results in larger welfare losses at lower levels of full wealth and, in both cases, this pattern is invariant to scale.

Table 8.14 decomposes the welfare losses across the demographic details of the 244 household types. These are summarized by the population-weighted averages within each group. Clearly, households containing three or more adults are generally better off than those with two adults, which in turn are better off than single-adult households. This is not surprising in that larger households generally are wealthier in terms of their lifetime spending on goods, services *and* leisure. Within these groups, the presence of children is of equal interest. Households with three or more adults are better off with three or more or no children and are worse off with one or two children. Households with two adults fare progressively worse the fewer children they have whereas the opposite occurs in households with only one adult. Among single-adult households and within each grouping based on the number of children, rural households headed by females fare worst.

In the sample, 18.9% of the household population resides in the Northeast, with 23.0, 36.5 and 21.6% residing in the Midwest, South and West, respectively. Most of the households with large welfare losses are located in the South or Midwest and the largest losses occur in the South. The households with the smallest proportional losses are in the West and, on average, this region fares the best followed by the Northeast, South and Midwest.

Households headed by non-white females comprise 7.4% of the sample population. Households headed by white females comprise 22.5% of the sample. Households headed by non-white and white males, comprise 10.3 and 59.8% of the sample, respectively. The household types with largest welfare losses are headed by females though, on average, there is not much difference between those headed by whites or non-whites. Male-headed households fare much better, owing to their greater wealth. Here, again, the average difference between the races is not large. Overall, the welfare gap across the sexes is much more significant than that across the races. The households with the largest losses are concentrated in rural areas. The larger

**Table 8.14** Household welfare effects, 25% target (population weighted-average equivalent variations as a % of full wealth)

| | Full wealth | | |
|---|---|---|---|
| | Half mean | Mean | Twice mean |
| Children, adults per household | | | |
| 3+, 3+ | −0.124 | −0.064 | −0.004 |
| 2, 3+ | −0.127 | −0.067 | −0.007 |
| 1, 3+ | −0.125 | −0.065 | −0.005 |
| 0, 3+ | −0.124 | −0.064 | −0.004 |
| 3+, 2 | −0.144 | −0.084 | −0.023 |
| 2, 2 | −0.146 | −0.086 | −0.026 |
| 1, 2 | −0.149 | −0.089 | −0.029 |
| 0, 2 | −0.152 | −0.092 | −0.032 |
| 3+, 1 | −0.222 | −0.162 | −0.102 |
| 2, 1 | −0.216 | −0.156 | −0.096 |
| 1, 1 | −0.213 | −0.153 | −0.093 |
| 0, 1 | −0.213 | −0.153 | −0.093 |
| Region of household | | | |
| Northeast | −0.165 | −0.105 | −0.045 |
| Midwest | −0.176 | −0.116 | −0.056 |
| South | −0.173 | −0.113 | −0.053 |
| West | −0.156 | −0.096 | −0.036 |
| Race and gender of household head | | | |
| Non-white female | −0.202 | −0.142 | −0.082 |
| White female | −0.201 | −0.141 | −0.081 |
| Non-white male | −0.160 | −0.100 | −0.040 |
| White male | −0.154 | −0.094 | −0.033 |
| Location of household | | | |
| Urban | −0.166 | −0.106 | −0.046 |
| Rural | −0.193 | −0.133 | −0.073 |
| Overall | −0.168 | −0.108 | −0.048 |

(92.1%), wealthier urban population fares better than the smaller (7.9%), poorer rural segment.

## 8.5.3 Effects of banking emissions allowances

A common provision in climate policy is the intertemporal transfer of emissions allowances through *borrowing* allowances for repayment in the future and *banking* allowances for future use. Significant borrowing requires an excess supply of allowances and relatively low in-kind interest rates governing their repayment. In US policy initiatives to date, these conditions are not met, generally because of the high borrowing costs in proposed legislation. Accordingly, we do not permit borrowing.

Banking of allowances is a common feature of proposals for climate policy (Environmental Protection Agency, 2012a). However, the rules governing the time horizon are often unclear. There appear to be three possibilities. (i) Banking is allowed to continue beyond the terminal policy date. In this case, policy assessment requires assumptions about the annual supply of allowances beyond the terminal date in order to determine the initial allowance price and the final year of banking drawdown. (ii) Banking expires at the terminal target date of the policy. Any remaining banked allowances would then be worthless and allowance prices would rise sharply to clear the market. (iii) Banking expires in the terminal date of the proposal. After expiration of banking, the allowance prices are set to avoid a sharp price spike. This is another form of so-called safety-valve pricing. Under these conditions, the climate proposal secures emissions certainty through its terminal date and price certainty thereafter.

For the purposes of this exercise, we adopt two of these approaches as alternatives to our central case involving the emissions target 25% below 2005 levels by 2050. First, banking is permitted, 2012–2050, but the covenant expires beginning in 2051. Under the conditions of optimal banking, allowance prices through 2050 grow annually by 5%, a rate common to many such assessments, from a starting price that ensures the same cumulative emissions, 2012–2050, as occur without banking. In 2051 and beyond, allowances prices then either revert to the non-banking price in 2050 or are held fixed in terms of GDP purchasing power at the 2050 banking price. We denote the first of these as banking with no safety valve and the second as banking with a safety valve.

Under banking, the effective allowance prices, shown in Figure 8.13, begin at just over $7 (2005 dollars) in 2012 and rise 5% annually to just under $48 by 2050. This time path of prices yields the same cumulative emissions of 241.4 $GtCO_2$-e as would occur without banking. As we will show, this is less harmful to the overall economy and household welfare. In 2051, banking is no longer permitted and the allowance price reverts to $109 per tonne (no safety valve) or remains at $48 per tonne indefinitely (safety valve). The transition to a yet another price-oriented policy from a quantity-focused one leads to still higher emissions than occur without banking; over the period 2051–2060, the cumulative emissions are 71.8 $GtCO_2$-e here versus 59.1 $GtCO_2$-e in our central case without banking (and versus the 54.0 $GtCO_2$-e that would occur were emissions held constant).

The mechanisms of adjustment described above apply equally to the no-banking and banking scenarios. However, it is clear from Tables 8.15 and 8.16 that banking reduces the economic costs of compliance. It is true that banking leads to larger economic losses from 2012 through 2030 but these are comparatively small. Banking leads to substantially smaller economic losses over the remainder of its existence. With the new safety valve, by 2050, the reduction in real GDP under banking is around half of that which occurs in its absence, 1.6 versus 3.0%. With no safety valve, the 2050 comparison is 1.8 versus 3.0% which is still substantial. Obviously, the longer term

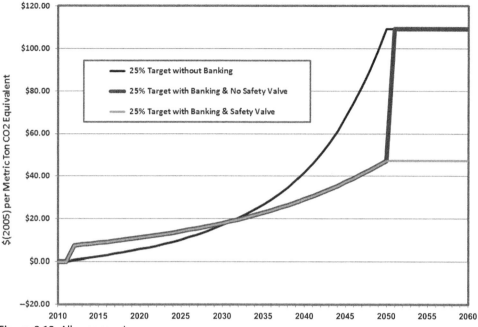

**Figure 8.13** Allowance prices.

benefits of banking depend on what happens post-2050. With price reversion, the 2060 loss in GDP is 2.9% whether or not banking was allowed, 2012–2050. The continuation of the 2050 banking price, 2051 and beyond, reduces this loss to 1.8%. Clearly, long-run policy specifications matter.

There is an interesting finding relating to the mix of abatement with and without banking. Over the period 2012–2050, both policies achieve the same level of cumulative emissions reductions. However, under banking, more of the abatement comes from reductions in coal use and less from petroleum, natural gas and other sources (Table 8.16). With banking, coal prices are higher from the beginning, leading to larger percentage reductions in coal use early on. By taking advantage of the arbitrage opportunity offered by banking, allowance prices then rise by 5% annually. This controls the increases in coal prices and comparatively large percentage reductions in coal use continue to occur, although less elastically.

Without banking, the increases in coal prices start small, leading to smaller reductions in coal use. Subsequently, coal price increases become much, much larger and further reductions in coal use are harder to achieve. This requires more abatement from reductions in the uses of oil and gas and from other emissions-generating activities. By the time the allowance price reaches $109 (2005 dollars) per tonne $CO_2$-e (as compared to $48 with banking), coal demand has fallen by over 90% and has become significantly inelastic, further shifting the burden of abatement to other sources.

**Table 8.15** Macroeconomic impacts (25% target)

| | No Banking | Banking Safety valve | No safety valve |
|---|---|---|---|
| Emissions ($GtCO_2$-e) | | | |
| Cumulative emissions target, 2012–2050 | 241.4 | 241.4 | 241.4 |
| Cumulative emissions outcome, 2051–2060 | 59.1 | 71.8 | 59.1 |
| Allowance prices ($\$(2005)$/tonne $CO_2$ equivalent) | | | |
| 2012 | 1 | 7 | 7 |
| 2050 | 109 | 48 | 48 |
| 2051 and beyond | 109 | 48 | 109 |
| Average % change from base case, 2010–2060 | | | |
| Real GDP | −1.4 | −1.0 | −1.3 |
| Consumption | −0.9 | −0.7 | −0.8 |
| Investment | −2.1 | −1.4 | −1.9 |
| Government | 0.0 | 0.0 | 0.0 |
| Exports | −2.9 | −2.1 | −2.7 |
| Imports | −2.6 | −1.8 | −2.4 |
| GDP prices | 1.4 | 1.0 | 1.2 |
| Consumption | 1.1 | 0.8 | 1.0 |
| Investment | 0.8 | 0.6 | 0.7 |
| Government | 0.6 | 0.4 | 0.5 |
| Exports | 1.6 | 1.2 | 1.4 |
| Imports | 1.1 | 0.8 | 1.0 |
| Household full consumption (goods, services and leisure) | −0.1 | −0.1 | −0.1 |
| Capital stock | −1.2 | −0.9 | −1.1 |
| Labor demand and supply | −0.7 | −0.5 | −0.7 |
| Leisure demand | 0.3 | 0.2 | 0.3 |
| Exchange rate ($\$$/foreign currency) | 1.1 | 0.8 | 1.0 |

Allowance banking gives rise to somewhat larger economic costs in the initial years following enactment. Subsequently, banking with or without safety-valve pricing secures more substantial cost savings. There is strong evidence that banking is preferred to non-banking as a policy covenant. This most certainly is true over the 2010–2060 period reported above. However, it is also true in terms of dynastic welfare over an infinite time horizon as is shown in Figure 8.14. On average, with no safety valve and at mean full wealth, climate policy under banking incurs a marginally smaller net welfare loss, −0.10% versus −0.11%. At half mean full wealth, the comparative figures are −0.16

**Table 8.16** Industry effects (25% target; average % change from base case, 2010–2060)

| | | No banking | | Banking | | | |
| | | Price | Output | With safety valve | | No safety valve | |
| | | | | Price | Output | Price | Output |
|---|---|---|---|---|---|---|---|
| 1 | Agriculture | 7.5 | −8.5 | 4.6 | −5.6 | 6.4 | −7.5 |
| 2 | Metal mining | 2.0 | −2.5 | 1.5 | −1.2 | 1.8 | −2.0 |
| 3 | Coal mining | 358.3 | −61.9 | 208.0 | −63.3 | 309.5 | −65.2 |
| 4 | Petroleum and gas | −2.1 | −0.6 | −1.2 | −0.4 | −1.8 | −0.5 |
| 5 | Non-metallic mining | 2.3 | −4.2 | 1.8 | −3.0 | 2.2 | −3.9 |
| 6 | Construction | 0.8 | −1.5 | 0.6 | −1.0 | 0.7 | −1.4 |
| 7 | Food products | 2.6 | −3.0 | 1.7 | −2.0 | 2.3 | −2.6 |
| 8 | Tobacco products | 1.2 | −1.7 | 0.8 | −1.2 | 1.0 | −1.5 |
| 9 | Textile mill products | 1.6 | −2.6 | 1.1 | −1.8 | 1.4 | −2.4 |
| 10 | Apparel and textiles | 0.9 | −1.1 | 0.7 | −0.8 | 0.8 | −1.0 |
| 11 | Lumber and wood | 1.3 | −2.2 | 0.9 | −1.5 | 1.2 | −2.0 |
| 12 | Furniture and fixtures | 0.9 | −1.6 | 0.7 | −1.1 | 0.9 | −1.5 |
| 13 | Paper products | 1.8 | −2.8 | 1.4 | −2.1 | 1.6 | −2.6 |
| 14 | Printing and publishing | 0.6 | −1.0 | 0.5 | −0.7 | 0.6 | −0.9 |
| 15 | Chemical products | 3.5 | −5.4 | 2.2 | −3.6 | 3.1 | −4.8 |
| 16 | Petroleum refining | 5.1 | −6.4 | 3.7 | −4.7 | 4.7 | −5.9 |
| 17 | Rubber and plastic | 1.9 | −3.5 | 1.3 | −2.6 | 1.7 | −3.2 |
| 18 | Leather products | 1.2 | −1.9 | 0.9 | −1.4 | 1.1 | −1.7 |
| 19 | Stone, clay and glass | 0.8 | −2.0 | −0.1 | −0.6 | 0.5 | −1.5 |
| 20 | Primary metals | 3.8 | −5.2 | 3.2 | −4.1 | 3.7 | −5.0 |
| 21 | Fabricated metals | 1.4 | −3.1 | 1.1 | −2.3 | 1.3 | −2.9 |
| 22 | Industrial machinery | 0.8 | −2.0 | 0.6 | −1.4 | 0.7 | −1.8 |
| 23 | Electronic and electric equipment | 0.8 | −1.8 | 0.6 | −1.2 | 0.7 | −1.6 |
| 24 | Motor vehicles | 1.1 | −2.8 | 0.9 | −2.0 | 1.0 | −2.6 |
| 25 | Other transportation equipment | 0.7 | −0.7 | 0.5 | −0.5 | 0.6 | −0.7 |
| 26 | Instruments | 0.4 | −1.2 | 0.4 | −0.8 | 0.4 | −1.1 |
| 27 | Miscellaneous manufacturing | 1.0 | −1.6 | 0.7 | −1.0 | 0.9 | −1.5 |
| 28 | Transport and warehouse | 1.2 | −2.7 | 0.9 | −2.0 | 1.1 | −2.5 |
| 29 | Communications | 0.6 | −1.4 | 0.4 | −1.0 | 0.5 | −1.2 |
| 30 | Electric utilities | 6.5 | −4.8 | 5.5 | −4.1 | 6.3 | −4.7 |
| 31 | Gas utilities | 13.9 | −11.4 | 8.9 | −7.7 | 12.3 | −10.2 |
| 32 | Trade | 0.8 | −1.6 | 0.6 | −1.1 | 0.7 | −1.4 |
| 33 | FIRE | 0.7 | −1.5 | 0.5 | −1.1 | 0.6 | −1.4 |
| 34 | Services | 0.6 | −1.3 | 0.5 | −0.9 | 0.6 | −1.2 |
| 35 | Government enterprises | 0.9 | −1.7 | 0.7 | −1.2 | 0.8 | −1.5 |

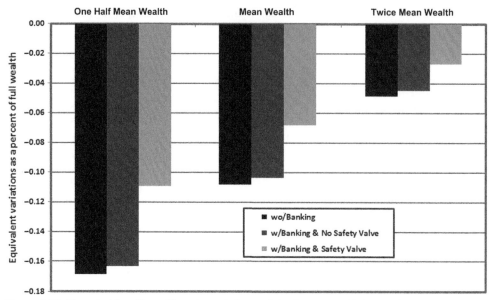

**Figure 8.14** Household welfare effects (population weighed average, 25% target).

versus −0.17% and, at twice mean full wealth, the welfare losses under banking are −0.04% of lifetime expenditure compared to −0.05% without it. With safety valve pricing post-2050, the improvements in welfare losses become more substantial. At mean full wealth, it is −0.07 versus −0.11%, at one half mean full wealth, it is −0.11 versus −0.17% and, at twice mean full wealth, it is −0.03 versus −0.05%.

Banking with or without safety valve pricing introduces a measure of progressivity in an otherwise regressive policy. In Figure 8.14, we observe the spread increasing with falling wealth (i.e. moving right to left) indicating that the benefits of banking increase as full wealth decreases across household types. We note, however, that the percentage welfare improvements from banking favor wealthier households. The absolute benefits of banking also increase as full wealth decreases within a household type. That is, the spread increases with falling wealth — twice mean to mean and then mean to half mean — for a given reference household. These findings certainly add merit to the inclusion of banking as a matter of policy.

## 8.6 CONCLUSIONS

Econometric general equilibrium modeling is a very important addition to economic methodologies for evaluating energy and environmental policies. The traditional approach originated by Johansen is based on calibration of the models of household and producer behavior to a single data point. This useful simplification is a severe limitation in the application of these models to the analysis of energy and environmental policies.

The estimates of the costs of these policies are dramatically increased by ignoring the possibilities for substitution among inputs and induced changes in technology in responding to policy changes.

Econometric general equilibrium models retain long-established principles of microeconomic theory in modeling producer and consumer behavior. Exact aggregation over models for individual households makes it possible to incorporate demographic characteristics that reflect the enormous heterogeneity of household behavior. The intertemporal price system embodied in IGEM since its introduction by Jorgenson and Wilcoxen (1998) is essential to overcome the Lucas (1976) critique of macroeconometric models, which applies equally to CGE models.

The progress of econometric general equilibrium modeling has been impeded by the lack of appropriate national accounting data, except for the US. With the completion of the EU KLEMS project in 2008 and the establishment of the World KLEMS Initiative in 2010 (http://www.worldklems.net), this obstacle has been substantially reduced. These data are now available in the official statistics for many countries and are updated regularly for countries included in the EU KLEMS project.

The industry-level production accounts employed by Jorgenson *et al.* (2005) and employed in IGEM are consistent with the *2008 System of National Accounts* (United Nations *et al.*, 2009) and the new architecture for the US national accounts proposed by Jorgenson *et al.* (2006). Using the econometric methodology presented in this chapter, it is possible to develop econometric general equilibrium models for the major advanced countries of the world. Data will soon be available to extend this approach to 40 or more economies, including the leading emerging economies like China and India.

The new version of IGEM for evaluation of alternative climate policies employed by the US Environmental Protection Agency (2000, 2010) incorporates a new model of household behavior developed by Jorgenson and Slesnick (2008). This model successfully incorporates labor—leisure choices, as well as choices among goods and services, into the evaluation of climate policy. The model also incorporates demographic characteristics of individual households that reflect the heterogeneity of the US population.

Like the models of household behavior used in previous versions of IGEM, the Jorgenson—Slesnick model encompasses all the restrictions implied by the theory of consumer behavior. The new model also satisfies the conditions required for exact aggregation, so that we construct a model of aggregate consumer behavior for IGEM by aggregating over individual households. We then recover money measures of the impact on household welfare of changes in climate policy.

We provide results for 244 different types of households distinguished by demographic characteristics. We confirm the findings of previous studies of climate policy, including the study of a carbon tax by Jorgenson *et al.* (1997b), that the impact of climate policy would be regressive and negative, but is a relatively small effect. Overall, our findings imply that incorporating labor—leisure choice into the evaluation of alternative climate policies is a very worthwhile addition to policy analysis. This can be done while preserving the well-established framework for policy evaluation introduced by Jorgenson *et al.* (1997b).

An important goal for future research on econometric general equilibrium modeling is the development of econometric methods for inferences about the outcomes of CGE models. These would include confidence intervals and tests of hypotheses based on measures of production, like GDP and levels of industrial output, and measures of individual and social welfare. Jorgenson *et al.* in Chapter 17 of this Handbook describe how this can be done and apply the results to outcomes from the IGEM model presented in this chapter.

## REFERENCES

Ayres, R.U., Kneese, A.V., 1969. Production, consumption, and externalities. Am. Econ. Rev. 59, 282–297.

Barro, R.J., Sala-i-Martin, X., 2004. Economic Growth, second ed. MIT Press, Cambridge, MA.

Bergman, L., 2005. CGE modeling of environmental policy and resource management. In: Maler, K.-G., Vincent, J.R. (Eds), Handbook of Environmental Economics, vol. 3. Elsevier, Amsterdam, pp. 1273–1306.

British Petroleum, 2011. BP Energy Outlook 2030. British Petroleum Global, London.

Brock, W.A., Scott Taylor, M., 2005. Economic growth and the environment: a review of theory and empirics. In: Aghion, P., Durlauf, S.M. (Eds), Handbook of Economic Growth, vol. 1. Elsevier, Amsterdam, pp. 1749–1821.

Browning, M., Hansen, L.P., Heckman, J.J., 1999. Micro data and general equilibrium models. In: Taylor, J.B., Woodford, M. (Eds), Handbook of Macroeconomics, vol. 1A. North-Holland, Amsterdam, pp. 543–637.

Bureau of Economic Analysis, 2007. US benchmark input-output accounts, *Survey of Current Business*. October, 19-48, Available at http://www.bea.gov/scb/pdf/2007/10%20October/1007_benchmark_io.pdf.

Bureau of Labor Statistics, 2012a. Consumer Expenditure Survey. US Department of Labor, Washington, DC. Available at http://www.bls.gov/cex/.

Bureau of Labor Statistics, 2012b. Consumer Price Index. US Department of Labor, Washington, DC. Available at http://www.bls.gov/cpi/.

Bureau of the Census, 2008. 2008 National Population Projections. US Department of Commerce, Washington, DC. Available at http://www.census.gov/population/www/projections/natproj.html.

Cass, D., 1965. Optimum growth in an aggregative model of capital accumulation. Rev. Econ. Stud. 32, 233–240.

Congressional Budget Office, 2010a. The Budget and Economic Outlook: Fiscal Years 2010 to 2020. US Government Printing Office, Washington, DC.

Congressional Budget Office, 2010b. The Long-Term Budget Outlook. US Government Printing Office, Washington, DC. Available at http://www.cbo.gov/doc.cfm?index=11579.

Dasgupta, P.S., Heal, G.M., 1979. Economic Theory and Exhaustible Resources. Cambridge University Press, Cambridge.

Dixon, P.B., Parmenter, B.R., 1996. Computable general equilibrium modeling for policy analysis and forecasting. In: Amman, H.M., Kendrick, D.A., Rust, J. (Eds), Handbook of Computational Economics, vol. 1. North-Holland, Amsterdam, pp. 3–86.

Dixon, P. B., and Rimmer, M. T., 2012. Johansen's legacy to CGE modeling: originator and guiding light for 50 years. J. Policy Model. forthcoming.

Dixon, P.B., Parmenter, B.R., Sutton, J., Vincent, D.P., 1982. ORANI: A Multisectoral Model of the Australian Economy. North-Holland, Amsterdam.

Dixon, P.B., Parmenter, B.R., Powell, A.A., Wilcoxen, P.J., 1992. Notes and Problems in Applied General Equilibrium Modeling. North-Holland, Amsterdam.

Energy Information Administration, 2010. Annual Energy Outlook 2010. US Department of Energy, Washington, DC. Available at http://www.eia.doe.gov/oiaf/archive/aeo10/index.html.

Environmental Protection Agency, 2000. Guidelines for Preparing Economic Analyses. US Environmental Protection Administration, Office of the Administrator, Washington, DC.

Environmental Protection Agency, 2010a. Guidelines for Preparing Economic Analyses. US Environmental Protection Agency, National Center for Environmental Economics, Washington, DC.

Environmental Protection Agency, 2010b. Inventory of US Greenhouse Gas Emissions and Sinks: 1990−2008. US Environmental Protection Agency, Office of Atmospheric Programs, Washington, DC. Available at http://www.epa.gov/climatechange/emissions/usgginv_archive.html.

Environmental Protection Agency, 2012a. Climate Change—Climate Economics. US Environmental Protection Agency, Washington, DC. Available at http://www.epa.gov/climatechange/economics/economicanalyses.html.

Environmental Protection Agency, 2012b. Climate Economic Modeling. US Environmental Protection Agency, Washington, DC. Available at http://www.epa.gov/climatechange/economics/modeling.html.

Fixler, D., Jaditz, T., 2002. An Examination of the Difference between the CPI and the PCE Deflator. BLS Working Paper 361. US Department of Labor, Washington, DC.

Frisch, R., 1959. A complete scheme for computing all direct and cross demand elasticities in a model with many sectors. Econometrica 27, 177−196.

Goettle, R.J., Fawcett, A.A., 2009. The structural effects of cap and trade climate policy. Energy Econ. 31 (Suppl. 2), S244−S253.

Holmøy, E., 2012. The development and use of CGE models in Norway. J. Policy Model. forthcoming.

International Monetary Fund, 2010. World Economic Outlook Available at http://www.imf.org/external/pubs/ft/weo/2010/02/index.htm.

Jin, H., Jorgenson, D.W., 2010. Econometric Modeling of technical change. J. .Econ. 152, 205−219.

Johansen, L., 1974. A Multi-Sectoral Study of Economic Growth, second ed. North-Holland, Amsterdam (first ed. 1960).

Jorgenson, D.W., Slesnick, D.T., 2008. Consumption and labor supply. J. Econ. 147, 326−335.

Jorgenson, D.W., Wilcoxen, P.J., 1998. Environmental regulation and US economic growth. In: Jorgenson, D.W. (Ed.), Energy, the Environment, and Economic Growth. MIT Press, Cambridge, MA, pp. 157−194 (originally published in 1990).

Jorgenson, D.W., Yun, K.-Y., 2001. Lifting the Burden: Tax Reform, the Cost of Capital and US Economic Growth. MIT Press, Cambridge, MA.

Jorgenson, D.W., Lau, L.J., Stoker, T.M., 1997a. The transcendental logarithmic model of aggregate consumer behavior. In: Jorgenson, D.W. (Ed.), Aggregate Consumer Behavior. MIT Press, Cambridge, MA, pp. 203−356 (originally published in 1982).

Jorgenson, D.W., Slesnick, D.T., Wilcoxen, P.J., 1997b. Carbon taxes and economic welfare. In: Jorgenson, D.W. (Ed.), Measuring Social Welfare. MIT Press, Cambridge, MA, pp. 361−400 (originally published in 1992).

Jorgenson, D.W., Ho, M.S., Stiroh, Kevin J., 2005. Information Technology and the American Growth Resurgence. MIT Press, Cambridge, MA.

Jorgenson, D.W., Landefeld, J.S., Nordhaus, W.D. (Eds), 2006. A New Architecture for the US National Accounts. Chicago University Press, Chicago, IL.

Jorgenson, D.W., Goettle, R.J., Ho, M.S., Wilcoxen, P.J., 2009a. Cap and trade climate policy and US economic adjustments. J. Policy Model. 31, 362−381.

Jorgenson, D.W., Goettle, R., Ho, M.S., Slesnick, D.T., Wilcoxen, P.J., 2009b. Analyzing Environmental Policies with IGEM, an Intertemporal General Equilibrium Model of US Growth and the Environment. US Environmental Protection, Office of Atmospheric Programs, Washington, DC. Available at http://www.epa.gov/climatechange/economics/modeling.html#intertemporal.

Jorgenson, D.W., Goettle, R.J., Ho, M.S., Slesnick, D.T., Wilcoxen, P.J., 2010. The distributional impact of climate policy. B.E. J. Econ. Anal.and Policy 10 (2), 1–26.

Jorgenson, Dale W. (Ed.), 1997a. Aggregate Consumer Behavior. MIT Press, Cambridge, MA.

Jorgenson, D.W. (Ed.), 1997b. Measuring Social Welfare. MIT Press, Cambridge, MA.

Jorgenson, D.W. (Ed.), 1998a. Econometric General Equilibrium Modeling. MIT Press, Cambridge, MA.

Jorgenson, D.W. (Ed.), 1998b. Energy, the Environment, and Economic Growth. MIT Press, Cambridge, MA.

Jorgenson, D.W. (Ed.), 2000. Econometric Modeling of Producer Behavior. MIT Press, Cambridge, MA.

Jorgenson, D.W. (Ed.), 2009. The Economics of Productivity. Edward Elgar, Northampton, MA.

Kneese, A.V., Ayres, R.U., d'Arge, R.C., 1970. Economics and the Environment: a Materials Balance Approach. Johns Hopkins University Press, Baltimore, MD.

Koopmans, T.C., 1967. Objectives, constraints, and outcomes in optimal growth. Econometrica 35, 1–15.

Lau, L.J., 1977. Existence Conditions for Aggregate Demand Functions: The Case of Multiple Indexes. Technical Report 248. Stanford, Institute for Mathematical Studies in the Social Sciences, Stanford University, Stanford, CA.

Leontief, W., 1951. The Structure of the American Economy, second ed. Oxford University Press, New York (first ed. 1941).

Leontief, W. (Ed.), 1953. Studies in the Structure of the American Economy. Oxford University Press, New York.

Lucas Jr., R.E., 1976. Econometric policy evaluation: a critique. In: Brunner, K., Meltzer, A.H. (Eds), The Phillips Curve and Labor Markets. Carnegie-Rochester Conference Series. Elsevier, Amsterdam, pp. 19–46.

Maler, K.-G., 1974. Environmental Economics: A Theoretical Inquiry. Johns Hopkins University Press, Baltimore, MD.

Maler, K.-G., 1976. Macroeconomic aspects of environmental policy. In: Mills, E.S. (Ed.), Economic Analysis of Environmental Problems. Columbia University Press, New York, pp. 27–56.

McKibbin, W.J., Wilcoxen, P.J., 1999. The theoretical and empirical structure of the G-Cubed model. Econ. Model. 16, 123–148.

Nordhaus, W.D., 2008. A Question of Balance: Weighing the Options on Global Warming Policies. Yale University Press, New Haven, CT.

Nordhaus, W.D., 2010. Economic aspects of global warming in a post-Copenhagen environment. Proc. Natl. Acad. Sci. 107, 11721–11726.

Samuelson, P.A., 1951. Abstract of a theorem concerning substitutability in open Leontief models. In: Koopmans, T.C. (Ed.), Activity Analysis of Production and Allocation. Wiley, New York, pp. 142–146.

Scarf, H.A., 1973. Computation of Economic Equilibria. Yale University Press, New Haven, CT.

Schipper, L., Meyers, S., Howarth, R.B., Steiner, R., 1992. Energy Efficiency and Human Activity. Cambridge University Press, Cambridge.

Solow, R.M., 1956. A contribution to the theory of economic growth. Q. J. Econ. 70, 65–94.

Solow, R.M., 1974a. The economics of resources or the resources of economics. Am. Econ. Rev. 64 (2), 1–14.

Solow, R.M., 1974b. Intergenerational equity and exhaustible resources. Rev. Econ. Stud. 41, 29–45.

Solow, R.M., 2005. Reflections on growth theory. In: Aghion, P., Durlauf, S.M. (Eds), Handbook of Economic Growth, Vol. 1. Elsevier, Amsterdam, pp. 3–10.

Teplin, A.M., Antoniewicz, R., Hume McIntosh, S., Palumbo, M.G., Solomon, G., Mead, C.I., Moses, K., Moulton, B., 2006. Integrated macroeconomic accounts for the United States: draft SNA-USA. In: Jorgenson, D.W., Landefeld, J.S., Nordhaus, W.D. (Eds), A New Architecture for the US National Accounts. Chicago University Press, Chicago, IL, pp. 471–540.

United Nations, Commission of the European Communities, International Monetary Fund, Organization for Economic Cooperation and Development, the World Bank, 2009. 2008 System of National Accounts. United Nations, New York.

Uzawa, H., 1975. Optimal investment in social overhead capital. In: Mills, E.S. (Ed.), Economic Analysis of Environmental Problems. Columbia University Press, New York, pp. 9–22.

Uzawa, H., 1988. Optimality, Equilibrium, and Growth. Tokyo University Press, Tokyo.

# CHAPTER 9

# Computable General Equilibrium Modeling of Environmental Issues in Australia: Economic Impacts of an Emissions Trading Scheme

**Philip D. Adams\*, Brian R. Parmenter\*\*,[†]**
\*Centre of Policy Studies, Monash University
\*\*Queensland Competition Authority

## Abstract

A key distinguishing characteristic of computable general equilibrium (CGE) modeling in Australia is its orientation to providing inputs to the policy-formation process. Policy makers require detail. They want to be able to identify convincingly which industries, which occupations, which regions and which households would benefit or lose from policy changes, and when the benefits or losses might be expected to flow. In this chapter, we explain how the necessary level of detail can be provided, using as an example analysis that was undertaken by Centre of Policy Studies (CoPS) and Frontier Economics of the potential economic impacts of a carbon price on the Australian economy. The Australian carbon price framework is assumed to be part of a global emissions trading scheme (ETS). Over time, the global ETS becomes the dominant greenhouse abatement policy for all countries including Australia. It sets the price for carbon permits and allocates the number of permits available to each country. A number of key findings emerge from the CGE simulations of the effects of the ETS policy. (i) Domestic abatement falls well short of targeted abatement, requiring significant amounts of permits to be imported. (ii) Despite the requirement for deep cuts in emissions, the ETS reduces Australia's GDP by only about 1.1% relative to the base case in 2030. The negative impact on real household consumption (the preferred measure of national welfare) is somewhat greater, reflecting the need to import permits. (iii) The national macroeconomic impacts of the ETS might be described as modest in the context of the policy task. However, this does not carry through to the industry and state/territory levels where some industries and regions prove particularly vulnerable in terms of potential lost employment. The need for detail is highlighted throughout the analysis. For example, a suitably detailed treatment of electricity supply is provided by linking CoPS' CGE model with Frontier's detailed bottom-up model of the stationary energy sector. Similarly, necessary detail on the effects of the global ETS on Australia's international trading conditions is provided by linking with a multicountry model.

## Keywords

Emissions trading, Australia, CGE modeling

## JEL classification codes

C68, Q52, Q58

---

[†] During drafting of this chapter, Brian Parmenter was working as a consultant with Frontier Economics. The chapter draws on collaborative work undertaken then between the Centre of Policy Studies and Frontier.

*Handbook of CGE Modeling - Vol. 1 SET*
ISSN 2211-6885, http://dx.doi.org/10.1016/B978-0-444-59568-3.00009-2

© 2013 Elsevier B.V.
All rights reserved.

## 9.1 INTRODUCTION

The key distinguishing characteristic of computable general equilibrium (CGE) modeling in Australia is its orientation to providing inputs to the policy-formation process. This reflects the history of the funding of CGE research. Australia's best-known CGE modeling group — the team now located in the Centre of Policy Studies (CoPS) at Monash University — was originally established in 1975 by the Australian Government under an interagency arrangement — the IMPACT Project — administered by the (then) Industry Commission (now the Productivity Commission). Since then, Australian government departments, principally the Productivity Commission and the Australian Bureau of Agricultural and Resource Economics and Sciences (ABARES), have continued to support CGE research and have maintained substantial in-house modeling capabilities. Universities, principally Monash University, have played an important role in the development of CGE models in Australia, but the focus of the work has always been as much on practical application of the models as on contributing to the academic literature.

Policy makers require detail. They want to be able to identify convincingly which industries, which occupations, which regions and which households would benefit or lose from policy changes, and when the benefits or losses might be expected to flow. Economic theory alone, or stylized general equilibrium analysis, is not well suited to meeting information demands at this level of detail. However, combining the theory in a CGE framework with disaggregated input–output data, labor force survey statistics, data on the sector composition of the regional economies, and household income and expenditure data provides the tool that policy makers require.

Starting in the early 1990s, greenhouse gas emissions, global warming and climate change emerged as prime policy concerns in Australia, culminating in 2007 with the Australian government's decision to ratify the Kyoto Protocol and to attempt to introduce a greenhouse gas emissions trading scheme (ETS). CGE modeling has played a prominent role in informing Australia's emissions policy debate.[1]

As in earlier policy debates (e.g. about trade liberalization), detail has been a key issue for economic modelers engaged in the emissions debate. In this context, modelers face a number of questions relating to model, data and simulation design.

- Stationary energy accounts for more than 50% of Australia's greenhouse gas emissions. At what level of detail must the stationary energy sector be modeled for the effects of policy on its emissions to be captured adequately? And is the required level of detail better provided by augmenting the representation of the sector inside the CGE model or by linking the CGE model with a detailed bottom-up model of the stationary energy sector?

---

[1] Academic contributions started with Dixon *et al.* (1990) and Dixon and Johnson (1990), followed by McDougall and Dixon (1996), and McKibbin and Pearce (1996).

- Investment in electricity generation (and many other branches of heavy industry, including energy-intensive minerals processing) is typically lumpy, not smooth. Is it necessary to include this lumpiness explicitly in CGE computations of the effects of climate change policy? To what aspects of the results does lumpiness matter?
- Concern about greenhouse gas emissions centers on a global externality problem. Does this mean that the consequences of emissions policy can only be investigated using a global model? In any case, the domestic effects of a particular country's policy will depend on what other countries do. If a single-country model is used to analyze the domestic policy effects, how can the effects of foreign countries' policies be included?
- Emissions policy is policy for the long term, with the underlying global externality and many abatement options involving complex dynamics. It is now common for CGE models to have dynamic or quasidynamic structures, but what dynamic mechanisms are required to make a meaningful input to decisions about emissions policy? For example, do we need agents with full intertemporal optimization or will recursive dynamics do?
- The possibility of international emissions leakage is a problem that proponents of unilateral emissions policy must face. What representation of a country's emissions-intensive trade-exposed industries (EITEIs) is required to handle this?
- The energy consumption of end users (including households) is conditioned by their investment decisions about energy-using equipment (appliances, vehicles, etc.) — another aspect of the dynamics of emissions policy. National-accounts-based models do not handle this well as far as households are concerned. How should energy usage be treated in the household consumption specification of a model to be used for the analysis of emissions policy?
- Emissions-intensive industries, especially in the energy sector, tend to be geographically concentrated, due mainly to the availability of primary energy sources — fossil or renewable. Hence, emissions policy could have significant regional effects. How can policy models inform policy makers about such effects?
- Carbon taxes and most ETSs would raise large amounts of government revenue and increase consumer prices. What effect will the recycling of this revenue have on the efficiency costs of the policy and on income distribution? To deal adequately with these issues, a policy model will need a detailed representation of the country's fiscal system and the ability to identify the income-distribution consequences of policy options.

In this chapter, how these issues have been handled by Australian CGE modelers is explained. This is done using an example: the analysis of the potential impacts on the Australian economy of a carbon price policy outlined in the Government's *Carbon Pollution Reduction Scheme Green Paper* (Department of Climate Change, 2008;

Department of Treasury, 2008) and the Garnaut Climate Change Review (Garnaut, 2008). The policy is assumed to apply as part of a global ETS. Over time, the global ETS becomes the dominant emissions abatement policy for all countries, including Australia. It sets the price for carbon permits and allocates the number of permits available to each country.

The analysis relies on a series of applications of three CGE models developed in Australia: the Global Trade and Environment Model (GTEM) (Pant, 2007), the G-Cubed model (McKibbin and Wilcoxen, 1998) and the Monash Multi-Regional Forecasting model (MMRF) (Adams *et al.*, 2011).[2] GTEM and G-Cubed are multi-country models. MMRF is a single-country multiregional model of Australia and its six states and two territories.

Much of the modeling of the global aspects of the ETS was undertaken using the GTEM model. Information from GTEM was then used to inform simulations of MMRF.[3] The role of MMRF was to supply estimates of the effects of the scheme on the Australian economy at the level of detail required by the policy makers. A key dimension was detail about the electricity system. To cover this, MMRF was linked to a specialized bottom-up model of the Australian electricity system. In the original work commissioned by the Treasury and the Garnaut Review, the electricity modeling was conducted by the consulting firm McLennan, Magasanik and Associates (MMA), using their probabilistic simulation model of the electricity market.[4] Subsequent studies were undertaken with the consulting firm Frontier Economics, using Frontier's *WHIRLYGIG* model of electricity supply (Frontier Economics, 2009). The latter studies also contained updated base-case assumptions and updated views about growth of Australia's trading partners with and without a global ETS. The results discussed in this Chapter are from these latter simulations.

The rest of the chapter is organized as follows. A brief general description of MMRF is given in Section 9.2. In Section 9.3 the enhancements of the general form of the model that were necessary for the ETS modeling are described. Specific items discussed are:

- linking with GTEM and with the detailed electricity model;
- modeling the free allocation of permits to shield emissions-intensive, trade-exposed industries during the period of transition to a full global ETS;
- modeling abatement of non-combustion emissions in response to an emissions price;
- land—land substitution in agriculture and forestry.

---

[2] MMRF and GTEM are solved using GEMPACK software (Harrison and Pearson, 1996). An overview of the current version of GEMPACK is given in Harrison and Pearson (2002).

[3] G-Cubed was broadly calibrated to the GTEM base-case scenario and provided comparative global cost estimates for the policy scenarios based on different rate-of-adjustment assumptions for global capital markets.

[4] An overview of MMA's suite of models covering the National Electricity Market (NEM), South West Interconnected System (SWIS) and the Darwin Katherine Interconnected System (DKIS) is given in MMA (2008).

Aspects of simulation design are given in Section 9.4 (the base case) and Section 9.5 (the policy simulation), including the exogenous shocks that drive the policy simulations. The effects of the shocks are given in Section 9.6 as deviations between the values of variables in the policy simulation and their values in the base case. The discussion of results in Section 9.6 focuses on explaining outcomes in a sequential way. National outcomes are dealt with first, then results for states and territories, and finally results for substate regions. The rationalization of macro results draws on a stylized model containing MMRF's principal macro mechanisms. An Appendix contains a description of the stylized model. Concluding remarks are in Section 9.7.

## 9.2 MMRF

### 9.2.1 Overview

MMRF is a dynamic, multisector, multiregion model of Australia. The current version of the model distinguishes 58 industries (Table 9.1), 63 products produced by the 58 industries, eight states/territories and 56 substate regions. At the state/territory level, it is

**Table 9.1** Industries in MMRF[a]

| Name | Description of major activity |
|---|---|
| 1. Sheep and beef cattle | Sheep and cattle production |
| 2. Dairy cattle | Raw milk and dairy cattle |
| 3. Other livestock | Activities associated with other animals |
| 4. Grains | Grains production |
| 5. Other agriculture | Other primary agricultural production |
| 6. Agricultural services, fishing, hunting | Agricultural services, fishing, hunting |
| 7. Forestry | Logging and forestry services |
| 8. Coal mining | Mining of coal |
| 9. Oil mining | Mining of oil |
| 10. Gas mining | Production of natural gas at well |
| 11. Iron ore mining | Mining of iron ore |
| 12. Non-ferrous ore mining | Mining of ore other than iron |
| 13. Other mining | Other mining activity |
| 14. Meat and meat products | Processed food related to animal |
| 15. Other food, beverages and tobacco | Other food and drink products |
| 16. Textiles, clothing and footwear | Textiles, clothing and footwear |
| 17. Wood products | Manufacture of wood products |
| 18. Paper products | Manufacture of paper products |
| 19. Printing and publishing | Printing and publishing |
| 20. Petroleum products | Manufacture of petroleum (refinery) products |
| 21. Basic chemicals | Manufacture of basic chemicals and paints |
| 22. Rubber and plastic products | Manufacture of plastic and rubber products |

*(Continued)*

**Table 9.1** Industries in MMRF[a]—cont'd

| Name | Description of major activity |
|---|---|
| 23. Non-metal construction products | Non-metallic building products excl. cement |
| 24. Cement | Manufacture of cement |
| 25. Iron and steel | Manufacture of primary iron and steel |
| 26. Alumina | Manufacture of alumina |
| 27. Aluminum | Manufacture of aluminum |
| 28. Other non-ferrous metals | Manufacture of other non-ferrous metals |
| 29. Metal products | Manufacture of metal products |
| 30. Motor vehicles and parts | Manufacture of motor vehicles and parts |
| 31. Other manufacturing | Manufacturing non elsewhere classified |
| 32. Electricity generation-coal | Electricity generation from coal |
| 33. Electricity generation-gas | Electricity generation from natural gas |
| 34. Electricity generation-oil products | Electricity generation from oil products |
| 35. Electricity generation-nuclear | Electricity generation from nuclear |
| 36. Electricity generation-hydro | Electricity generation from hydro |
| 37. Electricity generation-other | Electricity generation from other renewable |
| 38. Electricity supply | Distribution of electricity; generator to user |
| 39. Gas supply | Urban distribution of natural gas |
| 40. Water supply | Provision of water and sewerage services |
| 41. Construction services | Residential and other construction services |
| 42. Trade services | Provision of wholesale and retail trade services |
| 43. Accommodation, hotels and cafes | Accommodation, meal and drink services |
| 44. Road passenger transport | Provision of road transport services — passenger |
| 45. Road freight transport | Provision of road transport services — freight |
| 46. Rail passenger transport | Provision of rail transport services — passenger |
| 47. Rail freight transport | Provision of rail transport services — freight |
| 48. Water, pipeline and transport services | Provision of water transport services |
| 49. Air transport | Provision of air transport services |
| 50. Communication services | Provision of communication services |
| 51. Financial services | Provision of financial services |
| 52. Business services | Provision of business services |
| 53. Dwelling services | Provision of dwelling services |
| 54. Public services | Government and community services |
| 55. Other services | Provision of services not elsewhere classified |
| 56. Private transport services | Provision of services to households from the stock of motor vehicles |
| 57. Private electricity equipment services | Provision of services to households from the stock of electrical equipment |
| 58. Private heating services | Provision of services to households from the stock of heating equipment |

[a]For most of the industries identified in this table there is an obvious correspondence to one or more standard categories in the Australian and New Zealand Standard Industrial Classification (ANZSIC), 2006 version. The exceptions are: industries 32–38, which together comprise ANZSIC 26 *Electricity Supply*; industry 53, which is equivalent to the *Ownership of dwellings* industry in the industrial classification of the official Input/output statistics; and industries 56–58, which relate to the provision of services from the private stocks of motor vehicles, electrical equipment (not heating) and heating equipment.

a fully specified bottom-up system of interacting regional economies. A top-down approach is used to estimate the effects of the policy at the substate level.

Of the 58 industries, three produce primary fuels (coal, oil and gas), one produces refined fuel (petroleum products), six generate electricity and one supplies electricity to final customers. The six generation industries are defined according to primary source of fuel: *Electricity-coal* includes all coal-fired generation technologies; *Electricity-gas* includes all plants using turbines, cogeneration and combined cycle technologies driven by burning gas; *Electricity-oil products* covers all liquid-fuel generators; *Electricity-hydro* covers hydro generation; and *Electricity-other* covers the remaining forms of renewable generation from biomass, biogas, wind, etc. Nuclear power generation is not currently used in Australia, but *Electricity-nuclear* is included and could be triggered, if desired, at a specified emissions price.

Apart from *Grains* (industry 4) and *Petroleum products* (industry 20), industries produce single products. *Grains* produces grains for animal and human consumption and biofuel used as feedstock by *Petroleum products*. *Petroleum products* produces gasoline, (including gasoline-based biofuel blends), diesel (including diesel-based biofuel blends), LPG, aviation fuel and other refinery products (mainly heating oil).

## 9.2.2 General equilibrium core

### 9.2.2.1 Nature of markets

MMRF determines regional supplies and demands of commodities through optimizing behavior of agents in competitive markets. Optimizing behavior also determines industry demands for labor and capital. Labor supply at the national level is determined by demographic factors, while national capital supply responds to rates of return. Labor and capital can cross regional borders in response to relative regional employment opportunities and relative rates of return.

The assumption of competitive markets implies equality between the basic price (i.e. the price received by the producer) and marginal cost in each regional sector. Demand is assumed to equal supply in all markets other than the labor market (where excess-supply conditions can hold). The government intervenes in markets by imposing *ad valorem* sales taxes on commodities. This places wedges between the prices paid by purchasers and the basic prices received by producers. The model recognizes margin commodities (e.g. retail trade and road transport) that are required for the movement of a commodities from producers to the purchasers. The costs of the margins are included in purchasers' prices of goods and services.

### 9.2.2.2 Demands for inputs to be used in the production of commodities

MMRF recognizes two broad categories of inputs: intermediate inputs and primary factors. Firms in each regional sector are assumed to choose the mix of inputs that minimizes the costs of production for their levels of output. They are constrained in their choices by a three-level nested production technology. At the first level, intermediate-input bundles and a primary-factor bundle are used in fixed proportions to output.[5] These bundles are formed at the second level. Following Armington (1969), intermediate-input bundles are combinations of domestic goods and goods imported from overseas. The primary-factor bundle is a combination of labor, capital and land. At the third level, inputs of domestic goods are formed as combinations of goods sourced from each of the eight domestic regions and the input of labor is formed as a combination of inputs from nine occupational categories.

### 9.2.2.3 Domestic final demand: household, investment and government

In each region, the household buys bundles of goods to maximize a utility function subject to an expenditure constraint. The bundles are combinations of imported and domestic goods, with domestic goods being combinations of goods from each domestic region. A Keynesian consumption function is usually used to determine aggregate household expenditure as a function of household disposable income (HDI).

Capital creators for each regional sector combine inputs to form units of capital. In choosing these inputs, they minimize costs subject to a technology similar to that used for current production, with the main difference being that they do not use primary factors directly.

State/territory governments and the Federal government demand commodities from each region. In MMRF, there are several ways of handling these government demands, including:

- by a rule such as moving government expenditures with aggregate household expenditure, domestic absorption or GDP;
- as an instrument to accommodate an exogenously determined target such as a required level of government budget deficit;
- exogenous determination.

### 9.2.2.4 Foreign demand (international exports)

MMRF adopts the ORANI[6] specification of foreign demand. Each export-oriented sector in each state or territory faces its own downward-sloping foreign demand curve. Thus, a shock that reduces the unit costs of an export sector will increase the quantity exported, but reduce the foreign currency price. By assuming that the foreign demand schedules are specific to product and region of production, the

---

[5] A miscellaneous input category, *Other costs*, is also included and required in fixed proportion to output. The price of *Other costs* is indexed to the price of private consumption. It is assumed that the income from *Other costs* accrues to the government.

[6] MMRF and MONASH (Dixon and Rimmer, 2002) have evolved from the Australian ORANI model (Dixon et al., 1977, 1982).

model allows for differential movements in foreign currency prices across domestic regions.

### 9.2.2.5 Regional labor markets

The response of regional labor markets to policy shocks depends on the treatment of three key variables — regional labor supplies, regional unemployment rates and regional wage differentials. The main alternative treatments are:

- to set regional labor supplies and unemployment rates exogenously and determine regional wage differentials endogenously;
- to set regional wage differentials and regional unemployment rates exogenously and determine regional labor supplies endogenously (via interstate migration or changes in regional participation rates);
- to set regional labor supplies and wage differentials exogenously and determine regional unemployment rates endogenously.

The second treatment is the one adopted for the ETS simulations reported in this chapter, with regional participation rates exogenous. Under this treatment, workers move freely (and instantaneously) across state borders in response to changes in relative regional unemployment rates. With regional wage rates indexed to the national wage rate, regional employment is demand determined.

### 9.2.2.6 Physical capital accumulation

Investment undertaken in year $t$ is assumed to become operational at the start of year $t+1$. Under this assumption, capital in industry $i$ in region $q$ accumulates according to:

$$K_{i,q}(t+1) = (1 - DEP_{i,q}) \times K_{i,q}(t) + Y_{i,q}(t), \tag{9.1}$$

where $K_{i,q}(t)$ is the quantity of capital available in industry $i$ in region $q$ at the start of year $t$, $Y_{i,q}(t)$ is the quantity of new capital created in industry $i$ in region $q$ during year $t$ and $DEP_{i,q}$ is the rate of depreciation for industry $i$ in region $q$. Given a starting value for capital in $t=0$, and with a mechanism for explaining investment, equation (9.1) traces out the time paths of industries' capital stocks.

Following the approach taken in the MONASH model (Dixon and Rimmer, 2002, section 16), investment in year $t$ is explained via a mechanism of the form:

$$\frac{K_{i,q}(t+1)}{K_{i,q}(t)} = F_{i,q}\left[\frac{EROR_{i,q}(t)}{RROR_{i,q}(t)}\right], \tag{9.2}$$

where $EROR_{i,q}(t)$ is the expected rate of return in year $t$, $RROR_{i,q}(t)$ is the required rate of return on investment in year $t$ and $F_{i,q}$ is an increasing function of the ratio of expected to required rate of return. In standard closures of the model, *RROR* is an exogenous variable which can be moved to achieve a given growth rate in capital

In the current version of MMRF, it is assumed that investors take account only of current rentals and asset prices when forming expectations about rates of return (static expectations). An alternative treatment available in the MONASH model, but not currently for MMRF, allows investors to form expectations about rates of return that are consistent with model-determined present values of the rentals earned from investing $A1 in year t (rational expectations).[7]

### 9.2.2.7 Lagged adjustment process in the national labor market

The ETS simulations are year-to-year recursive-dynamic simulations, in which it is assumed that the national real wage rate deviates from its base-case level in inverse proportion to deviations in the national unemployment rate. That is, in response to a shock-induced increase (decrease) in the unemployment rate, the real wage rate declines (increases), stimulating (reducing) employment growth. The coefficient of adjustment is chosen so that effects of a shock on the unemployment rate are largely eliminated after about ten years. This is consistent with macroeconomic modeling in which the NAIRU (non-accelerating inflation rate of unemployment) is exogenous.

Given the treatment of regional labor markets outlined in Section 9.2.2.5, if the national real wage rate rises (falls) in response to a fall (rise) in the national unemployment rate, then wage rates in all regions rise (fall) by the same percentage amount, and regional employment adjusts immediately, with regional labor supplies adjusting to stabilize relative regional unemployment rates.

## 9.2.3 Environmental enhancements

In this subsection, the key environmental enhancements of MMRF to facilitate the ETS study are described. These are:

- an accounting module for energy and greenhouse gas emissions that covers each emitting agent, fuel and region recognized in the model;
- quantity-specific carbon taxes or prices;
- equations for interfuel substitution in transport and stationary energy;
- a representation of Australia's National Electricity Market (NEM);
- an improved treatment of energy-using equipment in private household demand.

### 9.2.3.1 Energy and emissions accounting

MMRF tracks emissions of greenhouse gases according to: emitting agent (58 industries and the household sector), emitting state or territory (8) and emitting

---

[7] The treatment of rational expectations in the MONASH model is discussed in Dixon *et al.* (2005).

activity (9). Most of the emitting activities are the burning of fuels (coal, natural gas and five types of petroleum products). A residual category, named *Activity*, covers non-combustion emissions such as emissions from mines and agricultural emissions not arising from fuel burning. *Activity* emissions are assumed to be proportional to the level of activity in the relevant industries (animal-related agriculture, gas mining, cement manufacture, etc.).

The resulting $59 \times 8 \times 9$ array of emissions is designed to include all emissions except those arising from land clearing. Emissions are measured in terms of carbon dioxide equivalents ($CO_2$-e). Table 9.2 summarizes MMRF's emission data for the starting year of the simulations — the financial year 2006. Note that MMRF accounts for domestic emissions only; emissions from combustion of Australian coal

**Table 9.2** Summary of MMRF emissions data for Australia, 2005–2006 (kt of $CO_2$-e)

| Fuel user | Source of emissions (fuel and non-fuel) | | | | |
| | Coal | Gas | Refinery | Non-fuel | Total |
|---|---|---|---|---|---|
| 1. Sheep and beef cattle | 0.0 | 1.3 | 1179.6 | 70179.0 | 71360.0 |
| 2. Dairy cattle | 0.0 | 0.4 | 483.8 | 9297.0 | 9781.3 |
| 3. Other livestock | 0.0 | 0.7 | 192.4 | 2983.0 | 3176.1 |
| 4. Grains | 0.0 | 0.8 | 1650.1 | 2399.0 | 4050.0 |
| 5. Other agriculture | 0.0 | 0.7 | 1248.3 | 3085.0 | 4333.9 |
| 6. Ag services, fishing, hunting | 0.0 | 1.2 | 1231.2 | 13.0 | 1245.5 |
| 7. Forestry | 0.0 | 0.0 | 473.6 | −19610.0 | −19136.4 |
| 8. Coal mining | 0.0 | 0.0 | 2761.5 | 21610.0 | 24371.5 |
| 9. Oil mining | 0.0 | 0.0 | 136.4 | 818.0 | 954.3 |
| 10. Gas mining | 0.0 | 8991.0 | 263.2 | 6360.0 | 15614.1 |
| 11. Iron ore mining | 37.1 | 312.0 | 321.8 | 0.0 | 670.9 |
| 12. Non-ferrous ore mining | 699.9 | 660.0 | 3699.9 | 1634.0 | 6693.7 |
| 13. Other mining | 0.0 | 0.0 | 926.4 | 0.0 | 926.4 |
| 14. Meat and meat products | 78.7 | 83.2 | 21.1 | 0.0 | 182.9 |
| 15. Other food and drink | 718.4 | 1529.8 | 124.8 | 0.0 | 2373.0 |
| 16. Textiles, clothing, footwear | 2.8 | 350.3 | 12.8 | 0.0 | 365.9 |
| 17. Wood products | 371.1 | 96.1 | 14.1 | 0.0 | 481.4 |
| 18. Paper products | 606.7 | 682.3 | 17.2 | 704.0 | 2010.3 |
| 19. Printing and publishing | 13.0 | 174.0 | 32.6 | 0.0 | 219.6 |
| 20. Petroleum products | 0.0 | 1255.1 | 4740.4 | 490.0 | 6485.5 |
| 21. Basic chemicals | 507.0 | 1332.2 | 2073.0 | 2513.0 | 6425.2 |
| 22. Rubber, plastic products | 27.0 | 982.9 | 398.0 | 0.0 | 1407.9 |
| 23. Other construction products | 404.2 | 1814.1 | 156.4 | 1499.0 | 3873.7 |
| 24. Cement | 2004.8 | 1011.9 | 406.5 | 4738.0 | 8161.2 |
| 25. Iron and steel | 3532.0 | 1295.0 | 170.4 | 8961.0 | 13958.5 |
| 26. Alumina | 3488.7 | 3023.6 | 1958.9 | 0.0 | 8471.2 |

*(Continued)*

**Table 9.2** Summary of MMRF emissions data for Australia, 2005–2006 (kt of $CO_2$-e)—cont'd

| Fuel user | Coal | Gas | Refinery | Non-fuel | Total |
|---|---|---|---|---|---|
| 27. Aluminum | 0.0 | 0.0 | 291.6 | 4642.0 | 4933.6 |
| 28. Other non-ferrous metals | 1778.1 | 3380.8 | 481.0 | 0.0 | 5640.0 |
| 29. Metal products | 0.0 | 76.6 | 25.6 | 0.0 | 102.2 |
| 30. Motor vehicles and parts | 0.0 | 62.1 | 20.5 | 0.0 | 82.5 |
| 31. Other manufacturing | 97.1 | 228.0 | 73.3 | 674.0 | 1072.4 |
| 32. Electricity-coal | 179163.0 | 0.0 | 0.0 | 0.0 | 179163.0 |
| 33. Electricity-gas | 0.0 | 14573.0 | 0.0 | 0.0 | 14573.0 |
| 34. Electricity-oil products | 0.0 | 0.0 | 1042.3 | 0.0 | 1042.3 |
| 35. Electricity-nuclear | 0.0 | 0.0 | 0.0 | 0.0 | 0.0 |
| 36. Electricity-hydro | 0.0 | 0.0 | 0.0 | 0.0 | 0.0 |
| 37. Electricity-other | 0.0 | 0.0 | 0.0 | 0.0 | 0.0 |
| 38. Electricity supply | 0.0 | 0.0 | 662.6 | 0.0 | 662.6 |
| 39. Gas supply | 0.0 | 0.0 | 15.5 | 2132.0 | 2147.5 |
| 40. Water supply | 0.0 | 0.0 | 307.4 | 0.0 | 307.4 |
| 41. Construction services | 0.0 | 159.3 | 1696.7 | 0.0 | 1856.0 |
| 42. Trade services | 0.0 | 1490.4 | 5299.0 | 361.0 | 7150.4 |
| 43. Accommodation, etc. | 0.0 | 232.9 | 705.3 | 302.0 | 1240.2 |
| 44. Road passenger transport | 0.0 | 5.6 | 2371.0 | 728.0 | 3104.7 |
| 45. Road freight transport | 0.0 | 71.5 | 22468.7 | 0.0 | 22540.3 |
| 46. Rail passenger transport | 0.0 | 0.0 | 341.3 | 0.0 | 341.3 |
| 47. Rail freight transport | 0.0 | 0.0 | 1793.6 | 0.0 | 1793.6 |
| 48. Water transport | 0.0 | 4.1 | 2657.8 | 0.0 | 2661.8 |
| 49. Air transport | 0.0 | 0.0 | 5136.3 | 0.0 | 5136.3 |
| 50. Communication services | 0.0 | 98.2 | 1574.1 | 0.0 | 1672.3 |
| 51. Financial services | 0.0 | 2.3 | 3.2 | 0.0 | 5.6 |
| 52. Business services | 0.0 | 262.3 | 1635.9 | 0.0 | 1898.2 |
| 53. Dwelling services | 0.0 | 5.4 | 18.5 | 0.0 | 23.9 |
| 54. Public services | 0.0 | 187.4 | 1867.9 | 0.0 | 2055.4 |
| 55. Other services | 0.0 | 44.1 | 1634.0 | 17037.0 | 18715.1 |
| 56. Private transport services | 0.0 | 0.0 | 36905.0 | 1613.0 | 38518.0 |
| 57. Private electricity equipment services | 0.0 | 0.0 | 0.0 | 835.0 | 835.0 |
| 58. Private heating services | 0.0 | 6983.6 | 0.0 | 0.0 | 6983.6 |
| Residential | 16.8 | 0.0 | 277.9 | 0.0 | 294.7 |
| Total | 193546.4 | 51466.3 | 114000.6 | 145997.0 | 505010.4 |

exports, say, are not included, but fugitive emissions from the mining of the coal are included.

According to Table 9.2, the burning of coal, gas and refinery products account for around 38%, 10% and 23% of Australia's total greenhouse emissions. The residual, about 29%, comes from non-combustion sources. The largest emitting industry is electricity generation, which contributes around 39% of total emissions. The next largest is animal-agriculture, which contributes 14%; agriculture in total contributes nearly 20%. Other large emitters are: transport (including private transport services) with about 10% of total emissions, coal mining with around 5% and other services (including waste dumps) with nearly 4%.

### 9.2.3.2 Carbon taxes and prices

MMRF treats the ETS price on emissions as a specific tax on emissions of $CO_2$-e. On emissions from fuel combustion, the tax is imposed as a sales tax on the use of fuel. On *Activity* emissions, it is imposed as a tax on production of the relevant industries.

In MMRF, sales taxes are generally assumed to be *ad valorem*, levied on the basic value of the underlying flow. Carbon taxes, however, are specific, levied on the quantity ($CO_2$-e) emitted by the associated flow. Hence, equations are required to translate a carbon tax, expressed per unit of $CO_2$-e, into *ad valorem* taxes, expressed as percentages of basic values. The $CO_2$-e taxes are specific but coupled to a single price index (typically the national price of consumption) to preserve the nominal homogeneity of the system. Suppressing indices, an item of $CO_2$-e tax revenue can be written as:

$$TAX = S \times E \times I, \tag{9.3}$$

where $S$ is the specific rate ($A per tonne of $CO_2$-e), $E$ is the emission quantity (tonne of $CO_2$-e) and $I$ is a price index (base year $= 1$) used to preserve nominal homogeneity.

*Ad valorem* taxes in MMRF raise revenue:

$$TAX = \frac{V \times P \times Q}{100}, \tag{9.4}$$

where $V$ is the percentage *ad valorem* rate, $P$ is the basic price of the underlying taxed flow and $Q$ is the quantity of the underlying taxed flow.

To translate from specific to *ad valorem* the right-hand sides of equations (9.3) and (9.4) are set equal to each other, yielding:

$$V = \frac{S \times E \times I \times 100}{P \times Q}. \tag{9.5}$$

As can be seen from equation (9.5), to convert specific $CO_2$-e taxes to *ad valorem* taxes frequent use is made of the ratio of the indexed-value of emissions ($E \times I$) to the value of the *ad valorem* tax base ($P \times Q$). Indeed, values for the ratio across all fuels and users and the matrix of specific tax rates are the primary additional data items added to MMRF for carbon tax/ETS modeling.

Production taxes in MMRF are also assumed to be *ad valorem*, and levied on the basic value of production. Accordingly, the linking equation for a $CO_2$-e tax on *Activity* emissions is:

$$V = \frac{S \times E \times I \times 100}{P \times Z}, \tag{9.6}$$

where $Z$ is the volume of production for which $P$ is the basic price.

### 9.2.3.3 Interfuel substitution

In the standard specification of MMRF, there is no price-responsive substitution between composite units of commodities or between composite commodities and the composite of primary factors.[8] With fuel–fuel and fuel–factor substitution ruled out, $CO_2$-e taxes could induce abatement only through activity effects.

We correct this in two ways:

**(i)** by introducing interfuel substitution in electricity generation using the 'technology bundle' approach;[9]

**(ii)** by introducing a weak form of input substitution in sectors other than electricity generation to mimic 'KLEM substitution'.[10]

Electricity-generating industries are distinguished based on the type of fuel used (Section 9.2.1 and Table 9.1). There is also an end-use supplier (*Electricity supply*) in each state and territory and a single dummy industry (*NEM*) covering the six regions that are included in Australia's NEM [New South Wales (NSW), Victoria (VIC), Queensland (QLD), South Australia (SA), the Australian Capital Territory (ACT) and Tasmania (TAS)]. Electricity flows to the local end-use supplier either directly from generators in the case of Western Australia (WA) and the Northern Territory (NT) or via *NEM* in the remaining regions. Further details of the operation of *NEM* are given in Section 9.2.3.4.

Purchasers of electricity from the generation industries (*NEM* in NEM regions or the *Electricity supply* industries in the non–NEM regions) can substitute between the different generation technologies in response to changes in generation costs. Such substitution is price-induced, with the elasticity of substitution between the technologies typically set at around 5.

---

[8] Composite commodities are constant elasticity of substitution (CES) aggregations of domestic and imported products with the same name. The composite of primary factors is a CES aggregation of labor, capital and land inputs – see Section 9.2.2.2.

[9] The technology bundle approach has its origins in the work done at the CoPS, Monash University in the early 1990s (McDougall, 1993) and at ABARES for the MEGABARE model (Hinchy and Hanslow, 1996).

[10] KLEM substitution allows for substitution between capital (K), labor (L), energy (E) and materials (M) for each sector: see Hudson and Jorgenson (1974), and Berndt and Wood (1975). Other substitution schemes used in Australian models are described in chapter 4 of Pezzy and Lambie (2001). A more general current overview is in Stern (2012).

For other energy-intensive commodities used by industries, MMRF allows for a weak form of input substitution. If the price of cement (say) rises by 10% relative to the average price of other inputs to construction, the construction industry will use 1% less cement, and a little more labor, capital and other materials. In most cases, as in the cement example, a substitution elasticity of 0.1 is imposed. For important energy goods (petroleum products, electricity supply and gas) the substitution elasticity in industrial use is 0.25. Being driven by price changes, this input substitution is especially important in an ETS scenario, where outputs of emitting industries are made more expensive.

### 9.2.3.4 NEM

The NEM is a wholesale market covering nearly all of the supply of electricity to retailers and large end-users in NEM regions. MMRF's represents the NEM as follows.

Final demand for electricity in each NEM region (Section 9.2.3.3) is determined within the CGE core of the model in the same manner as demand for all other goods and services. All end users of electricity in NEM regions purchase their supplies from their own-state *Electricity supply* industry. Each of the *Electricity supply* industries in the NEM regions sources its electricity from a dummy industry called *NEM*, which does not have a regional dimension; in effect *NEM* is a single industry that sells a single product (electricity) to the *Electricity supply* industry in each NEM region. *NEM* sources its electricity from generation industries in each NEM region. Its demand for electricity is price-sensitive. For example, if the price of hydro generation from TAS rises relative to the price of gas generation from NSW, then *NEM* demand will shift towards NSW gas generation and away from TAS hydro generation.

The explicit modeling of the NEM enables substitution between generation types in different NEM regions. It also allows for interstate trade in electricity, without having to trace explicitly the bilateral flows. Note that WA and NT are not part of the NEM, and electricity supply and generation in these regions is determined on a state-of-location basis.[11]

This modeling of the NEM is adequate for many MMRF simulations, but for the ETS simulations reported in this chapter much of it was overwritten by results from Frontier's detailed bottom-up model of the electricity system (Section 9.3.2). The MMRF electricity system structure described above provides a suitable basis for interfacing MMRF with the bottom-up model.

### 9.2.3.5 Services of energy-using equipment in private household demand

The final three industries shown in Table 9.1 are dummy industries that provide services of energy-using equipment to private households. These dummy industries enable

---

[11] Note that transmission costs are handled as margins associated with the delivery of electricity to *NEM* or to the *Electricity supply* industries of WA and the NT. Distribution costs in NEM regions are handled as margins on the sale of electricity from *NEM* to the relevant *Electricity supply* industries.

households to treat energy and energy-using equipment as complementary, which is not possible in MMRF's standard budget-allocation specification based on the linear expenditure system (LES).

Industry 56 provides private transport services to the household sector, using inputs of capital (private motor vehicles), automotive fuel and other inputs required for the day-to-day servicing and running of vehicles. Industry 57 provides the services of electrical equipment (including air conditioners) to households, using inputs of capital (electrical equipment) and electricity. Industry 58 provides the services of appliances used for heating and cooking, using inputs of capital (heating and cooking appliances), gas and electricity. Energy used by these three dummy industries accounts for all of the energy consumption of the residential sector.

Including these dummy industries improves the model's treatment of price-induced energy substitution and its treatment of the relationship between energy and energy equipment in household demand. For example, in the LES-based specification of household demand, if the price of electricity fell relative to the price of other goods and services, electricity would be substituted for other commodities, including electrical and heating appliances. However, under the dummy-industry specification, a change in the price of electricity induces substitution only through its effect on the prices of electrical equipment services and private heating services. If the change in the electricity price reduces the price of electrical equipment services relative to the price of other products, then electrical equipment services (including its inputs of appliances and energy) will be substituted for other items in the household budget.

## 9.3 ADDITIONAL ENHANCEMENT FOR ETS MODELING

In this section, enhancements to our modeling that are necessary for simulating the effects of a real-world ETS are explained. This involves:
- linking MMRF to GTEM, to enhance MMRF's handling of global aspects of the ETS and of changes to Australia's trading conditions;
- linking MMRF to Frontier's *WHIRLYGIG* electricity model, to enhance MMRF's electricity-supply detail;
- modeling transitional arrangements for EITEIs;
- modeling abatement of non-combustion emissions;
- modeling carbon sequestration in forest industries.

### 9.3.1 Linking with GTEM

Linking economic models with different economic structures is not straightforward. For example, MMRF and GTEM have similar production structures, but their industrial classifications are not the same (compare Table 9.1 with Table 9.3, which gives the

**Table 9.3** Industries and regions in the GTEM modeling

| Regions | Industries |
|---|---|
| Australia | Coal mining |
| US | Oil mining |
| EU | Gas mining |
| Japan | Petroleum and coal products |
| China | Electricity with 12 technologies: coal, oil, gas, nuclear, hydro, etc.) |
| India | Iron and steel with two technologies: electric arc and blast furnace |
| Indonesia | Non-ferrous metals |
| Other South and East Asia | Chemical, rubber and plastic products |
| Russia and CIS | Other mining |
| OPEC | Non-metallic minerals |
| Canada | Other manufacturing |
| South Africa | Air transport |
| Rest of World | Water transport |
| | Other transport with five technologies: rail, internal combustion road, advanced internal combustion road, hybrid road and non-fossil fuel vehicles |
| | Crops |
| | Livestock |
| | Fishing and forestry |
| | Food products |
| | Services |

industrial and regional classifications in the version of GTEM used for the ETS simulations). Also, the elasticities of supply and demand associated with comparable industries are not necessarily consistent across the two models.

In general, the degree of linking required will vary depending on the number and nature of variables that are common between the two models. For example, if the only common variables are exogenous in the primary model (MMRF), then a relatively simple top-down linking from the secondary model (GTEM) is sufficient. On the other hand, if there are many common variables with some endogenous to both systems, a more complex linking with two-way transmission of results may be necessary.

As discussed in Section 9.1, the simulations reported in this chapter relate to a global ETS, with a global cap, a global price and allocations of permits to participating countries. GTEM was used to model the global scheme. Projections were obtained from GTEM for the global permit price and the allocation of permits across regions for each global emissions target. The projections for the global permit price and Australia's emissions allocation were fed directly into MMRF. In MMRF, the global permit price and Australia's emissions allocation are naturally exogenous variables. Hence, a simple one-way link from GTEM to MMRF is sufficient.

GTEM also simulates changes in world trading conditions faced by Australia, with and without the global ETS. These are as represented in MMRF as changes in the positions of foreign export-demand and import-supply schedules. In MMRF, import supply is assumed to be perfectly elastic and foreign-currency import prices are naturally exogenous, once again allowing for one-way transmission from GTEM to MMRF.

For exports, however, foreign demand schedules are assumed to be downward sloping. In this case, one-way transmission is problematic because export prices and quantities are endogenous in both models. Despite the potential for feedback, the linking between GTEM and MMRF for export variables was done via one-way transmission from GTEM to MMRF. The main challenge was to deduce the changes in position of export-demand schedules in MMRF implied by the projected changes in export volumes and prices in GTEM.

In the remainder of this subsection we give a short overview of the GTEM model and then explain how changes in export demand schedules were transmitted to MMRF.

### 9.3.1.1 GTEM Overview

GTEM (Pant, 2007) and MMRF are based on a common theoretical framework — the ORANI model.[12] GTEM can be likened to a series of ORANI models, one for each national region, linked by a matrix of bilateral international trade flows. Similarly, MMRF can be likened to a series of ORANI models, one for each state and territory, linked by a matrix of interstate trade flows. However, unlike the static ORANI model, MMRF and GTEM are recursively dynamic models, developed to address long-term global policy issues, such as climate change mitigation costs.

GTEM models inter-regional linkages arising from the flows of tradable goods and services and of capital. In doing so it ensures that each region's total exports equal total imports of these goods by other regions.

Industry demands in each region in GTEM are derived from solutions to a cost-minimization problem involving a three-level production function like that used in MMRF. The only difference is that in GTEM regional substitution is between different national regions rather than different Australian states and territories. In GTEM, aggregate household expenditure in each region is determined as a constant share of total regional income.

The cost-minimizing capital creator in each region in GTEM combines inputs to assemble units of capital, subject to a nested production technology similar to that facing each sector for current production. Investment in each region is financed from a global pool of savings. Each region contributes a fixed proportion of its income to the

---

[12] GTEM was derived from MEGABARE and the static GTAP model (Hertel, 1997). Aspects of MEGABARE are described in Hinchy and Hanslow (1996), Kennedy et al. (1998), and Tulpule et al. (1999).

savings pool. In standard GTEM, there are two alternative ways of allocating this pool to investment in each region. The first makes investment in each region a fixed proportion of the overall size of the pool — if the pool increases by 10%, investment in each region increases by 10%. The second relates investment allocation to relative rates of return. Regions that experience increases in their rate of return relative to the global average will receive increased shares of the investment pool, whereas regions experiencing reductions in their rate of return relative to the global average will receive reduced shares.

### 9.3.1.2 Environmental enhancements in GTEM

GTEM contains a number of enhancements relative to the MEGABARE and GTAP systems to improve its capability for environmental analysis.

- It has a global emissions database that includes all major sources of greenhouse gases, except land-use change. This database is built primarily from data compiled for the GTAP-E model.[13]

- As in MMRF, in GTEM it is assumed that combustion emissions of $CO_2$-e are proportional to the quantity of fuel combusted, while *Activity* emissions are proportional to the level of production in the industry generating them.

- Emission response functions are defined for *Activity* emissions. These specify abatement as increasing functions of the rate of carbon tax and reflect the assumption that the marginal cost of abatement rises with the level of abatement.

- GTEM uses the 'technology-bundle' approach to model electricity generation, transport and steel manufacture. Under this approach, multiple technologies are specified for the production of the relevant output. The shares of the technologies in aggregate output depend on their relative profitabilities but there is no input substitution within technologies.

- Other industries can substitute between four energy commodities in determining their aggregate use of energy. Energy can then be combined with a primary factor composite. Finally, the energy/factor composite can be combined with other intermediate inputs in fixed proportions to produce a single good.

- For emerging electricity generation technologies, such as solar and geothermal, learning-by-doing mechanisms are added. These lower primary-factor input requirements per unit of output over time.

- In some mining industries, factor productivity is assumed to decline with increases in the cumulative level of resource extraction, reflecting increasing extraction costs as the resource base diminishes.

---

[13] GTAP-E is a version of the GTAP (Global Trade Analysis Project) model designed at the GTAP Center specifically for global greenhouse analysis. Its structure and database are outlined in Truong (1999), Burniaux and Truong (2002), and (latest database) McDougall and Golub (2009).

### 9.3.1.3 *Linking export variables*

As outlined earlier, GTEM projections for the international permit price, Australia's emissions' allocation and foreign-currency import prices can easily be taken in to MMRF via a simple one-way link.[14] However, for exports, GTEM must provide MMRF with changes in the positions of the individual (downward-sloping) export-demand schedules, not changes in quantities or foreign-currency prices.

Figure 9.1 shows the method by which changes in export prices and quantities projected in GTEM (Figure 9.1a) are translated into movements in export-demand schedules in MMRF (Figure 9.1b). In Figure 9.1(a), the initial export price-quantity point is A — at the intersection of the initial demand and supply schedules. In modeling the effects of a global ETS, demand moves from D to D′ and supply from S to S′, with the price-quantity point changing from A to B. The quantity exported changes by $q$ and export price by $p$. Note that the changes in demand and supply schedules are not directly observed — only the changes $p$ and $q$.

Figure 9.1(b) shows how the information from GTEM (Figure 9.1a) is used to deduce the shift in the export-demand schedule required for the MMRF simulation.

First note that the elasticity of the demand curve in MMRF is shown as being the same as in GTEM. This is not necessary for the top-down procedure to work, but it does help avoid unduly large differences in *ex post* outcomes for export quantities and prices. GTEM's import-substitution elasticities were adjusted to ensure consistency between its implied export-demand elasticities and the explicit elasticities in MMRF.

The values for $p$ and $q$ from the GTEM simulation are used to shift the export-demand schedule in MMRF in two directions. The schedule shifts horizontally by $q$ and vertically by $p$. If in MMRF the supply schedule had the same shape as in GTEM, and if it were to shift in the same way, then in MMRF the *ex post* outcomes for export price and volume would be the same as in GTEM. Typically though, this was not the case — for several commodities MMRF's supply response was quite different from the supply response in GTEM. Thus, even though the shifts in export demand were the same, the observed changes in export price and quantity were quite different.

## 9.3.2 Linking with *WHIRLYGIG*

The idea that environmental issues could be tackled effectively by linking a CGE model with a detailed bottom-up energy model has a long history with Australian modelers. The first attempts were in a joint CoPS/ABARES project using ORANI and MENSA, which is an Australian version of the International Energy Agency's generic MARKAL framework.

---

[14] The only complication is that GTEM has a more aggregated commodity classification than does MMRF, so the GTEM information must first be mapped to MMRF commodities.

**(a)**

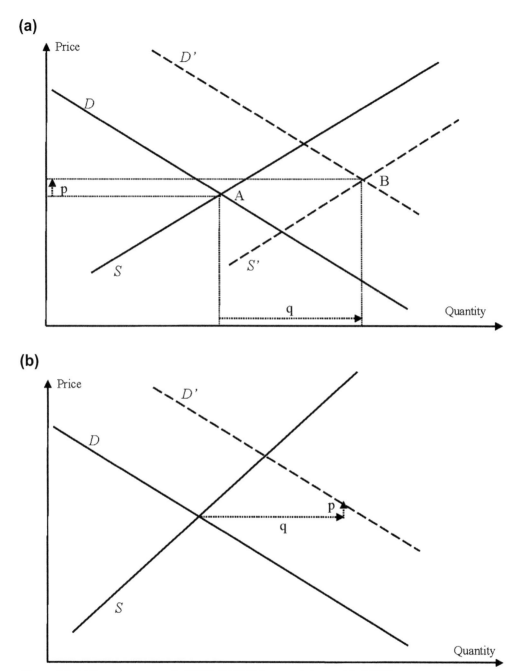

**(b)**

**Figure 9.1** (a) Export response in GTEM. (b) Shift in export demand in MMRF.

MENSA/MARKAL is an optimization model of the Australian energy system. Adams *et al.* (1992) provide an exposition in a form that makes it accessible to CGE modelers. Powell (1993) discusses methodological issues arising in attempts to link such a model with a CGE model and presents an ambitious agenda for complete two-way integration — an agenda that is still not met in current practice.

Frontier's *WHIRLYGIG* model simulates the least-cost expansion and operation of generation and transmission capacity in the Australian electricity system (Section 9.3.2.1). In linking MMRF to *WHIRLYGIG*, the electricity sector in MMRF (Sections 9.2.1, 9.2.3.3 and 9.2.3.5) is effectively replaced with *WHIRLYGIG's* specification. MMRF provides information on fuel prices and other electricity-sector costs, and on electricity demand from industrial, commercial and residential users. This is fed into *WHIRLYGIG*, which generates a detailed description of supply, covering generation by generation type, capacity by generation type, fuel use, emissions, and wholesale and retail electricity prices. Retail electricity prices are a key endogenous variable in both systems. Information is passed back and forth between the two models in a series of iterations that stop when the average retail price in the electricity model has stabilized. Experience suggests that up to three iterations for each year are necessary to achieve convergence.

There are a number of reasons to prefer linking to a detailed electricity model over the use of MMRF's standard treatment of electricity.

- *Technological detail.* MMRF recognizes six generation technologies (Table 9.1). *WHIRLYGIG* recognizes many hundreds, some of which are not fully proved and/or are not in operation. For example, MMRF recognizes one form of coal generation. *WHIRLYGIG* recognizes many forms, including cleaner gasification technologies and generation in combination with carbon capture and storage (CCS). Having all known technologies available for production now or in the future allows for greater realism in simulating the technological changes available in electricity generation in response to a price on emissions. *WHIRLYGIG* also captures details of the inter-relationships between generation types. A good example is the reliance by hydro generation on base-load power in off-peak periods to pump water utilized during peak periods back to the reservoir.

- *Changes in capacity.* MMRF treats investment in generation like all other forms of investment (Section 9.2.2.6). Capital supply is assumed to be a smooth increasing function of expected rates of return, which are set equal to current rates of return. Changes in generation capacity, however, are generally lumpy, not smooth, and investment decisions are forward looking, given long asset lives. *WHIRLYGIG* allows for lumpy investments and for realistic lead times between investment and capacity change. It also allows for forward-looking expectations, which aligns more with real-world experience than does MMRF's standard static assumption. The demand for electricity is exogenous in *WHIRLYGIG* but when demand is endogenized by running *WHIRLYGIG* linked to MMRF, investment in the electricity sector is essentially driven by model-consistent expectations.

- *Policy detail.* Currently, in Australia there are around 100 policies at the state, territory and commonwealth levels affecting electricity generation and supply. These include: market-based instruments to encourage increased use of renewable generation, regulations affecting the prices paid by final residential customers and regional policies that offer subsidies to attract certain generator types. Some of these policies interact with an ETS. For example, the market-based Renewable Energy Target (RET), which is designed to ensure that 20% of Australia's electricity supply will come from renewable sources by 2020, operates by requiring electricity retailers to acquire and surrender Renewable Energy Certificates (RECs). These RECs have a market price that will be sensitive to an ETS. Associated interactions and policy details are handled well in *WHIRLYGIG*, but are generally outside the scope of stand-alone modeling in MMRF.

- *Sector detail.* In MMRF, electricity production is undertaken by symbolic industries — *Electricity-coal Victoria, Electricity-gas NSW,* etc. In *WHIRLYGIG*, actual generation units are recognized — unit $x$ in power station $y$ located in region $z$. Thus, results from the detailed electricity model can be reported at a much finer level and in a way which industry experts fully understand. This adds to credibility in result reporting.

In the remainder of this section we describe further the Frontier electricity model and how it is used to inform MMRF.

### 9.3.2.1 WHIRLYGIG *overview*

Formally, *WHIRLYGIG* is a mixed integer linear programming model of Australia's electricity system. The objective function is the total cost (including fixed and variable costs) of the system. The model solves for optimal investment and generation to minimize total cost subject to constraints that include:

- system supply must meet system demand at all times;[15]
- minimum reserve requirements;
- generators cannot run more than allowed for by their physical capacity factors;
- certain generators must run for certain periods;
- some generators cannot run for specified periods;
- policy-related constraints, like that imposed by a price on emissions.

---

[15] *WHIRLYGIG* recognizes the (very high) price cap that is imposed in the NEM. This prevents prices rising to clear the market at extreme market conditions. To handle this, the objective function in *WHIRLYGIG* includes a valuation of the unmet demand (*lost load*) at the NEM price cap.

Inputs to *WHIRLYGIG* cover:

- general system data for electricity demand by region and the reserve capacity requirements for each region;
- data for the capacity of each inter-regional interconnector and for transmission losses;
- data on fixed and variable costs of production for each generation plant (existing and new), and on capacities and plant-commissioning timeframes;
- data on greenhouse gas emissions for each generation option.

Outputs are categorized as *decision* variables and *calculated* variables. The main decision variables are investment (or changes in capacity) for the various generation options, and production (or dispatch) from each available generation type. The key calculated variables are total costs of each plant, total system cost, wholesale and retail electricity prices, and greenhouse emissions and total greenhouse emission abatement.

*WHIRLYGIG*'s modeling of capacity changes takes account of establishment of new units and retirement of existing units. Its modeling of wholesale electricity prices is based on the long-run marginal cost of generation. Retail prices comprise the wholesale price (multiplied by the marginal loss factor in transmission) *plus* network fees *plus* gross retail margins, market fees and the cost of administering various government schemes to encourage the purchase of renewable generation.

### 9.3.2.2 Linking

The linking of *WHIRLYGIG* to MMRF proceeds as follows. For either a base-case or a policy simulation, an initial MMRF simulation is conducted, with the electricity system unconstrained. From this simulation come annual projections for:

1. electricity demand by industry and region in petajoules (PJ);
2. prices for labor, energy carriers such as coal and other relevant material inputs.

   These projections are supplied to *WHIRLYGIG*. The Frontier modelers take the annual demand projections, generate within-year load profiles, and update their estimates for the variable costs of generation for each option. The electricity model is then run (with appropriate constraints relating to $CO_2$-e emissions if necessary) to provide annual projections by region for:

3. sent-out generation (GWh) by type, aggregated to MMRF's level of detail;[16]
4. fuel usage by generation type (PJ), aggregated appropriately;
5. emissions by generation type (tonnes of $CO_2$-e), aggregated appropriately;
6. capacity by generation type (GW), aggregated appropriately;
7. wholesale electricity prices ($A/GWh);
8. retail electricity prices ($A/GWh).

---

[16] Three stages of electricity production are identified in *WHIRLYGIG* and MMRF. Generation sent out is raw generation net of electricity used in the generation process. Final-use electricity is electricity sent out less transmission and distribution losses. Any generation option in the detailed electricity model associated with the use of coal is aggregated into a single number for the MMRF industry *Electricity-coal*, etc.

**Table 9.4** Transfer of information from *WHIRLYGIG* to MMRF

| *WHIRLYGIG* variable | MMRF target | MMRF Instrument |
|---|---|---|
| 3. Sent-out generation by type and region | Sent-out generation by type and region | Cost-neutral shifts in input technologies of the electricity supply industry in each state |
| 4. Fuel usage by generation type and region | Fuel usage by generation type and region | Cost-neutral shifts in input technologies of the fossil fuel generation industries |
| 5. Emissions by generation type and region | Emissions per unit of fuel used by fossil fuel generation industries | Naturally exogenous |
| 6. Capacity by generation type and region | Capital stock in use by generation type and region | Shifts in the required rate of return on capital by generation type and region, which allows capital supply to be exogenous and set equal to achieve the targeted change in capacity (equation 9.2) |
| 7. Wholesale electricity prices by region | Average basic price of the output of generator industries in each region | Equiproportionate shifts in the price of 'other costs' of each generator in a region to mimic changes in unit pure profit |
| 8. Retail electricity prices by region | Basic price of the electricity supply industry in each region | Shifts in the price of 'other costs' of the electricity supply industry in each region |

Items 3–8 are then input to MMRF, enabled by closure changes that in effect turn off MMRF's treatment of electricity supply and investment. Details of the closure changes are given in Table 9.4. The first column shows the *WHIRLYGIG* variable being transferred. The second column shows the MMRF variable targeted. Most of these variables are naturally endogenous but must be made exogenous. The final column gives the MMRF variable — typically a naturally exogenous variable — endogenized to allow the targeted variable to be exogenized.

The changes in generation mix imposed on MMRF are initially cost-neutral and so have no effect on the average price of the *Electricity supply* industry. *WHIRLYGIG* estimates of changes in average wholesale price and in the retail prices of electricity in each region are introduced into MMRF via changes in *Other costs*[17] in MMRF's generation and electricity supply industries.

[17] See Section 9.2.2.2, especially footnote 5.

Imposing these *WHIRLYGIG* values in MMRF and rerunning completes the first iteration. Revised values for items 1 and 2 are passed to *WHIRLYGIG* which then recalculates values for variables 3–8. Iterations continue until between successive iterations the retail prices of electricity in each region stabilize.

### 9.3.3 Transitional arrangements

In the policy framework outlined in the Australian government's ETS design paper, certain EITEIs were to be shielded from some of the cost effects of the permit price during the initial years when a global ETS is being established. Shielding reduces the adverse effects of the carbon price on the EITEIs and limits the carbon leakage that imposing a carbon tax in Australia in advance of its adoption by major international trade competitors would otherwise induce.

In the ETS modeling reported in this chapter, shielding is implemented as a general production subsidy to offset the combined direct and indirect effects of the emissions price on an industry's average cost. The direct effects arise from the imposition of the emission price on the industry's combustion emissions or on the emissions directly associated with its activity (e.g. industrial and fugitive emissions); the indirect effects arise from the increased cost of electricity.

To offset the direct impacts of a carbon price, the proposed ETS specified shielding proportional to the emission price and the shielded industry's output level. The coefficient of proportionality reflects the coverage of the shielding scheme[18] and the industry's initial (2005–2006) emissions intensity, i.e.:

$$SHIELDING_{DIR} = -COVER \times T \times \left[\frac{QGAS}{OUTPUT}\right]_{INIT} \times OUTPUT, \qquad (9.7)$$

where $SHIELDING_{DIR}$ (a negative number) is the required offset to average cost, *COVER* is the rate of coverage (a number between 0 and 1.0), *T* is the effective carbon tax rate ($A per tonne of $CO_2$-e), *QGAS* is the number of tonnes of $CO_2$-e emissions, *OUTPUT* is the output of the industry and $[\ ]_{INIT}$ indicates the initial, 2005–2006, ratio of emissions to output.

For shielding to offset the increased cost of electricity:

$$SHIELDING_{IND} = -COVER \times \left[PETS - PREF\right] \times \left[\frac{ELEC}{OUTPUT}\right]_{INIT}$$
$$\times OUTPUT, \qquad (9.8)$$

---

[18] Under the Government's proposal two industry classes were considered for shielding — one deemed most exposed to the ETS and the other deemed less adversely affected, but still requiring shielding. The rates of shielding for the two categories start at 0.9 and 0.6, respectively, and then decline over time.

where $SHIELDING_{IND}$ (a negative number) is the required offset to average cost, $PETS$ is the price of a unit of electricity with the ETS in place $PREF$ is the price of electricity in the absence of the ETS, $ELEC$ is the number of units of electricity used and $[\ ]_{INIT}$ indicates the initial, 2005−2006, ratio of electricity to output.

Equation (9.8) is similar in structure to equation (9.7), with the emissions-price-induced increase in the electricity price in (9.8) replacing the permit price in (9.7).

Having determined the necessary offsets for the direct and indirect costs associated with emissions pricing, the model then applies the offset to each shielded industry via a production subsidy. The subsidy is paid for initially by the Federal government. However, since government budget balances are held fixed at base-case case levels in the ETS simulations via endogenous lump-sum payments to households, the shielding subsidy is ultimately paid by Australian households.

Shielding has a macro/welfare impact due to its role in recycling the revenue raised from the sale of emissions permits (or from the imposition of a carbon tax). Shielding payments reduce the lump-sum payments to households that are the default revenue-recycling method in the ETS simulation. By definition, lump-sum payments to households are non-distorting in the conventional public finance sense. Since the carbon tax is distorting and ignoring any environmental benefits that it might have, the policy of imposing the tax and recycling its revenue through lump-sum payments reduces GDP and conventionally measured economic welfare. Shielding represents a reduction in the effective energy tax impost associated with the ETS and a corresponding reduction in the lump-sum payments that are required to recycle the ETS revenue. This reduces the adverse effects on GDP and conventionally measured welfare. Proponents of the ETS or a carbon tax often argue that these adverse effects could be reduced further, or even eliminated, by using the revenue to reduce other distorting taxes − the so-called double-dividend argument.

## 9.3.4 Abatement of non-combustion emissions

Non-combustion (or *Activity*) emissions include: agricultural emissions (largely from animals), emissions from land-clearing or forestry, fugitive emissions (e.g. gas flaring); emissions from industrial processes (e.g. cement manufacture) and emissions from land-fill rubbish dumps. In modeling with MMRF, it is assumed that in the absence of an emissions price, non-combustion emissions move with industry output, so that non-combustion emissions intensity (emissions per unit of output) is fixed.

MMRF's theory of abatement of non-combustion emissions in the presence of an emissions price is similar to that developed for GTEM. It assumes that as the price of $CO_2$-e rises, *targeted* non-combustion emissions intensity (emissions per unit of output) falls (abatement per unit increases) through the planned introduction of less emission-intensive technologies. More specifically, for *Activity* emitter $i$ in region $q$ it is assumed that abatement per unit of output can be achieved at an increasing marginal cost according to a curve such as that shown in Figure 9.2(a). In Figure 9.2(a), units are chosen so that complete elimination of non-combustion emissions corresponds to an abatement level of 1. However, complete elimination is not possible. So, as shown in Figure 9.2(a), the marginal cost of abatement goes to infinity as the abatement level per unit of output reaches a maximum level, $1 - MIN$, where MIN is the proportion of non-combustion emissions that cannot be

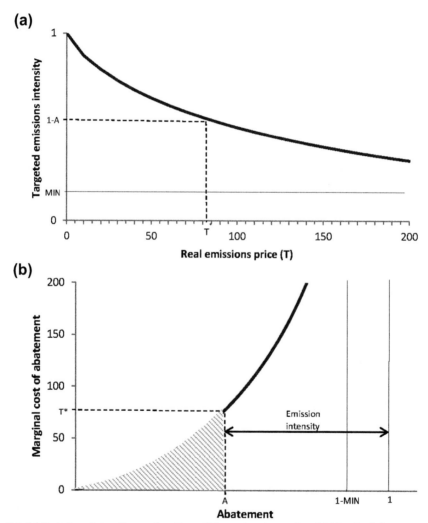

**Figure 9.2** (a) Emissions intensity as a function of the real carbon price. (b) Marginal abatement curve for the hypothetical industry.

removed. From Figure 9.2(a), an intensity function for emissions can be derived of the form:

$$Intensity_{i,q} = MAX_{i,q}\{MIN_{i,q}, F_{i,q}(T)\}, \tag{9.9}$$

where $Intensity_{i,q}$ is the target level of non–combustion emissions intensity, $MIN_{i,q}$ is the minimum possible level of emissions intensity and $F_{i,q}$ is a non–linear monotonic decreasing function of the real level of the emissions price, $T$ ($A per tonne of $CO_2$-e in constant 2010 prices).

This is illustrated in Figure 9.2(b), which shows for a typical *Activity* abater the relationship between targeted emissions intensity and emissions price, with intensity indexed to 1 for $T=0$.

To ensure that emissions intensities do not respond too vigorously to changes in the emissions price, especially at the start of a simulation in which the price of $CO_2$-e rises immediately from zero, a lagged adjustment mechanism is also put in place, allowing actual emissions intensity to adjust slowly towards targeted emissions intensity specified by (9.9).

In MMRF the abatement cost per unit of output (the shaded area in Figure 9.2a) is imposed as an all–input using technological deterioration in the production function of the abating industry.[19]

## 9.3.5 Land use in forestry

In MMRF, land is an input to production for the agricultural industries and forestry. Prior to the ETS project, the standard treatment had land industry specific and in fixed supply. Hence when a land-using industry expanded, the scarcity value of its land increased, leading to an increase in its rental price.

For the ETS simulations, land is considered region-specific, but not industry-specific, and there are regional supply constraints. This means that within a region, an industry can increase its land usage but that increase has to be met by reduced usage by other industries within the region. Land is assumed to be allocated between users to maximize the total return to land subject to a constant elasticity of transformation (CET) constraint defining production possibilities across the various land-using sectors. This is the same treatment as adopted in GTAP and GTEM. With this mechanism in place, if demand for biosequestration pushes up demand for land in the forestry sector, then forestry's use of land will increase, increasing the regionwide price of land and causing non-forestry industries to reduce their land usage and overall production.

---

[19] Here, the MMRF treatment differs from the treatment in GTEM where it is assumed that the change in technology necessary to achieve the reduction in emission intensity is costless.

## 9.4 BASE CASE

The base case is the control projection against which the policy scenario (with an ETS in place) is compared. For the ETS work, much importance was placed on establishing a detailed base case with a credible projection for emissions across regions and sectors. There were two reasons for this. (i) The cost of implementing the ETS in each year depends critically on the underlying level of base-case emissions (Weyant and Hill, 1999). (ii) Acceptance of the modeling outcomes, including the level of shielding necessary for emission-intensive industries, is reliant on the credibility of the base case.

In Section 9.4.1 we describe the key assumptions underlying the base case. Sections 9.4.2–9.4.5 contain base-case projections for macroeconomic variables, industry outputs, greenhouse gas emissions and electricity generation.

### 9.4.1 Key assumptions

The base case for the ETS simulation reported in this chapter incorporates a large amount of information from specialist forecasting agencies. MMRF traces out the implications of the specialists' forecasts at a fine level of industrial and regional detail. Information imposed on the model included:

- state/territory macroeconomic forecasts to 2014 based on information provided by Frontier Economics;
- national-level assumptions for changes in industry production technologies and in household preferences developed from MONASH and MMRF historical-decomposition modeling;[20]
- forecasts through to 2014 for the quantities of agricultural and mineral exports from a range of industry sources;
- estimates of changes in generation mix, generation capacity, fuel use, emissions and wholesale prices from Frontier Economics' electricity modeling;
- forecasts for state/territory populations and participation rates drawing, in part, on projections in the Treasury's *Intergenerational Report* (Department of Treasury, 2007);
- forecasts for land-use change and for forestry sequestration from experts at ABARES;
- forecasts for changes in Australia's aggregate terms of trade and for the foreign export and import prices for Australia's key traded goods in agriculture, mining and manufacturing drawn from simulations of GTEM undertaken for the Treasury.

To impose this information in MMRF, numerous naturally endogenous variables are made exogenous. To allow the naturally endogenous variables to be exogenous, an

---

[20] Historical decomposition modeling is discussed in Dixon and Rimmer (2002, chapter 5) and in Dixon *et al.* in Chapter 2 of this Handbook.

equal number of naturally exogenous variables are made endogenous. For example, to accommodate the exogenous setting of the aggregate terms of trade, an all-commodity and all-region shift variable, naturally exogenous in MMRF but endogenous in the base-case simulation, imparts an equi-proportionate change in the positions of foreign demand curves. Another example relates to private consumption. In the base case, real private consumption by state (a naturally endogenous variable) is set exogenously by allowing the average propensity to consume (APC) in each state to adjust endogenously.

## 9.4.2 Base-case projections for selected macroeconomic variables

Figure 9.3(a—c) shows base-case projections for selected national macroeconomic variables. The following are some key features.

- Real GDP (Figure 9.3a) grows at an average annual rate of 3.1% between 2010 and 2020, slowing to an average rate of 2.6% between 2020 and 2030. Average annual growth over the full projection period (2.9%) is consistent with the historical norm for Australia. Note that in the first 4 years after 2010, growth exceeds 3%, supported by strong growth in exports as the world recovers from the global financial crisis. Thereafter, GDP growth is projected to stabilize, eventually declining slowly in line with demographic projections from the *Intergenerational Report*.

- Although not shown in Figure 9.3(a), but in line with recent history, the export-oriented states — QLD and WA — are projected to be the fastest growing state economies, followed by NSW and VIC. SA and TAS are the slowest growing, although the gap between the slowest and fastest growing states and territories is a little less than in recent times.

- Real national private consumption (Figure 9.3a) grows at an average annual rate of 3.0% in the first half of the period and 2.9% in the second half. This time profile is similar to that for real GDP: initially strong, then stabilizing and eventually declining slowly.

- The regional pattern of growth for consumption is also similar to that for GDP: fastest growth occurs in QLD and WA, and slowest growth in TAS and SA.

- Over the 15 years leading up to 2010, the volumes of international exports and imports grew rapidly relative to real GDP. This reflects several factors — declining transport costs, improvements in communications, reductions in protection in Australia and overseas, and technological changes favoring the use of import-intensive goods such as computers and communication equipment.[21] All these factors

---

[21] The effects of changes in technology and preferences in explaining the rapid growth in trade are discussed in Dixon *et al.* (2000).

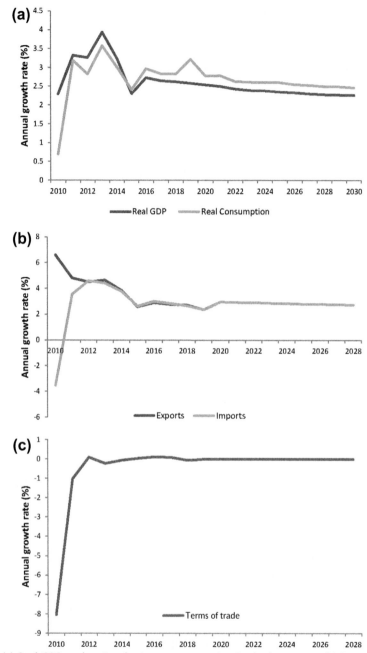

**Figure 9.3** (a) Real GDP and national private consumption in the base case. (b) Export and import volumes in the base case. (c) Terms of trade in the base case.

are extrapolated into the early years of the base case, but their influence is assumed to weaken over time (Figure 9.3b). On average, trade volumes grow relative to GDP by about 1.5% per year. Unlike in recent history, import growth is projected to be in line with export growth, implying little improvement in the current imbalance between export and import volumes.

• Australia's terms of trade are assumed to decline sharply in the first few years of the base case (Figure 9.3c), returning to a historically normal level by 2020 from their initial 50-year high.

## 9.4.3 Base-case projections for national industry production

Table 9.5 and Figures 9.4(a–i) show base-case projections for industry output at the national level.

Table 9.5 Projections for national industry output: base case (average annual percentage changes, ranked)

| Rank | Industry | 2010–2030 |
| --- | --- | --- |
| 1 | 37. Electricity generation-other | 7.3 |
| 2 | 7. Forestry | 7.0 |
| 3 | 49. Air transport | 5.2 |
| 4 | 50. Communication services | 4.6 |
| 5 | 52. Business services | 4.6 |
| 6 | 10. Gas mining | 4.2 |
| 7 | 8. Coal mining | 4.0 |
| 8 | 33. Electricity generation-gas | 4.0 |
| 9 | 47. Rail freight transport | 3.7 |
| 10 | 51. Financial services | 3.6 |
| 11 | 46. Rail passenger transport | 3.6 |
| 12 | 13. Other mining | 3.5 |
| 13 | 54. Public services | 3.4 |
| 14 | 44. Road passenger transport | 3.4 |
| 15 | 55. Other services | 3.1 |
| 16 | 12. Non-ferrous ore mining | 3.1 |
| 17 | 45. Road freight transport | 3.0 |
| 18 | 41. Construction services | 3.0 |
| 19 | 57. Private electricity equipment services | 3.0 |
| 20 | 48. Water, pipeline and transport services | 2.9 |
| 21 | 43. Accommodation, hotels and cafes | 2.9 |
| 22 | 53. Dwelling services | 2.8 |
| 23 | 11. Iron ore mining | 2.8 |
| 24 | 4. Grains | 2.7 |
| 25 | 39. Gas supply | 2.6 |
| 26 | 26. Alumina | 2.6 |

*(Continued)*

**Table 9.5** Projections for national industry output: base case (average annual percentage changes, ranked)—cont'd

| Rank | Industry | 2010–2030 |
|------|----------|-----------|
| 27 | 42. Trade services | 2.5 |
| 28 | 19. Printing and publishing | 2.3 |
| 29 | 24. Cement | 2.2 |
| 30 | 5. Other agriculture | 2.1 |
| 31 | 28. Other non-ferrous metals | 1.9 |
| 32 | 40. Water supply | 1.8 |
| 33 | 27. Aluminum | 1.8 |
| 34 | 56. Private transport services | 1.7 |
| 35 | 6. Agricultural services, fishing and hunting | 1.7 |
| 36 | 58. Private heating services | 1.7 |
| 37 | 38. Electricity supply | 1.7 |
| 38 | 1. Sheep and beef cattle | 1.6 |
| 39 | 20. Petroleum products | 1.5 |
| 40 | 23. Non-metal construction products | 1.5 |
| 41 | 3. Other livestock | 1.3 |
| 42 | 22. Rubber and plastic products | 1.3 |
| 43 | 17. Wood products | 1.3 |
| 44 | 29. Metal products | 1.2 |
| 45 | 15. Other food, beverages and tobacco | 1.1 |
| 46 | 14. Meat and meat products | 1.1 |
| 47 | 25. Iron and steel | 1.1 |
| 48 | 2. Dairy cattle | 0.9 |
| 49 | 18. Paper products | 0.9 |
| 50 | 9. Oil mining | 0.6 |
| 51 | 21. Basic chemicals | 0.5 |
| 52 | 32. Electricity generation-coal | 0.4 |
| 53 | 30. Motor vehicles and parts | 0.1 |
| 54 | 36. Electricity generation-hydro | 0.0 |
| 55 | 34. Electricity generation-oil products | 0.0 |
| 56 | 35. Electricity generation-nuclear | 0.0 |
| 57 | 31. Other manufacturing | −0.1 |
| 58 | 16. Textiles, clothing and footwear | −0.8 |

- *Electricity generation-other renewable* (industry 37) has the strongest growth prospects, with average annual growth of 7.3%, of which most occurs in the first half of the period. This industry generates electricity from renewable sources other than hydro. Its prospects are greatly enhanced by the Australian government's mandated target for the share of renewable energy in total electricity generation that is integrated into the modeling. Other forms of electricity generation have mixed prospects. Generation from gas (industry 33, rank 8) is projected to grow at a relatively strong average annual rate of 4.0%, supported by environmental policies at both the federal and state level.

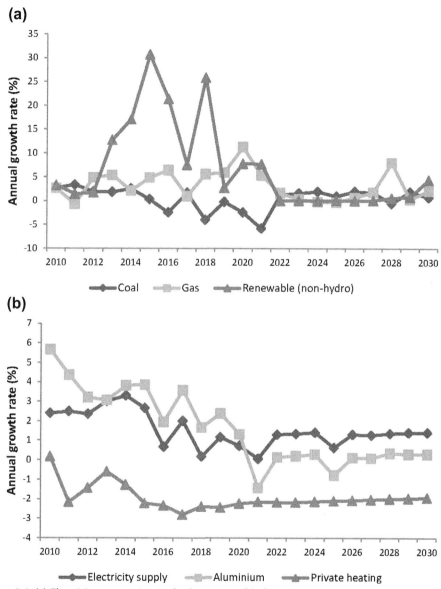

**Figure 9.4** (a) Electricity generation in the base case. (b) Electricity use and major customers in the base case. (c) Forestry and wood products in the base case. (d) Selected transport industries in the base case. (e) Communication, financial and business services in the base case. (f) Mining in the base case. (g) Agriculture in the base case. (h) Selected manufacturing industries in the base case. (i) Selected service industries in the base case.

**(c)**

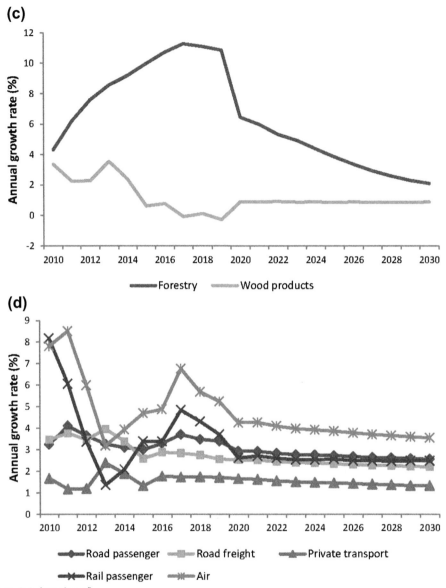

**Figure 9.4 (continued).**

The same policies restrict the average annual growth rate of emission-intensive coal generation (industry 32, rank 52) to 0.4%. It is assumed that generation from oil products (industry 34, rank 55) and hydro (industry 36, rank 54) will not change over the projection period. Production of hydroelectricity is constrained by environmental factors, while the detailed electricity sector modeling indicates little scope for oil-based generation to change.

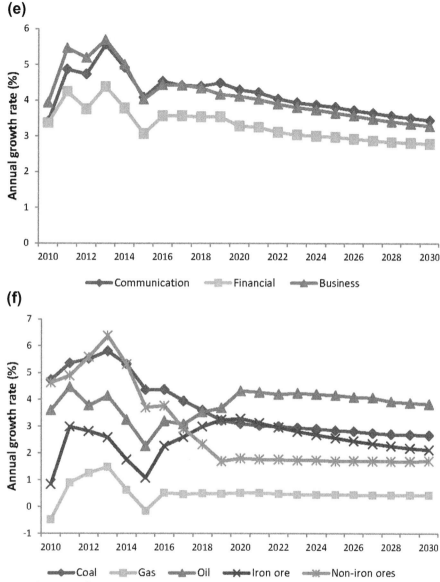

**(e)**

**(f)**

**Figure 9.4 (*continued*).**

- Figure 9.4(a) shows that the production of the key electricity generation sectors does not evolve smoothly over time. For example, annual growth for other renewable generation in the 4 years from 2014 to 2017 is 16.5%, 31.0%, 19.8% and 7.1%. These numbers come directly from the detailed electricity modeling which allows for large and discrete increases in renewal generation capacity. Similarly, there can be discrete changes in utilization of existing capacity.

**(g)**

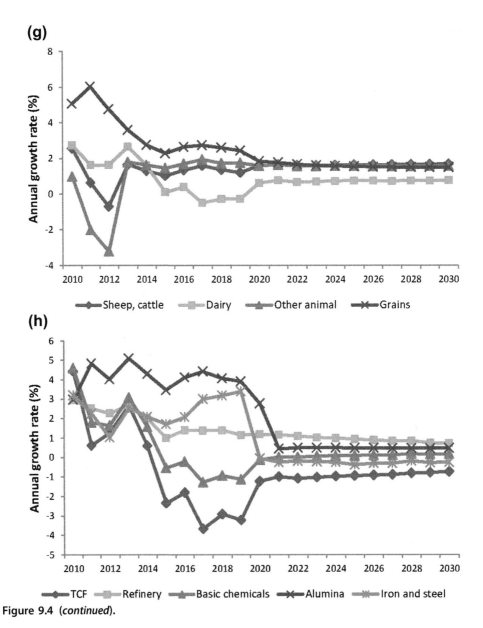

**Figure 9.4** (*continued*).

- Projected growth in overall *Electricity supply* (industry 38, rank 37) is relatively slow at 1.7% per annum (Figure 9.4b). In line with recent history, the base case includes an autonomous annual 0.5% rate of electricity-saving technological change in all forms of end-use demand. This, coupled with relatively slow average annual growth in two of the main electricity-using industries — *Aluminum* (1.8%) and *Private heating services* (1.7%) — explains the relatively slow growth projected for *Electricity supply.*

**(i)**

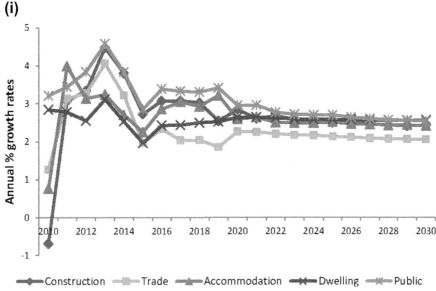

Figure 9.4 (*continued*).

- The fastest growing industry outside of the electricity sector is *Forestry* (industry 7), with a projected average annual growth rate of 7.0 per cent. This industry benefits from strong growth of softwood plantations on land previously used in marginal broad-acre agriculture The ABARES GTEM model projects significant growth in world demand for *Forestry* which absorbs much of the additional forestry supply with relatively little change in basic price. The expansion in exports explains how *Forestry* can expand strongly while its main domestic customer, *Wood products* (industry 17, rank 43), has a relatively low growth ranking (Figure 9.4c).
- *Air transport* is the third ranked industry, with a projected average annual growth rate of 5.2%. Prospects for this industry are good because of expected strong growth in inbound tourism, and the assumed continuation of a taste shift in household spending towards air and away from road as the preferred mode for long-distance travel.
- *Rail freight transport* (industry 47, rank 9) and *Rail passenger transport* (industry 46, rank 11) are each ranked in the top 15 industries by growth prospect. *Rail freight* is used mainly to transport bulk commodities (coal, iron ore and grains) to port for export. It grows strongly in the base case because of strong growth in coal exports. *Rail passenger transport* is dominated by urban rail services. It is assumed that road congestion in urban areas will intensify through the projection period, inducing commuters to substitute rail for road travel.
- Rapid growth in *Communication services*, *Business services* and *Financial services* (industries 50, 52 and 51, ranks 4, 5 and 10) reflects the assumption that changes in technology through the projection period will favor intermediate usage of these

services strongly and that comparatively rapid productivity growth will reduce their prices relative to consumer prices in general (see Figure 9.4e).

- *Gas mining* and *Coal mining* (industries 10 and 8, ranks 6 and 7) have good growth prospects (see Figure 9.4d), reflecting an assumption of very strong growth in exports of liquefied natural gas (LNG) and coal. Note that the main domestic users of gas and coal — *Gas supply* (industry 39, rank 25) and coal-fired electricity generation — have relatively low growth prospects. The former supplies town gas in the Eastern states, and is closely connected to *Private heating services*, which has projected average annual growth of just 1.7%. As noted above, base-case growth in coal-fired electricity generation is very weak.

- Prospects for the non-energy mining industries are governed by projections for world demand taken from GTEM. Production of *Oil* is expected to increase at an average annual rate of just 0.6%, reflecting estimates of supply availability from current reserves.

- Forecasts for the agricultural sector are, in the main, determined by the prospects of downstream food and beverage industries. These have below-average growth prospects, reflecting fairly weak growth in exports and expected increases in import penetration on local markets. *Grains* (industry 4, rank 24) has the best growth prospects of the agricultural industries, due mainly to relatively strong export-demand growth forecast by GTEM. *Agricultural services, fishing and hunting* (industry 6, rank 35) is projected to grow relatively slowly due to resource constraints on fishing stocks.

- Most manufacturing industries have weak growth prospects, due mainly to increases in import competition and weak growth in exports (see Figure 9.4e). The effects of increasing import competition are seen most clearly in the prospects for *Other manufacturing* (industry 31, rank 57) and *Textiles, clothing and footwear* (industry 16, rank 58), which are the only industries expected to contract over the projection period. Despite projected strong growth in exports, growth in output for the *Iron and steel* industry (25, rank 47) is projected to be weak due to slow growth in domestic demand. *Alumina* and *Aluminum* (26 and 27, ranks 26 and 33) have better growth prospects than *Iron and steel* because they have much larger export propensities and world demand for these products is expected to be stronger.

- Nearly all of the remaining industries have close to average growth prospects. The prospects for *Construction services* (industry 41, rank 18) reflect the model's projection for growth in real national investment. *Trade services* (industry 42, rank 27) sells widely throughout the economy. Its growth rate, though, is below that of real GDP because of adverse taste and technology shifts. *Public services* (industry 54, rank 13) and *Other services* (industry 55, rank 15) are oriented towards public consumption which moves in line with private consumption. *Dwelling services* (industry 53, rank 22) is projected to grow slightly slower than aggregate private consumption in the base case. Its expenditure elasticity is around 1.2 but this is offset by the prospect of the price of dwellings rising relative to the CPI.

### 9.4.4 Base-case projections: emissions by source

Figure 9.5 gives a year-to-year picture of the level of emissions at the national level. In line with Kyoto accounting principles, it covers all emissions except for emissions from land clearing. Table 9.6 gives region-specific details on the sources of emissions in the base case.

- In aggregate, emissions are projected to grow at an average annual rate of 1.8% between 2010 and 2020, 1.2% between 2020 and 2030, and 1.5% across the full projection period. By 2020, emissions are projected to be 19.6% higher than in 2010. Emission levels at 2030 are projected to be 34.5% above 2010 levels.
- The largest source of emissions is electricity generation, especially generation from coal combustion. In 2010, electricity contributed almost 36% to total emissions. However, the detailed electricity modeling indicates that average annual growth in emissions from electricity will be only 0.2% through the projection period. This is a little below the assumed growth rate in output (generation) of 0.4%, reflecting improved fuel efficiency.

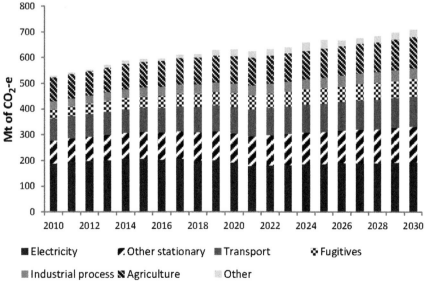

**Figure 9.5** Emissions by major source in the base case.

**Table 9.6** $CO_2$-e emissions by major source category: base case

|  | NSW | VIC | QLD | SA | WA | TAS | NT | ACT | AUS |
|---|---|---|---|---|---|---|---|---|---|
| *Average annual growth rates (%), 2010–2030* | | | | | | | | | |
| Energy sector, total | 1.0 | −0.1 | 1.8 | −2.0 | 3.6 | 0.9 | 2.2 | 1.5 | 1.3 |
| Fuel combustion | 0.7 | −0.1 | 1.6 | −1.8 | 3.0 | 0.9 | 2.2 | 1.5 | 1.1 |
| Stationary | 0.5 | −0.4 | 1.5 | −3.5 | 3.2 | 1.1 | 2.2 | 1.3 | 0.9 |
| Electricity | 0.3 | −0.9 | 1.1 | −8.8 | 1.2 | 1.2 | 2.2 | 0.0 | 0.2 |
| Other | 0.9 | 0.7 | 2.2 | −0.6 | 4.3 | 1.1 | 2.3 | 1.3 | 2.2 |
| Transport | 1.3 | 1.2 | 2.2 | 0.8 | 2.2 | 0.6 | 2.1 | 1.6 | 1.6 |
| Fugitive emissions | 2.4 | 0.5 | 3.3 | −3.6 | 7.4 | 0.5 | 3.1 | 2.1 | 3.3 |
| Industrial processes | 1.0 | 1.4 | 2.3 | 1.1 | 1.5 | 1.2 | 2.8 | 2.0 | 1.4 |
| Agriculture | 1.2 | 1.2 | 1.5 | 1.0 | 1.1 | 0.5 | 1.6 | 0.8 | 1.3 |
| Waste | 0.9 | 1.0 | 1.7 | 0.5 | 1.5 | 0.3 | 1.4 | 0.9 | 1.1 |
| Forestry | NA | NA | NA | NA | NA | NA | NA | NA | NA |
| Total | 1.1 | 0.4 | 1.8 | −0.5 | 3.6 | 2.0 | 2.0 | 1.7 | 1.5 |
| *Shares in Australia-wide total (%) 2010* | | | | | | | | | |
| Energy sector, total | 20.4 | 20.0 | 19.2 | 3.7 | 10.3 | 0.7 | 1.1 | 0.3 | 75.7 |
| Fuel combustion | 17.4 | 19.7 | 17.1 | 3.2 | 9.4 | 0.7 | 1.1 | 0.3 | 68.8 |
| Stationary | 12.9 | 15.9 | 13.4 | 2.2 | 7.1 | 0.3 | 0.8 | 0.1 | 52.8 |
| Electricity | 9.3 | 12.2 | 9.7 | 1.2 | 3.0 | 0.1 | 0.3 | 0.0 | 35.7 |
| Other | 3.6 | 3.7 | 3.8 | 1.0 | 4.2 | 0.3 | 0.5 | 0.1 | 17.0 |
| Transport | 4.5 | 3.8 | 3.7 | 1.0 | 2.3 | 0.4 | 0.3 | 0.2 | 16.0 |
| Fugitive emissions | 3.0 | 0.3 | 2.1 | 0.5 | 0.9 | 0.0 | 0.0 | 0.0 | 6.9 |
| Industrial processes | 2.5 | 0.7 | 0.9 | 0.5 | 1.0 | 0.2 | 0.1 | 0.0 | 5.9 |
| Agriculture | 3.6 | 3.5 | 5.4 | 1.1 | 2.3 | 0.5 | 1.3 | 0.0 | 17.7 |
| Waste | 1.2 | 0.8 | 0.7 | 0.2 | 0.4 | 0.1 | 0.0 | 0.0 | 3.5 |
| Forestry | −0.2 | −0.8 | 0.0 | −0.3 | −1.2 | −0.3 | 0.0 | 0.0 | −2.8 |
| Total | 27.5 | 24.3 | 26.3 | 5.1 | 12.9 | 1.2 | 2.4 | 0.4 | 100.0 |
| *2030* | | | | | | | | | |
| Energy sector, total | 18.5 | 14.6 | 20.5 | 1.9 | 15.4 | 0.6 | 1.3 | 0.3 | 73.1 |
| Fuel combustion | 14.9 | 14.4 | 17.6 | 1.7 | 12.6 | 0.6 | 1.2 | 0.3 | 63.3 |
| Stationary | 10.5 | 10.8 | 13.3 | 0.8 | 10.0 | 0.3 | 0.9 | 0.1 | 46.8 |
| Electricity | 7.4 | 7.7 | 9.0 | 0.1 | 2.8 | 0.1 | 0.3 | 0.0 | 27.4 |
| Other | 3.2 | 3.1 | 4.3 | 0.7 | 7.2 | 0.2 | 0.6 | 0.1 | 19.4 |
| Transport | 4.4 | 3.5 | 4.3 | 0.9 | 2.6 | 0.3 | 0.3 | 0.2 | 16.5 |
| Fugitive emissions | 3.6 | 0.3 | 2.9 | 0.2 | 2.8 | 0.0 | 0.1 | 0.0 | 9.8 |
| Industrial processes | 2.3 | 0.7 | 1.1 | 0.4 | 1.0 | 0.2 | 0.1 | 0.0 | 5.8 |
| Agriculture | 3.4 | 3.3 | 5.4 | 1.0 | 2.1 | 0.4 | 1.3 | 0.0 | 16.9 |
| Waste | 1.1 | 0.8 | 0.8 | 0.1 | 0.4 | 0.1 | 0.0 | 0.0 | 3.3 |
| Forestry | 0.0 | 0.2 | 0.0 | 0.1 | 0.5 | 0.1 | 0.0 | 0.0 | 0.9 |
| Total | 25.3 | 19.6 | 27.8 | 3.5 | 19.5 | 1.3 | 2.7 | 0.4 | 100.0 |
| *Total emissions (Mt of $CO_2$-e)* | | | | | | | | | |
| 2010 | 144.9 | 128.1 | 138.6 | 27.2 | 68.0 | 6.3 | 12.8 | 1.9 | 527.8 |
| 2030 | 179.3 | 138.8 | 197.6 | 24.8 | 138.3 | 9.4 | 18.9 | 2.7 | 709.8 |

- The second largest source of emissions is agriculture, with a 2010-share of 17.7%. In the Kyoto-accounting framework, most of Australia's agricultural emissions come from methane emitted by cattle and sheep. Base-case growth prospects for these livestock industries are well below GDP growth: *Sheep and beef cattle* (1.6% per annum), *Dairy cattle* (0.9%) and *Other livestock* (1.3%). Average annual growth in emissions from agriculture is 1.3%.
- Other stationary energy sources contribute 17.0% to total emissions in 2010. These include residential, industrial and commercial space heating. Emissions from other stationary sources are projected to grow at an average annual rate of 2.2%. This is below the growth rate of real GDP, reflecting the relatively slow growth of *Private heating services* (1.7% per annum) and *Other manufacturing* (−0.1%).
- Transport contributes 16.0% to total emissions in 2010 and has projected emissions growth of 1.6% per annum. Around 60% of transport emissions are due to *Private transport services*, which is projected to grow at an average annual rate of 1.7%. Much of the remaining transport emissions come from *Road freight transport*, which grows at an average annual rate of 3.0%. Emissions grow by less than output in these two key industries because it is assumed that use of bioproducts will increase.
- Of the remaining sources, growth in fugitive emissions is highest, reflecting rapid growth in the mining of gas and coal. Industrial process emissions are projected to grow at an average annual rate of 1.4%, reflecting growth in output from *Cement* and the metals manufacturing industries. Emissions of methane from landfill waste dumps are assumed to grow in line with recent history.
- The final category is *Forestry*. The modeling ignores all emissions from land-use change except for sequestration from forestation and reforestation in areas where the preceding vegetation or land use was not forest. For the base case, data on forestry sequestration were supplied by ABARES. The ABARES projections take account of the life cycle of individual forests established since 1990, accounting for carbon sequestered when the forest is planted and growing, and for carbon released when the forest is harvested. Note that this makes a negative contribution to emissions in 2010 but positive contributions in 2020 and 2030.

Aggregate emissions per $A of real GDP (national emissions intensity) is projected to fall, on average, by 1.4% per year. Much of this has been explained in our discussion of growth rates in emissions by source. In addition, there is a structural effect. The service industries, *Communication services*, *Financial and business services*, *Dwelling ownership*, *Public services* and *Other services*, together contribute around 40% of GDP, but emit relatively little (directly and indirectly via their use of electricity) per unit of real value added. In the base case, they contribute significantly to growth in real

GDP, but have little impact on growth in emissions, generating a fall in emissions per unit of GDP.

Table 9.6 shows that total emissions are projected to grow fastest in the states/ territories with the highest projected growth rates — NT, WA and QLD. Total emissions are highest in NSW and VIC up until 2015. Beyond 2015, QLD surpasses VIC. Emissions in WA increase by more than other states reflecting the high economic growth rates and the increase in mining, natural gas and mineral processing activities in that state.

### 9.4.5 Base-case projections: electricity generation sent out

Figure 9.6(a) shows base-case projections for the shares of generating technologies (other than oil) in aggregate generation (PJ). Figure 9.6(b) shows projections for shares in capacity (GW). Both figures are based on information provided by detailed electricity modeling in *WHIRLYGIG* and summarize the final information fed to MMRF (Section 9.3.2). Further detail is given in Table 9.7.

Total generation sent out is forecast to increase at an average annual rate of 1.5% over the forecast period, which is 1.3 percentage points higher than the growth rate in emissions from generation (Section 9.4.4).[22] The difference is due, in the main, to the federal and state policies included in the detailed electricity modeling that encourage non-coal generation and improved fuel efficiencies within the coal generation sector.

The national share of gas generation (Figure 9.6a) is projected to increase from 14.0% in 2010 to 17.7% in 2020 and to 19.7% in 2030. The total renewable share increases from 13.8% in 2010 to 18.9% in 2020 and increases slightly thereafter. Over the 20-year period, coal's share falls from 73.8% to 61.1%.

Figure 9.6(b) is broadly consistent with Figure 9.6(a). However, the pattern of capacity installation is lumpy, not smooth as the CGE model would have it were it not for the imposition of data from the bottom–up electricity model. Recall that changes in electricity capacity are accommodated in MMRF by shifts in required rates of return (see equation 2 and Table 9.4).

The share of coal in generation capacity declines, as does its share in aggregate sent-out generation. The capacity shares of gas and non-hydro renewables increase as do their generation shares. Note that the share of coal in total capacity (Figure 9.6b) is always less than its share in total generation (Figure 9.6a), reflecting the high rates of capacity utilization of base-load technologies. After 2022, coal's capacity share is fairly

---

[22] Growth in total generation sent out (Table 9.7) does not necessarily equal growth in the output of the *Electricity supply* industry. *Electricity supply* produces transmission, distribution and retail services. Growth in the volume of these services may differ from growth in generation sent out if, for example, there are improvements in the efficiency of distribution, which means more generation can be delivered with the same amount of distribution services.

**(a)**

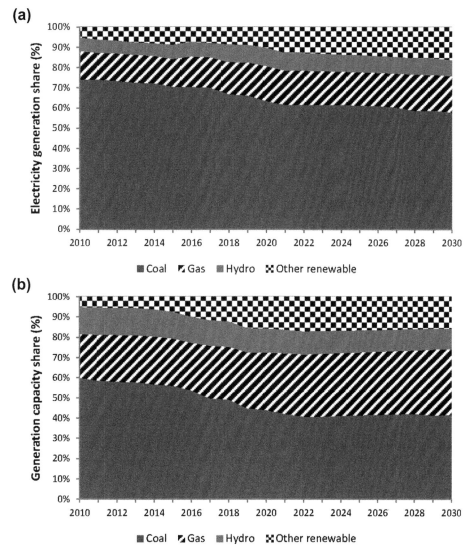

**Figure 9.6** (a) Generation sent out by type (shares) in the base case. (b) Generation capacity by type (shares) in the base case.

constant at around 45%, but its generation share continues to fall. In the detailed electricity modeling, there are no net additions to coal capacity after 2022, but the rate of utilization of older plants not being replaced declines. Capacity for gas generation increases by more than is suggested by the change in its generation share. This reflects, in part, forward-looking expectations in the detailed electricity model, which allow for new capacity to come on line even if initially it has a low utilization rate.

**Table 9.7** Generation sent out by generator type for Australia: base case

| | Levels (PJ) | | | | | | | | | Average annual percentage growth rates 2010 to 2030 |
|---|---|---|---|---|---|---|---|---|---|---|
| | NSW | VIC | QLD | SA | WA | TAS | NT | ACT | AUS | |
| *2010* | | | | | | | | | | |
| Electricity generation-coal | 205.5 | 186.6 | 200.6 | 19.1 | 42.9 | 0.0 | 0.0 | 0.0 | 654.7 | 0.5 |
| Electricity generation-gas | 14.1 | 12.1 | 41.9 | 4.2 | 37.9 | 1.8 | 12.3 | 0.0 | 124.4 | 3.2 |
| Electricity generation-oil products | 1.2 | 0.0 | 1.2 | 0.1 | 1.3 | 0.0 | 0.0 | 0.0 | 3.8 | 0.0 |
| Electricity generation-hydro | 10.7 | 11.4 | 3.5 | 0.0 | 0.0 | 34.5 | 0.0 | 0.0 | 60.1 | 0.0 |
| Electricity generation-other | 6.9 | 5.6 | 4.3 | 9.0 | 14.3 | 4.6 | 0.0 | 0.0 | 44.7 | 6.7 |
| Total | 238.4 | 215.8 | 251.5 | 32.4 | 96.5 | 40.9 | 12.3 | 0.0 | 887.7 | 1.5 |
| *2030* | | | | | | | | | | |
| Electricity generation-coal | 243.7 | 174.2 | 285.3 | 0.2 | 20.9 | 0.0 | 0.0 | 0.0 | 724.2 | |
| Electricity generation-gas | 25.8 | 16.4 | 41.9 | 10.0 | 117.0 | 2.5 | 20.0 | 0.0 | 233.6 | |
| Electricity generation-oil products | 1.2 | 0.0 | 1.2 | 0.1 | 1.3 | 0.0 | 0.0 | 0.0 | 3.8 | |
| Electricity generation-hydro | 10.7 | 11.4 | 3.5 | 0.0 | 0.0 | 34.5 | 0.0 | 0.0 | 60.1 | |
| Electricity generation-other | 24.5 | 47.8 | 21.8 | 49.4 | 15.9 | 4.8 | 0.0 | 0.0 | 164.1 | |
| Total | 305.9 | 249.8 | 353.6 | 59.6 | 155.1 | 41.8 | 20.0 | 0.0 | 1185.9 | |

## 9.5 ETS SIMULATION DESIGN

### 9.5.1 Introduction

In Section 9.6, we report MMRF simulations of a global ETS with a global allocation of permits sufficient to reduce global emissions in 2050 to 5% below their level in the year 2000.[23] The simulations examine the effects of this scheme out to 2030. The effects are reported as deviations from the values of variables in the base-case projection described in Section 9.4.

The main inputs to the MMRF policy simulation are projected effects of the scheme on:

- various aspects of electricity supply, as modeled by Frontier Economics;
- vehicle use by vehicle type, as modeled by the Australian Bureau of Infrastructure, Transport and Regional Economics (BITRE) and by the Commonwealth Scientific and Industrial Research Organization (CSIRO);
- forestry sequestration and plantation use of land from land-use experts at ABARES;
- foreign currency import prices and the positions of foreign export-demand schedules from the GTEM model;
- the global emissions price and Australia's allocation of global permits as specified by the Australian Treasury.

In the remainder of this section, we first outline the key features of the scheme (Section 9.5.2), including the permit price and Australia's allocation of emission permits. In Section 9.5.3 we discuss the other key inputs listed above. Key assumptions regarding the behavior of the macroeconomy in the MMRF simulations are discussed in Section 9.5.4.

### 9.5.2 Scheme design

Table 9.8 summaries design features of the modeled ETS scheme.

#### 9.5.2.1 Permit price

The GTEM projection of the international permit price, converted to real Australian dollars in MMRF, is given in Figure 9.7. The starting price is $A24.3 per tonne by the year 2012. Thereafter, it increases at an annual rate of around 4%, reaching $A33.3 per tonne in 2020 and $A49.3 per tonne in 2030.

In MMRF, the permit price is modeled as a tax imposed per unit of $CO_2$-e (Section 9.2.3.2). In keeping with the design of the scheme, initially the tax is imposed on all sources of emissions other than agriculture and transport. From 2012 onwards it is extended to transport, and from 2015 to agriculture. Thus, all emissions are priced at the same rate after 2015.

---

[23] This is the scheme identified by the Australian Treasury as the CPRS (Carbon Pollution Reduction Scheme)-5.

**Table 9.8** Features of the ETS scheme as modeled

| Assumption | Details |
| --- | --- |
| Timing and relationship to global action | Scheme starts in 2011 as a domestic scheme with a specified emissions price. From 2012 to 2020 it continues to operate as a domestic scheme, but with permits allowed to be purchased from overseas such as credits generated through projects under the Kyoto Protocol's Clean Development Mechanism (CDM). |
|  | From 2020 onwards, Australia's scheme is fully integrated into a single comprehensive global scheme. |
|  | Scheme price is specified for each year. The allocation of permits in Australia is specified from 2012 onwards. Emission price and permit allocation come from GTEM and are given in Sections 9.5.2.1 and 9.5.2.2. |
| Coverage | Phased coverage of sectors: |
|  | • All emissions other than from agriculture and transport from 2011 onwards. |
|  | • Transport emissions from 2012. |
|  | • Agricultural emissions from 2015. |
|  | All sectors covered by the scheme face the same emissions price. |
| Free permit allocation to generators | Limited free allocation of permits to electricity generators to 2020. Emission permits are allocated to offset net loss in profits. |
| Compensation for trade exposed, energy intensive industries | Energy-intensive trade exposed industries are compensated through to 2020 according to the shielding formulae (7) and (8). Category 1 industries are: Sheep and beef cattle (industry 1), Dairy cattle (2), Grains (4), Cement (24), Iron and steel (25) and Aluminum (27). Category 2 industries are: Other livestock (industry 3), Gas mining (10), Paper products (18), Basic chemicals (21), Non-metal construction products (23), Alumina (26) and Other non-ferrous metals (28). From 2020 onwards the shielding rates decline in a linear way to zero in 2025. |
| Recycling of surplus revenue | Remaining permits, beyond those used to compensate generators and trade-exposed energy sectors, were assumed to be auctioned, with surplus revenue recycled as a lump sum to households. |
| Other Australian mitigation policies | The MRET continues to operate through to 2020. Most other mitigation policies included in the base case cease with the exception of a QLD scheme designed to increase gas generation in that state to 15% of total generation. |
| Banking | Unconstrained banking is allowed, but no borrowing. The impact of banking is reflected in the Frontier modeling for the electricity generation sector and thus influences the permit price adopted in the MMRF modeling. Banking allows arbitrage between higher permit prices later in the ETS period and lower permit prices earlier. This has the effect of increasing the amount of (cheaper) abatement undertaken early, and reducing the amount of (more expensive) abatement later. |

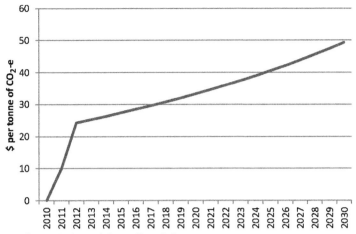

**Figure 9.7** Price of permits in real Australian dollars.

### 9.5.2.2 Australia's allocation of permits

Figure 9.8 shows Australia's allocation of permits under the global ETS. It also shows Australia's projected path for emissions in the base case where no ETS is in place. In the base case, emissions rise from 528 Mt of $CO_2$-e in 2010 to 710 Mt in 2030. Australia's permit allocation in 2030 is for emissions of 365 Mt of $CO_2$-e.

The gap between base-case emissions and permit allocation represents the international abatement obligation faced by Australia under the global ETS. As shown in Figure 9.8 the gap steadily widens over time, so that by 2030 the abatement obligation is

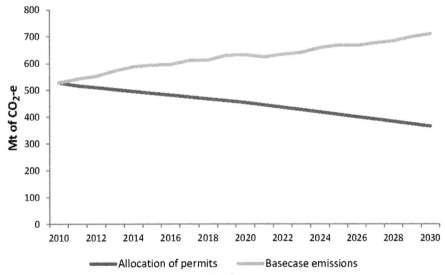

**Figure 9.8** Permit allocation and base case path of emissions.

345 ($=710-365$) Mt of $CO_2$-e. Australia can meet this in two ways: by domestic abatement in response to the emission price and by purchasing permits from overseas. As will be seen, based on the price profile in Figure 9.7, Australia ends up importing a large number of permits.

### 9.5.2.3 Electricity inputs from Frontier WHIRLYGIG

Following the iterative process described in Section 9.3.2.2, the Frontier electricity model provides projections (deviations from base-case values) for electricity generation, energy use, generation capacity, emissions and electricity prices. These projections are accommodated in the MMRF modeling via the closure changes given in Table 9.4.

In the Frontier modeling, the electricity sector responds to the permit price by switching technologies, changing the utilization of existing capacity, and replacing old plants with new more-efficient plants. The modeling also includes the reduction in electricity usage projected in MMRF's modeling of demand. These factors underlie the deviations from base plotted in Figure 9.9(a) (generation) and Figure 9.9(b) (capacity). Further detail on generation is given in Table 9.9.

Compared to the base case, the overall level of generation in 2030 is down by 6.9% and the mix of generation has changed appreciably away from coal and towards gas and non-hydro renewables. By assumption, there is no change in generation from oil products (not shown in Figure 9.9a) and hydro.

In the base case, the detailed electricity modeling tells a fairly straightforward story for the relationship between generation and capacity for each generation technology (Figure 9.6a and b). However, in the ETS-induced deviations from base case the relationships are more complicated. For coal, capacity declines at the same rate as it does in the base case through to 2020, yet generation falls significantly relative to base-case levels, reflecting reduced capacity utilization. From 2020 onwards, the emission price depresses expectations of long-run profit to such a degree that conventional coal capacity starts to decline — replacement investments in coal-fired capacity that occur in the base case are discouraged by the emissions price. In 2030, coal capacity is 28% below its base-case level, while coal generation is down by about 20%.

Capacity for gas generation, which expands in the base case, is below base-case levels from 2014 onwards. Units of gas generation are generally smaller than units of coal generation. Hence, in the detailed electricity modeling, gas generation capacity can be adjusted relatively quickly. Note that rate of capacity utilization for gas plant is above the base-case rate throughout the projection period. This is especially marked after 2019, due to the ETS bringing forward a large upgrade of an existing plant, reducing its unit operating costs.

Capacity for other-renewable generation initially falls relative to its base-case levels, before exceeding base-case levels from 2013 onwards. This postpones the rate at which

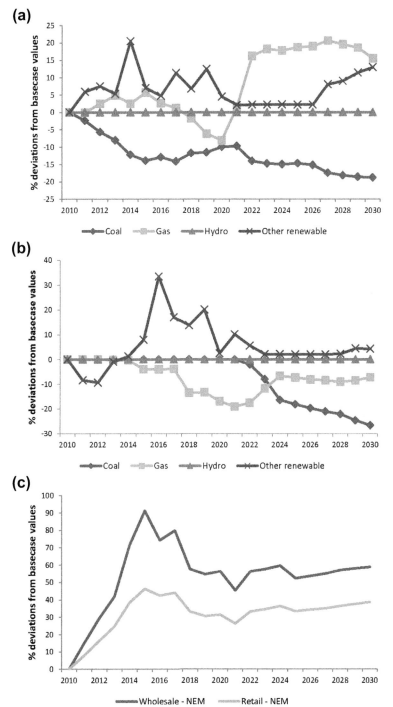

**Figure 9.9** (a) Electricity generation by type. (b) Electricity capacity by type. (c) NEM electricity prices.

**Table 9.9** Generation sent out by generator type for Australia: policy

| Percentage deviations from base-case values | 2015 | 2020 | 2030 |
|---|---|---|---|
| Electricity generation-coal | -13.0 | -9.8 | -18.0 |
| Electricity generation-gas | 6.6 | -5.7 | 11.5 |
| Electricity generation-oil products | 0.0 | 0.0 | 0.0 |
| Electricity generation-hydro | 0.0 | 0.0 | 0.0 |
| Electricity generation-other | 4.7 | 5.0 | 13.3 |
| Total | -8.0 | -6.5 | -6.9 |

| Changes in levels (PJ) | NSW | VIC | QLD | SA | WA | TAS | NT | ACT | AUS |
|---|---|---|---|---|---|---|---|---|---|
| *2015* | | | | | | | | | |
| Electricity generation-coal | -38.0 | -39.4 | -10.4 | -1.3 | -6.3 | 0.0 | 0.0 | 0.0 | -95.3 |
| Electricity generation-gas | -1.4 | -1.2 | 0.7 | 9.1 | 3.2 | -0.2 | -0.5 | 0.0 | 9.6 |
| Electricity generation-oil products | 0.0 | 0.0 | 0.0 | 0.0 | 0.0 | 0.0 | 0.0 | 0.0 | 0.0 |
| Electricity generation-hydro | 0.0 | 0.0 | 0.0 | 0.0 | 0.0 | 0.0 | 0.0 | 0.0 | 0.0 |
| Electricity generation-other | -0.1 | 20.8 | -10.2 | -7.8 | 0.9 | -0.1 | 0.0 | 0.0 | 3.7 |
| Total | -39.4 | -19.8 | -19.9 | 0.1 | -2.1 | -0.3 | -0.5 | 0.0 | -81.9 |
| *2030* | | | | | | | | | |
| Electricity generation-coal | -25.0 | -42.5 | -47.4 | -0.6 | -15.1 | 0.0 | 0.0 | 0.0 | -130.6 |
| Electricity generation-gas | 17.6 | -0.4 | 1.7 | -5.3 | 14.5 | -0.2 | -1.1 | 0.0 | 26.8 |
| Electricity generation-oil products | 0.0 | 0.0 | 0.0 | 0.0 | 0.0 | 0.0 | 0.0 | 0.0 | 0.0 |
| Electricity generation-hydro | 0.0 | 0.0 | 0.0 | 0.0 | 0.0 | 0.0 | 0.0 | 0.0 | 0.0 |
| Electricity generation-other | 0.0 | 8.1 | 10.7 | 3.0 | 0.0 | 0.0 | 0.0 | 0.0 | 21.8 |
| Total | -7.5 | -34.9 | -34.8 | -2.8 | -0.6 | -0.2 | -1.1 | 0.0 | -82.1 |

new renewable plant is installed relative to base-case assumptions. Note, however, that renewable generation is still replacing coal-fired generation in these early years. This is due to a rise in capacity utilization for renewable and a fall for coal. After 2013, capacity in the non-hydro renewable sector increases but unevenly, reflecting the detailed electricity model's handling of lumpy investments.

In the Frontier modeling, cleaner technologies for generating electricity from coal are adopted when the price on emissions makes it economical to do so. The uptake of such technologies is the reason that, as a percentage of base-case values, emissions from coal generation fall by more than generation levels. Relative to base case, coal generation falls by 13.0% (2015), 9.8% (2020) and 18.0% (2030), while emissions are down 14.5% (2015), 10.6% (2020) and 23.9% (2030).

In addition to generation and capacity, electricity prices are key variables imported into MMRF from *WHIRLYGIG*. Figure 9.9(c) gives deviations from base-case values for average wholesale and retail prices in the NEM.

With base-case emission intensities and the base-case composition of generation, the carbon price (Figure 9.7) would increase the average cost of generation in the NEM to about 80% above its base-case level in 2030. With wholesale electricity accounting for around 40% of the retail cost, we would then expect the retail price in 2030 to be about 30% above its base-case value. As shown in Figure 9.9(c), however, in the detailed electricity modeling the wholesale price jumps quickly to be about 90% above its base-case level, then declines in a jumpy way to about 60% above base in 2030. The retail price follows a similar pattern, ending up about 40% higher than its base-case level.

The initial increase in the wholesale price occurs because the carbon price increases the relative cost of Victorian brown-coal generation so that it becomes the marginal supply that sets the price in the early years, instead of being base-load plant. As the brown-coal generators set the price in the NEM and because they have high emission intensities (of greater than 1 t/MWh), electricity prices increase by the full amount of the increase in their short-run marginal cost. After 2015, the conventional brown-coal generators are phased out (though not immediately scrapped, as can be seen from Figure 9.9b) and the marginal generator changes to gas and renewable generation units with lower marginal costs. These changes continue until by 2030 with a carbon price of almost $A50 per tonne, the wholesale price has reached a level about 60% above its base-case value.

The increase in retail price is higher than would be expected given the increase in wholesale price. Higher network charges associated with the significant changes in type and location of generation account for this.

### 9.5.2.4 Road transport inputs from the BITRE and CSIRO

The BITRE and CSIRO provide data for changes away from base-case values in fuel use and emissions for private transport by region. The assumptions suggest that to 2030 the emissions price will have little impact on fuel choice and emissions in private transport.[24]

Projections for the use of gasoline, diesel and LPG in road transport are accommodated in MMRF by endogenous shifts in fuel-usage coefficients in industries' production functions. The BITRE/CSIRO emissions projections are accommodated by endogenous shifts in emissions per unit of fuel used.

### 9.5.2.5 Forestry land and biosequestration inputs from ABARES

According to the ABARES inputs, the global ETS would have a significant impact on forestry production and forest biosequestration, as shown in Figure 9.10. By 2030, forestry production has risen 80% above its base-case level and sequestration has risen by 30 Mt.

Corresponding changes in land under forestry are also imposed. With total land availability by region, fixed, land available for agriculture falls.

The ABARES estimates of the response of forestry sequestration to the emissions price is accommodated in MMRF by endogenous shifts in emissions per unit of forestry output.

### 9.5.2.6 Trade variables based on information from GTEM

Projections of changes in foreign-currency import prices and in the positions of foreign export-demand schedules for Australia in response to a global emissions price are sourced from GTEM modeling.[25] The GTEM projections are summarized by changes in the aggregate terms of trade shown in Figure 9.11.

The long-term effect of the ETS on Australia's terms of trade is negative. This is driven mainly by a reduction in the world price of coal as users switch to less emission-intensive fuels. However, when China joins the international coalition in 2015[26] there is a temporary jump in global coal prices as Chinese demand is diverted from local to foreign supplied product. This effect dissipates in 2020 when India and the rest of the world join the scheme and world coal demand falls.

### 9.5.2.7 Assumptions about gas reserves and gas prices from various industry sources

In the base-case and policy simulations, gas reserves in the eastern Australia gradually close down and are replaced by supplies from WA and the NT. WA and NT gas is produced for export as well as for local use and its price is set by the global gas price. Gas from eastern sources is produced for local demand and its price is determined, in the

---

[24] Note that the post-2030 ETS modeling reported by the Treasury has electric-powered cars taking significant market share away from vehicles relying on internal combustion technologies.

[25] The methodology used to introduce the GTEM results into MMRF is described in Section 9.3.1.

[26] The Treasury's CPRS assumed a multistage approach to international emissions trading. Developed countries act first, then developing countries join over time.

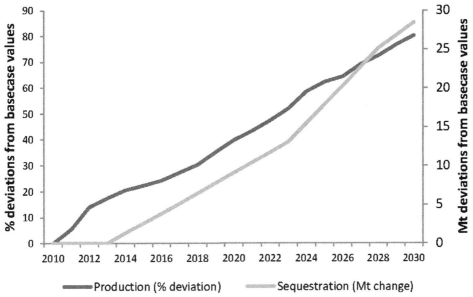

**Figure 9.10** Forestry production and sequestration.

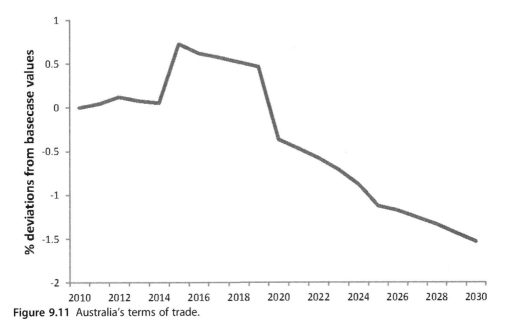

**Figure 9.11** Australia's terms of trade.

main, by domestic factors. As eastern fields are replaced by WA and NT gas, so the prices paid by customers in the eastern states move to international parity. In the base-case and policy simulations, it is assumed that eastern gas prices rise gradually to reach full international parity by 2030.

### 9.5.3 Assumptions for the macroeconomy in the policy scenarios

The following assumptions are made for key aspects of the macro economy in the policy (with-ETS) simulation.

#### 9.5.3.1 Labor markets

At the national level, lagged adjustment of the real-wage rate to changes in employment is assumed. Adoption of the ETS can cause employment to deviate from its base-case value initially, but thereafter, real wage adjustment steadily eliminates the short-run employment consequences of the emissions price. In the long run, the costs of emissions pricing are realized almost entirely as a fall in the national real wage rate, rather than as a fall in national employment. This labor-market assumption reflects the idea that in the long run national employment is determined by demographic factors, which are unaffected by the adoption of an emissions price.

At the regional level, labor is assumed to be mobile between state economies (Section 9.2.2.5). Labor is assumed to move between regions so as to maintain interstate unemployment-rate differentials at their base-case levels. Accordingly, regions that are relatively favorably affected by emissions pricing will experience increases in their labor forces as well as in employment, at the expense of regions that are relatively less favorably affected.

#### 9.5.3.2 Private consumption and investment

Private consumption expenditure is determined via a Keynesian consumption function that links nominal consumption to HDI. HDI includes the lump-sum return of permit income which is part of the ETS design. In the ETS simulations, the APC is an endogenous variable that moves to ensure that the balance on current account in the balance of payments remains at its base-case level. Thus, any change in aggregate investment brought about by the ETS is accommodated by a change in domestic saving, leaving Australia's call on foreign savings unchanged.

This treatment of domestic and foreign savings is sufficient, but more extreme than is necessary, to ensure that the long-run deviation in real private consumption from its base-case level is a valid measure of the impacts of the ETS on the welfare of Australians. A less extreme treatment would be to impose a foreign-debt constraint directly and allow the year-to-year pattern of aggregate consumption and the current account to reflect year-to-year changes in disposable income.

Investment in all but a few industries is allowed to deviate from its base-case value in line with deviations in expected rates of return on the industries' capital stocks. In the policy scenarios, MMRF allows for short-run divergences in rates of return from their base-case levels. These cause divergences in investment and hence capital stocks that gradually erode the initial divergences in rates of return. Provided there are no further shocks, rates of return revert to their base-case levels in the long run. An exception to this rule is the electricity generating industries, for which changes in capacity are taken from the detailed electricity model. The changes are accommodated by allowing the required rates of return on investment to shift endogenously.

### 9.5.3.3 Government consumption and fiscal balances

MMRF contains no theory to explain changes in real public consumption. In these simulations, public consumption is simply indexed to nominal GDP. The fiscal balances of each jurisdiction (federal, state and territory) as a share of nominal GDP are fixed at their values in the base case. Budget balance constraints are accommodated by endogenous movements in lump-sum payments to households.

### 9.5.3.4 Production technologies and household tastes

MMRF contains many variables to allow for shifts in technology and household preferences. In the policy scenarios, most of these variables are exogenous and have the same values as in the base-case projection. The exceptions are technology variables that are made endogenous to allow for:

- changes in the fuel intensity of electricity generation, based on data from the detailed electricity modeling;
- the new production technology required to achieve the reductions in emissions intensity implied by equation (9.9) (Section 9.3.4);
- the replacement of gasoline and diesel with cleaner (but more expensive) biofuels and electricity in the provision of private transport services. This is based on information from the detailed road-transport modeling (Section 9.5.2.4).

## 9.6 ECONOMIC EFFECTS OF THE ETS

### 9.6.1 Introduction

Figure 9.12 illustrates the interpretation of MMRF results for the effects of an ETS on a particular variable, e.g. real GDP. MMRF generates a base case, which is a projection through time for the variable without an ETS (Section 9.4). The base case is depicted as the path between points A and B. The model is also used to produce an alternative projection in which endogenous variables shift away from base-case trends to accommodate the exogenous shocks associated with the ETS (Section 9.5). A typical alternative projection for the variable considered in Figure 9.12 is shown as the path between points A and C.

Figure 9.12 has been drawn with the base-case path and the ETS path both smooth and with the deviation of the ETS path from the base-case path also growing smoothly. In this case, it is apparent that there are a number of options for reporting the effects of the ETS, all of which will tell a similar story.

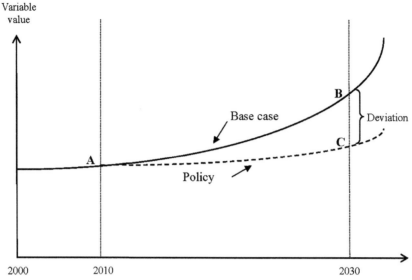

**Figure 9.12** Interpretation of results.

One option is to compare average annual growth in the base case with average annual growth in the ETS simulation. In terms of average annual rates between 2010 and 2030, we would be comparing:

$$100 \times \left\{ \left(\frac{B}{A}\right)^{1/20} - 1 \right\} \text{ with } 100 \times \left\{ \left(\frac{C}{A}\right)^{1/20} - 1 \right\}. \tag{9.10}$$

Note that in the smooth case shown in Figure 9.12, comparing average annual growth rates over shorter periods will not be seriously misleading relative to the whole-period comparison.

Alternatively, deviations can be reported by comparing the value of variables in a specific year in the ETS simulation with values in the base case. Deviations could be expressed as percentage changes from base-case values in the final year of the simulation period:

$$100 \times \left\{ \left(\frac{C}{B}\right) - 1 \right\}, \tag{9.11}$$

or as absolute ($A million or Mt, etc.) changes from base-case values:

$$(C - B). \tag{9.12}$$

Again, in the smooth case intermediate-year comparisons will not be seriously misleading relative to the final-period comparison.

Users of model-based projections of the effects the ETS policy have often been tempted to select their preferred reporting option according to how it is likely to be interpreted by non-specialists. Proponents of the ETS opt for measures that appear superficially to suggest that its cost will be small while opponents opt for measures that appear to suggest large costs.

To illustrate this, in Table 9.10 we report the effects of the ETS on Australian real GDP in 2020 and 2030 according to measures (9.10)–(9.12) and according to a fourth measure (9.13) that emphasizes that negative deviations from base-case values are compatible with continuing strong growth in an economy that would have been enjoying strong growth in the absence of the ETS. This fourth measure expresses the deviation as the number of months of base-case growth that are lost as a consequence of the ETS:

$$-12 \times \frac{\left\{ \left( \frac{C}{B} \right) - 1 \right\}}{\left\{ \left( \frac{B}{A} \right)^{1/20} - 1 \right\}}. \tag{9.13}$$

Unsurprisingly, proponents of the ETS usually opt for the first or fourth measure, while opponents tend to concentrate on the second or especially the third measure.

More fundamental than this cosmetic point is the question of how to report results in cases in which, unlike Figure 9.12, the base-case path or the ETS path or the deviation between the paths does not develop smoothly. As shown in Figures 9.9(a–c) and 9.11, when we incorporate results from a bottom-up model of the electricity system like *WHIRLYGIG* or a world-trade model like GTEM, the paths and deviations for electricity variables and the terms of trade may not develop smoothly. One option is to report a time profile of the deviations of base-case values from ETS values. Another is to use an aggregate measure that includes all the year-specific deviations. The present value of the deviations is an obvious choice.

## 9.6.2 Results

The rest of this section contains a discussion of deviations from base-case values in the ETS simulations (Tables 9.11–9.14). National impacts are dealt with first, followed by

**Table 9.10** Alternative interpretation of ETS impacts

| Equation | Description of measure | 2020 | 2030 |
|---|---|---|---|
| 10 | Average annual growth rates (%) | 2.91 (base)/ 2.87 (ETS) | 2.63 (base)/ 2.56 (ETS) |
| 11 | Deviations from base case (%) | −0.5 | −1.1 |
| 12 | Absolute deviations from base case ($Am) | −7268.7 | −20138.4 |
| 13 | Months of growth lost due to the ETS | 2.0 | 4.9 |

state and substate outcomes. Projected deviations for 2030 are given in Tables 9.11 (macro variables), 9.13 (national industry output) and 9.14 (emissions of $CO_2$-e). A series of charts provide time profiles of the deviations for key variables. In the discussion below, which focuses mainly on the final year (2030), subheadings headings outline the main features of the results.

Our explanations of the national-level macroeconomic results are informed by a stylized back-of-the-envelope (BOTE) macro model that we constructed to demonstrate the macroeconomic mechanisms underlying the MMRF results. Details of the stylized model are in the Appendix.

### 9.6.2.1 National variables

In the short run, the ETS reduces employment relative to its base-case level; over time, the employment deviation remains fairly constant as the national real wage rate adjusts downwards

The explanation of macro effects begins with the impacts on the national labor market. Figure 9.13 shows percentage deviations in national employment, the national real wage rate and the national real cost of labor. The real wage is defined as the ratio of the nominal wage rate to the price of consumption. The real cost of labor is defined as the ratio of the nominal wage rate to the national price of output (measured by the factor-cost GDP deflator). Assuming competitive markets, the equilibrium nominal wage will be equal to the value of the marginal product of labor.

According to the labor market specification in MMRF (Section 9.5.3.1), the real wage rate is sticky in the short run (i.e. the nominal wage moves with the price of consumption), but adjusts with a lag downwards (upwards) in response to a fall (rise) in employment. When the ETS starts up, the emissions price increases the price of spending (e.g. household consumption) relative to the price of output and hence moves the nominal wage above the value of the marginal product of labor in the short run. In

**Table 9.11** Macroeconomic variables (% changes from base-case values, 2030)

|          | Real GDP/GSP | Real consumption | Real international exports | Real international imports | Employment |
|----------|------|------|------|------|------|
| NSW      | −1.2 | −1.9 | 1.2  | −2.4 | −0.5 |
| VIC      | −0.9 | −2.0 | 6.9  | −1.6 | 0.1  |
| QLD      | −1.8 | −1.1 | −2.0 | −2.8 | −0.9 |
| SA       | −0.7 | −2.5 | 7.2  | −1.6 | 0.0  |
| WA       | −0.8 | 0.8  | −1.5 | −1.4 | 1.0  |
| TAS      | 3.3  | −1.8 | 21.4 | 1.6  | 3.1  |
| NT       | 1.5  | 2.2  | 3.3  | 1.0  | 2.2  |
| ACT      | −1.2 | −3.0 | 3.0  | −2.8 | −0.9 |
| National | −1.1 | −1.5 | 1.2  | −2.0 | −0.1 |

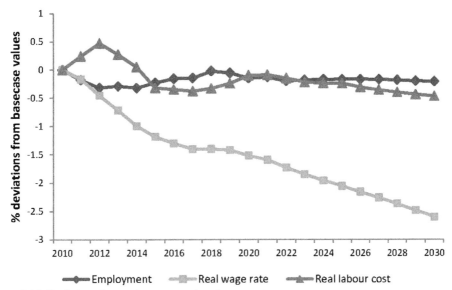

**Figure 9.13** Deviations in employment and real wage rates.

Figure 9.13 this shows as an increase in the real cost of labor relative to its base-case value and a fall in employment relative to base case.

If there were no further shocks, over time the real wage rate would progressively fall relative to base-case levels, reducing the real cost of labor and forcing employment back to its base-case level. In the ETS simulations, however, shocks continue with the permit price increasing under a progressively tighter regime of tradable permits. Hence, as shown in Figure 9.13, the employment deviation is never fully eliminated and the real wage rate declines steadily relative to its base-case value. In 2030, the employment deviation is −0.2%, while the real wage rate is down 2.6%.

Note that the deviations in employment and the real wage rate are not smooth, especially in the early years, despite the smoothness of the permit-price trajectory (Figure 9.7). This reflects a number of factors:
- the changing coverage of the ETS scheme, with transport industries entering in 2012 and agricultural industries entering in 2015 (Table 9.8);
- large changes in electricity generation and capacity by technology type projected by the detailed electricity modeling (Figure 9.9a and b);
- swings in the national terms of trade projected by GTEM (Figure 9.11).

The swings in the terms of trade have a significant impact on the labor market in the short run. An increase in the terms of trade causes the price of final domestic demand (which *includes* import prices but *excludes* export prices) to fall relative to the price of GDP (which *excludes* import prices but *includes* export prices), leading to downward pressure on the real cost of labor. Hence, relative to base, changes in the terms of trade

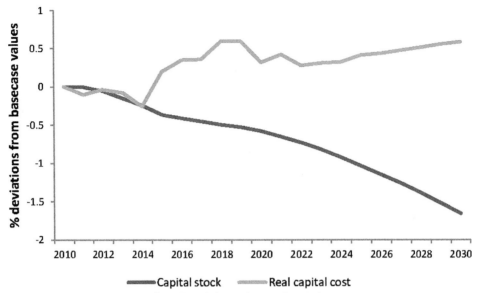

**Figure 9.14** Deviations in capital stock and the real cost of capital.

contribute positively to employment in the first few years of the projection when the terms of trade rise.

A final point to note is that even though the fall in national employment is fairly small, this does not mean that employment at the individual industry or regional level remains close to base-case values. In most industries and regions, there are significant permanent employment responses to the ETS, compounding or defusing existing (base-case) pressures for structural change.

### The ETS depresses the economy-wide labor/capital ratio

Figure 9.14 shows percentage deviations from base-case values for the national capital stock and the real cost of capital. The latter is defined as the ratio of the nominal rental cost of capital to the national price of output (measured by the factor-cost GDP deflator). In 2030, the capital stock deviation is −1.7%, implying an increase in the ratio of labor to capital of around 1.6%. In the same year, the real cost of capital is up 0.6% relative to its base case level.[27]

The reduction in capital is due, in part, to changes in relative factor prices. As the real cost of labor falls relative to the real cost of capital (compare Figure 9.13 with Figure 9.14), producers substitute labor for capital across the economy. In 2030, with the real cost of capital relative to the real cost of labor rising by around 1.1%, the shift in

---

[27] In general terms, as the real cost of labor falls, so the real cost of the other key factor of production (capital) will rise.

relative factor prices could be expected to contribute about $0.5 \times 3.0 = 1.5$ percentage points to the eventual 1.6% increase in the labor/capital ratio.[28] In addition, there is a compositional effect due to the fact that the energy-related mining and coal-fired electricity sectors that are suppressed by the ETS are capital-intensive.

### With little change in employment and technology, the reduction in capital leads to a fall in real GDP at factor cost

The percentage change in real GDP at factor cost is a share-weighted average of the percentage changes in quantities of factor inputs (labor, capital and agricultural land), with allowance for technological change. Figure 9.15(a) shows, in stacked annual columns, the contribution of each component other than land to the overall percentage deviation in real factor-cost GDP. Although land can be re-allocated between uses, its availability overall is fixed.

Real GDP at factor cost falls relative to its base-case level in all years of the simulation. In the final year it is down 0.9%. The possibility of achieving large cuts in emissions at a relatively mild macro-cost is a common theme in all of the analyses of carbon taxes and emission trading schemes undertaken at CoPS.

As Figure 9.15(a) shows, nearly all of the fall in factor-cost GDP is due to the reduction in capital. Labor's contribution in the final year is a little more than $-0.1$ percentage point.

The ETS does induce some technological change (Section 9.5.3.4), but its contribution to the deviation in real GDP is small. In the MMRF simulation, the carbon price leads to technological deterioration primarily through the adoption of more expensive, but less emission-intensive, production technologies (Section 9.3.4). This is evident in Figure 9.15(a) for the early years of the simulation period. In the later years it is offset and eventually dominated by a compositional factor. In dynamic policy simulations, deviations in real GDP are affected by induced changes in the composition of GDP (Dixon and Rimmer, 2002; Section 9.7.2). If the policy shock increases the shares in GDP of industries with rapid technological progress and reduces the shares of industries with less rapid technological progress, then real GDP growth will be elevated in the policy simulation relative to the base case.[29] In our base-case simulation, service industries are assumed to have stronger labor-saving technological progress than mining and manufacturing industries. As the carbon price shifts the composition of the economy towards services, this allows technological change to make a positive contribution to the deviation in real GDP from 2019 onwards.

---

[28] The capital to labor substitution elasticity is 0.5.

[29] Similar phenomena affect the measurement of other macro indices. For example, the path of real consumption in a policy simulation can deviate from its base-case path not only because of deviations in quantities consumed of each commodity, but also because of deviations in budget shares.

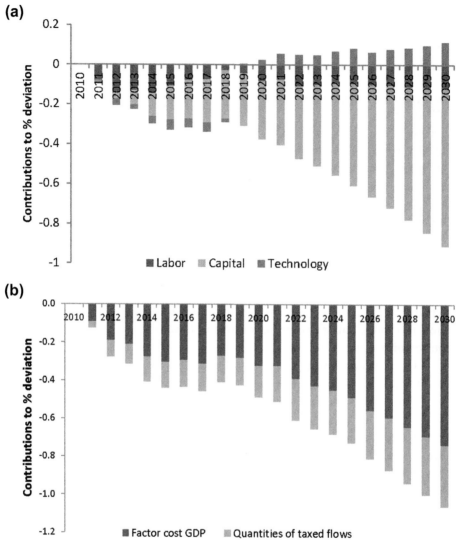

**Figure 9.15** (a) Contributions to percent deviation in real GDP at factor cost. (b) Contributions to percent deviation in real GDP at market prices.

**Real GDP at market prices falls by more than real GDP at factor cost, due to a contraction in real indirect-tax bases**

The percentage change in real GDP at market prices is a share-weighted average of the percentage change in real GDP at factor cost and real net-indirect-tax bases. As shown in Figure 9.15b, in line with the fall in factor-cost GDP, market-price GDP falls through the projection period to be 1.1% below its base-case value in 2030. Box 9.1 provides a plausibility check on this result.

## BOX 9.1 Check on reality via BOTE calculations

As noted above, by 2030 with an emissions price of close to $A50, real GDP at market prices is projected to be 1.1% lower than it otherwise would have been and emissions are projected around 25% lower.

Is this result plausible? To answer this question, CoPS modelers typically make use of BOTE calculations. This can be done in a formal way using a stylized model as demonstrated in the Appendix. Or it can be done less formally. For example, we know that the main $CO_2$-e emitting activities are the fossil fuel-based provision of electricity and transport services. According to the MMRF database, in 2011 these activities represent about 2.5% of market-price GDP and about 55% of total emissions. Based on the Frontier Economics electricity model and expert transport sector input, Australia can cut its emissions from these sectors by about 45% with roughly a 55% increase in the costs of electricity and motor fuels. As a BOTE calculation, this suggests that Australia could make a 25% cut in emissions at a cost of around 1.4% ($= 55\%$ of 2.5) of GDP. The projected outcome for real GDP is a little milder than this, suggesting that cheaper abatement opportunities exist than might be available from electricity and transport alone.

The contribution made by changes in real indirect-tax bases in 2030 is $-0.3$ percentage points. $CO_2$-e emissions, petroleum products and consumption are the principal bases on which indirect taxes are levied. All of these contract relative to their base-case values. More specifically, in 2030:

- Emissions are down 25.6%, contributing $-0.1$ percentage points to the gap of $-0.3$ percentage points between the deviation in market-price real GDP and factor-cost real GDP.
- Petroleum usage is down 3.8%, contributing $-0.03$ percentage points.
- Real consumption is down 1.5%, contributing $-0.04$ percentage points.

The residual of just over 0.1 percentage points is due to changes in the miscellaneous *Other-costs* category, which is treated as an indirect tax on production for GDP accounting purposes. *Other-costs* rates in the electricity generation and supply industries are endogenous variables in the policy simulation, adjusting to accommodate changes in wholesale and retail electricity prices taken from the detailed electricity modeling (Table 9.4, see also Figure 9.9c). To accommodate these changes, MMRF requires little change in the *Other-costs* rate for generation, but relatively large increases for electricity supply. MMRF does not fully capture the resource costs associated with using more expensive renewable forms of generation. Neither does it capture the impact on electricity network costs. Inputs from the detailed electricity modeling correct for this and in doing so force retail electricity prices in the MMRF simulation to increase by more than they would otherwise do in response to a carbon price. As demand for electricity falls, so does the production of the now heavily taxed electricity supply industries. This fall in the real *Other-costs* base contributes 0.1 percentage points to the overall fall in real market-price GDP.

### By 2030 Australia must import a significant quantity of permits to meet its global ETS obligation

Figure 9.16 repeats the plots of Australia's permit allocation and base-case emissions from Figure 9.8 and adds a plot of emissions permit imports from the ETS simulation. Permit imports fill the gap between the permit allocation and actual emissions under the ETS.

The permit price effectively stabilizes total emissions near to their 2010 levels. Hence, with Australia's allocation of permits progressively falling, there is an increasing need to purchase permits from overseas. In 2030, around 160 Mt of permits are required. At a price of nearly $A50 per tonne, this translates into an annual financing cost of close to $A8 billion.

This financing cost represents a reduction in domestic welfare in the form of a transfer to foreigners. An alternative way in which Australia might meet its emissions target would be to impose a domestic emissions tax on top of the international permit price. This would involve a transfer of tax revenue from the domestic private sector to the Australian government and a deadweight loss. The latter represents a reduction in domestic welfare and is additional to the loss represented by the purchase of permits from the international market under the scheme that we have simulated. Hence, relying on imported permits minimizes the global cost of abatement and the loss of domestic welfare.

### The ETS reduces HDI and real private consumption, but the fall in consumption is attenuated by an increase in the APC

Figure 9.17 shows percentage deviations from base-case values for real private consumption, consumer-price-deflated HDI and the national average APC. In 2030,

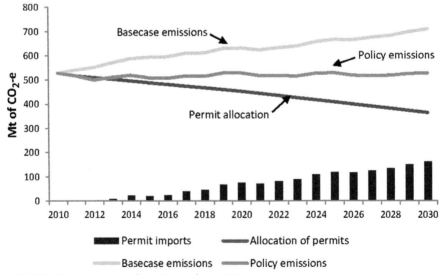

**Figure 9.16** Emissions, permit allocation and permit imports.

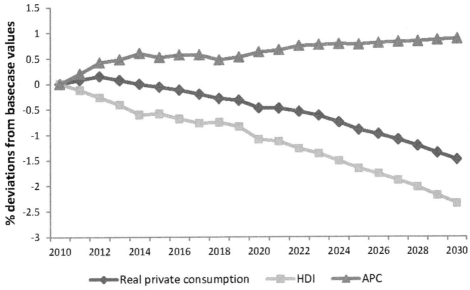

**Figure 9.17** Real private consumption, HDI and the propensity to consume.

HDI is down 2.3% relative to its base-case level, and real private consumption is down 1.5%. The difference is due to an increase in the APC of 0.9%.

The carbon charge reduces HDI by reducing the factor incomes (wages and profits, after income tax) that domestic residents receive from domestic enterprises. However, the charge does not reduce HDI by the entire amount of the gross revenue that it raises. Some of that revenue is required to purchase emissions permits from overseas, but some is returned to domestic households, either indirectly via shielding payments that are made to domestic EITEIs or directly via lump-sum recycling payments. In a partial equilibrium world, the lump-sum payments would be equal to the difference between the gross ETS revenue and the costs of shielding and international permit purchases. However, our general equilibrium calculations take account of the indirect effects that the ETS might have on the government budget balance. Lump-sum payments to households are then whatever is necessary to insulate the government budget balance (as a share of GDP) from the total effects of the ETS. The first part of Table 9.12 decomposes the change in HDI in 2030 into its components. Note that the excess of gross ETS revenue over the international permit cost is $A18.1 billion, but only $A14.5 billion of this is returned to household via lump-sum payments. The reason is that the indirect effects of the ETS on the government budget are negative — the ETS reduces income tax revenue, for example.

Recall from Section 9.5.3.2 that the APC is an endogenous variable, moving to ensure that the national balance on current account remains at its base-case level. To maintain an unchanged balance on current account, domestic savings (private *plus* public)

**Table 9.12** Household income, consumption, savings and investment (changes from base-case values, 2030)

|  | Deviation ($A billion) |
|---|---|
| Household disposable income |  |
|    Household income from labor and capital after income tax | −33.4 |
|    Permit price times emissions (gross permit tax) | 26.0 |
|    Minus value of permits purchased from overseas | −7.9 |
|    Minus value of shielding | 0.0[a] |
|    Government handout to maintain budget balances (ex permit income) | −14.5 |
|    Total HDI | −29.8 |
| Private consumption expenditure | −14.8 |
| Public consumption expenditure | −6.3 |
| Private saving ($\Delta$HDI − $\Delta$private consumption) | −15.1 |
| Public saving ($\Delta$government income − $\Delta$public consumption) | −3.4 |
| Investment | −18.1 |

[a]Shielding rates decline to zero after 2020.

must change to accommodate changes in aggregate investment. As shown in Table 9.12, the ETS generates an $A18.1 billion (or 3.4%) reduction in aggregate investment relative to base case. Public saving falls by $A3.4 billion. Hence, private saving must fall by around $A15 billion. Given a fall in total HDI of $A29.8 billion and a base-case value for the APC of 0.78, the APC must rise to achieve the necessary change in saving.

### Real gross national expenditure falls relative to real GDP leading to an improvement in the net volume of trade

Figure 9.18 shows percentage deviations from base-case values for real private consumption (C), real public consumption (G), real investment (I), real exports (X) and real imports (M). Deviations in C have already been discussed. Deviations in nominal G reflect deviations in nominal GDP (Section 9.5.3.3). Real government consumption rises relative to real GDP because the price of government spending (heavily influenced by the price of labor) relative to the price of GDP moves in line with the real wage rate. Deviations in I, which as noted above are particularly sharp, reflect the declines in gross investment necessary to accommodate the falls in capital shown in Figure 9.14.

On balance, real gross national expenditure ($= C + I + G$) falls by more than real GDP, implying an improvement in the net volume of trade ($X - M$). This sterilizes the impacts on the current account balance of deterioration in the terms of trade and the cost of purchasing global emissions permits.

To achieve the necessary improvement in net trade volumes, mild depreciation of the real exchange rate is necessary. This improves the competitiveness of export industries on foreign markets and the competitiveness of import-competing industries on local markets. In 2030, the real exchange rate is 2.5% below its base-case value.

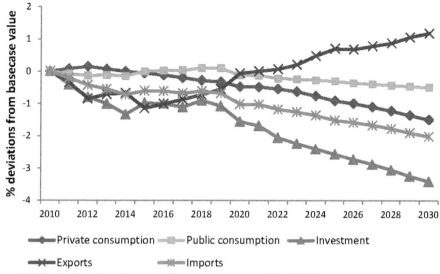

**Figure 9.18** Deviations in main expenditure components of real GDP.

## Production in some industries increases relative to base case, while production in other industries falls

Table 9.13 gives percentage deviations from base-case production levels for industries nationally in 2030. There are a number of industries for which the ETS raises output significantly. The most favorably affected industry is *Forestry* (industry 7), for which the carbon charge is effectively a production subsidy on biosequestration. Two other industries very favorably affected are *Electricity generation-other renewable* (industry 37, rank 3) and *Electricity generation-gas* (industry 33, rank 2). The carbon price causes substitution in favor of these industries at the expense of high-emissions *Electricity generation-coal* (industry 32, rank 58). Another negative factor for coal generation is the reduction in overall electricity demand due to the increased price of electricity to final customers. In Table 9.13, this shows up as a decline in production in the *Electricity supply* industry (industry 38, rank 55).

Table 9.13 shows significant increases in production for *Iron and steel* (industry 25, rank 4) and *Alumina* (industry 26, rank 6). Both are energy-intensive and trade-exposed, and under a unilateral ETS would contract, unless shielded. However, GTEM analysis of the multilateral aspects of the ETS projects trade diversion towards these Australian industries due to the availability of cheap energy abatement options in Australia that are not matched by competing suppliers. Another positive factor for these industries, and for all other traded-goods sectors, is the projected depreciation in the real exchange rate. A lower real exchange rate means that exports of industries such as the metal producers are more competitive on world markets.

**Table 9.13** National industry output (% changes from base-case values, 2030, ranked)

| Rank | Industry | 2030 |
|---|---|---|
| 1 | 7. Forestry | 80.2 |
| 2 | 33. Electricity generation–gas | 15.5 |
| 3 | 37. Electricity generation–other | 12.9 |
| 4 | 25. Iron and steel | 9.1 |
| 5 | 28. Other non-ferrous metals | 9.1 |
| 6 | 26. Alumina | 6.5 |
| 7 | 21. Basic chemicals | 3.8 |
| 8 | 3. Other livestock | 1.9 |
| 9 | 46. Rail passenger transport | 1.8 |
| 10 | 16. Textiles, clothing and footwear | 1.7 |
| 11 | 23. Non-metal construction products | 1.6 |
| 12 | 30. Motor vehicles and parts | 1.5 |
| 13 | 18. Paper products | 1.4 |
| 14 | 17. Wood products | 1.2 |
| 15 | 22. Rubber and plastic products | 1.0 |
| 16 | 2. Dairy cattle | 0.8 |
| 17 | 45. Road freight transport | 0.8 |
| 18 | 15. Other food, beverages and tobacco | 0.7 |
| 19 | 6. Agricultural services, fishing, hunting | 0.3 |
| 20 | 19. Printing and publishing | 0.2 |
| 21 | 34. Electricity generation-oil products | 0.0 |
| 22 | 36. Electricity generation-hydro | 0.0 |
| 23 | 35. Electricity generation-nuclear | 0.0 |
| 24 | 9. Oil mining | 0.0 |
| 25 | 1. Sheep and cattle | −0.1 |
| 26 | 31. Other manufacturing | −0.1 |
| 27 | 29. Metal products | −0.2 |
| 28 | 4. Grains | −0.2 |
| 29 | 53. Dwelling services | −0.2 |
| 30 | 54. Public services | −0.2 |
| 31 | 51. Financial services | −0.2 |
| 32 | 48. Water, pipeline and transport services | −0.2 |
| 33 | 42. Trade services | −0.3 |
| 34 | 52. Business services | −0.3 |
| 35 | 11. Iron ore mining | −0.4 |
| 36 | 12. Non-ferrous ore mining | −0.5 |
| 37 | 5. Other agriculture | −0.6 |
| 38 | 50. Communication services | −0.7 |
| 39 | 40. Water supply | −0.8 |
| 40 | 14. Meat and meat products | −0.8 |
| 41 | 39. Gas supply | −1.0 |
| 42 | 55. Other services | −1.2 |
| 43 | 43. Accommodation, hotels and cafes | −1.6 |

*(Continued)*

**Table 9.13** National industry output (% changes from base-case values, 2030, ranked)—cont'd

| Rank | Industry | 2030 |
|------|----------|------|
| 44 | 13. Other mining | −1.7 |
| 45 | 24. Cement | −1.7 |
| 46 | 47. Rail freight transport | −2.1 |
| 47 | 49. Air transport | −2.1 |
| 48 | 27. Aluminum | −2.4 |
| 49 | 56. Private transport services | −2.4 |
| 50 | 44. Road passenger transport | −2.4 |
| 51 | 41. Construction services | −3.1 |
| 52 | 58. Private heating services | −4.6 |
| 53 | 10. Gas mining | −5.8 |
| 54 | 20. Petroleum products | −5.9 |
| 55 | 38. Electricity supply | −6.8 |
| 56 | 57. Private electricity equipment services | −7.7 |
| 57 | 8. Coal mining | −12.8 |
| 58 | 32. Electricity generation-coal | −18.8 |

*Coal* (industry 8, rank 57) production is projected to fall by 12.8% compared to its base-case level. The imposition of the ETS adversely affects coal demand for electricity generation and steel production in Australia and overseas. Domestic demand for coal falls by 14.6%. Foreign demand, which contributes around 85% to overall demand, is down 12.5%. These projections are remarkably sanguine when compared to the dire predictions from coal industry representatives. In terms of average annual growth, the projections imply a reduction from 4.0% in the base case to 3.3% with the ETS in place. The key factor underlying this mild outcome is rapid uptake of clean-coal technologies for electricity generation. In Australia, the new technologies are mainly based on CCS. In the rest of the world, as modeled by GTEM, the new technologies include CCS and other less radical innovations that have already started to be used in Australia.

Contraction in export demand accounts for the 5.8% reduction in production of *Gas mining* (industry 10, rank 53).

Other adversely affected industries are *Private transport services* (industry 56, rank 49), *Private electricity equipment services* (industry 57, rank 56) and *Private heating services* (industry 58, rank 53). All three are affected by increases in the price of energy: automotive fuels for transport services, electricity for electrical equipment services and gas for heating services. Increased energy costs shift their supply schedules up, leading to adverse substitution in residential demand.

Most of the remaining industries suffer mild contractions in output relative to base-case levels, in line with the general shrinkage of the economy. General economic conditions are particularly influential for the service industries.

For most sectors, the effects of the ETS build smoothly over the projection period but there are exceptions. These generally reflect the influence of inputs taken in from the models to which MMRF was linked for the ETS simulations. Figure 9.19(a and b) gives some examples.

Figure 9.19(a) shows deviations from base-case production for the main electricity generation sectors. It is moreorless a repeat of Figure 9.9(a), which is based on PJ data

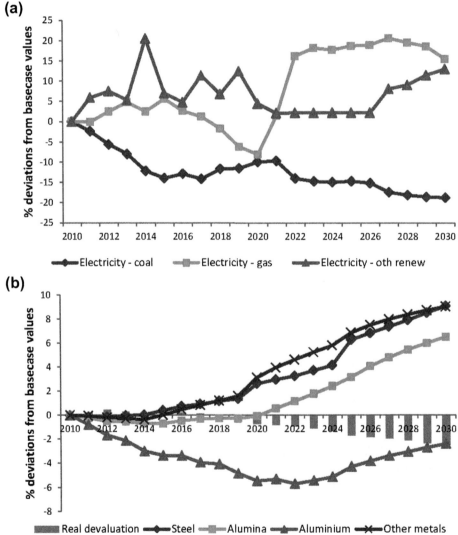

**Figure 9.19** (a) Deviations in production of electricity generation industries. (b) Deviations in production of metal manufacturing industries.

taken from the detailed electricity modeling and reflects particular sequences of the introduction of new types of capacity that are included in the detailed electricity model.

Figure 9.19(b) shows deviations in the production of the metal-manufacturing sectors, together with deviations in the real exchange rate ($local/$foreign). The metal-processing sectors are all highly trade-exposed. Nevertheless, after 2020 when shielding is removed and the terms of trade start to decline (Figure 9.11), their production responds positively to the carbon price due to the changes in the real exchange rate, also shown in Figure 9.19(b). As the need to import global permits intensifies, so the volume of net trade must improve. This requires increasing depreciation of the real exchange rate, which more than offsets the contraction in export demand imposed from GTEM, allowing export volumes for a number industries, such as the metals producers, to expand.

### Emissions from most sources fall

Table 9.14 shows deviations (in percentages and Mt of $CO_2$-e) from domestic base-case emissions. In 2030, total domestic emissions are down by 25.6%, or 181.8 Mt of $CO_2$-e. In addition, permits for 160 Mt of $CO_2$-e are imported, making Australia's total contribution to global emissions reduction about 342 Mt of $CO_2$-e.

Domestic emissions from stationary energy and fugitive sources deliver the bulk of the overall abatement. Emissions from stationary energy are down 47.5 Mt relative to their base-case levels, with emissions from electricity generation down by 37.4 Mt, and emissions from other forms of direct combustion down by 10.1 Mt. Fugitive emissions fall by 41.4% (28.6 Mt). Significant abatement also occurs in other areas, and in terms of percentage deviations are larger than abatement from stationary energy and fugitive sources. From waste, emissions are down by 75.9% (or 10.9 Mt of $CO_2$-e) relative to base-case levels, while emissions from industrial processes fall by 56.1%, (or 23.1 Mt of $CO_2$-e).

All of the emission reductions outside of electricity and transport occur via reductions in the output of the relevant emitting industry or reductions in emissions intensity brought about by the price-responsive mechanisms outlined in Section 9.3.4. The abatement from stationary energy and transport is achieved via industry activity effects, fuel switching and technology changes. The last-mentioned is most important for electricity where, according to the detailed electricity modeling, extensive abatement is achieved from the uptake of clean coal technologies, especially in the later part of the projection period.

### 9.6.2.2 State variables

#### Real gross state product falls relative to base case in all states/territories, except TAS and NT

Figure 9.20 shows projected percentage deviations from base-case levels of real gross state product (GSP). Percentage deviations in 2030 are given in Table 9.11.

**Table 9.14** CO$_2$-e emissions by major source category for Australia (changes from base-case values)

| | Percentage deviations from base-case values 2030 |
|---|---|
| Energy sector, total | −17.3 |
| Fuel combustion | −13.6 |
| Stationary | −14.3 |
| Electricity generation | −19.2 |
| Other | −7.3 |
| Transport | −11.7 |
| Fugitive emissions from fuels | −41.1 |
| Industrial processes | −56.1 |
| Agriculture | −17.6 |
| Waste | −75.9 |
| LUCF | NA |
| Total | −25.6 |

| | NSW | VIC | QLD | SA | WA | TAS | NT | ACT | AUS |
|---|---|---|---|---|---|---|---|---|---|
| *Change from base-case value (Mt of CO$_2$-e) 2015* | | | | | | | | | |
| Energy sector, total | −10.6 | −18.1 | −9.6 | −0.6 | −4.2 | −0.2 | −0.4 | −0.1 | −43.9 |
| Fuel combustion | −5.0 | −17.8 | −6.0 | −0.1 | −2.9 | −0.2 | −0.3 | −0.1 | −32.4 |
| Stationary | −3.2 | −16.3 | −4.4 | 0.3 | −1.9 | −0.1 | −0.2 | 0.0 | −25.8 |
| Electricity generation | −2.2 | −15.5 | −2.5 | 0.4 | −1.0 | 0.0 | −0.1 | 0.0 | −20.8 |
| Other | −0.9 | −0.8 | −1.9 | −0.2 | −1.0 | −0.1 | −0.1 | 0.0 | −5.0 |
| Transport | −1.8 | −1.5 | −1.6 | −0.4 | −1.0 | −0.1 | −0.1 | −0.1 | −6.6 |
| Fugitive emissions from fuels | −5.6 | −0.4 | −3.6 | −0.5 | −1.3 | 0.0 | −0.1 | 0.0 | −11.4 |
| Industrial processes | −6.1 | −1.7 | −2.4 | −1.2 | −2.3 | −0.4 | −0.1 | −0.1 | −14.2 |
| Agriculture | −2.5 | −2.5 | −4.0 | −0.8 | −1.7 | −0.4 | −1.1 | 0.0 | −13.0 |
| Waste | −3.7 | −2.6 | −2.4 | −0.5 | −1.4 | −0.2 | −0.1 | −0.1 | −10.9 |

| | | | | | | | | |
|---|---|---|---|---|---|---|---|---|
| LUCF | −0.4 | −1.0 | −0.1 | −0.4 | −1.4 | −0.3 | −0.2 | 0.0 | −3.8 |
| Total | −23.2 | −25.9 | −18.6 | −3.4 | −11.0 | −1.6 | −1.8 | −0.3 | −85.8 |

*Change from base-case value (Mt of CO$_2$-e)*

**2020**

| | | | | | | | | | |
|---|---|---|---|---|---|---|---|---|---|
| Energy sector, total | −12.2 | −10.5 | −13.5 | −2.4 | −7.0 | −0.2 | −0.5 | −0.1 | −46.5 |
| Fuel combustion | −4.7 | −10.1 | −8.6 | −1.9 | −4.7 | −0.2 | −0.4 | −0.1 | −30.8 |
| Stationary | −2.3 | −8.2 | −6.4 | −1.4 | −3.5 | −0.1 | −0.3 | 0.0 | −22.2 |
| Electricity generation | −1.3 | −7.5 | −4.0 | −1.2 | −2.0 | 0.0 | −0.1 | 0.0 | −16.1 |
| Other | −1.1 | −0.8 | −2.4 | −0.2 | −1.4 | −0.1 | −0.2 | 0.0 | −6.1 |
| Transport | −2.3 | −1.9 | −2.1 | −0.5 | −1.3 | −0.2 | −0.1 | −0.1 | −8.5 |
| Fugitive emissions from fuels | −7.5 | −0.4 | −4.9 | −0.5 | −2.3 | 0.0 | −0.1 | 0.0 | −15.7 |
| Industrial processes | −7.5 | −2.1 | −3.1 | −1.5 | −2.6 | −0.5 | −0.1 | −0.1 | −17.5 |
| Agriculture | −3.0 | −2.9 | −4.8 | −0.9 | −1.9 | −0.4 | −1.4 | 0.0 | −15.3 |
| Waste | −4.3 | −3.0 | −2.9 | −0.6 | −1.7 | −0.3 | −0.1 | −0.2 | −13.0 |
| LUCF | −0.8 | −2.5 | −0.2 | −0.9 | −5.0 | −0.8 | −0.2 | 0.0 | −10.4 |
| Total | −27.7 | −21.1 | −24.5 | −6.3 | −18.3 | −2.2 | −2.3 | −0.4 | −102.7 |

**2030**

| | | | | | | | | | |
|---|---|---|---|---|---|---|---|---|---|
| Energy sector, total | −29.5 | −16.4 | −26.1 | −2.0 | −14.8 | −0.1 | −0.5 | −0.2 | −89.7 |
| Fuel combustion | −17.0 | −15.8 | −17.6 | −1.7 | −8.3 | −0.1 | −0.4 | −0.2 | −61.2 |
| Stationary | −13.4 | −13.0 | −13.8 | −1.0 | −6.1 | 0.0 | −0.2 | 0.0 | −47.5 |
| Electricity generation | −11.9 | −12.0 | −10.4 | −0.8 | −2.2 | 0.0 | −0.1 | 0.0 | −37.4 |
| Other | −1.5 | −1.0 | −3.4 | −0.2 | −4.0 | 0.1 | −0.1 | 0.0 | −10.1 |
| Transport | −3.6 | −2.8 | −3.7 | −0.7 | −2.1 | −0.2 | −0.2 | −0.2 | −13.6 |
| Fugitive emissions from fuels | −12.5 | −0.5 | −8.6 | −0.3 | −6.5 | 0.0 | −0.1 | 0.0 | −28.6 |
| Industrial processes | −9.5 | −2.9 | −4.4 | −1.8 | −3.6 | −0.6 | −0.2 | −0.1 | −23.1 |
| Agriculture | −4.1 | −3.9 | −6.7 | −1.2 | −2.6 | −0.4 | −2.4 | 0.0 | −21.2 |
| Waste | −5.8 | −4.1 | −4.1 | −0.8 | −2.3 | −0.3 | −0.1 | −0.2 | −17.7 |
| LUCF | −2.6 | −7.5 | −0.7 | −2.6 | −12.9 | −2.6 | −1.0 | −0.1 | −30.1 |
| Total | −51.4 | −34.7 | −42.0 | −8.4 | −36.3 | −4.0 | −4.2 | −0.6 | −181.8 |

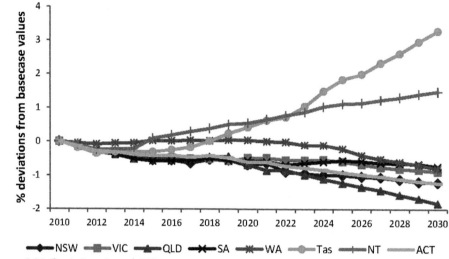

**Figure 9.20** Deviations in real GSP.

The pattern of impacts on real GSP in 2030 reflects the industry effects of the ETS (Table 9.13). Just as some industries experience output gains relative to the base case and some industries experience output loss, so some regions experience output gain and others output loss, with differences between regions explained by the differences in the industrial compositions of the regions.

QLD and to a lesser extent NSW have over-representations of *Coal mining* and *Coal-fired electricity generation*, which is the main reason why the ETS is expected to reduce their shares in the national economy. The ACT is the capital territory of Australia. Its economy is almost entirely service oriented, with an over-representation of energy-intensive providers of private transport, private electricity equipment and private heating services. This is the main reason why the territory is relatively adversely affected by the ETS.

WA is favored by an industrial composition with an over-representation of gas-fired generation, natural gas and trade-exposed industries that benefit from trade diversion under the global ETS (*Iron ore, Alumina* and *Other non-ferrous metals*).

As discussed earlier SA's coal-fired generation industry is phased out by 2015 in the base case and its gas industry ceases production by 2025. The absence of these two significantly adversely affected industries and an over-representation of agricultural industries, which do relatively well under the ETS, is enough to elevate SA's GDP share.

TAS does not have coal-fired generation or gas and coal mining. *Forestry* and agriculture are over represented. Hence, it gains share in the national economy. The NT has an over-representation of animal-agriculture and *Alumina* production. Thus, even though it has no *Forestry*, it too gains share in the national economy.

### 9.6.2.3 Substate results

MMRF includes a top-down facility for generating base-case prospects and the effects of ETS policies on gross regional product (GRP) and regional employment for 57 substate regions: the ABS statistical divisions.[30]

Under the top-down procedure, the model's 58 industry sectors are split into two groups: the group whose outputs are readily traded between regions and the group producing outputs (mainly services) that are not readily traded between regions. For an industry in the first group, our assumption is that the ETS policy has the same percentage effect on output and employment in a substate region as it has on output and employment overall in the industry in the state to which the substate region belongs. If this assumption were applied to all industries, then differences between substate regions in the estimated effects of the ETS would depend simply on differences between regions in industries' shares in output or employment. However, in addition to this, we recognize that for industries in the second (non-traded) group demand in a substate region will be met by output in that region. This means that changes in activity in a substate region arising from changes in activity in industries in the first group have local multiplier effects.

The key data input to our top-down method for generating output and employment results for the substate regions is a database showing gross value added and employment by industry and region. From this the shares of each region's GRP and employment accounted for by each industry can be calculated. These shares allow the implications for a region's gross product or employment of a change in an industry's activity level within the region to be inferred. In this section, we concentrate on employment.

An extract of the data is given in Figure 9.21. The extract refers to five industries that are particularly vulnerable to ETS policies and to 12 regions in which the six industries in total account for relatively large shares of gross product or employment. As a benchmark, we show in the last bar of the figure the industries' shares in aggregate national employment. For Australia as a whole, the five vulnerable industries account for less than 2% of aggregate employment. However, some substate regions are much more heavily dependent on the vulnerable industries. Hence, we should expect that these regions will be much more vulnerable to ETS policies than is the Australian economy overall.

One issue that arises in presenting substate regional employment results is the issue of scale. Scale is ignored if the results are presented as percentage deviations between the level of employment attained with the ETS policy in place and the base-case level of employment. For example, we might identify a region for which the ETS policy has a large adverse *percentage* effect, but which is very small so that the effect of the policy is small in terms of numbers employed. In such a case, although the ETS has a large effect

---

[30] A review of top-down regional models, and regional CGE models more generally, is given in Giesecke and Madden in Chapter 7 of this Handbook.

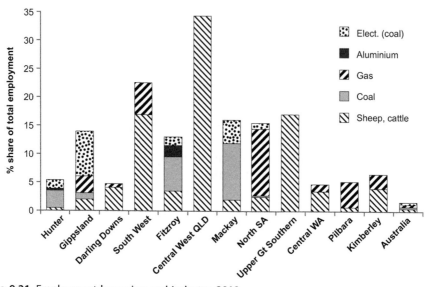

**Figure 9.21** Employment by region and industry, 2010.

from the point of view of the particular region, the significance of the effect from a wider (e.g. national or state) point of view would be small. An implication would be that any adjustment policy necessary to assist the region to cope with the effects of the policy might be manageable.

The scale issue is dealt with by reporting the regional employment effects of the ETS policy in two ways: as percentage deviations from base-case values and as numbers employed. Figures 9.22 and 9.23 provide examples. Figure 9.22 shows the eight regions most adversely affected by the ETS policy as measured by its percentage-point effect on total growth of employment over the period 2010–2030. Figure 9.23 shows the eight most favorably affected regions. In Figures 9.22 and 9.23 we deal with the scale issue by making the areas of the dots representing the regions proportional to the numbers of jobs lost on account of the ETS in 2030.

It is clear from Figure 9.22 that *Hunter NSW* is of particular significance: it has a large employment loss from the ETS in percentage terms and the largest loss in terms of numbers of jobs. As shown in Figure 9.21, *Coal mining* and *Coal-fired electricity generation* are both important industries in the *Hunter* region. The two central-coast QLD regions (*Fitzroy* and *Mackay*), are also face significant employment losses from the ETS.

The industries that contribute most strongly to the policy-induced expansions in the regions' employment growth shown in Figure 9.23 are mainly the industries (*Forestry* and *Electricity generation-other renewable*) that are identified in Table 9.13 as sectors that are favorably affected by the ETS policy.

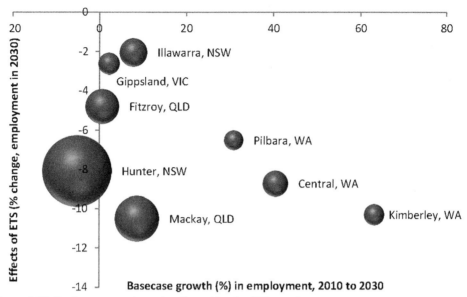

**Figure 9.22** Regions most adversely affected by the ETS: employment.

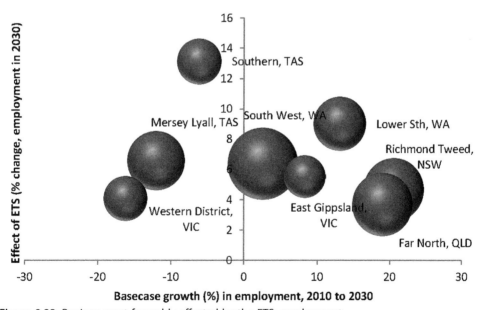

**Figure 9.23** Regions most favorably affected by the ETS: employment.

In Figures 9.22 and 9.23, we show regions' base-case growth prospects as well as the regional effects of the ETS. The reason is that the main policy interest in the regional results relates to structural adjustment. Structural adjustment problems are likely to be most severe for regions that are affected adversely by the ETS and already

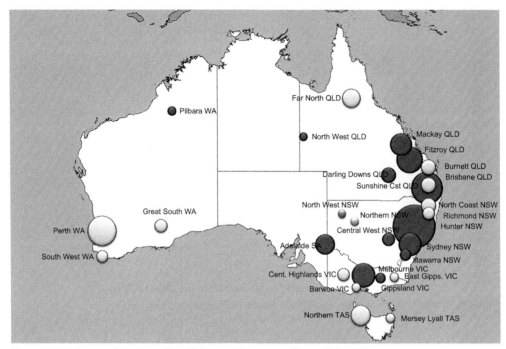

**Figure 9.24** Geographic dispersion of the employment effects of the ETS.

face poor or negative base-case growth prospects. A good example is the *Hunter* region.

Figure 9.24 provides a final perspective on the geographic aspect of the structural change that adoption of the ETS would require. The map is coded to show regions in which employment growth is reduced by the ETS (indicated by dark bubbles) and regions in which employment growth is stimulated by the ETS (indicated by light bubbles). As in Figures 9.22 and 9.23, the areas of the dots in Figure 9.24 are proportional to the numbers of jobs created or lost on account of the adoption of the ETS.

It is clear from Figure 9.24 that, in many cases, the stimulated regions are far from contiguous with the adversely affected regions. This suggests that there might be geographical adjustment problems to the extent that structural adjustment requires relocation of workers between adversely affected and stimulated regions.

## 9.7 CONCLUSION

In this chapter, we focus on issues that arise in using a CGE model of the Australian economy to provide advice to policy makers and other stakeholders about the effects of complex real-world policy proposals. To illustrate the issues, we use a study of the effects of the Australian government's 2008 emissions trading policy proposal (Table 9.8). The proposal integrates Australia into a global trading scheme by 2015 and requires Australia to progressively reduce emissions to around 40% below their base-case level by 2030. This reduction can be achieved by a mix of domestic abatement and purchases of emissions permits from the global market. The global price of permits rises from around $A25 per tonne in 2015 to around $A50 per tonne in 2030.

## 9.7.1 Main results

A number of key findings emerge from our simulations of the effects of the ETS policy.

(i) Domestic abatement falls well short of targeted abatement, requiring significant amounts of permits to be imported. As can be seen in Figure 9.16, in 2030 only about half of the required reduction in emissions is met from domestic abatement, leaving half to be met from foreign permit purchases.

(ii) Despite the requirement for deep cuts in emissions, the ETS reduces Australia's GDP by only just over 1.1% in 2030 relative to the base case (Figure 9.15b). In Section 9.6.1 (see especially Table 9.10) we discuss alternative ways in which this result can be presented.

(iii) The negative impact on real household consumption, which is the preferred measure of national welfare, is somewhat greater reflecting the need to import permits. The cost of imported permits reduces household income. Relative to its base-case level real household consumption is down by over 2.0% in 2030 (Figure 9.17).

(iv) While the national macroeconomic impacts of the ETS are modest in the context of the policy task, this does not carry through to the industry (Table 9.13) and regional (Figures 9.20–9.23) levels.

(v) Relative to base case, there are a number of industries for which the ETS significantly raises output in percentage terms. The most favorably affected industry is *Forestry*, for which the carbon charge effectively is a production subsidy. Within the electricity sector, non-hydro renewables and gas-fired generation gain at the expense of coal-fired generation. Somewhat surprisingly, production of *Iron and steel* and *Alumina* also increase due in part to overcompensation during the transition period, and in part to GTEM projection of trade diversion in favor of the Australian industries at the expense of other suppliers. Other adversely affected industries are *Private transport services*, *Private electricity equipment services* and *Private heating services*. All three are affected by increases in the price of energy: automotive fuels for transport services, electricity for electrical equipment services and gas for heating services.

(vi) The pattern of impacts on Australian regions in 2030 reflects the industry effects of the ETS. At the state/territory level, QLD is the most adversely affected region, due to its over representation of coal and coal-fired generation, and TAS is the most favorably affected, due to the importance of forestry.

Twelve (substate) regions are identified as particularly vulnerable in terms of potential loss of employment. These include coal-dependent regions such as Hunter in NSW, Fitzroy in QLD and Gippsland in VIC. On the other hand, eight regions are identified as potentially gaining employment. These regions generally have an over-representation of the sectors that expand due to the ETS, especially forestry and renewable electricity generation.

## 9.7.2 Including detail

In the introduction to this chapter, eight questions were posed regarding the level of detail required by policy makers and other stakeholders when considering CGE-based analyses of an ETS. Our experience from the Australian study suggests the following answers.

- *At what level of detail must the stationary-energy sector be modeled for the effects of policy on its emissions to be captured adequately?* For the credibility of results, we think that very fine detail is required, especially for the electricity sector. Even the BOTE explanation of GDP outcomes given in Box 9.1 relies on detailed understanding of the costs and abatement opportunities available in the future from the electricity sector. Our experience is that the required level of detail is best provided by linking with a detailed bottom-up model of the stationary energy sector. The alternative is to elaborate the representation of the sector inside the CGE model. While attractive from a pure theoretical point of view, this is much more difficult than our preferred option because of computational and data constraints.

- *Is it necessary to include the lumpiness of generation investment explicitly in CGE computations of the effects of climate change policy?* The issue here is really about the timing of results. If the stakeholder is interested only in broad-based analysis of outcomes for some far-off future year, or a net present value (NPV) calculation of effects across many years, then the answer is probably no, assuming that the existing treatment of investment is realistic for the projected long-run change in capital. On the other hand, if the focus is on year-to-year changes for investment and other variables, then incorporating lumpiness does matter, as illustrated in Figure 9.9(a and b) and the associated commentary.

- *Concern about greenhouse gas emissions centers on a global externality problem. Does this mean that the consequences of emissions policy can only be investigated using a global model?* Certainly for Australia, and probably for most other countries, changes in trading conditions brought about by global action on climate change will be significant and therefore should be incorporated into modeling the effects of reducing greenhouse emissions. In this chapter, we showed how this can be done via linking of a detailed country model with a multicountry system (GTEM). GTEM provides MMRF with a carbon price and projections of changes in Australia's trading environment for the base case and the ETS-inclusive projections.

- *In modeling the effects of an emissions policy, do we need agents with full intertemporal optimization or will recursive dynamics do?* An ETS is normally designed to ensure a measure of certainty — there will be a non-zero carbon price after a specified date, that price will probably increase given a scheme of increasing tightness of emission allocation, during the early transition period to a multinational arrangement certain EITEIs will be shielded, etc. Under such arrangements, investment in industries such as electricity generation, where asset lives are very long, would be expected to change in line with anticipated future changes in permit price, rather than in response to announcements. Thus, a degree of forward-looking expectations is important, especially in the early years of any arrangement. The modeling reported in this chapter generally assumes recursive dynamics (Sections 9.2.2.8 and 9.2.2.9). However, it does incorporate forward-looking expectations in electricity and transport via linking with the specialized bottom-up models that assume full intertemporal optimization. This improves the analysis considerably, particularly for the early years.

- *What representation of a country's EITEIs is required when early action against climate change is unilateral?* Unilateral action has the potential to disadvantage a country's EITEIs. Accordingly, nearly all unilateral schemes specify some form of assistance or shielding during the period of transition to a fully global ETS. Modeling such assistance is necessary if realistic projections of industry output and employment are required. In the modeling reported in this chapter, a detailed representation is put in place (Section 9.3.3). The influence of the associated shielding can be seen, for example, in Figure 9.16(b) where, for the early transition years to 2020 some of Australia's key ETIEIs suffer little if any production loss despite the significant direct increase in unit cost due to a domestic carbon price.

- *How should energy usage be treated in the household consumption specification of a model to be used for the analysis of emissions policy?* As explained in Section 9.2.3.5, we think that a traditional budget allocation model of household demand across standard budget categories, which identify energy and energy equipment as separate products leads to unrealistic projections of final demand for energy and equipment. Our preferred treatment allows for dummy industries that provide services of energy-using equipment to private households.

- *Can CGE modeling inform policy makers about the regional effects of emissions policy?* The answer to this question is yes, as evidenced in this chapter by our discussion of the regional implications of the ETS in Sections 9.6.2.2 and 9.6.2.3. Another related question is to what extent policy makers require projections of regional effects. Our experience of modeling the effects of an ETS in Australia, and our experience more generally across many countries, is that national and regional policy makers are very concerned with the regional dimension. Much of the current discussion in Australia regarding the impacts of the proposed ETS is based about the regional implications of the ETS where the impacts, as discussed in this chapter, could be highly significant. This has had a significant impact on public opinion regarding the policy.

- *What effect will the recycling of revenue from a carbon tax or sale of permits under an ETS have on the efficiency costs of the policy and on income distribution?* Revenue can be recycled in a number of ways, such as increasing government spending or transfer payments, or reducing other existing taxes. As noted in Section 9.3.3, the net welfare effects of the ETS depend on the extent to which recycling of the ETS revenue adds to or offsets the distortionary effects of the ETS charge. The double-dividend literature suggest that it is possible to recycle in such a way as achieve conventional resource allocation gains by using the revenue to reduce existing tax distortions. Another view is that the revenue churn associated with the ETS is likely to introduce inefficiencies.

- The issues here are complex, but are crucial to an understanding of the welfare implications of an emissions policy. To deal adequately with these issues, a policy model needs to have a detailed representation of the country's fiscal system and the ability to identify the income-distribution consequences of policy options. MMRF has this facility, though little use has made of it for the study reported in this chapter. Here, it is simply assumed that any revenue from the ETS in excess of that used for buying foreign emission permits or shielding domestic EITEIs is returned to households as a lump-sum payment.

### 9.7.3 Interpretation of results

To meet the needs of stakeholders engaging in real-world policy debates, the analysis requires, in addition to substantially more detail than is included in most CGE models, a detailed intuitive explanation of key results.

Users of economic models are often faced with skeptical audiences of policy advisors who may have some economic training, but have little knowledge of economic modeling. In this context, a key to modeling success is interpretation of results.

On the one hand, interpretation is about telling a story true to the modeling outcomes without referring to the technicalities of the modeling. This is difficult, but is essential for the general acceptance of the results. Section 9.6 contains an example of detailed explanation that aims to demonstrate the relatively simple economic mechanisms underlying the apparently complex results.

On the other hand, interpretation is about explaining results in quantitative detail. This aids credibility and acceptance of the modeling, but it is also a check on whether the modeling has been done correctly. To this end, CoPS modelers make extensive use of BOTE calculations, often supported by formal stylized models of the type described in the Appendix. There are three roles for such models (Dixon *et al.*, 1977, pp. 194–195). (i) With a model as large as MMRF, 'the onus is on the model builders to provide convincing evidence that the computations have been performed correctly, i.e. that the results do in fact follow from the theoretical structure and database'. (ii) Calculations with stylized models are the only way '... to understand the [full] model; to isolate those assumptions which cause particular results; and to assess the plausibility of particular results by seeing which real-world phenomena have been considered and which have been ignored'. (iii) By extending the stylized calculations, '... the reader will be able to obtain a reasonably accurate idea of how some of the projections would respond to various changes in the underlying assumptions and data'.

An example of the use of BOTE calculations is given in Box 9.1, which focuses on the plausibility of the headline finding — *big emission cuts at relatively mild macro-cost.* There it is shown that such a finding can be rationalized by considering the abatement opportunities available in only the key areas of electricity and transport.

## 9.7.4 Future work — integrated assessment modeling

The approach to environmental modeling described in this chapter — based on linking models of the electricity system (*WHIRLYGIG*) and world trade in emissions permits (*GTEM*) along with other models to a multiregion, multisector model of the Australian economy — has an obvious parallel with integrated assessment models (IAMs).[31] The latter also depend on linking models of different types, but unlike the system we have described, IAMs aim to deal with the benefit side of emissions control as well as its costs. An Australian example of this is work by ABARES to develop its global integrated assessment model (GIAM) model in collaboration with CSIRO (Gunasekera *et al.*, 2008). In the GIAM project, ABARES supplies economic modeling and CSIRO supplies physical climate modeling.

Figure 9.25 outlines the basic structure of GIAM. The ovals represent submodels and the rectangles represent the variables that connect the models. To project a base case with GIAM, an iterative procedure is used. It starts with a preliminary economic scenario for the period of interest, generated in the *Economy* submodel. This submodel includes a facility for projecting the path of greenhouse gas emissions associated with

---

[31] Early overviews of IAMs are given in Schneider (1997) and Goodess, *et al.* (2003). An up-to-date explanation is provided by Nordhaus in Chapter 16 of this Handbook. To our knowledge, most other IAMs used around the world use aggregated economic accounts. These include DICE, MERGE, WIAGEM and MiniCAM (see Mastrandrea, 2010).

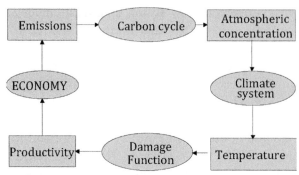

**Figure 9.25** Structure of GIAM.

economic activity: principally the use of fossil fuels in the generation of stationary energy and in transport. The emissions path from the preliminary economic scenario is fed into two climate submodules: a *Carbon-cycle* submodel that projects the accumulation of greenhouse gasses in the atmosphere and a *Climate-system* submodel that projects the development of the global climate on the basis of these atmospheric concentrations. Finally, a system of *Damage Functions* translates the projected climate change into changes in variables that are relevant to economic development (e.g. agricultural productivity).

As indicated in Figure 9.25, the output of the *Damage Functions* is fed back into the *Economy* submodel and the sequence is repeated until satisfactory convergence is achieved. The *Economy* submodel allows agents to adapt to the economic effects of climate change (e.g. to react to changes in relative prices induced by the damage effects), but in generating the base case no policy reactions are assumed.

GIAM provides an example of how an Australia-focused IAM can be constructed using readily available components, in particular drawing on computable general economic modeling techniques that have a long history in policy analysis in Australia. The GIAM results that have been published to date are preliminary and just illustrative of the capability of the model. In particular, the range of climate change effects included is not yet wide enough to provide a base case for assessment of the benefits and costs of greenhouse policy.

For the simulations discussed in this chapter, no effort is made to include the possible effects of climate change in the base-case projection. Not including climate change means that we do not account for any of the possible direct economic benefits arising from the abatement achieved by an ETS. Including the potential benefits, and hence being able to show a net economic gain from an ETS, is an important item for further research with MMRF. The way forward is likely to be through linking MMRF with a climate model, such as that developed at the CSIRO.

# APPENDIX: STYLIZED MODEL

## A.1 Introduction

The explanation of the deviations in macro variables given in Section 9.6 relied, but not explicitly, on a stylized macroeconomic model.[32] In this Appendix the model and its calibration in the context of the ETS simulations is described. The predictive power of the model is then demonstrated by comparing results computed using MMRF with those computed using the stylized system. The comparison also offers additional insight into the MMRF projections.

## A.2 Model

Equations of the stylized model are given in Table A1. The first part of the table shows the levels equations. The second part shows the equations linearized in the changes (percentage or otherwise) of the variables.

### A.2.1 Non-linear form in levels of variables

Equations (A)−(J) deal with real GDP (factor cost and market prices) and the main components of real expenditure. Equation (A) defines real GDP at market prices ($Y_{MP}$) as the sum of real consumption (C), real investment (I), real government consumption (G) and the net volume of trade (X − M). Ignoring changes in stocks, this is the standard expenditure-side definition for real GDP.

Equation (B) is the economy's production function, based on a constant returns to scale functional form (as assumed in MMRF). It relates real GDP at factor cost ($Y_{FC}$) to inputs of labor (L) and capital (K), with an allowance for technological change summarized by the variable $A$: an increase in $A$ means technological regress; a decrease means technological progress. There are many forms of technological change incorporated into the MMRF system, but in this stylized system we only allow for one − the overall technological regress (or cost) associated with the factors identified in Section 9.5.3.4. Note that in writing (B), and elsewhere in the stylized model, the existence of a third primary factor of production, agricultural land, is ignored.

Total emissions ($Q_{CO_2}$) is related positively to the size of the economy and negatively to the emissions price (T). This is shown in equation (C), which is a fairly crude

---

[32] The stylized model described here is similar to the model in Adams (2005) that was developed to explain results from a GTAP simulation. The idea of using stylized models as an aid to interpretation is discussed in detail in Dixon *et al.* (1984). The stylized model is based on the microeconomic theory underlying a conventional CGE model, like MMRF. It is comparative static, not dynamic. The model is designed to be as simple and transparent as possible. Adding dynamics would increase the complexity of the model, without enhancing significantly its explanatory power. As the stylized model is comparative static, we do not use it to analyze deviations through time. Instead, it is used to analyze deviations at specific points, typically in the first year of the simulation (short run) and after a long period of time (long run). Here, we assume that short run is 2011 and long run is 2030 (even though the economy is still adjusting to exogenous shocks).

**Table A1** Stylized macro model
**Levels equations**

$$Y_{MP} = C + I + G + (X - M) \tag{A}$$

$$Y_{FC} \times A = F_Y(L, K) \tag{B}$$

$$Q_{CO_2} = F_{Q_{CO_2}}\left(Y_{FC}, \frac{1}{T}\right) \tag{C}$$

$$A = F_A(T) \tag{D}$$

$$P_{GDP}^{MP} \times Y_{MP} = P_{GDP}^{FC} \times Y_{FC} + Q_{CO_2} \times T \tag{E}$$

$$P_C \times C = \left\{P_{GDP}^{MP} \times Y_{MP}\right\} \times \Omega \tag{F}$$

$$P_C \times RW \times G = P_{GDP}^{MP} \times Y_{MP} \times \Gamma \tag{G}$$

$$M = Y_{MP} \times F_M(RER) \tag{H}$$

$$X = F_X\left(\frac{1}{RER}\right) \times Y_{WORLD} \tag{I}$$

$$\frac{I}{K} = F_I\left(\frac{ROR}{ROR_{REQ}}\right) \tag{J}$$

$$RER = \frac{P_{GDP}^{MP}}{\Phi \times P_{WORLD}} \tag{K}$$

**Table A1** Stylized macro model—cont'd
**Levels equations**

$$P_{\text{GDP}}^{\text{MP}} = F_{P_{\text{GDP}}^{\text{FC}}}\left(P_{\text{GDP}}^{\text{FC}}, T\right) \tag{L}$$

$$TOT = \frac{F_{\text{TOT}}\left(\dfrac{1}{X}\right)}{P_{\text{WORLD}}} \tag{M}$$

$$\frac{P_C}{P_{\text{GDP}}^{\text{MP}}} = F_{P_{\text{GDP}}^{P_C}}\left(\frac{1}{TOT}, T\right) \tag{N}$$

$$\frac{K}{L} = F_{KL}\left(\frac{RP_{\text{L}}}{RP_{\text{K}}}\right) \tag{O}$$

$$(A \times RP_{\text{L}})^{S_{\text{L}}} = (A \times RP_{\text{K}})^{-S_{\text{K}}} \tag{P}$$

$$RP_{\text{L}} = F_{RP_{\text{L}}}\left(RW, \frac{1}{TOT}, T\right) \tag{Q}$$

$$RP_{\text{K}} = F_{RP_{\text{K}}}\left(ROR, \frac{1}{TOT}, T\right) \tag{R}$$

Linearized equations in the percentage changes of variables

$$y_{\text{mp}} = S_C c + S_I i + S_G g + \left(S_X x - S_M m\right) \tag{a}$$

$$y_{\text{fc}} = S_{\text{L}} l + S_{\text{K}} k - a \tag{b}$$

$$q_{\text{co}_2} = y_{\text{mp}} + \sigma_T \times d_{\_}T \tag{c}$$

*(Continued)*

**Table A1** Stylized macro model—cont'd
**Levels equations**

$$a = \sigma_A \times d\_T \tag{d}$$

$$y_{mp} = S_{GDP}^{FC} y_{fc} + S_T q_{co_2} \tag{e}$$

$$c = p_{gdp}^{mp} + y_{mp} + \omega - p_c \tag{f}$$

$$g = p_{gdp}^{mp} + y_{mp} + \gamma - \left(rw + p_c\right) \tag{g}$$

$$m = y_{mp} + \sigma_M rer \tag{h}$$

$$x = y_{world} + \sigma_X rer \tag{i}$$

$$i - k = \sigma_I \left(ror - ror_{req}\right) \tag{j}$$

$$rer = p_{gdp}^{mp} - \left(\varphi + p_{world}\right) \tag{k}$$

$$S_{GDP}^{FC} p_{gdp}^{fc} = p_{gdp}^{mp} - CO_2 ratio \times d\_T \tag{l}$$

$$tot = \frac{x}{\sigma_X} - p_{world} \tag{m}$$

$$p_{gdp}^{mp} = p_c + S_X tot \tag{n}$$

$$k - l = \sigma_{KL} \left\{ rp_l - rp_k \right\} \tag{o}$$

**Table A1** Stylized macro model—cont'd
**Levels equations**

$$rp_l = -\frac{S_K}{S_L}rp_k - \frac{1}{S_L}a \tag{p}$$

$$rp_l = rw - S_X tot + CO_2 ratio \times d\_T \tag{q}$$

$$rp_k = ror - S_X tot + CO_2 ratio \times d\_T \tag{r}$$

summary of the many abatement possibilities available in the full model. Equation (D) relates the technological change variable in equation (B) to the permit price to capture deadweight loss effects associated with an ETS.

The relationship between the value of GDP at market prices and the value of GDP at factor cost is explained in equation (E). $P_{GDP}^{MP}$ is the price of GDP at market prices. $P_{GDP}^{FC}$ is the price of GDP at factor cost. The emission price is the only form of indirect tax allowed for in the stylized system. The value of the emissions tax is the quantity of emissions (tonnes) times the emission price ($A per tonne).

Equation (F) is the economy's private consumption function, relating the value of consumption ($P_C C$) to the value of income via the Average Propensity to Consume (APC) ($\Omega$). In the stylized system, household income is proxied by GDP at market prices. Market-price GDP includes the total return to factors plus income from indirect taxes (the gross value of the emissions tax). Accordingly it does not account for factor income accruing to foreigners, neither does it account for income used to purchase permits from overseas.

The value of government consumption is explained in equation (G). $\Gamma$ is the ratio of public consumption expenditure to market-price GDP. Public consumption is labor intensive. Thus in (G) the price of public consumption is indexed to the wage rate, here defined as the product of the real wage rate ($RW$) and the price of consumption.

Equation (H) relates the volume of imports to the general level of real activity ($Y_{MP}$) and to the real exchange rate ($RER$). In the stylized system the real exchange rate is both an indicator of international competitiveness (+ means less competitive, − means more competitive) and a proxy for the ratio of the average price of domestic goods to the average price of foreign imported substitutes. Thus, equation (H) is consistent with the Armington specification of demand in the full model. As shown in equation (H), imports are an increasing function of the real exchange rate. Equation (I) is the corresponding export function. $Y_{\text{WORLD}}$ is an exogenous variable representing the general level of activity in the rest of the world. Exports are inversely related to the real exchange rate.

Equation (J) is the economy's investment function. This relates the ratio of investment to capital (or annual capital growth ignoring depreciation) to the rate of return on capital ($ROR$) relative to the rate of return required by investors ($ROR_{\text{REQ}}$). This approximates, in a comparative-static framework, the dynamic relationship between capital growth and the expected rate of return in MMRF (equation 9.2).

Equations (K)–(N) deal with relative prices. Equation (K) is MMRF's definition of the real exchange rate: the ratio of the price of GDP in the domestic economy (a proxy for local production costs) to the foreign currency price of GDP in the rest of the world ($P_{\text{WORLD}}$), converted to domestic currency by the nominal exchange rate ($\Phi$). The nominal exchange rate is defined as units of domestic currency per unit of foreign currency. The relationship between the price of GDP at market prices and the price of GDP at factor cost is given by equation (L).

Equation (M) relates the terms of trade ($TOT$) (i.e. the price of exports relative to the price of imports) negatively to the volume of exports, making allowance for exogenous changes in import prices ($P_{\text{WORLD}}$). The function $F_{\text{TOT}}\{\}$ is a decreasing function of $X$. Equation (M) is consistent with the assumption in MMRF that Australia is a small country with respect to imports, but faces downward-sloping demand curves for its exports.

Equation (N) explains the ratio of the price of consumption to the price of GDP at market prices as a decreasing function, $F_{\text{PGDP}}^{PC}\{\}$, of the terms of trade. A terms-of-trade improvement reduces the price of total domestic final expenditure (which includes imports, but not exports) relative to the market price of output (which includes exports, but not imports).[33]

The final block of equations, equations (O)–(R) relate to the prices and quantities of capital and labor. Equation (O) is the macro-equivalent of the industry-level CES relationship between relative factor inputs and relative factor prices. $RP_L$ is the real price of labor, defined as the nominal wage rate relative to the price of GDP at factor cost (i.e. to the price of output). $RP_K$ is the real price of capital, defined as the nominal rental on capital relative to the price of GDP at factor cost. Under equation (O), an increase in the real price of labor relative to the real price of capital will cause an increase in the capital intensity of the economy. Notice that with perfect competition, the real price of labor is equivalent to the marginal product of labor and the real price of capital is equivalent to the marginal product of capital.

---

[33] Note, though, that since imports of consumption goods are only part of total imports, not all terms-of-trade changes will lead to changes in the price of consumption goods relative to the GDP deflator. Moreover, consumption is only a part of total domestic final expenditure (GNE). Changes in other factors, such as the price of labor, may affect other GNE prices more than the price of consumption, leading to a change in the price of consumption relative to the GDP deflator which has nothing to do with the terms of trade.

Equation (P) is the relationship between marginal products and technological change at the industry level, carried over to the macro level in the stylized model. It is known as the factor-price frontier (Samuelson, 1962) and is consistent with the geometric average form:

$$P_{GDP}^{FC} = (A \times P_L)^{S_L} \times (A \times P_K)^{S_K}, \tag{9.14}$$

where $S_L$ and $S_K$ are the shares of labor and capital in the economy ($S_L + S_K = 1$), and $P_L$ and $P_K$ are the nominal wage rate and the nominal rental on capital. To obtain equation (P), divide both sides of (9.14) by the factor-cost price of GDP, redefine in terms of real prices and then rearrange.

Equation (Q) explains the real price of labor as a function of the real wage rate ($RW$) (i.e. the nominal wage rate deflated by the price of consumption), the inverse of the terms of trade, and the permit price. This is based on the following decomposition of the real cost of labor:

$$\frac{P_L}{P_{GDP}^{FC}} = \frac{P_L}{P_C} \times \frac{P_C}{P_{GDP}^{MP}} \times \frac{P_{GDP}^{MP}}{P_{GDP}^{FC}}. \tag{9.15}$$

On the right-hand side of (9.15), the first term is the real wage rate ($RW$), the second term is a function of the inverse of the terms of trade (equation N) and the third term is related to $T$ (equation L).

In deriving equation (R), note that for the real cost of capital:

$$\frac{P_K}{P_{GDP}^{FC}} = \frac{P_K}{P_I} \times \frac{P_I}{P_{GDP}^{MP}} \times \frac{P_{GDP}^{MP}}{P_{GDP}^{FC}}, \tag{9.16}$$

where $P_I$ is the price of investment. On the right hand side of (9.16), the first term can be interpreted as the economy's gross rate of return, $ROR$. The second term, like the corresponding term in (9.15), responds generally to changes in the inverse of the terms of trade.[34] The final term is an increasing function of $T$.

### A.2.2 Linearized form in changes of variables

The linearized forms of equations (A)−(R) are given in the second part of Table A1 as equations (a)−(r). In writing the equations, lowercase letters are used to identify percentage changes in variables written in the corresponding uppercase letters. The prefix '$d\_$' attached to a variable name indicates ordinary (not percentage) change. Only the permit price (or carbon tax) is expressed as an ordinary change variable because its value can pass through zero.

Variables in the linearized model are listed in Table A2, coefficients and parameters in Table A3. The derivations of the linear forms are generally straightforward. However, some explanation is necessary.

---

[34] The previous footnote, which relates to consumption goods, also applies to investment goods.

**Table A2** Variables, percentage change and otherwise, in the stylized model

| Symbol | Description | Naturally exogenous(X)/ endogenous (N) | Short run | Long run |
|---|---|---|---|---|
| $y_{mp}$ | Real GDP at market prices | N | | |
| C | Real private consumption | N | | |
| I | Real investment | N | | |
| G | Real public consumption | N | | |
| X | Real exports | N | | |
| M | Real imports | N | | |
| $y_{fc}$ | Real GDP at factor cost | N | | |
| a | Technological change | N | | |
| l | Employment | | N | X |
| k | Capital stock | | X | N |
| $d\_T$ | Emissions price | X | | |
| $q_{CO_2}$ | Quantity of emissions | N | | |
| $p_c$ | Price of consumption | X (numéraire) | | |
| $p_{gdp}^{fc}$ | GDP price (factor cost) | N | | |
| $p_{gdp}^{mp}$ | GDP price (market prices) | N | | |
| $\omega$ | APC | X | | |
| $\gamma$ | Public consumption share | X | | |
| rer | Real exchange rate | N | | |
| $p_{world}$ | World GDP price | N | | |
| $\varphi$ | Nominal exchange rate | N | | |
| $y_{world}$ | World GDP | X | | |
| ror | Rate of return on capital | | N | X |
| $ror_{req}$ | Required rate of return | X | | |
| tot | Terms of trade | X | | |
| $rp_l$ | Real price of labor | N | | |
| $rp_k$ | Real price of capital | N | | |
| rw | Real wage rate | | X | N |

All variables in this table are expressed as percentage changes except for the change in permit price, which expressed in $A per tonne of $CO_2$-e.

To obtain equation (c), the elasticity of emissions to the size of the economy is assumed to be one. The semielasticity with respect to the ordinary change in permit price $(d\_T)$ is given by the parameter $\sigma_T$. As a semielasticity, $\sigma_T$ has units: % $\Delta$emissions per $A. The value of $\sigma_T$ summarizes the percentage abatement impact of the permit price through the effects of fuel switching, land-use change, introduction of less-emission-intensive production technologies, etc. For the purpose of this chapter, the elasticity will be calibrated using results from the main model. Similar calibration is necessary for the semielasticity $\sigma_A$ in equation (d). $\sigma_A$ is expressed as % $\Delta$technological cost per $A.

**Table A3** Coefficients and parameters in the stylized model

| Symbol | Description | Indicative value[a] | |
| --- | --- | --- | --- |
| | | 2011 | 2030 |
| $S_C$ | Share of private consumption in GDP at market prices | 0.52 | 0.53 |
| $S_I$ | Share of investment in GDP at market prices | 0.29 | 0.28 |
| $S_G$ | Share of public consumption in GDP at market prices | 0.19 | 0.19 |
| $S_X$ | Share of exports in GDP at market prices | 0.22 | 0.23 |
| $S_M$ | Share of imports in GDP at market prices | 0.23 | 0.23 |
| $S_L$ | Share of the cost of labor in GDP at factor cost | 0.53 | 0.56 |
| $S_K$ | Share of the cost of capital in GDP at factor cost | 0.47 | 0.44 |
| $S_{GDP}^{FC}$ | Share of factor cost in GDP at market prices | 1.00 | 1.00 |
| $S_T$ | Share of indirect taxes in GDP at market prices | 0.00 | 0.00 |
| $\sigma_T$ | Semi elasticity: % $\Delta$ emissions to $A \Delta$ in permit price | −0.45 | −0.50 |
| $\sigma_A$ | Semi elasticity: % $\Delta$ technological cost to $A \Delta$ in permit price | 0.0020 | 0.002 |
| $\sigma_{KL}$ | Capital/labor substitution elasticity (+ number) | 0.5 | 0.5 |
| $\sigma_M$ | Average domestic/import substitution elasticity (+ number) | 2.6 | 2.6 |
| $\sigma_X$ | Price elasticity of world demand for exports (− number) | −5.0 | −5.0 |
| $\sigma_I$ | Elasticity of I/K to rate of return (+ number) | 1.0 | 1.0 |
| $CO_2 ratio$ | 100 times the ratio of emissions to GDP (Mt/$A m) | 0.0475 | 0.0386 |

[a]Data are from the model's base case for 2011 (short run) and 2030 (long run) with the exceptions of data for $\sigma_T$, $\sigma_A$ and $\sigma_I$. Values for each of these elasticities are inferred *ex post* from the MMRF modeling results reported in Section 9.6.

In writing equation (e), the first share on the right-hand side is the share of factor cost in market-price GDP. The second share is the share of indirect taxes (the value of permits) in market-price GDP. It is assumed that changes in the underlying quantity (emissions) directly affect real GDP. Changes in the tax rate only directly affect the price of GDP (equation l).

In equation (h), $\sigma_M$, a positive parameter, is the value of the average domestic/import substitution elasticity evaluated using data from MMRF. In equation (i), $\sigma_X$, a negative parameter, represents the average price elasticity of world demand for Australian exports. Again, its value comes from MMRF.

Equation (j) relates the percentage change in capital growth in the comparative-static year, to the percentage change in rate of return net of the required rate of return. The elasticity $\sigma_I$ is a positive parameter. As for $\sigma_T$ and $\sigma_A$, the value for $\sigma_I$ will be calibrated using results from the main model.

Equation (l) is generated by first noting that the percentage change in the price of GDP at market prices is a share weighted sum of the percentage changes in factor prices and in the price associated with indirect taxes (in this model, the permit price or carbon tax). In other words:

$$p_{gdp}^{mp} = S_{GDP}^{FC} p_{gdp}^{fc} + \frac{Q_{CO_2} T}{P_{GDP}^{MP} \times Y_{MP}} \times 100 \times \frac{d\_T}{T}. \tag{9.17}$$

Cancelling $T$ gives equation (l), with the economy's emission intensity ($\times 100$) given by:

$$CO_2 \; ratio = 100 \times \frac{Q_{CO_2}}{P_{GDP}^{MP} \times Y_{MP}}, \tag{9.18}$$

For equation (n), it is assumed that:

$$p_{gdp}^{mp} = S_C p_c + S_G p_g + S_I p_i + \left(S_X p_x - S_M p_m\right). \tag{9.19}$$

If the prices of private consumption, public consumption and investment move together, i.e.:

$$p_c = p_g = p_i, \tag{9.20}$$

and trade is initially balanced, i.e.:

$$S_X = S_M, \tag{9.21}$$

then:

$$p_{gdp}^{mp} - p_c = S_X\left(p_x - p_m\right) = S_X tot. \tag{9.22}$$

Equation (o) is an implication of the CES form for capital/labor substitution:

$$\frac{K}{L} = \left(\frac{P_L \times P_{GDP}^{FC}}{P_K \times P_{GDP}^{FC}}\right)^{\sigma_{KL}}. \tag{9.23}$$

where $\sigma_{KL}$ is a positive parameter, representing the capital/labor substitution elasticity.

The starting point for equation (q) is equation (9.15). This implies that the percentage change in real price of labor is the sum of: (i) the percentage change in the real wage rate (*rw*), (ii) the percentage change in the ratio of the consumption price to the market-price GDP deflator and (iii) the percentage change in the ratio of the market-price GDP deflator to the factor-cost GDP deflator. Component (ii) is explained by equation (n). Component (iii) is explained by equation (l). The derivation of equation (r) from equation (9.16) is analogous to the derivation of (q) from (9.15).

The number of variables (9.27) exceeds the number of equations (9.18) by nine. Thus, nine variables must be declared exogenous. Table A2 shows the exogenous/endogenous status of each variable in the short-run and long-run closures of the model. Seven variables are shown as exogenous in both cases. The price of consumption is the numéraire. The terms of trade is also exogenous, reflecting its status in the MMRF simulations. It is exogenized by making endogenous the world GDP price (the proxy for import prices).

This leaves two more variables to be made exogenous. As indicated in the final two columns of Table A1, in short-run comparative-static simulations, the capital stock and real wage rate are exogenous, allowing the model to determine values for employment and the rate of return on capital. In long-run comparative-static simulations, employment and the rate of return are exogenous, allowing the model to determine values for capital and the real wage rate.

In the next section, simulation results from MMRF are compared to results deduced using the stylized model.

## A.3 MMRF Projections compared with results from the stylized model

Table A4 compares Australia-wide results for the ETS as simulated by MMRF with those derived using the stylized model. In the column labeled 'Short (2011)', results from the first year (2011) of the MMRF simulation, expressed as deviations from base case, are compared with short-run comparative-static results from the stylized model. In the column labeled 'Long (2030)', results for the final simulation year (2030) of the MMRF simulation are compared with long-run comparative-static results from the stylized model. All simulations with the stylized model were run using the same multistep solution procedure as used for MMRF simulations.

First, the short-run results are compared. Generally, these are the easiest to understand in terms of known details about the underlying data, equations and closure. Then, the long-run results are examined. These are more easily understood once the short-run outcomes have been discussed.

### A.3.1 Short-run impacts

The MMRF simulation of the effects of the ETS in 2011 is reproduced in the stylized model by shocking the exogenous variables $d\_T$, $tot$, $rw$ and $\omega$, and setting all other exogenous variables to zero change (see the italic entries of Table 9.4). The values of the shocks are the deviations from base case imposed or simulated using the full model for 2011.

**Table A4** Values for variables compared

| Symbol | Description | Short (2011) | | Long (2030) | |
|---|---|---|---|---|---|
| | | Stylized | MMRF | Stylized | MMRF |
| $y_{mp}$ | Real GDP at market prices | −0.1 | −0.1 | −0.8 | −1.1 |
| c | Real private consumption | 0.1 | 0.1 | −1.3 | −1.5 |
| i | Real investment | −0.6 | −0.4 | −2.3 | −3.4 |
| g | Real public consumption | −0.1 | −0.1 | −1.2 | −0.5 |
| x | Real exports | 0.0 | −0.3 | 1.6 | 1.2 |
| m | Real imports | −0.1 | −0.2 | −1.6 | −2.0 |
| $y_{fc}$ | Real GDP at factor cost | −0.1 | −0.1 | −0.4 | −0.8 |
| a | Technological change | 0.0 | 0.0 | 0.0 | −0.1 |
| l | Employment | −0.2 | −0.2 | −0.1 | −0.1 |
| k | Capital stock | 0.0 | 0.0 | −0.5 | −1.7 |
| $d\_T$ | Emissions price ($A per tonne of $CO_2$-e) | 10.0 | 10.0 | 49.3 | 49.3 |
| $q_{co_2}$ | Quantity of emissions | −4.5 | −4.5 | −24.4 | −25.6 |
| $p_c$ | Price of consumption | 0.0 | 0.0 | 0.0 | 0.0 |
| $p_{gdp}^{fc}$ | GDP price (factor cost) | −0.3 | −0.4 | −1.6 | −2.1 |
| $p_{gdp}^{mp}$ | GDP price (market prices) | 0.0 | −0.1 | −0.4 | −0.8 |
| $\omega$ | APC | 0.2 | 0.2 | −0.1 | 0.9 |
| $\gamma$ | Public consumption share | 0.0 | 0.0 | 0.0 | 0.0 |
| rer | Real exchange rate | 0.0 | −0.2 | −0.3 | −2.5 |
| $p_{world}$ | World GDP price | 0.0 | NA | 1.3 | NA |
| $\varphi$ | Nominal exchange rate | 0.0 | −0.3 | −1.3 | 1.0 |
| $y_{world}$ | World GDP | 0.0 | NA | 0.0 | NA |
| ror | Rate of return on capital | −0.6 | −0.4 | −1.2 | −1.2 |
| $ror_{req}$ | Required rate of return | 0.0 | 0.0 | 0.0 | 0.0 |
| tot | Terms of trade | 0.0 | 0.0 | −1.5 | −1.5 |
| $rp_l$ | Real price of labor | 0.2 | 0.2 | −0.5 | −0.5 |
| $rp_k$ | Real price of capital | −0.2 | −0.1 | 0.4 | 0.6 |
| rw | Real wage rate | −0.2 | −0.2 | −2.1 | −2.6 |

NA indicates that the variable is not present in the full model.

According to equation (q), the imposition of a carbon price of $A10 per tonne of $CO_2$-e, combined with no change in the terms of trade and a real wage cut of 0.2%, causes the real price of labor ($RP_L$) to increase by 0.2%. The increase in real price of labor implies a decrease in the real price of capital ($RP_K$) (equation p). The stylized model projects a fall of 0.2%. In the full model, the real price of labor increases relative to its base-case value by 0.2% and the real price of capital falls by 0.1%. The stylized model overestimates the impact on the real price of capital mainly because it ignores the other factor fixed in the short-run, agricultural land. In the full model, the imposition of the carbon price in the short run causes the real price of land to fall by 0.9%. Land is about

5% of GDP. A weighted average of the changes in land and capital prices is −0.2%, as predicted in the stylized model.

An increase in the real price of labor relative to the real price of capital causes producers to substitute capital for labor. According to the CES equation (o), the ratio of capital to labor should increase by 0.2%. With capital exogenous and set to zero change in the short-run, employment falls by 0.2%. In this case the prediction of the stylized model is the same as the projection of the full system.

Via equation (b), in the absence of technological change, the fall in employment leads to a 0.1% decline in real GDP at factor cost. Real GDP in market prices falls by the same percentage amount (equation e). These are the same results projected in the full model. Compositional effects, which are not captured in the stylized model, appear to have had a negligible impact on the short-run results for employment and real GDP.[35]

The stylized model predicts that the price of GDP at market prices will be affected by less than 0.1% (see equation n).[36] This implies, via equation (l), a 0.3% reduction in the price of GDP at factor cost. In the full model, the price of GDP at market prices falls relative to base by 0.1% and the price of GDP at factor cost falls by 0.4%.

We now turn to the expenditure-side aggregates of real GDP. In the stylized model, the change in real private consumption is explained by equation (f). If there were no change in the APC ($\Omega$), then the stylized model would predict a 0.1% reduction in real consumption, in line with the fall in the value of GDP at market prices. However, the full model predicts a 0.2% increase in the APC to ensure that the balance on current account remains unchanged relative to its base case level. After taking this into account, the final predicated change in consumption is 0.1%, in line with the simulated deviation from the full model.

Equation (j) explains the percentage change in investment (with capital held fixed) as a function of the percentage change in the ratio of the actual to required rate of return. According to equation (r), based on the 0.2% fall in the real price of capital (already explained), the rate of return on capital will fall by 0.6%. Given a value of 1.0 for $\sigma_I$, the stylized model predicts a fall in investment of 0.6%, which is the same as the simulated deviation from base in the full model.

In the stylized model, the changes in real private consumption and investment, together with the assumption that public consumption moves with nominal GDP, imply a percentage change in real final domestic absorption (C + I + G) of:

$$S_C c + S_I i + S_G g = 0.52 \times 0.1 + 0.29 \times -0.6 + 0.19 \times -0.1 = -0.1\%.$$

[35] In a multisectoral model, the economy-wide ratio of capital to labor is affected not only by changes in the ratio of aggregate factor prices, but also by changes in the sectoral composition of GDP. For example, in the short-run the capital-to-labor ratio can fall because of changes in the composition of the economy away from capital-intensive industries. Conversely, it can rise with changes in composition towards capital-intensive industries.

[36] Recall, that the price of consumption is the numéraire, which is fixed at zero change.

This matches the predicted percentage change in real GDP at market prices. With the initial trade balance assumed to be slightly in deficit (Table A3), equal percentage changes in real GDP and real GNE requires the percentage change in import volume to be a little below the percentage change in export volume. This is consistent with the full model.

To generate the necessary changes in trade volumes, equations (h) and (i) suggest that no change in the real exchange rate is necessary. This is in contrast to the full model, where a real devaluation of 0.2% is projected. Without the devaluation, the carbon price, which has relatively adverse effects on export-oriented mining and manufacturing sectors, would shift the trade balance towards deficit. These compositional effects are not captured by the stylized model. Note, that with no change in the real exchange rate and no change in the world GDP price, there is no scope for change in the nominal exchange rate (equation k).

Based on the calibrated values for $\sigma_T$ and $\sigma_A$ of $-0.45$ and $0.02$, the emissions price of $A10 generates a changes in emissions and technological change consistent with the projections of the full model.

### A.3.2 Long-run impacts

The MMRF simulation of the effects of the ETS in 2030 is reproduced in the stylized model by shocking the exogenous variables $d\_T$, $tot$, $ror$, $\omega$ and $l$, and setting all other exogenous variables to zero change (see the entries of the last panel of numbers in Table A4). With one exception, the values of the shocks are the deviations from base case imposed or simulated using the full model for 2030. The exception is the shock to the APC ($\omega$). MMRF projects an increase of 0.9%. For the stylized model, this is adjusted down by 1.0 percentage points to $-0.1\%$ to account for the loss of consumption associated with the need to purchase global emissions permits from overseas ($A7.9 billion in 2030). It is assumed in the full and stylized modeling that these purchases are ultimately paid for by private households.

According to equation (r), the imposition of the tax ($A49.3 per tonne of $CO_2$-e), combined with the terms-of-trade deterioration of 1.5% and a fall of 1.2% in capital's rate of return, causes the real price of capital to increase by 0.4%. This leads to a fall in the real price of labor of 0.5% (equation p). In the full model, the real price of capital increases by 0.6% relative to base and the real price of labor falls by 0.5%.

The predicted change in real factor prices causes the ratio of capital to labor to fall by 0.4% (equation o). With employment down by 0.1%, this implies a 0.5% decline in capital. In the full model, relative to the stylized model the change in real factor prices is similar. However, the outcome for the ratio of capital to labor is different, with the full model projecting a change of $-1.6\%$, rather than $-0.4\%$. The difference is due to the long-run compositional effect mentioned in Section 9.6.2.1. The effect operates primarily in the long-run and allows the national ratio of capital to labor to fall with relatively little change in relative factor prices when the economy's composition moves away from capital-intensive sectors.

The stylized model predicts a 0.4% fall in real GDP at factor cost (equation b), while the full model projects a 0.8% fall. This is in line with the respective outcomes for labor and capital, which suggest a larger fall in the main model for factor-cost GDP. The stylized model predicts little change in technology. The full model projects technological improvement (a negative value for $a$) of 0.1%.

According to equation (e), with real GDP at factor cost down by 0.4% and a reduction in emissions of roughly 25%, the percentage change in real GDP at market prices will be −0.8%: the reduction in highly taxed emissions reduces real GDP by 0.4 percentage points. In the full model real GDP at market prices falls by 1.1%, with changes in the underlying volumes of taxed flows contributing −0.3 percentage points. Changes in the volumes of taxed flows are strongly influenced by compositional factors, which account for the different contributions in the two sets of model results.

The stylized model predicts that the price of GDP at market prices will fall relative to the price of consumption by 0.4%, driven by the 1.5% cut in terms of trade (equation n). The full model projects a fall of 0.8%. There are a number of compositional factors causing the stylized model to underestimate the change in price of GDP. A key factor is that it fails to take account of the composition of changes in foreign currency import prices that are based on projections from GTEM. In the GTEM shocks, the price of imported consumption goods fall relative to the average price of imported products, leading to a larger fall in the market-price GDP deflator relative to the consumption deflator than predicted by the stylized model. The stylized model also underestimates the fall in the factor-cost deflator. This is due, in the main, to the underestimation of the change in the market-price deflator.

We now turn to the expenditure side aggregates of real GDP. Given a 0.1% decrease in APC, the stylized model predicts a fall in real consumption of 1.3% (equation f). Given the fall in capital of 0.5%, a reduction in the rate of return on capital of 1.2%, the stylized model predicts a fall in investment of 2.3% (equation j). In the full model, real private consumption falls by 1.5% and real investment falls 3.4%.

In the stylized model, the changes in real private consumption, real public consumption and investment imply a 0.7% reduction in real domestic absorption relative to real GDP at market prices. Thus, the volume of imports must fall relative to the volume of exports. In the stylized model, imports fall by 1.6% and exports rise by 1.6%. In the full model, imports fall by 2.0% and exports increase by 1.2%. In the stylized model, mild depreciation of the real exchange rate is necessary to achieve the required outcome for the net volume of trade. In the full model, stronger real depreciation is required, in part to offset compositional shifts against traded-goods industries.

## A.4 Final remarks regarding the stylized model

The stylized model assists in identifying the principal theoretical mechanisms that underlie the projections from the full model. It also aids in highlighting the important elements of the database (Table A3). The extent of its predictive power is inversely proportional to the degree to which compositional changes, not allowed for in the stylized framework, influence the final simulation outcome. However, as shown in Sections A.3.1 and A.3.2 of this Appendix, even for the ETS simulations in which compositional effects are strong, the stylized model can aid interpretation by identifying the strength of specific compositional effects and in some cases the nature and location of those effects.

In addition to being interpretation aid, the stylized model can also be used to create summary reduced-form expressions for the short- and long-run impacts of an ETS on real GDP. These assist further with arguments about plausibility, etc. The reduced-form expressions are given below.

### A.4.1 Short-run

From equations (o)–(q), the following reduced-form expression for $(k-l)$ is obtained:

$$k - l = \frac{\sigma_{KL}}{S_K} \{ nv - S_X tot + CO_2 \; ratio \times d_-T + a \}. \tag{9.24}$$

Substituting equation (24) into (b) yields an expression for the deviation in real GDP at factor cost:

$$y_{fc} = -\frac{S_L \sigma_{KL}}{S_K} \{ nv - S_X tot + CO_2 \; ratio \times d_-T + a \} + k - a. \tag{9.25}$$

From (e) the following expression for real GDP at market prices is derived:

$$y_{mp} = S_{GDP}^{FC} \left[ -\frac{S_L \sigma_{KL}}{S_K} \{ nv - S_X tot + CO_2 \; ratio \times d_-T + a \} + k - a \right] + S_T q_{CO_2}. \tag{9.26}$$

The contribution of changes in factor inputs to the percentage change in real market-price GDP is given by the first of the two right-hand terms. The contribution from the efficiency effects associated with changes in the quantity of taxed flows is given by the second of the two right-hand terms.

If in the short-run there is no impact on capital and the real wage rate, and if there is no technological change, then carbon price's short-run effect on real GDP at factor cost reduces to:

$$\left[ -\frac{S_L \sigma_{KL}}{S_K} \{ - S_X tot + CO_2 \; ratio \times d_-T \} \right]. \tag{9.27}$$

$CO_2$ *ratio* $\times d\_T$ is the ratio of the emissions tax to GDP. Thus, ignoring compositional changes and terms-of-trade effects, the percentage effect on real GDP of a carbon tax is inversely proportional to the size of the tax relative to GDP. Based on the data in Table A3, in 2011 the short-run impact on real GDP of a \$A10 per tonne tax will be $-0.3\%$ (actual outcome $-0.1\%$).

### A.4.2 Long-run

The corresponding equations for the long run are:

$$k - l = \frac{\sigma_{KL}}{S_L} \{ror - S_X tot + CO_2 \ ratio \times d\_T + a\} \tag{9.28}$$

$$y_{fc} = -\frac{S_K \sigma_{KL}}{S_L} \{ror - S_X tot + CO_2 \ ratio \times d\_T + a\} + l - a \tag{9.29}$$

$$y_{mp} = S_{GDP}^{FC} \left[ -\frac{S_K \sigma_{KL}}{S_L} \{ror - S_X tot + CO_2 \ ratio \times d\_T + a\} + l - a \right] + S_T q_{CO_2}. \tag{9.30}$$

In the long run, assuming no change in rate of return and employment, and no technological change, then carbon price's short-run effect on real GDP at factor cost reduces to:

$$\left[ -\frac{S_K \sigma_{KL}}{S_L} \{ - S_X tot + CO_2 \ ratio \times d\_T \} \right]. \tag{9.31}$$

Evaluated at coefficient values for 2030 given in Table A3, and ignoring terms-of-trade changes, equation (9.31) yields an estimate of $-0.8\%$ for the long-run impact of a \$A49.3 carbon price on real factor-cost GDP (actual outcome $-0.8\%$).

## REFERENCES

Adams, P.D., 2005. Interpretation of results from CGE models such as GTAP. J. Policy Model. 27, 941–959.

Adams, P.D., Dixon, P.B., Jones, B., 1992. The MENSA Model: An Exposition. Centre of Policy Studies, Monash University.

Adams, P.D., Dixon, J., Giesecke, J., Horridge, M.J., 2011. MMRF: Monash multi-regional forecasting model: A dynamic multi-regional applied general equilibrium model of the Australian economy. Working Paper G-223. Centre of Policy Studies, Monash University.

Armington, P.S., 1969. The geographic pattern of trade and the effects of price changes. IMF Staff Papers 16, 179–199.

Berndt, E.R., Wood, D., 1975. Technology prices and the derived demand for energy. Rev. Econ. Stat. 56, 259–268.

Burniaux, J., Truong, T., 2002. GTAP-E: An energy-environmental version of the GTAP model. GTAP Technical Paper 16. Center for Global Trade Analysis, Purdue University, West Lafayette, IN.

Department of Climate Change, 2008. Carbon Pollution Reduction Scheme Green Paper. Australian Government, Canberra.

Department of Treasury, 2007. Intergenerational Report 2007. Australian Government, Canberra.

Department of Treasury, 2008. Australia's Low Pollution Future: The Economics of Climate Change Mitigation. Australian Government, Canberra.

Dixon, P.B., Johnson, D.T., 1990. Estimates of the macroeconomic effects on Australia of attempting to reduce $CO_2$ emissions by 20 per cent by 2005. In: Swaine, D.J. (Ed.), Greenhouse and Energy. CSIRO, Canberra, pp. 127–134.

Dixon, P.B., Rimmer, M.T., 2002. Dynamic General Equilibrium Modeling for Forecasting and Policy: A Practical Guide and Documentation of MONASH. Contributions to Economic Analysis 256. North-Holland, Amsterdam.

Dixon, P.B., Parmenter, B.R., Ryland, G.J., Sutton, J., 1977. ORANI, A General Equilibrium Model of the Australian Economy: Current Specification and Illustrations of Use for Policy Analysis, Volume 2 of the First Progress Report of the IMPACT Project. Australian Government Publishing Service, Canberra.

Dixon, P.B., Parmenter, B.R., Sutton, J., Vincent, D.P., 1982. ORANI: A Multisectoral Model of the Australian Economy. North-Holland, Amsterdam.

Dixon, P.B., Parmenter, B.R., Powell, A.A., 1984. The role of miniatures in computable general equilibrium modeling: Experience from ORANI. Econ. Model. 1, 421–428.

Dixon, P.B., Marks, R.E., Swan, P.L., McLennan, P., Schodde, R., Johnson, D.T., 1990. The cost of Australian carbon dioxide abatement. Energy J. 12, 135–152.

Dixon, P.B., Menon, J., Rimmer, M.T., 2000. Changes in technology and preferences: a general equilibrium explanation of rapid growth in trade. Aust. Econ. Pap. 39, 33–55.

Dixon, P.B., Pearson, K.R., Picton, M.R., Rimmer, M.T., 2005. Rational expectations for large CGE models: A practical algorithm and a policy application. Econ. Model. 22, 1001–1019.

Frontier Economics, 2009. Modeling Methodology and Assumptions: A Report for IPART. Frontier Economics, Melbourne. Available from www.frontier-economics.com/australia/au.

Garnaut, R., 2008. The Garnaut Climate Change Review. Cambridge University Press, Melbourne.

Goodess, C.M., Hanson, C., Hulme, M., Osborn, T.J., 2003. Representing climate and extreme weather events in integrated assessment models: A review of existing methods and options for development. Integr. Assess. 4, 145–171.

Gunasekera, D., Ford, M., Heyhoe, E., Gurney, A., Phipps, S.J., Harman, I., Finnigan, J.J., Brede, M., 2008. Global Integrated Assessment Model: A New Analytical Tool for Assessing Climate Change Risks and Policies. Australian Commodities 15 (1), March quarter, pp. 195–216.

Harrison, W.J., Pearson, K.R., 1996. Computing solutions for large general equilibrium models using GEMPACK. Comput. Econ. 9, 83–127.

Harrison, W.J., Pearson, K.R., 2002. Documentation of the GEMPACK Software System for Solving Large Economic Models. Available by writing to the GEMPACK Office. Centre of Policy Studies, Monash University.

Hertel, T.W., 1997. Global Trade Analysis: Modeling and Applications. Cambridge University Press, Cambridge.

Hinchy, M., Hanslow, K., 1996. The MEGABARE Model: Interim Documentation. Australian Bureau of Agricultural and Resource Economics, Canberra.

Hudson, E.A., Jorgenson, D.W., 1974. US energy policy and economic growth, 1975–2000. Bell J. Econ. Manage. Sci. 5, 461–514.

Kennedy, D., Brown, S., Graham, B., Fisher, B.S., 1998. Kyoto Protocol: Advantages of emissions trading over independent abatement. Aust. Commodities 5, 511–521.

Mastrandrea, M.D., 2010. Representation of climate impacts in integrated assessment models. Assessing the Benefits of Avoided Climate Change: Cost–Benefit Analysis and Beyond: Proceedings of Workshop on Assessing the Benefits of Avoided Climate Change. Available from http://www.pewclimate.org/events/2009/benefitsworkshop.

McDougall, R., 1993. Energy taxes and greenhouse gas emissions in Australia. CoPS/IMPACT General Paper G-104. Monash University.

McDougall, R.A., Dixon, P.B., 1996. Analyzing the economy-wide effects of an energy tax: Results for Australia from the ORANI-E model. In: Bouma, W., Pearman, G., Manning, M. (Eds.), Greenhouse: Coping With Climate Change. CSIRO, Canberra, pp. 607–619.

McDougall, R., Golub, A., 2009. GTAP-E release 6: A revised energy-environmental version of the GTAP model. GTAP Research Memorandum 15. Center for Global Trade Analysis, Purdue University, West Lafayette, IN.

McKibbin, W., Pearce, D., 1996. Global carbon taxes: An Australian perspective. In: Bouma, W., Pearman, G., Manning, M. (Eds.), Greenhouse: Coping With Climate Change. CSIRO, Canberra, pp. 570–585.

McKibbin, W., Wilcoxen, P., 1998. The theoretical and empirical structure of the G-Cubed model. Econ. Model. 16, 123–148.

MMA, 2008. Impacts of the carbon pollution reduction scheme on Australia's electricity markets. Report to Federal Treasury. Available from http://www.treasury.gov.au/lowpollutionfuture/consultants_report/downloads/Electricity_Sector_Modeling_Report_updated.pdf.

Pant, H., 2007. GTEM: Global Trade and Environment Model. Australian Bureau of Agricultural and Resource Economics, Canberra.

Pezzy, J.C.V., Lambie, N.R., 2001. Computable general equilibrium models for evaluating domestic greenhouse policies in Australia: A comparative analysis. Report to the Productivity Commission. AusInfo, Canberra.

Powell, A.A., 1993. Integrating econometric and environmetric modeling, Keynote address to the International Congress on Modeling and Simulation, University of Western Australia. Also available as *General Paper G-102* from the Centre of Policy Studies.

Samuelson, P.A., 1962. Parable and realism in capital theory: The surrogate production function. Rev. Econ. Stud. 29, 193–206.

Schneider, S.H., 1997. Integrated assessment modeling of global climate change: Transparent rational tool for policy making or opaque screen hiding value-laden assumptions? Environmental Modeling and Assessment 2, 229–242.

Stern, D.I., 2012. Interfuel substitution: A meta-analysis. J. Econ. Surv. 26, 307–331.

Truong, T.P., 1999. GTAP-E: Incorporating energy substitution into the GTAP model. GTAP Technical Paper 16. Center for Global Trade Analysis, Purdue University, West Lafayette, IN.

Tulpule, V., Brown, S., Lim, J., Polidano, C., Pant, H., Fisher, B.S., 1999. The Kyoto protocol: An economic analysis using GTEM. Energy J. (Kyoto Special Issue), 257–286.

Weyant, J.P., Hill, J., 1999. Introduction and overview. Energy J. (Kyoto Special Issue), viii–xliv.

# CHAPTER 10

# Taxation, Efficiency and Economic Growth

**Dale W. Jorgenson**[*], **Kun-Young Yun**[**]
[*]Harvard University
[**]Yonsei University

## Abstract

In this chapter we present a dynamic general equilibrium methodology for evaluating alternative proposals for tax reform. We illustrate this methodology by comparing alternative proposals that would remove barriers to efficient allocation of capital and labor inputs. These proposals are based on two broad approaches to reform: (i) Remove discrepancies in the tax treatment of different categories of income and (ii) shift the tax base from income to consumption. To illustrate our methodology we construct a dynamic general equilibrium model of the US economy. An intertemporal price system clears markets for outputs of consumption and investment, and inputs of capital and labor services. This price system links the past and the future through markets for investment goods and capital services. The government sector is coupled to the commodity markets through the tax system. We identify Efficient Taxation of Income as the most effective approach to tax reform. This involves equalizing tax burdens on business and household assets, especially owner-occupied housing. The graduated tax on labor income would be replaced by a proportional tax and equity would be preserved by different tax rates on capital and labor incomes. Another effective approach would be to substitute a proportional National Retail Sales Tax for the existing income tax, but this would involve a serious loss in equity.

## Keywords

Dynamic general equilibrium, tax reform, corporate taxation, individual taxation, efficiency, progressivity

## JEL classification codes

C01, C68, D58, D61, D90, E6, H21

## 10.1 INTRODUCTION

In June 2001, President George W. Bush signed the Economic Growth and Tax Relief and Reconciliation Act into law, initiating a multiyear program of reductions in taxes on individual income. In January 2003, President Bush approved the Jobs and Growth Tax Relief Reconciliation Act of 2003, substantially cutting taxes on business income. The tax legislation of 2001 and 2003 has led to major declines in federal revenue. In January 2005, President Bush convened the President's Advisory Panel on Federal Tax Reform.

*Handbook of CGE Modeling - Vol. 1 SET*
ISSN 2211-6885, http://dx.doi.org/10.1016/B978-0-444-59568-3.00010-9
© 2013 Elsevier B.V.
All rights reserved.

The Panel presented its report, *Simple, Fair, and Pro-Growth: proposals to Fix America's Tax System*, in November 2005.

The proposals of President Bush's Advisory Panel did not lead to further legislation. In February 2010, President Barack Obama established the National Commission on Fiscal Responsibility and Reform. The purpose of this Commission was "… to improve the fiscal situation in the medium term and to achieve fiscal sustainability in the long run."[1] These objectives were to be attained through reductions in government expenditures and increases in government revenues. The Commission's report, *The Moment of Truth*,[2] was released on 1 December 2010.

The National Commission's proposed tax reform would eliminate almost all "tax expenditures." These are provisions of tax law that provide relief from taxation for specific categories of transactions. Part of the increased government revenue would reduce the federal deficit and the remainder would reduce tax rates for individual and corporate income. On 17 December 2010, one week after the release of the National Commission's final report, President Obama signed into law the Tax Relief, Unemployment Insurance Reauthorization and Job Creation Act of 2010. This had the effect of extending the Bush tax cuts, scheduled to expire or "sunset" in 2010, for an additional two years.[3]

In this chapter we model the impact of tax reforms that would remove the barriers to efficient allocation of capital and labor. These barriers arise from disparities in the tax treatment of different forms of income. The centerpiece of the Bush Administration's 2003 tax cuts on business income was the reduction of taxes on dividend income at the individual level. This helped to mitigate one of the most glaring deficiencies of the US tax system, i.e. double taxation of corporate income.

In the US, as in most countries, corporate income is taxed (i) through the corporate income tax and (ii) through individual taxes on corporate distributions, such as dividends.

This leads to a disparity with the taxation of non-corporate income, which is taxed only at the individual level. President Bush's Advisory Panel[4] identified substantial differences between the tax treatment of corporate and non-corporate income that remained after the 2003 tax cuts.

The Bush Administration's tax legislation in 2001 and 2003 failed to address a second major barrier to efficient capital allocation. This is the exclusion of owner-occupied

---

[1] President's Advisory Panel on Tax Reform (2005). See: http://www.fiscalcommission.gov/.

[2] National Commission on Fiscal Responsibility and Reform (2010). See: http://www.fiscalcommission.gov/sites/fiscalcommission.gov/files/documents/TheMomentofTruth12_1_2010.pdf.

[3] A comprehensive review of proposals for tax reform, including the proposals of the Advisory Panel and the National Commission, is presented by the Tax Policy Center (2012). See: http://www.taxpolicycenter.org/taxtopics/Tax_Reform_Proposals.cfm.

[4] President's Advisory Panel on Tax Reform (2005, Figure 5.5, p. 71).

housing from the tax base. While income for non-corporate business is taxed at the individual level and corporate income is taxed at both corporate and individual levels, income from owner-occupied housing is not taxed at either level.

In Jorgenson and Yun (2005) we have shown that allowing owner-occupied housing to remain untaxed would sacrifice most of the gains in economic efficiency from tax reform. President Bush's instructions to the Advisory Panel on Tax Reform included "preservation of incentives for home ownership" — language intended to preserve the tax-free status of owner-occupied housing. Unfortunately, President Bush's instructions nullified most of the potential gains from tax reform at the outset.

In Jorgenson and Yun (2001) we have shown that progressivity of labor income taxation is another major source of inefficiency in the US tax system. This produces marginal tax rates on labor income that are far in excess of average tax rates. A high marginal tax rate results in a large wedge between the wages and salaries paid by employers and those received by households. A proportional tax on labor income would equalize marginal and average tax rates, and would sharply curtail the losses in economic efficiency due to high marginal rates.

An important challenge for tax reform is to eliminate the barriers to efficient capital allocation arising from "double" taxation of assets held in the corporate sector and the exclusion of owner-occupied housing from the tax base. A drastic, but effective, way of meeting this challenge is to shift the tax base from income to consumption. This would remove new investments from the tax base and add revenue from a consumption tax. As investments grow, taxation of income from capital would gradually be eliminated.

During the 1990s, the Committee on Ways and Means of the US House of Representatives held extensive hearings on proposals to shift the federal tax base from income to consumption. The proposals included replacing individual and corporate income taxes by one of three alternative consumption taxes — a European-style value-added tax, the Flat Tax proposed by Robert Hall and Alvin Rabushka (Hall and Rabushka, 1983, 1995), and a National Retail Sales Tax (NRST).

All three approaches to a consumption tax were considered by President Bush's Advisory Panel before settling on the Growth and Investment Tax Plan. This Plan is closely modeled on David Bradford's (Bradford, 2004) X-Tax — an approach to consumption taxation similar to the Hall—Rabushka Flat Tax. Bradford's X-Tax preserves the basic structure of the Flat Tax, described in more detail below, but would add a progressive tax on consumption.

A less drastic approach to removing barriers to efficient allocation of capital and labor inputs is to reform the existing income tax system. President Bush's Advisory Panel presented a Simplified Income Tax Plan that would eliminate double taxation of corporate income. Although the corporate income tax would remain, distributions of income subject to the tax, such as dividends, would be exempt from the individual income tax.

Integration of the individual and corporate income tax systems was proposed by the US Department of the Treasury (1992) in a widely cited study, *Integration of the Individual and Corporate Income Tax Systems: Taxing Business Income Once.* President Bush's Advisory Panel[5] pointed out that the Simplified Income Tax Plan would have only a modest impact on disparities in the tax treatment of corporate and non-corporate income. More important, it would exacerbate the differences between the tax treatment of business income and income from owner-occupied housing.

In Jorgenson and Yun (2005) we proposed to equalize the tax treatment of all forms of capital income. The key to this proposal, which we call Efficient Taxation of Income, is a system of investment tax credits. Each dollar of new investment would generate a credit against taxes on business income. These credits would be calibrated to equalize the tax burdens.

In order to remove the barriers to efficient allocation of capital, it is critically important to equalize tax burdens on business and household assets, especially owner-occupied housing but also consumers' durables like automobiles. Efficient Taxation of Income would include a system of prepayments of future taxes on household investments. This new source of revenue would precisely offset the new tax credits for business investment, preserving revenue neutrality.

To generate further gains in efficiency the graduated tax on labor income would be replaced by a proportional labor income tax. This would reduce the marginal tax rate to the much lower average tax rate. The combination of equal tax burdens on different types of capital and a proportional tax on labor income would produce gains in consumer welfare well in excess of the gains from substituting consumption for income as the tax base.

In modeling alternative proposals for tax reform we begin by describing the US tax system. We classify assets by three different legal forms of organization in order to capture the differences in taxation most relevant to modeling the impact of tax reforms. Income from assets held by households and non-profit institutions is not subject to tax at either individual or corporate levels, while income from assets held by non-corporate businesses is subject to tax at the individual level, but not the corporate level. Finally, income from corporate assets is subject to tax at both the individual and corporate levels.

We further subclassify assets within each of the three sectors — corporate business, non-corporate business, and households and non-profit institutions — between long-lived and short-lived assets. This reflects the fact that capital income from assets with different tax lifetimes are taxed differently. The description of the tax system in terms of this cross-classification of assets is an integral part of our modeling strategy.[6]

---

[5] President's Advisory Panel on Tax Reform (2005, Figure 5.5, p. 71).

[6] In Jorgenson and Yun (2001) we compare this classification of assets with others employed in the literature.

Our next step is to model the impact of alternative tax policies on US economic growth. To simplify this task we distinguish two categories of output, consumption and investment, and two categories of input, capital and labor. Investment and consumption make up the gross domestic product (GDP), while capital and labor comprise the gross domestic income (GDI). We model the allocation of capital among the three legal forms of organization and long-lived and short-lived assets.

Economic growth is the consequence of the growth of labor input, capital input and productivity. Growth of labor input takes place through increases in the labor force, and improvements in labor quality through education and experience. We project future growth in the labor force and labor quality, and model the supply of labor at each point of time. Growth of capital input occurs through investment in new assets. We model the growth of capital input as a consequence of this investment.

We describe our model of economic growth as a dynamic general equilibrium model. The model includes markets for the four commodity groups — investment, consumption, capital and labor. Supply and demand for these commodity groups is equilibrated through the four commodity prices. The market for capital input is linked to past investments, while the market for investment is linked to the future through the arbitrage between the price of new investment goods and future rental values of capital services.

The government sector is coupled to the commodity markets through the tax system. Transactions in the markets for outputs of investment and consumption goods, and inputs of capital and labor services generate government revenues. For example, a proportional tax on consumption produces revenues that depend on the value of consumption. Our model includes budget constraints for consumers, producers and governments. Combining demands and supplies for the four commodity groups with these budget constraints, we obtain a model of the growth of the US economy.

We refer to the alternative tax reform proposals as the policy cases. We compare the time path of economic growth under the policy cases with economic growth under the base case with no change in tax policy. Since the purpose of economic activity is to provide consumption in the form of goods and services and leisure, we focus on the time path of future consumption associated with the base case and each of the alternative policy cases.

We order the alternative policies in terms of the equivalent variation in wealth associated with each policy. The equivalent variation is a standard measure of economic welfare and answers the following question: how much additional wealth would be required at the prices of the base case to achieve the level of consumer welfare in the policy case? If the equivalent variation is positive, the tax reform of the policy case is preferred to the base case with no change in policy.

Since comparisons among tax policies are expressed in prices of the base case, the equivalent variation provides a consistent ranking of the policy cases. This ranking enables us to choose the policy that achieves the highest level of consumer welfare. An important advantage of the equivalent variation is that the ranking of alternative policies is expressed in monetary terms and provides a money metric of consumer welfare. This metric can be compared with other monetary magnitudes, such as the level of wealth of the economy.

In Jorgenson and Yun (1996a) we construct a dynamic general equilibrium model of the US economy. We employ this model to analyze the economic impact of the US tax reforms of 1981 in Jorgenson and Yun (1996b). In Jorgenson and Yun (1996c) we present an updated version of our model and use it to examine the impact of the Tax Reform Act of 1986.[7] Finally, in Jorgenson and Yun (2001), we present a new version of the model and analyze tax reforms like those considered below.

Our model of the US economy incorporates the main features of the US tax system and the alternative proposals for tax reform. These features require the distinctions among different types of assets that correspond to differences in taxation. We have radically simplified the description of consumer behavior by employing a single, representative consumer. Our measure of economic welfare — the equivalent variation in wealth — captures the change in efficiency that would result from each tax change, but not the change in equity.[8]

Debates about tax policies often include both efficiency and equity considerations. Measures of efficiency like the equivalent variation in wealth provide an indicator of potential consumer welfare. This is the welfare that could be attained through tax reform and a costless redistribution of income to maximize consumer welfare. Actual redistributions would require distorting taxes that would lower consumer welfare, so that our measure of efficiency provides an upper bound to the gains in welfare from a change in tax policy.

Measures of the distributional impact of specific tax policies, like those considered by President Bush's Advisory Panel and President Obama's National Commission, are available from the Tax Policy Center.[9] Official estimates of distributional impacts of specific legislative proposals are provided by the Joint Committee on Taxation in the US Congress and the Office of Tax Analysis in the US Department of the Treasury.[10] The TAXSIM model, maintained by the National Bureau of Economic Research, is a valuable resource for measuring the distributional impact of tax policies.[11]

---

[7] More details are given by Yun (2000).

[8] Jorgenson *et al.* in Chapter 8 of this Handbook present similar measures of welfare for individual households, and analyze the distributional impact of alternative energy and environmental policies, including tax policies. For further discussion of efficiency and equity, see Jorgenson (1997).

[9] See: http://www.taxpolicycenter.org/taxtopics/Tax_Reform_Proposals.cfm.

[10] See: http://www.jct.gov/ and http://www.treasury.gov/about/organizational-structure/offices/Pages/Office-of-Tax-Analysis.aspx.

[11] See: http://www.nber.org/~taxsim/.

In this chapter we summarize dynamic general equilibrium modeling of the two broad approaches to tax reform. The first is reform of the existing income tax by removing discrepancies among the tax treatments of different forms of capital income and different types of labor income. It is worth emphasizing that this does not entail equalizing the tax treatment of capital and labor incomes. The second broad approach to tax reform is to replace the income tax base for taxation by a consumption tax base.

Comprehensive treatments of tax reform are given in *The Benefit and the Burden: Tax Reform — Why We Need It and What It Will Take* by Bruce Bartlett (Bartlett, 2012) and *Corporate Tax Reform: Taxing Profits in the 21st Century* by Martin A. Sullivan (Sullivan, 2011). Both of these include extensive bibliographies on all aspects of tax reform, including recent tax policy changes in the US. Comprehensive and detailed descriptions of US tax policy are provided by Joel Slemrod and Jon Bakija (Slemrod and Bakija, 2008), Taxing Ourselves: *A Citizen's Guide to the Debate over Taxes*, and Steuerle (Steuerle, 2008), *Contemporary Tax Policy*.

We present our model of economic growth in Section 10.2. This is based on a dynamic general equilibrium model that incorporates demands and supplies for four commodity groups — consumption, investment, capital and labor — and budget constraints for three main actors — consumers, producers and governments. The mechanisms that generate economic growth are represented in neoclassical models of economic growth.[12] We incorporate tax policy through a description of the tax system that captures the distinction between individual and corporate income taxes, as well as taxes on commodities and taxes on property.

In Section 10.3 we present econometric models that describe the behavior of consumers and producers. In order to simplify the description of the US economy, our model of consumer behavior is based on a single, infinitely-lived, household. This representative household demands capital services from housing and consumers' durables, other goods and services, and leisure.[13] The household supplies capital and labor services. Our model of producer behavior is based on a single, representative firm. The representative firm demands capital and labor services and supplies investment and consumption goods. We incorporate the econometric models of Section 10.3 into the neoclassical model of economic growth in Section 10.2 to obtain our dynamic general equilibrium model of the US economy.

In Section 10.4 we present a methodology for evaluating the welfare effects of tax reform. For this purpose we design a computational algorithm for determining the growth of the economy following the reform. (i) We solve for the unique steady

---

[12] See, e.g. Barro and Sala-i-Martin (2004).

[13] This approach is standard in neo-classical models of economic growth, but sacrifices the heterogeneity of consumers captured by lifecycle models like those surveyed by Diamond and Zodrow in Chapter 11 of this Handbook. Distributional analyses of change in tax policy by the Tax Policy Center (http://www.taxpolicycenter.org/taxtopics/Tax_Reform_Proposals.cfm) are even more detailed.

state corresponding to any tax policy. (ii) We determine the transition path consistent with the steady-state and the initial conditions. We describe the dynamics of our general equilibrium model in terms of the saddle-point configuration of this transition path.

In Section 10.5 we estimate the gains to consumer welfare from Efficient Taxation of Income. This would combine equalizing the tax burden for all sources of capital income and replacing the progressive tax on labor income by a proportional labor income tax. The potential gain in welfare would be $7.0 trillion (2011 US$)! The additional wealth generated by corporate tax integration, the core of the Advisory Panel's Simplified Income Tax Plan, would be only $2.3 trillion, slightly less than a third of the gains from Efficient Taxation of Income.

Efficient Taxation of Income would also have a much greater impact on welfare than a revenue-neutral version of the Hall—Rabushka Flat Tax. In Section 10.6 we estimate that the Flat Tax would yield $3.8 trillion in additional wealth, a little over half the gains from Efficient Taxation of Income. President Bush's Advisory Panel has proposed a Growth and Investment Tax Plan similar to the Flat Tax. The gains would be diminished by the Panel's introduction of a substantial tax subsidy to owner-occupied housing and a progressive tax on consumption at the individual level.

Tax reform proposals, like cherry blossoms, are hardy perennials of the Washington scene. Occasionally, a new approach to tax reform appears and changes the course of the debate. President Reagan's proposal of May 1985 is the most recent example of a new approach to tax reform. Like the Reagan proposal, Efficient Taxation of Income retains the income tax rather than shifting to a consumption tax. In Section 10.7 we conclude that this remains the most rewarding direction for reform.

## 10.2 MODELING ECONOMIC GROWTH

In this section we present a new version of our dynamic general equilibrium model. This incorporates an updated description of the US tax system. In the following section we present econometric models of producer and consumer behavior based on data for the US economy for the period 1970—2010. In Section 10.2.1 we present a system of notation for demands and supplies of the four commodity groups included in our model — capital and labor services, and consumption and investment goods.

Equilibrium in our model is characterized by an intertemporal price system. The price system clears the markets for all four commodity groups in every time period. This price system links the past and the future through markets for investment goods and capital services. Assets are accumulated as a result of past investments, while asset prices are equal to present values of future capital services.

In Section 10.2.2 we present a model of producer behavior based on a production possibility frontier for the representative producer and the corresponding objective function. The first stage of the producer's optimization problem is to choose outputs of investment and consumption goods, and inputs of capital and labor services. In our model, inputs of corporate and non-corporate capital services are treated separately. The second stage is to allocate capital services within each of these sectors between long-lived and short-lived assets.

In Section 10.2.3 we present a model of household behavior based on an intertemporal welfare function for the representative consumer and the corresponding budget constraint. The first stage of the consumer's optimization problem is to allocate wealth among all time periods. The second stage is to allocate consumption in each time period among capital services, other goods and services, and leisure. We derive labor supply by subtracting leisure demand from the household's time endowment. The third and final stage is to allocate capital services between the services of long-lived and short-lived assets.

In Section 10.2.4 we present accounts for the government and rest-of-the-world sectors based on identities between income and expenditure. We first outline the generation of government revenue from taxes on consumption and investment goods and capital and labor services. We complete the government budget by generating purchases of consumption and investment goods and labor services. The deficit of the government sector is the difference between expenditure and revenue. Similarly, net foreign investment is equal to the difference between US imports and exports to the rest of the world.

Finally, we describe intertemporal equilibrium in our model in Section 10.2.5. Equilibrium requires that supply must be equal to demand for each of the four commodity groups — consumption goods, investment goods, capital services and labor services. We show that demand and supply functions satisfy Walras' law; one of the four market clearing conditions is implied by the three remaining conditions, together with identities between income and expenditure for the household, business, government and rest-of-the-world sectors. In addition, the model is homogeneous of degree zero in prices and nominal income and wealth.

## 10.2.1 Commodities

In our model the US economy is divided into household, business, government and rest-of-the-world sectors. The household sector includes both households and non-profit institutions, while the business sector includes both corporate and non-corporate businesses. Although we do not model production in the corporate and non-corporate sectors separately, we distinguish between assets and capital services in these two sectors. The government sector includes general government and government enterprises. Finally, the rest-of-the-world sector encompasses transactions between the US economy and the rest of the world.

Our model includes four commodity groups — consumption goods, investment goods, capital services and labor services. To represent the quantities of these commodity groups we introduce the following notation:

$C$       personal consumption expenditures, excluding household capital services

$I$       gross private domestic investment, including purchases of consumers' durables

$K$       private national capital stock, including the stock of household capital

$L$       labor services.

Consumption and investment correspond closely to the concepts employed in the US National Income and Product Accounts (NIPA).[14] However, purchases of consumers' durables are included in personal consumption expenditures and excluded from gross private domestic investment in the US national accounts. Our accounting system treats consumers' durables symmetrically with other forms of capital. To denote prices we place a $P$ before the corresponding symbol for quantity. For example, $PC$ is the price of private national consumption, excluding household capital services.

We require notation for the supply and demand of consumption goods, investment goods, and labor services by all four sectors. Private national consumption C represents purchases of consumption goods by the household sector. The remaining components of supply and demand for consumption goods are as follows:

$CE$       supply of consumption goods by government enterprises

$CG$       government purchases of consumption goods

$CR$       rest-of-the-world purchases of consumption goods

$CS$       supply of consumption goods by private enterprises.

Similarly, gross private domestic investment $I$ represents purchases of investment goods by the business and household sectors. The remaining components of supply and demand for investment goods are as follows:

$IG$       government purchases of investment goods

$IR$       rest-of-the-world purchases of investment goods

$IS$       supply of investment goods by private enterprise.

We distinguish among assets and capital services in the corporate, non-corporate and household sectors. We further distinguish between short-lived and long-lived assets within each sector. Short-lived assets include producers' and consumers' durable equipment, while long-lived assets include residential structures, non-residential

---

[14] Bureau of Economic Analysis (2011). See: http://www.bea.gov/national/pdf/NIPAchapters1-9.pdf.

structures, inventories and land. Altogether, we represent six types of assets, cross-classified by legal form of organization and durability, in the model.

The classification of assets by legal form of organization enables us to model differences in the tax treatment of capital income in the corporate, non-corporate and household sectors. The classification of assets differing in durability is useful in introducing the effects of asset-specific tax rules, such as the investment tax credit and capital consumption allowances. Ignoring the interasset tax wedges within the corporate and non-corporate sectors would omit an important source of tax distortions. Similarly, a classification of assets based only on differences in durability would neglect the impact of intersectoral tax wedges.[15]

We distinguish between debt and equity claims on capital income for corporate, non-corporate and household sectors. We take the debt–equity ratios to be fixed exogenously for all three sectors. Financial market equilibrium requires that after-tax rates of return to equity are equalized across the three sectors. In addition, rates of return on debt issued by the private sectors and the government must equal the market interest rate. Conditions for financial market equilibrium determine the allocation of capital among the sectors and the allocation of financial claims between debt and equity.

We have simplified the representation of technology in our model by introducing a single stock of capital at each point of time. Capital is perfectly malleable and allocated to equalize after tax rates of return to equity in the corporate, non-corporate and household sectors. Capital services, say *KD*, are proportional to private national capital stock *K*. A complete system of notation that includes the six classes of assets in our model is as follows:

| | |
|---|---|
| *HD* | household capital services |
| *HL* | household capital services from long-lived assets |
| *HS* | household capital services from short-lived assets |
| *MD* | non-corporate capital services |
| *ML* | non-corporate capital services from long-lived assets |
| *MS* | non-corporate capital services from short-lived assets |
| *QD* | corporate capital services |
| *QL* | corporate capital services from long-lived assets |
| *QS* | corporate capital services from short-lived assets. |

---

[15] In Jorgenson and Yun (2001, Chapter 2) we show how to incorporate past and current tax rules into the rental prices of assets. The proposals for tax reform discussed in Sections 10.4 and 10.5 below are also represented in terms of these prices.

The household sector is the only sector with a time endowment. Part of this endowment is consumed as leisure by the household sector. The rest is supplied as labor services to the business, government and rest-of-the-world sectors. The components of demand and supply for labor services are as follows:

| | |
|---|---|
| *LD* | private enterprise purchases of labor services |
| *LE* | government enterprise purchases of labor services |
| *LG* | general government purchases of labor services |
| *LH* | time endowment |
| *LJ* | leisure time |
| *LR* | rest-of-the-world purchases of labor services. |

## 10.2.2 Producer behavior

The business sector includes both corporate and non-corporate enterprises, so that we have divided capital services between corporate and non-corporate capital services. Similarly, we have divided capital services in each sector between long-lived and short-lived components to capture differences in the tax treatment of income from long-lived and short-lived assets. We model the tax treatment of capital income by incorporating specific features of the tax structure into the prices of capital services.

Our model of producer behavior provides a highly schematic representation of the US economy. This model is based on two-stage allocation. At the first stage a representative producer employs capital and labor services to produce outputs of consumption and investment goods. At the second stage the values of both types of capital services are allocated between long-lived and short-lived assets.

To represent our model of producer behavior we first require some notation. We denote the shares of outputs and inputs in the value of labor input as follows:

$$v_{CS} = \frac{PCS \cdot CS}{PLD \cdot LD}, v_{IS} = \frac{PIS \cdot IS}{PLD \cdot LD}, v_{MD} = -\frac{PMD \cdot MD}{PLD \cdot LD}, v_{QD} = -\frac{PQD \cdot QD}{PLD \cdot LD}.$$

The value shares for outputs are positive, while the value shares for inputs are negative. We also introduce the following notation:

$$v = (v_{CS}, v_{IS}, v_{MD}, v_{QD}) \qquad \text{vector of value shares}$$

$$\ln P = (\ln PCS, \ln PIS, \ln PMD, \ln PQD) \text{ vector of logarithms}$$

$$\text{of prices of outputs and inputs.}$$

We characterize the technology of the business sector in terms of labor requirements. Labor services are a function of consumption and investment goods outputs and corporate and non-corporate capital inputs. The technology is characterized by constant returns to scale. By modeling the substitution between consumption and investment goods in production, we introduce external costs of adjustment in the response of investment to changes in tax policy.[16]

Under constant returns to scale we can represent the technology in dual form through the price function, giving the price of labor services as a function of the prices of consumption and investment goods, corporate and non-corporate capital services, and time as an index of technology. The price function must be homogeneous of degree one, non-decreasing in the prices of outputs and non-increasing in the prices of inputs, and convex in the prices of outputs and inputs. We have incorporated these restrictions into the system of supply and demand functions presented in the following section. The rate of productivity growth is endogenous and depends on the prices of inputs and outputs.[17]

We employ the transcendental logarithmic or translog form of the price function:[18]

$$\ln PLD = \ln P' \alpha_P + \alpha_T T + \frac{1}{2} \ln P' B_{PP} \ln P + \ln P' \beta_{PT} T + \beta_{TT} T^2. \tag{10.1}$$

In this representation the scalars $\{\alpha_T, \beta_{TT}\}$, the vectors $\{\alpha_P, \beta_{PT}\}$, and the matrix $\{B_{PP}\}$ are constant parameters. This representation facilitates the expression of demands and supplies as functions of the prices of inputs and outputs. The parameters embody the elasticities of demand and supply that are critical for the evaluation of alternative tax policies.

A model of producer behavior based on the translog price function has an important advantage over models based on Cobb–Douglas or constant elasticity of substitution production functions. Although explicit demand and supply functions can be derived from these production functions, all elasticities of substitution must be same.[19] This frustrates the basic objective of determining the elasticities of demand and supply empirically in order to model the response of producer behavior to changes in tax policy.

The value shares for outputs and inputs can be expressed in terms of the logarithmic derivatives of the price function with respect to the logarithms of the prices of the output and input prices:

$$v = \alpha_P + B_{PP} \ln P + \beta_{PT} T. \tag{10.2}$$

---

[16] Models with internal costs of adjustment are surveyed by Hayashi (2000).

[17] Our approach to endogenous productivity growth was originated by Jorgenson and Fraumeni (2000).

[18] The translog price function was introduced by Christensen *et al.* (2000).

[19] McFadden (1963) and Uzawa (1962) have shown that this restriction is implicit in constant elasticity of substitution production functions.

The parameters $\{B_{PP}\}$ can be interpreted as *share elasticities* and represent the degree of substitutability among inputs and outputs, while the parameters $\{\beta_{PT}\}$ are *biases of productivity growth* and represent the impact of changes in productivity on the value shares.[20]

Similarly, the rate of productivity growth, say $v_T$, is the negative of the growth of the price of labor input, holding the prices of outputs and inputs constant:

$$-v_T = \alpha_T + \beta_{PT} \ln P + \beta_{TT} T. \tag{10.3}$$

The parameter $\beta_{TT}$ is the *deceleration* of productivity growth. To assure existence of a balanced growth equilibrium, we assume that productivity growth is labor-augmenting and takes place at a constant rate:

$$\beta_{PT} = 0, \; \beta_{TT} = 0.$$

To represent the second stage of our model of producer behavior we first denote the shares of long-lived and short-lived assets in the value of non-corporate and corporate capital as follows:

$$v_{ML} = \frac{PML \cdot ML}{PMD \cdot MD}, v_{MS} = \frac{PMS \cdot MS}{PMD \cdot MD}, v_{QL} = \frac{PQL \cdot QL}{PQD \cdot QD}, v_{QS} = \frac{PQS \cdot QS}{PQD \cdot QD}.$$

These value shares are positive. We also find it convenient to introduce the notation:

$v_M = (v_{ML}, v_{MS})$         vector of value shares in non-corporate capital input

$v_Q = (v_{QL}, v_{QS})$         vector of value shares in corporate capital input

$\ln PM = (\ln PML, \ln PMS)$    vector of logarithms of prices of capital

inputs in the non-corporate sector

$\ln PQ = (\ln PQL, \ln PQS)$    vector of logarithms of prices of capital inputs

in the corporate sector.

We represent the prices of corporate and non-corporate capital services as functions of the prices of their long-lived and short-lived components. These price functions must be homogeneous of degree one, non-decreasing in the prices of inputs, and concave in the input prices. We have incorporated these restrictions into the demand functions presented in the following section.

---

[20] For further discussion of share elasticities and biases of productivity growth, see Jorgenson (2000).

As before, we employ the translog form for the price functions:

$$\ln PMD = \ln PM' \alpha_{PM} + \frac{1}{2} \ln PM' B_{PM} \ln PM$$

$$\ln PQD = \ln PQ' \alpha_{PQ} + \frac{1}{2} \ln PQ' B_{PQ} \ln PQ. \qquad (10.4)$$

In this representation the matrices $\{B_{PM}, B_{PQ}\}$ are constant parameters that embody the elasticities of demand for capital inputs needed for analyzing the response of producer behavior to changes in tax policy.

The value shares can be expressed in terms of the logarithmic derivatives of the price functions with respect to the logarithms of the prices:

$$v_M = \alpha_{PM} + B_{PM} \ln PM$$

$$v_Q = \alpha_{PM} + B_{PQ} \ln PQ. \qquad (10.5)$$

The *share elasticities* $\{B_{PM}, B_{PQ}\}$ represent the degree of substitutability between the capital services of short-lived and long-lived assets within the non-corporate and corporate sectors. There is no role for productivity growth in the second stage of our model of producer behavior.

## 10.2.3 Consumer behavior

The household sector includes both households and non-profit institutions. This sector owns the private capital in the US economy, as well as having claims on the government and the rest of the world. Claims on the government sector represent liabilities owed by the government to its own citizens. Similarly, claims on the rest of the world correspond to liabilities owed by the rest of the world sector. Household wealth is the sum of tangible capital in the private sector and claims on the government and rest-of-the-world sectors.

Capital services from housing and consumers' durables are directly consumed by the household sector. We have divided these services between long-lived and short-lived components in order to capture differences in the tax treatment of income from these assets. We incorporate features of the tax structure specific to household assets into the prices of capital services.

Our model of consumer behavior is based on a representative consumer with an infinite time horizon. Barro (1974) has provided a rationale for the infinite-horizon representative consumer model in terms of intergenerational altruism. Our assumption is an alternative to the life-cycle theory in modeling consumer behavior. The implications are very different from those of the life-cycle theory, based on a finite lifetime for each consumer.[21]

---

[21] More details are given by Diamond and Zodrow in Chapter 11 of this Handbook.

The objective of the representative consumer is to maximize welfare through allocation of lifetime wealth. Our model is based on an intertemporally additive utility function that depends on levels of full consumption in all time periods. Full consumption is an aggregate of consumption goods, household capital services and leisure. To simplify the model we endow the representative consumer with perfect foresight about future prices and rates of return.[22]

To represent our model of consumer behavior we introduce the following notation:

$F_t$      full consumption *per capita* with population measured in efficiency units

$PF_t$      price of full consumption *per capita*

$n_t$      rate of population growth

$-\alpha_T$      rate of labor-augmenting productivity growth

$\rho$      nominal private rate of return.

Labor-augmenting productivity growth is incorporated into our representation of the technology. Since full consumption includes consumption goods, household capital services and leisure, we take the rate of productivity growth in both sectors to be the same. This assumption assures the existence of balanced growth equilibrium. We represent full consumption *per capita* in a time-invariant form by defining population in efficiency units, the number of individuals augmented by growth in productivity.

In our model of consumer behavior the representative consumer maximizes the *intertemporal welfare function*:

$$V = \frac{1}{1-\sigma} \sum_{t=0}^{\infty} \prod_{s=0}^{t} \left(\frac{1+n_s}{1+\gamma}\right) U_t^{1-\sigma}, \tag{10.6}$$

where $\sigma$ is the inverse of the intertemporal elasticity of substitution and $\gamma$ is the subjective rate of time preference.

The intertemporal welfare function is a discounted sum of products of total population, which grows at the rate $n_t$, and *per capita* welfare $U_t$ ($t = 0, 1, ...$). These depend on full consumption *per capita* $F_t$ with population measured in efficiency units:

$$U_t = F_t(1 - \alpha_T)^t, t = 0, 1, .... \tag{10.7}$$

The representative consumer maximizes the welfare function (10.6), subject to the *intertemporal budget constraint*:

---

[22] Perfect foresight models of tax incidence are presented by Chamley (1981), Diamond and Zodrow in Chapter 11 of this Handbook, and many others.

$$W = \sum_{t=0}^{\infty} \frac{PF_t F_t (1 - \alpha_T)^t \prod_{s=0}^{t} (1 + n_s)}{\prod_{s=0}^{t} (1 + \rho_s)}, \tag{10.8}$$

where $W$ is full wealth. Full wealth is the present value of full consumption over the future of the economy, where full consumption is discounted at the nominal private rate of return $\rho_s$.

The function $V$ is additively separable in the welfare functions $U_t$ ($t = 0, 1, \ldots$). These depend on the consumption of leisure, consumption goods and capital services, so that we can divide the representative consumer's optimization problem into two stages. The consumer first allocates full wealth among different time periods. In the second stage, the consumer allocates full consumption among leisure, consumption goods and household capital services in each period.

The necessary conditions for optimization are given by the discrete-time Euler equation:

$$\frac{F_t}{F_{t-1}} = \left[ \frac{PF_{t-1}}{PF_t} \frac{1 + \rho_t}{(1 + \gamma)(1 - \alpha_T)^\sigma} \right]^{\frac{1}{\sigma}}, \quad t = 1, 2, \ldots. \tag{10.9}$$

This describes the optimal time path of full consumption, given the sequence of prices and nominal rates of return. We refer this as the *transition equation* for full consumption. The growth rate of full consumption is given by the transition equation, so that the level of full consumption in any period determines the optimal time path.

In a steady state with no inflation, the level of full consumption *per capita* with population measured in efficiency units is constant. Therefore, the only private nominal rate of return consistent with the steady state, say $\tilde{\rho}$, is:

$$\tilde{\rho} = (1 + \gamma)(1 - \alpha_T)^\sigma - 1. \tag{10.10}$$

This depends on the rate of labor-augmenting productivity growth and the parameters of the intertemporal welfare function, but is independent of tax policy.

We denote the rate of inflation in the price of full consumption by $\pi_t$, where:

$$\pi_t = \frac{PF_t}{PF_{t-1}} - 1, \quad t = 1, 2, \ldots$$

In a steady state with a constant rate of inflation $\tilde{\pi}$ the nominal private rate of return is:

$$\tilde{\rho} = (1 + \gamma)(1 - \alpha_T)^\sigma (1 + \tilde{\pi}) - 1. \tag{10.11}$$

If we denote the real private rate of return by $r_t$, where:

$$r_t = \frac{PF_{t-1}}{PF_t} (1 + \rho_t) - 1, \quad t = 1, 2, \ldots.$$

the steady-state real private rate of return is:

$$\tilde{r} = (1+\gamma)(1-\alpha_T)^\sigma - 1. \tag{10.12}$$

This rate of return is independent of tax policy and the rate of inflation.

The transition equation for full consumption implies that if the real private rate of return exceeds the steady-state rate of return, full consumption rises; conversely, if the rate of return is below its steady-state value, full consumption falls. To show this we take the logarithm of both sides of the transition equation, obtaining:

$$\ln\frac{F_t}{F_{t-1}} = \frac{1}{\sigma}[\ln(1+r) - \ln(1+\tilde{r})]. \tag{10.13}$$

To a first-order approximation, the growth rate of full consumption is proportional to the difference between the real private rate of return and its steady-state value.[23] The constant of proportionality is the intertemporal elasticity of substitution $1/\sigma$. The greater this elasticity, the more rapidly full consumption approaches its steady-state level.

We have assumed that consumption decisions can be separated into three stages. At the first stage the value of full wealth is allocated among different time periods. At the second stage full consumption is allocated among nondurable consumption goods, household capital services and leisure. The third stage involves the allocation of household capital services between long-lived and short-lived assets.

To complete the representation of preferences of the household sector we require some additional notation. We denote the shares of consumption goods, household capital services and leisure in full consumption as follows:

$$v_C = \frac{PC\cdot C}{PF\cdot F}, v_{HD} = \frac{PHD\cdot HD}{PF\cdot F}, v_{LJ} = \frac{PLJ\cdot LJ}{PF\cdot F}.$$

Similarly, we denote the shares of long-lived and short-lived assets in household capital services as follows:

$$v_{HL} = \frac{PHL\cdot HL}{PHD\cdot HD}, v_{HS} = \frac{PHS\cdot HS}{PHD\cdot HD}.$$

These value shares are positive.

We find it convenient to introduce the notation:

---

[23] Chamley (1981) derives this formula in a continuous time framework with a single good and fixed labor supply.

$$v_D = (v_C, v_{HD}, v_{LJ})$$    vector of value shares of full consumption

$$v_H = (v_{HL}, v_{HS})$$    vector of value shares of household capital input

$$\ln PD = (\ln PC, \ln PHD, \ln PLJ^*)$$    vector of logarithms of prices of consumption

goods, household capital services and leisure,

where $PLJ^*$ is the price of leisure, defined

in terms of labor measured in efficiency units

$$\ln PH = (\ln PHL, \ln PHS)$$    vector of logarithms of prices of capital inputs

in the household sector.

By taking the preferences of the household sector to be homothetic, we can represent the second stage of our model by expressing the price of full consumption as a function of the prices of nondurable consumption goods, household capital services and leisure. This price function must be homogeneous of degree one, non–decreasing in the prices of the three commodity groups and concave in these prices. We have incorporated these restrictions into the demand functions presented in the following section.

As before, we employ the translog form for the price function:[24]

$$\ln PF = \ln PD'\alpha_{PD} + \frac{1}{2} \ln PD' B_{PD} \ln PD. \tag{10.14}$$

The parameters $B_{PD}$ embody elasticities of demand needed for analyzing the response of consumer behavior to changes in tax policy.

Similarly, we can express the price of household capital services as a function of its long–lived and short–lived components. This price function must also be homogeneous of degree one, non–decreasing in the prices of the two components and concave in these prices. We incorporate these restrictions into the model of consumer behavior presented in the following section. Employing the translog form for this price function:

$$\ln PHD = \ln PH'\alpha_{PH} + \frac{1}{2} \ln PH' B_{PH} \ln PH. \tag{10.15}$$

The matrix $B_{PH}$ is constant and embodies elasticities of demand for household capital services.

The value shares can be expressed in terms of logarithmic derivatives of the price functions with respect to the logarithms of the prices:

[24] The translog indirect utility function was introduced by Christensen *et al.* (1997).

$$v_D = \alpha_{PD} + B_{PD} \ln PD$$

$$v_H = \alpha_{PH} + B_{PH} \ln PH. \tag{10.16}$$

The *share elasticities* $B_{PD}$ and $B_{PH}$ represent the degree of substitutability among commodity groups within the household sector.

## 10.2.4 Government and rest of the world

We consolidate federal and the state and local governments into a single government sector. The government collects taxes from the household and business sectors, issues government debt to households to finance deficits, and spends its revenues on consumption goods, investment goods, labor services, interest on the government debt, and transfer payments to households and the rest of the world. Similarly, we consolidate the federal and state and local government enterprises into a single government enterprise sector. Government enterprises purchase labor services to produce consumption goods and turn over any surplus to the general government.

### 10.2.4.1 Government revenue

To represent the tax revenues of the government sector we introduce some additional notation. We use the symbol $R$ for government revenues and the symbol $t$ for tax rates. For sales taxes our notation is as follows:

| | |
|---|---|
| $R_C$ | sales tax revenues from consumption goods |
| $R_I$ | sales tax revenues from investment goods |
| $t_C$ | sales tax rate on consumption goods |
| $t_I$ | sales tax rate on investment goods. |

Government revenues from taxes on consumption goods and investment goods are generated by the following equations:

$$R_C = t_C PCS \cdot CS$$

$$R_I = t_I PIS \cdot IS. \tag{10.17}$$

Property taxes are levied on the lagged values of assets, so that we require the following notation:

| | |
|---|---|
| $R_q^p, R_m^p, R_h^p$ | property tax revenues from corporate, non-corporate and household assets |
| $t_q^p, t_m^p, t_h^p$ | property tax rates on corporate, non-corporate and household assets |
| $VQL, VML, VHL$ | lagged values of corporate, non-corporate and household assets |
| $VGL, VRL$ | lagged values of claims on government and rest of the world. |

Government revenues from property taxes are generated by:

$$R_q^p = t_q^p VQL$$

$$R_m^p = t_m^p VML$$

$$R_h^p = t_h^p VHL. \tag{10.18}$$

Wealth taxes include federal estate and gift taxes and state and local death and gift taxes. These taxes are levied on the lagged value of wealth, so that we require the notation:

$R_w$       wealth tax revenues

$WL$       lagged value of wealth

$t_w$       wealth tax rate.

The lagged value of wealth is the sum of the lagged values of corporate, non-corporate and household assets, together with the lagged values of claims on government and rest of the world sectors:

$$WL = VQL + VML + VHL + VGL + VRL.$$

Wealth tax revenues are generated by:

$$R_w = t_w WL. \tag{10.19}$$

### 10.2.4.2 Corporate income tax

Income from corporate capital is taxed both at the corporate level and the individual level. The base of the corporate income tax is corporate property compensation less depreciation allowances. At the federal level this is reduced by tax deductions for interest expenses, state and local property taxes, and state and local corporate income taxes. During part of the period covered by our study, tax liabilities were reduced by the investment tax credit.

Replicating the actual practice for calculating capital consumption allowances and investment tax credits would require a detailed description of tax law and vintage accounts of all depreciable assets. However, we can approximate the economic effects of these tax provisions very accurately by converting the allowances and credits into imputed flows that are proportional to the flow of capital services.

To represent the corporate income tax we require the following notation:

| $\alpha$ | dividend payout rate |
|---|---|
| $\beta_q$ | debt–capital ratio of the corporate sector |
| $\delta_q^s, \delta_q^l$ | economic depreciation rates on short-lived and long-lived corporate assets |
| $DC$ | proportion of nominal capital gains excluded from the individual income tax base |
| $DQ$ | imputed corporate capital consumption allowances |
| $DSLI$ | deduction of state and local income taxes for federal tax purposes |
| $DSLQ$ | deduction of state and local taxes on corporate property for federal tax purposes |
| $i$ | interest rate |
| $k_q^s, k_q^l$ | corporate investment tax credit rates on short-lived and long-lived assets |
| $ITCQ$ | imputed corporate investment tax credit rate |
| $r^e$ | real rate of return on corporate equity after corporate taxes |
| $r^q$ | nominal discount rate for corporate investment |
| $\rho^e$ | nominal private rate of return on corporate equity |
| $t_q^e$ | marginal tax rate on corporate dividends |
| $t_q^g$ | marginal tax rate on capital gains on corporate equity |
| $t_q$ | corporate income tax rate |
| $t_q^f, t_q^s$ | corporate income tax rates, federal and state and local |
| $VQL^s, VQL^l$ | lagged values of corporate capital stock of short-lived and long-lived assets |
| $z_q^s, z_q^l$ | present values of corporate capital consumption allowances on short-lived and long-lived assets. |

The base of corporate income tax $BQ$ is defined as:

$$BQ = PQD \cdot QD - DQ - [\beta_q(1 - DI)i + \alpha \cdot DD(1 - \beta_q)r^e]VQL$$
$$- \left[ t_q^s + t_q^f \left( DSLQ - DSLIt_q^s \right) \right] R_q^p / t_q, \tag{10.20}$$

where imputed corporate capital consumption allowances $DQ$ are:[25]

$$DQ = z_q^s \left[ r^q - \pi + (1 + \pi)\delta_q^s \right] VQL^s + z_q^l \left[ r^q - \pi + (1 + \pi)\delta_q^l \right] VQL^l.$$

The real rate of return on corporate equity after taxes is:

$$r^e = \frac{\rho^e - \pi \left[ 1 - (1 - DC)t_q^g \right]}{1 - \left[ \alpha t_q^e + (1 - \alpha)t_q^g \right]}.$$

---

[25] We give additional details in Jorgenson and Yun (2001, Chapter 2, especially section 2.7).

Equation (10.20) shows how the tax treatment of various types of corporate expenses affects the corporate tax burden. For example, when state and local taxes are fully deductible at the federal level, the term involving revenue from taxes on corporate property reduces to $R_q^p$. Similarly, if interest expenses are not indexed for inflation, so that $DI$ is equal to zero, all of nominal interest payments are deductible. If indexing of interest expenses is complete, then only real interest expenses can be deducted.

Finally, tax revenues from corporate taxes $R_q$ are generated by:

$$R_q = t_q \cdot BQ - ITCQ, \tag{10.21}$$

where the imputed corporate investment tax credit $ITCQ$ is defined as:

$$ITCQ = k_q^s \left[ r^q - \pi + (1 + \pi)\delta_q^s \right] VQL^s + k_q^l \left[ r^q - \pi + (1 + \pi)\delta_q^l \right] VQL^l.$$

### 10.2.4.3 Individual income tax

To represent the individual income tax we require the following notation:

| | |
|---|---|
| $\beta_m,\ \beta_h$ | debt-capital ratios of the non-corporate and household sectors |
| $\delta_m^s, \delta_m^l$ | economic depreciation rates on short-lived and long-lived non-corporate assets |
| $DHI$ | proportion of household interest expense deductible for tax purposes |
| $DM$ | imputed non-corporate capital consumption allowances |
| $DSLM$ | deduction of state and local taxes on non-corporate property for federal tax purposes |
| $DSLH$ | deduction of state and local taxes on household property for federal tax purposes |
| $HDI$ | proportion of the household interest payments deducted for indexation for inflation |
| $r^m$ | nominal discount rate for non-corporate investment |
| $t_m^e$ | marginal tax rate on income from non-corporate equity |
| $t_m^{ef},\ t_m^{es}$ | marginal tax rates on income from non-corporate equity, federal and state and local |
| $t_h^e$ | marginal tax rate for deductions from household equity income |
| $t_h^{ef},\ t_h^{es}$ | marginal tax rates for deductions from household equity income, federal and state and local |
| $t_m^g$ | marginal tax rate on capital gains on non-corporate assets |
| $t_h^g$ | marginal tax rate on capital gains on household assets |
| $VDQ$ | economic depreciation on corporate assets |
| $VML^s,\ VML^l$ | lagged values of non-corporate capital stock of short-lived and long-lived assets |
| $VHL^s,\ VHL^l$ | lagged values of household capital stock of short-lived and long-lived assets |
| $z_m^s,\ z_m^l$ | present values of non-corporate capital consumption allowances on short-lived and long-lived assets. |

In modeling the taxation of individual income, we distinguish between income from labor and capital. All labor compensation is included in the individual income tax base $BL$, defined as:

$$BL = PLD \cdot LD + PLE \cdot LE + PLG \cdot LG + PLR \cdot LR. \qquad (10.22)$$

Interest income is the sum of interest earned on corporate, non-corporate and household debt and on claims on government and the rest of the world. We assume that households own claims on the rest of the world through US corporations and that these corporations pay income taxes to the host countries on the earnings of US assets abroad. We assume, further, that the rate of return on these claims after corporate taxes is the same as on domestic corporate capital. Interest originating in the household sector is taxable to the creditor and deductible from the income of the debtor. Under these assumptions the interest income of individuals $BD$ is:

$$BD = [\beta_q(VQL + VRL) + \beta_m VML + \beta_h VHL + VGL](1 - DI)i, \qquad (10.23)$$

where $VQL$ is the value of lagged capital stock of both short-lived and long-lived corporate assets and $VML$ and $VHL$ are the values of lagged capital stock of the corresponding non-corporate and household assets, respectively.

Income from equity includes income from corporate and non-corporate assets. Income from equity in household assets is not taxed, but interest expenses and property taxes on these assets are deductible from the income of the owner. Since nominal capital gains on assets are taxed only on realization, we define the marginal tax rate on capital gains in such a way as to convert accrued capital gains to a realization basis.[26]

Taxable income from equity $BE$ includes corporate profits after taxes, together with earnings on claims on the rest of the world. This income also includes non-corporate property compensation — net of interest expenses, property taxes, and depreciation allowances — less property taxes and interest expenses on household assets. Finally, income from equity includes nominal capital gains on private capital. Taxable income from equity is defined as:

$$BE = PQD \cdot QD - R_q^p - R_q + (1 - \beta_q)r^e \cdot VRL - \beta_q(i - \pi)VQL - VDQ$$
$$+ PMD \cdot MD - DM - \beta_m VML \cdot (1 - DI)i - \left[t_m^{es} + t_m^{ef}\left(DSLM - DSLIt\,_m^{es}\right)\right]R_m^p/t_m^e$$
$$- DHI \cdot \beta_h(1 - HDI)VHL \cdot i - \left[t_h^{es} + t_h^{ef}\left(DSLH - DSLIt_h^{es}\right)\right]R_h^p/t_h^e +$$
$$\left[\left(1 - \beta_q\right)(VQL + VRL)t_q^g/t_q^e + (1 - \beta_m)VMLt_m^g/t_m^e + (1 - \beta_h)VHLt_h^g/t_h^e\right]\left(1 - DC\right)\pi,$$
$$\qquad (10.24)$$

where economic depreciation on corporate assets $VDQ$ is defined as:

---

[26] We give additional details in Jorgenson and Yun (2001, Chapter 2).

$$VDQ = (1 + \pi)\left[\delta_q^s VQL^s + \delta_q^l VQL^l\right],$$

and imputed non-corporate capital consumption allowances $DM$ are defined as:

$$DM = z_m^s\left[r^m - \pi + (1 + \pi)\delta_m^s\right] VML^s + z_m^l\left[r^m - \pi + (1 + \pi)\delta_m^l\right] VML^l.$$

To complete the representation of the individual income tax we require the following notation:

| | |
|---|---|
| $ITCH$ | imputed household investment tax credit |
| $ITCM$ | imputed non-corporate investment tax credit |
| $k_h^s$, $k_h^l$ | household investment tax credit rates on short-lived and long-lived assets |
| $k_m^s$, $k_m^l$ | non-corporate investment tax credit rates on short-lived and long-lived assets |
| $R_l$ | tax revenues from labor income |
| $R_e$ | tax revenues from equity income |
| $R_d$ | tax revenues from interest income |
| $t_L^a$ | average tax rate on labor income |
| $t_e^a$ | average tax rate on equity income |
| $t_d^a$ | average tax rate on interest income. |

Tax revenues from individual income taxes are generated by:

$$R_l = t_L^a BL$$
$$R_e = t_e^a BE - ITCM - ITCH \tag{10.25}$$
$$R_d = t_d^a BD,$$

where the imputed household and non-corporate investment tax credits $ITCH$ and $ITCM$ are defined as:

$$ITCH = k_h^s\left[r^h - \pi + (1 + \pi)\delta_h^s\right] VHL^s + k_h^s\left[r^h - \pi + (1 + \pi)\delta_h^l\right] VHL^l$$

$$ITCM = k_m^s\left[r^m - \pi + (1 + \pi)\delta_m^s\right] VML^s + k_m^s\left[r^m - \pi + (1 + \pi)\delta_m^l\right] VML^l.$$

Ordinarily, average tax rates on labor, equity, and interest incomes are the same.

To represent the government budget we require the following notation:

$t_L^m$       marginal tax rate on labor income

$t_g^d$       marginal tax rate on government interest payments

$t_t$       effective rate of non–tax payments

$DG$       government deficit

$EL$       government transfers to households

$ER$       government transfers to foreigners

$GS$       real government expenditures, net of interest payments

$PGS$       price deflator, government expenditures

$R$       government revenue

$R_{ge}$       surplus of government enterprises

$R_t$       revenue from non–tax payments

$R_{lum}$       government revenues from a lump–sum tax

$SGOV$       share of government expenditures in GDP

$SCE$       proportion of consumption goods produced by government enterprises to business sector production

$SLE$       proportion of the labor compensation of government enterprises in the value of labor supply

$SCG$       proportion of government purchases of consumption goods in government expenditures, net of interest payments

$SIG$       proportion of government purchases of investment goods in government expenditures, net of interest payments

$SLG$       proportion of government purchases of labor services in government expenditures, net of interest payments

$SEL$       proportion of transfers to households in government expenditures, net of interest payments

$SER$       proportion of transfers to foreigners in government expenditures, net of interest payments

$XPND$       government expenditures, including interest payments.

To complete the specification of the government budget we determine revenues from non-tax payments and government enterprises, as well as government expenditures. We assume that federal and state and local personal non-tax payments are given as a proportion of before-tax labor income, so that revenue from non-tax payments is generated by:

$$R_t = t_t BL. \tag{10.26}$$

We assume that the value of labor compensation from government enterprises is given as a proportion of the value of total labor compensation:

$$PLE \cdot LE = SLE \frac{PLH \cdot LH - PLJ \cdot LJ}{1 - t_L^m}. \tag{10.27}$$

Government enterprises employ labor to produce consumption goods; surpluses of these enterprises are revenues of the general government. We assume that the production of consumption goods by government enterprises $CE$ is proportional to business production of these goods:

$$CE = SCE \cdot CS. \tag{10.28}$$

The surplus of government enterprises $R_{ge}$ is the difference between the value of output and labor compensation:

$$R_{ge} = PC \cdot CE - PLE \cdot LE. \tag{10.29}$$

We assume that the government allocates total expenditures, net of interest payments on government debt, among consumption goods, investment goods, labor services and transfer payments to the household and rest-of-the-world sectors in the following proportions:

$$PC \cdot CG = SCG(XPND - VGL \cdot i)$$
$$PI \cdot IG = SIG(XPND - VGL \cdot i)$$
$$PLG \cdot LG = SLG(XPND - VGL \cdot i) \tag{10.30}$$
$$EL = SEL(XPND - VGL \cdot i)$$
$$ER = SER(XPND - VGL \cdot i).$$

Under our assumptions on the allocation of government expenditures, we can aggregate the five categories of government expenditures by means of a linear logarithmic or Cobb−Douglas price function. The price index for government expenditures is defined as:

$$\ln PGS = SCG \cdot \ln(PCG) + SIG \cdot \ln(PIG) + SLG \cdot \ln(PLG), \qquad (10.31)$$

where the price indexes of transfer payments to households and the rest of the world are equal to unity. The quantity of government expenditures net of interest payments is then defined as:

$$GS = \frac{XPND - VGL \cdot i}{PGS}. \qquad (10.32)$$

In some experiments with alternative tax policies, we control the paths of real government expenditures and government debt, and use a "lump-sum tax" levied on the household sector to generate government revenue. We can express the revenue of the government as the sum of tax revenues, including this lump-sum tax, non-tax receipts and the surplus of government enterprises. Government revenue is defined as:

$$R = R_C + R_I + R_q + R_l + R_e + R_d + R_{ge} + R_q^p + R_m^p + R_h^p + R_t + R_w + R_{lum}. \qquad (10.33)$$

We assume that government expenditures are a constant proportion of GDP:

$$XPND = SGOV \cdot GDP, \qquad (10.34)$$

where $GDP$ is defined below. The government budget constraint, including the government deficit, is defined by:

$$XPND = R + DG. \qquad (10.35)$$

### 10.2.4.4 Rest of the world
To represent the rest-of-the-world sector we require the following notation:

$DR$      current account deficit of the rest of the world

$SCR$      proportion of purchases of consumption goods by the rest of the world to domestic purchases

$SLR$      proportion of purchases of labor services by the rest of the world in the value of labor supply

$SIR$      proportion of purchases of investment goods by the rest of the world to domestic supply.

We assume that purchases of consumption goods, labor services, and investment goods by the rest of the world are given by:

$$CR = SCR(C + CG)$$

$$IR = SIR \cdot IS \tag{10.36}$$

$$PLR \cdot LR = SLR \frac{PLH \cdot LH - PLJ \cdot LJ}{1 - t_L^m}.$$

The value of net exports from the US, together with earnings from claims on the rest of the world, net of the government transfers to foreigners, is added to the US claims on the rest of the world. The deficit of the rest of the world or surplus of the US is given by:

$$DR = PC \cdot CR + PI \cdot IR + PLR \cdot LR + \left[(1 - \beta_q)r^e + \beta_q(i - \pi)\right]VLR - ER. \tag{10.37}$$

### 10.2.4.5 National income and wealth

To represent the national income and product accounts we require the following notation:

| | |
|---|---|
| $D$ | economic depreciation |
| $GDP$ | gross domestic product |
| $GNP$ | gross national product |
| $S$ | gross private national saving |
| $V$ | revaluation of domestic capital |
| $VK$ | value of private domestic capital |
| $Y$ | gross private national income. |

We define $GDP$ as the market value of goods and services produced domestically, which is equal to the sum of the value of domestically employed labor and capital services, indirect taxes, and the surplus of government enterprises. Gross national product $GNP$ is defined as the sum of $GDP$ and the value of labor and capital services employed abroad:

$$GDP = PLD \cdot LD + PLG \cdot LG + PLE \cdot LE$$

$$+ PQD \cdot QD + PMD \cdot MD + PHD \cdot HD + R_C + R_I + R_{ge}.$$

$$GNP = GDP + PLR \cdot LR + \left[(1 - \beta_q)r^e + \beta_q(i - \pi)\right]VRL. \tag{10.38}$$

Gross private national income $Y$ is the sum of labor and capital incomes after taxes:

$$Y = PLD \cdot LD + PLG \cdot LG + PLE \cdot LE + PLR \cdot LR - R_l$$
$$+ PQD \cdot QD + PMD \cdot MD + PHD \cdot HD + \left[ (1 - \beta_q) r^e + \beta_q (i - \pi) \right] VRL$$
$$+ VGL \cdot i - \left( R_q^p + R_m^p + R_h^p + R_q + R_e + R_d + R_w + R_t + R_{lum} \right).$$

$$(10.39)$$

Gross private domestic saving $S$ is defined as gross private national income plus government transfers to households, less household expenditures on consumption goods and capital services:

$$S = Y + EL - (PC \cdot C + PHD \cdot HD). \qquad (10.40)$$

Saving is used to finance gross private domestic investment and the deficits of the government and rest of the world:

$$S = PI \cdot ID + DG + DR. \qquad (10.41)$$

Private domestic investment is allocated among the six categories of private assets — short-lived and long-lived assets in the corporate, non-corporate and household sectors. We assume that tangible assets are perfectly malleable and can be transformed from one category to another. Under this assumption we can represent the accumulation of capital by:

$$VK = VKL + PI \cdot ID - D + V, \qquad (10.42)$$

where $VK$ is the current value of capital stock and $VKL$ is the lagged value. For each asset category the value of economic depreciation is the product of the rate of economic depreciation and the current value of lagged capital stock and revaluation is the difference between the current and lagged values of the lagged capital stock.

The accumulation of nominal government debt is represented as:

$$VG = DG + VGL, \qquad (10.43)$$

where $VG$ is the current value of outstanding government debt. Similarly, the accumulation of claims on the rest of the world is represented as:

$$VR = DR + (1 + \pi) VRL, \qquad (10.44)$$

where $VR$ is the current value of claims on the rest of the world.

## 10.2.5 Market equilibrium

We represent markets in the US economy corresponding to consumption goods, investment goods, labor services, and capital services. The business sector and government enterprises supply the consumption goods purchased by the household, government and rest-of-the-world sectors. The value of consumption goods supplied is equal to the value demanded:

$$(1 + t_C)PCS \cdot CS + PC \cdot CE = PC \cdot (C + CG + CR). \qquad (10.45)$$

We assume, further, that the products of the business sector and government enterprises are homogenous, so that balance between supply and demand implies:

$$CS + CE = C + CG + CR. \qquad (10.46)$$

Equivalently, we can replace this equation with the relationship between the producer and consumer prices:

$$PC = (1 + t_C)PCS.$$

We use the price deflator $PC$ for consumption goods produced by government enterprises and for purchases by the household, government and rest-of-the-world sectors.

The business sector supplies the investment goods purchased by the household, government and rest-of-the-world sectors. Since private domestic saving is used to finance private investment, as well as the deficits of government and rest of the world sectors, the demand for private investment is given by:

$$PI \cdot ID = S - DG - DR. \qquad (10.47)$$

The value of investment goods supplied is equal to the value demanded:

$$(1 + t_I)PIS \cdot IS = PI \cdot (ID + IG + IR), \qquad (10.48)$$

and the balance between supply and demand implies:

$$IS = ID + IG + IR. \qquad (10.49)$$

As before, we can replace this equation with the relationship between the producer and consumer prices:

$$PI = (1 + t_I)PIS. \qquad (10.50)$$

We assume that the consumer is endowed with a fixed amount of time, fourteen hours per day. This can be consumed as leisure or supplied as labor services. The remaining time is required for personal maintenance. Labor supply is the difference between the time endowment of the household sector and the consumption of leisure. This supply is allocated among the business, government, government enterprise and rest-of-the-world sectors. For the economy as a whole, we distinguish among individuals by sex, level of education and age, and allow for the fact that wage rates vary among individuals. Since the composition of the time endowment, leisure and employment in the various sectors of the economy differs, we use separate price indexes for the time endowment and its various uses.

The demand for labor originates from businesses, governments, government enterprises and the rest of the world. The value of labor supplied is equal to the value demanded:

$$PLH \cdot LH - PLJ \cdot LJ = (PLD \cdot LD + PLG \cdot LG + PLE \cdot LE + PLR \cdot LR)(1 - t_L^m).$$
$$(10.51)$$

Since we have no mechanism to determine the relative prices of the time endowment, the consumption of leisure and labor demanded, we take the relative prices to be exogenous. We find it convenient to express the prices of labor in terms of the price for labor demanded by the business sector:

$$PLH = (1 - t_L^m)A_{LH} \cdot PLD$$
$$PLJ = (1 - t_L^m)A_{LJ} \cdot PLD$$

$$PLG = A_{LG} \cdot PLD$$
$$PLE = A_{LE} \cdot PLD \qquad\qquad (10.52)$$
$$PLR = A_{LR} \cdot PLD,$$

where the factors of proportionality — $A_{LH}$, $A_{LJ}$, $A_{LG}$, $A_{LE}$ and $A_{LR}$ — are given exogenously.

Households are the sole suppliers of capital services and own all private capital. The demand side of the market includes corporate and non-corporate businesses, as well as households. As in the case of labor services, we take the relative prices of the six types of capital assets to be exogenous. Under the assumption of perfect malleability of capital any type of capital can be converted into any other type of capital with rates of transformation given by the relative prices. In order to describe the equilibrium of capital market, we introduce the following notation:

$K_{QS}$    quantity of short-lived corporate capital stock

$K_{QL}$    quantity of long-lived corporate capital stock

$K_{MS}$    quantity of short-lived non-corporate capital stock

$K_{ML}$    quantity of long-lived non-corporate capital stock

$K_{HS}$    quantity of short-lived household capital stock

$K_{HL}$    quantity of long-lived household capital stock.

We define capital services and capital stock in such a way that one unit of each of the six categories of capital stock generates one unit of capital services. The quantity index of the demand for capital services of a particular category is equal to the quantity index of the capital stock necessary to meet the demand for capital services, i.e., $K_{QS} = QS$,

$K_{QL} = QL$, $K_{MS} = MS$, $K_{ML} = ML$, $K_{HS} = HS$ and $K_{HL} = HL$. Given differences in tax rates, investment tax credits, capital consumption allowances, and economic rates of depreciation, a dollar's worth of assets in different categories of capital generates different amounts of capital services.

Equilibrium in the market for capital services is achieved when the total value of demands for all six categories of capital services is equal to the value of the capital stock available:

$$PK_{QS} \cdot QS + PK_{QL} \cdot QL + PK_{MS} \cdot MS + PK_{ML} \cdot ML + PK_{HS} \cdot HS + PK_{HL} \cdot HL$$
$$= (1 + \pi)VKL, \tag{10.53}$$

where $\pi$ is the rate of inflation in the price of capital assets, $PK_{QS}$ is the current price of short-lived corporate capital stock and $PK_{QL}$, the current price of long-lived corporate capital stock, and so on. The equilibrium values of economic depreciation $D$ and revaluation $V$ are based on the allocation of capital among the six categories of assets.

In order to express Walras' law we can define the value of excess demand, say $SXD$, as the sum of differences between the values of supply and demand in each of the four markets. Substituting the definitions of tax revenues and the surplus of government enterprises, we obtain the following expression for the value of excess demands:

$$SXD = PC(C + CG - CE) - (PCS \cdot CS + R_C) + PI(ID + IG) - (PIS \cdot IS + R_I)$$
$$+ (PLD \cdot LD + PLE \cdot LE + PLG \cdot LG) - \left[ \frac{PLH \cdot LH - PLJ \cdot LJ}{1 - t_L^m}(1 - t_L^a) + R_l \right]$$
$$+ (PQD \cdot QD + PMD \cdot MD + PHD \cdot HD) - (PQS \cdot K_{QS} + PQL \cdot K_{QL} + PMS \cdot K_{MS}$$
$$+ PML \cdot K_{ML} + PHS \cdot K_{HS} + PHL \cdot K_{HL}).$$
$$\tag{10.54}$$

where $K_{QS} = QS$, $K_{QL} = QL$, $K_{MS} = MS$, $K_{ML} = ML$, $K_{HS} = HS$ and $K_{HL} = HL$ are substituted from (10.53).

By successive substitutions we arrive at the following expression for the value of excess demand:

$$SXD = (PQD \cdot QD + PMD \cdot MD + PLD \cdot LD) - (PIS \cdot IS + PCS \cdot CS),$$

which is the zero profit condition of the business sector. Walras' law implies that the market clearing condition for one market is implied by the conditions for the other three markets and the budget constraints of the household, business, government and rest-of-the-world sectors. In solving the model, we drop the condition for equilibrium of the labor market.

In modeling the allocation of full consumption, production and the allocation of demand for capital services, we have imposed homogeneity of degree one on the price functions. For each of the six categories of capital services the price of capital services is homogeneous of degree one in the current and lagged prices of capital stock, given the rate of revaluation and the nominal rate of return. Finally, gross private national income and savings are homogenous of degree one in prices, given the nominal rate of return. We conclude that the model is homogeneous of degree zero in the prices and the nominal magnitudes, such as income and wealth, given the rate of inflation and the real private rate of return.

We normalize the prices by setting the current prices of capital assets and investment goods and the rate of inflation exogenously. Under this normalization, it is natural to define the rate of inflation as the rate of change in the price of capital assets and investment goods. As a consequence, we use the terms "rate of inflation" and "rate of revaluation" synonymously.

## 10.3 MODELING CONSUMER AND PRODUCER BEHAVIOR

In this section we present econometric estimates of the parameters of the models of consumer and producer behavior that we have introduced in the previous section. A more common methodology is to calibrate the parameter values to a single data point. Econometric methods are more burdensome from the computational point of view, but incorporate considerably more information.[27]

In order to estimate the parameters describing preferences in Section 10.3.1, we begin by specifying econometric models corresponding to the transition equation for full consumption and the share equations for allocating full consumption and household capital services within each time period. We impose the restrictions required for concavity of the underlying price functions at all data points in our sample. We combine the transition equation and the two sets of share equations and estimate the parameters simultaneously. The resulting parameter estimates generate our econometric model of consumer behavior.

We follow a similar strategy in estimating the parameters that describe technology. We first specify an econometric model corresponding to the share equations for outputs of consumption and investment goods and inputs of capital services from corporate and non-corporate assets. We then specify the share equations for allocating corporate and non-corporate capital services between short-lived and long-lived assets separately. We impose curvature restrictions on the underlying price functions at all data points in our sample. We estimate the three sets of equations simultaneously. The resulting estimates generate our econometric model of producer behavior in Section 10.3.2.

---

[27] More details on econometric methods for general equilibrium modeling are given by Jorgenson *et al.* in Chapter 17 of this Handbook.

We describe our econometric models of consumer and producer behavior in terms of price elasticities of demand and supply in Section 10.3.3. We present estimates of own-price and cross-price elasticities for each model. We also provide an estimate of the compensated elasticity of labor supply in our model of consumer behavior, holding consumer welfare constant. Finally, we provide estimates of the elasticities of substitution for both consumer and producer models. The intertemporal elasticity of substitution of full consumption is a constant parameter and we present an estimate of this elasticity as well.

We also assign values to the remaining parameters employed in our dynamic general equilibrium model in Section 10.3.4. We employ historical averages to represent debt—asset ratios in corporate, non-corporate and household sectors, the dividend pay-out ratio in the corporate sector, and the real interest rate. We use similar averages for the shares of different commodity groups in government expenditure, and the shares of the labor force employed by the rest of the world and government enterprises. Finally, we choose relative prices of different types of capital assets and investment goods and relative prices of different types of labor to coincide with historical relationships.

We choose values for the parameters that determine steady-state values for the debt of the government and rest of the world sectors to assure the existence of a viable long-run equilibrium of the US economy. The key parameter for the government sector is the share of government expenditures in GDP. For the rest-of-the-world sector the key parameters are net exports of consumption and investment goods as proportions of the domestic demand for consumption goods and domestic production of investment goods, respectively.

## 10.3.1 Consumer behavior

The lifetime budget constraint and the transition equation for full consumption determine the allocation of the household sector's wealth over time. To generate an econometric model for this allocation we add a disturbance term to the transition Equation (10.13), obtaining:

$$\ln\frac{F_t}{F_{t-1}} = \frac{1}{\sigma}[\ln(1 + r_t) - \ln(1 + \tilde{r})] + \varepsilon_{Ft}, \quad t = 1, 2, ..., T, \qquad (10.55)$$

where $r_t$ is the real private rate of return:

$$r_t = \frac{PF_{t-1}}{PF_t}(1 + \rho_t) - 1,$$

and $\tilde{r}$ is the steady-state value of this rate of return:

$$\tilde{r} = (1 + \gamma)(1 - \alpha_T)^{\sigma} - 1.$$

The parameter $\sigma$ is the inverse of the intertemporal elasticity of substitution and the parameter $\gamma$ is the subjective discount rate, as in (10.13). We estimate the parameter $\alpha_T$, the negative of the rate of labor-augmenting productivity growth, as part of the model of producer behavior described below. The disturbances $\varepsilon_{Ft}$ correspond to random deviations from the optimal allocation of full consumption as well as errors in measurement of the growth rate of consumption. We assume that the disturbance term is distributed independently over time with expected value zero and constant variance.

Under homotheticity of preferences we can describe the allocation of full consumption among different commodity groups by means of the price function (10.14). The value shares (10.16) sum to unity, since this function is homogeneous of degree one in the prices. In addition, the matrix of share elasticities $B_{PD}$ must be symmetric. We refer to these as the *summability* and *symmetry* restrictions. In addition, the value shares must be *non-negative*, since the price function is non–decreasing and the price function must be *concave* to guarantee the appropriate curvature.

To generate an econometric model for the allocation of full consumption we add a vector of random disturbances $\varepsilon_{Dt}$ to the equations for the value shares (10.16), obtaining:

$$v_{Dt} = \alpha_{PD} + B_{PD} \ \ln PD_t + \varepsilon_{Dt}, \quad t = 1, 2, ..., T, \tag{10.56}$$

where the parameters $\alpha_{PD}$ and $B_{PD}$ are the same as in (10.16), the variables $v_{Dt}$ and $\ln PD_t$ now have time subscripts, and the vector of disturbances $\varepsilon_{Dt}$ takes the form:

$$\varepsilon_{Dt} = \begin{bmatrix} \varepsilon_{Ct} \\ \varepsilon_{LJt} \\ \varepsilon_{HDt} \end{bmatrix}. \tag{10.57}$$

The disturbance vector corresponds to random deviations from the optimal allocation of full consumption within each time period and errors in measuring the value shares. We assume that the expected value of this vector is zero:

$$E(\varepsilon_{Dt}) = 0, \quad t = 1, 2, ..., T, \tag{10.58}$$

and the covariance matrix:

$$V(\varepsilon_{Dt}) = \sum\nolimits_{,t=1,2,...,T}, \tag{10.59}$$

is constant. We also assume that the disturbances of any two distinct time periods are distributed independently.

The summability restrictions imply that the value shares sum to unity, so that the sum of the corresponding disturbance terms must be zero:

$$i'\varepsilon_{Dt} = 0, t = 1, 2, ..., T \tag{10.60}$$

and the covariance matrix $\sum$ must be singular. We assume that this third-order matrix has rank two.

We incorporate symmetry and summability restrictions into our model of consumer behavior by imposing these restrictions on the parameter estimates for the share equations. To impose the concavity restrictions, we first consider the following transformation of the Hessian of the price function:

$$\frac{1}{PF}P'HP = B_{PD} + v_D v'_D - V_D, \tag{10.61}$$

where $H$ is the Hessian, $P$ is a diagonal matrix with prices of the three commodity groups along the main diagonal:

$$P = \begin{bmatrix} PC & 0 & 0 \\ 0 & PHD & 0 \\ 0 & 0 & PLJ \end{bmatrix},$$

$v_D$ is the vector of value shares of full consumption and $V_D$ is a diagonal matrix with these value shares along the main diagonal:

$$V_D = \begin{bmatrix} v_C & 0 & 0 \\ 0 & v_{HD} & 0 \\ 0 & 0 & v_{LJ} \end{bmatrix}.$$

Since the prices are non-negative, the Hessian $H$ is negative semidefinite if, and only if, the expression on the right-hand side of equation (10.61) is negative semidefinite.[28]

Our strategy is to estimate the share equations with the parameters constrained so that concavity holds at all data points. We require that the transformation of the Hessian of the price function given in equation (10.61) must be negative semidefinite for each data point. We represent this transformation of the Hessian in terms of its Cholesky factorization:

$$B_{PD} + v_D v'_D - V_D = LDL', \tag{10.62}$$

where $L$ is a lower triangular matrix and $D$ is a diagonal matrix.

Given the prices of consumption goods, leisure, and household capital services, estimates of the parameters $\alpha_{PD}$ and $B_{PD}$ are sufficient to determine the value shares, but the price level of full consumption is indeterminate. To fix the price level we add a constant term $\alpha_0^{PD}$ to the logarithmic price function and set its value at the average of:

$$\ln PF^* - \ln PD^{*'}\alpha_{PD}^* - \frac{1}{2}\ln PD^{*'}B_{PD}\ln PD^*,$$

---

[28] Further details are given by Jorgenson (2000).

for our sample period 1970–2010, where $\ln PF^*$ and $\ln PD^*$ are based on the price system consistent with our model. This assures that the fitted full consumption price tracks the historical path.[29]

To generate an econometric model for the allocation of household capital services we add a vector of random disturbances $\varepsilon_{Ht}$ to the equations for the value shares (10.16), obtaining:

$$v_{Ht} = \alpha_{PH} + B_{PH} \ln PH_t + \varepsilon_{H_t}, \quad t = 1, 2, \ldots, T, \tag{10.63}$$

where the parameters $\alpha_{PH}$ and $B_{PH}$ are the same as in (10.16), the variables $v_{Ht}$ and $\ln PH_t$ have time subscripts, and the vector of disturbances $\varepsilon_{Ht}$ takes the form:

$$\varepsilon_{Ht} = \begin{bmatrix} \varepsilon_{HLt} \\ \varepsilon_{HSt} \end{bmatrix}. \tag{10.64}$$

The disturbance vector corresponds to random deviations from the optimal allocation of household capital services within each time period, as well as errors in measuring the value shares. We assume that the expected value of this vector is zero, the covariance matrix is constant and the disturbances from distinct time periods are distributed independently. Summability implies that the value shares must sum to one, so that the disturbances must sum to zero and the covariance matrix is singular; we assume that this second-order matrix must have rank one.

We estimate all three components of our econometric model of consumer behavior simultaneously. The complete system of equations consists of the transition equation (10.55), two of the three equations for the allocation of full consumption (10.56) and one of the two equations for the allocation of household capital services (10.63). We estimate a total of 20 parameters — two in the transition equation, 12 in the allocation of full consumption and six in the allocation of household capital services. The symmetry and summability restrictions reduce the number of parameters in the four estimating equations to only nine.

In our model of the US economy these prices are endogenously determined by the interaction of supply and demand. The method of non-linear three-stage least squares (NL3SLS) is consistent and asymptotically efficient in the class of minimum distance estimators that employ the same set of instruments.[30] The NL3SLS estimator is invariant with respect to the choice of an equation to be dropped under the summability conditions.

We estimate our econometric model of consumer behavior by the method of NL3SLS, using the instrumental variables. The results are summarized in Table 10.1. The price function for household capital services satisfies the conditions for local concavity without imposing restrictions on the parameters. Cholesky values at each data point in the sample

---

[29] We similarly determine the levels of estimated logarithmic price functions for capital services of the household, corporate and non-corporate sectors, and labor requirement in the business sector.

[30] See Jorgenson and Laffont (2000).

**Table 10.1** Allocation of lifetime wealth, full consumption and household capital services: parameter estimates

| Parameter | Estimate | Standard error | t-Statistic |
|---|---|---|---|
| $\alpha_C$ | 0.292687 | 1.84E–03 | 159.112 |
| $\alpha_L$ | 0.626518 | 1.36E–03 | 459.697 |
| $\alpha_H$ | 0.080796 | 1.20E–03 | 67.3279 |
| $\beta_{CC}$ | 0.126598 | 4.91E–03 | 25.7708 |
| $\beta_{CL}$ | −0.149088 | 2.00E–03 | −74.5344 |
| $\beta_{CH}$ | 0.02249 | 2.96E–03 | 7.5919 |
| $\beta_{LC}$ | −0.149088 | 2.00E–03 | −74.5344 |
| $\beta_{LL}$ | 0.214793 | 3.45E–04 | 622.842 |
| $\beta_{LH}$ | −0.065705 | 1.86E–03 | −35.3796 |
| $\beta_{HC}$ | 0.02249 | 2.96E–03 | 7.5919 |
| $\beta_{HL}$ | −0.065705 | 1.86E–03 | −35.3796 |
| $\beta_{HH}$ | 0.043215 | 1.35E–03 | 32.0026 |
| $\delta_L$ | −0.0192 | 0 | 0 |
| $\lambda_{LH}$ | 0.785695 | 0.062624 | 12.5462 |
| $\delta_H$ | −0.0192 | 0 | 0 |
| $\alpha_o^{PD}$ | 0.18315 | | |
| $\alpha_C^*$ | 0.25077 | | |
| $\alpha_L^*$ | 0.6869 | | |
| $\alpha_H^*$ | 0.062325 | | |
| $\alpha_S^H$ | 0.554599 | 4.21E–03 | 131.657 |
| $\alpha_L^H$ | 0.445401 | 4.21E–03 | 105.734 |
| $\beta_{SS}^H$ | 0.054014 | 4.62E–03 | 11.6893 |
| $\beta_{SL}^H$ | −0.054014 | 4.62E+03 | −11.6893 |
| $\beta_{LL}^H$ | 0.054014 | 4.62E–03 | 11.6893 |
| $\delta_S^H$ | −0.193005 | 4.41E+03 | −43.7455 |
| $\alpha_0^{PH}$ | −0.0025794 | | |
| $\sigma$ | 2.24146 | 0.370072 | 6.05682 |
| $\gamma$ | 0.025545 | 6.82E–03 | 3.74696 |
| $SSR$ | 5.55175 | | |

$\delta_L$ and $\delta_H$ are constrained at −0.0192.

are given in Table 10.2. The non–negativity conditions hold at every data point in the sample. To interpret the implications of our estimates for consumer behavior we present price elasticities of demand and elasticities of substitution for this model in Section 10.3.3.

## 10.3.2 Producer behavior

There are many similarities between our models of the business sector and the household sector. We describe technology in terms of the labor requirements for producing outputs

**Table 10.2** Allocation of lifetime wealth, full consumption and household capital services: local Cholesky values

| Year | $\delta_L$ | $\delta_H$ | $\delta_S^H$ |
|------|-----------|-----------|-----------|
| 1970 | −0.0057291 | −0.0045918 | −0.18416 |
| 1971 | −0.006374 | −0.0080258 | −0.18411 |
| 1972 | −0.0097633 | −0.023913 | −0.18528 |
| 1973 | −0.01124 | −0.025123 | −0.18567 |
| 1974 | −0.0073066 | −0.0010157 | −0.18439 |
| 1975 | −0.0083358 | −0.00462 | −0.18351 |
| 1976 | −0.013836 | −0.03007 | −0.18627 |
| 1977 | −0.016158 | −0.034712 | −0.18686 |
| 1978 | −0.016819 | −0.035911 | −0.18746 |
| 1979 | −0.015738 | −0.031542 | −0.18716 |
| 1980 | −0.013559 | −0.023004 | −0.1863 |
| 1981 | −0.015616 | −0.029485 | −0.18741 |
| 1982 | −0.010566 | −0.021383 | −0.18856 |
| 1983 | −0.01367 | −0.030232 | −0.18929 |
| 1984 | −0.018305 | −0.039538 | −0.19018 |
| 1985 | −0.018049 | −0.037974 | −0.19035 |
| 1986 | −0.017541 | −0.035397 | −0.19019 |
| 1987 | −0.012517 | −0.027235 | −0.19057 |
| 1988 | −0.013113 | −0.02767 | −0.19072 |
| 1989 | −0.014155 | −0.028227 | −0.19077 |
| 1990 | −0.012881 | −0.023753 | −0.19089 |
| 1991 | −0.010276 | −0.014999 | −0.19081 |
| 1992 | −0.011373 | −0.017586 | −0.19088 |
| 1993 | −0.012257 | −0.017702 | −0.19045 |
| 1994 | −0.01288 | −0.021883 | −0.19095 |
| 1995 | −0.012854 | −0.021402 | −0.19093 |
| 1996 | −0.01594 | −0.029309 | −0.19155 |
| 1997 | −0.016894 | −0.030674 | −0.19186 |
| 1998 | −0.016711 | −0.028402 | −0.19186 |
| 1999 | −0.018661 | −0.030702 | −0.19217 |
| 2000 | −0.019045 | −0.028468 | −0.19207 |
| 2001 | −0.018381 | −0.02411 | −0.19196 |
| 2002 | −0.018896 | −0.025672 | −0.19262 |
| 2003 | −0.018652 | −0.022468 | −0.19275 |
| 2004 | −0.018556 | −0.017872 | −0.19245 |
| 2005 | −0.0192 | −0.0192 | −0.193 |
| 2006 | −0.02038 | −0.021011 | −0.1934 |
| 2007 | −0.021479 | −0.025349 | −0.19421 |
| 2008 | −0.020602 | −0.024391 | −0.19462 |
| 2009 | −0.020534 | −0.029333 | −0.19512 |
| 2010 | −0.022557 | −0.03295 | −0.19517 |

of consumption and investment goods, given inputs of corporate and non-corporate capital services. Our description of technology also expresses inputs of corporate and non-corporate capital services as functions of their long-lived and short-lived components. Finally, we impose conditions on the description of technology that imply the existence of balanced growth equilibrium for our dynamic general equilibrium model.

Under constant returns to scale we can describe the technology of the business sector through the price function for labor input (10.1). The value shares (10.2) derived from this price function sum to unity, since the function is homogeneous of degree one. The interpretation of this condition is that the value of the products is exhausted by the value of the factors of production. In addition, the matrix of share elasticities $B_{pp}$ must be symmetric. We refer to these as the product *exhaustion* and *symmetry* restrictions.

The theory of producer behavior implies two additional sets of restrictions on our description of technology. First, the value shares of outputs of consumption and investment goods must be non-negative and the shares of inputs of corporate and non-corporate capital services must be non-positive, since the price function is non-decreasing in the prices of outputs and non-increasing in the prices of inputs. Second, the price function must be *convex* in order to guarantee the appropriate curvature.

To generate an econometric model for the outputs of consumption and investment goods, and inputs of corporate and non-corporate capital services, we add a vector of random disturbances $\varepsilon_t$ to the equations for the value shares (10.2), obtaining:

$$v_t = \alpha_p + B_{pp} \ln P_t + \beta_{PT} T + \varepsilon_t, \qquad (10.65)$$

where the parameters $\alpha_p$, $B_{pp}$ and $\beta_{PT}$ are the same as in (10.2), the variables $v_t$ and $\ln P_t$ now have time subscripts, and the vector of disturbances $\varepsilon_t$ takes the form:

$$\varepsilon_t = \begin{bmatrix} \varepsilon_{CSt} \\ \varepsilon_{ISt} \\ \varepsilon_{MDt} \\ \varepsilon_{QDt} \end{bmatrix}, \qquad (10.66)$$

The disturbance vector corresponds to random deviations from the optimal allocation of outputs and inputs and errors in measuring the value shares. We assume that the expected value of this vector is zero, the covariance matrix is constant and the disturbances corresponding to any two distinct time periods are distributed independently. The product exhaustion condition implies that the value shares sum to unity, so that the sum of the corresponding disturbance terms must be zero and the covariance matrix must be singular. We assume that this fourth-order matrix has rank three.

The rate of productivity growth $v_T$ is the negative of the growth rate of the price of labor input, holding the prices of the two outputs and the two capital inputs constant. To generate an econometric model for the rate of productivity growth we add a random disturbance $\varepsilon_{Tt}$ to Equation (10.3):

$$- v_{Tt} = \alpha_T + \beta_{PT} \ln P_t + \beta_{TT} T + \varepsilon_{Tt}, \tag{10.67}$$

where the parameters $\alpha_T$, $\beta_{PT}$ and $\beta_{TT}$ are the same as in (10.3) and the variables $v_{Tt}$ and $\ln P_t$ have time subscripts. The disturbance $\varepsilon_{Tt}$ corresponds to random shocks in the rate of productivity growth and errors in measurement in this growth rate.

The parameters $\beta_{PT}$ and $\beta_{TT}$ must be equal to zero in (10.65) and (10.67). These are the balanced growth restrictions. There are 21 parameters to be estimated in the equations for the value shares and the rate of productivity growth. Symmetry of the matrix $B_{PP}$ reduces this number to 15 and product exhaustion reduces the number to 10. These restrictions also imply that the contemporaneous disturbances are linearly dependent and the covariance matrix is singular. Therefore, we drop the share equation for the output of consumption goods and estimate the parameters of the remaining four equations. As before, we employ the method of NL3SLS to obtain consistent estimates, using the instrumental variables.

The non-negativity and non-positivity restrictions on the share equations must be checked at each data point. To impose convexity restrictions on the price function for labor input, we consider the following transformation of the Hessian of the price function:

$$\left(\frac{1}{PLD}\right) P' H P = B_{PP} + vv' - V, \tag{10.68}$$

where $H$ is the Hessian and $P$ is a diagonal matrix with prices of the four inputs and outputs along the main diagonal:

$$P = \begin{bmatrix} PCS & 0 & 0 & 0 \\ 0 & PIS & 0 & 0 \\ 0 & 0 & PMD & 0 \\ 0 & 0 & 0 & PQD \end{bmatrix},$$

$v$ is the vector of value shares of the outputs and inputs and $V$ is a diagonal matrix with these value shares along the main diagonal:

$$V = \begin{bmatrix} v_{CS} & 0 & 0 & 0 \\ 0 & v_{IS} & 0 & 0 \\ 0 & 0 & v_{MD} & 0 \\ 0 & 0 & 0 & v_{QD} \end{bmatrix}.$$

Our strategy for imposing convexity on the price function for labor input is similar to the approach we have employed in our model of consumer behavior. We constrain the parameters of the share equations so that convexity holds at all data points in the sample. To impose convexity we require that the Hessian of the price function is positive semidefinite. We represent the transformation of the Hessian (10.68) in terms of its Cholesky factorization:

$$B_{PP} + v v' - V = LDL', \tag{10.69}$$

where $L$ is a lower triangular matrix and $D$ is a diagonal matrix.

Under convexity the diagonal elements of the matrix $D$, the Cholesky values, must be greater than or equal to zero. Since one of the Cholesky values is zero by product exhaustion, we impose inequality constraints on the three remaining values. The convexity restrictions are satisfied at all data points.

The rate of productivity growth cannot be measured directly. However, the translog price function (10.1) implies that the rate of productivity growth in any two periods can be expressed as *an exact index number*:[31]

$$\bar{v}_{Tt} = \Delta \ln PLD_t - \bar{v}_{Ct} \Delta \ln PCS_t - \bar{v}_{It} \ln PIS_t - \bar{v}_{Qt} \Delta \ln PQD_t - \bar{v}_{Mt} \Delta \ln PMD_t. \tag{10.70}$$

Under the balanced growth restrictions the negative of the average rate of productivity growth (10.70) in any two periods can be expressed as a constant plus the average of the disturbance terms in the two periods:

$$-\bar{v}_{Tt} = \alpha_T + \bar{\varepsilon}_{Tt}, \tag{10.71}$$

The covariance matrix of the transformed disturbances is the Laurent matrix:

$$\Omega = \begin{bmatrix} \dfrac{1}{2} & \dfrac{1}{4} & 0 & \cdots & 0 \\ \dfrac{1}{4} & \dfrac{1}{2} & \dfrac{1}{4} & \cdots & 0 \\ 0 & \dfrac{1}{4} & \dfrac{1}{2} & \cdots & 0 \\ \cdots & \cdots & \cdots & \cdots & \cdots \\ 0 & 0 & 0 & \cdots & \dfrac{1}{2} \end{bmatrix}.$$

[31] See Jorgenson (2000) for further details.

The subdiagonals above and below the main diagonal of the matrix $\Omega$ reflect the serial correlation induced by averaging the rate of productivity growth. To eliminate this serial correlation we express the matrix $\Omega^{-1}$ in terms of the Cholesky factorization:

$$\Omega^{-1} = LDL',$$

where $L$ is a lower triangular matrix and $D$ is a diagonal matrix.

We transform the matrix $\Omega$ by premultiplying this matrix by the matrix square root of $\Omega^{-1}$:

$$D^{\frac{1}{2}}L'\Omega LD^{\frac{1}{2}} = I,$$

where $I$ is an identity matrix of order $T-1$. We can transform the vector of observations in the equation for the average rate of productivity growth (10.71) by means of this matrix square root to eliminate serial correlation.

We treat the share equations (10.65) symmetrically with the average rate of productivity growth (10.71) by expressing the average of the value shares in any two periods as a function of the average of the logarithm of the prices in the two periods:

$$\bar{v}_t = \alpha_P + \beta_{PP}\overline{\ln P_t} + \bar{\varepsilon}_t.$$

This transformation induces serial correlation that can be eliminated by multiplying the vector of observations by the matrix square root of the matrix $\Omega^{-1}$.

Our strategy for estimation of the model of producer behavior is similar to the one we have used for the model of consumer behavior. However, we require that the price function for labor input is convex. We must also take account of serial correlation induced by construction of the exact index number for productivity growth. (i) We construct the variables by calculating 2-year averages of the value shares, the rate of productivity growth and the logarithms of prices. (ii) We transform the vector of dependent and independent variables by the matrix square root given above. (iii) We drop the share equation for consumption goods in order to incorporate the product exhaustion restrictions.

In estimating the parameters of producer behavior, $\alpha_P$, $\alpha_T$ and $B_{PP}$, we normalize the producer prices of consumption goods, investment goods, corporate and non-corporate capital services at unity in 2005, and simplify representation of the convexity restrictions. The estimate of $B_{PP}$ is not affected by the choice of the base year. To fix the level of producer price of labor services, we add a constant term $\alpha_0^P$ to the logarithmic producer price function of labor services, and set its value at the average of:

$$\ln PLD^* - \ln P^{*'}\alpha_P^* - \alpha_T T - \frac{1}{2}\ln P^{*'}, B_{PP}\ln P^*,$$

for 1970–2010, where $\ln PLD^*$ and $\ln P^*$ are based on the price system used in our dynamic general equilibrium model. This assures that the fitted value of labor price tracks the historical path.

In estimating models for the allocation of capital services between long-lived and short-lived assets in the corporate and non-corporate sectors, we follow the procedure employed for household capital services in Section 10.3.1. We pool the three components of our model of producer behavior by estimating the parameters simultaneously. By pooling observations we exploit the information in all three components of the model and take account of non-zero covariances among the disturbances.

In order to take account of the serial correlation induced by averaging the rate of productivity growth, we employ 2-year averages of both dependent and independent variables in all equations and eliminate the resulting serial correlation by transforming these averaged observations. Table 10.3 summarizes the estimates, which are used in our dynamic general equilibrium model. Table 10.4 gives the Cholesky values at each data point. As before, the fitted value shares satisfy appropriate non-negativity conditions for all data points.

## 10.3.3 Elasticities of demand and supply

The estimated values of the parameters in our models of consumer and producer behavior provide important information on the responses of consumers and producers to changes in tax policy. We supplement this information by deriving price elasticities of demand and supply implied by our parameter estimates, including the compensated price elasticity of supply for labor services. We also provide elasticities of substitution in consumption, including the intertemporal elasticity of substitution — a constant parameter in our model of consumer behavior.

We present own-price and cross-price elasticities of demand for consumption goods, leisure and household capital services, using pooled estimates for our model of consumer behavior and average shares for the period 1970—2010, in panel 2 of Table 10.5.

The average share of leisure is more than 64% of full consumption, while the share of consumption goods and services is slightly more than 27% and the share of household capital services is around 8.6%. The own-price elasticity of demand for consumption goods and services is 26%, while the own-price elasticity of demand for leisure is only 2.4% and the elasticity of demand for capital services is 41%.

The compensated elasticity of labor supply is, perhaps, a more familiar concept than the elasticity of demand for leisure. We employ the average ratio of the values of leisure and labor supply for the period 1970—2010 in estimating this elasticity; the result, given at the bottom of panel 2, Table 10.5, is 6.2%. The elasticity of intertemporal substitution in consumption is the inverse of $\sigma$, estimated from the transition equation for full consumption:

$$\ln \frac{F_t}{F_{t-1}} = \frac{1}{\sigma}\left[ \ln\left(1 + r_t\right) - \ln\left(1 + \tilde{r}\right)\right] + \varepsilon_{Ft}, \quad t = 1, 2, ..., T.$$

This describes the rate of adjustment of full consumption to the difference between the real private rate of return and its long-run equilibrium value. The estimate of this elasticity reported in panel 3 of Table 10.5, is 44.6%.

**Table 10.3** Production Frontier and the allocation of corporate and non-corporate capital services: parameter estimates

| Parameter | Estimate | Standard error | t-statistic |
|---|---|---|---|
| $\alpha_C$ | 1.08299 | 0.00700537 | 154.594 |
| $\alpha_I$ | 0.426091 | 0.00365921 | 116.444 |
| $\alpha_Q$ | −0.368551 | 0.0055957 | −65.8633 |
| $\alpha_M$ | −0.14053 | 0.00203508 | −69.0537 |
| $\alpha_T$ | 0.014622 | 0.013054 | 1.12008 |
| $\beta_{CC}$ | 0.580427 | 0.086049 | 6.74531 |
| $\beta_{CI}$ | −0.429505 | 0.016886 | −25.4353 |
| $\beta_{CQ}$ | −0.130724 | 0.069699 | −1.87555 |
| $\beta_{CM}$ | −0.020199 | 0.023259 | −0.868429 |
| $\beta_{IC}$ | −0.429505 | 0.016886 | −25.4353 |
| $\beta_{II}$ | 0.264538 | 0.000540894 | 489.075 |
| $\beta_{IQ}$ | 0.138956 | 0.015006 | 9.2603 |
| $\beta_{IM}$ | 0.026012 | 0.00237318 | 10.9607 |
| $\beta_{QC}$ | −0.130724 | 0.069699 | −1.87555 |
| $\beta_{QI}$ | 0.138956 | 0.015006 | 9.2603 |
| $\beta_{QQ}$ | −0.02263 | 0.059596 | −0.379722 |
| $\beta_{QM}$ | 0.014398 | 0.018498 | 0.778363 |
| $\beta_{MC}$ | −0.020199 | 0.023259 | −0.868429 |
| $\beta_{MI}$ | 0.026012 | 0.00237318 | 10.9607 |
| $\beta_{MQ}$ | 0.014398 | 0.018498 | 0.778363 |
| $\beta_{MM}$ | −0.020211 | 0.00718281 | −2.8138 |
| $\delta_I$ | 0.02 | 0 | 0 |
| $\lambda_{IQ}$ | −0.904055 | 0.727653 | −1.24243 |
| $\lambda_{IM}$ | −1.69335 | 0.11627 | −14.5639 |
| $\delta_Q$ | 0.465406 | 0.048976 | 9.5028 |
| $\lambda_{QM}$ | 0.076434 | 0.050949 | 1.50022 |
| $\delta_M$ | 0.08 | 0 | 0 |
| $\alpha_0^P$ | 0.04412 | | |
| $\alpha_C^*$ | −0.14024 | | |
| $\alpha_I^*$ | 1.09059 | | |
| $\alpha_Q^*$ | 0.41778 | | |
| $\alpha_M^*$ | −0.36814 | | |
| $\alpha_S^Q$ | 0.459123 | 0.00705052 | 65.119 |
| $\alpha_L^Q$ | 0.540877 | 0.00705052 | 76.7145 |
| $\beta_{SS}^Q$ | −0.02923 | 8.977486E−02 | −2.99117 |
| $\beta_{SL}^Q$ | 0.029238 | 0.00977486 | 2.99117 |
| $\beta_{LL}^Q$ | −0.02923 | 8.977486E−02 | −2.99117 |
| $\delta_S^Q$ | −0.27756 | 7.010253 | −27.0712 |
| $\alpha_0^{PQ}$ | 0.010036 | | |
| $\alpha_S^M$ | 0.173957 | 0.0031578 | 55.0879 |
| $\alpha_L^M$ | 0.826043 | 0.0031578 | 261.588 |
| $\beta_{SS}^M$ | 0.069115 | 0.00398289 | 17.3531 |
| $\beta_{SL}^M$ | −0.06911 | 5.398289E−02 | −17.3531 |
| $\beta_{LL}^M$ | 0.069115 | 0.00398289 | 17.3531 |
| $\delta_S^M$ | −0.07458 | 0.574420E−02 | −12.9836 |
| $\alpha_0^{PM}$ | −0.0045680 | | |
| SSR | 8.90669 | | |

$\delta_I$ and $\delta_M$ are constrained at 0.02 and 0.08, respectively.

**Table 10.4** Production Frontier and the allocation of corporate and non-corporate capital services: local Cholesky values

| Year | $\delta_I$ | $\delta_Q$ | $\delta_M$ | $\delta_S^Q$ | $\delta_S^M$ |
|------|-----------|-----------|-----------|-----------|-----------|
| 1970 | 0.022576 | 0.30062 | 0.025622 | −0.2741 | −0.12085 |
| 1971 | 0.02135 | 0.3047 | 0.024552 | −0.2738 | −0.12229 |
| 1972 | 0.021915 | 0.3022 | 0.024074 | −0.27412 | −0.11996 |
| 1973 | 0.021229 | 0.30304 | 0.021604 | −0.27461 | −0.11585 |
| 1974 | 0.019102 | 0.31108 | 0.019989 | −0.27476 | −0.11514 |
| 1975 | 0.018589 | 0.31428 | 0.023622 | −0.27463 | −0.12007 |
| 1976 | 0.020112 | 0.30821 | 0.024832 | −0.2746 | −0.12055 |
| 1977 | 0.021592 | 0.30343 | 0.023615 | −0.27477 | −0.11647 |
| 1978 | 0.022133 | 0.30132 | 0.023535 | −0.27502 | −0.11475 |
| 1979 | 0.021092 | 0.30481 | 0.022115 | −0.27508 | −0.11372 |
| 1980 | 0.01916 | 0.31323 | 0.021056 | −0.27492 | −0.11489 |
| 1981 | 0.018827 | 0.31514 | 0.02028 | −0.27486 | −0.11483 |
| 1982 | 0.018941 | 0.3152 | 0.018593 | −0.275 | −0.11248 |
| 1983 | 0.01809 | 0.31927 | 0.015847 | −0.27518 | −0.11055 |
| 1984 | 0.018215 | 0.31648 | 0.012395 | −0.27536 | −0.10807 |
| 1985 | 0.018055 | 0.31586 | 0.009426 | −0.2755 | −0.10493 |
| 1986 | 0.016734 | 0.32488 | 0.008492 | −0.27558 | −0.10302 |
| 1987 | 0.015963 | 0.33196 | 0.0078281 | −0.27534 | −0.10339 |
| 1988 | 0.01564 | 0.33443 | 0.0059678 | −0.27517 | −0.10328 |
| 1989 | 0.015171 | 0.34098 | 0.0069308 | −0.27532 | −0.10174 |
| 1990 | 0.014689 | 0.3549 | 0.012434 | −0.27536 | −0.1008 |
| 1991 | 0.014542 | 0.3718 | 0.021896 | −0.27532 | −0.10106 |
| 1992 | 0.014734 | 0.38608 | 0.031102 | −0.27532 | −0.10153 |
| 1993 | 0.014947 | 0.39378 | 0.036093 | −0.27539 | −0.10119 |
| 1994 | 0.014839 | 0.3904 | 0.032846 | −0.27557 | −0.099776 |
| 1995 | 0.014737 | 0.38601 | 0.029015 | −0.27576 | −0.098399 |
| 1996 | 0.014775 | 0.38744 | 0.029308 | −0.27592 | −0.097097 |
| 1997 | 0.014855 | 0.39033 | 0.0303 | −0.27613 | −0.094962 |
| 1998 | 0.015229 | 0.40255 | 0.038323 | −0.2763 | −0.093688 |
| 1999 | 0.015979 | 0.41909 | 0.049579 | −0.27644 | −0.092055 |
| 2000 | 0.017021 | 0.43425 | 0.060449 | −0.27654 | −0.090273 |
| 2001 | 0.018913 | 0.45057 | 0.073976 | −0.27658 | −0.089185 |
| 2002 | 0.020562 | 0.45953 | 0.08213 | −0.2767 | −0.08665 |
| 2003 | 0.021418 | 0.46592 | 0.0859 | −0.27693 | −0.083543 |
| 2004 | 0.021406 | 0.47018 | 0.086233 | −0.27723 | −0.080016 |
| 2005 | 0.02 | 0.46541 | 0.08 | −0.27757 | −0.07458 |
| 2006 | 0.018655 | 0.4562 | 0.07159 | −0.27786 | −0.067841 |
| 2007 | 0.019428 | 0.46231 | 0.076328 | −0.27796 | −0.065103 |
| 2008 | 0.02271 | 0.47975 | 0.091671 | −0.27784 | −0.068882 |
| 2009 | 0.026121 | 0.49207 | 0.10159 | −0.27767 | −0.075016 |
| 2010 | 0.026036 | 0.49881 | 0.10184 | −0.27772 | −0.077245 |

**Table 10.5** Elasticities of consumer behavior

1. Basic information
*Average shares (1970–2010)*

| | |
|---|---|
| $v_C$ | 0.27325 |
| $v_{LJ}$ | 0.64069 |
| $v_{HD}$ | 0.08605 |
| $v_{HS}$ | 0.57058 |

*Second-order coefficients*

| | |
|---|---|
| $\beta_{CC}$ | 0.1266 |
| $\beta_{CL}$ | −0.14909 |
| $\beta_{CH}$ | 0.02249 |
| $\beta_{LL}$ | 0.21479 |
| $\beta_{LH}$ | −0.065705 |
| $\beta_{HH}$ | 0.043215 |
| $\beta_{SS}^{H}$ | 0.054014 |

2. Compensated elasticities (with constant full consumption)
*Elasticities of demand*

| | |
|---|---|
| $\varepsilon_{CC}$ | −0.26344 |
| $\varepsilon_{CL}$ | 0.095086 |
| $\varepsilon_{CH}$ | 0.16836 |
| $\varepsilon_{LC}$ | 0.040554 |
| $\varepsilon_{LL}$ | −0.02406 |
| $\varepsilon_{LH}$ | −0.016502 |
| $\varepsilon_{HC}$ | 0.53461 |
| $\varepsilon_{HL}$ | −0.12286 |
| $\varepsilon_{HH}$ | −0.41175 |

*Elasticity of labor supply*

| | |
|---|---|
| $\varepsilon_{LL}^{S}$ | 0.06248 |

3. Elasticity of intertemporal substitution

| | |
|---|---|
| $\sigma^{-1}$ | 0.44614 |

4. Elasticities of intratemporal substitution

| | |
|---|---|
| $e_{CL}$ | −0.24873 |
| $e_{CH}$ | −0.6323 |
| $e_{LH}$ | −0.33675 |
| $e_{HD}$ | −0.77955 |

The elasticity of substitution between two consumption goods is defined as the ratio of the proportional change in the ratio of the quantities consumed relative to the proportional change in the corresponding price ratio. The prices of other components are held constant, while the quantities are allowed to adjust to relative price changes. Our estimates of elasticities of substitution are based on parameter values from the pooled estimation of the model of consumer behavior, using average shares for 1970–2010. We report estimates of these elasticities in panel 4 of Table 10.5. The elasticity of substitution between the services of the long-lived and short-lived household assets is presented at the bottom of panel 4, Table 10.5. All of these elasticities are considerably less than one in absolute value, so that the corresponding value shares rise with an increase in price.

As in our model of consumer behavior, we define elasticities of substitution in production by allowing the relative quantities to adjust to changes in relative prices, while holding the prices of other inputs and outputs constant. We derive these elasticities from the pooled estimation of our model of producer behavior and the average value shares for 1970–2010. We report the results in panel 2 of Table 10.6.

**Table 10.6** Elasticities of producer behavior

1. Basic information
*Average shares (1970–2010)*

| | |
|---|---|
| $v_{CS}$ | 0.95513 |
| $v_{IS}$ | 0.50823 |
| $v_{QD}$ | −0.3342 |
| $v_{MD}$ | −0.12913 |
| $v_{QS}$ | 0.44533 |
| $v_{MS}$ | 0.21496 |

*Second-order coefficients*

| | |
|---|---|
| $\beta_{CC}$ | 0.58043 |
| $\beta_{CI}$ | −0.4295 |
| $\beta_{CQ}$ | −0.13072 |
| $\beta_{CM}$ | −0.0202 |
| $\beta_{II}$ | 0.26454 |
| $\beta_{IQ}$ | 0.13896 |
| $\beta_{IM}$ | 0.026012 |
| $\beta_{QQ}$ | −0.02263 |
| $\beta_{QM}$ | 0.014398 |
| $\beta_{MM}$ | −0.02021 |
| $\beta_{SS}^{Q}$ | −0.02924 |
| $\beta_{SS}^{M}$ | 0.069115 |

2. Elasticities of substitution

| | |
|---|---|
| $e_{CL}$ | 12.54486 |
| $e_{IL}$ | 0.058447 |
| $e_{QL}$ | −0.94925 |
| $e_{ML}$ | −0.86138 |
| $e_{CI}$ | 0.13778 |
| $e_{CQ}$ | −0.80182 |
| $e_{CM}$ | −0.86509 |
| $e_{IQ}$ | −3.39865 |
| $e_{IM}$ | −1.10465 |
| $e_{QM}$ | −0.8061 |
| $e_{QD}$ | −1.11837 |
| $e_{MD}$ | −0.59043 |

We also give the elasticities of substitution between the capital services from the short-lived and long-lived assets in the corporate and non-corporate sectors. The relative value shares of labor and the two capital inputs rise with a price increase if the elasticities of substitution are less than unity in absolute value and fall with a price increase if the elasticities are greater than unity in absolute value. The elasticities of substitution among inputs are less than unity in absolute value. However, the elasticities of substitution between labor and corporate capital, labor and non-corporate capital, and the two types of capital are only slightly less than one.

### 10.3.4 Non-tax parameters

We conclude this section by assigning values to the parameters of our model of the US economy that cannot be estimated econometrically. These include the ratio of government expenditures to GDP, *SGOV*, and the shares of government expenditures, net of interest payments on government debt, *SCG*, *SIG*, *SLG*, *SEL* and *SER*. These parameters are given in the first three panels of Table 10.7.

The next group of parameters includes the proportions of labor employed by government enterprises and net exports of labor services to the total labor supply, *SLE* and *SLR*. It also includes the production of consumption goods by government enterprises as a proportion of the total consumption goods produced by the business sector *SCE*. Finally, this group includes net exports of consumption goods as a proportion of the total domestic demand for consumption goods, *SCR*, and net exports of investment goods as a proportion of the total domestic production of investment goods, *SIR*. The parameters are given in panels 4 and 5 of Table 10.7.

The third group of parameters includes the dividend pay-out ratio of the corporate sector, $\alpha$, the debt—asset ratios of the corporate, non-corporate and household sectors, $\beta_q$, $\beta_m$ and $\beta_h$, and the real interest rate. This group of parameters is given in the sixth panel of Table 10.7. The parameters — *SGOV*, *SCR* and *SIR* — are used to calibrate the size of the government debt and claims on the rest of the world in the steady state of our model of the US economy. All other parameter values are set at the averages for the sample period, 1970—2010.

The fourth group of parameters is given in panels 7 and 8 of Table 10.7. This group includes the steady-state values of government debt and claims on the rest of the world, relative to the US GDP. The time endowment, *LH*, is set at the historical value in 2011. The growth of this time endowment reflects the growth of population as well as changes in the quality of labor.

Our population projections are based on the official projections by the Bureau of the Census for 2009.[32] Population growth and changes in labor quality will decline in the

---

[32] See: http://www.census.gov/population/www/projections/2009projections.html.

**Table 10.7** Non-tax parameters

1. Size of government
   $SGOV = 0.20168$          government expenditure including debt service/GDP

2. Unemployment
   $SLU = 0.0$          share of unemployed time in total labor supply

3. Allocation of government expenditure, net of interest payments (1970–2010 averages)
   $SCG = 0.16883$          share of consumption goods
   $SIG = 0.17814$          share of investment goods
   $SLG = 0.47807$          share of labor services
   $SEL = 0.16208$          share of transfer payments
   $SER = 0.012887$          share of transfer to foreigners

4. Government enterprises (1970–2010 averages)
   $SLE = 0.018781$          share of labor used by government
                                          enterprises
   $SCE = 0.028954$          ratio of consumption goods produced by government
                                          enterprises and the private sector

5. Export–import
   $SCR = -0.0007$          net export of consumption goods as a fraction of total
                                          domestic demand for consumption goods
   $SIR = -0.0022$          net export of investment goods as a fraction of total
                                          production of investment goods
   $SLR = -0.00048489$          share of exported labor
   (1970–2010 average)

6. Financial variables (1970–2010 averages)
   $\alpha = 0.47855$          dividend pay-out ratio
   $\beta_q = 0.098245$          debt–capital ratio in the corporate sector
   $\beta_m = 0.22618$          debt–capital ratio in the noncorporate sector
   $\beta_h = 0.33152$          debt–capital ratio in the household sector
   $i_o = 0.046576$          real interest rate

7. Other parameters
   $LH_{2011} = 27820$          total time endowment in efficiency units of 2011

8. Wealth composition (steady state of the Base Case)
   Government debt/
   GDP = 0.40
   Claims on the rest of the
   world/GDP = 0.05

9. Rates of economic depreciation
   $\delta_q^S = 0.1554$          short-lived corporate asset
   $\delta_q^L = 0.0186$          long-lived corporate asset
   $\delta_m^S = 0.1578$          short-lived noncorporate asset

*(Continued)*

**Table 10.7** Non-tax parameters—cont'd

| | |
|---|---|
| $\delta_m^L = 0.0122$ | long-lived noncorporate asset |
| $\delta_h^S = 0.1895$ | short-lived household asset |
| $\delta_h^L = 0.0132$ | long-lived household asset |

10. Prices of asset and investment goods (2011 values)

| | |
|---|---|
| $PK_q^S = 4.410$ | short-lived corporate asset |
| $PK_q^L = 8.665$ | long-lived corporate asset |
| $PK_m^S = 5.006$ | short-lived noncorporate asset |
| $PK_m^L = 9.773$ | long-lived noncorporate asset |
| $PK_h^S = 4.386$ | short-lived household asset |
| $PK_h^L = 23.867$ | long-lived household asset |
| $PI = 1.0473$ | investment goods |

11. Relative prices of labor

| | |
|---|---|
| $A_{LH} = 1.04411$ | time endowment (before tax) |
| (1970−2010 average) | |
| $A_{LJ} = 1.06406$ | leisure (before tax) |
| (1970−2010 average) | |
| $A_{LG} = 0.93698$ | labor employed in general government |
| (1970−2010 average) | |
| $A_{LE} = 0.97045$ | labor employed in government enterprises |
| (1970−2010 average) | |
| $A_{LR} = 1.0$ | exported labor (assumption) |
| $A_{LU} = 1.0$ | unemployed time (assumption) |

future. The initial values of the quantity indexes of the capital stock, government debt and claims on the rest of the world are set at their historical values in 2011. This procedure guarantees that the size of our simulated economy is equal to that of the US economy in 2011.

The ratio of government debt to the US GDP has shown a distinct downward trend after the two World Wars. In view of the recent rise of the government debt/GDP ratio, we set the ratio at 65% of the GDP in 2011. In the same spirit, we set its steady-state value at 0.4. We set the steady-state ratio of the US claims on the rest of the world to the GDP at 0.05. We treat the paths of government debt and claims on the rest of the world as exogenous.

Our fifth group of parameters includes the rates of economic depreciation. We distinguish among corporate, non-corporate and household sectors and two types of assets, short-lived and long-lived, within each sector. For the corporate and non-corporate sectors the short-lived asset includes producers' durable equipment, while the long-lived asset includes structures, inventories, and land. For the household sector the short-lived asset includes 28 types of consumers' durables, while the long-lived asset includes structures and land.

The rates of economic depreciation of the six classes of assets, two classes within each of the three sectors, are weighted averages of their components with capital stocks at the end of 2010 as weights. For example, the rate of economic depreciation of the long-lived corporate asset is the average depreciation rate of 29 categories of non-residential structures, residential structures, non-farm inventories and land employed in the corporate sector. Economic depreciation rates for the six categories of assets are shown in panels 9 of Table 10.7.

Finally, we present two sets of relative prices in panels 10 and 11 of Table 10.7. The relative prices of the six categories of assets in the corporate, non-corporate and household sectors and the price of investment goods are the first of these. We set the relative prices of the six categories of assets and investment goods at their 2011 values, adjusted for the inflation of 2011. The relative prices of the time endowment, leisure, and labor employed in the various sectors of the economy and the rest of the world are set at historical averages for the period 1970–2010.

## 10.4 ECONOMIC IMPACT OF TAX REFORM

The objective of this section is to develop a methodology for evaluating the welfare effects of tax reform. For this purpose we design a computational algorithm for determining the time path of the economy following the reform. This algorithm is composed of two parts. First, we solve for the unique steady state of the economy corresponding to any tax policy. We then determine the unique transition path that is consistent with both the steady-state and the initial conditions. We describe the dynamics of our dynamic general equilibrium model of the US economy in terms of the saddle-point configuration of this transition path.

The plan of this section is as follows. In Section 10.4.1 we describe the dynamics of our model of the US economy. In Section 10.4.2 we present a methodology for comparing welfare levels for alternative tax policies. In Section 10.4.3 we outline our computational algorithm for determining the transition path to a new balanced growth equilibrium following tax reform. In the following section we evaluate the economic impact of alternative tax reform proposals.

### 10.4.1 Perfect foresight dynamics

In a world of perfect foresight the transition path of the economy from an initial state to the steady state is unique. It is also self-validating in the sense that expectations on the future course of the economy are actually realized. Suppose that the economy is initially at a steady state, indicated by point A in Figure 10.1. At the

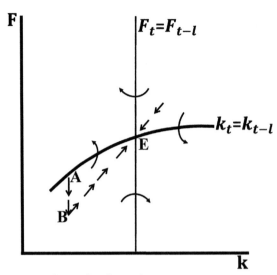

**Figure 10.1** Transition path under perfect foresight.

steady state, the real private rate of return on capital is constant at the value determined by (10.12):

$$\tilde{r} = (1+\gamma)(1-\alpha_T)^\sigma - 1, \qquad (10.72)$$

where $\gamma$ is the rate of time preference, $-\alpha_T$ is the rate of labor-augmenting productivity growth and $\sigma$ is the inverse of intertemporal elasticity of substitution. The steady-state value of the rate of return is independent of tax policy.

For expository purposes we first assume that the supply of labor is fixed and that full consumption includes only a single homogeneous good, measured in the same units as capital. We also assume that government rebates all the tax revenues to the household sector and that net exports are zero. We suppose that a new tax policy is introduced in order to improve the efficiency of capital allocation. The short run impact of this policy is that the nominal rate of return $\rho$ rises above the steady-state level $\tilde{\rho}$. The transition path for full consumption is described by equation (10.9), so that:

$$F_t = F_{t-1} \left[ \frac{PF_{t-1}}{PF_t} \frac{1 + \rho_t}{(1+\gamma)(1-\alpha_T)^\sigma} \right]^{\frac{1}{\sigma}}, \qquad (10.73)$$

where $F$ is full consumption *per capita* with population expressed in efficiency units and $PF$ is the price of full consumption. Immediately after the introduction of the new policy the level of full consumption rises over time. The intuition is that with a higher rate of return future consumption is cheaper relative to current consumption, so that the consumer can attain a higher level of welfare by saving more now in order to consume more in the future.

When the rate of return exceeds its long-run equilibrium level, capital intensity in the new steady state is higher than in the initial state. As the economy moves along the transition path, capital intensity rises and the rate of return is brought down, gradually, to the steady-state level. In the new steady state, represented by point E in Figure 10.1, both the level of full consumption and capital intensity are higher than at the starting point of the transition path, given by point B.

In order to understand the dynamics of the transition to a new steady state, it is useful to examine changes in the level of full consumption and capital intensity. At the beginning of period $t$ the capital stock is the sum of capital stock at the beginning of period $t - 1$ and investment during period $t - 1$. In period $t$, this capital stock must be allocated among the total labor force. As a consequence, *capital intensity*, defined as the ratio of capital stock to labor in efficiency units, grows according to the equation:

$$k_t = \frac{[k_{t-1} + h(k_{t-1}) - F_t]}{(1 - \alpha_T)(1 + n_t)}, \tag{10.74}$$

where $k_{t-1}$ is the capital intensity at the end of period $t - 1$, $h$ is the production function in intensive form, representing output *per capita* as a function of capital intensity, and $n$ is the rate of population growth.

The locus of points at which capital intensity remains constant is characterized by $k_t = k_{t-1}$. In the steady state $n_t = n$. By substituting these conditions into (10.74), we obtain:

$$F_t = h(k_{t-1}) - ((1 - \alpha_T)(1 + n) - 1)k_{t-1}. \tag{10.75}$$

Similarly, the locus of the points at which full consumption *per capita* remains constant is obtained by substituting $F_t = F_{t-1}$ into (10.73):

$$\tilde{\rho} = \rho_t. \tag{10.76}$$

Making use of Equations (10.73)–(10.76), we can illustrate the dynamics of our model of the US economy. In Figure 10.1 the arrows indicate directions of movement. If the new policy improves efficiency of the economy, the locus of $k_t = k_{t-1}$ shifts upward and the initial steady state at point A lies below the curve along which capital intensity is constant under the new policy. At the beginning of the transition the economy has to jump to point B by adjusting the level of full consumption downward. After this level of full consumption is known, we can describe the entire transition path of the economy with Equations (10.73) and (10.74). The only path that leads to the new steady state is $\overline{BE}$. Along this transition path the markets for goods and for labor and capital services clear in each period.

## 10.4.2 Comparison of welfare levels

In order to evaluate alternative tax policies, we compare the levels of social welfare associated with each of these policies. We can translate welfare comparisons into monetary terms by introducing the equivalent variation in wealth. We express the full wealth required to achieve a given level of welfare in terms of the time path of all future prices of full consumption and rates of return. We refer to this expression as *the intertemporal expenditure function*. Using the expenditure function, we can express differences in welfare in terms of differences in wealth.

To derive the intertemporal expenditure function we first express the time path of full consumption in terms of the initial level and future real private rates of return:

$$\frac{F_t}{F_0} = \prod_{s=0}^{t} \left[ \frac{1 + r_s}{(1 + \gamma)(1 - \alpha_T)^{\sigma}} \right]^{\frac{1}{\sigma}}, (t = 1, 2, \ldots),$$  (10.77)

Using this expression, we can write the intertemporal welfare function as:

$$V = \frac{F_0^{1-\sigma}}{1 - \sigma} D,$$  (10.78)

where:

$$D = \sum_{t=0}^{\infty} \left[ \frac{1}{(1 + \gamma)^{\frac{1}{\sigma}}} \right]^{t} \prod_{s=0}^{t} (1 + n_s)(1 + r_s)^{\frac{1-\sigma}{\sigma}}.$$

The function $D$ summarizes the effect of all future prices and rates of return on the initial level of full consumption $F_0$ associated with a given level of welfare $V$.

Since the optimal time path for full consumption must satisfy the intertemporal budget constraint, we can express the initial level of full consumption in terms of full wealth and all future real private rates of return:

$$F_0 = \frac{W}{PF_0} \frac{1}{D}.$$

Combining this expression with (10.78) and solving for full wealth, we obtain the intertemporal expenditure function, say $W(PF_0, D, V)$, where:

$$W\left( PF_0, D, V \right) = PF_0 \left[ \frac{(1 - \sigma)V}{D^{\sigma}} \right]^{\frac{1}{1-\sigma}}.$$  (10.79)

We employ the intertemporal expenditure function to provide a money measure of differences in levels of welfare associated with alternative tax policies. For this purpose we first calculate the solution to our dynamic general equilibrium model of the US economy for the base case. We denote the resulting prices and discount rates by $PF_0$ and $D_0$ and the corresponding level of welfare by $V_0$. We then solve the model for a policy case and denote the resulting level of welfare by $V_1$. Finally, we calculate the *equivalent variation in full wealth*, say $\Delta W$, where:

$$\Delta W = W(PF_0, D_0, V_1) - W(PF_0, D_0, V_0)$$
$$= W(PF_0, D_0, V_1) - W_0. \tag{10.80}$$

The equivalent variation in full wealth (10.80) is the difference between the wealth required to attain the level of welfare associated with the policy case at prices of the base case, $W(PF_0, D_0, V_1)$, less the wealth required for the base case $W_0$. If the equivalent variation is positive, a change in policy produces a gain in welfare; otherwise, the policy change results in a welfare loss. The equivalent variations in full wealth enable us to rank the base case and any number of policy cases in terms of a money metric of the corresponding welfare levels.[33]

### 10.4.3 Computational algorithm

The computational algorithm for determining the solution of our dynamic general equilibrium model of the US economy has two stages. In the first stage we determine the steady state consistent with a given tax policy. In the second stage we find the transition path that is consistent with this steady state and the initial conditions at the time the tax policy is introduced.

The evolution of the economy from one period to the next is determined by the transition equation for full consumption and the accumulation equations for capital stock, government debt and claims on the rest of the world. The paths of government debt and claims on the rest of the world are predetermined and the initial value of capital stock is given. The second stage reduces to finding the initial level of full consumption that is consistent with convergence to the steady state of the economy.

Along the transition path, as well as in the steady state, the time endowment in efficiency units grows at the rate $(1 - \alpha_T)(1 + n_t) - 1$. We find it convenient to use the property of constant returns in order to scale the solution of the model to the time endowment. When the economy moves from one period to the next, we rescale the economy by dividing the three stock variables — capital stock, government debt and claims on the rest of the world — at the end of the period by the factor $(1 - \alpha_T)(1 + n_t)$ in order to obtain the stocks available at the beginning of the next period.

With a rate of inflation different from zero we set the prices of the six categories of assets and the price of investment goods at the values shown in panel 10 of Table 10.7. For capital stock, government debt and claims on the rest of the world, we set the current prices at unity and the lagged prices at $1/(1 + \pi)$. After the normalized equilibrium of the economy is determined, conversion to the actual size of the economy with the absolute price level is straightforward.

---

[33] The approach proposed by Ballard *et al.* (1985, Chapter 7) is based on the difference between present values of time paths of full consumption associated with alternative tax policies, rather than the equivalent variation in full wealth. Although there are important similarities between comparisons of present values of full consumption and the equivalent variation, the two approaches do not coincide.

We next describe the algorithm for computing market equilibrium for our model of the US economy. The model is in balanced growth equilibrium when all the quantities grow at the same rate $(1 - \alpha_T)(1 + n)$ and relative prices are constant. This is a steady state in the sense that the relative prices and quantities per unit of labor expressed in efficiency units are constant. In each period the relative prices and the allocation of the capital stock and the time endowment are determined so that all the markets clear, producers maximize profit and consumers maximize utility.

We can characterize the steady state of the economy by three conditions. (i) Capital stock, government debt and claims on the rest of the world grow at the same rate as the time endowment in efficiency unit:

$$VK = VKL - D + V + (S - DG - GR) = VKL(1 - \alpha_T)(1 + n)(1 + \pi)$$

(10.81a)

$$VG = VGL + DG = VGL(1 - \alpha_T)(1 + n)(1 + \pi)$$    (10.81b)

$$VR = VRL(1 + \pi) + DR = VRL(1 - \alpha_T)(1 + n)(1 + \pi).$$    (10.81c)

Equation (10.81a) shows that the nominal value of private capital decreases by the value of depreciation ($D$) and increases by revaluation of the capital remaining ($V$) and gross investment. Investment equals gross private saving ($S$), net of the accumulation of government debt ($DG$) and claims on the rest of the world ($DR$). Equation (10.81b) shows that the outstanding government debt grows at the rate of government budget deficit ($DG$). Equation (10.81c) shows that growth of the claims on the rest of the world is the sum of the trade deficit ($DR$) and the revaluation of the outstanding claims. In a steady state with a constant rate of inflation, the nominal value of private capital ($VKL$), government debt ($VGL$) and claims on the rest of the world ($VRL$) all grow at the same rate and the quantities of these variables per unit of labor in efficiency units remain constant. (ii) Full consumption per unit of labor in efficiency units remains constant:

$$F_t = F_{t-1}.$$    (10.82)

Together with (10.72) and (10.73), Equation (10.82) implies that that the nominal rate of return $\rho$ is equal to its steady-state value $\tilde{\rho}$. (iii) Every market must clear in the steady state. By invoking Walras' law we can ignore the labor market, and consider clearing of markets for consumption goods, investment goods and capital services.

In the steady state all the endogenous variables can be expressed in terms of the seven variables: $F$, $KL$, $GL$, $RL$, $PC$, $PLD$ and $LD$, where $KL$, $GL$ and $RL$ are quantity indexes of capital stock, government debt, and claims on the rest of the world, respectively.[34]

---

[34] The quantity indexes are implicitly defined by $VKL = KL \cdot PKL$, $VGL = GL \cdot PGL$ and $VRL = RL \cdot PRL$.

Thus, we have seven unknowns and six equations. The system is closed by the price possibility frontier (10.1) of the business sector:

$$\ln PLD \; = \; \ln P'\alpha_p + \alpha_T \cdot T + \frac{1}{2} \ln P' B_{PP} \ln P. \qquad (10.83)$$

This form of the price possibility frontier is consistent with the existence of balanced growth equilibrium. We solve the equation system by Newton's method.[35]

To solve for the steady state, we set the prices of investment goods, capital stock, government debt and claims on the rest of the world exogenously. The prices of aggregate capital stock, government debt and claims on the rest of the world are set at unity. The producers' price of investment goods is obtained from:

$$PIS \; = \; \frac{PI}{1 + t_{\mathrm{I}}}.$$

Since the real private rate of return $r$ is equal to the value $\tilde{r}$ in the steady state, the nominal private rate of return is defined as:

$$\rho \; = \; (1 + \tilde{r})(1 + \pi) - 1, \qquad (10.84)$$

and the nominal private rate of return on equity, say $\rho^e$, is obtained from the definition of $\rho$:

$$\rho\left(VKL + VGL + VRL\right) \; = \; \left((1 - \beta)\rho^e + \beta i_k\right)\left(VKL + VRL\right) + i_g \cdot VGL, \qquad (10.85)$$

where $\beta$ is the average debt–asset ratio of private national wealth, including private assets and claims on the rest of the world, $i_k$ is the average after-tax nominal interest rate on private national wealth, and $i_g$ is the after-tax nominal interest rate on government debt, defined as:

$$i_g \; = \; \left[1 - (1 - D1)t_g^d\right] \cdot i.$$

The nominal interest rate $i$ is determined according to the strict version of Fisher's law:

$$i \; = \; i_0 + \pi,$$

where $i_0$ is the real interest rate, given exogenously. Given the nominal private rate of return to equity, the real rates of return for investments in the corporate, non-corporate and household sectors ($r^q$, $r^m$ and $r^h$) can be calculated from the equations:

$$r^q - \pi \; = \; (1 - \beta_q)\frac{\left[\rho^e - \pi\left(1 - (1 - DC)t_q^g\right)\right]\left(1 - \alpha DDt_q\right)}{1 - \left[\alpha t_q^e + (1 - \alpha)t_q^g\right]}$$

$$\qquad (10.86a)$$

$$+ \beta_q\left[\left(1 - (1 - DI)t_q\right)i - \pi\right]$$

---

[35] More details on the computational procedure for applying Newton's method to our seven equation system for the steady state under the Base Case are presented in Chapter 7 of Jorgenson and Yun (2001).

$$r^{m} - \pi = (1 - \beta_{m})\left[\rho^{e} - \pi\left(1 - (1 - DC)t_{m}^{g}\right)\right] + \beta_{m}\left[\left(1 - (1 - DI)t_{m}^{e}\right)i - \pi\right]$$
$$(10.86b)$$

$$r^{h} - \pi = (1 - \beta_{h})\left[\rho^{e} - \pi\left(1 - (1 - DC)t_{h}^{g}\right)\right] + \beta_{h}\left[\left(1 - DHI(1 - HDI)t_{h}^{e}\right)i - \pi\right].$$
$$(10.86c)$$

The nominal private rate of return on equity $\rho^{e}$ can be calculated from (10.85) if the average debt–asset ratio of private national wealth $\beta$ and the average after-tax nominal interest rate $i_{k}$ are known. However, $\beta$ and $i_{k}$ depend on the allocation of capital among the corporate, non-corporate and household sectors, which in turn depends on $\rho^{e}$ through the discount rates for investment in the three private sectors as defined in (10.86a)–(10.86c). In order to simplify the algorithm, we include the nominal private rate of return to equity $\rho^{e}$ in the list of unknowns and Equation (10.85) to the simultaneous equation system to be solved.

The remaining problem is to find the transition path consistent with the steady-state and the initial conditions of the economy. After the steady state of the economy is determined, the paths of government debt and claims on the rest of the world are also determined, so that capital stock and full consumption remain the essential determinants of the dynamics of the economy along the transition path. Given the level of full consumption in the first year on the transition path, the complete time path of full consumption is determined by the model. For this purpose we employ the method of multiple shooting.[36] It is convenient to assume that the economy has been under a new policy regime in period 0, one period before the policy is actually introduced. The computational procedures are similar to those of the steady-state solution except that we now take $FS_{0}$ as one of the unknowns and $K_{0}$, $G_{0}$ and $R_{0}$ as given where $FS_{0} = F_{0} \cdot PF_{0}^{1/\sigma}$. The current and lagged prices of assets, and the producer and purchaser's price of investment goods are determined as before.

We have assumed that the allocation of total government expenditure, net of the interest payments on government debt, among consumption goods ($CG$), investment goods ($IG$), labor ($LG$), and transfer payments to US citizens ($EL$) and to foreigners ($ER$) can be represented by a Cobb–Douglas price function (10.31):

$$\ln PGS = SCG \ln PC + SIG \ln PI + SLG \ln PLG + SEL \ln PEL + SER \ln PER,$$

where $PGS$ is the price index of aggregate government spending, and $SCG$, $SIG$, $SLG$, $SEL$ and $SER$ are the exogenously given shares of government expenditure. Under an appropriate normalization of the indirect utility function of the government, the benefits derived from government spending are equal to the quantity of government spending ($GS$).

---

[36] For a systematic treatment of the multiple shooting technique, see Lipton *et al.* (1982).

In the base case, we set the steady-state level of government spending equal to a fixed proportion *SGOV* of the GDP. Along the transition path the level of government spending is determined as the sum of the tax revenue and budget deficit. When we solve the model under the policy cases, we control the level of welfare derived from government spending by setting the quantity of government spending in each period at the value in the base case.

In a dynamic setting the budget constraint of the government requires that the present value of government spending equals the present value of government receipts plus the net worth of the government. Under this budget constraint, the government can finance a given amount of spending either by taxation or by issuing debt, followed by a tax increase to service and eventually repay the debt. However, this is not to say that tax financing and debt financing are equivalent in terms of their economic impact.

We require that the budget deficit of the government and government tax revenue must follow the same path under all the policies being compared. We assume that the level of government debt reaches its steady-state value in 39 years after the introduction of the new policy. We close the gap between the initial and the steady-state levels of the government debts at the annual rate of $1/34$ during the first 29 years and then at the annual rate of $1/68$ for the remaining 10 years. The steady-state value is reached in year 40. We apply the same procedure to determine the path of claims on the rest of the world.

Since the time paths of real government spending and the government budget deficit are predetermined, the level of tax revenue under an alternative tax policy must be adjusted to meet the budget constraint. In order to adjust the tax revenues, we consider four alternative approaches. These include the adjustments of a hypothetical lump-sum tax, sales taxes, the labor income tax and the individual income tax. In each period we have to find the size of tax adjustment along with other endogenous variables. When the lump-sum tax is adjusted to meet the government budget constraint, $R_{lum}$ is added to government tax revenue and is subtracted from private national income.

Under the labor income tax adjustment we adjust the average and marginal tax rates on labor income either by the same percentage points or by the same proportion. These adjustment methods are referred to the *additive adjustment* and *proportional adjustment*, respectively. Under the sales tax adjustment, we adjust the tax rates on consumption goods and investment goods by the same percentage points. When the sales taxes are flat and the tax rates are identical, additive and proportional adjustments are equivalent. Finally, when the individual income tax is adjusted, we adjust the average and marginal tax rates on labor income either by the same percentage points or by the same proportion.

If the average and marginal tax rates on labor income are adjusted by the same percentage points, the average tax rate on capital income is also adjusted by the same percentage points, but the marginal tax rates on capital income are adjusted in the same proportion as the marginal tax rate on labor income. If the average and marginal tax rates on labor income are adjusted in the same proportion, the average and marginal tax rates on capital income are also adjusted in this proportion. We represent the size of tax adjustment by *ADJ* and to close the equation system for the equilibrium of the economy, we add the budget constraint of the government (10.35) as one of the balancing equations. The algorithm used to solve for the steady state for a policy case is similar to the one used for the base case.

In our model of the US economy trade with the rest of the world need not be balanced. However, capital employed abroad does not generate corporate tax revenues. Second, this capital is not combined with domestic labor in production, so that domestic labor productivity is unaffected. Therefore, we control the path of the claims on the rest of the world in the same way as government debt. In order to keep the trade deficit on a path implied by claims on the rest of the world, we adjust net exports of consumption and investment goods and labor services.

## 10.5 INCOME TAX REFORM

We next employ our dynamic general equilibrium model to evaluate the economic impact of alternative tax reform proposals. The economy is characterized by a price system that clears markets for labor and capital services and for consumption and investment goods. These prices link past and future through markets for investment goods and capital services. Assets are accumulated through past investments, while asset prices equal the present values of future capital services.

In this section we evaluate tax reforms that remove barriers to efficiency of the existing income tax system. In Section 10.5.1 we present the base case for our tax policy evaluations, based on the tax laws of 2010. We then consider policy cases involving the elimination of tax wedges among streams of capital income received from different classes of assets and different legal forms of organization. Finally, we consider Efficient Taxation of Income, which involves the elimination of all tax wedges among different forms of capital income and substitutes a proportional tax on labor income from a graduated or "progressive" tax on labor income.

### 10.5.1 Tax law of 2010

In order to evaluate the economic impact of alternative tax reforms we require a reference economy to serve as a base case. We take the US economy under the tax laws effective in 2010 as the point of reference. We take 1 January 2011 as the starting point for our simulations we consider. This takes place after the end of the Great Recession of 2007–2009. The simulated growth path of the US economy is the base case for our analysis of the economic impact of alternative tax reforms.

The growth of the population determines the time endowment available for work and leisure. We assume that the distribution of individuals by age, sex and education will evolve in accord with demographic projections. Hence, the quality of the time endowment, leisure and the labor employed in the various sectors of the economy will also change. We also assume that the efficiency of a given quality of labor improves at the rate of productivity growth.

In Table 10.8 we present the tax rates that describe the US tax system in 2010. These include: the marginal tax rates on individual capital income, the corporate income tax rate, the marginal tax rate on labor income and the average tax rate on personal income. The tax rates also include sales and property taxes, personal non-taxes, and wealth taxes.

**Table 10.8** Tax rates (2010)

1. Marginal tax rates on individual income

| Inflation rate | 0 | 0.04 | 0.08 |
|---|---|---|---|
| $t_q^e$ | 0.19124 | 0.19185 | 0.19224 |
| $t_m^e$ | 0.29027 | 0.29027 | 0.29027 |
| $t_h^e$ | 0.29027 | 0.29027 | 0.29027 |
| $t_q^g$ | 0.053 | 0.053 | 0.053 |
| $t_m^g$ | 0.07257 | 0.07257 | 0.07257 |
| $t_h^g$ | 0 | 0 | 0 |
| $t_q^d$ | 0.16589 | 0.17681 | 0.18397 |
| $t_m^d$ | 0.24493 | 0.24882 | 0.25138 |
| $t_h^d$ | 0.27575 | 0.27589 | 0.27598 |
| $t_g^d$ | 0.19384 | 0.19678 | 0.19871 |

2. Corporate income tax rate

| | |
|---|---|
| $t_q$ | 0.38765 |

3. Marginal tax rate on labor income

| | |
|---|---|
| $t_L^m$ | 0.25094 |

4. Average tax rates on personal income

| | |
|---|---|
| $t_L^a$ | 0.095 |
| $t_e^a$ | 0.15218 |
| $t_d^a$ | 0.15218 |

5. Sales tax rates

| | |
|---|---|
| $t_C$ | 0.0537 |
| $t_I$ | 0.0537 |

6. Property tax rates

| | |
|---|---|
| $t_q^p$ | 0.01295 |
| $t_m^p$ | 0.01705 |
| $t_h^p$ | 0.00731 |

7. Others

| | |
|---|---|
| $t_t$ | 0.0111 |
| $t_w$ | 0.00034 |

*(Continued)*

**Table 10.8** Tax rates (2010)—cont'd

*Notations:*

| | |
|---|---|
| $t_q^e, t_m^e, t_h^e$ : | Average marginal tax rates of individual income accruing to corporate, noncorporate and household equities, respectively |
| $t_q^g, t_m^g, t_h^g$ : | Average marginal tax rates of capital gains accruing to corporate, noncorporate and household equities, respectively |
| $t_q^d, t_m^d, t_h^d, t_g^d$ : | Average marginal tax rates of interest income accruing to corporate, noncorporate, household, and government debts, respectively |
| $t_q$ : | Corporate income tax rate (federal + state and local) |
| $t_L^m$ : | Average marginal tax rate of labor income |
| $t_L^a$ : | Average tax rate of labor income |
| $t_e^a, t_d^a$ : | Average tax rates of personal capital income from equity and debt |
| $t_c, t_I$ : | Sales tax rates of consumption and investment goods |
| $t_q^p, t_m^p, t_h^p$ : | Property tax rates of corporate, noncorporate and household assets, respectively |
| $t_t$ : | Rate of personal non-taxes |
| $t_w$ : | Effective rate of wealth taxation |

*Note:* We set $t_h^e = t_m^e$ and $t_h^g = 0$.

Non-taxes are payments to the government sector that do not take the form of taxes, e.g. fees for government services provided to the private sector. Capital consumption allowances are permitted only for corporate and non-corporate business sectors.

In Table 10.9 we give the present values of the capital consumption allowances for short-lived and long-lived assets in 2010 under alternative rates of inflation. We calculate present values of the capital consumption allowances from the statutory depreciation schedules. We employ the after-tax nominal interest rate for discounting these allowances to the present.

Inflation is exogenous to our model. Under the 2010 tax law inflation increases the tax burden of corporate assets faster than that of non-corporate assets and the burden of non-corporate assets faster than that of household assets. Table 10.10 shows the impact of inflation on the performance of the US economy under a lump-sum tax adjustment, labor income tax, sales tax and individual income tax adjustments.

**Table 10.9** Present value of capital consumption allowances (2010)

| Inflation rate | Corporate | | Non-corporate | |
|---|---|---|---|---|
| | Short | Long | Short | Long |
| 0.00 | 0.9364 | 0.5907 | 0.9408 | 0.4914 |
| 0.04 | 0.8887 | 0.4811 | 0.896 | 0.3819 |
| 0.08 | 0.8465 | 0.4054 | 0.8558 | 0.3091 |

**Table 10.10** Welfare effects of inflation under the 2010 law (billions of 2011 US$)

| Rate of inflation | Revenue adjustment | Welfare effect |
|---|---|---|
| 0.00 | Lump-sum tax | 1473.0 |
| | Labor income tax | 1092.2 |
| | Sales tax | 809.8 |
| | Individual income tax | 953 |
| 0.04 | Lump-sum tax | 0 |
| | Labor income tax | 0 |
| | Sales tax | 0 |
| | Individual income tax | 0 |
| 0.08 | Lump-sum tax | −1339.7 |
| | Labor income tax | −1061.8 |
| | Sales tax | −813.3 |
| | Individual income tax | −860.3 |

In 2011, GDP and the private national wealth (i.e., the sum of the real private assets in the corporate, non-corporate, and household sectors and the claims on the rest of the world at the beginning of the year) were $15,094 and 50,767 billion dollars, respectively.

## 10.5.2 Elimination of tax wedges

The economic impact of tax distortions can be measured by the improvement in economic welfare when the tax wedges are eliminated. We first analyze the impact of distortions resulting from the taxation of income from capital. We consider the elimination of tax wedges among assets and among sectors. We also consider the elimination of wedges between rates of return before and after taxes. Specifically, we measure the gains from the following changes in the 2010 tax system:

(i) Eliminate tax wedges between short-lived and long-lived assets within each sector.

(ii) Eliminate tax wedges between short-lived and long-lived assets in the business sector — corporate and non-corporate.

(iii) Eliminate tax wedges for short-lived and long-lived assets among all sectors — corporate, non-corporate and household.

(iv) Eliminate all tax wedges in the business sector.

(v) Eliminate all tax wedges in the private sector.

(vi) Corporate tax integration.

(vii) Eliminate taxation of income from capital

(viii) Eliminate capital income taxes and sales tax on investment goods.

(ix) Eliminate capital income taxes and property taxes.

(x) Eliminate capital income taxes, sales tax on investment goods and property taxes.

The social rate of return is the rate of return before all taxes, adjusted for inflation. This is calculated by subtracting the rate of depreciation from the price of capital services. The

**Table 10.11** Steady state of the base case (rate of inflation: 4%)

|  | Corporate | | Non-corporate | | Household | |
|---|---|---|---|---|---|---|
|  | Short | Long | Short | Long | Short | Long |
| $w$ | 0.1062 | 0.2325 | 0.0169 | 0.1683 | 0.1157 | 0.3603 |
| $z$ | 0.8887 | 0.4811 | 0.896 | 0.3819 | 0 | 0 |
| $\delta$ | 0.1554 | 0.0186 | 0.1578 | 0.0122 | 0.1895 | 0.0132 |
| PKS | 0.2722 | 0.1457 | 0.2562 | 0.1148 | 0.2597 | 0.0764 |

$w$: Share of capital stock.
$z$: Present value of capital consumption allowances.
$\delta$: Economic depreciation rate.
PKS: Price of capital services.

social rate of return includes the inflation-adjusted rate of return after all taxes, together with the tax burdens due to corporate income taxes, individual income taxes and property taxes. The tax burdens are partly offset by capital consumption allowances. In order to eliminate tax wedges among asset categories, we equalize the social rates to return by assigning an appropriate investment tax credit to each category of assets.

Table 10.11 shows the present values of capital consumption allowances $z$ and the rates of economic depreciation $\delta$. Capital consumption allowances are deductions from income for tax purposes and must be distinguished from tax credits, which are deductions from tax liabilities. Table 10.11 also shows the steady-state allocation of capital stock $\omega$ and prices of capital services PKS for the base case corresponding to the 2010 tax system. The tax credits required for the first six sets of changes in the 2010 tax system are presented in panel 2 of Table 10.12, along with the corresponding social rates of return and effective tax rates. For comparison base case figures are presented in panel 1.

The welfare effects of the 10 tax reform proposals are summarized in Table 10.13. We begin with simulations based on a lump-sum tax adjustment to achieve revenue neutrality. This provides a standard of comparison for more realistic policies that achieve revenue neutrality by adjusting distorting taxes, such as labor income taxes, sales taxes and individual income taxes. We find that the welfare gain from the elimination of the tax wedges within the three sectors is $479.0 billion (2011 US$). Under lump-sum tax adjustment, elimination of tax wedges between the corporate and non-corporate sectors yields a welfare gain of only $40.7 billion.

The economic impact of our third tax reform proposal illustrates the substantial welfare gains from eliminating tax wedges between the business and household sectors. This is intuitively plausible, given the size of the tax wedges between these sectors. The estimated gain is $5347.8 billion. By contrast, the welfare gain from eliminating all tax wedges among business assets alone is only $303.9 billion. The fifth simulation eliminates all the tax wedges among sectors and assets, leading to efficient allocation of capital

**Table 10.12** Elimination of interasset and intertemporal tax wedges (rate of inflation: 4%)

| | Corporate | | Non-corporate | | Household | |
|---|---|---|---|---|---|---|
| | Short | Long | Short | Long | Short | Long |
| **1. Base case** | | | | | | |
| $\sigma - \pi$ | 0.1106 | 0.1264 | 0.0921 | 0.1021 | 0.0626 | 0.0626 |
| $e$ | 0.3584 | 0.4384 | 0.3061 | 0.3738 | 0.0761 | 0.0761 |
| $k$ | 0 | 0 | 0 | 0 | 0 | 0 |
| **2. Alternative policies** | | | | | | |
| *(i) No interasset wedges: corporate and non-corporate* | | | | | | |
| $\sigma - \pi$ | 0.1214 | 0.1214 | 0.1012 | 0.1012 | 0.0626 | 0.0626 |
| $e$ | 0.4155 | 0.4155 | 0.3682 | 0.3682 | 0.0761 | 0.0761 |
| $k$ | −0.0273 | 0.0303 | −0.028 | 0.0083 | 0 | 0 |
| *(ii) No intersector wedges: corporate and non-corporate* | | | | | | |
| $\sigma - \pi$ | 0.1081 | 0.1162 | 0.1081 | 0.1162 | 0.0626 | 0.0626 |
| $e$ | 0.3433 | 0.3891 | 0.4085 | 0.4497 | 0.0761 | 0.0761 |
| $k$ | 0.0064 | 0.0625 | −0.0493 | −0.128 | 0 | 0 |
| *(iii) No intersector wedges: all sectors* | | | | | | |
| $\sigma - \pi$ | 0.0861 | 0.0908 | 0.0861 | 0.0908 | 0.0861 | 0.0908 |
| $e$ | 0.1753 | 0.2186 | 0.2571 | 0.2961 | 0.3277 | 0.363 |
| $k$ | 0.0621 | 0.2179 | 0.0188 | 0.1025 | −0.0921 | −0.3962 |
| *(iv) No interasset and intersector wedges: all assets, corporate and non-corporate* | | | | | | |
| $\sigma - \pi$ | 0.1143 | 0.1143 | 0.1143 | 0.1143 | 0.0626 | 0.0626 |
| $e$ | 0.3789 | 0.3789 | 0.4406 | 0.4406 | 0.0761 | 0.0761 |
| $k$ | −0.0092 | 0.0741 | −0.0685 | −0.1107 | 0 | 0 |
| *(v) No interasset and intersector wedges: all assets, all sectors* | | | | | | |
| $\sigma - \pi$ | 0.0897 | 0.0897 | 0.0897 | 0.0897 | 0.0897 | 0.0897 |
| $e$ | 0.2086 | 0.2086 | 0.2872 | 0.2872 | 0.3549 | 0.3549 |
| $k$ | 0.0529 | 0.2249 | 0.0075 | 0.1129 | −0.1063 | −0.3802 |
| *(vi) Corporate tax integration* | | | | | | |
| $\sigma - \pi$ | 0.0921 | 0.1021 | 0.0921 | 0.1021 | 0.0626 | 0.0626 |
| $e$ | 0.2296 | 0.3048 | 0.3061 | 0.3738 | 0.0761 | 0.0761 |
| $k$ | 0.0468 | 0.1488 | 0 | 0 | 0 | 0 |

$\sigma - \pi$: Social rate of return.
$e$: Effective tax rate.
$k$: Investment tax credit.
$\pi$: Inflation rate.

within each time period. The welfare gain is estimated to be $5567.0 billion. Most of this can be attributed to the elimination of tax wedges between business and household sectors, as in the third simulation.

The sixth simulation, corporate tax integration, is the key to President Bush's Advisory Panel's Simplified Income Tax Plan. In this simulation we eliminate tax wedges between the assets in the corporate and non-corporate assets by setting the

**Table 10.13** Welfare effects of tax distortion: 2010 tax law (billions of 2011 US$)[a]

| Eliminated wedges and method of revenue adjustment | Welfare effect | |
|---|---|---|
| | Additive[b] | Proportional[c] |
| (i) Within sector interasset distortion | | |
| Lump–sum tax adjustment | 479.0 | 479.0 |
| Labor income tax adjustment | 473.7 | 551.6 |
| Sales tax adjustment | 483.2 | 483.2 |
| Individual income tax adjustment | 474.3 | 570.0 |
| (ii) Intersector distortion: corporate and non-corporate sectors | | |
| Lump–sum tax adjustment | 40.7 | 40.7 |
| Labor income tax adjustment | −27.4 | −62.8 |
| Sales tax adjustment | −70.5 | −70.5 |
| Individual income tax adjustment | −63.4 | −100.9 |
| (iii) Intersector distortion: all sectors | | |
| Lump–sum tax adjustment | 5347.8 | 5347.8 |
| Labor income tax adjustment | 5326.2 | 5367.5 |
| Sales tax adjustment | 5313.2 | 5313.2 |
| Individual income tax adjustment | 5313.0 | 5364.2 |
| (iv) Interasset and intersector distortion: corporate and non-corporate sectors, all assets | | |
| Lump–sum tax adjustment | 303.9 | 303.9 |
| Labor income tax adjustment | 253.9 | 248.1 |
| Sales tax adjustment | 223.0 | 223.0 |
| Individual income tax adjustment | 227.6 | 226.9 |
| (v) Interasset and intersector distortion: all sectors, all assets | | |
| Lump–sum tax adjustment | 5567.0 | 5567.0 |
| Labor income tax adjustment | 5558.1 | 5619.4 |
| Sales tax adjustment | 5550.3 | 5550.3 |
| Individual income tax adjustment | 5545.4 | 5612.6 |
| (vi) Corporate tax integration (set $\sigma^q = \sigma^m$) | | |
| Lump–sum tax adjustment | 2320.2 | 2320.2 |
| Labor income tax adjustment | 1715.4 | 398.3 |
| Sales tax adjustment | 1237.6 | 1237.6 |
| Individual income tax adjustment | 1422.4 | 100.0 |
| (vii) Capital income taxes (business and personal) | | |
| Lump–sum tax adjustment | 5176.7 | 5177.0 |
| Labor income tax adjustment | 3858.5 | −1104.7 |
| Sales tax adjustment | 3138.3 | 3138.3 |
| Individual income tax adjustment | 3858.5 | −1104.7 |
| (viii) Capital income taxes and sales tax on investment goods | | |
| Lump–sum tax adjustment | 5628.2 | 5628.4 |
| Labor income tax adjustment | 3997.9 | −3799.3 |

*(Continued)*

**Table 10.13** Welfare effects of tax distortion: 2010 tax law (billions of 2011 US$)[a]—cont'd

| Eliminated wedges and method of revenue adjustment | Welfare effect | |
| --- | --- | --- |
| | Additive[b] | Proportional[c] |
| Sales tax adjustment | 2996.1 | 2995.5 |
| Individual income tax adjustment | 3997.9 | −3799.3 |
| (ix) Capital income taxes and property taxes | | |
| Lump-sum tax adjustment | 6054.0 | 6054.0 |
| Labor income tax adjustment | 3490.1 | −18738.7 |
| Sales tax adjustment | 2557.6 | 2557.8 |
| Individual income tax adjustment | 3490.1 | −18738.7 |
| (x) Capital income taxes, sales tax on investment goods, and property taxes | | |
| Lump-sum tax adjustment | 6421.8 | 6422.1 |
| Labor income tax adjustment | 3543.4 | −25441.2 |
| Sales tax adjustment | 2280.6 | 2280.4 |
| Individual income tax adjustment | 3543.4 | −25441.2 |

[a]Inflation is fixed at 4% per year.
[b]Under the additive tax adjustment, the average and marginal tax rates of labor income and the average tax rates of individual capital income are adjusted in the same percentage points. The marginal tax rates of individual capital income are adjusted in the same proportion as the marginal tax rate of labor income.
[c]Under the proportional tax adjustment, average and marginal tax rates are adjusted in the same proportion.

social rates of return of corporate assets equal to the corresponding rates on non-corporate assets. The tax burdens on the corporate assets are unambiguously reduced without an offsetting increase in other marginal tax rates. The estimated welfare gains are $2320.2 billion, less than half the gains from eliminating all tax wedges among sectors and assets.

In the first six simulations we have focused on the distorting impact of tax wedges among sectors and assets. In the following four simulations, we estimate the welfare cost of tax distortions resulting from wedges between before- and after-tax rates of return. We eliminate the distortions caused by the taxes on capital income, including property taxes and sales taxes on investment goods. In the seventh simulation we set the effective tax rates on all forms of capital equal to be zero.

We find that elimination of capital income taxes at both individual and corporate levels generates a welfare gain of $5176.7 billion. Eliminating sales taxes on investment goods as well increases this gain to $5628.2 billion. Eliminating capital income taxes and property taxes produces a gain of $6054.0 billion, while eliminating taxes on investment goods as well generates a gain of $6421.8 billion.

Table 10.13 also shows that the magnitudes of welfare gains under alternative tax adjustments. Since the elimination of tax wedges is not revenue-neutral, changes in tax rates to generate the missing revenue can produce significant distortions. For this reason the welfare effects are very sensitive to the method for revenue adjustment. These effects are most sensitive to the choice between lump–sum tax adjustment and the distorting tax adjustments. The results are also somewhat sensitive to choices among the distorting tax adjustments, especially when the required revenue is large.

## 10.5.3 Efficient Taxation of Income

Our final simulation is intended to measure the distortions associated with progressivity of the tax on labor income. A progressive tax on labor income produces marginal tax rates far in excess of average tax rates. Our point of departure is the elimination of all tax distortions in panel (v) of Table 10.13. In Table 10.14 we replace the progressive labor income tax by a proportional labor income tax. Under a lump–sum tax adjustment this generates a welfare gain of $6963.6 billion — a substantial increase over the gain from eliminating all capital income distortions.

We conclude that a tax reform that would combine elimination of tax wedges among all sectors and assets with substitution of a proportional tax on labor income for a graduated tax would produce the greatest gain in consumer welfare. Elimination of the tax wedges would remove barriers to efficient allocation of capital. The lower marginal tax rate on labor income would substantially reduce distortions from labor income taxes.

Table 10.14 describes the new approach to tax reform that we call Efficient Taxation of Income. This would avoid a drastic shift in tax burdens by introducing different tax rates for property-type income and earned income from work — a distinction that existed in the US tax code between 1969 and 1982. An important advantage of Efficient Taxation of Income is that the tax bases would be defined exactly as in the existing tax code, so that no cumbersome transition rules would be required.

The key to Efficient Taxation of Income is the system of investment tax credits presented in Table 10.12. These credits would equalize the tax burdens on all sources of business income. The average tax credits for corporations would be 5.3% on equipment and 22.5% on structures. Non-corporate business would receive smaller credits of 0.8% on equipment and 11.3% on structures. In order to equalize tax burdens on business and

**Table 10.14** Welfare cost of labor tax progressivity under efficient capital allocation (billions of 2011 US$)

| | Revenue adjustment | | |
|---|---|---|---|
| | Progressive | | Proportional |
| | Additive | Proportional | Additive |
| Lump–sum tax | 5567 | 5567 | 6963.6 |
| Labor income tax | 5558.1 | 5619.4 | 6961.1 |
| Sales tax | 5550.3 | 5550.3 | 6988.2 |
| Individual income tax | 5545.4 | 5612.6 | 6980.7 |

1. Inflation is fixed at 4% per year.
2. The figures for the progressive labor income tax are the same as in Panel (v) of Table 10.13.

household assets, prepayments of taxes on new investments by households would be required. The prepayment rates given in Table 10.12 would be 10.6% on new durables and 38% on new housing. The additional revenue from these prepayments would precisely offset the tax credits for business investment, preserving revenue neutrality.

Under Efficient Taxation of Income individuals would continue to file the familiar Form 1040 for individual income, while corporations would file corporate income tax returns. Deductions from taxable income, as well as tax credits and exemptions, would be unaffected. Businesses would continue to claim depreciation on past investments, as well as tax deductions for interest paid on debt. Mortgage interest and property taxes would be deductible from individual income for tax purposes. The tax treatment of Social Security and Medicare would remain the same, and the private pension fund industry would not be eviscerated.

It is important to emphasize that prepayments would apply only to new investments in owner-occupied housing and consumers' durables. Owners of existing homes and consumer durables would be deemed to have prepaid all taxes at the time of their original purchase. No additional taxes would be imposed on housing or durables already in the hands of households. This is essential for enactment, since 65% of households own their homes. Home owners are also voters who can express their concerns about maintaining the value of their property and new taxes on existing homes at the ballot box.

The prepayments under Efficient Taxation of Income are essential to protect property values after tax reform is enacted. The cost of new housing reflects the cost of capital to businesses, including the taxes paid on capital income. These taxes would be reduced sharply for corporations and substantially for non-corporate businesses. Without tax prepayments in place, the price of new housing would plummet. This price decline would erode the price structure for existing housing, leading to capital losses for home owners. After introduction of Efficient Taxation of Income most existing home owners would enjoy a modest capital gain.

A second point to emphasize is that tax credits for new investments in structures by corporations and non-corporate businesses would apply to new rental housing. These credits would provide incentives for real estate developers to expand the construction of rental housing. The added supply of rental housing would provide existing renters with more attractive and affordable options. It would also substantially reduce housing costs for newly formed households.

In summary, Efficient Taxation of Income would preserve all the features of the existing tax code that have been carefully crafted by generations of lawmakers since adoption of the Federal income tax in 1912. At the same time this new approach to tax reform would remedy the conspicuous deficiencies in our income tax system. These arise from differential taxation of corporate income and exclusion of owner-occupied housing, as well as consumers' durables, from the income tax base. In addition, substantial gains would arise from replacing the progressive taxation of labor income by a proportional labor income tax. We turn next to tax reforms that would shift the tax base from income to consumption.

## 10.6 CONSUMPTION TAX REFORM

A useful starting point for the definition of consumption for tax purposes is personal consumption expenditures (PCE), as defined in the US NIPA.[37] However, the taxation of the services of household capital poses significant administrative problems, reviewed in the US Department of the Treasury (1984) monograph on tax reform. The services of owner-occupied housing and consumers' durables could be taxed by the "prepayment method" described by Bradford (1986). Taxes on these capital services would be prepaid by including investment rather than consumption in the tax base, as in Efficient Taxation of Income.

Proposals to replace income by consumption as a tax base in the US were revived during the 1990s. We compare the economic impact of consumption tax proposals, taking the 2010 Tax Law as a point of departure. In Section 10.6.1 we consider impact of the Hall–Rabushka proposal and the closely related Armey–Shelby Proposal. These are similar to the Growth and Investment Plan of President Bush's Advisory Panel (2005). In Section 10.6.2 we analyze the economic impact of replacing the existing tax system by a National Retail Sales Tax (NRST). We consider combinations of consumption and labor income taxes and evaluate the cost of progressivity by comparing proportional or "flat" taxes with graduated or "progressive" taxes.

### 10.6.1 Alternative proposals

The "subtraction method" for implementing a consumption tax is the basis for the ingenious Flat Tax proposed by Hall and Rabushka (1983, 1995). The Hall–Rabushka proposal divides tax collections between firms and households. Firms would expense or "subtract" the cost of all purchases from other businesses, including investment goods. Firms would also deduct purchases of labor services, so that labor compensation — wages and salaries, health insurance, pension contributions, and other supplements — could be taxed at the individual level. This facilitates the introduction of personal allowances for low-income taxpayers in order to achieve progressivity.

Taxation of business firms under the Hall–Rabushka proposal is different from the current income tax system in three ways. (i) A constant tax rate would be applied to the tax base, hence the identification of this proposal as a Flat Tax. (ii) Interest paid by the firm would no longer be tax deductible. (iii) Investment spending would be recovered through immediate write-offs, so that the effective tax rate on new investments would be zero. The inclusion of interest payments in the tax base eliminates the differential tax

---

[37] See Bureau of Economic Analysis (2011).

treatment of debt and equity, insuring financial neutrality of the tax system. These features of the Flat Tax have been incorporated into President Bush's Advisory Panel's Growth and Investment Plan.

The Armey–Shelby proposal, introduced in the 104th Congress by former Representative Richard Armey and Senator Dick Shelby, is a variant of the Hall–Rabushka Flat Tax proposal.[38] The Armey–Shelby proposal is more generous to the taxpayer than the Hall–Rabushka proposal, since the tax rate is lower after the first two years and the family allowances are higher. The natural question is, would the Armey–Shelby proposal achieve revenue neutrality? Since Hall and Rabushka have set the Flat Tax rate to make the Hall–Rabushka proposal revenue-neutral, it is clear that tax revenue under the Armey–Shelby would fall short of neutrality. We will show, however, that neither proposal would achieve revenue neutrality.

A proposal for replacing the income tax system with a NRST has been introduced by former Representatives Dan Schaefer, Bill Tauzin and others.[39] The Schaefer–Tauzin proposal replaces personal and corporate income taxes, estate and gift taxes, and some excise taxes with a 15% national retail sales tax on a tax-inclusive consumption base. On this definition the tax base would include sales tax revenues as well as the value of retail sales to consumers. The Schaefer–Tauzin proposal allows for a family consumption refund in order to achieve progressivity.

To achieve revenue neutrality through a NRST, we consider a number of alternatives to the Schaefer–Tauzin proposal. In all of these alternatives, new investment would be excluded from the tax base. We first construct a prototype NRST, and then develop alternative proposals by varying the degree of progressivity and the division of revenues between the sales tax and a labor income tax. The labor tax may be flat or proportional to the tax base, or may be graduated by introducing a system of family allowances.

## 10.6.2 Modeling the tax reform proposals

We maintain the role of the property tax in the existing US tax system in all of our simulations. However, we consider alternative treatments of existing sales taxes on consumption and investment goods. The key tax parameter of the Hall–Rabushka and Armey–Shelby proposals is the Flat Tax rate. If investment is expensed, the effective tax rate on new investment is zero, whatever the Flat Tax rate, so that the choice of this rate does not affect intertemporal resource allocation. However, the Flat Tax rate plays a very important role in the labor–leisure choice by households. It also affects the tax burden on capital assets already accumulated at the time of the reform.

---

[38] Armey and Shelby (1995).

[39] The Schaefer–Tauzin proposal was first introduced in the 104th Congress of 1996 and again in the 105th Congress in 1997. See Schaefer (1997). An alternative national sales tax proposal was introduced by former Representative John Linder (2005).

Since compensation for labor input would be excluded from a business firm's tax base, the marginal and average tax rates are the same as the statutory flat rate, unless value added by the firm falls short of the compensation for labor input. However, a substantial proportion of households are exempt from taxation due to personal allowances, so that marginal and average tax rates on labor income are very different.

Under the Hall–Rabushka proposal the statutory Flat Tax rate is 19%. Under the Armey–Shelby proposal a Flat Tax rate of 20% applies in the first two years after the tax reform, followed by a lower rate of 17% thereafter. These rates are chosen in order to replace federal tax revenues. In our model all three levels of government — federal, state and local — are combined into a single government sector. If the federal income tax is replaced by a Flat Tax, we assume that the state and local income taxes are also replaced by a Flat Tax. In addition, we assume that the state and local Flat Tax is deductible at the federal level. In order to determine the federal and state and local Flat Tax rates for corporations, we calibrate the Flat Tax rates to the 2010 federal and state and local corporate income tax revenues.

The average marginal tax rate for labor income is defined as a weighted average of the marginal tax rates of individual taxpayers, where the share of labor income for each taxpayer in total labor income is used as the weight. The average tax rate is simply the total tax revenue divided by total labor income. Using the same NIPA for 1993 as Hall and Rabushka,[40] we estimate that the average labor income tax rate is 0.0855 for the Hall–Rabushka Flat Tax proposal.

In order to determine the average marginal tax rates for the Hall–Rabushka and Armey–Shelby proposals on a consistent basis, we require the distribution of labor income by the marginal tax rate of the individual taxpayer. We use the Current Population Survey to estimate the average and the average marginal federal tax rates on labor income for both the Hall–Rabushka and Armey–Shelby Flat Tax proposals.[41]

In order to determine the average marginal tax rate on labor income for the government sector as a whole, we follow the same procedure as in calculating the federal and state and local Flat Tax rates for corporations. In place of the corporate income tax revenues, we use the individual income tax revenues for 2010. The results are that the average marginal tax rate is 0.2214 for Hall–Rabushka and 0.1924 for Armey–Shelby. The corresponding figure for the Tax Law of 2010 is 0.2509. Our estimate of the average tax rate is 0.0902 for Hall–Rabushka and 0.0704 for Armey–Shelby. These figures may be compared with the corresponding figure of 0.0950 for the 2010 Tax Law, or with the federal tax rate of 0.0855 estimated by Hall and Rabushka.

We can summarize the tax rates as follows:
- Hall–Rabushka:
  - Business tax rate, average and marginal: 0.2162

---

[40] Hall and Rabushka (1995, p. 57, Table 3.1).
[41] We are indebted to M. S. Ho for these calculations. For more details, see Ho and Stiroh (1998).

- Labor income tax rate, marginal: 0.2214
- Labor income tax rate, average: 0.0902
- Armey—Shelby:
  - Business tax rate, average and marginal: 0.1941
  - Labor income tax rate, marginal: 0.1924
  - Labor income tax rate, average: 0.0704
- Tax Law of 2010:
  - Corporate income tax rate: 0.3877
  - Labor income tax rate, marginal: 0.2509
  - Labor income tax rate, average: 0.0950

We develop alternative plans for the NRST by combining a sales tax on consumption and a labor income tax. Taxation of capital income is eliminated in all these plans. Although the existing sales taxes on investment may or may not be abolished as part of tax reform, we prefer the policies with no sales taxes on investment. As before, property taxes are left unchanged in our simulations. The alternative proposals differ in progressivity. They also differ in the revenue-raising roles of the sales tax and the labor income tax. This has the effect of altering the relative tax burden between labor income and capital accumulated prior to reform.

We first construct prototype sales tax and labor income taxes. The labor income tax is based on the Hall—Rabushka Flat Tax proposal. The sales tax is a Flat Tax rate with personal exemptions. We set the proportion of total exemptions in retail sales equal to the proportion of total exemptions in Hall—Rabushka, which is 0.3516. Assuming that the federal sales tax rate is 17%, as in Aaron and Gale (1996, Table 1.1), we estimate that the corresponding average tax rate is 11.02%. In order to represent the current sales taxes, used mainly by the state and local government, we add a Flat Tax of 5.37% to the progressive tax system we have derived.

We construct eight alternative NRST plans. Each plan consists of two parts — a sales tax and a labor income tax. The first two plans are limited to a sales tax, while the last two consist of a labor income tax alone.[42] Although these two plans are not sales taxes in the usual sense, they provide benchmarks for analyzing the economic impacts of the NRST plans. We evaluate the impacts on efficiency of resource allocation for all eight plans.

In Plan 1, a progressive NRST replaces the capital and labor income taxes. Since the revenue requirement is very large in relation to the sales tax base, we start with marginal and average tax rates twice as high as those of the prototype consumption tax. These sales tax rates serve as the starting values of our simulations, but are adjusted to achieve revenue neutrality. In Plan 2, we remove the progressivity from the sales tax of Plan 1 and set the marginal tax rate equal to the average tax rate.

---

[42] We discuss the equivalence of consumption and labor income taxes in Jorgenson and Yun (2001, section 8.4, pp. 353—364).

In Plan 3, we introduce a prototype labor income tax from the Hall–Rabushka Flat Tax proposal and combine this with a prototype sales tax with the progressivity removed. As a consequence, the sales tax is flat or proportional while the labor income tax has the same progressivity as Hall–Rabushka. Compared with Plan 1, the role of the sales tax as an instrument for tax collection and redistribution is substantially reduced.

In Plan 4, we replace the current income tax system with the combination of a flat sales tax and a flat labor income tax. Since no attempt is made to achieve progressivity, this plan would be politically unpopular. On the other hand, the efficiency loss is minimal, so that Plan 4 provides a useful benchmark for evaluation of the potential cost of trading off efficiency against equity.

Plan 5 combines a progressive sales tax with a flat labor income tax. The sales tax rates are the same as in the prototype sales tax plan and the rate of the labor income tax is set at the average tax rate of the Hall–Rabushka proposal. Plan 6 combines the prototype sales tax with the labor income tax of the Hall–Rabushka proposal. Since both segments of the plan are progressive, the sacrifice of efficiency could be substantial.

Plan 7, the labor income tax is flat or proportional and there is no sales tax. The average and marginal tax rates of labor income are equal. Since all the tax revenue is raised by the tax on labor, we start with a labor income tax rate twice that of the Hall–Rabushka Flat Tax proposal. Finally, in Plan 8, we introduce an element of progressivity into Plan 7 by setting the average and the average marginal tax rate of labor income at twice the level in the Hall–Rabushka proposal.

We preserve revenue neutrality by requiring the government sector to follow the same time paths of real spending and government debt under all tax reform proposals. We also fix the time paths of the claims on the rest of the world. These assumptions are necessary to separate the economic impacts of alternative tax policies from the effects of changes in the government budget and the balance of payments. Government revenues must be adjusted through changes in the tax policy instruments in order to satisfy the government budget constraints in every period along the transition path to a steady state.

Investment spending on household assets is included in the sales tax base under the Schaefer–Tauzin proposal. The most important type of investment spending is the purchase of owner-occupied housing. We model the sales tax on household investment by imposing taxes on sales to the household sector. At the same time we increase the price of capital services by the amount of the sales tax. This is equivalent to prepayment of the consumption tax on household capital services.

### 10.6.3 Welfare impact of consumption taxation

In Table 10.15 we present two sets of welfare impacts. In the first set of simulations the corporate and individual income taxes of 2010 are replaced by the Hall–Rabushka

**Table 10.15** Welfare effects of fundamental tax reform—flat tax (billions of 2011 US$)[a]

| Tax reform proposal and revenue adjustment | Welfare effect | |
|---|---|---|
| | $t_C = t_C^a = t_I = 0.0537$ | $t_C = t_C^a = t_I = 0.0$ |
| 1. Hall—Rabushka | | |
| Lump-sum tax | 5111.8 | 6308.2 |
| Flat tax | 3789.8 | 2819.6 |
| Sales taxes | 4064.6 | — |
| Flat tax and sales taxes | 3912.0 | — |
| 2. Armey—Shelby | | |
| Lump-sum tax | 5444.3 | 6541.5 |
| Flat tax | 3299 | 1806.7 |
| Sales taxes | 3912.1 | — |
| Flat tax and sales taxes | 3626.8 | — |

[a]Inflation is fixed at 4% per year.
$t_C$: Marginal sales tax rate on consumption goods.
$t_C^a$: Average sales tax rate on consumption goods.
$t_I$: Sales tax rate on investment goods.

or Armey—Shelby Flat Tax, while sales taxes on consumption and investment goods remain unchanged Column (2). In the second set of simulations we replace the sales taxes as well, so that marginal and average consumption taxes, as well as taxes on investment are zero. In these simulations, all tax distortions, except for the property tax, are eliminated.

If both income taxes and sales taxes are replaced by a Flat Tax, and a lump-sum tax is used to compensate for the revenue shortfall, the welfare gains are very substantial, $5111.8 billion US dollars of 2011 for Hall—Rabushka and $5444.3 billion for Armey—Shelby. If sales taxes, as well as a corporate and individual income taxes, are replaced with a Flat Tax and a lump-sum tax is used to raise the additional revenue, the gains are even larger — $6308.2 billion for Hall—Rabushka and $6541.5 billion for Armey—Shelby.

The welfare gains from the Flat Tax proposals are lower when distorting taxes are increased to meet the revenue requirement. If the Flat Tax rate is adjusted to make up the revenue shortfall, substitution of the Hall—Rabushka Flat Tax for corporate and individual income taxes would produce a welfare gain of only $3789.8 billion. If sales taxes are also replaced the gain falls to $2819.6 billion. The corresponding welfare gains for the Armey—Shelby Flat Tax are $3299.0 billion for replacement of income taxes and $1806.7 billion for replacement of sales taxes as well. These results imply that the distortions resulting from the Flat Tax are worse than those from sales taxes.[43]

---

[43] A high Flat Tax rate implies a heavy lump-sum tax on "old" capital, offsetting the distorting effects of the tax on labor.

President Bush's Advisory Panel has proposed a Growth and Investment Tax Plan that would permit the expensing of business investment and disallow interest deductions from corporate income. However, the Growth and Investment Tax Plan would retain mortgage interest tax deductions at the individual level, introducing a substantial subsidy for owner-occupied housing.[44] This has the advantage of preserving incentives for home ownership, as requested by President Bush. However, it undercuts the equalization of tax burdens on business assets and owner-occupied housing associated with consumption taxes, such as the Hall—Rabushka and Armey—Shelby Flat Tax proposals.

Table 10.16 reports the welfare effects of the six plans for replacing the corporate and individual income taxes with an NRST and the two additional plans for replacing income taxes with a labor income tax. We present two sets of simulations — one with the sales tax on investment goods and the other without. First, note that the case without a sales tax on investment goods is more in the spirit of the NRST, which exempts sales taxes on investment goods from taxation.

Second, in Plans 1—6 a sales tax is included as a part of the replacement tax policy. These sales taxes on consumption goods together with sales taxes on investment goods generate revenue surpluses and require either a negative lump-sum tax adjustment or a decrease in tax rates. This explains the fact that welfare gains under the lump-sum tax adjustment are lower than under other tax adjustments.[45] Plan 4 with flat sales and labor income taxes and no tax on investment goods attains a welfare gain of $6574.9 billion. However, Plan 2 and Plan 7 are not far behind in terms of gains in welfare. Finally, the welfare gains attainable with the progressive Plans 1, 3 and 5 are also quite high.

A second set of comparisons highly relevant to deliberations about tax reform is the cost of progressivity. One of the most attractive features of the Hall—Rabushka and Armey—Shelby Flat Tax proposals is the possibility of introducing a system of family allowances in order to preserve the progressivity of the existing US tax system. Plan 1 for the NRST retains this feature, but generates welfare gains of $6090.8 billion with a distorting sales tax adjustment, more than doubling the gains of the Hall—Rabushka Flat Tax proposal with a distorting flat tax adjustment. The NRST is clearly superior to the Flat Tax as an approach to tax reform.

The costs of progressivity can be ascertained by comparing the welfare gains between Plan 1, a progressive sales tax, with Plan 2, a flat sales tax. With no sales tax on investment goods and adjustment of the sales tax on consumption goods to achieve revenue neutrality, the gain in welfare from eliminating progressivity is $530 billion. When this is added to the welfare gain of a progressive sales tax of $6090.8 billion, the overall gain is $6620.8 billion. Other comparisons between progressive and flat tax versions on the

---

[44] See President's Advisory Panel (2005, Figure 7.3, p. 165).
[45] Revenue shortfalls occur in Plan 7.

**Table 10.16** Welfare effects of fundamental tax reform—national retail sales tax (billions of 2011 US$)[a]

| Tax reform proposal and revenue adjustment | Welfare effect | |
|---|---|---|
| | $t_l = 0.0537$ | $t_l = 0.0$ |
| **1. Progressive sales, no labor income tax** | | |
| Lump-sum tax | 4807.7 | 5332.4 |
| Labor income tax | — | — |
| Sales taxes | 5959.2 | 6090.8 |
| Labor income tax and sales taxes | — | — |
| **2. Flat sales, no labor income tax** | | |
| Lump-sum tax | 5748.7 | 6180.8 |
| Labor income tax | — | — |
| Sales taxes | 6460.0 | 6620.8 |
| Labor income tax and sales taxes | — | — |
| **3. Flat sales tax, progressive labor income tax** | | |
| Lump-sum tax | 4880.1 | 5395.0 |
| Labor income tax | 5817.3 | 5633.8 |
| Sales taxes | 5256.4 | 5471.4 |
| Labor income tax and sales taxes | 5465.7 | 5531.2 |
| **4. Flat sales, flat labor income tax** | | |
| Lump-sum tax | 6196.8 | 6574.9 |
| Labor income tax | 6408.3 | 6639.8 |
| Sales taxes | 6450.4 | 6638.6 |
| Labor income tax and sales taxes | 6437.7 | 6639.3 |
| **5. Progressive sales tax, flat labor income tax** | | |
| Lump-sum tax | 5799.3 | 6226.9 |
| Labor income tax | 6053.4 | 6297.0 |
| Sales taxes | 6163.8 | 6317.8 |
| Labor income tax and sales taxes | 6128.0 | 6309.8 |
| **6. Progressive sales tax, progressive labor income tax** | | |
| Lump-sum tax | 4215.3 | 4790.1 |
| Labor income tax | 5272.4 | 4995.5 |
| Sales taxes | 4726.3 | 4875.7 |
| Labor income tax and sales taxes | 4927.6 | 4919.8 |
| **7. No sales, flat labor income tax** | | |
| Lump-sum tax | 6499.9 | 6814.5 |
| Labor income tax | 6288.9 | 6489.4 |
| Sales taxes | — | — |
| Labor income tax and sales taxes | — | — |
| **8. No sales, progressive labor tax** | | |
| Lump-sum tax | 2248.2 | 2918.4 |

*(Continued)*

**Table 10.16** Welfare effects of fundamental tax reform—national retail sales tax (billions of 2011 US$)[a]—cont'd

| Tax reform proposal and revenue adjustment | Welfare effect | |
|---|---|---|
| | $t_I = 0.0537$ | $t_I = 0.0$ |
| Labor income tax | −3343.5 | −6564.4 |
| Sales taxes | — | — |
| Labor income tax and sales taxes | — | — |

[a]Inflation is fixed at 4% per year.
$t_I$: Sales tax rate on investment goods.

NRST given in Table 10.16 generate estimates of the cost of progressivity that are similar in magnitude.

Since tax wedges distort resource allocation, a critical requirement for comparisons among alternative tax reform proposals is that all proposals must raise the same amount of revenue. The authors of the Hall—Rabushka Flat Tax proposal have calibrated their tax rates to the NIPA for 1993 so that the resulting tax regime is revenue-neutral. It is clear that the Armey—Shelby proposal falls short of revenue neutrality because it is more generous in personal allowances and applies a lower tax rate than the Hall—Rabushka proposal. However, the Hall—Rabushka proposal also fails the test of revenue neutrality.

The need for a major upward adjustment in the Flat Tax rate conflicts with the claim by Hall and Rabushka that their proposal is designed to be revenue-neutral. The explanation is that the dataset employed by Hall and Rabushka, the US NIPA of 1993, was generated under a tax system with a significant tax burden on capital.[46] Although the Flat Tax imposed a lump-sum tax on "old" capital accumulated before the tax reform, the Flat Tax does not impose any tax burden on "new" capital accumulated through investment after the reform. The tax base of the business portion of the tax shrinks dramatically and a large revenue shortfall emerges, requiring an increase in the Flat Tax rate.

From the point of view of efficiency the most attractive approach to tax reform we have considered is Plan 4 for the NRST, which combines a flat sales tax with a flat labor income tax and eliminates sales taxes on investment goods. The welfare gain would be diminished relatively little by shifting the burden toward the labor income tax, as in Plan 7. The combination of an NRST collected at the retail level and a labor income tax collected as at present would also be administratively attractive.

---

[46] In 1993, the corporate income taxes were $138.3 billion for the Federal Government and $26.9 billion for the state and local governments. In the same year, the Federal Government collected $508.1 billion of income tax from individuals, and the state and local governments collected $124.2 billion.

## 10.7 CONCLUSIONS

Our overall conclusion is that the most substantial gains from tax reform are associated with equalizing tax burdens on all assets and all sectors and eliminating the progressive taxation of labor income. Efficient Taxation of Income produces the largest welfare gains of any proposal that we consider. Since the definitions of individual and corporate income would be unchanged, no cumbersome transition rules would be required. Efficient Taxation of Income could be enacted today and implemented tomorrow.

Integration of corporate and individual taxes is a key objective of President Bush's Advisory Panel's Simplified Income Tax Plan. The purpose of this proposal is to eliminate the double taxation of corporate income. The Advisory Panel's plan would leave a substantial tax wedge between corporate and non-corporate income, and would actually increase the wedge between business income and owner-occupied housing.

We have shown that the most popular Flat Tax proposals would generate substantial welfare gains. President Bush's Advisory Panel's Growth and Investment Plan would follow the subtraction approach to consumption taxation for business income employed by Hall and Rabushka. However, this Plan would introduce a substantial tax subsidy for owner-occupied housing and would fail to achieve the benefits of equalizing the tax burdens on business assets and owner-occupied housing.

A NRST with the same progressivity as the Hall—Rabushka Flat Tax would produce welfare gains that are 50% higher. This would require a marginal sales tax rate of around 34% and an average sales tax rate of more than 25% for revenue neutrality. These rates would provide substantial incentives for tax evasion and erosion of the tax base, boosting the required marginal and average tax rates even further. The Advisory Panel's selection of the subtraction method of the Flat Tax for its consumption tax proposal undoubtedly reflects these administrative issues associated with a progressive NRST.

The cost of maintaining a progressive rate structure within the framework of the NRST is substantial. This is due to the increase in the marginal tax rate on consumption required to compensate for the loss of portions of the tax base that are required to achieve progressivity. However, the benefits of a NRST with a flat rate structure are double those of a Flat Tax. These welfare gains are nearly comparable with the largest gains from Efficient Taxation of Income. However, gains from combining Efficient Taxation of Income with a proportional tax on labor income would be much greater.

We conclude that the frontier for economic analysis of tax and spending programs is to combine estimates of social rates of return for alternative tax policies with estimates of substitution possibilities by businesses and households. This can be done by means of a dynamic general equilibrium model like the one that we have presented in this chapter. This model also facilitates the evaluation of alternative tax reforms programs in terms of their impact on economic welfare.

We have illustrated the dynamic general equilibrium methodology for evaluating alternative proposals for a variety of tax reforms. These are based on two broad approaches to reform. (i) Reform the existing income tax, as in Efficient Taxation of Income. (ii) Replace income by consumption as a tax base. Our detailed illustrations can serve as a guide for policy makers who share our goal of making the allocation of capital and labor inputs within a market economy more efficient.

## ACKNOWLEDGMENTS

We are indebted to Peter Dixon for editorial suggestions and Stefan Boeters for detailed comments on an earlier draft. We appreciate the help of Jon Samuels in developing the dataset used in the econometric work and the description of the US tax system. We are grateful to Trina Ott for editing and preparing the manuscript. Financial support was provided by the Alliance for Competitive Taxation.

## REFERENCES

Aaron, H.J., Gale, W.G. (Eds.), 1996. Economic Effects of Fundamental Tax Reform. Brookings Institution, Washington, DC.
Armey, D., Shelby, R., 1995. Freedom and Fairness Restoration Act of 1995, H.R.2060 and S. 1050. Bill Summary and Status for 104th Congress. House of Representatives, U.S. Congress, Washington, DC.
Ballard, C.L., Fullerton, D., Shoven, J.B., Whalley, J., 1985. A General Equilibrium Model for Tax Policy Evaluation. University of Chicago Press, Chicago, IL.
Barro, R.J., 1974. Are government bonds net wealth? J. Polit. Econ. 82, 1095–1117.
Barro, R.J., Sala-i-Martin, X., 2004. Economic Growth, second ed. MIT Press, Cambridge, MA.
Bartlett, B., 2012. The Benefit and the Burden: Tax Reform—Why We Need It and What It Will Take. Simon & Schuster, New York.
Bradford, David F, 1986. Untangling the Income Tax. Harvard University Press, Cambridge, MA.
Bradford, David F, 2004. The X-Tax in the World Economy: Going Global with a Simple, Progressive Tax. AEI Press, Washington, DC.
Bureau of Economic Analysis, 2011. Concepts and Methods of the US National Income and Product Accounts. US Department of Commerce, Washington, DC. Available at http://www.bea.gov/national/pdf/NIPAchapters1-9.pdf.
Chamley, C., 1981. The welfare cost of capital income taxation in a growing economy. J. Polit. Econ. 89, 468–496.
Christensen, L.R., Jorgenson, D.W., Lau, L.J., 1997. Transcendental Logarithmic Production Frontiers. In: Jorgenson, D.W. (Ed.), Measuring Social Welfare. MIT Press, Cambridge, MA, pp. 125–158.
Christensen, L.R., Jorgenson, D.W., Lau, L.J., 2000. Transcendental Logarithmic Utility Functions. In: Jorgenson, D.W. (Ed.), Aggregate Consumer Behavior. MIT Press, Cambridge, MA, pp. 1–28.
Congress of the United States, 2010. Tax Relief, Unemployment Insurance Reauthorization and Job Creation Act of 2010. Government Printing Office, Washington, DC.
Dixon, P.B., Jorgenson, D.W. (Eds.), 2012. Handbook of Computable General Equilibrium Modeling. North-Holland, Amsterdam.
Hall, R.E., Rabushka, A., 1983. Low Tax, Simple Tax, Fair Tax. McGraw-Hill, New York.
Hall, R.E., Rabushka, A., 1995. The Flat Tax, second ed. Hoover Institution Press, Stanford, CA.
Hayashi, F., 2000. The Cost of Capital, Q, and the Theory of Investment Demand. In: Lau, L.J. (Ed.), Econometrics and the Cost of Capital. MIT Press, Cambridge, MA, pp. 55–84.
Ho, M.S., Stiroh, K.J., 1998. Revenue, progressivity, and the flat tax. Contemp. Econ. Policy 45, 85–97.
Internal Revenue Service, 2001. Economic Growth and Tax Relief and Reconciliation Act of 2001: Public Law 107-16. Government Printing Office, Washington, DC.

Internal Revenue Service, 2003. Jobs and Growth Tax Relief Reconciliation Act of 2003. Government Printing Office, Washington, DC.

Jorgenson, D.W., 1996. Tax Policy and the Cost of Capital. MIT Press, Cambridge, MA.

Jorgenson, D.W., 1997. Aggregate Consumer Behavior and the Measurement of Social Welfare. In: Jorgenson, D.W. (Ed.), Measuring Social Welfare. MIT Press, Cambridge, MA, pp. 1–38.

Jorgenson, D.W. (Ed.), 2000. Econometric Modeling of Producer Behavior. MIT Press, Cambridge, MA.

Jorgenson, D.W., Fraumeni, B.M., 2000. Relative Prices and Technical Change. In: Jorgenson, D.W. (Ed.), Econometric Modeling of Producer Behavior. MIT Press, Cambridge, MA, pp. 341–373.

Jorgenson, D.W., Laffont, J.-J., 2000. Efficient Estimation of Nonlinear Simultaneous Equations with Additive Disturbances. In: Jorgenson, D.W. (Ed.), Econometric Modeling of Producer Behavior. MIT Press, Cambridge, MA, pp. 209–240.

Jorgenson, D.W., Yun, K.-Y., 1996a. The Efficiency of Capital Allocation. In: Jorgenson, D.W. (Ed.), Tax Policy and the Cost of Capital. MIT Press, Cambridge, MA, pp. 299–320.

Jorgenson, D.W., Yun, K.-Y., 1996b. Tax Policy and Capital Allocation. In: Jorgenson, D.W. (Ed.), Tax Policy and the Cost of Capital. MIT Press, Cambridge, MA, pp. 321–364.

Jorgenson, D.W., Yun, K.-Y., 1996c. Tax Reform and US Economic Growth. In: Jorgenson, D.W. (Ed.), Tax Policy and the Cost of Capital. MIT Press, Cambridge, MA, pp. 365–410.

Jorgenson, D.W., Yun, K.-Y., 2001. Lifting the Burden: Tax Reform, the Cost of Capital, and US Economic Growth. MIT Press, Cambridge, MA.

Jorgenson, D.W., Yun, K.-Y., 2005. Efficient taxation of income. In: Kehoe, T.J., Srinivasan, T.N., Whalley, J. (Eds.), Frontiers in Applied General Equilibrium Modeling. Cambridge University Press, Cambridge, pp. 173–218.

Lau, L.J. (Ed.), 2005. Econometrics and the Cost of Capital. MIT Press, Cambridge, MA.

Linder, J., 2005. To Promote Freedom, Fairness, and Economic Opportunity by Repealing the Income Tax and Other Taxes, Abolishing the Internal Revenue Service, and Enacting a National Sales Tax to Be Administered Primarily by the States, H.R.25, January 4. House of Representatives, U.S. Congress, Washington, DC.

Lipton, D., Poterba, J., Sachs, J., Summers, L.H., 1982. Multiple shooting in rational expectations models. Econometrica 51, 1329–1333.

McFadden, D.L., 1963. Further results on CES production functions. Rev. Econ. Stud. 30 (2), 73–83.

National Commission on Fiscal Responsibility and Reform. 2010. The Moment of Truth, Washington, DC, Executive Office of the President. Available at http://www.fiscalcommission.gov/sites/fiscalcommission.gov/files/documents/TheMomentofTruth12_1_2010.pdf.

President's Advisory Panel on Federal Tax Reform. 2005. Simple, Fair, & Pro-Growth: Proposals to Fix America's Tax System, President's Advisory Panel on Federal Tax Reform. Washington, DC, November 1. See: http://govinfo.library.unt.edu/taxreformpanel/index-2.html

Schaefer, D., et al., 1997. National Retail Sales Act of 1996, H.R.3039 introduced in the 104th Congress, March 6, 1996. Also: National Retail Sales Tax Act of 1997, H.R.2001 introduced in the 105th Congress, June 19, 1997. House of Representatives, U.S. Congress, Washington, DC.

Slemrod, J., Bakija, J., 2008. Taxing Ourselves: A Citizen's Guide to the Debate over Taxes, fourth ed. MIT Press, Cambridge, MA (1st edition 1996).

Steuerle, E., 2008. Contemporary Tax Policy, second ed. Urban Institute Press, Washington, DC (1st edition 2004).

Sullivan, M.A., 2011. Corporate Tax Reform: Taxing Profits in the 21st Century. Apress, New York.

Tax Policy Center. 2012. Tax Reform Proposals. Available at http://www.taxpolicycenter.org/taxtopics/Tax_Reform_Proposals.cfm.

US Department of the Treasury, 1984. Tax Reform for Simplicity, Fairness, and Economic Growth, 3 vol. US Government Printing Office, Washington, DC.

US Department of the Treasury, 1992. Integration of the Individual and Corporate Tax Systems: Taxing Income Once. US Department of the Treasury, Office of Tax Analysis, Washington, DC.

Uzawa, H., 1962. Production functions with constant elasticities of substitution. Rev. Econ. Stud. 29, 291–299.

Yun, K.-Y., 2000. The Cost of Capital and Intertemporal General Equilibrium Modeling of Tax Policy Effects. In: Lau, L.J. (Ed.), Econometrics and the Cost of Capital. MIT Press, Cambridge, MA, pp. 227–272.

# CHAPTER 11

# Dynamic Overlapping Generations Computable General Equilibrium Models and the Analysis of Tax Policy: The Diamond–Zodrow Model

**George R. Zodrow\*, John W. Diamond\*\***

\*Economics Department and Tax and Expenditure Policy Program, Baker Institute for Public Policy, Rice University and Centre for Business Taxation, Oxford University
\*\*Tax and Expenditure Policy Program, Baker Institute for Public Policy, Rice University

## Abstract

We examine the use of dynamic overlapping generations (OLG) computable general equilibrium (CGE) models to analyze the economic effects of tax reforms, using as a paradigm our Diamond–Zodrow (DZ) model. Such models are especially well-suited to analyzing both the short-run transitional and the long-run dynamic macroeconomic effects of tax reforms, including the time paths of reform-induced changes in labor supply, saving, and investment, as well as the redistributional effects of reforms across and within generations. We begin with a brief overview of the use of OLG-CGE models in the analysis of tax reform, focusing on the seminal contribution of Auerbach and Kotlikoff (1987). We then consider a variety of extensions of this work, including the multiple-good, multiple-individual model constructed by Fullerton and Rogers (1993), as well as the addition of open economy factors, human capital accumulation and uncertainty. Many of the applications of these models have focused on changes in capital income taxation or, more generally, the replacement of an income tax system that fully taxes capital income with a consumption-based tax system that exempts normal returns to capital, and we focus on such reforms. We describe in considerable detail the DZ model, which is characterized by 55 cohorts, 12 income groups within each cohort, four production sectors and explicit calculation of reform-induced changes in asset values. We conclude by describing numerous applications of the DZ model, ranging from incremental reforms of the income tax system including deficit-financed tax cuts to 'fundamental tax reforms' that involve replacing the income tax with a consumption-based tax system, to the implementation of a value-added tax imposed in addition to the income tax as a means of reducing current deficits and the national debt in the US.

## Keywords

Computable general equilibrium, overlapping generations, dynamic modeling, tax reform simulation, incidence analysis, redistributive effects of tax reform, macroeconomic modeling

## JEL classification codes

C630, C680, H200, H220

*Handbook of CGE Modeling - Vol. 1 SET*
ISSN 2211-6885, http://dx.doi.org/10.1016/B978-0-444-59568-3.00011-0

© 2013 Elsevier B.V.
All rights reserved.

## 11.1 INTRODUCTION

The use of computable general equilibrium (CGE) models to analyze the effects of changes in economic policy has become widespread, as vividly demonstrated by the wide range of applications discussed in this Handbook. In this chapter, we focus on the use of dynamic overlapping generations (OLG) life-cycle CGE models to analyze the economic effects of tax reforms. Such models are characterized by a large number of adult cohorts and sometimes also have multiple types of individuals with varying lifetime incomes within each cohort. These models are especially well-suited to analyzing both the short-run transitional and the long-run dynamic macroeconomic effects of tax reforms, especially the time paths of reform-induced changes in labor supply, saving and investment, as well as the redistributional effects of reforms, including the changes in the prices of existing assets, across and within generations. The analysis of the effects of such behavioral responses and all of their complex interactions in a completely specified general equilibrium framework distinguishes the OLG-CGE approach from the alternative 'static' or 'microsimulation' approach that distributes the effects of tax reforms without taking into account such responses.[1] We examine both the structure of OLG-CGE models and their applications to analyzing tax reforms in this chapter, using as a paradigm a model that we have constructed, the Diamond–Zodrow (DZ) model.

The chapter is organized as follows. In the next section, we provide a brief overview of the use of OLG-CGE models in the analysis of tax reform, focusing on the seminal contribution of Auerbach and Kotlikoff (1987) who, following the path breaking work of Summers (1981), constructed a dynamic OLG-CGE model that has spawned a vast literature. We also consider a variety of subsequent extensions of this work, including the multiple-good, multiple-individual model constructed by Fullerton and Rogers (1993), and many other extensions including the addition of open economy factors, human capital accumulation, uncertainty, and age-dependent taxes.[2] Many of the applications of these models have focused on the effects of changes in capital income taxation or, more generally, the replacement of an income tax system that fully taxes capital income with a consumption-based tax system that exempts normal returns to capital and we focus on such reforms in our review of this literature. In Section 11.3, we describe the DZ model, which is characterized by 55 cohorts, 12 income groups within each cohort and four production sectors (a corporate and a non-corporate composite non-housing consumption good, and owner-occupied and rental residential housing), and explicit

---

[1] On the other hand, the microsimulation approach is able to model the tax system in much more detail than the stylized approach used in OLG-CGE models. For further elaboration, see the discussions of 'dynamic scoring' of tax reforms by Auerbach (2005) and Altshuler et al. (2005).

[2] We focus on the historical development of OLG-CGE models, especially models that significantly extended the model of Auerbach and Kotlikoff; for a complementary literature review, see Fehr et al. in Chapter 27 of this Handbook, which focuses on recent extensions that emphasize demographic changes in an international context, endogenous retirement decisions, and uncertainty.

calculation of reform-induced changes in all asset values. We then describe several applications of the DZ model in Section 11.4.[3] Finally, Section 11.5 offers some conclusions.

## 11.2 BRIEF HISTORY OF OLG-CGE MODELING OF TAX REFORM

### 11.2.1 Early (non-OLG) models

Most discussions of general equilibrium tax incidence models begin with the celebrated contribution of Harberger (1962) — although some antecedents are in Musgrave (1953, 1959). Harberger constructed a two-sector model to analyze the incidence of the corporate income tax, but assumed a static framework in which aggregate supplies of labor and capital were fixed, although both factors were mobile across the production sectors. Within this context, he showed that the corporate income tax tended to be borne entirely by all owners of the taxed factor, as capital migrated from the taxed corporate sector to the untaxed non-corporate sector, depressing the overall return to capital. Although this result was based on a differential analysis and thus strictly applicable to only small tax increases, Shoven and Whalley (1972) constructed the first CGE analog to the Harberger model and confirmed his result for large tax changes.

The Harberger model is an excellent tool to study issues related to tax-induced reallocations of fixed total supplies of capital and labor, but it ignores the central question of the effects of tax-induced reductions on the rate of return to capital on saving and investment behavior and thus on capital accumulation. Early studies of this issue simply added taxes to the neoclassical growth model, with saving a function of income and perhaps the rate of return to capital. In these models, capital income taxation reduces saving, which in turn lowers the equilibrium capital–labor ratio; as a result, labor productivity falls and wages decline, implying that the tax has been at least partially shifted from capital to labor, typically by about one-third to one-half (Krzyzaniak, 1967; Feldstein, 1974; Mankiw and Weinzierl, 2005).

The extension to a variable capital stock — and to multiple consumption and production goods — was also examined in the CGE literature by Ballard et al. (1985), who assumed that individual utility was a function of current consumption and a composite good that captured all future consumption; this model also implied that saving was a function of the after-tax rate of return to capital, so that capital income taxes were partially or fully shifted to labor. This approach was a precursor to the more formal models of saving behavior in which individuals are effectively infinitely-lived

---

[3] As will be described in detail below, these applications often use somewhat different versions of the DZ model, reflecting both the evolution over time of the model and extensions that were added to address specific issues that were the focus of a particular analysis. The simulation results in the various applications are thus not strictly comparable.

that are analyzed in Chapter 8 by Jorgenson and Yun as well as many others in this Handbook.

By comparison, in this chapter we focus on analyses in which individual behavior with respect to saving and labor supply follows a many-period life-cycle model, supplemented with a bequest motive. In a typical version of the model, the economy is characterized by many overlapping generations that are alive at any given point in time, so that the effects of tax reforms can be determined in the aggregate and then distributed both across and within generations — results that cannot be captured when individuals are infinitely-lived.

## 11.2.2 Summers OLG Model

The use of the OLG model to analyze tax reforms was pioneered by Summers (1981) who analyzes the replacement of an income tax with two different forms of consumption-based taxation — an expenditure tax and a wage tax — using a continuous-time, single-good OLG model characterized by life-cycle savers with fixed labor supply and myopic expectations. Summers, following Hall (1968), stresses that a many-period approach, rather than the traditional two-period life-cycle model with labor earnings occurring only in the first period, is essential to modeling life-cycle effects accurately because only the former approach captures the fact that an increase in the tax rate on capital income reduces the after-tax discount rate individuals use in estimating their human wealth when making consumption and savings decisions. The resulting increase in human wealth prompts greater consumption early in life, i.e. less saving.

The simulations reported by Summers suggest that this human wealth effect results in large reductions in savings (savings elasticities with respect to the after-tax rate of return on the order of 1—3), which in turn implies that the enactment of a consumption tax reform results in large steady-state welfare gains. For example, in one central case, the enactment of a cash flow consumption tax results in a steady-state welfare gain equal to 11.2% of lifetime income. The enactment of a wage tax in the Summers model also increases steady-state welfare, but to a significantly smaller extent (7.0% of lifetime income) since existing capital is not subject to tax. This highlights the often-noted point that a significant fraction of the efficiency gains obtained from a consumption tax reform may be attributable to a one-time reduction in the value of existing capital; moreover, this 'capital levy' primarily affects the elderly generations alive at the time of enactment since they own the vast majority of existing capital — an effect that can only be captured in life-cycle OLG models.

The Summers dynamic OLG model sparked a great deal of interest. Much of the subsequent research focused on the extent to which its savings responses are sensitive to various choices about model structure, especially the treatment of bequests and parameter values (Evans, 1983; Starrett, 1988), and appear to be implausibly large, given the empirical literature (Ballard, 1990, 2002; Gravelle, 2002). In addition, Summers assumes an inelastic labor supply and wages that increase exponentially over the life cycle — assumptions that tend to inflate the human wealth effect that is the focus of his analysis and are thus especially problematical.

## 11.2.3 Seminal model of Auerbach and Kotlikoff

These and many other issues raised by the Summers study were addressed in the model constructed by Auerbach and Kotlikoff (1987), hereafter the AK model, which is the seminal contribution in the vast OLG-CGE literature; the book by Auerbach and Kotlikoff (1987) builds on an earlier article by Auerbach et al. (1983) and recent extensions of the model are described in Kotlikoff (1998). Following Summers, Auerbach and Kotlikoff model a closed economy that produces a single good with a single representative individual in each adult cohort alive at any given point in time. However, the AK model differs in five important ways from the Summers model, all of which have been followed by most subsequent researchers (including ourselves).

The first and arguably most important innovation in the AK model is that, rather than assuming myopic expectations, Auerbach and Kotlikoff assume that individuals (and firms, in some applications of the model) have perfect foresight. This naturally makes solving the model far more difficult from a computational standpoint, since all prices in the current and all future years must be determined simultaneously. However, the assumption of perfect foresight implies that firms and households systematically and rationally form expectations about the future, including all of the future effects of tax reforms — a significant improvement over earlier models that is now the standard approach in general equilibrium modeling of tax policy.[4] In particular, the assumption of perfect foresight generally results in more reasonable behavioral responses, as it implies that individuals and firms do not over-react to temporary price increases that will be reversed over time (e.g. temporary tax-induced increases in the rate of return to capital that dissipate over time with capital accumulation).

Second, rather than assuming exogenous labor supply, Auerbach and Kotlikoff allow labor—leisure choices in each period; as a result, labor income taxation distorts labor supply decisions (rather than acting as a lump sum tax) both within a given period and across the life cycle. Third, rather than assuming exponentially growing wages, Auerbach and Kotlikoff assume a 'hump-backed' wage profile over the life cycle, based on estimates from the labor economics literature. Fourth, in some applications, Auerbach and Kotlikoff assume that firms incur convex costs of adjustment when altering their capital stocks; this allows the calculation of an optimal path for investment in response to changes in the tax structure, which in turn implies the model can be used to track the

---

[4] The Auerbach and Kotlikoff approach is thus consistent with the micro-foundations approach to dynamic macroeconomic modeling sparked in large part by the famous Lucas (1976) critique of macroeconomic policy modeling.

economy in each period following reform until it reaches a new steady state (rather than simply comparing the steady states before and after reform). This allows a thorough analysis of the transitional effects of reform. Finally, Auerbach and Kotlikoff generally use more conservative parameter values than those utilized by Summers; among other things, their choices dampen the sensitivity of savings in response to changes in the after-tax rate of return, which addresses a common criticism of the Summers model — that it implies unreasonably large savings elasticities.

Auerbach and Kotlikoff also consider the effects of a movement from an income tax to a consumption-based tax system in their model. As a result of the five changes described above and other more minor differences from the Summers model, the welfare gains obtained from the enactment of a consumption tax reform in the AK model are more moderate. For example, in their base case analysis, the replacement of an income tax with a cash flow expenditure tax increases steady-state welfare by 2.3% of the present value of 'lifetime resources' (which is a broader measure of welfare than that used by Summers as it includes the value of leisure). By comparison — and for the same reasons as in the Summers model — the enactment of a wage tax (again without a complementary business tax) reduces steady-state welfare by 0.9% of the present value of lifetime resources. They also calculate the efficiency gains from such reforms, under the assumption that lump-sum redistributions are used so that the utility levels of all generations existing at the time of reform are held constant and all subsequent efficiency gains or losses are distributed so that future generations experience an equal percentage change in utility. Under these circumstances, enacting a cash flow expenditure tax results in an efficiency gain of 1.7% of lifetime resources, while enactment of a wage tax results in an efficiency loss of 2.3%. They note that these efficiency calculations imply that roughly 60% of the difference in the long-run welfare gains that occur with expenditure tax and wage tax reforms in the absence of such redistributions are attributable to intergenerational redistributions.

Auerbach and Kotlikoff also use their model to analyze a variety of other issues in their book. In particular, they examine the effects of increasing business tax incentives, which they show reduces the welfare of the elderly by reducing the value of their holdings of old capital (which does not benefit from the incentives), although this effect is mitigated by the presence of adjustment costs which imply that old capital earns above-normal returns until the economy reaches a new steady-state equilibrium. Auerbach and Kotlikoff also use their model to examine the efficiency costs of increased income tax progressivity, as well as the long-run effects of deficit-financed income tax cuts.

More recently, Auerbach (1996) and Jokisch and Kotlikoff (2007) have used updated versions of the AK model to analyze the effects of several consumption tax reform proposals. For example, Auerbach estimates that enactment of a flat rate comprehensive retail sales tax or a value-added tax (VAT) would increase economic efficiency by more than twice as much as enactment of the Hall–Rabushka Flat Tax with its standard deductions and personal exemptions. He also shows that adding transition rules to the Flat Tax in the form of allowing continued deductions for depreciation on existing assets further reduces long-run efficiency gains. Thus, a central message of Auerbach's analysis is that reform-induced efficiency gains vary significantly across consumption tax reforms, and are negatively affected by adding progressivity and transition rules. Indeed, Auerbach also estimates that the efficiency gains associated with implementing the USA Tax — a form of cash flow expenditure tax that provides for transition rules and multiple individual tax rates that range up to 40% as well as a variety of other features (Weidenbaum, 1996) — are negligible.

## 11.2.4 Extensions of the AK model

We conclude our overview of OLG-CGE models by providing a necessarily selective overview of some of the many extensions of the AK model. The models and extensions discussed are summarized in Table 11.1.

### 11.2.4.1 Many goods and many incomes: Fullerton and Rogers model

Two of the most important extensions of the AK model are due to Fullerton and Rogers (1993), hereafter the FR model. First, following Ballard *et al.* (1985), Fullerton and Rogers include many consumption goods (17) and production goods (19) in their model; the consumption goods are linked to the production goods with a fixed coefficients input-output matrix. This disaggregation allows the decomposition of the effects of tax reforms into those that are specific to certain industries and consumer goods. Fullerton and Rogers also require minimum purchases of each good in their formulation of individual tastes; they stress that this limits the amount of discretionary income that can be reallocated across periods and thus results in smaller savings elasticities that are more consistent with empirical evidence. They also allow five types of capital — equipment, structures, land, inventories and intangible assets — and include a simple foreign trade sector (although they ignore international factor flows).

Second, and perhaps most important, rather than assuming a single representative individual in each generation, Fullerton and Rogers include 12 representative individuals in each cohort. The 12 groups correspond to each decile of the lifetime income distribution, with the top (bottom) decile split into the top (bottom) 2% and the remaining 8%, in order to focus on the effects of reform at the very top and bottom of the income distribution. For each income and age group, Fullerton and Rogers estimate (i) wage profiles over the life cycle and across lifetime income groups, (ii) an income tax function with marginal tax rates that are constant within groups but vary across group, and (iii) a profile of government transfers received over the life cycle and across lifetime income groups. Given this detailed intragenerational framework, the FR model allows a much richer analysis of the intragenerational redistributive effects of tax

**Table 11.1** Selected models based on the AK model (Auerbach and Kotlikoff, 1987)

| Study | Key extensions and limitations (relative to the AK model) |
|---|---|
| Fullerton and Rogers (1993) | Multiple goods, multiple individuals in each cohort, a target bequest, minimum purchase requirements, multiple types of capital, foreign trade in goods, but myopic expectations and no adjustment costs |
| Auerbach (1996) | Open economy |
| Altig *et al.* (2001) | Multiple individuals in each cohort and a joy of giving bequest |
| Goulder and Summers (1989) | Explicit modeling of firm behavior, following Tobin's *q*-theory of investment, Kueschnigg (1990, 1991) explicit modeling of firm values, risk premium (Goulder and Summers, 1989), variable debt—equity ratio (Kueschnigg, 1990) |
| Engen and Gale (1996) | Uncertain earnings, an uncertain time of death and precautionary saving |
| Davies and Whalley (1991); Taber (2002) | Human capital accumulation |
| de Mooij and Devereux (2010); Bettendorf *et al.* (2010) | Open economy modeling of multiple regions, with trade and capital mobility, with two-period OLG structure |
| Fehr *et al.* (Chapter 27 in this Handbook) | Open economy modeling with trade and capital/labor mobility, multiple regions, multiple goods, variable population growth, endogenous retirement decisions, and uncertain earnings and lifespan |

The AK model is characterized by perfect foresight, variable savings and variable labor supply with an exogenous wage profile, no bequests, progressive labor income taxation, convex costs of adjusting the capital stock, a closed economy, a single good, a single type of capital, and a single representative individual in each cohort.

reforms, while still capturing the intergenerational redistributions stressed by Auerbach and Kotlikoff.

These extensions of course significantly complicate the model. To facilitate its solution, Fullerton and Rogers assume myopic expectations for firms and consumers, no adjustment costs (so that firms reallocate factors costlessly each period), investment that is solely determined by individuals savings decisions rather than firm optimization over time, and calculate equilibria every 5 years rather than on an annual basis.

Within this context, Fullerton and Rogers examine the lifetime incidence of the US tax system as well as the effects of several tax reforms. They find that the overall tax system is quite progressive with respect to the lifetime burdens borne by the very top and very bottom lifetime income groups, with the burden on the top group (as a fraction of lifetime income) more than three times the burden on the bottom group. However, they find that the overall tax system is roughly proportional or only slightly progressive over the remaining 10 lifetime income groups.

Fullerton and Rogers (1996) use their model to analyze the effects of various fundamental tax reforms, stressing the intragenerational redistributions associated with implementing consumption tax reforms as well as their intergenerational burdens. For example, they note that the implementation of a comprehensive proportional wage tax increases saving more than does the implementation of a comprehensive proportional consumption tax (a VAT). As noted above, intergenerational redistributions imply a smaller increase in saving under a wage tax because it does not include the 'hit' on old capital that is owned primarily by the elderly who tend to consume relatively more in the latter stages of their life cycle. However, Fullerton and Rogers note that the capital levy under the consumption tax hits the lifetime rich more than the lifetime poor and the lifetime rich have a relatively high propensity to save, so that avoiding this hit under the wage tax increases saving and, in their model, this intragenerational effect more than offsets the traditional intergenerational effect. Fullerton and Rogers also show that, not surprisingly, moving to a flat rate consumption tax is a regressive reform, although much of that regressivity can be eliminated at the low end of the lifetime income distribution with a modest tax exemption. They also show that despite the intergenerational saving effect noted above, the implementation of a consumption tax generates larger efficiency gains than enacting a wage tax; these gains are on the order of 1% of lifetime income, but disappear if the intertemporal elasticity is sufficiently low.

### 11.2.4.2 AK model revisited, with many income groups and perfect foresight

Following Fullerton and Rogers, the AK model has been extended to include 12 income groups in each generation in Altig *et al.* (2001), hereafter the AAKSW model, while maintaining the assumptions of perfect foresight by consumers and a one-year period structure. Altig *et al.* also examine a wide variety of consumption tax reforms. Of particular interest is their analysis of the 'X-Tax' devised by Bradford (1986, 2005). The X-Tax is a multiple-rate progressive version of the Hall and Rabushka (1983, 1995) Flat Tax; the latter is a flat rate tax on labor compensation with standard deductions and personal exemptions coupled with a cash flow business tax that was the model for the 'Progressive Consumption Tax' discussed at length — but ultimately not recommended — in the report of the President's Advisory Panel on Federal Tax Reform (2005). The Altig *et al.* simulations indicate that replacement of the current income tax with an X-Tax with a top marginal rate of 30% would result in a long-run increase in output of 6.4%, coupled with long-run welfare increases for each of the 12 lifetime income classes in their model of between 1 and 2% of full lifetime resources. The Altig *et al.* results thus suggest that a progressive consumption tax reform could be designed without causing huge long-run redistributions of income across income classes.

These long-run gains, however, are accompanied by transitional losses for the elderly at the time of reform that range between 1 and 2% of remaining lifetime utility. Altig *et al.* do not analyze the effects of adding transition relief to mitigate these losses. However, they do analyze the effects of the Flat Tax, with and without transition relief in the form of allowing continued depreciation deductions on existing capital assets; they estimate that adding transition relief reduces the long-run increase in output from 4.5% to 1.9%. This suggests that adding transition relief to the X-Tax would significantly reduce, and perhaps even reverse, its long-run steady-state welfare gains, especially since the windfall loss due to the capital levy imposed on the elderly under the X-Tax is relatively large since they face a relatively high marginal tax rate.

### 11.2.4.3 Including explicit calculation of firm values and financial markets

Several models extend the standard OLG-CGE model to include explicit calculation of firm values, taking into account the current values of existing capital assets given the depreciation deductions taken previously on such assets (Goulder and Summers, 1989; Kueschnigg, 1990, 1991). This approach is based on the '*q*'-theory of investment developed by Tobin (1969), under which firms' investment decisions are related to the ratio of the market value to the replacement value of capital, as extended to include the costs of adjusting the capital stock by Hayashi (1982). Firms with perfect foresight are assumed to choose an optimal investment path to maximize firm value, which is defined as the discounted value of future after-tax cash flows. The debt—equity ratio is typically assumed to be fixed, although in some formulations the degree of leverage is endogenous and typically depends on a balancing of the tax advantages of debt in the form of deductible interest against the agency costs (diminished control over managers) of higher leverage (Kueschnigg, 1990).

Such models are especially well-suited to analyzing the transitional effects of reform, as firm values and thus individual asset holdings are calculated explicitly. In addition, since depreciation on existing assets is calculated explicitly, the effects of different transition rules can be analyzed explicitly. For example, the implementation of a 'pure' consumption tax would include the denial of all depreciation deductions on existing capital (Hall and Rabushka, 1983, 1995). Such a policy is likely to be too harsh to be politically feasible, and models that calculate firm values explicitly can determine the macroeconomic and distributional effects of alternative transition rules, such as full or partial continuation of such allowances.

### 11.2.4.4 Adding a precautionary saving motive: Engen and Gale model

As noted above, one common criticism of OLG-CGE models (that is invoked to an even greater extent with infinite-horizon models) is that they are characterized by savings responses to changes in after-tax rates of return that some perceive to be implausibly large. These responses arise because individuals are assumed to have perfect foresight, so that even small changes in the after-tax rate of return are compounded into large changes in the prices of future consumption goods, generating relatively large savings responses (Judd, 1985; Chamley, 1986).

One response to this issue has been to assume that individuals have motives for saving other than to finance retirement. In particular, Engen and Gale (1996) argue that much saving reflects a precautionary motive, as individuals attempt to protect themselves against fluctuations in earnings (note that this could also be interpreted as earnings net of uninsured medical expenses) and an uncertain lifetime. They augment a standard OLG-CGE model to include uncertain earnings, an uncertain time of death and precautionary saving, stressing that such saving is far less sensitive to rates of return than life-cycle saving; indeed, in the case of 'target' saving where individuals want to accumulate a fixed 'buffer stock' of saving, saving is inversely related to the rate of return since target savings can be more easily attained with a higher rate of return. They note that the saving elasticity with respect to the after-tax rate of return in their model is in the neighborhood of 0.25−0.40, which is far smaller than typically observed in an OLG-CGE model; they argue that such small elasticities are consistent with the empirical literature. Engen and Gale also stress that the current tax system is not a pure income tax, but a hybrid with many important features of a consumption tax, especially the treatment of much retirement saving and investments in owner-occupied housing. They argue that this implies that roughly half of saving is tax preferred (taxed as it would be under a consumption tax) under the income tax. As a result, moving toward a consumption-based tax does not represent as much of a change as it would if the initial equilibrium were a true income tax.

Within this context, Engen and Gale simulate the effects of the implementation of a flat rate consumption tax. Although this reform still generates efficiency gains, these gains — which are on the order of 1% of lifetime income in the long run — are significantly smaller than in alternative analyses that do not consider precautionary saving; they also show that allowing transition relief in the form of allowing continued depreciation deductions for existing capital reduces this efficiency gain by approximately one-half. The Engen and Gale results clearly imply that the efficiency case for consumption tax reform is weaker if the precautionary motive is a dominant factor in determining saving behavior (and to the extent that the current income tax already has consumption tax features). On the other hand, the relative importance of precautionary saving is open to debate; for example, Kennickel and Lusardi (2004) estimate that precautionary saving represents only 8% of total net worth.

### 11.2.4.5 Adding human capital

Another strand of this literature adds human capital to the OLG-CGE model, thus allowing life-cycle saving in the form of both physical and human capital accumulation and making future wages endogenous. This extension was prompted in part by the early partial equilibrium work of Driffill and Rosen (1983) who simulated the effects of moving from a proportional income tax to a proportional consumption-based tax within the context of a partial equilibrium life-cycle model (the rate of return to capital was assumed to be fixed) with both human capital accumulation and variable labor supply in each period. They argued that the focus of the standard OLG-CGE model on the changes in labor supply induced by such tax reforms was misplaced, as the distortions of human capital accumulation were likely to be more important. Driffill and Rosen assume that all the costs of human capital accumulation are foregone earnings, which are implicitly deductible, implying that individuals effectively receive cash flow tax treatment of human capital investment under either tax system, which in turn implies a non-distortionary marginal effective tax rate of zero on such investment. By comparison, investment in physical capital is fully taxed under an income tax and untaxed at the margin under a consumption-based tax, which implies that the income tax creates a tax bias favoring investment in human capital while the consumption tax is neutral between investment in human and physical capital. The simulations of a consumption tax reform conducted by Driffill and Rosen suggest that the efficiency costs associated with the distortion of both labor supply and human capital accumulation decisions under the income tax are roughly seven times as large as the distortion of the labor supply decision considered in isolation (35% versus 5% of revenues). The authors suggest that this provides a compelling argument for consumption-based tax reforms.

Subsequent general equilibrium analyses with endogenous rates of return on physical capital, however, have cast doubt on this conclusion. In particular, Davies and Whalley (1991) show that although the short-run negative effects on human capital accumulation of replacing a proportional income tax with a proportional consumption (or a wage) tax are significant as the relative after-tax return to physical capital spikes initially, this effect dissipates rapidly, as the after-tax rate of return to physical capital quickly falls back to roughly its initial level with additional physical capital accumulation. As a result, the tax-reform-induced effects on human capital accumulation are small in the intermediate and long runs, and the incremental efficiency gains from adding a human capital accumulation decision to the life-cycle model are small.[5]

Taber (2002) obtains broadly similar results in a model that considers progressive as well as proportional taxes. In principle, progressive taxes create a tax bias against human capital accumulation, since the implicit deductions for foregone earnings are taken at relatively low rates (since income is relatively low during human capital accumulation) while some of the subsequent returns in the form of higher future wages are taxed at relatively high rates. However, Taber finds that progressivity has relatively small effects on

---

[5] Similar results are obtained by Lord (1989) in an analysis of the replacement of a payroll or wage tax with a consumption tax.

human capital accumulation; he also confirms the Davies and Whalley result that consumption tax reforms have only short-run effects on human capital accumulation that dissipate rather quickly.

### 11.2.4.6 Adding international flows of goods and factors

Much of the analysis of tax reforms using OLG-CGE models has been done within either a closed economy framework, or one in which trade in outputs and/or international factor mobility is modeled in a fairly ad hoc way. For example, the AK model is closed and the FR model includes a simple form of trade in goods but has no international movements of capital or labor. Auerbach (1996) includes some simulations in which the US economy is simply modeled as a small open economy (the international rate of return to capital is assumed to be fixed).

The need to consider open economy issues, especially international capital flows, is highlighted by the ongoing debate regarding the incidence of the corporate income tax. For example, Harberger (1995, 2008) constructs a four-sector general equilibrium model, characterized by perfectly mobile capital and tradable goods with prices that are determined on international markets, in which a tax on capital income is typically shifted more than 100% to labor. This result, however, has been questioned by Gravelle and Smetters (2006), who argue that, even if capital is perfectly mobile internationally, capital in the US will bear more of the burden of the corporate income tax than the US share of world output if domestic goods and imports are not perfect substitutes; indeed, they show that the capital share of the tax burden increases dramatically as the substitutability between domestic goods and imports falls. By comparison, Randolph (2006) shows that extending the Gravelle–Smetters model to allow a domestic corporate sector that produces two types of traded goods — some that are perfect substitutes for imports and others that are imperfectly substitutable — greatly reduces the importance of imperfect product substitutability.

Although none of these models includes an OLG structure, the issues of the appropriate way to model international factor mobility and international trade, as well as the magnitudes of the key parameters, are obviously relevant to OLG-CGE modeling as well — an issue to which we return in our discussion of the DZ model below. One recent example of explicit modeling of international capital flows in an OLG-CGE framework is de Mooij and Devereux (2010), who model the effects of various tax reforms in the EU. Their model has a simple two-period OLG structure, but is essentially a model of a 'world' economy that includes the 27 countries of the EU plus the US and Japan. Although labor is assumed to be immobile internationally, capital is perfectly mobile across all countries in the model (the overall world supply of capital is determined by the saving of each country) and the single production good in the model is traded on perfectly competitive world markets. They also consider an extension to the model in another form of capital 'mobility' — income shifting to tax havens — is allowed with the extent of income shifting determined by differences in statutory tax rates in the EU countries relative to the tax havens.

Within this context, de Mooij and Devereux analyze the effects of various EU-coordinated and single-country reforms that would eliminate current tax distinctions between debt and equity financed investments. These include the enactment of an 'allowance for corporate equity' or ACE business tax, which allows firms an extra deduction for the cost of equity, and a 'comprehensive business income tax' (CBIT) that would deny firms deductions for business interest expense. In their benchmark model, they show that a coordinated ACE reform would increase welfare in each of the EU countries, by amounts that range from 0.2 to 0.8% of GDP; however, these gains are largely or fully offset if tax havens are added to the model, as the higher ACE rate (required to maintain revenues, given the new deduction for equity capital) results in significant income shifting out of the EU. By comparison, in their benchmark model, most EU countries experience a welfare loss with a coordinated CBIT reform due to the resulting increase in the cost of capital; however, such a reform tends to increase welfare in most countries when tax havens are allowed, as the extent of income shifting declines due to the reduction in the tax rate made possible by the denial of interest deductions under the CBIT regime. The de Mooij–Devereux analysis provides an excellent example of how the standard OLG-CGE model might be extended to incorporate international trade and factor flows, even if only in the context of a two-country model of the US and the 'rest of the world'.[6]

## 11.3 OVERVIEW OF THE DZ MODEL

In this section, we provide an overview of the DZ model, which is a large-scale dynamic OLG-CGE model that can be used to analyze both the short-run and long-run macroeconomic and distributional effects of tax reforms. A detailed description is provided in the Appendix. We describe a fairly general version of the model; however, all of the features of the model described are not necessarily used in all applications. In particular, we describe a version of the model in which there are 12 lifetime income groups within each generation, but in many applications we assume a single representative individual in each generation.

The basic features of the model are as follows. Consumers are assumed to have perfect foresight and to maximize utility over a 55-year adult life, consisting of 45 working years

---

[6] See also Bettendorf *et al.* (2010), who use a similar model to analyze the effects of corporate income tax harmonization (the Common Consolidated Corporate Tax Base with formula apportionment) in the EU. See also the comprehensive multiregional model with internationally mobile capital and labor, variable population growth, multiple goods, uncertain earnings and lifespan, and endogenous retirement decisions by Fehr *et al.* in Chapter 27 of this Handbook.

followed by a 10-year retirement.[7] The model is constructed in discrete time, with each period corresponding to 1 year. Individual lifetime utility is the discounted sum of annual utility in each of the 55 periods. Annual utility is a function of leisure and an aggregate consumption good, which is in turn a composite of four goods — a non-housing composite consumption good produced by the corporate sector, a non-housing composite consumption good produced by the non-corporate sector, owner-occupied housing and rental housing. The model also includes relatively simple representations of bequests and inheritances, and tax-deferred saving under the current income tax. There are 12 lifetime income groups within each generation, each characterized by its own profiles for lifetime earnings and lifetime transfers received.[8]

Firm managers are also characterized by perfect foresight. Firms are assumed to maximize firm value and thus the discounted value of future profits. Following the well-known $q$-theory of investment behavior formulated by Tobin (1969), firm managers calculate the optimal time path of investment in response to any changes in the tax structure, taking into account convex costs of adjusting investment from its initial steady-state level. Firm behavior is modeled separately for each of the four production sectors, with individuals who own their own homes treated as the owners of private 'firms' that produce housing and then rent it to their owners (themselves), taking into account the income tax advantages of home ownership. The debt—capital ratio is assumed to be fixed in each industry.

The government must finance an exogenously specified time path of public services, which are assumed to be separable from the individual lifetime utility function, as well as income transfers, which are included in individual income. This fairly standard 'differential incidence' approach significantly simplifies the model while still allowing us to analyze a wide range of tax substitutions, as well as changes in government spending that take the form of changes in transfers payments, which are fully accounted for in the individual budget constraint. However, we cannot conduct 'balanced budget incidence' analyses, i.e. we cannot analyze an increase in government services (other than transfer payments) that is financed with a tax increase. Such an analysis would of course require a complete specification of how all government services enter individual utility functions, by age and by income group. We leave this interesting but complex extension to further research.

---

[7] Following most of the models in this literature, we consider an economy characterized by perfect certainty. This admittedly strong assumption has been relaxed in the dynamic stochastic general equilibrium literature (see, e.g. the discussion in Kocherlakota, 2010).

[8] The individual utility functions, however, are identical across the various lifetime income groups, which implies that the parameters that determine behavioral responses, including those associated with changes in labor supply and saving, are identical across the various lifetime income groups; allowing variation by lifetime income group of these parameters in order to better capture differences in their behavioral responses is a topic of future research.

The basic version of the DZ model follows the AK model in assuming a closed economy. This simplifying assumption is acceptable for some reforms that are unlikely to have large effects on rates of return to capital and thus on international capital flows, or if one believes that international capital mobility, especially with respect to capital flows in and out of the US, is less than often asserted.[9] Nevertheless, because such capital flows are of great importance in the modern economy, in several of our analyses with the DZ model, we have modified the model to allow a simple representation of capital flows, as described below.

In the initial steady-state equilibrium, the government's tax instruments include a corporate income tax and an income tax with a progressive wage income tax structure and constant rate capital income taxes. The model can be used to analyze the short-run and long-run effects of both reforms of the existing income tax system, such as base-broadening, rate-reducing reforms (BBRR) or various approaches to business–personal income tax integration, as well as various types of consumption tax reforms, including the Hall–Rabushka Flat Tax and its variants such as the Bradford X-Tax, cash flow expenditure taxes, national retail sales taxes and VATs. In general, the government must satisfy an annual budget constraint. However, the model can also accommodate federal government debt, and the government can issue debt for a finite period and then satisfy the annual budget constraint from that point forward, paying interest on the accumulated debt.

All markets are assumed to be perfectly competitive. Market equilibrium in the model requires that total consumer demand, obtained by aggregating the demands of each of the 12 types of individuals within each of the 55 generations alive at any single point in time, must equal aggregate supply in each of the four production sectors. In addition, factor demands must equal factor supplies in the labor and capital markets, the total amounts of debt and equity held as individual wealth must equal firm stocks of debt and equity, and both individual and firm expectations regarding the time paths of future prices must be satisfied. In all applications including those with government debt, the model must arrive at a steady-state equilibrium, in which all key macroeconomic variables, including GDP and output in the various sectors, the capital stock, the effective labor force, any government debt held by the public, etc., grow at the steady-state growth rate, which is defined as the sum of the long-run population growth rate and the rate of labor-augmenting technological progress, both of which are specified exogenously and assumed to remain constant. Note that because we assume a constant rate of population growth in our model, we cannot analyze the effects of demographic changes, including the fiscal imbalances that currently plague the US and many other countries due to an aging population. The model can, however, be extended to allow varying rates of population growth for a finite time period, as long as population growth eventually

---

[9] See, for example, Feldstein and Horioka (1980) and the voluminous subsequent literature, reviewed in Zodrow (2010).

returns to a constant steady-state growth rate; for example, Auerbach and Kotlikoff make such a modification in their analysis of reform of the social security system in the US, and Fehr *et al.* in their multiregional model in Chapter 27 of this Handbook analyze demographic changes in great detail.

The model calculates asset values in all four markets explicitly for each period after the enactment of a reform, taking into account both the effects of all changes in the tax treatment of existing capital assets, as well as their previous tax treatment under the existing tax system. As noted above, the model is thus especially well suited to analyzing the transitional effects of reform, including reform-induced changes in asset prices in all four sectors, as well as the associated redistributions within and across all generations alive at the time of reform. The model can also be used to calculate the long-run economic effects of reform, including the welfare effects of reform on future generations.

## 11.4 APPLICATIONS OF THE DZ MODEL

In this section, we describe the results of using the DZ model to analyze five types of potential tax reforms, including (i) fundamental tax reform in the form of replacing the income tax with a consumption-based tax (the Flat Tax), (ii) the implementation of a Flat Tax supplemented by the taxation of capital income at the individual level, (iii) reform of the existing income tax in the form of a BBRR corporate income tax reform, (iv) implementing a new VAT designed to reduce current deficits and the US national debt, and (v) deficit-financed tax reductions. The initial equilibrium for evaluating these reforms is a stylized representation of the US economy, characterized by numerous tax-induced inefficiencies that offer the potential for efficiency-enhancing reforms. These inefficiencies include the taxation of corporate income with double taxation at the business and individual levels of corporate equity income, the taxation of saving at both the business and individual levels, the taxation of labor income, and differential taxation of the corporate and non-corporate sectors as well as differential taxation of the business and housing sectors.[10] Typical parameter values used in constructing the initial equilibrium are shown in Table 11.2; for a detailed discussion of parameter choices, see Gunning *et al.* (2008).

### 11.4.1 Consumption-based tax reforms

In Diamond and Zodrow (2008a), we examine the short-run and long-run effects of fundamental tax reform, focusing on the transitional effects of replacing the current

---

[10] Note that most of these distortions would be reduced or eliminated with the replacement of the existing income tax with a consumption-based tax, especially if its base were broad enough to reduce the effective tax rates applied to labor income; as noted above, this is the main reason many of the reforms analyzed in the OLG-CGE literature examine the effects of such reforms.

**Table 11.2** Typical parameter values used in the DZ model

| Symbol | Description | Value |
|---|---|---|
| *Utility function parameters* | | |
| $\rho$ | Rate of time preference | 0.004–0.01 |
| $\sigma_U$ | Intertemporal elasticity of substitution | 0.25–0.35 |
| $\sigma_C$ | Intratemporal elasticity of substitution | 0.60–0.80 |
| $\sigma_H$ | Elasticity of substitution between composite good, housing | 0.33–0.50 |
| $\sigma_N$ | Elasticity of substitution between corporate, non-corporate good | 5.0 |
| $\sigma_R$ | Elasticity of substitution between rental, owner housing | 0.80 |
| $\alpha_C$ | Utility weight on the composite consumption good | 0.70 |
| $\alpha_H$ | Utility weight on non-housing consumption good | 0.72 |
| $\alpha_N$ | Utility weight on corporate good | 0.75 |
| $\alpha_R$ | Utility weight on owner-occupied housing | 0.78 |
| *Production function parameters* | | |
| $\epsilon_C$ | Elasticity of substitution for corporate good | 0.5–1.0 |
| $\epsilon_N$ | Elasticity of substitution for non-corporate good | 0.5–1.0 |
| $\epsilon_H, \epsilon_R$ | Elasticities of substitution for owner and rental housing | 0.25–0.80 |
| $\gamma_C$ | Capital share for corporate good | 0.25–0.35 |
| $\gamma_N$ | Capital share for non-corporate good | 0.25–0.50 |
| $\gamma_H, \gamma_R$ | Capital share for owner and rental housing | 0.99 |
| $\beta_X, \beta_N, \beta_H$ | Adjustment cost parameters | 0–15 |
| $\zeta$ | Dividend payout ratio in corporate sector | 0.68 |
| $b_C, b_N, b_H, b_R$ | Debt–asset ratio | 0.35 |
| $\delta_C, \delta_N$ | Depreciation rates in the corporate and non-corporate sectors | 0.088 |
| $\delta_H, \delta_R$ | Depreciation rates in the owner and rental housing sectors | 0.019 |

income tax with a Hall–Rabushka Flat Tax.[11] Transitional issues have played an important and controversial role in the tax reform debate. Some observers argue that the prospect of large reform-induced windfall losses creates a huge impediment to the enactment of reform, while others stress that such losses, which are typically concentrated among high-lifetime-income capital owners, create the potential for larger long-run reform-induced efficiency gains while simultaneously mitigating the distributional problems associated with the lower marginal tax rates at the top of the income distribution and the generous treatment of capital income that characterize a consumption tax.

In particular, we focus on two specific transitional issues that often arise in discussions of the feasibility of consumption tax reforms. The first is the potential one-time windfall loss imposed on the owners of existing capital assets (other than owner-occupied housing). For example, under the Flat Tax, allowing expensing is equivalent in present

---

[11] See Diamond and Zodrow (2007b) for a similar analysis of the effects of implementing a national retail sales tax.

value to exempting from taxation the normal rate of return on all new investments. However, in the absence of transition rules under the Flat Tax, firms would not be allowed to deduct the remaining basis of existing assets, although the returns earned by such assets (and the proceeds of asset sales) would be included in the tax base. As a result, the rate of return on existing assets would fall relative to the return on new investments, and arbitrage across new and existing assets would imply that the value of existing assets would fall; Gravelle (1996) constructs a simple model in which the decline is proportional to the rate of tax. Moreover, in the likely event that the general price level remains unchanged under the Flat Tax, lenders would be insulated from this loss since the nominal value of outstanding bonds would be fixed; thus, the entire reform-induced one-time windfall loss would be borne by business equity holders.

However, as described by Zodrow (2002), this analysis ignores a wide variety of other factors associated with the implementation of a Flat Tax that would also affect existing business capital owners, most of which would act to reduce the one-time windfall tax on existing assets or offset its negative welfare effects. A partial list of these factors — all of which are considered in the DZ model — includes: (i) the costs of adjusting the capital stock, which would allow the owners of capital to earn above-normal returns on both existing assets and new investments during the period of transition to the new postreform equilibrium; (ii) a short-run (and perhaps a long-run) increase in the after-tax rate of interest, which would allow the owners of capital to earn a higher after-tax rate of return on existing assets and new investments; (iii) the reduction under a lower-rate flat tax of the expected tax on assets that were allowed accelerated depreciation allowances, including 'bonus depreciation' and expensing of investments in research and development or advertising, under the current income tax (Lyon and Merrill, 2001); and (iv) the efficiency gains obtained from eliminating distortions of saving and investment decisions and reducing distortions of the labor—leisure choices, as well as from improvements in the allocation of capital across business sectors.[12] Thus, the magnitudes of such reform-induced reductions in the prices of business equity assets are far from clear, and results presented in Auerbach (1996) and Altig et al. (2001) suggest they are smaller than those obtained in the Gravelle (1996) analysis.

---

[12] The model tends to overstate transitional losses for two additional reasons. (i) To the extent the 'new view' of dividend taxation is accurate, the enactment of a consumption tax reform would benefit existing assets by removing individual level taxation of dividends that is capitalized into current asset prices (Auerbach, 1996). As the model is based on the 'traditional' view of dividend taxation, it does not capture this effect. One potential extension of the model is to allow some 'traditional view' firms and some 'new view' firms, consistent with the evidence presented in Auerbach and Hassett (2003). (ii) As stressed by Hubbard (2002), the primary difference between income and consumption taxes is that only the latter exempts normal returns to capital; by comparison, above-normal returns and the returns to risk-taking are treated similarly under income and consumption taxes. Since the model is characterized by perfect competition and certainty, it does not consider these factors. In particular, as discussed by Auerbach (2008), treating all of the return to capital as normal returns may significantly overstate the gains that could be achieved with a consumption tax reform.

The second potential windfall loss from implementing a Flat Tax is its potentially negative effect on the price of owner-occupied housing. This price decline is due to a reform-induced increase in the user cost of housing, as perceived by the owner-occupier, which arises primarily because (i) normal returns to business equity investments are effectively untaxed under the Flat Tax, making such investments relatively more attractive and raising the opportunity cost of equity-financed investment in owner-occupied housing, and (ii) deductions for mortgage interest and property taxes are eliminated. This increase in the user cost of owner-occupied housing would tend to reduce the demand for owner-occupied housing, which in turn would tend to result in a decline in the price of owner-occupied housing in the short run. In the long run, the quantity of housing and the cost of housing would return to an equilibrium reflecting production costs, including the cost of land, and the absence of taxation.

Several analysts have commented on the impact of consumption tax reforms on housing prices, and the range of predicted effects is large. An analysis conducted by Data Resources Incorporated (Brinner et al., 1995) predicts that the present value of the loss of mortgage interest and property tax deductions alone would cause the aggregate value of owner-occupied housing to decline by 15%. Capozza et al. (1996) predict that implementing a Flat Tax would reduce owner-occupied housing prices by an average of 20%, assuming that interest rates fall by one percentage point. By comparison, Gravelle (1996), Bruce and Holtz-Eakin (1999), and Hall (1997) argue that both the short-run and the long-run effects of a Flat Tax on housing prices would be fairly small.

The housing component of the DZ model captures most of the important factors affecting the housing market discussed in these studies. The model explicitly accounts for changes in the level of new investment and the reallocation of the existing capital stock across the business and both owner-occupied and rental housing sectors, and examines the effects of the costs of adjusting the capital stock. In addition, changes in consumer demands across rental and owner-occupied housing, including those changes attributable to the elimination of deductibility of home mortgage interest and property taxes, as well as changes in demands for the composite good, are considered. It should be noted, however, that a weakness of the approach used in the model is that land is not modeled explicitly. Instead, the difficulties of converting land used initially for owner-occupied housing to other uses are captured indirectly by including the costs of adjusting the housing capital stock in the analysis. These costs are assumed to be symmetric (i.e. to follow the same quadratic pattern for both declines and increases in investment, relative to the steady-state level), and reflect the costs of reducing the level of new investment, reducing the level of replacement investment, converting owner-occupied housing to rental housing and finally, if necessary, converting owner-occupied housing to production of the composite good.

Finally, we focus on the Flat Tax because it is among the most often-discussed consumption tax proposals [e.g. the progressive 'X-Tax' variant of the Flat Tax was the consumption tax option discussed at length in the report of the President's Advisory Panel on Federal Tax Reform (2005)], its enactment is believed to raise the most troublesome transitional issues among the various consumption-based tax reform options and it is the main reform analyzed in existing studies of the effects of fundamental reform on the housing values (Capozza *et al.*, 1996; Gravelle, 1996).

The version of the DZ model used in this analysis has only three production sectors (the 'composite good' sector reflects a combination of the corporate and non-corporate sectors) and only a single representative individual in each generation, and the bequest motive assumes a target bequest (following Fullerton and Rogers). Since adjustment costs are uncertain, but are critical for analyzing transitional effects, the simulations include sensitivity analysis for various adjustment costs.

The reform simulated is the replacement of the federal income tax system with a revenue neutral Hall–Rabushka (1985, 1995) Flat Tax that applies a constant tax rate to (i) a comprehensive measure of household labor incomes, with an exemption amount that is initially set at $20,000 per household, and (ii) business real cash flow, which allows expensing of all non-financial business purchases and ignores financial flows and thus does not allow deductions for interest expense. The assumption of a comprehensive Flat Tax base, which follows the admittedly highly optimistic Hall and Rabushka approach of assuming full taxation of all fringe benefits, elimination of all deductions, and elimination of the Earned Income Tax Credit, implies that the required flat tax rate is relatively low — it ranges from 21.0% to 22.3% in the year of reform, depending on the level of adjustment costs, and gradually declines to a steady-state value of 20.1%. The reform is assumed to be unanticipated and enacted immediately.

The results of the simulations, which are presented in Table 11.3, can be summarized as follows. The enactment of the Flat Tax results in a longrun increase in GDP of nearly 5%, long-run increases in investment that range from about 2% in owner-occupied housing to 15–17% in the composite good and rental housing production sectors, a long-run increase in labor supply of roughly 1.8%, and a long-run increase in welfare of nearly 3%. The increase in labor supply occurs immediately, while the increase in the capital stock occurs slowly over time, with the capital–labor ratio nearly 9% higher, and wages 4% higher in the long run. Note that part of the increase in labor supply is attributable to the reform-induced reallocation of capital from owner-occupied housing into the much more labor-intensive production of the composite good, which stimulates the demand for labor.

Although one of the economic benefits of fundamental tax reform is a more efficient allocation of capital across the housing and composite good sectors, this naturally comes only with a reduction in investment in owner-occupied housing during a transition period following reform. The capital stocks in the composite good and rental housing sectors increase in every year after the enactment of reform, and are 16.9% and 15.0% larger, respectively, in the long run. By comparison, in the owner-occupied housing sector, the stock of capital declines initially, as capital is reallocated from the

**Table 11.3** Simulation results: Flat Tax reform (% changes in variables)

| | Years after reform | | | | | |
|---|---|---|---|---|---|---|
| | 2 | 5 | 10 | 20 | 50 | 150 |
| GDP | 2.3 | 3.7 | 4.2 | 4.7 | 4.9 | 4.9 |
| Output − X | 2.6 | 3.9 | 4.5 | 5.0 | 5.2 | 5.2 |
| Output − R | −0.3 | 0.5 | 0.7 | 1.1 | 1.2 | 1.2 |
| Output − H | 0.7 | 2.5 | 3.0 | 3.5 | 3.6 | 3.7 |
| Capital stock − X | 8.0 | 12.9 | 14.6 | 16.5 | 16.9 | 16.9 |
| Capital stock − R | 4.0 | 8.5 | 11.0 | 14.1 | 14.9 | 15.0 |
| Capital stock − H | −5.8 | −4.6 | −1.9 | 1.4 | 2.2 | 2.3 |
| Investment − X | 21.7 | 18.8 | 17.7 | 16.9 | 17.0 | 16.9 |
| Investment − R | 33.1 | 27.9 | 24.2 | 18.0 | 15.4 | 15.0 |
| Investment − H | −18.2 | 1.1 | 6.4 | 5.1 | 2.6 | 2.3 |
| Labor supply | 2.0 | 2.0 | 1.9 | 1.8 | 1.8 | 1.8 |
| Asset prices − X | −11.6 | −9.2 | −7.5 | −5.7 | −5.0 | −4.9 |
| Asset prices − R | −26.6 | −23.6 | −21.6 | −19.3 | −18.4 | −18.3 |
| Asset prices − H | −5.2 | −3.1 | −1.2 | 1.2 | 2.2 | 2.3 |

X = corporate and non-corporate sector, R = rental housing sector, H = owner-occupied housing sector.

owner-occupied housing to the rental housing and composite good sectors. Five years after the reform is enacted, the capital stock in the owner-occupied housing sector is 1.0–6.1% smaller than in the initial steady state, depending on the level of adjustment costs, although it is 2.3% larger in the long run. (By comparison, in results not shown, in the high adjustment costs case ($\beta_x = 10$ and $\beta_h = 2$) the owner-occupied housing stock falls by 9.3% 10 years after reform, and the ensuing reform-induced growth effects are spread out over a longer transition period.) Output is 5.2% larger in the composite good sector and 1.2% larger in the rental housing sector in the long run; in the owner-occupied housing sector, the change in output ranges from 0.1 to −1.5 in the short run, but is 3.6% larger in the long-run steady state.

As discussed above, the Flat Tax results in changes in the prices of assets at the time of its enactment. The declines in the value of business equity range from 0.1% to 16.5%, depending on the size of adjustment costs, while the average value of equity in the rental housing sector (where remaining basis is relatively large) decreases by 19.9–29.9%. The effects of reform on the value of equity in the owner-occupied sector are much more modest, where home equity values initially fall by 5.1–2.9% which, with a debt-asset ratio of 0.35, is equivalent to a 3.3–1.9% decline in the total value of owner-occupied housing; equity values return to their initial levels by the fourth year after the reform. This suggests that the negative effects on house values of reducing tax preferences for owner-occupied housing under a Flat Tax would be relatively small, at least in the aggregate, once all general equilibrium effects are taken into account. Instead, the biggest transitional issue arises in the rental housing sector (and in general for long-lived assets with significant amounts of remaining basis), where a reasonably strong case can be made for transitional relief.

The gains described above come at the expense of one-time windfall losses experienced by the (primarily elderly) owners of business equity, which are moderated as adjustment costs increase. For example, the generation of age 54 in the year of enactment experiences a net welfare loss that ranges from 1.8% to 11.3% of remaining lifetime utility. These losses are larger than those predicted in some other recent studies, but not nearly as large as those predicted by partial equilibrium models that ignore a wide variety of factors that tend to mitigate asset price declines in an OLG-CGE model. In our view, these results suggest that special transition rules should be used with caution when implementing fundamental tax reform, especially since they significantly reduce the long-run gains obtained with such a reform.

Finally, it is interesting to note that the effects of adjustment costs — at least if they are symmetric across production sectors — tend to cancel, as higher adjustment costs mitigate the fall in the value of business equity but exacerbate declines in the values of owner-occupied housing, in both cases by slowing down the reallocation of capital from owner-occupied housing to the other production sectors. Thus, explicitly accounting for such differential asset price effects is essential to accurately estimating the welfare effects of fundamental tax reform.

## 11.4.2 Effects of a capital income tax add-on to a flat tax

Moving completely to the consumption-based Flat Tax (or its progressive variant, the X-Tax) implies completely exempting all of the normal returns to capital from taxation at the individual level. Such a reform may be undesirable for a variety of both economic and political reasons. Indeed, the 'Growth and Investment Tax' (GIT) proposed by the President's Advisory Panel on Federal Tax Reform (2005) provided for a consumption-based tax at the firm level (since expensing was allowed and deductions for interest expense were denied), but included an 'add-on' tax on capital income at the individual level.[13] In Diamond and Zodrow (2007a), we examine the economic effects of adding an individual level capital income tax to the Flat Tax.

The use of an add-on capital income tax reflects the current state of the debate regarding the relative desirability of income-based and consumption-based direct taxes. Specifically, there is widespread agreement that an 'ideal' or comprehensive 'Schanz–Haig–Simons' accrual-based tax on real economic income is not administrable,

---

[13] The GIT included an individual level tax on labor compensation assessed at rates of 15%, 25% and 30%, supplemented with a 15% 'add-on' capital income tax at the individual level. The DZ model was used to provide some of the simulations of the economic effects of the three tax reform proposals discussed by the tax reform panel; see the appendix to the report of the President's Advisory Panel on Federal Tax Reform (2005). Another variant of this approach is the 'dual income tax' used in the Nordic countries and elsewhere, which is characterized by a progressive tax on labor income, but taxes capital income at the lowest positive rate applied to labor income (see Sorensen, 2007).

as it would require current taxation of all changes in wealth (i.e. accrual taxation of all capital gains and losses). Moreover, there is less but still considerable agreement that the taxation of the normal returns to capital inherent to an income tax is relatively undesirable, as it creates an inefficient tax bias favoring current consumption over saving, discriminates against savers (i.e. individuals who have the same lifetime income, but save more over their life cycle, would pay more tax under an income tax), and creates considerable complexity in administration and compliance, especially given the significant difficulties in accurately measuring real capital income.[14] On the other hand, many observers remain unconvinced that movement to a full-fledged consumption tax is desirable or could be implemented, citing its distributional implications, as well as uncertainty about the magnitudes of the associated efficiency gains, improvements in administrative and compliance simplicity, and transitional problems.[15] The add-on capital income tax represents a reasonable compromise between these two ends of the tax reform spectrum.

The model we use to analyze the add-on capital income tax is essentially the same as in Diamond and Zodrow (2008a), except that bequests are modeled assuming that donors are motivated by the 'joy of giving.' We compare two reform options, involving the replacement of the current federal income tax system with either (i) a revenue-neutral Hall-Rabushka Flat Tax (hereafter the FT plan) that applies the same constant tax rate to both a comprehensive measure of household labor incomes, with an exemption amount that is initially set at $20,000 per household, and business real cash flow (which allows expensing of all non-financial business purchases and ignores financial flows including interest expense), or (ii) a revenue-neutral tax system that includes a flat tax on wages and business cash flow supplemented with a relatively low flat rate 'add-on' capital income tax at the individual level on interest, dividends, and capital gains (hereafter the AT plan).

As in the previous analysis, the assumption of a truly comprehensive FT base implies that the required tax rate under the FT plan is quite low, equal to 21.1–22.1% in the year of reform, depending on the level of adjustment costs, and gradually declines to a steady-state value of 20.2%. Under the alternative AT plan, the capital income tax rate is assumed to be 10%, roughly half of the wage tax rate,[16] which is 20.0–20.8% in the year of reform, depending on adjustment costs, and declines to a steady-state value of 19.3%.[17]

---

[14]  See Zodrow (2007) for a review of these arguments.

[15]  For recent collections of articles that reflect the current status of the debate on these issues, see Diamond and Zodrow (2008b), Aaron et al. (2007), Auerbach and Hassett (2005), and Zodrow and Mieszkowski (2002).

[16]  Note that this 10% 'flat rate' is the statutory tax rate applied to all capital income under the AT plan, rather than the effective tax rate. In the model, the annual accrual individual-level capital gains tax rate, taking into account the advantages of deferral and tax exemption of death and the disadvantage of the taxation of inflationary gains, is assumed to be 3.3%. All capital income tax rates are assumed to be fixed for all years after the enactment of reform.

[17]  Note that the lower rates under the AT plan are due to its taxation of capital income, which results in a somewhat broader base than under the FT plan.

The general patterns of the economic effects of implementing the FT plan, which are shown in Table 11.4, are of course quite similar to that described in the previous section. Accordingly, we focus our discussion on a comparison of the effects of the AT plan, relative to the FT plan. The reform-induced increase in labor supply is slightly larger under the AT plan because its additional layer of capital income taxation implies a somewhat lower tax rate on labor income and thus a higher after-tax wage rate; this effect, however, is tempered by the higher long-run capital—labor ratio and thus higher gross wages under the FT plan (the increase in wages is about 18% greater) due to its lower overall level of capital taxation. Investment responses are muted somewhat under the AT plan relative to the FT plan, as its individual level taxation of capital income implies smaller reductions in the cost of capital; this translates into a long-run increase in GDP that is 0.4 percentage points greater under the AT plan than under the FT plan. The general pattern of changes in investment is the same — large increases in investment in the composite good and rental housing sectors, but an initial decline and ultimately only a small increase in investment in the owner-occupied housing sector — but the magnitudes of these changes are reduced by as much as 15% relative to the FT plan, with similar reductions in the long-run changes in the capital stocks in each sector.

With respect to asset price changes, the tax treatment of capital income is less generous under the AT plan, which implies that the differences between the treatment of old and new business assets, including rental housing, before and after reform is smaller than under the FT plan. As a result, the changes in the prices of these assets are less

**Table 11.4** Simulation results: capital income tax add-on to Flat Tax reform (% changes in variables)

|  | Years after reform | | | | | |
|---|---|---|---|---|---|---|
|  | 2 | 5 | 10 | 20 | 50 | 150 |
| GDP | 1.9 | 2.5 | 2.8 | 3.4 | 3.8 | 3.9 |
| Output − X | 2.0 | 2.6 | 3.0 | 3.6 | 4.0 | 4.1 |
| Output − R | 1.0 | 1.3 | 1.4 | 1.6 | 1.7 | 1.6 |
| Output − H | 1.4 | 2.1 | 2.4 | 3.0 | 3.3 | 3.3 |
| Capital stock − X | 1.5 | 4.0 | 5.8 | 8.5 | 10.5 | 10.9 |
| Capital stock − R | 1.0 | 2.8 | 4.3 | 6.9 | 9.3 | 9.9 |
| Capital stock − H | −0.3 | −0.4 | −0.3 | 0.4 | 1.7 | 2.2 |
| Investment − X | 8.0 | 8.7 | 9.4 | 10.1 | 10.8 | 10.9 |
| Investment − R | 13.4 | 13.1 | 12.9 | 11.5 | 10.3 | 9.9 |
| Investment − H | −2.5 | −0.3 | 1.2 | 2.3 | 2.5 | 2.3 |
| Labor supply | 2.1 | 2.1 | 2.1 | 2.0 | 2.1 | 2.1 |
| Asset prices − X | −2.9 | −3.6 | −3.9 | −4.6 | −4.9 | −4.9 |
| Asset prices − R | −16.1 | −15.6 | −15.2 | −15.0 | −15.0 | −14.9 |
| Asset prices − H | −2.1 | −0.7 | 0.4 | 1.6 | 2.2 | 2.3 |

X = corporate and non-corporate sector, R = rental housing sector, H = owner-occupied housing sector.

pronounced. With adjustment costs, this effect is small, except for rental housing, where the decline in average equity prices is about 15% less than under the FT plan; by comparison, without adjustment costs, the declines in the equity values of all three assets are smaller by roughly 13–15% under the AT plan. In particular, this implies that implementing the AT plan would decrease the total value of owner-occupied housing by less than 3% initially. However, as discussed in the previous section, the declines in the values of rental housing are relatively large under all scenarios, suggesting the case for transition relief is strongest for rental housing. In marked contrast, with the higher level of adjustment costs, equity asset prices in the composite good sector rise slightly – reversing the 13% decline that occurs in the absence of such costs – in which case for transition relief is much weaker. The more modest changes in asset prices (and thus smaller windfall losses) under the AT plan suggest that while an add-on tax promises smaller increases in investment and capital accumulation, it is likely to be politically more feasible.

### 11.4.3 Corporate income tax rate reduction

Although there has been considerable interest in recent years in fundamental tax reform in the US, experience suggests that incremental reform of the existing income tax system is a much more likely possibility. In particular, there has been much recent discussion of corporate income tax reform, especially a BBRR reform along the lines of the much celebrated Tax Reform Act of 1986.[18] Diamond *et al.* (2011) uses the DZ model to examine the economic effects of such a corporate income tax reform.

The case for a BBRR corporate income tax reform is well-known: by eliminating tax preferences for certain forms of investment and lowering statutory rates, such a reform reduces costly distortions of economic decisions, and thus promotes economic growth and economic efficiency in resource allocation, simplifies tax administration and compliance, reduces incentives for tax evasion and tax avoidance, and creates both the perception and the reality of a fairer tax system. These arguments are especially compelling in the case of the corporate income tax, which has often been characterized as a singularly complex and inefficient tax instrument, as it significantly distorts a wide variety of decisions, including those regarding asset mix and thus the allocation of investment across different industries, the method of finance (debt versus equity in the form of retained earnings or new share issues), organizational form (corporate versus non-corporate), and the mix of retentions, dividends paid and share repurchases (Gravelle, 1994; US Department of the Treasury, 2007; Nicodème, 2008). Moreover, in the case of equity finance, the magnitude of these distortions is increased to the extent that the effective tax rate on corporate income is increased by the double taxation of such

---

[18] See McLure and Zodrow (1987) for a discussion of the Tax Reform Act of 1986 as well as its predecessor, the plan prepared by the US Department of the Treasury known as 'Treasury-I'.

income at both the business level under the corporate tax and then again at the individual level as dividends or capital gains (and, to an increasingly limited extent, under the estate tax). The taxation of capital income inherent in the corporate income tax also reduces saving and investment, which in turn reduces the size of the capital stock, labor productivity, and wage growth.

Many recent proposals for corporate income tax reform have also focused on international issues, especially increasing international capital mobility, international tax competition and aggressive tax avoidance on the part of US multinationals. Proponents of such reforms argue that both statutory tax rates and the overall tax burden on capital income in the US are quite high by international standards, and that the corporate income tax should be reformed in the interest of attracting and retaining mobile capital, promoting economic growth, improving economic efficiency, reducing opportunities for tax avoidance and evasion, and reducing administrative and compliance costs. The ongoing process of globalization also implies that the tax system increasingly has important effects on the competitiveness of US multinationals and on the investment decisions of multinationals based in both the US and in other countries. All of these factors suggest that the corporate income tax is ripe for reform.

The direction that such a reform should take is, however, not obvious. Although the BBRR approach is the traditional one, a question that inevitably arises in discussions of lowering the corporate tax rate is whether maintaining a high statutory rate, coupled with investment incentives such as an investment tax credit or more accelerated depreciation allowances (including partial expensing) for new investment, is not preferable. The investment incentive approach is often touted as having more 'bang for the buck' in that the revenue cost per dollar of induced investment is lower than with a rate reduction (US Department of the Treasury, 2007), i.e. revenue losses are comparatively small because the new tax incentives apply only to new investment while the relatively high statutory rate continues to apply to the income earned by old investments.[19] In addition, the use of investment incentives implies that the effective marginal tax rate applied to normal returns is reduced, while above normal returns, including those attributable to location-specific rents, are still taxed at the statutory rate. By comparison, revenue losses are argued to be significantly higher under a reduction in the statutory tax rate because the rate reduction applies to both the income earned by old investments and by investments that generate above normal returns. Finally, to the extent that a lower statutory corporate tax rate increases a positive rate differential between the personal and corporate income tax rates, it creates incentives for shifting income from the personal tax base to the corporate tax base (Gordon and Slemrod, 2000).

---

[19] Note, however, that even in this case, much of the incentives for new investments will nevertheless be inframarginal and will reduce revenues for investments that would have been made without the incentive.

Although each of these arguments has some validity, there are important counter-arguments. (i) The 'bang for the buck' from rate reduction may not be as small as sometimes envisioned, because the rate cut reduces the taxation of above-normal returns that reflect firm-specific rents attributable to highly mobile investments in invention and innovation or firm-created intangible assets, and thus attracts such investments by lowering the average effective tax on such returns — a result that does not obtain under investment incentives. Thus, the desirability of taxing above-normal returns depends on whether they reflect relatively mobile firm-specific rents or relatively immobile location-specific rents. (ii) The relatively high statutory corporate tax rate under the 'tax incentives' approach encourages multinational firms to use transfer pricing and other tax planning strategies, including debt reallocation and relocation of patents and other intangible assets, to reduce the share of taxable income realized in relatively high-tax countries like the US, while increasing the share of taxable income realized in relatively low-tax countries. Such 'financial reallocation', which is much easier to put into effect than physical reallocation of capital assets, can significantly reduce taxable incomes reported in the US and thus government tax revenues. Much empirical evidence confirms that such income shifting is become increasingly prevalent (Diamond et al., 2011), with one study suggesting that that the revenue increase from a unilateral increase in the statutory tax rate is on average reduced by roughly more than 65% due to income shifting solely in the form of transfer pricing (Bartelsman and Beetsma, 2003). In addition, it is difficult in practice to design an investment incentive system that is neutral across business assets, tax incentives for new investment may be perceived as unfair by firms that invested under the previous tax system and tax incentives may have a limited effect on investment if they are received by firms in a loss position that must carry forward their benefits without interest. The desirability of the traditional BBRR corporate income tax reform is thus open to question, and we attempt to shed some light on this difficult issue by simulating its economic effects.

We extend our model in several ways in order to evaluate the arguments outlined above. (i) We account explicitly for a wide variety of business tax expenditures, including rate-reducing preferences, production incentives, investment incentives, and lump sum deductions, as described by the Joint Committee on Taxation (2008), modeling in detail how their elimination would affect the cost of capital in the corporate and non-corporate sectors. (ii) In order to account for the taxation of economic rents, we extend the model to include an imperfectly competitive sector in which investments permanently earn above normal returns.[20] This is accomplished by splitting the corporate sector into two production sectors — a perfectly competitive sector characterized by normal returns and

---

[20] Note that, in contrast to the basic model, the extension to an imperfectly competitive sector implies that the initial equilibrium is characterized by inefficiencies other than those related to taxes and a reallocation of resources from the imperfectly competitive sector will generate an efficiency gain.

an imperfectly competitive corporate sector characterized by above-normal returns, even in the long-run steady-state equilibrium. The above-normal returns in the imperfectly competitive sector are assumed to reflect a fixed markup of the price of the goods produced in that sector. The extent of imperfect competition in the US economy — and thus the appropriate way to model the corporate sector — is of course a subject of much debate. We assume that the imperfectly competitive sector consists of large multinational corporations, which account for slightly over 20% of the US economy; also, following Bayoumi *et al.* (2004), we assume a price markup of 20%. Second, to examine the effects of corporate tax reform on international capital flows (including into the imperfectly competitive sector), we adopt an approach used by Goulder *et al.* (1983) and assume that the elasticity of supply of international capital with respect to the difference between the US and world rates of return is constant; based on the discussion in Gravelle and Smetters (2006) we make the relatively conservative assumption that this elasticity is unitary. (iii) In order to capture the benefit of a lower statutory corporate income tax rate in reducing incentives for income shifting abroad by US multinationals, we assume that one-half of the static revenue reduction in the imperfectly competitive sector that would occur with a rate reduction in the absence of income shifting is offset by reduced income shifting abroad.

We perform numerous simulations of a BBRR corporate income tax reform within the context of this expanded version of the DZ model, focusing on the macroeconomic effects of reform, especially the effects on long-run GDP (rather than aggregate efficiency gains or losses); the results of several of these simulations are reported in Table 11.5. We begin with a pure BBRR reform that eliminates all business tax expenditures (nearly $100 billion) using all the revenues for rate reduction. This reform allows a reduction in the corporate rate from 35% to roughly 20% in the long run. The effects of such a reform on GDP, however, are moderately negative in the long run, as GDP decreases by 0.56%. This reflects the classic problem with a BBRR reform of the corporate income tax: the combination of reducing the rate and eliminating tax expenditures (the vast majority of which are assumed to reduce the cost of capital at the margin in our analysis) has roughly offsetting effects on the incentives for new investment, but the rate reduction reduces revenues on income earned by existing capital. The resulting relatively large statutory rate implies a higher effective tax rate on capital, reducing investment, the capital stock, labor productivity, wages and labor supply, generating a long reduction in GDP.

These negative macroeconomic effects are exacerbated when an imperfectly competitive sector is added to the model, as the corporate rate reduction applies to the above-normal returns earned in this sector, further driving down revenues and thus further limiting the rate reductions that can be achieved with a revenue neutral reform. In this case, the corporate tax rate falls to 21.9% in the long run and GDP falls by 0.84%.

**Table 11.5** Simulation results: corporate income tax rate reduction (% changes in variables)

| | Years after reform | | | | | |
|---|---|---|---|---|---|---|
| | 2 | 5 | 10 | 20 | 50 | 150 |
| *Benchmark case: base broadening* | | | | | | |
| GDP | 0.08 | −0.01 | −0.14 | −0.30 | −0.51 | −0.56 |
| Capital stock | −0.19 | −0.64 | −1.15 | −1.72 | −2.22 | −2.35 |
| Investment | −2.57 | −2.65 | −2.76 | −2.81 | −2.95 | −2.99 |
| Labor supply | 2.1 | 2.1 | 2.1 | 2.0 | 2.1 | 2.1 |
| Consumption | 0.26 | 0.03 | −0.19 | −0.33 | −0.17 | −0.14 |
| *Base broadening with imperfectly competitive sector, foreign capital flows and income shifting* | | | | | | |
| GDP | 0.07 | −0.04 | −0.20 | −0.40 | −0.60 | −0.63 |
| Capital stock | −0.01 | −0.83 | −1.42 | −1.66 | −2.00 | −2.05 |
| Investment | −2.08 | −2.48 | −2.84 | −2.85 | −2.94 | −2.95 |
| Labor supply | −0.09 | −0.12 | −0.13 | −0.11 | −0.10 | −0.10 |
| Consumption | 0.30 | 0.00 | −0.21 | −0.29 | −0.15 | −0.16 |
| *Base broadening to reach 25% rate, keep accelerated depreciation and 80% investment credits* | | | | | | |
| GDP | 0.09 | 0.20 | 0.31 | 0.48 | 0.60 | 0.62 |
| Capital stock | 0.22 | −0.03 | −0.09 | 0.27 | 0.46 | 0.51 |
| Investment | −0.34 | −0.24 | −0.11 | 0.36 | 0.45 | 0.48 |
| Labor supply | −0.02 | −0.04 | −0.04 | −0.03 | −0.04 | −0.04 |
| Consumption | 0.16 | 0.04 | −0.01 | 0.12 | 0.59 | 0.80 |

As discussed above, several factors might mitigate these negative macroeconomic effects of a BBRR reform. However, these effects are fairly modest in our simulations. In principle, allowing for an elastic supply of foreign capital might increase the amount of reform-induced investment, especially in the imperfectly competitive sector where above-normal returns would be taxed at lower rates. However, the net effect of the reform on after-tax interest rates is very small, as the negative effects of eliminating tax expenditures that benefit capital investment roughly offset the beneficial effects of the rate cut. This in turn implies that changes in capital inflows and outflows, which are assumed to be determined by differences in relative after-tax interest rates, are similarly very small. As a result, 'opening up' the economy has virtually no effect on the results.

Somewhat more positive results occur when reform-induced reductions in income shifting are added to the model, which result in higher revenues at each tax rate. For example, in the version of the model with an imperfectly competitive and a closed economy, adding income shifting results in a long-run decline in GDP of 0.63% (rather than 0.84%).

These results may appear to be surprising, given the negligible or slightly positive effects on GDP from a BBRR reform reported by the US Department of the Treasury (2007). Although our analyses differ in numerous respects, the most important difference is that the Treasury analysis is based on the questionable assumption that all tax expenditures other than accelerated depreciation have no effects on marginal investment decisions, i.e. they do not affect the cost of capital and thus the level of investment. For purposes of comparison, we perform a simulation in which we follow Treasury in assuming a perfectly competitive, closed economy with no income shifting. In this case, the effects of eliminating all business tax expenditures and lowering the corporate tax rate are, unsurprisingly, much more positive, as GDP increases in the long run by 0.52%. However, when we extend the model to include an imperfectly competitive sector, foreign capital flows, and the income shifting response, the long-run increase in GDP declines to 0.20%.[21]

To sum up, our simulations of the economic effects of a traditional BBRR reform suggests that it results in modest declines in long-run GDP, even when one takes into account the taxation of economic rents in an imperfectly competitive sector, the possibility of international capital flows, and the potential for reduced income shifting due to a lower statutory corporate tax rate in the US. However, it is important to stress that our simulations do not fully capture one of the key benefits of a BBRR reform — the improved allocation of capital across industries within the corporate and non-corporate sectors due to the elimination of tax preferences for certain industries. Thus, one could interpret our results as suggestive of the magnitudes of the efficiency gains that would need to be obtained from such reallocations of investment and capital to generate long-run increases in economic growth.

## 11.4.4 Implementing a VAT for deficit reduction

All of the tax reforms considered thus far have been revenue neutral, raising the same amount of revenue as the current income tax system. However, much recent attention has been focused on the unsustainable fiscal imbalance faced by the US under currently projected spending and tax policies. For example, Auerbach and Gale (2011), drawing on the recent report of the Congressional Budget Office (2011) as well as the latest projections by the actuaries of the Social Security and Medicare programs, estimate that federal deficits will be in excess of 6% of GDP by late in the decade even with a relatively strong economy, with the debt—GDP ratio approaching 100% by 2021. The long-term budget outlook is even worse. Although the magnitude of the long-term fiscal imbalance depends on a wide variety of factors, especially the pattern of healthcare spending, Auerbach and Gale estimate that even under the most optimistic assumptions, the long-term fiscal gap, defined as the immediate and permanent increase in taxes or reduction in spending required to maintain the long-term debt—GDP ratio at its current level, will be between 6% and 7% of GDP. These projections demonstrate clearly that the US faces

---

[21] We also show that greater GDP growth can be obtained with more carefully designed BBRR reforms, including (i) focusing on eliminating only rate-reducing, production, and lump-sum tax preferences, rather than direct investment incentives, and (ii) replacing the revenues lost with corporate tax rate reduction with higher taxes on wages.

fiscal problems of unprecedented proportions and that dramatic actions must be taken relatively quickly to avoid a catastrophic outcome (Burman *et al.*, 2010).

The reports of several recent commissions focusing on deficit and debt reduction, including the report of the National Commission on Fiscal Responsibility and Reform (the Bowles–Simpson report) and the alternative proposed by the Bipartisan Policy Center's Debt Reduction Task Force (the Rivlin–Domenici plan), have examined potential solutions to these fiscal problems. Although they differ considerably in their details, both reports recognize that additional tax revenues are assuredly going to have to play some role in solving our nation's looming fiscal problems, even if this role is secondary to spending reductions and cost-saving reforms of the Social Security, Medicare, and Medicaid programs (Diamond and Zodrow, 2011).

One often-cited proposal for partially addressing the deficit and debt problems in the US is the enactment of a new federal VAT — not as a substitute for the existing income tax as in the proposals for fundamental tax reform discussed above, but as an 'add-on' tax designed to reduce the deficit and, over time, the debt. Cline *et al.* (2010) examine the effects of such a policy using the DZ model.

We make several modifications to the basic model (which in this case assumes a target bequest) to facilitate the analysis of a deficit-reducing add-on VAT. Most importantly, we add government debt. In a steady-state equilibrium in the model — both before enactment of the add-on VAT and once the economy has fully adjusted to the VAT — the debt must grow at the steady-state growth rate of the economy; in this analysis, the model assumes a fixed population growth rate of 1.1% and a fixed productivity growth rate of 2.3%, which equal the average population and productivity growth rates in the US over both the past 50 and the past 20 years (Council of Economic Advisors, 2010). Thus, federal government debt owned by the public must grow at a 3.4% rate to maintain a constant ratio of government debt to GDP in the steady state. This in turn implies that the steady-state annual increment in the debt — the government's annual budget deficit — must equal the product of the growth rate and the steady-state level of debt.

However, the model can accommodate annual deficits and debt levels that differ from steady-state values during the transition period following the enactment of the add-on VAT. In the simulations, we assume an initial steady state with 2007 as our benchmark year and then superimpose on that year a relatively large steady-state debt of roughly 90% of GDP — as predicted by Congressional Budget Office (2010) to occur by 2020 under the Obama administration proposals — which in turn implies a steady-state deficit of 3.1% of GDP. We then introduce an add-on VAT that raises roughly 2.0% of GDP and thus, at least initially, reduces the deficit from approximately 3.1%–1.1% of GDP; the exact amounts of deficit reduction vary primarily because interest payments on the debt decline as the reduction in the deficit reduces debt accumulation.

We maintain this deficit-reducing VAT for 20 years, during which time the debt–GDP ratio declines by roughly 2–3 percentage points of GDP per year, until it reaches a level roughly half of the initial level, declining from roughly 90% to about 45% of GDP. At this point, we have to 'close' the model so that we can return to a steady-state equilibrium, i.e. we cannot continue to reduce the debt–GDP ratio indefinitely and reach a steady state, and instead have to alter fiscal policy to ensure that the deficit is consistent with a steady-state debt of 45% of GDP, which implies a steady-state deficit of roughly 1.5% of GDP.

Although this could be done in many ways, we close the model 20 years after the enactment of the VAT by increasing government transfer payments, by roughly 3.3% of GDP, to achieve the steady-state level of the deficit. This seems to be a reasonable approach, given projected increases in government transfers through the Medicare, Medicaid, and Social Security programs; in particular, we assume that these transfers are distributed uniformly on a *per capita* basis, which could be argued as corresponding roughly to the effects of a deficit-financed increase in the Medicare program. Thus, the 'add-on VAT' in the model is best interpreted as financing an approximate halving of government debt relative to GDP and then financing an increase in transfer payments that are distributed on a lump-sum basis. Our simulation results calculate the economic and distributional effects of this specific add-on VAT, relative to a baseline equilibrium in which the debt–GDP ratio is constant at 90% and the deficit–GDP ratio is constant at 3.1%.[22]

We examine several different VAT structures in our analysis, which differ in the broadness of the base and the existence of a means-tested rebate. In principle, a VAT should include all personal consumption expenditures and exclude all investment purchases, with any distributional concerns regarding the effects of the taxation of necessities addressed with a VAT rebate in the form of means-tested income transfers that refund VAT paid on consumption purchases by the poor. In practice, even in the presence of rebates, the VAT base is seldom applied to all consumption expenditures, with a variety of goods excluded from the base or given rate preferences, typically to relieve the tax burden on the poor; in addition, for social reasons, tax is often reduced or eliminated on goods such as food consumed at home, education or health care services. In our analysis, we follow Toder and Rosenberg (2010) in considering two potential bases for a US VAT — a 'Broader' base that includes all of personal consumption that might reasonably be expected to be subject to tax and includes approximately 73% of all consumption, and a 'Narrow' base that includes several additional exemptions and includes roughly 46% of consumption. We also consider a rebate that would refund tax paid on the poverty level of consumption and phases out as household income increases.

---

[22] Note, however, that the analysis assumes that a debt–GDP ratio of 90% is sustainable in the long run, which very well may not be the case. Our analysis thus does not capture the perhaps significant benefits of moving from an unsustainable situation to a sustainable growth path.

**Table 11.6** Simulation results: effects of add-on value-added tax (% changes in variables)

| | Years after reform | | | | | |
|---|---|---|---|---|---|---|
| | 2 | 5 | 10 | 20 | 50 | 150 |
| *Broader base VAT* | | | | | | |
| GDP | −0.12 | −0.04 | 0.20 | 0.69 | 1.34 | 1.43 |
| Investment | 3.40 | 4.05 | 5.34 | 6.97 | 8.36 | 8.25 |
| Employment/aggregate labor | −0.64 | −0.63 | −0.62 | −0.64 | −0.79 | −0.82 |
| Consumption | −1.08 | −1.17 | −1.24 | −1.09 | −0.71 | −0.58 |
| Debt−GDP | 91.24 | 85.83 | 75.81 | 55.24 | 54.89 | 54.84 |
| *Narrow base VAT* | | | | | | |
| GDP | −0.12 | −0.03 | 0.20 | 0.68 | 1.32 | 1.42 |
| Investment | 3.52 | 4.12 | 5.37 | 6.97 | 8.34 | 8.23 |
| Employment/aggregate labor | −0.63 | −0.62 | −0.62 | −0.63 | −0.78 | −0.81 |
| Consumption | −1.11 | −1.19 | −1.26 | −1.10 | −0.73 | −0.59 |
| Debt−GDP | 91.21 | 85.86 | 75.96 | 55.60 | 55.25 | 55.20 |

The results of our simulations, which are shown in Table 11.6, can be summarized as follows. With respect to macroeconomic effects, the VAT reduces the need for deficit finance by roughly 2% of GDP over a 20-year period in which the debt is roughly cut in half, with the deficit-reducing effect magnified over time with the decline of the debt and the associated reduction in government interest payments. Most of the private saving in the model that formerly was allocated to government bonds and used to finance government consumption or transfer payments is now diverted to private saving and used to finance investment. As a result, investment surges, as the classic 'crowding out' effect of government debt is reversed.

This effect is reinforced by (i) the eventual decline in interest rates that occurs because the government's demand for debt is reduced, which in turn reduces the cost of capital, (ii) the decline in income tax rates that occurs because government revenue needs decline as interest payments decline with the reduction in the level of government debt and (iii) the fact that the VAT discourages consumption relative to saving.[23] At the same time, the government expenditures that were formerly financed with debt are now financed with the consumption-based VAT, which is assumed to be fully shifted forward as higher consumer prices.[24] As a result, private consumption falls. Moreover, by

---

[23] This pattern is also reinforced in the short run to the extent that elderly owners of capital, who have a relatively high propensity to consume in their retirement years, suffer a windfall loss due to the implementation of the VAT, as the real value of their capital assets declines due to VAT-induced increases in consumer prices.

[24] In our view, this is the most reasonable assumption regarding the incidence of the VAT; see Zodrow et al. (2011) for further discussion. Note that we adjust transfer payments for the VAT so that their real value is held constant, i.e. the VAT is increased to both cover this increase in transfer payments and reduce the deficit by 2% of GDP.

increasing consumer prices, the VAT reduces the real wage, causing labor supply to fall. Whether these negative effects on consumption and labor supply are offset in the long run depends on the strength of the investment effect; in any case, overall GDP is likely to increase in the long run due to efficiency gains, as the increase in investment is larger than any reduction in consumption. These effects, however, are secondary — the primary effect of the add-on VAT is to increase private saving and investment at the expense of private consumption by substituting government revenues that come from a consumption-based tax for revenues that were raised with deficit finance. Finally, 20 years after enactment of the VAT, government transfer payments are increased on a *per capita* basis to increase the deficit to the 1.5% of GDP level consistent with a steady-state debt of about 45% of GDP. This increases consumption, but also reduces labor supply as it has purely an income effect, increasing the demand for leisure.

With respect to distributional effects, a VAT tends to be regressive relative to annual income since consumption is a larger fraction of annual income for the poor, although this effect is mitigated by the rebate, and to a much smaller extent, any exemptions under the tax. Moreover, the VAT is less regressive when measured with respect to lifetime income, the approach we take in our analysis. This occurs because consumption and thus VAT paid relative to income is higher during youth and in old age, when income is relatively low, than it is during the prime saving years of middle age, when income is relatively high and consumption and VAT paid are relatively low; these factors imply that any annual snapshot of the incidence of a consumption-based tax relative to income will overstate regressivity, relative to our measure, which compares lifetime taxes to lifetime income (Fullerton and Rogers, 1993).

Within this context, the incidence of the VAT in our model is determined primarily by three factors. (i) As a consumption-based tax, the burden of the VAT in isolation is slightly regressive in a lifetime context (due to difference in bequest motives), but this regressivity is largely or fully offset by the rebate and, to a much smaller extent, by any exemptions. As a result, the VAT tends to be moderately progressive over the lower and middle lifetime income ranges. (ii) VAT-induced changes in interest rates have a large effect on the distribution of the burden of the VAT policy. Individuals who are near death benefit significantly from the initial short-run increase in the interest rate since it has a large positive impact on the income from their assets. Over time, however, interest rates decline, which has a negative effect on the wealthy — an effect that dominates the direct effect of the VAT, since interest rates in the simulations eventually decline by roughly a quarter. As a result, wealthy individuals who are elderly at the time of enactment of the VAT tend to benefit, but wealthy individuals who are younger tend to be hurt by the reform. (iii) The significant increase in government transfers that occurs 20 years after the enactment of the VAT (that we have chosen to close the model to return it to a steady-state equilibrium) tends to drive the incidence results for those who live long enough to benefit from the transfers. As the transfers are distributed on a *per capita* basis, they disproportionately benefit the poor and make the 'VAT plus eventual increase in transfers' policy quite progressive.

We close by reporting some of the detailed results for our simulation of the effects enacting the 'Broader' VAT with a means-tested rebate. Consumption falls immediately, by 1.4% initially, with the declines gradually increasing in absolute value, to 1.7% 10 years after enactment, and then declining moderately to 1.3% in the long run, reflecting the effects of VAT-induced capital accumulation. As described above, this decline in consumption is accompanied by an increase in investment, as private saving is diverted from purchases of government debt to private investment. Investment initially increases by 4.5% and gradually continues to rise, with an ultimate increase of 10.1% in the long run. Labor supply falls due to the reduction in the real wage, with declines of 0.6% in the short run, and 0.8% in the long run. Nevertheless, GDP still rises after enactment of the VAT, as it initially increases by slightly less than 0.3% and then gradually continues to rise, with an increase of 1.4% in the long run.

Over the 20 years of deficit reduction, government debt falls from 93.5% to 46.3% of GDP, while the deficit falls from 3.2% to 1.9% of GDP initially, and then turns to a slight surplus, before jumping to its steady-state value of 1.5% of GDP 20 years after enactment of the VAT when *per capita* transfers increase by 3.4% to close the model. Although the interest rate initially increases, from 5.4% to 6.4%,[25] the increase in the supply of private saving available for private investment quickly puts downward pressure on the interest rate, which declines to 5.1% 5 years after enactment of the VAT and to 4.1% in the long run.[26] The decline in interest rates, when coupled with the decline in debt, implies that interest payments on the debt fall considerably, enhancing the amount of deficit reduction obtained under the VAT. Specifically, interest on the debt rises initially from 5.0% to 6.0% of GDP, but quickly falls to 4.4% of GDP 5 years after enactment and to 1.9% of GDP in the long run.

The distributional analysis of the broad-based VAT with a rebate (Figure 11.1) shows the net effects of the three primary factors determining incidence in the model discussed above (the direct effects of the VAT, the indirect effects on interest rates and the eventual increase in transfers 20 years after enactment of the VAT). Note first that the very wealthy and very elderly benefit primarily from the initial reform-induced increase in interest rates; for example, for individuals of economic age 54 at the time of reform, the 11th income group experiences a gain of 3.0% of remaining lifetime

[25] The initial increase in the interest rate reflects two purely transitional factors: a short period of time during which existing capital earns above-normal rents due to costs in adjusting the capital stock to its new higher level and anticipated capital gains as the value of the capital stock initially declines due to the enactment of a consumption-based tax that favors new capital over capital (which is assumed not to receive any transitional relief, e.g. in the form of expensing of existing basis), but then increases in value with time. For further discussion, see Zodrow (2002) and Auerbach and Kotlikoff (1987).

[26] Note that these figures reflect the before-tax interest rate on debt in the model; in this version of the model, we incorporate an equity premium of 5%, following Goulder and Summers (1989).

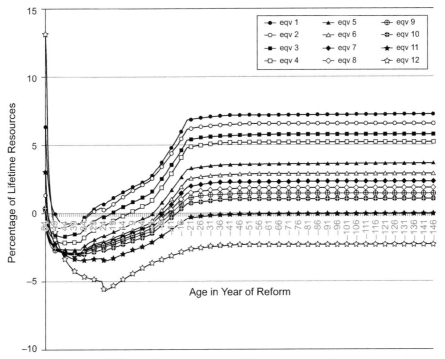

**Figure 11.1** Distributional effects of a broader-base VAT with a rebate. *(Source: Authors' calculations based on results presented in Carroll et al. (2010).)*

resources and the 12th income group (the top 2%) experience an increase of 13.1% of lifetime resources. At the same time, individuals of age 54 in the first four income groups also benefit from reform, primarily because their government transfers are fully indexed and they receive VAT rebates, and also because their assets, while small in absolute terms, are large relative to income so that they benefit from the initial increase in the interest rate.

These positive effects, however, diminish rapidly as individuals live longer after reform. For example, for individuals age 51 at the time of reform, the poorest group benefits slightly (0.5% of remaining lifetime resources) and the incidence of the tax is progressive throughout lifetime income group 6, but then turns regressive due to the lingering effects of the initial increase in the interest rate. By comparison, for individuals of age 46 at the time of enactment, the incidence of the tax is progressive for the low- and high-lifetime-income groups, and roughly proportional for the middle-income groups, with losses ranging from 0.7% of remaining lifetime resources for the lowest income group to 2.8% of lifetime resources for the highest income group. Looking at an even younger group — those age 35 at the time of enactment — the tax is progressive over the entire income range except for the first two income groups (although it is still roughly proportional for the middle-income groups) with losses ranging from 0.5% of remaining lifetime resources for the lowest income group to 4.6% of lifetime resources for the highest income group. Once individuals start receiving transfers 20 years after enactment of reform (those of age 34 or less), the net effect of the fiscal policy on the low-income groups is more likely to be positive, while middle- and upper-income groups still lose from reform. In the long run, the capital accumulation benefits of the VAT increase wages modestly. For example, for individuals born 10 years after reform, individuals in the first eight income groups benefit from reform, while individuals in the top four groups are net losers, with the gains ranging from 4.2% of lifetime resources to −3.2%. In the long run, only the top two income groups lose from the reform and the tax policy is progressive at all but the very lowest income levels, with the gains ranging from 7.2% to −2.3% of lifetime resources.

In summary, our analysis provides several insights regarding the effects of implementing an add-on VAT for deficit reduction. Most importantly, it shows that reducing the deficit is a difficult task, even if the instrument used is a relatively efficient tax. The use of an add-on VAT diverts private saving from government debt to private investment and is successful in reducing the deficit and ultimately the level of debt, reducing interest rates and increasing private saving. However, these benefits come at the cost of reducing consumption in both the short run and, to only a slightly smaller extent, in the long run. Moreover, the reduction in the real wage associated with the VAT reduces labor supply, again both the short run and, to a slightly smaller extent, in the long run. These are simply costs associated with using a consumption-based tax to replace deficit-financed government spending. In addition, although most individuals ultimately benefit from the VAT reform, these benefits are long delayed, accruing primarily to those not yet alive at the time of reform — a result that demonstrates the political difficulty of dealing with the deficit problem.

The enactment of a VAT is also often believed to problematical from a distributional standpoint. Our simulation results suggest that this concern is largely misplaced, as long as the VAT includes a rebate designed to relieve its burden on the poor. Indeed, because the replacement of deficit finance with the VAT reduces interest rates over time, much of its burden is borne by the wealthy.[27]

Our results are generally consistent with a recent study by the International Monetary Fund (2010), which provides both empirical and simulation evidence that fiscal consolidation has a negative macroeconomic impact in the short run. However, the International Monetary Fund study suggests that the fact that we assume a closed economy to simplify our analysis implies that our results may overstate the increases in

---

[27] Results not reported confirm the conventional wisdom that the use of an income-conditioned rebate is superior to using VAT exemptions to protect the poor; indeed, to a first approximation, the distributional benefits of the broad-based VAT with a rebate can be matched by a narrow-based VAT only if also includes a rebate.

domestic investment that would occur with an add-on VAT. In an open-economy context, some of current and projected future deficits are financed with borrowing from abroad, which is associated with a trade deficit. Introduction of the VAT would reduce the government deficit, thus increasing national saving and reducing the need to borrow abroad. However, some of the reduction in the deficit would be reflected in an improvement in the trade balance, i.e. an increase in net exports rather than an increase in domestic investment; thus, domestic investment would increase less (and interest rates would decline less) than under our closed-economy scenario.

## 11.4.5 Macroeconomic effects of tax cuts and the financing decision

Tax cuts are often adopted with no explicit provisions for offsetting the resulting revenue losses, with the most recent examples being the Bush administration tax cuts enacted in 2001 and 2003. In this section we discuss several studies that use OLG-CGE models to analyze the effects of such tax cuts, including some using the DZ model.

### 11.4.5.1 Overview

The decrease in revenue from deficit-financed tax cuts initially increases the stock of government debt. However, the government's infinite-horizon budget constraint requires that measures must ultimately be adopted to service or retire that debt. Deficit-financed tax cuts have been controversial, with supporters highlighting the beneficial economic effects from reductions in distortionary taxes and opponents stressing the adverse economic effects of deficits.

In view of these conflicting economic effects, the assessment of deficit-financed tax cuts requires an estimate of the magnitudes of their various effects, including their impacts on output, consumption, labor supply and the capital stock. In addition, it is important to examine the impact of deficit-financed tax cuts on the welfare of various generations in an overlapping generations framework, and OLG-CGE models offer a natural way to obtain such estimates. As noted above, Auerbach and Kotlikoff (1987) is the pioneering work in the use of OLG-CGE models to examine the effects of deficit-financed tax cuts, as they analyze the effects of broad-based income tax cuts that last 1, 5, and 20 years, followed by income-tax increases that maintain the debt—output ratio stabilized at its new, higher level. A number of other studies have also examined the impact of deficit-financed tax cuts.[28] In general, these studies find that both the form of

---

[28] The Office of Tax Analysis, US Department of the Treasury (2007), the Joint Committee on Taxation (2006) and the Congressional Budget Office (2007) have all produced estimates of the effects of deficit-financed tax cuts. The Office of Tax Analysis, US Department of the Treasury (2006) uses a version of the DZ model, among others, to examine the permanent extension of the 2001 and 2003 tax cuts. The Joint Committee on Taxation (2006) also uses the DZ model to consider a rate reduction in individual income taxes accompanied by base-broadening measures, assuming two different offsets to finance the deficit, one involving changes in transfer payments and the other involving changes in individual income tax rates.

the initial tax cut and the financing method matter. An increase in steady-state output is most likely if the initial tax cut is targeted toward marginal-rate reduction, if the financing method does not raise marginal rates and has income effects that encourage work (with transfer payment reductions being ideal), and if financing is implemented quickly.

One of the major issues confronting tax policy makers is related to whether the tax provisions in the Economic Growth and Tax Reduction Reconciliation Act of 2001 (EGTRRA) and the Jobs and Growth Tax Relief Reconciliation Act of 2003 (JGTRRA) should be extended permanently. In addition, the Alternative Minimum Tax (AMT) is a subject that has been receiving widespread attention since a large number of taxpayers, including many that earn less than $100,000, will be affected by the AMT in the next several years if changes are not enacted.

The debate over permanent extension of EGTRRA and JGTRRA focuses primarily on issues of economic growth, equity, and affordability. Proponents of permanently extending the tax cuts argue that a permanent reduction in tax rates will increase individual incentives to work and save. They argue that if the extension of the 2001 and 2003 tax packages were combined with tight spending controls, then the tax-induced economic growth and the reduction in the growth of spending would reduce the size of the deficit relative to GDP to a sustainable level. The opponents of permanently extending the tax cuts argue that given the current US budget deficit the tax cuts are unaffordable. They contend that the tax cuts are unlikely to increase economic output because larger deficits would lead to higher interest rates and debt-servicing costs, thereby offsetting the potential long-run gains from tax-induced increases in labor supply and personal saving. Given this, they believe that extending the tax cuts would be detrimental to the government's ability to solve other pressing budget issues, such as the need to reform the AMT and deal with the predicted budget shortfalls related to demographic changes in the population. In addition, many of the opponents believe that the tax cuts are unfairly distributed, with most of the benefits accruing to higher income taxpayers.

Auerbach (2002) examines the effects of extending the 2001 and 2003 tax cuts. He considers a somewhat different policy experiment than most other studies, which generally assume permanent tax cuts and then add a financing mechanism to pay for the tax cuts. (Of course, when the financing mechanism is a tax rate increase, layering on the tax increase effectively undoes the tax cuts in whole or in part.) Following Auerbach and Kotlikoff (1987), Auerbach instead considers experiments in which the 2001 and 2003 tax cuts last 10, 15, or 20 years before expiring, after which the debt−output ratio is stabilized using either increases in wage taxes or capital income taxes. Output increases while the tax cuts are in effect, but falls after the tax cuts expire. The long-run output decline is greater when the tax cut lasts longer, causing more debt to be accumulated, and when the financing is done through higher taxes on capital income. These negative effects are diminished if government purchases are reduced during the time the tax cuts are in effect to offset part of the revenue loss.

### 11.4.5.2 Diamond (2005) analysis

Diamond (2005) uses the DZ model (with a target bequest motive) to simulate the impact on the federal deficit and economic growth of permanently extending most of the provisions in EGTRRA and JGTRRA, assuming that the baseline is present law modified to include AMT relief.[29] In 2005, permanently extending the 2001 and 2003 income tax cuts roughly corresponded to a delayed tax cut on labor income since the bulk of the reduction in income tax rates would have occurred after 2010. The capital income tax cuts were also delayed since the tax rate reductions on dividends and capital gains were effective for taxable years beginning after 2008, and the most significant tax rate reductions on interest income and non-corporate business income would have occurred for taxable years after 2010.

In addition, an offsetting federal fiscal policy must be assumed to achieve a constant debt–GDP ratio in the long run. There are an infinite number of fiscal policies that could achieve this goal, and the choice of policy has an important effect on the simulation results. The three main fiscal policy responses considered by Diamond are: (i) a cut in government transfer payments after 10 years that achieves a constant debt–GDP ratio, (ii) an increase in federal income taxes after 10 years that achieves a constant debt–GDP ratio and (iii) a federal fiscal policy that assumes the growth in real discretionary government spending increases at the population growth rate instead of the growth rate of real GDP (under this assumption an additional offsetting income tax adjustment may also be necessary to achieve a constant debt–GDP ratio). The first two scenarios are often assumed by the Joint Committee on Taxation and Congressional Budget Office in analyses of the effects of changes in tax policy. Feldstein (2004) suggests a policy similar to the third fiscal policy alternative in a commentary that supported permanent extension of the 2001 and 2003 tax cuts. By comparison, the Joint Committee on Taxation (2003) and Congressional Budget Office (2003) assume that changes in income tax rates or government consumption (or transfer payments) are implemented after 2014 — the end of the federal budget window — to insure a stable long-run equilibrium growth path.

---

[29] The percentage changes in the average and marginal tax rates for different sources of taxable income are calculated using the Joint Committee on Taxation's individual tax model. Marginal tax rates are calculated on an income-weighted basis. Tax rates with similar patterns and percentage changes are averaged across adjacent years to simplify the presentation. From 2005 to 2010, the average wage tax rate decreases by 4%, the marginal wage tax rate decreases by 1% and the tax rate on interest income decreases by 2%. From 2011 to 2014, the average wage tax rate decreases by 20%, the marginal wage tax rate decreases by 12% and the tax rate on interest income decreases by 15%. From 2009 to 2014, the dividend tax rate decreases by 54% and capital gains tax rate decreases by 23% (there is no change in dividend or capital gains tax rates before 2009).

**Table 11.7** Simulation results: permanent extension of 2001 and 2003 tax cuts with different financing options (% changes in variables)

| | Years after reform | | | | | |
| --- | --- | --- | --- | --- | --- | --- |
| | 2005–2009 | 2010–2014 | 2015–2019 | 2020–2024 | 2035–2044 | 2095 |
| *Transfer offset after 2014* | | | | | | |
| GDP | 0.1 | 0.6 | 0.8 | 0.9 | 0.8 | 0.8 |
| Capital stock | 0.1 | 0.4 | 0.8 | 0.9 | 1.0 | 0.4 |
| Investment | 0.9 | 1.5 | 1.4 | 1.2 | 0.6 | 0.4 |
| Labor supply | 0.1 | 0.7 | 0.8 | 0.8 | 0.8 | 0.9 |
| Consumption | −0.1 | 0.4 | 0.6 | 0.7 | 0.8 | 0.8 |
| *Transfers increase at population growth rate 2005–2045 then income tax rates adjust* | | | | | | |
| GDP | 0.1 | 0.6 | 0.8 | 0.8 | 1.2 | 1.2 |
| Capital stock | 0.1 | 0.5 | 0.8 | 0.9 | 1.0 | 4.0 |
| Investment | 1.0 | 1.6 | 1.3 | 1.1 | 3.6 | 4.0 |
| Labor supply | 0.1 | 0.7 | 0.8 | 0.8 | 0.9 | 1.2 |
| Consumption | −0.1 | 0.4 | 0.7 | 0.8 | 0.8 | 2.1 |

The results of Diamond's simulations are reported in Table 11.7. He finds that permanently extending the 2001 and 2003 income tax cuts assuming that transfer payments are reduced after 2014 would increase employment and output by 0.1% and investment by 0.9% over the 5-year period after enactment. These effects occur because individuals increase saving in response to the lower tax rates and to offset the decrease in transfer payments in 2014 and thereafter.[30] In the long run, the permanent extension of the tax cuts increases employment and output by more than 0.8% relative to the baseline. In the long run, the capital stock increases by 0.7% and private consumption increases by 0.8%.

Beginning in 2015, transfer payments, which are 4.4% of GDP in the baseline, are reduced by roughly 44% to reach a stable fiscal policy. The remaining items that make up government spending are held constant at their baseline levels, except for net interest payments, which increase from 2 to 2.5% of GDP in the long run. This policy increases the debt-GDP ratio from 38% in 2005 to 47% in 2014 and beyond. Net interest payments increase by roughly $70 billion in 2014. A $262 billion reduction in real transfer payments is necessary to hold the debt-GDP ratio constant in 2015. This corresponds to a change in all real non-interesting outlays of $314 billion.

The net welfare effects, however, paint a much different picture than do the aggregate macroeconomic variables, such as GDP, labor supply, and investment. The net welfare effects show that current old and future generations would suffer a net welfare loss if the

---

[30] Note that individuals are fully aware of the pending cut in transfer payments under the assumption of perfect foresight.

2001 and 2003 tax cuts were permanently extended and transfer payments were cut after 2014. The oldest six generations (of economic ages 49–55) at the time of enactment would experience a net welfare change of −0.2% to −0.5% of remaining lifetime utility. Current young and middle aged generations would experience a net welfare gain ranging from 0.1% to 0.3% of remaining lifetime utility, with the largest net welfare gains occurring for individuals of economic age six (or roughly 30 years old) in the year of enactment. Generations born more than eight years after enactment would experience a net welfare change ranging from −0.1% to −0.4% of lifetime utility. These welfare losses demonstrate the negative effects of the larger federal deficits that occur before the enactment of offsetting fiscal policy actions in 2014. If the fiscal policy response occurred in 2005, the net welfare effects would reflect gains that range from 0% to 0.4% for all generations that are younger than age 24 at the time of enactment. The labor supply responses are roughly equivalent whether the fiscal policy response occurs immediately or is delayed for 10 years. However, the investment response when the fiscal policy response is delayed is mitigated considerably. For example, in the long run, investment increases by 3.2% with an immediate fiscal policy response rather than 0.4% if the fiscal policy response is delayed 10 years. This shows the importance of enacting offsetting fiscal policy responses in a timely manner.

Diamond also shows the effects of permanently extending the 2001 and 2003 income tax cuts assuming that increases in income tax rates are enacted in 2014 to reach a stable fiscal policy. In this case, employment increases in both the short and long run. In the short run, households supply more labor because tax rates are expected to increase in the future.[31] In the long run, households must work more to maintain the same level of consumption since the burden of increased debt service costs and the reduction in the private capital stock reduces after-tax disposable income. The capital stock declines by 1.2% relative to the baseline as a result of government debt crowding out private capital.

Because the fiscal offset is not enacted until after 2014, government debt increases in the period from 2005 to 2014, as tax revenues are reduced and government expenditures net of interest payments are unchanged relative to the baseline values. The debt–GDP ratio increases from 38% in 2005 to 47% in 2014. Net interest payments on the debt increase as the government accumulates more debt, although a decline in the interest rate in the first 5 years mitigates this effect slightly in the short run. Households increase private consumption immediately by effectively borrowing from future generations. Household consumption of private goods would be roughly constant after 2020 as the increase in income tax rates, lower wage rates, and an increase in labor supply would have offsetting effects on disposable income. Current young and middle-aged generations receive small welfare benefits from the extension of the tax cuts, while older and future

---

[31] This result is similar to the behavioral response to a delayed tax cut found in House and Shapiro (2006).

generations suffer a net welfare loss. The net welfare loss of future generations is approximately 0.4% of their remaining lifetime utility.

In the 5-year period 2015—2019, income tax rates increase by 16.5% from 2015 to 2019 levels and by approximately 19% thereafter. The net effect of the 2001 and 2003 tax cuts and the income tax increase in 2014 is different for each source of income. The net effect on dividend and capital gains tax rates is a net decrease. Interest income and the general business tax rate increase after 2014 relative to the baseline. In the long run, the marginal tax rate on wages falls by roughly 1% and the average tax rate on wages is unchanged. Thus, this could be viewed as a scenario similar to allowing the tax cuts to sunset in 2010, although the period that federal debt is accumulated would be four years shorter.

Diamond also examines the effect of assuming that the growth rates of real transfer payments and government spending, excluding Social Security and Medicare programs, are equal to the population growth rate for 50 years (after this 50-year period they grow at the growth rate of GDP).[32] In the baseline, transfer payments and government consumption are assumed to grow at the growth rate of GDP, which is determined by the growth rate of the population and technological growth.[33] Thus, this fiscal policy reduces the growth rate of real transfer payments and government spending from 2% to 1% per year for 50 years after the enactment of the permanent extension of the 2001 and 2003 income tax cuts. After 40 years, the income tax rates are allowed to adjust to stabilize the debt—GDP ratio.

The immediate impacts of this fiscal policy on labor supply and GDP are insignificant in the first 5 years after enactment. After that 5-year period, labor supply increases permanently by 0.3—0.5% relative to the baseline. GDP increases in the 15-year period from 2010 to 2024; however, this increase slowly diminishes as the stock of capital declines as the increase in the deficit relative to GDP increases interest rates and thus crowds out private investment. As the effect of moderate spending controls strengthens slowly over time, the deficit is reduced and private investment rebounds. In the long run, permanent extension of the 2001 and 2003 income tax cuts increases investment, labor supply, and GDP. In 2095, the capital stock is 1.7% higher relative to the baseline. Private consumption is higher in every period relative to the baseline.

The reductions in transfer spending and government consumption are equivalent to reductions in real non–interest spending of 6% in 2015, 16% in 2035 and 25% in the long run. The deficit—GDP ratio in the period from 2010—2034 increases above the baseline level as current generations borrow from future generations. In the long run, the

---

[32] The 50-year period is chosen arbitrarily. Periods shorter than 50 years will decrease the gains in economic output and periods longer than 50 years will increase the gains in economic output.

[33] However, it is important to note that actual transfer payments and government consumption currently are growing slower than GDP; thus, the offsetting spending cuts will reduce *per capita* spending over time.

debt–GDP ratio is roughly 9 percentage points higher than in the baseline. However, note that the income tax rate adjustment to stabilize the debt–GDP ratio, which occurs 40 years after enactment, reduces income tax rates by an additional 11.3% in the period from 2045 to 2054 and 15.4% in the long run.[34]

The simulation results presented by Diamond (2005) suggest that extending the 2001 and 2003 income tax cuts and reducing the growth rate of government spending, excluding Social Security and Medicare, would increase investment, employment, and output. In this case, the net welfare of the oldest generations alive at the time of enactment would decrease, while the net welfare of future generations would likely increase. By comparison, adopting the other fiscal policy offsets considered would decrease the net welfare of future generations. For, example, increasing future taxes to finance the 2001 and 2003 tax cuts will impose significant net welfare losses on future generations.

### 11.4.5.3 Diamond and Viard (2008) analysis

Diamond and Viard (2008) also use the DZ model to examine the macroeconomic and welfare effects of several alternative tax cuts under a number of different financing options. The magnitude of the tax reduction is chosen so that the decrease in revenue over the 10-year period following enactment is $500 billion with no behavioral responses. The tax cuts are permanent, unanticipated, and enacted immediately. The three main financing methods, which are announced at the time of enactment, are: (i) government transfers (other than social security benefits) are reduced immediately to finance the tax cut, (ii) government debt is used to finance the tax cut for 10 years and then government transfers (other than social security benefits) are reduced so that government debt grows at the steady-state rate of growth, and (iii) government debt is used to finance the tax cut for 10 years and then all personal income tax rates (wage, interest, dividends, and capital gains) are increased proportionately so that government debt grows at the steady-state growth rate.

Diamond and Viard (2008) simulate the macroeconomic effects of five different tax cuts paired with one of the three financing methods. The five tax cuts examined are a 3.9% reduction in average and marginal wage tax rates, a 22.1% reduction in the effective tax rate on interest income, a 50.6% reduction in the effective tax rate on dividend income, a 12.3% reduction in the effective tax rate on corporate income, and a 41% increase in personal tax credits. Some representative results of these simulations are presented in Table 11.8.

All four of the reductions in distortionary taxes increase long-run GDP when they are offset by an immediate reduction in transfer payments. The increase in GDP is largest for reductions in dividend and corporate taxes, because those taxes are more distortionary.

---

[34] This tax rate reduction affects wages, interest income, dividends, capital gains and pass-through business entities.

**Table 11.8** Simulation results: effects of the financing decision (% changes in variables)

| | Years after reform | | | | | |
|---|---|---|---|---|---|---|
| | **2** | **5** | **10** | **20** | **50** | **150** |
| *Wage tax cut with immediate transfer offset* | | | | | | |
| GDP | 0.3 | 0.3 | 0.4 | 0.4 | 0.4 | 0.4 |
| Investment − X | 0.4 | 0.4 | 0.5 | 0.5 | 0.5 | 0.5 |
| Investment − R | 0.8 | 0.8 | 0.8 | 0.6 | 0.5 | 0.5 |
| Investment − H | 0.8 | 0.8 | 0.8 | 0.6 | 0.5 | 0.5 |
| Labor supply | 0.4 | 0.4 | 0.4 | 0.4 | 0.4 | 0.4 |
| Consumption | 0.2 | 0.3 | 0.3 | 0.3 | 0.4 | 0.4 |
| *Wage tax cut with transfer offset after 10 years* | | | | | | |
| GDP | 0.3 | 0.3 | 0.3 | 0.3 | 0.3 | 0.3 |
| Investment − X | 0.2 | 0.2 | 0.1 | 0.0 | −0.2 | −0.2 |
| Investment − R | 0.5 | 0.4 | 0.2 | 0.0 | −0.2 | −0.2 |
| Investment − H | 0.5 | 0.4 | 0.2 | 0.0 | −0.2 | −0.1 |
| Labor supply | 0.4 | 0.4 | 0.4 | 0.4 | 0.4 | 0.4 |
| Consumption | 0.3 | 0.3 | 0.3 | 0.4 | 0.4 | 0.4 |
| *Wage tax cut with tax offset after 10 years* | | | | | | |
| GDP | 0.3 | 0.3 | 0.3 | −0.1 | −0.2 | −0.3 |
| Investment − X | 0.0 | −0.2 | −0.7 | −1.1 | −1.5 | −1.6 |
| Investment − R | 0.3 | 0.1 | −0.3 | −1.3 | −1.4 | −1.3 |
| Investment − H | 0.6 | 0.5 | 0.6 | −0.6 | −0.8 | −0.7 |
| Labor supply | 0.4 | 0.4 | 0.4 | 0.1 | 0.1 | 0.1 |
| Consumption | 0.3 | 0.4 | 0.4 | 0.1 | 0.0 | −0.1 |

X = corporate and non-corporate sector, R = rental housing sector, H = owner-occupied housing sector.

If the tax rate on wage income is reduced, GDP increases by 0.3% in the year of reform and by 0.4% in the long run. If the tax rate on interest income tax is reduced, GDP is unchanged in the short run and increases by 0.1% in the long run. GDP does not increase in the case of an increase in personal tax credits.

With an immediate reduction in transfer payments, the macroeconomic effects of reducing the dividend and corporate tax rates are similar.[35] The before-tax interest rate increases by 24 (48) basis points in the year the dividend (corporate) tax rate is cut and then gradually declines to a level that is 4 (5) basis points higher than in the initial steady state. Under both the dividend and corporate rate cuts, labor supply increases by 0.1% in every year after enactment. Under the dividend (corporate) rate cut, the before-tax wage rate is initially unchanged and increases by 0.7 (0.5)% in the long run as the capital stock increases by 2.7 (2.1)%. Non-housing investment increases by 2.6 (1.9)% in the year of enactment under the dividend (corporate) tax cut. In the long run, investment in the

---

[35] Recall that the DZ model assumes the validity of the traditional view of the effects of dividend taxation.

non-housing sector increases by 2.7 (2.1)% under the dividend (corporate) rate cut. Investment in the owner and rental housing sectors decreases by 2.3–3.2% in the year of enactment, and is roughly unchanged in the long run. Consumption decreases by 0.1–0.2% in the year of enactment, but increases by 0.3–0.4% in the long run. In this case, cutting the dividend (corporate) tax rate increases GDP by 0.7 (0.5)% in the long run.

When the reduction in transfer payments is delayed by 10 years, however, the long-run effects are less beneficial. In each case, the increase in GDP is diminished by 0.1 or 0.2 percentage points. This implies that the reduction in the tax rate on interest income has no effect or a slightly negative effect on GDP; however, a noticeable increase in GDP still occurs if corporate, dividend, or wage tax rates are reduced. The long-run gains are smaller because the increase in debt crowds out private investment (there is virtually no change in labor supply). Notably, long-run non-housing investment is increased by cuts in wage taxes and interest taxes when the transfer payment cut is immediate, but such investment is reduced in the case of a 10-year deficit financing strategy. The dividend and corporate rate cuts, which are more directly targeted to investment, still increase long-run non-housing investment with 10-year deficit financing, but by significantly less than with an immediate transfer cut to hold the deficit constant.

The macroeconomic effects are much worse if an across-the-board tax increase is enacted after ten years to finance the deficit and increased interest costs. In the long run, GDP is unchanged if the dividend tax rate is reduced, decreases by 0.2% if the corporate tax rate is reduced, decreases by 0.5% if the tax rate on interest income is reduced, and decreases by 0.8% if personal tax credits are increased. Non-housing investment falls in every case, except the dividend tax cut. Long-run labor supply falls in every case, except for the wage-tax reduction. With the across-the-board tax increase used as the method of financing, the distortionary effects of the tax increases reinforce crowding out.

Estimates of the macroeconomic effects of tax policy changes have become an important tool for tax policy analysts in the 2000s. However, macroeconomic aggregates are not always reliable indicators of whether certain policies make individuals better off, are not sufficient to compare alternative policies, and do not allow policy makers to examine the effects of policies across various income or age groups. Diamond and Viard (2008) present estimates of the intergenerational welfare effects of the various policies they examine. They show that welfare gains for the generations alive at the time of reform, assuming that government transfers are cut immediately so that government debt grows at the steady-state rate of the economy, are largest under the corporate rate cut, the dividend rate cut, and the interest income tax cut. With the immediate cut in transfer payments, the well-being of future generations is increased under all of the policies except for the decrease in the tax rate on interest income. Notably, the increase in the well-being of future generations is 4–8 times larger (measured as a percentage of lifetime resources) under a decrease in the wage tax rate than under the alternative tax decreases.

The deficit-financed tax cuts uniformly reduce the well-being of future generations — a result that occurs even though these generations benefit from a more efficient tax system — as deficit financing redistributes income from current generations to future generations. As expected, deficit-financed tax cuts almost uniformly benefit the generations alive at the time of the reform. Diamond and Viard also calculate the intergenerational welfare effects of reducing the wage and dividend tax rates when government transfers are reduced 20 years after the reform rather than 10. In this case, welfare losses are much larger for future generations. For the wage tax cut, the long-run welfare loss is 2% of lifetime resources instead of the 0.08% loss for the 10-year deficit finance approach. For the dividend tax cut, the long-run welfare loss is 2.4% of lifetime resources instead of 0.32%. Confirming the findings of Auerbach and Kotlikoff (1987), these welfare losses increase non-linearly with the period of deficit finance.

Diamond and Viard conclude that deficit-financed tax cuts can increase long-run output if the financing mechanism is less distortionary than the tax that is initially reduced and if the financing begins relatively soon after the tax cut is adopted. Even then, however, the shift in fiscal burdens generally reduces the well-being of future generations while increasing that of current generations.

## 11.5 CONCLUSION

In this chapter, we have examined the use of dynamic, OLG-CGE models to analyze the macroeconomic and distributional effects of tax reforms, using as a paradigm a model that we have constructed — the DZ model. Although the use of such models is not without controversy — as illustrated by the exchange between Gravelle (2006) and Diamond and Zodrow (2006) — in our view, OLG-CGE models are an excellent tool for illustrating the potential effects of tax reforms in a general equilibrium setting. In particular, OLG-CGE models characterized by perfect foresight are especially well-suited to analyzing both the short-run transitional and the long-run dynamic macroeconomic effects of tax reforms, including the time paths of reform-induced changes in labor supply, saving and investment, as well as the redistributional effects of reforms both across and within generations. Our paper provides both a historical overview of the development of OLG-CGE models for tax analysis and a discussion of numerous applications of such models, using as a paradigm our own DZ model.

Analyses using OLG-CGE models have thus provided policy makers with much useful information for gauging the effects of various tax reforms. However, much remains to be done, especially in terms of treating in a single model all of the issues of most current concern to policy analysts, including complete specifications of international trade and factor flows, involuntary unemployment, business financial decisions, and the role of financial institutions in the world economy. It is clear that OLG-CGE modeling will be a fruitful research area for many years to come.

## APPENDIX

In this Appendix, we provide a fairly detailed description of the DZ model. We begin with a discussion of timing conventions, and then consider in turn the behavior of households, firms, and the government, and the nature of the market equilibrium in the model.

## A.1 Timing conventions

It will be useful to begin by specifying the timing conventions used in the model, which is constructed in discrete time, with each period reflecting a year. In each period, all flow variables, including labor supply, saving, consumption, investment, and the associated issuance of debt and new equity shares, government spending, taxation, and the accumulation of any deficits, occur at the end of the period. Individual utility levels, which are based on current and future flows of consumption and leisure, are thus calculated at the end of the period, as is the lifetime budget constraint. The prices related to all flow variables are also determined at the end of the period. In contrast, all stock variables, including capital stocks in all four sectors, individual wealth including all asset values, and the stocks of private and public debt are measured at the beginning of the period. That is, stock values at the beginning of a period reflect the effects of the flow values that occurred at the end of the previous period.

Births and deaths occur at the beginning of the period, as do inheritances and bequests. Thus, an individual is of age zero all of the birth period and age one all of the following period. Age $a$ is defined at the beginning of a specific time period $t$ and thus changes with time. For example, an individual of age $a = 10$ at the beginning of period $t = 1$ is age $a = 30$ at the beginning of period $t = 21$. In general, individual age is specified with respect to period $t = 1$, as the enactment of reform is typically assumed to occur at the beginning of period $t = 1$. Since the enactment of reform is assumed to be unexpected, reform affects only consumption $C_1$, saving $S_1$ and investment $I_1$ decisions made at the end of period $t = 1$ and thereafter, but has no effect on these values in the initial pretax equilibrium in period $t = 0$. Thus, period zero $C_0$, $S_0$, $I_0$, capital stock $K_0$, asset value $A_0$ and period $t = 1$ capital stock $K_1$ are all determined in the initial income tax equilibrium. The first postreform values are thus flows $C_1$, $S_1$, and $I_1$, and the capital stock $K_2$. However, asset values $A_1$, which are calculated when reform is announced at the beginning of period $t = 1$, instantaneously reflects the anticipated effects of the reform.

## A.2 Individual behavior

### A.2.1 Setting up the life-cycle optimization problem

Individual behavior is modeled using an overlapping generations framework that consists of 55 cohorts, with an exogenous population growth rate $n$. Individual cohorts alive at the time of reform $t = 1$ are identified by ages that range from $a = 0$ to $a = 54$, as the economic life span, which is assumed to begin at age 23, is known (with certainty) to be 55 years, reflecting an average life expectancy of 78 years. Each individual works for the first 45 years of the 55-year economic lifespan and is retired for the last 10 years. Generations who are unborn at the time of reform $t = 1$ are identified by negative ages.[36]

All individuals share the same utility function. In the multi-income-group version of the model, each generation is divided into 12 different types of individuals, classified by lifetime income, with $y = 1$ representing the bottom 2% of population cohort $a$ in terms of lifetime income, $y = 2$ representing the rest of the first lifetime income decile, $y = 3$ through $y = 10$ representing the next eight deciles by lifetime income, $y = 11$ representing the bottom four-fifths of the top decile, and $y = 12$ representing the top 2% of individuals in the cohort. Each type of individual within a cohort has a unique exogenous endowment of human capital and a 'humped-back' dynamic wage profile over the lifetime.[37]

An individual of age $a$ and lifetime income type $y$ at the beginning of any period $t$ over the life cycle has assets $A_t(a,y)$ that have been accumulated from the time of 'economic birth' and are used to help finance both consumption over the subsequent years of the individual's lifetime, including during the retirement period and the making of a bequest. Accumulated assets include inheritances received (or the present value of anticipated inheritances), which are assumed to be received at economic age $a = 25$ (actual age $a = 48$). Bequests are given at the time of death (age $a = 55$) and total assets at death $A_t(55,y)$ are just sufficient to fund the bequest $BQ_t(55,y)$, which becomes the inheritance of the recipient $INH_t(25,y)$. Following Altig et al. — and consistent with the empirical results of Kopczuk and Lupton (2007) — the model utilizes the 'joy of giving' model of bequests, under which individuals receive utility directly from the making of bequests.[38]

The model assumes that individuals have perfect foresight and optimize over their life cycles. The (remaining) lifetime utility of an individual of age $a$ and lifetime income type $y$ calculated at the end of period $t$, $LU_t(a,y)$, is assumed to be a time-separable aggregation of individual utility in each period over the remainder of the life cycle and the bequest, or:

---

[36] For individuals who are not yet born at the time of reform, the $t$ subscript in the expressions derived below should be interpreted as their year of birth.

[37] As will be discussed further below, endowments and wages vary across individuals, and individual wages are a multiplicative function of a single economy-wide equilibrium wage. We use the wage profiles estimated by Altig et al., which imply that wages peak around ages 45–50, and the peak wages of the highest income group are approximately 20 times the peak wages of the lowest income group. In the single-income-group version of the model, there is a single value of $y$ for each generation.

[38] One can interpret the joy of giving bequest motive as including the benefits from holding wealth while accumulating resources sufficient to finance the bequest.

$$
LU_t(a, \gamma) = \frac{1}{(1 - 1/\sigma_U)} \left[ \begin{array}{c} \sum_{s=t}^{t+54-a} \left( \dfrac{U_s(a, \gamma)^{(1-1/\sigma_U)}}{(1+\rho)^{s-t}} \right) \\[2em] + \dfrac{1}{(1+\rho)^{54-a}} [\alpha_B(\gamma)] [BQ_{t+54-a}(a, \gamma)]^{1-1/\sigma_U} \end{array} \right], \quad (11.1)
$$

where $\sigma_U$ is the intertemporal elasticity of substitution, $\rho$ is the pure rate of time preference, $U_s(a,\gamma)$ is utility in period $s$ of an individual of age $a$ of lifetime income type $\gamma$, $\alpha_B(\gamma)$ is the utility function weight placed on bequests due to the joy of giving bequest motive by an individual of lifetime income type $\gamma$ and $BQ_{t+54-a}(a,\gamma)$ is the bequest that will be made in period $t + 54 - a$ by an individual of lifetime income type $\gamma$ who is of age $a$ at the time of enactment of reform.

Utility within each period (other than that attributable to the bequest) is defined as $U_s(a,\gamma)$ and is modeled as a constant elasticity of substitution (CES) function of a composite consumption good (which aggregates all non-housing consumption goods and housing services) $CH_s(a,\gamma)$ and leisure $LE_s(a,\gamma)$:

$$
\begin{aligned}
U_s(a, \gamma) &= \left[ (\alpha_C)^{1/\sigma_C} CH_s(a, \gamma)^{(\sigma_C-1)/\sigma_C} + (1 - \alpha_C)^{1/\sigma_C} LE_s(a, \gamma)^{(\sigma_C-1)/\sigma_C} \right]^{\sigma_C/(\sigma_C-1)} \\
&= \left[ U_s^*(a, \gamma) \right]^{\sigma_C/(\sigma_C-1)},
\end{aligned}
$$

$$(11.2)$$

where $\sigma_C$ is the intratemporal elasticity of substitution between the composite consumption good and leisure in any period, $\alpha_C$ and $(1 - \alpha_C)$ are the utility weights on the composite consumption good and leisure, and leisure is defined as $LE_s(a,\gamma) = HT_s(a,\gamma) - L_s(a,\gamma)$, where $HT_s(a,\gamma)$ is the time endowment or the total number of hours available in period $s$ for either labor supply $L_s(a,\gamma)$ or leisure. The time endowment $HT_s(a,\gamma)$ varies across individuals of different lifetime income types, reflecting differences in initial human capital. To keep the ratio of labor supply to time endowment constant in the steady state, the time endowment for each generation is assumed to be larger by a factor equal to $(1+g)$, where $g$ is the exogenous productivity growth rate. The $[U_s^*(a, \gamma)]$ notation, and similar notation defined below, is introduced simply to facilitate exposition.

The composite consumption good is modeled as a CES function of (non-housing) consumption goods and housing services:

$$
\begin{aligned}
CH_s(a, \gamma) &= \left\{ \begin{array}{l} (\alpha_H)^{1/\sigma_H} [CN_s(a, \gamma)]^{(\sigma_H-1)/\sigma_H} \\ + (1 - \alpha_H)^{1/\sigma_H} [HR_s(a, \gamma)]^{(\sigma_H-1)/\sigma_H} \end{array} \right\}^{\sigma_H/(\sigma_H-1)} \\
&= \left[ CH_s^*(a, \gamma) \right]^{\sigma_H/(\sigma_H-1)},
\end{aligned}
\quad (11.3)
$$

where $CN_s(a,y)$ is consumption of non-housing consumption goods in period $s$ by individuals of age $a$ and lifetime income type $y$, $HR_s(a,y)$ is the analogous consumption of housing services, $\alpha_H$ and $(1 - \alpha_H)$ are the utility weights on the non-housing consumption goods and housing services, and $\sigma_H$ is the elasticity of substitution between consumption goods and housing.

The non-housing consumption good is modeled as a CES function of consumption in period $s$ by individuals of age $a$ and lifetime income type $y$ of the goods produced by the corporate sector $C_s(a,y)$ and the goods produced by the non-corporate sector $N_s(a,y)$, with the option of specifying minimum required purchases of each good for each type of individual, $b_s^C(a, y)$ and $b_s^N(a, y)$ (which are assumed to grow at the productivity growth rate $g$), or:

$$
\begin{aligned}
CN_s(a, y) &= \left\{ \begin{array}{l} (\alpha_N)^{1/\sigma_N} \left[ C_s(a, y) - b_s^C(a, y) \right]^{(\sigma_N-1)/\sigma_N} \\ + (1 - \alpha_N)^{1/\sigma_N} \left[ N_s(a, y) - b_s^N(a, y) \right]^{(\sigma_N-1)/\sigma_N} \end{array} \right\}^{\sigma_N/(\sigma_N-1)} \\
&= \left[ CN_s^*(a, y) \right]^{\sigma_N/(\sigma_N-1)},
\end{aligned}
\tag{11.4}
$$

where $\alpha_N$ and $(1 - \alpha_H)$ are the utility weights for corporate and non-corporate goods, and $\sigma_N$ is the elasticity of substitution between above-minimum quantities of the corporate and non-corporate goods.

Housing services $HR_s(a,y)$ are also modeled as a CES function of the quantities of owner-occupied housing services $H_s(a,y)$ and rental housing services $R_s(a,y)$, in excess of the minimum required purchases $b_s^H(a,y)$ and $b_s^R(a,y)$:

$$
\dot{HR}_s(a, y) = \left\{ \begin{array}{l} (\alpha_R)^{1/\sigma_R} \left[ H_s(a, y) - b_s^H(a, y) \right]^{(\sigma_R-1)/\sigma_R} \\ + (1 - \alpha_R)^{1/\sigma_R} \left[ R_s(a, y) - b_s^R(a, y) \right]^{(\sigma_R-1)/\sigma_R} \end{array} \right\}^{\sigma_R/(\sigma_R-1)},
\tag{11.5}
$$

where $\sigma_R$ is the elasticity of substitution between the discretionary or above-minimum quantities of owner-occupied housing and rental housing services, and $\alpha_R$ and $(1 - \alpha_R)$ are the utility weights for owner-occupied and rental housing.

We turn next to the lifetime budget constraint, simplifying notation by dropping the age and lifetime income type subscripts where it is possible to do so without creating ambiguity. Individuals are assumed to discount future cash flows at the after-tax interest rate $r_u$ for the relevant period $u$, which implies that marginal savings are taxable (and that marginal borrowing is deductible, e.g. investment interest or borrowing in the form of a home mortgage or a home equity loan), $r_u = i_u(1 - \tau_{iu})$, where $\tau_{iu}$ is the tax rate on interest income under the income tax in future period $u$. In principle, marginal tax rates on capital income should vary with income. However, primarily for analytical tractability, the model assumes the various elements of capital income are taxed at differing proportional rates that do not vary across income types, an approach that ensures that all individuals use the same discount rate. This approach is justifiable because most saving is done by individuals in the top bracket, and the differentials in effective capital income tax rates across income types are relatively moderate due to the narrowing of marginal income tax rates since the 1980s, the recent reductions in tax rates on capital gains and dividends, and the greater access to tax sheltering opportunities available to the wealthy, which lowers their effective capital income tax rates; this approach follows the FR and AAKSW models.

Each individual maximizes lifetime utility subject to a lifetime budget constraint:

$$TDW_t(a,y) = TDE_t(a,y) = \sum_{s=t}^{t+54-a} \frac{p_s^c\left(1+\tau_{vs}^c\right)\left(C_s - b_s^c\right) + p_s^n\left(1+\tau_{vs}^n\right)\left(N_s - b_s^n\right)}{\Pi_{u=t+1}^s\left(1+r_u\right)}$$

$$+ \sum_{s=t}^{t+54-a} \frac{p_s^h\left(1+\tau_{vs}^h\right)\left(H_s - b_s^h\right) + p_s^r\left(1+\tau_{vs}^r\right)\left(R_s - b_s^r\right)}{\Pi_{u=t+1}^s\left(1+r_u\right)} + \frac{\left(1+\tau_{vs}^b\right)BQ_{t+54-a}}{\Pi_{u=t+1}^{t+54-a}\left(1+r_u\right)},$$

(11.6)

where $TDW_t(a,y)$ is the total discretionary wealth for an individual of age $a$ and income type $y$ at the end of period $t$ that is available to spend on total discretionary expenditures $TDE_t(a,y)$, defined as the present value of lifetime consumption of the four goods in excess of minimum required levels and the bequest $BQ_{t+54-a}$, $p_s^c$ is the producer price of the corporate good, which is chosen to be the numéraire so that $p_s^c = 1$ in each period $s$, $p_s^n$ is the producer price of the non-corporate good, $p_s^h$ is the unit price of owner-occupied housing services received by individuals in their role as producers of owner-occupied housing and $p_s^r$ is the unit price of rental housing services received by the producers of rental housing.

Note that consumer prices include any sales or VATs imposed on a destination basis by either the national or subnational governments, as reflected in the various $\tau_v$ terms. For example, the consumer price of the corporate good is $p_s^c(1+\tau_{vs}^c)$, $\tau_{vs}^c = \tau_{vs}f_{vs}^c$, where $f_{vs}^c$ is the fraction of the corporate consumption good that is included in the VAT base (under a comprehensive VAT $f_{vs}^c = 1$, but VATs typically exempt certain goods for administrative, social or political reasons). Similarly, $p_s^n(1+\tau_{vs}^n)$, $\tau_{vs}^n = \tau_{vs}f_{vs}^n$, $p_s^h(1+\tau_{vs}^h)$, $\tau_{vs}^h = \tau_{vs}f_{vs}^h$, and $p_s^r(1+\tau_{vs}^r)$, $\tau_{vs}^r = \tau_{vs}f_{vs}^r$. In the case of owner-occupied housing, if $f_{vs}^h$ is non-zero, it is typically defined as the ratio of purchases of new housing to the imputed rental value of the existing stock of owner-occupied housing (Carroll et al., 2010). The denominator of this expression reflects the theoretically correct VAT base — the value of the housing services generated by the existing stock of housing. However, taxing this imputed value is widely believed to be impossible for both administrative and political reasons. It may, however, be possible to apply some tax to the services provided by owner-occupied housing by taxing new housing construction, which effectively taxes currently all the future rents that will be generated by such housing. The value of $f_{vs}^h$ simply reflects the fraction of imputed rents on existing housing captured by this indirect approach to taxing owner-occupied housing.

To define total discretionary wealth, options for saving must be specified. Individuals can save to accumulate both taxable assets $A_t(a,y)$ and tax-preferred 'total retirement assets' $TRA_t(a,y)$ that accumulate at the after-tax interest rate $i_u$. 'Retirement saving' is assumed to be mechanical, both because pension saving is relatively non-discretionary and because in many cases our primary concern is simply to determine the extent of tax-favored assets held in the initial equilibrium. Specifically, retirement saving is assumed to consist of a fixed annual contribution that varies by lifetime income level, with all discretionary saving and dis-saving occurring in taxable accounts. Individuals are assumed to allocate a fixed dollar amount $RS_s(y) = RS$ to retirement saving each year of their working lives, ages $0 \leq a \leq 44$, with all additional saving going into taxable accounts.

Total retirement assets $TRA_t(a, y)$ consist primarily of tax-deferred assets $\text{TDA}_t(a, y)$, such as pension plans (assumed to be owned by the individual), traditional IRAs, and 401(k) and 403(b) plans, all of which receive cash flow or 'tax postpaid' treatment, i.e. contributions are deductible and all withdrawals are fully taxable, by assumption at a proportional rate specific to each income type $\tau_{rt}(y)$. However, individuals can also save in the form of 'tax prepaid' assets $TPA_t(a,y)$, such as Roth IRAs, for which contributions are not deductible and all withdrawals are tax free, so that at the time of the enactment of reform $t = 1$, individuals will have accumulated $TRA_t(a,y) = TDA_t(a,y) + TPA_t(a,y)$. The ratio of retirement saving in each period in tax-deferred assets to total retirement assets $s_d(y)$ is assumed to be constant for individuals at each lifetime income level.

Withdrawals $WD_s(a,y)$ from retirement accounts in period $s$ start upon reaching retirement at age $a = 45$. These withdrawals are assumed to occur at the end of the period in each of the 10 years of retirement in the following pattern. For a person who is in the first year of retirement in period $s$ at age $a = 45$, one-tenth of the balance of both tax-deferred and tax-prepaid accounts is assumed to be withdrawn. At the end of the second year of retirement, at age $a = 46$, one-ninth of the remaining balance of the retirement account is withdrawn, and this process continues until all of the remaining balance of the retirement account is spent at the end of the period when the individual is age $a = 54$.

Total discretionary wealth at the end of period $t$, $TDW_t(a,y)$, is defined as the total physical and human wealth, net of current and future taxes, available over the rest of the lifetime for discretionary lifetime consumption expenditures (those in excess of any minimum required consumption expenditures) and for the bequest, or:

$$TDW_t(a, y) = A_t(a, y)(1 + r_t) + [TRA_t(a, y)](1 + i_t)$$

$$+ \sum_{s=t}^{t+54-a} \frac{w_s(a, y)[HT_s(a, y) - LE_s(a, y)] - LIT_s(a, y) - SST_s(a, y)}{\Pi_{u=t+1}^s (1 + r_u)}$$

$$+ \sum_{s=t}^{t+54-a} \frac{SSB_s(a, y)[1 - \tau_{bs}(y)] - RS_s(a, y)}{\Pi_{u=t+1}^s (1 + r_u)}$$

$$+ \sum_{s=t}^{t+54-a} \frac{WD_s(a, y)[(1 - s_d \tau_{rs}(y)] + TR_s(a, y) + LSR_s(a, y)}{\Pi_{u=t+1}^s (1 + r_u)}$$

$$- \sum_{s=t}^{t+54-a} \frac{p_s^c (1 + \tau_{vs}^c) b_s^c + p_s^n (1 + \tau_{vs}^n) b_s^n + p_s^h (1 + \tau_{vs}^h) b_s^h + p_s^r (1 + \tau_{vs}^r) b_s^r}{\Pi_{u=t+1}^s (1 + r_u)},$$

$$(11.7)$$

where $A_t(a,y)$ is the value of taxable assets including the present value of the inheritance if not yet received and the value of individual ownership of business equity and debt and government debt in period $t$ for an individual age $a$ and income type $y$, $TRA_t(a,y)$ is the value of tax-preferred retirement assets at the beginning of period $t$, $LIT_s(a,y)$ is the labor income tax component of the individual income tax for an individual of age $a$ and income type $y$ in period $s$, $SST_s(a,y)$ is the social security payroll tax paid on labor income, $SSB_s(a,y)$ represents any social security benefits received which are subject to tax at rate $\tau_{bs}(y)$, $TR_s(a,y)$ is transfers received, $LSR_s(a,y)$ equals any lump sum rebates received (which may include VAT rebates, which for simplicity are assumed to be lump sum and uniform across each lifetime income group and declining as lifetime income increases), and $p_s^i b_s^i$ is the cost, including the VAT, of meeting the minimum purchase requirement for the consumption good $i = c, n, h, r$ in period $s$.

The individual income tax is modeled as a progressive tax on labor income, coupled with the taxation of the various forms of capital income as described above. The AMT is modeled implicitly as changes in the tax rates applied to labor income at each income level. The calculation of the labor income base $LIB_s(a,y)$ begins with total wage income $w_s(a,y)[HT_s(a,y) - LE_s(a,y)]$, defined broadly to include all labor compensation including fringe benefits. This base is then reduced by $DED_s(a,y)$, which reflects the standard deduction and other itemized deductions (other than home mortgage interest or property taxes, which are treated in the calculation of capital income earned in the owner-occupied housing production sector described below), personal exemptions and exclusions from income including fringe benefits such as employer-provided health insurance. Individual tax credits, the most important of which is the earned income tax credit, are modeled implicitly by adjusting the labor income tax rates. The base of the tax on labor income is also reduced by saving in the tax-deferred component of retirement savings, $s_d[RS_s(a,y)]$, so that the labor income base is:

$$LIB_s(a, y) = w_s[HT_s(a, y) - LE_s(a, y)] - DED_s(a, y) - s_d[RS_s(a, y)]. \qquad (11.8)$$

Taxable labor income is assumed to be taxed at progressive rates. Following Fullerton and Rogers (1993), we approximate the existing progressive income tax system as a piecewise linear system characterized by a constant marginal tax rate $\tau_{wms}(y)$ for each lifetime income group, with marginal tax rates that increase with lifetime income. Specifically, revenues from labor income taxation of an individual of age $a$ and lifetime income type $y$ in period $s$ are:

$$LIT_s(a, y) = \psi_s LIB_s(a, y) + (\chi_s/2)[LIB_s(a, y)]^2, \qquad (11.9)$$

where $\tau_{wms}(y) = \chi_s(y) > 0$ and $\psi_s(y) > 0$ is set so that the average revenue collected from the income group $y$ in period $s$ is correct.

Capital income is assumed to be taxed at flat rates $\tau_{ds}$ on dividends, $\tau_{is}$ on interest, and $\tau_{gs}$ on capital gains. The tax rate on capital gains is an effective annual accrual rate, taking into account the benefits of tax deferral until gains are realized and the tax exemption of gains transferred at death, as well as the cost in an inflationary environment of taxing nominal rather than real gains. The tax rate on withdrawals from the retirement saving account is $\tau_{rs}(a,y)$. The effective social security tax rate is $\tau_{ss}$ and the tax rate on social security benefits is $\tau_{bs}(y)$; the modeling of social security is discussed further below.

Substituting from the definitions of the various components of $TDW_t(a,y)$, isolating the $LE_s$ terms, and dropping the age and lifetime income subscripts to simplify notation yields:

$$
\begin{aligned}
TDW_t ={}& A_t(1 + r_t) + TRA_t(1 + i_t) + \sum_{s=t}^{t+54-a} \frac{w_s HT_s}{\Pi_{u=t+1}^{s}(1 + r_u)} \\[4pt]
& - \sum_{s=t}^{t+54-a} \frac{\chi_s[w_s HT_s - DED_s - s_d RS_s] - \psi_s}{\Pi_{u=t+1}^{s}(1 + r_u)} - \sum_{s=t}^{t+54-a} \frac{\tau_{ss}[w_s HT_s - DED_s - s_d RS_s]}{\Pi_{u=t+1}^{s}(1 + r_u)} \\[4pt]
& + \sum_{s=t}^{t+54-a} \frac{SSB_s(1 - \tau_{bs}) - RS_s + WD_s[(1 - s_d\tau_{rs}(y))] + TR_s + LSR_s}{\Pi_{u=t+1}^{s}(1 + r_u)} \\[4pt]
& - \sum_{s=t}^{t+54-a} \frac{p_s^c(1 + \tau_{vs}^c)b_s^c + p_s^n(1 + \tau_{vs}^n)b_s^n + p_s^h(1 + \tau_{vs}^h)b_s^h + p_s^r(1 + \tau_{vs}^r)b_s^r}{\Pi_{u=t+1}^{s}(1 + r_u)} \\[4pt]
& - \sum_{s=t}^{t+54-a} \frac{w_s LE_s(1 - \chi_s - \tau_{ss})}{\Pi_{u=t+1}^{s}(1 + r_u)} \\[4pt]
={}& TDEW_t - \sum_{s=t}^{t+54-a} \frac{w_s LE_s(1 - \chi_s - \tau_{ss})}{\Pi_{u=t+1}^{s}(1 + r_u)},
\end{aligned}
$$

$$(11.10)$$

where $TDEW_t$ is total discretionary *endowment* wealth, including the value of leisure, and is a function only of variables and parameters that are exogenous to the individual optimization problem in period $t$.

Following the FR and AAKSW models, the wage rate for an individual of age $a$ and lifetime income $y$ is defined as $w_s(a,y) = (weq_s)[h(a,y)]$, where $weq_s$ is the economy-wide equilibrium wage in period $s$ and $h(a,y)$ is a labor efficiency parameter that reflects both the exogenous accumulation of individual human capital and the exogenous rate of economy-wide productivity growth. The labor efficiency parameter varies in a 'hump-backed' fashion over the individual life cycle, reflecting increasing productivity during middle age and decreasing productivity in the final earning years, as described above. Exogenous productivity growth over time at rate $g$ is modeled as exogenous growth of the time endowment $HT_s(a,y)$, so that the economy-wide equilibrium wage $weq_s$ exhibits no time trend.

### A.2.2 Individual behavior: solving the optimization problem

The individual consumer demand functions for the four consumer goods are calculated under the assumption of maximization of the nested individual lifetime utility function subject to the lifetime budget constraint. Solving the first order conditions with respect to $C_s$ and $N_s$ in the innermost nest of the individual utility function yields:

$$\left(C_s - b_s^c\right) = \frac{F_s^c\, CN_s}{p_s^c} \tag{11.11}$$

$$\left(N_s - b_s^n\right) = \frac{F_s^n\, CN_s}{p_s^n}, \tag{11.12}$$

where:

$$F_s^c = \frac{(\alpha_N)\left[\left(p_s^c\right)^{1-\sigma_N}\right]}{\left[(\alpha_N)\left(p_s^c\right)^{(1-\sigma_N)}+(1-\alpha_N)\left(p_s^n\right)^{(1-\sigma_N)}\right]^{\sigma_N/(\sigma_N-1)}}$$

$$F_s^n = \frac{(1-\alpha_N)\left[\left(p_s^n\right)^{1-\sigma_N}\right]}{\left[(\alpha_N)\left(p_s^c\right)^{(1-\sigma_N)}+(1-\alpha_N)\left(p_s^n\right)^{(1-\sigma_N)}\right]^{\sigma_N/(1-\sigma_N)}},$$

are factors that are functions only of prices and tastes and are thus exogenous to the consumer. Note that if $p_s^c = p_s^n$, $(F_s^c + F_s^n)$ reduces to $p_s^c$. More generally:

$$F_s^{c+n} = F_s^c + F_s^n = \left[(\alpha_N)\left(p_s^c\right)^{(1-\sigma_N)}+(1-\alpha_N)\left(p_s^n\right)^{(1-\sigma_N)}\right]^{1/(1-\sigma_N)}.$$

The analogous derivations for $H_s$ and $R_s$ imply:

$$\left(H_s - b_s^{\mathrm{h}}\right) = \frac{F_s^{\mathrm{h}} HR_s}{p_s^{\mathrm{h}}} \tag{11.13}$$

$$\left(R_s - b_s^{\mathrm{r}}\right) = \frac{F_s^{\mathrm{r}} HR_s}{p_s^{\mathrm{r}}}, \tag{11.14}$$

where:

$$F_s^{\mathrm{h}} = \frac{(\alpha_{\mathrm{R}})\left(p_s^{\mathrm{h}}\right)^{(1-\sigma_{\mathrm{R}})}}{\left[(\alpha_{\mathrm{R}})\left(p_s^{\mathrm{h}}\right)^{(1-\sigma_{\mathrm{R}})}+(1-\alpha_{\mathrm{R}})\left(p_s^{\mathrm{r}}\right)^{(1-\sigma_{\mathrm{R}})}\right]^{\sigma_{\mathrm{R}}/(\sigma_{\mathrm{R}}-1)}}$$

$$F_s^{\mathrm{r}} = \frac{(1-\alpha_{\mathrm{R}})\left(p_s^{\mathrm{r}}\right)^{(1-\sigma_{\mathrm{R}})}}{\left[(\alpha_{\mathrm{R}})\left(p_s^{\mathrm{h}}\right)^{(1-\sigma_{\mathrm{R}})}+(1-\alpha_{\mathrm{R}})\left(p_s^{\mathrm{r}}\right)^{(1-\sigma_{\mathrm{R}})}\right]^{\sigma_{\mathrm{R}}/(\sigma_{\mathrm{R}}-1)}}$$

$$F_s^{\mathrm{h+r}} = F_s^{\mathrm{h}} + F_s^{\mathrm{r}} = \left[(\alpha_{\mathrm{R}})\left(p_s^{\mathrm{h}}\right)^{(1-\sigma_{\mathrm{R}})}+(1-\alpha_{\mathrm{R}})\left(p_s^{\mathrm{r}}\right)^{(1-\sigma_{\mathrm{R}})}\right]^{1/(1-\sigma_{\mathrm{R}})}.$$

The determination of the optimal amounts of the non-housing and housing composite goods, obtained by maximizing lifetime utility with respect to $CN_s$ and $HR_s$, yield:

$$CN_s = \frac{\left(F_s^{cn}\right)CH_s}{\left(F_s^{c+n}\right)} \tag{11.15}$$

$$HR_s = \frac{\left(F_s^{hr}\right)CH_s}{\left(F_s^{h+r}\right)}, \tag{11.16}$$

where:

$$F_s^{cn} = \frac{(\alpha_{\mathrm{H}})\left(F_s^{c+n}\right)^{(1-\sigma_{\mathrm{H}})}}{\left[(\alpha_{\mathrm{H}})\left(F_s^{c+n}\right)^{(1-\sigma_{\mathrm{H}})}+(1-\alpha_{\mathrm{H}})\left(F_s^{h+r}\right)^{(1-\sigma_{\mathrm{H}})}\right]^{\sigma_{\mathrm{H}}/(\sigma_{\mathrm{H}}-1)}}$$

$$F_s^{hr} = \frac{(1-\alpha_{\mathrm{H}})\left(F_s^{h+r}\right)^{(1-\sigma_{\mathrm{H}})}}{\left[(\alpha_{\mathrm{H}})\left(F_s^{c+n}\right)^{(1-\sigma_{\mathrm{H}})}+(1-\alpha_{\mathrm{H}})\left(F_s^{h+r}\right)^{(1-\sigma_{\mathrm{H}})}\right]^{\sigma_{\mathrm{H}}/(\sigma_{\mathrm{H}}-1)}}.$$

Substituting into the expression for total discretionary expenditures yields:

$$TDE_t = \left[ \sum_{s=t}^{t+54-a} \frac{\left(F_s^{c+h}\right) CH_s}{\Pi_{u=t+1}^{s}(1+r_u)} \right] + \frac{BQ_{t+54-a}}{\Pi_{u=t+1}^{t+54-a}(1+r_u)},$$

where:

$$F_s^{c+h} = F_s^{cn} + F_s^{hr} = \left[ (\alpha_H) \left( F_s^{c+n} \right)^{(1-\sigma_H)} + (1-\alpha_H) \left( F_s^{h+r} \right)^{(1-\sigma_H)} \right]^{1/(1-\sigma_H)}.$$

Finally, optimizing lifetime utility with respect to the aggregate consumption good $CH_s$, leisure $LE_s$ (and thus labor supply $L_s = HT_s - LE_s$), and the bequest $BQ_{t+54-a}$ yields

$$CH_t(a, y) = \Psi_t^{ch}(a, y) TDEW_t(a, y) \tag{11.17}$$

$$LE_s = \Psi_t^{le}(a, y) TDEW_t(a, y) \tag{11.18}$$

$$BQ = \Psi_t^{b}(a, y) TDEW_t(a, y), \tag{11.19}$$

where

$$F_s^b = \left[ \left( F_s^u \right)^{(1/\sigma_U - 1/\sigma_C)(\sigma_C/(\sigma_C - 1))} \left( F_s^{c+h} \right) \frac{(\alpha_B)}{(\alpha_C)^{1/\sigma_C}} \frac{(1+\rho)^{s-t}}{(1+\rho)^{54-a}} \prod_{u=s}^{t+54-a} (1+r_u) \right]^{\sigma_U}$$

$$F_s^{le} = \frac{(1-\alpha_C)}{(\alpha_C)} \left[ \frac{F_s^{c+h}}{w_s(1 - \chi_s - \tau_{ss})} \right]^{\sigma_C}$$

$$\Psi_t^{ch}(a, y) = \left[ \sum_{s=t}^{t+54-a} \frac{\left( F_s^{c+h} \right)}{\Pi_{u=t+1}^{s}(1+r_u)} + \sum_{s=t}^{t+54-a} \frac{w_s(1 - \chi_s - \tau_{ss})}{\Pi_{u=t+1}^{s}(1+r_u)} \left( F_s^{le} \right) \right.$$
$$\left. + \frac{\left( F_t^b \right)}{\Pi_{u=t+1}^{t+54-a}(1+r_u)} \right]^{-1},$$

i.e. that all consumer demands are multiplicative functions of $TDEW_t(a,y)$.

Given individual labor supply, the aggregate effective labor force $(EL_s)$ depends on the exogenous population growth rate $n$. Thus, the size of the population of age $a$ in years, $P_s(a)$, is $P_s(a) = P_t(a)(1+n)^{s-t}$, where $P_t(a)$ is the size of this population in some reference time period, typically the initial period $(t = 0)$. This implies that in any period $s$, the total effective labor force is:

$$EL_s = \sum_{a=0}^{44} P_s(a) L_s(a), \tag{11.20}$$

where $L_s(a)$ is labor supply of an individual of age $a$ in period $s$. Initial values for $EL_s$ and $K_s$ are established at the beginning of period zero ($s = 0$) as the steady-state values under the existing tax system.

### A.2.3 Modeling the social security program

The DZ model includes a simple if somewhat unrealistic modeling of Social Security. Social Security taxes paid $SST_s(a,y)$ are assumed to be assessed on the same base as the labor income component of the personal income tax base $LIB_s(a,y)$. With an effective Social Security tax rate of $\tau_{ss}$, this implies that the Social Security taxes paid by an individual of age a and lifetime income level y are $SST_s(a,y) = \tau_{ss}[LIB_s(a,y)]$. Social security benefits $SSB_s(a,y)$ are received by individuals of lifetime income y who reach an economic age $a = 45$ in years and continue until death at age $a = 54$.

The model assumes that social security is financed on a 'pay-as-you-go' basis; any accumulation or decumulation of the Social Security trust fund is ignored, as is any link between marginal additional taxes paid and additional future benefits.[39] To calculate the budget constraint of the Social Security system, recall that population growth at rate $n$ is assumed to be uniform across all types of individuals.[40] Thus, the population of age $a$ of lifetime income group y in period s is $P_s(a,y) = P_t(a,y)(1 + n)^{s-t}$, where $P_t(a,y)$ is the size of this population in some reference time period, typically the initial period ($t = 0$), just before the enactment of reform at the beginning of period one ($t = 1$). Hence, assuming that the revenues raised from taxing social security benefits go into general revenues, the government's social security budget constraint requires that annual social security taxes must equal annual benefit payments or:

$$\sum_{a=0}^{44} \sum_{y=1}^{12} P_s(a, y) SST_s(a, y) = \sum_{a=45}^{54} \sum_{y=1}^{12} P_s(a, y) SSB_s(a, y). \qquad (11.21)$$

This expression determines the social security tax rate $\tau_{ss}$. Social security benefits are then allocated across the lifetime income groups so that the fraction received by each lifetime income group is consistent with current data.

## A.3 Firm behavior

The DZ model has four production sectors, which use all of the supplies of capital and labor, as derived above. Production of all goods other than housing is divided into two sectors, the 'corporate' sector ($X^c$) and the 'non-corporate' sector ($X^n$). Both sectors are assumed to have CES production functions. A third sector comprised of landlords, who

---

[39] This link is fairly minimal; for example, AK argue that additional benefits offset only 25% of marginal Social Security taxes.

[40] Thus in its current form the DZ model cannot be used to analyze the problems faced by the Social Security system due to an aging population.

are also non-corporate entities, produces rental housing ($X^r$), and the fourth sector is individual home owners who effectively produce (and consume) owner-occupied housing ($X^h$). Both types of housing are produced with the same CES production function.

In each sector, the model assumes that firm managers, including landlords and the owners of owner-occupied housing, act to maximize the value of their firm in a perfectly competitive environment in the absence of uncertainty. The approach utilized is based on Tobin's '$q$'-theory of investment, as extended to include investment adjustment costs by Hayashi (1982). The firm modeling approach is similar to those utilized by Goulder and Summers (1989) and Kueschnigg (1990).

### A.3.1 Corporate sector

The corporate sector is characterized by a CES production function:

$$X_s^c = \left[(\gamma_c)^{1/\epsilon_c}\left(K_s^c\right)^{(\epsilon_c-1)/\epsilon_c} + (1-\gamma_c)^{1/\epsilon_c}\left(EL_s^c\right)^{(\epsilon_c-1)/\epsilon_c}\right]^{\epsilon_c/(\epsilon_c-1)}, \qquad (11.22)$$

where $K_s^c$ denotes inputs of capital used for corporate production in period $s$, $EL_s^c$ denotes effective labor used for corporate production in period $s$ and $\gamma_C$ is the capital weighting parameter in the CES production function in the corporate sector.

Gross investment in the corporate sector in period $s$, $I_s^c$, equals:

$$I_s^c = K_{s+1}^c - (1-\delta^c)K_s^c, \qquad (11.23)$$

where $\delta^c$ is the rate of depreciation of the capital stock in the corporate sector. The investment good and the corporate good are assumed to be identical. The price of the corporate good $p_s^c$ is assumed to be the numéraire, or $p_s^c = 1$.

Following Goulder and Summers (1989), adjustment costs per unit of investment are:

$$\Phi_s^c\left(I_s^c/K_s^c\right) = \frac{p_s^c(\beta^c/2)\left(I_s^c/K_s^c - \mu^c\right)^2}{\left(I_s^c/K_s^c\right)}, \qquad (11.24)$$

where $\beta^c$ and $\mu^c$ are adjustment cost parameters that are specific to the corporate sector. The parameter $\mu^c$ is equal to the steady-state ratio of gross investment to capital in the corporate sector; that is, $\mu^c = \delta^c + n + g + ng$.

Investment can be financed with either debt or equity. Firms in the corporate sector are assumed to maintain a constant debt-capital ratio, $b^c$, so that:

$$B_s^c = b^c K_s^c, \qquad (11.25)$$

where $B_s^c$ is the stock of outstanding corporate sector debt at time $s$. New bond issues in the corporate sector in period $s$, $BN_s^c$, are the difference in bonds outstanding in two consecutive periods, or $BN_s^c = B_{s+1}^c - B_s^c$, which implies:

$$BN_s^c = b^c\left(K_{s+1}^c - K_s^c\right) = b^c\left(I_s^c - \delta^c K_s^c\right). \qquad (11.26)$$

Note that this implies that existing loans are repaid at the rate of depreciation of the existing capital stock, so that the existing stock of outstanding corporate debt always equals $b^c K_s^c$.

Total gross equity earnings in the corporate sector (before depreciation and corporate taxes, but after local property taxes assessed at rate $\tau^{pc}$) in period $s$, $EARN_s^c$, are:

$$EARN_s^c = p_s^c X_s^c - w_s EL_s^c - i_s B_s^c - \tau^{pc} K_s^c. \tag{11.27}$$

Dividends paid are assumed to equal a constant fraction ($\zeta^c$) of the corporation's after-tax earnings net of economic depreciation, or:

$$DIV_s^c = \zeta^c \left( EARN_s^c - TE_s^c - p_s^c \delta^c K_s^c \right), \tag{11.28}$$

where $TE_s^c$ denotes total corporate taxes paid in period $s$. Assuming that adjustment costs are fully deductible and that the corporate business tax rate is $\tau_{bs}$, total corporate taxes are defined as:

$$TE_s^c = \tau_{bs} \left[ p_s^c X_s^c - w_s EL_s^c - f_e I_s^c - \Phi_s^c I_s^c - f_i i_s B_s^c - f_p \delta^c b^c K_s^c \right. $$
$$\left. + f_b b^c I_s^c - f_d \delta^{\tau c} K_s^{\tau c} - \tau^{pc} K_s^c \right], \tag{11.29}$$

where $\delta^{\tau c}$ is the depreciation rate for tax purposes in the corporate sector and $K_s^{\tau c}$ is tax basis under the corporate income tax. This formulation accommodates a wide variety of alternative income-based or consumption-based tax regimes, depending on the values of the various $f$ parameters, which equal zero or one. Assuming no cash accumulation on the part of the corporation, cash inflows in period $s$ must equal total disbursements, or:

$$EARN_s^c + BN_s^c + VN_s^c = DIV_s^c + I_s^c (1 + \Phi_s^c) + TE_s^c, \tag{11.30}$$

where $VN_s^c$ is corporate new share issues in period $s$.

Following Auerbach and Kotlikoff and Fullerton and Rogers, the model assumes individual level arbitrage. The after-tax nominal return on bonds is $r_s = (1 - \tau_{is}) i_s$ so that individual level arbitrage[41] implies:

$$r_s = (1 - \tau_{is}) i_s = \frac{(1 - \tau_{ds}) DIV_s^c + (1 - \tau_{gs}) \left( V_{s+1}^c - V_s^c - VN_s^c \right)}{V_s^c}, \tag{11.31}$$

where $V_s^c$ is the value of the firm, $(V_{s+1}^c - V_s^c - VN_s^c)$ is the capital gain on outstanding shares, and $DIV_s^c$ is dividends paid; note that the return on equity income is the sum of the return on dividends after dividend taxation at rate $\tau_{ds}$ and the return on capital gains, after capital gains taxation at an annual accrual tax rate $\tau_{gs}$. This treatment of equity

---

[41] In this formulation, after-tax returns to debt and equity are identical. However, it is straightforward to add an equity premium, which in principle could vary across sectors (Goulder and Summers, 1989); such an approach facilitates calibrating the model as it realistically allows after-tax returns to equity to exceed after-tax returns to debt.

finance follows the traditional view of the effects of dividend taxes, which are assumed to increase the cost of capital for investment financed with retained earnings. As noted above, dividends are a fixed fraction of earnings after taxes and depreciation. Investments are financed from the remaining retained earnings, or with new share issues if retained earnings are insufficient to finance the desired level of investment. (If desired investment is less than retained earnings, the firm repurchases shares without paying a dividend tax). Rearranging and simplifying yields:

$$V_{s+1}^c = V_s^c(1 + \theta_s) + VN_s^c - \left(\frac{1 - \tau_{ds}}{1 - \tau_{gs}}\right)DIV_s^c, \tag{11.32}$$

where $\theta_s = (1 - \tau_{is})i_s/(1 - \tau_{gs})$.

This expression can be used to obtain the value of the firm by repeatedly substituting for $V_{s+i-1}^c$ and solving for $V_s^c$, imposing the transversality condition, and substituting to yield:

$$V_s^c = \sum_{u=s}^{\infty}\left\{\left[\prod_{v=s}^{u}\frac{1}{(1 + \theta_v)}\right]\begin{bmatrix}(1 - \tau_{bs})\Omega_u^c(p_s^c X_s^c - w_s L_s^c) - (1 - \tau_{bs}f_i)\Omega_u^c i_s b^c K_s^c \\ + f_e\tau_{bs}\Omega_u^c I_s^c(1 + \Phi_s^c) - f_b\tau_{bs}\Omega_u^c b^c I_s^c \\ + f_p\tau_{bs}\Omega_u^c\delta^c b^c K_s^c + f_d\tau_{bs}\Omega_u^c\delta^{\tau c} K_s^{\tau c} - p_s^c\Omega_u^c\delta^c K_s^c \end{bmatrix} \right. $$
$$\left. - I_u^c(1 + \Phi_u) + \delta^c K_u^c + b^c(I_u^c - \delta^c K_u^c)\right\}, \tag{11.33}$$

where:

$$\Omega_u^c = [\zeta^c(1 - \tau_{du}) + (1 - \zeta^c)(1 - \tau_{gu})]/(1 - \tau_{gu}).$$

The term $f_d\tau_{bs}\Omega_u^c\delta^{\tau c}K_s^{\tau c}$ reflects the tax savings from depreciation allowances, which include both those attributable to past investments and those attributable to future investments made after time $t$. It is useful to distinguish between the present value of depreciation allowances on old capital, which are irrelevant to the investment decision, and the present value of depreciation allowances on future investments. Separating these two effects yields:

$$V_s^c = \sum_{u=s}^{\infty}\prod_{v=s}^{u}\frac{1}{(1 + \theta_v)}\Gamma_u^c + f_d X_t^c, \tag{11.34}$$

where:

$$\Gamma_u^c = (1 - \tau_{bu})\Omega_u^c[p_u^c X_u^c - w_u L_u^c]$$
$$- K_u^c\left\{\Omega_u^c(1 - \tau_{bu}f_i)i_u b^c - \delta^c\left[1 - b^c - \Omega_u^c\left(1 - f_p\tau_{bs}b^c\right)\right]\right\}$$
$$- I_u^c[1 - b^c - \Omega_u^c\tau_{bs}(f_e - f_b b^c)] - f_d Z_u^c + \Phi_u^c(1 - \tau_{bu}\Omega_u^c)]$$

$$Z_j^c = \sum_{u=j}^{\infty} \left[ \tau_{bu} \Omega_u^c \delta^{\tau c} (1 - \delta^{\tau c})^{u-j} \prod_{v=j}^{u} \frac{1}{(1 + \theta_v)} \right],$$

where $X_t^c = Z_t^c K_t^{\tau c}$ is the value of future depreciation deductions on old capital existing at the time of enactment of reform.

The corporation maximizes firm value subject to $K_{s+1}^c = I_s^c + (1 - \delta^c) K_s^c$ and $\lim_{T \to \infty} K_T^c \geq 0$. Defining $(q_{u+1}^c)^* = \prod_{v=s}^{u} [1/(1 + \theta_v)] q_{u+1}^c$, the necessary conditions for a maximum are:

$$w_s = p_s^c F_{uL}^c, \qquad (11.35)$$

i.e. the wage rate must equal the value of the marginal product of labor, $p_s^c F_{uL}^c$, and:

$$q_{s+1}^c = 1 - b^c - f_d Z_{s+1}^c - \Omega_u^c \tau_{bs} (f_e - f_b b^c) + (1 - \tau_{bs} \Omega_s^c) \left[ \Phi_s^c + (I_s^c / K_s^c)(\Phi_s^c)' \right], \qquad (11.36)$$

which describes the variable commonly known as Tobin's $q$, the ratio of the market value of a marginal unit of capital to its replacement cost. Thus, the shadow price of additional capital goods $(q_{s+1}^c)$ must equal the after-tax marginal cost of capital goods (the right-hand side). Since the investment good is the numéraire, the first term in the equation indicates that the shadow price is simply one in the absence of debt and taxes. The second term reflects the financing of a fraction $b^c$ of the cost of the investment with debt. The third term reflects the reduction in the shadow price of new capital goods due to tax deductions for depreciation. The fourth term reflects the effects of either expensing or the inclusion of the proceeds of debt under the consumption tax options. The last term reflects the costs of installing new capital goods with immediate expensing of adjustment costs. This expression yields the standard optimal investment equation for the firm, expressed as a function of Tobin's $q$, or:

$$\frac{I_s^c}{K_s^c} = \frac{q_{s+1}^c - 1 + b^c + f_d Z_{s+1}^c + \Omega_u^c \tau_{bs}(f_e - f_b b^c)}{p_s^c \beta^c (1 - \tau_{bs} \Omega_s^c)} + \mu^c \qquad (11.37)$$

It is, however, convenient to express investment demand as a function of the value of the corporation, $V_s^c$, rather than of $q_{s+1}^c$. To do this, note that, as shown by Hayashi (1982), the relationship between marginal $q$ and average $q$ denoted as $Q$, is:

$$q_s = \frac{[V_s - X_s]}{K_s}, \qquad Q_s = \frac{V_s}{K_s}. \qquad (11.38)$$

Thus, the investment demand function can be written as:

$$\frac{I_s^c}{K_s^c} = \frac{(V_{s+1}^c - X_{s+1}^c)/K_{s+1}^c - 1 + b^c + f_d Z_{s+1}^c + \Omega_u^c \tau_{bs}(f_e - f_b b^c)}{p_s^c \beta^c (1 - \tau_{bs} \Omega_s^c)} + \mu^c \qquad (11.39)$$

The third necessary condition is the Euler equation:

$$
i_s = \frac{\Omega_s^c(1 - \tau_{bs})p_s^c\dfrac{\partial F_s^c}{\partial K_s^c} + \delta^c\left[1 - b - \Omega_s^c\left(1 - f_p\tau_{bs}b^c\right)\right] + q_{s+1}^c(1 - \delta^c) - q_s^c}{\Omega_s^c(1 - \tau_{bs}f_i)b^c + q_s^c(1 - \tau_{is})/(1 - \tau_{gs})}
$$

(11.40)

$$
+ \frac{(1 - \tau_{bs}\Omega_s^c)p_s^c(\beta^c/2)\left[\left(I_s^c/K_s^c\right)^2 - \mu^2\right]}{\Omega_s^c(1 - \tau_{bs}f_i)b^c + q_s^c(1 - \tau_{is})/(1 - \tau_{gs})},
$$

which can be written as a difference equation in $q_s^c$, and solved to yield:

$$
q_s^c = \sum_{u=s}^{\infty}\left\{\begin{array}{l}\displaystyle\prod_{v=s}^{u}\frac{1}{(1 + \theta_v)}(1 - \delta^c)^{u-t}\left[\Omega_u^c(1 - \tau_{bu})\ p_u^c\frac{\partial F_s^c}{\partial K_s^c} - \Omega_u^c(1 - \tau_{bu}f_i)i_ub^c\right]\\[12pt]+ \delta^c\left(1 - b^c - \Omega_u^c\left(1 - f_p\tau_{bs}b^c\right)\right) + (1 - \tau_{bu}\Omega_u^c)p_u^c(\beta/2)\left[\left(I_s^c/K_s^c\right)^2 - (\mu^c)^2\right]\end{array}\right\}.
$$

(11.41)

This equation implies that the shadow price of new capital in the corporate sector, $q_s^c$, equals the present value of future income, reflecting the productivity of the asset, depreciation allowances, savings future installation costs and future interest payments. From, $Q_s^c = q_s^c + X_s^c/K_s^c$, that is, average $Q$ equals marginal $q$ plus an adjustment for future depreciation deductions on existing assets. Also, can be solved for the user cost of capital developed by Jorgenson (1963), the minimum return an investment must yield in order to provide the investor with the same rate of return that would be received from lending at the after-tax interest rate, or:

$$
\frac{\partial F_u^c}{\partial K_u^c} = \frac{\Omega_u^c(1 - \tau_{bu}f_i)i_ub^c - \delta^c\left[1 - b^c - \Omega_u^c\left(1 - f_p\tau_{bs}b^c\right)\right] + q_s^c(1 + \theta_s)}{\Omega_s^c(1 - \tau_{bs})p_s^c}
$$

(11.42)

$$
+ \frac{-q_{s+1}^c(1 - \delta^c) - (1 - \tau_{bu}\Omega_u^c)p_u^c(\beta/2)\left[\left(I_s^c/K_s^c\right)^2 - (\mu^c)^2\right]}{\Omega_s^c(1 - \tau_{bs})p_s^c}.
$$

Finally, the optimal solution must satisfy:

$$
\lim_{T\to\infty} K_{T+1}^c \geq 0,\quad \lim_{T\to\infty}\left(q_{T+1}^c\right)^* \geq 0,\quad \text{and}\quad \lim_{T\to\infty} K_{T+1}^c\left(q_{T+1}^c\right)^* = 0.
$$

(11.43)

The equations for the remaining three production sectors in the DZ model are generally similar to those for the corporate sector, and are thus not replicated in detail below. The following three subsections highlight the special features of each of these sectors.

### A.3.2 Non-corporate sector

The primary difference between the corporate and non-corporate sectors is that dividends and new share issues are not modeled explicitly. Instead, the value of the non-corporate firm is determined by the net cash flow (NCF) accruing to the owners of the business in each period, defined as gross equity earnings less the individual-level business taxes paid by the owners of the non-corporate business and less the portion of new investment that is financed with new equity contributions by the owners. Letting 'n' superscripts denote the non-corporate sector and defining all variables as above, net cash flow is:

$$NCF_s^n = EARN_s^n - TE_s^n - \left[I_s^n(1 + \Phi_s^n) - BN_s^n\right]. \tag{11.44}$$

This term replaces the dividend term in the numerator of the non-corporate analog of the expression defining the value of the firm, with new share issues by definition equal to zero. The business tax rate is the average individual tax rate applied to business income that is 'passed through' to individual owners of non-corporate business owners. Thus, although in reality all non-corporate earnings are passed through to individual owners, in the model these earnings are nominally taxed at the business level, but at the appropriate individual tax rate.

### A.3.3 Two housing sectors

The framework for determining the value of housing services to homeowners or landlords is similar to that utilized for the non-corporate firm. In particular, housing sector 'dividends' take the form of the service flows from the housing stock and thus are paid out in full, as either imputed or actual rents; in addition, new share issues are assumed to be unavailable. Thus, investment in the housing sector is all financed by either debt or equity in the form of retained earnings (or new equity if retained earnings are insufficient). Homeowners and landlords maintain constant debt to capital ratios, and existing loans are repaid at the rate of depreciation of the housing existing capital stock.

Earnings in the owner-occupied and rental housing sectors are defined as the value of housing services less labor cost (used in the production or maintenance of the capital that generates housing services), real interest payments on total indebtedness, and property tax payments. However, the tax treatment of housing differs across the owner-occupied and rental housing sectors. Earnings in the owner-occupied housing sector (imputed rents) are not taxed, but owner-occupiers who are itemizers receive income tax deductions for mortgage interest and property tax payments (but not for maintenance and repair expenditures). The net service flow of owner-occupied or rental housing, $S_s^j$, is:

$$S_s^j = EARN_s^j + BN_s^j - I_s^j(1 + \Phi_s^j) - TE_s^j, \tag{11.45}$$

where variables are defined as above, and the $j - h$, r superscripts refer to housing that is owner-occupied and rental housing.

## A.4 Market equilibria

Finally, prices must adjust so that equilibrium is obtained in all periods in all markets. This requires that aggregate demand (including investment demands, inclusive of adjustment costs, and government demands) equal aggregate supply for all four goods, that aggregate demand equal aggregate supply in the markets for capital and labor, and that the government budget (including both national and state governments) be balanced in each period (with the option of increasing government debt for a finite period). Asset market equilibrium requires that the total equity holdings of individuals equals total firm values for all four types of firms and that the total debt holdings of individuals equals the amount of debt issued by all four types of firms. Implicit in the calculation of these equilibria is that the expectations regarding all future prices by all individuals and firms must be satisfied.

The model is solved using the method developed by Fair and Taylor (1983). This method uses an initial guess to calculate actual values for all forward looking variables, and then updates the guess using a combination of the initial guess and the actual value. This procedure iterates until the model converges to a fixed point, where the difference between the revised guess and actual value is sufficiently small for each endogenous variable.

## REFERENCES

Aaron, H.J., Burman, L.E., Steuerle, C.E. (Eds.), 2007. Taxing Capital Income. Urban Institute Press, Washington, DC.

Altshuler, R., Bull, N., Diamond, J.W., Dowd, T., Moomau, P., 2005. The role of dynamic scoring in the federal budget process: Closing the gap between theory and practice. Am. Econ. Rev. 95, 432–436.

Altig, D., Auerbach, A.J., Kotlikoff, L.J., Smetters, K.A., Walliser, J., 2001. Simulating fundamental tax reform in the United States. Am. Econ. Rev. 91, 574–595.

Auerbach, A.J., 1996. Tax reform, capital allocation, efficiency, and growth. In: Aaron, H.J., Gale, W.G. (Eds.), Economic Effects of Fundamental Tax Reform. Brookings Institution, Washington, DC, pp. 29–81.

Auerbach, A.J., 2002. The Bush tax cut and national saving. Natl. Tax J. 55, 387–407.

Auerbach, A.J., 2005. Dynamic scoring: An introduction to the issues. Am. Econ. Rev. 95 (2), 421–425.

Auerbach, A.J., 2008. Tax reform in the 21st century. In: Diamond, J.W., Zodrow, G.R. (Eds.), Fundamental Tax Reform: Issues, Choices and Implications. MIT Press, Cambridge, MA, pp. 27–74.

Auerbach, A.J., Gale, W.G., 2011. Tempting fate: The latest federal budget outlook. Working Paper. Brookings Institution, Washington, DC.

Auerbach, A.J., Hassett, K.A., 2003. On the marginal source of investment funds. J. Pub. Econ. 87, 205–232.

Auerbach, A.J., Hassett, K.A. (Eds.), 2005. Toward Fundamental Tax Reform. AEI Press, Washington, DC.

Auerbach, A.J., Kotlikoff, L.J., 1987. Dynamic Fiscal Policy. Cambridge University Press, Cambridge.

Auerbach, A.J., Kotlikoff, L.J., Skinner, J., 1983. The efficiency gains from dynamic tax reform. Int. Econ. Rev. 24, 81–100.

Ballard, C.L., 1990. On the specification of simulation models for evaluating income and consumption taxes. In: Rose, M. (Ed.), Proceedings of the Heidelberg Congress on Taxing Consumption. Springer, Berlin, pp. 147–188.

Ballard, C.L., 2002. International aspects of fundamental tax reform. In: Zodrow, G.R., Mieszkowski, P. (Eds.), United States Tax Reform in the 21st Century. Cambridge University Press, Cambridge, pp. 109–139.

Ballard, C.L., Fullerton, D., Shoven, J.B., Whalley, J., 1985. A General Equilibrium Model for Tax Policy Evaluation. University of Chicago Press, Chicago, IL.

Bartelsman, Eric J., Beetsma, R.M.W.J., 2003. Why pay more? Corporate tax avoidance through transfer pricing in OECD countries. J. Pub. Econ. 87, 2225–2252.

Bayoumi, T., Laxton, D., Pesenti, P., 2004. Benefits and spillovers of greater competition in Europe: A macroeconomic assessment. NBER Working Paper 10416. National Bureau of Economic Research, Cambridge, MA.

Bettendorf, L., Devereux, M.P., van der Horst, A., Loretz, S., de Mooij, R., 2010. Corporate tax harmonization in the European Union. Economic Policy 25, 537–590.

Bradford, D.F., 1986. Untangling the Income Tax. Harvard University Press, Cambridge MA.

Bradford, D.F., 2005. A tax system for the twenty-first century. In: Auerbach, A.J., Hassett, Kevin A. (Eds.), Toward Fundamental Tax Reform. AEI Press, Washington, DC, pp. 81–94.

Brinner, R., Lansky, M., Wyss, D., 1995. Market Impacts of Flat Tax Legislation. DRI/McGraw-Hill. US Review, June.

Bruce, D., Holtz-Eakin, D., 1999. Fundamental tax reform and residential housing. J. Hous. Econ. 8, 249–271.

Burman, L.E., Rohaly, J., Rosenberg, J., Lim, K.C., 2010. Catastrophic budget failure. Natl. Tax J. 63, 561–583.

Capozza, D.R., Green, R.K., Hendershott, P.H., 1996. Taxes, mortgage borrowing and residential land prices. In: Aaron, H.J., Gale, W.G. (Eds.), Economic Effects of Fundamental Tax Reform. Brookings Institution, Washington, DC.

Chamley, C., 1986. Optimal taxation of capital income in general equilibrium with infinite lives. Econometrica 54, 607–622.

Carroll, R.J., Cline, R.J., Diamond, J.W., Neubig, T.S., Zodrow, G.R., 2010. The Macroeconomic Effects of an Add-On Value-Added Tax. Ernst and Young LLP, Washington, DC.

Congressional Budget Office, 2003. How CBO Analyzed the Macroeconomic Effects of the President's Budget. Congressional Budget Office, Washington, DC.

Congressional Budget Office, 2007. An Analysis of the President's Budgetary Proposals for Fiscal Year 2008. Congressional Budget Office, Washington, DC.

Congressional Budget Office, 2010. An Analysis of the President's Budgetary Proposals for Fiscal Year 2011. Congressional Budget Office, Washington, DC.

Congressional Budget Office, 2011. The Budget and Economic Outlook: Fiscal Years 2011–2021. Congressional Budget Office, Washington, DC.

Council of Economic Advisors, 2010. Economic Report of the President, 2010. US Government Printing Office, Washington, DC.

Davies, J., Whalley, J., 1991. Taxes and capital formation: How important is human capital? In: Bernheim, B.D., Shoven, J.B. (Eds.), National Saving and Economic Performance. University of Chicago Press, Chicago, IL, pp. 163–200.

De Mooij, R.A., Devereux, M.P., 2010. Alternative systems of business tax in Europe: An applied analysis of ACE and CBIT reforms. Taxation Papers Working Paper 17-2009. European Commission, Brussels.

Diamond, J.W., 2005. Dynamic effects of extending the 2001 and 2003 income tax cuts. Int. Tax Pub. Finance 12, 165–192.

Diamond, J.W., Viard, A.D., 2008. Welfare and macroeconomic effects of deficit − financed tax cuts: Lessons from CGE Models. In: Viard, A.D. (Ed.), Tax Policy Lessons from the 2000s. AEI Press, Washington, DC, pp. 145–193.

Diamond, J., Zodrow, G. R., 2006. Reflections on the use of life-cycle computable general equilibrium models in analyzing the effects of tax reform. NTA Network, April, 3–4.

Diamond, J.W., Zodrow, G.R., 2007a. Economic effects of a personal capital income tax add-on to a consumption tax. Finanzarchiv 63, 374–395.

Diamond, J.W., Zodrow, G.R., 2007b. Effects of the FairTax on Housing. National Association of Home Builders, Washington, DC.

Diamond, J.W., Zodrow, G.R., 2008a. Consumption tax reform: Changes in business equity and housing prices. In: Diamond, J.W., Zodrow, G.R. (Eds.), Fundamental Tax Reform: Issues, Choices and Implications. MIT Press, Cambridge, MA, pp. 227−280.

Diamond, J.W., Zodrow, G.R., 2008b. Fundamental Tax Reform: Issues, Choices and Implications. MIT Press, Cambridge, MA.

Diamond, J.W., Zodrow, G.R., 2011. Fundamental tax reform: Then and now. Baker Institute Working Paper. Baker Institute for Public Policy, Houston, TX.

Diamond, J. W., Zodrow, G. R., Neubig, T. S., Carroll, R. J., 2011. The dynamic economic effects of a US corporate income tax rate reduction. Paper presented at the Conference on Defusing the Debt Bomb − Economic and Fiscal Reform, October, sponsored by the Baker Institute for Public Policy, Houston, TX.

Driffill, E.J., Rosen, H., 1983. Taxation and excess burden: A life cycle perspective. Int. Econ. Rev. 24, 671−683.

Engen, E.M., Gale, W.G., 1996. The effects of fundamental tax reform on saving. In: Aaron, H.J., W.G.G. (Eds.), Economic Effects of Fundamental Tax Reform. Brookings Institution, Washington, DC, pp. 83−121.

Evans, O.J., 1983. Tax policy, the interest elasticity of saving, and capital accumulation: Numerical analysis of theoretical models. Am. Econ. Rev. 73, 398−410.

Fair, R.C., Taylor, J.B., 1983. Solution and maximum likelihood estimation of dynamic nonlinear rational expectation models. Econometrica 51, 1169−1185.

Feldstein, M.S., 1974. Incidence of a capital income tax in a growing economy with variable savings rates. Rev. Econ. Stud. 41, 505−513.

Feldstein, M., 2004. Here are the facts. Wall Street J., A12. February 12.

Feldstein, M., Horioka, C., 1980. Domestic savings and international capital flows. Econ. J. 90, 314−329.

Fullerton, D., Rogers, D. Lim, 1993. Who Bears the Lifetime Tax Burden? Brookings Institution, Washington, DC.

Fullerton, D., Rogers, D. Lim, 1996. Lifetime effects of fundamental tax reform. In: Aaron, H.J., William, G.G. (Eds.), Economic Effects of Fundamental Tax Reform. Brookings Institution, Washington, DC, pp. 321−354.

Gordon, R.H., Slemrod, J.B., 2000. Are 'real' responses to taxes simply income shifting between corporate and personal income tax bases? In: Slemrod, J.B. (Ed.), Does Atlas Shrug? The Economic Consequences of Taxing the Rich. Russell Sage Foundation, New York/Harvard University Press, Cambridge, MA, pp. 240−280.

Goulder, L.H., Shoven, J.B., Whalley, J., 1983. Domestic tax policy and the foreign sector: The importance of alternative foreign sector formulations to results from a general equilibrium tax analysis model. In: Feldstein, M. (Ed.), Behavioral Simulation Methods in Tax Policy Analysis. University of Chicago Press, Chicago, IL, pp. 333−368.

Goulder, L.H., Summers, L.H., 1989. Tax policy, asset prices, and growth: A general equilibrium analysis. J. Pub. Econ. 38, 265−296.

Gravelle, J.G., 1994. The Economic Effects of Taxing Capital Income. MIT Press, Cambridge, MA.

Gravelle, J.G., 1996. The Flat Tax and Other Proposals: Effects on Housing. Congressional Research Service Report for Congress Number 96−379E. Congressional Research Service, Washington, DC.

Gravelle, J.G., 2002. Behavioral responses to a consumption tax. In: Zodrow, G.R., Mieszkowski, P. (Eds.), United States Tax Reform in the 21st Century. Cambridge University Press, Cambridge, pp. 25−54.

Gravelle, J.G., 2006. Feasible but hard-to-believe models: Computable general equilibrium intertemporal Models. NTA Network. National Tax Association. January 20063−4.

Gravelle, J.G., Smetters, K.A., 2006. Does the open economy assumption really mean that labor bears the burden of a capital income tax? Ad. Econ. Anal. Pol.y 6 Article 3.

Gunning, T.S., Diamond, J.W., Zodrow, G.R., 2008. Selecting parameter values for general equilibrium model simulations. Proceedings of the 100th Annual Conference on Taxation. National Tax Association, Washington, DC.

Hall, R.E., 1968. Consumption taxes versus income taxes: Implications for economic growth. Proceedings of the 61st Annual Conference on Taxation. National Tax Association, Columbus, OH, 125–145.

Hall, R.E., 1997. The effects of tax reform on prices and asset values. In: Poterba, J.M. (Ed.), Tax Policy and the Economy. National Bureau of Economic Research, Cambridge, MA, pp. 71–88.

Hall, R.E., Rabushka, A., 1983. Low Tax, Simple Tax, Flat Tax. McGraw-Hill, New York.

Hall, R.E., Rabushka, A., 1995. The Flat Tax. Hoover Institution Press, Stanford, CA (second ed.).

Harberger, A.C., 1962. The incidence of the corporate income tax. J. Polit. Econ. 70, 215–240.

Harberger, A.C., 1995. The ABCs of corporate tax incidence: Insights into the open-economy case. In: American Council for Capital Formation (Ed.), Tax Policy and Economic Growth. ACCF Center for Policy Research, Washington, DC, pp. 51–73.

Harberger, A.C., 2008. Corporation tax incidence: Reflections on what is known, unknown and unknowable. In: Diamond, J.W., Zodrow, G.R. (Eds.), Fundamental Tax Reform: Issues, Choices and Implications. MIT Press, Cambridge, MA, pp. 283–317.

Hayashi, F., 1982. Tobin's marginal $q$ and average $q$: A neoclassical interpretation. Econometrica 50, 213–224.

Hubbard, R.G., 2002. Capital income taxation in tax reform: implications for analysis of distribution and efficiency. In: Zodrow, G.R., Mieszkowski, P. (Eds.), United States Tax Reform in the 21st Century. Cambridge University Press, Cambridge, pp. 89–108.

House, C., Shapiro, M.D., 2006. Phased-in tax cuts and economic activity. Amer. Econ. Rev. 96, 1835–1949.

International Monetary Fund, 2010. Will it hurt? Macroeconomic effects of fiscal consolidation. In: World Economic Outlook: Recovery, Risk, and Rebalancing. International Monetary Fund, Washington, DC, pp. 93–124.

Joint Committee on Taxation, 2003. Macroeconomic analysis of H. R. 2, the Jobs and Growth Reconciliation Tax Act of 2003. Congressional Record, May 8, H3829. US Government Printing Office, Washington, DC.

Joint Committee on Taxation, 2006. Macroeconomic Analysis of a Proposal to Broaden The Individual Income Tax Base and Lower Individual Income Tax Rates. JCX-53-06. Joint Committee on Taxation, Washington, DC.

Joint Committee on Taxation, 2008. Estimates of Federal Tax Expenditures for Fiscal Years 2008–2012. JCT Report JCS-2-08. Joint Committee on Taxation, Washington, DC.

Jorgenson, D., 1963. Capital theory and investment behavior. Am. Econ. Rev. 53, 247–259.

Jokisch, S., Kotlikoff, L.J., 2007. Simulating the dynamic macroeconomic and microeconomic effects of the FairTax. Nat. Tax. J. 60, 225–252.

Judd, K.L., 1985. Redistributive income in a simple perfect foresight model. J. Publ. Econ. 28, 59–83.

Kennickel, A., Lusardi, A., 2004. Disentangling the importance of the precautionary saving motive. Working Paper. Board of Governors of the Federal Reserve System, Washington, DC.

Kocherlakota, N.R., 2010. The New Dynamic Public Finance. Princeton University Press, Princeton, NJ.

Kopczuk, W., Lupton, J., 2007. To leave or not to leave: the distribution of bequest motives. Rev. Econ. Stud. 74, 206–235.

Kotlikoff, L.J., 1998. The A–K model—its past, present, and future. NBER Working Paper 6684. National Bureau of Economic Research, Cambridge, MA.

Krzyzaniak, M., 1967. Long Run Burden of a General Tax on Profits in a Neoclassical World, vol. 22. Public Finance. 472–491.

Kueschnigg, C., 1990. Corporate taxation and growth: Dynamic general equilibrium simulation study. In: Brunner, J., Petersen, H.-G. (Eds.), Simulation Models in Tax and Transfer Policy. Campus Verlag, New York, pp. 245–278.

Kueschnigg, C., 1991. The transition to a cash flow income tax. Swiss. J. Econ. Stat. 127, 113–140.

Lord, W., 1989. The transition from payroll to consumption receipts taxes with endogenous human capital. J. Publ. Econ. 38, 53–73.

Lucas Jr., R.E., 1976. Econometric policy evaluation: A critique. In: Brunner, K., Meltzer, A. (Eds.), The Phillips Curve and Labor Markets. Carnegie-Rochester Conference Series on Public Policy 1. Elsevier, New York, pp. 19–46.

Lyon, A.B., Merrill, P.R., 2001. Asset price effects of fundamental tax reform. In: Hassett, K.A., Hubbard, R.G. (Eds.), Transition Costs of Fundamental Tax Reform. AEI Press, Washington, DC, pp. 58–95.

Mankiw, N.G., Weinzierl, M., 2005. Dynamic scoring: A back-of-the-envelope guide. J. Publ. Econ. 90, 1415–1433.

McLure Jr., C.E., Zodrow, G.R., 1987. Treasury I and the Tax Reform Act of 1986: The economics and politics of tax reform. J. Econ. Perspect. 1, 37–58.

Musgrave, R.A., 1953. General equilibrium aspects of incidence theory. Am. Econ. Rev. 43, 504–517.

Musgrave, R.A., 1959. The Theory of Public Finance. McGraw-Hill, New York.

Nicodème, G., 2008. Corporate income tax and economic distortions. CESifo Working Paper 2477. CESifo, Munich.

Office of Tax Analysis, 2006. A Dynamic Analysis of Permanent Extension of the President's Tax Relief. US Department of the Treasury, Washington, DC.

President's Advisory Panel on Federal Tax Reform, 2005. Simple, Fair, and Pro-Growth: Proposals to Fix America's Tax System. US Government Printing Office, Washington, DC.

Randolph, W.C., 2006. International burdens of the corporate income tax. CBO Working Paper 2006–09. Congressional Budget Office, Washington, DC.

Shoven, J.B., Whalley, J., 1972. A general equilibrium calculation of the effects of differential taxation of income from capital in the United States. J. Public Econ. 1, 281–321.

Sorensen, P.B., 2007. The Nordic dual income tax: Principles, practices, and relevance for Canada. Can. Tax. J. 55, 557–602.

Starrett, D.A., 1988. Effects of taxes on saving. In: Aaron, H.J., Galper, H., Pechman, J. (Eds.), Uneasy Compromise: Problems of a Hybrid Income–Consumption Tax. Brookings Institution, Washington, DC, pp. 237–259.

Summers, L.H., 1981. Capital taxation and accumulation in a life cycle growth model. Am. Econ. Rev. 71, 533–544.

Taber, C., 2002. Tax reform and human capital accumulation: Evidence from an empirical general equilibrium model of skill formation. Advances in Economic Analysis and Policy 2, article 3.

Tobin, J., 1969. A general equilibrium approach to monetary theory. J. Money Credit Bank. 1, 15–29.

Toder, E., Rosenberg, J., 2010. Effects of Imposing a Value-Added Tax to Replace Payroll Taxes or Corporate Taxes. Tax Policy Center, Urban Institute and Brookings Institution, Washington, DC.

US Department of the Treasury, 2007. Approaches to Improve the Competitiveness of the US Business Tax System for the 21st Century. US Department of the Treasury Office of Tax Policy, Washington, DC.

Weidenbaum, M., 1996. The Nunn–Domenici USA tax: Analysis and comparisons. In: Boskin, M.J. (Ed.), Frontiers of Tax Reform. Hoover Institution Press, Stanford, CA, pp. 54–69.

Zodrow, G.R., 2002. Transitional issues in the implementation of a flat tax or a national retail sales tax. In: Zodrow, G.R., Mieszkowski, P. (Eds.), United States Tax Reform in the 21st Century. Cambridge University Press, Cambridge, pp. 245–283.

Zodrow, G.R., 2007. Should capital income be subject to consumption-based taxation? In: Aaron, H.J., Leonard, E.B., Steuerle, E.C. (Eds.), Taxing Capital Income. Urban Institute Press, Washington, DC, pp. 49–81.

Zodrow, G.R., 2010. Capital mobility and capital tax competition. Natl. Tax J. 63, 865–901.

Zodrow, G.R., Mieszkowski, P. (Eds.), 2002. United States Tax Reform in the 21st Century. Cambridge University Press, Cambridge.

Zodrow, G. R., Neubig, T. S., Diamond, J. W., Cline, R. J., Carroll, R. J., 2011. Price effects of implementing a VAT in the United States. In Proceedings of the 103rd Annual Conference on Taxation. National Tax Association, Washington, DC, pp. 56–63.

*Note*: Page numbers followed by "f" and "t" indicate figures and tables respectively

*Note*: Page numbers followed by "f" and "t" indicate figures and tables respectively

Printed and bound by CPI Group (UK) Ltd, Croydon, CR0 4YY

08/05/2025

01864815-0005